THE LIBRARY

OF

LITERARY CRITICISM

OF

ENGLISH AND AMERICAN AUTHORS

VOLUME II
1639 – 1729

EDITED BY CHARLES WELLS MOULTON
ASSISTED BY A CORPS OF ABLE CONTRIBUTORS

GLOUCESTER, MASS.
PETER SMITH
1959

To

Right Honorable James Bryce, D. C. L., L. L. D., F. R. S.

INTRODUCTION.

THE CRITIC.

'Tis hard to say, if greater want of skill
Appear in writing or in judging ill;
But, of the two, less dang'rous is th' offence
To tire our patience, than mislead our sense.
Some few in that, but numbers err in this,
Ten censure wrong for one who writes amiss;
A fool might once himself alone expose,
Now one in verse makes many more in prose.
'Tis with our judgments as our watches, none
Go just alike, yet each believes his own.
In Poets as true genius is but rare,
True Taste as seldom is the Critic's share;
Both must alike from Heav'n derive their
    light,
These born to judge, as well as those to
    write.
Let such teach others who themselves excel,
And censure freely who have written well.
Authors are partial to their wit, 'tis true,
But are not Critics to their judgment too?
—POPE, ALEXANDER, 1709, *An Essay on
Criticism, v.* 1-18.

There is nothing more absurd, than for a Man to set up for a Critick, without a good insight into all parts of learning. . . . One great Mark by which you may discover a Critick who has neither Taste nor Learning, is this, that he seldom ventures to praise any passage in an Author which has not been before received and applauded by the Public, and that his Criticism turns wholly upon little Faults and Errors. . . . A true Critick ought to dwell rather upon Excellences than Imperfections, to discover the concealed Beauties of a Writer and communicate to the World such things as are worth their Observation. The most exquisite words, and finest Strokes of an Author, are those which very often appear the most doubtful and exceptionable to a man who wants a Relish for polite Learning; and they are these which a sour undistinguishing Critick generally attacks with the greatest Violence.—ADDISON, JOSEPH, 1711-12, *The Spectator, No.* 291.

On a superficial view we may seem to differ very widely from each other in our reasonings, and no less in our pleasures: but, notwithstanding this difference, which I think to be rather apparent than real, it is probable that the standard both of reason and taste is the same in all human creatures. . . . The cause of a wrong taste is a defect of judgment. And this may arise from a natural weakness of understanding (in whatever the strength of that faculty may consist), or, which is much more commonly the case, it may arise from a want of a proper and well-directed exercise, which alone can make it strong and ready. Besides, that ignorance, inattention, prejudice, rashness, levity, obstinacy, in short, all those passions, and all those vices, which pervert the judgment in other matters, prejudice it no less in this its more refined and elegant province.—BURKE, EDMUND, 1756-57, *The Sublime and Beautiful, Introduction.*

Wit certainly is the property of those who have it, nor should we be displeased if it is the only property a man sometimes has. We must not underrate him who uses it for subsistence, and flies from the ingratitude of the age even to a bookseller for redress. If the profession of an author is to be laughed at by the stupid, it is certainly better to be contemptibly rich than contemptibly poor. For all the wit that ever adorned the human mind will at present no more shield the author's poverty from ridicule, than his high-topped gloves conceal the unavoidable omissions of his laundress.—GOLDSMITH, OLIVER, 1759, *Enquiry into the Present State of Polite Learning.*

The science of rational criticism tends to improve the heart no less than the understanding. It tends, in the first place, to moderate the selfish affections. By sweetening and harmonizing the temper, it is a strong antidote to the turbulence of passion, and violence of pursuit. It procures, to a man, so much mental enjoyment, that, in order to be occupied, he is not tempted to deliver up his youth to hunting, gaming, drinking; nor his middle age to ambition, nor his old age to avarice. Pride and envy, two disgustful passions, find in the constitution no enemy more formidable than a delicate and discerning taste.— HOME, HENRY (LORD KAMES), 1762–63, *Elements of Criticism.*

This age may be best characterised as the age of criticism—a criticism to which everything must submit. Religion, on the ground of its sanctity, and law, on the ground of its majesty, often resist this sifting of their claims. But in so doing, they inevitably awake a not unjust suspicion that their claims are ill-founded, and they can no longer expect the unfeigned homage paid by reason to that which has shown itself able to stand the test of free inquiry.—KANT, IMMANUEL, 1781, *Critique of Pure Reason.*

True criticism is the application of taste and of good sense to the several fine arts. The object which it proposes is, to distinguish what is beautiful and what is faulty in every performance; from particular instances to ascend to general principles; and so to form rules or conclusions concerning the several kinds of beauty in works of genius. The rules of criticism are not formed by any induction *à priori*, as it is called; that is, they are not formed by a train of abstract reasoning, independent of facts and observations. Criticism is an art founded wholly on experience.—BLAIR, HUGH, 1783, *Lectures on Rhetoric and Belles-Lettres, ed. Mills, Lecture* iii.

To regulate our intellectual pleasures, to free literature from the tyranny of the notion that there is no disputing about tastes, to constitute an exact science, intent rather on guiding than gratifying the mind.—NISARD, JEAN MARIE NAPOLÉON DÉSIRÉ, 1844, *Historie de la Littérature Française, vol.* I.

Those who consider the science of criticism as nothing more than a collection of arbitrary rules, and the art of criticism but their dextrous or declamatory application, rejoice in a system of admirable simplicity and barren results. It has the advantage of judging every thing and accounting for nothing, thus gratifying the pride of intellect without enjoining any intellectual exertion. By a steady adherence to its doctrines, a dunce may exalt himself to a pinnacle of judgment, from which the first authors of the world appear as splendid madmen, whose enormous writhings and contortions, as they occasionally blunder into grace and grandeur of motion, show an undisciplined strength, which would, if subjected to rule, produce great effects. A Bond-street exquisite complacently surveying a thunder-scarred Titan through an opera-glass, is but a type of a Grub-street critic, measuring a Milton or a Shakspeare with his three-foot rule.—WHIPPLE, EDWIN PERCY, 1848, *Shakspeare's Critics, Essays and Reviews, vol.* II, *p.* 248.

The following brief remarks on the critical faculty are chiefly intended to show that, for the most part, there is no such thing. It is a *rara avis;* almost as rare, indeed, as the phœnix, which appears only once in five hundred years. . . . The preceptive critical taste is, so to speak, the female analogue to the male quality of productive talent or genius. Not capable of *begetting* great work itself, it consists in a capacity of *reception,* that is to say, of recognising as such what is right, fit, beautiful, or the reverse; in other words, of discriminating the good from the bad, or discovering and appreciating the one and condemning the other. . . . That which distinguishes genius, and should be the standard for judging it, is the height to which it is able to soar when it is in the proper mood and finds a fitting occasion—a height always out of the reach of ordinary talent. . . . There are critics who severally think that it rests with each one of them what shall be accounted good, and what bad. They all mistake their own toy-trumpets for the trombones of fame. A drug does not affect its purpose if the dose is too large; and it is the same with censure and adverse criticism when it exceeds the measure of justice. — SCHOPENHAUER, ARTHUR, 1851–91, *The Art of Literature*, *tr. Saunders, pp.* 87, 88.

The Supreme Critic on the errors of the past and the present, and the only prophet of that which must be, is the great nature in which we rest as the earth lies in the soft arms of the atmosphere; that Unity, that Over-soul, within which every man's particular being is contained and made one with all other; that common heart of which all sincere conversation is the worship, to which all right action is submission; that overpowering reality which confutes our tricks and talents, and constrains every one to pass for what he is, and to speak from his character and not from his tongue, and which evermore tends to pass into our thought and hand and become wisdom and virtue and power and beauty.—EMERSON, RALPH WALDO, 1856–83, *The Over-Soul, Essays, First Series; Complete Works, Riverside ed., vol.* II, *p.* 252.

Each order of greatness has its own eminence and should not be contrasted with another. . . . The critical sense is not inoculated in an hour; he who has not cultivated it by a long scientific and intellectual discipline will always find adverse arguments to oppose to the more delicate inductions. . . . Criticism displaces admiration, but does not destroy it. . . . That delicate feeling for shades of thought which we call criticism, without which there is no insight into the past and consequently no extended understanding of human affairs. — RENAN, JOSEPH ERNEST, 1859–64, *Studies of Religious History and Criticism, tr.* Frothingham, *pp.* 40, 217, 263, 310.

It is of the last importance that English criticism should clearly discern what rule for its course, in order to avail itself of the field now opening to it, and to produce fruit to the future, it ought to take. The rule may be summed up in one word, — *disinterestedness.* And how is criticism to show disinterestedness? By keeping aloof from practice; by resolutely following the law of its own nature, which is to be a free play of the mind on all subjects which it touches; by steadily refusing to lend itself to any of those ulterior, political, practical considerations about ideas which plenty of people will be sure to attach to them, which perhaps ought often to be attached to them which in this country at any rate are certain to be attached to them quite sufficiently, but which criticism has really nothing to do with. Its business is, as I have said, simply to know the best that is known and thought in the world, and, by in its turn making this known, to create a current of true and fresh ideas. Its business is to do this with inflexible honesty, with due ability; but its business is to do no more, and to leave alone all questions of practical consequences and applications, questions which will never fail to have due prominence given to them. . . . It is because criticism has so little kept in the pure intellectual sphere, has so little detached itself from practice, has been so directly polemical and controversial, that it has so ill accomplished, in this country, its best spiritual work; which is to keep man from a self-satisfaction which is retarding and vulgarizing, to lead him towards perfection, by making his mind dwell upon what is excellent in itself, and the absolute beauty and fitness of things. — ARNOLD, MATTHEW, 1865, *The Function of Criticism at the Present Time, Essays in Criticism.*

Good composition is **far less dependent**

upon acquaintance with its laws, than upon practice and natural aptitude. A clear head, a quick imagination, and a sensitive ear, will go far towards making all rhetorical precepts needless.—SPEN-CER, HERBERT, 1871, *The Philosophy of Style*.

Though a thousand critics determine that a book ought not to live, if it is a real book it lives, without the slightest reference to their opinions and protests. What the critics prove by their work is, simply their lack of power to comprehend and appreciate it. They prove nothing against the book whatever. There has not lived a great British author within the last century whose works have not been subjected to the most scorching criticisms and the most slashing and sweeping condemnations. Yet those criticisms and condemnations have passed for nothing. The criticisms, often profoundly ingenious, and full of learning and power, die, and the books live. They are often exceedingly creditable productions—so creditable, indeed, that they form the basis of great personal reputations—but they accomplish absolutely nothing except the revelation of the men who produce them. Criticism thus becomes a form of personal expression, and is just as thoroughly individualized as if it were poetry, or picture, or sculpture. The critic takes a book in one hand, and uses the other to paint himself with. When his work is done we may fail to find the book in it, but we are sure to find him.—HOLLAND, JOSIAH GILBERT, 1876, *Every-Day Topics, First Series, p.* 58.

It is difficult to strike the balance between the educational needs of passivity or receptivity, and independent selection. We should learn nothing without the tendency to implicit acceptance; but there must clearly be a limit to such mental submission, else we should come to a stand-still. The human mind would be no better than a dried specimen, representing an unchangeable type. When the assimilation of new matters ceases, decay must begin. In a reasoned self-restraining deference there is as much energy as in rebellion; but among the less capable, one must admit that the superior energy is on the side of the rebels. And certainly a man who dares to say that he finds an eminent classic feeble here, extravagant there, and in general overrated, may chance to give an opinion which has some genuine discrimination in it concerning a new work or a living thinker—an opinion such as can hardly ever be got from the reputed judge who is a correct echo of the most approved phrases concerning those who have been already canonised.— ELIOT, GEORGE, 1880-83, *Leaves from a Note Book, Essays, p.* 365.

Only of late have we begun to look for criticism which applies both knowledge and self-knowledge to the test; which is penetrative and dexterous, but probes only to cure; which enters into the soul and purpose of a work, and considers every factor that makes it what it is;— the criticism which, above all, esteems it a cardinal sin to suffer a verdict to be tainted by private dislike, or by partisanship and the instinct of battle with an opposing clique or school.—STEDMAN, EDMUND CLARENCE, 1885, *Poets of America, p.* 25.

The whole history of criticism has been a triumph of authors over critics.—MOUL-TON, RICHARD GREEN, 1885, *Shakespeare as a Dramatic Artist*.

Our true critic renounces idiosyncratic whims and partialities, striving to enter with firm purpose into the understanding of universal goodness and beauty. In so far as he finds truth in Angelico and Rubens, will he be appreciative of both. —SYMONDS, JOHN ADDINGTON, 1886, *Renaissance in Italy, The Catholic Reaction, vol.* II, *p.* 397.

Learn your trade, gentlemen, or your art, if it be an art, before you attempt to practise it. Science points you the path, not whim or conceit or vain glory. It is a strait path, but a clear one. And its first foothold, if I mistake not, is humane courtesy.—FAWCETT, EDGAR, 1887, *Should Critics be Gentlemen? Lippincott's Magazine, vol.* 39, *p.* 177.

Our criticism is disabled by the unwillingness of the critic to learn from an author, and his readiness to mistrust him. A writer passes his whole life in fitting himself for a certain kind of performance; the critic does not ask why, or whether the performance is good or bad, but if he does not like the kind, he instructs the writer to go off and do some other sort of thing—usually the sort that has been done already, and done sufficiently. If he could once understand that a man who has written the book he dislikes, probably, knows infinitely more about its kind and his own fitness for doing it than any one else, the critic might learn something, and might help the reader to learn; but by putting himself in a false position, a position of superiority, he is of no use.— HOWELLS, WILLIAM DEAN, 1887, *Editor's Study, Harper's Magazine, vol.* 75, *p.* 156.

In the matter of literary criticism we need to guard against those scientific methods which assume that culture is mainly a thing of the head, and that the interpretation of literature is a thing to be acquired by the same methods as the ability to demonstrate Euclid. An age of speculation is not an age of faith, nor is an age of criticism an age of creation. A system has prevailed by which the critic is constituted a supreme judge, who, sitting apart, without sympathy or reverence, is to pronounce sentence upon the culprit who has dared to violate the judicial standard. In his charge he uses those maxims and doctrines which have become the commonest furniture of the commonest minds; he pronounces the style obscure, affected, or classical, the method involved, and the matter puerile or unintelligible, but does not explain

what he means by these terms; "if he would only give us the law by which we might be prevented from writing or speaking anything that is not simple, natural, and manly " what a blessing he would confer!—GEORGE, ANDREW J., 1889, *ed., Selections from Wordsworth, Preface, p.* vii.

No student or even reader of the world's literature can afford to despise the world's traditions about its great books. —HARDY, ARTHUR SHERBURNE, 1890, *Letters and Life, Andover Review, vol.* 14, *p.* 522.

Where is Burke on the Sublime, and where is Mr. Morritt's "Vindication of Homer," and Blackwell's treatise on the same author? Quite a mild little poem or a third-rate play outlives and outlasts most of our Criticisms, and the critic's lot, on the whole, is not a happy one.— LANG, ANDREW, 1891, *The Science of Criticism, The New Review, vol.* 4, *p.* 408.

The great writers, whose names are identified with criticism, have not been drawn to the work of other men by force of the scholarly instinct; they have sought and found in the study of literature a revelation of the soul and of the laws of life and art. The survey of literature as a whole has disclosed the deep unity of the human mind in the mind and art of many races, and the unity of literature as an expression of that mind. As a result of this broad and comprehensive study of literature we are fast discovering the secrets of race inheritance, temperament, and genius; the characteristics of each family of races; the political, spiritual, and social forces which dominated each literary epoch; and the fact or facts of experience, the stage or process of vital change and growth behind each great literary form.—MABIE, HAMILTON WRIGHT, 1891, *Short Studies in Literature, p.* 174.

The critical sense is so far from frequent that it is absolutely rare and that the possession of the cluster of qualities that minister to it is one of the highest distinctions. It is a gift inestimably precious and beautiful; therefore, so far from thinking that it passes overmuch from hand to hand, one knows that one has only to stand by the counter an hour to see that business is done with baser coin. We have too many small schoolmasters; yet not only do I not question in literature the high utility of criticism, but I should be tempted to say that the part it plays may be the supremely beneficent one when it proceeds from deep sources, from the efficient combination of experience and perception. In this light one sees the critic as the real helper of mankind, a torch-bearing outrider, the interpreter *par excellence.*—JAMES, HENRY, 1891, *The Science of Criticism, The New Review, vol.* 4, *p.* 401.

We cannot believe that he criticiseth best who loveth best all styles both great and small. Surely the best critic is he who, neither ashamed of admiring when he can, nor afraid of reprehending when he ought, does not ask the reader to take his admiration or reprehension on trust, but vindicates both, by adducing such reasons as in all ages have sufficed to demonstrate why masterpieces are masterpieces, and why failures are failures.— WATSON, WILLIAM, 1893, *Excursions in Criticism, p.* 88.

Popular objection to criticism is, however, senseless, because it is through criticism—that is, through discrimination between two things, customs, or courses that the race has managed to come out of the woods and lead a civilized life. The man who objected to the general nakedness, and advised his fellows to put on clothes, was the first critic. All genuine criticism consists in comparison between two ways of doing something, and it is by such comparison that the world has advanced.— GODKIN, EDWIN LAURENCE, 1894, *The Duty of Educated Men in a Democracy, The Forum, vol.* 17, *p.* 45.

In the sight of a picture, in the sight of a building, in the sound of music, although there is æsthetic pleasure, yet the æsthetic pleasure is directly dependent upon the senses, since it arises immediately from a sense-perception and ceases to be felt when the external stimulus is removed. The class of æsthetic pleasures with which literature is concerned do not depend upon any external stimuli except those which convey the symbols of thought to eye or ear. The enjoyment, therefore, which comes from the simulation of sensations or perceptions through the thoughts of others, or through the co-operation of the thoughts of others with our own memory and imagination, is the highest, though by no means the most complete or intense form of æsthetic enjoyment. It is the most independent of external stimuli, and therefore the most remote from physical impulse, and the most closely connected with the mind of the individual. Such pleasures are in the highest degree free; they can be enjoyed almost without reference to external circumstances, and they are in a peculiar sense the property of the individual himself: indeed they become part of his personality, a rich possession of which nothing short of the decay of his mental powers can deprive him.—WORSFOLD, W. BASIL, 1897, *The Principles of Criticism, p.* 13.

As the principles of literary judgment are akin to all æsthetic principles, are, in fact, only the application in a particular field of the general laws of art, so the methods by which these principles shall be applied in the process of critical appraisement are the adaptation to given conditions, and to a given end, of the critical method that characterizes the larger science of Discrimination.—GAYLEY, CHARLES MILLS, AND SCOTT, FRED NEWTON, 1899, *An Introduction to the Methods and Materials of Literary Criticism, Preface, p.* iv.

CONTENTS.

ENGRAVINGS.

SIR HENRY WOTTON

*From the Original of Cornelius Jansen
in the Bodleian Gallery, Oxford.
Engraving by W. Holl.*

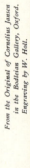

SIR WILLIAM ALEXANDER

*From a Rare Print by Marshall. Drawing
by J. Thurston. Engraving by C. Pye.*

The
Library of Literary Criticism

of

English and American Authors

VOLUME II

Sir Henry Wotton

1568–1639

Born, at Boughton Malherbe, Kent, 30 March 1568. Early education at Winchester College. Matric. New College, Oxford, 5 June 1584. Removed to Queen's College; B. A., 8 June 1588. Travelled on Continent, 1588–95. Student of Middle Temple, 1595. Sec. to Earl of Essex, 1595–1601. In Italy, 1601–03. Knighted, 1603. M. P. for Appleby, 1614; for Sandwich, 1625. Served on various embassies abroad. Provost of Eton, 1624–39. Died, at Eton, Dec. 1639. Buried there. *Works:* "The Elements of Architecture," 1604; "Epistola ad Marcum Velserum Duumvirum," 1612; "Epistola de Caspare Scioppio," 1613; "Ad Regeme Scotia reducem . . . Plausus," 1633. *Posthumous:* "Parallel between Robert, late Earl of Essex, and George, late Duke of Buckingham," 1641; "Short View of the Life and Death of George Villiers, Duke of Buckingham," 1642; "A Panegyrick of King Charles," 1649; "Reliquiæ Wottonianæ," ed. by Izaak Walton, 1651; "The State of Christendom," 1657; "Letters to Sir Edmund Baker," 1661; "Letters to the Lord Zouch," 1685. *Collected Works:* "Poems," ed. by A. Dyce, 1843.—SHARP, R. FARQUHARSON, 1897, *A Dictionary of English Authors,* p. 305.

PERSONAL

So well he understood the most and best
Of tongues that Babel sent into the West,
Spoke them so truly, that he had (you'd swear)
Not only liv'd, but been born ev'ry where.
Justly each nation's speech to him was known,
Who for the world was made, not us alone.
Nor ought the language of that man be less,
Who in his breast had all things to express.
We say that learning's endless, and blame Fate
For not allowing life a longer date.
He did the utmost bounds of Knowledge find,
He found them not so large as was his mind.
But, like the brave Pellæan youth, did moan,
Because that Art had no more worlds than one.
And when he saw that he through all had past,
He dy'd, lest he should idle grow at last.
—COWLEY, ABRAHAM, 1639, *On the Death of Sir Henry Wotton.*

And thus the circle of Sir Henry Wotton's life—that circle which began at Bocton, and in the circumference thereof did first touch at Winchester School, then at Oxford, and after upon so many remarkable parts and passages in Christendom—that circle of his Life was by Death thus closed up and completed, in the seventy and second year of his age, at Eton College; where, according to his Will, he now lies buried, with his motto on a plain Grave-stone over him: dying worthy of his name and family, worthy of the love and favour of so many Princes, and persons of eminent wisdom and learning, worthy of the trust committed unto him, for the service of his Prince and Country.
—WALTON, ISAAC, 1651, *The Life of Sir Henry Wotton.*

On the 15 July 1619, he returned from his Embassy at Venice with a vain hope

2A

of obtaining the office of Secretary of State, but missing his design, I cannot yet tell to the contrary but that he was sent to Venice again. ˙Sure 'tis, that about 1623 he had the Provostship of Eaton Coll. confer'd upon him, which he kept to his dying day, being all the reward he had for the great services he had done the Crown of England.—WOOD, ANTHONY, 1691–1721, *Athenæ Oxonienses, vol.* I, *f.* 623.

Sir Henry Wotton had the happiness to possess one of those rare characters in which it is difficult to say whether the useful or the agreeable was most to be observed. He was equally remarkable for a keen and sober sagacity, a brilliant wit, and a lively and jocose humour. He was not only a profound scholar, but well skilled also in all those elegant and delicate arts a just judgment in which has acquired since his time the appellation of taste. The severity of his studies, and the abstract forms of an academical life, had not prevented him from being one of the best bred men in England. . . . He lived beloved, respected, and admired; and descended into the grave with a character wholly unimpeached, and without leaving a single enemy.—LODGE, EDMUND, 1821–34, *Portraits of Illustrious Personages of Great Britain, vol.* IV, *p.* 27.

It appears to have been the peculiar privilege of sir Henry Wotton, and may be regarded by posterity as the most conclusive evidence of his merits, to have secured to himself through life, and amid all the vicissitudes of his fortune, the affection, the esteem and the cooperation of the master-spirits of the age in which he flourished.—AIKIN, LUCY, 1822, *Memoirs of the Court of King James the First, vol.* I.

Eton has never seen within her walls a more accomplished gentleman in the best sense of the word, or a more judicious ruler, than she received in 1625, when Sir Henry Wotton became her Provost.—CREASY, SIR EDWARD, 1850–75, *Memoirs of Eminent Etonians, p.* 100.

In the afternoons he had always a hospitable table, at which there was a perpetual succession of guests to keep up nice philosophic talk; and on these occasions two or three of the most hopeful pupils of the College were always present. His wit and his great store of reminiscences

made his own conversation delightful. He had seen or known intimately not only Essex, Raleigh, and the other Elizabethan statesmen, but also most of the great foreigners of the age—Beza, Casaubon, Guarini, Sarpi, Arminius, Kepler, and princes and artists without number. Bacon had not disdained to pick up anecdotes from his cousin Wotton, and even to register his apothegms; and, among Wotton's most interesting letters, is one to Bacon, thanking him for a gift of three copies of his "Organum," and promising to send one of them to Kepler. When any one within the circle of his acquaintance was going abroad, nothing pleased him better than to furnish the necessary advices and letters of introduction. One of his amusements in summer was angling; and Walton speaks of his delight when the month of May came and he could go out with his rod. . . . All in all, he deserved his reputation as one of the most accomplished and benevolent old gentlemen of his time; and it is pleasant yet to look at his portrait, representing him seated in his furred and embroidered gown, as Provost of Eton, leaning against a table, his head resting on his left hand, and his wise, kind face looking straight towards you, as if listening so courteously. —MASSON, DAVID, 1858, *The Life of John Milton, vol.* I, *ch.* vi.

He is the type of the successful all-round man, trying his hand at the education of boys. That one of the most distinguished diplomatists in his latter days should undertake the control of a school and the study of pedagogics, is an experiment little likely in our days or in the future to be repeated. If, therefore, the attempt, from the side of the accomplished gentleman, to become a schoolmaster has become impossible from the specialisation which now characterizes or is destined apparently to characterize teaching, it only remains for the schoolmasters to know their own work thoroughly, and to endeavour to approach Sir Henry Wotton by their grace of bearing, their culture, not only of learning, but of arts, of actions, of conversation, and of piety. He is accurately described as Sir Henry Wotton, Gentleman and Schoolmaster. Schoolmasters have before them still the desirability of the same combination. The circumstances of the age may demand the reversal of the order. Now it is school-master and gentleman. The combination is essential for high work, and no example would more pointedly illustrate this than that of Sir Henry Wotton.—WATSON, FOSTER, 1892, *Sir Henry Wotton: Gentle-man and Schoolmaster, The Gentleman's Magazine, vol.* 272, *p.* 289.

GENERAL

Sir Edward (Henry) Wotton's verses of a happie lyfe, he hath by heart.—DRUM-MOND, WILLIAM, 1619, *Notes on Ben Jon-son's Conversation.*

Though he was justly esteemed an ele-gant scholar, and an able critic, his works abound with exotic idioms; nor has he es-caped censure for his pedantry. But it should be considered that he wrote in an age, when, to write like a pedant, was to write like a gentleman; or, to speak more properly, like a king.—GRANGER, JAMES, 1769–1824, *Biographical History of England, vol.* III, *p.* 157.

The poetry of Wotton, though chiefly written for the amusement of his leisure, and through the excitement of casual cir-cumstances, possesses the invaluable at-tractions of energy, simplicity, and the most touching morality; it comes warm from the heart, and whether employed on an amatory or didactic subject, makes its appropriate impression with an air of sin-cerity which never fails to delight.—DRAKE, NATHAN, 1817, *Shakspeare and his Times, vol.* I, *p.* 672.

There is a vein of quiet self-respect running through this piece of profound and yet stately homage,—this distant and restrained adulation of a royal lady.* It is in no way unworthy of the man who, in his last years of peaceful retirement at his beautiful manor of Bocton, wrote that admirable hymn, happily never yet suf-fered to drop out of our memories and hymnals:—

"How happy is he born or taught,
  Who serveth not another's will," etc.
—PRESTON, HARRIET W., 1879, *The Latest Songs of Chivalry, Atlantic Monthly, vol.* 43, *p.* 18.

Of poetry he wrote but little; but of that little two pieces at least have ob-tained a permanent place in English liter-ature, his "Character of a Happy Life," written probably circ. 1614; and the lines,

*Queen of Bohemia.

"On his mistress the Queen of Bohemia," circ. 1620. Of the apophthegm "the style is of the man," it would be difficult to find better illustrations. As in a mirror, they reflect the high refined nature of one who, living in the world, and a master of its ways and courtesies, was yet never of it—was never a worldling.—HALES, JOHN W., 1880, *English Poets, ed. Ward, vol.* II, *p.* 108.

The spirit of "The State of Christen-dom" written shortly before the death of Queen Elizabeth, and the largest and most important of Wotton's extant prose writings, is that of a self-confident aggressiveness without *arrièrepensèes.*—WARD, ADOLPHUS WILLIAM, 1893, *English Prose, ed. Craik, vol.* II, *p.* 76.

The poem, ["Elizabeth of Bohemia,"] first appeared (with music), in 1624, in Michael Este's "Sixt Set of Bookes," etc.: was afterwards printed in "Wit's Recrea-tions," 1640, in "Wit's Interpreter," 1671, and in "Songs and Fancies to Sev-erall Musicall parts, both apt for Voices and Viols," Aberdeen, 1682. It also found its way, with variations, among Montrose's "Poems;" and Robert Cham-bers (ignorant of Wotton's claim to the authorship) printed it in his "Scottish Songs" as "written by Darnley in praise of the beauty of Queen Mary before their marriage." It has been a favourite mark for the second-rate imitator; and "addi-tional verses" are common. . . . "How happy is he born and taught." These lines were printed by Percy from the "Reliquiæ Wottonianæ:" believed to have been first printed in 1614. Ben Jonson admired and had them by heart, and in 1619 quoted them to Drummond as Wot-ton's. They are also said to be almost identical with a German poem of the same age. . . . Wotton may have seen the original in one of his several embassies to Germany on behalf of Elizabeth of Bohe-mia.—QUILLER-COUCH, A. T., 1894, *The Golden Pomp, pp.* 342, 358, *notes.*

Wotton was an amiable dilettante or literary amateur, with a growing inclina-tion to idleness in his later years. . . . Wotton's literary occupations at Eton led to little practical result. His history of England did not progress beyond the ac-cumulation of a few notes on the charac-ters of William I and Henry VI. . . . He contemplated a life of Martin Luther, but never began it, and he promised, shortly after Donne's death in 1631, to write a life of the dean as introduction to "Eighty Sermons" by Donne. The publication was delayed until Wotton's life should be ready. Wotton applied to Izaak Walton, whose acquaintance he had made through Donne, to collect materials, and Walton says that he "did but prepare them in a readiness to be augmented, and rectified by Wotton's powerful pen" (1640), but Wotton never worked upon Walton's draft, and Walton's biography of Donne alone survives. . . . Wotton's poems are the most valuable of his literary remains.—LEE, SIDNEY, 1900, *Dictionary of National Biography, vol.* LXIII, *pp.* 54, 56.

Thomas Carew

1589?–1639?

A poet of the reign of Charles I., descended from an old family in Gloucestershire, was born 1589. Having been educated at Oxford, he traveled abroad for some time, and on his return was received at court, and patronized by Charles I. Carew deserves mention chiefly as the precursor and representative of what may be called the courtier and conventional school of poetry, whose chief characteristic was scholarly ease and elegance, with a spice of indelicacy, and even indecency. Carew's poems, mostly lyrical, and treating of trifling subjects, are among the best of their kind, and exhibit much fancy and tenderness. He died 1639. Several editions of his poems, which first appeared in 1640, have been published.—PECK, HARRY THURSTON, ed., 1898, *The International Cyclopædia, vol.* III, *p.* 451.

PERSONAL

His glory was, that after fifty years of his life, spent with less severity or exactness than it ought to have been, he died with the greatest manifestations of Christianity, that his best friends could desire.—CLARENDON, LORD (EDWARD HYDE), 1674? *Life, p.* 9.

Then was told this by Mr. Anthony Faringdon, and have heard it discourst by others, that Mr. Thomas Cary, a poet of note, and a great libertine in his life and talke, and one that had in his youth bein acquainted with Mr. Ha., sent for Mr. Hales to come to him in a dangerous fit of sickness, and desired his advice and absolution, which Mr. Hales, upon a promise of amendment, gave him, (this was I think in the country). But Mr. Cary came to London, fell to his old company, and into a more visible scandalous life, and especially in his discourse, and be (being?) taken very sick, that which proved his last, and being much trowbled in mind, procured Mr. Ha. to come to him in this his sickness and agony of minde, desyring earnestly, after a confession of many of his sins, to have his prayers and his absolution. Mr. Ha. told him he shoold have his prayers, but woold by noe meanes give him then either the sacrament or absolution.—WALTON, ISAAC, 1683? *MSS. Collections for the Life of Hales, Fulman MSS., Corpus Christi* College, *Oxford; Notes and Queries, 2d Series, vol.* 6, *p.* 12.

He became reckon'd among the chiefest of his time for delicacy of wit and poetic fancy. About which time being taken into the Royal Court for his most admirable ingenuity, was made Gentleman of the Privy Chamber and Sewer in Ordinary to K. Ch. I. who always esteemed him to the last one of the most celebrated wits in his Court, and therefore by him as highly valued, so afterwards grieved at his untimely death. He was much respected, if not ador'd by the poets of his time, especially by Ben Johnson.—WOOD, ANTHONY, 1691–1721, *Athenæ Oxonienses, vol.* I, *f.* 630.

As an amatory poet, he is far superior to Waller: he had equal smoothness and fancy, and much more variety, tenderness, and earnestness; if his love was less ambitiously, and even less honourably placed, it was, at least, more deep seated, and far more fervent. The real name of the lady he has celebrated under the poetical appellation of Celia, is not known—it is only certain that she was no "fabled fair," —and that his love was repaid with falsehood.—JAMESON, ANNA BROWNELL, 1829, *The Loves of the Poets, vol.* II, *p.* 4.

The writings of Carew abound with conceits, but, unlike the conceits of some of his less noted contemporaries, they generally reconcile themselves to us by good taste in the treatment and delicacy of execution. We look back with changed feelings and different eyes upon these things; time has wrought a powerful alteration in the position before the world of old Sir Matthew Carew, the respectable and ill-fated Master in Chancery: his gallant son Sir Matthew, who was doubtless viewed as the hope and mainstay of the family: and the scapegrace youth to whom no one would have anything to say, and of whom his relatives despaired. For while the lives and fortunes of the high judicial functionary and the brave young knight-banneret are forgotten, while the persons of rank, fashion and influence with whom they mixed have passed, for the most part, completely away, and while even Sir Dudley Carleton is familiar only to a few antiquaries, the lustre which one man of genius has shed on the name of Carew remains unfaded, and can never decline.—HAZLITT, W. CAREW, 1870, ed., *The Poems of Thomas Carew, p.* xlviii.

There is an uncertainty about the time of Carew's death. It looks as if his life had been shortened by his irregular habits. When he was stricken down by mortal sickness, he sent for Hales of Eton to administer to him the consolations of religion. Hales seems to have thought very meanly of him, and made no secret of his low opinion. Carew has left some wretched attempts at versifying a few of the Psalms; these Mr. Hazlitt has printed. They have not a single merit. Carew probably died in 1639, but no entry of his burial has been found. The illness that led him to a maudlin kind of repentance seems to have come upon him when he was in the country. If he recovered enough from it to return to London, he probably died at his house in King Street, St. James's.—JESSOPP, AUGUSTUS, 1887, *Dictionary of National Biography, vol.* IX, *p.* 63.

GENERAL

Poems. | *By* | Thomas Carew | Esquire. | One of the Gentlemen of the | Privie-Chamber, and Sewer in | Ordinary to His Majesty. | London, | Printed by I. D. for *Thomas Walkley,* | and are to be sold at the signe of the | flying Horse, betweene Brittains | Burse, and York-House. | 1640.—TITLE PAGE OF FIRST EDITION.

Tom Carew was next, but he had a fault
That would not well stand with a laureat;
His muse was hide-bound, and the issue of 's brain
Was seldom brought forth but with trouble and pain.

And

All that were present there did agree,
A laureate muse should be easy and free,
Yet sure 'twas not that, but 'twas thought that, his grace
Considered, he was well he had a cup-bearer's place.

—SUCKLING, SIR JOHN, 1637, *A Sessions of the Poets.*

He was a person of a pleasant and facetious wit, and made many poems, especially in the amorous way, which, for the sharpness of the fancy, and the elegancy of the language in which that fancy was spread, were at least equal, if not superior to any of that time.—CLARENDON, LORD (EDWARD HYDE), 1674? *Life, p.* 9.

One of the famed poets of his time for the charming sweetness of his lyric odes and amorous sonnets. . . . By the strength of his curious fancy hath written many things which still maintain their fame amidst the curious of the present age.—WOOD, ANTHONY, 1691–1721, *Athenæ Oxonienses, vol.* I, *f.* 630.

This elegant and almost forgotten writer, whose poems have been deservedly revived.—PERCY, THOMAS, 1765, *Reliques of Ancient English Poetry.*

The consummate elegance of this gentleman entitles him to very considerable attention. Sprightly, polished, and perspicuous, every part of his works displays the man of sense, gallantry and breeding. Indeed, many of his productions have a certain happy finish, and betray a dexterity both of thought and expression much superior to any thing of his contemporaries, and (on similar subjects) rarely surpassed by his successors. Carew has the ease without the pedantry of Waller, and perhaps less conceit. He reminds us of the best manner of Lord Lyttelton. Waller is too exclusively considered as the first man who brought versification to any thing like its present standard. Carew's pretensions to the same merit are seldom sufficiently either considered or allowed. Though Love had long before softened us into civility, yet it was of a formal, ostentatious and romantic cast; and, with a very few exceptions, its effects on composition were similar to those on manners. Something more light, unaffected, and alluring was still wanting; in everything but sincerity of intention it (Poetry) was deficient. . . . Carew and Waller jointly began to remedy these defects. In them Gallantry, for the first time was accompanied by the Graces.—HEADLEY, HENRY, 1787, *Select Beauties of Ancient English Poetry, vol.* I.

The want of boldness and expansion in Carew's thoughts and subjects, excludes him from rivalship with *great* poetical names; nor is it difficult, even within the narrow pale of his works, to discover some faults of affectation, and of still more objectionable indelicacy. But among the poets who have walked in the same limited path, he is pre-eminently beautiful, and deservedly ranks among the earliest of those who gave a cultivated grace to our lyrical strains. His slowness in composition was evidently that sort of care in the poet, which saves trouble to his reader. His poems have touches of elegance and refinement, which their trifling subjects could not have yielded without a delicate and deliberate exercise of the fancy; and he unites the point and polish of later times with many of the genial and warm tints of the elder muse. Like Waller, he is by no means free from conceit; and one regrets to find him addressing the surgeon bleeding Celia, in order to tell him that the blood which he draws proceeds not from the fair one's arm, but from the lover's heart. But of such frigid thoughts he is more sparing than Waller; and his conceptions, compared to that poet's, are like fruits of a richer flavour, that have been cultured with the same assiduity.—CAMPBELL, THOMAS, 1819, *Specimens of the British Poets.*

Carew was an elegant court trifler.—HAZLITT, WILLIAM, 1820, *Lectures on the Literature of the Age of Elizabeth, p.* 192.

More of a poet than Corbet, and accounted the prince of the amorous versifiers of his day, was Thomas Carew. . . . There is a light French spirit in his love poems, a grace and even a tenderness of sentiment, and a lucid softness of style, that make them peculiarly pleasing and that, even when he becomes licentious, help to save him. . . . Spenser and Shakspeare seem to have been his favorites for private reading, and he seems to

have formed his style partly from them and partly from the light artificial French poets with whom he had become acquainted in his travels.—MASSON, DAVID, 1858, *The Life of John Milton, vol.* I, *ch.* vi.

No one touches dangerous themes with so light and glove-guarded a hand.—GILFILLAN, GEORGE, 1860, *Specimens of the Less-Known British Poets, vol.* I, *p.* 270.

In polish and evenness of movement, combined with a diction elevated indeed in its tone, as it must needs be by the very necessities of verse, above that of mere good conversation, but yet in ease, lucidity, and directness rivalling the language of ordinary life, Carew's poetry is not inferior to Waller's; and, while his expression is as correct and natural, and his numbers as harmonious, the music of his verse is richer, and his imagination is warmer and more florid. But the texture of his composition is in general extremely slight, the substance of most of his pieces consisting merely of the elaboration of some single idea; and, if he has more tenderness than Waller, he is far from having so much dignity, variety, or power of sustained effort.—CRAIK, GEORGE L., 1861, *A Compendious History of English Literature and of The English Language, vol.* II, *p.* 25.

Among the Royalist lyrists of the seventeenth century Carew takes a foremost place. In genius he is surpassed by Herrick only, and in age he is the first of that gallant band of cavalier song-writers of whom Rochester is the last. Born in the flush of the Elizabethan summer, when the whole garden of English poetry was ablaze with blossom, he lived to hand down to his followers a tradition of perfume and dainty form, that vivified the autumn of the century with a little Martin's summer of his own. . . . Carew was far too indolent to trouble himself with the rhetoric of the schools or to speculate upon the conduct of the mind. He loved wine, and roses, and fair florid women, to whom he could indite joyous or pensive poems about their beauty, adoring it while it lasted, regretting it when it faded. . . . The claim of Carew to a place among the artificers of our language must not be overlooked. In his hands English verse took a smooth and flexible character that had neither the splendours nor the discords of the great Elizabethan school, but formed an admirable medium for gentle thought and florid reverie. The praise that Voltaire gave to Waller might be transferred to Carew if it were not that to give such praise to any one writer is uncritical. But Waller might never have written, and the development of English verse would be still unbroken, whereas Carew is a necessary link between the Elizabethans and Prior. He represents the main stream of one of the great rivers of poetic influence proceeding from Ben Jonson, and he contrived to do so much because he remained so close to that master and yet in his particular vein excelled him.—GOSSE, EDMUND, 1880, *English Poets*, ed. Ward, vol. II, pp. 111, 112, 113.

He is one of the most perfect masters of lyrical form in English poetry. He possesses a command of the overlapped heroic couplet, which for sweep and rush of rhythm cannot be surpassed anywhere. He has, perhaps in a greater degree than any poet of that time of conceits, the knack of modulating the extravagances of fancy by the control of reason, so that he never falls into the unbelieveableness of Donne, or Crashaw, or Cleveland. He had a delicacy, when he chose to be delicate, which is quintessential, and a vigour which is thoroughly manly. Best of all, perhaps, he had the intelligence and the self-restraint to make all his poems wholes, and not mere congeries of verses. There is always, both in the scheme of his meaning and the scheme of his metre, a definite plan of rise and fall, a concerted effect. That these great merits were accompanied by not inconsiderable defects is true. Carew lacks the dewy freshness, the unstudied grace of Herrick. He is even more frankly and uncontrolledly sensual, and has paid the usual and inevitable penalty that his best poem, "The Rapture," is, for the most part, unquotable, while another, if he carried out its principles in this present year of grace, would run him the risk of imprisonment with hard labour. His largest attempt—the masque called "Cœlum Britannicum"—is heavy. His smaller poems, beautiful as they are, suffer somewhat from want of variety of subject. There is just so much truth in Suckling's impertinence that the reader of Carew sometimes catches himself repeating the lines of Carew's master,

"Still to be neat, still to be drest," not indeed in full agreement with them, but not in exact disagreement. One misses the "wild civility" of Herrick. This acknowledgment, I trust, will save me from any charge of overvaluing Carew.— SAINTSBURY, GEORGE, 1887, *History of Elizabethan Literature*, p. 360.

It was Carew, indeed, who first sounded these "courtly amorous strains" throughout the English land; who first taught his fellow-poets that to sing of love was not the occasional pastime, but the serious occupation of their lives. Yet what an easy, indolent suitor he is! What lazy raptures over Celia's eyes and lips! What finely poised compliments, delicate as rose leaves, and well fitted for the inconstant beauty who listened, with faint blushes and transient interest, to the song!—REPPLIER, AGNES, 1891, *English Love-Songs, Points of View*, p. 36.

Instead of Carew's poetry being characteristically euphuistic, licentious, trivial, and sporadic, the exact opposite is the truth. It is true that he has his concetti, like the other poets of his day, but they are relatively to the whole of his verse but a small proportion. . . . With a very slight deduction, his volume is good throughout. There are few pages on which one is not struck by something fine. Carew was an artist as well as a poet. If he in some slight degree misses the gay, artless charm of Suckling, he has a more serious attractiveness. There is a richness and dignity, likewise an intellectual force, in his verse which lifts him to the rank of a serious poet, and makes one regret that, with such natural gifts and artistic acquirements, he did not devote himself to poetry more continuously and of set purpose. For, to a considerable degree, he shared with Waller the gift of the stately line, and his verse has that body and glamour in which for the most part Waller's is deficient. There was indeed a drop of the ruddy Elizabethan blood in Carew.—LE GALLIENNE, RICHARD, 1894–95, *Retrospective Reviews*, vol. II, pp. 77, 79.

Carew has been unjustly condemned by Hazlitt as "an elegant Court trifler" in poetry. But it must be granted that he was a master of lyrical form, and that he had a rare sense of delicacy, which he combined too seldom with a manly glow and vigor of passion. He just misses being the equal of Herrick.—ROBERTSON, J. LOGIE, 1894, *A History of English Literature, p.* 106.

Carew's largest work was the masque, "Coelum Britannicum," with the production of which the court had tried, in 1634, to outrival the magnificance of the performance of Shirley's "Triumph of Peace" at the Inns of Court. It is of but slight literary interest, the words being subordinated to elaborate scenic effects. But Carew also wrote a small number of poems, almost all short, in the style of amorous addresses then coming into vogue; and it is on these that his claim to a high place among lyrical poets rests. They are polished with the utmost care, and are marked by a cultivated grace exceeding that of most, if not all, the lyrical poets of his time. They are also "reasonable," in a sense in which those of Donne or Crawshaw are not. . . . It is true that in Carew's verses there is little of Herrick's freshness and unstudied grace, but there is a self-restraint and balance that is almost, if not quite, an adequate compensation.—MASTERMAN, J. HOWARD B., 1897, *The Age of Milton, pp.* 95, 96.

John Spotiswood

1565–1639

John Spotswood (Spotiswood), Scotch prelate; born at Mid-Calder, near Edinburgh, 1565; died in London, Dec. 26, 1639. He was educated at Glasgow University, and succeeded his father as Parson at Calder, in 1583, when only eighteen. In 1601 he accompanied the Duke of Lennox as chaplain in his embassy to France, and in 1603 James VI. to England. In 1603 he was made Archbishop of Glasgow, and privy-councillor for Scotland. In 1615 he was transferred to St. Andrews, so that he became primate and metropolitan. On June 18, 1633, he crowned Charles I. at Holyrood. In 1635 he was made chancellor of Scotland. He was the leader in the movement to introduce the Liturgy into the church of Scotland, which occasioned the rebellion (1637). When the Covenant was signed (1638), he retired in disappointment to London. He wrote "The History of the Church and State of Scotland" (203-1625), London, 1655; best ed., Edinburgh, 1847-51, 3 vols., with life of the Author.— SCHAFF-HERZOG, 1883, *Encyclopœdia of Religious Knowledge, vol.* III, *p.* 2232.

PERSONAL

In prosperity his behaviour was without moderation, in adversity without dignity; but the character of a leading, aspiring prelate has either been unduly extolled, or unjustly degraded. As a scholar and an historian he excelled his contemporaries; and it was his peculiar felicity, that his erudition was neither infected with the pedantry, nor confined to the polemical disputes, of the age. His abilities recommended him first to preferment; but his ambitious views were chiefly promoted by the supple, insinuating habits of craft and intrigue. His revenge was formidable to the nobility and officers of state, oppressive to the clergy, and, joined with an inordinate ambition, ultimately ruinous to his own order. At an happier period, when no temptation was presented to his inordinate ambition, the same talents might have rendered him a distinguished ornament to that church, which his disregard of the gloomy decorum exacted by fanatics, was supposed to disgrace.— LAING, MALCOLM, 1800-4, *The History of Scotland, vol.* III, *p.* 154.

HISTORY OF SCOTLAND

Archbishop Spotiswoode was author of the "History of Scotland," a work compiled from scanty materials, but with great impartiality. There is throughout the whole an air of probity and candour, which was the peculiar character of the writer. This history was undertaken by the command of James I. who had a high opinion of the author's abilities. Upon expressing a diffidence to James about that part of it which relates to his mother, and which had been the stumbling-block of former historians, he replied, "Speak the truth, man, and spare not."— GRANGER, JAMES, 1769-1824, *Biographical History of England, vol.* II, *p.* 342.

Archbishop Spotswood's "Church History" was penned at the special command of K. James the Sixth; who, being told that some passages in it might possibly bear too hard upon the memory of his Majesty's mother, bid him "write the truth and spare not:" and yet he ventured not so far with a commission as Buchanan did without one.—NICOLSON, WILLIAM, 1696-1714, *Scottish Historical Library.*

Is considered to be, on the whole, a faithful and impartial narrative of the events of which it treats.—MILLS, ABRAHAM, 1851, *Literature and Literary Men of Great Britain and Ireland, vol.* I, *p.* 467.

It is an honest book, written by a strong upholder of Episcopacy.—MORLEY, HENRY, 1873, *A First Sketch of English Literature, p.* 566.

If he was a courtier, he had all the graces, and far more than the virtues, of the Court. It is natural to compare his work with that of Knox. Readers will declare for or against the sentiments of either according to their prepossessions.

In energy, in narrative power, and in the general impression of genius produced, the earlier writer must be pronounced by far the superior. Spottiswoode's merits are of a different order. His style is smooth, but seldom strikes any high note. There is no display of enthusiasm; the reader is rarely warmed into strong approval or censure; the tone is that of gentlemanly compromise or bland remonstrance. The really notable point about the book is the breadth of its charity. In this Christian virtue it must be acknowledged that the earlier Scottish Reformers were sadly deficient. Knox was most intolerant of opposition. Spottiswoode, in the whole of his "History," has not a bitter word for foe or friend, unless it be one about Andrew Melville, who had indeed been a sore thorn in His Grace's flesh.—DODDS, JAMES MILLER, 1893, *English Prose, ed. Craik, vol.* II, *p.* 68.

John Ford

Fl. 1639

Born at Ilsington, Devonshire, England, 1586 (baptized April 17): died after 1639. An English dramatist. Little is known of his life except that he was a member of the Middle Temple and not dependent on his pen for his living, and that he was popular with playgoers. He apparently retired to Ilsington to end his days. His principal plays are "The Lover's Melancholy" (printed 1629), "'Tis Pity She's a Whore" (1633), "The Broken Heart" (1633), "Love's Sacrifice" (1633), "The Chronicle History of Perkin Warbeck" (1634), "The Fancies Chaste and Noble" (1638), "The Lady's Trial" (1639), "The Sun's Darling" (with Dekker, 1656), "The Witch of Edmonton" (with Dekker, Rowley, etc., 1658). His works were collected by Weber in 1811, by Gifford in 1827, and by Dyce (Gifford) in 1869.—SMITH, BENJAMIN E., *ed.,* 1894–97, *The Century Cyclopedia of Names, p.* 400.

PERSONAL

A Gentleman of the *Middle-Temple,* who liv'd in the Reign of King *Charles* the First: Who was a Well-wisher to the Muses, and a Friend and Acquaintance of most of the Poets of his Time.—LANGBAINE, GERARD, 1691, *An Account of the English Dramatick Poets, p.* 219.

Of his social habits there little can be told with certainty. There is sufficient, however, to show that he lived, if not familiarly, yet friendlily, with the dramatic writers of his day, and neither provoked nor felt personal enmities. He speaks, indeed, of opposition; but this is merely the language of the stage; opposition is experienced by every dramatic writer worth criticism, and has nothing in common with ordinary hostility. In truth, with the exception of an allusion to the

"voluminous" and rancorous Prynne, nothing can be more general than his complaints. Yet Ford looked not much to the brighter side of life; he could, like Jaques, "suck melancholy out of a song as a weasel sucks eggs;" but he was unable, like this wonderful creation of our great poet, to extract mirth from it. When he touched a lighter string, the tones, though pleasingly modulated, were still sedate; and it must, I think, be admitted that his poetry is rather that of a placid and serene than of a happy mind: he was in truth, an amiable ascetic amidst a busy world.—GIFFORD, WILLIAM, 1827, *ed. Dramatic Works of John Ford, Introduction.*

He seems to have been a proud, reserved, austere kind of man, of few and warm attachments, with but slender gifts in the way of ebullient spirits or social flow. He was a barrister, with a respectable ancestry to look back to; and though he wrote several plays, and did not disdain to work in conjunction with such a professional playwright as Dekker, he was nervously anxious lest it should be supposed that he made his living by playwriting. In his first Prologue he spoke contemptuously of such as made poetry a trade, and he took more than one opportunity of protesting that his plays were the fruits of leisure, the issue of less serious hours. Some of his plays he dedicated to noblemen, but he was careful to assure them that it was not his habit to court greatness, and that his dedication was a simple offering of respect without mercenary motive.—MINTO, WILLIAM, 1874–85, *Characteristics of English Poets*, p. 360.

Ford drops from sight after the publication of the "Ladies Trial" in 1639; but in Gifford's time "faint traditions in the neighbourhood of his birth-place" led to the supposition that, having obtained a competency from his professional practice, he retired to Devonshire to end his days. In the "Time-Poets" ("Choice Drollery," 1656) occurs the couplet—

Deep in a dump John Forde was alone got,
With folded arms and melancholy hat.

—BULLEN, A. H., 1889, *Dictionary of National Biography, vol.* XIX, *p.* 421.

THE LOVER'S MELANCHOLY
1628–29

"The Lover's Melancholy; Contention of a Bird and a Musician."—This Story, which is originally to be met with in Strada's Prolusions, has been paraphrased in rhyme by Crashaw, Ambrose Philips, and others: but none of those versions can at all compare for harmony and grace with this blank verse of Ford's. It is as fine as anything in Beaumont and Fletcher; and almost equals the strife which it celebrates.—LAMB, CHARLES, 1808, *Specimens of Dramatic Poets.*

"The Lover's Melancholy" has been to almost all its critics a kind of lute-case for the very pretty version of Strada's fancy about the nightingale, which Crashaw did better; otherwise it is naught.—SAINTSBURY, GEORGE, 1887, *History of Elizabethan Literature, p.* 403.

Gifford rightly pronounces the comic portions of "The Lovers Melancholy" to be despicable; but it contains some choice poetry, notably the description (after Strada) of the contention between the nightingale and the musician.—BULLEN, A. H., 1889, *Dictionary of National Biography, vol.* XIX, *p.* 420.

'TIS PITY SHE'S A WHORE
1633

Thence to Salisbury Court play house, where was acted the first time "'Tis Pity She's a Whore," a simple play and ill acted, only it was my fortune to sit by a most pretty and most ingenious lady which pleased me much.—PEPYS, SAMUEL, 1661, *Diary, Sept.* 9.

All we can say in favour of Ford is, to wish he had employed his beautiful writing to a more laudable purpose.—DIBDIN, CHARLES, 1795, *A Complete History of the Stage, vol.* III, *p.* 280.

Ford was of the first order of poets. He sought for sublimity, not by parcels, in metaphors or visible images, but directly where she has her full residence in the heart of man; in the actions and sufferings of the greatest minds. There is a grandeur of the soul above mountains, seas, and the elements. Even in the poor perverted reason of Giovanni and Annabella, in the play which stands at the head of the modern collection of the works of this author, we discern traces of that fiery particle, which, in the irregular starting from out the road of beaten action, discovers something of a right line even in obliquity, and shows hints of an improvable greatness in the lowest descents and degradations of our nature.—LAMB, CHARLES, 1808, *Specimens of Dramatic Poets.*

It has been lamented that the play of his which has been most admired (" 'Tis Pity She's a Whore") had not a less exceptionable subject. I do not know, but I suspect that the exceptionableness of the subject is that which constitutes the chief merit of the play. The repulsiveness of the story is what gives it its critical interest; for it is a studiously prosaic statement of facts, and naked declaration of passions. It was not the least of Shakspeare's praise, that he never tampered with unfair subjects. His genius was above it; his taste kept aloof from it. I do not deny the power of simple painting and polished style in this tragedy in general, and of a great deal more in some few of the scenes, particularly in the quarrel between Annabella and her husband, which is wrought up to a pitch of demoniac scorn and phrensy with consummate art and knowledge; but I do not find much other power in the author (generally speaking) than that of playing with edged tools, and knowing the use of poisoned weapons.—HAZLITT, WILLIAM, 1820, *Lectures on the Literature of the Age of Elizabeth, p.* 136.

It is not easy to speak too favourably of the poetry of this play in the more impassioned passages; it is in truth too seductive for the subject, and flings a soft and soothing light over what in its natural state would glare with salutary and repulsive horror.—GIFFORD, WILLIAM, 1827, ed., *Dramatic Works of John Ford, Introduction.*

In spite of the harsh, affected, and offensive levity of the title, is Ford's masterpiece,—the play that justifies Mr. Swinburne's eloquent panegyric, and will always be most in the critic's mind in all attempts to fix Ford's place among the dramatists.—MINTO, WILLIAM, 1874–85, *Characteristics of English Poets, p.* 362.

It is somewhat unfortunate that the very title of Ford's masterpiece should sound so strangely in the ears of a generation "whose ears are the chastest part about them." For of these great twin tragedies the first-born is on the whole the greater. The subtleties and varieties of individual character do not usually lie well within the reach of Ford's handling; but in the part of Giovanni we find more of this power than elsewhere. Here the poet has put forth all his strength; the figure of his protagonist stands out complete and clear. There is more ease and life in it than in his other sculptures; though here as always Ford is rather a sculptor of character than a painter. But the completeness, the consistency of design is here all the worthier of remark, that we too often find this the most needful quality for a dramatist wanting in him as in other great writers of his time.—SWINBURNE, ALGERNON CHARLES, 1875, *John Ford, Essays and Studies, p.* 278.

Never has genius more miserably misused its gifts. If, as the title of "'Tis Pity She's a Whore" implies, this tragedy be intended to awaken a feeling akin to sympathy, or bordering upon it, on behalf of the heroine of its story of incest, the endeavour, so far as I can judge, fails in achieving the purpose insinuated. In truth, the dramatist's desire is to leave an impression far other and more perilous than that of a mere feeling of compassion for a fair sinner;—his purpose is to persuade us that passion is irresistible. But his efforts are vain, and so too is the sophistry of those who seek to explain away their chief force; for while recognising their charm, the soul revolts against the fatalism which, in spite of the Friar's preaching and Annabella's repentance, the sum-total of the action of this drama implies.—WARD, ADOLPHUS WILLIAM, 1875–99, *A History of English Dramatic Literature, vol.* III, *p.* 78.

English poets have given us the right key to the Italian temperament. . . . The love of Giovanni and Annabella in Ford's tragedy is rightly depicted as more imaginative than sensual.—SYMONDS, JOHN ADDINGTON, 1875, *Renaissance in Italy, vol.* I, *p.* 412.

The man who thus conceived the horrors of the Italian Renaissance in the spirit in which they were committed is Ford. In his great play he has caught the very tone of the Italian Renaissance: the abominableness of the play consisting not in the coarse slaughter scenes added merely to please the cockpit of an English theatre, but in the superficial innocence of tone; in its making evil lose its appearance of evil, even as it did to the men of the Renaissance.—LEE, VERNON, 1884, *Euphorion, vol.* I, *p.* 99.

After repeated readings and very careful weighings of what has been said, I come back to my first opinion—to wit, that the Annabella and Giovanni scenes, with all their perversity, all their availing themselves of what Hazlitt, with his unerring instinct, called "unfair attractions," are among the very best things of their kind. Of what may be thought unfair in them I shall speak a little later; but allowing for this, the sheer effects of passion—the "All for love and the world well lost," the shutting out, not instinctively or stupidly, but deliberately, and with full knowledge, of all other considerations except the dictates of desire— have never been so rendered in English except in "Romeo and Juliet" and "Antony and Cleopatra." The comparison of course brings out Ford's weakness, not merely in execution, but in design; not merely in accomplishment, but in the choice of means for accomplishment. Shakespere had no need of the *haut goût* of incest, of the unnatural horrors of the heart on the dagger. But Ford had; and he in a way (I do not say fully) justified his use of these means.—SAINTSBURY, GEORGE, 1887, *History of Elizabethan Literature, p.* 404.

Unlike most of his Elizabethan brethren, was ever a deliberate, cool, calculating literary workman, and while he is weaving this story of abnormal passion and investing it with all the grace and charm at his command, it is manifest that he is nowise carried away by the imaginative contemplation of it himself, but is all the while curiously studying the monstrous growth of his own diseased fancy in a cold anatomical fashion that rouses our moral repugnance in direct proportion as it excites our æsthetic admiration. He is always the craftsman, possessing a faculty of self-criticism rare among his compeers of that age.—WATSON, WILLIAM, 1893, *Excursions in Criticism, p.* 10.

Here Ford is at his best—and worst. He is the dramatist of passion—passion that neither inspires or ennobles; but drives on its victims with the awful force of irresistible destiny. Lost souls, struggling in the mælstrom of over-mastering fate, with no issue possible but self-destruction; and here and there a "despicable buffoon" to make coarse and insane jests—these are the elements of Ford's tragedy. The theme of the play is repulsive; it affords the most characteristic example of that straining after the fantastic and extraordinary, which marked the close of a literary period that seemed to have exhausted the simpler possibilities of tragedy.—MASTERMAN, J. HOWARD B., 1897, *The Age of Milton, p.* 81.

THE WITCH OF EDMONTON
1622?–58

It is very easy to sneer at the supernatural portions of this play . . . I consider creditable to the talents and feelings of both poets. I believe in witchcraft no more than the critics; neither, perhaps, did Ford and Decker, but they dealt with those who did; and we are less

concerned with the visionary creed of our forefathers than with the skill and dexterity of those who wrote in conformity to it, and the moral or ethical maxims which they enable us to draw from it. The serious part of this drama is sweetly written. The character of Susan is delineated in Ford's* happiest manner; pure, affectionate, confiding, faithful, and forgiving; anxious as a wife to prove her love, but fearful to offend, there is a mixture of warmth and pudency in her language, particularly in the concluding scene of the second act, which cannot fail to please the most fastidious reader. Winnifrede is only second to her unfortunate rival; for, though highly culpable before marriage, she redeems her character as a wife, and insensibly steals upon our pity and regard. Even Katherine with any other sister would not pass unnoticed.—GIFFORD, WILLIAM, 1827, *ed., Dramatic Works of John Ford.*

"The Witch of Edmonton" is a play of rare beauty and importance both on poetical and social grounds. It is perhaps the first protest of the stage against the horrors and brutalities of vulgar superstition; a protest all the more precious for the absolute faith in witchcraft and deviltry which goes hand in hand with compassion for the instruments as well as the victims of magic.—SWINBURNE, ALGERNON CHARLES, 1875, *John Ford, Essays and Studies, p.* 300.

This remarkable play . . . was when first published attributed to the joint authorship of Dekker, Ford, Rowley, "&c."—safety being evidently sought in numbers; but critical opinion has agreed in ascribing it in the main to Dekker and Ford. I confess at the same time that it is not obvious to me why the supposition should be excluded that William Rowley, whose literary identity seems to admit of so easy a treatment, had a substantial share in the play. In any case, there cannot be much likelihood of mistake in assuming Ford to have written at all events the earlier scenes, treating of the woes of Frank, Winnifrede and Susan. And assuredly the English drama includes very few domestic tragedies more harrowing than this play, of which its authors doubtless owed the immediate suggestion to a topic of the day, but which furnished

*(?)

Ford with an opportunity such as he would never have found by searching for it.— WARD, ADOLPHUS WILLIAM, 1875–99, *A History of English Dramatic Literature, vol.* III, *p.* 74.

THE SUN'S DARLING
1623–57

Is he, then, found? Phœbus, make holiday,
Tie up thy steeds, and let the Cyclops play;
Mulciber, leave thy anvil, and be trim,
Comb thy black muzzle, be no longer grim;
Mercury, be quick, with mirth furnish the
   heavens;
Jove, this day let all run at six and sevens;
And, Ganymede, be nimble, to the brim
Fill bowls of nectar, that the gods may swim,
To solemnise their healths that did discover
The obscure being of the Sun's fond lover;
That from th' example of their liberal mirth
We may enjoy like freedom (here) on earth.
—TATHAM, JOHN, 1640? *Upon the Sun's Darling.*

I know not on what authority Langbaine speaks, but he expressly attributes the greater part of this moral masque to Ford. As far as concerns the last two acts, I agree with him; and a long and clear examination of this poet's manner enables me to speak with some degree of confidence. But I trace Decker perpetually in the other three acts, and through the whole of the comic part. I think well of this poet, and should pause before I admitted the inferiority of his genius—as far, at least, as imagination is concerned—to that of Ford: but his rough vigour and his irregular metre generally enable us to mark the line between him and his more harmonious coadjutor. —GIFFORD, WILLIAM, 1827, *ed., Dramatic Works of John Ford.*

The greater part of the masque as we have it, or at all events the last two acts, have been thought attributable to Ford; but the ground is unsafe, the more so as the partial inconsistency of the allegory favours the notion of the work having been subjected to a revision. Much of the dialogue is very beautiful; the lyrics —in so far as they are original—seem to me less excellent.—WARD, ADOLPHUS WILLIAM, 1875–99, *A History of English Dramatic Literature, vol.* III, *p.* 75.

`THE BROKEN HEART
1633

I do not know where to find, in any play, a catastrophe so grand, so solemn,

and so surprising as in this. . . . What a noble thing is the soul in its strengths and its weaknesses! Who would be less weak than Calantha? Who can be so strong? The expression of this transcendent scene almost bears us in imagination to Calvary and the Cross; and we seem to perceive some analogy between the scenical sufferings which we are here contemplating, and the real agonies of that final completion to which we dare no more than hint a reference.—LAMB, CHARLES, 1808, *Specimens of Dramatic Poets.*

Except the last scene of the "Broken Heart" (which I think extravagant— others may think it sublime, and be right) they are merely exercises of style and effusions of wire-drawn sentiment.—HAZLITT, WILLIAM, 1820, *Lectures on the Literature of the Age of Elizabeth, p.* 137.

The "Broken Heart" has generally been reckoned his finest tragedy; and if the last act had been better prepared, by bringing the love of Calantha for Ithocles more fully before the reader in the earlier part of the play, there would be very few passages of deeper pathos in our dramatic literature.—HALLAM, HENRY, 1837–39, *Introduction to the Literature of Europe, pt.* iii, *ch.* vi, *par.* 97.

Ford can fill the ear and soul singly, with the trumpet-note of his pathos; and in its pauses you shall hear the murmuring voices of nature,—such a nightingale, for instance, as never sang on a common night. Then that death scene in the "Broken Heart!" who has equalled *that?* It is single in the drama,—the tragic of tragedy and the sublime of grief.— BROWNING, ELIZABETH BARRETT, 1842–63, *The Book of the Poets.*

Even in that single play of Ford's which comes nearest to the true pathetic, "The Broken Heart," there is too much apparent artifice, and Charles Lamb's comment on its closing scene is worth more than all Ford ever wrote. But a critic must look at it *minus* Charles Lamb. We may read as much of ourselves into a great poet as we will; we shall never cancel our debt to him. In the interests of true literature we should not honor fraudulent drafts upon our imagination.—LOWELL, JAMES RUSSELL, 1887–92, *Massinger and Ford, The Old English Dramatists, ed. Norton, p.* 129.

LOVE'S SACRIFICE
1633

Unto this altar, rich with thy own spice,
I bring one grain to thy "Love's Sacrifice;"
And boast to see thy flames ascending, while
Perfumes enrich our air from thy sweet pile.
Look here, thou that hast malice to the stage,
And impudence enough for the whole age;
Voluminously-ignorant, be vext
To read this tragedy, and thy own be next.
—SHIRLEY, JAMES, 1633? *To my Friend,
Master John Ford.*

Thou cheat'st us, Ford; mak'st one seem two
    by art:
What is Love's Sacrifice but the Broken
    Heart?
—CRASHAW, RICHARD, 1646, *The Delights
of the Muses.*

From the "high-tuned poem,"* as he
justly calls it, which he had here put
forth in evidence of his higher and purer
part of power, the fall, or collapse rather,
in his next work was singular enough. I
trust that I shall not be liable to any
charge of Puritan prudery though I avow
that this play of "Love's Sacrifice" is
to me intolerable. In the literal and
genuine sense of the word, it is utterly
indecent, unseemly and unfit for handling.
The conception is essentially foul because
it is essentially false; and in the sight of
art nothing is so foul as falsehood.—
SWINBURNE, ALGERNON CHARLES, 1875,
John Ford, Essays and Studies, p. 287.

Its theme is a tissue of passion and
revenge, into which too many coarse
threads are allowed to enter. . . .
The dramatist has drawn so wavering a
line between sin and self-restraint, guilt
and innocence, that he may be suspected
of having wished to leave unsettled the
"problem" which he proposes. If so, he
stands from every point of view self-con-
demned. The bye-plot of the play is
utterly revolting, and in the character of
d'Avolos, and the passages in which he
excites the jealousy of the Duke against
Fernando, Ford has most palpably copied
Iago.—WARD, ADOLPHUS WILLIAM, 1875-
99, *A History of English Dramatic Literature, vol.* III, *p.* 82.

PERKIN WARBECK
1634

It is indeed the best specimen of the
historic drama to be found out of Shakspeare; and, as a compact consecutive

* "The Broken Heart."

representation of a portion of English
history, excels King John or the two Parts
of Henry IV. It has as much unity as the
dramatic history admits or requires; a
clearly defined catastrophe, to which every
incident contributes, and every scene advances. Ford showed great judgment in
selecting a manageable episode of history,
instead of a reign or a "life and death,"
which no one but Shakspeare could ever
make practicable.—COLERIDGE, HARTLEY,
1840, *The Dramatic Works of Massinger
and Ford, Introduction, p.* lviii.

As the last attempt at historical drama
it suffers by contrast with the masterpieces of Shakespeare, but its merits are
considerable, and entirely different from
those of Ford's other works. The tragedy
is founded on Bacon's "Life of Henry the
Seventh," and the character of the monarch is developed with skill and discretion.
The play, interesting, dignified and occasionally humorous, seems to indicate
that Ford's genius was capable of a wider
range than his prevailing melancholy
allowed. We doubt, indeed, whether more
to wonder that he should have written
one such play, or that, having written one,
he should have written no more.—MASTER-
MAN, J. HOWARD B., 1897, *The Age of
Milton, p.* 82.

GENERAL

The author has not much of the oratorical stateliness and imposing flow of
Massinger; nor a great deal of the smooth
and flexible diction, the wandering fancy,
and romantic sweetness of Beaumont and
Fletcher; and yet he comes nearer to these
qualities than to any of the distinguishing characteristics of Jonson or Shakespeare. He excels most in representing
the pride and gallantry, and high-toned
honour of youth, and the enchanting softness, or the mild and graceful magnanimity of female character. There is a
certain melancholy air about his most
striking representations; and, in the
tender and afflicting pathetic, he appears
to us occasionally to be second only to
him who has never yet had an equal. The
greater part of every play, however, is
bad; and there is not one which does not
contain faults sufficient to justify the
derision even of those who are incapable
of comprehending its contrasted beauties.
The diction we think for the most part
beautiful, and worthy of the inspired age

which produced it.—JEFFREY, FRANCIS, 1811–44, *Contributions to the Edinburgh Review, vol.* II, *p.* 301.

Ford possesses nothing of the energy and majesty of Massinger, and but little of the playful gaiety and picturesque fancy of Fletcher, yet scarcely Shakspeare himself has exceeded him in the excitement of pathetic emotion. Of this, his two Tragedies of "'Tis Pity She's a Whore," and the "Broken Heart," bear the most overpowering testimony. Though too much loaded in their fable with a wildness and horror often felt as repulsive, they are noble specimens of dramatic genius; and who that has a heart to feel, or an eye to weep, can, in the first of these productions, view even the unhallowed loves of Giovanni and Annabella; or in the second, the hapless and unmerited fates of Calantha and Penthea, with a cheek unbathed in tears!—DRAKE, NATHAN, 1817, *Shakspeare and His Times, vol.* II, *p.* 563.

He has no great body of poetry, and has interested us in no other passion except that of love; but in that he displays a peculiar depth and delicacy of romantic feeling.—CAMPBELL, THOMAS, 1819, *An Essay on English Poetry.*

Ford is not so great a favorite with me as with some others, from whose judgment I dissent with diffidence.—HAZLITT, WILLIAM, 1820, *Lectures on the Literature of the Age of Elizabeth, p.* 135.

I know few things more difficult to account for than the deep and lasting impression made by the more tragic portions of Ford's poetry. Whence does it derive that resistless power which all confess, of afflicting, I had almost said harassing, the better feelings? It is not from any peculiar beauty of language,—for in this he is equalled by his contemporaries, and by some of them surpassed; nor is it from any classical or mythological allusions happily recollected and skilfully applied,—for of these he seldom avails himself: it is not from any picturesque views presented to the mind,—for of imaginative poetry he has little or nothing; he cannot conjure up a succession of images, whether grave or gay, to flit across the fancy or play in the eye. Yet it is hardly possible to peruse his passionate scenes without the most painful interest, the most heart-thrilling delight. This can only arise—at least I can conceive nothing else adequate to the excitement of such sensations—from the overwhelming efficacy of intense thought devoted to the embodying of conceptions adapted to the awful situations in which he has, imperceptibly and with matchless felicity, placed his principal characters.—GIFFORD, WILLIAM, 1827, *ed., Dramatic Works of John Ford, Introduction.*

Ford, with none of the moral beauty and elevation of Massinger, has, in a much higher degree, the power over tears: we smypathize even with his vicious characters, with Giovanni and Annabella and Bianca. Love, and love in guilt or sorrow, is almost exclusively the emotion he portrays: no heroic passion, no sober dignity, will be found in his tragedies. But he conducts his stories well and without confusion; his scenes are often highly wrought and effective; his characters, with no striking novelty, are well supported; he is seldom extravagant or regardless of probability.—HALLAM, HENRY, 1837–39, *Introduction to the Literature of Europe, pt.* iii, *ch.* vi, *par.* 97.

It would be unfair . . . to conclude that he delighted in the contemplation of vice and misery as vice and misery. He delighted in the sensation of intellectual power, he found himself strong in the imagination of crime and of agony; his moral sense was gratified by indignation at the dark possibilities of sin, by compassion for rare extremes of suffering. He abhorred vice—he admired virtue; but ordinary vice or modern virtue were, to him, as light wine to a dram drinker. His genius was a telescope, ill-adapted for neighbouring objects, but powerful to bring within the sphere of vision, what nature has wisely placed at an unsociable distance. Passion must be incestuous or adulterous; grief must be something more than martyrdom, before he could make them big enough to be seen. Unquestionably he displayed great *power* in these horrors, which was all he desired; but had he been "of the first order of poets," he would have found and displayed superior power in "familiar matter of to-day," in failings to which all are liable, virtues which all may practise, and sorrows for which all may be the better.—COLERIDGE, HARTLEY, 1840, *The Dramatic Works of Massinger and Ford, Introduction, p.* lviii.

His most splendid successes are in the handling of subjects which are, in themselves, unwritten tragedies—the deepest distresses of the heart and the terrible aberrations of the passions. His works make a sad, deep, and abiding impression on the mind, though hardly one that is pleasing or healthy. He had little of that stalwart strength of mind, and heedless daring, which characterize the earlier dramatists.—WHIPPLE, EDWIN P., 1846, *Old English Dramatists, Essays and Reviews, vol.* II, *p.* 70.

In fulness and fine equability Ford was far below Massinger; but in intensity, in the power of making an audience miserable and moving them to tears, he was thought to excel him. Indeed the reputation of lugubriousness had attached itself to him personally.—MASSON, DAVID, 1858, *The Life of John Milton, vol.* I, *ch.* vi.

By Ford, incidents of the most revolting kind are laid down as the foundation of his plots, upon which he wastes a pathos and tenderness deeper than is elsewhere found in the drama.—BOTTA, ANNE C. LYNCH, 1860–84, *Hand-Book of Universal Literature, p.* 481.

Ford's blank verse is not so imposing as Massinger's; but it has often a delicate beauty, sometimes a warbling wildness and richness, beyond anything in Massinger's fuller swell.—CRAIK, GEORGE L., 1861, *A Compendious History of English Literature and of The English Language, vol.* I, *p.* 606.

He would not seem to have looked at his plays from the point of view of his audience, or to have exerted himself to stir their interest or to keep it from flagging. There is a certain haughtiness of touch even in his language; sometimes a repudiation of emphasis, as if he did not care to be impressive on a slight occasion; sometimes a wilful abstruseness, as if it mattered nothing though his words were misunderstood. This alone is often the cause of considerable reaches of dull dialogue—dull, that is to say, for the purposes of the stage.—MINTO, WILLIAM, 1874–85, *Characteristics of English Poets, p.* 361.

He stands apart among his fellows, without master or follower; he has learnt little from Shakespeare or Marlowe, Jonson or Fletcher. . . . The poetry of Ford is no branch or arm of that illimitable sea; it might rather be likened to a mountain lake shut in by solitary highlands, without visible outlet or inlet, seen fitlier by starlight than by sunlight; much such an one as the Lac de Gaube above Cauterets, steel-blue and sombre, with a strange attraction for the swimmer in its cold smooth reticence and breathless calm. For nothing is more noticeable in this poet than the passionless reason and equable tone of style with which in his greatest works he treats of the deepest and most fiery passions, the quiet eye with which he searches out the darkest issues of emotion, the quiet hand with which he notes them down. At all times his verse is even and regular, accurate and composed; never specially flexible or melodious, always admirable for precision, vigour, and purity. . . . No poet is less forgetable than Ford; none fastens (as it were) the fangs of his genius and his will more deeply in your memory. You cannot shake hands with him and pass by; you cannot fall in with him and out again at pleasure; if he touch you once he takes you, and what he takes he keeps his hold of; his work becomes part of your thought and parcel of your spiritual furniture for ever; he signs himself upon you as with a seal of deliberate and decisive power. His force is never the force of accident; the casual divinity of beauty which falls as though direct from heaven upon stray lines and phrases of some poets falls never by any such heavenly chance on his; his strength of impulse is matched by his strength of will; he never works more by instinct than by resolution. . . . By the might of a great will seconded by the force of a great hand he won the place he holds against all odds of rivalry in a race of rival giants. In that gallery of monumental men and mighty memories, among or above the fellows of his godlike craft, the high figure of Ford stands steadily erect; his name is ineffaceable from the scroll of our great writers; it is one of the loftier landmarks of English poetry.—SWINBURNE, ALGERNON CHARLES, 1875, *John Ford, Essays and Studies, pp.* 276, 277, 312.

He carried to an extreme the tendency of the drama to unnatural and horrible subjects, but he did so with very great power. He has no comic humour, but no man has described better the worn and tortured human heart.—Brooke, Stopford, 1876, *English Literature Primer*, p. 92.

What Ford especially imitated from Greene was the art of writing romantic tales with plenty of adventures, unexpected meetings and discoveries, much love, and improbabilities enough to enchant Elizabethan readers and sell the book up to any number of editions. In this he rivalled his model very successfully, and his romances were among the most popular of the time of Shakespeare. The number of their editions was extraordinary, and they were renewed at almost regular intervals up to the eighteenth century; there was a far greater demand for them than for any play of Shakespeare.—Jusserand, J. J., 1890, *The English Novel in the Time of Shakespeare*, p. 193.

He, too, was borne down by enslavement to the red splendors of crime; his very titles carry such foretaste of foulness we do not name them. There are bloody horrors and moral ones. Few read him for love. Murder makes room for incest, and incest sharpens knives for murder. Animal passions run riot; the riot is often splendid, but never—to my mind—making head in such grand dramatic utterance as crowns the gory numbers of Webster. There are strong passages, indeed, gleaming out of the red riotings like blades of steel; now and then some fine touch of pathos—of quiet contemplative brooding—lying amid the fiery wrack, like a violet on banks drenched with turbid floods; but they are rare, and do not compensate—at least do not compensate me—for the wadings through bloody, foul quagmires to reach them.—Mitchell, Donald G., 1890, *English Lands Letters and Kings, From Elizabeth to Anne*, p. 91.

In reading him again after a long interval, with elements of wider comparison, and provided with more trustworthy tests, I find that the greater part of what I once took on trust as precious is really paste and pinchbeck. His plays seem to me now to be chiefly remarkable for that filigree-work of sentiment which we call sentimentality. The word "alchemy" once had a double meaning. It was used to signify both the process by which lead could be transmuted into gold, and the alloy of baser metal by which gold could be adulterated without losing so much of its specious semblance as to be readily detected. The ring of the true metal can be partially imitated, and for a while its glow, but the counterfeit grows duller as the genuine grows brighter with wear. The greater poets have found out the ennobling secret, the lesser ones the trick of falsification. Ford seems to me to have been a master in it. He abounds especially in mock pathos. I remember when he thoroughly imposed on me.—Lowell, James Russell, 1892, *Massinger and Ford, The Old English Dramatists, ed. Norton*, p. 128.

In the delineation of the strongest human passions—love, grief, revenge—Ford is without a peer among the later Elizabethan dramatists. He seeks, in own words, to

"Sing out a lamentable tale of things,
Done long ago, and ill done; and when sighs
Are wearied, piece up what remains behind
With weeping eyes and hearts that bleed to death."

He has no dramatic reserve, and shrinks from no touch of horror that can add intensity to the situation. It is in this that his want of due restraint betrays itself. A sane and healthy mind revolts instinctively from such scenes as that in which the reaking heart of Annabella is borne into the banquet-hall on the dagger of Giovanni; they awaken neither pity nor indignation, nor that purifying rest in accompished purpose, which is the highest end of tragedy. We are first stunned, then repelled, by the morbid fatalism of his greatest tragedies; they are like the hospital-museums where human deformities and distortions are catalogued and exhibited, and from which we long to escape into the fresh air and sunshine.—Masterman, J. Howard B., 1897, *The Age of Milton*, p. 83.

Last of all, in a final brief blaze of the sinking embers, we encounter John Ford, perhaps as genuine a tragic poet as any one of his forerunners, Shakespeare alone excepted, reverting for a moment to the old splendid diction, the haughty disregard of convention, the contempt for ethical restrictions. And so the brief and magnificent school of English drama, begun by Marlowe scarcely more than a generation before, having blazed and crackled like a forest fire fed with resinous branches, sinks almost in a moment, and lingers only as a heap of white ash and glowing charcoal.—GOSSE, EDMUND, 1897, *Short History of Modern English Literature, p.* 138.

Sir William Alexander
Earl of Stirling
1567?–1640

William Alexander, Earl of Sterling minor Scottish poet, born about 1567 at Menstrie House, Alva, studied at Glasgow and Leyden, travelled in France, Spain, and Italy, and published his "Tragedie of Darius" (1603), "Aurora" (sonnets, 1604), "Crœsus" (1604), "The Alexandræan" (1605), and "Julius Cæsar" (1607). He was knighted by 1609; in 1613 was attached to the household of Prince Charles; in 1614 was made Master of Requests for Scotland, and published part i. of his huge poem "Doomesday" (part ii. 1637). He received in 1621 the grant of "Nova Scotia" a vast tract in Canada and what now is United States; in 1631 he was made sole printer of King James's version of the Psalms. From 1626 till his death he was the (unpopular) Secretary of State for Scotland; and in 1627-31 he was also made Keeper of the Signet, a Commissioner of Exchequer, and a Judge of the Court of Session. The French pushed their conquests in America, and Alexander's grant of lands became valueless. In 1630 he was created Viscount and in 1633 Earl of Stirling, in 1639 also Earl of Dovan, but he died insolvent in London, 12th September 1640.—PATRICK AND GROOME, 1897, *ed., Chambers's Biographical Dictionary, p.* 885.

PERSONAL

As to my long stay in these parts, ye shall impute it [rather] to so sociable a company, from whom I am even loth to depart, than to a wilful neglect of promised coming to you. Fortune this last day was so favourable as by plain blindness to acquaint me with that most excellent spirit and rarest gem of our North, S. W. A. [Sir William Alexander]; for, coming near his house, I had almost been a Christian father to one of his children. He accepted me so kindly, and made me so good an entertainment (which, whatsomever, with him I could not have thought but good), that I cannot well show. Tables removed, after Homer's fashion well satiate, he honoured me so much as to show me his books and papers. This much I will say, and perchance not without reason dare say: he hath done more in one *day* than Tasso did all his *life* and Bartas in his two *weeks*, though both one and the other be most praiseworthy. I esteemed of him, before I was acquaint with him, because of his works; but I protest henceforth I will esteem of his works because of his own good, courteous, meek disposition. He entreated me to have made longer stay; and, believe me, I was as sorry to depart as a new enamoured lover would be from his mistress.—DRUMMOND, WILLIAM, 1614, *Letter, Life by Masson, p.* 41.

So Scotland sent us hither for our own
That man whose name I ever would have known
To stand by mine, that most ingenious knight,
My Alexander, to whom in his right
I want extremely, yet in speaking thus
I do but show the love that was 'twixt us,
And not his numbers, which were brave and high,
So like his mind was his clear poesie.
—DRAYTON, MICHAEL, c 1627, *Of Poets and Poesie.*

The purity of this gentleman's vein was quite spoiled by the corruptness of his courtiership; and so much the greater pity; for by all appearance, had he been contented with that mediocrity of fortune he was born unto, and not aspired to those grandeurs of the court, which could not without pride be prosecuted, nor maintained without covetousness, he might have made a far better account of himself. It did not satisfie his ambition to have a laurel from the Muses, and to be esteemed a king amongst poets, but he must be king of some new-found-land; and, like another Alexander indeed, searching after new worlds, have the sovaraignty of Nova Scotia.—URQUHART, SIR THOMAS, 1652, Σκκνβαλαυρον: *or, the Discovery of a most exquisite Jewel, p.* 207.

So this the end of our long acquaintance with Alexander of Menstrie. On the whole, we must pronounce him about the most unfortunate Scot of his time. Better for his memory had he died long ago, when he was still only Alexander of Menstrie, or at least no more than that Sir William Alexander, "the rarest gem of our north," with whom it had been such a delight to Drummond to have that first meeting in the Clackmannanshire mansion in 1614, when they revelled over books and papers, and became Damon and Alexis to each other. What had all the intermediate courtiership and climbing, with the Scottish Secretaryship, the Novia Scotia Charter, the Viscountcy, the Earldom, the splendid new family edifice at Stirling, been really worth? It had been all *per metre, per turners,* all by a dirty application of talent, all at the expense of the growing hatred of his countrymen at every step, and, what was worst, with no such countervailing consciousness of right, nor even such iron wilfulness in wrong, as have borne up better or stronger men through that form of calamity. If the hatred had lessened at the end, it had only been because much of it had been turned into contemptuous pity. Broken down by the loss of two of his sons, deep in debt, and with the future of his family overclouded, he had persevered through the First Bishop's War in the routine of his fatal Secretaryship, to become a kind of underling at last of Hamilton and Traquair in arranging the new onslaught on Scotland which the King had decreed. That was his final appearance in the world. All that one sees more is the ship toiling along the eastern coast with the leaden coffin in her hold, and the farther conveyance of the same up the windings of the Forth, to be laid, at dead of night, beside the other coffins in the vault in Stirling Church. There he lies, I suppose, to this day, vaguely remembered as the second-rate Scottish sycophant of an inglorious despotism, and the author of a larger quantity of fluent and stately English verse which no one reads.—MASSON, DAVID, 1873, *Drummond of Hawthornden, p. 328.*

GENERAL

Thy Phœnix-Muse still wing'd with wonders flyes,
Praise of our brookes, staine to old Pindus' springs,
And who thee follow would, scarce with their eyes
Can reach the sphere where thou most sweetly sings.

Though string'd with starres heavens Orpheus' harpe enrolle,
More worthy thine to blaze about the Pole.
—DRUMMOND, WILLIAM, 1614, *To Sir William Alexander, Verses Prefixed to Doomesday.*

The Occasion of his being mention'd in our Catalogue, is, from "four Monarchick Tragedies," (as he stiles them,) which are in print under his Name, *viz.* "The Alexandræan Tragedy," "Crœsus," "Darius," and "Julius Cæsar." These Plays seem to be writ with great Judgment, and (if I mistake not) the Author has propos'd the Ancients, for his Pattern; by bringing in the *Chorus* between the Acts. They are grave, and sententious, throughout, like the Tragedies of *Seneca;* and yet where the softer, and more tender Passions are touch't, they seem as moving, as the Plays so much in vogue with the Ladies of this Age. The greatest objection that I know against them, is the Choice the Author has made of his Verse, which is alternate, like the *Quatrains* of the French Poet *Pibrach;* or Sr. *William Davenant's* Heroick Poem, call'd "Gondibert."—LANGBAINE, GERARD, 1691, *An Account of the English Dramatick Poets.*

Enjoyed a higher reputation than Drummond in his time. His monarchical tragedies are full of ostentatious morality, diffused through smooth, rhetorical stanzas, without a single spark of celestial fire.—LAING, MALCOLM, 1800-4, *The History of Scotland, vol.* III, *p.* 477.

Wrote some very heavy tragedies; but there is elegance of expression in a few of his shorter pieces.—CAMPBELL, THOMAS, 1819, *Specimens of the British Poets.*

He is rather the poet of sentiment than of imagination: his works are less frequently distinguished by bold flights of fancy, than by a philosophical vein of reflection; but he often displays considerable vigour of conception, and expresses his thoughts with suitable force and dignity. The Earl of Orford has characterized him as a poet "greatly superior to the age;" and if we compare him with such writers as Donne and Cowley, he certainly appears to no small advantage. His style, though not entirely free from Scoticisms, and from harsh combinations, is frequently conspicuous for its nervous simplicity.—IRVING, DAVID, 1861, *History of Scotish Poetry, ed. Carlyle, p.* 522.

The chief literary beauties of these plays consist in their lyrical passages, which however are unequal in excellence, and weary by the sameness of their themes. The cadence of the quatrains which build up the dialogue is frequently pleasing, and its turns are often felicitous; but the general effect remains that of a volume of speech extremely prolix, and marred by affectations of style as well as by defects of construction and by occasional lapses into baldness of expression. The aid of antithesis and of alliteration is frequently called in, without any signal advantage being gained in the way of variety of effect. Elevated in tone, and often vigorous as well as dignified in sentiment, and manifesting the operation of an observing mind together with the influence of a carefully trained taste, these tragedies retain no interest for anybody but the literary student, whom alone they can be supposed to have been originally intended to please.—WARD, ADOLPHUS WILLIAM, 1875–99, *A History of English Dramatic Literature, vol.* II, *p.* 625.

Broadly, his poems are weighty with thought after the type of Fulk Greville, Lord Brooke, though scarcely so obscure as his. His tragedies have "brave translunary things," if laboured and dull as a whole. His "Avrora" and minor pieces are elegant and musical. There is less of conceit in the merely conceitful sense than was common with contemporaries, and if you only persevere, opalescent hues edge long passages otherwise comparable with mist and fog. As a man he grows in our regard the nearer one gets at the facts. Manlier speech never was addressed to kings than by him in his "Parænesis" and "Tragedies" and elsewhere. His "noble poverty" is the best vindication of his integrity. He stands above any contemporary Scot, alike in many-sidedness and strenuousness of character. —GROSART, A. B., 1885, *Dictionary of National Biography, vol.* I, *p.* 280.

Alexander had indeed more power of sustained versification than his friend Drummond, though he hardly touches the latter in point of the poetical merit of short isolated passages and poems.— SAINTSBURY, GEORGE, 1887, *History of Elizabethan Literature, p.* 311.

The sonnets never reach a high level. They betray in numerous ingenuities of fancy and expression the "conceitie braine," and have all the artificiality and more than all the monotony to be looked for in so long a series devoted to the praises of a mistress and lamentations of her cruelty. . . . The "Monarchicke Tragedies" are of all dramas the least dramatic. They are slow in movement, full of repetitions, destitute of living human characters, unfit alike for the stage and the study. Little or nothing is given as enacted; there is not even vigorous and progressive narrative, but, instead, windy commonplace reflections. . . . They stand apart from the true Elizabethan play with its abounding life, its vigorous action, its fulness of present interest. As little, perhaps even less, have they any vital relation to the classical drama. . . . If Alexander suggests anybody in the annals of dramatic composition it is Lorde Brooke; and that because of common defects rather than common merits. The works of both are equally preposterous as plays; but Alexander's have not the power and weight of thought which half redeems Lord Brooke's tragedies. . . . "Parænesis to Prince Henry," a poem of considerable length on the duties of a king. It has been extravagantly praised; but the grounds of the panegyric are hard to discover. There is evidence of considerable learning, of keen intelligence, and on the whole of more independence of mind than was to be expected from a courtier in the court of James. . . . "Doomesday," which in length almost rivals the other works of its author collectively and in dreariness, surpasses all.—WALKER, HUGH, 1893, *Three Centuries of Scottish Literature, vol.* I, *pp.* 135, 136, 137, 138.

An undue neglect has hitherto been Alexander's fortune at the hands of literary appraisers. For this the great extent of his writings is largely to blame, hiding the grains of gold in an earthen bed. But the insight, wisdom, and independent spirit, apart from the frequent beauties of his work, must always make even his longest poems worth perusal, and among the monuments of his time and of Scotland a niche of high honour of his own must remain to the Earl of Stirling as distinctively the poet-counsellor of kings.— EYRE-TODD, GEORGE, 1895, *Scottish Poetry of the Seventeenth Century, p.* 74.

Robert Burton

1577-1640

Robert Burton, author of the "Anatomy of Melancholy," was born at Lindley, Leicestershire, on the 8th February 1576. He attended the grammar schools of Nuneaton and Sutton Coldfields, and at the age of seventeen entered Brasenose College, Oxford. In 1599 he was elected student of Christ Church, and in 1614 took the degree of B. D. In 1616 he was presented to the vicarage of St. Thomas, and in 1636 to the rectory of Segrave. He died on the 25th of January 1639-40. "The Anatomy of Melancholy, what it is, with all the kinds, causes, symptoms, prognostics, and several cures of it: In three partitions, with their several sections, members, and sub-sections, philosophically, medicinally, historically opened and cut up: By Democritus Junior, with a satyrical preface conducing to the following discourse," was published in 1621. Our information with regard to the strange author of this strange book is very scanty.—BAYNES, THOMAS SPENCER, 1875, ed., Encyclopædia Britannica, Ninth ed., vol. IV, p. 571.

PERSONAL

He was an exact mathematician, a curious calculator of nativities, a general read scholar, a thoro'-pac'd philologist, and one that understood the surveying of lands well. As he was by many accounted a severe student, a devourer of authors, a melancholy and humorous person; so by others, who knew him well, a person of great honesty, plain dealing and charity. I have heard some of the ancients of Ch. Ch. often say that his company was very merry, facete and juvenile, and no man in his time did surpass him for his ready and dexterous interlarding his common discourses among them with verses from the poets or sentences from classical authors. Which being then all the fashion in the university, made his company more acceptable. . . . He the said R. Burton paid his last debt to nature, in his chamber in Ch. Ch. at, or very near that time, which he had some years before foretold from the calculation of his own nativity. Which being exact, several of the students did not forbear to whisper among themselves, that rather than there should be a mistake in the calculation, he sent up his soul to heaven thro' a slip about his neck. His body was afterwards with due solemnity buried near that of Dr. Rob. Weston, in the north aisle which joyns next to the choir of the Cath. of Ch. Church, on the 27 of January in sixteen hundred thirty and nine. Over his grave was soon after erected a comely monument on the upper pillar of the said isle, with his bust painted to the life: On the right hand of which, is the calculation of his nativity, and under the bust this inscription made by himself; all put up by the care of William Burton his brother. *Paucis notus, paucioribus ignotus, hic jacet Democritus junior, cui vitam dedit, &c., mortem Melancholia. Obiit viii. Id. Jan. A. C. M. DCXXXIX.* He left behind him a very choice library of books, many of which he bequeathed to that of Bodley, and a hundred pounds to buy five pounds yearly for the supplying of Ch. Ch. library with books.—WOOD, ANTHONY, 1691-1721, Athenæ Oxonienses, vol. I, f. 628.

The earl of Southampton went into a shop and inquired of the bookseller for Burton's "Anatomy of Melancholly." Mr. Burton sate in a corner of the shop at that time. Says the bookseller, My lord, if you please, I can shew you the author. He did so. *Mr. Burton*, says the earl, *your servant. Mr. Southampton*, says Mr. Burton, *your servant*, and away he went. —HEARNE, THOMAS, 1713, Reliquiæ Hearnianæ, ed. Bliss, Aug. 2, vol. I, p. 282.

Mr. Burton was one of the most facetious and pleasant companions of that age, but his conversation was very innocent. It was the way then to mix a great deal of Latin in discoursing, at which he was wonderfull ready, (in the manner his book is wrote,) which is now looked upon as pedantry. Ant. à Wood was a great admirer of Mr. Burton, and of the books he bequeathed to the Bodleian library, a great many of which were little historicall diverting pamphlets, now grown wonderfull scarce, which Mr. Burton used to divert himself with, as he did with other little merry books, of which there are many in his benefaction, one of which is "The History of Tom Thumb."—HEARNE, THOMAS, 1733-34, Reliquiæ Hearnianæ, ed. Bliss, Jan. 28, vol. III, p. 115.

ANATOMY OF MELANCHOLY
1621

Wherein he hath piled up variety of much excellent Learning. . . . Scarce any Book of Philology in our Land hath in so short a time passed so many *Impressions.*—FULLER, THOMAS, 1662, *The Worthies of England, ed. Nichols, vol.* I, *p.* 571.

'Tis a book so full of variety of reading, that gentlemen who have lost their time and are put to a push for invention, may furnish themselves with matter for common or scholastical discourse and writing. Several authors have unmercifully stolen matter from the said book without any acknowledgment.—WOOD, ANTHONY, 1691–1721, *Athenæ Oxonienses, vol.* I, *f.* 628.

If you never saw Burton upon Melancholy, printed 1676, pray look into it, and read the ninth page of his Preface, "Democritus to the Reader." There is something there which touches the point we are upon; but I mention the author to you, as the pleasantest, the most learned, and the most full of sterling sense. The wits of Queen Anne's reign, and the beginning of George the First, were not a little beholden to him.—HERRING, THOMAS, 1728–57, *Letters to William Duncombe.*

Jan. 23. No book sold better formerly than Burton's "Anatomy of Melancholy," in which there is great variety of learning, so that it hath been a common-place for filchers. It hath a great many impressions, and the bookseller got an estate by it; but now 'tis disregarded, and a good fair perfect copy (altho' of the 7th impression) may be purchased for one shilling, well bound, which occasion'd a gentleman yesterday (who observ'd how many books, that were topping books formerly, and were greedily bought at great prices, were turn'd to wast paper) to say, that sir Isaac Newton he believ'd, would also in time be turned to wast paper; an observation which is very likely to prove true.—HEARNE, THOMAS, 1733–34, *Reliquiæ Hearnianæ, vol.* III, *p.* 113.

He compiled "The Anatomy of Melancholy," a book which has been universally read and admired. This work is, for the most part, what the author himself styles it "a Cento;" but it is a very ingenious one. His quotations, which abound in every page, are pertinent; but if he had made more use of his invention, and less

of his common-place book, his work would perhaps have been more valuable than it is. He is generally free from the affected language, and ridiculous metaphors, which disgrace most of the books of his time.—GRANGER, JAMES, 1769–1824, *Biographical History of England, vol.* II, *p.* 70.

Burton's "Anatomy of Melancholy," he said, was the only book that ever took him out of bed two hours sooner than he wished to rise.—JOHNSON, SAMUEL, 1770, *Life by Boswell, vol.* III, *ch.* v.

It will be no detraction from the power of Milton's original genius and invention, to remark, that he seems to have borrowed the subject of "L'Allegro" and "Il Penseroso," together with some particular thoughts, expressions, and rhymes, more especially the idea of a contrast between these two dispositions, from a forgotten poem prefixed to the first edition of Burton's Anatomy of Melancholy, entitled, "The Author's Abstract of Melancholy; or, A Dialogue between Pleasure and Pain." Here pain is Melancholy. It was written, as I conjecture, about the year 1600. I will make no apology for abstracting and citing as much of this poem as will be sufficient to prove, to a discerning reader, how far it had taken possession of Milton's mind. The measure will appear to be the same; and that our author was at least an attentive reader of Burton's book, may be already concluded from the traces of resemblance which I have incidentally noticed in passing through the "L'Allegro" and "Il Penseroso." . . . As to the very elaborate work to which these visionary verses are no unsuitable introduction, the writer's variety of learning, his quotations from scarce and curious books, his pedantry sparkling with rude wit and shapeless elegance, miscellaneous matter, intermixture of agreeable tales and illustrations, and, perhaps, above all, the singularities of his feelings, clothed in an uncommon quaintness of style, have contributed to render it, even to modern readers, a valuable repository of amusement and information.—WARTON, THOMAS, 1785, *ed. Milton's Poems on several occasions, p.* 94.

The book, in my opinion, most useful to a man who wishes to acquire the reputation of being well read, with the least trouble, is Burton's "Anatomy of Melancholy," the most amusing and instructive medley of quotations and classical anecdotes I ever perused. But a superficial reader must take care, or his intricacies will bewilder him. If, however, he has patience to go through his volumes, he will be more improved for literary conversation than by the perusal of any twenty other works with which I am acquainted,—at least in the English language.—BYRON, LORD, 1807, *Life, Letters and Journals, ed. Moore, p.* 48.

After all, we know little or nothing of the extraordinary author of this extraordinary production—which, it has been said, was the only work that could force Dr. Johnson from his bed two hours earlier than he wished to rise. This might have happened once—in his life : for Burton's book is, in a great measure, a *task* to peruse. You can scarcely travel through thirty pages, without taking at least a good long breathing pause. The multiplicity, the redundancy, the faint forced analogy, of the quotations—the utter absurdity of the physical illustrations—and the limited knowledge of pathology, are heavy clogs to a free and unrestrained perusal.— DIBDIN, THOMAS FROGNALL, 1824, *The Library Companion, p.* 599, *note.*

Mary bids me warn you not to read the "Anatomy of Melancholy" in your present *low way.* You'll fancy yourself a pipkin or a headless bear, as Burton speaks of. You'll be lost in a maze of remedies for a labyrinth of diseasements—a plethora of cures.—LAMB, CHARLES, 1826, *Letter to J. B. Dibdin, Letters, ed. Ainger, vol.* II.

He is clogged by excess of reading, like others of his age ; and we may peruse entire chapters without finding more than a few lines that belong to himself. This becomes a wearisome style ; and, for my own part, I have not found much pleasure in glancing over the "Anatomy of Melancholy." It may be added, that he has been a collector of stories, far more strange than true, from those records of figments, the old medical writers of the sixteenth century, and other equally deceitful sources.—HALLAM, HENRY, 1837-39, *Introduction to the Literature of Europe, pt.* iii, *ch.* vii, *par.* 38.

The book was, in truth, no mere literary feat, but the genuine counterpart, in a strange literary form, of a mind as unusual. Burton's place is in that extraordinary class of humorists, of which, in modern times, Rabelais, Swift, and Jean Paul are, though with obvious mutual differences, the other best known examples.—MASSON, DAVID, 1858, *The Life of John Milton, vol.* I, *ch.* vi.

As a writer, Burton ranks, in some points, with Montaigne, and in others with Sir Thomas Browne. He resembles the first in simplicity, *bonhommie*, and miscellaneous learning, and the other in rambling manner, quaint phraseology, and fantastic imagination. Neither of the three could be said to write books, but they accumulated vast storehouses, whence thousands of volumes might be, and have been compiled. There is nothing in Burton so low as in many of the "Essays" of Montaigne, but there is nothing so lofty as in passages of Browne's "Religio Medici" and "Urn-Burial." Burton has been a favourite quarry to literary thieves, among whom Sterne, in his "Tristram Shandy," stands pre-eminent.—GILFILLAN, GEORGE, 1860, *ed., Specimens of the Less-Known British Poets, vol.* I, *p.* 267.

It is an extraordinary accumulation of out-of-the-way learning, interspersed, somewhat in the manner of Montaigne's "Essays," with original matter, but with this among other differences,—that in Montaigne the quotations have the air of being introduced, as we know that in fact they were, to illustrate the original matter, which is the web of the discourse, they but the embroidery ; whereas in Burton the learning is rather the web, upon which what he has got to say of his own is worked in by way of forming a sort of decorative figure. Burton is far from having the variety or abundance of Montaigne ; but there is considerable point and penetration in his style, and he says many striking things in a sort of half-splenetic, half-jocular humor, which many readers have found wonderfully stimulating.— CRAIK, GEORGE L., 1861, *A Compendious History of English Literature and of the English Language, vol.* I, *p.* 618.

Burton had an odd sort of humor, and an idle hour may be whiled away pleasantly enough by opening his book almost anywhere ; but, as for science, it is not to writers of his stamp that one must go for that.—ARNOLD, THOMAS, 1862-87, *A Manual of English Literature, p.* 123.

An ecclesiastic and university recluse,

who passed his life in libraries, and dabbled in all the sciences, as learned as Rabelais, of an inexhaustible and overflowing memory; unequal, moreover, gifted with enthusiasm, and spasmodically gay, but as a rule sad and morose, to the extent of confessing in his epitaph that melancholy made up his life and his death; in the first place original, enamoured of his own intelligence, and one of the earliest models of that singular English mood which, withdrawing man within himself, develops in him, at one time imagination, at another scrupulousness, at another oddity, and makes of him, according to circumstances, a poet, and eccentric, a humorist, a madman, or a puritan. He read on for thirty years, put an encyclopædia into his head, and now, to amuse and relieve himself, takes a folio of blank paper. Twenty lines of a poet, a dozen lines of a treatise on agriculture, a folio column of heraldry, the patience, the record of the fever fits of hypochondria, the history of the particle *que*, a scrap of metaphysics,—this is what passes through his brain in a quarter of an hour: it is a carnival of ideas and phrases, Greek, Latin, German, French, Italian, philosophical, geometrical, medical, poetical, astrological, musical, pedagogic, heaped one on the other; an enormous medley, a prodigious mass of jumbled quotations, jostling thoughts with the vivacity and the transport of a feast of unreason.—TAINE, H. A., 1871, *History of English Literature*, tr. *Van Laun, vol.* I, *bk.* ii, *ch.* i, *p.* 209.

One of the most fascinating books in literature. . . . Commonplace writers have described the "Anatomy" as a mere collection of quotations, a piece of patchwork. The description is utterly untrue. On every page is the impress of a singularly deep and original genius. As a humorist Burton bears some resemblance to Sir Thomas Browne; this vein of semiserious humour is, to his admirers, one of the chief attractions of his style.—BULLEN, A. H., 1886, *Dictionary of National Biography, vol.* VIII, *pp.* 12, 14.

An excellent book to steal from—whether quotations or crusty notions of the author's own.—MITCHELL, DONALD G., 1890, *English Lands Letters and Kings, From Elizabeth to Anne, p.* 144, *note.*

Burton occupied rather more than twenty years, from the time of his election to a position of learned ease, in shaping his book for its first appearance in 1621: he spent rather less than another twenty in refashioning and perfecting the work. Frequently as it has been reprinted, no attempt has ever yet been made to execute a critical edition, indicating the variations which were thus introduced by him on the four occasions when reissues were called for in his own lifetime. These alterations and additions are very numerous and very considerable, and the author not unfrequently draws attention to them in the text. But he has never, in making them, broken through the singular unity and control of treatment which the book shows. As far as the *minutiæ* of style are concerned, Burton's characteristics are well marked, and not very numerous. His method of quotation obliges him of necessity to immense sentences, or rather clauseheaps. But it is noteworthy that when he intermits citation and narrates or argues in his own person he is less, not more, given than his contemporaries to the long sentence, and frequenlty has a distinctly terse and crisp arrangement of the members of his paragraph.—SAINTSBURY, GEORGE, 1893, *English Prose, ed. Craik, vol.* II, *p.* 116.

There is entertainment in old Burton, because the man sometimes gets the better of his memory.—MABIE, HAMILTON WRIGHT, 1896, *My Study Fire, Second Series, p.* 30.

It is in his consolatory chapters that Burton's true worth shines forth, and compels our admiration. He is here no longer the disappointed, churlish cynic, nor does he in these pages, as he often seems to do elsewhere, exhibit a longing, Paracelsus-like, to save mankind, while he yet tramples on it, but, throwing off his ill-fitting disguise, shows himself the good honest fellow he really is—a comforter of the distressed, a sympathiser with the afflicted, a compassionate friend, a true, staunch champion of the oppressed and sorrowful.—ADAMS, EDWARD W., 1896, *Robert Burton, Gentleman's Magazine, vol.* 281, *p.* 53.

Accumulates epithets and multiplies quotations, until it is these, and not his theme, that engage the amused and bewildered mind.—TOVEY, DUNCAN C., 1897, *Reviews and Essays in English Literature, p.* 39.

Philip Massinger
1583–1640

Born, at Salisbury, 1583; baptised 24 Nov. Possibly page to Earl of Pembroke in boyhood, Matric., St. Alban Hall, Oxford, 14 May 1602. Left Oxford, 1606; took no degree. To London; took to writing plays. Collaborated with Nathaniel Field, Cyril Tourneur, Daborne and others; with Fletcher, 1613–25. Wrote plays for King's Company of Players, 1616–23, 1625–40; for Queen's Company, 1623–25. Married. Died, suddenly, in London, March 1640; buried, in St. Saviour's, Southwark, 18 March. *Works:* "The Virgin Martir" (with T. Dekker), 1622; "The Duke of Millaine," 1623; "The Bondman," 1624; "The Roman Actor," 1629; "The Picture," 1630; "The Renegado," 1630; "The Emperor of the East," 1632; "The Maid of Honour," 1632; "The Fatal Dowry" (with N. Field; anon.), 1632; "A New Way to pay Old Debts," 1633; "The Great Duke of Florence," 1636; "The Unnaturall Combat," 1639. (Several plays known to have been printed are lost.) *Posthumous:* "Three new Playes; viz., The Bashful Lover, Guardian, Very Woman," 1655; "The Old Law" (with Middleton and Rowley), 1656; "The City Madam," 1658; "The Parliament of Love," ed. by Gifford, 1805; "Believe as You List," ed. for Percy Soc., 1849. *Collected Works:* ed. by Coxeter (4 vols.), 1759; ed. by Monck Mason (4 vols.,) 1779; ed. by Gifford (4 vols.), 1805.—SHARP, R. FARQUHARSON, 1897, *A Dictionary of English Authors, p.* 190.

PERSONAL

Buried, Philip Massinger, a stranger.—PARISH REGISTER, *Church of St. Saviour's, March* 20, 1640.

This day I searched the register of St. Saviour's, Southwark, by the playhouse then there, vulgo St. Mary's Overy's; and find Philip Massinger buryed March 18th, 1639. I am enformed at the place where he dyed, which was by the Bankes side neer the then playhouse, that he was buryed about the middle of the Bullhead-churchyard—i. e. that churchyard (for there are four) which is next the Bullhead taverne, from whence it has its denomination. He dyed about the 66th yeare of his age: went to bed well, and dyed suddenly—but not of the plague.—AUBREY, JOHN, 1669–96, *Brief Lives, ed. Clark, vol.* II, *p.* 55.

As for our author Ph. Massinger, he made his last exit very suddenly, in his house on the Bank-side in Southwark, near to the then Play-House, for he went to bed well and was dead before morning. Whereupon his body, being accompanied by comedians, was buried about the middle of that Ch. Yard belonging to S. Saviours Church there, commonly called the Bullhead Ch. Yard, that is, in that which joyns to the Bull-head Tavern (for there are in all four yards belonging to that Church) on the 18 day of March in sixteen hundred thirty and nine.—WOOD, ANTHONY, 1691–1721, *Athenæ Oxonienses, vol.* I.

Of his private life literally nothing can be said to be known, except that his dedications bespeak incessant distress and dependence, while the recommendatory poems prefixed to his plays address him with attributes of virtue, which are seldom lavished with flattery or falsehood on those who are poor. . . . Of all his admirers only Sir Aston Cokayne dedicated a line to his memory. Even posterity did him long injustice: Rowe, who had discovered his merits in the depth of their neglect, forbore to be his editor, in the hopes of concealing his plagiarism from the "Fatal Dowry"; and he seemed on the eve of oblivion, when Dodsley's reprint of our old plays brought him faintly into that light of reputation, which has been made perfectly distinct by Mr. Gifford's edition of his works.—CAMPBELL, THOMAS, 1819, *Specimens of the British Poets.*

We draw to a close. After "The King and Subject," so happy in its timely expurgation, Massinger produced two dramas "Alexius, or the Chaste Lover," and "The Fair Anchoress of Pausilippo." It is a pity they are both lost, for the titles promise much in his best way. The last was acted in January, 1640. On the 16th March, in the same year, he went to bed in apparent health, and was found dead in the morning in his house on the Bankside. Such is the received account; but he seems to have had none to care for him, none to mark his symptoms, or to detect the slow decay which he might conceal in despair of sympathy. Poorly, poor man, he lived—poorly, poor man, he died.

He was buried in the churchyard of St. Saviour's, and the comedians were his only mourners—perhaps half envious of his escape from the storm that was already grumbling afar, and sending ahead its herald billows. No stone marked his neglected resting-place, but in the parish register appears this brief memorial, "March 20, 1639-40—buried Philip Massinger, a STRANGER." His sepulchre was like his life, obscure; like the nightingale, he sung darkling—it is to be feared, like the nightingale of the fable, with his breast against a thorn.—COLERIDGE, HARTLEY, 1840, *The Dramatic Works of Massinger and Ford, Introduction*, p. liv.

It may safely be asserted that, little as we know of Massinger's life, few personalities in the gallery of our old dramatists are recognisable with greater distinctness in their works, and few commend themselves more signally to high-minded sympathy and esteem.—WARD, ADOLPHUS WILLIAM, 1875-99, *A History of English Dramatic Literature*, vol. III, p. 2.

THE OLD LAW

There is an exquisiteness of moral sensiblity, making one's eyes to gush out tears of delight, and a poetical strangeness in the circumstances of this sweet tragi-comedy, which are unlike anything in the dramas which Massinger wrote alone. The pathos is of a subtler edge. Middleton and Rowley, who assisted in it, had both of them finer geniuses than their associate.—LAMB, CHARLES, 1808, *Specimens of Dramatic Poets*.

THE VIRGIN MARTYR
1622

Read the first four acts of Massinger's "Virgin Martyr," and Gifford's very agreeably written "Introduction." The merits of the poet are certainly great; though, as usual, rather exaggerated by the editor. The style is most elegant; and, as has often been observed, modern to a miracle. There is great moral grandeur in the conception of the principal character, but no probability, no decorum, a grossness so rank as to be perfectly disgusting.—MACKINTOSH, SIR JAMES, 1807, *Journal, Oct.* 26-27, *Life, ed. Mackintosh*, vol. I, *ch.* vii.

The "Virgin Martyr" is nothing but a tissue of instantaneous conversions to and from Paganism and Christianity. The only scenes of any real beauty and tenderness in this play are those between Dorothea and Angelo, her supposed friendless beggar-boy, but her guardian-angel in disguise, which are understood to be by Decker.—HAZLITT, WILLIAM, 1820, *Lectures on the Literature of the Age of Elizabeth, Lecture* iv.

The first act of the "Virign Martyr" is as fine an act as I remember in any play.—COLERIDGE, SAMUEL TAYLOR, 1833, *Table Talk, April* 5.

In the "Virgin Martyr," he has followed the Spanish model of religious Autos, with many graces of language and a beautiful display of Christian heroism in Dorothea; but the tragedy is in many respects unpleasing.—HALLAM, HENRY, 1837-39, *Introduction to the Literature of Europe*, pt. iii, *ch.* vi, *par.* 95.

Massinger's account of Theophilus's conversion, will, we fear, make those who know any thing of that great crisis of the human spirit, suspect that Massinger's experience thereof was but small: the fact which is most interesting is, the "Virgin Martyr" is one of the foulest plays known. Every pains has been taken to prove that the indecent scenes in the play were not written by Massinger, but by Dekker; on what grounds we know not. If Dekker assisted Massinger in the play, as he is said to have done, we are aware of no cannons of internal criticism, which will enable us to decide, as boldly as Mr. Gifford does, that all the indecency is Dekker's, and all the poetry Massinger's. He confesses (as indeed he is forced to do) that "Massinger himself is not free from dialogues of low wit and buffoonery;" and. then, after calling the scenes in question "detestable ribaldry," "a loathsome sorterkin, engendered of filth and dulness," recommends them to the reader's supreme scorn and contempt,—with which feelings the reader will doubtless regard them; but will also, if he be a thinking man, draw from them the following conclusions: that even if they be Dekker's, (of which there is no proof,) Massinger was forced, in order to the success of his play, to pander to the public taste, by allowing Dekker to interpolate these villainies; that the play which, above all others of the seventeenth century, contains the most supra-lunar rosepink of piety, devotion, and purity, also contains the stupidest abominations of any extant play; and lastly, that those who reprinted it for its rosepink piety and purity, as a sample of the Christianity of that past golden age of High-churchmanship had to leave out about one third of the play, for fear of becoming amenable to the laws against abominable publications.—KINGS-LEY, CHARLES, 1859, *Plays and Puritans, Miscellanies, p.* 99.

Though it seems to have been popular at the time, the modern reader will probably think that, in this case at least, the religious element is a little out of place. An angel and a devil take an acitve part in the performance; miracles are worked on the stage; the unbelievers are so shockingly wicked, and the Christians so obtrusively good, that we—the worldly-minded—are sensible of a little recalcitration, unless we are disarmed by the simplicity of the whole performance.—STEPHEN, LESLIE, 1874–79, *Hours in a Library, vol.* II, *p.* 153.

Dekker seems to have contributed the larger part of the play, including some very beautiful poetry as well as some grossly ribald talk. The action is simplicity itself; nor is there the slightest attempt at refining upon the clear purpose of the fable.—WARD, ADOLPHUS WILLIAM, 1875–99, *A History of English Dramatic Literature, vol.* III, *p.* 12.

The grace and tenderness of the Virgin's part are much more in accordance with what is certainly Dekker's than with what is certainly Massinger's, and that either was quite capable of the Hircius and Spungius passages which have excited so much disgust and indignation—disgust and indignation which perhaps overlook the fact that they were no doubt inserted with the express purpose of heightening, by however clumsily designed a contrast, the virgin purity of Dorothea the saint.—SAINTSBURY, GEORGE, 1887, *History of Elizabethan Literature, p.* 203.

THE UNNATURAL COMBAT
1639

We read, with the strongest feelings of admiration, horror, and disgust, Massinger's Tragedy of the "Unnatural Combat." It is surprising that a poet of so much taste and judgment in his style, should have none in his story, characters, or manners.

But it was with Massinger's taste, as with Shakspeare's genius, which is displayed with such prodigal magnificence in the parts, but never employed in the construction of the whole. No Englishman, after this play, ought ever to speak of the horrors of the German stage.—MACKIN-TOSH, SIR JAMES, 1807, *Journal, Nov.* 5, *Life, ed. Mackintosh, vol.* I, *ch.* vii.

The battle between the Father and Son, in the "Unnatural Combat," and the dreadful parley which precedes it, are as powerfully expressed as they are imagined. Indeed, the genius of Massinger is, perhaps, more conspicuous in this Play, with all its faults, than in any other.—NEELE, HENRY, 1827–29, *Lectures on English Poetry, Lecture* iv.

In the "Unnatural Combat," probably among the earliest of Massinger's works, we find a greater energy, a bolder strain of figurative poetry, more command of terror, and perhaps of pity, than in any other of his dramas. But the dark shadows of crime and misery which overspread this tragedy belong to rather an earlier period of the English stage than that of Massinger, and were not congenial to his temper.—HALLAM, HENRY, 1837–39, *Introduction to the Literature of Europe, pt.* iii, *ch.* vi, *par.* 95.

THE DUKE OF MILAN
1623

The most poetical of Massinger's productions.—HAZLITT, WILLIAM, 1820, *Lectures on the Literature of the Age of Elizabeth, Lecture* iv.

Among the tragedies of Massinger, I should incline to prefer the "Duke of Milan." The plot borrows enough from history to give it dignity, and to counterbalance in some measure the predominance of the passion of love which the invented parts of the drama exhibit. The characters of Sforza, Marcelia, and Francesco, are in Massinger's best manner; the story is skilfully and not improbably developed; the pathos is deeper than we generally find in his writings; the eloquence of language, especially in the celebrated speech of Sforza before the Emperor has never been surpassed by him.—HALLAM, HENRY, 1837–39, *Introduction to the Literature of Europe, pt.* iii, *ch.* vi, *par.* 95.

Although unrelieved either by pathos or

by humour, this tragedy powerfully depicts the operation of strong passions,
while suggesting a novel intermixture of
public and private motives of conduct.—
WARD, ADOLPHUS WILLIAM, 1875-99, *A
History of English Dramatic Literature,
vol. III, p.* 14.

THE BONDMAN
1623–38

Of Massinger's rhetorical ability this
play furnishes abundant evidence; and it
is at the same time the first among his
works that suggests a deliberate intention on the part of the dramatist to provoke an application to current events and
characters of the invective put by him
into the mouths of his characters.—WARD,
ADOLPHUS WILLIAM, 1875-99, *A History
of English Dramatic Literature, vol. III,
p.* 16.

THE ROMAN ACTOR
1626–29

Is, I think, Massinger's best tragic
effort; and the scene where Domitian murders Paris, with his tyrannical explanation
of the deed, shows a greater conception
of tragic poetry—a little cold and stately,
a little Racinish or at least Cornelian
rather than Shakesperian, but still passionate and worthy of the tragic stage—
than anything that Massinger has done.—
SAINTSBURY, GEORGE, 1887, *History of
Elizabethan Literature, p.* 400.

THE MAID OF HONOUR
1632

I think, that he really shows, by the
best means in his power, a strong sense
of the dignity of womanhood, and that his
catastrophe is more satisfactory than the
violent death or the consignment to an
inferior lover which would have commended themselves to most Elizabethan
dramatists.—STEPHEN, LESLIE, 1874-79,
Hours in a Library, vol. II, p. 169.

"The Maid of Honour" is beyond doubt
to be reckoned among Massinger's most
attractive productions and those best according with the bent of his own nature.
The comic character of "Signior Sylli, a
foolish self-lover," is at the same time
unusually diverting, especially in his references to his family traditions. The Page
is a specimen of a type for which Massinger had a special predilection.—WARD,
ADOLPHUS WILLIAM, 1875-99, *A History of
English Dramatic Literature, vol. III, p.* 20.

I was so enchanted with these plays of
Massinger's, but more especially with the
one called "The Maid of Honor," that I
never rested till I had obtained from the
management its revival on the stage.
The part of Camiola is the only one that
I ever selected for myself. "The Maid of
Honor" succeeded on its first representation, but failed to attract audiences.
Though less defective than most of the
contemporaneous dramatic compositions,
the play was still too deficient in interest
to retain the favor of the public. The
character of Camiola is extremely noble
and striking, but that of her lover so unworthy of her that the interest she excites personally fails to inspire one with
sympathy for her passion for him. The
piece in this respect has a sort of moral
incoherency, which appears to me, indeed,
not an infrequent defect in the compositions of these great dramatic pre-Shake-
spearites.—KEMBLE, FRANCES ANN, 1878,
Records of a Girlhood, p. 255.

THE PICTURE
1629–30

The good sense, rational fondness, and
chastised feeling, of the dialogue in which
Matthias, a knight of Bohemia, going to
the wars, in parting with his wife, shows
her substantial reasons why he should go
—make it more valuable than many of
those scenes in which this writer has attempted a deeper passion and more tragical interest.—LAMB, CHARLES, 1808, *Specimens of Dramatic Poets.*

THE FATAL DOWRY
1632

A novelty of much interest, in the revival of Massinger's tragedy of "The
Fatal Dowry," produced Wednesday, January 5th, 1825. The original work is one
of very great power, but unhappily disfigured by scenes too gross for presentation
before an audience making pretension to
any degree of refinement. Sheil undertook the task of its purification, and in its
adaptation, whilst maintaining the strictest fidelity to the story, substituted scenes
which, in energy, passion, and dramatic
power, fully equalled those on which they
were grafted. The parts of Rochfort and
Charolois were very well represented by
Terry and Wallack, and in Romont opportunities were afforded for the display of
energy and lofty bearing, to the full

height of which I laboured, not unsuccessfully, to reach; but though a great writer says *"Il n'y a point de hasard,"* we often find results under the sway of casualties. The play was well acted, and enthusiastically applauded: its repetition for the following Tuesday was hailed most rapturously.—MACREADY, WILLIAM CHARLES, 1825-67-75, *Reminiscences, ed. Pollock.*

My performance of "The Fair Penitent" was entirely ineffective, and did neither me nor the theater any service; the play itself is a feeble adaptation of Massinger's powerful drama of "The Fatal Dowry," and, as generally happens with such attempts to fit our old plays to our modern stage, the fundamentally objectionable nature of the story could not be reformed without much of the vigorous and terrible effect of the original treatment evaporating in the refining process. Mr. Macready revived Massinger's fine play with considerable success, but both the matter and the manner of our dramatic ancestors is too robust for the audiences of our day, who nevertheless will go and see "Diane de Lys," by a French company of actors, without wincing.—KEMBLE, FRANCES ANN, 1878, *Records of a Girlhood, p.* 318.

"The Fatal Dowry" is Massinger's highest effort in tragedy, and is—putting Shakespeare on one side—perhaps the most pathetic and most powerful of the plays written and produced in the great day of the drama in England. Seldom has there been seen upon the stage a story of more woe than that of Charalois. He is raised from abject misery, suddenly and unexpectedly, to most dazzling heights of prosperity, and then, by a revolution of the wheel of fortune, is plunged into such desperate and cureless ruin, and into such an untimely death; and all his woe is caused by the vile, fair woman who had been given to him as wife. Oh, the pity of it all! It is true tragedy. In Charalois a great, fine character is driven by dishonour into piteous, undeserved wreck. —WILSON, H. SCHÜTZ, 1899, *Fatal Dowry, Gentleman's Magazine, vol.* 287, *p.* 188.

THE NEW WAY TO PAY OLD DEBTS
1633

Pardon, I beseech you, my boldness in presuming to shelter this comedy under the wings of your Lordship's favour and protection. I am not ignorant (having never yet deserved you in my service) that it cannot but meet with a severe construction if, in the clemency of your noble disposition, you fashion not a better defence for me than I can fancy for myself . . . nor am I wholly lost in my hopes, but that your Honour (who have ever expressed yourself a favourer and friend to the Muses) may vouchsafe, in your gracious acceptance of this trifle, to give me encouragement to present you with some laboured works, and of a higher strain, hereafter. I was born a devoted servant to the thrice noble family of your incomparable lady, and am most ambitious, but with a becoming distance, to be known to your Lordship, which, if you will please to admit, I shall embrace it as a bounty, that while I live shall oblige me to acknowledge you for my noble patron, and profess myself to be

Your Honour's true servant,
—MASSINGER, PHILIP, 1833, *New Way to Pay Old Debts, Dedication to Earl of Caernarvon.*

It has been several times revived, particularly at Drury Lane, and since at Covent Garden, to assist Henderson, who performed sir Giles Overreach with judgment; but injudicious pruning always wounds a good tree, and this kind of stab did the reputation of Massinger sustain in both this case and in other cases.—DIBDIN, CHARLES, 1795, *A Complete History of the Stage, vol.* III, *p.* 237.

There is, it is true, one remarkable exception to the general weakness of Massinger's characters. The vigour with which Sir Giles Overreach is set forth has made him the one well-known figure in Massinger's gallery, and the "New Way to Pay Old Debts" showed, in consequence, more vitality than any of his other plays. Much praise has been given, and not more than enough, to the originality and force of the conception. The conventional miser is elevated into a great man by a kind of inverse heroism, and made terrible instead of contemptible. But it is equally plain that here, too, Massinger fails to project himself fairly into his villain. His rants are singularly forcible, but they are clearly what other people would think about him, not what he would really think, still less what he would say, of himself — STEPHEN, LESLIE, 1874-79, *Hours in a Library, vol.* II, *p.* 165.

His "New Way to pay Old Debts" is a very effective play, though in the reading far less interesting and pleasing than most of the others. Yet there are power and passion in it, even if the power be somewhat melodramatic, and the passion of an ignoble type. In one respect he was truly a poet—his conceptions of character were ideal; but his diction, though full of dignity and never commonplace, lacks the charm of the inspired and inspiring word, the relief of the picturesque image that comes so naturally to the help of Fletcher. —LOWELL, JAMES RUSSELL, 1887-92, *Massinger and Ford, The Old English Dramatists, ed. Norton, p.* 127.

Is the example of the entire Elizabethan and Jacobean drama outside Shakespeare which has longest held its place on the modern stage.—GOSSE, EDMUND, 1894, *The Jacobean Poets, p.* 213.

Has deservedly retained its popularity for theatrical purposes to our own day. Much of this popularity is due to the character of Sir Giles Overreach, whose prosperity and overthrow give just that kind of dramatic satisfaction which is wanting in most of the later Elizabethan plays. The old miser, watching with grim satisfaction the victims struggling in the meshes of his net, is a powerfully drawn and intensely living personality. Overreach's madness is too incidental to be an adequate close to the drama, the general moral purpose of which is set forth in Lord Lovel's speech.—MASTERMAN, J. HOWARD B., 1897, *The Age of Milton, p.* 75.

THE CITY MADAM
1632-59

This bitter satire against the city women for aping the fashions of the court ladies must have been peculiarly gratifying to the females of the Herbert family and the rest of Massinger's noble patrons and patronesses.—LAMB, CHARLES, 1808, *Specimens of Dramatic Poets.*

I cannot agree with the contention that either the versification or any other internal indication points to the authorship of any other writer than Massinger; nor bring myself to believe that this play was not written by the author of "A New Way to Pay Old Debts," with which it is distinctly congate in sentiment.—WARD, ADOLPHUS WILLIAM, 1875-99, *A History of English Dramatic Literature, vol.* III, *p.* 34.

A VERY WOMAN
1634-55

The "Very Woman" is, I think, one of the most perfect plays we have.—COLERIDGE, SAMUEL TAYLOR, 1833, *Table Talk, April* 5.

THE BASHFUL LOVER
1636-55

No other of Massinger's plays commends itself by a more effective mixture of abundant incident and noble sentiment than this romantic drama, which from a theatrical point of view well deserved the success it achieved. . . . The elevation of sentiment that marks Massinger's last work justly entitles it to a more than passing notice among the productions of the later Elisabethan drama.—WARD, ADOLPHUS WILLIAM, 1875-99, *A History of English Dramatic Literature, vol.* III, *p.* 36.

GENERAL

Notwithstanding my partiality for this kind of reading, and some pains I had taken to gratify it, I never heard of Massinger till about two years ago, when a friend of mine, who knew my inclination, lent me a copy of his works!—MASON, JOHN MONCK, 1779, *ed. Massinger.*

If, in Beaumont and Fletcher, we lament that authors sometimes attempt too much, in Massinger, we have a proof that they may do too little. This very charming writer has seldom been allowed the merit he possessed, perhaps, because he was a stranger to presumption, vanity, and those other qualities which often procure for an author more fame than he deserves; posterity, however, generally sets the matter right; which, in the opinions of all judges of genius and taste, has placed Massinger very little behind Jonson, and far before Beaumont and Fletcher.—DIBDIN, CHARLES, 1795, *A Complete History of the Stage, vol.* III, *p.* 231.

Who approached to Shakespeare in dignity?—SCOTT, SIR WALTER, 1805, *The Life of John Dryden.*

Massinger had not the higher requisites of his art in anything like the degree in which they were possessed by Ford, Webster, Tourneur, Heywood, and others. He never shakes or disturbs the mind with grief. He is read with composure and placid delight. He wrote with that equability of all the passions, which made his English style the purest and most free from violent metaphors and harsh constructions, of any of the dramatists who were his contemporaries.—LAMB, CHARLES, 1808, *Specimens of Dramatic Poets.*

The fame of Massinger has lately been revived by an edition of his works. Some literary men wish to rank him above Beaumont and Fletcher, as if he had approached more closely to the excellence of Shakspeare. I cannot find this. He appears to me to have the greatest resemblance to Beaumont and Fletcher in the plan of the pieces, in the tone of manners, and even in the language and negligences of versification. I would not undertake to decide, from internal symptoms, whether a play belonged to Massinger, or Beaumont and Fletcher.— SCHLEGEL, AUGUSTUS WILLIAM, 1809, *Dramatic Art and Literature, Lecture* xiii, tr. *Black, p.* 392.

Massinger, like Fletcher, pursued the path in which Shakspeare had preceded him with such imperishable glory; but he wants the tenderness and wit of the former, and that splendour of imagination and that dominion over the passions, which characterise the latter. He has, however, qualities of his own, sufficiently great and attractive, to gift him with the envied lot of being contemplated, in union with these two bards, as one of the chief pillars and supporters of the *Romantic drama.* He exhibits, in the first place, a perfectibility, both in diction and versification, of which we have, in dramatic poesy at least, no corresponding example. There is a transparency and perspicuity in the texture of his composition, a sweetness, harmony, and ductility, together with a blended strength and ease in the structure of his metre, which, in his best performances, delight, and never satiate the ear. To this, in some degree technical merit, must be added a spirit of commanding *eloquence,* a dignity and force of thought, which, while they approach the precincts of sublimity, and indicate great depth and clearness of intellect, show, by the nervous elegance of language in which they are clothed, a combination and comprehension of talent of very unfrequent occurrence.—DRAKE, NATHAN, 1817, *Shakspeare and His Times, vol.* II, p. 561.

With regard to Massinger, observe. 1. The vein of satire on the times; but this is not as in Shakspere, where the natures evolve themselves according to their incidental disproportions, from excess, deficiency, or mislocation, of one or more of the component elements; but is merely satire on what is attributed to them by others. 2. His excellent metre—a better model for dramatists in general to imitate than Shakspere's,—even if a dramatic taste existed in the frequenters of the stage, and could be gratified in the present size and management, or rather mismanagement, of the two patent theatres. I do not mean that Massinger's verse is superior to Shakspere's or equal to it. Far from it; but it is much more easily constructed and may be more successfully adopted by writers in the present day. It is the nearest approach to the language of real life at all compatible with a fixed metre. . . . I like Massinger's comedies better than his tragedies, although where the situation requires it, he often rises into the truly tragic and pathetic. He excels in narration, and for the most part displays his mere story with skill. But he is not a poet of high imagination; he is like a Flemish painter, in whose delineations objects appear as they do in nature, have the same force and truth, and produce the same effect upon the spectator.—COLERIDGE, SAMUEL TAYLOR, 1818, *Notes on Jonson, Beaumont, Fletcher and Massinger, ed. Ashe, pp.* 403, 406.

Massinger is distinguished for the harmony and dignity of his dramatic eloquence. Many of his plots, it is true, are liable to heavy exceptions. . . . In a general view, nevertheless, Massinger has more art and judgment in the serious drama than any of the other successors of Shakspeare. His incidents are less entangled than those of Fletcher, and the scene of his action is more clearly thrown open for the free evolution of character. Fletcher strikes the imagination with more vivacity, but more irregularly, and amidst embarrassing positions of his own choosing. Massinger puts forth his strength more collectively. Fletcher has more action and character in his drama, and leaves a greater variety of impressions upon the mind. His fancy is more volatile and surprising, but then he often blends disappointment with our surprise, and parts with the consistency of his characters even to the occasionally apparent loss of their identity. This is not the case with Massinger. It is true that Massinger excels more in description and declamation than in the forcible utterance of the heart, and in giving character the warm colouring of passion. Still, not to speak of his one distinguished hero in comedy, he has delineated several tragic characters with strong and interesting traits. They are chiefly proud spirits. Poor himself, and struggling under the rich man's contumely, we may conceive it to have been the solace of his neglected existence to picture worth and magnanimity breaking through external disadvantages, and making their way to love and admiration.—CAMPBELL, THOMAS, 1819, *An Essay on English Poetry.*

Massinger makes an impression by hardness and repulsiveness of manner. In the intellectual processes which he delights to describe, "reason panders will;" he fixes arbitrarily on some object which there is no motive to pursue, or every motive combined against it, and then by screwing up his heroes or heroines to the deliberate and blind accomplishment of this, thinks to arrive at "the true pathos and sublime of human life." That is not the way. He seldom touches the heart or kindles the fancy. It is in vain to hope to excite much sympathy with convulsive efforts of the will, or intricate contrivances of the understanding, to obtain that which is better left alone, and where the interest arises principally from the conflict between the absurdity of the passion and the obstinacy with which it is persisted in. For the most part, his villains are a sort of *lusus naturæ;* his impassioned characters are like drunkards or madmen. Their conduct is extreme and outrageous, their motives unaccountable and weak; their misfortunes are without necessity, and their crimes without temptation, to ordinary apprehensions. I do not say that this is invariably the case in all Massinger's scenes, but I think it will be found that a principle of playing at cross-purposes is the ruling passion throughout most of them.—HAZLITT, WILLIAM, 1820, *Lectures on the Literature of the Age of Elizabeth, p.* 131.

The public are much better acquainted with the writings of Massinger than with those of most of his contemporaries: for which distinction he is mainly indebted to the admirable manner in which he has been edited by Mr. Gifford, and to the circumstance of some of his Plays having been illustrated on the Stage by the talents of a popular Actor. I cannot, however, quite agree with Mr. Gifford, when he ranks this Author immediately after Shakspeare. He certainly yields in versatility of talent to Beaumont and Fletcher, whose Comic genius was very great; and in feeling and nature, I by no means think his Tragedies equal theirs, or to Ford's, or Webster's. Massinger excelled in working up a single scene forcibly and effectively, rather than in managing his plots skilfully, or in delineating characters faithfully, and naturally. His catastrophes are sometimes brought about in a very improbable and unnatural manner. . . . The sweetness and purity of his style, was not surpassed even in his own days. His choice and management of imagery is generally very happy; excepting that he is apt to pursue a favourite idea too long. His descriptive powers were also very considerable, the clearness and distinctness with which he places objects before our eyes, might furnish models for a Painter.—NEELE, HENRY, 1827–29, *Lectures on English Poetry, Lecture* iv.

The most striking excellence of this poet is his conception of character; and in this I must incline to place him above Fletcher, and, if I may venture to say it, even above Jonson. He is free from the hard outline of the one, and the negligent looseness of the other. He has indeed no great variety, and sometimes repeats, with such bare modifications as the story demands, the type of his first design. . . . The poetical talents of Massinger were very considerable, his taste superior to that of his contemporaries; the coloring of his imagery is rarely overcharged; a certain redundancy, as some may account it, gives fulness, or what the painters call *impasto,* to his style, and, if it might not always conduce to effect on the stage, is on the whole suitable to the character of his composition. The comic powers of this writer are not on a level with the serious: with some degree of humorous conception, he is too apt to aim at exciting ridicule by caricature; and his dialogue wants altogether the sparkling wit of Shakspeare and Fletcher. . . . Massinger, as a tragic writer, appears to me second only to Shakspeare: in the higher comedy, I can hardly think him inferior to Jonson. In wit and sprightly dialogue, as well as in knowledge of theatrical effect, he falls very much below Fletcher.—HALLAM, HENRY, 1837-39, *Introduction to the Literature of Europe, pt.* iii, *ch.* vi, *par.* 91, 93-4, 97.

There can be no doubt that Massinger admired and studied Shakspeare. In the haste of composition, his mind turned up many thoughts and phrases of the elder writer, in a more or less perfect state of preservation, but he was neither a plagiarist nor an imitator. His style, conduct, characterization, and metre, are perfectly distinct. No serious dramatist of the age owed Shakspeare so little. . . . Massinger's excellence—a great and beautiful excellence it is—was in the expression of virtue, in its probation, its strife, its victory. He could not, like Shakspeare, invest the perverted will with the terrors of a magnificent intellect, or bestow the cestus of poetry on simple unconscious loveliness.—COLERIDGE, HARTLEY, 1840, *The Dramatic Works of Massinger and Ford, Introduction, pp.* xlviii, liv.

Writes all like a giant—a dry-eyed giant. He is too ostentatiously strong for flexibility, and too heavy for rapidity, and monotonous through his perpetual final trochee; his gesture and enunciation are slow and majestic.—BROWNING, ELIZABETH BARRETT, 1842-63, *The Book of the Poets.*

In expressing the dignity of virtue, and in showing greatness of soul rising superior to circumstance and fate, Massinger exhibits so peculiar a vigour and felicity, that it is impossible not to conceive such delineations (in which the poet delighted) to be a reflection of his own proud and patient soul, and perhaps, too, but too true a memorial of "the rich man's scorn, the proud man's contumely," which he had himself undergone. In the tender and pathetic Massinger had no mastery; in the moral gloom of guilt, in the crowded agony of remorse, in painting the storm and tempest of the moral atmosphere, he is undoubtedly a great and mighty artist; and in expressing the sentiments of dignity and virtue, cast down but not humbled by undeserved misfortune,

he is almost unequalled. His versification, though never flowingly harmonious, is skilful and learned, an appropriate vehicle for the elevation of the sentiments; and in the description of rich and splendid scenes he is peculiarly powerful and impressive.—SHAW, THOMAS B., 1847, *Outlines of English Literature, p.* 129.

When Fox was a young man, a copy of Massinger accidentally fell into his hands: he read it, and, for some time after, could talk of nothing but Massinger.—ROGERS, SAMUEL, 1855, *Recollections of the Table-Talk of Samuel Rogers, p.* 90.

Of the Jacoban, as distinct from the Elizabethan dramatists, the greatest surviving representative was undoubtedly Massinger,—the modest and manly Massinger.—MASSON, DAVID, 1858, *The Life of John Milton, vol.* I, *ch.* vi.

Massinger possessed a large though not especially poetic mind, and a temperament equable rather than energetic. He lacked strong passions, vivid conceptions, creative imagination. In reading him we feel that the exulting, vigorous life of the drama of the age has begun to decay. But though he has been excelled by obscurer writers in special qualities of genius, he still attaches us by the harmony of his powers, and the uniformity of his excellence. The plot, style, and characters of one of his dramas all conduce to a common interest. His plays, indeed, are novels in dialogue. They rarely thrill, startle, or kindle us, but, as Lamb says, "are read with composure and placid delight." . . . Massinger's style, though it does not evince a single great quality of the poet, has always charmed English readers by its dignity, flexibility, elegance, clearness, and ease. His metre and rhythm Coleridge pronounces incomparably good. Still his verse, with all its merits, is smooth rather than melodious; the thoughts are not born in music, but mechanically set to a tune; and even its majestic flow is frequently purchased at the expense of dramatic closeness to character and passion.—WHIPPLE, EDWIN P., 1859-68, *The Literature of the Age of Elizabeth, pp.* 181, 182.

After Shakspeare, Beaumont and Fletcher, and Jonson, the next great name in our drama is that of Philip Massinger. . . . Massinger, like Jonson, had received a learned education, and his classic reading has colored his style and manner; but he had scarcely so much originality of genius as Jonson. He is a very eloquent writer, but has little power of high imagination or pathos, and still less wit or comic power.—CRAIK, GEORGE L., 1861, *A Compendious History of English Literature and of the English Language, vol.* I, *p.* 605.

The reader who peruses Massinger can hardly fail to be charmed with the force and chaste elegance of his language, happily yet sparingly enriched with choice classical allusions, and none of his contemporaries knew so well the art of developing his plot in such a way as to surprise and delight the spectator, while meting out strict poetical justice to all. His declamatory speeches are very fine models of their kind; and some of his characters, especially his females, are elaborated with great care. Massinger's style and versification are strongly marked with his own peculiar manner; yet so little is that manner known, even to professed scholars, that in most of the current manuals and books of "specimens," a scene from "The Virgin Martyr," undoubtedly written by Decker, is given as an example of his brother poet's composition!—FRISWELL, JAMES HAIN, 1869, *Essays on English Writers, p.* 160.

The greatest master of characterization of that age next to Shakespeare is certainly Massinger. Sir Giles Overreach and Luke are both real men. Luke is a true piece of nature, not all black-souled, nor all white, but of a mixed complexion. But the area which Massinger could make his own was of limited dimensions. When he stepped across its limits, his strength failed him, and he was even as other men.—HALES, JOHN W., 1873, *Notes and Essays on Shakespeare, p.* 67.

His view of life, indeed, is not only grave, but has a distinct religious colouring. . . . He is throughout a sentimentalist and a rhetorician. He is not, like the greatest men, dominated by thoughts and emotions which force him to give them external embodiment in life-like symbols. He is rather a man of much real feeling and extraordinary facility of utterance, who finds in his stories convenient occasions for indulging in elaborate didactic utterances upon moral topics. . . . When we turn to Massinger,

this boundless vigour has disappeared. The blood has grown cool. The tyrant no longer forces us to admiration by the fulness of his vitality, and the magnificence of his contempt for law. Whether for good or bad, he is comparatively a poor creature. He has developed an uneasy conscience, and even whilst affecting to defy the law, trembles at the thought of an approaching retribution. His boasts have a shrill, querulous note in them. His creator does not fully sympathise with his passion. Massinger cannot throw himself into the situation; and is anxious to dwell upon the obvious moral considerations which prove such characters to be decidedly inconvenient members of society for their tamer neighbours. He is of course the more in accordance with a correct code of morality, but fails correspondingly in dramatic force and brilliance of colour. . . . Massinger's remarkable flow of genuine eloquence, his real dignity of sentiment, his sympathy for virtuous motive, entitle him to respect; but we cannot be blind to the defect which keeps his work below the level of his greatest contemporaries. It is, in one word, a want of vital force.—STEPHEN, LESLIE, 1874-79, *Hours in a Library, vol.* II, *pp.* 153, 154, 160, 175.

He was the Gray of his generation—greater than Gray, inasmuch as his generation was greater than Gray's—a man of large, open, fertile, and versatile mind. . . . All Massinger's characteristics are those of a widely sympathetic man, with a genial propensity to laughter. He has written several very obscene passages, such as the courtship of Asotus by Corisca in "The Bondman," but they are all pervaded by genuine humour; and a countless number of his scenes, such as that between Wellborn and Marrall in "A New Way to Pay Old Debts," are irresistibly laughable. It may perhaps be said with justice that there is often a certain serious motive underlying Massinger's humour, which connects itself with the earnestness of his distressed life; but humour he undoubtedly had, and that of the most ebullient and irrepressible sort.—MINTO, WILLIAM, 1874-85, *Characteristics of English Poets, pp.* 363, 365.

Amongst the Caroline dramatists Massinger takes a high place. If it cannot be said of his works, that

"Every word is thought
And every thought is pure,"

his coarseness is merely adventitious. The main intention of his work is moral. He never descends to paint immoral intention as virtuous because it does not succeed in converting itself into vicious act. It will probably be a surprise even to those who are far better acquainted with the history of literature than I can pretend to be, that in many of Massinger's plays we have a treatment of the politics of the day so plain and transparent, that any one who possesses only a slight acquaintance with the history of the reigns of the first two Stuarts can read it at a glance. It is quite unintelligible to me that, with the exception of a few cursory words in Mr. Ward's "History of Dramatic Literature," no previous inquirer should have stumbled on a fact so obvious.—GARDINER, S. R., 1876, *The Political Element in Massinger, The Contemporary Review, vol.* 28, *p.* 495.

Clouds here and there arisen an hour past
noon
Checkered our English heaven with length-
ening bars
And shadow and sound of wheel-winged
thunder-cars
Assembling strength to put forth tempest
soon,
When the clear still warm concord of thy
tune
Rose under skies unscared by reddening
Mars,
Yet, like a sound of silver speech of stars,
With full mild flame as of the mellowing
moon,
Grave and great-hearted Massinger, thy face
High melancholy lights with loftier grace
Than gilds the brows of revel: sad and
wise,
The spirit of thought that moved thy deeper
song,
Sorrow serene in soft calm scorn of wrong,
Speaks patience yet from thy majestic eyes.
—SWINBURNE, ALGERNON CHARLES, 1882, *Philip Massinger*.

He had a high, a varied, and a fertile imagination. He had, and was the last to have, an extensive and versatile command of blank verse, never perhaps reaching the most perfect mastery of Marlowe or of Shakespere, but singularly free from monotony, and often both harmonious and dignified. He could deal, and deal well, with a large range of subjects; and if he never ascends to the height of a De Flores or a Bellafront, he never descends to the

depths in which both Middleton and Dekker too often complacently wallow. Unless we are to count by mere flashes, he must, I think, rank after Shakespere, Fletcher, and Jonson among his fellows; and this I say, honestly avowing that I have nothing like the enthusiasm for him that I have for Webster, or for Dekker, or for Middleton. We may no doubt allow too much for bulk of work, for sustained excellence at a certain level, and for general competence as against momentary excellence. But we may also allow far too little; and this has perhaps been the general tendency of later criticism in regard to Massinger. It is unfortunate that he never succeeded in making as perfect a single expression of his tragic ability as he did of his comic, for the former was, I incline to think, the higher of the two. But many of his plays are lost, and many of those which remain come near to such excellence. It is by no means impossible that Massinger may have lost incomparably by the misdeeds of the constantly execrated, but never to be execrated enough, minion of that careless herald.—SAINTS-BURY, GEORGE, 1887, *History of Elizabethan Literature, p.* 401.

To me Massinger is one of the most interesting as well as one of the most delightful of the old dramatists, not so much for his passion or power, though at times he reaches both, as for the love he shows for those things that are lovely and of good report in human nature, for his sympathy with what is generous and high-minded and honorable, and for his equable flow of a good every-day kind of poetry with few rapids or cataracts, but singularly soothing and companionable. The Latin adjective for gentleman, *generosus*, fits him aptly. His plots are generally excellent; his versification masterly, with skilful breaks and pauses, capable of every needful variety of emotion; and his dialogue easy, natural, and sprightly, subsiding in the proper places to a refreshing conversational tone. This graceful art was one seldom learned by any of those who may be fairly put in comparison with him.—LOWELL, JAMES RUSSELL, 1887-92, *Massinger and Ford, The Old English Dramatists, ed. Norton, p.* 122.

The Massinger weak line, which often is as hard to distinguish from measured prose as the iambics of Dickens or Musæus are from "Thalaba" or "Queen Mab" verse.—FLEAY, FREDERICK GARD, 1890, *A Chronicle History of the London Stage*, p. 256.

Generally speaking, he gives an impression of hardness, and seldom deviates into tender pathos. But his most characteristic trait is a peculiarly corrupt tone of thought, even in his heroines when they are intended as models of virtue. Their morality lies entirely in obedience to outward observances, and in no inner principle. Purity is not to be found in his world, and his obscenity seems often purposeless. The warning in his "Roman Actor," i. 3, that his portrayal of evil was intended to convey a wholesome reproof to the evil-minded, is unconvincing. Massinger's language is generally full and flowing, with more of a rhetorical than a dramatic character. In a contemporary poem "On the Time-Poets" ("*Choyce Drollery*, 1656") it is said of him that his

Easy Pegasus will amble o'er
Some threescore miles of Fancy in an hour.

. . . In his early work he introduces very much prose and rhyme, but in his later work he confines himself to blank verse. His blank verse shows a larger proportion of run-on lines and double endings in harmonious union than any contemporary author. Cartwright and Tourneur have more run-on lines, but not so many double endings. Fletcher has more double endings, but very few run-on lines. Shakespeare and Beaumont alone exhibit a somewhat similar metrical style.— BOYLE, ROBERT, 1894, *Dictionary of National Biography, vol.* XXXVII, *p.* 12.

Nothing exemplifies more curiously the rapidity of development in poetical literature at the opening of the seventeenth century than the fact that the same brief reign which saw the last perfection placed on the edifice of Elizabethan drama saw also the products of the pen of Massinger. For, however much we may respect the activity of this remarkable man, however warmly we may acknowledge the power of his invention, the skill and energy with which he composed, and however agreeable his plays may appear to us if we compare them with what succeeded them in a single generation, there can be no question that the decline in the essential parts of poetry from Webster or Tourneur, to go no further back, to Massinger is very

abrupt. Mr. Leslie Stephen has noted in this playwright "a certain hectic flush, symptomatic of approaching decay," and we may even go further and discover in him a leaden pallor, the sign of decreasing vitality. The "hectic flush" seems to me to belong more properly to his immediate successors, who do not come within the scope of this volume, to Ford, with his morbid sensibility, and to Shirley, with his mechanical ornament, than to Massinger, where the decline chiefly shows itself in the negation of qualities, the absence of what is brilliant, eccentric, and passionate. The sentimental and rhetorical drama of Massinger has its excellent points, but it is dominated by the feeling that the burning summer of poetry is over, and that a russet season is letting us down gently towards the dull uniformity of winter. Interesting and specious as Massinger is, we cannot avoid the impression that he is preparing us for that dramatic destitution which was to accompany the Commonwealth.—GOSSE, EDMUND, 1894, *The Jacobean Poets, p.* 202.

His versification and language are flexible and strong, "and seem to rise out of the passions he describes." He speaks the tongue of real life. He is greater than he seems to be. Like Fletcher, there is a steady equality in his work. Coarse, even foul as he is in speech, he is the most moral of the secondary dramatists. Nowhere is his work so forcible as when he represents the brave man struggling through trial to victory, the pure woman suffering for the sake of truth and love; or when he describes the terrors that conscience brings on injustice and cruelty.—BROOKE, STOPFORD A., 1896, *English Literature, p.* 147.

Massinger's wide range of subjects, the ingenuity and skill with which most of his plays are constructed, and the forcible rhetoric of his dialogues, entitle him to a high place in the group of dramatists that includes Webster, Middleton, and Dekker. The claim to a higher place, which has sometimes been put forward on his behalf, may not improbably have arisen from the fact that his works were efficiently edited earlier than those of most of the later Elizabethan dramatists. If he rarely sinks below a certain level of excellence, he seldom startles us with any sudden flash of inspiration. A tone of sombreness, which passes at times into one of sadness, pervades his entire work; and even in his comedies it is but a transient smile that flickers at rare intervals over the face of one whose moral purpose has grown through the discipline of poverty. A certain didactic aim is indeed rarely absent, although seldom unduly prominent, and if it is undeniable that his dramas are at times grossly indecent and overstrained in their delineation of vice and villainy, we are conscious that behind them there is a sane and healthy mind with a manly respect for virtue and goodness.—MASTERMAN, J. HOWARD B., 1897, *The Age of Milton*, p. 77.

We possess fifteen plays, written, with some aid, by Massinger, and know of the existence of eighteen others which are irrevocably lost. This loss occurred through the criminal carelessness of one John Warburton, F.R.S., F.S.A., Somerset Herald, and an ex-exciseman, who had collected fifty-five genuine unpublished dramas, of the best period, which he gave into the custody of his cook, who used them for coverings for pastry, or for lighting the kitchen fire. This abominable holocaust of such priceless material occurred in the middle of last century. Warburton, a mean, illiterate man, deserves almost more obloquy than does the infamous Gastrell, who destroyed New Place, and cut down Shakespeare's mulberry-tree.—WILSON, H. S., 1899, *The Fatal Dowry, Gentleman's Magazine, vol.* 287.

Sir Henry Spelman

1564?–1641

Sir Henry Spelman (born 1562 died 1641), a Norfork squire, was an eminent antiquary, whose learned works are still useful. Such are his "Glossarium Archæologicum," his treatise on "Knight's Tenures," his "History of English Councils," etc. A very strong Angelican, Spelman, wrote a "History of Sacrilege" to show the fate which holders of church lands were likely to incur, a "Treatise concerning Tithes," and a book "De Non temerandis Ecclesiis." The "Reliquiæ Spelmannianæ" contain a large number of his posthumous works. Spelman's intimate knowledge of the works of earlier writers, and his acquaintance with the intricacies of English law and legal custom in the period in which he lived, make his works of considerable value to the student and antiquarian.—LOW AND PULLING, 1884, *eds., Dictionary of English History*, p. 963.

PERSONAL

From George Lee:—he was a handsome gentleman (as appeares by his picture in Bibliotheca Cottoniana), strong and valiant, and wore allwayes his sword, till he was about 70 or +, when, finding his legges to faulter through feeblenes as he was walking, "Now," said he, "'tis time to leave off my sword." . . . He lies buried in the south crosse-aisle of Westminister abbey, at the foot of the pillar opposite to Mr. Camden's monument, but without any word of inscription or monument hitherto (1680). I very well remember his penon that hung-up there, but it was either taken downe or fell downe when the scaffolds were putt up at the coronation of his majestie King Charles II. Sir William Dugdale knew Sir Henry Spelman, and sayes he was as tall as his grandson, Harry Spelman.—AUBREY, JOHN, 1669-96, *Brief Lives, ed. Clark, vol.* II, *pp.* 231, 232.

United the learning of a profound antiquary to the superstition of a narrow bigot.—ROGERS, JAMES E. THOROLD, 1870, *William Laud, Historical Gleanings, Second Series*, p. 95.

He was an orthodox antiquary, who had written in behalf of tithes when John Selden got into trouble for his account of them, and left behind him a valuable archæological glossary, and a collection in two folios, the first published in 1639, the second after his death, of British Ecclesiastical Laws, *Concilia, Decreta, Leges, Constitutiones in Re Ecclesiastica Orbis Britannici.* He had a son, Sir John Spelman, who inherited his tastes, wrote a life of King Alfred, and survived his father but two years. In 1640, Sir Henry Spelman, then eighty years old, founded a lectureship at Cambridge for the study of Anglo-Saxon or First English.—MORLEY, HENRY, 1873, *A First Sketch of English Literature*, p. 586.

GENERAL

Spleman's "Glossary" is a very useful and learned book.—LOCKE, JOHN, 1704? *Some Thoughts Concerning Reading and Study.*

This learned and industrious antiquary, to whom every writer of English history, since his time, is indebted, was one of the Antiquarian Society in the reign of James I. and the intimate friend of Camden and Sir Robert Cotton. He was not only well skilled in the learned languages, but was also a great master of the Saxon tongue; of which he is justly esteemed a chief restorer, and for which he settled a lecture in the university of Cambridge. His principal works, which are in Latin, will last as long as the language in which they are written: of these his "English Councils," and his "Glossary," hold the first place.—GRANGER, JAMES, 1769-1824, *Biographical History of England, vol. III, p. 150.*

Of all the writers on etymology whose works I have read or consulted, Spelman and Lluyd are almost the only ones in whose deductions much confidence can be placed.—WEBSTER, NOAH, 1828, *Dictionary of the English Language, Introduction.*

His works are almost all upon legal and ecclesiastical antiquities. Having, in the course of his investigations, found it necessary to study the Saxon Language, he embodied the fruits of his labour in his great work called "Glossarium Archæologicum," the object of which is the explanation of obsolete words occurring in the laws of England. . . . The writings of this author have furnished valuable materials to English historians, and he is considered as the restorer of Saxon literature, both by means of his own studies, and by founding a Saxon professorship at Cambridge.—CHAMBERS, ROBERT, 1876, *Cyclopædia of English Literature, ed. Carruthers.*

Arthur Johnston

1587–1641

Physician and poet, was born in 1587, near Aberdeen, and was educated at the university of that city, on leaving which he went to Padua, where he took his doctor's degree, and then settled in Paris. After an absence of nearly forty years, chiefly spent in travel, he returned to Aberdeen, and became Principal of the university till Archbishop Laud invited him to London, and obtained for him the appointment of physician in ordinary to Charles I. He published a collection of Latin epigrams, an elegant parapharse of the Psalms in Latin verse, and a selection of the works of Scottish writers, entitled "Poetarum Scoticorum Deliciæ." Died, 1641.—CATES, WILLIAM L. R., 1867, *ed., Dictionary of General Biography, p. 571.*

GENERAL

Would have done honour to any country.—JOHNSON, SAMUEL, 1775, *A Journey to the Western Isles of Scotland.*

Arthur Johnston is not so verbose, and has, of course, more vigour; but his choice of a couplet, which keeps the reader always in mind of the puerile epistles of Ovid, was singularly injudicious.—BEATTIE, JAMES, 1783, *Dissertations.*

The Scots certainly wrote Latin with a good ear, and considerable elegance of phrase. A sort of critical controversy was carried on in the last century as to the versions of the Psalms by Buchanan and Jonston. Though the national honor may seem equally secure by the superiority of either, it has, I believe, been usual in Scotland to maintain the older poet against all the world. I am nevertheless inclined to think, that Jonston's Psalms, all of which are in elegiac metre, do not fall short of those of Buchanan, either in elegance of style or in correctness of Latinity.—HALLAM, HENRY, 1837-39, *Introduction to the Literature of Europe, pt. iii, ch. v, par. 72.*

As a latin poet, Arthur Johnston was all but the equal of Buchanan; and the literary reputation of Scotland depended abroad, if not in England, more on his Latin poetry than on the English poetry of his friends Drummond, Aytoun, and Alexander.—MASSON, DAVID, 1858, *The Life of John Milton, vol. I, ch. vi.*

His own poetical merits have perhaps been better recognised by English than by Scottish critics.—GORDON, ALEXANDER, 1892, *Dictionary of National Biography, vol. XXX, p. 59.*

Thomas Dekker

1570?-1641?

Born, in London, 1570 (?). Practically nothing known of life except constant literary activity. Wrote a number of plays from 1598 onwards. Died, 1641 (?). *Works:* "Canaans Calamitie," 1578; "The Shoemaker's Holiday" (anon.), 1600; "The Pleasant Comedie of Old Fortunatus" (anon.), 1600; "Satiromastix," 1602; "The Wonderfull Yeare, 1603" (anon.),1603; "The Batchelar's Banquet" (anon.), 1603: "Patient Grissil" (with Haughton and Chettle), 1603; "Magnificent Entertainment given to King James," 1604; "The Honest Whore," 1604; "The Seven Deadly Sinnes of London," 1606; "Newes from Hell," 1606; "The Double P. P." (anon.), 1606; "A Knight's Conjuring," 1607; "Westward Ho" (with Webster), 1607; "Northward Ho" (with Webster), 1607; "The Whore of Babylon," 1607; "The Famous History of Sir Thomas Wyat" (with Webster), 1607; "The Dead Tearme," 1608; "The Belman of London" (anon.), 1608; "Lanthorne and Candlelight," 1608 (2nd and 3rd edns., 1609; 4th, anon., entitled "O per se O," 1612); "The Ravens [Raven's] Almanacke," 1609; "The Guls Horne-booke," 1609; "Work for Armourers," 1609; "Fowre Birds of Noah's Arke," 1609; "The Roaring Girle" (with Middleton), 1611; "If it be not good, etc.," 1612; "Troia-Nova Triumphans," 1612; "A Strange Horse Race," 1613; "Villanies Discovered" (anon.), 1616; "Dekker his Dreame," 1620; "Greevous Grones for the Poore" (anon.), 1621; "The Virgin Martyr" (with Massinger), 1622; "A Rod for Run-Awayes," 1625; "Warres, Warres, Warres," 1628; "Britannia's Honour," 1628; "London's Tempe," 1629; "Second Part of The Honest Whore," 1630; "Match Mee in London," 1631; "The Wonder of a Kingdome," 1636. *Posthumous:* "The Sun's Darling" (with Ford), 1656; "The Witch of Edmonton" (with Ford and Rowley), 1658. *Collected Works:* Dramatic Works, with memoir, in 4 vols., 1873; Non-Dramatic Works, ed. by A. B. Grosart (5 vols.), 1884–86.—SHARP, R. FARQUHARSON, 1897, *A Dictionary of English Authors, p.* 76.

PERSONAL

That Sharpham, Day, Dicker, were all rogues. — DRUMMOND, WILLIAM, 1619, *Notes on Ben Jonson's Conversations.*

This quarrel is a splendid instance how genius of the first order, lavishing its satirical powers on a number of contemporaries, may discover, among the crowd, some individual who may return with a right aim the weapon he has himself used, and who will not want for encouragement to attack the common assailant: the greater genius is thus mortified by a victory conceded to the inferior, which he himself had taught the meaner one to obtain over him.—DISRAELI, ISAAC, 1812–13, *Jonson and Decker, Quarrels of Authors.*

The little that is known of Dekker's history, independent of his quarrel with Jonson, is unfortunate. His talents were prolific, and not contemptible; but he was goaded on by want to hasty productions— acquainted with spunging-houses, and an inmate of the King's Bench prison.— CAMPBELL, THOMAS, 1819, *Specimens of the British Poets.*

He was a playwright of great celebrity some years before the death of Queen Elizabeth, and had written most of his pieces for companies with which Alleyn and Henslowe were connected. Like many of his class, he seems to have been a man of careless habits, as regarded his pecuniary affairs, living from hand to mouth, by turns affluent and needy, and supplying his pressing wants by the produce of his prolific pen. — COLLIER, JOHN PAYNE, 1841, *ed., Memoirs of Edward Alleyn, p.* 131.

A man whose inborn sweetness and gleefulness of soul carried him through vexations and miseries which would have crushed a spirit less hopeful, cheerful, and humane. . . . Whatever may have been the effect of his vagabond habits on his principles, they did not stain the sweetness and purity of his sentiments. There is an innocency in his very coarseness, and a brisk, bright good-nature chirps in his very scurrility. In the midst of distresses of all kinds, he still seems, like his own Fortunatus, "all felicity up to the brims."—WHIPPLE, EDWIN P., 1859-68, *The Literature of the Age of Elizabeth, pp.* 131, 132.

O sweetest heart of all thy time save one,
Star seen for love's sake nearest to the sun,
  Hung lamplike o'er a dense and doleful
  city,
Not Shakespeare's very spirit, howe'er more
  great,
Than thine toward man was more compas-
  sionate,
  Nor gave Christ praise from lips more
  sweet with pity.
—SWINBURNE, ALGERNON CHARLES, 1882,
Thomas Decker, p. 629.

More than ordinarily tantalizing and disappointing has been the outcome of prolonged and earnest search in all likely sources and by all likely helpers for light on the long-dimmed story of Thomas Dekker. It is no new experience to such Worker as myself in Elizabethan-Jacobean literary-biographical fields. None the less is it trying to find one who demonstrably was in many men's mouths, and was noticeably and continuously a popular writer, so utterly overlooked by those from whom loving memories might have been counted on: *e. g.*, associated intimately as he was with the Playwrights of his period, from Ben Jonson to Massinger and Ford, and George Wilkins, it seems inexplicable that not one of all their superabundant productions yields a single distinct personal reference.— GROSART, ALEXANDER B., 1886, *ed., The Non-Dramatic Works of Thomas Dekker, Memorial Introduction, vol.* v, *p.* ix.

We have four goodly volumes of his plays and five of his other works; yet of Thomas Dekker, the man, we know absolutely less than of any one of his shadowy fellows. We do not know when he was born, when he died, what he did other than writing in the certainly long space between the two unknown dates. In 1637 he was by his own words a man of threescore, which, as it has been justly remarked, may mean anything between fifty-five and seventy. He was in circumstances a complete contrast to his fellow-victim in Jonson's satire, Marston. Marston was apparently a gentleman born and bred, well connected, well educated, possessed of some property, able to make testamentary dispositions, and probably in the latter part of his life, when Dekker was still toiling at journalism of various kinds, a beneficed clergyman in country retirement. Dekker was, it is to be feared, what the arrogance of certain members of

the literary profession has called, and calls, a gutter-journalist—a man who had no regular preparation for the literary career, and who never produced anything but hand-to-mouth work. Jonson went so far as to say that he was a "rogue;" but Ben, though certainly not a rogue, was himself not to be trusted when he spoke of people that he did not like; and if there was any but innocent roguery in Dekker he has contrived to leave exactly the opposite impression stamped on every piece of his work.—SAINTSBURY, GEORGE, 1887, *History of Elizabethan Literature*, p. 200.

In despite of his rare occasional spurts or outbreaks of self-assertion or of satire, he seems to stand before us as a man of gentle, modest, shiftless and careless nature, irritable and placable, eager and unsteady, full of excitable kindliness and deficient in strenuous principle; loving the art which he professionally followed, and enjoying the work which he occasionally neglected.—SWINBURNE, ALGERNON CHARLES, 1887, *Thomas Dekker, The Nineteenth Century, vol.* 21, *p.* 102.

OLD FORTUNATUS
1600

The humour of a frantic lover, in the scene where Orleans to his friend Galloway defends the passion with which himself, being a prisoner in the English king's court, is enamoured to frenzy of the king's daughter Agripyna, is done to the life. Orleans is as passionate an inamorato as any which Shakespeare ever drew. He is just such another adept in Love's reasons. The sober people of the world are with him

  A swarm of fools
Crowding together to be counted wise.

He talks "pure Biron and Romeo," he is almost as poetical as they, quite as philosophical, only a little madder. After all, Love's secretaries are a reason unto themselves. We have gone retrograde to the noble heresy, since the days when Sidney proselyted our nation to this mixed health and disease; the kindliest symptom, yet the most alarming crisis in the ticklish state of youth; the nourisher and the destroyer of hopeful wits; the mother of twin births, wisdom and folly, valour and weakness; the servitude above freedom; the gentle mind's religion; the liberal superstition. — LAMB, CHARLES, 1808, *Specimens of Dramatic Poets.*

Altogether this romantic comedy attracts by a singular vigour and freshness; but its principal charm lies in the appropriately *naïf* treatment of its simple, not to say childlike, theme.—WARD, ADOLPHUS WILLIAM, 1875-99, *A History of English Dramatic Literature, vol.* II. *p.* 459.

SATIROMASTRIX
1602

Dekker had very much the best of the contest. From Gifford's saying that "Dekker writes in downright passion, and foams through every page," we should infer that he had never read "Satiromastrix," were it not the case that he makes mistakes equally gross concerning plays that he must have read. Dekker writes with the greatest possible lightness of heart, easy mockery, and free abuse. It is absurd to say that he "makes no pretensions to invention, but takes up the characters of his predecessor, and turns them the seamy side without." Tucca is the only character that he borrows, and a very ingenious idea it is—one of the best parts of the joke—to set Jonson's own free-spoken swaggerer to abuse himself. Dekker's Tucca is much more ably wrought out than Jonson's; he has a much finer command of what Widow Minever calls "horrible ungodly names;" and his devices to obtain money are equally shameless and amusing. All the other characters, and what plot there is, are Dekker's own; he, of course, uses the names Horace, Crispinus, and Demetrius, otherwise there would have been no point in his reply—but he gives them very different characters. —MINTO, WILLIAM, 1874-85, *Characteristics of English Poets, p.* 344.

The controversial part of the play is so utterly alien from the romantic part that it is impossible to regard them as component factors of the same original plot. It seems to me unquestionable that Dekker must have conceived the design, and probable that he must have begun the composition, of a serious play on the subject of William Rufus and Sir Walter Tyrrel, before the appearance of Ben Jonson's "Poetaster" impelled or instigated him to some immediate attempt at rejoinder; and that being in a feverish hurry to retort the blow inflicted on him by a heavier hand than his own he devised—perhaps between jest and earnest — the preposterously

incoherent plan of piecing out his farcical and satirical design by patching and stitching it into his unfinished scheme of tragedy. It may be assumed, and it is much to be hoped, that there never existed another poet capable of imagining—much less of perpetrating—an incongruity so monstrous and so perverse. . . . That Dekker was unable to hold his own against Jonson when it came to sheer hard hitting—that on the ground or platform of personal satire he was as a light weight pitted against a heavy weight—is of course too plain, from the very first round, to require any further demonstration. But it is not less plain that in delicacy and simplicity and sweetness of inspiration the poet who could write the scene in which the bride takes poison (as she believes) from the hand of her father, in presence of her bridegroom, as a refuge from the passion of the king, was as far above Jonson as Jonson was above him in the robuster qualities of intellect or genius. This most lovely scene, for pathos tempered with fancy and for passion distilled in melody, is comparable only with higher work, of rarer composition and poetry more pure, than Jonson's: it is a very treasure-house of verses like jewels, bright as tears and sweet as flowers. When Dekker writes like this, then truly we seem to see his right hand in the left hand of Shakespeare.—SWINBURNE, ALGERNON CHARLES, 1887, *Thomas Dekker, The Nineteenth Century, vol.* 21, *pp.* 84, 85.

THE HONEST WHORE
1604–1630

There is in the second part of this play, where Bellafront, a reclaimed harlot, recounts some of the miseries of her profession, a simple picture of honour and shame, contrasted without violence, and expressed without immodesty, which is worth all the *strong lines* against the harlot's profession, with which both parts of this play are offensively crowded.— LAMB, CHARLES, 1808, *Specimens of Dramatic Poets.*

Old honest Decker's Signor Orlando Friscobaldo I shall never forget! I became only of late acquainted with this last-mentioned worthy character; but the bargain between us is, I trust, for life. We sometimes regret that we had not sooner met with characters like these, that seem to raise, revive, and give a new zest to our being. Vain the complaint! We should never have known their value, if we had not known them always: they are old, very old acquaintance, or we should not recognise them at first sight. We only find in books what is already written within "the red-leaved tables of our hearts."—HAZLITT, WILLIAM, 1820, *Lectures on the Literature of the Age of Elizabeth.*

In this play, which to my mind has every mark of being essentially his, Dekker has treated with powerful simplicity the most terrible of the sins of a great city, and although I am by no means inclined to assign to "The Honest Whore," from a literary point of view, the highest eminence among his dramatic works, the depth of its general conception and the broad effectiveness of its execution have justly caused this to be regarded as one of the most interesting productions of the popular Elisabethan drama. . . . Dekker's age, whatever its vices and weaknesses, had not lost the power of holding up to them a true and uncompromising mirror; and it must be allowed that in "The Honest Whore" the main lesson of the action is brought home not merely with the utmost directness of speech, but also with unmistakeable integrity of purpose.—WARD, ADOLPHUS WILLIAM, 1875-99, *A History of English Dramatic Literature, vol. II, p. 462.*

His smypathy with sinful and sorrowing humanity was genuine and deep; but his poignant feelings sometimes found expression in language which seems to have the air of insincerity. In the fine scenes where Hippolito implores Bellafront to abandon her vicious course of life, and again where he strives to undo the effect of his former teaching, one feels that the arguments and illustrations are enforced with over-heated vehemence. This note of exaggeration is never absent from Dekker's work; he let his fancy have full swing and did not write "with slower pen." But he was the most natural of writers, lovable at all points, full of simplicity and tenderness. The character of Orlando Friscobaldo is drawn in Dekker's cheeriest, sunniest manner. . . . Had Middleton's share in "The Honest Whore" been at all considerable, we may be tolerably sure that his name would not

have been omitted from the title-page.—BULLEN, A. H., 1885, *ed., The Works of Thomas Middleton, Introduction, vol. I, p. xxv, xxvii.*

My own reason for preferring it to almost all the non-tragical work of the time out of Shakespere, is the wonderful character of Bellafront, both in her unreclaimed and her reclaimed condition. In both she is a very woman—not as conventional satirists and conventional encomiasts praise or rail at women, but as women are. If her language in her unregenerate days is sometimes coarser than is altogether pleasant, it does not disguise her nature,—the very nature of such a woman misled by giddiness, by curiosity, by love of pleasure, by love of admiration, but in no thorough sense depraved. Her selection of Matheo not as the instrument of her being "made an honest woman," not apparently because she had any love for him left, or had ever had much, but because he was her first seducer, is exactly what, after a sudden convincing of sin, such a woman would have done; and if her patience under the long trial of her husband's thoughtlessness and occasional brutality seem excessive, it will only seem so to one who has been unlucky in his experience. Matheo indeed is a thorough good-for-nothing, and the natural man longs that Bellafront might have been better parted; but Dekker was a very moral person in his own way, and apparently he would not entirely let her—Imogen gone astray as she is—off her penance. — SAINTSBURY, GEORGE, 1887, *History of Elizabethan Literature, p. 205.*

Of all Dekker's works, "The Honest Whore" comes nearest to some reasonable degree of unity and harmony in conception and construction: his besetting vice of reckless and sluttish incoherence has here done less than usual to deform the proportions and deface the impression of his design.—SWINBURNE, ALGERNON CHARLES, 1887, *Thomas Dekker, The Nineteenth Century, vol. 21, p. 87.*

GENERAL

Quick Anti-Horace.—CHETTLE, HENRY, 1603, *England's Mourning Garment.*

Why, sir, sayd I, there is a booke called "Greenes Ghost haunts Conycatchers;" another called "Legerdemaine," and "The Blacke Dog of Newgate;" but the most wittiest, elegantest and eloquentest peece (Master Dekkers, the true heire of Appolo composed) called "The Bell-man of London," have already set foorth the vices of the time so vively, that it is unpossible the Anchor of any other mans braine can sound the sea of a more deepe and dreadful mischeefe.—FENNOR, WILLIAM, 1617, *The Compter's Commonwealth.*

A high-flier in wit, even against Ben Jonson himself, in his Comedy called "The Untrussing of the Humourous Poet."— PHILLIPS, EDWARD, 1675, *Theatrum Poetarum Anglicanorum,* ed. Brydges, p. 237.

A Poet that liv'd in the Reign of King *James* the First, and was Contemporary with that admirable *Laureat,* Mr. *Benjamin Johnson.* He was more famous for the contention he had with him for the Bays, than for any great Reputation he had gain'd by his own Writings. Yet even in that Age, he wanted not his Admirers, nor his Friends amongst the Poets: in which number I reckon the Ingenious Mr. *Richard Brome;* who always stil'd him by the Title of *Father.* He clubb'd with *Webster* in writing Three Plays; and with *Rowley* and *Ford* in another: and I think I may venture to say, that these Plays as far exceed those of his own Brain, as a platted Whipcord exceeds a single Thread in strength. Of those which he writ alone, I know none of much Esteem, except "The Untrussing the Humourous Poet," and that chiefly on account of the Subject of it, which was the Witty *Ben Johnson.*—LANGBAINE, GERARD, 1691, *An Account of the English Dramatick Poets,* p. 121.

Upon the whole, Decker cannot be ranked with Chapman and Heywood, and it is very probable that he could not have been half so well respected as he was, had not the envy of Jonson, who had he possessed an atom of good sense would have smiled and passed by him, lifted him into a consequence, not only fancied by him but credited by the world.—DIBDIN, CHARLES, 1795, *A Complete History of the Stage,* vol. III, p. 260.

Decker was a very popular writer, whose numerous tracts exhibit to posterity a more detailed narrative of the manners of the town in the Elizabethan age than is elsewhere to be found.—DISRAELI, ISAAC, 1812–13, *Jonson and Decker, Quarrels of Authors.*

On the same elevation with Middleton, as to dramatic merit, may we place the name of Thomas Decker, who, if he has not equalled his contemporary in the faculty of imagination, has, in some instances, exceeded him, in the vigorous conception of his characters, and the skilful management of his fable.—DRAKE, NATHAN, 1817, *Shakspeare and His Times,* vol. II, p. 566.

Yet more versatile, whimsical, and even prolific than either of the foregoing writers (perhaps not excepting Greene) was Thomas Dekker.—DIBDIN, THOMAS FROGNALL, 1824, *The Library Companion, note,* p. 594.

I take Webster and Decker to have been the two greatest of the Shakspeare men, for unstudied genius, next after Beaumont and Fletcher; and in some respects they surpassed them. Beaumont and Fletcher have no such terror as Webster, nor any such piece of hearty, good, affecting human clay as Decker's "Old Signior Orland Friscobaldo." Is there any such man even in Shakspeare?—any such exaltation of that most delightful of all things, *bonhomie?* Webster sometimes overdoes his terror; nay, often. He not only riots, he debauches in it; and Decker, full of heart and delicacy as he is, and qualified to teach refinement to the refined, condescends to an astounding coarseness. Beaumont and Fletcher's good company saved them from that, in words. In spirit they are full of it. But Decker never mixes up (at least not as far as I can remember) any such revolting and impossible contradictions in the same character as they do. Neither does he bring a doubt on his virtues by exaggerating them. He believes heartily in what he does believe, and you love him in consequence.—HUNT, LEIGH, 1844, *Imagination and Fancy,* p. 197.

One of the most fascinating dramatists of his generation, and, with much vulgarity and trash, has passages worthy of the greatest. He is light, airy, sportive, humane, forgetive, and possesses both animal and intellectual spirits to perfection. He seems flushed and heated with the very wine of life; throws off the sunniest morsels of wit and wisdom with a beautiful heedlessness and unstudied ease: and in his intense enjoyment of life and motion appears continually to exclaim, with his own Matheo, "Do we not fly high?"—WHIPPLE, EDWIN P., 1846, *Old English Dramatists, Essays and Reviews, vol.* II, *p.* 39.

He appears to have been by no means destitute of imagination, of pathos, or of humour; though his genius has always appeared to us rather lyric than dramatic.—SHAW, THOMAS B., 1847, *Outlines of English Literature, p.* 130.

Dekker must not be estimated from Jonson's character of him. He wrote a great number of plays, and was joined in several by Webster, Ford, and others. His pieces are remarkably unequal. His plots are not always well chosen, and are generally careless in construction. But in occasional scenes he rises to an unexpected height of power, and exhibits a range of fancy that fairly entitles him to take rank with the majority of his contemporaries.—BELL, ROBERT, 1867? *ed., Songs from the Dramatists, p.* 176.

I am not certain whether I may not now be calling up a singer whose song will appear hardly to justify his presence in the choir. But its teaching is of high import, namely, of content and cheerfulness and courage, and being both worthy and melodious, it gravitates heavenward. The singer is yet another dramatist: I presume him to be Thomas Dekker. I cannot be certain, because others were concerned with him in the writing of the drama from which I take it.—MACDONALD, GEORGE, 1868, *England's Antiphon, p.* 140.

Though his lyrical gifts were of a rare quality, though he was master of a vigorous if not elevated rhetoric, and though his natural humour, which shows itself at its height already in his earliest extant comedy, seems to have been constantly fed by lively observation, he produced no one dramatic work of a high order. It is in scattered scenes and passages rather than in the working out of characters or plots that he displays elements of real tragic power; for at times his pathos is singularly sudden and direct. A fuller measure of success he commands only within a limited sphere. Inside of this, although the grossness of his realism makes it impossible for a more refined age to dwell with unalloyed pleasure on his pictures of contemporary life, the unaffected healthiness of his spirit and the vigour of his comic genius are beyond dispute.—WARD, ADOLPHUS WILLIAM, 1875–99, *A History of English Dramatic Literature, vol.* II, *p.* 471.

Dekker had several qualities which made him a desirable coadjutor in playwriting. He was a master of the craft of the stage. A man of quick sympathies, unconquerable buoyancy of spirit, infinite readiness and resource, he had lived among the people who filled the theatres, and took a genuine delight in moving them by the exhibition of common joys and sorrows. His whole heart went with his audience, and, though he had not the loftiness of aim of his greatest contemporaries, none of them had a finer dramatic instinct. He knew London as well as Dickens, and had something of the same affection for its oddities and its outcasts. The humour which lights up its miseries, the sunshine which plays over its tears, the simple virtues of the poor and unfortunate, patience, forgiveness, mirthfulness, were the favourite themes of this tender-hearted dramatist. His plays are full of life and movement, of pathos that is never maudlin and humour that is never harsh. Vice always gets the worst of it, hardness of heart above all never goes unpunished, but relenting leniency always comes in to keep retribution within gentle bounds. Virtue is always triumphant, but it is discovered in the most fantastic shapes and the least conventional habiliments.—MINTO, WILLIAM, 1880, *English Poets, ed. Ward, vol.* II, *p.* 55.

A hopeful, cheerful, humane spirit, who turned vexations and miseries into commodities.—WELSH, ALFRED H., 1882, *Development of English Literature and Language, vol.* I, *p.* 425, *note.*

Dekker would have taken a high place among the finest if not among the greatest of English poets if he had but had the sense of form—the instinct of composition. Whether it was modesty, indolence, indifference or incompetence, some drawback or short-coming there was which so far impaired the quality of his strong and delicate genius that it is impossible for his most ardent and cordial admirer to say or think of his very best work that it really in this does him justice—that it adequately represents the fullness of his unquestionable powers.—SWINBURNE, ALGERNON CHARLES, 1886, *Thomas Middleton, The Nineteenth Century, vol.* 19, *p.* 143.

Honest Dekker, with his easy-going sensibilities and facile touch on human feeling.—SYMONDS, JOHN ADDINGTON, 1887, *Marlowe, (Mermaid Series), General Introduction to the Drama, p.* xxiv.

When all deductions have been made on the score of inartistic and reckless workmanship, Dekker's best plays rank with the masterpieces of the Elizabethan drama; and his numerous tracts, apart from their sterling literary interest, are simply invaluable for the information that they afford concerning the social life of Elizabethan and Jacobean times.—BULLEN, A. H., 1888, *Dictionary of National Biography, vol.* XIV, *p.* 300.

There is good meat in what Dekker wrote: he had humor; he had pluck; he had gift for using words—to sting or to praise—or to beguile one. There are traces not only of a Dickens flavor in him, but of a Lamb flavor as well; and there is reason to believe that, like both these later humorists, he made his conquests without the support of a university training. Swinburne characterizes him as a "modest, shiftless, careless nature:" but he was keen to thrust a pin into one who had offended his sensibilities; in his plays he warmed into pretty lyrical outbreaks, but never seriously measured out a work of large proportions, or entered upon execution of such with a calm, persevering temper. He was many-sided, not only literary-wise, but also conscience-wise. It seems incredible that one who should write the coarse things which appear in his "Bachelor's Banquet" should also have elaborated, with a pious unction (that reminds of Jeremy Taylor) the saintly invocations of the "Foure Birds of Noah's Ark:" and as for his "Dreame" it shows in parts a luridness of color which reminds of our own Wigglesworth—as if this New England poet of fifty years later may have dipped his brush into the same paint-pot.—MITCHELL, DONALD G., 1889, *English Lands Letters and Kings, From Celt to Tudor, p.* 287.

A marked difference between Dekker and Nash resulted from the fact that Dekker had not only a love of poetry, but a poetical faculty of a high order. He went far beyond the picturesqueness of Nash's word-painting, and reached in his prose as well as in his verse true lyrical emotion and pathos; he had, said Lamb, "poetry enough for anything;" and while Nash's gaiety, true and hearty as it is, takes often and naturally a bitter satirical turn, Dekker's gaiety though sometimes bitter, more usually takes a pretty, graceful, and fanciful turn. . . . Dekker did not write novels properly so called, but his prose works abound with scenes that seem detached from novels, and that were so well fitted for that kind of writing that we find them again in the works of professional novelists of his or of a later time.—JUSSERAND, J. J., 1890, *The English Novel in the Time of Shakespeare, pp.* 332, 335.

Is unrivalled in short pathetic scenes, has a tenderness that is all his own, combines with a sweet fancy a rare lyrical gift, but is excessively unequal as a craftsman, and mars some of his finest efforts by his impatience, his incoherence, and his carelessness. It is difficult to understand how it can be possible that the author of the detestable stuff called "If it be not good, the Devil is in it," could have turned away to contribute to Massinger's "Virgin Martyr" the exquisite episode between the heroine and the angel. This extravagant inequality, ever recurring, creates the standing difficulty about the literary position of Dekker.—GOSSE, EDMUND, 1894, *The Jacobean Poets, p.* 22.

Dekker is the complement of Chapman, with whom, as with Jonson and Marston, he was conjoined in a series of now inextricable literary friendships and quarrels. Chapman was a scholar and a ripe one; Dekker is not known to have had any education. Chapman had a rugged obscurity and a native force tending to extravagance as his chief gifts; Dekker combines sweetness, which is never cloying or merely sentimental, with a curious limpidity and fluency of diction. He wrote, so far as we know, no poems of note, save the charming lyrics inserted in his plays; but his prose is a sort of manual of the lower London life of the times of Elizabeth and James; and his best plays, "Old Fortunatus" and "The Honest Whore," exalt pathos, which is never maudlin or conventional, to nearly its highest pitch. A parallel contrast between Dekker and Dickens would be very instructive; I do not know that it has ever been drawn.—SAINTSBURY, GEORGE, 1895, *Social England, ed. Traill, vol.* IV, *p.* 108.

Though a cloud hangs over the birth and death of Thomas Dekker, and though the details of his personal career be obscured, yet through his pamphlets and plays he has supplied us with some of the most vivid existing pictures of the days in which he lived. We wander among the narrow streets of old London, beneath the gabled houses with their creaking signs; look in at the booth-like shops, and listen by day to the 'prentice call of "What d'ye lack?" or watch the mercers roll up their silks and velvets at nightfall and the goldsmiths put away their plate; we stroll beneath the Gothic arches of old St. Paul's, and see the gallants flaunt their cloaks; we float along the river, or pass beyond the city walls, in the days when the Moor-gate really led to moors, and when Fins-bury had its swampy fens; we visit the ordinaries, the taverns, the theatre; we behold the plague-stricken city, and watch the deadcart pass, and see the bodies "tumbled into their euerlasting lodgings (ten in one heape and twenty in another) as if all the roomes vpon earth had bin full;" we become familiar with the haunts of sin and vice, and may find ourselves with Dekker within the walls of one of those "thirteene strong houses of sorrow where the prisoner hath his heart wasting away." Dekker's homely pictures of this bygone life have all the realism of Dutch paintings; deficient as they are in composition and execution, we trace behind them a kindly human heart, like that of Steele or Goldsmith, which draws us to the writer despite evident faults of style and flaws of character.—MORLEY, HENRY AND GRIFFIN, W. HALL, 1895, *English Writers, vol.* XI, *p.* 290.

Marston, the respectable country parson, who, with his coarseness and his savage force, makes a strange contrast to his friend Dekker the vagabond, who had such a wonderful lyric faculty, and wrote with so much humour, pathos, and tenderness.—FIELD, LILIAN F., 1898, *An Introduction to the Study of the Renaissance, p.* 166.

Sir John Suckling
1609–1642

Sir John Suckling (1609–42), poet, was born at Whitton in Middlesex, the son of a secretary of state to James I. In 1623 he entered Trinity College, Cambridge, in 1628 went on his travels, and served for some time under Gustavus Adolphus. He returned about 1632, became famous at court for his wit and prodigality, and in 1639 raised a troop of 100 horse to aid the king against the Scots. Suckling was returned to the Long Parliament, joined in the abortive plot to rescue Strafford from the Tower, and in more desperate plots still against the liberties of the kingdom, but his schemes being discovered fled to the Continent. Impoverished and disgraced, he almost certainly poisoned himself at Paris. The works of Suckling consist of four plays, "Aglaura," "The Goblins," "Brennoralt," and "The Sad One," now forgotten; a prose treatise, "An Account of Religion by Reason;" a few "Letters;" and a series of miscellaneous poems, beginning with "A Sessions of the Poets" (1637), which is happily descriptive of the author's contemporaries. But the fame of Suckling rests on his ballads and songs such as the "Ballad upon a Wedding" and "Why so pale and wan, fond lover?" See the Rev. A. Suckling's "Selections, with a Life" (1836), reproduced by W. C. Hazlitt (1874; new ed. 1893); also the Memoir prefixed to F. A. Stokes's edition (New York, 1885).—PATRICK AND GROOME, *eds.,* 1897, *Chambers's Biographical Dictionary, p.* 891.

PERSONAL

Suckling next was called, but did not appear,
But straight one whispered Apollo i' th' ear,
That of all men living he cared not for 't,
He loved not the Muses so well as his sport.
And prized black eyes, or a lucky hit
At bowls, above all the trophies of wit;
But Apollo was angry, and publicly said,
'Twere fit that a fine were set upon 's head.
—SUCKLING, SIR JOHN, 1637, *A Sessions of the Poets.*

Suckling, whose numbers could invite
Alike to wonder and delight;
And with new spirit did inspire
The Thespian scene and Delphic lyre:
Is thus express'd in either part
Above the humble reach of art.
Drawn by the pencil, here you find
His form—by his own pen, his mind.
—STANLEY, THOMAS, 1646, *Lines beneath Marshall's Portrait, Suckling's Works.*

He was the greatest gallant of his

SIR JOHN SUCKLING

After the Painting by Vandyke.
Etching by J. S. King.

JOHN CLEVELAND

From a Picture by Fuller. Drawing by
T. Uwins. Engraving by R. Rhodes.

time, and the greatest gamester, both for bowling and cards, so that no shopkeeper would trust him for 6*d*., as to-day, for instance, he might, by winning, be worth 200 *li*., the next day he might not be worth half so much, or perhaps be sometimes *minus nihilo.* Sir William [Davenant] (who was his intimate friend, and loved him intirely) would say that Sir John, when he was at his lowest ebbe in gameing, I meane when unfortunate, then would make himselfe most glorious in apparell, and sayd that it exalted his spirits, and that he had then best luck when he was most gallant, and his spirits were highest. . . . He was of middle stature and slight strength, brisque round eie, reddish fac't and red nose (ill liver), his head not very big, his hayre a kind of sand colour; his beard turnd-up naturally, so that he had brisk and gracefull looke. He died a batchelour. . . . Sir John Suckling —from Mr. William Beeston—invented the game of cribbidge.—AUBREY, JOHN, 1669-96, *Brief Lives, ed. Clark, vol.* II, *pp.* 240, 242, 245.

He had so pregnant a Genius that he spoke *Latin* at Five Years Old, and writ it at Nine Years of Age. His Skill in Languages, and *Musick*, was Remarkable; but above all his *Poetry*, took with all the People, whose Souls were polished by the Charms of the *Muses:* And tho' *War* did not so well agree with his Constitution; yet in his Travels he made a Campaign under the Famous *Gustavus*, where he was present at three Battles, five Sieges, and as many Skirmishes: and if his Valour was not so Remarkable, in the North in the beginning of the Wars; yet his Loyalty was conspicuous, by his Expence in the Troop of Horse, which he rais'd, whose Equipage, *viz.* Horses, Arms and Clothes, were provided all at his own Charge, and stood him in 12000 *l*.—LANGBAINE, GERARD, 1691, *An Account of the English Dramatick Poets, p.* 496.

Sir John Suckling was an immoral man, as well as debauched. The story of the French cards was told me by the late Duke of Buckingham; and he had it from old Lady Dorset herself. That lady took a very odd pride in boasting of her familiarities with Sir John Suckling. She is the Mistress and Goddess in his poems; and several of those pieces were given by herself to the printer. This the Duke of Buckingham used to give as one instance of the fondness she had to let the world know how well they were acquainted.— POPE, ALEXANDER, 1728-30, *Spence's Anecdotes, ed. Singer, p.* 2.

Sir John Suckling, a poet of great vivacity, and some elegance, was one of the finest gentlemen of his time.—GRANGER, JAMES, 1769-1824, *Biographical History of England, vol.* III, *p.* 128.

The active life of our poet was now drawing rapidly towards its closing scene. Time, as it rolled in its unceasing course, brought no prospect of a national reunion, while the interdict against his safety continued in full validity. Reduced, at length, in fortune, and dreading to encounter poverty, which his habits and temper were little calculated to endure— hurled from his rank in society—an alien, and perhaps friendless—his energies at length gave way to the complicated wretchedness of his situation, and he contemplated an act which he had himself condemned in others. Purchasing poison of an apothecary at Paris, he produced death, says Aubrey, by violent fits of vomiting. Some writers, with great tenderness to his character, have attributed his end to other causes and dissimilar means; but, I regret to add, family tradition confirms the first and most revolting narration. . . . Thus perished immaturely, and in a land of strangers, the accomplished subject of this memoir; marked indeed by early levity and indiscretions, but happily more distinguished by devoted loyalty and intellectual refinement. If he be charged with want of prudence in the direction of his great abilities to his own advancement, they were at least ever exerted in favour of the learned and the deserving. If his earlier years were stained by habits of intemperance and frivolity, he has amply redeemed himself by the exertions of his maturer age. To a kind and amiable temper he united a generous and a friendly disposition; while the proofs of his patriotism and loyalty have been so fully developed in the progress of this essay, that, with all his imperfections, he is entitled to rank with the most distinguished characters of his day.—SUCKLING, ALFRED, 1836-74, *ed., Suckling's Works.*

The delight of the Court and the darling of the Muses, Suckling was one of the sweetest poets, the most refined gentleman, and perhaps the wildest and most reckless cavalier of the age in which he lived.—JESSE, JOHN HENEAGE, 1839-57, *Memoirs of the Court of England During the Reign of the Stuarts, Including the Protectorate, vol.* II, *p.* 215.

He comes among a herd of scented fops with careless natural grace, and an odour of morning flowers upon him. You know not which would have been most delighted with his compliments, the dairy maid or the duchess. He was thrown too early upon a town life; otherwise a serious passion for some estimable woman, which (to judge from his graver poetry) he was very capable of entertaining, might have been the salvation of him. As it was, he died early, and, it is said, not happily; but this may have been the report of envy or party-spirit; for he was a great loyalist. It is probable, however, that he excelled less as a partizan than as a poet and a man of fashion. He is said to have given a supper to the ladies of his acquaintance, the last course of which consisted of millinery and trinkets. The great Nelson's mother was a Suckling of the same stock, in Norfolk.—HUNT, LEIGH, 1846, *Wit and Humour, p.* 216.

Considering the early age at which he passed away, and what he has left behind him in print, not to name his political exploits, it will be allowed, no doubt, that Suckling was a man of no ordinary genius, nor have we it in our power, we apprehend, to raise a better monument to him, than a faithful text of his authentic writings.—HAZLITT, W. CAREW, 1874, *ed., Poems, Plays and Other Romances of Suckling, Introduction, vol.* I, *p.* vi.

The feverish life of Suckling never fulfilled its true issues. Expatriated and disgraced, his sun went down in a foreign land, ere almost it had reached its meridian. . . . To the allurements of a court at first brilliant and trifling, then sensual and devilish, we owe in great measure the failure of Sucking's life, and the extinction of his fine genius. But, when all deductions have been made, there still remain substantial reasons for classing the poet honourably amongst the distinguished men of his age.—SMITH, GEORGE BARNETT, 1878, *Sir John Suckling, The Gentleman's Magazine, vol.* 243, *p.* 439.

No English poet has lived a life so public, so adventurous and so full of vicissitude as his. Nothing short of an irresistible bias towards the art of poetry could have induced so busy and so fortunate a man to write in verse at all. Beautiful and vigorous in body, educated in all the accomplishments that grace a gentleman, endowed from earliest youth with the prestige of a soldier and a popular courtier, his enormous wealth enabled him to indulge every whim that a fondness for what was splendid or eccentric in dress, architecture and pageantry could devise. Such a life could present no void which literary ambition could fill, and Suckling's scorn for poetic fame was well known to his contemporaries.—GOSSE, EDMUND, 1880, *English Poets, ed. Ward, vol.* II, *p.* 170.

Sir John Suckling was a gay courtier, much addicted to gambling, like many others who, by the side of the grave decorum of Charles's domestic life, anticipated the loose profligacies of the Whitehall of Charles II. As a writer of sparkling verses he secured the admiration of his contemporaries, and has retained the admiration of later generations. His conversation was as easy and brilliant as his verse, and he readily made himself acceptable to the ladies of the Court, who thought it no shame to listen to the airy doctrine that constancy in married life was a fit object of scorn, and that modesty was but an empty name. Amongst men he was much respected. Once in his life he had thought of marrying a lady whose attractions were to be found in the weight of her purse. A rival, strong of arm, cudgelled him till he agreed to renounce all claims upon the golden prize.—GARDINER, SAMUEL R., 1883, *History of England from the Accession of James I. to the Outbreak of the Civil War, vol.* IX, *p.* 311.

. . . thou, whom Muses crowned with
        every gift,
While yet a boy—tho' in achievement man
And monarch—young in years yet ripe in
    fame, ...
    .   .   .   .
Tender and great, true poet, dauntless heart,
We cannot see with eyes as clear as thine.
A sordid time dwarfs down the race of men
They may not touch the lute or draw the
    sword
As thou didst, half immortal.
—DE TABLEY, LORD JOHN, 1893, *On a Portrait of Sir John Suckling.*

GENERAL

Among the highest and most refined wits of the nation, this gentle and princely poet took his generous rise from the Court, where, having flourished with splendour and reputation, he lived only long enough to see the sunset of that majesty from whose auspicious beams he derived his lustre, and with whose declining state his own loyal fortunes were obscured. But after the several changes of those times, being sequestered from the more serene contentments of his native country, he first took care to secure the dearest and choicest of his papers in the several cabinets of his noble and faithful friends, and among other testimonies of his worth, these elegant and florid pieces of his fancy were preserved in the custody of his truly honourable and virtuous sister, with whose free permission they were transcribed, and now published exactly according to the originals. This might be sufficient to make you acknowledge that these are the real and genuine works of Sir John Suckling; but if you can yet doubt, let any judicious soul seriously consider the freedom of the fancy, richness of the conceipt, proper expression, with that air and spirit diffused through every part, and he will find such a perfect resemblance with what hath been formerly known, that he cannot with modesty doubt them to be his. I could tell you further (for I myself am the best witness of it), what a thirst and general inquiry hath been after what I here present you, by all that have either seen or heard of them. And by that time you have read them, you will believe me, who have, now for many years, anually published the productions of the best wits of our own and foreign nations.—MOSELEY, HUMPHREY, 1646, *Suckling's Poems, The Stationer to the Reader.*

Full of flowers, ["Aglaura"] but rather stuck in than growing there.—FLECKNOE, RICHARD, 1664, *Short Discourse on the English Stage.*

His poems are clear, sprightly, and natural,—his plays well-humoured and taking,—his letters fragrant and sparkling.—LLOYD, DAVID, 1668, *Memoirs of Excellent Personages.*

The grace and elegance of his songs and ballads are inimitable.—ELLIS, GEORGE, 1790-1845, *Specimens of the Early English Poets.*

Sir John Suckling is acknowledged to have left far behind him all former writers of song in gayety and ease : it is not equally clear that he has ever since been surpassed. His poetry aims at no higher praise : he shows no sentiment or imagination, either because he had them not, or because he did not require either in the style he chose. Perhaps the Italians may have poetry in that style equal to Suckling's ; I do not know that they have, nor do I believe that there is any in French : that there is none in Latin I am convinced. —HALLAM, HENRY, 1837-39, *Introduction to the Literature of Europe, pt.* iii, *ch.* v, *par.* 56.

For one who now reads anything of Carew there are twenty who know by heart some verses of his friend and brother-courtier, Sir John Suckling. His ballad upon a wedding, with the necessary omission of a verse or two, is in all our books of poetic extracts.—MASSON, DAVID, 1858, *The Life of John Milton, vol.* I, *ch.* vi.

Has none of the pathos of Lovelace or Carew, but he equals them in fluency and natural grace of manner, and he has besides a sprightliness and buoyancy which is all his own. His poetry has a more impulsive air than theirs ; and while, in reference to the greater part of what he has produced, he must be classed along with them and Waller as an adherent to the French school of propriety and precision, some of the happiest of his effusions are remarkable for a cordiality and impetuosity of manner which has nothing foreign about it, but is altogether English, although there is not much resembling it in any of his predecessors any more than of his contemporaries, unless perhaps in some of Skelton's pieces. His famous ballad of "The Wedding" is the very perfection of gayety and archness in verse ; and his "Session of the Poets," in which he scatters about his wit and humor in a more careless style, may be considered as constituting him the founder of a species of satire, which Cleveland and Marvel and other subsequent writers carried into new applications, and which only expired among us with Swift.—CRAIK, GEORGE L., 1861, *A Compendious History of English Literature and of the English Language, vol.* II, *p.* 28.

They turn eloquent phrases in order to

be applauded, and flattering exaggerations in order to please. The divine faces, the serious or profound looks, the virgin or impassioned expressions which burst forth at every step in the early poets, have disappeared; here we see nothing but agreeable countenances, painted in agreeable verses. Blackguardism is not far off; we meet with it as early as in Suckling, and crudity to boot, and prosaic epicurism.—TAINE, H. A., 1871, *English Literature*, tr. *Van Laun, vol.* I, *bk.* ii, *ch.* i, *p.* 201.

Suckling—strange as it may appear to those who only know his career as a poet—wrote a brief religious treatise, entitled "An Account of Religion by Reason." There is little of thought or genuine argument in the treatise. It is the work of an elegant *litterateur* handling a subject which he knows imperfectly, and only from the outside. But the mere fact is a testimony to the theological excitement which then everywhere pervaded society, and indicates the desire there must have been in many minds, besides those whose writings and speculations have come to the surface, to examine the subject of religion rationally. Suckling avows that he feared the charge of Socinianism in his undertaking.—TULLOCH, JOHN, 1872, *Rational Theology and Christian Philosophy in England in the Seventeenth Century, vol.* I, *p.* 112.

A production ["The Goblins"] which defies—and as a drama hardly deserves—analysis. The conduct of its plot is at once dragging and breathless. . . . One finds some little difficulty in understanding how this sprightly fancy could have stood the test of stage-performance; but the rapid succession of scenes and the intermixture of lively dialogue with music, songs, and a superabundance of action may have taken away the breath of the spectators, and carried them on with victorious speed to the rather calmer close of the piece.—WARD, ADOLPHUS WILLIAM, 1875-99, *A History of English Dramatic Literature, vol.* III, *pp.* 144, 145.

While it is true that Suckling is devoid of imagination—in the higher sense of that word—it is a little unjust to deny him the presence of sentiment. But when a writer cannot be a great dramatist, it is something to be a true lyric poet, and this distinction Suckling rightfully enjoys. There is no finer poem of its kind than the "Ballad upon a Wedding," while many of the shorter pieces of this writer will compare favourably with the lyrics of Herrick and Waller. Many poets have written lyrics with ease and freedom; but Suckling cut cameos, and some of them are almost worthy of standing alone. . . . The poet was, in the first place, unequal to a great or extended conception; and in the second, lacked the power, which distinguishes the true dramatist, of giving breadth of treatment to such conceptions as he had. "Aglaura" is said to have been the poet's favourite drama. . . . "Aglaura" is studded with beautiful lines, and now and then there is even a sustained passage, but on the whole we are obliged to confess that the drama is stilted and unnatural. . . . His "Brennoralt" is generally regarded as his best dramatic work. . . . The versification of "Brennoralt" is almost as crude and halting as that of "Aglaura," though, as a whole, the former must take precedence for its superior dramatic qualities. Yet the lyrics in "Aglaura" are far superior to those found in the later drama. Suckling's comedy of "The Goblins" need not detain us.—SMITH, GEORGE BARNETT, 1878, *Sir John Suckling, The Gentleman's Magazine, vol.* 243, *pp.* 431, 435, 437.

Sir John Suckling is never to be trusted for good behavior through many stanzas, but how enchantingly gay he is! The utter frankness of his hilarity does something toward atoning for its coarseness. We are quite sure that he is never worse than his words, and even suspect that he is not altogether so desperate a rake as he sometimes pretends. If his courtesy seem scant, there is, at all events, no craft lurking beneath it; and so far from hating or discrediting the object of his bold advances because she had repelled them, he treats her with a mixture of petulant astonishment and whimsical respect altogether *naïf* and amusing.—PRESTON, HARRIET W., 1879, *The Latest Songs of Chivalry, Atlantic Monthly, vol.* 43, *p.* 20.

A worse playwright is scarcely to be found, even in that miserable period, among the Gomersalls, Lowers, and Killigrews. "Aglaura," a monster of tedious pageantry, was arranged with a tragic and a comic ending, according to choice: but this was not so unique as has been supposed, for we find the same silly contrivance in Howard's "Vestal Virgin" and in the "Pandora" of Sir William Killigrew. The only drama of Suckling's which is at all readable is "Brennoralt," which is incoherent enough, but does contain some fine tragic writing. The only real merit of these plays however consists in the beautiful songs they harbour.— GOSSE, EDMUND, 1880, *English Poets, ed. Ward, vol.* II, *p.* 171.

The selectors seem to have been afraid of giving the whole of this most delicious ballad, ["A Ballad of a Wedding"] a ballad "of twenty-two incomparable verses, of wonderful brightness and sweetness," fairly so described by Mr. Gosse in his excellent introduction of the poet, in Ward's "English Poets." Even there we have sixteen only of the "incomparable verses," one as of old incorrect and out of place; and what is yet worse, the fragment printed as if whole, without notice of excision except the few words I quote, not necessarily seen by readers of the Ballad. But the omitted stanzas may (my readers can judge for themselves) be "not in harmony with modern manners," as Mr. Palgrave so prettily phraseth it, and as some Rev. Mr. Suckling would seem also to have imagined, who gives with a Memoir of the Poet only the usual sixteen stanzas, without note or apology. A fastidiousness scarcely honest while Shakspere, not yet out of harmony, is on every gentleman's table.—LINTON, W. J., 1882, *ed., Rare Poems of the Sixteenth and Seventeenth Centuries, p.* 245, *note.*

> The blithest throat that ever carrolled love
>   In music made of morning's merriest heart,
> Glad Suckling stumbled from his seat above,
> And reeled on slippery roads of alien art.

—SWINBURNE, ALGERNON CHARLES, 1882, *James Shirley*

In the garden of Suckling's verse, side by side with rare blossoms of delightful fragrance, grew unsightly and noisome weeds. Of course they were affected by their surroundings and by the unnatural light of his court and his time; but some of his writings outrage the taste or morality of to-day. He is, however, although not as widely read or known as he should be, one of the immortals in literature, and had he written nothing but "A Ballad

upon a Wedding" and the song beginning "Why so pale and wan, fond lover," he would have earned his immortality. Their simplicity, grace, and wit are unmatched and are peculiarly his own. Their flavor is most rare : it delights at once, and is never forgotten. The path which Suckling's verse takes never scales sublime heights, but runs through fields where music and laughter are heard, where beauty is seen, and where there are occasional stormy days. His imagination never awes, nor does his feeling stir us deeply; but his fancy pleases us, his wit and gayety provoke a smile, and his careless ease and grace charm us.—STOKES, FREDERICK A., 1886, *ed., The Poems of Sir John Suckling, Preface, p.* xiii.

We go to him for his easy grace, his agreeable impudence, his scandalous mock-disloyalty (for it is only mock-disloyalty after all) to the "Lord of Terrible Aspect," whom all his elder contemporaries worshipped so piously. Suckling's inconstancy and Lovelace's constancy may or may not be equally poetical,— there is some reason for thinking that the lover of Althea was actually driven to something like despair by the loss of his mistress. But that matters to us very little. The songs remain, and remain yet unsurpassed, as the most perfect celebrations, in one case of chivalrous devotion, in the other of the coxcomb side of gallantry, that literature contains or is likely ever to contain.—SAINTSBURY, GEORGE, 1887, *History of Elizabethan Literature, p.* 376.

I admire Suckling's graceful audacity. It is luckier to do a little thing surpassingly well than a larger thing indifferently so.—LOCKER-LAMPSON, FREDERICK, 1896, *My Confidences, p.* 181.

His poems were collected and published five years after his death. They are, like their author, full of careless grace and light-hearted gallantry; but slovenly, and only too often unquotable. . . . There is nothing in his poems of the chivalrous devotion that dignifies Lovelace's two great songs; impudent frankness and careless *bonhomie* are their special characteristics. He might, perhaps, have produced better poetry if he had abandoned his favourite doctrine that a gentleman ought not to take trouble over verse-writing.— MASTERMAN, J. HOWARD B., 1897, *The Age of Milton, p.* 100.

William Rowley

1585?–1642?

William Rowley, 1585 (?)–1642 (?). Born, 1585 (?). For many years an actor and dramatist. Collaborated frequently with Middleton. Probably retired from stage about 1630. Married Isabel Tooley, 1637. Died 1642(?). *Works:* "The Travailes of the Three English Brothers" (with Wilkins and Day), 1607; "A Search for Money," 1609; "A Fair Quarrel" (with Middleton), 1617; "A Courtly Masque: the device called, The World Tost at Tennis" (with Middleton), (1620); "A Farewell Elegie on the Death of Hugh Atwell," 1621; "A New Wonder: a Woman Never Vext," 1632; "All's Lost by Lust," 1633; "A Match at Midnight," 1633; "A Shoomaker a Gentleman," 1638; "The Changeling" (with Middleton), 1653; "The Spanish Gipsy" (with Middleton), 1653; "Fortune by Land and Sea" (with Heywood), 1655; "The Excellent Comedy called the Old Law" (with Massinger and Middleton), 1656; "The Witch of Edmonton" (with Dekker, Ford, and others), 1658; "A Cure for a Cuckold" (with Webster), 1661; "The Thracian Wonder," 1661; "The Birth of Merlin" (pubd. as by Shakespeare and Rowley, but written by Rowley alone), 1662.—SHARP, R. FARQUHARSON, 1897, *A Dictionary of English Authors*, p. 242.

PERSONAL

An Author that flourish'd in the Reign of King *Charles* the First; and was sometime a Member of *Pembroke* Hall in *Cambridge*. I can say nothing further of his Life or Country: but as to his Poetry, and his intimate Acquaintance with the prime Poets of that Age, I can speak at large. He was not only beloved by those Great Men, *Shakespear*, *Fletcher* and *Johnson;* but likewise writ with the former, "The Birth of Merlin." Besides what he joyned in writing with Poets of the second Magnitude, as *Heywood*, *Middleton*, *Day* and *Webster;* as you may see under each of their Names; our Author has four Plays in print of his own Writing.—LANGBAINE, GERARD, 1691, *An Account of the English Dramatick Poets*, p. 428.

GENERAL

That a writer who was deemed a worthy assistant in such plays as "The Witch of Edmonton," "The Thracian Wonder," and "The Spanish Gipsey," must have possessed no very inferior abilities, can admit of little doubt, and is confirmed indeed by his own exclusive compositions; for "A Match at Midnight," and "All's Lost by Lust," the former in the comic, and the latter in the tragic, department of his art, evince, in incident and humour, in character and in pathos, powers which repel the charge of mediocrity. Upon the whole, however, we consider him as ranking last in the roll of worthies who have thus far graced our pages.—DRAKE, NATHAN, 1817, *Shakspeare and His Times*, vol. II, p. 570.

Though his name is found in one instance affixed to a piece conjointly with Shakespeare's, he is generally classed only in the third rank of our dramatists. His Muse is evidently a plebeian nymph, and had not been educated in the school of the Graces. His most tolerable production is the "New Wonder, or a Woman never vext." Its drafts of citizen life and manners have an air of reality and honest truth—the situations and characters are forcible, and the sentiments earnest and unaffected.—CAMPBELL, THOMAS, 1819, *Specimens of the British Poets*.

Rowley and Le Tourneur, especially the former, have occasionally good lines; but we cannot say that they were very superior dramatists. Rowley, however, was often in comic partnership with Massinger.—HALLAM, HENRY, 1837-39, *Introduction to the Literature of Europe*, pt. iii, ch. vi, par. 103.

He has his share of the cordial and straightforward manner of our old dramatists; but not a great deal more that is of much value. Of the style of his comedy a judgment may be formed from the fact, recorded by Langbaine, that certain of the scenes of one of his pieces, "A Shoemaker's a Gentleman," used to be commonly performed by the strolling actors at Bartholomew and Southwark fairs.—CRAIK, GEORGE L., 1861, *A Compendious History of English Literature and of the English Language*, vol. I, p. 598.

William Rowley, like certain other authors of merit in other departments or periods of our literature, seems to have cared but little for the kind of reputation which is made by the arts of *réclame*. No doubt there is justice in the demand:

"In full recompensacioun
Of good worke, give us good renoun."

But William Rowley would seem to have been one of that minority among men of letters to whom, even before the days of journalism and its compensations, a personal literary reputation has always been more or less a matter of indifference. At all events, he cared little or nothing for the undivided empire of a title-page. . . . This comedy ["A New Wonder"] was evidently intended to appeal to the sympathies of the sort of audience for whom plays dealing with traditions of the City of London were as a rule, primarily at all events, designed. It is, however, a noteworthy play, which would of itself prove its author to have been a dramatist deficient neither in skill nor in power. . . . The pathos is by no means deep, and the humour the reverse of refined; while the change in the disposition of the scapegrace uncle is too sudden to leave any moral impression. But the action as a whole is brisk, the tone healthy, and the writing vigorous. — WARD, ADOLPHUS WILLIAM, 1875-99, *A History of English Dramatic Literature, vol.* II, *pp.* 540, 543, 544.

In the underplot of "A Fair Quarrel" Rowley's besetting faults of coarseness and quaintness, stiffness and roughness, are so flagrant and obtrusive that we cannot avoid a feeling of regret and irritation at such untimely and inharmonious evidence of his partnership with a poet of finer if not of sturdier genius. . . . But here ["The Honest Whore"] we may assert with fair confidence that the first and the last scenes of the play bear the indisputable sign-manual of William Rowley. His vigorous and vivid genius, his somewhat hard and curt directness of style and manner, his clear and trenchant power of straightforward presentation or exposition, may be traced in every line as plainly as the hand of Middleton must be recognized in the main part of the tragic action intervening. To Rowley therefore must be assigned the very high credit of introducing and of dismissing with adequate and even triumphant effect the strangely original tragic figure which owes its fullest and finest development to the genius of Middleton.—SWINBURNE,

ALGERNON CHARLES, 1886, *Thomas Middleton, Nineteenth Century, vol.* 19, *pp.* 145, 152.

It is very difficult to form an opinion with regard to his talent. He is a kitchen-maid rather than a cook, and it is impossible to be certain what share he has had in the preparation of any comic feast that is set before us. So far, however, as we are able to form an opinion, we are apt to consider that the influence of Rowley upon Middleton was an unwholesome one. Middleton was strangely compacted of gold and clay, of the highest gifts and of the lowest subterfuges of the playwright. In Rowley, all that was not clay was iron, and it is difficult to believe that he sympathized with or encouraged his friend's ethereal eccentricities. That Rowley had a hand in the underplot of several of Middleton's noblest productions does not alter our conviction that his own sentiments were rather brutal and squalid, and that he cared for little but to pander to the sensational instincts of the groundlings. The mutual attitude of these friends has been compared to that of Beaumont and Fletcher, but it is hard to think of Middleton in any other light than as a poet unequally yoked with one whose temper was essentially prosaic.—GOSSE, EDMUND, 1894, *The Jacobean Poets, p.* 131.

A tradition handed down by Langbaine records that Rowley was beloved by those great men, Shakespeare, Fletcher, and Jonson; while his partnership in so many plays by a variety of writers has been regarded as proof of the amiability of his character. As a useful and safe collaborator he seems to have been only less in demand than Dekker. His hand is often difficult to identify, though his verse may generally be detected by its metrical harshness and irregularity. His style is disfigured by a monotonously extravagant emphasis, and he is sadly wanting in artistic form and refinement. He had, however, a rare vein of whimsical humour (cf. the episode of Gnotho in the "Old Law," iii.1), and occasionally he shows an unexpected mastery of tragic pathos. Drake ranks him in the same class with Massinger, Middleton, Heywood, Ford, Dekker, and Webster, but puts him last in this category.—SECCOMBE, THOMAS, 1897, *Dictionary of National Biography, vol.* XLIX, *p.* 363.

William Cartwright

1611–1643

An English poet of some reputation in his day, was born at Northway, near Tewkesbury, September, 1611. He studied at Oxford, and having taken orders, became a preacher of note in the university—one of his sermons finding a place, as a specimen of university preaching, in a volume of Five Sermons in Five several Styles or Ways of Preaching. In 1642 he received an appointment to an office in the church of Salisbury, and was in the same year made one of the Oxford council of war, appointed to provide for the king's troops stationed in the town. In 1643 he was chosen junior proctor in the university, and reader in metaphysics; but he did not long hold these offices, for he died in December of the same year. He had attained very great reputation, and was spoken of in terms of the highest commendation by Ben Jonson and others of his time. His works are now scarcely remembered. His "Comedies, Tragi-Comedies, and other Poems," appeared in 1647, and again in 1651. Wood praises his scholarship, and mentions that he wrote "Poemata Græca et Latina."—BROWN, JAMES, 1866, *Imperial Dictionary of Universal Biography, vol.* II, *p.* 920.

PERSONAL

'Tis not to be forgott that king Charles 1st dropt a teare at the newes of his death. William Cartwright was buried in the south aisle in Christ Church, Oxon. Pitty 'tis so famous a bard should lye without an inscription.—AUBREY, JOHN, 1669-96, *Brief Lives, ed. Clark, vol.* I, *p.* 148.

A Person as Eminent for Loyalty and Learning, (his years consider'd) as any this Age has produc'd. One, whose Character has been written by several Pens; and therefore has afforded me, (who fetch my knowledge from Books, more than verbal Information) the larger subject to expatiate on. . . . He was extremely remarkable both for his outward, and inward Endowments; his Body being as handsome as his Soul. He was an expert Linguist, understanding not only Greek and Latine, but French and Italian, as perfectly as his Mother-tonuge. He was an excellent Orator, and yet an admirable Poet, a Quality which *Cicero* with all his pains could not attain to. Nor was *Aristotle* less known to him than *Cicero* and *Virgil:* and those who heard his Metaphysical Lectures, gave him the Preference to all his Predecessors, the present Bishop of *Lincoln* excepted. His Sermons were as much admired as his other Composures, and One fitly applied to our Author, that Saying of *Aristotle* concerning *Æschron* the Poet, that *He could not tell what* Æschron *could not do.* In a word he was of so sweet a disposition, and so replete with all Virtues, that he was beloved by all Learned Men that knew him,

and admired by all Strangers.—LANGBAINE, GERARD, 1691, *An Account of the English Dramatick Poets, pp.* 51, 52.

He was another Tully and Virgil, as being most excellent for oratory and poetry, in which faculties, as also in the Greek tongue, he was so full and absolute, that those that best knew him, knew not in which he most excelled. . . . If the wits read his poems, divines his sermons, and philosophers his lectures on Aristotle's metaphysics, they would scarce believe that he died at a little above thirty years of age.—WOOD, ANTHONY, 1691-1721, *Athenæ Oxonienses, vol.* ii, *f.* 35.

William Cartwright not only wrote some of the best poems and plays of his time, and preached some of the best sermons, but as reader of metaphysics in his University he earned especial praise. King Charles wore black on the day of his funeral, and fifty wits and poets of the time supplied their tributary verses to the volume, first published in 1651 of "Comedies, Tragi-Comedies, with other Poems, by Mr. William Cartwright, late Student of Christ Church in Oxford, and Proctor of the University. The Airs and Songs set by Mr. Henry Lawes." There is in this book a touching portrait of young Cartwright, evidently a true likeness, with two rows of books over his head, and his elbow upon the open volume of Aristotle's metaphysics. He rests on his hand a young head, in which the full under-lip and downy beard are harmonized to a face made spiritual by intensity of thought. Cartwright died, in his thirty-second year, of a camp fever that killed many in

Oxford.—MORLEY, HENRY, 1868, *ed., The King and the Commons, Introduction, p.* viii.

GENERAL

I did but see thee! and how vain it is
To vex thee for it with remonstrances,
Though things in fashion; let those judge,
    who sit
Their twelve pence out, to clap their hands
    at wit.
I fear to sin thus near thee; for—great
    saint!—
'Tis known true beauty hath no need of paint.
Yet, since a label fix'd to thy fair hearse
Is all the mode, and tears put into verse
Can teach posterity our present grief
And their own loss, but never give relief;
I'll tell them—and a truth which needs no
    pass—
That wit in Cartwright at her zenith was.
Arts, fancy, language, all conven'd in thee,
With those grand miracles which deify
The old world's writings, kept yet from the
    fire
Because they force these worst times to ad-
    mire.
Thy matchless genius, in all thou didst write,
Like the sun, wrought with such staid heat
    and light,
That not a line—to the most critic he—
Offends with flashes, or obscurity.
—VAUGHAN, HENRY, 1651, *Upon the Poems and Plays of the Ever-Memorable Mr. William Cartwright.*

Cartwright, rare Cartwright, to whom all
    must bow,
That was best preacher, and best poet too;
Whose learned fancy never was at rest,
But always labouring, yet labour'd least.
—LEIGH, JOHN, 1651, *Prefixed to Cartwright's Plays and Poems.*

To have the same person cast his net and catch souls as well in the pulpit as on the stage! . . . A miracle of industry and wit, sitting sixteen hours a day at all manner of knowledge, an excellent preacher in whom hallowed fancies and reason grew visions and holy passions, raptures and extasies, and all this at thirty years of age!—LLOYD, DAVID, 1668, *Memoirs of Excellent Personages.*

In noticing the catalogue of poets ranged under the title of "Amatory and Miscellaneous," it is impossible not to be struck with the mutability of popular applause. Cowley and Cartwright were the favourites of their times, were considered as the first of poets, celebrated by their literary contemporaries in loud and repeated panegyrics, and their names familiar in every class of society. What is now their fate? To be utterly neglected, and, except to those who justly think it necessary to be intimate with every stage of our literature, nearly unknown. Have they deserved this? Let the patient reader wade through their numerous works, and he will probably answer, Yes.—DRAKE, NATHAN, 1798, *Literary Hours, No.* xxviii, *p.* 97.

Perhaps there is no instance in the annals of English literature of an author more admired by his contemporaries of distinction than Cartwright appears to have been. Indeed, he is now better known by the praises of others than by his own works. These, with the exception of his plays, which are now entirely neglected, consist principally of political addresses to distinguished characters of the day.—ALLIBONE, S. AUSTIN, 1854-58, *Dictionary of English Literature, vol.* I, *p.* 350.

The specific gravity of the poems, so to speak, is far greater than that of any of his contemporaries; everywhere is thought, fancy, force, varied learning. He is never weak or dull; though he fails often enough, is often enough wrong-headed, fantastical, affected, and has never laid bare the deeper arteries of humanity, for good or for evil. Neither is he altogether an original thinker; as one would expect he has over-read himself; but then he has done so to good purpose. If he imitates, he generally equals. The table of fare in "The Ordinary" smacks of Rabelais or Aristophanes, but then it is worthy of either; and if one cannot help suspecting that, "The Ordinary" never would have been written had not Ben Jonson written "The Alchemist," one confesses that Ben Jonson need not have been ashamed to have written the play himself: although the plot, as all Cartwright's are, is somewhat confused and inconsequent. . . . The "Royal Slave," too, is a gallant play, right-hearted and lofty from beginning to end, though enacted in an impossible court-cloud world akin to that in which the classic heroes and heroines of Corneille and Racine call each other Monsieur and Madame. . . . The "Royal Slave" seems to have been considered, both by the Court and by his contemporaries, his

masterpiece. And justly so. . . . The
songs are excellent, as are all Cartwright's; for grace, simplicity, and sweetness, equal to any (save Shakspeare's)
which the seventeenth century produced:
but, curiously enough, his lyric faculty
seems to have exhausted itself in these
half-dozen songs. His minor poems are
utterly worthless, out-Cowleying Cowley
in frigid and fantastic conceits; and his
various addresses to the king and queen
are as bombastic, and stupid, and artificial, as any thing which disgraced the
reigns of Charles II. or his brother.—
KINGSLEY, CHARLES, 1859, *Plays and
Puritans, Miscellanies.*

It was of William Cartwright Ben Jonson said, "My son Cartwright writes like
a man." He has not left much behind to
justify this eulogium; but his minor poems
exhibit evidences of taste and scholarship
which sufficiently explain the esteem and
respect in which he was held by his contemporaries.—BELL, ROBERT, 1867? *ed.,
Songs from the Dramatists, p.* 215.

Cartwright, whom his academical and
literary contemporaries regarded as a
phenomenon, is to us chiefly interesting
as a type. If it be allowable to regard
as extravagant the tendencies represented
by him in both his life and his poetry, he
may justly be remembered by a sufficiently
prominent title among English poets—

that of the typically extravagant Oxford
resident of his period. . . . He possessed a real rhetorical inventiveness, and
an extraordinary felicity of expression.
These gifts he was able to display on
occasions of the most opposite and diverse
character, great and small, public and
private,—from the occurrence of an unexampled frost to the publication of a
treatise on the art of vaulting. Yet even
with a panegyrical poet of the Fantastic
School the relations between his theme
and his own tastes and sentiments are of
the highest importance.—WARD, ADOL-
PHUS WILLIAM, 1880, *English Poets, ed.
Ward, vol.* II, *pp.* 227, 228.

He was a man of learning as well as of
zeal; and his admirable English style was
well fitted to add to the favour with which
his writings were received.—DOWDEN,
JOHN, 1897, *Outlines of the History of the
Theological Literature of The Church of
England, p.* 50.

Nothing in the writings that he has left
justify the warm admiration that his personality seems to have evoked. He is a
facile verse writer, especially of panegyric
addresses, and a few of his shorter poems
are pleasant enough of their kind—
academic exercises in amorous verse such
as the minor poets of the age were accustomed to produce.—MASTERMAN, J. HOW-
ARD B., 1897, *The Age of Milton, p.* 121.

William Browne
1591–1643?

William Browne was born at Tavistock in 1588, and died, probably, in the year
1643. He went to Oxford as a member of Exeter College; entered the Inner Temple
in 1612; published his elegy on Prince Henry in a volume along with another by his
friend Christopher Brooke 1613; the first book of his "Britannia's Pastorals" in the
same year; his "Shepherd's Pipe" in 1614; and the second book of his "Pastorals" in
1616, the year of the death of Shakespeare. The third book of his "Britannia's
Pastorals" was unknown till 1851, when it was published for the Percy Society from
a manuscript in the Cathedral Library at Salisbury. The most complete edition of
Browne is that published in the Roxburghe Library by Mr. W. Carew Hazlitt in 1868.
—WARD, THOMAS HUMPHREY, 1880, *ed., English Poets, vol.* II, *p.* 65.

An excellent edition of Browne is available in the Muses' Library, edited by Gordon
Goodwin, with an introduction by A. H. Bullen, in 1894.—MOULTON, CHARLES WELLS,
1901.

PERSONAL

In the same year he was actually created
Master of Arts, as I shall tell you elsewhere in the *Fasti,* and after he had left
the Coll. with his pupil, he became a retainer to the Pembrochian family, was

beloved by that generous Count, William
E. of Pembroke, and got wealth and purchased an estate, which is all I know of
him hitherto, only that as he had a little
body, so a great mind. In my searches I
find that one Will Browne of Ottery S.

Mary in Devon. died in the winter time 1645. Whether the same with the poet, I am hitherto ignorant. After the time of the said poet, appeared another person of both his names, author of two common law-books, written in English.—WOOD, ANTHONY, 1691–1721, *Athenæ Oxonienses. vol.* I, *f.* 493.

Browne was fortunate in his friends. His life at the Inner Temple brought him into contact not only with his intimate friend Wither and Charles Brooke, but also with such a man as Selden, who wrote commendatory verses to the first book of his "Pastorals." He was too, apparently, one of that knot of brilliant young men who called themselves the "sons" of Ben Jonson, and there are some interesting verses, of warm yet not extravagant praise, prefixed by Ben Jonson to the second book of the same poem. With Drayton he appears to have been on cordial and intimate terms. Some verses by Browne are prefixed to the second edition of the "Polyolbion," and some of the most charming commendatory verses that were ever written were penned by Drayton in honour of "Britannia's Pastorals." Chapman too, "the learned Shepherd of fair Hitching Hill," was, as more than one indication sufficiently proves, intimate with our poet, and Browne was not only familiar with his friend's Iliad and Odyssey, but also, we may be very sure, knew well that golden book of poetry, the "Hero and Leander." With such contemporary influences, and with the fullest knowledge of and reverence for such of his predecessors as Sidney and Spenser, Browne had every advantage given to his genius, and every help to enable him to float in the full and central stream of poetic tradition.—ARNOLD, W. T., 1880, *English Poets, ed. Ward, vol.* II, *p.* 65.

BRITANNIA'S PASTORALS

1613–1616–1852

Drive forth thy flock, young pastor, to that plain
Where our old shepherds wont their flocks to feed;
To those clear walks where many a skilful swain
To'ards the calm ev'ning tun'd his pleasant reed. . . .
. . . .
So may thy sheep like, so thy lambs increase,
And from the wolf feed ever safe and free!

So may'st thou thrive, among the learned prease,
As thou young shepherd art belov'd of me!
—DRAYTON, MICHAEL, 1613, *Commendatory Verses in Britannia's Pastorals.*

So much a stranger my severer Muse
Is not to love-strains, or a shepward's reed,
But that she knows some rites of Phœbus' dues,
Of Pan, of Pallas, and her Sisters' meed.
Read and commend she durst these tun'd essays
Of him that loves her. (She hath ever found
Her studies as one circle.) Next she prays
His readers be with rose and myrtle crown'd!
No willow touch them! As his bays are free
From wrong of bolts, so may their chaplets be.
—SELDEN, JOHN, 1613, *Commendatory Verses in Britannia's Pastorals.*

Some men, of books or friends not speaking right,
May hurt them more with praise than foes with spite.
But I have seen thy work, and I know thee:
And, if thou list thyself, what thou canst be.
For though but early in these paths thou tread,
I find thee write most worthy to be read.
It must be thine own judgment yet that sends
This thy work forth: that judgment mine commends
—JONSON, BEN, 1616, *Commendatory Verses in Britannia's Pastorals, Second Book.*

Thus do I spur thee on with sharpest praise,
To use thy gifts of Nature and of skill,
To double-gild Apollo's brows and bays,
Yet make great Nature Art's true sov'reign still.
So Fame shall ever say, to thy renown,
The shepherd's-star, or bright'st in sky, is Browne!
—DAVIES, JOHN, 1616, *Commendatory Verses in Britannia's Pastorals, Second Book.*

　　　　I feel an envious touch,
And tell thee, swain, that at thy fame I grutch,
Wishing the art that makes this poem shine,
And this thy work (wert not thou wronged) mine.
For when detraction shall forgotten be,
This will continue to eternize thee;
And if hereafter any busy wit
Should, wronging thy conceit, miscensure it,
Though seeming learn'd or wise: here he shall see,
'Tis prais'd by wiser and more learn'd than he.
—WITHER, GEORGE, 1616, *Commendatory Verses in Britannia's Pastorals, Second Book.*

Many inferior faculties are yet left, wherein our Devon hath displaied her abilities as well as in the former, as in Philosophers, Historians, Oratours and Poets, the blazoning of whom to the life, especially the last, I had rather leave to my worthy friend Mr. W. Browne, who, as hee hath already honoured his countrie in his elegant and sweet "Pastoralls," so questionles will easily be intreated a little farther to grace it by drawing out the line of his Poeticke Auncesters, beginning in Josephus Iscanus and ending in himselfe.—CARPENTER, NATHANIEL, 1625, *Geography Delineated Forth in Two Books, p.* 263.

Esteemed then, by judicious persons, to be written in a sublime strain, and for subject amorous and very pleasing.—WOOD, ANTHONY, 1691–1721, *Athenæ Oxonienses, vol.* I, *f.* 492.

Browne was a pastoral poet, with much natural tenderness and sweetness, and a good deal of allegorical quaintness and prolixity.—HAZLITT, WILLIAM, 1820, *Lectures on the Literature of the Age of Elizabeth, p.* 192.

Brown is one of the sweetest Pastoral Writers in the world.—NEELE, HENRY, 1827–29, *Lectures on English Poetry, Lecture* v.

His "Britannia's Pastorals" appear to have been much read then by persons of fine taste; nor could persons of the same class find now, among the books of that time, a more pleasant book of the kind for a day or two of peculiar leisure. The plan of the book is that of a story of shepherds and shepherdesses, with allegorical personages introduced into their society, wandering in quest of their loves and adventures, through scenes of English rural nature; but the narrative is throughout subordinate to the descriptions for which it gives occasion. A rich and sweet, and yet varied sensuousness, characterizes these descriptions. . . . The mood is generally calm and quiet, like that of a painter of actual scenery; there is generally the faintest possible breath of human interest; but now and then the sensuous takes the hue of the ideal, and the strain rises in vigor. In the course of the poem Spenser is several times acknowledged as the poet whose genius the author venerates most. The influence of other poets may, however, be traced, and especially that of Du Bartas. . . . Browne is a far more cultured versifier than Sylvester, and his lines are linked together with an artist's fondness for truth of phrase and rhyme, and for natural ease of cadence.—MASSON, DAVID, 1858, *The Life of John Milton, vol.* I, *ch.* vi.

Browne has no constructive power, and no human interest in his pastorals, but he has an eye for nature.—GILFILLAN, GEORGE, 1860, *ed. Specimens of the Less-Known British Poets, vol.* I, *p.* 288.

Browne was absolutely devoid of all epic or dramatic talent. His maids and shepherds have none of the sweet plausibility which enlivens the long recitals of Spenser. They outrage all canons of common sense. When a distracted mother wants to know if a man has seen her lost child, she makes the inquiry in nineteen lines of deliberate poetry. An air of silliness broods over the whole conception. Marina meets a lovely shepherd, whose snowy buskins display a still silkier leg, and she asks of him her way to the marish; he misunderstands her to say "marriage," and tells her that the way is through love; she misunderstands him to refer to some village so entitled, and the languid comedy of errors winds on through pages. The best of the poem consists in its close and pretty pictures of country scenes. At his best, Browne is a sort of Bewick, and provides us with vignettes of the squirrel at play, a group of wrens, truant schoolboys, or a country girl,

When she upon her breast, love's sweet repose,
Doth bring the Queen of Flowers, the English Rose.

But these happy "bits" are set in a terrible waste of what is not prose, but poetry and water, foolish babbling about altars and anagrams, long lists of blooms and trees and birds, scarcely characterized at all, soft rhyming verse meandering about in a vaguely pretty fashion to no obvious purpose.—GOSSE, EDMUND, 1894, *The Jacobean Poets, p.* 154.

INNER TEMPLE MASQUE

It was not only by the parade of processions, and the decorations of scenery, that these spectacles were recommended. Some of them, in point of poetical composition, were eminently beautiful and elegant. Among these may be mentioned a masque on the story of Circe and Ulysses, called the "Inner Temple Masque," written by William Brown, a student of that society, about the year 1620. From this piece, as a specimen of the temple-masques in this view, I make no apology for my anticipation in transcribing the following ode, which Circe sings as a charm to drive away sleep from Ulysses, who is discovered reposing under a large tree. . . . In praise of this song it will be sufficient to say, that it reminds us of some favourite touches in Milton's "Comus," to which it perhaps gave birth. Indeed one cannot help observing here in general although the observation more properly belongs to another place, that a masque thus recently exhibited on the story of Circe, which there is reason to think had acquired some popularity, suggested to Milton the hint of a masque on the story of Comus. It would be superfluous to point out minutely the absolute similarity of the two characters: they both deal in incantations conducted by the same mode of operation, and producing effects exactly parallel.— WARTON, THOMAS, 1778–81, *History of English Poetry, Sec.* xxxiv.

A masque has come down to us written by William Browne, a disciple of Spenser, expressly for the society of which he was a member, and entitled the "Inner Temple Masque." It is upon the story of Circe and Ulysses, and is worthy of the school of poetry out of which he came.— HUNT, LEIGH, 1858, *The Town, p.* 105.

GENERAL

It appears to us, that sufficient justice has not, since the era of Milton, been paid to his talents; for, though it be true, as Mr. Headley has observed, that puerilities, forced allusions, and conceits, have frequently debased his materials; yet are these amply atoned for by some of the highest excellencies of his art; by an imagination ardent and fertile, and sometimes sublime; by a vivid personification of passion; by a minute and truly faithful delineation of rural scenery; by a peculiar vein of tenderness which runs through the whole of his pastorals, and by a versification uncommonly varied and melodious. With these are combined a species of romantic extravagancy which sometimes heightens, but more frequently degrades, the effect of his pictures. Had he exhibited greater judgment in the selection of

his imagery, and greater simplicity in his style, his claim on posterity had been valid, had been general and undisputed. —DRAKE, NATHAN, 1817, *Shakspeare and his Times, vol.* I, *p.* 605.

His poetry is not without beauty; but it is the beauty of mere landscape and allegory, without the manners and passions that constitute human interest.—CAMPBELL, THOMAS, 1819, *Specimens of the British Poets.*

Among these historical poets I should incline to class William Browne, author of a poem with the quaint title of "Britannia's Pastorals;" though his story, one of little interest, seems to have been invented by himself. Browne, indeed, is of no distinct school among the writers of that age: he seems to recognize Spenser as his master; but his own manner is more to be traced among later than earlier poets. . . . Browne is truly a poet, full of imagination, grace, and sweetness, though not very nervous or rapid. I know not why Headley, favorable enough for the most part to this generation of the sons of song, has spoken of Browne with unfair contempt. Justice, however, has been done to him by later critics. But I have not observed that they take notice of what is remarkable in the history of our poetical literature, that Browne is an early model of ease and variety in the regular couplet. Many passages in his unequal poem are hardly excelled, in this respect, by the fables of Dryden. It is manifest that Milton was well acquainted with the writings of Browne.—HALLAM, HENRY, 1837–39, *Introduction to the Literature of Europe, pt.* iii, *ch.* v, *par.* 45.

Browne is one of those poets whom few but children and poets will either like or love.—COLERIDGE, HARTLEY, 1849–51, *Essays and Marginalia, p.* 278.

His facility of rhyming and command of harmonious expression are very great; and, within their proper sphere, his invention and fancy are also extremely active and fertile. His strength, however, lies chiefly in description, not the thing for which poetry or language is best fitted, and a species of writing which cannot be carried on long without becoming tiresome; he is also an elegant didactic declaimer; but of passion, or indeed of any breath of actual living humanity, his poetry has almost none. This, no doubt, was the cause of the neglect into which after a short time it was allowed to drop; and this limited quality of his genius may also very probably have been the reason why he so soon ceased to write and publish.—CRAIK, GEORGE L., 1861, *A Compendious History of English Literature and of the English Language, vol.* II, *p.* 55.

It is rare in literary history that so much promise is found so inexplicably stunted and silenced by time.—SARGENT, EPES, 1881, *ed., Harper's Cyclopædia of British and American Poetry, p.* 53.

He will never again be popular as he was unquestionably in his lifetime; but he will, I think, be always read by poets and students of poetry. The task of reading his works is not wholly pleasurable. If he charms us on one page, he wearies us on another; if he delights us one moment with a genuine bit of nature, in the next he is involved in the subtleties of allegory, and becomes unreadable if not unintelligible. When at his best his poetry is like a breath of sweet country air, or the scent of newly mown grass. His similes, drawn from what we are wont to call common objects, are often singularly happy; he gives us fresh draughts from nature, and his verse is frequently marked by an Arcadian simplicity, contrasting pleasurably with the classical conceits and forced allusions over which, in other portions, the reader is doomed to groan.—DENNIS, JOHN, 1883, *Heroes of Literature, p.* 95.

It is fair to say that there is in him no trace of the mawkish silliness which (blasphemy as the assertion may seem to some adorers of Keats) disfigures occasionally the work of that great poet. But Browne, like Keats, had that kind of love of Nature which is really the love of a lover, not of a mere artist, or a mere man of science, or a mere preacher; and he had, like Keats, a wonderful gift of expression of his love. When he tried other themes he was not generally successful, but his success, such as it is, is great; and, close student of poetry as Browne has been admitted to be, it must be added that, like Keats, who was also a close student in his way, he never smells of the lamp. It is evident that he would at any time and in any circumstances have sung, and that his studies have only to some extent coloured and conditioned the manner of

his singing. . . . He may never reach the highest poetry, but he is always a poet.—SAINTSBURY, GEORGE, 1887, *History of Elizabethan Literature, pp.* 301, 302.

What so pleasant as to read of Maygames, true-love knots, and shepherds piping in the shade? of pixies and fairy-circles? of rustic bridals and junketings? of angling, hunting the squirrel, nut-gathering? Of such-like subjects William Browne treats, singing like the shepherd in the "Arcadia" as though he would never grow old. He was a happy poet. It was his good fortune to grow up among wholesome surroundings, whose gracious influences sank into his spirit. He loved the hills and dales round Tavistock, and lovingly described them in his verse. Frequently he indulges in descriptions of sunrise and sunset; they leave no vivid impression, but charm the reader by their quiet beauty. It cannot be denied that his fondness for simple, homely images sometimes led him into sheer fatuity; and candid admirers must also admit that, despite his study of simplicity, he could not refrain from hunting (as the manner was) after far-fetched outrageous conceits. Browne had nothing of that restless energy which inspired the old dramatists; he was all for a pastoral contentment. Assuredly he was not a great poet, but he was a true poet, and a modest.—BULLEN, A. H., 1893, *The Poems of William Browne of Tavistock, Introduction, vol.* I, *p.* xxviii.

"*On the Countess Dowager of Pembroke.*" These famous lines occur in exactly the same form in the middle seventeenth-century MS. in the Library of Trinity College, Dublin, and are there signed "William Browne." They appear to have been first printed in Osborne's "Traditional Memoirs on the Reign of King James," in 1658 (p. 78), and were also included in the "Poems" of the Countess's son, William, Earl of Pembroke, and Sir Benjamin Rudyerd in 1660 (p. 66); but in neither volume is there any indication of the authorship. Writing about the same time Aubrey, in his "Natural History of Wiltshire" (ed. Britton, 1847, p. 90), cited the first sextain, and stated that the verses were "made by Mr. Browne, who wrote the "Pastorals." But in 1756 Peter Whalley printed a garbled version of the first six lines in his edition of Ben Jonson's "Works" (vi. 297), giving as

GEORGE SANDYS

FRANCIS QUARLES

his reason that they were "universally assigned" to Jonson, and they appear in all editions of Jonson since Whalley's time, and are commonly attributed to him. The epitaph is certainly more effective as a single sextain; and Mr. Hazlitt suggests that "Whoever composed the original sextain, the addition is the work of another pen, namely, Lord Pembroke's." Still, it must be remembered that Browne has occasionally marred his work by not knowing when to stay his hand, and the epitaph, as it appears in the Lansdowne and Dublin MSS., reflects him at his best and at his worst. It may be worth noting that Browne thus pointedly refers to this very epitaph in his "Elegy" on Charles, Lord Herbert of Cardiff and Shurland (p. 257), which is written in the same metre:—

"And since my weak and saddest verse
Was worthy thought thy grandam's horse;
Accept of this !'

—GOODWIN, GORDON, 1894, ed., *The Poems of William Browne of Tavistock, vol.* II, *p.* 350, *note.*

William Browne is perhaps the easiest figure in our literature. He lived easily, he wrote easily, and no doubt he died easily. He no more expected to be read through at a sitting than he tried to write all the story of Marina at a sitting. He took up his pen and composed: when he felt tired he went off to bed, like a sensible man: and when you are tired of reading he expects you to be sensible and do the same.—QUILLER-COUCH, A. T., 1894, *Adventures in Criticism, p.* 61.

Either wanted power to condense, or did injustice to a pretty talent by fluency "long drawn out," by want of taste and of proportion. His natural descriptions are apt to be in the old catalogue fashion; as if determined to outdo Chaucer or Spenser, he gives twenty-six lines to enumerate the trees in an imagined forest. Yet amongst his wearisome shepherd tales we have occasional glimpses of true landscape. —PALGRAVE FRANCIS, TURNER, 1896, *Landscape in Poetry, p.* 152.

The idyllic and objective spirit of the early period is better reproduced in Browne, who is often admirably suave and melodious, but whose manner tends to a more than lyrical profusion and length.— CARPENTER, FREDERIC IVES, 1897, *English Lyric Poetry, 1500-1700, Introduction, p.* liii.

Francis Quarles

1592-1644

Francis Quarles. An English sacred poet; born in Rumford, Essex, in 1592; died September 1644. He was educated at Cambridge, and studied for a lawyer. He received several appointments from the Crown, and finally held the position of city chronologer. His leading works were: "Emblems Divine and Moral" (1635); "Argalus and Parthenia" (1621); and the "Enchiridion" (1640) in prose. Frequent fine expressions redeem much commonplace.—WARNER, CHARLES DUDLEY, 1897, *ed., Library of the World's Best Literature, Biographical Dictionary of Authors, vol.* XXIX, *p.* 447.

EMBLEMS DIVINE AND MORAL
1635

Tinnit, inane est; with the picture of one ringing on the globe with his finger, is the best thing I have the luck to remember, in that great poet Quarles.— POPE, ALEXANDER, 1721-22, *Letter to Dr. Atterbury, March* 19.

His "Emblems," which have been serviceable to allure children to read, have been often printed, and are not yet forgotten. We sometimes stumble upon a pretty thought among many trivial ones in this book; and now and then meet with poetry in mechanism in the prints.— GRANGER, JAMES, 1769-1824, *Biographical History of England, vol.* III, *p.* 135.

"Quarles' Emblems," my childhood's pet book.—BROWNING, ROBERT, 1846, *Letters of Robert Browning and Elizabeth Barrett, vol.* II, *p.* 444.

His best known work is his "Emblems," through which a bitter melancholy vein runs, and in which the most extravagant notions on the misery of human life, and the sin and corruption of nature are to be found.—PERRY, GEORGE G., 1861, *History of the Church of England, vol.* I, *p.* 648.

These "Emblems" were illustrated in the first editions by most ridiculous prints; and yet, as Southey has noted, it is the prints that have been most popular, while the poems have been neglected. It is owing to both, however, that Quarles became so early what Philips, Milton's nephew, calls him, "the darling of our plebeian judgments." After the Restoration Quarles was completely forgotten, and Pope even gives him a place in the "Dunciad." The better taste, or, as Campbell says, the more charitable criticism, of modern times has admitted him into "the laurelled fraternity of the poets," and he is now admired for his quaintness, vigour, and occasional beauty.—ANGUS, JOSEPH, 1865, *The Handbook of English Literature, p.* 159.

It is difficult to conceive of any poet who could produce verse of a high order of merit in close on a hundred and fifty short poems written to order on as many pictures; and the author of the "Emblems" has certainly written nothing that can be classed with the best of Crashaw or Vaughan. But he has here kept a level of poetic excellence in his verse considerably above that to which it sometimes sank.—MASTERMAN, J. HOWARD B., 1897, *The Age of Milton, p.* 117.

GENERAL

Had he been contemporary with Plato (that great back-friend to Poets), he would not onely have allowed him to live, but advanced him to an office in his Commonwealth. Some Poets, if debarr'd profaness, wantoness, and satyricalness (that they may neither abuse God, themselves, nor their neighbours), have their tongues cut out in effect. Others onely trade in wit at the second hand, being all for translations, nothing for invention. Our Quarles was free from the faults of the first, as if he had drank of Jordan instead of Helicon, and slept on Mount Olivet for his Parnassus : and was happy in his own invention. His visible Poetry (I mean his "Emblems") is excellent, catching therein the eye and fancy at one draught, so that he hath out-Alciated therein, in some men's judgement. His Verses on Job are done to the life, so that the Reader may see his sores, and through them the anguish of his soul. —FULLER, THOMAS, 1662, *Worthies of England, ed. Nichols, vol.* I, *p* 354.

Milton was forced to wait till the world had done admiring Quarles.—WALPOLE, HORACE, 1757, *Letters, ed. Cunningham, vol.* III, *p.* 99.

Examples of bad writing might no doubt be produced, on almost any occasion, from Quarles and Blackmore; but as no body reads their works, no body is liable to be misled by them.—BEATTIE, JAMES, 1776–79, *An Essay on Poetry and Music, p.* 15, *note.*

The charitable criticism of the present age has done justice to Quarles, in contrasting his merits with his acknowledged deformities. . . . A considerable resemblance to Young may be traced in the blended strength and extravagance, and ill-assorted wit and devotion of Quarles. Like Young, he wrote vigorous prose— witness his "Enchiridion." In the parallel, however, it is due to the purity of Young to acknowledge, that he never was guilty of such indecency as that which disgraces the "Argalus and Parthenia" of our pious author.—CAMPBELL, THOMAS, 1819, *Specimens of the British Poets.*

I have been reading lately what of Quarles's poetry I could get. He was a contemporary of Herbert, and a kindred spirit. I think you would like him. It is rare to find one who was so much of a poet and so little of an artist. He wrote long poems, almost epics for length, about Jonah, Esther, Job, Samson, and Solomon, interspersed with meditations after a quite original plan,—Shepherd's Oracles, Comedies, Romancies, Fancies, and Meditations,—the quintessence of meditation,— and Enchiridions of Meditation all divine, —and what he calls his Morning Muse; besides prose works as curious as the rest. He was an unwearied Christian, and a reformer of some old school withal. Hopelessly quaint, as if he lived all alone and knew nobody but his wife, who appears to have reverenced him. He never doubts his genius; it is only he and his God in all the world. He uses language sometimes as greatly as Shakespeare; and though there is not much straight grain in him, there is plenty of tough, crooked timber. In an age when Herbert is revived, Quarles surely ought not to be forgotten.— THOREAU, HENRY DAVID, 1843, *Letter to Mrs. Emerson, Familiar Letters, ed. Sanborn, p.* 134.

As a poet he has been somewhat **hardly**

dealt with; having been judged more by the evidence of his conceits, absurdities, and false taste, than by his striking and original images, his noble and manly thoughts, and the exceeding fertility of his language. It is not surprising that posterity has failed to reverse the unjust judgment passed upon him by his contemporaries. . . . No writer is either more affected or more obscure. It is only by raking that we can gather the gold; yet it is such as will reward the seeker who has courage to undertake the search. His sagacity and good sense are unquestionable, and occasionally there is a rich outbreak of fancy; while at times he startles us by compressing, as it were, a volume into a single line.—HALL, SAMUEL CARTER, 1848, *Book of Gems.*

He has not so much of beauty and elegance as some of his contemporaries; his taste is coarser than even that of his time; but the ruggedly sublime knows and loves him well. . . . Besides the qualities we have chiefly ascribed to this poet, namely, grandeur and deep-hearted Christian earnestness, he has some minor but interesting qualities. He possesses a style, manly, nervous, generally clear, and more modern than that of almost any poet in his age. He has a keen discrimination of human nature, a copious supply of apt and bold imagery, and adds to this, extensive reading, particularly in the ancient fathers of the Church. Being a layman, too, his piety and zeal tell much better in favour of Christianity than had he been a minister; and Quarles ranks with Grotius, Addison, Pascal, Johnson, Coleridge, and Isaac Taylor, as one of the emnient "lay brothers" in the Christian Church, whose testimony is above all challenge, and whose talents lift their religion above all contempt.—GILFILLAN, GEORGE, 1857, *ed. Quarles Emblems*, pp. 191, 196.

His verses are characterized by ingenuity rather than fancy, but, although often absurd, he is seldom dull or languid. There is a good deal of spirit and coarse vigor in some of his pieces.—CRAIK, GEORGE L., 1861, *A Compendious History of English Literature and of the English Language, vol.* II, *p.* 19.

With honoured, thrice honoured George Herbert waiting at the door, I cannot ask Francis Quarles to remain longer: I can part with him without regret, worthy man and fair poet as he is.—MACDONALD, GEORGE, 1868, *England's Antiphon, p.* 173.

His poems, like those of so many others in this and the preceding age, bespeak a full mind and a meditative temper.—ARNOLD, THOMAS, 1868-75, *Chaucer to Wordsworth, p.* 193.

Whose name is preserved from oblivion by a touch of originality in his most characteristic productions.—WARD, ADOLPHUS WILLIAM, 1875-99, *A History of English Dramatic Literature, vol.* III, *p.* 286.

Like Byrom in the next century, like not a few poets in the Middle Ages, Quarles was a kind of journalist to whom the vehicle of verse came more easily than the vehicle of prose, and the dangers of that state of things are well known. . . . All Quarles's work is journey-work, but it is only fair to note the frequent wealth of fancy, the occasional felicity of expression, which illustrate this wilderness. I should not like to be challenged to produce twenty good lines of his in verse or prose written consecutively, yet it might be a still more dangerous challenge to produce any journalist in verse or prose of the present day who has written so much, and in whom the occasional flashes—the signs of poetical power in the individual and of what may be called poetical atmosphere in his "surroundings"—are more frequent.—SAINTSBURY, GEORGE, 1887, *History of Elizabethan Literature, p.* 378.

The wretchedness of man's earthly existence was the main topic of Quarles' muse, and it was exclusively in religous circles that the bulk of his work has been welcomed with any enthusiasm. In his own day he found very few admirers among persons of literary cultivation, and critics of a later age treated his literary pretentions with contempt. Anthony á Wood sneered at him as "an old puritanicall poet . . . the sometime darling of our plebeian judgment." Phillips, in his "Theatrum Poetarum" (1675), wrote that his verses "have been ever, and still are, in wonderful veneration among the vulgar;" Pope who criticised his "Emblems" in detail in a letter to Atterbury, denounces the books in the "Dunciad" (bk. i. ii., 139-40) as one
Where the pictures for the page atone,
And Quarles is saved by beauties not his own.

Horace Walpole wrote that "Milton was forced to wait till the world had done admiring Quarles." But Quarles is not quite so contemptible as his seventeenth-and-eighteenth-century critics assumed. Most of his verse is diffuse and dull; he abounds in fantastic, tortuous and irrational conceits, and he often sinks into ludicrous bathos; but there is no volume of his verse which is not illumined by occasional flashes of poetic fire. Charles Lamb was undecided whether to prefer him to Wither, and finally reached the conclusion that Quarles was the wittier writer, although Wither "lays more hold of the heart" ("Letters," ed. Ainger, i., 95). Pope deemed Wither a better poet but a less honest man. Quarles's most distinguished admirer of the present century was the American writer, H. D. Thoreau, who asserted, not unjustly, that "he uses language sometimes as greatly as Shakespeare" ("Letters" 1865.) Quarles's "Enchiridion," his most popular prose work, contains many aphorisms forcibly expressed.—LEE, SIDNEY, 1896, *Dictionary of National Biography*, vol. XLVII, p. 96.

George Sandys

1578–1644

Born in England; went to Oxford in 1589; traveled in the east, 1610–12, and published in 1615 an account of his travels in a work entitled a "Relation of a Journey in Four Books, containing a description of the Turkish Empire, of Egypt, of the Holy Land, etc." In 1621 he removed to America, succeeding his brother as treasurer to the English colony of Virginia. He was much interested in the welfare of the colony, establishing iron-works and introducing ship-building. The Virginia company broke up in 1624, and he returned to England. He published translations of Ovid's "Metamorphoses," the first translation of a classic to appear in America; also poetical versions of the *Psalms, Job, Ecclesiastes*, etc.—PECK, HARRY THURSTON, *ed.*, 1898, *The International Cyclopaedia, vol.* XIII, *p.* 105.

PERSONAL

SACRED
TO THE MEMORY
OF
GEORGE SANDYS, ESQ.

EMINENT AS A TRAVELLER, A DIVINE POET, AND A GOOD MAN,

WHO DIED MARCH IV. MDCXLIII AT BOXLEY ABBEY,

AGED LXVI,

AND LIES BURIED IN THE CHANCEL OF THIS CHURCH.

HIS LIFE

WAS THROUGHOUT BLAMELESS, AND NEVER UNUSEFUL:

ITS EARLIER PART WAS SOMETIMES PASS'D IN OBSERVING HIS

FELLOW MEN IN FOREIGN LANDS; AND ITS LATTER AT HOME

IN CELEBRATING THE PRAISES OF HIS GOD AND ATTUNING THE "SONGS OF ZION"

TO THE BRITISH LYRE.

"Thou brought'st me home in safety; that this earth
Might bury me, which fed me from my birth.
Blest with a healthful age; a quiet mind,
Content with little; to this work design'd,
Which I at length have finish'd by Thy aid;
And now my vows have at Thy altar paid."

ERECTED MDCCCXLVIII:

By an admirer of talents, piety, and virtue, His humble emulator in his latter task.
—MONTAGU, MATTHEW, 1848, *Inscription on Monument.*

He lived to be a very aged man, whom I saw in the Savoy, anno 1641, having a youthful soul in a decayed body; and I believe he dyed soon after.—FULLER, THOMAS, 1662, *Worthies of England*, ed. Nichols, vol. II, *p.* 519.

I happened to speake with his niece, my lady Wyat, at whose howse, viz. at Boxley abbey, he dyed. She saies he told her a little before he dyed that he was about 63. He lies buried in the chancel neer the dore of the south side, but without any remembrance of stone—which is pitty so sweet a swan should lye so ingloriously. He had something in divinity ready for the presse, which my lady lost in the warres—the title of it shee does not remember.—AUBREY, JOHN, 1669–96, *Brief Lives*, ed. Clark, vol. II, *p.* 212.

The Author upon his return in 1612 or after, being improved in several respects by this his large journey, became an accomplish'd Gent. as being Master of several Languages, of a fluent and ready discourse and excellent Comportment. He had also naturally a poetical fancy, and a zealous inclination to all human learning, which made his Company desir'd, and acceptable to most virtuous Men and Scholars of his time. . . . Was buried in the Chancel of the Parish Church there, near to the Door, on the South side, but hath no remembrance at all over his Grave, nor anything at that place, only this which stands in the common Register belonging to the said Church. *Georgius Sandys Poetarum Anglorum sui sœculi facile princeps, sepultus fuit Martii* 7 *stilo Anglic. an. dom.* 1643.—WOOD, ANTHONY, 1691–1721, *Athenæ Oxonienses, vol.* II, *ff.* 46, 47.

It would be injurious to the memory of Sandys, to dismiss his life without informing the reader that the worthy author stood high in the opinion of that most accomplished young nobleman the lord viscount Falkland, by whom to be praised, is the highest compliment that can be paid to merit; his lordship addresses a copy of verses to Grotius, occasioned by his "Christus Patiens," in which he introduces Mr. Sandys, and says of him, that he had seen as much as Grotius had read; he bestows upon him likewise the epithet of a fine gentleman, and observes, that though he had travelled to foreign countries to read life, and acquire knowledge, yet he was worthy, like another Livy, of having men of eminence from every country come to visit him.—CIBBER, THEOPHILUS, 1753, *Lives of the Poets, vol.* I, *p.* 284.

A RELATION OF A JOURNEY
1615

He studied the genius, the tempers, the religion, and the governing principles of the people he visited.—CIBBER, THEOPHILUS, 1753, *Lives of the Poets, vol.* I, *p.* 282.

That judicious traveller.—GIBBON, EDWARD, 1776–78, *Decline and Fall of the Roman Empire, ch.* xvii, *note.*

Sandys was an accomplished gentleman, well prepared by previous study for his travels, which are distinguished by erudition, sagacity, and a love of truth, and

are written in a pleasant style.—KERR, ROBERT, 1811–24, *General History and Collection of Voyages and Travels.*

Like Sir John Mandeville, the first English prose writer, Sandys was a distinguished traveller, and his book on the countries of the Mediterranean and the Holy Land enjoyed great popularity. It is said that Addison, in the history of his Italian tour took Sandys as his model. Sandys seems to have been one of the first to quote the allusions of the ancient poets to the places through which he passed, a plan so successfully adopted by Dodwell in his Classical Tour through Greece, and by Eustace in his Classical Tour through Italy.—JENKINS, O. L., 1876, *The Student's Handbook of British and American Literature, p.* 393.

OVID'S METAMORPHOSES
1621–26

It needeth more than a single denization, being a double stranger. Sprung from the stock of ancients Romanes, but bred in the New World, of the sadness whereof it can but participate; especially having wars and tumult to bring it to light instead of the Muses; . . . snatcht from the howers of night and repose, for the day was not mine, but dedicated to the service of your Great Father, and yourselfe.—SANDYS, GEORGE, 1621, *Ovid's Metamorphoses, Dedication to Charles I.*

Dainty Sands, that hath to English done
Smooth-sliding Ovid, and hath made him run
With so much sweetness and unusual grace,
As though the neatness of the English pace
Should tell the jetting Latin that it came
But slowly after, as though stiff and lame.
—DRAYTON, MICHAEL, c 1627, *Of Poets and Poesie.*

He most elegantly translated "Ovid's Metamorphoses" into English verse; so that, as the soul of Aristotle was said to have transmigrated into Thomas Aquinas (because rendring his sense so naturally), Ovid's genius may seem to have passed into Master Sandys. He was a servant, but no slave, to his subject; well knowing that a Translatour is a person in Free Custody; Custody, being bound to give the true sense of the Author he translated; Free, left at liberty to cloath it in his own expression. . . . Indeed some men are better Nurses then Mothers of a Poem; good only to feed and foster the Fancies of others; whereas Master Sandys was altogether as dexterous at inventing as translating; and his own Poems as sprite-full, vigorous, and masculine.—FULLER, THOMAS, 1662, *Worthies of England, ed. Nichols, vol.* II, *pp.* 518, 519.

'Twas a wonderfull helpe to my phansie, my reading of Ovid's "Metamorphy" in English by Sandys, which made me understand the Latin the better.—AUBREY, JOHN, 1669-96, *Brief Lives, ed. Clark, vol.* I, *p.* 36.

And no better has Ovid been served by the so-much admired Sandys. This is at least the idea which I have remaining of his translation; for I never read him since I was a boy. They who take him upon content, from the praises which their fathers gave him, may inform their judgment by reading him again, and see (if they understand the original) what is become of Ovid's poetry in his version; whether it be not all, or the greatest part of it, evaporated. But this proceeded from the wrong judgment of the age in which he lived. They neither knew good verse, nor loved it; they were scholars, it is true, but they were pedants; and for a just reward of their pedantic pains, all their translations want to be translated into English.—DRYDEN, JOHN, 1693, *Third Miscellany, Dedication.*

One of the earliest literary productions of the English colonists in America, of which we have any notice.—HOLMES, ABEL, 1829, *Annals of America, vol.* I, *p.* 184.

This production, handed down to us in stately form through two centuries and a half, is the very first expression of elaborate poetry, it is the first utterance of the conscious literary spirit, articulated in America. The writings which preceded this book in our literary history—the writings of Captain John Smith, of Percy, of Strachey, of Whitaker, of Poey—were all produced for some immediate practical purpose, and not with any avowed literary intentions. This book may well have for us a sort of sacredness, as being the first monument of English poetry, of classical scholarship, and of deliberate literary art, reared on these shores. And when we open the book, and examine it with reference to its merits, first, as a faithful rendering of the Latin text, and second, as a specimen of fluent, idiomatic, and musical English poetry, we find that

in both particulars it is a work that we may be proud to claim as in some sense our own, and to honor as the morning-star at once of poetry and of scholarship in the new world.—TYLER, MOSES COIT, 1878, *A History of American Literature, 1607–1676, vol.* I, *p.* 54.

Rendering of Ovid's "Metamorphoses" has chiefly preserved his name in literary circles. A writer in "Wits Recreations" (1640) congratulated Ovid on "the sumptous bravery of that rich attire" in which Sandys had clad the Latin poet's work. He followed his text closely, and managed to compress his rendering into the same number of lines as the original—a feat involving some injury to the poetic quality and intelligibility of the English. But Sandys possessed exceptional metrical dexterity, and the refinement with which he handled the couplet entitles him to a place beside Denham and Waller. In a larger measure than either of them, he probably helped to develop the capacity of heroic rhyme. He was almost the first writer to vary the cæsura efficiently, and, by adroitly balancing one couplet against another, he anticipated some of the effects which Dryden and Pope brought to perfection. Both Dryden and Pope read Sandys's Ovid in boyhood.—LEE, SIDNEY, 1897, *Dictionary of National Biography, vol.* L, *p.* 292.

DIVINE POEMS AND PSALMS
1636-38-40

Nor may you fear the poet's common lot,
Read and commended, and then quite forgot.
The brazen mines and marble rocks shall waste,
When your foundation will unshaken last.
'Tis Fame's best pay, that you your labours see
By their immortal subject crownéd be.
For ne'er was author in oblivion hid,
Who firm'd his name on such a pyramid.

—KING, BISHOP HENRY, 1638, *Verses Prefixed to a Paraphrase upon the Divine Poems by George Sandys.*

Say, sacred bard, what could bestow
Courage on thee to soar so high?
Tell me, brave friend, what help'd thee so
To shake off all mortality?
To light this torch thou hast climb'd higher
Than he who stole celestial fire.

—WALLER, EDMUND, 1638, *Verses Prefixed to a Paraphrase upon the Divine Poems by George Sandys.*

Others translate, but you the beams collect
Of your inspiréd authors, and reflect
Those heavenly rays with new and strong
effect.
Yet human language only can restore
What human language had impair'd before,
And, when that once is done, can give no
more.
Sir, I forbear to add to what is said,
Lest to your burnish'd gold I bring my lead,
And with what is immortal mix the dead.
—GODOLPHIN, SIDNEY, 1638, *Verses Prefixed to a Paraphrase upon the Divine Poems by George Sandys.*

Such is the verse thou writ'st, that who reads
thine
Can never be content to suffer mine;
Such is the verse I write, that, reading mine,
I hardly can believe I have read thine;
And wonder that, their excellence once
known,
I nor correct nor yet conceal mine own.
Yet though I danger fear than censure less,
Nor apprehend a breach like to a press,
Thy merits, now the second time, inflame
To sacrifice the remnant of my shame.
—FALKLAND, LORD, 1638, *Verses Prefixed to a Paraphrase upon the Divine Poems, by George Sandys.*

I presse not to the quire, nor dare I greet
The holy Place with my unhallowed feet;
My unwasht Muse pollutes not things
divine,
Nor mingles her prophaner notes with
thine:
Here humbly at the Porch she listning
stayes,
And with glad eares sucks in thy Sacred
Layes
—CAREW, THOMAS, 1638, *To my Worthy Friend, Master George Sandys, on his Translation of the Psalmes.*

Infinitely superior ["Psalms"] to any other both for fidelity, music, and strength of versification.—BOWLES, WILLIAM LISLE, 1807, *ed. Pope's Works, vol.* III, *p.* 359.

When Sir Philip Sidney was about twenty-three years old, George Sandys was born; and about fifty years after Sidney's early death, Sandys' version of the Psalms was published. It is difficult to believe that so brief a period separated the versions of the two men. Sidney's rhymes are for the most part rough and halting, while Sandys' verse, masculine and careful in construction, glides smoothly along and delights the ear with its music.—DENNIS, JOHN, 1883, *Heroes of Literature, p.* 83.

GENERAL

This Play ["Christ's Passion"] is translated from the *Latin* Original writ by *Hugo Grotius.* This Subject was handled before in *Greek,* by that Venerable Person, *Apollinarius* of *Laodicea,* Bishop of *Hierapolis;* and after him *Gregory Nazianzen:* tho' this of *Hugo Grotius,* (in our Author's Opinion) transcends all on this Argument. As to the Translator, I doubt not but he will be allow'd an Excellent Artist, by Learned Judges; and as he has follow'd *Horace's* Advice of Avoiding a servile Translation,
Nec verbum verbó curabis reddere fidus Interpres:
So he comes so near the Sence of the Author, that nothing is lost, no Spirits evaporate in the decanting of it into *English;* and if there be any Sediment, it is left behind.—LANGBAINE, GERARD, 1691, *An Account of the English Dramatick Poets, p.* 437.

Sandys' "Metamorphoses of Ovid," and his "Metrical Translations from Scripture," are poetically pleasing: and they have a merit in diction and versification which has been acknowledged thankfully by later poets.—SPALDING, WILLIAM, 1852-82, *A History of English Literature, p.* 276.

Sandys was happily taken away before his friend Lord Falkland fell, and he was spared the miseries of the civil troubles which culminated in the murder of his much-loved master. Of his private character no more need be said than that he seems to have been universally reverenced and beloved. As a poet, he has been too much overlooked, probably from his giving us so few original poems; but I trust that the republication of his works will show that his Paraphrases are not mere servile translations, but have all the freedom of original composition, are singularly sweet and harmonious in versification, and for richness and grandeur of language and imagery, and for true devotional spirit, may justly be ranked amongst the choicest specimens of sacred poetry.—HOOPER, RICHARD, 1872, *ed., The Poetical Works of George Sandys, vol.* I, *p.* liii.

His classical translations are not equal to his scriptural paraphrases, and if he had finished the Æneid Dryden would have left it alone. Like Dryden he did his best work late: he was fifty-nine when he published the Psalms. It does not do to compare Sandys with the authorised version of the Bible. Wherever the original is peculiarly striking he is disappointing: he gives his reader no such compensation for his temerity as Sternhold's version of the Theophany in the 18th Psalm or the close of the 24th, or as Watts's equally well-known paraphrase of the 90th. Even Tate and Brady at their best, as in the 139th Psalm, come very near to Sandys' highest level; but he is much more equable; he never subsides, like Sternhold and Hopkins, into doggerel; he never subsides, like Tate and Brady, into diffuse platitudes. He always grasps the meaning for himself; he seems to work, if not always from the Hebrew, from an ancient version, and he sometimes exhibits a really masterly power of condensation, as in the 119th and the 150th Psalms. Apart from the strictly relative praise due to the versification, the paraphrase on Job is appallingly tame.—SIMCOX, G. A., 1880, *English Poets, ed. Ward, vol.* II, *p.* 192.

In 1620, when Waller was but fourteen, "the learned and ingenious Mr. Sandys" had written lines which, if we modernize the spelling, we might easily pass off upon the unwary reader as Pope's heroics. And in spite of Pope's obligations to the large genius of Dryden, it is to his early delight in Sandys's translation of the Metamorphoses that he owed that ease and harmony of numbers which was his from first to last.—TOVEY, DUNCAN C., 1897, *Reviews and Essays in English Literature, p.* 89.

William Chillingworth
1602–1644

William Chillingworth, theologian, was born at Oxford in 1602, the son of a prosperous citizen, and in 1618 became a scholar, in 1628 a fellow of Trinity. Through the arguments of an able Jesuit, "John Fisher," he embraced Catholicism, and in 1630 went to Douay, where, urged to write an account of his conversion, he was led to renounce that faith by examination of the questions at issue. He became thereafter involved in controversies with several Catholic divines, and his answers are contained in his "Additional Discourses." In the quiet of Lord Falkland's house at Great Tew in Oxfordshire he wrote his famous book, "The Religion of Protestants a safe Way to Salvation" (1637)—a demonstration of the sole authority of the Bible in the matter of salvation, and of the free right of the individual conscience to interpret it. His conclusion is, in his own oft-quoted words: "The Bible, I say, the Bible only, is the religion of Protestants." He left also nine sermons, and a fragment on the apostolical institution of episcopacy. In 1638 he took orders, and was made Chancellor of Salisbury, with the prebend of Brixworth in Notts annexed. In the Civil War he accompanied the king's forces, and before Gloucester devised a seige-engine like the old Roman *testudo.* At Arundel Castle he fell ill, and after the surrender was lodged in the bishop's palace at Chichester, where he died, 30th January 1643.—PATRICK AND GROOME, *eds.,* 1897, *Chambers's Biographical Dictionary, p.* 212.

PERSONAL

Virtuti sacrum.
Spe certissimae resurrectionis
Hic reducem expectat animam
GULIELMVS CHILLINGWORTH,
S. T. P.
Oxonii natus et educatus,
Collegii S^tae *Trinitatis olim*
Socius, Decus et Gloria.
Omni Literarum genere celeberrimus,
Ecclesiae Anglicanae adversus Romano-
Catholicam
Propugnator invictissimus
Ecclesiae Sarisburiensis Praecentor dignis-
simus;
Sine Exequiis,
Furentis cujusdam Theologastri,
Doctoris Cheynell,
Diris et maledictione sepultus:
Honoris et Amicitiae ergò,
Ab OLIVERO WHITBY,
Brevi hoc monimento,
Posterorum memoriae consecratus,
Anno Salutis,
1672.

—WHITBY, OLIVER, 1672, *Inscription on Monument.*

Chillingworthi Novissima: or the sickness, heresy, death, and burial of William Chillingworth; (in his own phrase) Clerk of Oxford, and in the conceit of his fellow-soldiers, the Queen's *Arch Engineer* and *Grand Intelligencer*. Set forth in a letter to his eminent and learned friends. A relation of his apprehension at Arundel, a discovery of his errors in a brief catechism, and a short oration at the burial of his heretical book, by Francis Cheynell, late Fellow of Merton College.—CHEYNELL, FRANCIS, 1644, *Title Page*.

He was a litlte man, blackish haire, of a saturnine complexion. The lord Falkland (vide [life of] lord Falkland) and he had such extraordinary clear reasons, that they were wont to say at Oxon that if the great Turke were to be converted by naturall reason, these two were the persons to convert him. He lies buried in the south side of the cloysters at Chichester, where he dyed of the *morbus castrensis* after the taking of Arundel castle by the parliament: wherin he was very much blamed by the king's soldiers for his advice in military affaires there, and they curst *that little priest* and imputed the losse of the castle to his advice. In his sicknesse he was inhumanely treated by Dr. Cheynell, who, when he was to be buryed, threw his booke into the grave with him, saying, "Rott with the rotten; let the dead bury the dead." Vide a pamphlet of about 6 sheets writt by Dr. Cheynell (maliciously enough) where he gives an account of his life.—AUBREY, JOHN, 1669-96, *Brief Lives, ed. Clark, vol.* I, *p.* 172.

He was then observed to be no drudge at his Study, but being a Man of great Parts would do much in a little time when he settled to it. He would often walk in the College Grove and contemplate, but when he met with any Scholar there, he would enter into discourse, and dispute with him, purposely to facilitate and make the way of wrangling common with him; which was a fashion used in those days, especially among the disputing Theologists, or among those that set themselves apart purposely for Divinity. But upon the change of the Times, occasion'd by the Puritan, that way forsooth was accounted boyish and pedagogical. . . . He was a most noted Philosopher and Orator, and without doubt a Poet also, otherwise Sir Joh. Suckling would not have brought him into his poem called "The Session of Poets;" and had such an admirable Faculty in reclaiming Schismatics, and confuting Papists, that none in his time went beyond him. He had also very

great skill in Mathematics, and his Aid and Council was often used in making Fortifications for the King's Garrisons, especially those of the City of Gloucester, and Arundell Castle in Sussex.—WOOD, ANTHONY, 1691-1721, *Athenæ Oxonienses, vol.* II, *ff.* 40, 42.

RELIGION OF PROTESTANTS
1637

"The Religion of Protestants a safe way to Salvation," against Mr. Knot the Jesuit: I will not say, "Malo nodo malus quærendus est cuneus," but affirm no person better qualified than this Author, with all necessary accomplishments to encounter a Jesuit. It is commonly reported that Dr. Prideaux compared his book to a Lamprey; fit for food, if the venomous string were taken out of the back thereof: a passage, in my opinion, inconsistent with the Doctor's approbation, prefixed in the beginning of his book.—FULLER, THOMAS, 1662, *Worthies of England, ed. Nichols, vol.* II, *p.* 233.

Besides perspicuity, there must be also right reasoning, without which perspicuity serves but to expose the speaker. And for attaining of this, I should propose the constant reading of Chillingworth, who, by his example, will teach both perspicuity and the way of right reasoning, better than any book that I know, and therefore will deserve to be read upon that account over and over again, not to say any thing of his argument.—LOCKE, JOHN, 1704? *Some Thoughts Concerning Reading and Study for a Gentleman.*

Knott is by no means a despicable writer: he is concise, polished, and places in an advantageous light the great leading arguments of his church. Chillingworth, with a more diffuse and less elegant style, is greatly superior in impetuosity and warmth. In his long parenthetical periods, as in those of other old English writers, in his copiousness, which is never empty or tautological, there is an inartificial eloquence, springing from strength of intellect, and sincerity of feeling, that cannot fail to impress the reader. But his chief excellence is the close reasoning which avoids every dangerous admission, and yields to no ambiguousness of language. He perceived, and maintained with great courage, considering the times in which he wrote and the temper of those whom he was not unwilling to keep as friends, his favorite tenet,—that all things necessary to be believed are clearly laid down in Scripture.—HALLAM, HENRY, 1837-39, *Introduction to the Literature of Europe, pt.* iii, *ch.* ii, *par.* 26.

The celebrated work by Chillingworth on the "Religion of Protestants," is generally admitted to be the best defence which the Reformers have been able to make against the church of Rome. It was published in 1637, and the position of the author would induce us to look for the fullest display of bigotry that was consistent with the spirit of his time. Chillingworth had recently abandoned the creed which he now came forward to attack; and he, therefore, might be expected to have that natural inclination to dogmatize with which apostasy is usually accompanied. . . . If we turn now to the work that was written under these auspices, we can scarcely believe that it was produced in the same generation, and in the same country, where, only twenty-six years before, two men had been publicly burned because they advocated opinions different to those of the established church. It is, indeed, a most remarkable proof of the prodigious energy of that great movement which was now going on, that its pressure should be felt under circumstances the most hostile to it which can possibly be conceived; and that a friend of Laud, and a fellow of Oxford, should, in a grave theological treatise, lay down principles utterly subversive of that theological spirit which for many centuries had enslaved the whole of Europe. In this great work, all authority in matters of religion is openly set at defiance.— BUCKLE, HENRY THOMAS, 1857, *History of Civilization in England, vol.* I. *pp.* 251, 252.

This is one of the most closely and keenly argued polemical treatises ever written: the style in which Chillingworth presses his reasoning home is like a charge with the bayonet.—CRAIK, GEORGE L., 1861, *A Compendious History of English Literature and of the English Language, vol.* II, *p.* 64.

His style is, indeed, admirably suited at once to the matter and to the form of his work. He commands a considerable vocabulary, and although his sentences are often loosely constructed, he writes, when he is at his best, with point and carefully chosen phrase. His rhetorical weapons are retort and homely illustration. His manner of building up an argument is, indeed, worthy of Locke's encomium. If he desires to deal a specially heavy blow he reduces his reasoning to a formal syllogism, and crushes his opponent with it. He has a keen scent for a fallacy, and exposes one when he finds it with trenchant humour. He never condescends to quibbling, but all throughout an argument maintains a dignity which, more than anything else, gave him his strength in debate. It was a mind of no common order that could give unity to a work constructed on such a plan as "The Religion of Protestants." Even in the graces of composition, Chillingworth excels his contemporaries. The flexibility and pointedness of his style are virtues as great as the richness and power of Hooker's and Bacon's, and, for his purpose, of greater value. The heat of debate sometimes hurries him into undue vehemence, but he never loses his temper. His other works are not important.—WALLACE, W., 1893, *English Prose, ed. Craik, vol.* II, *p.* 261.

His great book was a strong plea for liberty. While it made a strong protest against the all-embracing dogmatism of Rome, and accepted the "religion of Protestants" as exemplified in the English Church as a "safe way of salvation," it was content to accept the guidance of a free and rational inquiry, which, though it might lead to some errors, was strong in the sanction of intellectual honesty, and the absence of exclusive and narrowing definitions. It was the work of an academic thinker not very intimately in touch with the problems of life, but it had that force of initiation which belongs not infrequently to scholastic speculation. Its free and rational appeal gave a new basis to Anglicanism, and started philosophic inquiry on a fruitful quest.—HUTTON, WILLIAM HOLDEN, 1895, *Social England, ed. Traill, vol.* IV, *p.* 289.

The book is an admirable controversial exercise, the logical accuracy of which won a warm eulogy from Locke. It is in reality an overgrown pamphlet, free indeed from the worst blemishes of contemporary pamphlet literature, and full of careful argument and wide learning, but not rising far enough above its temporary purpose to become a monumental work like Butler's "Analogy" or Hooker's "Ecclesiastical Polity." Its style, though clear and vigorous, is not marked by strong individuality, and its line of argument is academic rather than popular.—MASTERMAN, J. HOWARD B., 1897, *The Age of Milton, p.* 190.

GENERAL

Was justly esteemed the acutest and closest disputant of his time.—GRANGER, JAMES, 1769-1824, *Biographical History of England, vol.* II, *p.* 350.

His frequent changes proceeded from too nice an inquisition into truth. His doubts grew out of himself; he assisted them with all the strength of his reason; he was then too hard for himself; but finding as little quiet and repose in those victories, he quickly recovered by a new appeal to his own judgment, so that in all his sallies and retreats he was, in fact, his own convert.—GIBBON, EDWARD, 1793, *Autobiography, ed. Murray, p.* 90.

A notably militant and loyal mind, the most exact, the most penetrating, and the most convincing of controversialists, first Protestant, then Catholic, then Protestant again and for ever, has the courage to say that these great changes, wrought in himself and by himself, through study and research, are, of all his actions, those which satisfy him most. He maintains that reason applied to Scripture alone ought to persuade men; that authority has no claim in it; "that nothing is more against religion than to force religion;" that the great principle of the Reformation is liberty of conscience; and that if the doctrines of the different Protestants sects are not absolutely true, at least they are free from all impiety and from all error damnable in itself, or destructive of salvation. Thus is developed a new school of polemics, a theology, a solid and rational apologetics, rigorous in its arguments, capable of expansion, confirmed by science, and which, authorizing independence of personal judgment at the same time with the intervention of the natural reason, leaves religion in amity with the world and the establishments of the past.—TAINE, H. A., 1871, *English Literature, tr. Van Laun, vol.* I, *bk.* ii, *ch.* v, *p.* 381.

The style of Chillingworth is the natural expression of his thought—simple, strong, and earnest, occasionally rugged and vehement. Particularly like his thought, it is without any artifice. He is concerned with what he has to say, not with his mode of saying it; and having thrown aside almost all the scholastic pedantries which in his time still clung to theological style, he gives fair play to his native sense and vigour. His vehemence is apt to hurry him into disorder, but also often breaks into passages of lofty and powerful eloquence. If we compare his style with that of Hooker or Bacon, it is inferior in richness, compass, and power, but superior in flexibility, rapidity, and point. It turns and doubles upon his adversary with an impetuosity and energy that carry the reader along, and serve to relieve the tedious levels of the argument. If he must be ranked, upon the whole, greatly below such writers as we have mentioned, he is yet in this, as in other respects, much above most of his contemporary divines. The pages of Laud, or of his biographer Heylin, or even of Hammond, are barren and unreadable beside those of "The Religion of Protestants;" and even the richer beauties of Taylor, embedded amidst many pedantries and affectations, pall in comparison with his robust simplicity and energy.—TULLOCH, JOHN, 1872, *Rational Theology and Christian Philosophy in England in the Seventeenth Century, vol.* I, *p.* 316.

Chillingworth did little more than put in a clearer and more logical form, with all its excrescences stripped away, the contention of Laud in the conference with Fisher. That which marks the pre-eminence of the younger writer is his clear sense of the subordination of intellectual conviction to moral effort. . . . It is not given to any one man, even if he be a Chillingworth, to make out with complete fulness the remedies needed for the evils of his age. . . . Chillingworth's mind was too purely intellectual to enable him to understand how any given ritual could either raïse admiration or provoke hostility.—GARDINER, SAMUEL R., 1883, *History of England from the Accession of James I. to The Outbreak of the Civil War, vol.* VIII, *pp.* 262, 263, 264.

On the purely literary side the merits of Chillingworth are very great. His argumentative clearness was regarded by

Locke as a model, and although his book is the criticism of another treatise, he has contrived to give it unity by the impress of the order of his own mind. Sustained and dignified his argument moves steadily on; he is never captious nor sophistical; he never strains a point against his adversary, but overwhelms him by the massiveness of his learning and the loftiness of his intellectual attitude. Yet Chillingworth's learning never overmasters him, and there is no display of erudition; in fact he does not rest on precedents, but on the reasonableness of his conclusions in themselves. . . . In fact, Chillingworth's views, as lofty as they were, laboured under the defects of an academic thinker whose experience of intellectual problems was larger than his knowledge of the world and of human nature. Still, he put forward a conception of rationalism which was destined to influence other branches of speculation besides theology, and he stated an idea of toleration which was soon fruitful of results.—CREIGHTON, MANDELL, 1887, *Dictionary of National Biography, vol. x, pp.* 256, 257.

If *laudari a laudato* be a safe rule for estimating a writer's merits, the name of Chillingworth ought to stand nearly as high in English ecclesiastical literature as those of Hooker and Butler. . . . Chillingworth's style, indeed, is not only one of the greatest attractions of his book, but is also perhaps the strongest indication which it supplies of the extraordinary qualities of his mind. Its naked severity and nervous simplicity are occasionally dashed by a vein of eloquence which breaks out unexpectedly and with prodigious effect, especially as it depends neither upon a musical ear nor upon pleasure in ornament, but upon the excitement of strong masculine feeling roused by an adequate cause—the feeling, generally speaking, of indignation against oppression, sophistry, and falsehood. An earnest and indeed passionate love of truth was the great characteristic of Chillingworth's mind.—STEPHEN, SIR JAMES FITZJAMES, 1892, *Horae Sabbaticae, First Series, pp.* 187, 192.

It seems to me that the chief value of Chillingworth for our day is to be found in the moral impetus given by the study of his writings, in the influence of his transparent love of truth and his ardour in its search, which with honest hearts is infectious. Nor can one fail to admire his resolve to bring himself into a strict relation with facts. If evidence be insufficient, he never will allow his desires to add one grain to the scale.—DOWDEN, JOHN, 1897, *Outlines of the History of the Theological Literature of The Church of England, p.* 121.

This divine was somewhat slighted in his own age, as giving little show of learning in his discourses; but the perspicuity of his style and the force of his reasoning commended him to the Anglican divines of the Restoration. It is characteristic that Tillotson had a great admiration for this humane latitudinarian, and that Locke wrote, "If you would have your son reason well, let him read Chillingworth." The masterpiece of Chillingworth stands almost alone, in a sort of underwood of Theophrastian character-sketches.—GOSSE, EDMUND, 1897, *Short History of Modern English Literature, p.* 135.

William Laud

1573–1645

Laud was born at Reading, 5th October 1573. He was elected Fellow of St. John's College, Oxford, in 1593. After holding different livings, he was elected President of his College in 1611, and was made Chaplain to James I. In 1615 he became Archdeacon of Huntingdon; in 1621 Bishop of St. David's. In 1622 he had his famous controversy with the Jesuit Fisher; and in 1624 he was put into the High Commission Court. In 1626 he was made Bishop of Bath and Wells, in 1628 Bishop of London. In 1630 he became Chancellor of the University of Oxford, and in August 1633 he became Archbishop of Canterbury. From this time till the meeting of the Long Parliament he was nearly in the position of a Prime Minister, and was the chief agent in all the arbitrary acts of the time, such as the High Commission prosecutions, the introduction of the Liturgy into Scotland, the licensing of books, and the like. One of the first acts of the Long Parliament was to send him to the Tower in March 1641. His goods

were plundered by various violent proceedings. He was brought to trial March 1644, for high treason. The proceedings lasted, under one form or another, till January 1645, when he was beheaded, in the seventy-second year of his age. . . .
Writings: They consist of seven sermons; a report of the Conference with Fisher the Jesuit, held for the instruction of the Duke of Buckingham's mother; the Diary, of which Lord Macaulay spoke so contemptuously, and a small volume of private devotions; a variety of official papers connected with his duties as Chancellor of Oxford; reports of several of his speeches, especially of speeches at the Council Board and at the Court of High Commission; a history of his troubles and his trial; and a great mass of correspondence with various persons, of whom Strafford is the most remarkable.—STEPHEN, SIR JAMES FITZJAMES, 1892, *Horae Sabbaticae, First Series, pp.* 169, 170.

PERSONAL

It is true the roughness of his uncourtly nature sent most men discontented from him, yet would he often (of himself) find ways and means to sweeten many of them again when they least looked for it.—DEARING, SIR EDWARD, 1642, *Speeches in Matters of Religion, Preface, p.* 5.

Of apprehension he was quick and sudden, of a very sociable wit and a pleasant humour; and one that knew as well how to put off the gravity of his place and person when he saw occasion, as any man living; accessible enough at all times, but when he was tired out with multiplicity and vexation of business, which some, who did not understand him, ascribed unto the natural ruggedness of his disposition . . . constant not only to the public prayers in his chapel, but to his private devotions in his closet.—HEYLIN, PETER, 1644, *Cyprianus Anglicus; or, the Life and Death of Archbishop Laud, p.* 542.

My very pockets searched; my Diary, my very Prayer-book taken from me, and after used against me; and that in some cases not to prove but to make a charge. Yet I am thus far glad, even for this sad accident. For by my Diary your Lordships have seen the passages of my life; and by my Prayer-book the greatest secrets between God and my soul; so that you may be sure you have me at the very bottom: yet, blessed be God, no disloyalty is found in the one, no Popery in the other.—LAUD, WILLIAM, 1645, *Speech before House of Lords.*

A man vigilant enough, of an active or rather of a restless mind, more ambitious to undertake than politic to carry on, of a disposition too fierce and cruel for his coat which notwithstanding he was so far from concealing in a subtle way that he increased the envy of it by insolence. He had few vulgar and private vices, as

being neither taxed of covetousness, intemperance nor incontinence, and, in a word, a man not altogether so bad in his personal character as unfit for the state of England.—MAY, THOMAS, 1647, *History of the Long Parliament.*

A little, low, red-faced man.—D'EWES, SIR SYMONDS, 1650? *Autobiography, vol.* II, *p.* 100.

He was a man of great parts, and very exemplar virtues, allayed and discredited by some unpopular natural infirmities; the greatest of which was, (besides a hasty, sharp way of expressing himself,) that he believed innocence of heart, and integrity of manners, was a guard strong enough to secure any man in his voyage through this world, in what company soever he travelled, and through what ways soever he was to pass: and sure never any man was better supplied with that provision.—CLARENDON, LORD (EDWARD HYDE), 1674? *History of the Rebellion and Civil Wars in England, bk.* i, *par.* 189.

Thus died and was buried the king's and Church's martyr, a man of such integrity, learning, devotion and courage, as had he lived in the primitive times, would have given him another name: whom tho' the cheated multitude were taught to misconceive (for those honoured him most who best knew him) yet impartial posterity will know how to value him, when they hear the rebels sentenced him on the same day they voted down the liturgy of the Church of England.—WOOD, ANTHONY, 1691-1721, *Athenæ Oxonienses, vol.* II, *f.* 70.

A dream cometh through the multitude of business. That which the fancy is troubled with most in the day, it reincounters in the night, yet without any deliberation of reason; and therefore must be most groundless to collect an observation from it of any act that hath an intellectual touch in it. I except the infusions of prophetical inspiration, which commonly who can suppose he hath attained without enthusiastical presumption? Juggling astrologers, that will fly at any game for profit and credit, held the people in a dream, how they could interpret dreams which would hit, and which not, by the planet: as Salmasius says (*Clymact.* p. 789), that it was Hephæstion's profession to unfold . . . in what nights of every moon they will happen to be true. But he that *records his dreams*, as if he weighed a thing so light in the balance of observation, his wits are built upon fairy ground and needs no other astrology to deceive him but his own superstition.— HACKET, JOHN, 1693, *Scrinia Reserta: the Life of Archbishop Williams, vol.* II, *p.* 86.

A man of such admirable judgment and learning, that he knew what danger the nation was in, and whence it proceeded, and did declare, that if they would take his advise, he could heal all breaches; which the fanaticks (or *puritans*, as Joyner calls them) well perceiving, they dispatched him as soon as possible; which when they had done, they used these words,

All praise and glory to the Lord,
And *Laud* unto the devil.

—HEARNE, THOMAS, 1705, *Reliquiæ Hearnianæ, ed. Bliss, Nov.* 17, *vol.* I, *p.* 56.

The very enemies of the unfortunate archbishop admitted that he was learned and pious, attentive to his duties and unexceptionable in his morals: on the other hand his friends could not deny that he was hasty and vindictive, positive in his opinions, and inexorable in his enmities. To excuse his participation in the arbitrary measures of the council, and his concurrence in the severe decrees of the star-chamber, he alleged that he was only one among many; and that it was cruel to visit on the head of a single victim the common faults of the whole board. But it was replied, with great appearance of truth that "though only one, he was the chief;" that his authority and influence swayed the opinions both of his sovereign and his colleagues; and that he must not expect to escape the just reward of his crimes, because he had possessed the ingenuity to make others his associates in guilt. Yet I am of opinion that it was religious, and not political rancour, which led him to the

block. Could the zealots have forgiven his conduct as archbishop, he might have lingered out the remainder of his life in the tower. There was, however, little difference in this respect between them and their victim. Both were equally obstinate, equally infallible, equally intolerant.—LINGARD, JOHN, 1819-30, *A History of England, vol.* X, *ch.* ii.

Prejudged by foes determined not to spare,
An old weak Man for vengeance thrown aside,
Laud, "in the painful art of dying" tried,
(Like a poor bird entangled in a snare
Whose heart still flutters, though his wings forbear
To stir in useless struggle) hath relied
On hope that conscious innocence supplied,
And in his prison breathes celestial air.
Why tarries then thy chariot? Wherefore stay,
O Death! the ensanguined yet triumphant wheels,
Which thou prepar'st, full often, to convey
(What time a State with madding faction reels)
The Saint or Patriot to the world that heals
All wounds, all perturbations doth allay?
—WORDSWORTH, WILLIAM, 1821-22, *Ecclesiastical Sonnets, Part II,* XLV.

The friend of Strafford, archbishop Laud, with less worldly passions, and a more disinterested ardour, brought into the council the same feelings, the same designs. Austere in his conduct, simple in his life, power, whether he served it or himself wielded it, inspired in his mind a fanatical devotion. To prescribe and to punish, this was in his eyes to establish order, and order ever seemed to him justice. His activity was indefatigable, but narrow in its views, violent, and harsh. Alike incapable of conciliating opposing interests, and of respecting rights, he rushed, with head down and eyes closed, at once against liberties and abuses; opposing to the latter his rigid probity, to the former his furious hate, he was as abrupt and uncompromising with the courtiers as with the citizens; seeking no man's friendship, anticipating and able to bear no resistance, persuaded, in short, that power is all-sufficient in pure hands; and constantly the prey of some fixed idea, which ruled him with all the violence of passion, and all the authority of duty.— GUIZOT, FRANCOIS PIERRE GUILLAUME, 1826-41, *History of the English Revolution of* 1640, *tr. Hazlitt, p.* 39.

For the individual, indeed, we entertain a more unmitigated contempt than for any other character in our history. The fondness with which a portion of the church regards his memory, can be compared only to that perversity of affection which sometimes lead a mother to select the monster or the idiot of the family as the object of her especial favour. . . . The severest punishment which the two Houses could have inflicted on him would have been to set him at liberty, and send him to Oxford. There he might have stayed, tortured by his own diabolical temper, hungering for Puritans to pillory and mangle, plaguing the Cavaliers, for want of somebody else to plague, with his peevishness and absurdity, performing grimaces and antics in the cathedral, continuing that incomparable diary, which we never see without forgetting the vices of his heart in the abject imbecility of his intellect; minuting down his dreams, counting the drops of blood which fell from his nose, watching the direction of the salt, and listening for the note of the screech-owl! Contemptuous mercy was the only vengeance which it became the Parliament to take on such a ridiculous old bigot.—MACAULAY, THOMAS BABINGTON, 1827, *Hallam's Constitutional History, Essays.*

Cast in a mould of proportions that are much above our own, and of stature akin to the elder days of the Church.—NEWMAN, JOHN HENRY, 1839, *Laud's Diary, Preface.*

Stranger Primate of all England I have never in my life fallen in with. And it is a clean-brushed, cultivated man, well-read in the Fathers and Church history; a rational, at least much-reasoning, extremely logical man. He will prove it for thee by never-ending logic, and the most riveting arguments, if thou hast patience to listen. What he means, what he can possibly mean? . . . Human scepticism will not go the length of disbelieving that he lived; and yet alas, in what way; how could a human figure, with warm red blood in him consent to live in that manner? It is, and continues, very difficult to say! Future ages, if they do not, as is likelier, totally forget "W. Cant.," will range him under the category of Incredibilities. Not again in the dead strata which lie under men's feet, will such a fossil be dug up.

The wonderful wonder of wonders, were it not even this, A zealous Chief Priest, at once persecutor and martyr, who has no discoverable religion of his own? Or why not leave Laud very much on his own basis? Let the dead bury their dead. Laud is little to me.—CARLYLE, THOMAS, 1844-49-98, *Historical Sketches of Notable Persons and Events in the Reigns of James I. and Charles I., p.* 278.

Laud is regarded too generally in the one light of a zealous champion of forms and ceremonies, an uncompromising advocate of rubrical uniformity. He was certainly this; but he was a great many other things too; and in the department of character additions tell more than simply arithmetically; they enlarge, elevate, alter the whole nature of a man. The political department, *e. g.* in Laud, throws depth on the ecclesiastical, and each benefits the other. But the biographer is afraid of the politician. The combination of bishop and politician has a worldly look, and seems to give an advantage to Puritans. The politician is accordingly put in the background: the pious upholder of vestments and the Church-service is presented to us. The age catches the character, and expresses it in its own way; and the stickler for obsolete forms, the obstinate old zealot about trifles, becomes the one popular figure of Laud.—MOZLEY, J. B., 1845-78, *Archbishop Laud; Essays Historical and Theological, vol.* I, *p.* 107.

The church of All-Hallows, Barking, happened to stand open, much to my satisfaction, as I was threading a very narrow and old-fashioned street near the Tower; and I entered, with a thrill of emotion, to behold the venerable interior, where the service for the burial of the dead was read over the bleeding corpse of Archbishop Laud, as it was brought in just after the axe had made him a martyr, and here temporarily interred. I remember that Southey remarks that the Prayer-Book itself seemed to share in his funeral, for on the same day, the Parliament made it a crime to use it in any solemnity whatever; and I endeavored to recall the scene of desolation which must then have smitten to the heart any true son of the Church of England who was its spectator, beholding, as he did, the Primate of all England going down into the sepulchre, as the last, apparently, of his dignity and order; the Church herself beheaded, if not destroyed, with him; and the Prayer-Book reading its own burial! Thank God, there I stood, two hundred years later, a living witness of the resurrection of that Church and its ritual, and of its powerful life, in the new world of the West.—COXE, ARTHUR CLEVELAND, 1856, *Impressions of England, p.* 81.

Whose memory is still loathed, as the meanest, the most cruel, and the most narrow-minded man who ever sat on the episcopal bench.—BUCKLE, HENRY THOMAS, 1857, *History of the Civilization in England, vol.* I, *p.* 251.

The little restless, ubiquitous, statesman-priest, who so grievously mistook and under-rated the forces with which he had to deal, and the times in which he had fallen—Laud.—BENSON, ARTHUR CHRISTOPHER, 1896, *Essays, p.* 7.

GENERAL

Laud seems to have been an imitator, or follower, of Bishop Andrewes: and in some particulars the resemblance holds. The seven sermons contained few doctrinal allusions, with the exception of an important discussion on the future state of the Jews in Sermon I.; and they are chiefly remarkable as expositions *ad populum* of Laud's high views of the regal office. Thus they show him as a statesman more than as a theologian, and their value is rather in relation to the political than to the ecclesiastical or controversial history of the Caroline era. Public, and especially State, occasions, almost necessitate a stiff and artificial manner, as well as a confined range of thought; and it is much to be regretted that none of the many Sermons Laud preached in the ordinary course of his ministry have been preserved. That he was a theologian, and had read extensively and accurately, is proved both by his "Conference" and "Defence." That he was a frequent preacher his Diary abundantly testifies: and that his religion was eminently deep and earnest, we know from his published Devotions, as well as from his patient endurance of persecution and suffering. But neither as a divine, nor in other respects, must his character be altogether measured by these Sermons.—SCOTT, WILLIAM, 1847, *ed., The Works of William Laud, Preface to Sermons, vol.* I, *p.* vii.

Laud, largely as he figures in the social history of his period, is a less figure in our ordinary literary histories than Herrick, who would have licked his shoe.—MASSON, DAVID, 1858, *The Life of John Milton, vol.* I, *ch.* vi.

He was no mean theologian, and while his style of writing is far from attractive, it certainly has the merit of being vigorous and pithy. But better far than all mental gifts and stores of learning, it can be said of Laud, with strictest truth, that he was a man of prayer. The distractions of the times, the multiplicity of occupation, the troubles of his position, prevented not the communion of his soul with his heavenly Father. Seven times a day did he pour out his confessions, prayers, thanksgivings, at the thorne of grace; nor were the dark and silent watches of the night unprovided in his manual with suitable devotions, the language of which is remarkably scriptural, and showed a mind deeply imbued with knowledge of Holy Writ. The same book contains special prayers for prosperity, for adversity, for the State, the King, the Church, the Clergy.—NORTON, JOHN N., 1864, *Life of Archbishop Laud, p.* 263.

Laud's highest praise lies in his patronage of Letters.—ROGERS, JAMES E. THOROLD, 1870, *William Laud, Historical Gleanings, Second Series, p.* 89.

No one who has studied with care the devotions and the "Diary" of William Laud can doubt that his religion was personal, deep and strong; that his sympathies were wide and his ideals high; that the ceremonial which he advocated was dear to him only so far as it stimulated a more intimate knowledge and love of God; and that his personal sanctity must have played a notable part in the events of his disturbed and difficult life.—SIMPKINSON, C. H., 1894, *Life and Times of William Laud, p.* 290.

Laud's reputation, good or ill, as an ecclesiastical statesman has almost entirely obscured his fame as a theologian. His sermons are almost unknown even to students of the seventeenth-century pulpit, and his Controversy with Fisher is rarely, if ever, referred to by modern controversialists who contend over the same field and not infrequently, though perhaps unconsciously, use the same weapons. Two hundred years ago men thought differently.

The sermons were reprinted even in the dark days of the suppression of the Church, and the Conference, republished four times in the seventeenth century, became the authoritative statement of the position of Anglicanism in opposition to the Roman claims. . . . For the oblivion into which Laud's pulpit discourses have fallen many reasons might be assigned. They are probably not even typical of his style. He was a constant, and, from the demand, apparently an admired preacher. He preached as willingly and as often in little country churches as in London or at Court. But he seems to have intentionally avoided all ostentation and as far as possible all record of his pulpit ministry. Not until comparatively late in his career did he notice in his Diary even his most important discourses; and he never suffered any of his sermons to be printed except by direct royal command. In his will he left the publication entirely in the hands of his executors.—HUTTON, WILLIAM HOLDEN, 1895, *William Laud, p.* 138.

The "Conference with Fisher" is marked throughout by a reasonableness and masculine good sense which might not be expected by those who know Laud only through the partisan pages of certain popular historians. Laud was learned, but he was no mere "bookman," to use a word of his own; and in this controversy he does not suffer from being a man of the world, accustomed to observe, to consider, and to judge the facts of life and history. But, it seems to me, the chief interest that now attaches to the "Conference," is the light that it throws on the general attitude of mind, and particular beliefs, of the most prominent high-churchman of his day.—DOWDEN, JOHN, 1897, *Outlines of the History of the Theological Literature of The Church of England, p.* 115.

Sir Richard Baker
1568–1645

Born at Sissinghurst, in Kent, about 1568: died at London, in the Fleet Prison, Feb. 18, 1645. An English writer, author of "Chronicle of the Kings of England" (1641), and of various devotional and other works. He died in destitution due to his becoming surety for debts owed by relatives of his wife. His literary work was all done in the Fleet.—SMITH, BENJAMIN E., 1894-97, *The Century Cyclopedia of Names, p.* 110.

PERSONAL

He received the honour of Knighthood from K. Jam. I. at Theobalds; at which time this our Author (who lived at Highgate near London) was esteem'd a most compleat and learned Person: the benefit of which he reaped in his old Age, when his considerable Estate, was, thro' suretiship, very much impaired. In 1620 he was High Sheriff of Oxfordshire, being then Lord of Middle Aston, and of other Lands therein, and, if I mistake not, a Justice of the Peace. He was a Person tall and comely, of a good disposition and admirable discourse, religious, and well read in various Faculties, especially in Div. and Hist. as it may appear by these Books following, which he mostly composed when he was forced to fly for shelter to his Studies and Devotions.—WOOD, ANTHONY, 1691-1721, *Athenæ Oxonienses, vol.* II, *f.* 72.

GENERAL

"Chronicle of the Kings of England from the time of the Roman Government, unto the death of K. Jam." &c. Lond. 1641. &c. fol. Which Chronicle, as the Author saith, "was collected with so great care and diligence, that if all other of our Chronicles were lost, this only would be sufficient to inform posterity of all passages memorable or worthy to be known, &c. However the Reader must know, that it being reduced to method, and not according to time, purposely to please Gentlemen and Novices, many chief things to be observed therein, as name, time, &c. are egregiously false, and consequently breed a great deal of confusion in the Peruser, especially if he be curious or critical.—WOOD, ANTHONY, 1691-1721, *Athenæ Oxonienses, vol.* II, *f.* 72.

My friend Sir Roger de Coverley told me t'other night, that he had been reading my paper upon Westminster-abbey, in which, says he, there are a great many ingenious fancies. He told me at the same time, that he observed I had promised another paper upon the tombs, and that he should be glad to go and see them with me, not having visited them since he had read history. I could not imagine how this came into the knight's head, till I recollected that he had been very busy all last summer upon Baker's "Chronicle," which he has quoted several times in his disputes with Sir Andrew Freeport since his last coming to town. Accordingly I promised to call upon him the next morning, that we might go together to the abbey. . . . The glorious names of Henry the Fifth and queen Elizabeth gave the knight great opportunities of shining, and of doing justice to Sir Richard Baker, who, as our knight observed with some surprise, had a great many kings in him, whose monuments he had not seen in the abbey.—ADDISON, JOSEPH, 1711-12, *The Spectator, No.* 329.

He wrote "Meditations and Disquisitions on the Lord's Prayer," and on several of the Psalms, "Apology for a Layman's writing Divinity," and a poem called "Cato's Moral Distiches." His chief work, however, and the only one by which he is at all known, is "Chronicle of the Kings of England." . . . About the only history that Englishmen had until the publication of Rapin. The critics denounced it as unscholarly and inaccurate. But it was written in a pleasant, entertaining style, and it continued for a long time to be published and read, holding its place in the old-fashioned chimney-corners, on the same shelf with the Family Bible and Fox's Book of Martyrs.—HART, JOHN S., 1872, *A Manual of English Literature, p.* 106.

Baker's name, though not his fame, has been kept alive by his connection with Sir Roger de Coverley in the "Spectator:" Addison, ridiculing the simple ignorance of the Tory squires in the person of Sir Roger, makes him quote Sir Richard Baker as a great authority. Poor Sir Richard is visited quite as bitterly as his rustic admirer:—"The glorious names of Henry the Fifth and Queen Elizabeth gave the Knight great opportunities of shining, and doing justice to *Sir Richard Baker, who, as our Knight observed with some surprise, had a great many kings in him whose monuments he had not seen in the Abbey."* Baker's popularity with country gentlemen was probably due to his style, which is praised by such an authority as Sir Henry Wotton—"full of sweet raptures and researching conceits, nothing borrowed, nothing vulgar, and yet all glowing with a certain equal facility."—MINTO, WILLIAM, 1872-80, *Manual of English Prose Literature, p.* 256.

Its reputation with the learned never stood very high. Thomas Blount published at Oxford in 1672 "Animadversions upon Sr Richard Baker's 'Chronicle,' and its continuation," where eighty-two errors are noticed, but many of these are mere typographical mistakes. The serious errors imputed to the volume are enough, however, to prove that Baker was little of an historical scholar, and depended on very suspicious authorities.—LEE, SIDNEY, 1885, *Dictionary of National Biography, vol.* III, *p.* 16.

Thomas Nabbes

1600?–1645?

Thomas Nabbes, died about 1645, is called by Langbaine a third-rate poet, and by Cibber a fifth-rate poet. Sir John Suckling, his patron, and other wits of the day, either thought better of his plays or liked the author for his personal merits. Among the best-known of his pieces are: 1. "Microcosmus; a Morall Masque," London, 1637, 4to. . . . 2. "Hannibal and Scipio; a Tragedy," 1637, 4to. 3. "Covent-Garden; a Comedy," 1638, '39, 4to. 4. "The Unfortunate Mother; a Tragedy," 1640, 4to. A volume of his Plays, Masks, Epigrams, Elegies, and Epithalamiums was published 1639, 4to.—ALLIBONE, S. AUSTIN, 1870, *Dictionary of English Literature, vol.* II, *p.* 1397.

GENERAL

A writer in the Reign of *Charles* the First, who we may reckon amongst Poets of the Third-rate; and One who was pretty much respected by the Poets of those Times; Mr. *Richard Brome,* and Mr. *Robert Chamberlain,* (before mention'd) having publickly profest themselves his Friends; and Sir *John Suckling* being his Patron.—LANGBAINE, GERARD, 1691, *An Account of the English Dramatick Poets, p.* 379.

A Writer in the reign of Charles I,

whom we may reckon, says Langbaine, among poets of the third rate, but who in strict justice cannot rise above a fifth. He was patronized by Sir John Suckling. He has seven plays and masks extant, besides other poems, which Mr. Langbaine says, are entirely his own, and that he has had recourse to no preceding author for assistance, and in this respect deserves pardon if not applause from the critic. . . As he was in some degree of esteem in his time, we thought it improper to omit him.—CIBBER, THEOPHILUS, 1753, *Lives of the Poets, vol.* II, *p.* 24.

Nabbes, a member of the Tribe of Ben, and a man of easy talent, was successful in comedy only, though he also attempted tragedy. "Microcosmus" (1637), his best-known work, is half-masque, half-

morality, and has considerable merit in a difficult kind. "The Bride," "Covent Garden," "Tottenham Court," range with the already characterised work of Brome, but somewhat lower. — SAINTSBURY, GEORGE, 1887, *History of Elizabethan Literature, p.* 422.

Nabbes displays a satisfactory command of the niceties of dramatic blank verse, in which all his plays, excluding the two earliest comedies, were mainly written. Although he was far more refined in sentiment than most of his contemporaries, he is capable at times of considerable coarseness. As a writer of masques Nabbes deserves more consideration. His touch was usually light and his machinery ingenious.—LEE, SIDNEY, 1894, *Dictionary of National Biography, vol.* XL, *p.* 18.

Edward Lord Herbert

1583–1648

Edward Herbert, Baron : usually styled Lord Herbert of Cherbury ; soldier, statesman, philosopher, and author ; born of an ancient family at Eyton in Shropshire, in 1583 ; educated at University College, Oxford ; served with renown in the Netherlands ; became a gentleman of the court of James I. ; was ambassador to France 1618–24 ; entered the Irish peerage in 1625, and the English in 1630. His deistical "Tractatus de Veritate" appear in 1624, and the "De Religione Gentilium" was added in 1645. His philosophical writings are somewhat obscure, but he maintained the existence of innate ideas and of a personal Deity, and taught that the mind of the devout seeker for truth may become illuminated by an inward light. The indistinctness of his expressions and the somewhat mystical subtlety of his notions have caused him to be little read or understood. Died in London, Aug. 20, 1648.—ADAMS, CHARLES KENDALL, *ed.,* 1897, *Johnson's Universal Cyclopædia, vol.* IV, *p.* 243.

PERSONAL

Sir Edward Herbert, afterward lord Cherbery, etc., dyed at his house, in Queen street, in the parish of St. Giles in the fields, London, and lies interred in the chancell, under the lord Stanhope's inscription. On a black marble grave-stone thus :

> Heic inhumatur corpus
> Edvardi Herbert, Equitis
> Balnei, Baronis de Cherbury
> et Castle-Island. Auctoris Libri
> cui titulus est *De Veritate*
> Reddor ut herbae,
> Vicessimo die Augusti,
> Anno Domini 1648.

—AUBREY, JOHN, 1669–96, *Brief Lives,* ed. *Clark, vol.* I, *p.* 308.

He was a Person well studied in the Arts and Languages, a good Philosopher and Historian, and understood Men as well as Books, as it evidently appears in his

Writings. . . . He surrendered up his last breath in his House in Queenstreet near London in sixteen hundred forty and eight, and was buried in the Chancel of S. Giles's Church in the Fields. Over his Grave, which is under the South Wall, was laid a flat Marble Stone with this Inscription engraven thereon, *Heic inhumatur corpus Edwardi Herbert, Equitis Balnei, Baronis de Cherbury &c Castle Island, auctoris libri cui titulus est* De veritate. *Reddor ut herbæ ; vicesimo die Augusti anno Domini,* 1648.—WOOD, ANTHONY, 1691-1721, *Athenæ Oxonienses, vol.* II, *f.* 117.

As a soldier, he won the esteem of those great captains the Prince of Orange and the Constable de Montmorency ; as a knight, his chivalry was drawn from the purest founts. Had he been ambitious, the beauty of his person would have carried him as far as any gentle knight can aspire to go. As a public minister, he supported the dignity of his country, even when its prince disgraced it; and that he was qualified to write its annals as well as to ennoble them, the history I have mentioned proves, and must make us lament that he did not complete, or that we have lost, the account he purposed to give of his embassy. These busy scenes were blended with, and terminated by, meditation and philosophic inquiries. Strip each period of its excesses and errors, and it will not be easy to trace out, or dispose the life of a man of quality into a succession of employments which would better become him. Valour and military activity in youth; business of state in the middle age; contemplation and labours for the information of posterity in the calmer scenes of closing life: this was Lord Herbert. — WALPOLE, HORACE, 1764, *ed., Autobiography of Edward Lord Herbert of Cherbury, Advertisement.*

Lord Herbert stands in the first rank of the public ministers, historians, and philosophers of his age. It is hard to say whether his person, his understanding, or his courage, was the most extraordinary; as the fair, the learned, and the brave, held him in equal admiration. But the same man was wise and capricious; redressed wrongs and quarrelled for punctilios; hated bigotry in religion, and was himself a bigot to philosophy. He exposed himself to such dangers, as other men of courage would have carefully declined; and called in question the fundamentals of religion which none had the hardiness to dispute beside himself.— GRANGER, JAMES, 1769-1824, *Biographical History of England, vol. ii, p.* 319.

The life of Lord Herbert of Cherbury, written by himself, is one of the most curious works of the kind that has ever issued from the press. Who can read without delight a narrative, and such a narrative too, of the private foibles and most secret thoughts of the soldier, the statesman, the wit, and the philosopher. That he was truth itself is undoubted; and if his vanity sometimes occasions a smile, we must bear in mind the peculiar features of the period in which he lived. We must remember that chivalry was not then extinct, and that the smiles of beauty and the honours of battle were considered as indispensable in conferring not only

reputation, but respect. Gifted by nature with wit, beauty, and talent, and possessing courage almost amounting to a fault, can we wonder, that in a martial and romantic age Lord Herbert should have engaged the hearts of women, almost as universally as he won for himself the respect of men. If he speaks somewhat ostentatiously of his own merits, at least with equal candour he lays open to us his faults.—JESSE, JOHN HENEAGE, 1839-57, *Memoirs of the Court of England during the Reign of the Stuarts, Including the Protectorate, vol.* i, *p.* 299.

Lord Edward Herbert was one of the handsomest men of his day, of a beauty alike stately, chivalric and intellectual. His person and features were cultivated by all the disciplines of a time when courtly graces were not insignificant, because a monarch mind informed the court, nor warlike customs, rude or mechanical, for individual nature had free play in the field, except as restrained by the laws of courtesy and honor. The steel glove became his hand, and the spur his heel; neither can we fancy him out of his place, for any place he would have made his own. But all this grace and dignity of the man of the world was in him subordinated to that of the man, for in his eye, and in the brooding sense of all his countenance, was felt the life of one who, while he deemed that his present honour lay in playing well the part assigned him by destiny, never forgot that it was but a part, and fed steadily his forces on that within that passes show.— OSSOLI, MARGARET FULLER, 1846, *Papers on Literature and Art.*

Still less heroic, and much less great, was Lord Herbert of Cherbury, who, however, had more literary power than Selden, and was even more double-faced.— SAINTSBURY, GEORGE, 1895, *Social England, ed. Traill, vol.* iv, *p.* 98.

KING HENRY VIII.
1649

Above all, Edward, Lord Herbert, of Cherbury, may be truly said to have written the life and reign of King Henry the Eight; having acquitted himself with the like reputation as the Lord-Chancellor Bacon gained by that of Henry the Seventh. For, in the politic and martial part of this honourable author has been admirably particular and exact, from the best records that were extant; though, as to the ecclesiastical, he seems to have looked upon it as a thing out of his province, and an undertaking more proper for men of another profession.—NICOLSON, WILLIAM, 1696-1714, *English Historical Library.*

His reign of Henry VIII. is allowed to be a masterpiece of historic biography.—WALPOLE, HORACE, 1764, *ed., Autobiography of Edward Lord Herbert of Cherbury, Advertisement.*

Has been ever esteemed one of the best histories in the English language: but there is not in it that perfect candour which one would wish, or expect to see, in so celebrated an historian.—GRANGER, JAMES, 1769-1824, *Biographical History of England, vol.* III, *p.* 145.

A book of good authority, relatively at least to any that preceded, and written in a manly and judicious spirit.—HALLAM, HENRY, 1837-39, *Introduction to the Literature of Europe, pt.* iii, *ch.* ix, *par.* 36.

Undoubtedly the best work of its kind before the Restoration: the English is a model of purity, and perhaps the very best prose, in the sense of being most comprehensible to modern ears, before Dryden's; the periods are well constructed, though not quite so abundant in antithesis as those of Bacon.—FLETCHER, C. R. L., 1881, *The Development of English Prose Style, p.* 11.

The "History" was intended to challenge comparison with Bacon's "Henry VII.," but all the labour of its author failed to secure for it anything like the spring and liveliness of Bacon's narrative. —KER, W. P., 1893, *English Prose, ed. Craik, vol.* II, *p.* 175.

AUTOBIOGRAPHY

Being written when Lord Herbert was past sixty, the work was probably never completed. The spelling is in general given as in the MS. but some obvious mistakes it was necessary to correct, and a few notes have been added, to point out the most remarkable persons mentioned in the text. The style is remarkably good for that age, which coming between the nervous and expressive manliness of the preceding century, and the purity of the present standard, partook of neither. His lordship's observations are new and acute,

some very shrewd; his discourse on the Reformation very wise. . . . Nothing is more marked than the air of veracity or persuasion which runs through the whole narrative. If he makes us wonder, and wonder makes us doubt, the charm of his ingenuous integrity dispels our hesitation. The whole relation throws singular light on the manners of the age, though the gleams are transient.—WALPOLE, HORACE, 1764, *ed., Autobiography of Edward Lord Herbert of Cherbury, Advertisement.*

In many passages the autobiography of Lord Herbert is of a style so charming, and of a manner and matter so singularly characteristic of his order, age, and nation, that one might easily believe it written by some skilful student of the period, with a tacit modern consciousness of the wonderful artistic success of the study. As you read, you cannot help thinking now and then that Thackeray himself could not have done it better, if he had been minded to portray a gentleman of the first James's time. Yet this picture, so frank, so boldly colored, so full of the very life of a young English noble, is one of the most remarkable instances of self-portraiture in any language, in the absence of that consciousness which the momentarily bewildered sense attributes to it; its great value to the reader of our day is, that the author sits to himself as unconstrainedly as if posterity should never come to look over his shoulder, and all his attitudes and expressions are those of natural ease. A rare sincerity marks the whole memoir, and gives it the grace of an antique simplicity.—HOWELLS, WILLIAM DEAN, 1877, *ed., Life of Lord Herbert of Cherbury, p.* 1.

It may be doubted whether there is any more astounding monument of coxcombry in literature. Herbert is sometimes cited as a model of a modern knight-errant, of an Amadis born too late. Certainly, according to his own account, all women loved and all men feared him; but for the former fact we have nothing but his own authority, and in regard to the latter we have counter evidence which renders it exceedingly doubtful. He was, according to his own account, a desperate duellist. But even by this account his duels had a curious habit of being interrupted in the immortal phrase of Mr. Winkle by "several police constables;" while in regard to actual war the exploits of his youth seem not to have been great, and those of his age were wholly discreditable, inasmuch as being by profession an ardent Royalist, he took the first opportunity to make, without striking a blow, a profitable composition with the Parliament. Nevertheless, despite the drawbacks of subject-matter, the autobiography is a very interesting piece of English prose.—SAINTS-BURY, GEORGE, 1887, *History of Elizabethan Literature, p.* 439.

Herbert is best known to modern readers by his autobiography. Childlike vanity is the chief characteristic of the narrative. He represents himself mainly as a gay Lothario, the hero of innumerable duels, whose handsome face and world-wide reputation as a soldier gained for him the passionate adoration of all the ladies of his acquaintance and the respect of all men of distinction. He enters into minute details about his person and habits. He declares that he grew in height when nearly forty years old, that he had a pulse in his head, that he never felt cold in his life, and that he took to tobacco in his later years with good effect on his health. But Herbert's veracity even on such points is disputable; his accounts of his literary friends and his mother are very incomplete, his dates are conflicting, and he does himself an injustice by omitting almost all mention of his serious studies, which give him an important place in the history of English philosophy and poetry. He only shows the serious side of his character in a long digression on education in the early part of his memoirs, where he recommends a year's reading in philosophy and six months' study of logic, although "I am confident," he adds, "a man may have quickly more than he needs of these arts." Botany he praises as "a fine study," and "worthy of a gentleman," and he has some sensible remarks on moral and physical training. At the end of his autobiography he states that he had written a work on truth, which he had shown to two great scholars, Tilenus and Grotius, who had exhorted him to print it, and that a miraculous sign to the same effect had been vouchsafed him from heaven in answer to a prayer.—LEE, SIDNEY, 1891, *Dictionary of National Biography, vol.* XXVI, *p.* 178.

The "Life of Lord Herbert" is full of adventures and of encounters with great personages. The adventures are well told; there is seldom anything very striking in the descriptions of people. King Louis XIII. and the fair maid of an inn are described more particularly than the rest: the writer has little to say of Casaubon or Grotius, of Henry IV. or Queen Margaret. Spinola, though there is not much about him, is represented as a soldier and a gallant gentleman, whom Herbert offered to follow "if ever he did lead an army against the infidels." The fortunes and the ideas of Herbert are generally sufficient for him: he is not much interested in other people. The story comes to an end in 1624; the writer did not go on to tell of his difficulty in understanding what the civil war of England was all about, and of the inconvenience which it caused him.—KER, W. P., 1893, *English Prose, ed. Craik, vol.* II, *p.* 176.

POEMS

I have no wish to rob Oblivion of its legitimate prey. Some of Lord Herbert's poems are, I freely admit, not worth resuscitation, but many of them, or portions at least of many of them, seem to me authentic poetry. In almost all of them we find originality and vigour, however fantastic the conception, however rough the execution. But were their merits even less than they are, no cultivated man could regard them with indifference. The name of their writer would be a sufficient passport to indulgent attention. . . . In my estimate of Lord Herbert's poems I have hitherto stood alone. . . . It is strange that in his "Autobiography" Lord Herbert makes no mention of his Poems, the existence of which seems not to have been suspected by any of his distinguished contemporaries. They were evidently jotted down in moments of leisure, as occasion offered. Some of them were the work of his youth, some of his middle age; the last was written four years before his death. . . . But Herbert's greatest metrical triumph is that he was the first to discover the harmony of that stanza with which the most celebrated poet of our own day has familiarised us. The glory of having invented it belongs indeed to another, but the glory of having passed it almost perfect into Mr. Tennyson's hands belongs unquestionably to Herbert. And it is due also to

Herbert to say that he not only revealed its sweetness and beauty, but that he anticipated some of its most exquisite effects and variations. . . . The Latin poems of Herbert are scarcely likely to find favour in the eyes of modern scholars. Their diction is, as a rule, involved and obscure; they teem with forced and un-classical expressions. His hendecasyl-labics are intolerably harsh, and violate almost every metrical canon. His Elegiacs are not more successful; indeed, the only tolerable copy among the poemata are the verses on a Dial, for the epigrams are below contempt.—COLLINS, JOHN CHUR-TON, 1881, *ed., The Poems of Lord Herbert of Cherbury, pp.* xviii, xx, xxx, xxxiii.

As a poet he was a disciple of Donne, and excelled his master in obscurity and ruggedness. Ben Jonson was impressed by his "obscureness." His satires are very poor, but some of his lyrics have the true poetic ring, and at times suggest Her-rick. He often employs the metre which was brought to perfection by Tennyson in "In Memoriam." His Latin verses are scholarly, and chiefly deal with philosophic subjects.—LEE, SIDNEY, 1891, *Dictionary of National Biography, vol.* XXVI, *p.* 180.

GENERAL

He was a most excellent Artist and rare Linguist, studied both in Books and Men, and himself the Author of two Works most remarkable, viz. "A Treatise of Truth," written in French, so highly prized beyond the Seas, that (as I am told) it is extant at this day with great Honour in the Pope's Vatican.—FULLER, THOMAS, 1662, *Worthies of England, ed.* Nichols, *vol.* II, *p.* 601.

His lordship sems to have been one of the first that formed Deism into a system, and asserted the sufficiency, universality, and absolute perfection of natural re-ligion, with a view to discard all extraor-dinary revelation as useless and needless. He seems to assume to himself the glory of having accomplished it with great labour and a diligent inspection into all religions, and applauds himself for it as happier than any Archimedes.—LELAND, JOHN, 1754-56, *A View of the Deistical Writers.*

Too much space may seem to have been bestowed on a writer who cannot be ranked high among metaphysicians. But Lord

Herbert was not only a distinguished name, but may claim the priority among those philosophers in England. If his treatise "De Veritate" is not, as an entire work, very successful, or founded always upon principles which have stood the test of severe reflection, it is still a monument of an original, independent thinker, with-out rhapsodies of imagination, without pedantic technicalities, and, above all, bearing witness to a sincere love of the truth he sought to apprehend. The am-bitious expectation that the real essences of things might be discovered, if it were truly his, as Gassendi seems to sup-pose, could not be warranted by any thing, at least, within the knowledge of that age. But, from some expressions of Herbert, I should infer that he did not think our faculties competent to solve the whole problem of *quiddity,* as the logicians called it, or the real nature of any thing, at least, objectively without us. He is, indeed, so obscure, that I will not vouch for his entire consistency. It has been an additional motive to say as much as I have done concerning Lord Herbert, that I know not where any account of his treatise "De Veritate" will be found. Brucker is strangely silent about this writer, and Buhle has merely adverted to the letter of Gassendi. Descartes has spoken of Lord Herbert's book with much respect, though several of their leading principles were far from the same.—HALLAM, HENRY, 1837-39, *Introduction to the Literature of Europe, pt.* iii, *ch.* iii, *par.* 28.

Vain and eccentric Lord Herbert. . . . His celebrated treatise "*De Veritate, prout distinguitur a Revelatione, a Verisimili, a Possibili et a Falso,*"—a book, as he says himself, "so different from anything which had been written before," that he had not dared to publish it, till, in answer to his prayers, he had received a supernatural sign from heaven. He had circulated copies of the book among the continental thinkers, "without suffering it to be divulged to others;" but, satisfied with the result, he was now preparing a second edition to be published in London. When this edition appeared (1633,) it bore the "imprimatur" of Laud's domestic chap-lain, stating that nothing had been found in it "contrary to good morals or the truth of the Faith." It is the custom now, however, to regard the book as the **first**

English Deistical treatise, and the author as the first English Deist. It may be doubted whether this judgment is, in any respect, correct; nay, whether, if the conspicuous heads of that day were carefully counted, there might not be found among them one or two whose speculations passed the bounds of any form of Theism whatever.—MASSON, DAVID, 1858, *The Life of John Milton, vol.* I, *ch.* vi.

With Lord Herbert appeared a systematic deism.—TAINE, H. A. 1871, *English Literature, tr. Van Laun, vol.* I, *bk.* ii, *ch.* i, *p.* 207.

William Drummond
1585–1649

William Drummond, 1585–1649. Born, at Hawthornden, 13 Dec. 1585. Educated at Edinburgh High School till 1601; at Edinburgh University, 1601–05; M. A., 27 July 1605. To London, 1606. In France, studying law at Bourges and Paris, 1607–08. In Scotland, 1609. In London, 1610. Returned to Hawthornden as laird, same year, at father's death. Betrothed to Miss Cunningham of Barns, 1614 (?); she died, 1615. Severe illness, 1620. Took out a patent for mechanical appliances, mostly military, Dec. 1627. Presented library to Edinburgh University, 1627. Married Elizabeth Logan, 1632. Political activity 1638–49. Died, 4 Dec. 1649, at Hawthornden. Buried in Lasswade Church. *Works:* "Tears on the Death of Meliades," 1613; "Mausoleum" (a collection of elegies by various writers), 1613; "Poems" (anon.) 1616; "Forth Feasting" (anon.), 1617; "Flowers of Zion," 1623; "The Cypresse Grove," 1625; Sonnet on the Death of King James, 1625; "A Pastorall Elegie," 1638; "A Speech to the Noblemen, etc." 1639; "Considerations to the Parliament," 1639; "Speech for Edinburgh to the King," 1641; "Σκιαμαχια" 1642; "Remoras for the National League," 1643; "Objections against the Scots answered," 1646; "Vindication of the Hamiltons," 1648. *Posthumous:* "The History of Scotland," 1655; "Poems," 1656; "Polemo-Middenia" (anon.; attrib. to Drummond), 1683; Extracts from MSS. (ed. by Laing in "Archæologica Scotica"), 1827. "Conversations with Jonson," 1842. *Collected Works:* "Poems," 1711; "Poems," ed. by W. S. Ward (4 vols.), 1894. *Life:* by Prof. Masson, 1873.—SHARP, R. FARQUHARSON, 1897, *A Dictionary of English Authors, p.* 87.

PERSONAL

My dear Drummond, to whom much I owe
For his much love, and proud I was to know
His poesie: for which two worthy men
I Menstry still shall love, and Hawthornden.
—DRAYTON, MICHAEL, c 1627, *Of Poets and Poesie.*

Mr. Drummond, though a scholar and a man of genius, did not think it beneath him to improve himself in those gay accomplishments which are so peculiar to the French, and which never fail to set off wit and parts to the best advantage. He studied music, and is reported to have possessed the genteel accomplishment of dancing, to no inconsiderable degree.—CIBBER, THEOPHILUS, 1753, *Lives of the Poets, vol.* I, *p.* 305.

I have no doubt that Drummond, a valetudinarian and "minor poet," was thoroughly borne down by the superior powers, physical and mental, of Jonson, and heartily glad when he saw the last of his somewhat boisterous and somewhat arrogant guest. The picture drawn by one who thus felt himself "sat upon" at every turn was not likely to be a flattering one, and yet there is nothing in the "Conversations" to lead us to expect that the portrait given at the end of them would be composed almost entirely of shadows.—GIFFORD, WILLIAM, 1816, *ed., The Works of Ben Jonson, vol.* IX, *p.* 416

He loved a beautiful girl of the noble family of Cunningham, who is the Lesbia of his poetry. After a fervent courtship, he succeeded in securing her affections; but she died, "in the fresh April of her years," and when their marriage-day had been fixed. Drummond has left us a most charming picture of his mistress; of her modesty, her retiring sweetness, her accomplishments, and her tenderness for him. . . . He travelled for eight years, seeking, in change of place and scene, some solace for his wounded peace. There was a kind of constancy even in Drummond's inconstancy; for meeting many years afterwards with an amiable girl, who bore the most striking resemblance to his lost mistress, he loved her for that very resemblance, and married her. Her name was Margaret Logan.—JAMESON, ANNA BROWNELL, 1829, *The Loves of the Poets, vol.* I, *pp.* 267, 269.

Whose chief value to posterity is as the Boswell of Ben Jonson.—LOWELL, JAMES RUSSELL, 1858-64-90, *Library of Old Authors, Prose Works, Riverside ed., vol.* I, *p.* 252.

Drummond was evidently a man of superior talents and accomplishments. We are informed that he was familiarly acquainted with the best Greek and Latin authors: his long residence on the Continent afforded him an excellent opportunity of acquiring a knowledge of the living languages: and he is said to have spoken French, Italian, and Spanish as fluently as his native tongue. To his graver qualifications he added no mean proficiency in music; and he occasionally sought a relaxation of his studies by playing on the lute, "which he did to admiration." He seems to have devoted a considerable portion of his time to the invention or improvement of various instruments and machines, applicable to various purposes of peace or war. They are curiously enumerated, to the extent of sixteen, in a patent which he obtained in the year 1627, and which secured to him the sole right and property within the kingdom of Scotland for the space of twenty-one years.—IRVING, DAVID, 1861, *History of Scotish Poetry, ed. Carlyle, p.* 540.

The church and churchyard of Lasswade are on a height overlooking the village, and about two miles and a half from Hawthornden. The present church was built about a hundred years ago; but, in a portion of the well-kept churchyard, railed in separately from the rest, as more select and important, there is the fragmentary outline of the smaller old church, with some of the sepulchral monuments that belonged to it. Drummond's own aisle, abutting from one part of the ruined wall, is still perfect, a small arched space of stone-work, with a roofing of strong stone slabs, and a grating of iron for door-way. Within that small arched space Drummond's ashes certainly lie, though there is no inscription to mark the precise spot as distinct from the graves of some of his latest descendants who are also buried there, and to one of whom there is a commemorative tablet. The small arched aisle itself is his monument, and it is a sufficient one. There could hardly be a more peaceful rustic burying-ground than that in which it stands, the church and the manse close to it on the height, with only steep descending lanes from them to Lasswade village and to the road leading from Lasswade to Edinburgh.—MASSON, DAVID, 1873, *Drummond of Hawthornden, p.* 456.

The natural beauties of Hawthornden make it a fit scene where fancy may sport at will with the poets' memories; and the associations of a later minstrel have added fresh charms to the romantic dell, fragrant in olden times with the scent of the hawthorn bloom, through which the North Esk still wends its way past Roslin Castle, Drummond's tower, and Melville Grove, mid scenes of ancient song and story, to the meeting of the waters under Dalkeith palace.—WILSON, DANIEL, 1878, *Reminiscences of Old Edinburgh, vol.* II, *p.* 216.

He was a man of varied culture, and his writings in poetry and prose were widely read. He was the foremost of that band of men which broke the tradition that Scottish literature ought to be written in the Scottish national tongue, and which strove to express their thoughts in the language which had served the purposes of Shakspeare and Jonson, and was one day to serve the purposes of Scott and Campbell. He was withal an upright and honest man, craving for philosophic and literary culture rather than for Calvinistic orthodoxy, and fearing the inquisitive meddling of the Presbyterian clergy who would be sure to bear hard upon one of his tastes and opinions. He was one who, like Patrick Forbes, had formed part of that wave of liberal reaction, which, through the blunders of James and Charles, had already spent its force.—GARDINER, SAMUEL R., 1883, *History of England from the Accession of James I. to The Outbreak of the Civil War, vol.* VII, *p.* 295.

If Drummond, as he sat under his sycamore-tree that memorable afternoon, watching Jonson's approach, did not cry, "Welcome, welcome, royal Ben," and if Jonson did not reply on the instant, "Thank'e, thank'e, Hawthornden," as tradition has ever since asserted, there can be no question that the welcome was a right royal one. Jonson might not have been so free with his thanks and his speech, however, if he had known that his "Hawthornden" was to become, at his expense, the inventor of interviewing.— HUTTON, LAWRENCE, 1891, *Literary Landmarks of Edinburgh, p.* 17.

Drummond of Hawthornden lives in literature rather by the picturesque beauty of his name than by the intrinsic merit of his poetry, real as that is. Drummond of Hawthornden! There is a pleasant murmur in the very syllables, as of the humming of bees on Mount Hybla.—LE GALLIENNE, RICHARD, 1894-95, *Retrospective Reviews, vol.* II, *p.* 157.

CYPRESS GROVE
1625

"A Cypress Grove" is a remarkable, and in some respects unique, example of sonorous poetic prose. Detached passages of similar eloquence are to be found in the prose of Drummond's contemporaries and immediate successors; none of them has maintained the same height of imaginative contemplation throughout a piece of equal length. "A Cypress Grove" is the first original work in which an English writer has deliberately set himself to make prose do service for poetry. It is a dignified "Meditation upon Death," tinged with melancholy; and the whole has unity of tone and conception. . . . The most characteristic qualities of Drummond's style are wealth of imagery, variety of sentence-structure, and rhythmic flow. His metaphors are apt and pregnant; he uses similes less frequently than the writers of his age, and seldom draws them out beyond a line. The antithesis of some of the apophthegms which break the continuity of his periods is not overstrained. Two cases of word-play occur, but they are venial. The composition, though carefully elaborated, is seldom laboured or overcharged with ornament; and his ear is rarely, if ever, betrayed into a preference of sound to sense. The even pitch of subdued eloquence at which the style is maintained would prove monotonous but for the ever-changing and contrasting formation of the sentences. This skilful variation of construction, by diversifying the length and cadence of the clauses, gives to the pages of "A Cypress Grove" the peculiar charm of richly modulated music.—M'CORMICK, W. S., 1893, *English Prose, ed. Craik, vol.* II, *pp.* 191, 192.

SONNETS

Without ostentatious praise (which is always to be suspected) it is but truth to observe that many of his sonnets, those more especially which are divested of Italian conceits, resemble the best Greek epigrams in their best taste, in that exquisite delicacy of sentiment, and simplicity of expression, for which our language has no single term, but which is known to all classical readers by the word αφετεια. It is in vain we lament the fate of many of our poets, who have undeservedly fallen victims to a premature oblivion, when the finished productions of this man are little known, and still less read.—HEADLEY, HENRY, 1787, *Select Beauties of Ancient English Poetry.*

His sonnets are in the highest degree elegant, harmonious, and striking. It appears to me that they are more in the manner of Petrarch than any others that we have, with a certain intenseness in the sentiment, an occasional glitter of thought and uniform terseness of expression.— HAZLITT, WILLIAM, 1820, *Lectures on the Literature of the Age of Elizabeth, p.* 177.

Drummond's sonnets, for the most part, are not only of the legitimate order, but they are the earliest in the language that breathe what may be called the habit of mind observable in the best Italian writers of sonnets; that is to say, a mixture of tenderness, elegance, love of country, seclusion, and conscious sweetness of verse. We scent his "muskèd eglantines," listen to his birds, and catch glimpses of the "sweet hermitress" whose loss he deplored. Drummond was not without the faults of prototypes inferior to those writers. His Italian scholarship in some measure seduced, as well as inspired him; but upon the whole his taste was excellent; and he leaves upon his readers the impression of an elegant-minded and affectionate man.—HUNT, LEIGH, 1859-67, *An Essay on the Sonnet, ed. Lee, vol.* I, *p.* 78.

As a poet in the broadest sense of the word, Drummond of Hawthornden ranks far below Spenser; but in the "sonnet's scanty plot" he rules as of right divine, and even the lord of the world of faery must stand uncovered before him. There is not the same weight of matter in his sonnets that there is in the irregular sonnets of Shakspeare, nor is there the same penetrative vigour of language; but there are qualities equally precious if not equally impressive—exquisite keenness of sensibility, attested by peculiar delicacy of touch; imaginative vision and notable power of rendering it; native spontaneousness happily allied with fine mastery of the secrets of metre and melody; and the rare art—carried to perfection in the sonnets of Mr. Rossetti—of making his verse the expression, not of crude passion, which, as Edgar Poe pointed out, is not genuine poetic material, but rather the reflection of passion in the still deeps of imaginative reverie.—NOBLE, JAMES ASH-CROFT, 1880-92, *The Sonnet in England*, p. 22.

Some of Drummond's sonnets are—one *must* use the word—simply adorable; and if this sounds extravagant there are "Be as thou wast, my Lute," and "Dear Quir-ister who from these shadows sends," and twenty more, to speak for themselves in such wise as no man may gainsay.—LA-NIER, SIDNEY, 1880, *A Forgotten English Poet, Music and Poetry*, p. 121.

Their most distinguishing quality is elegance of expression,—a tender pensiveness of sentiment, and a vein of meditation that bespeaks a serious thinker.—STODD-ARD, RICHARD HENRY, 1881, *The Sonnet in English Poetry, Scribner's Monthly*, vol. 22, p. 914.

What poems of Drummond do we remember as we remember those which record how he loved and lamented Mary Cunningham?—DOWDEN, EDWARD, 1881, ed., *The Sonnets of William Shakespeare, Introduction*, p. xviii.

Drummond said that Drayton seemed rather to love his muse than his mistress, judging by his many artificial similes, which showed the quality of his mind, but not the depth of his passion. Perhaps Drummond alone of the poets of his period, excepting Shakspeare only, had just license to write so, for what he says with truth of Drayton might with equal appropriateness have been urged against all his other contemporaries save one. . . . Drummond also was free from excess of the kind that marred contemporaries possessed of more vital impulse; for much

that reality of absorbing passion did for Shakspeare in preserving him from the artificial expression of affected suffering, time itself, acting healingly on a great sorrow, did for him. After the early book in which he told the story of his life's one loss, Drummond seemed to sit above the need of that languishing craving for love-experience which was the will-o'-the-wisp which led his contemporaries into one knows not what quagmires of poetic mockery. Drummond's sonnets are wholly devoid of those excellences of conception and phrase which, where they exist in the best of his brother poets, seem to be delved out of the full depth of a deep nature, but they are distinguished by a healthful seriousness and enlarged view of life and its operative relationships, such as must have come to him equally from his patient submission to untoward circumstance, and from the distance at which he stood removed from the irritating atmosphere of small rivalries, which in London narrowed the sympathies of men so much above him in original gift as Ben Jonson.—CAINE, HALL, 1882, ed., *Sonnets of Three Centuries*, p. 277, *note*.

A graceful poet, but assuredly not the master he has again and again been represented to be. His essential weakness may be seen in his inability to adopt any pure mould: his sonnets may either be regarded as English bastards of Italian parentage, or as Italian refugees disguised in a semi-insular costume.—SHARP, WILLIAM, 1886, ed., *Sonnets of This Century*, p. xlix.

A more important event in Drummond's life, the most important perhaps of all for literature, was his meeting with a daughter of Cunningham of Barns, which seems to have taken place about this time. He fell in love with the lady, wooed and won her; the marriage day was fixed, but before it came she died of a fever. Drummond's genuine and deep affection for her and the tragic close of their love had a profound effect upon his poetry. It strengthened and confirmed the melancholy which, implanted by nature, had been nourished by the quietude of Hawthornden. It fed his mystic idealism; it gave him, both during the lady's life and after she was dead, a real subject for his muse; and thus it did much to save him from that tendency to conceits which was

creeping like a canker into English poetry.
. . . These poems are Drummond's
most valuable contribution to literature.
The series of pieces commemorating his
love is divided into two parts, one prior,
the other subsequent to her death. Together they contain most of what is truly
excellent in the author's poetry; only occasionally in later years did he rise as
high. . . . The best of Drummond's
pieces entitle him to a place in the first
rank of English sonneteers; and it is to
be wondered that he has not, in virtue of
these exquisite poems, taken a higher
place in the rolls of literature.—WALKER,
HUGH, 1893, *Three Centuries of Scottish
Literature, vol. I, pp.* 150, 151.

THE HISTORY OF SCOTLAND
1655

Had there been nothing extant of him
but his "History of Scotland," consider
but the language, how florid and ornate it
is, consider the order and the prudent
conduct of the story, and you will rank
him in the number of the best writers, and
compare him even with Thuanus himself.
—PHILLIPS, EDWARD, 1656, *ed., Poems by
that most famous Wit, William Drummond
of Hawthornden, Preface.*

He was universally esteemed one of the
best poets of his age, and stands in the
first rank of modern historians. He, for
his excellence in telling a story, and interesting his reader in what he relates, is
thought to be comparable to Livy.—
GRANGER, JAMES, 1769-1824, *Biographical History of England, vol. III, p.* 142.

To take what came to hand in any easily
accessible form—the mere first tea-leaves,
let us say, that had already yielded three
or four infusions calling themselves Histories; to get from these, by his art as a
stylist, yet another weak dilution, which
he could tinge with his doctrine of kingly
prerogative; thus, in the guise of a new
History, to inculcate the same Drummondism in politics which he had expounded
more openly in his pamphlets: such was
Drummond's method, and such his purpose. Even the literary ability shown in
the execution of the task is not great.
There is nothing graphic in the book; you
are in a haze as you read; you cannot,
except at a point or two, discern a group
of faces, or see things happening.—MAS-
SON, DAVID, 1873, *Drummond of Hawthornden, p.* 470.

GENERAL

His censure of my verses was: That they
were all good, especiallie my Epitaphe of
the Prince, save that they smelled too
much of the Schooles, and were not after
the fancie of the tyme: for a child (sayes
he) may writte after the fashion of the
Greeks and Latine verses in running; yett
that he wished, to please the King, that
piece of Forth Feasting had been his
owne.—DRUMMOND, WILLIAM, 1619, *Notes
on Ben Jonson's Conversations.*

To say that these Poems are the effects
of a genius the most polite and verdant
that ever the Scottish nation produced,
although it be a commendation not to be
rejected (for it is well known that that
country hath afforded many rare and admirable wits), yet it is not the highest
that may be given him; for, should I affirm
that neither Tasso, nor Guarini, nor any
of the most neat and refined spirits of
Italy, nor even the choicest of our English
Poets, can challenge to themselves any
advantage above him, it could not be
judged any attribute superior to what he
deserves, nor shall I think it any arrogance
to maintain that among all the several
fancies that in these times have exercised
the most nice and curious judgments there
hath not come forth anything that deserves
to be welcomed into the world with
greater estimation and applause.—PHIL-
LIPS, EDWARD, 1656, *ed., Poems by that
most famous Wit, William Drummond of
Hawthornden, Preface.*

During the reign of King James and
Charles I. we have met with no poet who
seems to have had a better ear, or felt
more intimately the passion he describes.
—CIBBER, THEOPHILUS, 1753, *Lives of the
Poets, vol. I, p.* 304.

The earliest piece of Waller is that to
the King on his Navy, in 1625. The piece
in which Sir John Denham's greatest force
lies, "Cooper's Hill," was not written
till 1640. The harmony of Drummond
therefore at a time when those who are
usually called the first introducers of a
smooth and polished versification, had not
yet begun to write, is an honour to him
that should never be forgotten. Nor is
his excellence half enough praised or acknowledged.— LE NEVE, PHILIP, 1789,
*Cursory Remarks on Some of the Ancient
English Poets, particularly Milton.*

It is not easy to determine, whether a

dead language, in which men had been initiated, and of which the purest models had been studied, from their earliest years, or a foreign dialect which, the tongue was unable to pronounce, and to the purity and precision of which the mind was unaccustomed, imposed the severest constraint upon original genius. Yet at a time when the rugged numbers of Donne and Johnson prevailed in poetry, Drummond of Hawthornden gave the first specimen of a rich and melodious versification, and discovered a vein of tender, unaffected sentiment which succeeding poets have not disdained to imitate. His taste was formed in the Italian school; and he preceded Denham and Waller in the refinement of our numbers; though his poetry, like theirs, is neither always equal, nor always correct.—LAING, MALCOLM, 1800-4, *The History of Scotland, vol.* III, *p.* 476.

The Scottish Court of James the Sixth, in the midst of pedantry, scholastic jargon, and polemic theology, produced several poets by no means devoid of genius. Some possessed quaintness of wit, some easy versification, and some the power of affecting the emotions of the heart; but the various talents of the poets were seldom concentrated in the same person. The rays of poetical light were refracted and divided among several poets. In Drummond alone were they united, and displayed the solar radiance of fancy.—LEYDEN, JOHN, 1803, *Scottish Descriptive Poems, p.* 254.

I have long sought a copy of Drummond's works, and I have sought it in vain; but from specimens which I have casually met with, in quotations, I am forcibly inclined to favour the idea, that, as they possess natural and pathetic sentiments, clothed in tolerably harmonious language, they are entitled to the praise which has been so liberally bestowed on them.—WHITE, HENRY KIRKE, 1806, *Melancholy Hours, Remains, vol.* II, *p.* 247.

The elegance of Drummond's sonnets, and the humour of his Scotch and Latin macaronics, have been at least sufficiently praised: but when Milton has been described as essentially obliged to him, the compliment to his genius is stretched too far.—CAMPBELL, THOMAS, 1819, *Specimens of the British Poets.*

Drummond, the over-praised and under-praised,—a passive poet, if we may use the phraseology,—who was not careful to achieve greatness, but whose natural pulses beat music, and with whom the consciousness of life was the sentiment of beauty.—BROWNING, ELIZABETH BARRETT, 1842-63, *The Book of the Poets.*

And Mr. Drummond was a genius? I expect his singing will differ a little from that of the old Iliad Homerides,—merging direct with fiery veracity towards the fact, melting into music by the very truth and fire of it. Alas, yes, from the Greek Homerides, from the Norse Skalds, from the English or Scotch ballad-singer, from all men that ever at any time sang truly. The true singer hurries direct—towards the fact, intent on that alone, melts into music by the very fire of his veracity. Drummond's genius one would say is that of an accomplished Upholsterer rather. Different from Homer's—as a pair of the costliest slashed puff-breeches, stuffed broader than a bushel with nothing in them, may differ from a pair of Grecian Hippolytus' limbs with nothing superflous on them, but good Mr. Drummond is a type of his age. His monstrous unveracious puff-breeches ovation is the emblem of so much other unveracity.—CARLYLE, THOMAS, 1844-49-98, *Historical Sketches of Noble Persons and Events in the Reigns of James I. and Charles I., p.* 260.

Through the greater part of his verse we hear a certain muffled tone of the sweetest, like the music that ever threatens to break out clear from the brook, from the pines, from the rain-shower,—never does break out clear, but remains a suggested, etherially vanishing tone. His is a *voix voilée*, or veiled voice of song.—MACDONALD, GEORGE, 1868, *England's Antiphon, p.* 146.

Scotland, underneath all her apparent unanimity for the Covenant during the last two years, and her exultation in the new Presbyterian order of things, yet contained, as may be readily guessed, a good deal of lurking or diffused *Drummondism.* That was not the name by which it was known at the time; it was called Malignancy by the Covenanters, and Loyalty and the like by its professors; but *Drummondism* is the best name for us, and we are quite entitled to introduce it into the language of this portion of Scottish History. For, though Drummond was only a private man, no one had expressed, or was capable of expressing, so eloquently and energetically as he had done, in his "Irene" and subsequent tracts, the very essence of all the antipathy to the established order of things existing anywhere among his countrymen. These tracts were, in fact, the best unpublished manifestoes, if such a phrase may pass, of the scattered, diffused, and suppressed discontent. All the disaffected in Scotland were virtual Drummondists. So far as words went, Drummond was their universal representative. — MASSON, DAVID, 1873, *Drummond of Hawthornden, p.* 342.

His poetry lacks fire and force, and emotional power; but on the other hand, he had a cultured taste, fancy, and a command of descriptive imagery. Some of his sacred poems exhibit poetical imagery and an easy flow of versification.—MACKINTOSH, JOHN, 1878-92, *History of Civilisation in Scotland, vol.* III, *p.* 366.

Good as are some of the love-sonnets and madrigals, Drummond is best where he is most serious. His deepest interests are metaphysical and religious; he is for ever taking refuge from the ills of the present in meditations on Death, Eternity, the Christian Doctrine. The Universe, "this All" as he calls it,—that conception of the earth with its concentric spheres which belonged to the older astronomy, —is an idea on which he dwells in almost monotonous fashion. The finest of all his writings, the prose tract called "The Cypresse Grove," is a discourse upon Death, reminding us, as Mr. Masson well says, of the best work of Sir Thomas Browne; the most striking of his poems are certainly those where, as in the sonnet "For the Baptist," he presents in his own rich language the severer portions of the Christian history, or the inexhaustible theme of the shortness and the mystery of life. What saves him from becoming wearisome is partly the nobility of his verse at its best, its stateliness and sonorous music; partly his evident sincerity, and his emancipation, speaking generally, from the evil influences that were creeping in to corrupt English poetry at that time.—WARD, THOMAS HUMPHRY, 1880, *English Poets, vol.* II, *p.* 26.

Drummond is a learned poet, and is at his best in his sonnets. Italian influence is always perceptible, and his indebtedness to Guarini is very pronounced. Yet sonnets like those on "Sleep" and the "Nightingale" possess enough natural grace and feeling to give them immortality, and borrowed conceits are often so cleverly handled by Drummond that he deserves more praise than their inventor. His madrigals show a rare command of difficult metres, but are less sprightly than could be wished. The elegy on Prince Henry, which has been compared with "Lycidas," is solemnly pathetic. Drummond anticipated Milton in using the metre of the "Hymn of the Nativity." The prose of "The Cypresse-Grove" is majestic and suggests Sir Thomas Browne, but the historical and political tracts are not noticeable for their style. Drummond's political epigrams and satires are dull and often pointless.—LEE, SIDNEY, 1888, *Dictionary of National Biography, vol.* XVI, *p.* 48.

His sonnets, a form in which he is peculiarly successful, approach more nearly to perfection of rhyme-structure than any of those of his contemporaries, except perhaps Donne's; but he is barely able to resist the tempting error of the final couplet. One or two long and glowing odes of great merit he styles "songs." This first collection of his poems contains many lyrics that are admirable, and few that are without dignity and skill. He uses flowers and pure colours like a Tuscan painter, and strikes us as most fantastic when he essays to write in dispraise of beauty, since no poet of his time is so resolute a worshipper of physical loveliness as he is. In Drummond's voluptuous and gorgeous verse there is no trace of the Elizabethan *naiveté* or dramatic passion. It is the deliberate poetry of an accomplished scholar-artist.—GOSSE, EDMUND, 1894, *The Jacobean Poets, p.* 103.

With one exception the Scottish poets of mark of the Jacobean period were something more than simply men of letters. Courtiers, statesmen, or, as in the case of the later Montrose, soldiers, the main interests of their lives lay in the world of action, and poetry was with them either the solace of hours of retirement or the outcome of experience gained in active life. William Drummond, alone of them all, can be said to have lived a life devoted to the art of poetry. To this circumstance may possibly, to some extent, be attributed the fact that of all the

Scottish poets of that time he, without question, holds the highest place. . . . Drummond's poetry, though it is limited in range, was certainly the finest English poetry of its time. . . . The chief characteristics of Drummond's verse are its lustrous beauty and its melodious sweetness. For these qualities it has been termed Spenserian, but Spenser was not its model. . . . If he appears to lack vigour and originality, as has sometimes been said, that lack is more than atoned for by the wonderful sensuous richness and perfection of his work. His genius, it is true, seems to have been unfitted for the production of any long-sustained composition, but so also, later, was the genius of Robert Burns, and it may well be doubted whether the yard-measure serves as any very valuable criterion of poetic merits.—EYRE-TODD, GEORGE, 1895, *Scottish Poetry of the Seventeenth Century, pp.* 139, 151, 152.

His landscape is generalised: Hawthornden and its lovely scenery have no distinct place in it. But the passion which burned in his heart was true and tender as Petrarch's; and this has given a vivifying power, a peculiar colour to his descriptions.—PALGRAVE, FRANCIS T., 1896, *Landscape in Poetry, p.* 153.

The imagination of Drummond aspires to Spenser's rich standard of association and contrast; he has a refined poetic sensuousness and delight in objective imagery; his sentiment is romantic, melancholy, and musical; but the new subjective and meditative emotion which pervades his verse, and a slight involuntary tendency to the new conceits and metaphysical quiddities mark him also as one of the new age.—CARPENTER, FREDERIC IVES, 1897, *English Lyric Poetry,* 1500–1700, *Introduction, p.* liii.

Drummond of Hawthornden's "Forth Feasting," 1617, bought by Ouvry at Sotheby's in 1858 for £8, 15s. (bound in morocco), fetched £60 at Ouvry's sale in 1882.—WHEATLEY, HENRY B., 1898, *Prices of Books, p.* 218.

John Winthrop

1588–1649

John Winthrop, colonist, b. Edwardston, near Groton, Suffolk, England, 12 Jan., 1588. Studied at Cambridge university. Succeeded his father as lord of Groton Manor. Gave up or lost his position as an attorney of the court of wards in London, perhaps through his non-conformist sympathies, and was elected governor of the Massachusetts Company, 20 Oct., 1629. Sailed from Yarmouth in the *Arbella* with the company's second supply, arriving at Salem, 12 June, 1630, and bringing the charter with him. Settled first at Charlestown, but had removed to Boston by November. Was active in the banishment of the so-called Antinomians in 1637, holding that the colony's existence depended on its religious unity. Had previously taken part in Roger Williams's banishment, but continued his private relations with the founder of Rhode Island, and was his life-long correspondent. In 1638 saved the colony's charter, which had been called for from England, by a diplomatic letter excusing the sending of it. In 1643 headed the commissioners of Massachusetts who met with others from the Plymouth, Connecticut, and New Haven colonies and formed the old New England Union and Confederation, of which Winthrop was the originator and first president. Was elected governor of Massachusetts eleven times, and held many other important offices. His "Modell of Christian Charity," written on the voyage from England, was first printed by the Mass. Hist. Society. The "History of New England," a fount of information concerning events in Massachusetts for the period it covers, was written as a daily journal in three manuscript volumes. Of these the first two were copied and printed in 1790. On the discovery of the third in the tower of the old South church in 1816, the whole work was edited and printed by James Savage in 1825–6 (revised ed. 1853). "Life and Letters," by Robert C. Winthrop, appeared in 1866. Winthrop's speech defining civil liberty, made after his acquital from charges of unduly exercising his power as a magistrate, has become a classic. Died, Boston, Mass., 26 Mar., 1649.—STEDMAN, ARTHUR, 1890, *A Library of American Literature, Short Biographies, vol.* XI, *p.* 611.

PERSONAL

Upon this occasion we are now to attend
to this duty for a governour. . . .
who has been unto us a brother; not
usurping authority over the church; often
speaking his advice, and often contradicted, even by young men, and some of
low degree; yet not replying, but offering
satisfaction also when any supposed offences have arisen; a governour who has
been unto us as a mother, parent-like distributing his goods to brethren and neighbours at his first coming; and gently bearing our infirmities without taking notice
of them.—MATHER, COTTON, 1649, *Sermon.*

Governor Winthrop had five sons living
at the time of his decease, all of whom,
notwithstanding the reduction of his fortune, acquired and possessed large property, and were persons of eminence. The
high reputation of the first Governor of
Massachusetts, has been well sustained by
succeeding generations of his family; and
no name, perhaps, in the history of New
England has been more richly adorned by
exalted public and private character, or
more generally respected, than that of
Winthrop.—MOORE, JACOB, 1848, *Lives
of the Governors of New Plymouth and Massachusetts Bay, p.* 272.

Certain is it that, among the millions
of living men descended from those whom
he ruled, there is not one who does not —
through efficient influences, transmitted
in society and in thought along the intervening generations—owe much of what is
best within him and in the circumstances
about him to the benevolent and courageous wisdom of John Winthrop.—PAL-
FREY, JOHN GORHAM, 1860, *History of
New England, vol.* II, *p.* 266.

Born at Groton, in Suffolk, of a family
honored in that neighborhood for its high
character and its wealth, he had been
trained to the law, as his father and
his grandfather had been before him. He
was a man of good books and of good
manners; catholic in opinion and sympathy; a deeply conscientious man; not
willing that his life should be a thing of
extemporized policies and make-shifts,
but building it up clear from the foundation on solid principle. . . . The
native qualities of the man were lofty,
self-respecting, grave; by culture and
habit he expressed himself spontaneously

in dignified and calm words; and at times
when the thought lifted him, he rose to a
stately unconscious eloquence. He was
no artist, only a thinker and a doer.
Of course he never aimed at effect.
His moral qualities are plainly stamped
upon his manner of expression—moderation, disinterestedness, reverence, pity,
dignity, love of truth and of justice.
The prevailing tone is judicial: he tells
the truth squarely, even against himself.
The greatest incidents in the life of the
colony are reported; also the least. The
pathos, and heroism, and pettiness of
their life, all are here.—TYLER, MOSES
COIT, 1878, *A History of American Literature, 1607-1676, vol.* I, *pp.* 129, 131.

His public statues in Boston and in the
National Capital present him with the
Holy Bible in one hand and the Charter of
Massachusetts in the other. No emblem-
atic expression could be more true.
Without question he was primarily a man
of religion. To himself the main purport
of the work he wrought was religious. In
his eyes Massachusetts was ever, before
all things else, a Church. The State was for
the sake of the Church, incident and subordinate to it. And this probably is the reason
why he so quietly accepted and adjusted
himself to changes in the interior civil
polity of the commonwealth that were adverse to his judgment. They concerned the
secondary interest. While in his political
principles he was liberal in that large sense
in which Puritanism was liberal, in his
practical view of government, as between
aristocracy and democracy he inclined to
the former. Yet his temper was such as to
make him a potent mediator between the
aristocratic and democratic elements that
were ever in conflict around him. By the
moderating influence of his self-control,
humility, disinterestedness, patriotism,
the strife of rival parties was again and
again so restrained as to save the State
from serious detriment. In this respect
he was a prototype of Abraham Lincoln.
The particular service with which, above
all his contemporaries, he stands identified
is that of the defence of the Charter.
Which is to say that he was the pre-
eminent representative in the Massachusetts colony of the idea of independent
self-government. — TWITCHELL, JOSEPH
HOPKINS, 1891, *John Winthrop (Makers
of America), p.* 232.

Winthrop's own personality comes out well in his Journal. He was a born leader of men, a *conditor imperii*, just, moderate, patient, wise.—BEERS, HENRY A., 1895, *Initial Studies in American Letters*, p. 26.

JOURNAL

The antiquarian considered it a Godsend, and the lovers of American literature at large were much delighted at this discovery. Here was something authentick; a history written day by day, as the events transpired, by one who knew the whole matter, and in which he acted no small part: a journal not written to please any set of men, or to assist the designs of a party.—KNAPP, SAMUEL L., 1829, *Lectures on American Literature*, p. 46.

The Massachusetts Company proper, with their charter, had not left their final anchorage at the Cowes, near the Isle of Wight, in 1630, before the governor of that colony—John Winthrop—had made the first entry in a journal or history, which he continued from day to day, and from year to year, until his death in 1648-9. That work, too, remained in perishable manuscript for a century and a half. The original was in three volumes; the first two of which were printed, for the first time, at Hartford, in 1790, from an inaccurate copy, which had been commenced by Governor Trumbull, with a preface and dedication by the great lexicographer, Noah Webster, who subsequently confessed that he had never even read the original manuscript. It remained for one whom we now recognize, since the death of our veteran Quincy, as the venerable senior member of our Society, and its former President,—James Savage,—to decipher and annotate and edit the whole; for lo! in 1816, the third volume, of which nothing had been seen or heard for more than sixty years, turned up in the tower of the Old South Meeting-house! The Rev. Thomas Prince, the pastor of that church, who kept his library in that tower, and is known to have had all three of the volumes in 1755, died without returning this third volume to the family of the author, from whom I have the best reason to think they were all borrowed. And so in 1825-6, one hundred and ninety-five years after that first entry, on that Easter Monday, while the "Arabella" was "riding at the Cowes," these annals of the first nineteen years of the Massachusetts colony were published in a correct and complete form. But as if to illustrate the risks to which they had been so long exposed, and to signalize the perils they had so providentially escaped, one of the original volumes was destroyed by a memorable fire in Court Street, before Mr. Savage had finished the laborious corrections and annotations to which he had devoted himself.—WINTHROP, ROBERT C., 1869, *Massachusetts and Its Early History, Addresses and Speeches*, p. 18.

Is a treasure beyond price among our early historic memorials. . . . For almost twenty years the story went forward, from 1630 until a few weeks before the writer's death in 1649. It is quite evident that Winthrop wrote what he did with the full purpose of having it published as a history; but he wrote it amid the hurry and weariness of his unloitering life, with no anxiety about style, with no other purpose than to tell the truth in plain and honest fashion.—TYLER, MOSES COIT, 1878, *A History of American Literature, 1607-1676, vol.* I, *pp.* 130, 131.

These journals, by the most prominent men in the two colonies, naturally invite comparison. Bradford's work is without doubt the better of the two. It is readable, and its literary style is excellent. Winthrop's history is dull and often unreadable. It has more historical value than Bradford's, simply because the Colony of Massachusetts Bay became of more importance than the Plymouth Plantation. Winthrop delights in recording miracles, apparitions, and monstrosities. He dwells on the darker side of Puritanism, while Bradford constantly aims to display its brighter phases. Winthrop's history has proved a rich mine for later writers. Hawthorne probably conceived of his "Scarlet Letter" while perusing its pages. —PATTEE, FRED LEWIS, 1896, *A History of American Literature*, p. 31.

The "Journal," to give it its original and appropriate title, is an invaluable document, no less for its historical detail than as a revelation of puritan modes of thought and administration.—SECCOMBE, THOMAS, 1900, *Dictionary of National Biography, vol.* LXII, *p.* 230.

GENERAL

The author of two works: "A Model of Christian Charity," written on board the

Arabella, on the Atlantic Ocean; and "A Journal of the Public Occurrences in the Massachusetts Colony." . . . . Its value as an original historical document is extremely great. It is entitled to consideration also for its literary merits.—HART, JOHN S., 1872, *A Manual of American Literature, p.* 34.

Governor John Winthrop's "History of New England" is, on the whole. less graphic and picturesque than Governor William Bradford's "History of Plymouth Plantation;" but it has a smoother and more finished style. . . . Winthrop's best treatise, "A Model of Christian Charity," written on shipboard, need not long detain the literary student. It was one

of the many religious tracts produced during the Puritan revival in England and America, and it surpassed some of its fellows in spirit and execution. . . . Winthrop was an intelligent man, and familiar with some part of the English literature of his day; thus he called George Wither "our modern spirit of poetry;" and he did not do discredit to the general spirit of intelligence which pervaded the Puritan movement. His letters—even those of affection—were written in a somewhat stately style, and abounded in religious allusions and Biblical quotations.—RICHARDSON, CHARLES F., 1887, *American Literature,* 1607-1885, *vol.* I, *pp.* 89, 91.

Richard Crashaw
1613?-1649

Richard Crashaw, religious poet, was born in London about 1613, the only son of the Puritan poet and clergyman, William Crashaw, (1572-1626). From the Charterhouse he proceeded in 1631 to Pembroke Hall, Cambridge, and in 1637 became a fellow of Peterhouse. His Catholic leanings prevented him from receiving Anglican orders, and in 1644 he lost his fellowship for refusing to take the Covenant. He went to Paris, embraced Catholicism, and suffered great distress, until after 1646, through Cowley, he was introduced to Queen Henrietta Maria, who recommended him at Rome; and in April 1649 he became a sub-canon at Loretto, but died four months afterwards. In 1634 Crashaw published a volume of Latin poems *Epigrammatum Sacroium Liber* (2d ed. 1670), in which occurs the famous line on the miracle at Cana: *"Nympha pudica Deum vidit et erubuit"* (the modest water saw its God and blushed); in 1646 appeared his "Steps to the Temple," republished at Paris in 1652, under the title "Carmen deo Nostro," with 12 vignette engravings designed by Crashaw. His works have been edited by Turnbull (1858), Grosart (1872), and Tutin (Hull, 1893).—PATRICK AND GROOME, *eds.,* 1897, *Chambers's Biographical Dictionary, p.* 258.

PERSONAL

His faith perhaps in some nice tenets might
Be wrong; his life, I'm sure,was in the right.
And I myself a Catholic will be,
So far at least, great Saint, to pray to thee.
Hail bard triumphant! and some care bestow
On us, the poets militant below!
. . . .
And when my Muse soars with so strong a wing,
'Twill learn of things divine, and first of thee, to sing.
—COWLEY, ABRAHAM, 1650, *On the Death of Mr. Crashaw.*

Was Car then Crashawe; or was Crashawe Car,
Since both within one name combined are?
Yes, Car's Crawshawe, he Car; 'tis loue alone
Which melts two harts, of both composing one.
So Crashaw's still the same: so much desired
By strongest witts; so honor'd, so admired;

Car was but he that enter'd as a friend
With whom he shar'd his thoughts, and did commend
(While yet he liu'd) this worke; they lou'd each other:
Sweete Crashawe was his friend; he Crashawe's brother.
So Car hath title then; 'twas his intent
That what his riches pen'd, poore Car should print;
Nor feares he checke, praysing that happie one
Who was belou'd by all; disprais'd by none:
To witt, being pleas'd with all things, he pleas'd all,
Nor would he giue, nor take offence.
—CAR, THOMAS, 1652, *ed. Carmen Deo Nostro.*

If Crashaw was not generally popular, and if his detractors malignantly defamed him as a "small poet," a "slip of the times, " and as a "peevish, silly seeker, who glided away from his principles in a poetical vein of fancy and an impertinent curiosity," he enjoyed, on the other hand, the praise of some applauded men, and a general "sweet savour" of renown in his day and generation. He is said to have been a universal scholar—versed in the Hebrew, Greek, Latin, Spanish, and Italian languages—to have made the Grecian and Roman poets his study—and to have possessed, besides, the accomplishments of music, drawing, engraving, and painting. In his habits, too, he was temperate to severity; indeed, had he not been so, his poetry would have sunk from a panegyric on God into a bitter, unintentional satire on himself.—GILFILLAN, GEORGE, 1857, *ed. The Poetical Works of Richard Crashaw, p.* vii.

His position in history, his manhood spent in the last years of the reign of "Thorough," and in the very forefront of the crisis, give him a greater claim upon us than Herbert, who died before Laud succeeded to the Primacy, or Vaughan, who was still a boy when Strafford was executed. There are many other points of view from which Crashaw is of special interest; his works present the only important contribution to English literature made by a pronounced Catholic, embodying Catholic doctrine, during the whole of the seventeenth century, while as a poet, although extremely unequal, he rises, at his best, to a mounting fervour which is quite electrical, and hardly rivalled in its kind before or since. Nor is the story of his life, brief and vague though its outline may be, unworthy of having inspired, as it has evidently done, that noble romance of "John Inglesant" which all the world has been reading with so much curiosity and delight.—GOSSE, EDMUND, 1883, *Seventeenth-Century Studies, p.* 143.

GENERAL

I take this poet to have writ like a gentleman, that is, at leisure hours, and more to keep out of idleness than to establish a reputation, so that nothing regular or just can be expected from him.—POPE, ALEXANDER, 1710, *Letter to H. Cromwell, Dec.* 17, *Pope's Works, ed. Courthope and Elwin, vol.* VI.

Crashawe possessed the requisites of a genuine poet, enthusiasm and sublimity; but he never undertook any grand or original work.—DRAKE, NATHAN, 1798, *Literary Hours, No.* xxviii.

Crashaw formed his style on the most quaint and conceited school of Italian poetry, that of Marino; and there is a prevalent harshness and strained expression in his verses; but there are also many touches of beauty and solemnity, and the strength of his thoughts sometimes appears even in their distortion.—CAMPBELL, THOMAS, 1819, *Specimens of the British Poets.*

Crashaw was a hectic enthusiast in religion and in poetry, and erroneous in both.—HAZLITT, WILLIAM, 1820, *Lectures on the Literature of the Age of Elizabeth.*

These verses were ever present to my mind whilst writing the second part of "Christabel"; if indeed, by some subtle process of the mind, they did not suggest the first thought of the whole poem.—COLERIDGE, SAMUEL TAYLOR, 1836, *Letters and Conversation.*

I can only mention to you Quarles, a great favorite with my uncle Southey, and Crashaw, whose sacred poetry I think more truly poetical than any other, except Milton and Dante. I asked Mr. Wordsworth what he thought of it, and whether he did not admire it; to which he responded very warmly. My father, I recollect, admired Crashaw; but then neither Quarles nor Crashaw would be much liked by the modern general reader. They would be thought queer and extravagant.—COLERIDGE, SARA, 1847, *Memoir and Letters, p.* 320.

Had Milton, before leaving Christ's College, become acquainted with the younger versifier of Pembroke, and read his "Music's Duel," his "Elegies on the Death of Mr. Herrys," and such other pieces of verse, original or translated, as he then had to show, he would have found in them a sensuous beauty of style and sweetness of rhythm quite to his taste. . . On the whole, there was a richer vein of poetical genius in Crashaw than in Herbert. . . . Apart from the modified intellectual assent expressly accorded by Donne, by Ferrar, and by others, to some of the Catholic doctrines which Crashaw seems to have made his spiritual diet, we trace a more occult effect of the same influence in a rhetorical peculiarity common to many of the writers of this theological school. We cannot define the peculiarity better than by saying that it consists in a certain flowing effeminacy of expression, a certain languid sensualism of fancy, or, to be still more particular, an almost cloying use of the words, "sweet," "dear," and their cognates, in reference to all kinds of objects.—MASSON, DAVID, 1858, *The Life of John Milton, vol.* I, *ch.* vi.

As a poet, his works have ever been appreciated by those most qualified to decide upon their sterling beauties, and have suggested to others (too frequently without acknowledgment) some of their finest imageries. In every volume of any pretensions to taste, designed to offer specimens of English poetry, extracts are to be found; yet, with the exception of being partially, and by no means accurately, printed in the bulky and inconvenient collections of Chalmers and Anderson, it is somewhat remarkable that, in an age when familiarity with our Old English Authors is so eagerly sought, a full reprint should have been deferred till now. —TURNBULL, WILLIAM B., 1858, *ed., Complete Works of Richard Crashaw, Preliminary Observations, p.* x.

Having said so much on this subject, I fear I cannot point out as much in detail as I would wish, a very striking peculiarity in Crashaw's lyrical poems which seems deserving of special attention. I refer to the extraordinary resemblance both in structure, sentiment, and occasionally in expression, which many passages (that are comparatively less spoiled than others by the prevailing bad taste of Crashaw's time) bear to the lyrics of that first of England's *poet*-lyrists,—I of course mean Shelley. Strange as it may appear, there are many things in common between them. They both, at great personal sacrifices, and with equal disinterestedness, embraced what they conceived to be the truth. Fortunately, in Crashaw's case, Truth and Faith were synonymous; unhappily with Shelley the Abnegation of Faith seemed to be of more importance than the reception of any tangible or intelligible substitute. Both were persecuted, neglected, and misunderstood; and both terminated their brief lives, at about the same age, on opposite shores of the same beautiful country, whither even at that early period "The Swans of Albion" had begun to resort, there perchance in a moment of peace

to sing one immortal death-song, and so die.—M'CARTHY, D. F., 1858, *Crashaw and Shelley, Notes and Queries, June* 5, 2*d Series, vol.* 5, *p.* 449.

He is perhaps, after Donne, the greatest of these religious poets of the early part of the seventeenth century. He belongs in manner to the same school with Donne and Herrick, and in his lighter pieces he has much of their lyrical sweetness and delicacy; but there is often a force and even occasionally what may be called a grandeur of imagination in his more solemn poetry which Herrick never either reaches or aspires to.—CRAIK, GEORGE L., 1861, *A Compendious History of English Literature and of the English Language, vol.* II, *p.* 20.

Like "charity" for "love," the word "sensuous" has deteriorated in our day. It is, I fear, more than in sound and root confused with "sensual," in its base application. I use it as Milton did, in the well-known passage when he defined Poetry to be "simple, *sensuous*, and passionate;" and I qualify "sensuousness" with "imaginative," that I may express our Poet's peculiar gift of looking at everything with a full, open, penetrative eye, yet through his imagination; his imagination not being as spectacles (coloured) astride the nose, but as a light of white glory all over his intellect and entire faculties. Only Wordsworth and Shelley, and recently Rossetti and Jean Ingelow are comparable with him in this. You can scarcely err in opening on any page in your out-look for it.—GROSART, ALEXANDER B., 1873, *ed., The Complete Works of Richard Crashaw, vol.* II, *p.* lxii.

Crashaw is full of diffuseness and repetition; in the "Wishes for his Mistress" he puts in every fantastic way possible the hope that she will not paint; often the variations are so insignificant that he can hardly have read the poem through before sending it to press. . . . He spins the 23rd psalm into three dozen couplets. The Stabat Mater is very far from being the severest of mediæval hymns, but there is no appropriateness in Crashaw's own title for his paraphrase "A Pathetical descant on the devout Plain Song of the Church," as though he were a pianist performing variations upon a classical air. He extemporises at ease in his rooms at Peterhouse, then the ritualistic college of

Cambridge. Like Herbert he was a piece of a courtier, but he did not go to court to seek his fortune, he found nothing there but materials for a sketch of the supposed mistress who never disturbed his pious vigils.—SIMCOX, G. A., 1880, *English Poets, ed. Ward, pp.* 195, 196.

Crashaw had the softened fire of Southwell with the placid sweetness of Habington. He possessed a wider range than either of them; the fact that he was at his best in paraphrases shows that he did not own the force and power which Habington had in less degree than Southwell, or that his fluency of diction and copiousness of imagery easily led him to ornament the work of others rather than to carve out his own.—EGAN, MAURICE FRANCIS, 1880-89, *Lectures on English Literature, p.* 87.

But if the azure cherubim of introspection are the dominant muses of English sacred verse, the flame-coloured seraph of worship reigns in that of Crashaw. He has made himself familiar with all the amorous phraseology of the Catholic metaphysicians; he has read the passionate canticles of St. John of the Cross, the books of the Carmelite nun, St. Teresa, and all the other rosy and fiery contributions to ecclesiastical literature laid by Spain at the feet of the Pope during the closing decades of the sixteenth century. The virginal courage and ardour of St. Teresa inspire Crashaw with his loveliest and most faultless verses. . . . He is the solitary representative of the poetry of Catholic psychology which England possessed until our own days; and Germany has one no less unique in Friedrich Spe.—GOSSE, EDMUND, 1883, *Seventeenth-Century Studies, pp.* 153, 154.

Crashaw's verse is marked by some of the highest qualities of poetry. He has strong affinities to two of our great nineteenth-century poets; he has the rich imagination and sensuousness of Keats, and the subtlety of thought and exquisite lyrical flow of Shelley. Crashaw is essentially a sacred poet, and, compared with George Herbert, is his superior, judged from the purely poetic standpoint. Herbert is, in a limited degree, a popular poet; Crashaw is not, and has never been so. One of the reasons for this is (probably) the taste for artificial poetry of the school of Waller, Dryden, Pope, &c., during the seventeenth and eighteenth

centuries. The fact of his being a Catholic would also deter many readers from studying his works; but, poetical thought now being wider, and religious intolerance almost a thing of the past, it may be hoped that Crashaw will soon receive the recognition which is his due.—TUTIN, J. R., 1887, *ed., Poems of Richard Crashaw, Preface, p.* viii.

There is not in his work the slightest sign of the exercise of any critical faculty before, during, or after production. His masterpiece, one of the most astonishing things in English or any other literature, comes without warning at the end of "The Flaming Heart." For page after page the poet has been poorly playing on some trifling conceits suggested by the picture of Saint Theresa and a seraph. First he thinks the painter ought to have changed the attributes; then he doubts whether a lesser change will not do; and always he treats his subject in a vein of grovelling and grotesque conceit which the boy Dryden in the stage of his elegy on Lord Hastings would have disdained. And then in a moment, in the twinkling of an eye, without warning of any sort, the metre changes, the poet's inspiration catches fire, and there rushes up into the heaven of poetry this marvellous rocket of song. . . . Often, as in verse after verse of "The Weeper," it has an unearthly delicacy and witchery which only Blake, in a few snatches, has ever equalled; while at other times the poet seems to invent, in the most casual and unthinking fashion, new metrical effects and new jewelries of diction which the greatest lyric poets since—Coleridge, Shelley, Lord Tennyson, Mr. Swinburne—have rather deliberately imitated than spontaneously recovered. Yet to all this charm there is no small drawback. The very maddest and most methodless of the "Metaphysicals" cannot touch Crashaw in his tasteless use of conceits.—SAINTSBURY, GEORGE, 1887, *History of Elizabethan Literature, pp.* 364, 369

Crashaw's sacred poems breathe a passionate fervour of devotion, which finds its outlet in imagery of a richness seldom surpassed in our language. . . . Diffuseness and intricate conceit, which at times become grotesque, are the defects of Crashaw's poetry. His metrical effects, often magnificent, are very unequal.

He has little of the simple tenderness of Herbert, whom he admired, and to whom he acknowledged his indebtedness. —LEE, SIDNEY, 1888, *Dictionary of National Biography, vol.* XIII, *pp.* 35, 36.

Crashaw represents sensuous Mysticism . . . . Like Quarles, (though not to the same degree), he quits the ideal point of view, the high Platonic aether. We cannot say of him, as has been said of that "Son of Light," Origen, the great founder of Christian Mysticism, that he "is never betrayed into the imagery of earthly passion used by the monastic writers," and which also marked the style of the Italian Marino, from whose "Herod" Crashaw has left a brilliant paraphrase. Yet this mode of feeling has its place; it also demands and deserves its compartment in a Sacred Anthology. Crashaw's work in poetry, as a whole, is incomplete and irregular; Pope, whilst praising him, was correct in recognizing that he was an amateur rather than an artist. It was the same with Marvell:— neither, one would say, did justice to his fine natural gift. But Crashaw has a charm so unique, an imagination so nimble and subtle, phrases of such sweet and passionate felicity, that readers who . . . turn to his little book, will find themselves surprised and delighted, in proportion to their sympathetic sense of Poetry, when touched to its rarer and finer issues.—PALGRAVE, FRANCIS TURNER, 1889, *The Treasury of Sacred Song, Note, p.* 342.

Crashaw is remarkable among poets for the extraordinary inequality of his work. It is impossible to open a page of his poems without being rewarded by some charming novelty of metre or language, some sudden turn of expression of melodious cadence of rhythm. But the music flags, and the moment or inspiration passes, and Crashaw sinks to earth, the child of Marini and Gongora, the weaver of trivial conceits and over-elaborate fancies. It is this inequality that has made his poetry less read than it deserves to be. Poets of as widely different schools as Pope, Coleridge, and Shelley— have each acknowledged their indebtedness to him; and Mr. Swinburne has in our own day restored some of his lyrical measures to English verse.—MASTERMAN, J. HOWARD B., 1897, *The Age of Milton.*

Crashaw is in poetry as in religion an emotional ritualist; a rich and sensuous pathos characterizes his diction and his rhythms, and redeems from tastelessness conceits over-subtle and symbolical, and marked by all the extravagance of the rococo vein.—CARPENTER, FREDERIC IVES, 1897, *English Lyric Poetry,* 1500-1700, *Introduction, p.* lix.

His age gave the preference to Cowley, in whose odes there is unlimited ostentation of dominating ardour without the reality, the result being mere capricious and unmeaning dislocation of form. Too much of the like is there in Crashaw; but every now and again he ascends into real fervour, such as makes metre and diction plastic to its own shaping spirit of inevitable rightness. This is the eminent praise of Crashaw, that he marks an epoch, a turn of the tide in English lyric, though the crest of the tide was not to come till long after, though—like all first innovators—he not only suffered present neglect, but has been overshadowed by those who came a century after him. He is fraught with suggestion—infinite suggestion. More than one poet has drawn much from him, yet much remains to be drawn. But it is not only for poets he exists. Those who read for enjoyment can find in him abundant delight, if they will be content (as they are content with Wordsworth) to grope through his plenteous infelicity. He is no poet of the human and household emotions; he has not pathos, or warm love, or any of the qualities which come home to the natural kindly race of men. But how fecund is his brilliant imagery, rapturous ethereality. He has, at his best, an extraordinary cunning of diction, cleaving like gold-leaf to its object. In such a poem as "The Musician and the Nightingale" the marvel of diction becomes even too conscious; in the moment of wondering at the miracle, we feel that the miracle is too researched: it is the feat of an amazing gymnast in words rather than of an unpremeditating angel. Yet this poem is an extraordinary verbal achievement, and there are numerous other examples in which the miracle seems as unconscious as admirable. —THOMPSON, FRANCIS, 1897, *Excursions in Criticism, The Academy, vol.* 52, *p.* 427.

Phineas Fletcher

1582–1650

Phineas Fletcher: poet, born in England in 1582; entered Cambridge University in 1600, and became rector of Hilgay, Norfolk, in 1621. He wrote various poems— "The Locustœ, or Apollyonists," a satire against the Jesuits (1627), rare; "Sicelides, a Dramatic Piece" (1631); "Joy in Tribulation," (1632); "The Purple Island, or The Isle of Man," together with "Piscatoric Eclogues and other Poetical Miscellanies" (1633), etc. Died at Hilgay in 1650. He was a cousin of Fletcher, the dramatist, and a brother of Giles Fletcher (1588–1623), a clergyman, and author of the fine poem "Christ's Victory and Triumph."—ADAMS, CHARLES KENDALL, ed., 1897, *Johnson's Universal Cyclopœdia, vol. III, p. 417.*

PERSONAL

Phineas was what honest Walton would have called "a true brother of the nangle," and his master-passion betrays itself in the most unexpected places. It appears even in the characters and subject of his only dramatic work, which he describes oñ the title-page as "A Piscatory."—BELL, ROBERT, 1867? ed., *Songs from the Dramatists, p. 216.*

Our little life-Story is well-nigh told. I regret that after search and research utterly disproportionate to the result, the circumstances and date of his death remain uncertain. My predecessors have given—Archdeacon Todd in his Milton "1649" and George Ellis in his "Specimens," and most "1650" for his death: but no evidence is adduced, and I do not see that it can be accurate. There is no entry of his death and interment at Hilgay: no memorial whatever of his having either died or been buried there; while the last "record" by him in the Register is in "1648." I fear the conclusion is inevitable that he was among the fugitives and a "Sufferer" of the Church (of England), though Walker who has [mis] chronicled so many other worthless names, names not him.—GROSART, ALEXANDER B., 1869, ed., *Poems of Phineas Fletcher, Memoir, vol. I, p. cli.*

PURPLE ISLAND
1633

THE | PURPLE | ISLAND, | or | The Isle of Man: | together with | Piscatorie Eclogs, | and other | Poeticall Miscellanies. | By P. F. | Hinc lucem et pocula sacra. | Alma mater. | Printed by the Printers to the Universitie | of Cambridge. 1633. (40).—TITLE PAGE OF FIRST EDITION.

. . . Thou art Poet borne: who know
thee, know it:
Thy brother, sire, thy very name's a Poet:

Thy very name will make these Poems take,
These very Poems else thy name will make.
—BENLOWES, W., 1633, *Lines prefixed to The Purple Island.*

He that would learn Theologie, must first studie Autologie. The way to God is by ourselves. It is a blinde and dirty way. It hath many windings, and is easie to be lost. This Poem will make thee understand that way: and therefore my desire is, that thou maist understand this Poem. Peruse it as thou shouldst thyself, from thy first sheet to thy last. The first view, perchance, may runne thy judgement in debt; the second will promise payment; and the third will perform promise. Thou shalt finde here Philosophie and Moralitie, two curious handmaids, dressing the King's daughter, whose garments "smell of Myrrhe and Cassia," and being "wrought with needlework and gold," shall make thee take pleasure in her beautie. Here are no blocks for the purblinde, no snares for the timerous, no dangers for the bold. I invite all sorts to be readers, all readers to be understanders, all understanders to be happie.—FEATLY, DANIEL, 1633, *The Purple Island, To the Readers.*

If . . . these dull times
Should want the present strength to prize
thy rhymes,
The time-instructed children of the next
Shall fill thy margent and admire the text;
Whose well-read lines will teach them how
to be
The happy knowers of themselves and thee.
—QUARLES, FRANCES, 1633, *To the Spencer of this Age.*

I much thank you for your visits, and other fair respects you shew me; 'specially that you have enlarg'd my quarters 'mong these melancholy walks by sending me a whole Isle to walk in, I mean that delicate *purple Island* I receiv'd from you, where

I meet with *Apollo* himself and all his daughters, with other excellent society. I stumble also there often upon myself, and grow better acquainted with what I have within me and without me: Insomuch that you could not make choice of a fitter ground for a Prisoner, as I am, to pass over, than of that *purple Isle*, that *Isle of Man* you sent me; which, as the Ingenious Author hath made it, is a far more dainty soil than that *Scarlet* Island which lies near the *Baltic* Sea.—HOWELL, JAMES, 1645, *Familiar Letters, vol.* II, *p.* 189.

Amid such profusion of images many are distinguished by a boldness of outline, a majesty of manner, a brilliancy of colouring, a distinctness and propriety of attribute, and an air of life, that we look for in vain in modern productions, and that rival, if not surpass, what we meet with of the kind even in Spenser, from whom our author caught his inspiration. —HEADLEY, HENRY, 1787, *Select Beauties of Ancient English Poetry.*

The conclusion of the "Purple Island" sinks into such absurdity and adulation, that we could gladly wish the poet back again to allegorizing the bladder and kidneys.—CAMPBELL, THOMAS, 1819, *Specimens of the British Poets.*

From its nature, it is insuperably wearisome; yet his language is often very poetical, his versification harmonious, his invention fertile. But that perpetual monotony of allegorical persons, which sometimes displeases us even in Spenser, is seldom relieved in Fletcher; the understanding revolts at the confused crowd of inconceivable beings in a philosophical poem; and the justness of analogy, which had given us some pleasure in the anatomical cantos, is lost in tedious descriptions of all possible moral qualities, each of them personified, which can never co-exist in the Purple Island of one individual.— HALLAM, HENRY, 1837-39, *Introduction to the Literature of Europe, pt.* iii, *ch.* v, *par.* 32.

"The Purple Island" of the younger brother, Phineas, is the nearest thing we have to an imitation of Spenser; but it is hardly worthy of its fame. It is an undisguised and wearisome allegory, symbolizing all parts and functions both of man's body and of his mind; and it is redeemed only by the poetical spirit of some of the passages.—SPALDING, WILLIAM, 1852-82 *A History of English Literature, p.* 277.

About the sixth canto,—where the poet passes from technical anatomy and physiology into what may be called the psychology of his subject, and begins to enumerate and marshall the faculties, habits, and passions of man, each under a separate personification, with a view to the great battle of the virtuous powers of the list under their leader Eclecta, or Choice, against the vices,—then the genius of the poet, already more than indicated even in the former cantos, takes wing into a freer element, which it fills, in the remaining six cantos, with beauty and sublimity in ill-devised profusion. Some of the personifications, in the latter part of the "Purple Island," are not surpassed in Spenser; and, on the whole, the poetry, though still wearisome from the unflagging strain of the abominable allegory, is richer than in his brother's shorter production, if not so serenely solemn.—MASSON, DAVID, 1858, *The Life of John Milton, vol.* I, *ch.* vi.

The "Purple Island" is rather a production of the same species with Dr. Darwin's "Botanic Garden;" but, forced and false enough as Darwin's style is in many respects, it would be doing an injustice to his poem to compare it with Phineas Fletcher's, either in regard to the degree in which nature and propriety are violated in the principle and manner of the composition, or in regard to the spirit and general success of the execution. Of course, there is a good deal of ingenuity shown in Fletcher's poem; and it is not unimpregnated by poetic feeling, nor without some passages of considerable merit. But in many other parts it is quite grotesque; and, on the whole, it is fantastic, puerile, and wearisome.—CRAIK, GEORGE L., 1861, *A Compendious History of English Literature and of the English Language, vol.* II, *p.* 18.

Of all the strange poems in existence, surely this is the strangest. . . . And yet the poem is full of poetry. He triumphs over his difficulties partly by audacity, partly by seriousness, partly by the enchantment of song. But the poem will never be read through except by students of English literature. It is a whole; its members are well-fitted; it is full of beauties—in parts they swarm like fireflies; and *yet* it is not a good poem. It is like a well-shaped house, built of mud, and stuck full of precious stones. . . . Never was there a more incongruous dragon of allegory.—MACDONALD, GEORGE 1868, *England's Antiphon, pp.* 155, 156.

Starting with Headley, and reaching to Campbell in his "Specimens" . . . it is vulgarly imagined that Phineas Fletcher is a simple imitator if not copyist, of Spenser. Never was there more ignorant and egregious representation. Like Giles he had a splendid faculty of Impersonation, and by the requirements of the ground-idea of his "Purple Island" these play a frequent and controlling part in his great Poem: but unless you are to make Spenser the inventor of Impersonation and Allegory, and ignore his translating into English of the classic mythology and of Ariosto and of other predecessors, you must allow that the selection of Impersonation and Allegory by our Fletchers, as the vehicle for the expression of their thick-coming thoughts and fancies, in nowise involves Spenserian or other "imitation."—GROSART, ALEXANDER B., 1869, *ed., Poems of Phineas Fletcher, Essay, vol.* I, *p.* ccxxvi.

A poem which reminds us of the "Faery Queen" by the supreme tediousness of its allegory, but in nothing else.—LOWELL, JAMES RUSSELL, 1875, *Spenser, Works, Riverside ed., vol.* IV, *p.* 297.

Fletcher's allegory is overloaded with detail, and as a whole is clumsy and intricate. His diction is, however, singularly rich, and his versification melodious. Incidental descriptions of rural scenes with which he was well acquainted are charmingly simple, and there is a majesty in his personification of some vices and virtues which suggest Milton, who knew Fletcher's works well.—LEE, SIDNEY, 1889, *Dictionary of National Biography, vol.* XIX, *p.* 316.

GENERAL

It is to his honour that Milton read and imitated him, as every attentive reader of both poets must soon discover. He is eminently entitled to a very high rank among our old English classics.—HEADLEY, HENRY, 1787, *Select Beauties of Ancient English Poetry.*

The "Piscatory Eclogues," to novelty of scenery, add many passages of genuine and delightful poetry, and the music of the verse is often highly gratifying to the ear; but many of the same faults are discernible in these pieces, which we remarked in the "Purple Island;" pedantry and forced conceits occasionally intrude, and, though the poet has not injured the effect of his delineations by coarseness, or rusticity of expression, he has sometimes forgotten the simple elegance which should designate the pastoral muse.—DRAKE, NATHAN, 1817, *Shakspeare and his Times, vol.* I, *p.* 623.

From the handful of books that usually lay strewn about wherever we two sat, I took up one he had lately got, with no small pains I was sure, and had had bound in its own proper colour, and presented it to me—"The Purple Island" and "Sicelides" of Phineas Fletcher. People seldom read this wise, tender, and sweet-voiced old fellow now; so I will even copy the verses I found for John to read.—CRAIK, DINAH M., 1857, *John Halifax, Gentleman, ch.* ix.

The so-called "Piscatory Eclogues" of Phineas Fletcher differ from Spenserian pastorals only in this, that the occupations of Thyrsilis, Thelgon, Dorus, Thomalin, and the rest, are those of fishermen rather than shepherds. Otherwise the fiction is the same; and, following his simple fisher-lads down the Cam, or the Thames, or the Medway, or out at sea in their skiffs along the rocky coasts, the poet, just as in the other case, but with more of watery than of sylvan circumstance, expresses his own feelings and makes his own plaint.—MASSON, DAVID, 1858, *The Life of John Milton, vol.* I, *ch.* vi.

He may without injustice to his brother Giles be said to be the most distinguished Spenserian in our seventeenth-century literature. . . . Of characterisation this pastoral ["Sicelides"] contains as little as other examples of the species; the charm of its diction, however, is not only great, but remarkably varied. A poem is assuredly worth study, which is made beautiful by descriptive passages of the sweetest simplicity, and of a rare contemplative stillness; by a dialogue at times instinct with the fire and the dolours of the passion of love; by truly dramatic narratives; by bursts of lyric emotion; as well as by single lines or couplets of pregnant force or enshrining figures of irresistible charm.—WARD, ADOLPHUS WILLIAM, 1875-99, *A History of English Dramatic Literature, vol.* III, *pp.* 180, 181.

The relation of Phineas Fletcher to Spenser is very close, but the former possesses a distinct individuality. He is enamoured to excess of the art of personification, and the allegorical figures he creates in so great abundance are distinct and coherent, with, as a rule, more of Sackville than of Spenser in the evolution of their types. In his eclogues he imitates Sannazaro, but not without a reminiscence of "The Shepherd's Calendar." Nevertheless, Spenser is the very head and fount of his being, and the source of some of his worst mistakes, for so bound is Phineas to the Spenserian tradition that he clings to it even where it is manifestly unfitted to the subject he has in hand.—GOSSE, EDMUND, 1894, *The Jacobean Poets.*

Thomas May

1595–1650

He was the son of Sir Thomas May of Mayfield, Sussex, and was born in 1594. A Fellow-commoner of Sidney Sussex College, Cambridge, a student at Gray's Inn, and a courtier, he occupied his leisure in penning tragedies, comedies, descriptive poems, and translations from Virgil and Lucan. During the Civil Wars he was employed as secretary and historiographer to the Long Parliament. In this capacity he published in 1647 his "History of the Parliament of England, which began 3rd Nov. 1640." This work however only extends to the battle of Newbury in 1643. In a "Breviary" of the same history, published in 1650, he carries the story some years further. May's "History" was reprinted by Baron Maseres in 1812, and by the Clarendon Press in 1854; his "Breviary" is included in Maseres' "Select Tracts relating to the Civil Wars" (1815). His comedies are, "The Heir" and "The Old Couple:" his tragedies, "Cleopatra," "Agrippina," and "Antigone." To these Mr. Fleay would add the anonymous play of "Nero," and if this be really May's it is his masterpiece. There exists a rare book entitled "An Epitome of the English History by Thomas May, Esq., a late Member of Parliament," 3rd ed. 1690; but as this is written in an anti-Cromwellian vein, and as the events narrated go down to 1660, it can hardly be the work of our author, who died in 1650.—CRAIK, HENRY, 1893, *ed., English Prose. vol. II, p.* 225.

PERSONAL

Sure I am, if he were a biassed and partiall Writer, he lieth buried near a good and true Historian indeed (I mean Mr. Camden) in the West side of the North Isle of Westminster Abby, dying suddenly in the night, anno Domini 1652, in the 55th year of his age.—FULLER, THOMAS, 1662, *Worthies of England, ed. Nichols, vol. II, p. 396.*

As to Tom May, Mr. Edmund Wyld told me that he was acquainted with him when he was young, and then he was as other young men of this towne are, scil. he said he was debaucht *ad omnia:* but doe not by any meanes take notice of it—for we have all been young. But Mr. Marvel in his poems upon Tom May's death falls very severe upon him. He was choaked by tyeing his cap.—AUBREY, JOHN, 1669–96, *Brief Lives, ed. Clark, vol. II. p,* 56.

Since his fortune could not raise his mind, he brought his mind down to his fortune by a great modesty and humility in his nature, which was not affected, but very well became an imperfection in his speech, which was great mortification to him, and kept him from entering upon any discourse but in the company of his very friends. His parts of art and nature were very good.—CLARENDON, LORD (EDWARD HYDE), 1674? *Life, vol. I.*

As one put drunk into the packet-boat,
Tom May was hurried hence and did not
　　know't.

—MARVELL, ANDREW, 1681, *Tom May's Death, Poems.*

While James was still King, he had earned a place in letters by a comedy called "The Heir," acted in 1620, though not published till 1633, and by a translation of Virgil's Georgics. Remaining about the court on a footing of intercourse with Charles, he had added to his reputation by three tragedies, a translation of Lucan's Pharsalia (1630), and other works; and now, at the age of thirty-seven, somewhat fat and with an impediment in his speech, he had some established celebrity as a dramatist and poet, which was to be curiously obscured afterwards when he became better known as Thomas May, the parliamentarian secretary and authorized historian of the Long Parliament. With no such twist in the end of his career as yet anticipated, he was still loyal Tom May, a "chosen friend" of Ben Jonson, and looking, it was said, for the laureateship, in the event of Ben's death.—MASSON, DAVID, 1858, *The Life of John Milton, vol.* I, *ch.* vi.

May had no reason for rejoicing in his early intimacy with Clarendon, whose portrait of him is more enduring than brass.—WARD, ADOLPHUS WILLIAM, 1875-99, *A History of English Dramatic Literature, vol.* iii, *p.* 142.

HISTORY OF THE PARLIAMENT
1650

Impartially true . . . saving some little mistakes in his own judgment, and misinformations which some vain people gave of the state, and more indulgence to the king's guilt than can justly be allowed.—HUTCHINSON, MRS. LUCY, 1664? *Memoirs of Colonel Hutchinson.*

May's "History of the Parliament" is a good model of genuine English; he is plain, terse, and vigorous, never slovenly, though with few remarkable passages, and is, in style as well as substance, a kind of contrast to Clarendon.—HALLAM, HENRY, 1837-39, *Introduction to the Literature of Europe, pt.* iii, *ch.* vii, *par.* 36.

A work which is less polished or eloquent than the author's poetical tastes might have led us to expect.—SPALDING, WILLIAM, 1852-82, *A History of English Literature, p.* 240.

Their histories, like May's for instance, are flat and heavy.—TAINE, H. A., 1871, *History of English Literature, tr. Van Laun, vol.* I, *bk.* ii, *ch.* v, *p.* 398.

May is a man of letters playing the historian. He flaunts you his Latin at every turn, decking his narrative with quotations from Claudian, Petronius, Lucan, and stopping to translate them with superfluous nicety. He conceives of history rather as an art than a science; his object is to instruct ignorance, not to assist investigation; he will insert a document here and there, but for the most part you must take his word for his authorities.

And, as is the wont of literary men, it is the personal note that attracts him most, not as with the modern school, analysis of hidden cause and obvious effect; so that the best part of his book is to be found in the touches of characterisation, in the sketches of Pym, of Strafford. As a describer of battles he is hardly vigorous or picturesque enough. Indeed to style in writing he never attains. He has not the gift of the paragraph; page after page is a string of disconnected notes. And his diction is so far Latinised as to become bald, without catching the felicities which Latinisms sometimes convey.—CHAMBERS, EDMUND K., 1893, *English Prose, ed. Craik, vol.* II, *p.* 225.

As a prose writer May's reputation rests on his "History of the Long Parliament." It is written in a flowing and elegant style, abounding, like all May's writings, with quotations and parallels from Latin literature. Strafford is compared to Curio, Marie de Medicis to Agrippina. May bases his history on the newspapers and on the official manifestos of the two parties. He keeps himself studiously in the background, avoids, as far as possible, any expression of his own opinion, and is silent about his own reminiscences. He professes to relate facts without rhetoric or invective, to recall to the minds of his readers the judgments passed at the time on the facts he records, and to inform the world of the right nature, causes, and growth of the civil strife. Secret motives or hidden causes he makes no attempt to explain.—FIRTH, C. H., 1894, *Dictionary of National Biography, vol.* XXXVII, *p.* 145.

On the whole, May's "History" is a colourless production, though the style is easy and fluent. He is generally content to narrate events without comment or criticism, and is equally unmoved by animosity or enthusiasm. Indeed, the personal opinions of the writer only very rarely appear in the course of the record, a fact which seems to indicate either indifference or strong self-repression. May is sometimes happy in his references to Roman history, but, considering his high reputation for learning, the volume is very little "ornamented" with quotations or illustrations. All this seems to show that the writer's task was perfunctory and uncongenial, and that the work was written like Milton's "Eikonoklastes," to order, not by choice, but was not inspired, like Milton's pamphlet, with the fire and fervour of strong convictions.—MASTERMAN, J. HOWARD B., 1897, *The Age of Milton, p.* 204.

GENERAL

The Heire, being borne, was in his tender age
Rockt in the Cradle of a private Stage,
Where, lifted up by many a willing hand,
The child did from the first day fairely stand;
Since, having gather'd strength, he dares preferre
His steps into the publike Theater,
The World: where he despaires not but to find
A doome from men more able, not lesse kind.
—CAREW, THOMAS, 1633, *To my Honoured Friend, Master Thomas May, upon his Comedie, The Heire.*

I am sure his Enemies must allow him to be a good Poet, tho' possibly he fell short of Sir *William D'Avenant:* and tho' I no ways abet his self Opinion, yet I learn from *Horace,* that even Ill Poets, set a value on their Writings, tho' they are despis'd by others;

*Ridentur mala qui componunt Carmina, verùm
Gaudent Scribentes, & se venerantur, & ultrò,
Si taceas, laudant, quicquid scripsere beati.*

And therefore I hope the moderate Critick will bear with the Frailty of our Author: and I doubt not but if they will read his Works with Candor, and especially his Plays, they will find he had some Reason for his Opinion of what he writ.—LANGBAINE, GERARD, 1691, *An Account of the English Dramatick Poets, p.* 361.

His battle-pieces highly merit being brought forward to notice; they possess the requisites in a considerable degree to interest the feelings of an Englishman, while in accuracy they vie with a gazette, they are managed with such dexterity as to busy the mind with unceasing agitation, with scenes highly diversified and impassioned by striking character, minute incident, and alarming situations.—HEADLEY, HENRY, 1787, *Select Beauties of Ancient English Poetry.*

Of May and Beaumont it is not necessary to say much: the former is occasionally nervous and energic, and their national subjects might enhance their reputation; their poems, however, are but too often little superior to gazettes in rhyme.—DRAKE, NATHAN, 1798, *Literary Hours, No.* xxviii.

He has ventured in narrative poetry on a similar difficulty to that Shakspeare encountered in the historical drama, but it is unnecessary to show with how much less success. Even in that department, he has scarcely equalled Daniel or Drayton.—CAMPBELL, THOMAS, 1819, *Specimens of the British Poets.*

The first Latin poetry which England can vaunt is May's "Supplement to Lucan," in seven books, which carry down the history of the Pharsalia to the death of Cæsar. This is not only a very spirited poem, but, in many places at least, an excellent imitation. The versification, though it frequently reminds us of his model, is somewhat more negligent. May seems rarely to fall into Lucan's tumid extravagances, or to emulate his philosophical grandeur: but the narration is almost as impetuous and rapid, the images as thronged; and sometimes we have rather a happy imitation of the ingenious sophisms Lucan is apt to employ. The death of Cato and that of Cæsar are among the passages well worthy of praise. In some lines on Cleopatra's intrigue with Cæsar, while married to her brother, he has seized, with felicitous effect, not only the broken cadences, but the love of moral paradox, we find in Lucan.—HALLAM, HENRY, 1837-39, *Introduction to the Literature of Europe, pt.* iii, *ch.* v, *par.*74.

"Nero" is, . . . manifestly the work of a highly accomplished scholar, such as May undoubtedly was, and the theme must have had special interest for the translator and continuer of Lucan. It is, moreover, the work of a dramatic poet capable of writing admirable blank verse of the stronger sort, and often pithy in the substance of his diction. The canvas is crowded with characters, but they are graphically distinguished, and the whole picture of the feather-brained despot and his strangely-assorted surroundings is, without any slavish dependence on Tacitus and the other classical authorities, skilful in the choice and disposition of its details as well as striking in its total effect.—WARD, ADOLPHUS WILLIAM, 1875-99, *A History of English Dramatic Literature, vol.* III, *p.* 143.

His verse is fluent and sometimes musical, but apart from this his plays possess no special merit.—MASTERMAN, J. HOWARD B., 1897, *The Age of Milton, p.* 93.

James Graham
Marquis of Montrose
1612–1650

James Graham, fifth Earl and first Marquis of Montrose. Born in 1612: died May 21, 1650. A noted Scottish statesman and soldier. He served in the Presbyterian army at the beginning of the civil war, but afterward joined the king, by whom he was made lieutenant-general in Scotland in 1644. He defeated the Covenanters at Tippermuir Sept. 1, and at Aberdeen Sept. 13, 1644, and at Inverlochy Feb. 2, Auldearn May 9, Alford July 2, and Kilsyth Aug. 15, 1645. He was defeated by David Leslie at Philiphaugh, Sept. 13, 1645, and expelled from Scotland. He afterward entered the service of the emperor Ferdinand III., by whom he was made a field-marshal. In 1650 he conducted an abortive Royalist descent on Scotland, and was captured and executed.—SMITH, BENJAMIN E., 1894–97, *The Century Cyclopedia of Names, p.* 452.

PERSONAL

I know I need no arguments to induce you to my service. Duty and loyalty are sufficient to *a man of so much honour as I know you to be:* Yet as I think this of you, so I will have you to believe of me, that I would not invite you to share of my hard fortune, if I intended you not to be a plentiful partaker of my good. The bearer will acquaint you of my designs, whom I have commanded to follow your directions in the pursuit of them. I will say no more but that I am your assured friend.—CHARLES, KING, 1642, *Letter to Montrose, May* 7.

In his down-going, from the Tolbooth to the place of execution, he was very richly clad in fine scarlet, laid over with rich silver-lace,—his hat in his hand,—his bands and cuffs exceeding rich,—his delicate white gloves on his hands,—his stockings of incarnate (flesh-coloured) silk,—and his shoes with their ribbands (roses) on his feet,—and sarks, (embroidered linen,) provided for him, with pearling (lace) about, above ten pund the elne. All these were provided for him by his friends, and a pretty cassock put on upon him, upon the scaffold, wherein he was hanged. To be short, nothing was here deficient to honour his poor carcase, more beseeming a bridegroom, nor (than) a criminal going to the gallows.—NICHOLL, JOHN, 1650, *Diary, by Napier, Memoirs, vol.* II, *p.* 547.

He was a gentleman of a very ancient extraction, many of whose ancestors had exercised the highest charges under the king in that kingdom, and had been allied to the crown itself. He was of very good parts, which were improved by a good education: he had always a great emulation, or rather a great contempt of the marquis of Argyle, (as he was too apt to contemn those he did not love), who wanted nothing but honesty and courage to be a very extraordinary man, having all other good talents in a great degree. Mountrose was in his nature fearless of danger, and never declined any enterprise for the difficulty of going through with it, but exceedingly affected those which seemed desperate to other men, and did believe somewhat to be in himself which other men were not acquainted with, which made him live more easily towards those who were, or were willing to be, inferior to him (and towards whom he exercised wonderful civility and generosity), than with his superiors or equals. He was naturally jealous, and suspected those who did not concur with him in the way, not to mean so well as he. He was not without vanity, but his virtues were much superior, and he well deserved to have his memory preserved and celebrated amongst the most illustrious persons of the age in which he lived.—CLARENDON, LORD (EDWARD HYDE), 1674? *History of the Rebellion and Civil Wars in England, bk.* xii, *par.* 142.

GENERAL

But a poet who lived slightly anterior to those we mentioned, the brilliant Marquis of Montrose—who was even still readier with the sword—appears to have excelled them all, with the exception of Lovelace—that is, in the poetry of love. —SMITH, GEORGE BARNETT, 1875, *English Fugitive Poets, Poets and Novelists, p.* 387.

Montrose was a poet as well as a warrior and statesman. His poems have a political purpose, but, unlike most political verses, they have a poetic vigour which would have given them life apart from the intention with which they were written. —GARDINER, S. R., 1890, *Dictionary of National Biography, vol.* XXII, *p.* 319.

The poems of Montrose are exactly such as might have been expected from a character like that of the Marquis. Ardent and somewhat unequal, they are the production of the man of action rather than the man of letters, the work of one who cared more for the thought than for its manner of expression, yet whose thought is of itself so noble that in spite of all shortcomings the verse lives and must always live in the national mind and heart. —EYRE-TODD, GEORGE, 1895, *Scottish Poetry of the Seventeenth Century, p.* 232.

Thomas Heywood
1575?–1650?

Born, in Lincolnshire, 1575 [?]. Probably educated at Peterhouse, Camb. A member of Henslowe's company of players; of Earl of Southampton's company; and of Earl of Worcester's (afterwards the Queen's) company. Voluminous writer of plays. Translated several Latin classical works. Died, 1650 [?]. *Works:* "If you know not me, you know nobody" (2 pts.), 1606; "A Woman kilde with Kindnesse," 1607; "The Fair Maid of the Exchange" (anon.), 1607; "The Rape of Lucrece," 1608; "Troia Britannica," 1609; "The Golden Age," 1611; "An Apology for Actors," 1612; "A Funeral Elegy on the Death of Prince Henry," 1613; "The first and second parts of King Edward the Fourth" (anon.), 1613; "A Marriage Triumph" on the Nuptials of the Prince Palatine, 1613; "The Silver Age," 1613; "The Brazen Age," 1613; "The Four Prentices of London," 1615; "The Captives," 1624; "Γυναικειον" 1624; "England's Elizabeth," 1631; "The Fair Maid of the West," 1631; "Eromena," 1632; "The Iron Age," 1632; "The English Traveller," 1633; "A Maidenhead Well Lost," 1634; "The Late Lancashire Witches" (with R. Brome), 1634; "The Hierarchy of the Blessed Angels," 1635; "Philocothonista," 1635; "Love's Maistresse," 1636; "A Challenge for Beauty," 1636; "The Royall King," 1637; "A True Description of His Majesty's Royal Ship," 1637; "A Curtain Lecture" (under initials: T. H.), 1637; "Pleasant Dialogues and Dramas," 1637; "The Royal King and the Loyal King," 1637; "Porta Pietatis," 1638; "The Wise Woman of Hogsdon," 1638; "Londini Status Placatus," 1639; "The Exemplary Lives . . of Nine of the most worthy Women of the World," 1640; "The Life of Merlin," 1641; "Machiavel" (anon) 1641; "Fortune by Land and Sea" (with Rowley), 1655. He *translated:* "Two . . . notable Histories" of Sallust, 1608; and *edited:* Lydgate's "Life and Death of Hector," 1614; Cooke's "Greene's Tu Quoque," 1622; Sir R. Barckley's "Felicitie of Man," 1631; Marlowe's "Jew of Malta," 1633. *Collected Works:* in 6 vols., with memoir, 1874.—SHARP, R. FARQUHARSON, 1897, *A Dictionary of English Authors, p.* 132.

PERSONAL

Md. that this 25 of marche 1598, Thomas Hawoode came and hiered hime seallfe with me as a covenante searvante for ij yeares, by the Recevinge of ij synell pence, acordinge to the statute of winchester, and to begine at the daye above written, and not to playe any wher publicke abowt London not whille thes ij yeares be exspired, but in my howsse: yf he do, then he dothe forfette unto me, by the Recevinge of these ij⁴, fortie powndes, and wittnes to this

ANTONY MONDAY,	WM. BORNE,
GABRELL SPENCER,	THOMS DOWTON,
ROBART SHAWE,	RICHARD JONNES,
RICHARD ALLEYN.	

—HENSLOWE, PHILIP, 1598, *Diary, ed. Collier, p.* 260.

An Author that liv'd in the Time of Queen *Elizabeth*, and the Reign of King *James* the First. Tho' he were but an Actor, as is manifest by Mr. *Kirkman's* Testimony, and apparent from a Piece writ by him, call'd "The Actors Vindication;" yet his Plays were in those Days accounted of the Second-Rate. He was the most Voluminous Writer that ever handled Dramatick Poetry in our Language; and I know none but the Famous "Spaniard," Lopez de Vega," that can vye with him; if at least we give Credit to his own Attestation, in the Preface to One of his Plays.—LANGBAINE, GERARD, 1691, *An Account of the English Dramatick Poets, p.* 256.

Little as we know of his life, his dedications and prefaces make us better acquainted with his personality than we are with that of much more famous men. —SAINTSBURY, GEORGE, 1887, *History of Elizabethan Literature, p.* 284.

A WOMAN KILLED WITH KINDNESS
1602-7

Pd at the apoyntment of the company, the 6 of marche 1602, unto Thomas Hewode, in fulle payment for his playe called a womon Kyld with Kyndnes, the some of . . . . iij[ij].

. . . .

Pd at the apoyntment of Thomas Blackewod, the 7 of marche 1602, unto the tayller which made the blacke saten sewt for the womon Kyld with Kyndnes, the some of . . . . X[s]. —HENSLOWE, PHILIP, 1602, *Dairy, ed. Collier, pp.* 249, 250.

Heywood is a sort of *prose* Shakespeare. His scenes are to the full as natural and affecting. But we miss *the poet*, that which in Shakespeare always appears out and above the surface of *the nature*. Heywood's characters in this play, for instance, his country gentlemen, &c., are exactly what we see, but of the best kind of what we see in life. Shakespeare makes us believe, while we are among his lovely creations, that they are nothing but what we are familiar with, as in dreams new things seem old; but we awake, and sigh for the difference.—LAMB, CHARLES, 1808, *Specimens of Dramatic Poets.*

The winding up of this play is rather awkwardly managed, and the moral is, according to established usage, equivocal. It required only Frankford's reconciliation to his wife, as well as his forgiveness of her, for the highest breach of matrimonial duty, to have made "A Woman Killed with Kindness" a complete anticipation of "The Stranger." Heywood, however, was in that respect but half a Kotzebue! —HAZLITT, WILLIAM, 1820, *Lectures on the Literature of the Age of Elizabeth, Lecture* ii.

The language is not much raised above that of comedy; but we can hardly rank a tale of guilt, sorrow, and death, in that dramatic category. It may be read with interest and approbation at this day; being quite free from extravagance either in manner or language, the besetting sin of our earlier dramatists, and equally so from buffoonery. The subject resembles

that of Kotzebue's drama, "The Stranger," but is managed with a nobler tone of morality. It is true that Mrs. Frankfort's immediate surrender to her seducer, like that of Beaumelé in the "Fatal Dowry," makes her contemptible; but this, though it might possibly have originated in the necessity created by the narrow limits of theatrical time, has the good effect of preventing that sympathy with her guilt which is reserved for her penitence.— HALLAM, HENRY, 1837-39, *Introduction to the Literature of Europe, pt.* ii, *ch.* vi, *par.* 33.

The play, therefore, was finished when Henslowe paid £3 for it; and we may conclude, perhaps, that the "black satin suit" was worn by the hero after the fall of his wife, and when she was dying, in consequence of the undeserved tenderness with which she had been treated by her forgiving husband. Nothing can be more tragically touching than the whole of this part of this fine moral play, and we are not ashamed to own, after having read it many times previously, that we could not go through the mechanical process of correcting the proofs, without a degree of emotion that almost disqualified us for the duty.—COLLIER, JOHN PAYNE, 1850, *ed., A Woman Killed With Kindness, Introduction, p.* viii.

His masterpiece, "The Woman Killed with Kindness" (in which a deceived husband, coming to the knowledge of his shame, drives his rival to repentance, and his wife to repentance and death, by his charity), is not wholly admirable. Shakespere would have felt, more fully than Heywood, the danger of presenting his hero as something of a wittol without sufficient passion of religion or affection to justify his tolerance. But the pathos is so great, the sense of "the pity of it" is so simply and unaffectedly rendered, that it is impossible not to rank Heywood very high.—SAINTSBURY, GEORGE, 1887, *History of Elizabethan Literature, p.* 280.

In the centre of the choir, but quite invisible, stands the figure of Thomas Heywood, a voluble secondary writer in the class of Shakespeare and Fletcher, claiming "an entire hand, or at least a main finger," in no fewer than 220 plays. He is remarkable chiefly for a pleasing mediocrity in picturesqueness, a prosaic, even spirit of flowing romance. Heywood rises once to real force of emotion in the naked, sombre atonement of "A Woman Killed with Kindness."—GOSSE, EDMUND, 1897, *Short History of Modern English Literature* p. 118.

THE ENGLISH TRAVELLER
1633

Heywood's preface to this play is interesting, as it shows the heroic indifference about the opinion of posterity, which some of these great writers seem to have felt. There is a magnanimity in authorship as in everything else. His ambition seems to have been confined to the pleasure of hearing the players speak his lines while he lived. It does not appear that he ever contemplated the possibility of being read by after-ages. What a slender pittance of fame was motive sufficient to the production of such plays as the "English Traveller," the "Challenge for Beauty," and the "Woman Killed with Kindness"! Posterity is bound to take care that a writer loses nothing by such a noble modesty.—LAMB, CHARLES, 1808, *Specimens of Dramatic Poets.*

This play is written in verse, and with that ease and perspicuity, seldom rising to passion or figurative poetry, which distinguishes this dramatist. Young Geraldine is a beautiful specimen of the Platonic, or rather inflexibly virtuous lover, whom the writers of this age delighted to portray. On the other hand, it is difficult to pronounce whether the lady is a thorough-paced hypocrite in the first acts, or falls from virtue, like Mrs. Frankfort, on the first solicitation of a stranger. In either case, the character is unpleasing, and, we may hope, improbable. The underplot of this play is largely borrowed from the "Mostellaria" of Plautus, and is diverting, though somewhat absurd.—HALLAM, HENRY, 1837-39, *Introduction to the Literature of Europe, pt.* iii, *ch.* vi, *par.* 99.

The plot of "The English Traveller" is especially good: and in reading few works of fiction do we receive a greater shock of surprise than in Geraldine's discovery of the infidelity of Wincott's wife, whom he loves with a Platonic devotion. It is as unanticipated as the discovery, in Jonson's "Silent Woman," that Epicœne is no woman at all, while at the same time it has less the appearance of artifice, and is more the result of

natural causes. —WHIPPLE, EDWIN P., 1859-68, *The Literature of the Age of Elizabeth, p.* 123.

The hero of "The English Traveller," however worthy to stand beside him as a typical sample of English manhood at its noblest and gentlest, cannot be said to occupy so predominant a place in the conduct of the action or the memory of the reader. The comic Plautine underplot— Plautus always brought good luck to Heywood—is so incomparably preferable to the ugly and unnatural though striking and original under plot of "A Woman Killed with Kindness" as well nigh to counterbalance the comparative lack of interest, plausibility and propriety in the main action.—SWINBURNE, ALGERNON CHARLES, 1895, *The Plays of Thomas Heywood, The Nineteenth Century, vol.* 38, *p.* 404.

THE FAIR MAID OF THE WEST
1631

The versification is varied and harmonious; but it is necessary to remark that Heywood appears to have been, in this particular, a somewhat careless writer, heeding little how his lines were divided in the printed copy, as long as they came agreeably or forcibly from the mouths of the actors. It seems to have been his great aim (like that of most, if not all, of his contemporaries) to satisfy on the stage, without thinking of the reader: the printer, too, has not unfrequently done his verse injustice; and we wonder that, as the sheets went through the author's hands, he did not himself regulate the lines, in many places, differently. This consideration has frequently checked us, when otherwise we should have felt disposed to make some changes, merely of location, in order to render the blank verse more conformable to ordinary rule: upon a few, and very few, changes we have ventured; but it is quite evident in many places, which we need not point out, that the omission or insertion of a monosyllable would sometimes have restored the measure, injured perhaps by the imperfectness of the memory, or of the ear, of the performer. We have never felt ourselves at liberty to make the slightest insertion or omission, without either placing the added word within brackets, or distinctly mentioning in a note the exclusion of a particle.—COLLIER, JOHN PAYNE, 1850, ed., *The Fair Maid of the West, Introduction, p.* x.

"The Fair Maid of the West" is one of Heywood's most characteristic works, and one of his most delightful plays. Inartistic as this sort of dramatic poem may seem to the lovers of theatrical composition and sensational arrangement, of emotional calculations and premeditated shocks, it has a place of its own, and a place of honour, among the incomparably various forms of noble and serious drama which English poets of the Shakespearean age conceived, created, and left as models impossible to reproduce or to rival in any generation of poets or readers, actors or spectators, after the decadent forces of English genius in its own most natural and representative form of popular and creative activity had finally shrivelled up and shuddered into everlasting inanition under the withering blast of Puritanism. —SWINBURNE, ALGERNON CHARLES, 1895, *The Plays of Thomas Heywood, The Nineteenth Century, vol.* 38, *p.* 404.

GENERAL

But tho' many of these Plays being written loosely in Taverns as Mr. *Kirkman* observes, might occasion their being so mean; yet it did not in probability much contribute to their loss, as Mr. *Winstanley* would have it. To do our Author justice, I cannot allow that his Plays are so mean as Mr. *Kirkman* has represented them: for he was a general Scholar, and an indifferent Linguist, as his several Translations from *Lucian, Erasmus, Textor, Beza, Buchanan,* and other Latine and Italian *Authors,* sufficiently manifest. Nay, further in several of his Plays he has borrow'd many Ornaments from the Ancients; as more particularly in his Plays call'd "The Ages," he has intersperst several Things, borrow'd from *Homer, Virgil, Ovid, Seneca, Plautus, &c.,* which extreamly set them off.—LANGBAINE, GERARD, 1691, *An Account of the English Dramatick Poets, p.* 258.

The prodigious quantity he wrote, for which he ransacked the ancients without mercy, whatever might have been his real merit had he taken time to correct and polish his works, rendered it impossible for him to turn any thing out of hand likely to secure him a solid reputation;

and thus we have a list of twenty-four pieces, out of two hundred and twenty which he himself says he either wrote or was concerned in, little more known at this moment than by their titles.—DIBDIN, CHARLES, 1795, *A Complete History of the Stage, vol.* III, *p.* 106.

If I were to be consulted as to a Reprint of our Old English Dramatists, I should advise to begin with the collected Plays of Heywood. He was a fellow Actor, and fellow Dramatist, with Shakespeare. He possessed not the imagination of the latter; but in all those qualities which gained for Shakespeare the attribute of *gentle,* he was not inferior to him. Generosity, courtesy, temperance in the depths of passion; sweetness, in a word, and gentleness; Christianism; and true hearty Anglicism of feelings, shaping that Christianism; shine throughout his beautiful writings in a manner more conspicuous than in those of Shakespeare, but only more conspicuous, inasmuch as in Heywood these qualities are primary, in the other subordinate to poetry. I love them both equally, but Shakespeare has most of my wonder. Heywood should be known to his countrymen, as he deserves. His plots are almost invariably English. I am sometimes jealous, that Shakespeare laid so few of his scenes at home.—LAMB, CHARLES, 1808, *Specimens of Dramatic Poets.*

Though Heywood had little of the enthusiasm of fancy of the genuine poet, there are in several of the pieces which remain, an unaffected ease and simplicity, and a power of touching the heart, which merit preservation in no common degree. He abounds, too, in pictures of domestic life very minutely finished, correct without being cold, and effective without being overcharged.—DRAKE, NATHAN, 1817, *Shakspeare and His Times, vol.* II, *p.* 568.

He possesses considerable power of interesting the affections, by placing his plain and familiar characters in affecting situations. The worst of him is, that his commonplace sentiments and plain incidents fall not only beneath the ideal beauty of art, but are often more fatiguing than what we meet with in the ordinary and unselected circumstances of life. When he has hit upon those occasions where the passions should obviously rise with accumulated expression, he lingers on through the scene with a dull and level indifference. The term artlessness may be applied to Heywood in two very opposite senses. His pathos is often artless in the better meaning of the word, because its objects are true to life, and their feelings naturally expressed. But he betrays still more frequently an artlessness, or we should rather call it, a want of art, in deficiency of contrivance.—CAMPBELL, THOMAS, 1819, *Specimens of the British Poets.*

As Marlowe's imagination glows like a furnace, Heywood's is a gentle, lambent flame that purifies without consuming. His manner is simplicity itself. There is nothing supernatural, nothing startling or terrific. He makes use of the commonest circumstances of every-day life, and of the easiest tempers, to show the workings, or rather the inefficacy of the passions, the *vis inertiæ* of tragedy. His incidents strike from their very familiarity, and the distresses he paints invite our sympathy, from the calmness and resignation with which they are borne. The pathos might be deemed purer from its having no mixture of turbulence or vindictiveness in it; and in proportion as the sufferers are made to deserve a better fate. In the midst of the most untoward reverses and cutting injuries, good nature and good sense keep their accustomed sway. He describes men's errors with tenderness, and their duties only with zeal, and the heightenings of a poetic fancy. His style is equally natural, simple, and unconstrained.—HAZLITT, WILLIAM, 1820, *Lectures on the Literature of the Age of Elizabeth, Lecture* ii.

Heywood seldom rises to much vigor of poetry; but his dramatic invention is ready, his style is easy, his characters do not transgress the boundaries of nature, and it is not surprising that he was popular in his own age.—HALLAM, HENRY, 1837-39, *Introduction to the Literature of Europe, pt.* iii, *ch.* vi, *par.* 99.

Perhaps Shakespeare would not have left untouched so pathetic a tragedy as that of Jane Shore, if he had not seen it so well handled by Heywood.—FIELD, BARRON, 1842, *The First and Second Parts of King Edward IV., Introduction, p.* v.

The most profuse, but perhaps the least poetic of these dramatists, was Thomas Heywood, of whom little is known, except

that he was one of the most prolific writers the world has ever seen. . . . Heywood's best plays evince large observation, considerable dramatic skill, a sweet and humane spirit, and an easy command of language. His style, indeed, is singularly simple, pure, clear, and straightforward; but it conveys the impression of a mind so diffused as almost to be characterless, and incapable of flashing its thoughts through the images of imaginative passion. He is more prosaic, closer to ordinary life and character, than his contemporaries.—WHIPPLE, EDWIN P., 1859-68, *The Literature of the Age of Elizabeth, pp.* 121, 122.

His plays, however, are for the greater part in verse, which at least has ease of flow enough; and he may be styled not only a prose Shakspeare, but a more poetical Richardson. If he has not quite the power of Lillo in what has been called the domestic tragedy, which is the species to which his best pieces belong, he excels that modern dramatist both in facility and variety.—CRAIK, GEORGE L., 1861, *A Compendious History of English Literature, and of The English Language, vol.* I, *p.* 599.

Considering how much he wrote, and the circumstances under which he appears to have written, it is no slight merit to have produced scenes as natural and affecting, and characters as true to life as those of Shakespeare, even without the power idealizing his conceptions.—BELL, ROBERT, 1867? *ed., Songs for the Dramatists, p.* 193.

It would grieve me to seem unjust towards a writer to whom I have long felt very specially attracted—and this by no means only because of a pious although perhaps more or less apocryphal bond. Yet the highest praise which it seems right to bestow upon Thomas Heywood is that which was happily expressed by Tieck when he described him as "the model of a light and rapid talent." Carried, it may be, by fortune or by choice from the tranquil court of Peterhouse to a very different scene of intellectual effort, he worked during a long and laborious life with an energy in itself deserving of respect, and manifestly also with a facility attesting no ordinary natural endowment. His creative power was, however, of that secondary order which is content with accommodating itself to conditions imposed by the prevailing tastes of the day. It may be merely his 'prentice hand that he tried on a dramatic reproduction of chronicles and popular story-books; but though even here the simplicity of his workmanship was due to a natural directness of touch by no means to be confounded with rudeness of hand, he cannot be said to have done much to revive a species which though still locally popular was already doomed to decay. . . . Of humour he had his share—or he would have been no master of pathos; but he cannot be said to have excelled in humorous characterisation; there is as a rule little individuality in his comic figures at large, and his clowns, although good examples of their kind, are made to order. Indeed, the inferior sort of wit—which of all writers dramatists most readily acquire as a literary accomplishment—his practised inventiveness displays with the utmost abundance; of all the Elisabethan playwrights he is one of the most unwearied, and to my mind one of the most intolerable punsters. In outward form he is nearly as Protean as in choice of subject and of treatment; his earlier plays more especially abound with rimes; in general, fluent verse and easy prose are freely intermixed. But—apart from the pathetic force of particular passages and scenes, and a straightforward naturalness which lends an irresistible charm to a writer as it does to a friend in real life—his strength lies in a dramatic insight which goes far towards the making of a master of the playwright's art, while it has undoubtedly been possessed by some not entitled to rank as dramatic poets.—WARD, ADOLPHUS WILLIAM, 1875-99, *A History of English Dramatic Literature, vol.* II, *pp.* 585, 586.

The play which resulted,—the "Lancashire Witches,"—is interesting partly because it combines the two kinds of dramatic incident in which Heywood was most at home,—the domestic and the mythological. It unites a motive akin to that of the "Woman killed with Kindness" and the "English Traveller" with others drawn from that world of superstition and occult art of which Heywood had all his life been a persevering student and in which he was probably more deeply versed than any of his fellow dramatists. The

character of the erring and repentant wife he had made his own; and the peculiar tenderness with which he repeatedly touched it was evidently something more than the stock pathos of a clever playwright. Mrs. Generous in the "Lancashire ·Witches" is the sister of the erring wives in the "Woman killed with Kindness" and the "English Traveller." She is not seduced from her husband, as they are, by a human lover; but she yields to the fascination of the powers of darkness and becomes a witch. Generous, her husband, views her fault like his earlier counterparts, more in sorrow than in anger, and when she meets him after the commission of her fault and confesses her guilt he forgives her in a scene little inferior to the corresponding scenes in which Mr. Frankford and Young Geraldine receive the last penitent confessions of another sort of guilt.—HERFORD, CHARLES H., 1886, *Studies in The Literary Relations of England and Germany in the Sixteenth Century, p.* 238.

Never sinking to the lowest depth of the Elizabethan playwright, including some great ones, Heywood never rises to anything like the highest height. His chronicle plays are very weak, showing no grasp of heroic character, and a most lamentable slovenliness of rhythm.— SAINTSBURY, GEORGE, 1887, *History of Elizabethan Literature, p.* 282.

Heywood, the master of homely English life, the gentlest of all poets who have swept the chords of passion.—SYMONDS, JOHN ADDINGTON, 1887, *Marlowe (Mermaid Series), General Introduction to the Drama, p.* xxv.

Since his resuscitation he has suffered from a fresh injustice, the cause of which it is not easy to discover. Those who have complained of his flatness, rudeness, want of poetic art, have themselves increased these qualities in tacitly considering him as one of the latest of the great dramatic group. He is usually placed in chronological arrangement after Massinger, after Ford, with only Shirley and Jasper Mayne behind him. It is true that he lived till all but these were gone, but not on that account ought he to be considered as one of the latest of the group. The proper position of Heywood is in the center, at the climax of the drama. That miraculous decade (1590–1600) in which the green undergrowth of English literature, as if in a single tropical night, burst into wave after wave of sudden blossom, produced so much and developed so rapidly that the closest study is needed to detect the stages of poetic progress. . . . Heywood was not one of those poets on whom the gaze of all critics turns, as to a star whose beams lend themselves to infinite analysis; it is easy enough to divide the clear rays in his one pencil of light. He is a poet who will never, in future, want his friends, but who will scarcely claim one lover. It is not possible to be enthusiastic over the memory of a gossip so cheerful, garrulous, and superficial as this haunter of the Strand and the Exchange. He has a thousand entertaining things to tell us about the shops and the shop-girls; about the handsome young gallants, and the shocking way in which they waste their money; about the affectations of citizen fathers, and the tempers of citizen mothers. He is the most confirmed button-holer of our poetical acquaintance; and if he were only a little more monotonous, he would be universally voted a bore. Somehow or other, he has a little group of listeners always around him; it is not easy to drag one's self away till his stories are finished. His voice trembles as he tells us the strangest, saddest tale of how this or that poor girl came to shame and sorrow—of how such a noble gentleman, whom we must have often seen in the streets, lost all his estate, and died in want; and though there is nothing new in what he tells us, and though he hurries with characteristic timidity over every embarrassing or painful detail, we cannot help paying his loquacity the tribute of our laughter and our tears.—GOSSE, EDMUND, 1894, *The Jacobean Poets, pp.* 117, 122.

Facile and most productive of dramatists, visited at moments by the golden touch of lyric inspiration.—SCHELLING,

FELIX E., 1895, *A Book of Elizabethan Lyrics, p.* xxix.

As a historical or mythological playwright, working on material derived from classic legends or from English annals, he shows signs now and then, as occasion offers, of the sweet tempered manliness, the noble kindliness, which won the heart of Lamb: something too there is in these plays of his pathos, and something of his humour: but if this were all we had of him we should know comparatively little of what we now most prize in him. Of this we find most in the plays dealing with English life in his own day: but there is more of it in his romantic tragicomedies than in his chronicle histories or his legendary compilations and variations on the antique. . . . He is English of the English in his quiet, frank, spontaneous expression, suppression is no longer either possible or proper, of all noble and gentle and natural emotion. . . . His prose, if never to be called masterly, may generally be called good and pure: its occasional pedantries and pretentions are rather signs of the century than faults of the author: and he can tell a story, especially a short story, as well if not better than many a better-known writer. I fear, however, that it is not the poetical quality of his undramatic verse which can ever be said to make it worth reading: it is, as far as I know, of the very homeliest homespun ever turned out by the very humblest of workmen. His poetry, it would be pretty safe to wager, must be looked for exclusively in his plays: but there, if not remarkable for depth or height of imagination or of passion, it will be found memorable for unsurpassed excellence of unpretentious elevation in treatment of character.—SWINBURNE, ALGERNON CHARLES, 1895, *The Plays of Thomas Heywood, The Nineteenth Century, vol.* 38, *pp.* 397, 402, 410.

Arthur Wilson

1596-1652

Arthur Wilson was secretary to Robert, Earl of Essex, the Parliamentary general in the Civil Wars; and afterwards became steward to the Earl of Warwick. He left in manuscript a work on "The Life and Reign of King James I.," which was published in 1653. A comedy of his, entitled "The Inconstant Lady," was printed at Oxford, edited by Dr. Bliss, in 1814.—CHAMBERS, ROBERT, 1876 *Cyclopœdia of English Literature, ed. Carruthers.*

HISTORY OF KING JAMES I.

A most infamous pasquil. . . . It is not easy to judge whether the matter be more false or the style more reproachful in all parts thereof.—HEYLIN, PETER, 1658, *Examen Historicum, Preface.*

Had a great command of the English tongue, as well in writing as speaking, and had he bestowed his endeavours on another subject than that of history, they would have without doubt seemed better. For in those things which he hath done, are wanting the principal matters conducing to the completion of that faculty, *viz.:* matter from record, exact time, name and place; which by his endeavouring too much to set out his bare collections in an affected and bombastic stile, are much neglected.—WOOD, ANTHONY, 1691-1721, *Athenæ Oxonienses, vol.* II, *f.* 155.

Among minor historical works may be mentioned a "History of King James I.," by Arthur Wilson, a Suffolk gentleman who held for some time the position of Secretary to the Earl of Essex, through whose influence he gained access to many important documents. His history is a work of some merit, and has the advantage of being nearly contemporary with the period with which it deals.—MASTERMAN, J. HOWARD B., 1897, *The Age of Milton, p.* 207.

As an historian Wilson is very strongly prejudiced against the rule of the Stuarts, but his work is of value because it records contemporary impressions and reminiscences which are of considerable interest. At times he speaks as an eye-witness, especially in his account of the foreign expeditions in which he took part.—FIRTH, C. H., 1900, *Dictionary of National Biography, vol.* LXII, *p.* 82.

Nathaniel Ward

1578-1652

Nathaniel Ward, a son of Samuel Ward, D. D., Ipswich (*infra*), was born at Haverhill, Suffolk, England, about 1570; entered of Emmanuel College, Cambridge, 1596, and received his degree of A. M., 1603; for a time practised law, and then travelled on the Continent; became preacher at St. James's, Duke Place, London, 1626, and was afterwards Rector of Standon Massaye; was suspended by Laud for nonconformity, 1633, and in 1634 became pastor of Agawam, or Ipswich, Massachusetts; was the author of the "Body of Liberties," the first code of laws established in New England, (adopted in 1641;) returned to England in 1645, became minister of Shenfield, Essex, and retained this connection until his death, in 1653, 1. "The Simple Cobler of Agavvam in America, Willing to help mend his Native Country, lamentably tattered, both in the upper-Leather and Sole, with all the honest stitches he can take," &c. . . . 2. "Mercurius Anti-mechanicus, or the Simple Cobbler's Boy with his Lap-full of Caveats," &c.; by Theodore de la Guarden, Lon, 1648, 4to.—ALLIBONE, S. AUSTIN, 1871, *Dictionary of English Literature, vol.* III, *p.* 2575.

SIMPLE COBLER OF AGAWAM

1647

The Simple Cobler of Aggawam in America, willing to help 'mend his native country, lamentably tattered, both in the upper-leather and sole, with all the honest stitches he can take. And as willing never to be paid for his work, by old English wonted pay.

It is his trade to patch all the year long, gratis, Therefore I pray, Gentlemen, keep your purses.

By Theodore de la Guard. *In rebus arduis ac tenui spe, fortissima quaque consilia tutissima sunt.* Cic. In English,

When bootes and shoes are torne up to the lefts,
Coblers must thrust their awls up to the hefts,
This is no time to feare *Apelles gramm:*
Ne Sutor quidem ultra crepidam.
London: Printed by J. D. & R. I. for Stephen Bowtell, at the signe of the Bible in Pope's Head Alley, 1647.—TITLE PAGE TO FIRST EDITION.

One of them, (Samuel Ward's sons,) lately dead, was beneficed in Essex, and, following the counsel of the poet,
Ridentem dicere verum
Quis vetat?
"What doth forbid but one may smile
And also tell the Truth the while?"

hath in a jesting way, in some of his Books, delivered much Smart-Truth of this present times.—FULLER, THOMAS, 1662, *Worthies of England, ed. Nichols, vol.* II, *p.* 344.

The celebrated Nathaniel Ward, whose wit made him known to more Englands than one.—MATHER, COTTON, 1702, *Magnalia Christi Americana.*

This work is in its manner one of the most quaint and pedantick of a period when quaintness and pedantry were the fashion; and in its principles one of the most violent and enthusiastick of an age when violence and enthusiasm were almost universal. . . . This book had several editions in England and in this country; it is now scarce, and costs in England about thirty shillings.—TUDOR, WILLIAM, 1815, *North American Review.*

The most quaint and far fetched in vigorous expression of the early political and religious tracts generated in New England, is that piece of pedantic growling at toleration, and pungent advice to British Royalty, inclosing a satire on the fashionable ladies of the day, the production of Nathaniel Ward, Pastor of the Church at Ipswich, which is entitled the "Simple Cobler of Agawam."—DUYCKINCK, EVERT A. AND GEORGE L., 1855-65-75, *Cyclopœdia of American Literature, ed. Simons, vol.* I, *p.* 23.

It is a tremendous partisan pamphlet, intensely vital even yet, full of fire, wit, whim, eloquence, sarcasm, invective, patriotism, bigotry. One would have to search long among the rubbish of books thrown forth to the public during those hot and teeming days, to find one more authentically representing the stir, the earnestness, the intolerance, the hope, and the wrath of the times than does this book.—TYLER, MOSES COIT, 1878, *A History of American Literature, 1607-1676, vol.* I, *p.* 230.

This early New England Sartor Resartus spoke freely that which he thought, and satirized sharply those thoughts, words, and deeds, in Old and New England, which he deemed harmful. He was not always polished, temperate, consistent, fair, or even funny; but he contrived to say some things effectively and nearly all things plainly, notwithstanding a cumbrous, punning, and pedantic style. He was a pseudo Hans Sachs in prose, talking from his cobbler's bench, and trying to mend manners and morals. This literary device, however, proved rather burdensome, and was not constantly kept in mind. Ward felt that he was writing in earthquaking times, and he outspoke as a warning guide and prophet. A theoretical believer in religious and political freedom, he was as much afraid of anarchy and free-thought as he was of priestcraft and oppression. He wanted to whip others, while saving his own back. The moral which the Anglican drew from the book must have been: See what your Puritanism amounts to! Ward's moral was: Crush dissent from our dissent; make our social laws still more rigid. He goes so far, indeed, that we half believe the whole thing a *reductio ad absurdum*, written in the interests of episcopacy and monarchy. "I am not tolerant," he seems to shout to his English accusers; "I am as anxious to get rid of those who disagree with me, as you are to get rid of me."—RICHARDSON, CHARLES F., 1887, *American Literature, 1607-1885, vol.* I, *p.* 101.

This pungent satire, published at London in 1647, inveighs, sometimes with a caustic drollery, sometimes with a right manly vehemence, against the principle of religious toleration, the vanities of womankind, and the state of contemporary English politics.—BATES, KATHARINE LEE, 1897, *American Literature, p.* 28.

William Basse
1583?-1653?

He was probably born about 1583, probably born and schooled at Northampton, probably a page to Lady Wenman, of Thame Park, and certainly a retainer of the family, probably at Oxford, probably a friend (as certainly a disciple of Spenser, probably a musician as well as a poet, almost certainly married, burying "Helinor ye wife of Willia Basse," 23rd Sept., 1637, and probably died at Thame some time during 1653.—LE GALLIENNE, RICHARD, 1893-95, *Retrospective Reviews, vol.* I, *p.* 257.

GENERAL

CORIDON: I will sing a song, if anybody will sing another; else, to be plain with you, I will sing none: I am none of those that sing for meat, but for company: I say, "'Tis merry in hall, when men sing all."

PISCATOR: I'll promise you I'll sing a song that was lately made at my request, by Mr. William Basse, one that hath made the choice songs of the Hunter in his Career, and of Tom of Bedlam, and many others of note; and this that I will sing is in praise of angling.—WALTON, ISAAC, 1653, *The Complete Angler, ch.* v.

Basse's poetry is characterised by a pleasant homeliness of language and versification and by an enthusiastic love of country life. It derives an historical interest from Izaak Walton's honourable mention of it, and from the homage paid to Shakespeare by its author. The long interval of fifty-one years between the production of the first and last poems bearing Basse's signature has led Mr. J. P. Collier to conjecture that there were two poets of the same name, and he attributes to an elder William Basse the works published in 1602, and to a younger William Basse all those published later. The internal evidence offered by the poems fails, however, to support this conclusion.—LEE, SIDNEY, 1885, *Dictionary of National Biography, vol.* III, *p.* 374.

The fate of Basse is perhaps one of the most pathetic, paradoxically speaking, in the history of oblivion. Forgotten poets, or rather poets remembered by a very few, are plentiful. The number of quite forgotten poets it is obviously impossible to estimate. Evidently Basse does not belong to those, else we should not be speaking of him. But he is as near to them as a man may well be. A breath nearer and he had tumbled over into the pitchy darkness. His singularity is this, that whereas the nearly forgotten poet was usually somewhat of a figure in his own day, and had at least the pleasure of seeing his name on a title-page, Basse, though occasionally referred to by his contemporaries, and evidently of some account amongst them, was certainly not a figure, and his best work, that which he had so carefully filed and polished, has lain in manuscript for two hundred and forty

years. So had they gone on lying had it not occurred to Messrs. Ellis and Elvey, who possess the manuscripts, to ask Mr. Warwick Bond to edit them, and to publish them in the sumptuous volume before me. It was a sweet, charitable act. Poor Basse! if he could only know. How would he exclaim, with Herrick (whom he probably lived long enough to read), "Like to a bride come forth my book at last!" Of course, his publishers will have sent him a copy!—LE GALLIENNE, RICHARD, 1893-95, *Retrospective Reviews, vol.* I, *p.* 256.

Basse, though an elaborate is a very tame and tedious rhymer, whose vein of Spenserian richness soon wore out, and left nothing but an awkward and voluble affectation behind it.—GOSSE, EDMUND, 1894, *The Jacobean Poets, p.* 157.

On the whole, however, it is impossible to regard him as anything but a diluted Spenserian. His flat pastoral fertility is more curious than edifying, and prompts the suspicion that there must have been just a touch of friendly log-rolling about Walton's praise of his lyric gift, since it is not greatly conspicuous in the pair of pieces mentioned, neither of which excels the "Angler's Song."—DOBSON AUSTIN, 1894, *Old English Songs, Introduction, p.* xii.

One of the feebler of Spenser's imitators, published "Three Pastoral Elegies of Anander, Anetor, and Muridella" (1602), and left at his death the manuscript of nine other "Eclogues." . . . Basse is perhaps better known as the author of an "Elegy" on Shakespeare, and of an "Angler's Song," quoted in Walton's "Compleat Angler."—CHAMBERS, EDMUND K., 1895, *English Pastorals, p.* 178.

His initials, "W. B.," have led to some confusion with Browne, whose friend he was, to whose "Pastorals" he wrote commendatory verses, and whom he a good deal resembles in his own poems of the same kind, his "Urania," his "Polyhymnia" (only surviving in fragments), and other pieces. But he is only a curiosity, and a very weak poet, though it may be a little stronger than any other outsider of the Browne-Wither group, Christopher Brooke, whose poems have also been printed.—SAINTSBURY, GEORGE, 1898, *A Short History of English Literature, p.* 363.

John Taylor

1580-1654

One of the most voluminous of city rhymsters and chroniclers was John Taylor (*circa* 1580-1654), a London waterman, who styled himself "The King's Majesty's Water Poet." Taylor was a native of Gloucester, and having served an apprenticeship to a waterman in London, continued to ply on the Thames, besides keeping a public-house. The most memorable incident in his career was travelling on foot from London to Edinburgh, "not carrying any money to or fro, neither begging, borrowing, or asking meat, drink, or lodging." He took with him, however, a servant on horseback, who carried some provisions and provender, and having met Ben Jonson at Leith, he received from Ben a present of "a piece of gold of two and twenty shillings to drink his health in England." Of this journey, Taylor wrote an account, entitled "The Penniless Pilgrimage, or the Moneyless Perambulation of John Taylor, alias the King's Majesty's Water Poet," &c. 1618. This tract is partly in prose and partly in verse. . . . Various journeys and voyages were made by Taylor, and duly described by him in short occasional tracts. In 1630, he made a collection of these pieces: "All the Workes of John Taylor, the Water Poet; being Sixty and Three in Number." He continued, however, to write during more than twenty years after this period, and ultimately his works consisted of not less than 138 separate publications.—CHAMBERS, ROBERT, 1876, *Cyclopædia of English Literature, ed. Carruthers.*

PERSONAL

He was very facetious and diverting company; and for stories and lively telling them, few could out-doe him. Anno 1643, at the Act time, I sawe him at Oxon. I guesse he was then neer 50. I remember he was of middle stature, had a good quick looke, a black velvet, a plush-gippe and silver shoulder-belt; was much made of by the scholars, and was often with Josias Howe at Trinity College. He had heretofore in the long peace severall figgaries, e.g. he came from London to Salisbury in his skuller. He went so to Calais. He went to Scotland (I think round Great Britaine) *littus legens* in his skuller. Ever since the beginning of the civill warres he lived in Turne-stile-alley in Long Acre, about the middle on the east side over against the Goate (now), where he sold ale. His conversation was incomparable for three or four mornings' draughts. But afterwards you were entertained with *crambe bis coeta.* His signe was his owne head, and very like him, which about 22 yeares since was removed to the alehowse, the corner howse opposite to Clarendon howse. Under his picture are these verses; on one side :—

There's many a head stands for a signe.
Then, gentle reader, why not mine?

On the other :—

Though I deserve not, I desire
The laurell wreath, the poet's hire.

This picture is now almost worne out.— AUBREY, JOHN, 1669-96, *Brief Lives, ed. Clark, vol. II, p. 253.*

There is a protrait of him bearing date 1655, by his nephew, who was a painter at Oxford, and presented it to the Bodleian, where it was thought not unworthy of a place. He is represented in a black scull-cap, and black gown or rather cloak. The countenance is described to me as one of "well-fed rotundity; the eyes small, with an expression of cunning, into which their natural shrewdness had probably been deteriorated by the painter; their colour seems to have been hazel: there is scarcely any appearance of eye-brows; the lips have a slight cast of playfulness or satire. The brow is wrinkled, and he is in the fashion of mustachios with a tuft of beard under the lip. The portrait now is, like the building in which it has thus long been preserved, in a state of rapid decay. . . . If the Water Poet had been in a higher grade of society, and bred to some regular profession, he would probably have been a much less distinguished person in his generation. No spoon could have suited his mouth so well as the wooden one to which he was born. His way of life was best suited to his character, nor could any regular education so fully have brought out the sort of talent which he possessed. Fortunately, also, he came into the world at the right time, and lived in an age when Kings and Queens condescended to notice him, nobles and archbishops admitted him to their table, and mayors and corporations received him with civic honours. The next of our uneducated poets was composed of very different clay,—and did not moisten it so well.—SOUTHEY, ROBERT, 1836, *Lives of Uneducated Poets, pp.* 84, 86.

Taylor therefore sought to increase his earnings by turning to account his knack of easy rhyming. He was ready at the shortest notice and on the most reasonable terms to celebrate any one of the three principal events in human life—with a birthday ode, epithalamium, or funeral elegy. Various wagering journeys were also undertaken by him with the same object, and as he was an acute observer of character, custom, and incident, and could express himself in rollicking prose as well as rhyme, his descriptive tours were largely subscribed for when issued in book form. Previous to starting on any journey it was Taylor's custom to issue a vast number of prospectuses, or "Taylor's bills" as he called them, announcing the conditions under which he travelled, in the hope of inducing his friends either to pay down a sum of money at once, or to sign their names as promising to do so on the completion of the "adventure." Most of his brochures were printed at his own cost, and were "presented" by him to distinguished persons. In this way he acquired not only money but numerous patrons of all degrees. Ben Jonson, Nicholas Breton, Samuel Rowlands, Thomas Dekker, and other men of genius took kindly notice of him.— GOODWIN, GORDON, 1898, *Dictionary of National Biography, vol.* LV, *p.* 431.

GENERAL

If lord ship, lady-ship, or court-ship fight,
Friend-ship and fellow-ship will do thee
   right
And wor-ship will assist to make a peace;
Whilst surety-ship stands bound the wars
   should cease.
Thus was that battle ended, but thy praise
Hath raised a crew which will outlast thy
   days;
Steer on thy course then, let thy fertile brain
Plough up the deep which will run o'er the
   main
In such a fleet of sweet conceited matter,
Which sails by land more swifter than by
   water,
That whilst the ocean doth contain a billow
Thou and thy book shall never have a fellow.
—MASON, F., 1627, *In John Taylor's An Armado, or Nauye.*

Nay, if it were put to the question of

the Water-rimer's works, against Spenser's, I doubt not but they would find more suffrages; because the most favour common vices, out of a prerogative the vulgar have to lose their judgments, and like that which is naught.—JONSON, BEN, 1630-37, *Timber, or Discoveries.*

The works of Taylor, which are not destitute of natural humour, abound with low jingling wit, which pleased and prevailed in the reign of James I. and which too often bordered, at least, upon bombast and nonsense. He was countenanced by a few persons of rank and ingenuity, but was the darling and admiration of numbers of the rabble. He was himself the father of some cant words, and he had adopted others which were only in the mouths of the lowest vulgar. His rhyming spirit did not evaporate with his youth; he held the pen much longer than he did the oar, and was the poetaster of half a century.—GRANGER, JAMES, 1769-1824, *Biographical History of England, vol.* II, *p.* 135.

There is nothing of John Taylor's which deserves preservation for its intrinsic merit alone, but in the collection of his pieces which I have perused there is a great deal to illustrate the manners of his age; and as he lived more than twenty years after this collection was printed, and continued publishing till the last, there is probably much in his uncollected works also which for the same reason ought to be preserved. A curious and useful volume of selections might be formed from them.—SOUTHEY, ROBERT, 1836, *Lives of Uneducated Poets, p.* 86.

Confident in his popularity, the Sculler had had the audacity to print, or bind together for sale, in 1630, a folio edition of his collected "Works," including all that he had written in prose or in verse up to that date. He was to live four-and-twenty years after the publication, and, besides distinguishing himself by his sturdy loyalty during the civil wars, was to pen a farther quantity of prose and verse, enough to make a second folio, had all been collected.—MASSON, DAVID, 1858, *The Life of John Milton, vol.* I, *ch.* vi.

He had a knack of rapid versification, but no claim to the rank of a true poet, and Ben Jonson contrasts him with Spenser: he often wrote to supply temporary necessity.—COLLIER, JOHN PAYNE, 1865, *A Bibliographical and Critical Account of the Rarest Books in the English Language, vol.* II, *p.* 416.

As literature his books—many of them coarse and brutal—are contemptible; but his pieces accurately mirror his age, and are of great value to the historian and antiquary.—GOODWIN, GORDON, 1898, *Dictionary of National Biography, vol.* LV, *p.* 433.

William Habington

1605–1654

William Habington, poet, was born at Hindlip, Worcestershire, 4th November 1605. His family was Catholic; his uncle was executed, and his father, the antiquary, Thomas Habington (1560–1647), lay six years in the Tower for complicity in Babington's plot. He was educated at St. Omer, but declined to become a Jesuit, and was next sent to Paris. He married Lucy Herbert, daughter of the first Lord Powis, and has immortalised her in his "Castara" (1634), a collection of lyrical poems, some of rare beauty and sweetness, and stamped with a purity then unusual. He died 30th November 1654. Other works were "The Historie of Edward the Fourth" (1640); "The Queene of Aragon, a Tragi-comedie" (1640); and "Observations upon Historie" (1641).—PATRICK AND GROOME, *eds.,* 1897, *Chambers's Biographical Dictionary, p.* 448.

PERSONAL

"And when I'm lost in death's cold night,
Who will remember now I write?"

So wrote William Habington, nearly two centuries and a half ago, foreboding, perhaps, the neglect which was so soon to settle on his name. His was not a genius of that robust and cheerful temper which calmly forestalls the verdict of posterity and usurps immortality as its birthright, the royal purple of the sovereigns of song. His premonition, if such it were, had speedy fulfilment. So popular during his lifetime that no less than three editions of his poems were called for in the short space of five years, he seems, upon his death, to have dropped out of notice as quietly and quickly as a pebble tossed into a stream. So far as we can learn, not even a single buble of elegy—and a prodigious quantity of such "airy nothings" the drowning poets of his day were wont to set afloat, to show for a little where they had sunk in the Lethean river—marked his exit.—CASSERLY, D. A., 1877, *A Catholic Poet of the Seventeenth Century, American Catholic Quarterly Review, vol.* 2, *p.* 614.

Habington devotes as many of his poems to his wife, as to his mistress, and in them reaches a higher level of poetic accomplishment than he elsewhere attains. It is pleasant to contemplate the happy course of this pure and honourable affection, and it is impossible not to feel a kind of liking for so constant a wooer, so good a friend, and so upright a man. We must not complain if, like Evelyn, Habington seems to have gone through the Civil War without taking a decided part one way or the other. The man was no hero, nor born to shine in public life. What political sympathies his writings reveal were strongly Royalist; he himself came of an old Catholic stock, and was educated at St. Omer; and we may be sure that as far as he took any side at all, he took part against those whom he would regard as rebels and schismatics. Habington—as revealed to us by his own verses—was something of a dreamer, something of an ascetic, something even of a bigot. His was just the sort of life and character which could live through, as not of them, the din and turmoil and passion of those stirring years. He was not of those who are great among the sons of men; nevertheless the interest that his work arouses is likely rather to increase than diminish, for though narrow in scope it is intense in feeling, and though in parts feeble and one-sided, it is as a whole made vital by the impress of a distinct and original personality.—ARNOLD, W. T., 1880, *English Poets, ed. Ward, vol.* II, *p.* 158.

CASTARA

1635

If not too indulgent to what is my owne, I think even these verses will have that proportion in the world's opinion that heaven hath allotted me in fortune; not so high as to be wondered at, nor so low as to be contemned.—HABINGTON, WILLIAM, 1635, *Castara, Preface.*

The author of poems which came forth above twenty years since under title of "Castara," the feigned name, no doubt, of that humane goddess who inspired them; but better known by the history of the Reign of King (Edward) the Fourth, in which he hath a style sufficiently florid, and perhaps better becoming a poet than historian. . . . In respect of his poems they are almost forgotten. He may be ranked, in my opinion, with those who deserve neither the highest nor lowest seat in the Theatre of Fame.—PHILLIPS, EDWARD, 1675, *Theatrum Poetarum Anglicanorum.*

They possess much elegance, much poetical fancy; and are almost everywhere tinged with a deep moral cast, which ought to have made their fame permanent. Indeed I cannot easily account for the neglect of them.—BRYDGES, SAMUEL EGERTON, 1805–9, *Censura Literaria.*

One of the most elegant monuments ever raised by genius to conjugal affection, was Habington's "Castara."—JAMESON, ANNA BROWNELL, 1829, *The Loves of the Poet, vol.* II, *p.* 110.

The poetry of Habington is that of a pure and amiable mind, turned to versification by the custom of the age, during a real passion for a lady of birth and virtue, the Castara whom he afterwards married; but it displays no great original power, nor is it by any means exempt from the ordinary blemishes of hyperbolical compliment and far-fetched imagery.—HALLAM, HENRY, 1837-39, *Introduction to the Literature of Europe, pt.* III, *ch.* V, *par.* 55.

Faith and purity go hand-in-hand. If "Castara" were studied in this age it might almost make chastity fashionable among men. This virtue of Sir Galahad was not common in Habington's time, and it has always required much courage in a man of the world to proclaim that he possesses a quality which is generally regarded as the crowning attribute of womanhood. To this poet, who dared to dedicate, in a licentious age, his work to the woman who was to him as the church to Christ, we owe honor; it was his Catholic faith and practice that made him so noble among the men of his time. Habington ought to be studied by all young Catholics. Americans have inherited his poems along with that language which was forced on the ancestors of some of us, but

which is none the less our own. His faults of *technique,* so glaringly apparent in this day of almost perfect *technique* in poetry, offer lessons in themselves. No man can read "Castara" without feeling better and purer; and of how many poets can this be said? Since Pope taught the critics to place execution above conception Habington has found no place. It remains for the rising generation of young Catholics who read and think to give him a niche that will not be unworthy of the poet of that chaste love which was born from Christianity.—EGAN, MAURICE FRANCIS, 1880, *Three Catholic Poets, Catholic World, vol.* 32, *p.* 138.

"Castara" is a real instance of what some foreign critics very unjustly charge on English literature as a whole—a foolish and almost canting prudery. The poet dins the chastity of his mistress into his readers' heads until the readers in self-defence are driven to say, "Sir, did any one doubt it?" He protests the freedom of his own passion from any admixture of fleshly influence, till half a suspicion of hypocrisy and more than half a feeling of contempt force themselves on the hearer. SAINTSBURY, GEORGE, 1887, *History of Elizabethan Literature, p.* 382.

Habington claims credit in his preface for the purity of his muse. "In all those flames," he writes, "in which I burned I never felt a wanton heate, nor was my invention ever sinister from the straite way of chastity." He also dwells upon Castara's chastity with wearisome iteration. Though they are wanting in ardour, the love-verses are elegantly written; and the elegies on his kinsman Talbot are tender and sincere.—BULLEN, A. H., 1890, *Dictionary of National Biography, vol.* XXIII, *p.* 415.

William Habbington, who sings to us with such monotonous sweetness of Castara's innocent joys, surpasses Lodge alike in the charm of his descriptions and in the extravagance of his follies. In reading him we are sharply reminded of Klopstock's warning, that "a man should speak of his wife as seldom and with as much modesty as of himself;" for Habbington, who glories in the fairness and the chastity of his spouse, becomes unduly boastful now and then in vaunting these perfections to the world. He, at least, being safely married to Castara, feels none of that haunting insecurity which disturbs his fellow-poets.

"All her vows religious be,
And her love she vows to me,"

he says complacently, and then stops to assure us in plain prose that she is "so unvitiated by conversation with the world that the subtle-minded of her sex would deem it ignorance." Even to her husband-lover she is "thrifty of a kiss," and in the marble coldness and purity of her breast his glowing roses find a chilly sepulchre. Cupid, perishing, it would seem, from a mere description of her merits, or, as Habbington singularly expresses it,—

"But if you, when this you hear,
Fall down murdered through your ear,"

is, by way of compensation, decently interred in the dimpled cheek which has so often been his lurking-place.—REPPLIER, AGNES, 1891, *English Love-Songs, Points of View*, p. 50.

"*They meet but with unwholesome springs.*" Habington, who sang long and loud of the "Chaste Castara" in an age when ladies of her icy temperament were not so much in the fashion as they have become of later years, devotes this not very convincing poem to the praise of women; but the song contains a couplet which is perhaps more absolutely poetical, in design and form, than any two lines written in this or the following reign—

"They hear but when the mermaid sings,
And only see the falling star."

—CRAWFURD, OSWALD, 1896, *ed., Lyrical Verse from Elizabeth to Victoria*, p. 427, note.

The religious verses included in the collection are devout expressions of religious feeling, and those in praise of the virtues of Castara are pleasing and sincere, never sinking below but seldom rising above mediocrity.—MASTERMAN, J. HOWARD B., 1897, *The Age of Milton*, p. 119.

GENERAL

By many ["Edward IV"] esteemed to have a stile sufficiently florid, and better becoming a poetical, than historical, subject.—WOOD, ANTHONY, 1691-1721, *Athenæ Oxoniensis, vol.* II, *f.* 110.

Some of his pieces deserve being revived.—HEADLEY, HENRY, 1787, *Select Beauties of Ancient English Poetry*.

There is no very ardent sensibility in his lyrics, but they denote a mind of elegant and chaste sentiments. He is free as any of the minor poets of his age from the impurities which were then considered as wit. He is indeed rather ostentatiously platonic, but his love language is far from being so elaborate as the complimentary gallantry of the preceding age. A respectable gravity of thought, and succinct fluency of expression, are observable in the poems of his later life.—CAMPBELL, THOMAS, 1819, *Specimens of the British Poets*.

A kind of sweet, modest punctiliosity is the virtue he strives to paint and inculcate in his ideal woman.—MASSON, DAVID, 1858, *The Life of John Milton, vol.* I, *ch.* vi.

His religion is a further reason why to Catholic readers he should be better known than he is. Habington is, in all respects, a Catholic poet, not only like Lodge, a Catholic, who chanced to be a poet, or like Pope, a poet who chanced to be a Catholic, but rather like Aubrey de Vere, one in whom faith and genius are so interfused and blended that he seems to be a poet because he is a Catholic, and a Catholic because he is a poet. In a man of Habington's nature, his religion is not a social form or a sentimental fancy, but a deep and pervading influence in his life and work.—CASSERLY, D. A., 1877, *A Catholic Poet of the Seventeenth Century, American Catholic Quarterly Review, vol.* II, *p.* 618.

Many pleasing thoughts and lines. His purity is worthy of the highest praise.—LAWRENCE, EUGENE, 1878, *English Literature Primers, Classical Period*, p. 48.

From a purely literary point of view, Habington only rarely reaches high water mark in poetry. There are no glaring faults in his verse, and few conceits. The mass of his work is fluent, ingenious, tolerable poetry. It does not often attain to the inner music which can only proceed from a born singer, or to the flawless expression of a noble thought. Perfect literary tact Habington does not possess; he will follow up a fine stanza with a lame and halting one, apparently without sense of the incongruity. It takes a strong *furor poeticus* to uplift him wholly, and keep him at a high level throughout an entire poem, however short. . . . His inadequate sense of poetic form does not allow him often to attain to a perfect whole. He is too fond of awkward

EDWARD HYDE

From a Drawing by Freeman.

JOHN SELDEN

From a Picture attributed to Sir Peter Lely, in the Bodleian Library, Oxford

elisions, and endeavours to force more into a line than it will fairly hold. His sonnets, one or two of which rank among the best efforts, are, formally speaking, not sonnets at all, but strings of seven rhyming couplets. He does not sufficiently know, he has not sufficiently laboured at,

the technical business of his art.—ARNOLD, W. T., 1880, *English Poets, ed. Ward, vol.* II, *pp.* 161, 162.

If not born a singer, was yet so near the divine voice as to catch some exquisite echoes.—EGAN, MAURICE FRANCIS, 1889, *Lectures on English Literature, p.* 75.

John Selden
1584–1654

Born at Salvington, Sussex, Dec. 16, 1584: died at London, Nov. 30, 1654. An English jurist, antiquary, Orientalist, and author. At about 16 years of age he entered Hart Hall, Oxford, and in 1603 Clifford's Inn, London; in 1604 he migrated to the Inner Temple. He was intimately associated with Ben Jonson, Drayton, Edward Lyttleton, Henry Rolle, Edward Herbert, and Thomas Gardener. He was first employed by Sir Robert Cotton to copy and abridge parliamentary records in the Tower. He established a large and lucrative practice, but his chief reputation was made as a writer and scholar. In 1610 he published "England's Epinomis" and "Janus Anglorum, Facies Altera," which treated of English law down to Henry II. These were followed by "Titles of Honour" (1614), "Analecton Anglo-Britannicon" (1615), "De Diis Syriis" (1617). The "History of Tithes," published in 1618, was suppressed. He was the instigator of the "protestation" of Dec. 18, 1621, and was committed to the Tower. In 1623 he entered Parliament as member for Lancaster, and in 1628 helped to draw up and carry the Petition of Right. In 1635 he dedicated his "Mare Clausum" to the king (Charles I.), and seems to have inclined to the court party. He was returned to the Long Parliament (1640) for the University of Oxford, and was a member of the committee which impeached Archbishop Laud. In 1646 he became master of Trinity Hall, Cambridge. Besides the works already mentioned, he was the author of "De Juri Naturali, etc." (1640) "Privileges of the Baronage of England, etc." (1642), and "Table-Talk," his best-known work (1689).—SMITH, BENJAMIN E., 1894-97, *The Century Cyclopedia of Names, p.* 915.

PERSONAL

He never owned the mariage with the countesse of Kent till after her death, upon some lawe account. He never kept any servant peculiar, but my ladie's were all at his command; he lived with her *in Aedibus Carmeliticis* (White Fryers), which was, before the conflagration, a noble dwelling. . . . He was temperate in eating and drinking. He had a slight stuffe, or silke, kind of false carpet to cast over the table where he read and his papers lay, when a stranger came-in, so that he needed not to displace his bookes or papers. . . . When he was neer death, the minister (Mr. [Richard] Johnson) was comeing to him to assoile him: Mr. Hobbes happened then to be there; sayd he, "What, will you that have wrote like a man, now dye like a woman?" So the minister was not let in. . . . He was very tall, I guesse about 6 foot high; sharp ovall face; head not very big; long nose inclining to one side; full

popping eie (gray).—AUBREY, JOHN, 1669-96, *Brief Lives, ed. Clark, vol.* II.

Selden was a person whom no character can flatter, or transmit in any expressions equal to his merit and virtue. He was of so stupendous learning in all kinds and in all languages (as may appear in his excellent and transcendent writings) that a man would have thought he had been entirely conversant amongst books, and had never spent an hour but in reading and writing; yet his humanity, courtesy, and affability was such that he would have been thought to have been bred in the best courts but that his good nature, charity, and delight in doing good, and in communicating all he knew, exceeded that breeding. His style in all his writings seems harsh and sometimes obscure, which is not wholly to be imputed to the abstruse subjects of which he commonly treated out of the paths trod by other men, but to a little undervaluing the beauty of a style, and too much propensity to the language of antiquity; but in his conversation he was the most clear discourser, and had the best faculty in making hard things easy, and presenting them to the understanding of any man that hath been known. Mr. Hyde was wont to say that he valued himself upon nothing more than upon having had Mr. Selden's acquaintance from the time he was very young, and held it with great delight as long as they were suffered to continue together in London; and he was very much troubled always when he heard him blamed, censured, and reproached for staying in London and in the parliament after they were in rebellion, and in the worst times, which his age obliged him to do; and how wicked soever the actions were which were every day done, he was confident he had not given his consent to them, but would have hindered them if he could with his own safety, to which he was always enough indulgent. If he had some infirmities with other men, they were weighed down with wonderful and prodigious abilities and excellencies in the other scale.—CLARENDON, LORD (EDWARD HYDE), 1674? *Life, pt.* i, *p.* 16.

I know you are acquainted, how greatly he (Sir M. Hale) valued Mr. *Selden*, being one of his Executors; his Books and Picture being still near him. I think it meet therefore to remember, that because many *Hobbists* do report, that Mr. Selden was at the heart an Infidel, and inclined to the Opinions of *Hobbs*, I desired him (Sir M. Hale) to tell me the truth herein; And he oft professed to me, that Mr. Selden was a resolved serious Christian; and that he was a great adversary to *Hobbs* his errors; and that he had seen him openly oppose him so earnestly, as either to depart from him, or drive him out of the Room.— BAXTER, RICHARD, 1682, *Additional Notes on the Life and Death of Sir Matthew Hale, p.* 8.

That he was regarded with extraordinary veneration and esteem by his contemporaries of different parties, we have the fullest evidence: indeed, the man who reckoned among his friends and admirers Whitelock and Clarendon, Usher and Hale, must have possessed no ordinary share of moral, as well as intellectual, excellence. —AIKIN, JOHN, 1812, *The Lives of John Selden, Esq., and Archbishop Usher, p.* 208.

Mr. Selden was certainly the most learned, and perhaps the most honest Englishman of his time. He was actually a patriot, for his continued efforts to serve his country, however frequently he might have mistaken the means, seem never for a moment to have incurred even a suspicion of selfishness. Wealth, power, and dignities, had been laid at his feet, and refused by him. Firm in his occasional resistance to that royal prerogative, the limits of which no man could so well define as himself; incapable of private resentment for public causes; indifferent to popularity, and despising the hypocritical fanaticism by which it was then the fashion to court it; he stood almost alone, a perfect example of public integrity. His patriotism extended to, and guided even his literary studies. The final object of all his works was to improve the history of the religion, the laws, the government, or the liberties, of his country. In the prosecution of his profound inquiries he disdained conjecture, and avoided argument. Devoted by his nature to the love of truth, he could not rest on his way till he had arrived at facts; and influenced by the habit of his profession, he considered those only as facts which he could prove by the most rigid evidence.—LODGE, EDMUND, 1821-34, *Portraits of Illustrious Personages of Great Britain, vol.* v, *p.* 47.

No reputation stood higher than that of Selden. He was respected on all sides as an honest man, and as a constitutional lawyer to whom there was no rival. He had little mind to be a martyr, but he had still less a mind to be a knave.—ROGERS, JAMES E. THOROLD, 1870, *William Laud, Historical Gleanings, Second Series, p.* 102.

He was the first and greatest of the "Trimmers" who enlisted during this stormy century so large a contingent of our nation's strength. As long as personal sovereignty menaced the traditional privileges of Englishmen he was distinctly popular in sympathy, and even stood a certain amount of persecution in the popular cause. When that cause had got the upper hand and began to presume, Selden drew back. He was an Oxford man; but the greatest Cambridge poet of our time has exactly summarised Selden's idea, without probably thinking of Selden, in the well-known lines about

　　Freedom slowly broadening down
　　From precedent to precedent.

He was thus very horrible to "high-fliers"

and men in a hurry on either side; and indeed to the present day there is a certain cold-bloodedness about him. He had the lawyer's—especially the English lawyer's—dislike of ecclesiasticism; he had the scholar's dislike of democracy. He was almost a great man; but he was not in the least a hero.—SAINTSBURY, GEORGE, 1895, *Social England, ed. Traill, vol.* IV, *p.* 98.

In politics, if Selden did not exhibit the character of a hero, a martyr, or a saint, he played the part of an honest man. The fact that he was consulted alike by the commons on their rights and by the lords on their privileges is a remarkable testimony not only to his learning, but to his freedom from party bias. He seems in all cases to have maintained what he believed to be the right, and to have been diverted from this course neither by the hope of popular applause nor by the favour of the court, nor by resentment for wrongs by which many men would have been soured. His desire was for an ordered liberty, and that he thought was to be found in the ancient constitution of the country. He had no democratic feeling, and no admiration for the great mass of mankind.—FRY, SIR EDWARD, 1897, *Dictionary of National Biography, vol.* LI, *p.* 222.

TITLES OF HONOUR
1614

J. Selden liveth on his owne, is the Law book of the Judges of England, the bravest man in all languages; his booke "Titles of Honour," written to his chamber-fellow Heyward.—DRUMMOND, WILLIAM, 1619, *Notes on Ben Jonson's Conversations.*

As to what concerns our nobility and gentry, all that come within either of those lists, will allow that Mr. Selden's "Titles of Honour" ought first to be well perused, for the gaining of a general notion of the distinction of degrees, from an emperor, down to a country gentleman.—NICOLSON, WILLIAM, 1696-1714, *English Historical Library.*

Selden's "Titles of Honour" a gentleman should not be without.—LOCKE, JOHN, 1704? *Some Thoughts concerning Reading and Study for a Gentleman.*

DE DIIS SYRIIS
1617

For the enumeration of the Syrian and Arabian deities, it may be observed that Milton has comprised in one hundred and thirty very beautiful lines the two large and learned syntagmas which Selden had composed on that abstruse subject.—GIBBON, EDWARD, 1776-78, *Decline and Fall of the Roman Empire, ch.* xv, *note.*

This was Selden's celebrated work, which placed him at once in the rank of the first scholars of the age. The primary purpose was to treat on the false gods mentioned in the Old Testament, but with which he joined an inquiry into the Syrian idolatry in general, and an occasional illustration of the ancient Theology of the other Heathen nations.—AIKIN, JOHN, 1812, *The Lives of John Selden, Esq., and Archbishop Usher.*

Remark Milton's wonderful sublimity, not merely in his central figure of him who had not "lost his original brightness," who was "not less than archangel ruined;" but in his creation, it may almost be said, out of Selden's book and the few allusions in the Old Testament, of a new Demonology. . . . I owe the germ of this observation, perhaps more than the germ, to my friend Mr. Macaulay.—MILMAN, HENRY HART, 1855-*History of Latin Christianity, vol.* VI, *bk.* xiv, *ch.* ii, *note.*

HISTORY OF TITHES
1618

Mr. Selden's "History of Tithes," was what, most of all his works, blasted his credit, and exposed him to penance, as well as censure.—NICOLSON, WILLIAM, 1696-1714, *English Historical Library.*

Though often attacked, and the author compelled to make an apology for writing it, it has never been answered. His doctrines on the subject are now, I believe, very generally received.—ORME, WILLIAM, 1824, *Bibliotheca Biblica, p.* 394.

His work "De Decimis," in which he tried to prove that the giving of tithes was not ordered by any Divine command, excited much contention, and aroused the animosity of the clergy. In consequence of this in 1621 he was imprisoned, and remained in custody for five years. On the dissolution of Parliament in 1629, being obnoxious to the royal party, he was sent to the Tower, and then confined in a house of correction for pirates. But as a compensation for his injuries in 1647 he received £5,000 from the public purse and became a member of the Long Parliament. —DITCHFIELD, P. H., 1894, *Books Fatal to their Authors, p.* 134.

When published the book aroused a fierce storm. The author was summoned to answer for his opinions before some of the lords of the court of high commission and some of the privy council, and he acknowledged his error in a few lines in writing. The submission contained, as Selden contended, no confession of mistakes in the book, and expressed no change of opinion, but merely regret at the publication of the work. The form of the submission was probably a matter of arrangement between himself and those of his judges who seemed to favour him. The book itself was suppressed by public authority, and by some command, probably of the king, he was forbidden to print any reply to his numerous antagonists, a restraint of which he bitterly complained to the Marquis of Buckingham in May 1620.—FRY, SIR EDWARD, 1897, *Dictionary of National Biography, vol.* LI, *p.* 213.

DE JURI NATURALI, ETC.
1640

Let him hasten to be acquainted with that noble volume written by our learned Selden, "Of the Law of Nature and of Nations," a work more useful and more worthy to be perused by whoever studies to be a great man in wisdom, equity, and justice, than all those "decretals and sumless sums" which the pontifical clerks have doted on, ever since that unfortunate mother famously sinned thrice, and died impenitent of her bringing into the world those two mis-begotten infants, Lombard and Gratian.—MILTON, JOHN, 1643, *The Doctrine and Discipline of Divorce, ch.* xxii.

The whole work belongs far more to theological than to philosophical investigation; and I have placed it here chiefly out of conformity to usage: for undoubtedly Selden, though a man of very strong reasoning faculties, had not greatly turned them to the principles of natural law. His reliance on the testimony of Jewish writers, many of them by no means ancient, for those primeval traditions as to the sons of Noah, was in the character of his times; but it will scarcely suit the more rigid criticism of our own. His book, however, is excellent for its proper purpose, that of representing Jewish opinion; and is

among the greatest achievements in erudition that any English writer has performed.—HALLAM, HENRY, 1837-39, *Introduction to the Literature of Europe, pt.* iii, *ch.* iv, *par.* 28.

TABLE TALK
1689

Table-Talk: | Being the | DISCOURSES| of | John Selden, Esq. | Being His *Sense* of various *Matters* of | Weight and high Consequence; | relating especially to | RELIGION and STATE. | *Distingue Tempora.* | LONDON: | Printed for E. Smith, in the Year | M DC LXXXIX.—TITLE PAGE OF FIRST EDITION.

Were you not Executors to that Person, who (while he liv'd) was the Glory of the Nation, yet I am Confident anything of his would find Acceptance with you; and truly the Sense and Notion here is wholly his, and most of the Words. I had the opportunity to hear his Discourse twenty Years together; and lest all those Excellent things that usually fell from him might be lost, some of them from time to time I faithfully committed to Writing, which here digested into this Method, I humbly present to your Hands. You will quickly perceive them to be his by the familiar Illustrations wherewith they are set off, and in which way you know he was so happy, in that, with a marvellous delight to those that heard him, he would presently convey the highest Points of Religion, and the most important Affairs of State, to an ordinary apprehension. In reading be pleased to distinguish Times, and in your Fancy carry along with you, the *When* and the *Why* many of these things were spoken; this will give them the more Life, and the smarter Relish. —MILWARD, RICHARD, 1689, *Table Talk of John Selden, Dedication to Sir Matthew Hale and others.*

There can scarcely be a less disputable mark of integrity and worthiness in an individual than his succeeding in securing the "golden opinions" of parties opposed to each other in contending for the same object, and concerning which object that individual is known by them to differ from them both. Now of all contentions, history affords uniform testimony that none are so jealous and implacable as those in which are involved the religious opinions and the temporal pre-eminence of the disputants. Mingling in such contentions,

Selden passed his life a prominent actor in them all, and yet so moderate, consistent, and talented was his course, that although occasionally supporting and opposing each, the extremes of the conflicting parties looked up to him and sought the aid of his abilities.—JOHNSON, GEORGE W., 1835, *Memoirs of Selden, p.* 342.

There is more weighty bullion sense in this book than I ever found in the same number of pages of any uninspired writer. . . . O! to have been with Selden over his glass of wine, making every accident an outlet and a vehicle of wisdom.— COLERIDGE, SAMUEL TAYLOR, 1836, *Notes on Books and Authors; Miscellanies, Æsthetic and Literary ed. Ashe, p.* 297.

This very short and small volume which gives, perhaps, a more exalted notion of Selden's natural talents than any of his learned writings. . . . Full of vigor, raciness, and a kind of scorn of the half-learned, far less rude, but more cutting, than that of Scaliger. It has been said that the "Table-Talk" of Selden is worth all the Ana of the Continent. In this I should be disposed to concur; but they are not exactly works of the same class.—HALLAM, HENRY, 1837-39, *Introduction to the Literature of Europe, pt.* iii, *ch.* iv, *par.* 37.

He died in 1654, and his "Table-Talk" was published by his amanuensis Richard Milward in 1689. Lucky the scholar who can talk and who has a discriminating "Richard Milward;" for, otherwise, how many readers would John Selden now boast in England? Most men of letters, indeed, have had occasion to make some acquaintance with his writings—let us say with the "Titles of Honour" for instance—and have bowed reverently to the immensely learned man, of whom Ben Jonson said "he was the law book of the Judges." But is the Selden of the "Titles of Honour" the same person as the Selden of the "Table-Talk"? One scarcely believes it. Dry, grave, and almost crabbed in his writings—his conversation is homely, humorous, shrewd, vivid, even delightful! He is still the great scholar and the tough parliamentarian, but merry, playful, and witty. The ἀνήριθμον γεηασμα is on the sea of his vast intellect. He writes like the opponent of Grotius; he talks like the friend of Ben Jonson.—HANNAY, JAMES, 1856, *Essays from the Quarterly Review, p.* 20

These Discourses show somewhat of the mind, but not the whole mind of Selden, even in the subjects treated of. What must have been the fulness of information, the aptness of illustration, the love of truth, the justness of reasoning, when such fragments as these could be picked up by a casual hearer? Bacon's "Essays" are most carefully finished compositions: Selden's "Table-Talk" is the spontaneous incidental outpouring of an overflowing mind; and yet it may not unworthily compare with the former.—ARBER, EDWARD, 1868, *ed., Selden's Table-Talk, English Reprints, Introduction, p.* 10.

His homely, familiar manner, has its attractions as well for the scholar as for the common reader; pregnant as are his sentences with his great good sense, rare learning, bringing abstruse subjects home to the affairs of life in a style at once perspicuous and agreeable.—ALCOTT, A. BRONSON, 1869, *Concord Days, p.* 249.

Selden's style is crabbed and sometimes obscure, while most of his treatises are overweighted with the ponderous learning of their author. Clarendon, while admitting the harshness and obscurity of his writings, records that "in his conversation he was a most clear discourser." His "Table Talk" bears out this description. It is full of quaint humour and pleasant satire, combined with much admirable common sense. Many of the sententious remarks in the volume indicate Selden's strong resentment against religious bigotry and intolerance, but there is no malice in the whimsical anecdotes and allusions in which the book abounds. Altogether, the "Table Talk" shows Selden as a genial, shrewd, and sensible observer of men and things, whose mind had neither been soured by theological controversies, nor warped by legal studies. —MASTERMAN, J. HOWARD B., 1897 *The Age of Milton, p.* 233.

GENERAL

You that have been
Ever at home, yet have all countries seen;
And like a compass, keeping one foot still
Upon your centre, do your circle fill
Of general knowledge; watch'd men, manners too,
Heard what times past have said, seen what ours do!
Which grace shall I make love to first? your skill

Or faith in things? or is't your wealth and
　　will
T' inform and teach? or your unwearied pain
Of gathering? bounty in pouring out again?
What fables have you vex'd, what truth re-
　　deem'd,
Antiquities search'd, opinions disesteem'd,
Impostures branded, and authorities urg'd!
What blots and errors have you watched and
　　purg'd
Records and authors of! how rectified
Times, manners, customs! innovations spied!
Sought out the fountains, sources, creeks,
　　paths, ways,
And noted the beginnings and decays!
Where is that nominal mark, or real rite,
Form, act, or ensign, that hath 'scaped your
　　sight?
　—JONSON, BEN, 1614, *To his Honor'd
Friend, Mr. John Selden.*

The chief of learned men reputed in
this land.—MILTON, JOHN, 1644, *Areopagitica.*

Lo! such was Selden, and his learned fame
All polish'd nations would be proud to claim.
The gods, nay, e'en the stones, their voice
　　would raise,
Should men by silence dare withhold their
　　praise.
　—LANGBAINE, GERARD, 1692? *Written
under the Portrait of Selden.*

His style in all his writings seems harsh,
and sometimes obscure; which is not
wholly to be imputed to the abstract subjects of which he commonly treated, out
of the paths trod by other men, but to a
little undervaluing the beauty of a style,
and too much propensity to the language
of antiquity: but in his conversation he
was the most clear discourser, and had the
best faculty in making hard things and
present to the understanding, of any man
that hath been known.—CLARENDON, LORD
(EDWARD HYDE), 1674? *Life.*

The most learned Mr. Selden, one of the
greatest men that any age has produced.
—BURNET, GILBERT, 1679-1715, *The History of the Reformation of the Church of
England, bk.* iii.

The famous Dr. Pocock assisted Mr.
Selden very much, as Selden himself is
pleased to acknowledge in several places,
particularly in his edition of Eutychius'
"Origines Ecclesiæ Alexandrinæ," which
Origines is only a small inconsiderable
fragment of Eutychius' "Annales" that
Pocock himself afterwards published in
Arabic and Latin. Indeed Selden, not-
withstanding his great pretences, had

but little skill in Arabic, and he made use
of others' help in that, as in many other
things. His design of printing these
Annals was purely out of his hatred to
episcopacy. His Commentary upon them,
which is large, is a mere rhapsody, learned
indeed and full of reading, but generally
like his other performances injudicious.
His efforts against episcopacy are but
weak, and yet he did what he was able.—
HEARNE, THOMAS, 1726-27, *Reliquiæ
Hearnianæ, ed. Bliss, Jan.* 24, *vol.* II, *p.*
287.

John Selden, sometimes styled "The
great dictator of learning of the English
nation," and pronounced by Grotius, his
antagonist, to be the glory of it, was a man
of as extensive and profound knowledge
as any of his age. He was thoroughly
skilled in every thing that related to his
own profession; but the general bent of
his studies was to sacred and profane
antiquity. The greater part of his works
are on uncommon subjects. Like a man
of genius, he was not content with walking
in the beaten track of learning, but was
for striking out new paths, and enlarging
the territories of science.—GRANGER,
JAMES, 1769-1824, *Biographical History
of England, vol.* III, *p.* 27.

Certainly the most philosophical as well
as learned inquirer into antiquity who had
yet appeared in the country.—AIKIN,
LUCY, 1822, *Memoirs of the Court of King
James the First, vol.* I, *p.* 129.

His literary merit was liberally acknowledged by those continental scholars
best able to appreciate it; Grotius,
Salmasius Bochart, G. Vossius, Gronovius
and Daniel Heinsius are a few among the
distinguished list of his encomiasts, and
though his works are probably little read
at the present day, because the additions
he made to the stock of learning have
been made available by modern writers
and compilers, he must ever be accounted
one of the chief literary ornaments of
this country, nor has perhaps Europe
produced a scholar of more profound and
varied erudition.—SINGER, S. W., 1855,
ed., The Table Talk of John Selden, p. 85.

The only man in the British Islands who
was allowed to be more than a match for
Usher in miscellaneous erudition was his
friend and correspondent, the English
lawyer, Selden. No man in that age is
more worthy of note than this superb

scholar. His life, though simple in its tenor, had already been full of important incidents. . . . After some minor exhibitions of his learning in legal tracts and in notes to a portion of Drayton's "Polyolbion," he had published, in 1614, when in his thirtieth year, his work on "Titles of Honor," still one of our great authorities in all matters of heraldry. . . . A memorable singularity about Selden is that, while perhaps the greatest scholar of his day in England, he was yet one of its freest and most conspicuously skeptical thinkers. With a memory full of all that had happened since the Flood, he reasoned on current questions as if, the pressure of his recollections on all sides being equal, the result, for his judgment, was absolute equilibrium. — MASSON, DAVID, 1858, *The Life of John Milton, vol.* I, *ch.* vi.

John Selden, unsurpassed for learning and ability in the whole splendid history of the English bar, on every book of whose library was written, "Before every thing, Liberty!" — SUMNER, CHARLES, 1863, *Speech on our Foreign Relations, Sept.* 10.

Selden's learning, prudence, and polite affable manner, made him perhaps the most generally respected man of his time—respected alike by Royalist and by Puritan. As a writer of English, he is known by his "History of Tithes" (1618), which offended the clergy by denying their divine right to such revenue; but chiefly by his "Table-Talk," published after his death. The style of his writings is harsh, obscure, and antiquated; in conversation he seems to have been more felicitous, dealing in pointed sententious aphorisms and witty turns. The "Table-Talk" is full of worldly wisdom and sarcasms against clerical bigotry.—MINTO, WILLIAM, 1872-80, *A Manual of English Prose Literature, p.* 257.

Selden has the limitations of one whose feet are always planted firmly on solid earth. He is a guide, a critic; not a leader, an inspirer. As he is untouched by the fanaticisms, he is incapable of the fine enthusiasms of his days. . . . In his writings his sentences are usually ponderous, and often involved—a striking contrast to the homeliness and lucidity of his conversations, which, however, show also carelessness as to form. Yet in both there is an entire absence of pedantry.—M'CORMICK, W. S., 1893, *English Prose, ed Craik, vol.* II, *p.* 168.

Joseph Hall
1574–1656

Joseph Hall, born 1st July 1574 at Ashby-de-la-Zouch, became a fellow of Emmanuel College, Cambridge, in 1595, incumbent of Halstead and Waltham, and dean of Worcester (1617). In that year he accompanied James I. to Scotland to help establish Episcopacy, and he was one of the English deputies to the synod of Dort. He became Bishop of Exeter in 1627, and as such on suspicion of Puritanism incurred Laud's enmity, though he zealously defended Episcopacy. In 1641 he was translated to Norwich, and having with other prelates protested against the validity of laws passed during their enforced absence from Parliament, was committed to the Tower, but liberated at the end of seven months, on finding bail for £5000. Shortly after his return to Norwich his revenues were sequestrated and his property pillaged. He retired to a small farm at Higham in 1647, and died 8th September 1656. His works, including "Contemplations," "Christian Meditations," "Episcopacy," and "Mundus Alter et Idem," a Latin satirical romance, were edited by Pratt (1808), by Peter Hall, a descendant (1837–39), and by Wynter (1863). His poetical "Satires: "Virgidemiarum" (1597-98) Pope calls "the best poetry and the truest satire in the English language."—PATRICK AND GROOME, *eds.*, 1897, *Chambers's Biographical Dictionary, p.* 453.

PERSONAL

Not out of a vain affectation of my own glory, which I know how little it can avail me when I am gone hence, but out of a sincere desire to give glory to my God, whose wonderful providence I have noted in all my ways, have I recorded some remarkable passages of my fore-past life. What I have done is worthy of nothing but silence and forgetfulness; but what God hath done for me is worthy of everlasting and thankful memory.—HALL,

JOSEPH, 1641-2? *Observations of Some Specialties of Divine Providence in the Life of Joseph Hall, Works*, ed. *Wynter, vol.* I, *p.* xi.

He was noted for a singular wit from his youth: a most acute rhetorician and an elegant poet. He understood many tongues; and in the rhetorick of his own he was second to none that lived in his time.—WHITEFOOTE, JOHN, 1656, *Bishop Hall's Funeral Sermon, Sept.* 30.

So soon almost as Emanuel Colledge was admitted into Cambridge, he was admitted into that Colledge, within few years after the first foundation thereof. He passed all his degrees with great applause. First, noted in the University, for his ingenuous maintaining (be it Truth, or Paradox) that *Mundus senescit*, "The World groweth old." Yet, in some sort, his position confuteth his position, the wit and quickness whereof did argue an increase rather than a decay of parts in this latter age. . . . He may be said to have dyed with his pen in his hand, whose Writing and Living expired together.—FULLER, THOMAS, 1662, *Worthies of England*, ed. *Nichols, vol.* I, *p.* 566.

Seems to have been very credulous in his disposition, rather religious than wise, or possessing any attainments equal to the dignity to which he rose.—CIBBER, THEOPHILUS, 1753, *Lives of the Poets, vol.* I, *p.* 320.

Joseph Hall, styled the Christian Seneca, from his sententious manner of writing, was justly celebrated for his piety, wit, learning, and extensive knowledge of mankind.—GRANGER, JAMES, 1769-1824, *Biographical History of England, vol.* II, *p.* 337.

Both as a writer and as a preacher his reputation stands high. With less scholarship and wit than Andrewes, and less original power than Donne or Taylor, he writes with great fluency and energy, and with much better taste than any of these writers. Some have called him the best preacher of that century—no small honour among such giants; and undoubtedly, for pulpit oratory, his strong feelings and fluent expression, guided by superior taste, would be more effective than the undisciplined profusion and originality of his great rivals.—MINTO, WILLIAM, 1872-80, *A Manual of English Prose Literature, p.* 254.

He is thus, more than any other man of his time, the personification of a great intellectual and spiritual movement. A character of which this could be said would hardly be one of great intellectual force; and, in fact, there is no trace in him of any individual opposition to the ideas floating in the circles in which he moved. His ecclesiastical opinions were the same as those of Laud; he had the same reverence for authority, and the same notion of the position of the king in the constitution. There is nothing to show that he was capable of contributing a single useful thought to avert the dangers which threatened his party and his country. Hall's highest qualities, in truth, were moral rather than intellectual. Whatever doctrine he held, he did not push it to extremes; and, whatever order he enforced, he not only tried persuasion first, but he had the knack of persuading persuasively. If he had been Archbishop of Canterbury instead of Laud, he would have maintained much the same principles as Laud did, but he would have caused far less irritation.—GARDINER, SAMUEL R., 1886, *The Academy, vol.* 29, *p.* 267.

VIRGIDEMIARUM

1597-98

They are full of spirit and poetry, as much of the first as Dr. Donne, and far more of the latter.—GRAY, THOMAS, 1752, *Letter to Dr. Wharton.*

These satires are marked with a classical precision, to which English poetry had yet rarely attained. They are replete with animation of style and sentiment. The indignation of the satirist is always the result of good sense. Nor are the thorns of severe invective unmixed with the flowers of pure poetry. The characters are delineated in strong and lively colouring, and their discriminations are touched with the masterly traces of genuine humour. The versification is equally energetic and elegant, and the fabric of the couplets approaches to the modern standard. It is no inconsiderable proof of a genius predominating over the general taste of an age when every preacher was a punster, to have written verses, where laughter was to be raised, and the reader to be entertained with sallies of pleasantry, without quibbles and conceits. His chief fault is obscurity, arising from a remote phraseology, constrained combinations, unfamiliar allusions, elliptical apostrophes, and abruptness of expression.—WARTON, THOMAS, 1778-81, *History of English Poetry.*

The "Satires" of Hall exhibit a very minute and curious picture of the literature and manners, the follies and vices of his times, and numerous quotations in the course of our work will amply prove the wit, the sagacity, and the elegance of his Muse.—DRAKE, NATHAN, 1817, *Shakspeare and his Times, vol.* I, *p.* 629.

In his "Satires," which were published at the age of twenty-three, he discovered not only the early vigour of his own genious, but the powers and pliability of his native tongue. Unfortunately, perhaps unconsciously, he caught, from studying Juvenal and Persius as his models, an elliptical manner and an antique allusion, which cast obscurity over his otherwise spirited and amusing traits of English manners; though the satirist himself was so far from anticipating this objection, that he formally apologizes for *"too much stooping to the low reach of the vulgar."* But in many instances he redeems the antiquity of his allusions by their ingenious adaptation to modern manners; and this is but a small part of his praise; for in the point and volubility, and vigour of Hall's numbers, we might frequently imagine ourselves perusing Dryden.—CAMPBELL, THOMAS, 1819, *Specimens of the British Poets.*

This powerful and truly original writer is the earliest professed Satirist among our Poets; and he has himself alluded to that fact with a proud and pardonable egotism:
"I first adventure, follow me who list,
And be the Second English Satirist."
His Satires, beside their own intrinsic poetical excellencies, are valuable to the Antiquary as presenting a most vivid and faithful picture of the manners of our ancestors; their fashions, follies, vices, and peculiarities. These Hall has touched with a powerful and unsparing hand. Scribblers, Lawyers, Parsons, Physicians, all those unfortunate classes of men, who have, from time immemorial, enjoyed the unenvied privilege of attracting the peculiar notice of the Satiric Muse, are by him laid bare and shrinking to the scorn and hatred of Mankind.—NEELE, HENRY, 1827, *Lectures on English Poetry, Lecture* V.

Hall is in fact not only so harsh and rugged, that he cannot be read with much pleasure, but so obscure in very many places, that he cannot be understood at all; his lines frequently bearing no visible connection in sense or grammar with their neighbors. The stream is powerful, but turbid and often choked.—HALLAM, HENRY, 1837-39, *Introduction to the Literature of Europe, pt.* ii, *ch.* v, *par.* 71.

The first book of the "Toothless Satires" was directed against the faults, literary and other, of the poets of the age; the second treated of academical abuses; the third of public manners and morality, which also form the matter of the "Biting Satires." The author's acknowledged models are Juvenal and Persius; and he professes that it was to their nervous and crabbed style of poetry, rather than to the imitation of Virgil and Spenser, that his genius inclined him.
"Rather had I, albe in careless rhymes,
Check the misordered world and lawless times."
What Hall's satires did towards "checking the misordered world" may not have been much; but, as compositions of the satirical order, they have kept a place in our literature.—MASSON, DAVID, 1858, *The Life of John Milton, vol.* I, *ch.* vi.

Have little to recommend them to the modern reader of English Verse, for they are disfigured with affected expressions, archaic phrases, and a curious obscurity of thought. Resolute in intention, and merciless in execution, his energy never flags, and his invectives never give out. The virtue with which he plies the lash, and which gives him such a savage delight, is a vice in disguise. His hatred of vice is more monstrous than vice itself. So thought the Archbishop of Canterbury and Bishop of London, the censors of the press, who forthwith ordered that the satires should be burnt.—STODDARD, RICHARD HENRY, 1883, *English Verse, Chaucer to Burns, Introduction, p.* xxxii.

His Satires belong to his early Cambridge days, and to the last decade of the sixteenth century. They have on the whole been rather overpraised, though the variety of their matter and the abundance of reference to interesting social traits of the time to some extent redeem them. The worst point about them, as already noted, is the stale and commonplace impertinence with which their author, unlike the best breed of young poets and men of letters, attempts to satirise his literary betters; while they are to some extent at any rate tarred with the other two brushes of corrupt imitation of the ancients, and of sham moral indignation. Indeed the want of sincerity—the evidence of the literary exercise—injures Hall's satirical work in different ways throughout. We do not, as we read him, in the least believe in his attitude of Hebrew prophet crossed with Roman satirist, and the occasional presence of a vigorous couplet or a lively metaphor hardly redeems this disbelief. Nevertheless, Hall is here as always a literary artist—a writer who took some trouble with his writings.—SAINTSBURY, GEORGE, 1887, *History of Elizabethan Literature, p.* 152.

EPISTLES
1608–11

An able inquirer into the literature of this period has affirmed that Hall's Epistles, written before the year 1613, are the first example of epistolary composition which England had seen. "Bishop Hall," he says, "was not only our first satirist, but was the first who brought epistolary writing to the view of the public; which was common in that age to other parts of Europe, but not practiced in England till he published his own Epistles." And Hall himself in the Dedication of his Epistles to Prince Henry observes, "Your grace shall herein perceiue a new fashion of discourse by Epistles, new to our language, vsuall to others: and, as nouelty is neuer without plea of vse, more free, more familiar."—WARTON, THOMAS, 1778–81, *History of English Poetry, sec.* lxiv.

CONTEMPLATIONS
1612–15

Why have I travelled thus far on the road of Divinity without mentioning the "Contemplations" of *Bishop Hall?* a prelate and a poet, of very distinguished attainments. A vein of piety, and even of an original cast of observation, runs through the greater part of his performances: and his "Contemplations," in particular, breathe the fire of poetry as well as of devotion. His works have been long and justly held in very general esteem. —DIBDIN, THOMAS FROGNALL, 1824, *The Library Companion, p.* 55.

The first and last terms are justly applied, but not the middle one; as there is very little criticism, in the proper meaning of the term, in any of the works of Hall. . . . There is a great variety of sentiment, and great richness of thought and expression, in these "Contemplations." The historical passages are often very happily illustrated; and a pure and elevated devotion, combined with a fine imagination, pervades the whole.— ORME, WILLIAM, 1824, *Bibliotheca Biblica.*

"The Contemplations" of Hall are among his most celebrated works. They are prolix, and without much of that vivacity or striking novelty we meet with in the devotional writings of his contemporary, but are perhaps more practical and generally edifying.—HALLAM, HENRY, 1837–39, *Introduction to the Literature of Europe, pt.* iii, *ch.* ii, *par.* 72.

Very devotional and useful.—BICKERSTETH, EDWARD, 1844, *The Christian Student.*

CHRISTIAN MEDITATIONS
1640

These satires, however, striking as they are for their compactness of language and vigor of characterization, convey but an inadequate idea of the depth, devoutness, and largeness of soul displayed in Hall's theological writings. His "Meditations," especially, have been read by thousands who never heard of him as a tart and caustic wit. But the one characteristic of sententiousness marks equally the sarcasm of the youthful satirist and the raptures of the aged saint. —WHIPPLE, EDWIN P. 1859-68, *The Literature of the Age of Elizabeth, p.* 242.

MUNDUS ALTER ET IDEM
1643

"Mundus Alter et Idem" . . . is a witty and ingenious Invention of a Learned Prelate, writ by him in his younger days (but well enough becoming the austerity of the gravest Head), in which he distinguisheth the Vices, Passions, Humours, and ill Affections most commonly incident to mankind into several Provinces; gives us the Character of each, as in the descriptions of a Country, People, and chief Cities of it, and sets them forth unto the Eye in such lively Colours, that the Vitious man may see therein his own Deformities, and the well-minded man his own Imperfections. The Scene of this Design is laid by the Reverend Author in this *Terra Australis;* the *Decorum* happily preserved in the whole Discovery; the style acutely clear, in the invention singular.—HEYLYN, PETER, 1652, *Cosmography, bk.* iv.

With Hall's satires should be ranked his "Mundus Alter et Idem," an ingenious satirical fiction in prose, where, under a pretended description of the Terra Australis, he forms a pleasant invective against the characteristic vices of various nations, and is remarkably severe on the Church of Rome. This piece was written about the year 1600, before he had quitted the classics for the fathers, and published some years afterwards against his consent. —WARTON, THOMAS, 1778-81, *History of English Poetry, sec.* lxiv.

I can only produce two books by English authors, in this first part of the seventeenth century, which fall properly under the class of novels or romances; and, of these, one is written in Latin. This is the "Mundus Alter et Idem" of Bishop Hall, an imitation of the latter and weaker volumes of Rabelais. A country in Terra Australis is divided into four regions,— Crapulia, Viraginia, Moronea, and Lavernia. Maps of the whole land and of particular regions are given; and the nature of the satire, not much of which has any especial reference to England, may easily be collected. It is not a very successful effort.—HALLAM, HENRY, 1837-39, *Introduction to the Literature of Europe, pt.* iii, *ch.* vii, *par.* 59.

Other circumstances, already recited, which connect the work with Gentili are its dedication to the Earl of Huntingdon and its publication at the cost of Ascanio Rinialme, both members of Gentili's Inn, and further coincidence that the improved edition, Hanau, 1607, bears the same imprint as at least four others of Gentili's acknowledged works. Assuming the preface to be *bona fide,* Knight, as an Oxford M.A. may have been as much the friend of Gentili as of Hall. For Hall there is (*a*) the address of "J. H., the translator, to J. H., the author," (*b*) the translator's apology to the "reverend man" to whose muse some few attributed the little book from Frankfort, (*c*) Heylyn's assignment of it to a "learned prelate"—unquestionably Hall is intended—and (*d*) the Bodleian

Catalogue (1674) referring "Mercurius Britannicus" to Hall. Upon which an advocate for Gentili might further argue that, accepting all that the critics say about the book, there is nothing in it of which a scholar need be ashamed; (*e*) Hall never claimed it himself, as far as is known; (*f*) His friend James did not claim it ·for him in the Bodleian Catalogue of 1620, while (*g*) Gentili is mentioned as the author in the table of contents prefixed to the book; and (*h*) his name appears as author of it upon the title-page of the German translation (1613) within eight years of the original publication, not more than five years after Gentili's death, three years before the death of his brother, Scipio Gentili, and without his or Hall's contradiction (?).—PETHERICK, EDWARD A., 1896, *Mundus Alter et Idem, Gentleman's Magazine, vol.* 281, *p.* 86.

GENERAL

He was commonly called our English Seneca, for the purenesse, plainesse, and fulnesse of his style. Not unhappy at Controversies, more happy at Comments, very good in his Characters, better in his Sermons, best of all in his Meditations. —FULLER, THOMAS, 1662, *Worthies of England, ed. Nichols, vol.* I, *p.* 566.

Monsieur Balzac exceedingly admired him and often quotes him: vide Balzac's "Apologie."—AUBREY, JOHN, 1669-96, *Brief Lives, ed. Clark, vol.* I, *p.* 282.

The wit of Hall is levelled against the ribaldry and bombast of the stage, the puritanical and religious poetry of the Precisians; and the extravagance of romantic and legendary poems. Spenser alone is excepted, from the general censure bestowed on the latter class of authors. Spenser was the only great poet contemporary with Hall, whose reputation, at the time his satires were published, was established.—HIPPISLEY, J. H., 1837, *Chapters on Early English Literature, p.* 309.

Imaginative and copious eloquence, terse and pointed sentences, full of piety and devotion. Few writers more likely to be useful to (Divinity) students. Let them thoroughly read and digest such a writer, and they will be furnished for most of the calls upon them.—BICKERSTETH, EDWARD, 1844, *The Christian Student.*

Most of Hall's prose writings, had

a merit which might have been expected from the author of the "Satires," and which distinguished them from the mass of the theological writings of their day—the merit of careful literary execution. . . . Has still a place in the history of English theological prose between Hooker and Jeremy Taylor; and there are modern critics who, comparing Hall and Taylor, and pointing out their differences in the midst of some obvious similarities, seem to waver in their choice between them. With much of Taylor's rich fancy and rhetorical copiousness, however, there is more in Hall of a certain mechanical hardness of purpose, more of astringency and of mean temper. Even in his "Meditations" there is less of a genuine meditative disposition than of a cultured tendency to ethical sententiousness. —MASSON, DAVID, 1858, *The Life of John Milton, vol.* I, *ch.* vi.

In naming Hall, indeed, we name a prince and chief among our English divines—equally good at all weapons, equally surpassing in every department of theology. . . . The highest tribute to the merits of Bishop Hall's writings is their great and unceasing popularity with the unlearned and poor. Side by side with the writings of Bunyan and Defoe, portions of them are to be found on many a cottage shelf; and the pious contemplations of the witty and eloquent bishop have gladdened and strengthened many a soul in sickness, sorrow, and pain. Do we seek the cause of this? It will be found in the fact that Joseph Hall had not only earnest, practical piety, great learning, great zeal, but also the invaluable gift of genuine wit and humour. Resembling Bishop Andrewes in the raciness, point, and piquancy of his imaginings, he far surpassed him in his power of expressing, in nervous and telling words, the products of his brain. His style is eminently happy, effective, graphic, and genuine. His mind was stored with learning. He had studied men and things under many circumstances, in various lands. His power of illustration is inexhaustible; his wit always fresh and telling; his knowledge of Scripture profound; his sense of the wants, dangers, and difficulties of men deep and practical; his charity and loving spirit abundant. With these qualifications he could scarcely fail of addressing himself effectively to men. And he shone in all subjects. His satires are the best imitations of the Juvenalian vein which we possess; his letters some of the most charming specimens of earnestness, without dulness.—PERRY, GEORGE G., 1861, *History of the Church of England, vol.* I, *p.* 629.

The poetic temperament of Hall reveals itself, in his prose as well as in his verse, by the fervor of his piety, and the forcible and often picturesque character of his style, in which it has been thought he made Seneca his model. . . . Both in style and in mind Hall and Donne were altogether opposed; neither in his prose nor in his verse has the former the originality of the latter, or the fineness of thought that will often break out in a sudden streak of light from the midst of his dark sayings; but, on the other hand, he is perfectly free from the dominant vices of Donne's manner, his conceits, his quaintness, his remote and fantastic analogies, his obscurity, his harshness, his parade of a useless and encumbering erudition.— —CRAIK, GEORGE L., 1861, *A Compendious History of English Literature and of the English Language, vol.* I, *p.* 612.

Hall writes with skill and with spirit. It can scarcely be said of him: *Facit indignatio versum.* He finds a pleasure in imitating, and in some sort reproducing, his Latin models; and this is rather his inspiration than any moral fervour. And the chief value of his work is its vigorous picture of Elizabethan ways and manners. Whatever the old comedy did for Athens in the way of illustrating the old Athenian life, that satire did for Rome, and with inferior, but yet no mean force, Hall did for Elizabethan London. It is no contemptible service to have helped to keep alive for us an age so fascinating, so glorious, so momentous. Whoever would picture to himself the very town in the midst of which Shakespeare moved, its lights and shadows, its whims and phantasies and follies—"a mad world, my masters"—see "the very age and body of the time, his form and presence," and learn what were its daily thoughts, interests, cares, credulities, passions—will find truly valuable aid in Hall's satires.—HALES, JOHN W., 1881, *Bishop Hall, The Antiquary, vol.* 4, *p.* 190.

In language the "Satires" are artificially archaic: and the tone that pervades them has very little in common with the spirit of his later work. But they brought a freedom and a vigour to his prose style which it never lost, and the practice which they gave him in his early years not only added force and liveliness to his later controversial style, but also gave to his religious writings the quick movement, the variety and the lavish illustration, which are their chief characteristics. Hall thus combined some elements which are rarely found in combination. Educated amongst puritanic influences and under the shadow of a religion that regarded each individual accident as brought about by the special intervention of providence; passing from this to the classical influences of the University, and finding his models in antiquity; thrusting himself as a youth into the literary struggles of the day—he brought to his later work as a divine some unique qualities. His earliest religious writings are devout and earnest, but they borrow their illustrations largely from secular sources; they have no strongly marked dogmatic features, and their language has a freedom and a force that are peculiar.—CRAIK, HENRY, 1893, *ed., English Prose, vol.* II, *p.* 134.

John Hales

1584–1656

John Hales, 1584–1656. Born, in Bath, 19 April 1584. Educated at Bath Grammar School. To Corpus Christi College, Oxford, as scholar, 16 April 1597; B. A., 9 July 1603; Fellow of Merton College, 1605; M. A., 20 June 1609; Lecturer in Greek to University, 1612. Fellow of Eton College, 24 May 1613 to April 1649. To Holland with Sir Dudley Carleton, as Chaplain, 1616. To Eton, 1619. Canon of Windsor, 23 May, 1639; installed, 27 June; deprived of canonry by Parliamentary Committee, 1642. Tutor to William Salter, in Buckinghamshire, 1649. Returned to Eton. Died there, 19 May 1656. Buried there. *Works:* "Oratio Funebris" (on Sir Thomas Bodley), 1613; "A Sermon," 1617; "Anonymi dissertatio de pace et concordia Ecclesiæ," 1630; "The way towards the finding of a Decision of the Chief Controversie, etc.," (anon.), 1641; "A Tract concerning Schisme," 1642 (anon.; 2nd. edn. same year); "Of the Blasphemie againste the Holy Ghost" (anon.; attrib. to Hales), 1646. *Posthumous:* "Golden Remains," 1659; "Sermons preached at Eton," 1660; "Several Tracts," 1677. *Collected Works:* ed. by Lord Hailes (3 vols.), 1765. —SHARP, R. FARQUHARSON, 1897, *A Dictionary of English Authors, p.* 121.

PERSONAL

Hales, set by himself most gravely did smile
To see them about nothing keep such a coil;
Apollo had spied him, but, knowing his mind,
Past by, and called Falkland that sat just
    behind.
—SUCKLING, SIR JOHN, 1637, *Sessions of the Poets.*

His industry did strive, if it were possible, to equal the largeness of his capacity, whereby he became as great a master of polite, various, and universal learning, as ever yet conversed with books. Proportionate to his reading was his meditation, which furnished him with a judgment beyond the vulgar reach of man, built upon unordinary notions, raised out of strange observations, and comprehensive thoughts within himself. So that he really was a most prodigious example of an acute and piercing wit, of a vast and illimited knowledge, of a severe and profound judgment.—PEARSON, JOHN, 1659, *ed., Golden Remains, Preface.*

At Eaton he lodged (after his sequestration) at the next house (to) the Christopher (inne), where I sawe him, a prettie little man, sanguine, of a cheerfull countenance, very gentile, and courteous; I was received by him with much humanity: he was in a kind of violet-coloured cloath gowne, with buttons and loopes (he wore not a black gowne), and was reading Thomas à Kempis; it was within a yeare before he deceased. He loved Canarie; but moderately, to refresh his spirits. He had a bountifull mind. . . . He lies buried in the church yard at Eaton, under an altar monument of black marble, erected at the sole chardge of Mr. . . . Curwyn, with a too long epitaph. He was no kiff or kin to him.—AUBREY, JOHN, 1669-96, *Brief Lives, ed. Clark, vol.* I, *pp.* 279, 280.

He had read more and carried more about him, in his excellent memory, than any man I ever knew; he was one of the least men in the kingdom, and one of the greatest scholars in Europe.—CLARENDON, LORD (EDWARD HYDE), 1674? *Life*.

Thro' the whole course of his bachelorship there was never any one in the then memory of man (so I have been informed by certain seniors of that coll. at my first coming thereunto) that ever went beyond him for subtle disputations in philosophy, for his eloquent declamations and orations, as also his exact knowledge in the Greek tongue, evidently demonstrated afterwards, not only when he read the Greek lecture in that coll., but also the public lecture of that tongue in the schools. . . . He was a man highly esteemed by learned men beyond and within the seas, from whom he seldom fail'd to receive letters every week, wherein his judgment was desir'd as to several points of learning.—WOOD, ANTHONY, 1691-1721, *Athenæ Oxonienses*.

His great learning and "profound judgment" were combined with the most punctilious integrity and the utmost modesty of demeanor; so that there was no man of the day of whom more people spoke well.—MASSON, DAVID, 1858, *The Life of John Milton, vol.* I, *ch.* vi.

We can readily realise from the whole tenor of his life, as well as of his writings, the picture suggested by Clarendon of a modest, sensitive, yet profound and discerning spirit—hating religious controversy, yet apt and keen in religious argument when once engaged in it—honest and open-minded to a fault, yet with a great power of reserve in him before the unwise and unreflective—loving peace, yet detesting tyranny—and severe to himself, while kind and charitable in all his thoughts of others.—TULLOCH, JOHN, 1872, *Rational Theology and Christian Philosophy in England in the Seventeenth Century, vol.* I, *p.* 218.

There are several Etonians of this century who acquired distinction as churchmen and scholars, whom I have not yet spoken of, but I must not omit in this chapter. First, I will revert to

THE EVER-MEMORABLE JOHN HALES.

Such was the title given by his friends and contemporaries to a learned, ingenious, pious, and kind-hearted man, who became a Fellow of Eton in 1613. The sounding title of "ever-memorable," applied to one whose works now seldom find

a reader, and whose name is rarely mentioned by any modern writer, reminds one of the epithets "Angelic," "Seraphic," "Irrefragable," and the like, which were so liberally bestowed on the once idolized but now neglected Schoolmen. In truth, the reputation of Hales in his own age seems to have been due not so much to any proof of gigantic genius or stupendous learning, as to pleasing powers of conversation, and affability of temper, combined with a fair share of natural ability and an unusual share of industrious energy. Every age has its John Hales.—CREASY, SIR EDWARD, 1876, *Memoirs of Eminent Etonians, p.* 222.

The genial recluse, with his prodigious memory and his keen, rapier-like thrust of argument, was the most loving and tenderhearted of men.—GARDINER, SAMUEL R., 1883, *History of England from the Accession of James I. to the Outbreak of the Civil War, vol.* VIII, *p.* 265.

Pure-minded, simple-hearted little man, reading Thomas-à-Kempis in his violet gown; poor, degraded, but not dishonoured; what a strong, grave protest your quiet, exiled life, self-contained and serious is, against the crude follies, the boisterous energies of the revolution seething and mantling all about you! the clearsighted soul can adopt no party cries, swears allegiance to no frantic school; enlightened, at the mercy of no tendency or prejudice, it resigns all that gave dignity to blessed quiet, and takes the peace without the pomp; with unobtrusive, unpretentious hopes and prospects shattered in the general wreck, the true life-philosopher still finds his treasures in the old books, the eternal thoughts and the kindly offices of retired life.—BENSON, ARTHUR CHRISTOPHER, 1896, *Essays, p.* 17.

GENERAL

Their [Hale's Works] merits are unequal. The best seems to be his discourse on Schism, that on the abuse of hard places of Scripture, and his letters to Sir Dudley Carleton, from the Synod of Dort, in which he gives a good account of that far-famed convention. He was evidently a man superior to many of the prejudices of his age; but if the reader's expectations are raised very greatly by his highsounding title and the testimonies referred to, he will probably be disappointed even by his Golden Remains.—ORME, WILLIAM, 1824, *Biblotheca Biblica.*

John Hales was a man whose reputation was far higher among his contemporaries than his *Remains* (rather unmeaningly called *Golden*) seem to justify. He was admittedly the first Greek scholar of his day. Sir Henry Savill's grand edition of Chrysostom was in reality his work, but the one was Warden, the other Fellow of Merton, and the name of higher position was affixed to the work. In religious principles he was a latitudinarian, like Chillingworth.—PERRY, GEORGE G., 1861, *History of the Church of England, vol.* I, *p.* 566.

If by its political structure the English Church is persecuting, by its doctrinal structure it is tolerant; it needs the reason of the laity too much to refuse it liberty; it lives in a world too cultivated and thoughtful to proscribe thought and culture. John Hales, its eminent doctor, declared several times that he would renounce the Church of England to-morrow, if she insisted on the doctrine that other Christians would be damned; and that men believe other people to be damned only when they desire them to be so. It was he again, a theologian, a prebendary, who advises men to trust to themselves alone in religious matters; to leave nothing for authority, or antiquity, or the majority; to use their own reason in believing, as they use "their own legs in walking;" to act and be men in mind as well as in the rest; and to regard as cowardly and impious the borrowing of doctrine and sloth of thought.—TAINE, H. A., 1871, *History of English Literature, tr.* Van Laun, *vol.* I, *bk.* ii, *ch.* v, *p.* 381.

There is in all our author's writings exactly that which so many theological writings want, the light of a bright, open-eyed, candid intelligence, which sees frequently far beyond the range of the most powerful systematic intellect straight to the truth—"an acute and piercing wit," a wise, calm, and "profound judgment." . . . His accumulated knowledge of books and systems never encumbers him. He never, or rarely, uses it as materials of exposition, or stuff for dilating and parading arguments in themselves worthless, after the prevailing fashion. But all his knowledge has become an enriching basis of his own thought, and raises him above "the vulgar reach of man" to see

for himself clearly and widely. It has entered into the very life of his quick and genial intellect, and contributes to the wealth of his meditative insight, and his tolerant, comprehensive, and sweetly-tempered genius. The simplicity and breadth of his religious thought are astonishing for his time. He goes to the heart of controversies, and distinguishes with a delicate and summary skill the essential from the accidental in religion as in other things. . . . In freedom of thought and clearness of faith, he greatly excels the mere professional divine of any age. He is evangelical without dogmatism, and preaches grace without despising philosophy. At once conservative in feeling, and liberal in opinion, he hates all extremes, as of the nature of falsehood, and a prolific source of wrong. He is the representative—the next after Hooker—of that catholicity yet rationality of Christian sentiment which has been the peculiar glory of the Church of England.—TULLOCH, JOHN, 1872, *Rational Theology and Christian Philosophy in England in the* 17th *Century, vol.* I, *pp.* 221, 222, 260.

Andrew Marvel justly describes Hales as "one of the clearest heads and best prepared breasts in Christendom." The richness of his learning impresses us even less than his felicity in using it. His humour enables him to treat disturbing questions with attractive lightness of touch. His strength lies in an invincible core of common sense, always blended with good feeling, and issuing in a wise and thoughtful charity.—GORDON, ALEXANDER, 1890, *Dictionary of National Biography, vol.* xxiv, *p.* 32.

Hales's literary style is, in the main, the reflection of his lucid manner of thinking. When he argues, he goes straight to the point, and, barring a certain looseness in the construction of his sentences, he is a master of exposition. His illustrations, though copious, never weary the reader, being always the natural overflow of a mind well stocked with learning, and not a mere display of pedantry. There runs through his writings a thin thread of humour characteristic of the man—himself in earnest, but scorning the earnestness about non-essentials which he discovers in others.—WALLACE, W., 1893, *English Prose, ed. Craik, vol.* II, *p.* 185.

The large and generous current of

Hales' human sympathy, and his appreciation of all that is good wherever it is to be found, are characteristic features of his writings, and make him one of the most delightful, stimulating, and wholesome of the divines of the seventeenth century. He appears as quite unconnected historically with the School of Cambridge divines who came, at a later time, to be spoken of as the "Latitude-men," though his tone is in many respects similar to theirs.—DOWDEN, JOHN, 1897, *Outlines of the History of the Theological Literature of the Church of England*, p. 165.

James Usher

1580–1656

James Usher, or Ussher, D. D., born at Dublin, Ireland, Jan. 4, 1580, educated at Trinity Coll., Dublin, where he became a fellow; took orders in the Church of England 1601; became chancellor of the cathedral of St. Patrick 1607; was professor of divinity at the University of Dublin 1607–20; drew up the Articles of Faith of the Irish Church 1615; became bishop of Meath 1620, archbishop of Armagh and primate of Ireland 1623; had his house destroyed by the Irish rebels 1641, while visiting England, in which country he thenceforth remained; was appointed by Charles I. bishop of Carlisle, and was preacher of Lincoln's Inn 1647–54, residing chiefly at Oxford. Author of numerous theological treatises, mostly in Latin. His *Annales Veteris et Novi Testamenti* contain a scheme of biblical chronology, since printed in the margin of the authorized version of the Bible, though now admitted to be inexact. Died March 21, 1656.—BARNARD AND GUYOT, 1885, *eds.*, *Johnson's New General Cyclopædia*, vol. II, p. 1412.

Wrote "Annales V. et N. Testamenti, à primâ Mundi Origine deducta ad extremum Reipubliæ Judaiccæ Excidium Ecclesiarum"; "Gravissimæ Questionis de Christianarum in Occidentis præsertim partibus" (1613); "Answer to a Challenge of a Jesuit in Ireland" [William Malone] (1624); "A Discourse of the Religion anciently professed by the Irish and British" (1622); "Britannicarum Ecclesiarum Antiquitates et Primordia" (1639); "The Original of Bishops and Metropolitans" (1641); "Direction concerning the Lyturgy and Episcopal Government" (1642); "Vox Hiberniæ: or, rather the Voyce of the Lord from Ireland" (1642); "Immanuel: or, the Mystery of the Incarnation of the Son of God" (1638); "The Principles of the Christian Religion" (1644); "Chronologia Sacra et de Romanæ Ecclesiæ Symbolo Apostolico Vetere" (1660); "Episcopal and Presbyterian Government conjoyned" (1679); and many other *Works:* the whole of which were collected and published, with a "Life of the author, by Dr. Ebrington, 1847.—ADAMS, W. DAVENPORT, 1877, *Dictionary of English Literature*, p. 724.

PERSONAL

I heard the Common Prayer (a rare thing in these days) in St. Peter's at Paul's Wharf, London; and in ye morning the Archbishop of Armagh, that pious person and learned man, Usher, in Lincoln's Inn Chapel.—EVELYN, JOHN, 1649, *Diary*, *March 25.*

He was easy, affable, and chearful in conversation, and extremely charitable. He was of so sweet a temper that I never heard he did an ill office to any one man, or revenged any of those that had been done to him. He envied no man's happiness, or vilified their persons or parts; nor was he apt to censure or condemn any man upon bare reports. Though he could rebuke sharply in the cause of virtue and religion, yet he was not easily provoked to passion.—PARR, RICHARD, 1686, *Life of Usher.*

Talking of the Irish Clergy, he said, "Swift was a man of great parts, and the instrument of much good to his country. Berkeley was a profound scholar, as well as a man of fine imagination; but "Usher," he said, "was the great luminary of the Irish Church; and a greater," he added, "no church could boast of; at least in modern times."—JOHNSON, SAMUEL, 1770, *Life by Boswell.*

His mildness of disposition, and the faculty of seeing the defects of all parties which belongs to the student, prevented his exercising the influence which his talents would have warranted. It is as a scholar that he is remembered, and it is in that that he is linked to the leaders of the Caroline Church. Men of both parties turned from the turmoil of the war and of political change to talk of Ussher's manuscripts, of the Septuagint, the Samaritan Pentateuch, and the Syriac version, of the history of Episcopacy, and of the Ignatian letters. Literature, indeed, in him as in many others of the King's party, prevented the rift between the men of King and Parliament being very deep or lasting.—HUTTON, WILLIAM HOLDEN, 1895, *Social England, ed. Traill, vol.* IV, *p.* 291.

Cromwell required that a public funeral should be accorded to the great Archbishop, and that he should be buried with all honours in Westminster Abbey. The spot chosen for his final resting-place was in St. Paul's Chapel, close to the monument of his first teacher, Fullerton, and near the steps leading to Henry Seventh's Chapel. We are told that a large concourse of people met the funeral *cortège*, including many of the nobility and London clergy. So great was the concourse that a military guard was found necessary. Only on this occasion was the Burial Service of the Church of England read within the Abbey walls during the entire period of the Commonwealth. The sermon was preached by the Archbishop's chaplain, Dr. Bernard, and afterwards published. He took for his text the suitable words, "And Samuel died, and all Israel were gathered together and lamented him, and buried him." No stone marks the spot where the Archbishop sleeps. The funeral expenses, it may be observed, reached a far higher sum than the £200 voted for the purpose by Cromwell, and the deficit was made good by his family, who could ill spare the expense.—CARR, J. A., 1895, *The Life and Times of James Ussher, p.* 370.

ANNALS

1650-54

I have with no small eagerness and delight turned over these your learned and accurate "Annals," wondering not a little at that your indefatigable labour which you have bestowed on a work fetched together out of such a world of monuments of antiquity; whereby your Grace hath better merited the title of χαλκευτερος and φυλοπονος than those on whom it

was formerly bestowed.—HALL, JOSEPH, 1650? *Letter to Archbishop Usher.*

Along with the reading of the historical books of the Scripture I would recommend Usher's Annals, which is a work perfect in its kind, and which well digested will give a very sound knowledge of the history of the world, sacred and profane, to the destruction of the second temple; which knowledge will upon innumerable occasions be of unspeakable use.—WOTTON, WILLIAM, 1726-34? *Thoughts Concerning a Proper Method of Studying Divinity.*

This is a work of great labour and research, which has been followed by the greater part of modern chronologers, though the system of Dr. Hales is perhaps more correct.—ORME, WILLIAM, 1824, *Bibliotheca Biblica, p.* 442.

Our learned Archbishop Usher might there have been named, since the first part of his "Annals of the Old Testament," which goes down to the year of the world 3828, was published in 1650. The second part followed in 1654. This has been the chronology generally adopted by English historians, as well as by Bossuet, Calmet, and Rollin, so that for many years it might be called the orthodox scheme of Europe. No former annals of the world has been so exact in marking dates, and collating sacred history with profane. It was therefore exceedingly convenient for those, who, possessing no sufficient leisure or learning for these inquiries, might very reasonably confide in such authority.—HALLAM, HENRY, 1837-39, *Introduction to the Literature of Europe, pt.* iv, *ch.* i, *par.* 23.

GENERAL

Archbishop Usher, that prodigy of learning and industry.—NICOLSON, WILLIAM, 1724, *Irish Historical Library, Appendix.*

All that learning can extract from the rubbish of the Dark Ages is copiously stated by Archbishop Usher in his "Britannicarum Ecclesiarum Antiquitates."— GIBBON, EDWARD, 1776-78, *Decline and Fall of the Roman Empire, ch.* xxxvii, *note.*

The first writer who instituted a systematic inquiry into the Septuagint version was Archbishop Usher. . . . This is a work of great merit; it displays much original inquiry, and may be regarded as the ground-work of later publications on the Septuagint.—MARSH, HERBERT, 1809-11, *Lectures on Divinity, Part II., Lectures* xii, *p.* 121.

The writings of our Irish primate, Usher, who maintained the antiquity of his order, but not upon such high ground as many in England would have desired, are known for their extraordinary learning, in which he has perhaps never been surpassed by an English writer. But for judgement, and calm appreciation of evidence, the name of Usher has not been altogether so much respected by posterity as it was by his contemporaries.— HALLAM, HENRY, 1837-39, *Introduction to the Literature of Europe, pt.* iii, *ch.* ii, *par.* 66.

He was one of the most wonderful men of that wonderful age. . . . His writings . . . contain an invaluable mass of historical and ecclesiastical information and of controversial and practical divinity.—BICKERSTETH, EDWARD, 1844, *The Christian Student, pp.* 245, 246.

His preference had been for the lighter forms of literature. He knew Spenser, and did not think it impossible that he might himself be a poet. As he grew older, Nature corrected the mistake. Struck one day by Cicero's saying: "*Nescire quid antea quam natus sis acciderit, id est semper esse puerum*" (" Not to know what happened before you were born, is to be always a child"), he found his genius revealed to him in the fascination of the phrase, and from that day devoted himself to history. Before he had reached his thirtieth year he was profound in universal chronology, and known to Camden and other English scholars as the most learned of Irishmen. . . . It was the pride of the English Calvinists about the year 1632, when the learning of Laud and other prelates of his school was mentioned, to point across the Channel to the great Calvinistic Primate as a scholar who outweighed them all.—MASSON, DAVID, 1858, *The Life of John Milton, vol.* I, *ch.* vi.

Usher's works are numerous, and were regarded by his contemporaries as marvels of research. It may be said of the majority of them, however, that the growth of knowledge has thrown them decidedly into the shade.—HART, JOHN S., 1872, *A Manual of English Literature, p.* 169.

Argument means for Ussher the accumulation of authorities; authorities, indeed, weighed with precision, criticised as to their authenticity, but in the last result accepted as authoritative. And with this is connected his renunciation of style; for to style the abundance of quotations must needs be fatal. Fragments pieced together from other men's works, even where translation is freely used, cannot but lack the unity which the impress of a single personality gives. Ussher's writing is always a mosaic of quotations. His learning is immense. At an early age, so his biographers tell us, he sat down and read the fathers straight through. Chroniclers, schoolmen, the writers of Greece and Rome, all are at his fingers' ends. He has wandered in the byeways of Celtic and Scandinavian lore. And in this he was happy, that by his time the sum-total of things knowable had not so swelled as to be beyond the compass of one intellect; so that he does not appear a mere specialist, but a true scholar, with a wide sweep and an adequate survey of knowledge. Moreover, he has at least one gift—an architectonic gift—of style.—CHAMBERS, EDMUND K., 1893, *English Prose, ed. Craik, vol.* II, *p.* 158.

Selden calls him "learned to a miracle" ("ad miraculum doctus"). To estimate his labours aright would be the work of a company of experts. His learning was for use; and his topics were suggested by the controversies of his age, which he was resolved to probe to their roots in the ground of history. . . . As a writer, his passion for exactness (which made him extremely sensitive on the subject of unauthorised publication) exhibits itself in his use of materials. He lets his sources tell their story in their own words, incorporating them into his text with clear but sparing comment. Few faults have been found with his accuracy; his conclusions have been mended by further application of his own methods. His merits as an investigator of early Irish history are acknowledged by his countrymen of all parties; his contributions to the history of the creed and to the treatment of the Ignatian problem are recognised by modern scholars as of primary value; his chronology is still the standard adopted in editions of the English Bible.—GORDON, ALEXANDER, 1899, *Dictionary of National Biography, vol.* LVIII, *p.* 70.

William Harvey

1578–1657

Born at Folkestone, Kent, April 1, 1578: died at London, June 3, 1657. A celebrated English physician, physiologist, and anatomist: the discoverer of the circulation of the blood. He was educated at Canterbury and Cambridge (Gonville and Caius College), where he graduated in 1597; studied at Padua; took the degree of doctor of medicine at Cambridge in 1602; became physician of St. Bartholomew's Hospital in 1609; was Lumleian lecturer at the College of Physicians 1615–56; and became physician extraordinary to James I. in 1618. During the civil war he sided with the Royalists, was at the battle of Edgehill, and went to Oxford with the king. His chief works are "Exercitatio de motu cordis et sanguinis" ("Essay on the Motion of the Heart and the Blood," 1628), "Exercitationes de generatione animliaum" (1651). —SMITH, BENJAMIN E., 1894–97, *The Century Cyclopedia of Names, p.* 484.

PERSONAL

He did delight to be in the darke, and told me he could then best contemplate. He had a house heretofore at Combe, in Surrey, a good aire and prospect, where he had caves made in the earth, in which in summer time he delighted to meditate. —He was pretty well versed in the Mathematiques, and had made himselfe master of Mr. Oughtred's Clavis Math. in his old age; and I have seen him perusing it, and working problems, not long before he dyed, and that booke was alwayes in his meditating apartment. . . . He was not tall; but of the lowest stature, round faced, olivaster complexion; little eie, round, very black, full of spirit; his haire was black as a raven, but quite white 20 yeares before he dyed. . . . I have heard him say, that after his booke of the Circulation of the Blood came-out, that he fell mightily in his practize, and that 'twas beleeved by the vulgar that he was crack-brained; and all the physitians were against his opinion, and envyed him; many wrote against him, as Dr. Primige, Paracisanus, etc. (vide Sir George Ent's booke). With much adoe at last, in about 20 or 30 yeares time, it was received in all the Universities in the world; and, as Mr. Hobbes sayes in his book "De Corpore," *he is the only man, perhaps, that ever lived to see his owne doctrine established in his life time.* He understood Greek and Latin pretty well, but was no critique, and he wrote very bad Latin. . . . All his profession would allowe him to be an excellent anatomist, but I never heard of any that admired his therapeutique way. I knew severall practisers in London that would not have given 3*d*. for one of his bills; and that a man could hardly tell by one of his bills what he did

aime at.—AUBREY, JOHN, 1669–96, *Brief Lives, ed. Clark, vol.* I, *pp.* 298, 300, 302.

Dr. Harvey was not only an excellent physician; he was also an excellent man: his modesty, candour, and piety, were equal to his knowledge: the farther he penetrated into the wonders of nature, the more was he inclined to venerate the author of it.—GRANGER, JAMES, 1769–1824, *Biographical History of England, vol.* III, *p.* 115.

Twice in the past thirty years, I have visited the vault at Hempstead, and viewed the receptacle that holds, like an Egyptian mummy-case, the remains. In 1848 the leaden case was lying with several others —there are over forty of them—near one of the open gratings of the vault. There were many loose stones upon it, and a large hole in the lead, which let in water. In 1859 Drs. Quain and Stewart, who went to the vault by request of the fellows of the Royal College of Physicians, found the remains in even a worse state, for the leaden case was then almost full of dirty water. In 1868 I found the case removed from its previous position, and lying apart in the vault, which had been repaired. In the case there was still an opening, but the water had either been removed or had escaped by evaporation. I was able to throw a reflected light into this opening, but I could see no remains, and I think that there is little left of what was once the bodily form of our greatest English anatomist. I would that what there may be, were safely placed in the mausoleum of the illustrious,—the Abbey of Westminster. John Hunter and David Livingstone were nobly companioned by William Harvey.—RICHARDSON, BENJAMIN W., 1878, *William Harvey, The Gentleman's Magazine, vol.* 242, *p.* 477.

GENERAL

Devoting myself to discern the use and utility of the movements of the heart in animals, in a great number of vivisections, I found at first the subject so full of difficulties that I thought for a long time, with Fracastor, that the secret was known to God alone. I could distinguish neither in what manner the systole and diastole took place, nor at what moment the dilatation and constriction occurred, owing to the celerity of the movements of the heart, which in most animals is executed in the twinkling of an eye, or like the flash of lightning. I floated undecided, without knowing on what opinion to rest. Finally, from redoubled care and attention, by multiplying and varying my experiments, and by comparing the various results, I believed I had put my finger on the truth, and commenced unravelling the labyrinth. I believed I had seized the correct idea of the movement of the heart and arteries, as well as their true use. From that time I did not cease to communicate my views either to my friends, or to the public in my academical course.— HARVEY, WILLIAM, 1628, *Essay on the Motion of the Heart and the Blood.*

Thus Harvey sought for truth in truth's own book,
The creatures, which by God Himself was writ ;
And wisely thought 'twas fit
Not to read comments only upon it,
  But on th' original itself to look.
Methinks in art's great circle others stand
Lock'd up together hand in hand,
  Ev'ry one leads as he is led ;
  The same bare path they tread,
And dance, like fairies, a fantastick round,
With neither change of motion, nor their ground :
  Had Harvey to this road confin'd his wit,
  His noble circle of the blood, had been untrodden yet

—COWLEY, ABRAHAM, 1656? *Ode.*

Harvey is entitled to the glory of having made, by reasoning alone, without any mixture of accident, a capital discovery in one of the most important branches of science. He had also the happiness of establishing at once his theory on the most solid and convincing proofs ; and posterity has added little to the arguments suggested by his industry and ingenuity. His treatise of the circulation of the blood is farther embellished by that warmth and spirit which so naturally accompany the genius of invention.—HUME, DAVID, 1762, *The History of England, The Commonwealth.*

It may indeed be thought wonderful, that Servetus, Columbus, or Cæsalpin should not have more distinctly apprehended the consequences of what they maintained, since it seems difficult to conceive the lesser circulation without the greater ; but the defectiveness of their views is not to be alleged as a counterbalance to the more steady sagacity of Harvey. The solution of their falling so short is, that they were right, not indeed quite by guess, but upon insufficient proof : and that the consciousness of this, embarrassing their minds, prevented them from deducing inferences which now appear irresistible. In every department of philosophy, the researches of the first inquirers have often been arrested by similar causes. Harvey is the author of a treatise on generation, wherein he maintains that all animals, including men, are derived from an egg. In this book we first find an argument maintained against spontaneous generation, which, in the case of the lower animals, had been generally received. Sprengel thinks this treatise prolix, and not equal to the author's reputation. It was first published in 1651.— HALLAM, HENRY, 1837-39, *Introduction to the Literature of Europe*, pt. III, *ch.* ix, *par.* 18, 19.

In truth, the great intellectual achievement of Harvey consisted precisely in the fact that his discovery was made without even that degree of ocular verification (imperfect though it be) which subsequent inquiry has rendered possible. The difficulty that confronted him, and of which his theory failed to take account, was the mode in which the blood passed from the small arteries into the small veins. These vessels he and others could see and recognise by dissection of a dead animal's body. But the union of an artery and a vein he could never see. That in some unexplained manner the blood did pass from the final branching of an artery to the final branching of a vein he felt as scientifically certain as though his eye had seen it ; but the fine network of capillary tubes which unite the two systems of vessels was reserved for Malpighi's microscope. — BRIDGES, J. H., 1876, *Harvey and Vivisection, Fortnightly Review*, N. S., *vol.* 20, *p.* 15.

Harvey was the favoured friend of his sovereign, the honoured Nestor of his profession, the pride of his countrymen. If he lived now, and were guilty of serving mankind to the same extent and in the same way, so far from any such marks of favour reaching him, he would find himself to be a mark of a different kind—a mark, I mean, for immeasurable calumny and scandalous vituperation; and, though his professional brethren would surely pay him all honour, so far from being the pride of his countrymen, a goodly number of them, of all grades in the social scale, would be spending a world of energy in the endeavour to give him the legal status of a burglar.—HUXLEY, THOMAS HENRY, 1878, *William Harvey, Fortnightly Review*, N. S., *vol.* 23, *p.* 189.

From the MS. volume of Harvey's lectures, in the British Museum, which, after having been lost sight of, has been recently rediscovered, he appears to have fully established his doctrines in 1616, but first promulgated them in his lectures in 1619, after reiterated experiments and long and patient study. His immortal "Treatise on the Motion of the Heart and Blood," dedicated to Charles I, was published at Frankfort in 1628, when he had attained his fiftieth year, when his reputation as a physician had been long established, and when his brilliant discoveries were the theme of discussion and admiration in all the seats of learning throughout Europe—not that his doctrine was accepted without opposition and even scorn and contempt—for he did not escape the opprobrium and contradictory treatment that has befallen most other great discoverers. At first his doctrines were denied and repudiated, subsequently it was affirmed that they contained nothing that was not already known.—BENNETT, JAMES RISDON, 1880, *William Harvey, Leisure Hour, vol.* 29, *p.* 710.

The modern controversy (Dr. George Johnson, "Harveian Oration," 1882; Willis, "William Harvey, a History of the Discovery of the Circulation of the Blood," 1878) as to whether the discovery was taken from some previous author is sufficiently refuted by the opinion of the opponents of his views in his own time, who agreed in denouncing the doctrine as new; by the laborious method of gradual demonstration obvious in his book and lectures; and, lastly, by the complete absence of lucid demonstration of the action of the heart and course of the blood in Cæsalpinus, Servetus, and all others who have been suggested as possible originals of the discovery. It remains to this day the greatest of the discoveries of physiology, and its whole honour belongs to Harvey. —MOORE, NORMAN, 1891, *Dictionary of National Biography, vol.* XXV, *p.* 97.

His other celebrated work, the "De Generatione," belongs to the next period. Though this work has not the importance of the "De Motu Cordis," it is remarkable that the doctrine of "epigenesis" expounded in it—the theory that the development of the embryo takes place by the successive addition of parts, not by the unfolding of a complete miniature present from the first—is substantially that which is now held.—WHITTAKER, T. 1895, *Social England, ed. Traill, vol.* IV. *p.* 83.

William Bradford
1590-1657

Governor of the Plymouth Colony, 1621-57. He left in manuscript a "History of Plymouth Plantation," the leisurely composition of 20 years, which was drawn from by Morton, Prince, and Hutchinson as a basis for their respective histories, and after being lost for nearly a century was found in the library of the Bishop of London in 1855, and published soon after. He was the earliest American historian, and his work exhibits judicial impartiality, broad conceptions, and a direct, vigorous style. —ADAMS, OSCAR FAY, 1897, *A Dictionary of American Authors, p.* 35.

HISTORY OF PLYMOUTH PLANTATION

Governor Bradford's reputation as an author is decidedly of a posthumous character. He left a MS. history, in a folio volume of 270 pages, of the Plymouth colony, from the formation of their church in 1602 to 1647. It furnished the material for Morton's Memorial, was used by Prince and Governor Hutchinson in the preparation of their histories, and deposited, with the collection of papers of the former, in the library of the Old South Church, in Boston. During the desecration of this edifice as a riding-school by the British in the Revolutionary war, the MS. disappeared. A copy of a portion closing with the year 1620, in the handwriting of Nathaniel Morton, was discovered by the Rev. Alexander Young in the library of the First Church, at Plymouth, and printed in his "Chronicles of the Pilgrim Fathers of the Colony of Plymouth," in 1841. A "letterbook," in which Bradford preserved copies of his correspondence, met with a similar fate, a portion only having been rescued from a grocer's shop in Halifax, and published in the Collections of the Massachusetts Historical Society, in 1794, vol. iii. of the first series of Collections, with a fragment of a poem on New England. These, with two other specimens of a few lines each, first published by the same Society in 1838, form, with the exception of some slight controversial pieces, the whole of his literary productions.—DUYCKINCK, EVERT A. AND GEORGE L., 1855-65-75, *Cyclopædia of American Literature, ed. Simons, vol.* I, *p.* 35.

William Bradford, of the Mayflower and Plymouth Rock, deserves the pre-eminence of being called the father of American history. We pay to him also that homage which we tender to those authors who even by their writings give to us the impression that, admirable as they may be in authorship, behind their authorship is something still more admirable— their own manliness. . . . Governor Bradford wrote of events that had passed under his own eye, and that had been shaped by his own hand; and he had every qualification of a trustworthy narrator. His mind was placid, grave, well-poised; he was a student of many books and of many languages; and being thus developed both by letters and by experience, he was able to tell well the truth of history as it had unfolded itself during his own strenuous and benignant career. His history is an orderly, lucid, and most instructive work; it contains many tokens of its author's appreciation of the nature and requirements of historical writing; and though so recently published in a perfect form, it must henceforward take its true place at the head of American historical literature, and win for its author the patristic dignity that we have ascribed to him.—TYLER, MOSES COIT, 1878, *A History of American Literature, 1607-1676, vol.* I, *pp.* 116, 118.

Though not enjoying special educational advantages in early life, Bradford possessed more literary culture than was common among those of similar occupation to himself. He had some knowledge of Latin and Greek, and knew sufficient Hebrew to enable him to "see with his own eyes the ancient oracles of God in their native beauty." He was also well read in history and philosophy, and an adept in the theological discussion peculiar to the time. He employed much of his leisure in literary composition.—HENDERSON, T. F., 1886, *Dictionary of National Biography, vol.* VI, *p.* 163.

Bradford was a forerunner of literature, not a historian. He stands not as an early Palfrey or Bancroft, but ranks with the useful company of annalists, diarists, and autobiographers, few of whom have equalled him in strength of character and fidelity of purpose. He was the first Pilgrim writer in America, the first recorder of doings in New England, and a storyteller of considerable power, as well as of absolute truthfulness in matters of fact. —RICHARDSON, CHARLES F., 1887, *American Literature, 1607-1885, vol.* I, *p.* 75.

John Cleveland

1613-1658

A native of Loughborough, Leicestershire, was educated at Christ's College, and St. John's College, Cambridge. He had the honour of being the first poetical champion of the royal cause, and suffered imprisonment when the opposition prevailed. He was for some time a tutor at St. John's College, and subsequently lived in chambers at Gray's Inn, where he died in 1659. "The King's Disguise," 1646, 4to. "A London Diurnal-maker," &c., 1647, '54, 4to. "The Rustic Rampant," 1658, 8vo. "Poems, Orations, and Epistles," 1660, 12mo. "Petition to the Lord Protector for the Scots Rebel; a satirical Poem." "Works," 1687, 8vo.—ALLIBONE, S. AUSTIN, 1854-58, *Dictionary of English Literature, vol.* I, *p.* 394.

PERSONAL

He was a fellow of St. John's Colledge in Cambridge, where he was more taken notice of for his being an eminent disputant, than a good poet. Being turned out of his fellowship for a malignant he came to Oxford, where the king's army was, and was much caressed by them. He went thence to the garrison at Newark upon Trent, where upon some occasion of drawing of articles, or some writing, he would needs add a short conclusion, viz. "and hereunto we annex our lives, as a labell to our trust." After the king was beaten out of the field, he came to London, and retired in Grayes Inne. He, and Sam. Butler, &c. of Grayes Inne, had a clubb every night. He was a comely plump man, good curled haire, darke browne. Dyed of the scurvy, and lies buried in St. Andrew's church, in Holborne, anno Domini 165. .—AUBREY, JOHN, 1669-96, *Brief Lives, ed. Clark, vol.* I, *p.* 174.

In the character of Cleveland there is much to admire. He was steadfast in his principles when such men as Waller cringed and vacillated; he entered into the thick of the conflict with arm and pen while Cowley and Davenant fled to the French court, serving the cause far away from the actual scenes of struggle and distress.—SCOLLARD, CLINTON, 1893, *A Forgotten Poet, The Dial, vol.* 14, *p.* 270.

GENERAL

Admired Cleveland.—DANIEL, GEORGE, 1647, *A Vindication of Poesy.*

He was justly esteemed a man of wit; but his writings abound with strained and far-fetched metaphors, which is a fault objected to Butler himself. That great poet has condescended to imitate, or copy Cleveland, in more instances than occurred to Dr Grey in his notes upon "Hudibras." —GRANGER, JAMES, 1769-1824, *Biographical History of England, vol,* iii, *p.* 127.

Of all the cavalier poets, the one who did his cause the heartiest and stoutest service, and who, notwithstanding much carelessness or ruggedness of execution, possessed perhaps, even considered simply as a poet, the richest and most various faculty was John Cleveland, the most popular verse-writer of his own day, the most neglected of all his contemporaries ever since. Among the one hundred and sixty-one poets, from Robert of Gloucester to Sir Francis Fane, whose choicest relics furnish out Ellis's three volumes of Specimens, the name of Cleveland does not occur. Nor is his poetry included either in Anderson's or in Chalmers's collection. Yet for nearly twenty years he was held to be the greatest among living English poets. . . . Cleveland is commonly regarded as a mere dealer in satire and invective, and as having no higher qualities than a somewhat rude force and vehemence. His prevailing fault is a straining after vigor and concentration of expression; and few of his pieces are free from a good deal of obscurity, harshness, or other disfigurement, occasioned by this habit or tendency working in association with an alert, ingenious, and fertile fancy, a neglect of and apparently a contempt for neatness of finish, and the turn for quaintness and quibbling characteristic of the school to which he belongs—for Cleveland must be considered as essentially one of the old wit poets. Most of his poems seem to have been thrown off in haste, and never to have been afterwards corrected or revised. There are, however, among them some that are not without vivacity and sprightliness; and others of his more solemn verses have all the dignity that might be expected from his prose letter to Cromwell.—CRAIK, GEORGE L., 1861, *A Compendious History of English Literature and of the English Language, vol.* II, *pp.* 33, 35.

A boisterous, turbulent royalist.— ARNOLD, THOMAS, 1868-75, *Chaucer to Wordsworth, p.* 204.

The Cavalier Poet. A name given to John Cleveland, at one time a favorite and successful English poet, but now almost forgotten.—FREY, ALBERT R., 1888, *Sobriquets and Nicknames, p.* 60.

Though the perusal of Cleveland's work is likely to afford but little pleasure, there are reasons why he should not fall into utter oblivion. He was one of those men in whom lay the possibilities of more than ordinary, if not of great, achievement. The spirit of the age into which he was born was adverse to the development of his finest powers. He saw dimly,—never clearly,—that the poetic tide was setting toward wrong channels, yet he had not the force to stem it. Had kindlier influences been brought to bear upon his life, had peace instead of turmoil surrounded him in his mature years, he might have made a strong resistance to the growing flood, though he never could more than slightly have diverted it, so irresistible was its impetus. . . . Cleveland was probably the first English poet to make deliberate use of the dactyl and anapest,—that is, if we do not take into account the pre-Chaucerian rhymesters. Here was his opportunity of winning for himself a permanent place in literature; and had he not been turned aside by force of circumstances, those ear-catching measures that have so delighted latter-day readers and poets might have been given to the language more than a century earlier. In some of Cleveland's political pieces is heard the trip of the anapest, and also in a rollicking poem reminiscent of the poet's early Cambridge days. In a fantastic, impetuous lyric, "Mark Antony," the dactyls go madly chasing one another. In form this is the precise counterpart of Scott's famous song in the "Lady of the Lake,"—

"Row, vassals, row for the pride of the highlands."

May it not be possible that Scott, poring over an unearthed copy of Cleveland's poems (almost as little known in Scott's time as now), came upon and was fascinated by the stanza in which the whimsical poem is cast, and adopted it for his own uses?—Scollard, Clinton, 1893, *A Forgotten Poet, The Dial, vol.* 14, *pp.* 268, 269.

Besides his numerous satires, Cleveland wrote several fulsome panegyrics on Prince Rupert, Laud, and other leaders of the royalist party. More notable than these are his non-political verses. Though disfigured often by extravagant conceits, and not unfrequently by grossness, they are melodious and polished effusions, comparatively free from the careless disregard of metre and rhyme that spoils much of the work of Cartwright, Suckling, and other Caroline poets.—Masterman, J. Howard B., 1897, *The Age of Milton, p.* 140.

Richard Lovelace

1618-1658

Richard Lovelace was born in Woolwich, Kent, England, in 1618. He was graduated at Oxford in 1636, and went to court. Anthony Wood praises him extravagantly for beauty and amiability. He entered the royal service, and rose to the rank of colonel. For delivering to the Long Parliament a petition for the restoration of the king he was thrown into prison until he could procure heavy bail. He entered the French service in 1646, and was wounded at the siege of Dunkirk. He died in 1658, in extreme poverty, having spent a fortune in the royalist cause. He published "The Scholar," a comedy; "The Soldier," a tragedy (both of which are lost); and two volumes of lyrics addressed to Lucasta.—Johnson Rossiter, 1875, *Little Classics. Authors, p.* 159.

PERSONAL

He was an extraordinary handsome man, but prowd.—Aubrey, John, 1669-96, *Brief Lives, ed. Clark, vol.* II, *p.* 37.

Being then accounted the most amiable and beautiful person that ever eye beheld, a person also of innate modesty, virtue and courtly deportment, which made him then, but especially after, when he retired to the great city, much admired and adored by the female sex. In 1636, when the King and Queen were for some days entertained at Oxon, he was, at the request of a great Lady belonging to the Queen, made to the Archb. of Cant. then Chancellor of the University, actually created, among other persons of quality, Master of

Arts, tho' but of two years standing; at which time his conversation being made public, and consequently his ingenuity and generous soul discovered, he became as much admired by the male, as before by the female, sex. . . . He died in a very mean lodging in Gun-powder Alley near Shoe-lane, and was buried at the West-end of the Church of S. Bride alias Bridget in London, near to the body of his kinsman Will. Lovelace of Greys-Inn Esq; in sixteen hundred fifty and eight, having before been accounted by all those that well knew him, to have been a person well vers'd in the Greek and Lat. poets, in music whether practical or theoretical, instrumental or vocal, and in other things befitting a gentleman.—WOOD, ANTHONY, 1691–1721, *Athenæ Oxonienses, vol.* II, *ff.* 228, 229.

The most notable instance of inconstancy related in the "loves of the poets" is that of Lucy Sacheverell, to whom Col. Lovelace, the Philip Sidney of Charles I's court, was warmly attached. He celebrated her accomplishments in some exquisite poetry; but, on his being taken prisoner in one of the wars of the time, and reported to be dead, she hastily married another. He soon returned to his native land, imprecated divers anathemas on the sex, and declined into a vagabond, —dying perhaps of a malady, common enough in dark ages, but now happily banished from genteel society, a broken heart. —WHIPPLE, EDWIN P., 1847–71, *Authors in their Relation to Life, Literature and Life, p.* 32.

Aubrey says that Lovelace's death took place in a cellar in Long Acre, and adds: "Mr. Edm. Wylde, etc., had made a collection for him and given him money." But Aubrey's authority is not valued against Wood's. He is to be read like a proper gossip, whose accounts we may pretty safely reject or believe as it suits other testimony.—HUNT, LEIGH, 1848, *The Town, ch.* iii, *note.*

Faults and virtues, Richard Lovelace, as a man and as a writer, may be taken as an impersonation of the cavalier of the civil wars, with much to charm the reader, and still more to captivate the fair.— MITFORD, MARY RUSSELL, 1851, *Recollections of A Literary Life, p.* 295.

Lucy Sacheverell married another, on a false report that Richard Lovelace had fallen in foreign war, and he was twice for years in prison, and died miserably at forty; but somehow we cannot think that the bright essence of the most ideal of English knights, after Sir Philip Sidney, was permanently subdued by adverse fate. Who shall say that the mystical reunion foreshadowed in that last stanza may not actually have taken place far outside of these mundane conditions, which the poet invariably treated with a kind of angelic scorn?—PRESTON, HARRIET W., 1879, *The Latest Songs of Chivalry, Atlantic Monthly, vol.* 43, *p.* 21.

There is no reason to suppose that Richard Lovelace, the poet of Bethersden, was ever married. He played an active part in the stormy drama of the great English Rebellion, his natural extravagance and unswerving loyalty, at a period when loyalty was more expensive than any extravagance, must have brought him at an early period into serious pecuniary difficulties, and for a part of his brief career he was probably, like his father, a soldier of fortune. When not actually in military service he was either plotting or in prison, and his romantic life closed in obscurity and wretchedness. In the short period of his Court life he was apparently a great favourite with women; we have the assurance of Wood that he was the handsomest man of his time; and to the exterior graces of his person were united a cultivated and brilliant mind, a refined courtesy of manner, and a disposition at once gentle and heroic. Lucasta and Althea are the subjects of his amorous verses; a third, Amarantha, seems to have been another name for Lucasta, to whom we may conclude, from the evidence of the poems themselves, that he was actually betrothed. The seeds of future domestic happiness were therefore sown, and in a happier time might have borne rich fruit to the unhappy poet. As it is, there is no evidence forthcoming to contradict the story preserved by Wood, and which has been already referred to, except the fact that the posthumous poems of Richard Lovelace contain no reference to Lucasta's broken troth.—WAITE, ARTHUR E., 1884, *Richard Lovelace, Gentleman's Magazine, vol.* 257, *p.* 474.

Lovelace was buried in St. Bride's Church, Fleet Street, "at the west end of the church;" but the building was destroyed in the Great Fire of 1666. The present St. Bride's was built by Wren, and contains no memorial to the poet.— HUTTON, LAURENCE, 1885, *Literary Landmarks of London, p.* 199.

GENERAL

"Lucasta:" Epodes, Odes, Sonnets, Songs, &c. Lond. 1649, Oct. The reason why he gave that title was, because, some time before, he had made his amours to a gentlewoman of great beauty and fortune named Lucy Sacheverel, whom he usually called *Lux casta;* but she upon a strong report that Lovelace was dead of his wound received at Dunkirk, soon after married.—WOOD, ANTHONY, 1691–1721, *Athenæ Oxonienses, vol.* II, *f.* 228.

His pieces, which are light and easy, had been models in their way were their simplicity but equal to their spirit: they were the offerings of gallantry and amusement, and, as such, are not to be reduced to the test of serious criticism.—HEADLEY, HENRY, 1787, *Select Beauties of Ancient English Poetry, vol.* I, *pp* lvi, lvii.

Lovelace is chiefly known by a single song: his other poetry is much inferior; and indeed it may be generally remarked, that the flowers of our early verse, both in the Elizabethan and the subsequent age, have been well culled by good taste and a friendly spirit of selection. We must not judge of them very favorably, by the extracts of Headley or Ellis.—HALLAM, HENRY, 1837–39, *Introduction to the Literature of Europe, pt.* iii, *ch.* v, *par.* 56.

It was worth while, perhaps, to reprint Lovelace, if only to show what dull verses may be written by a man who has made one lucky hit. . . . He is to be classed with the *lucky* authors who, without great powers, have written one or two pieces so facile in thought and fortunate in phrase as to be carried lightly in the memory, poems in which analysis finds little, but which are charming in their frail completeness.—LOWELL, JAMES RUSSELL, 1858-64-90, *Library of Old Authors, Prose Works, Riverside ed., vol.* I, *pp.* 254, 302.

We see the gallant cavalier in the happy moods when he was true to his natural feelings, and wrote as men with any power at all always write when unfettered by a system, unprejudiced by a theory. In prison his poetry was freer than when he himself was at liberty. The fetters on his body seemed not only not to chain his mind, but to leave it more elastic and buoyant to roam in the fairy-land of love and poetry. What would have overcome less self-reliant and heroic men, and bound them down until they became equal to the degrading circumstances which oppressed them, only raised the poet and made him what men, strong and heroic men always are, superior to those circumstances—their lord and master. . . . When in the stone walls of his cell he lifts up his voice and sings in honour of love, of constancy, of loyalty and truth, he strikes a chord so true, so national and so universal, that we cheerfully lend him our ear; willingly give ourselves up to the delight of his verse; and yield him our warmest praise. A more generous, chivalrous, and noble-hearted man than Richard Lovelace never made a prison famous, or glorified a dungeon by the power of song.—LANGFORD, JOHN ALFRED, 1861, *Prison Books and Their Authors, pp.* 212, 213.

Party feeling did not blind Wither or Marvell to the genius of Lovelace. A living poet had the living fellowship of his competitors, a dead poet their praise.—MORLEY, HENRY, 1868, *ed., The King and the Commons, Introduction, p.* vii.

It may safely be said that of all the Royalist lyrists Lovelace has been overestimated the most, as Carew has been the most neglected. The reason of this is not hard to find. Carew was a poet of great art and study, whose pieces reach a high but comparatively uniform standard, while Lovelace was an improvisatore who wrote two of the best songs in the language by accident, and whose other work is of much inferior quality. A more slovenly poet than Lovelace it would be difficult to find; his verses have reached us in the condition of unrevised proofs sent out by a careless compositor; but it is plain that not to the printer only is due the lax and irregular form of the poems. It did not always occur to Lovelace to find a rhyme, or to persist in a measure, and his ear seems to have been singularly defective. To these technical faults he added a radical tastelessness of fancy, and an excess of the tendency of all his contemporaries to dwell on the surroundings of a subject rather than on the subject itself. . . . There are high qualities in the verses of Lovelace, though he rarely allows us to see them unalloyed. His language has an heroic ring about it; he employs fine epithets and gallant phrases, two at least of which have secured the popular ear, and become part of our common speech. "Going to the Wars," his best poem, contains no line or part of a line that could by any possibility be improved; "To Althea" is less perfect, but belongs to a higher order of poetry. The first and fourth stanzas of this exquisite lyric would do honour to the most illustrious name, and form one of the treasures of our literature.—GOSSE, EDMUND, 1880, *English Poets, ed. Ward, vol.* II, *pp.* 181, 182.

It is not quite true that Lovelace left nothing worth reading but the two immortal songs, "To Lucasta on going to the Wars" and "To Althea from Prison;" and it is only fair to say that the corrupt condition of his text is evidently due, at least in part, to incompetent printing and the absence of revision. "The Grasshopper" is almost worthy of the two better-known pieces, and there are others not far below it. But on the whole any one who knows those two (and who does not?) may neglect Lovelace with safety.
—SAINTSBURY, GEORGE, 1887, *History of Elizabethan Literature, p.* 375.

Whether we think of Lovelace as the spoiled darling of a voluptuous court, or as dying of want in a cellar; whether we picture him as sighing at the feet of beauty, or as fighting stoutly for his country and his king; whether he is winning all hearts by the resistless charms of voice and presence, or returning broken from battle to suffer the bitterness of poverty and desertion, we know that in his two famous lyrics we possess the real and perfect fruit, the golden harvest, of that troubled and many-sided existence.
—REPPLIER, AGNES, 1891, *English Love-Songs, Points of View, p.* 41.

As a poet Lovelace is known almost exclusively by his best lyrics. Popularly his name is more familiar than those of his contemporaries, Carew, Suckling, Randolph, and Waller, who are at most points his superiors. This is due partially, no doubt, to the fact that his poems not being very accessible except in anthologies, few have courted disappointment by perusing his minor pieces. . . . Whether Lovelace is a mere reckless improvisatore, or the most fastidious of the concettists, may be open to argument, but it is tolerably certain that to the majority of readers

his minor lyrics will remain as poetry unintelligible. If none of his song-writing contemporaries, with the possible exception of Wither, could have surpassed the exquisite "Tell me not (sweet) I am unkind," few could have written short pieces so inelegant or so vapid as some of the "Posthume Poems." On a surer foundation than the permanence of his poetry rests the chivalrous repute in which his life has been held. The Adonis of the court, "the handsomest man of his time," he rejected a courtier's career for the profession of arms, and his heroism, rather than his rhyme, challenged the oft-quoted comparison with Sir Philip Sidney.
—SECCOMBE, THOMAS, 1893, *Dictionary of National Biography, vol.* XXXIV, *p.* 171.

True love's own talisman, which here
Shakespeare and Sidney failed to teach,
A steel-and-velvet Cavalier
Gave to our Saxon speech:
Chief miracle of theme and touch
That upstart enviers adore:
*I could not love thee, dear, so much,
Loved I not Honour more.*
   .   .   .   .   .   .
'Twas virtue's breath inflamed your lyre,
Heroic from the heart it ran;
Nor for the shedding of such fire
Lives since a manlier man.
And till your strophe sweet and bold
So lovely aye, so lonely long,
Love's self outdo, dear Lovelace! hold
The pinnacles of song.
—GUINEY, LOUISE IMOGEN, 1893, *A Roadside Harp, pp.* 39, 40.

Much of Lovelace's verse is almost hopelessly obscure, but it is hard to say whether this obscurity is due to over-elaboration, or to want of care. The earlier editions abound in printer's errors, which it is now impossible to correct.
—MASTERMAN, J. HOWARD B., 1897, *The Age of Milton, p.* 98.

Sir Thomas Urquhart

1611–1660

Sir Thomas Urquhart, of Cromarty (c. 1605–60), eldest son of Sir Thomas Urquhart, studied at king's College, Aberdeen, and travelled in France, Spain, and Italy. On his return he took up arms against the Covenanting party in the north, but was worsted and forced to fly to England. Becoming attached to the court, he was knighted in 1641. The same year he published his "Epigrams Divine and Moral." On succeeding his father he went abroad. At Cromarty, though much troubled by his creditors, he produced his "Trissotetras;" or a most exquisite Table for resolving Triangles, &c. (1645). In 1649 his library was seized and sold. He again took up arms in the royal cause, and was present at Worcester, where he lost most of his MSS. At London, through Cromwell's influence, he was allowed considerable liberty, and in 1652 published "The Pedigree" and "The Jewel." The first was an exact account of the Urquhart family, in which they were traced back to Adam; the second is chiefly a panegyric on the Scots nation. In 1653 he issued his "Introduction to the Universal Language" and the first two books of that English classic, his version of "Rabelais." The third was not issued till after his death, which is said to have occurred abroad, in a fit of mirth on hearing of the Restoration. His learning was vast, his scholarship defective. Crazy with conceit, he yet evinces a true appreciation of all that is noble, and has many phrases of quaint felicity, many passages of great power. See his "Works" in the Maitland Club series (1834).—PATRICK AND GROOME, *ed.*, 1897, *Chambers's Biographical Dictionary, p.* 932.

PERSONAL

It is impossible to mistake the small dark profile which he has left us, small and dark though it be, for the profile of any mind except his own. . . . His ingenious but unfortunate work, "The Universal Language." . . . Laborious as this work must have proved, it was only one of a hundred great works completed by Sir Thomas before he had attained his thirty-eight year, and all in a style so exquisitely original, that neither in subject nor manner had he been anticipated in so much as one of them. He had designed, and in part digested, four hundred more. A complete list of these, with such a description of each as I have here attempted of his Universal Language, would be, perhaps, one of the greatest literary curiosities ever exhibited to the world; but so unfortunate was he, as an author, that the very names of the greater number of the works he finished have died with himself, while the names of his projected ones were, probably, never known to any one else. . . . When we look at his literary character in one of its phases, and see how unconsciously he lays himself open to ridicule, we wonder how a writer of such general ingenuity should be so totally devoid of that sense of the incongruous which constitutes the perception of wit. . . . And his moral character seems to have been equally anomalous. He would sooner have died in prison than have concealed, by a single falsehood, the respect which he entertained for the exiled Prince, at the very time when he was fabricating a thousand for the honour of his family. Must we not regard him as a kind of intellectual monster—a sort of moral centaur! His character is wonderful, not in any of its single parts, but in its incongruity as a whole. The horse is formed like other animals of the same species, and the man much like other men; but it is truly marvellous to find them united.—MILLER, HUGH, 1834, *Scenes and Legends of The North of Scotland, pp.* 86, 88, 90, 103.

Urquhart translated Rabelais, and, had they had been of the same century, Rabelais would have flouted the hero who gave him a second life. For as in style Urquhart was the last of the Elizabethans, so in science he resumed the fallacies of the Middle Ages. He regarded with a childish reverence the many problems at which Rabelais laughed from the comfortable depths of his easy chair. And there is a delightful irony in the truth that this perfect translator was in his own original essays nothing else than Rabelais stripped of humour. He would discuss the interminable stupidities of the schoolmen with a grave face and ceaseless ingenuity. He had no interest in aught save the unattainable. To square the circle and perfect the Universal Language were the least of his enterprises. And so we touch the tragedy of his life. He was like the man he met at Venice: "who believed he was Sovereign of the whole Adriatic Sea, and sole owner of all the ships that came from the Levant." His madness—for it was nothing less—inspired him with the confidence that all things were possible to his genius. He was Don Quixote with a yet wilder courage. . . . . Urquhart's misery is the more acute for the greater height of his aspiration. His life was marred by broken ambitions and made by one surpassing masterpiece. His manifold schemes of progress and of scholarship died with the brain which they inhabited. The Italian artificers and French professors whom he bade to Cromarty never obeyed his invitation; the castle which stood upon the South Suter, was so fiercely demolished that the place of its foundation is left unmarked. The vulgar reputation of Hugh Miller has persuaded the town whereof Urquhart was sheriff to forget that it was the birthplace of a great man. But the translation of Rabelais remains, and that will only die with the death of Pantagruel himself.—Whibley, Charles, 1897, *Sir Thomas Urquhart, New Review, vol.* 17, *pp.* 36, 38.

GENERAL

We believe, that the expectation of posthumous fame which commonly animates the secret breast of the author, and which the poet sometimes boldly anticipates in his verses, was never more egregiously disappointed than in the case of Sir Thomas Urquhart, of Cromartie, Knight. In the opinion of his contemporaries, he must have been accounted a remarkable man; his works possess a considerable portion of a wild and irregular talent, and, if we may be allowed to gather from his remaining writings the estimation in which he held them and himself, very different, indeed, ought to have been the treatment of posterity. . . . His translation of "Rabelais" is accounted by the best judges to be the most perfect version of any author whatever—which is no mean praise, when we call to mind the obscurity, singularity, and difficulty of the original, in despite of which he has managed to transfuse the spirit of his author with undiminished force and vigour. . . . The style of Sir Thomas is of so singular a kind, he possesses such a copious fund of sesquipedalian eloquence, and stalks along his subject with such a rapid and gigantic stride, that we can ensure our readers a certain portion of amusement, at least; and from the curious subject of one of the extracts, perhaps some share of information.—Southern, H., 1822, *Sir Thomas Urquhart's Jewel, Retrospective Review, vol.* 6, *pp.* 177, 178, 179.

The epigrams of this redoubtable knight of Cromarty have very little to recommend them: the thoughts are not sufficiently ingenious to support themselves without the aid of more skilful versification; and his fancy and vivacity are more conspicuously displayed in his Jewel, and in his translation of Rabelais.—Irving, David, 1861, *History of Scotish Poetry, ed. Carlyle, p.* 539, *note.*

It may be suspected that Urquhart, like some others whose naturally fantastic brains were superheated by those troublous times, was not entirely sane. But his learning, or at least his reading, was thoroughly genuine: the "Trissotetras" is not unworthy of a countryman and contemporary of Napier, and the "Logopandecteision" in the midst of its exuberant oddities displays acuteness enough. In language Urquhart is merely an extreme example of the deliberately extravagant quaintness which characterised his time, but it must be admitted that he is one of the most extreme, and that it would be nearly impossible to go beyond him. How far the study of Rabelais, and perhaps of other French writers of the same school encouraged his natural tendencies, and how far these tendencies inclined him to the study of Rabelais, are questions which in the absence of data it is not very profitable to discuss. But he is certainly one of our greatest translators, despite the liberties which he sometimes takes with his text.—Saintsbury, George, 1893, *English Prose, ed. Craik, vol.* ii, *p.* 306.

Despite its obvious extravagance, Urquhart's "Jewel" has not only many graphic and humorous touches, but much truth of observation; while its inimitable quaintness justifies its title in the eyes of lovers of recondite literature. . . . The same year (1653) saw the appearance of Urquhart's admirable translation of the first book of Rabelais—"one of the most perfect transfusions of an author from one language into another that ever man accomplished." In point of style Urquhart was Rabelais incarnate, and in his employment of the verbal resources, whether of science and pseudo-science or slang, he almost surpassed Rabelais himself. As for his mistakes, they are truly "condoned by their magnificence." He often met the difficulty of finding the exact equivalent of a French word by emptying all the synonyms given by Cotgrave into his version; thus on one occasion a list of thirteen synonyms in Rabelais is expanded by the inventive Urquhart into thirty-six. Some of the chapters are in this way almost doubled in length. . . . Urquhart was a Scottish euphuist, with a brain at least as fertile and inventive as that of the Marquis of Worcester (many of whose hundred projects he anticipated). His sketch of a universal language exhibits rare ingenuity, learning, and critical acumen. Hugh Miller pointed out that the modern chemical vocabulary, with all its philosophical ingenuity, is constructed on principles exactly similar to those which Urquhart divulged more than a hundred years prior to its invention in the preface to his "Universal Language." His fantastic and eccentric diction, which accurately reflects his personality, obscures in much of his writing his learning and his alertness of intellect. Urquhart's singularities of mind and style found, however, their affinity in Rabelais, and conspired to make his translation of the great French classic a universally acknowledged "monument of literary genius."—SECCOMBE, THOMAS, 1899, *Dictionary of National Biography, vol.* LVIII, *pp.* 48, 49.

Samuel Rutherford
1600–1661

Rutherford was born near Jedburgh in 1600, and educated at Edinburgh University, where he became Professor of Humanity in 1623. In 1625 he left the University, and from 1627 to 1639 (with a temporary ejection for non-conformity), he was minister of Anwoth in Galloway. In 1639 he was appointed Professor of Divinity at St. Andrews. From 1642 to 1647 he was in London as a member of the Westminster Assembly of Divines. On his return he became Principal of the New College in St. Andrews, and subsequently Rector of the University. He died in 1661. His principal works were "Exercitationes Apologeticæ" (Amsterdam, 1636), "Plea for Paul's Presbytery in Scotland" (1646), "The Due Right of Presbyteries," and "Lex, Rex" (1644), "The Trial and Triumph of Faith" (sermons 1645), "Divine Right of Church Government and Excommunication' (1646), "Christ Dying and Drawing Sinners to Himself" (sermons, 1647), "A Survey of the Spiritual Antichrist" (1648), "A Free Disputation against Pretended Liberty of Conscience" (1649), "The Covenant of Life Opened" (1655), "Influences of the Life of Grace" (1659), and "An Examination of Arminianism," and the "Letters" (dating from 1639 to 1661), both of which were published posthumously. Several editions of the "Letters" have been issued in the present century, and at least one of "Lex, Rex."—CRAIK, HENRY, 1893, *ed., English Prose, vol.* II, *p.* 267.

PERSONAL

Rutherford does not indeed stand on a level with the Church leaders of an earlier date. He cannot be compared with Melville or with Knox. He was not the greatest man in the country or the Church even of his own day: but he has always, even in quarters where we should least expect it, been regarded by some with a veneration and an affection which the greater men have ceased to evoke. To his admirers he was, in varying figures, "the renowned eagle," "one of the most resplendent lights that ever arose in this horizon," "that Flower of the Church, famous Mr. Samuel Rutherford," "a most profound, learned man, a most plain and painful minister, and a most heavenly Christian." When he had gone to his last resting-place, men desired that, after their death, they might be laid beside him. Even at the beginning of the present century, there was a nobleman who always reverently lifted his hat when he passed the supposed birthplace of Rutherford. Even within the last sixty years, masons have chosen rather to be dismissed from their employment than pull down the house in which he had lived. Even within the last twenty years, enthusiasts have lain all night upon that grave in the churchyard of the Cathedral of St. Andrews, in the hope of catching inspiration from him whose remains were buried there two centuries before. He is the only Covenanting divine whose writings can now lay any claim to popularity.—MUIR, PEARSON M'ADAM, 1883, *St. Giles' Lectures*.

He was a "little fair man," and is said to have been "naturally of a hot and fiery temper." He was certainly one of the most perfervid of Scotsmen, but seems to have had little of that humour which was seldom wanting in the grimmest of his contemporaries. "In the pulpit he had" (says a friend) "a strange utterance, a kind of skreigh that I never heard the like. Many a time I thought he would have flown out of the pulpit when he came to speak of Jesus Christ.'' His abilities were of a high order, but as a church leader by his narrowness he helped to degrade and destroy presbyterianism which he loved so well, and in controversy he was too often bitter and scurrilous. With all his faults, his honesty, his steadfast zeal, and his freedom from personal ambition give him some claim to the title that has been given him of the "saint of the covenant."—SPROTT, REV. G. W., 1897, *Dictionary of National Biography, vol.* L, *p.* 9.

GENERAL

The excellent Rutherford. . . . A very powerful, awakening, and heart-stirring writer.—BICKERSTETH, EDWARD, 1844, *The Christian Student.*

In Rutherford, indeed, both the poetry and the logic must be admitted to be of very inferior quality. Yet the same contrast of mental character is presented. He is scarcely the same writer in his "Letters," the only productions of his pen now known, and in his argumentative treatises. The "Letters" are marked by the extravagances of a fancy lawless in its exuberance. The treatises are dull, barren, operose, and unillumined in argument to a frightful degree. Nobody without an effort can read them.—TULLOCH, JOHN, 1872, *Rational Theology and Christian Philosophy in England in the Seventeenth Century, vol.* I, *p.* 350.

You have, speaking generally, such assumption of personal infallibility, such fierceness of contradiction, such unmeasured vituperation, such extreme narrowness of sectarian orthodoxy, and such suspicion of all who differed from him, as is alike wonderful and sorrowful.—GROSART, ALEXANDER B., 1879, *Representative Nonconformists, p.* 202.

Few men have so remarkably combined the qualities of a keen and able controversialist and a fervid and loving saint. No doubt tyranny and persecution had tinged him with bigotry and intolerance in matters which, in a happier age of liberty, we deem non-essential. But the chord of Christian love was ever the dominant one in his heart.—MACHAR, AGNES MAULE, 1886, *A Scottish Mystic, The Andover Review, vol.* 6, *p.* 394.

We have not to do with him here as a man or as an author, but as a preacher, yet it is scarcely possible for us to ignore the two former in the third; and when we include them we are at once startled and perplexed, for I frankly confess that no character even in that stormy time seems to me so difficult to regard as a unit as that of Rutherford. There were two men in him, and the two were so distinct that you could hardly call him a "strange mixture," for they did not mix. The one of them seemed to have no effect in conditioning or qualifying the other, but each was just as unshaded by the other as if it had stood alone.—TAYLOR, WILLIAM M., 1887, *The Scottish Pulpit, p,* 90.

Rutherford is a writer most of whose books have a memorial only in the graveyard of history. . . . We pass from the brawls of the market-place to the cloistered, star-lit seclusion of those "Letters," which the evangelical succession, from Baxter to Spurgeon, has united to declare seraphic and divine. Like Knox, Rutherford was a great fatherconfessor or director of souls. Knox, however, was no mystic. Rutherford had a quasi-oriental faculty of self-absorption in his ideal of "heavenly love." This quality received partial expression in his sermons, but it is in his letters, where he was under no restraint, that its full development appears. The letters are the unstringing of a bent bow, the channel by which he delivered his soul. They are full of sympathy, rather of an angel writing from the seventh heaven than of a fellowman. . . . The exceptionol metaphors that give an air of alternate extravagance and quaintness to nearly every page of the "Letters" are borrowed, somewhat incongruously, from the imagery of the Song of Solomon, and from the devious practice of old Scots Law. . . . The "Letters," as a Puritan classic, deserve a place beside "The Saint's Rest" and "The Pilgrim's Progress."—DODDS, JAMES MILLER, 1893, *English Prose, ed.* Craik, *vol.* II, *pp.* 267, 268, 270.

Samuel Rutherford, the Presbyterian Thomas Aquinas, with his learning, his theological acumen, his piety—at once a great Church leader and a saint, equally at home among the tomes of the fathers, writing a letter of comfort to a poor widow, or praying in the hovels of his parishioners.—HURST, JOHN FLETCHER, 1900, *History of the Christian Church, vol.* II, *p.* 724.

Thomas Fuller

1608–1661

Born, at Aldwincle, Northamptonshire, June 1606. Educated at village school and by his father. To Queen's Coll., Cambridge, 29 June 1621; B. A., 1625; M. A., 1628; B. D., 11 June 1635. Ordained, 1630; Perpetual Curate to St. Benet's, Cambridge, 1630–33. Prebend of Netherbury, 18 June 1631 to 1641. Rector of Broadwindsor, Dorsetshire, 1634–41. Married, 1637 [?]. Proctor for Diocese of Bristol, 1640. Settled in London after wife's death, 1641. Curate of Savoy, 1641–43. Removed to Oxford, 1643. Chaplain to Sir Ralph Hopton, 1643–1644. Entered Princess Henrietta's household at Exeter, 1644. Bodley Lecturer at Exeter, 21 March 1646. To London, April 1646. Perpetual Curate of Waltham Abbey, 1648 [or 1649?]. Married Hon. Mary Roper, 1651. Rector of Cranford, March 1658. Created D. D. by Royal Letters Patent, Aug. 1660. Died, in London, 16 Aug. 1661. Buried at Cranford. *Works:* [besides a number of separate sermons] "David's Hanious Sinne," 1631; "The History of the Holy Warre," 1639; "Joseph's Party-coloured Coat" (under initials T. F.), 1640; "The Holy State" and "The Profane State," 1642; "Truth Maintained," 1643; "Good Thoughts in Bad Times," 1645; "Andronicus," 1646 (2nd and 3rd edns. same year); "The Cause and Cure of a Wounded Conscience," 1647; "Good Thoughts in Worse Times,' 1647; "A Pisgahsight of Palestine," 1650; contrib. to "Abel Redivivus," 1651; "A Comment on Matt. iv. 1–11," 1652; "The Infant's Advocate," 1652; "A Comment on Ruth" (anon), 1654; "Ephemeris Parliamentaria" (anon.), 1654; "A Triple Reconciler," 1654; "The Church History of Britain," 1655; "History of the University of Cambridge," 1655; "History of Waltham Abbey," 1655; "A Collection of Sermons" (5 pts.), 1656–57; "The Best Name on Earth," 1657; "The Appeal of Injured Innocence," 1659; "An Alarum to the Counties of England and Wales" (anon.), 1660 (2nd and 3rd edns. same year); "Mixt Contemplations in Better Times," 1660; "A Panegyrick to His Majesty," 1660. *Posthumous:* "The History of the Worthies of England" (ed. by J. Fuller), 1662; "Collected Sermons" (ed. by J. E. Bailey and W. E. A. Axton), 1891. He *edited:* Rev. H. Smith's "Sermons," 1657; J. Spencer's "Καινα και Παλαια,"1658.—SHARP, R. FARQUHARSON, 1897, *A Dictionary of English Authors, p.* 105.

PERSONAL

He was a boy of a pregnant witt, and when the bishop and his father were discoursing, he would be by and hearken, and now and then putt in, and sometimes beyond expectation, or his yeares. He was of a middle stature; strong sett; curled haire; a very working head, in so much that, walking and meditating before dinner, he would eate-up a penny loafe, not knowing that he did it. His naturall memorie was very great, to which he had added the *art of memorie:* he would repeate to you forwards and backwards all the signes from Ludgate to Charingcrosse. . . . He was a pleasant facetious person, and a *bonus socius.*—AUBREY, JOHN, 1669–96, *Brief Lives, ed. Clark, vol.* I, *pp.* 257, 258.

In a moral and religious point of view, the character of Fuller is entitled to our veneration, and is altogether one of the most attractive and interesting which that age exhibits to us. His buoyant temper, and his perpetual mirthfulness, were altogether at variance with that austerity and rigour which characterized so many of the religionists of his time; but his life and conduct bore ample testimony that he possessed genuine and habitual piety. Amidst all his levity of manner, there was still the gravity of the heart—deep veneration for all things sacred; and while his wit clothed even his religious thoughts and feelings with irresistible pleasantry, his manner is as different from that of the scorner, as the innocent laugh of childhood from the malignant chuckle of a demon. In all the relations of domestic and social life, his conduct was most exemplary. In one point, especially, does he appear in honourable contrast with the bigots of all parties in that age of strife —he had learnt, partly from his natural benevolence, and partly from a higher principle, the lessons of "that charity which thinketh no evil," and which so few of his contemporaries knew how to practise.—ROGERS, HENRY, 1842, *Thomas Fuller, Edinburgh Review, vol.* 74, *p.* 356.

Fuller is described as tall and bulky, though not corpulent, well made, almost "majestical," with light curly hair, rather slovenly in dress and often absent-minded, and careless "to seeming inurbanity" in his manners. He was sparing in diet and in sleep. He seldom took any exercise except riding. His powers of memory were astonishing, and gave occasion for many anecdotes. He could, it was said, repeat five hundred strange names after two or three hearings, and recollect all the signs after walking from one end of London to the other. His anonymous biographer declares that he used to write the first words of every line in a sheet and then fill up all the spaces, which Mr. Bailey thinks "not a bad method."—STEPHEN, LESLIE, 1889, *Dictionary of National Biography, vol. xx, p.* 318.

Shrewd Dr. Fuller, and a man not to be forgotten! He was a "Cavalier parson" through the Civil-War days; was born down in Northamptonshire in the same town where John Dryden, twenty-three years later, first saw the light. He was full of wit, and full of knowledges; people called him—as so many have been and are called—"a walking library;" and his stout figure was to be seen many a time, in the Commonwealth days, striding through Fleet Street, and by Paul's Walk, to Cheapside. There is quaint humor in his books, and quaintness and aptness of language.—MITCHELL, DONALD G., 1890, *English Lands Letters and Kings. From Elizabeth to Anne, p.* 221.

A PISGAHSIGHT OF PALESTINE
1650

This is one of the most curious works ever written on the Scriptures. . . . The View of Palestine is not a mere geographical work; it contains many things relating to Jewish antiquities, and to the manners and customs of the poeple, and incidentally illustrates a number of passages of Scripture.—ORME, WILLIAM, 1824, *Biblotheca Biblica.*

His book really answers to its title. He might be thought to have seen the "Good Land," so graphic are some of its sketches, so lively his observations, and so pleasantly does he keep the eyes and hearts of his hearers. He is as painstaking, acute, discriminating, and cautious as Dr. Robinson himself; but where this tedious Doctor is dull, dry, and monotonous, our old Fuller is all life and buoyancy, enticing you by his company into long rambles over scenes which he knows all about, and upon which he looks lovingly, about which he talks charmingly, and which he really photographs upon your very soul by the light of his genial wit and hallowed fancy. His wit, however, is never out of tune with pure and simple faith; his intellectual brightness never loses its devout warmth, nor does any affectation of science ever mar the loveliness of his meek and reverent spirit. —CHRISTOPHERS, SAMUEL WOOLCOCK, 1873, *Homes of Old English Writers.*

THE CHURCH HISTORY OF BRITAIN
1655

An ingenious gentleman some months since in jest-earnest advised me to make haste with my History of the church of England; "for fear," said he, "lest the church of England be ended before the History thereof." This History is now, though late, (all church-work is slow,) brought with much difficulty to an end. And, blessed be God! the church of England is still (and long may it be) in being, though disturbed, distempered, distracted. God help and heal her most sad condition! The three first books of this volume were for the main written in the reign of the late king, as appeareth by the passages then proper for the government. The other nine books we made since *monarchy* was turned into a *state.* May God alone have the glory, and the ingenuous reader the benefit, of my endeavours! which is the hearty desire of Thy servant in Jesus Christ.—*From my Chamber in Sion College.*—FULLER, THOMAS, 1655, *The Church History of Britain, To the Reader.*

Proceed we in the next place to verses and old ends of poetry, scattered and dispersed in all parts of the history, from one end to the other; for which he hath no precedent in any historian, Greek or Latin, or any of the national histories of these latter times. . . . By his interlarding of his prose with so many verses he makes the book look rather like a Church-romance (our late romancers being much given to such kind of mixtures) than a well-built ecclesiastical history. And if it be a matter so unconvenient to put a new piece of cloth on an old garment; the putting of so many old patches on a new piece of cloth must be more un-fashionable. Besides that, many of those old ends are so light and ludicrous, so little pertinent to the business which he has in hand, that they serve only to make sport for children (*ut pueris placeas et declamatio fias*), and for nothing else.—HEYLIN, PETER, 1658–59, *Examen Historicum.*

It is divided into eleven books, whereof the sixth gives the history of the abbies of England, from the first rise of monkery, to the final eradication of it under Henry the Eighth. These are subdivided into lesser sections, which are severally dedicated to such patrons as were most likely to make their due acknowledgements to the author. Nor were these infant lords and rich aldermen the only people he desired to flatter. He was to make his court to the powers then in fashion; and, he well knew, nothing would be more grateful to them, than squinting reflections on the management of the late King's chief ministers of state, eminent churchmen, &c. For such misbehaviour as this, he was severely taken to task by Peter Heylin, in his "Examen Historicum;" to which was added Dr. Cosin's Apology, in answer to some passages in that history, which concerned himself. . . . Even the most serious and most authentic parts of it are so interlaced with pun and quibble, that it looks as if the man had designed to ridicule the annals of our church into fable and romance. . . . There are in it some things of moment, hardly to be had elsewhere, which may often illustrate dark passages in more serious writers.—NICOLSON, WILLIAM, 1696–1714, *English Historical Library, pp.* 96, 97.

There are only two writers of the genuine History of our Church who deserve the name of historians, Collier and Fuller.—WARBURTON, WILLIAM, 1779? *Directions for the Study of Theology.*

Quaint and witty, but sensible, pious, candid, and useful; an invaluable body of information to the death of Charles the First.—BICKERSTETH, EDWARD 1844, *The Christian Student.*

All the charms of Southey's prose may please you in his "Book of the Church"; on turning to the old church historian, Thomas Fuller, you may find in his "History of the Church in Great Britain" (one of the most remarkable works in the language) the varied powers of learning,

sagacity, pathos, an overflowing wit, humour, and imagination, all animating the pages of a church history.—REED, HENRY, 1885, *Lectures on English Literature, p.* 203.

The desire of authors to obtain more pay for their work set them thinking of the best means to increase it. Fuller's "Church History" has twelve title-pages, besides the general one, with as many particular dedications, and no less than fifty or sixty inscriptions addressed to benefactors.—WHEATLEY, HENRY B., 1887, *The Dedication of Books, p.* 16.

No man of his times was more witty or more popular for his wit. Edition after edition of his books was issued even during the days when it was dangerous to write of the Church's doings. No one could tell a story as he could, yet no one was so free from bitterness. His sharpness, and indeed much of his humour too, lay upon the surface. He sought, and he achieved, the praise of being a moderate man; and though he did not escape slander, he was secure in the affections of his readers. "No stationer ever lost by me," he said. He was, in fact, unquestionably the most popular of all the writers of his day. From him and such as he men learned that the Church was a larger home than Puritanism.—HUTTON, WILLIAM HOLDEN, 1895, *Social England*, ed. Traill, vol. IV, p. 292.

WORTHIES OF ENGLAND
1662

I met with Dr. Thomas Fuller. He tells me of his last and great book that is coming out: that is, the "History of all the Families in England;" and could tell me more of my own than I knew myself. And also to what perfection he hath now brought the art of memory; that he did lately to four eminently great scholars dictate together in Latin, upon different subjects of their proposing, faster than they were able to write, till they were tired; and that the best way of beginning a sentence, if a man should be out and forget his last sentence (which he never was), that then his last refuge is to begin with an *Utcunque.*—PEPYS, SAMUEL, 1660–61, *Diary, Jan.* 22nd.

It was huddled up in haste, for the procurement of some moderate profit for the author, though he did not live to see it published. It corrects many mistakes in his ecclesiastical story; but makes more new ones in their stead.—NICOLSON, WILLIAM, 1696–1714, *English Historical Library, p.* 5.

It is a most fascinating storehouse of gossiping, anecdote, and quaintness; a most delightful medley of interchanged amusement, presenting entertainment as varied as it is inexhaustible.—CROSSLEY, JAMES, 1821, *Fuller's Holy and Profane States, Retrospective Review, vol.* III, *p.* 54.

Fuller must be always read with a certain degree of caution; for he was fond of a joke, and often picked up intelligence in a slovenly manner.—DIBDIN, THOMAS FROGNALL, 1824, *The Library Companion, note, p.* 507.

GENERAL

His writings are very facetious, and (where he is careful) judicious. His "Pisgah Sight" is the exactest; his "Holy War and State," the wittiest; his "Church History," the unhappiest,— written in such a time when he could not do the truth right with safety, nor wrong it with honour; and his "Worthies," not finished at his death, the most imperfect. As for his other works, he that shall but read FULLER'S name unto them will not think them otherwise but worthy of that praise and respect which the whole nation afforded unto the author. —WINSTANLEY, WILLIAM, 1660, *England's Worthies.*

The writings of Fuller are usually designated by the title of quaint, and with sufficient reason; for such was his natural bias to conceits, that I doubt not upon most occasions it would have been going out of his way to have expressed himself out of them. But his wit is not always a *lumen siccum,* a dry faculty of surprising; on the contrary, his conceits are oftentimes deeply steeped in human feeling and passion. Above all, his way of telling a story, for its eager liveliness, and the perpetual running commentary of the narrator happily blended with the narration, is perhaps unequalled.—LAMB, CHARLES, 1811, *Specimens from the writings of Fuller.*

If ever there was an amusing writer in this world the facetious Thomas Fuller was one.—There was in him a combination of those qualities which minister to our entertainment, such as few have ever possessed in an equal degree. He was, first of all, a man of extensive and multifarious reading; of great and digested knowledge, which an extraordinary retentiveness of memory preserved ever ready for use, and considerable accuracy of judgment enabled him successfully to apply. He was also, if we may use the term, a very great anecdote-monger; an indefatigable collector of the traditionary stories related of eminent characters, to gather which, his biographers inform us, he would listen contentedly for hours to the garrulity of the aged country people whom he encountered in his progresses with the king's army. With such plenitude and diversity of information, he had an inexhaustible fund for the purposes of illustration, and this he knew well how to turn to the best advantage. Unlike his tasteless contemporaries he did not bring forth or display his erudition on unnecessary occasions or pile extract on extract and cento on cento with industry as misapplied as it was disgusting. . . . So well does he vary his treasures of memory and observation, so judiciously does he interweave his anecdotes, quotations, and remarks, that it is impossible to conceive a more delightful chequer-work of acute thought and apposite illustration, of original and extracted sentiment, than is presented in his works. As a story-teller, he was most consummately felicitous. The relation which we have seen for the hundredth time, when introduced in his productions, assumes all the freshness of novelty, and comes out of his hands instinct with fresh life and glowing with vitality and spirit.—CROSSLEY, JAMES, 1821, *Fuller's Holy and Profane States, Retrospective Review, vol.* III, *pp.* 50, 51.

Next to Shakspeare, I am not certain whether Thomas Fuller, beyond all other writers, does not excite in me the sense and emotion of the marvellous;—the degree in which any given faculty or combination of faculties is possessed and manifested, so far surpassing what one would have thought possible in a single mind, as to give one's admiration the flavour and quality of wonder! Wit was the staff and substance of Fuller's intellect. It was the element, the earthen base, the material which he worked in, and this very circumstance has defrauded him of his due praise for the practical wisdom of the thoughts, for the beauty and variety of the truths, into which he shaped the stuff. Fuller was incomparably the most sensible, the least prejudiced, great man of an age that boasted a galaxy of great men. He is a very voluminous writer, and yet, in all his numerous volumes on so many different subjects, it is scarcely too much to say, that you will hardly find a page in which some one sentence out of every three does not deserve to be quoted for itself—as motto or as maxim.—COLE-RIDGE, SAMUEL TAYLOR, 1829, *Miscellanies*, ed. *Ashe, p.* 327.

Fuller is one of the few voluminous authors who is never tedious. . . . Of all the forms of wit, Fuller affects that of the satirist least. Though he can be caustic, and sometimes is so, he does not often indulge the propensity; and when he does it is without bitterness—a sly irony, a good-humoured gibe, at which even its object could hardly have helped laughing, is all he ventures upon. . . . So exuberant is Fuller's wit, that, as his very melancholy is mirthful, so his very wisdom wears motley. But it is wisdom notwithstanding; nor are there many authors, in whom we shall find so much solid sense and practical sagacity, in spite of the grotesque disguise in which they masque themselves.—ROGERS, HENRY, 1842, *Life and Writings of Thomas Fuller, Edinburgh Review, vol.* 74, *pp.* 334, 340, 343.

Of a sanguine, happy, easy temperament, a jolly Protestant father confessor, and this attracted him to the side of the laughing muse. Yet he abounds in quiet, beautiful touches both of poetry and pathos.—GILFILLAN, GEORGE, 1855, *A Third Gallery of Portraits, p.* 393.

One of the liveliest and yet, in the inmost heart of him, one of the most serious writers one can meet with. I speak of this writer partly because there is no one who is so resolute that we should treat him as a friend, and not as a solemn dictator. By some unexpected jest, or comical turn of expression, he disappoints your purpose of receiving his words as if they were fixed in print, and asserts his right to talk with you, and convey his subtle wisdom in his own quaint and peculiar dialect.—MAURICE, FREDERICK DEN-ISON, 1856–74, *The Friendship of Books and Other Lectures, ed. Hughes, p.* 18.

The wise old Fuller, whom no lover of wit, truth, beauty, and goodness can ever tire of reading.—MARSH, GEORGE P., 1859, *Lectures on the English Language, First Series, p.* 58.

He is the most singular writer, full of verbal quibbling and quaintness of all kinds, but by far the most amusing and engaging of all the rhetoricians of this school, inasmuch as his conceits are rarely mere elaborate feats of ingenuity, but are usually informed either by a strong spirit of very peculiar humor and drollery, or sometimes even by a warmth and depth of feeling, of which too, strange as it may appear, the oddity of his phraseology is often a not ineffective exponent. He was certainly one of the greatest and truest wits that ever lived: he is witty not by any sort of effort at all, but as it were in spite of himself, or because he cannot help it. . . . No man ever (in writing at least) made so many jokes, good, bad, and indifferent; be the subject what it may, it does not matter; in season and out of season he is equally facetious; he cannot let slip an occasion of saying a good thing any more than a man who is tripped can keep himself from falling; the habit is as irresistible with him as the habit of breathing; and yet there is probably neither an ill-natured nor a profane witticism to be found in all that he has written. It is the sweetest-blooded wit that was ever infused into man or book. And how strong and weighty, as well as how gentle and beautiful, much of his writing is!—CRAIK, GEORGE L., 1861, *A Compendious History of English Literature and of the English Language, vol.* II, *pp.* 65, 72.

Quaint but full and sufficient.—FRIS-WELL, JAMES HAIN, 1869, *Essays on English Writers, p.* 12.

For one reason or another Fuller has become a kind of privileged pet amongst those traders in literary curiosities whose favourite hunting ground is amongst the great writers of the seventeenth century. He is the spoilt child of criticism whose most audacious revolts against the respectable laws of taste have an irresistible claim. Some of their eulogies rather tax our credulity. . . . He was the most buoyant of mankind; and if he ever knew what it was to be melancholy, he could find relief in lamentations so lively as to sound like an effusion of exuberant spirits. The wonder is that we feel this boyish exhilaration to be significant of true feeling. Some men shed tears when they are deeply moved; Fuller pours forth a string of quibbles. It is a singular idiosyncrasy which inverts the conventional modes of expressing devotion, and makes jokes, good, bad, and indifferent, do duty for sighs. But nobody should read Fuller who cannot more or less understand the frame of mind to which such fantastic freaks are congenial; and those who do will learn that, if in one sense he is the most childlike, in another he is amongst the most manly writers. He enjoys a sort of rude intellectual health, which enables him to relish childish amusements to the end of his days; and it is difficult to imagine a more enviable accomplishment, though it must be admitted that it leads to some rather startling literary phenomena.—STEPHEN, LESLIE, 1872, *Hours in a Library, Cornhill Magazine, vol.* 25, *pp.* 33, 44

The Quaintness of the seventeenth century is commonly linked with the name of Thomas Fuller, not because he is the most glaring example, but rather because he is one of the few high class writers in whom this quality is conspicuous. For in fact, although quaintness is best known to the modern reader through his writings, yet he does not afford a true example of the fault of quaintness. His quaintness is a sort, a droll sort perhaps, of beauty; because the language is a true vesture to the thought, and Fuller is quaint in his very thought. The quaintness which is blamable rises when a writer is more curious about his diction than careful to have something to say before he covers paper with decorated words. The Quaintness of the Seventeenth century is a phenomenon of the same nature as the Euphuism of the Sixteenth. It is like the secular return of an epidemic enthusiasm.—EARLE, JOHN, 1890, *English Prose, p.* 452.

Fuller perhaps has, and it may possibly be due to a sort of feeling of this that, though he has never wanted for fervent admirers, they seem always rather to have shrunk from paying him the greatest and the most necessary, if the most trying, honour that can be paid to an author by issuing a complete edition of his works. There are many curious contradictions in Fuller's character, both personal and literary, and it is not impossible that the presence of them communicates to his personality and his literature the almost unmatched piquancy which both possess, and which have never failed to attract fit persons. A Puritan Cavalier (Dr. Jessopp calls him a Puritan, and though I should hardly go so far myself, there is no doubt that Fuller leaned far more to the extreme Protestant side than most of his comrades in loyalty), a man of the sincerest and most unaffected piety, who never could resist a joke, an early member of the exact or antiquarian school of historians, who was certainly not a very profound or wide scholar, and who constantly laid himself open to the animadversions of others by his defects in scholarship—Fuller is a most appetising bundle of contradictions. But his contradictions undoubtedly sometimes disgust; and perhaps even some almost insatiable lovers of "the humour of it" may occasionally think that he carries the humour of it too far.—SAINTSBURY, GEORGE, 1893, *English Prose,* ed. Craik, vol. II, p. 374.

Without endorsing the extravagant praise of Coleridge, we must acknowledge that the wit of Fuller was amazing, if he produced too many examples of it in forms a little too desultory for modern taste.—GOSSE, EDMUND 1897, *Short History of Modern English Literature, p.* 152.

Of all our many English writers whom it is customary to designate as quaint, perhaps Fuller exhibits a quaintness which savours least of antiquity, of affectations now quite obsolete.—TOVEY, DUNCAN C., 1897, *Reviews and Essays in English Literature, p.* 39.

As a theological writer, Fuller is distinguished by earnest piety and indomitable cheerfulness rather than by sublimity of thought or intensity of emotion. Though his moderate attitude on the burning questions of the day did not entirely satisfy either of the great religious parties, it enabled him to continue his ministry through all the vicissitudes of the Commonwealth without any of those vacillations of principle by which other men purchased the toleration of the ruling powers. His temperament unfitted him for entering into the war of invective and vituperation that was raging around him. He rarely displays either enthusiasm or indignation, preferring to interest and amuse rather than to rouse or convince. The homely imagery, of which his sermons and devotional writings are full, laid him open to the charge of levity; but though his similes are often grotesque, they are seldom actually ludicrous, while their very incongruity sometimes gives an added force to the comparison.—MASTERMAN, J. H. B., 1897, *The Age of Milton*, p. 172.

Peter Heylin

1600–1662

Peter Heylin, D. D., 1600–1662, a learned divine of the English Church, educated at Oxford, who took part with the royalists, was deprived by the republicans, and again reinstated in his ecclesiastical dignities on the restoration of the Stuarts. His writings are very numerous, and are mostly historical and polemical. Thirty-seven of his publications are enumerated. The following are some of them: "History of the Reformation of the Church of Scotland," fol.; "History of the Reformation Church of England," fol.; "History of the Presbyterians," fol.; "Life and Death of Archbishop Laud," fol., etc.—HART, JOHN S., 1872, *A Manual of English Literature*, p. 175.

PERSONAL

He was a person endowed with singular gifts, of a sharp and pregnant wit, solid and clear judgment. In his younger years he was accounted an excellent poet, but very conceited and pragmatical, in his elder, a better historian, a noted preacher, and a ready or extemporanean speaker.—WOOD, ANTHONY, 1691–1721, *Athenæ Oxonienses, vol.* II, *f.* 279.

LIFE OF LAUD

1644

Laud's Life has been described by Peter Heylin, D. D.; the man known usually in Presbyterian Polemics by the name of "Lying Peter." He is an alert, logical, metaphorical, most swift, ingenious man; alive every inch of him, Episcopal to the very finger-ends. This present writer has read the old dim folio, every word of it, with faithful industry, with truest wish to understand. A hope did dawn on him that he of all Adam's posterity would be the last that undertook such a trouble; some one of Adam's sons was fated to be the last; why not he? It had been too sad a task otherwise. For if the truth must be told, this unfortunate last reader found that properly he did not "understand" it in the least, that though the thing lay plain, patent as the turnpike highway, no man would ever more understand it. For the mournful truth is, that the human brain in this stage of its progress, refuses any longer to concern itself with Peter Heylin. The result was, no increase of knowledge at all. Read him not, O reader of this nineteenth century, let no pedant persuade you to read him. Spectres and air-phantos of altars in the East, half-paces, communion-rails, shovel-hatteries, and mummeries and genuflexions; I for one, O Peter, have forever lost the talent of taking any interest in them, this way or that. As good to say it free out. My sight strains itself looking at them; discerns them to be verily phantoms, air-woven, brain-woven; disowned by Nature, noxious to health and life,—dreary as an aged cobweb full of dust and dead flies. Peter, my friend, it is enough to sit two centuries as an incubus upon the human soul; thou wouldst not continue it into the third century? Thou art requested in terms of civilty to disappear. Incubuses have one duty to do: withdraw. Were Peter's Book well burnt and not a copy of it left, this therefore were the balance of accounts: human knowledge where it was, and two weeks of time and misery saved to many men. On these terms, this last reader will not grudge having read.—CARLYLE, THOMAS, 1844–49–98, *Historical Sketches of Noble Persons and Events in the Reigns of James I. and Charles I.*, p. 274.

We must pay our tribute, however, to the contemporary historian, to the vivid, amusing, clever Heylin. Heylin was one of those persons whom Laud picked up in the course of his administration (as he did many others), and set to work in the Church cause. He wrote books and pamphlets when Laud wanted them, and supplied the Archbishop with university and clerical information. It was Laud's character to be most good-natured and familiar with his subordinates—with any who worked under him, and did what he told them; and Heylin thoroughly enjoyed and relished his good graces. There is an amusing under-stream of self-congratulation throughout his biography, at his participation of the great man's patronage. He seems to have been occasionally told secrets and let behind the scenes—a matter of great pride to him. He communicates the information, with a kind of sly, invisible smirk in the background, and a nudge under the table to the reader —to remind him of the Archbishop's cleverness, not forgetting the biographer's. The former would not have been particularly obliged, on one or two occasions, for the candid display of his strategics, and bits of necessary statecraft, in his devoted admirer's pages.— MOZLEY, J. B., 1845-78, *Archbishop Laud*, *Essays Historical and Theological, vol.* I, *p.* 107.

GENERAL

(1) I knew him a man of able parts and learning; God sanctify both to his Glory and the Church's good! (2) Of an eager spirit, with him of whom it was said, *Quicquid voluit, valde voluit.* (3) Of a tart and smart style, endeavouring to down with all which stood betwixt him and his opinion. (4) Not over dutiful in his language to the Fathers of the Church (what then may children expect of him?), if contrary in judgment to him. Lastly, and chiefly: One, the edge of whose keenness is not taken off by the death of his adversary; witness his writing against the Archbishops of York and Armagh [who both died in 1656]. The fable tells me that the tanner was the worst of all masters to his cattle, as who would not only load them soundly whilst living, but tan their hides when dead; and none could blame one if unwilling to exasperate such a pen, which, if surviving, would prosecute his adversary into his grave. The premises made me, though not servilely fearful (which, praise God, I am not of any writer) yet generally cautious not to give him any personal provocation, knowing that though both our pens were long, the world was wide enough for them without crossing each other.—FULLER, THOMAS, 1659, *The Appeal of Injured Innocence.*

His knowledge in history and divinity was extensive; but he wrote with more ease than elegance; and his memory, which was very extraordinary, was better than his judgment. He is not free from the leaven and acrimony of party-prejudice. The generality of his writings are in no great esteem at present; but his "Help to History," which is a work of great utility, deserves particular commendation. —GRANGER, JAMES, 1769-1824, *Biographical History of England, vol.* V, *p.* 40.

Heylin, in his history of the *Puritans* and the *Presbyterians*, blackens them for political devils. He is the Spagnolet of history, delighting himself with horrors at which the painter himself must have started. He tells of their "oppositions" to monarchical and episcopal government; their "innovations" in the church; and their "embroilments" of the kingdoms. The sword rages in their hands; treason, sacrilege, plunder; while "more of the blood of Englishmen had poured like water within the space of four years, than had been shed in the civil wars of York and Lancaster, in four centuries!"—DISRAELI, ISAAC, 1791-1824, "*Political Religionism,*" *Curiosities of Literature.*

A party writer, to be read with caution. He perverts and misrepresents.—BICKER-STETH, EDWARD, 1844, *The Christian Student.*

As an historian, he displays too much of the spirits of a partisan and bigot, and stands among the defenders of civil and ecclesiastical tyranny. His works, though now almost forgotten, were much read in the seventeenth century, and portions of them may still be perused with pleasure. —CHAMBERS, ROBERT, 1876, *Cyclopædia of English Literature, ed. Carruthers.*

Heylyn was a man of undoubted sincerity, of quick and active, if somewhat superficial, intellect, and of a temper which found satisfaction only in controversy. If, in his triumph, he often pressed the advantage hard against his antagonists, he accepted, with undaunted spirit, the fate of the conquered, and throughout his life he neither gave nor asked for quarter. His memory was enormous, and his learning various, although ill digested: and while he grasped clearly and tenaciously the principles of Laud's policy, and frequently had the best of his antagonists in arguments, he was without judgment, imagination, or any sense of proportion. He did not altogether lack wit, but his sarcasm is rough and boisterous rather than keen. . . . Like all his contemporaries, Heylyn always avoids a slipshod style: and we are never allowed to forget that he belonged to a school which followed, as closely as it might, the classical models, and aimed at least, if it did not always succeed in its aim, at giving to history a worthy and dignified literary dress.—CRAIK, HENRY, 1893, *ed., English Prose, vol. ii, pp.* 247, 248.

John Gauden
1605-1662

Born at Mayland, Essex, 1605: died Sept. 20, 1662. An English prelate, appointed bishop of Exeter in 1660, and translated to the see of Worcester in May, 1662. He graduated at Oxford; became vicar of Chippenham in 1640; was chaplain to the Earl of Warwick; was appointed dean of Bocking, Essex, in 1641; and was chosen a member of the Assembly of Divines in 1643, but was not allowed to take his seat. He wrote "Cromwell's Bloody Slaughter House, etc." (1660), "Tears of the Church" (1659), "Ἱερὰ Δάκρυα Ecclesiæ Anglicanæ Suspiria, or the Tears, Sighs, Complaints, and Prayers of the Church of England," etc.—SMITH, BENJAMIN E., 1894-97, *The Century Cyclopedia of Names, p.* 427.

ICON BASILIKE

The particular which you often renewed I do confess was imparted to me under secrecy, and of which I did not take myself to be at liberty to take notice, and truly when it ceases to be a sceret I know nobody will be glad of it except Mr. Milton. I have very often wished I had never been trusted with it.—CLARENDON, LORD (EDWARD HYDE), 1661, *Letter to John Gauden, Clarendon State Papers,* iii, *Supplement, pp.* xxvi, xxxii.

It may be expected that we should here mention the "Icon Basiliké," a work published in the king's name a few days after his execution. It seems almost impossible, in the controverted parts of history, to say anything which will satisfy the zealots of both parties: but with regard to the genuineness of that production, it is not easy for an historian to fix any opinion which will be entirely to his own satisfaction. The proofs brought to evince that this work is or is not the king's are so convincing, that if an impartial reader peruse any one side apart, he will think it impossible that arguments could be produced sufficient to counterbalance so strong an evidence; and when he compares both sides, he will be some time at a loss to fix any determination. Should an absolute suspense of judgment be found difficult or disagreeable in so interesting a question, I must confess that I much incline to give the preference to the arguments of the royalists. The testimonies which prove that performance to be the king's, are more numerous, certain, and direct, than those on the other side. This is the case, even if we consider the external evidence; but when we weigh the internal, derived from the style and composition, there is no manner of comparison. These meditations resemble, in elegance, purity, neatness, and simplicity, the genius of those performances which we know with certainty to have flowed from the royal pen; but are so unlike the bombast, perplexed, rhetorical and corrupt style of Dr. Gauden, to whom they are ascribed, that no human testimony seems sufficient to convince us that he was the author. Yet all the evidences which would rob the king of that honour, tend to prove that Dr. Gauden had the merit of writing so fine a performance, and the infamy of imposing it on the world for the king's.—HUME, DAVID, 1762, *The History of England, Charles I.*

He had a hand in the publication of the "Eikon Basilike," and has been reputed the author of it; but that he actually wrote it is abundantly disproved by external and internal evidence. . . . Whoever examines the writings of the royal and reverend authors, will find them specifically different; and must, from taste and sentiment, conclude, as well as from the peculiar circumstances of both writers, that Charles could no more descend to write like Gauden, than Gauden could rise to the purity and dignity of Charles. The style of the divine is more debased with the pedantry, than embellished with the elegancies of learning.—GRANGER, JAMES, 1769–1824, *Biographical History of England, vol.* III, *p.* 321.

Like the spurious political legacies, however, of other statesmen, the "Icon Basilike" contained nothing beyond the familiar meditations and the limited observation of a court divine; and, if more chaste and correct than Gauden's, the style appeared, when impartially examined, to be far more elegant and diffusive than that of the king.—LAING, MALCOLM, 1800–4, *The History of Scotland, vol.* III, *p.* 407.

There is much in the "ΕΙΚΩΝ ΒΑΣΙΛΙΚΗ" itself which forbids me to believe that Charles was the real author; though the latter, whoever he were, may have occasionally consulted and copied the royal papers; and the claim of Gauden appears too firmly established to be shaken by the imperfect and conjectural improbabilities which have hitherto been produced against it.—LINGARD, JOHN, 1809–44, *A History of England, vol.* X, *p.* 482, *note.*

One topic however remains, on which the biographer of Charles appears called upon to declare an opinion, —the authenticity of the work entitled "Icon Basilike," published in the name of the king immediately after his death. On a patient examination of the evidence adduced on both sides, she has no hesitation in stating her entire conviction that Dr. Gauden was, as he affirmed himself to be, the real author of that book, for which he was rewarded by Charles II. with a bishopric; and the composition of which Clarendon, with every facility for ascertaining the truth, has carefully abstained from claiming for the king, whose character it was the express purpose of his History to vindicate and to exalt.—AIKIN, LUCY, 1833, *Memoirs of The Court of King Charles the First, vol.* II, *p.* 376.

The famous "Icon Basilice," ascribed to Charles I., may deserve a place in literary history. If we could trust its panegyrists, few books in our language have done it more credit by dignity of sentiment, and beauty of style. It can hardly be necessary for me to express my unhesitating conviction, that it was solely written by Bishop Gauden, who, after the Restoration, unequivocally claimed it as his own. The folly and impudence of such

a claim, if it could not be substantiated, are not to be presumed to as to any man of good understanding, fair character, and high station, without stronger evidence than has been alleged on the other side; especially when we find that those who had the best means of inquiry, at a time when it seems impossible that the falsehood of Gauden's assertion should not have been demonstrated, if it were false, acquiesced in his pretensions. We have very little to place against this, except secondary testimony; vague, for the most part, in itself and collected by those whose veracity has not been put to the test like that of Gauden. The style also of the "Icon Basilice" has been identified by Mr. Todd with that of Gauden by the use of several phrases so peculiar, that we can hardly conceive them to have suggested themselves to more than one person. It is, nevertheless, superior to his acknowledged writings. A strain of majestic melancholy is well kept up; but the personated sovereign is rather too theatrical for real nature, the language is too rhetorical and amplified, the periods too artificially elaborated. None but scholars and practised writers employ such a style as this.— HALLAM, HENRY, 1837–39, *Introduction to the Literature of Europe, pt.* iii, *ch.* vii, *par.* 37.

In that year (1692) an honest old clergyman named Walker, who had, in the time of the Commonwealth, been Gauden's curate, wrote a book which convinced all sensible and dispassionate readers that Gauden, and not Charles the First, was the author of the "Icon Basilike."—MACAULAY, THOMAS BABINGTON, 1855, *History of England, ch.* xix.

The death of Charles gave fresh vigor to the Royalist cause, and the new loyalty was stirred to enthusiasm by the publication of the "Eikon Basilike," a work really due to the ingenuity of Dr. Gauden, a Presbyterian minister, but which was believed to have been composed by the King himself in his later hours of captivity, and which reflected with admirable skill the hopes, the suffering, and the piety of the Royal "martyr."—GREEN, JOHN RICHARD, 1874, *A Short History of the English People, ch.* viii, *sec.* ix.

The most important in its influence of all the books brought out during the period of the Church's proscription was unquestionably the "Eikon Basilike," a "portraiture of his Sacred Majesty in his sufferings." The skilful work of Dr. Gauden, one of Charles's chaplains, it expressed with extraordinary fidelity, and at the same time idealised with masterly art, the feelings that had moved the king when his conscience spoke most clearly. The love of his people and the love of God, the steadfast determination not to impair his own prerogative or imperil the fabric of the Church, personal abasement and moral grandeur, these were interwoven with rare delicacy and insight. No book had ever been so popular. It was impossible to suppress it: equally impossible to answer. Forty-seven editions of it were soon exhausted; and if it contained arguments for kingship, it contained ten times as many indirectly for Anglicanism and the system of Laud. The horror and pity which it evoked made Charles a saint and Laud a martyr, and enlisted all the sentiment of the age on the side of the Monarchy and the Church.—HUTTON, W. H., 1895, *Social England, ed. Traill, vol.* IV, *p.* 288.

Robert Sanderson

1587–1663

Robert Sanderson, greatest of English casuists, was born 19th September 1587, either at Sheffield or at his father's seat, Gilthwaite Hall near Rotherham. From Rotherham grammar-school he passed in his thirteenth year to Lincoln College, Oxford, of which he became a fellow (1606), reader of logic (1608), and thrice subrector (1613–16), in the last year being also chosen senior proctor. In 1631 he became king's chaplain, was created D. D. in 1636, in 1646–48 filled the regius chair of Divinity at Oxford, and was parson of Boothby-Pagnell for upwards of forty years (1619–60), even through all the Great Rebellion. In 1660 he became Bishop of Lincoln. To him are due the present preface to the Prayer-book and the General Confession. He died at his palace of Buckden, Hunts, 29th Jan. 1663. His works (6 vols. 1854) comprise, besides sermons, the "Logicæ Artis Compendium" (1615), "De Obligatione Conscientiae Prælectiones" (1647); new ed. by Whewell, (1851), "Nine Cases of Conscience Resolved" (1628–78), and "Episcopacy not Prejudicial to the Regal Power" (1661).—PATRICK AND GROOME, *eds.*, 1897, *Chambers's Biographical Dictionary, p.* 822.

PERSONAL

He was a lover of musique, and was wont to play on his base violl, and also to sing to it. He was a lover of heraldry, and gave it in chardge in his articles of enquiry; but the clergie-men made him such a lamentable imperfect returne that it signified nothing. The very Parliamentarians reverenced him for his learning and his vertue, so that he always kept his living, quod N. B. (the information in the Oxon. Antiq. was false). He had no great memorie, I am certaine not a sure one; when I was a fresh-man and heard him read his first lecture, he was out in the Lord's Prayer. He alwayes read his sermons and lectures. Had his memorie been greater his judgement had been lesse: they are like two well-bucketts.—AUBREY, JOHN, 1669–96, *Brief Lives, ed. Clark, vol.* II, *p.* 212.

He was moderately tall: his behaviour had in it much of a plain comeliness, and very little, yet enough, of ceremony or courtship; his looks and motion manifested affability and mildness, and yet he had with these a calm, but so matchless a fortitude, as secured him from complying with any of those many Parliament injunctions, that interfered with a doubtful conscience. His learning was methodical and exact, his wisdom useful, his integrity visible, and his whole life so unspotted, that all ought to be preserved as copies for posterity to write after; the Clergy especially, who with impure hands ought not to offer sacrifice to that God, whose pure eyes abhor iniquity. There was in his Sermons no improper rhetoric, nor such perplexed divisions, as may be said to be like too much light, that so dazzles the eyes, that the sight becomes less perfect: but there was therein no want of useful matter, nor waste of words; and yet such clear distinctions as dispelled all confused notions, and made his hearers depart both wiser, and more confirmed in virtuous resolutions. His memory was so matchless and firm, as 'twas only overcome by his bashfulness; for he alone, or to a friend, could repeat all the Odes of Horace, all Tully's Offices, and much of Juvenal and Persius, without book: and would say, "the repetition of one of the Odes of Horace to himself, was to him such music, as a lesson on the viol was to others, when they played it to themselves or friends."—WALTON, IZAAK, 1678, *The Life of Dr. Robert Sanderson.*

Whether you consider him in his writings or conversation, from his first book of logic to his divinity lectures, sermons and other excellent discourses, the vastness of his judgment, the variety of his learning, all laid out for public benefit, his unparalleled meekness, humility and constancy, you cannot but confess that the Church of England could not lose a greater pillar, a better man, and more accomplished divine.—WOOD, ANTHONY, 1691-1721, *Athenæ Oxonienses, vol.* II, *f.* 322

GENERAL

Dr. Sanderson, who stands at the head of all casuists, ancient and modern, was frequently consulted by Charles I. . . . His Sermons still maintain their reputation for *clearness of reason,* and a purity of style, which seems to be the effect of it.—GRANGER, JAMES, 1769-1824, *Biographical History of England, vol.* V, *p.* 78.

Sanderson was the greatest casuist in the world.—WALFORD, JOHN, 1741, *Memorials and Characters.*

Sanderson was the most celebrated of the English casuists.—HALLAM, HENRY, 1837-39, *Introduction to the Literature of Europe, pt.* iii, *ch.* iv, *par.* 24.

His works, though not abounding with the grace of the gospel, do not, as far as we have read them, present views opposing that grace. . . . His sermons are rather dry and repulsive, but more correct than some later writers.—BICKERSTETH, EDWARD, 1844, *The Christian Student, pp.* 247, 495.

Katherine Philips
1631-1664

Katherine Philips, 1631-1664. Born [Katherine Fowler], in London, 1 Jan. 1631. Educated in London. Married to James Philips, 1647. After her marriage, formed society of persons known by fanciful names; herself adopting that of Orinda. Tragedy, "Pompey" (from Corneille), produced at Smock-Alley Theatre, Dublin, Feb. 1663. Died, in London, 22 June 1664. Buried in church of St. Benet Sherehog. *Works:* "Pompey" (anon.), 1663 (3rd edn., same year); "Poems" (unauthorized edition), 1664. *Posthumous:* "Poems," ed. by Sir C. Cotterel, 1667; "Letters of Orinda to Poliarchus," 1705.—SHARP, R. FARQUHARSON, 1897, *A Dictionary of English Authors, p.* 227.

PERSONAL

From her cosen Blacket, who lived with her from her swadling cloutes to eight, and taught her to read:—She informes me viz.—when a child she was mighty apt to learne, and she assures me that she had read the Bible through before she was full four yeares old; she could have sayd I know not how many places of Scripture and chapters. She was a frequent hearer of sermons; had an excellent memory and could have brought away a sermon in her memory. Very good-natured; not at all high-minded; pretty fatt; not tall; reddish faced.—AUBREY, JOHN, 1669-96, *Brief Lives, ed. Clark, vol.* II, *p.* 154.

As few ladies ever lived more happy in her friends than our poetess, so those friends have done justice to her memory,

and celebrated her, when dead, for those virtues they admired, when living. Mr. Dryden more than once mentions her with honour, and Mr. Cowley has written an excellent Ode upon her death.—CIBBER, THEOPHILUS, 1753, *Lives of the Poets, vol.* II, *p.* 156.

It was not until the second half of the seventeenth century that women began to be considered competent to undertake literature as a profession. In the crowded galaxy of Elizabethan and Jacobean poets there is no female star even of the seventh magnitude. But with the Restoration, the wives and daughters, who had learned during the years of exile to act in political and diplomatic intrigue with independence and skill, took upon themselves to write independently too, and the last forty years of the century are crowded with the names of "celebrated scribbling women." Among all these the Matchless Orinda takes the foremost place—not exactly by merit, for Aphra Behn surpassed her in genius, Margaret, Duchess of Newcastle, in versatility, and Catherine Trotter in professional zeal; but by the moral eminence which she attained through her elevated public career, and which she sealed by her tragical death. When the seventeenth century thought of a poetess, it naturally thought of Orinda; her figure overtopped those of her literary sisters; she was more dignified, more regal in her attitude to the public, than they were; and, in fine, she presents us with the best type we possess of the woman of letters in the seventeenth century.—GOSSE, EDMUND, 1883, *Seventeenth-Century Studies*, p. 205.

GENERAL

Thou dost my wonder, wouldst my envy
　　raise,
If to be prais'd I lov'd more than to praise;
　　Where'er I see an excellence,
I must admire to see thy well-knit sense,
Thy numbers gentle, and thy Fancies high:
Those as thy forehead smooth, these spark-
　　ling as thine eye.
　　　'Tis solid, and 'tis manly all,
　　　Or rather 'tis Angelical;
　　　For as in Angels, we
　　　Do in thy Verses see
Both improv'd Sexes eminently meet;
They are than Man more strong, and more
　　than Woman sweet.
—COWLEY, ABRAHAM, 1663, *On Orinda's Poems*.

. . . soft Orinda, whose bright shining
　　Name,
Stands next great Sappho's in the Ranks of
　　Fame: . . .
—OLDHAM, JOHN, 1681, *A Pastoral on the Death of the Earl of Rochester*.

A woman's Poems, the Lady Catherine Philips, are far above contempt; but that is best to me which is most holy.—BAXTER, RICHARD, 1681, *Poetical Fragments, Prefatory Address*.

She was author of several poems, which are more to be admired for propriety and beauty of thought, than for harmony of versification, in which she was generally deficient.—GRANGER, JAMES, 1769–1824, *Biographical History of England, vol.* IV, p. 45.

Cannot be said to have been a woman of genius; but her verses betoken an interesting and placid enthusiasm of heart,

and a cultivated taste, that form a beautiful specimen of female character.—CAMPBELL, THOMAS, 1819, *Specimens of the British Poets*, p. 265.

Some of the verses of Katherine Philips, . . . have an easy though antithetical style, like the lighter ones of Cowley, or the verses of Sheffield and his French contemporaries.—HUNT, LEIGH, 1847, *Specimens of British Poetesses; Men, Women, and Books*.

Mrs. Philips has always seemed to me to be one of the best of our Female Poets. Her versification, though often careless, is chaste and harmonious, and her sentiments extremely pure and excellent.—ROWTON, FREDERIC, 1848, *The Female Poets of Great Britain*, p. 67.

Orinda, though not exactly "matchless," must have been a very gifted woman—of elevated mind and character, warm attachments, and no inconsiderable poetic endowment: she was full mistress of the faculty of nervous and direct expression in verse.—ROSSETTI, WILLIAM MICHAEL, 1872–78, *ed., Humorous Poems*, p. 149.

Did much to acclimatize in England the refinements, elegancies, and heroism à *panache* of her French neighbours. With the help of her friends she translated some of the plays of Corneille, not without adding something to the original to make it look more heroical.—JUSSERAND, J. J., 1890, *The English Novel in the Time of Shakespeare*, p. 370.

Modern criticism has entirely neglected her. I cannot find that any writer of authority has mentioned her name with interest since Keats, in 1817, when he was writing "Endymion," came across her poems at Oxford, and in writing to Reynolds remarked that he found "a most delicate fancy of the Fletcher kind" in her poems, and quoted one piece of ten stanzas to prove it. . . . Nor was she, like so many of her contemporaries, an absurd, or preposterous, or unclean writer: her muse was uniformly pure and reasonable; her influence, which was very great, was exercised wholly in favour of what was beautiful and good; and if she failed, it is rather by the same accident by which so many poets of less intelligence have unexpectedly succeeded.—GOSSE, EDMUND, 1883, *Seventeenth-Century Studies, pp.* 205, 206.

Her poetry is not very interesting to the modern reader. It is affected. There is little heart-beating to be felt in it. Even to the extent of sickly prudery, she eschews the romance of love as a theme, and versifies platonically on the delights of friendship, generally friendship between one woman and another. Some of her strongest thinking is expended on political poems which have lost all savour now; and stilted use of stale classical metaphor is abundant. . . . Two things have to be borne in mind when we judge her. In the first place, we have to recollect the recognition she deserves as being the first English woman with sufficient imagination (and confidence in it) to adopt pliant verse as the habitual vehicle for her thinking, in defiance of the almost vested right in it which male writers had till then preserved. Her courage may be compared to that of a woman who should make herself as skilful with the rapier as a man. Over form of verse Orinda exhibits as much command as any author of her time. And, as our first poetess, she at any rate should obtain rank relatively as high as that which we accord to Cædmon, our first poet.—ROBERTSON, ERIC S., 1883, *English Poetesses, p. 4.*

Sir Kenelm Digby

1603-1665

An Everard Digby, who died in 1592, wrote curious books; his son, Sir Everard, knighted by James I., was hanged, drawn, and quartered for giving fifteen hundred pounds towards expenses of the Gunpowder Plot. The eldest son of that Sir Everard was Sir Kenelm Digby, born in 1603, and educated at Oxford. He travelled in Spain, discovered, as he supposed, a sympathetic powder for cure of wounds, was knighted in 1623, was sent with a fleet into the Mediterranean in 1628, and returned to the faith of his fathers as a Roman Catholic in 1636. In the civil wars he helped the king among the Roman Catholics, and was then exile in France until Cromwell's supremacy gave him liberty to revisit England; but he returned to France. He published, in 1644, a mystical interpretation of "The 22d Stanza in the 9th Canto of the 2d Book of Spenser's Faery Queen;" in 1645, "Two Treatises on the Nature of Bodies and of Man's Soul;" took lively interest in Palingenesis; wrote "Observations upon Sir T. Browne's Religio Medici," and was ingenious in the pursuit of forms of learning which have proved to be more curious than true. He died in 1665.—MORLEY, HENRY, 1879, *A Manual of English Literature, ed. Tyler, p. 469.*

PERSONAL

He doth excel
In honour, courtesy and all the parts
Court can call hers, or man could call his arts.
He's prudent, valiant, just and temperate:
In him all virtue is beheld in state;
And he is built like some imperial room
For that to dwell in, and be still at home.
His breast is a brave palace, a broad street,
Where all heroic ample thoughts do meet:
Where nature such a large survey hath ta'en,
As other souls, to his, dwelt in a lane.

—JONSON, BEN, 1635? *An Epigram to my Muse, the Lady Digby, on her husband, sir Kenelm Digby, Works, ed. Gifford and Cunningham, vol.* IX, *p. 33.*

He was a great traveller, and understood 10 or 12 languages. He was not only master of a good and gracefull judicious stile, but he also wrote a delicate hand, both fast-hand and Roman. . . . He was such a goodly handsome person, gigantique and great voice, and had so gracefull elocution and noble addresse, etc., that had he been drop't out of the clowdes in any part of the world, he would have made himselfe respected. But the Jesuites spake spitefully, and sayd 'twas true, but then he must not stay there above six weekes. He was envoyé from Henrietta Maria (then Queen-mother) to Pope (Innocent X) where at first sight he was mightily admired; but after some time he grew high, and hectored with his holinesse, and gave him the lye. The pope sayd he was mad. He was well versed in all kinds of learning And he had also this vertue, that no man *knew better how to abound, and to be abased,* and either was indifferent to him. No man became grandeur better; sometimes again he would live only with a lackey, and horse with a foote-cloath. . . . He was a person of very extraordinary strength . . . he was of an undaunted courage, yet not apt in the least to give offence. His conversation was both ingeniose and innocent.—AUBREY, JOHN, 1669-96, *Brief Lives*, ed. *Clark, vol.* I, *pp.* 225, 227.

His knowledge, though various and extensive, appeared to be greater than it really was; as he had all the powers of elocution and address to recommend it. He knew how to shine in a circle of ladies, or philosophers; and was as much attended to when he spoke on the most trivial subjects, as when he spoke on the most important. He was remarkably robust, and of a very uncommon size, but moved with peculiar grace and dignity. Though he applied himself to experiment, he was sometimes hypothetical in his philosophy; and there are instances of his being very bold and paradoxical in his conjectures: hence he was called the "Pliny of his age for lying."—GRANGER, JAMES, 1769-1824, *Biographical History of England, vol.* III, *p.* 155.

One of the most attractive figures visible on that imaginary line where the eve of chivalry and the dawn of science unite to form a mysterious yet beautiful twilight, is that of Sir Kenelm Digby. To our imagination he represents the knight of old before the characteristics of that romantic style of manhood were diffused in the complexed developments of modern society, and the philosopher of the epoch when fancy and superstition held sway over the domain of the exact sciences. Bravery, devotion to the sex, and a thirst for glory, nobleness of disposition and grace of manner, traditional qualities of the genuine cavalier, signalized Sir Kenelm, not less than an ardent love of knowledge, a habitude of speculation, and literary accomplishment; but his courage and his gallantry partook of the poetic enthusiasm of the days of Bayard, and his opinions and researches were something akin to those of the alchemists. High birth and a handsome person gave emphasis to these traits; and we have complete and authentic memorials whereby he is distinctly reproduced to our minds.—TUCKERMAN, HENRY T., 1856, *The Modern Knight; Essays, Biographical and Critical, p.* 75.

The fact seems to be that, with striking superficial qualities and an imposing air of ability, Sir Kenelm Digby was a man distinguished more by a certain restless liveliness of nature than by any higher attributes of head or heart.—TULLOCH, JOHN, 1872, *Rational Theology and Christian Philosophy in England, vol.* I, *p.* 108.

Amongst the many strange personalities of the 17th century, there are few whose character it is more difficult to gauge than that of Kenelm Digby. He played his part as courtier, man of fashion, romancer, critic, soldier, virtuoso, and philosopher; and although he was distinguished in each, there was no sphere in which some suspicion of charlatanism did not attach to him. It is indeed difficult to avoid the conclusion that an element of madness entered into his composition, or at least that his versatility was united to an abnormal eccentricity, which, if it partly relieves him of the worst charges, yet explains how small his influence was in any single sphere of activity. His vanity was prodigious, and is naturally most conspicuous where his writings (as is frequently the case) relate to his own actions.—CRAIK, HENRY, 1893, *ed., English Prose, vol.* II, *p.* 291.

GENERAL

Deserves a word among the half-mystic, half-scientific men of his time. He was a strange compound of dashing soldier, accomplished courtier, successful lover, and occult philosopher.—MINTO, WILLIAM, 1872-80, *Manual of English Prose Literature, p.* 306.

He has not the boldness or the mastery of language which invents new expressions or clothes new thoughts in words. But he writes with the polished ease and grace which in his carriage and his manner so vividly impressed all his contemporaries, even when they were compelled to admit his total want of veracity. He has the confidence, and, at the same time, the breadth of view, acquired by converse with every phase of life. His prose has not the quaint turns, and the sympathetic subtlety of Browne's. . . . He can rise occasionally to very lofty heights of dignity and eloquence. With all this, however, there is a pervading impression of artificiality, as of one whose character was above all things theatrical; and of superficial confidence, as of one to whom philosophical lucubrations were only a phase of eccentric and ill-balanced restlessness.—CRAIK, HENRY, 1893, *ed., English Prose, vol.* II, *p.* 293.

His friendship with Descartes, Hobbes and other leaders of the new philosophy invested his erratic speculations with an importance that they little deserved. Though he was in close intercourse with the chief men of science of the time, his writings are a singular medley of Aristotelian Philosophy, Astrology, Alchemy, and absurd superstitions. His romantic courtship of Venetia Stanley—the history of which is recorded in his "Private Memoirs," published in 1827—his successful privateering expedition in 1627, and the various confidential missions in which he was engaged on behalf of the Queen, and subsequently in the service of the Protector, all serve to perpetuate the memory of one of the most picturesque and eccentric characters of the period.—MASTERMAN, J. H. B., 1897, *The Age of Milton*, p. 236.

John Earle

1601?–1665

John Earle or Earles, 1601–1665, entered at Merton Coll., Oxford, 1620, became chaplain and tutor to Prince Charles, and accompanied him in his exile. On the Restoration he was made Dean of Westminster, consecrated Bishop of Worcester in 1662, and transferred to Salisbury in 1663. "Microcosmographie; or, A Peece of the World discovered in Essayes and Characters," Lon., 1628, 8vo; 6th ed., 1630, 12mo; 10th ed., Salisbury, 1786. New ed. (78 characters) with Notes and Appendix, by Philip Bliss, Lon., 1811, sm. 8vo. This ed. contains a Catalogue of the various Writers of Character to the year 1700. . . . "An Elegy upon Francis Beaumont," by Bishop Earle, will be found printed at the end of Beaumont's Poems, 1640. He trans. into Latin the Eikon Basilike, (Hague, 1649), and Hooker's "Ecclesiastical Polity;" the last was destroyed by the carelessness of his servants. The character of Bishop Earle was most exemplary.—ALLIBONE, S. AUSTIN, 1854–58, *Dictionary of English Literature, vol.* I, *p.*539.

PERSONAL

Doctor Earles was at that Time Chaplain in the House to the Earl of Pembroke, Lord Chamberlain of his Majesty's Household, and had a Lodging in the Court under that Relation: He was a Person very notable for his Elegance in the Greek and Latin Tongues; and being Fellow of Merton College in Oxford, and having been Proctor of the University, and some very witty, and sharp Discourses being published in Print without his Consent, though known to be his, He grew suddenly into a very general Esteem with all Men; being a Man of great Piety and Devotion; a most eloquent and powerful Preacher; and of a Conversation so pleasant and delightful, so very innocent, and so very facetious, that no Man's Company was more desired, and more loved. No man was more negligent in his Dress, and Habit, and Mien; no Man more wary, and cultivated, in his Behaviour, and Discourse; insomuch as He had the greater Advantage when He was known, by promising so little before He was known. He was an excellent Poet both in Latin, Greek, and English, as appears by many Pieces yet abroad; though He suppressed Many More himself, especially of English, incomparably good, out of an Austerity to those Sallies of his Youth. . . . He was amongst the few excellent Men who never had, nor never could have an Enemy, but such a one, who was an Enemy to all Learning, and Virtue, and therefore would never make himselfe known.—CLARENDON, LORD (EDWARD HYDE), 1674? *Life.*

He was the man of all the Clergy for whom the King had the greatest esteem. He had been his sub-tutor, and had followed him in all his exile with so clear a Character, that the King could never see or hear of any one thing amiss in him. So he, who had a secret pleasure in finding out any thing that lessened a man esteemed eminent for piety, yet had a value for him beyond all the men of his order.—BURNET GILBERT, 1715–34, *History of My Own Time.*

GENERAL

Perhaps the most valuable collection of characters, previous to the year 1700, is that published by Bishop Earle, in 1628, under the title of "Microcosmography," and which may be considered as a pretty faithful delineation of many classes of characters as they existed during the close of the sixteenth, and commencement of the seventeenth century.—DRAKE, NATHAN, 1817, *Shakspeare and His Times.*

In some of these short characters, Earle is worthy of comparison with La Bruyère; in others, perhaps the greater part, he has contented himself with pictures of ordinary manners, such as the varieties of occupation, rather than of intrinsic character, supply. In all, however, we find an acute observation and a happy humor of expression. The chapter entitled the Sceptic is best known: it is witty, but an insult throughout on the honest searcher after truth, which could have come only from one that was content to take up his own opinions for ease or profit. Earle is always gay, and quick to catch the ridiculous, especially that of exterior appearances: his style is short, describing well with a few words, but with much of the affected quaintness of that age. It is one of those books which give us a picturesque idea of the manners of our fathers at a period now become remote; and for this reason, were there no other, it would deserve to be read.—HALLAM, HENRY, 1837–39, *Introduction to the Literature of Europe, pt.* iii, *ch.* vii, *par.* 39.

Earle is preserved from pedantry by the liveliness of his wit, while his wit itself has in it a salt nobler than the Attic—the savour of pure and unaffected piety.—WARD, ADOLPHUS WILLIAM, 1893, *English Prose, ed. Craik, vol.* II, *p.* 279.

The one strain in character which throughout afflicts him most, and for which he reserves his most distilled contempt, is the strain of unreality—the affectation whose sin is always to please, and which fails so singularly of its object. Hypocrisy, pretension, falseness—against everything which has that lack of simplicity so fatal to true life he sets his face. For the rest he can hardly read the enigma; he only states it reverently.—BENSON, ARTHUR CHRISTOPHER, 1896, *Essays, p.* 34.

Sir Richard Fanshawe

1608–1666

Mr. (afterwards Sir Richard) Fanshawe was born June 1608,—in 1630, was appointed Secretary to Lord Aston's embassy to Spain, where he remained as Chargé d'Affaires after Lord Aston's recall—returned to England about 1638—obtained, in 1641, the office of Remembrancer of the Court of Exchequer—attended Charles I. to Oxford during the early part of the civil war—in March, 1645, was appointed Secretary to the Prince of Wales, and accompanied him in the west—resigned his employment on the Prince quitting Jersey—compounded, and returned to England about the end of 1646, and quitted it again the following year—went on a mission to Spain in February, 1650, from whence he returned unsuccessful in October—was created a baronet, September 2, 1650—afterwards joined Charles II. in Scotland—was taken prisoner at the battle of Worcester—after the Restoration, was M. P. for the University of Cambridge—was sent to Portugal in 1661, on a complimentary mission to the Princess Katherine—in 1662, was made Privy Councillor for Ireland—in 1663, was sent on another mission to Portugal—in 1664, went ambassador to Madrid, from whence he was recalled, but, before he could return, he died at Madrid, June 26, 1666.—LISTER, T. H., 1837, *Life and Administration of Edward, First Earl of Clarendon, vol.* III, *p.* 18, *note.*

PERSONAL

He was an exact critic in the Latin tongue, spoke the Spanish with ease and propriety, and perfectly understood the Italian. The politeness of his manners, and the integrity of his life, did not only procure him the love and esteem of his own countrymen, but gained him unusual favour and respect in Spain; among a people notorious for their disregard to strangers, and too apt to overlook all merit but their own.—GRANGER, JAMES, 1769–1824, *Biographical History of England, vol.* V, *p.* 103.

GENERAL

At present we are only to consider his Scholarship, which will sufficiently appear by the several Translations which he has publisht, particularly those which are Dramatick: the first of which in Order, and the most Eminent, is stil'd *Il Pastor Fido, The Faithful Shepherd,* a Pastoral, printed 4° Lond. 1646, and dedicated to the Hope and Lustre of three Kingdoms, *Charles* Prince of *Wales*. This Piece is translated from the *Italian* of the Famous *Guarini*. . . . Sir *John Denham* in his Verses on this Translation, infinitely commends it: and tho' he seems to assent to our Author's Notions, touching Translations in general: yet he shews that Sir *Richard* has admirably succeeded in this particular Attempt; as the Reader may see by the following Lines; where after having blam'd servile Translators, he goes on thus;

"A new and nobler Way thou dost pursue
To make Translations, and Translators too
They but preserve the Ashes, thou the Flame,
True to his Sense, but truer to his Fame."

—LANGBAINE, GERARD, 1691, *An Account of the English Dramatick Poets, p.* 191.

Sir Richard's version ["The Lusiad"] is quaint, flat, and harsh; and he has interwoven many ridiculously conceited expressions which are foreign both to the spirit and style of his original; but in general it is closer than the modern translation to the literal meaning of Camoens. Altogether, Fanshawe's representation of the Portuguese poem may be compared to the wrong side of the tapestry.—CAMPBELL, THOMAS, 1819, *Specimens of the British Poets.*

To my taste this ["Querer por Solo Querer"] is fine, elegant, queen-like raillery; a second part of "Love's Labour's Lost," to which title this extraordinary play has still better pretensions than even Shakespeare's; for after leading three pair of royal lovers through endless mazes of doubts, difficulties; oppositions of dead fathers' wills; a labyrinth of losings and findings; jealousies; enchantments; conflicts with giants, and single-handed against armies; to the exact state in which all the lovers might with the greatest propriety indulge their reciprocal wishes—when, the duce is in it, you think, but they must all be married now—suddenly the three ladies turn upon their lovers; and, as an exemplification of the moral of the play, "Loving for loving's sake," and a hyperplatonic, truly Spanish proof of their affections—demand that the lovers shall consent to their mistresses' taking upon them the vow of a single life! to which the gallants, with becoming refinement, can do no less than consent.—

The fact is that it was a court play, in which the characters—males, giants, and all—were played by females, and those of the highest order of Grandeeship. No nobleman might be permitted amongst them; and it was against the forms, that a great court lady of Spain should consent to such an unrefined motion, as that of wedlock, though but in a play.—LAMB, CHARLES, 1827, *Notes on the Garrick Plays, p.* 287.

Sir Richard Fanshawe is the author of versions of Camoens's "Lusiad," of Guarini's Pastor Fido, of the Fourth Book of the Æneid, of the Odes of Horace, and of the Querer por Solo Querer (To love for love's sake) of the Spanish dramatist Mendoza. Some passages from the last-mentioned work, which was published in 1649, may be found in Lamb's "Specimens," the ease and flowing gayety of which never have been excelled even in original writing. The "Pastor Fido" is also rendered with much spirit and elegance. Fanshawe is, besides, the author of a Latin translation of Fletcher's "Faithful Shepherdess," and of some original poetry. His genius, however, was sprightly and elegant rather than lofty, and perhaps he does not succeed so well in translating poetry of a more serious style.—CRAIK, GEORGE L., 1861, *A Compendious History of English Literature and of the English Language, vol.* I, *p.* 576.

His writings show a scholar's acquaintance with the best ancient and modern poets. In all he wrote a good deal, but the greater part consists of translations from the Italian, Spanish and Portuguese. He is one of the many translators who have wasted themselves over the hopeless tediousness of the "Lusiad." But, besides a little graceful original work, his reputation rests chiefly on his beautiful translation of the "Pastor Fido," on a small volume of translations from Virgil and Horace, and on a curious and clever piece of work, a rendering in Latin verse of Fletcher's "Faithful Shepherdess."—MACKAIL, J. W., 1888, *Sir Richard Fanshawe, Macmillan's Magazine, vol.* 59, *p.* 111.

The translations of Horace's "Odes" deserve to rank among the most successful efforts of the kind. Most of the subtle turns of the original are given with rare felicity, and there is throughout an ease and elegance which prove the translator to be a skilled literary workman. His classical scholarship was also shown to advantage in his translation of Fletcher's "Faithful Shepherdess" into Latin hexameters and hendecasyllabics. Fanshawe's few surviving original English poems exhibit rare literary faculty, and it is to be regretted that they are so few. —LEE, SIDNEY, 1889, *Dictionary of National Biography, vol.* XVIII, *p.* 189.

James Howell
1594?–1666

James Howell, born near Brecknock about 1594, was educated at Jesus College, Oxford. He was appointed manager of a patent glass manufactory in London, and travelled on the continent from 1619 to 1621, in which year he was elected a fellow of Jesus College. He became secretary to Lord Scrope in 1626, secretary to an extraordinary embassy to Denmark in 1632, and having filled various appointments, obtained the clerkship of the Council at Whitehall in 1640. Howell, sent to the Fleet in 1643, was liberated soon after the execution of Charles I., and at the Restoration was appointed historiographer royal. He died Nov. 1666, and was buried in the Temple Church. Howell was a prolific writer. His best known works are "Dendrologia, Dodona's Grove, or the Vocal Forest," a poem published in 1640, and the "Epistolæ Ho-Elianæ: Familiar Letters, Domestic and Foreign, &c." of which the first volume appeared in 1645, and the second in 1655.—TOWNSEND, GEORGE H., 1870, *ed. The Every-Day Book of Modern Literature, vol.* I, *p.* 177.

PERSONAL

Multofarious indeed were Howell's acquirements. He was one of the best modern linguists of his day: sometimes he figures at the court of Denmark, delivering Latin speeches before the king: then in Ireland, under Wentworth, afterwards Earl of Strafford—with whose death Howell's hopes sank. He had long been a kind of poet of a low standard; and he consoled himself on mediocrity by presenting to Charles the First his "Vote," a poem which procured him a place as Clerk of the Council, and gave him a suite of apartments at Whitehall. — THOMPSON, KATHERINE (GRACE WHARTON), 1862, *The Literature of Society, vol.* I, *p.* 232,

A thorough Welshman, Howell became a celebrated English author in his day. He was past forty years of age before his first book was published. Then for the remaining twenty odd years of his life, with an incessant and unwearying industry, he wrote, compiled, or translated book after book, each varying greatly in subject. Lastly, he is one of the earliest instances of a literary man successfully maintaining himself with the fruits of his pen.—ARBER, EDWARD, 1869, *Howell's Instructions, Preface.*

Howell has been accused of being a prig, which is harsh, and of being a coxcomb, which is true enough; and he has other qualities which are not in themselves gifts or graces. But his pedantry, his egotism, his adroit, if seldom quite abject flattery of the great, his spice of ill-nature now and then, his self-seeking and intriguing, present, as they are reflected in his style and matter, a spectacle by no means ugly, and very decidedly lively.—SAINTSBURY, GEORGE, 1893, *English Prose, ed. Craik, vol.* II, *p.* 236.

DODONA'S GROVE
1640

This is a strange allegory, without any ingenuity in maintaining the analogy between the outer and inner story, which alone can give a reader any pleasure in allegorical writing. The subject is the state of Europe, especially of England, about 1640, under the guise of animated trees in a forest. The style is like the following: "The next morning the royal olives sent some prime elms to attend Prince Rocolino in quality of officers of state; and, a little after, he was brought to the royal palace in the same state Elaiana's kings use to be attended the day of their coronation." The contrivance is all along so clumsy and unintelligible, the invention so poor and absurd, the story, if story there be, so dull an echo of well-known events, that it is impossible to reckon "Dodona's Grove" any thing but an entire failure. Howell has no wit; but he has abundance of conceits, flat and commonplace enough. With all this, he was

a man of some sense and observation.—
HALLAM, HENRY, 1837–39, *Introduction
to the Literature of Europe, pt.* iii, *ch.* vii,
par. 61.

The great bibliographer Haller was de-
ceived into including the title of James
Howell's "Dendrologia, or Dodona's
Grove" (1640), in his "Bibliotheca
Botanica."—WHEATLEY, HENRY B.,1893,
Literary Blunders, p. 75.

FAMILIAR LETTERS

James Howell published his "Ho-
Elianæ" for which he indeed was laughed
at (not for his letters which acquainted
us with a number of passages worthy to
be known and had never else been preserved) but which, were the language enlightened with that sort of exercise and
conversation, I should not question its
being equal to any of the most celebrated
abroad.—EVELYN, JOHN, 1668, *Letter to
Lord Spencer.*

He had a singular command of his pen,
whether in verse or in prose, and was well
read in modern Histories, especially in
those of the Countries wherein he had
travelled, had a parabolical and allusive
fancy, according to his motto *Senesco non
Segnesco.* But the Reader is to know that
his writings have been only to gain a
livelihood, and by their dedications to
flatter great and noble persons, are very
trite and empty, stolen from other authors
without acknowledgment, and fitted only
to please the humours of novices. . . .
Many of the said Letters were never
written before the Author of them was in
the Fleet, as he pretends they were, only
feigned, (no time being kept with their
dates) and purposely published to gain
money to relieve his necessities, yet give
a tolerable history of those times.—WOOD,
ANTHONY, 1691–1721, *Athenæ Oxonienses.*

I believe the second published correspondence of this kind, and, in our language
at least, of any importance after Hall, will
be found to be "Epistolæ Hoelianæ, or the
Letters of James Howell," a great traveller, an intimate friend of Jonson, and the
first who bore the office of the royal historiographer, which discover a variety of literature, and abound with much entertaining and useful information.—WARTON,
THOMAS, 1778–81, *History of English
Poetry, sec.* lxiv.

A work containing numberless anecdotes
and historical narratives, and forming one
of the most amusing and instructive
volumes of the seventeenth century.—
BRYDGES, SIR EGERTON, 1808, *Censura
Literaria.*

These letters were written in England,
but are not the *coinage* of British soil.
They are amusing and instructive, and
have deservedly gone through half a score
of editions. The account in them of the
assassination of Henry IV. of France is
minutely curious.—DIBDIN, THOMAS FROG-
NALL, 1824, *The Library Companion, p.*
601, *note.*

Montaigne and "Howel's *Letters*" are
my bedside books. If I wake at night, I
have one or other of them to prattle me
to sleep again. They talk about themselves for ever and don't weary me. I
like to hear them tell their old stories
over and over again. I read them in the
dozy hours and only half remember them.
I am informed that both of them tell
coarse stories. I don't heed them. It
was the custom of their time, as it is of
Highlanders and Hottentots, to dispense
with a part of dress which we all wear in
cities. . . . I love, I say, and scarcely
ever tire of hearing, the artless prattle
of those two dear old friends, the Peri-
gourdin gentleman and the priggish little
Clerk of King Charles's Council.—THACK-
ERAY, WILLIAM MAKEPEACE, 1862, *On
Two Children in Black, Roundabout
Papers.*

To the list of writers whom it is impossible to use with confidence must, I am
afraid, be added that agreeable letter-
writer Howell. But there can be no doubt
that many of his letters are mere products of the bookmaker's skill, drawn up
from memory long afterwards [e. g. I. ii.
12]. On the other hand, some of the
letters have all the look of being what
they purport to be, actually written at
the time, but even then, the dates at the
end are frequently incorrectly given.—
GARDINER, SAMUEL RAWSON, 1864, *Prince
Charles and the Spanish Marriage, Preface,
p.* xiv.

He may be called the Father of Epistolary Literature, the first writer, that is
to say, of letters which addressed to individuals, were intended for publication.
A style animated, racy, and picturesque;
keen powers of observation; great literary
skill; an eager, restless, curious spirit;

some humour and much wit; and a catholicity of sympathy very unusual with the
writers of his age—are his chief claims
to distinction.—SCOONES, W. BAPTISTE,
1880, *Four Centuries of English Letters*,
p. 71.

It is strange that no new edition of
Howell's "Letters" has appeared for the
last 130 years. In the century after
their first appearance, no less than a dozen
editions testified to their continued
vitality, and stray allusions prove that
they have never passed beyond the ken of
the true lovers of books. A work which
Thackeray has praised so highly, and
Scott, Browning, and Kingsley have used
for some of their most popular effects,
cannot be said to have ever lost its chances
of revival. Perhaps the supply of the
second-hand copies of twelve editions has
hitherto been sufficient to satisfy the demand. But the avidity of our American
cousins is fast causing this source to fail,
and the time seems opportune for Howell
to make a fresh bid for the popularity he
deserves.—JACOBS, JOSEPH, 1892, *ed.*, *The
Familiar Letters of James Howell, Preface*,
p. ix.

Surpassed all previous letter-writers in
the ease and livelienss of his letters.—
GOSSE, EDMUND, 1897, *Short History of
Modern English Literature*, *p.* 152.

Has survived in English literature as a
retailer of lively and agreeable gossip and
anecdotage. . . . Howell's style is
careless and colloquial, but his "Letters"
will always retain their interest as a record of the life of the time, and for their
genuine literary merit.—MASTERMAN, J.
HOWARD B., 1897, *The Age of Milton*, *pp.*
238, 239.

GENERAL

Not to know the Author of these Poems,
were an ignorance beyond *Barbarism*. . . .
He may be called the prodigie of his Age,
for the variety of his Volumes; for from
his Δενδϸολογία or "Parly of Trees"
[1640], to his Θηϸολογία or "Parly of
beasts" [1660] (not inferior to the other),
there hath pass'd the Press above forty of
his Works on various subjects; useful not
only to the present times, but to all posterity. And 'tis observed that in all his
Writings there is somthing still *New*
either in the *Matter, Method* or *Fancy*,
and in an untrodded Tract. Moreover,
one may discover a kinde of Vein of *Poesie*

to run through the body of his *Prose*, in
the Continuity and succinctness thereof
all along. He teacheth a new way of
Epistolizing; and that "Familiar Letters"
may not only consist of Words and a
bombast of Compliments, but that they
are capable of the highest Speculations
and solidest kind of Knowledge.—FISHER,
PAYNE, 1664, *Mr. Howel's Poems, Preface*.

He had a great knowledge in modern
histories, especiall y in those of the countries in which he had travelled, and he
seems, by his letters, to have been no
contemptible politician: As to his poetry,
it is smoother, and more harmonious, than
was very common with the bards of his
time. As he introduced the trade of
writing for bread, so he also is charged
with venal flattery, than which nothing
can be more ignoble and base.—CIBBER,
THEOPHILUS, 1753, *Lives of the Poets, vol.*
II, *p.* 34.

In the time of the civil war, he was
commited a close prisoner to the Fleet,
where he continued for many years. The
greatest part of his works were written
for his support during his confinement;
and he indeed appears, in several of his
hasty productions, to have been more
anxious to satisfy his stomach, than to do
justice to his fame. His "Dodona's
Grove," which was published in the reign
of Charles I. gained him a considerable
reputation. But of all his performances,
his "Letters" are the most esteemed,
though, as Mr. Wood justly observes,
many of them were never written till he
was in prison.—GRANGER, JAMES, 1769–
1824, *Biographical History of England,
vol.* IV, *p.* 51.

Notable because he wrote so much; and
I specially name him because he was the
earliest and best type of what we should
call a hackwriter; ready for anything; a
shrewd salesman, too, of all he did write;
travelling largely—having modern instincts, I think; making small capital—
whether of learning or money—reach
enormously. He was immensely popular,
too, in his day; a Welshman by birth, and
never wrote at all till past forty; but
afterward he kept at it with a terrible
pertinacity. —MITCHELL, DONALD G.,
1890, *English Lands Letters and Kings,
from Elizabeth to Anne*, *p.* 107.

Howell is one of the earliest Englishmen
who made a livelihood out of literature.

He wrote with a light pen; and although he shows little power of imagination in his excursions into pure literature, his pamphlets and his occasional verse exhibit exceptional faculty of observation, a lively interest in current affairs, and a rare mastery of modern languages, including his native Welsh. His attempts at spelling reform on roughly phonetic lines are also interesting. He urged the suppression of redundant letters like the *e* in done or the *u* in honour (cf. *Epist. Ho—el.* ed. Jacobs, p. 510; *Parley of Beasts*, advt. at end). But it is in his "Epistolæ Hoelianæ: Familiar Letters, Domestic and Foreign, divided into Sundry Sections, partly Historical, Political, and Philosophical," that his literary power is displayed at its best. Philosophic reflection, political, social, and domestic anecdote, scientific speculation, are all intermingled with attractive ease in the correspondence which he professes to have addressed to men of all ranks and degrees of intimacy. . . . Most of Howell's letters were in all probability written expressly for publication "to relieve his necessities" while he was in the Fleet—LEE, SIDNEY, 1891, *Dictionary of National Biography, vol.* XXVIII, *pp.* 112, 113.

A busy "polygraph" as the French say, and a professional man of letters who had travelled much, and tried many irons in many fires, has filled his letters (his miscellaneous writings are mostly unread) with such vivid and interesting details— gossip, anecdote, description, and what not—as have altogether bribed many good judges, and have not failed to produce an effect even upon the most incorruptible. —SAINTSBURY, GEORGE, 1895, *Social England, ed. Traill, vol.* IV, *p.* 101.

James Shirley

1596–1666

Born, in London, 18 Sept. 1596. At Merchant Taylors' School, Oct. 1608 to June 1612. Matric., St. John's Coll., Oxford, 1612. Removed to Catherine Hall, Cambridge. B. A., 1617. Ordained Curate of parish near St. Albans. Resigned Curacy on becoming a Roman Catholic. Kept a Grammar school at St. Albans, 1623–24. This failing, he removed to London; devoted himself to literature. Mem. of Gray's Inn, 1634. Wrote many plays till 1640. Valet of Chamber to Queen Henrietta Maria. Kept a school in White Friars, 1640–46. Resumed career of dramatist, 1646. Died, in London, Oct. 1666. Buried in church of St. Giles'-in-the-Fields, 29 Oct. *Works:* "Eccho" (no copy known), 1618 (another end., called: "Narcissus, or the Self-Lover," 1646); "The Wedding," 1629; "The Greatful Servant," 1630; "The School of Complement" (also known as "Love Tricks"), 1631; "Changes," 1632; "The Wittie Fair One," 1633; "A Contention for Honour and Riches," 1633; "The Bird in a Cage," 1633; "The triumph of Peace," 1633; "The Traytor," 1635; "Hide Park," 1637; "The Young Admirall," 1637; "The Gamester," 1637; "The Example," 1637; "The Lady of Pleasure," 1637; "The Royall Master," 1638; "The Duke's Mistris," 1638; "The Maide's Revenge," 1639; "The Ball" (with Chapman), 1639; "Chabot, Admiral of France" (with Chapman), 1639; "The Opportunitie," 1640; "The Coronation" (pubd. under Fletcher's name), 1640; "St. Patrick for Ireland," 1640; "The Constant Maid," 1640 (another end., called: "Love will finde out the Way," 1661); "The Humorous Courtier," 1640; "The Arcadia," 1640; "Poems," 1646; "The Triumph of Beautie," 1646; "The Way made Plain to the Latin Tongue," 1649; "Grammatica Anglo-Latina," 1651; "The Cardinal," 1652; "Six New Playes," 1653 [1652]; "Cupid and Death" (under initials: J. S.), 1653; "The Gentleman of Venise," 1655; "The Polititian," 1655; "The Rudiments of Grammar," 1656; "Εισαγωγη," 1656; "Honour and Mammon; and, the Contention of Ajax and Ulysses," 1659; "Andromana" (under initials: J. S.), 1660. *Posthumous:* "An Essay towards an Universal and Rational Grammar," ed. by J. T. Phillipps, 1726; "Double Falsehood" (pubd. under Shakespeare's name; probably by Shirley), 1728; "Jenkin of Wales," ed. by J. O. Halliwell, 1861. *Collected Works:* "Dramatic Works and Poems," ed., with memoir, by A. Dyce (6 vols.), 1833.—SHARP, R. FARQUHARSON, 1897, *A Dictionary of English Authors,* p. 256.

PERSONAL

James, thou and I did spend some precious
　　yeeres
At Katherine-Hall; since when, we some-
　　times feele
In our poetick braines, (as plaine appeares)
A whirling tricke, then caught from Kather-
　　ine's wheele.
—BANCROFT, THOMAS, 1639, *Two Bookes
of Epigrammes.*

He was educated at St. John's College,
in Oxford, where he was taken great
notice of by Dr. Laud, then president of
that house. He entered into holy orders;
though he was much discouraged from it,
by his friend the president, on account of
a large mole on his left cheek; and was
some time a parish priest in Hertfordshire.
He afterward turned Roman Catholic, and
kept a school at St. Alban's, but soon grew
tired of that employment, and going to
London commenced poet. He wrote no
less than thirty dramatic pieces, some of
which were acted with great applause. In
the Interregnum, he was necessitated to
return to his former profession of schoolmaster; in which he became eminent, and
wrote several grammatical books for the
use of his scholars.—GRANGER, JAMES,
1769–1824, *Biographical History of England, vol.* III, *p.* 130.

GENERAL

In the play of the Ball written by
Shirley and acted by the Queen's players
there were divers personated so naturally
both of lords and others in the Court that
I took it ill and would have forbidden the
play but that Beeston promised many
things which I found fault withall should
be left out, and that he would not suffer
it to be done by the poet any more, who
deserves to be punished: and the first who
offends in this kind of poets or players
shall be sure of public punishment.—
HERBERT, SIR HENRY, 1632, *Master of the
Revels Office Book,* Nov. 18.

Heywood and Shirley were but types of thee,
Thou last great prophet of tautology.
—DRYDEN, JOHN, 1682, *Mac Flecknoe.*

One of such Incomparable parts, that
he was the Chief of the Second-rate Poets:
and by some has been thought even equal
to *Fletcher* himself. . . . I need not
take pains to shew his Intimacy, not only
with the Poets of his Time; but even the
Value and Admiration that Persons of the

first Rank had for him; since the Verses
before several of his Works, and his
Epistles Dedicatory sufficiently shew it.
He has writ several *Dramatick Pieces,* to
the Number of 37, which are in print:
besides others which are in Manuscript.—
LANGBAINE, GERARD, 1691, *An Account
of the English Dramatick Poets, pp.* 474,
475.

Think, ye vain scribbling tribe of Shirley's
　　fate,
You that write farce, and you that farce
　　translate;
Shirley, the scandal of the ancient stage
Shirley, the very Durfey of his age;
Think how he lies in Ducklane shops forlorn,
And never mention'd but with utmost scorn;
Think that the end of all your boasted skill,
As I presume to prophecy it will
Justly,—for many of you write as ill.
—GOULD, ROBERT, 1709, *The Play House,
a Satire.*

Claims a place amongst the worthies of
this period, not so much for any transcendent talent in himself, as that he was the
last of a great race, all of whom spoke
nearly the same language, and had a set
of moral feelings and notions in common.
A new language, and quite a new turn of
tragic and comic interest, came in with
the Restoration.—LAMB, CHARLES, 1808,
Specimens of Dramatic Poets.

Shirley was the last of our good old
dramatists. When his works shall be
given to the public, they will undoubtedly
enrich our popular literature. His language sparkles with the most exquisite
images. Keeping some occasional pruri-
ences apart, the fault of his age rather
than of himself, he speaks the most polished and refined dialect of the stage; and
even some of his over-heightened scenes
of voluptuousness are meant, though with
a very mistaken judgment, to inculcate
morality. I consider his genius, indeed,
as rather brilliant and elegant than
strong or lofty. His tragedies are defective in fire, grandeur, and passion; and
we must *select* his comedies, to have any
favourable idea of his humour. His finest
poetry comes forth in situations rather
more familiar than tragedy and more
grave than comedy, which I should call
sentimental comedy, if the name were not
associated with ideas of modern insipidity.
That he was capable, however, of pure
and excellent comedy will be felt by those
who have yet in reserve the amusement

of reading his "Gamester," "Hyde-park," and "Lady of Pleasure." In the first and last of these there is a subtle ingenuity in producing comic effect and surprise, which might be termed Attic, if it did not surpass any thing that is left us in Athenian comedy. I shall leave to others the more special enumeration of his faults, only observing, that the airy touches of his expression, the delicacy of his sentiments, and the beauty of his similes, are often found where the poet survives the dramatist, and where he has not power to transfuse life and strong individuality through the numerous characters of his voluminous drama.—CAMPBELL, THOMAS, 1819, *An Essay on English Poetry, p.* 49.

Shirley's facility in composition is proved by the number of his plays; and doubtless they would have swelled into an ampler catalogue, had not the antipoetic spirit of Puritanism suppressed the stage, while the vigour of his genius was yet unimpaired. No single writer, among the early English dramatists, with the exception of Shakespeare, has bequeathed so many regular five-act pieces to posterity. . . . His fine moral feeling rejected those unhallowed themes, on which some of his contemporaries boldly ventured; he offends us by no glowing pictures of incestuous love. His writings are soiled, in a certain degree, by gross and immodest allusions; but whoever is conversant with our ancient drama will admit that the Muse of Shirley is comparatively chaste. . . . He abounds in brilliant thoughts, in noble and majestic sentiments, yet exhibits little of profound reflexion. His imagination seldom takes a lofty flight: he loves to crowd his dramas with events of romantic beauty; but he shews no fondness for the ideal world, its ghosts, and magic wonders.—DYCE, ALEXANDER, 1833, *ed., Dramatic Works and Poems of James Shirley, vol.* I, *pp.* lxiii, lxv.

Shirley has no originality, no force in conceiving or delineating character, little of pathos, and less perhaps of wit: his dramas produce no deep impression in reading, and of course can leave none in the memory. But his mind was poetical; his better characters, especially females, express pure thoughts in pure language; he is never tumid or affected, and seldom obscure; the incidents succeed rapidly; the personages are numerous; and there is a general animation in the scenes, which causes us to read him with some pleasure. No very good play, nor possibly any very good scene, could be found in Shirley; but he has many lines of considerable beauty. Among his comedies, the "Gamesters" may be reckoned the best. Charles I. is said to have declared, that it was "the best play he had seen these seven years;" and it has even been added, that the story was of his royal suggestion. It certainly deserves praise both for language and construction of the plot, and it has the advantage of exposing vice to ridicule; but the ladies of that court, the fair forms whom Vandyke has immortalized, must have been very different indeed from their posterity if they could sit it through.—HALLAM, HENRY, 1837–39, *Introduction to the Literature of Europe, pt.* iii, *ch.* vi, *par.* 98.

An inferior writer, though touched, to our fancy, with something, of a finer ray and closing, in worthy purple, the procession of the Elizabethan men.—BROWNING, ELIZABETH BARRETT, 1842–63, *The Book of the Poets.*

He has not much pathos, it is true, nor much knowledge of the heart; but there are few dramatists whose works give a more agreeable and unforced transcript of the ordinary scenes of life, conveyed in more graceful language. His humour, though not very profound, is true and fanciful, and his plays may always be read with pleasure, and often with profit.—SHAW, THOMAS B., 1847, *Outlines of English Literature, p.* 133.

Of the group of play-writers belonging more properly to Charles's own reign, the most important was James Shirley.—MASSON, DAVID, 1858, *The Life of John Milton, vol.* I, *ch.* vi.

He was the last of a race of giants. . . . Vigour and variety of expression, and richness of imagery are amongst his conspicuous merits; and, making reasonable allowance for occasional confusion in the "imbroglio" of his more complicated fables, arising, no doubt, from hasty composition, the action of his dramas is generally contrived and evolved with considerable skill.—BELL, ROBERT, 1867? *ed., Songs from the Dramatists, pp.* 221, 222.

He was not a great man in himself, but an essentially small man inspired by the creations of great men. Fletcher was his master and exemplar, as Shakespeare was Massinger's; but he imitated much more closely, was much more completely carried away by this model than Massinger was. And although his language and moral feelings and notions (even as regards female types and kings) are Fletcher's, and he had most ambition to emulate Fletcher's dashing and brilliant manner, yet Shirley's plays contain frequent echoes of other dramatists. One great interest in reading him is that he reminds us so often of the situations and characters of his predecessors. It is good for the critic, if for nobody else, to read Shirley, because there he finds emphasised all that told most effectively on the playgoers of the period. We read Greene and Marlowe to know what the Elizabethan drama was in its powerful but awkward youth; Shirley to know what it was in its declining but facile and still powerful old age.—MINTO, WILLIAM, 1874-85, *Characteristics of English Poets*, p. 367

In Shirley, last of the great race, the fire and passion of the grand old era passes away. Imagination is driven from its last asylum. The sword is drawn, and the theatres are closed. Dramatists are stigmatized, actors are arrested; and when, after the lapse of a few years, they return to their old haunts, it is as roisterers under a foreign yoke.—WELSH, ALFRED H., 1882, *Development of English Literature and Language, vol.* i, *p.* 427.

The dusk of day's decline was hard on dark
  When evening trembled round thy glow-worm lamp
  That shone across her shades and dewy damp,
A small clear beacon whose benignant spark
Was gracious yet for loiterers' eyes to mark,
  Though changed the watchword of our English camp
  Since the outposts rang round Marlowe's lion ramp,
When thy steed's pace went ambling round Hyde Park
—SWINBURNE, ALGERNON CHARLES, 1882, *James Shirley.*

Shirley, with more of genial inspiration and a richer vein, follows the same track as Massinger.—SYMONDS, JOHN ADDINGTON, 1887, *Marlowe* (*Mermaid Series*), *General Introduction on the Drama, p.* xxv.

Shirley was neither a very great nor a very strong man; and without originals to follow it is probable that he would have done nothing. But with Fletcher and Jonson before him he was able to strike out a certain line of half-humorous, half-romantic drama, and to follow it with curious equality through his long list of plays, hardly one of which is very much better than any other, hardly one of which falls below a very respectable standard. He has few or no single scenes or passages of such high and sustained excellence as to be specially quotable; and there is throughout him an indefinable flavour as of study of his elders and betters, and appearance as of a highly competent and gifted pupil in a school, not as of a master and leader in a movement.—SAINTSBURY, GEORGE, 1887, *History of Elizabethan Literature, p.* 410.

Shirley is in complete contrast with Ford in that he neither sought for overstrained and unnatural situations as a stimulus for his tragedy, nor allowed his comedy to degenerate into coarse buffoonery. Writing at the close of an extraordinarily prolific dramatic period, and at a time when the works of the great dramatists of that period were being made accessible in collected form, he drew freely from them for characters, situations, and ideas. But though there is little originality in his dramas, he shews great dexterity in the management of his material, and a facility of poetic expression which is pleasing until it grows monotonous. The plots of many of his plays are ingenious and interesting, and, as in the case of Massinger, a healthy moral tone underlies his occasional grossness. Shirley's masques are of considerable literary value, and the few lyrics he wrote show him to be a lyric poet of no mean power.—MASTERMAN, J. HOWARD B., 1897, *The Age of Milton, p.* 87.

Remarkably alive to the danger of distracting the spectator's interest from the main plot of the action of a play, he displayed in tragic as well as in comic actions a curious presentiment of the modern theatrical principle that everything depends on the success of one great scene (*la scène à faire*). His tragedies of "The Traitor" and "The Cardinal," his tragic-comedy of "The Royal Master," and his comedy of "The Gamester," may be instanced as signal examples of his constructive skill. His excellence seems to lie less in the depiction of the comic than in that of serious scenes and characters; but, as is shown in all his comedies from the earliest onwards, but more especially by his "Hyde Park" and by the less attractive comedy of "The Ball," in which he collaborated with Chapman, he was an acute observer and at times a humorous delineator of the vagaries of contemporary manners, whether in town or country. . . . But what chiefly entitles Shirley to hold the place to which he has been restored among our great dramatists is the spirit of poetry which adorns and elevates so many of his plays. He was one of the last of our seventeenth-century playwrights who interspersed their dialogue with passages of poetic beauty, at once appropriate to the sentiment of the situation and capable of carrying their audience to a higher imaginative level. Nor was he merely the last of the group; few members of it, besides Shakespeare himself, have surpassed Shirley in the exercise of the rare power of ennobling his dramatic diction by images which, while they "would surpass the life," spring without effort from the infinitude of the suggestions offered by it to creative fancy.— WARD, ADOLPHUS WILLIAM, 1897, *Dictionary of National Biography, vol.* LII, *p.* 130.

Abraham Cowley

1618–1667

Born, in London, 1618. King's Scholar at Westminster School, 1628 [?]–1636. First poems published, 1633. Scholar of Trinity Coll., Cambridge, 14 June 1637; B. A., 1639; Minor Fellow, 30 Oct., 1640; M. A., 1642; Major Fellow, 1642. Latin Comedy, "Naufragium Joculare" performed before University, 2 Feb. 1638. "The Guardian" performed, 12 March 1641; rewritten and produced at Lincoln's Inn Fields as "The Cutter of Coleman Street," 16 Dec. 1661. Ejected from Cambridge as a Royalist, and removed to St. John's Coll., Oxford, 1664. Afterwards in household of Earl of St. Alban's, and in Court of exiled Queen in France. Engaged on diplomatic services. Returned to England, 1656. Studied Medicine. M. D., Oxford, 2 Dec. 1657. Removed to Chertsey, April 1665. Died there, 28 July 1667. Buried in Westminster Abbey. *Works:* "Poetical Blossoms" (anon.), 1633; "Love's Riddle," 1638; "Naufragium Joculare," 1638; "A Satyre: the Puritan and the Papist," 1643 [?]; "Ad Populum" (anon.), 1644; "The Mistress," 1647; "The Foure Ages of England" (anon.), 1648; "The Guardian," 1650 (second version, entitled: "The Cutter of Coleman Street," 1663); "Poems," 1656; "Ode upon the Blessed Restoration," 1660; "Vision concerning . . . Cromwell the Wicked," 1661; "A Proposal for the Advancement of Experimental Philosophy," 1661; "A. Couleii Plantarum libri duo," 1662; "Verses upon several Occasions," 1663; "Verses lately written," 1663. *Posthumous:* "A Poem on the late Civil War," 1679; "Love's Chronicle" (anon.), [1730?]. He *translated:* "Anacreon" (anon., with Willis, Wood and Oldham), 1683. *Collected Works:* ed., with *life*, by T. Sprat, 1668 (subsequent ends., some enlarged, 1689–1721); ed., with *life* by Grosart, 1880–81.— SHARP, R. FARQUHARSON, 1897 *A Dictionary of English Authors, p.* 67.

PERSONAL

Even when I was a very young boy at school, instead of running about on holydays and playing with my fellows, I was wont to steal from them, and walk into the fields, either alone with a book, or with some one companion, if I could find any of the same temper. I was then, too, so much an enemy to all constraint, that my masters could never prevail on me, by any persuasions or encouragements, to learn without book the common rules of grammar; in which they dispensed with me alone, because they found I made a shift to do the usual exercise out of my own reading and observation. That I was then of the same mind as I am now (which, I confess, I wonder at, myself) may appear by the latter end of an ode, which I made when I was but thirteen years old, and which was then printed, with many other verses. The beginning of it is boyish; but of this part, which I here set down (if a very little were corrected), I should hardly now be much ashamed.—COWLEY, ABRAHAM, 1667? *On Myself, Essays*

Went to Mr. Cowley's funerall, whose corps lay at Wallingford House, and was thence convey'd to Westminster Abbey, in a hearse with six horses, and all funeral decency; neeare an hundred coaches of noblemen and persons of qualitie following; among these all the witts of the towne, divers bishops and cleargymen.—EVELYN, JOHN, 1667, *Diary, August* 3.

In the thirteenth Year of his Age there came forth a little Book under his Name, in which there were many things that might well become the Vigour and Force of a manly Wit. The first beginning of his studies, was a Familiarity with the most solid and unaffected Authors of Antiquary, which he fully digested not only in his Memory, but his Judgment. By this Advantage he leanr'd nothing while a Boy, that he needed to forget or forsake, when he came to be a Man. His Mind was rightly season'd at first, and he had nothing to do, but still to proceed on the same Foundation on which he began. He was wont to relate, that he had this Defect in his Memory at that time, that his Teachers could never bring it to retain the ordinary Rules of Grammar. However he supply'd that want, by conversing with the Books themselves, from whence those Rules had been drawn.—SPRAT, THOMAS, 1668, *An Account of the Life of Mr. Abraham Cowley.*

He lies interred at Westminster Abbey, next to Sir Jeffrey Chaucer, N., where the duke of Bucks has putt a neate monument of white marble, viz. a faire pedestall, wheron the inscription:—

ABRAHAMUS COULEIUS,

ANGLORUM PINDARUS, FLACCUS, MARO,

DELICIAE, DECUS, DESIDERIUM AEVI SUI,

HIC JUXTA SITUS EST.

AUREA DUM VOLITANT LATÈ TUA SCRIPTA PER ORBEM,

ET FAMÂ AETERNÙM VIVIS, DIVINE POETA,

HIC PLACIDÂ JACEAS REQUIE; CUSTODIAT URNAM

CANA FIDES, VIGILENTQUE PERENNI LAMPADE MUSAE;

SIT SACER ISTE LOCUS. NEC QUIS TEMERARIUS AUSIT

SACRILEGÂ TURBARE MANU VENERABILE BUSTUM.

INTACTI MANEANT, MANEANT PER SECULA, DULCIS

COULEI CINERES SERVENTQUE IMMOBILE SAXUM.

SIC VOVET,

VOTUMQUE SUUM APUD POSTEROS SACRATUM ESSE VOLUIT, QUI VIRO INCOMPARABILI POSUIT SEPULCRALE MARMOR, GEORGIUS DUX BUCKINGHAMIAE.

ABRAHAM COWLEY EXCESSIT E VITÂ ANNO AETATIS SUAE 49; ET, HONORIFICÂ POMPÂ ELATUS EX AEDIBUS BUCKINGHAMIANIS, VIRIS ILLUSTRIBUS OMNIUM ORDINUM EXEQUIAS CELEBRANTIBUS, SEPULTUS EST DIE 3 MENSIS AUGUSTI ANNU DOMINI 1667. Above that a very faire urne, with a kind of ghirland of ivy about it. The inscription was made by Dr. (Thomas) Spratt, his grace's chapellane: the Latin verses were made, or mended, by Dr. (Thomas) Gale. On his very noble gravestone, his scutcheon, and Abrahamus Couleius H. S. E. 1667.—AUBREY, JOHN, 1669-96, *Brief Lives, ed. Clark, vol.* I, *p.* 189.

He was not so much respected by the cavaliers as he ought to have been, upon the restauration, which much troubled him, and made him fly off something, as appears partly from the preface to his poems. He was however a good natured man, of great candor and humanity, and no party ever spoke ill against him upon that score.—HEARNE, THOMAS, 1706, *Reliquiæ Hearnianæ, ed. Bliss, May* 18, *vol.* I, *p.* 108.

Cowley's allowance was, at last, not above three hundred a year. He died at Chertsey; and his death was occasioned by a mean accident, whilst his great friend, Dean Sprat, was with him on a visit there. They had been together to see a neighbour at Cowley's; who (according to the fashion of those times) made them too welcome. They did not set out for their walk home till it was too late; and had drank so deep, that they lay out in the fields all night. This gave Cowley the fever that carried him off. The parish still talk of the drunken Dean.—POPE, ALEXANDER, 1728-30, *Spence's Anecdotes, ed. Singer, p.* 10.

When Cowley grew sick of the court, he took a house first at Battersea, then at Barnes; and then at Chertsey: always farther and farther from town. In the latter part of his life, he showed a sort of aversion for women; and would leave the room when they came in: 'twas probably from a disappointment in love. He was much in love with his Leonora; who is mentioned at the end of that good ballad of his, on his different mistresses. She was married to Dean Sprat's brother; and Cowley never was in love with anybody after. —POPE, ALEXANDER, 1742–43, *Spence's Anecdotes, ed. Singer, p.* 216.

Of Cowley, we are told by Barnes, who had means enough of information, that, whatever he may talk of his own inflammability, and the variety of characters by which his heart was divided, he in reality was in love but once, and then never had resolution to tell his passion.—JOHNSON, SAMUEL, 1779, *Abraham Cowley, Lives of the English Poets.*

We suspect, from the portraits of Cowley, that his blood was not very healthy by nature. . . . Cowley and Thomson were alike in their persons, their dispositions, and their fortunes. They were both fat men, not handsome; very amiable and sociable; no enemies to a bottle; taking interest both in politics and retirement; passionately fond of external nature, of fields, woods, gardens, &c.; bachelors,—in love, and disappointed; faulty in style, yet true poets in *themselves,* if not always the best in their writings, that is to say, seeing everything in its poetical light; childlike in their ways; and, finally, they were both made easy in their circumstances by the party whom they served; both went to live at a little distance from London, and on the banks of the Thames; and both died of a cold and fever, originating in a careless exposure to the weather, not without more than a suspicion of previous "jollification" with "the Dean," on Cowley's part, and great probability of a like vivacity on that of Thomson, who had been visiting his friends in London. Thomson could push the bottle like a regular *bon vivant:* and Cowley's death is attributed to his having forgotten his proper bed, and slept in a field all night, in company with his reverend and jovial friend Sprat.— HUNT, LEIGH, 1847, *Men, Women, and Books, vol.* II, *p.* 50.

Cowley House . . . in which Cowley spent his last days, is on the west side of Guildford Street near the railway station. . . It was a little house, with ample gardens and pleasant meadows attached. Not of brick indeed, but half timber, with a fine old oak staircase and balusters, and one or two wainscoted chambers, which yet remain much as when Cowley dwelt there, as do also the poet's study, a small closet with a view meadow-ward to St. Anne's Hill, and the room, overlooking the road, in which he died. He lived here little more than two years in all.—THORNE, JAMES, 1876, *Hand-Book to the Environs of London, Chertsey.*

JUVENILE POEMS

We are even more pleased with some of the earliest of his juvenile poems, than with many of his later performances; as there is not every where in them that redundancy of wit; and where there is, we are more inclined to admire, than be offended at in the productions of a boy. His passion for studious retirement, which was still increasing with his years, discovered itself at thirteen, in an ode which a good judge thinks equal to that of Pope on a similar subject, and which was written about the same era of his life. The tenderness of some of his juvenile verses shews, that he was no stranger to another passion; and it is not improbable but Margarita, or one of her successors, might at fifteen, have had a full possession of his heart.—GRANGER, JAMES, 1769–1824, *Biographical History of England, vol.* III, *p.* 124.

Let any reader of "Pyramus and Thisbe" consider how naïve, artless, and infantine are the writings of the very cleverest child of ten that he has ever known when compared with this first work of Cowley's. After more than two hundred years it remains still readable— much more readable, in fact, than many of its author's more elaborate poems of maturity. . . "Pyramus and Thisbe" is a work which few of the adult poets of that day would have been ashamed of writing. It contains mistakes of rhyme, and grammar that might be so easily corrected that they form an interesting proof that the poem was not touched up for the press by older hands, but in other respects it is smooth and singularly mature. The heroic verse in which it is written is nerveless, but correct, and the story is told in a straightforward way, and with a regular progress, that are extraordinary in so young a child.—GOSSE, EDMUND, 1883, *Seventeenth-Century Studies, pp.* 174, 175.

THE CUTTER OF COLEMAN STREET
1641–63

We are therefore wonderful wise men, and have a fine business of it; we, who spend our time in poetry. I do sometimes laugh, and am often angry with myself, when I think on it; and if I had a son inclined by nature to the same folly, I believe I should bind him from it by the strictest conjurations of a paternal blessing. For what can be more ridiculous than to labour to give men delight, whilst they labour, on their part, most earnestly to take offence?—COWLEY, ABRAHAM, 1663, *Cutter of Coleman Street, Preface.*

The comedy, as acted in 1661, seems to have subjected Cowley to censure as having been intended for abuse and satire of the Royalists, besides being guilty of profaneness. In his Preface, which is well worth reading, he accordingly defends himself with effective indignation against both charges—and this he could upon the whole well afford to do. What enraged these injudicious assailants, proves to us the moral courage of the poet. As a tried friend of the monarchy he rendered a real service to its cause, and to that of social order at large, by thus boldly and bravely satirising the scum of the loyal party at the very time when its ignobler elements were actively striving to remain at the top; and for the sake of the spirit of manliness which pervades this comedy we may readily pardon its occasional coarseness and the farcical improbabilities of its plot.—WARD, ADOLPHUS WILLIAM, 1875–99, *A History of English Dramatic Literature, vol.* III, *p.* 327.

THE MISTRESS
1647

Considered as the verses of a lover, no man that has ever loved will much commend them. They are neither courtly nor pathetic, have neither gallantry nor fondness. His praises are too far sought, and too hyperbolical, either to express love, or to excite it; every stanza is crowded with darts and flames, with wounds and death, with mingled souls, and with broken hearts.—JOHNSON, SAMUEL, 1779, *Abraham Cowley, Lives of the English Poets.*

In the next year, 1647, Cowley's "Mistress" appeared; the most celebrated performance of the miscalled metaphysical poets. It is a series of short amatory poems, in the Italian style of the age, full of analogies that have no semblance of truth, except from the double sense of words and thoughts that unite the coldness of subtility with the hyperbolical extravagance of counterfeited passion.—HALLAM, HENRY, 1837–39, *Introduction to the Literature of Europe, pt.* iii, *ch.* v, *par.* 41.

It is as though in the course of a hundred years the worst fancies which Wyatt had borrowed from Petrarch had become fossilized, and were yet brought out by Cowley to do duty for living thoughts. What is love? he seems to ask: it is an interchange of hearts, a flame, a worship, a river to be frozen by disdain—he has a hundred such physical and psychological images of it; and the poetry consists in taking the images one by one and developing them in merciless disregard of taste and truth of feeling.—WARD, THOMAS HUMPHRY, 1880, *English Poets, vol.* II, *p.* 237.

DAVIDEIS

His "Davideis" was wholly written in so young an Age; that if we shall reflect on the vastness of the Argument, and his manner of handling it, he may seem like one of the Miracles, that he there adorns, like a Boy attempting *Goliah.*—SPRAT, THOMAS, 1668, *An Account of the Life of Mr. Abraham Cowley.*

The "Davideis" is much more disfigured by far-fetched conceits than even his Odes; and they offend still more against good Taste, when we find them mixed up with the sobriety of narration, than when they mingle in his Pindaric ecstacies. The narrative itself is also heavy and uninteresting; there are no strongly drawn or predominating characters; and the Allegorical personages, who are the chief actors, do not, of course, excite any strong interest, or greatly arrest the attention. Still there are many scattered beauties throughout the Poem; many original ideas, and much brilliant versification.—NEELE, HENRY, 1827–29, *Lectures on English Poetry, Lecture* ii.

His epic attempt, "Davideis," was not successful.—SCHERR, J., 1874–82, *A History of English Literature, p.* 115.

The "Davideis" is a school exercise, no more.—WARD, THOMAS HUMPHRY, 1880, *English Poets, vol.* II, *p.* 241.

ESSAYS

In all our comparisons of taste, I do not know whether I have ever heard your opinion of a poet, very dear to me,—the now-out-of-fashion Cowley. Favour me with your judgment of him, and tell me if his prose essays, in particular, as well as no inconsiderable part of his verse, be not delicious. I prefer the graceful rambling of his essays, even to the courtly elegance and ease of Addison; abstracting from this the latter's exquisite humour.—LAMB, CHARLES, 1797, *Letter to Coleridge, Letters, ed. Ainger, vol. I, p. 64*.

Spent the two hours that remained before dinner, in skimming the "Prose Essays" of Cowley, which I had often heard very highly commended for the style; in this respect I was so much gratified, by the genuine vein of English idiom, as well as by what appeared to my ear, in many passages, a sweet and flowing melody of composition, that I have resolved to read the volume over again three or four times, till I fix some of those beauties in my memory, and accustom my ear to the tune. —HORNER, FRANCIS, 1802, *Memoirs and Correspondence, vol. I, p. 204*.

They are eminently distinguished for the grace, the finish, and the clearness which his verse too often wants. That there is one cry which pervades them—vanity of vanities! all is vanity!—that there is an almost ostentatious longing for obscurity and retirement, may be accounted for by the fact that at an early age Cowley was thrown among the cavaliers of the civil wars. sharing the exile and the return of the Stuarts, and doubtless disgusted, as so pure a writer was pretty sure to be, by a dissolute Court, with whom he would find it easier to sympathize in its misery than in its triumph. —MITFORD, MARY RUSSELL, 1851, *Recollections of A Literary Life, p. 36*.

His prose is as easy and sensible as his poetry is contorted and unreasonable. A polished man, writing for polished men, pretty much as he would speak to them in a drawing-room,—this I take to be the idea which they had of a good author in the seventeenth century. It is the idea which Cowley's "Essays" leave of his character; it is the kind of talent which the writers of the coming age take for their model; and he is the first of that grave and amiable group which, continued in

Temple, reaches so far as to include Addison.—TAINE, H. A., 1871, *History of English Literature, tr. Van Laun, vol. I, bk. ii, ch. i, p. 205*.

Cowley holds perhaps a higher rank among prose writers than among poets. His "Essays," written for the most part after the Restoration, mark an advance in the art of prose composition. The construction of the sentences is often stumbling and awkward, but the diction shows an increasing command over the language. No previous writer, not even Fuller, is so felicitous as Cowley in the combination of words. His prose has none of the extravagance of his poetry.—MINTO, WILLIAM, 1872-80, *Manual of English Prose Literature, p. 286*.

Cowley's prose essays, it must be acknowledged, have held their ground in our literature, but as a poet he is a dead name, or living only in depreciation and ridicule. We hope to show that, however great his faults, this depreciation is unjust and this ridicule absurd, and in doing so it will be necessary to solve two questions—why Cowley ever attained so immense a poetic reputation, and why, having once gained it, he has so completely lost it.—GOSSE, EDMUND, 1883, *Seventeenth-Century Studies, p. 172*.

The familiar ease, never descending into what would misbecome either the man of breeding or the man of letters, is the true cause of the pleasure which cultivated readers have never ceased to derive from these "Essays;" and to enjoy this pleasure to the full, we should pace with their author the whole length of his modest garden walks; for his estate was not on the scale of his friend John Evelyn's. —WARD, ADOLPHUS WILLIAM, 1893, *English Prose, ed. Craik, vol. II, p. 575*.

This test of re-reading is, of course, only an approximate one. So great an authority as Hume said it was sufficient to read Cowley over, but that Parnell after the fiftieth reading was as fresh as at the first. Now, for my part, I have to go to the encyclopedia to find out who Parnell was, but of Cowley even desultory readers like myself know something. His essays one can not only read, but re-read. They make one of the unpretentious minor books that one can put in his pocket and take with him on a walk to the woods, and nibble at under a tree or by a waterfall.

Solitude seems to bring out its quality, as it does that of some people.—BUR-ROUGHS, JOHN, 1897, *On the Re-reading of Books, The Century, vol.* 55, *p.* 147.

LOVE'S CHRONICLE

"The Chronicle" was written two hundred years ago. Ladies, dear ladies, if one could be sure that no man would open this book, if we were altogether in (female) parliament assembled, without a single male creature within hearing, might we not acknowledge that the sex, especially that part of it formerly called coquette, and now known by the name of flirt, is very little altered since the days of the Merry Monarch? and that a similar list compiled by some gay bachelor of Belgravia might, allowing for differences of custom and of costume, serve very well as a companion to Master Cowley's catalogue? I would not have a man read this admission for the world.—MITFORD, MARY RUSSELL, 1851, *Recollections of A Literary Life, p.* 46.

GENERAL

To him no author was unknown,
Yet what he wrote was all his own;
He melted not the ancient gold,
Nor with Ben Jonson, did make bold
To plunder all the Roman stores
Of poets and of orators.
Horace's wit and Virgil's state,
He did not steal, but emulate;
And when he would like them appear,
Their garb, but not their clothes, did wear.
He not from Rome alone, but Greece,
Like Jason, brought the golden fleece.
—DENHAM, SIR JOHN, c 1667, *On Mr. Abraham Cowley's Death, and Burial amongst the Ancient Poets.*

These times have produced many excellent poets, among whom, for strength of wit, Dr. Abraham Cowley justly bears the bell.—BAXTER, RICHARD, 1681, *Poetical Fragments, Prefatory Address.*

The darling of my youth.—DRYDEN, JOHN, 1692, *Essay on Satire, Works, ed. Scott and Saintsbury, vol.* XIII, *p.* 116.

Great Cowley then, a mighty genius, wrote,
O'er run with wit, and lavish of his thought:
His turns too closely on the reader press:
He more had pleased us, had he pleased us less.
One glittering thought no sooner strikes our eyes
With silent wonder, but new wonders rise;
As in the milky-way a shining white
O'erflows the heavens with one continued light,

That not a single star can show his rays,
Whilst jointly all promote the common blaze.
Pardon, great poet, that I dare to name
The unnumber'd beauties of thy verse with blame;
Thy fault is only wit in its excess.
—ADDISON, JOSEPH, 1694, *An Account of the Greatest English Poets.*

One of our late great poets is sunk in his reputation, because he could never forgive any conceit which came in his way; but swept, like a drag-net, great and small. There was plenty enough—but the dishes were ill sorted; whole pyramids of sweetmeats for boys and women, but little of solid meat for men. All this proceeded not from any want of knowledge, but of judgment. Neither did he want that in discerning the beauties and faults of other poets, but only indulged himself in the luxury of writing; and perhaps knew it was a fault, and hoped to find it. For this reason, though he must always be thought a great poet, he is no longer esteemed a good writer; and for ten impressions which his works have had in so many successive years, yet at present a hundred books are scarcely purchased once a twelvemonth; for, as my last Lord Rochester said, though somewhat profanely, "Not being of God, he could not stand."—DRYDEN, JOHN, 1700, *Preface to The Fables.*

Never any poet left a greater reputation behind him than Mr. Cowley, while Milton remained obscure, and known but to few.—DENNIS, JOHN, 1721, *Letters.*

Who now reads Cowley? If he pleases yet,
His moral pleases, not his pointed wit:
Forgot his Epic, nay Pindaric art
But still I love the language of his heart.
—POPE, ALEXANDER, 1733, *First Epistle of the Second Book of Horace.*

Cowley is a fine poet, in spite of all his faults.—He, as well as Davenant, borrowed his metaphysical style from Donne.—POPE, ALEXANDER, 1734–36, *Spence's Anecdotes, ed. Singer, p.* 130.

The time seems to be at hand when justice will be done to Mr. Cowley's prose, as well as poetical writings; and though his friend Doctor Sprat, bishop of Rochester, in his diction falls far short of the abilities for which he has been celebrated; yet there is some times a happy flow in his periods, something that looks like eloquence.—GOLDSMITH, OLIVER, 1759, *The Bee No.* 8, *Nov.* 24.

Cowley is an author extremely corrupted by the bad taste of his age; but had he lived even in the purest times of Greece or Rome, he must always have been a very indifferent poet. He had no ear for harmony; and his verses are only known to be such by the rhyme which terminates them. In his rugged untunable numbers are conveyed sentiments the most strained and distorted, long-spun allegories, distant allusions, and forced conceits. Great ingenuity, however, and vigour of thought, sometimes break out midst those unnatural conceptions; a few anacreontics surprise us by their ease and gaiety: his prose writings please, by the honesty and goodness which they express, and even by their spleen and melancholy. This author was much more praised and admired during his lifetime, and celebrated after his death, than the great Milton.—HUME, DAVID, 1762, *The History of England, The Commonwealth, vol.* v.

Botany in the mind of Cowley turned into poetry. . . . The power of Cowley is not so much to move the affections, as to exercise the understanding. . . . A mind capacious by nature, and replenished by study. In the general review of Cowley's poetry it will be found that he wrote with abundant fertility, but negligent or unskilful selection; with much thought but with little imagery; that he is never pathetic, and rarely sublime; but always either ingenious or learned, either acute or profound. . . . His manner he had in common with others; but his sentiments were his own. Upon every subject he thought for himself; and such was his copiousness of knowledge that something at once remote and applicable rushed into his mind; yet it is not likely that he always rejected a commodious idea merely because another had used it; his known wealth was so great, that he might have borrowed without loss of credit. . . . He makes no selection of words, nor seeks any neatness of phrase: he has no elegance, either lucky or elaborate, as his endeavours were rather to impress sentences upon the understanding than images on the fancy, he has few epithets, and those scattered without peculiar propriety of nice adaptation.—JOHNSON, SAMUEL, 1779, *Abraham Cowley, Lives of the English Poets.*

Cowley, at all times harsh, is doubly so in his Pindaric compositions. In his Anacreontic odes, he is much happier. They are smooth and elegant; and indeed the most agreeable and the most perfect in their kind, of all Mr. Cowley's Poems.—BLAIR, HUGH, 1783, *Lectures on Rhetoric and Belles Letters, ed. Mills, p.* 446.

Ingenious Cowley! and though now, reclaim'd
By modern lights from an erroneous taste,
I cannot but lament thy splendid wit
Entangled in the cobwebs of the schools.
I still revere thee, courtly though retired;
Though stretch'd at ease in Chertsey's silent bowers
Not unemploy'd, and finding rich amends
For a lost world in solitude and verse.
—COWPER, WILLIAM, 1784, *The Task, The Winter Evening.*

Cowley, I think, would have had grace (for his mind was graceful) if he had had any ear, or if his taste had not been vitiated by the pursuit of wit; which, when it does not offer itself naturally, degenerates into tinsel or pertness.—WALPOLE, HORACE, 1785, *Letters, ed. Cunningham, vol.* VIII, *p.* 564.

To speak of this neglected writer, as a poet. He had a quick and ready conception; the true enthusiasm of genius, and vast materials, with which learning as well as fancy had supplied him for it to work upon. He had besides a prodigious command of expression, and a natural and copious flow of eloquence on every occasion, and understood our language in all its force and energy. Yet betwixt the native exuberance of his wit, which hurried him frequently on conceits, and the epidemical contagion of that time, which possessed all writers with the love of points, of affected turns, and hard unnatural allusion, there are few of his poems which a man of just taste will read with admiration, or even with pleasure. Some few there are and enough to save his name from oblivion, or rather to consecrate it, with those of the master spirits of our country, to immortality.—HURD, RICHARD, 1808? *Commonplace Book, ed. Kilvert, p.* 240.

The mind of Cowley was beautiful, but a querulous tenderness in his nature breathes not only through his works, but influenced his habits and his views of human affairs.—DISRAELI, ISAAC, 1812–13, *Quarrels of Authors.*

The metre of Pindar is regular, that of

Cowley is utterly lawless; and his perpetual straining after points of wit, seems to show that he had formed no correcter notion of his *manner* than of his *style*.— GIFFORD, WILLIAM, 1816, *ed., The Works of Ben Jonson, vol.* IX, *p.* 8.

For mere ease and grace, is Cowley inferior to Addison, being as he is so much more thoughtful and full of fancy? Cowley, with the omission of a quaintness here and there, is probably the best model of style for modern imitation in general.— COLERIDGE, SAMUEL TAYLOR, 1818, *Style; Miscellanies, Æsthetic and Literary, ed. Ashe, p.* 181.

He wrote verses while yet a child; and amidst his best poetry as well as his worst, in his touching and tender as well as extravagant passages, there is always something that reminds us of childhood in Cowley. . . . Misanthropy, as far as so gentle a nature could cherish it, naturally strengthened his love of retirement, and increased that passion for a country life which breathes in the fancy of his poetry, and in the eloquence of his prose.—CAMPBELL, THOMAS, 1819, *Specimens of the British Poets*.

Cowley, with all his admirable wit and ingenuity, had little imagination; nor indeed do we think his classical diction comparable to that of Milton.—MACAULAY, THOMAS BABINGTON, 1825, *Milton, Edinburgh Review, Essays*.

The Pindaric odes of Cowley were not published within this period. But it is not worth while to defer mention of them. They contain, like all his poetry, from time to time, very beautiful lines; but the faults are still of the same kind: his sensibility and good sense, nor has any poet more, are choked by false taste; and it would be difficult to fix on any one poem in which the beauties are more frequent than the blemishes. Johnson has selected the elegy on Crashaw as the finest of Cowley's works. It begins with a very beautiful couplet, but I confess that little else seems, to my taste, of much value. "The Complaint," probably better known than any other poem, appears to me the best in itself. His disappointed hopes give a not unpleasing melancholy to several passages. But his Latin ode in a similar strain is much more perfect. Cowley, perhaps, upon the whole, has had a reputation more above his deserts than any

English poet; yet it is very easy to perceive that some, who wrote better than he, did not possess so fine a genius.—HALLAM, HENRY, 1837–39, *Introduction to the Literature of Europe, pt.* iii, *ch.* v, *par.* 41.

Cowley was coarsely curious: he went to the shamoles for his chambers of imagery, and very often through the mud. All which faults appear to us attributable to his coldness of temperament, and his defectiveness in the instinct towards Beauty; to having the intellect only of a great poet, not the sensibility. . . . Yet his influence was for good rather than for evil, by inciting to a struggle backward, a delay in the revolutionary movement: and this, although a wide gulf yawned between him and the former age, and his heart's impulse was not strong enough to cast him across it. For his actual influence, he lifts us up and casts us down— charms, and goes nigh to disgust us—does all but make us love and weep.—BROWNING, ELIZABETH BARRETT, 1842–63, *The Book of the Poets*.

On the other side of the corner of Chancery Lane was born a man of genius and benevolence, who would not have hurt a fly—Abraham Cowley. His father was a grocer; himself, one of the kindest, wisest, and truest gentlemen that ever graced humanity. He has been pronounced by one, competent to judge, to have been "if not a great poet, a great man." But his poetry is what every other man's poetry is, the flower of what was in him; and it is at least so far good poetry, as it is the quintessence of amiable and deep reflection, not without a more festive strain, the result of his sociality. Pope says of him—

"Forgot his epic, nay pindaric art;
Yet still we love the language of his heart."

His prose is admirable, and his character of Cromwell a masterpiece of honest enmity, more creditable to both parties than the zealous royalist was aware. Cowley, notwithstanding the active part he took in politics, never ceased to be a child at heart. His mind lived in books and bowers—in the sequestered "places of thought;" and he wondered and lamented to the last, that he had not realised the people he found there. His consolation should have been, that what he found in himself was an evidence that the people exist.—HUNT, LEIGH, 1858, *The Town, p.* 116.

His imagination is tinsel, or mere surface gilding, compared to Donne's solid gold; his wit little better than word-catching, to the profound meditative quaintness of the elder poet; and of passion, with which all Donne's finest lines are tremulous, Cowley has none. Considerable grace and dignity occasionally distinguish his Pindaric Odes (which, however, are Pindaric only in name); and he has shown much elegant playfulness of style and fancy in his translations from and imitations of Anacreon, and in some other verses written in the same manner. As for what he intends for love verses, some of them are pretty enough frost-work; but the only sort of love there is in them is the love of point and sparkle.—CRAIK, GEORGE L., 1861, *A Compendious History of English Literature and of the English Language, vol.* II, *p.* 99.

Cowley's "Essays" are delightful reading. Nor shall I forgive his biographer for destroying the letters of a man of whom King Charles said at his interment in Westminster Abbey, "Mr. Cowley has not left a better in England." The friend and correspondent of the most distinguished poets, statesmen, and gentlemen of his day, his letters must have been most interesting and important, and but for the unsettled temper of affairs, would doubtless have been added to our polite literature.—ALCOTT, A. BRONSON, 1869-72, *Concord Days, p.* 62.

On this boundary line of a closing and a dawning literature a poet appeared, one of the most fanciful and illustrious of his time, Abraham Cowley, a precocious child, a reader and a versifier like Pope, having known passions less than books, busied himself less about things than about words. Literary exhaustion has seldom been more manifest. He possesses all the capacity to say whatever pleases him, but he has just nothing to say. The substance has vanished, leaving in its place a hollow shadow. In vain he tries the epic, the Pindaric strophe, all kinds of stanzas, odes, little lines, long lines; in vain he calls to his assistance botanical and philosophical similes, all the erudition of the university, all the relics of antiquity, all the ideas of new science: we yawn as we read him. Except in a few descriptive verses, two or three graceful tendernesses, he feels nothing, he speaks only; he is a poet of the brain. His collection of amorous pieces is but a vehicle for a scientific test, and serves to show that he has read the authors, that he knows his geography, that he is well versed in anatomy, that he has a dash of medicine and astronomy, that he has at his service references and allusions enough to break the head of his readers.—TAINE, H. A., 1871, *History of English Literature, tr. Van Laun, vol.* I, *bk.* ii, *ch.* i, *p.* 204.

Cowley is one of the poets of remote and brilliant turns of thought, and elaborated literary distinction. One does not love his poetry; but one can admire it often —if only one would read it.—ROSSETTI, WILLIAM MICHAEL, 1872-78, *ed., Humorous Poems, p.* 132.

Cowley is defective through a redundancy of wit.—SMITH, GEORGE BARNETT, 1875, *Poets and Novelists, English Fugitive Poets, p.* 374.

Except for a few students like Lamb and Sir Egerton Brydges, Cowley's verse is in this century unread and unreadable. Not even the antiquarian curiosity of an age which reprints Brathwaite and Crowne has yet availed to present him in a new edition. The reasons of this extraordinary decline in a poetical reputation are not difficult to find; Dryden absorbed all that was best in Cowley, and superseded him for the readers of the eighteenth century, and the nineteenth century, which reads Dryden little, naturally reads Cowley less. Yet criticism has to justify great names. There must be something in a man who was regarded by his age, and that an age which boasted of having outgrown all illusions, as the most profound and ingenious of its writers.—WARD, THOMAS HUMPHRY, 1880, *English Poets, vol.* II, *p.* 235.

What a change from the musical songs of Shakespeare, Beaumont, and Ben Jonson, or from the dainty love-lyrics of Cowley's contemporary, Robert Herrick, to these painful and mechanical efforts! The student who wishes to see how a poetic judgment may be perverted—for Cowley unquestionably was a poet—should read the passages given in Dr. Johnson's masterly criticism, which is the more interesting inasmuch as it shows that the intellectual vice of Cowley was not peculiar to that poet. Earlier writers had been infected by it, later versemen were not wholly free from it. These quiddities and once fashionable follies proved Cowley's death-warrant as a poet, for although some of his verses have a vital force and beauty, the great body of his poetry is as dead as that of Sir Richard Blackmore, or the once popular Cleveland.—DENNIS, JOHN, 1883, *Heroes of Literature, p.* 112.

The period of English poetry which lies between the decline of Ben Jonson and the rise of Dryden was ruled with undisputed sway by a man whose works are now as little read as those of any fifth-rate Elizabethan dramatist. During the whole life time of Milton, the fame of that glorious poet was obscured and dwarfed by the exaggerated reputation of this writer, and so general and so unshaken was the belief in the lyrist of the day, that a Royalist gentleman of Cambridge or an exiled courtier at Paris in the year 1650 would have laughed in your face, had you suggested that time could ever wither the deathless laurels of Mr. Cowley, or untune the harmonies of his majestic numbers. Yet in a very short space this work of destruction was most thoroughly done. The generation of Dryden admired his genius passionately, but not without criticism. The generation of Pope praised him coldly, but without reading him, and within fifty years of his own decease this nonpariel of the Restoration fell into total disfavour and oblivion. With the revival of naturalistic poetry, the lyrists and dramatists of the reign of Charles I. came once more into favour. Crashaw, Quarles, Lovelace, martyrs, pietists, and rakes, all the true children of the Muses, whatever their mode or matter, were restored and reprinted.— GOSSE, EDMUND, 1883, *Seventeenth-Century Studies, p.* 171.

Cowley was still mentioned with high respect during the eighteenth century, and was the first poet in the collection to which Johnson contributed prefaces. Johnson's life in that collection was famous for its criticism of the "metaphysical" poets, the hint of which is given in Dryden's "Essay on Satire." It assigns the obvious cause for the decline of Cowley's fame. The "metaphysical poets" are courtier pedants. They represent the intrusion into poetry of the love of dialectical subtlety encouraged by the still prevalent system of scholastic disputation. In Cowley's poems, as in Donne's, there are many examples of the technical language of the schools, and the habit of thought is perceptible throughout. In the next generation the method became obsolete and then offensive. Cowley can only be said to survive in the few pieces where he condescends to be unaffected, and especially in the prose of his essays, which are among the earliest examples in the language of simple and graceful prose, with some charming poetry interspersed.—STEPHEN, LESLIE, 1887, *Dictionary of National Biography, vol.* XII, *p.* 382.

But cleverness and sense, both of which he has to a very high degree, when wanting good taste and that indescribable something which eternally severs poetry from verse, have long since placed him amongst those writers who are rarely read, but never read without profit.—PALGRAVE, FRANCIS T., 1889, *The Treasury of Sacred Song, note, p.* 347.

A constitutional sentiment for ease permeates all his prose works. His poems are labored and more prosy than his prose. —EMERY, FRED PARKER, 1891, *Notes on English Literature, p.* 43.

A rhetorician rather than a poet, without passion, without imagination, but rich in fancy and rich in thought, his style insensibly took its colour from the temper of his genius.—COLLINS, JOHN CHURTON, 1895, *Essays and Studies, p.* 16.

In Abraham Cowley we are presented with a striking example of original genius breaking through the restraints of the traditional methods of his time.—MASTERMAN, J. HOWARD B., 1897, *The Age of Milton, p.* 129.

His somewhat voluminous poems contain many passages that are well worth perusal.—PAINTER, F. V. N., 1899, *A History of English Literature, p.* 166.

He introduced the form known as the irregular or Pindaric ode, based on a misconception of the meter of the Greek poet, which Cowley did not perceive to consist of groups of three stanzas of definite forms. Cowley's epic "The Davideis" is unfinished, and his verse has not life enough to be of interest to any but special students of the period.—JOHNSON, CHARLES F., 1900, *Outline History of English and American Literature, p.* 200.

ISAAC BARROW

From the Original Picture by Isaac Wood at

JEREMY TAYLOR

Jeremy Taylor

1613–1667

Jeremy Taylor, *Bishop of Down, Connor and Dronmore*, 1613–1667. Born, at Cambridge, 15 Aug. 1613. At Cambridge Free School, 1616–26. Sizar, Gonville and Caius Coll., Camb., 18 Aug. 1626; matric., 17 March 1627; B. A., 1631; M. A., 1634; Incorp. Fellow of All Souls Coll., Oxford, 20 Oct. 1635. Ordained chaplain to Archbishop Laud. Chaplain to Charles I., 1638. Rector of Uppingham, 1638–42. Married Phoebe Landisdale, 27 May 1639. Created D. D. from Brasenose Coll. Oxford, 1 Nov. 1642. With the King, as Chaplain, during Civil War. Kept a school in Wales, with W. Nicholson and W. Wyatt, 1646–47. Chaplain to Earl of Carbery, at Golden Grove, Carmarthenshire, 1647–57. Settled in Ireland, as Rector of Lisburn and Portmore, 1658. Bishop of Down and Connor, Jan. 1661. Privy Councillor, Ireland, Feb. 1661. Bishop of Dronmore, June 1661. Vice-Chancellor, Dublin Univ., 1661. Died, at Lisburn, 13 Aug. 1667. Buried in Dronmore Cathedral. *Works:* "A Sermon preached . . . in Oxford, upon the Anniversary of the Gunpowder Treason," 1638; "Of the Sacred Order and Offices of Episcopacy," 1642; "A Discourse concerning Prayer Extempore" (anon.), 1646; "A New and Easie Institution of Grammar," 1647; "Θεολια Ἐκλεκτικη," 1647; "Treatises" (4 pts.), 1648; "An Apology for . . . set forms of Liturgie," 1649; "The Great Exemplar," 1649; "The Martyrdom of King Charles I.," 1649; "Sermon at the Funeral of Frances, Countess of Carbery," 1650; "The Rule and Exercises of Holy Living," 1650; "The Rule and Exercises of Holy Dying," 1651; "Twenty-eight Sermons," 1651; "A Short Catechism" (anon.), 1652; "A Discourse of Baptism," 1652; "The Real Presence," 1654; "Ἐνιαυτος," (3 pts.), 1653–55; "The Golden Grove" (anon.), 1655; "Unum Necessarium," 1655; "Deus Justificatus," 1656; "An Answer to a Letter written by the Bishop of Rochester," 1656; "A Discourse of Auxiliary Beauty" (anon.), 1656; "A Discourse of . . . Friendship" (under initials: J. T., D. D.), 1657 (2nd edn., called: "The Measure and Offices of Friendship," same year); "Συμβολον'Ηθικη-Πολεμικον," 1657; "The Ephesian Matron" (anon.), 1659; "Ductor Dubitantium," 1660; "The Worthy Communicant," 1660; "Sermon preached at the Consecration of two Archbishops, etc.," 1661; "Rules and Advices to the Clergy of Down and Connor," 1661; "A Sermon preached at the Opening of Parliament," 1661; "Via Intelligentiæ," 1662; "Sermon preached at the Funeral of the Archbishop of Armagh," 1663; "Ἑβδομας Ἐμβολιμαιος" (6 pts.,) 1661–63; "A Dissuasive from Popery," 1664; (3rd edn. same year); "Second Part" of preceding, 1667. *Posthumous:* Συμβολον Θεολογικον, 1673–74; "Christ's Yoke an Easy Yoke," 1675; "Contemplations of the State of Man," 1684; "A Discourse on the Lord's Supper," 1792. He *edited:* "The Psalter of David," 1644. *Collected Works:* in 15 vols., ed. by Bishop Heber, 1822. *Life:* by H. K. Bonney, 1815.—SHARP, R. FARQUHARSON, 1897, *A Dictionary of English Authors, p.* 275.

PERSONAL

To these advantages of nature, and excellency of his spirit, he added an indefatigable industry, and God gave a plentiful benediction; for there were very few kinds of learning but he was a *mystes* and a great master in them. He was a rare Humanist, and hugely versed in all the polite parts of Learning, and thoroughly concocted all the antient Moralists, Greek and Roman Poets and Orators, and was not unacquainted with the refined wits of the latter ages, whether French or Italian. . . . This great prelate had the good humour of a gentleman, the eloquence of an orator, the fancy of a poet, the acuteness of a Schoolman, the profoundness of a Philosopher, the wisdom of a Counsellor, the sagacity of a Prophet, the reason of an angel, and the piety of a Saint: he had devotion enough for a Cloister, learning enough for an University, and wit enough for a College of Virtuosi: and, had his parts and endowments been parcelled out among his poor Clergy that he left behind him, it would, perhaps, have made one of the best dioceses in the world.—RUST, GEORGE, 1667, *Funeral Sermon.*

He was esteemed by the generality of persons a compleat artist, accurate logician, exquisite, quick and acute in his reasonings, a person of great fluency in his language and of prodigious readiness in his learning. A noted Presbyterian [Hen. Jeanes, in his Epist. to the Reader before Certain Letters between him and Jer. Taylor, 1660, fol.] also (his antagonist) doth ingeniously confess that Dr. Taylor is a man of admirable wit, great parts, hath a quick and elegant pen, is of abilities in critical learning and of profound skill in antiquity.—WOOD, ANTHONY, 1691–1721, *Athenæ Oxonienses, vol.* II, *f.* 401.

Those who have looked at Taylor's portraits will have been struck by the beauty and grace of his personal appearance. There is a ripe and somewhat soft freshness of health in his face, "with his hair long and gracefully curling on his cheeks, large dark eyes full of sweetness, an aquiline nose," and an open earnest expression. He is said not to have been without consciousness of his personal beauty, and to have frequently introduced his portraits in different attitudes in his various writings.—TULLOCH, JOHN, 1872, *Rational Theology and Christian Philosophy in England in the Seventeenth Century, vol.* I, *p.* 371.

THE LIBERTY OF PROPHESYING
1647

The most curious, and, perhaps, the ablest of all his compositions,—his admirable "Liberty of Prophesying"; composed, as he tells his patron, Lord Hatton, . . . under a host of grievous disadvantages; in adversity and want; without books or leisure; and with no other resources than those which were supplied by a long familiarity with the sacred volume, and a powerful mind, imbued with all the learning of past ages.—HEBER, REGINALD, 1822, *Life of Jeremy Taylor.*

Taylor's was a great and lovely mind; yet how much and injuriously was it perverted by his being a favourite and follower of Laud, and by his intensely popish feelings of church authority. His "Liberty of Prophesying" is a work of wonderful eloquence and skill; but if we believe the argument, what do we come to? Why to nothing more or less than this, that—so much can be said for every opinion and sect,—so impossible is it to settle anything by reasoning or authority of Scripture,—we must appeal to some positive jurisdiction on earth, *ut sit finis controversiarum.* . . I fear you will think me harsh, when I say that I believe Taylor was, perhaps unconsciously, half a

Socinian in heart. Such a strange inconsistency would not be impossible.—COLERIDGE, SAMUEL TAYLOR, 1830, *Table Talk, ed. Ashe, June* 4, *pp.* 92, 93.

This celebrated work was written, according to Taylor's dedication, during his retirement in Wales, whither he was driven, as he expresses it, "by this great storm which hath dashed the vessel of the church all in pieces;" and published in 1647. He speaks of himself as without access to books: it is evident, however, from the abundance of his quotations, that he was not much in want of them; and from this, as well as other strong indications, we may reasonably believe that a considerable part of his treatise had been committed to paper long before. The argument of this important book rests on one leading maxim, derived from the Arminian divines, as it was in them from Erasmus and Acontius, that the fundamental truths of Christianity are comprised in narrow compass, not beyond the Apostles' Creed in its literal meaning; that all the rest is matter of disputation, and too uncertain, for the most part, to warrant our condemning those who differ from us, as if their error must be criminal. —HALLAM, HENRY, 1837–39, *Introduction to the Literature of Europe, pt.* iii, *ch.* ii, *par.* 52, 53.

HOLY LIVING AND HOLY DYING
1650–51

His "Holy Living and Dying" is a divine pastoral. He writes to the faithful followers of Christ, as the shepherd pipes to his flock. He introduces touching and heartfelt appeals to familiar life; condescends to men of low estate; and his pious page blushes with modesty and beauty. His style is prismatic. It unfolds the colours of the rainbow; it floats like the bubble through the air; it is like innumerable dew-drops that glitter on the face of morning, and tremble as they glitter. He does not dig his way underground, but slides upon ice, borne on the winged car of fancy. The dancing light he throws upon objects is like an Aurora Borealis, playing betwixt heaven and earth.—HAZLITT, WILLIAM, 1820, *Lectures on the Literature of the Age of Elizabeth.*

His masterpiece. A series of sermons in simple paragraphs, eloquent and persuasive, exhorting to an upright and holy life. It has been a popular book even to the present time. All of Taylor's writings are marred by the style prevalent in his time, but accentuated and exaggerated by him; Latinized, but careless, florid, gorgeous, rapid, opulent of words.— EMERY, FRED PARKER, 1896, *Notes on English Literature, p.* 42.

Even Jeremy Taylor suffers from the imperfections of contemporary taste. His unction is too long-drawn, his graces too elaborate and gorgeous, and modern readers turn from the sermons which his own age thought so consummate in their beauty to those more colloquial treatises of Christian exposition and exhortation of which the "Holy Living" and the "Holy Dying" are the types.—GOSSE, EDMUND, 1897, *Short History of Modern English Literature, p.* 152.

UNUM NECESSARIUM
1655

In another, the "Unum Necessarium," or Discourse on Repentance, his looseness of statement and want of care in driving several horses at once, involved him in a charge of Pelagianism, or something like it, which he wrote much to disprove, but which has so far lasted as to justify modern theologians in regarding his ideas on this and other theological points as, to say the least, confused.—SAINTSBURY, GEORGE, 1887, *History of Elizabethan Literature, p.* 331.

DUCTOR DUBITANTIUM
1660

A brilliancy of imagination appears in all his writings; but his "Ductor Dubitantium" is a signal proof of his judgment. —GRANGER, JAMES, 1769–1824, *Biographical History of England, vol.* v, *p.* 22.

The best work of the sort, perhaps, that ever was published, and the most elaborate and exquisite of all his own writings. —HURD, RICHARD, 1808? *Commonplace Book, ed. Kilvert, p.* 277.

Of this largest and most laborious of Bishop Taylor's works it has been said, without exaggeration, that it is the production of retentive memory and laborious research, of learning various and profound, and of reasoning close and dispassionate.—HEBER, REGINALD, 1822, *Life of Jeremy Taylor.*

The most extensive and learned work **on** casuistry which has appeared in the English language is the "Ductor Dubitantium" of Jeremy Taylor, published in 1660. This, as its title shows, treats of subjective morality, or the guidance of the conscience. But this cannot be much discussed without establishing some principles of objective right and wrong, some standard by which the conscience is to be ruled. . . . The heterogeneous combination of things so different in nature and authority, as if they were all expressions of the law of God, does not augur well for the distinctness of Taylor's moral philosophy, and would be disadvantageously compared with the "Ecclesiastical Polity" of Hooker. Nor are we deceived in the anticipations we might draw. With many of Taylor's excellences, his vast fertility and his frequent acuteness, the "Ductor Dubitantium" exhibits his characteristic defects: the waste of quotations is even greater than in his other writings, and his own exuberance of mind degenerates into an intolerable prolixity. His solution of moral difficulties is often unsatisfactory: after an accumulation of arguments and authorities, we have the disappointment to perceive that the knot is neither untied nor cut; there seems a want of close investigation of principles, a frequent confusion and obscurity, which Taylor's two chief faults—excessive display of erudition, and redundancy of language—conspire to produce. Paley is no doubt often superficial, and sometimes mistaken; yet in clearness, in conciseness, in freedom from impertinent reference to authority, he is far superior to Taylor.— HALLAM, HENRY, 1837–39, *Introduction to the Literature of Europe, pt.* iv, *ch.* iv, *par.* 3, 4.

Illustrating, better almost than any other book in the language, a remarkable point in the history of speculation—the transition from moral theology to moral philosophy, from the textbooks of the confessional to the works of writers on morals, regarded as a matter of ordinary speculation.—STEPHEN, SIR JAMES FITZJAMES, 1892, *Horæ Sabbaticæ.*

The style of the book is prolix and hazy, overloaded with quotations and references, and only rarely enriched by illustration or eloquence, for which, indeed, the subject gives little scope.—MASTERMAN, J. HOWARD B., 1897, *The Age of Milton, p.* 183.

SERMONS

Borrowed Dr. Taylor's "Sermons," and is a most excellent booke and worth my buying.—PEPYS, SAMUEL, 1655, *Diary,* Nov. 28.

His excellent discourses, which are enough of themselves to furnish a library, and will be famous to all succeeding generations for the exactness of wit, profoundness of judgment, richness of fancy, clearness of expression, copiousness of invention, and general usefulness to all the purposes of a Christian.—WOOD, ANTHONY, 1691–1721, *Athenæ Oxonienses, vol.* II.

Taylor and Barrow are incomparably the greatest preachers and divines of their age. But my predilection is for Taylor. He has all the abundance and solidity of the other, with a ray of lightening of his own, which, if he did not derive it from Demosthenes and Tully, has, at least, as generous and noble an original. It is true they are both *incompti,* or rather exuberant. But it is for such little writers as the Preacher of Lincoln's Inn [himself] to hide their barrenness by the finicalness of culture.—WARBURTON, WILLIAM, 1777–1808, *Letters from a Late Eminent Prelate, Letter L, note.*

As essays for the closet, and as intended for those into whose hands they usually fall, few compositions can be named so eminently distinguished by fancy, by judgment, by learning, and by powers of reasoning; few, where the mind is so irresistibly allured, . . . or where so much luxuriance of imagination, and so much mellowness of style, are made the vehicles of divinity so sound, and holiness so practical.—HEBER, REGINALD, 1822, *Life of Jeremy Taylor.*

It seems very certain that he was preeminently a poet amongst preachers. This apology and allowance must be made for him, that no other pulpit name is associated with so rich and rare a poetic exuberance. The epithet of the modern, or the English Chrysostom seems scarcely a fitting one; Chrysostom was essentially an orator. We do not think of Jeremy Taylor as an orator. We have already said, we cannot conceive those sermons preached to vast audiences; he who cannot preach to vast audiences is no orator; he may be a most delightful preacher with the audience fit and few, and the charm of cryptic thought and feeling; and this is the attraction and the pleasure of the devotions and contemplations of Jeremy Taylor.—HOOD, E. PAXTON, 1885, *The Throne of Eloquence, p.* 154.

It is generally admitted that the literary genius of Taylor is seen at its best in his sermons. A passage in a sermon by South (30 April 1668) is evidently aimed at the pulpit style of Taylor, whose "starched similitudes" he caricatures. But while Taylor's imagination travels far and wide, takes daring flights, and again treads homely ground, he employs his gift in real elucidation of his point; and by the vividness of his own conceptions redeems from commonplace the preacher's most obvious themes. Apart from the play of fancy, the singular neatness of his workmanship gives beauty to his writing. The appalling length of his periods is very much a matter of punctuation. His style is not involved; few writers have been better artists in clear and striking sentences. It is true that he is wanting in some of the higher qualities of eloquence. He arrests and delights rather than moves his reader, for he is not himself carried away. In the midst of splendours he never rises into passion, and bounds his meaning with even cautious care. In his piety there is little fervour, but all his writings give the deep impression of a chastened and consecrated spirit of devotion.—GORDON, ALEXANDER, 1898, *Dictionary of National Biography, vol.* LV, *p.* 428.

GENERAL

We see the Reverend Doctor's Treatises standing, as it were, in the front of this order of authors, and as the foremost of those *Good Books* used by the politest and most refined *Devotees* of either sex. They maintain the principal place in the study of almost every elegant and high *Divine.* They stand in folios and other volumes, adorned with variety of pictures, gildings, and other decorations, on the advanced shelves or glass cupboards of the *ladies'* closets. They are in use at all seasons, and for all places; as well for church service as closet-preparation; and, in short, may vie with any devotional books in *British Christendom.*—SHAFTESBURY, EARL OF (ANTHONY ASHBY COOPER), 1711, *Characteristics of Men, Manners, and Opinions, vol.* III.

In learning he was scarcely inferior to any theologian whatever; and in richness of imagination he is superior to all. On the subject of original sin, and of the justification of man before God, his sentiments differed from those of the established church of which he was a member; but on other points of Christian verity his views were generally correct. He is one of those few authors "the dust of whose works is gold;" and as long as the English language is understood, his volumes will constitute some of its choicest treasures. Through the whole of his numerous writings the flame of genius and of devotion burns with unabated and unexampled strength.—WILLIAMS, EDWARD, 1800–43, *The Christian Preacher, 5th ed., p.* 363.

Doctor Jeremy Taylor, late Lord Bishop of Down and Connor in Ireland, and Administrator of the See of Dromore; such are the titles which his sounding title pages give him, and I love the man, and I love his paraphernalia, and I like to name him with all his attributions and additions. If you are yet but lightly acquainted with his real manner, take up and read the whole first chapter of the "Holy Dying"; in particular turn to the first paragraph of the 2 sect. of that chapter for a simile of a rose, or the more truly many similes within simile; for such were the riches of his fancy, that when a beauteous image offered, before he could stay to expand it into all its capacities, throngs of new coming images came up, and jostled out the first, or blended in disorder with it, which imitates the order of every rapid mind. But read all of the first chapter by my advice. . . . . Or for another specimen . . . . turn to the story of the Ephesian Matron in the second section of the 5th chapter . . . read it yourself and show it to Plumstead with my Love, and . . . ask him if Willy* himself has ever told a story with more circumstances of Fancy and Humor. The paragraph begins, "But that which is to be faulted," and the story not long after follows. Make these references while P. is with you, that you may stir him him up to the Love of Jeremy Taylor, and make a convertite of him. Coleridge was the man who first solemnly exhorted me to "study" the works of Dr. Jeremy Taylor, and I have had reason to bless

* Shakespeare.

the hour in which he did it.—LAMB, CHARLES, 1801, *Letter, Charles Lamb and the Lloyds, ed. Lucas, pp.* 148, 149, 150.

From this venerable and learned writer's Polemical Discourses, the Theological Student must derive the soundest instruction and most important advantages. It may not perhaps be generally known, but its nevertheless true, that partly from the 44th section or discourse of Dr. Taylor, and partly from Stillingfleet's Irenicum, Mr. Locke borrowed the plan of his Letters on Toleration.—BELOE, WILLIAM, 1806, *Anecdotes of Literature and Scarce Books, vol.* I, *p.* 180.

There is in any one of the prose folios of Jeremy Taylor more fine fancy and original imagery—more brilliant conceptions and glowing expressions—more new figures, and new applications of old figures —more, in short, of the body and the soul of poetry, than in all the odes and the epics that have since been produced in Europe. —JEFFREY, FRANCIS, 1811–44, *Contributions to the Edinburgh Review, vol.* II, *p.* 287.

It would be worth your while to read Taylor's "Letter on Original Sin," and what follows. I compare it to an old statue of Janus, with one of the faces, that which looks towards his opponents, the controversial phiz in highest preservation,—the force of a mighty one, all power, all life,—the face of a God rushing on to battle, and, in the same moment, enjoying at once both contest and triumph; the other, that which should have been the countenance that looks toward his followers, that with which he substitutes his own opinion, all weather eaten, dim, useless, a *Ghost* in *marble,* such as you may have seen represented in many of Piranesi's astounding engravings from Rome and the Campus Martius. Jer. Taylor's discursive intellect dazzle-darkened his intuition. The principle of becoming all things to all men, if by *any* means he might save *any,* with him as with Burke, thickened the protecting epidermis of the tact-nerve of truth into something like a callus. But take him all in all, such a miraculous combination of erudition, broad, deep, and omnigenous; of logic subtle as well as acute, and as robust as agile; of psychological insight, so fine yet so secure! of public prudence and practical *sageness* that one ray of *creative Faith* would have lit up and transfigured into wisdom, and of genuine imagination, with its streaming face unifying all at one moment like that of the setting sun when, through an interspace of blue sky no larger than itself, it emerges from the cloud to sink behind the mountain, but a face seen only at *starts*, when some breeze from the higher air scatters, for a moment, the cloud of butterfly fancies, which flutter around him like a morning-garment of ten thousand colours—(now how shall I get out of this sentence? the tail is too big to be taken up into the coiler's mouth)—well, as I was saying, I believe such a complete man hardly shall we meet again.—COLERIDGE, SAMUEL TAYLOR, 1814, *Letters, ed. E. H. Coleridge, vol.* II, *p.* 640.

Jeremy Taylor was a writer as different from Sir Thomas Browne as it was possible for one writer to be from another. He was a dignitary of the church, and except in matters of casuistry and controverted points, could not be supposed to enter upon speculative doubts, or give a loose to a sort of dogmatical scepticism. He had less thought, less "stuff of the conscience," less "to give us pause," in his impetuous oratory, but he had equal fancy —not the same vastness and profundity, but more richness and beauty, more warmth and tenderness. He is as rapid, as flowing and endless, as the other is stately, abrupt, and concentrated. The eloquence of the one is like a river, that of the other is more like an aqueduct. The one is as sanguine as the other is saturnine in the temper of his mind. Jeremy Taylor took obvious and admitted truths for granted, and illustrated them with an inexhaustible display of new and enchanting imagery. Sir Thomas Browne talks in sum-totals: Jeremy Taylor enumerates all the particulars of a subject. He gives every aspect it will bear, and never "cloys with sameness." His characteristic is enthusiastic and delightful amplification. Sir Thomas Browne gives the beginning and end of things, that you may judge of their place and magnitude: Jeremy Taylor describes their qualities and texture, and enters into all the items of the debtor and creditor account between life and death, grace and nature, faith and good works. He puts his heart into his fancy. He does not pretend to annihilate the passions and pursuits of mankind in the pride

of philosophic indifference, but treats them as serious and momentous things, warring with conscience and the soul's health, or furnishing the means of grace and hopes of glory. In his writings, the frail stalk of human life reclines on the bosom of eternity.—HAZLITT, WILLIAM, 1820, *Lectures on the Literature of the Age of Elizabeth.*

From whose mind of its treasures redundant Streams of eloquence flowed, like an inexhaustible fountain.
—SOUTHEY, ROBERT, 1821, *A Vision of Judgment,* ix.

I have already had occasion to point out the versatility of his talents, which, though uniformly exerted on subjects appropriate to his profession, are distinguished, where such weapons are needed, by irony and caustic humour, as well as by those milder and sublimer beauties of style and sentiment which are his more familiar and distinguishing characteristics. Yet to such weapons he has never recourse either wantonly or rashly. Nor do I recollect any instance in which he has employed them in the cause of private, or personal, or even polemical hostility; or any occasion where their fullest severity was not justified and called for by crimes, by cruelty, by interested superstition, or base and sordid hypocrisy. His satire was always kept in check by the depth and fervour of his religious feelings, his charity, and his humility.—HEBER, REGINALD, 1822, *Life of Jeremy Taylor.*

The heavenly-mindedness of Jeremy Taylor threw such a charm over his diction—exhibited such proofs of genius and of piety—that that great man may be considered as the founder of a school, (even of the opposite persuasion), in which enthusiasm was mistaken for inspiration, and where there was an equal glow of piety, but unsupported by such flights of genius and such demonstrations of learning.—DIBDIN, THOMAS FROGNALL, 1824, *The Library Companion, p.* 49.

Jeremy Taylor, restless, fervid, aspiring, scattering abroad a prodigality of life, not unfolding but creating, with the energy and the "myriad-mindedness" of Shakspere. . . . As to Jeremy Taylor, we would as readily undertake to put a belt about the ocean as to characterize him adequately within the space at our command. . . . The only very obvious defects of Taylor were in the mechanical part of his art, in the mere *technique.* He writes like one who never revises, nor tries the effect upon his ear of his periods as musical wholes, and in the syntax and connexion of the parts seems to have been habitually careless of slight blemishes.— De Quincey Thomas, 1828–59, *Rhetoric, Collected Writings, ed. Masson, vol.* x, *pp.* 105, 106, 108.

With all his genius, learning, and industry, Jeremy Taylor never could be a poet, because he never went beyond himself—beside himself, if you will. He has put the question beyond doubt : he tried verse ; but his lines are like petrifications, glittering, and hard, and cold ; formed by a slow but certain process in the laboratory of abstract thought ; not like flowers, springing spontaneously from a kindly soil, fresh, and fragrant, and blooming in open day. The erudite divine is always in his study.—Montgomery, James, 1833, *Lectures on General Literature, p.* 83.

What a man he is ! He has such a knowledge of the nature of man, and such powers of expressing its properties, that I sometimes feel as if he had had some exact counterpart of my own individual character under his eye, when he lays open the depths of the heart, or traces some sin to its root. The eye of his portrait expresses this keen intuition : and I think I should less like to have stood with a lie on my tongue before him, than before any other I know of.—Fitzgerald, Edward, 1835, *Letters, vol.* I, *p.* 29.

When Jeremy Taylor wishes to prove the insensible progress of "a man's life and reason," he does not set about it by a syllogism, but a picture. He is not contented with a simple illustration—he raises up an elaborate landscape.—Lytton, Lord Edward George Lytton Bulwer, 1836, *Sir Thomas Browne, Edinburgh Review, vol.* 64, *p.* 11.

"The crowded, yet clear and luminous, galaxies of imagery diffused through the works of Bishop Taylor," are mentioned in glowing terms by Dr. Parr. It must, however, be admitted that his warmth of imagination is sometimes more conspicuous than his sobriety of judgment. His style is distinguished by its vivacity, and is more fluent and unencumberd than that of his most eminent predecessors in English literature. His popularity continues

unimpaired.—Irving, David, 1842, *Life of Taylor, Encyclopædia Britannica,* 7th *ed., vol.* XXI, *p.* 126.

Jeremy Taylor stands altogether alone among churchmen. Who has ever manifested any portion of that exquisite intermixture of a yearning love with a heavenly fancy, which enabled him to embody and render palpable the holy charities of his religion in the loveliest and most delicate images ? Who has ever so encrusted his subjects with candied words ; or has seemed, like him, to take away the sting of death with "rich conceit ;" or has, like him, half persuaded his hearers to believe that they heard the voice of pitying angels ?—Talfourd, Thomas Noon, 1842, *On Pulpit Oratory, Critical and Miscellaneous Writings, p.* 226.

Bishop Taylor is a writer of the first-rate powers, with a fine imagination, and much devotion, holiness, and humility. Yet he is too ascetic, and has too little of the good tidings of the gospel. . . . He fell into something of Pelagian errors, and, like Warburton, did not consider the immortality of the soul revealed to the Patriarchs. It is also to be regretted that prayers for the dead have received countenance from some passages in his writings. . . . A fine, rich imagination, with great devotion, but a tone of divinity below that of the Reformers, and in some material points erroneous.—Bickersteth, Edward, 1844, *The Christian Student.*

Nor are the boldness and the fancy, the endless variety and unexpected sallies of Taylor, to be matched by other divines, any more than they are to be ventured upon by such as duly regard the severe taste which the solemnity of the occasion prescribes.—Brougham, Henry Lord, 1856, *Contributions to Edinburgh Review, vol.* I, *p.* 128.

The Pelagian Jeremy Taylor.—Pattison, Mark, 1860, *Essays, vol.* II, *p.* 61.

Taylor, the Shakspeare of divines. —Emerson, R. W., 1865? *The Problem.*

His very style—like the murmur of a deep sea, bathed in the sun—so richly coloured by an imagination that was never disunited from the affections, and at the same time so sweetly cadenced, so full of gentle and varied melodies, reflects his character ; and nòt the less so because of a certain want of nervousness and consistency, a certain vagueness and almost feebleness which it occasionally displays. —LECKY, WILLIAM EDWARD HARTPOLE, 1865, *Spirit of Rationalism in Europe.*

At the head of our English divines stands Jeremy Taylor at least as regards eloquence and brilliancy of imagination. He has been by some called the Spenser, by others the Shakespeare, of our theological literature; and he deserves both titles. He is as learned, as sweet, and as alluring as Spenser, and he has sometimes the tragic force and power, now and then a glimpse of the humour, and in some degree the fertile imagery and copiousness of diction of Shakespeare.—FRISWELL, JAMES HAIN, 1869, *Essays on English Writers, p.* 182.

A writer of genius appears amongst these, a prose-poet, gifted with imagination like Spenser and Shakspeare,— Jeremy Taylor, who, from the bent of his mind as well as from circumstances, was destined to present the alliance of the Renaissance with the Reformation, and to carry into the pulpit the ornate style of the court. . . . There was never a better or more upright man, more zealous in his duties, more tolerant by principle; . . . Taylor imagines objects, not vaguely and feebly, by some indistinct general conception, but precisely, entire, as they are, with their sensible colour, their proper form, the multitude of true and particular details which distinguish them in their species.—TAINE, H. A., 1871, *History of English Literature, tr.* Van Laun, *vol.* I, *bk.* ii, *ch.* v, *pp.* 382, 383.

Taylor is medieval, ascetic, casuistic in his mature type of thought. He is a scholastic in argument, a pietist in feeling, a poet in fancy and expression; he is not a thinker. He seldom moves in an atmosphere of purely rational light; and even when his instincts are liberal and his reasoning highly rational in its results, he brings but a slight force of thought, of luminous and direct comprehension, to bear upon his work.—TULLOCH, JOHN, 1872, *Rational Theology and Christian Philosophy in England in the Seventeenth Century, vol.* I, *p.* 347.

A kind of Spenser in a cassock.—LOWELL, JAMES RUSSELL, 1875, *Spenser, Works, Riverside ed., vol.* IV, *p.* 325, *note.*

But Taylor's theology, it must be admitted, is without symmetry; it is not a noble building; a very large portion of his writings reads like the essays and confession of Montaigne, expressed in most dazzling and ambitious language. His most religious writings are what we have called them, Divine contemplations; thought, in the more strict comprehension of the term, we have little or none; imagination and emotion we have in abundance. After a time we find the understanding is not firm beneath us, and we begin to perceive that if we demand from our author argumentative coherence, we shall deal unjustly with him, while we cut ourselves off from the possession of much pleasure. We learn that his gift is to teach us rather as a seer than as a philosopher; to lift us at once to the spiritual rather than debate with us the material reasons of things. When he attempts the latter we become angry with him; always, when he attempts the former, it is as if at his touch the tabernacle of the testimony is opened in heaven.—HOOD, E. PAXTON, 1885, *The Throne of Eloquence, p.* 163.

It is not true that, except by great complaisance of the reader, Jeremy Taylor's long sentences are at once understandable. They may, of course, and generally can be understood *kata to semainsmenon,* as a telegram with half the words left out may at the other end of the scale be understood. But they constantly withstand even a generous parser, even one who is to the fullest extent ready to allow for idiom and individuality. They abuse in particular the conjunction to a most enormous extent— coupling by its means propositions which have no legal connection, which start entirely different trains of thought, and which are only united because carelessness and fashion combined made it unnecessary for the writer to take the little extra trouble necessary for their separation. Taylor will, in the very middle of his finest passages, and with hardly so much as a comma's break, change *oratio obliqua* to *oratio recta,* interrupt the sequence of tenses, make his verbs agree with the nearest noun, irrespective of the connection, and in short, though he was, while in Wales, a schoolmaster for some time, and author of a grammatical treatise, will break Priscian's head with the calmest unconcern.—SAINTSBURY, GEORGE, 1887, *History of Elizabethan Literature, p.* 332.

He united learning and fervent eloquence perhaps more than any other English writer. —PALGRAVE, FRANCIS TURNER, 1889, *The Treasury of Sacred Song, note, p.* 345.

He was saturated through and through with learning and with piety; and they gurgled from him together in a great tide of mellifluous language. The ardors and fervors of Elizabethan days seem to have lapped over upon him in that welter of the Commonwealth wars. He has been called the Shakespeare of the pulpit; I should rather say the Spenser—there is such unchecked, and uncheckable, affluence of language and illustration; thought and speech struggling together for precedence, and stretching on and on, in ever so sweet and harmonious jangle of silvery sounds.—MITCHELL, DONALD G., 1890, *English Lands Letters and Kings, Elizabeth to Anne, p.* 139.

Those who claim for the Church of England one of the highest places amongst Christian bodies for literary eminence, would naturally put forward Jeremy Taylor as one of the leading witnesses in favour of their proposition; and certainly it may be doubted whether any English ecclesiastical writer would be entitled to take precedence of him in a literary point of view, though he has been surpassed again and again by writers on special subjects whose eloquence, versatility, learning, dexterity were greatly inferior to his.—STEPHEN, SIR JAMES FITZJAMES, 1892, *Horae Sabbaticae, First Series, p.* 209.

On the whole the elements of greatest hopefulness for English prose—its earnestness, its dignity, its conscious grace—were perhaps best summed up, in that age, in Jeremy Taylor: and to him more than to any other may be ascribed the handing on of the torch from the preceding to the next generation, and the preserving of its flame clear and undimmed amidst the heated struggles and cloudy controversies of the time. — CRAIK, HENRY, 1893, *English Prose. Introduction, vol.* II, *p.* 7

As a preacher and devotional writer, Bishop Jeremy Taylor stands in the very first rank among the great divines of the golden period of English theology. His sermons are, of their kind, unrivalled. They differ widely from those of his great contemporaries, Barrow, Sanderson, and South; but they are, in their way, quite equal to any of them. In wealth of illustration, exuberance of fancy, grandeur of diction and style, it would be difficult to find their equals in the English language. . . . One of his great merits as a devotional writer is the very rare faculty he possessed of composing prayers. His prayers are some of the very few which can bear a moment's comparison with those in the Book of Common Prayer. —OVERTON, J. H., 1893, *English Prose, ed. Craik, vol.* II, *pp.* 525, 527.

Few theologians have left more mark on English religion than Jeremy Taylor. His sermons combine many of the merits of Andrewes and of William Law. They are extraordinarily fertile in conceit and in appropriate illustration, they are searching and intimate in their application, and removed from all possibility of dulness by their sparkling and abundant imagination. His controversial writings are less easy, but their style is vigorous. His "Ductor Dubitantium" is almost the only treatise on casuistry written by an English Churchman, and it has all the honesty, and more than the skill, that might be expected. Books such as these belong to the armoury of the theologians, but the prayers of the "Golden Grove" and the admonitions of "Holy Living" and "Holy Dying" belong by right to every man that can appreciate either literature or religion. Certainly no religious works in English possess the same rare combination of merits, and none have more powerfully affected English life. The acute insight and the intimate knowledge of human nature which they show on every page are only equalled by the marvellous imagination which illuminates the style as well as the matter. Of all English prose writers, Jeremy Taylor is the richest.—HUTTON, WILLIAM HOLDEN, 1895, *Social England, ed. Traill, vol.* IV, *p.* 292.

Taylor was the most eloquent of men, and the most facile of orators. Laden with thought, his books are read for their sweet and deep devotion (a quality which also belonged to his fellow-writer, Lancelot Andrewes), even more than for their impassioned and convoluted outbreaks of beautiful words.—BROOKE, STOPFORD A., 1896, *English Literature, p.* 153.

George Wither

1588-1667

Born, at Bentworth, Hants, 11 June 1588. Early education at a school at Colemore. Matric. Magdalen Coll., Oxford, 1604 [?]. Left Oxford after about three years. Imprisoned for libel, 1614. Student of Lincoln's Inn, 1615. Served as Captain in cavalry regiment under Charles I., 1639. Served in Parliamentary Army, 1642; obtained rank of Major. Governor of Farnham Castle, Oct. to Dec., 1642. J. P. for Hampshire, Surrey and Essex, 1642-58. Major-General of Forces in Surrey, 1643 [?]. Master of the Statute Office, 1655 [?]. Imprisoned for libel, March 1662 to 1665. Died, in London, 2 May 1667. Buried in the Savoy Church. *Works:* "Prince Henrie's Obsequies," 1612; "Epithalamia," 1612; "Abuses Stript and Whipt," 1613; "A Satyre, dedicated to His Most Excellent Majestie," 1614; "The Shepheards Hunting," 1615; "Fidelia," 1617; "A Preparation to the Psalter," 1619; "Workes," 1620; "Exercises upon the first Psalme," 1620; "The Songs of the Old Testament," 1621; "Wither's Motto," 1621; "Juvenilia," 1622; "Faire-Virtue," 1622; "The Hymnes and Songs of the Church," 1623; "The Scholler's Purgatory" [1625?]; "Britain's Remembrance," 1628; "The Psalmes of David translated into Lyrick verse," 1632; "Collection of Emblemes," 1634-35; "Read and Wonder" (anon.; ascribed to Wither), 1641; "Halelujah," 1641; "Campo-Musæ," 1643; "Se Defendo" [1643]; "Mercurius Rusticus" (anon.), 1643; "The Speech without Doore," 1644; "The Two Incomparable Generalissimos," 1644; "Letters of Advice," 1645 [1644]; "Vox Pacifica," 1645; "The Great Assizes holden in Parnassus" (anon.), 1645; "The Speech without Doore defended," 1646; "Justiciarus Justificatus," 1646; "What Peace to the Wicked?" (anon.), 1646; "Opobalsamum Anglicanum," 1646; "Major Wither's Disclaimer," 1647; "Carmen Expostulatorium," 1647; "Amygdale Britannica" (anon.), 1647; "Prosopopœia Britannica," 1648; "Carmen Eucharisticon," 1649; "Respublica Anglicana," 1650; "The British Appeals," 1651; "Three Grains of Spiritual Frankincense," 1651; The Dark Lantern," 1653; "Westrow Revived," 1653; "Vaticinum Casuale," 1655; "Rapture at the Protector's Recovery," 1655; "Three Private Meditations," 1655; "The Protector," 1655; "Boni Ominis Votum," 1656; "A Suddain Flash" (anon.), 1657; "Salt upon Salt," 1659; "A Cordial Confection," 1659; "Epistolium Vagum-Prosa-Metricum," 1659; "Petition and Narrative" [1659]; "Furor Poeticus," 1660; "Speculum Speculativum," 1660; "Fides-Anglicana," 1660; "An Improvement of Imprisonment," 1661; "A Triple Paradox," 1661; "The Prisoner's Plea," 1661; "A Proclamation in the Name of the King of Kings," 1662; "Verses Intended to the King's Majesty," 1662; "Parallellogrammaton," 1662; "Tuba Pacifica," 1664; "A Memorandum to London," 1665; "Meditations upon the Lord's Prayer," 1665; "Echoes from the Sixth Trumpet" [1666]; "Sighs for the Pitchers," 1666; "Vaticina Poetica," 1666. *Posthumous:* "Divine Poems on the Ten Commandments," ed. by his daughter, 1688. He *translated:* Nemesius' "The Nature of Man," 1636. *Collected Works:* "Poems," ed. by H. Morley, 1891.—SHARP, R. FARQUHARSON, 1897, *A Dictionary of English Authors, p.* 302.

PERSONAL

In the time of the civill warres, George Withers, the poet, begged Sir John Denham's estate at Egham of the Parliament, in whose cause he was a captaine of horse. It (happened) that G. W. was taken prisoner, and was in danger of his life, having written severely against the king, &c. Sir John Denham went to the king, and desired his majestie not to hang him, for that whilest G. W. lived he should not be the worst poet in England.—AUBREY, JOHN, 1669-96, *Brief Lives, ed. Clark, vol.* I, *p.* 221.

At this day it is hard to discover what parts in the poem here particularly alluded to, "Abuses Stript and Whipt," could have occasioned the imprisonment of the author. Was Vice in High Places more suspicious than now? had she more power; or more leisure to listen after ill reports? That a man should be convicted of a libel when he named no names but Hate and Envy, and Lust, and Avarice, is like one of the indictments in the "Pilgrim's Progress," where Faithful is arraigned for having "railed on our noble Prince Beelzebub, and spoken contemptibly of his honourable friends, the Lord Old Man, the Lord Carnel Delight, and the Lord Luxurious.'' What unlucky jealousy could have tempted the great men of those days to appropriate such innocent abstractions to themselves! Wither seems to have contemplated to a degree of idolatry his own possible virtue. He is for ever anticipating persecution and martyrdom; fingering, as it were, the flames, to try how he can bear them. Perhaps his premature defiance sometimes made him obnoxious to censures, which he would otherwise have slipped by. — LAMB, CHARLES, 1818, *George Wither's Poetical Works*.

Wither, though a man of very high character, seems to have had all his life what men of high character not unfrequently have, a certain facility for getting into what is vulgarly called hot-water.— SAINTSBURY, GEORGE, 1887, *History of Elizabethan Literature, p.* 303.

Wither was no exception to the general rule that those who abandon for public life the studies of poetry and philosophy suffer a steady degeneration, partaking like brooks and rivers, as Landor finely says, ''the nature of that vast body whereunto they run, its dreariness, its bitterness, its foam, its storms, its everlasting noise and commotion.'' Not that Wither ever became quite the fanatic that he has been represented to have been. . . . His own charitableness was considerably tempered by an ineradicable contentiousness. He lived under eleven different forms of government, and he managed to be more or less at loggerheads with them all.— FYVIE, JOHN, 1890, *George Wither, Macmillan's Magazine, vol.* 62, *p.* 44.

GENERAL

George Wither, a most profuse pourer forth of English rhime, not without great pretence to a poetical zeal against the vices of his times, in his ''Motto,'' his ''Remembrancer,'' and other such like satirical works. . . . But the most of poetical fancy which I remember to have found in any of his writings is a little piece of pastoral poetry called ''The Shepherd's Huntings.''—PHILLIPS, EDWARD, 1675, *Theatrum Poetarum Anglicanorum*.

Honest George Withers, though a rustic poet, hath been very acceptable; as to some for his prophecies, so to others, for his plain country honesty.—BAXTER, RICHARD, 1681, *Poetical Fragments*.

Wretched Withers.—POPE, ALEXANDER, 1728, *Dunciad, bk.* i, *v.* 296.

This beautiful old song [''The Shepherd's Resolution''] was written by a poet, whose name would have been utterly forgotten, if it had not been preserved by Swift, as a term of contempt. ''Dryden and Wither'' are coupled by him like the ''Bavius and Mævius'' of Virgil. Dryden however has had justice done him by posterity: and as for Wither, though of subordinate merit, that he was not altogether devoid of genius, will be judged from the following stanzas. The truth is, Wither was a very voluminous partywriter: had as his political and satirical strokes rendered him extremely popular in his lifetime: so afterwards, when these were no longer relished, they totally consigned his writings to oblivion.—PERCY, THOMAS, 1765, *Reliques of Ancient English Poetry, p.* 381.

George Wither, began to display his rhyming talent, which he exercised for a long course of years, and had many admirers among readers of a lower class. He was, in several respects, an unsuccessful, but was ever a persevering writer.— GRANGER, JAMES, 1769-1824, *Biographical History of England, vol.* II, *p.* 133.

Amongst his numerous verses, which he seems to have scribbled with endless profusion, and with a total disregard to the art of blotting, there are entire compositions, which could not have proceeded, but from one, who was endowed with a strong poetical spirit. In those instances he is generally characterized by an easy elegance, and a copiousness of unaffected sentiment. A man of real taste, who has an opportunity of comparing all his publications, many of which can now seldom be met with, would do an acceptable service to the literary world, by giving a judicious selection from them.—BRYDGES, SAMUEL EGERTON, 1806, *Censura Literaria, Preface, vol.* II, *p.* x.

Dismissing with contempt the puerilities and conceits which deformed the pages of so many of his contemporaries, he cultivated, with almost uniform assiduity, a simplicity of style, and an expression of natural sentiment and feeling, which have occasioned the revival of his choicest compositions in the nineteenth century, and will for ever stamp them with a permanent value.—DRAKE, NATHAN, 1817, *Shakspeare and his Times, vol.* I, *p.* 668.

From youth to age George continued to pour forth his lucubrations, in prophesy, remonstrance, complaint, and triumph, through good and evil report, through all vicissitudes of fortune: at one time in command among the saints, and at another scrawling his thoughts in jail, when pen and ink were denied him, with red ochre upon a trencher. It is generally allowed that his taste and genius for poetry did not improve in the political contest. Some of his earliest pieces display the native amenity of a poet's imagination but as he mixed with the turbulent times, his fancy grew muddy with the stream. While Milton in the same cause brought his learning and zeal as a partisan, he left the Muse behind him, as a mistress too sacred to be introduced into party brawlings; Wither, on the contrary, took his Muse along with him to the camp and the congregation, and it is little to be wondered at that her cap should have been torn and her voice made hoarse in the confusion.—CAMPBELL, THOMAS, 1819, *Specimens of the British Poets.*

George Wither, by siding with the less poetical though more prosperous party in the civil war, and by a profusion of temporary writings to serve the ends of faction and folly, has left a name which we were accustomed to despise, till Ellis did justice to "that playful fancy, pure taste, and artless delicacy of sentiment, which distinguish the poetry of his early youth." His best poems were published in 1622, with the title, "Mistress of Philarete." Some of them are highly beautiful, and bespeak a mind above the grovelling Puritanism into which he afterwards fell. I think there is hardly any thing in our lyric poetry of this period equal to Wither's lines on his Muse, published by Ellis.—HALLAM, HENRY, 1837–39, *Introduction to the Literature of Europe, pt.* iii, *ch.* v, *par.* 54.

Wither, who wrote of poetry like a poet, and in return has been dishonored and misprised by some of his own kind— a true sincere poet of blessed oracles!— BROWNING, ELIZABETH BARRETT, 1842–63, *The Book of the Poets.*

From among the host of writers using verse for social purposes, one stands out very conspicuously as the popular satirist of the day. This was George Wither, whose poetry had been all but forgotten. . . . With his self-satisfaction he conjoined some real strength of brain, a certain elevation of aim, and a perfect dauntlessness of spirit. In his very first writings he had come forward as a plain man who was to speak truth and care for nobody. . . . And so, through the world, from that time forward, he continues to go, self-labelled as "Wither, the man that would not flatter." His "Motto," published in 1618, was, as we have said, a detailed exhibition of his character to the public in this light. He had had his portrait painted; under it he had written the motto *"Nec habeo, nec careo, nec curo;"* this motto he had adopted as his impress. . . . Wither, in addition to his satires, his pastoral narrations, and his devotional hymns, had written, chiefly as interspersed lyrics in his earlier poems, some really good secular songs. One of these is still to be heard occasionally in drawing-rooms; and a very good song it is:

'Shall I, wasting in despair
Die because a woman's fair?

—MASSON, DAVID, 1858, *The Life of John Milton, vol.* I, *ch.* vi,

It would have been very well to have republished the "Fair Virtue," and "Shepherd's Hunting" of George Wither, which contain all the true poetry he ever wrote; but we can imagine nothing more dreary than the seven hundred pages of his "Hymns and Songs," whose only use, that we can conceive of, would be as penal reading for incorrigible poetasters. —LOWELL, JAMES RUSSELL, 1858–64–90, *Library of Old Authors, Prose Works, Riverside ed*

One excellence for which all Wither's writings are eminent, his prose as well as his verse, is their genuine English. His unaffected diction, even now, has scarcely a stain of age upon it,—but flows on, ever fresh and transparent, like a pebbled rill. —CRAIK, GEORGE L., 1861, *A Compendious History of English Literature and of the English Language, vol.* II, *p.* 45.

Throughout it is distinguished by a certain straightforward simplicity of good English thought and English word. His hymns remind me, in the form of their speech, of Gascoigne.—MACDONALD, GEORGE, 1868, *England's Antiphon, p.* 159.

It is somewhat difficult to tell the student what may be considered the chief production of George Wither. His "Shepheards' Hunting" is generally associated with his name. But he was the author of more than a hundred works besides, the collection together of which no one has as yet been found sufficiently courageous to undertake. Very many of these productions are of a political nature. He was also the author of a number of religious pieces, of some very graceful songs and poems, and of some very biting satires under the title "Abuses Stript and Whipt." "Britain's Remembrancer" is a long and able poem, written by him in London, during the plague of 1627, and is by some considered the most valuable of all his writings.—FRISWELL, JAMES HAIN, 1869, *Essays on English Writers, p.* 76.

Braithwaite wrote in 1615—
"And long may England's Thespian springs be known
By lovely Wither and by bonny Browne."
But the wish has hardly been fulfilled, and there are few readers who would not be a little surprised by the epithet here applied to the Puritan poet. No real lover of poetry will however grudge it him. He is one of the few masters of octosyllabic verse in our language. Lamb has dwelt lovingly on its curious felicities, and for compass and variety it would not be easy to name its superior. It is the one form of verse pre-eminently suited to Wither, who has achieved no such triumphs with the heroic couplet. But it is not only for beauty of poetic form that Wither deserved Braithwaite's enthusiastic epithet. Like the Charmides of Plato's dialogue, he has "what is much more important, a beautiful soul." Never was there a purer or more honourable spirit, or one which kept closer to the best it knew, and as Wither has revealed himself in his works in a way in which few poets have done, it is natural to read him not only with admiration but with sympathy.—ARNOLD, W. T., 1880, *English Poets, ed. Ward, vol.* II, *p.* 89.

The time has passed when this voluminous writer can be treated by any competent critic with the contempt of the age of Anne. The scorn of Pope still clings, however, to the "wretched Withers," whose name is misspelt, and of whose works he had probably seen nothing but the satires. Nor would it be safe, on the score of exquisite beauties discoverable in the early lyrics of Wither, to overlook the radical faults of his style. One or two generous appreciators of Jacobean verse have done this, and have claimed for Wither a very high place in English poetry. But proportion, judgment, taste must count for something, and in these qualities this lyrist was deplorably deficient. The careful student, not of excerpts made by loving and partial hands, but of the bulk of his published writings, will be inclined to hesitate before he admits that Wither was a great poet. He will rather call him a very curious and perhaps unique instance of a tiresome and verbose scribbler, to whom in his youth there came unconsidered flashes of most genuine and exquisite poetry.—GOSSE, EDMUND, 1894, *The Jacobean Poets, p.* 181.

His heights and depths approach the heights and depths of Wordsworth; whilst his fecundity is no less amazing than his metrical facility. Would that we had one more lyric like the immortal "Shall I wasting in despair" for many pages of eclogues and satires, excellent although many of them undoubtedly are.—SCHELLING, FELIX E., 1895, *A Book of Elizabethan Lyrics, p.* xxxiv.

It is now universally recognised that Wither was a poet of exquisite grace, although only for a short season in his long career. Had his last work been his "Faire Virtue," he would have figured in literary history in the single capacity of a fascinating lyric poet. He was one of the few masters in English of heptasyllabic couplet, and disclosed almost all its curious felicities. But his fine gifts failed him after 1622, and during the last forty-five years of his life his verse is mainly remarkable for its mass, fluidity, and flatness. It usually lacks any genuine literary quality and often sinks into imbecile dogerel. Ceasing to be a poet, Wither became in middle life a garrulous and tedious preacher, in platitudinous prose and verse, of the political and religious creeds of the commonplace middle-class puritan.—LEE, SIDNEY, 1900, *Dictionary of National Biography, vol.* LXII, *p.* 268.

Sir William D'Avenant

1606-1668

Born, at Oxford, Feb. 1606. Educated at Magdalen College School, Oxford; and at Lincoln College, 1620 [?]-22[?]. Page to Duchess of Richmond; afterwards to Fulke Greville, Lord Brooke. Play, "The Cruel Brother," performed, 1630. Appointed Poet Laureate, 13 Dec. 1638. Governor of King and Queen's Company of Players, 27 June 1639. Active part in Civil War; escaped imprisonment and took refuge in France. Knighted after Siege of Gloucester, Sept. 1643. Returned to France after King's defeat. Became Roman Catholic. Sent on private mission from Queen to King, 1646. Returned to Paris. Sent by Queen on mission to Virginia, 1650. Captured by Parliament ship soon after start, and imprisoned in Cowes Castle; thence to London for trial. Imprisoned in the Tower, 1651-53. First wife, Anne, died, 1655. Was twice married. Licensed to give dramatic entertainments at Rutland House, 1656 ("The Siege of Rhodes" produced there, 1656), and at the Cockpit, in Drury Lane, 1658. Imprisoned for short time in 1659 on account of implication in Sir George Booth's insurrection. At Restoration, license granted him to maintain a company of players, 1660. These acted at Salisbury Court Theatre, or at Cockpit, Nov. 1660 to Spring of 1662. Under patronage of Duke of York, the company was installed in new Lincoln's Inn Fields Theatre, March or April 1662. Successful production of plays. Died, in Lincoln's Inn Fields, 7 April 1668. Buried in Westminster Abbey. *Works:* "The Tragedy of Albovine," 1629; "The Cruel Brother," 1630; "The Just Italian," 1630; "The Temple of Love" (with Inigo Jones), 1634; "The Triumphs of the Prince d'Amour" (anon.), 1635; "The Platonick Lovers," 1636; "The Witts," 1636; "Britannia Triumphans" (with Inigo Jones), 1637; "Madagascar," 1638; "Ode in Remembrance of Master Shakespeare," 1638; "Salmacida Spolia," 1639; "To the honorable . . . House of Commons," [1641]; "The Unfortunate Lovers," 1643; "London," 1648; "Love and Honour," 1649; "Gondibert," 1651; "The Siege of Rhodes," 1656 (revised and altered edn., 1663); "The First Dayes Entertainment at Rutland House" (anon.), 1657; "The Cruelty of the Spaniards in Peru" (anon.), 1658; "The History of Sir Francis Drake" (anon.) 1659; "Poem to the King's most sacred Majesty," 1660; "Poem upon his sacred Majestie's most happy return," 1660; "The Rivals" (anon.; altered from "The Two Noble Kinsmen"), 1668. *Posthumous:* "The Man's the Master," 1669; "The Tempest" (with Dryden), 1670; "New Academy of Complements" (anon., with Lord Buckhurst and Sir Chas. Sedley), 1671; "Macbeth . . . with all the Alterations, etc.," 1673. *Collected Works:* in 3 pts., ed. by his widow, 1673; in 5 vols., ed. by Laing and Maidment ("Dramatists of the Restoration" series), with *Life*, 1872-74.—SHARP, R. FARQUHARSON, 1897, *A Dictionary of English Authors, p.* 74.

PERSONAL

Will Davenant, ashamed of a foolish mis-
chance,
That he had got lately travelling in France,
Modestly hoped the handsomeness of's muse
Might any deformity about him excuse.
                And
Surely the company would have been content,
If they could have found any precedent;
But in all their records either in verse or
prose,
There was not one laureate without a nose.
—SUCKLING, SIR JOHN, 1637, *Sessions of the Poets.*

Up and down to the Duke of York's play-house, there to see, which I did, Sir W. Davenant's corpse carried out towards Westminster, there to be buried. Here were many coaches and six horses, and many hacknies, that made it look, methought, as if it were the buriall of a poor poet. He seemed to have many children, by five or six in the first mourning coach, all boys.—PEPYS, SAMUEL, 1668, *Diary, April* 9.

I was at his funerall He had a coffin of walnutt-tree; Sir Jonn Denham sayd 'twas the finest coffin that ever he sawe. His body was carried in a hearse from the play-house to Westminster-Abbey, where, at the great west dore, he was received by the sing (ing) men and choristers, who sang the service of the church ("I am the Resurrection, &c.") to his grave, which is in the south crosse aisle, on which, on a paving stone of marble, is writt, in imitation of that on Ben Johnson, "*O rare

Sir Will. Davenant." . . . That sweet swan of Iris, Sir William Davenant, dyed the seaventh day of April last, and lies buried amongst the poets in Westminster abbey, by his anatgonist, Mr. Thomas May, whose inscription of whose marble was taken away by order since the king came in. Sir William was Poet Laureat· and Mr. John Dryden hath his place. But me thought it had been proper that a laurell should have been sett on his coffin —which was not donne.—AUBREY, JOHN, 1669-96, *Brief Lives, ed. Clark, vol.* I, *pp.* 208, 209.

His mother was a very beautiful woman, of a good wit and conversation, in which she was imitated by none of her children, but by this William. The father, who was a very good and discreet citizen, (yet an admirer and lover of plays and playmakers, especially Shakespeare, who frequented his house in his journies between Warwickshire and London,) was of a melancholic disposition, and was seldom or never seen to laugh. . . . As for William, whom we are farther to mention, and may justly stile "the sweet swan of Isis," he was educated in grammar learning under Edw. Sylvester, whom I shall elsewhere mention, and in academical in Linc. Coll. under the care of Mr. Dan. Hough, in 1620, or 21, or thereabouts, and obtained there some smattering in logic; but his geny which was always opposite to it, lead him in the pleasant paths of poetry, so that tho' he wanted much of university learning, yet he made as high and noble flights in the poetical faculty, as fancy could advance, without it.—WOOD, ANTHONY, 1691-1721, *Athenœ Oxonienses.*

That notion of Sir William Davenant being more than a poetical child only of Shakespeare, was common in town; and Sir William himself seemed fond of having it taken for truth.—POPE, ALEXANDER, 1728-30, *Spence's Anecdotes, ed. Singer, p.* 18.

Was a great favourite of the Earl of Newcastle, who appointed him lieutenant-general of his ordnance; but it was thought that he might easily have found a person much better qualified for that command. We read, that Alexander took Homer's Works with him in his expeditions; but it is not probable that he would have taken the poet himself, if he had

been living. Voltaire informs us, that Lewis XIV. in his pompous expedition to Flanders, was attended by Vander Meulen the painter, and Pelisson the historian, to design and record his victories; but he does not say that he took Boileau with him to sing them; and, if he did, he knew better how to employ him than to make him a lieutenant-general.—GRANGER, JAMES, 1769-1824, *Biographical History of England, vol.* III, *p.* 35.

A princess in any degree more delicate than Henrietta must have shrunk with loathing from affording her patronage to a man whose licentious conduct had become matter of such very peculiar notoriety.—AIKIN, LUCY, 1833, *Memoirs of The Court of King Charles the First, vol.* II, *p.* 36.

GONDIBERT
1650

Now to thy matchless book,
Where in those few that can with judgment look,
May find old love in pure fresh language told,
Like new-stampt coin made out of Angel-gold.
Such truth in love as the antique world did know,
In such a style as courts may boast of now;
Which no bold tales of gods or monsters swell,
But human passions, such as with us dwell.
Man is thy theme, his virtue, or his rage,
Drawn to the life in each elaborate page.
—WALLER, EDMUND, 1650, *To Sir William Davenant upon his two first books of Gondibert, finished before his voyage to America.*

The prince of poets and of lovers too.
—VAUGHAN, HENRY, 1650, *To Sir William Davenent upon his Gondibert.*

Thy Fancy, like a Flame its way does make,
And leaves bright Tracks for following Pens to take.
—COWLEY, ABRAHAM, 1650, *To Sir Will. Davenant upon his two first books of Gondibert, finished before his voyage to America.*

The sort of verse he made choice of, might, I suppose, contribute much to the vitiating of his stile; for thereby he obliges himself to stretch every period to the end of four lines. Thus the sense is broken perpetually with parentheses, the words jumbl'd in confusion, and a darkness spread over all; that the sense is either not discern'd, or found not sufficient for one just verse, which is sprinkl'd on the whole tretrastick.—RYMER, THOMAS, 1694, *Preface to Rapin's Reflections on Aristotle's Treatise of Poesie.*

Sir William Davenant's "Gondibert" is not a good poem, if you take it in the whole; but there are a great many good things in it.—He is a scholar of Donne's, and took his sententiousness and metaphysics from him.—POPE, ALEXANDER, 1734–36, *Spence's Anecdotes, ed. Singer, p.* 128.

He distinguished himself by a bold, but unsuccessful attempt to enlarge the sphere of poetry. He composed an heroic poem, called "Gondibert," in five books, after the model of the drama; applauded himself greatly upon this invention; and looked upon the followers of Homer as a timorous, servile herd, that were afraid to leave the beaten track. This performance, which is rather a string of epigrams than an epic poem, was not without its admirers, among whom were Waller and Cowley. But the success did not answer his expectation. When the novelty of it was over, it presently sunk into contempt; and he at length found, that when he strayed from Homer he deviated from nature.—GRANGER, JAMES, 1769–1824, *Biographical History of England, vol.* v, *p.* 246.

His heroic poem of "Gondibert" has, no doubt, great imperfections; but it intimates everywhere a mind above those laborious triflers, who called that poetry which was only verse; and very often exhibits a majestic, dignified, and manly simplicity, equally superior to the metaphysical school, by the doctrines of which Davenant was occasionally misled. Yet, if that author too frequently imitated their quaint affectations of uncommon sentiment and associations, he had at least the merit of couching them in stately and harmonious verse.—SCOTT, SIR WALTER, 1805, *The Life of John Dryden.*

More than a century and a half have elapsed since the first publication of "Gondibert," and its merits are still a subject of controversy; an indubitable proof of some inherent excellence not willingly forgotten. The critics are marshalled on each side, one against the other, while between these formidable lines stands the poet, with a few scattered readers; but what is more surprising in the history of the "Gondibert," the poet

is a great poet, the work imperishable!—DISRAELI, ISAAC, 1812–13, *D'Avenant and a Club of Wits, Quarrels of Authors.*

Davenant's "Gondibert" is a tissue of stanzas, all aiming to be wise and witty, each containing something in itself, and the whole together amounting to nothing. The thoughts separately require so much attention to understand them, and arise so little out of the narrative, that they with difficulty sink into the mind, and have no common feeling of interest to recall or link them together afterwards.—HAZLITT, WILLIAM, 1818, *Lectures on the English Comic Writers, p.* 60.

It wants the charm of free and forcible narration; the life-pulse of interest is incessantly stopped by solemn pauses of reflection, and the story works its way through an intricacy of superfluous fancies, some beautiful and others conceited, but all as they are united, tending to divert the interest, like a multitude of weeds upon a stream, that entangle its course while they seem to adorn it.—CAMPBELL, THOMAS, 1819, *Specimens of the British Poets.*

As for "Gondibert," those may criticise it who can read it.—MACAULAY, THOMAS BABINGTON, 1828, *Dryden, Edinburgh Review, Critical and Miscellaneous Essays.*

The narrative is diffuse, the action without unity, the events are complicated, and the language often obscure. Instead of naïve perception and lofty inspiration, we find reflection and elegant phraseology, nay even epigrammatic turns, upon which D'Israeli, strangely enough, bestows especial praise, and designates the poet as a poetical Rochefoucauld. The metre also is unhappily chosen, as the four-lined stanza is stiff and wearisome, and leaves no room for the flow of the narrative or for the minuteness of description, such as is offered by the hexameter, the blank verse, or by the ottava rima. Davenant in his preface considers it an advantage of this metre, that the end of each stanza requires a pause or conclusion to the thought, that the alternate rhyme is suited to stately music, and that the shortness of the stanza makes it more convenient to the singer. If only the contents were in any way singable!—ELZE, KARL, 1869, *Sir William Davenant, Essays on Shakespeare, tr. Schmitz, p.* 329.

GENERAL

Thou hast redeemed us, Will., and future times
Shall not account unto the age's crimes
Dearth of pure wit: since the great lord of it,
Donne, parted hence, no man has ever writ
So near him in's own way: I would commend
Particulars; but then, how should I end
Without a volume? every line of thine
Would ask, to praise it right, twenty of mine.

—SUCKLING, SIR JOHN, 1638, *To my Friend Will. Davenant, on his other Poems.*

In the time I writ with him, I had the opportunity to observe somewhat more nearly of him than I had formerly done, when I had only a bare acquaintance with him: I found him then of so quick a fancy, that nothing was proposed to him, on which he could not suddenly produce a thought, extreamly pleasant and surprising: and those first thoughts of his, contrary to the old Latin proverb, were not always the least happy. And as his fancy was quick, so likewise were the products of it remote and new. He borrowed not of any other; and his imaginations were such as could not easily enter into any other man. His corrections were sober and judicious: and he corrected his own writings much more severely than those of another man, bestowing twice the time and labour in polishing, which he used in invention.—DRYDEN, JOHN, 1669, *Preface to The Tempest, or The Enchanted Island, by Sir William D'Avenant and John Dryden.*

'Twas observ'd, that at his Funeral his Coffin wanted the Ornament of his *Laureats Crown,* which by the Law of Heraldry justly appertain'd to him: but this omission is sufficiently recompenc'd by an Eternal Fame, which will always accompany his Memory; he having been the first Introducer of all that is splendid in our English *Opera's,* and 'tis by his means and industry, that our Stage at present rivals the Italian Theatre.—LANGBAINE, GERARD, 1691, *An Account of the English Dramatick Poets, p.* 115.

He was amongst the first who refined our poetry, and did more for the interest of the drama, than any who ever wrote for the stage.—CIBBER, THEOPHILUS, 1753, *Lives of the Poets, vol.* II, *p.* 63.

Davenant was a sort of adventurer and wit, and in every manner worthy of the royal favour, to enjoy which dignity of character was never considered as a necessary requisite. He set himself to work in every way which the want of a rich theatrical repertory may render necessary; he made alterations of old pieces, wrote himself plays, operas, prologues, &c. But of all his writings nothing has escaped a merited oblivion.—SCHLEGEL, AUGUSTUS WILLIAM, 1809, *Dramatic Art and Literature, Lecture* xiii, *tr. Black, p.* 395.

Devoid of all higher original genius, D'Avenant applied himself, in no vulgar spirit nor without taking full advantage of such lights as were vouchsafed to him, to the task of satisfying what to him was the supreme criterion of merit, viz. the most cultivated taste (or what appeared to him such) of his age. . . . As a dramatist, D'Avenant may, in the earlier series of his plays, be described as a limb of Fletcher.—WARD, ADOLPHUS WILLIAM, 1875–99, *A History of English Dramatic Literatvre, vol.* III, *pp.* 167, 169.

There is not a more hopelessly faded laurel on the slopes of the English Parnassus than that which once flourished so bravely around the grotesque head of Davenant. The enormous folio edition of his works, brought out in 1673 in direct emulation of Ben Jonson, is probably the most deplorable collection of verses anywhere to be found, dead and dusty beyond the wont of forgotten classics.—GOSSE, EDMUND, 1880, *English Poets, ed. Ward, vol.* II, *p.* 289.

Dryden's practice shows clearly enough that his earlier critical creed was modelled on the teaching of his friend and predecessor, the inventor of the heroic play, the best exponent of heroic doctrine, Sir William Davenant.—RALEIGH, WALTER, 1894, *The English Novel, p.* 104.

Of Davenant's numerous plays it would be impossible to speak in detail. They are energetic and bold in construction, show novelty in imagery, and often originality in the analysis of character. They teem with philosophical reflections and condensed epigrams, and yet they lack passion and fire, and have not the exalted view of human nature and of the earnestness of human life which is shown in "Gondibert." Even with Davenant the stage began to take its downward course. And this, in spite of the great and undeniable services he rendered it. With all his talent, Davenant had not the moral force to stem the tide of his age. He could not dictate to it like Jonson, nor was he unworldly enough, like Milton, to go serenely on, unmindful of its applause and its alluring rewards.—WEST, KENYON, 1895, *The Laureates of England, p. 22.*

His plays are full of incident and careless melody, but do not show any real power of drawing characters or developing situations.—MASTERMAN, J. HOWARD B., 1897, *The Age of Milton p. 90.*

Sir John Denham
1615–1668

Born, in Dublin, 1615. At school in London. Entered at Lincoln's Inn, 28 April 1631; called to Bar, 1638. Matriculated Trinity Coll., Oxford, 18 Nov. 1631. Married Ann Cotton, 25 June 1634. Inherited family estates on father's death, 1638. Took King's side in Civil War, being High Sheriff of Surrey. Governor of Farnham Castle, 1642. Taken prisoner and sent to London. Lived at Oxford, 1643–47. In attendance on Charles I., Henrietta Maria, and Charles II., respectively, till 1651. Returned to England, winter of 1651. Forbidden to live in London, 1655; settled at Bury, Suffolk, 1658. Abroad with Earl of Pembroke, 1659. Surveyor-General of Works, June 1660. Arranged Coronation Ceremony for Charles II., 1661; created Knight of the Bath. Married Margaret Brooke, 25 May 1665. She died, 6 Jan. 1667. He died, in London, March 1669. Buried in Westminster Abbey. *Works:* "The Sophy" (anon.), 1642; "Cooper's Hill" (anon.), 1642; a verse adaptation of Cicero's "Cato Major," 1648; "Anatomy of Play" (anon.), 1651 "The Destruction of Troy" (anon.; trans. from "Virgil's Æneid," Book II.), 1656; "Panegyrick on . . . . Gen. George Monck" (anon., attrib. to Denham), 1659; "A Relation of a Quaker" (anon., attrib. to Denham), 1659; "Second and Third Advices to a Painter," 1667 (another edn. same year); "The Famous Battel of the Catts" (anon.), 1668; "Poems and Translations," 1668. *Posthumous:* "The Gaming Humour considered" (anon.), 1684; "A Version of the Psalms of David," 1714 —SHARP. R. FARQUHARSON, 1897, *A Dictionary of English Authors, p. 77.*

PERSONAL

Sir John Denham was unpolished with the small-pox: otherwise a fine complexion. . . . He delighted much in bowles, and did bowle very well. He was of the tallest, but a little incurvetting at his shoulders, not very robust. His haire was but thin and flaxen, with a moist curle. His gate was slow, and was rather a stalking (he had long legges), which was wont to putt me in mind of Horace, *De Arte Poetica:*—

"Hic, dum sublimes versus ructatur, et errat
Si veluti merulis intentus decidit auceps
In puteum foveamve."—

His eie was a kind of light goose-gray, not big; but it had a strange piercingness, not as to shining and glory, but (like a Momus) when he conversed with you he look't into your very thoughts. He was generally temperate as to drinking.—AUBREY, JOHN, 1669–96, *Brief Lives, ed. Clark, vol.* I, *pp.* 216, 220.

But being looked upon as a slow and dreaming young man by his seniors and contemporaries, and given more to cards and dice, than his study, they could never

then in the least imagine, that he could ever inrich the world with his fancy, or issue of his brain, as he afterwards did. —WOOD, ANTHONY, 1691–1721, *Athenæ Oxonienses, vol.* II, *f.* 422.

THE SOPHY
1642

At last, viz. 1640, his play of "The Sophy" came out, which did take extremely: Mr. Edmund Waller sayd then of him, that he *broke-out like the Irish Rebellion—threescore thousand strong,* before any body was aware.—AUBREY, JOHN, 1669–96, *Brief Lives, ed. Clark, vol.* I, *p.* 217.

He has writ but one Play, but by that Specimen we may judge of his ability in Dramatick, as well as Epick Poesy; this Play being generally commended.—LANGBAINE, GERARD, 1691, *An Account of the English Dramatick Poets, p. 128.*

"The Sophy" on its production met with extraordinary praise. Its celebrity is no doubt attributable in part to the impressive character of its versification. . . . The style of this production is rhetorical, but sustained; its value was overrated by Denham's contemporaries, but it is certainly one of the best tragedies of its time, and had doubtless been produced under the inspiration of worthy models. In the political wisdom which it teaches in one of its most striking scenes, something nobler than party spirit reveals itself; and a lesson is enforced deserving the attention both of kings and of rebels who misuse religion as an instrument or as a pretext.—WARD, ADOLPHUS WILLIAM, 1875-99, *A History of English Dramatic Literature, vol. III, pp.* 148-49.

COOPER'S HILL
1642

. . . he whose Song rais'd "Cooper's Hill" so high,
As made its Glory with Parnassus vie; . . .
—OLDHAM, SIR JOHN, 1684? *A Pastoral on the Death of the Earl of Rochester.*

Nor, Denham, must we e'er forget thy strains,
While "Cooper's Hill" commands the neigh-b'ring plains.
—ADDISON, JOSEPH, 1694, *An Account of the Greatest English Poets.*

SIR John Denham, in his "Cooper's Hill," (for none of his other poems merit attention), has a loftiness and vigour which had not before him been attained by any English poet who wrote in rhyme. The mechanical difficulties of that measure retarded its improvement. Shakspeare, whose tragic scenes are sometimes so wonderfully forcible and expressive, is a very indifferent poet when he attempts to rhyme. Precision and neatness are chiefly wanting in Denham.—HUME, DAVID, 1762, *The History of England, The Commonwealth.*

This poem, by Denham, though it may have been exceeded by later attempts in description, yet deserves the highest applause, as it far surpasses all that went before it: the concluding part, though a little too much crowded is very masterly.—GOLDSMITH, OLIVER, 1767, *The Beauties of English Poetry.*

"Cooper's Hill" if it be maliciously inspected, will not be found without its faults. The digressions are too long, the morality too frequent, and the sentiments sometimes such as will not bear a rigorous enquiry. . . . It has beauty peculiar to itself, and must be numbered among those felicities which cannot be produced

at will by wit and labour, but must arise unexpectedly in some hour propitious to poetry.—JOHNSON, SAMUEL, 1779, *Sir John Denham, Lives of the English Poets.*

The plan is original, as far as our poetry is concerned; and I do not recollect any exception in other languages. Placing himself upon an eminence not distant from Windsor, he takes a survey of the scene; he finds the tower of St. Paul's on its farthest horizon, the Castle much nearer, and the Thames at his feet. These, with the ruins of an abbey, supply, in turn, materials for a reflecting rather than imaginative mind, and, with a stag-hunt, which he has very well described, fill up the canvas of a poem of no great length, but once of no trifling reputation. The epithet, *majestic* Denham, conferred by Pope, conveys rather too much; but "Cooper's Hill" is no ordinary poem. It is nearly the first instance of vigorous and rhythmical couplets; for Denham is incomparably less feeble than Browne, and less prosaic than Beaumont. Close in thought, and nervous in language like Davies, he is less hard and less monotonous; his cadences are animated and various, perhaps a little beyond the regularity that metre demands; they have been the guide to the finer ear of Dryden. Those who cannot endure the philosophic poetry must ever be dissatisfied with "Cooper's Hill"; no personification, no ardent words, few metaphors beyond the common use of speech, nothing that warms or melts or fascinates the heart. It is rare to find lines of eminent beauty in Denham; and equally so to be struck by any one as feeble or low. His language is always well chosen and perspicuous, free from those strange turns of expression, frequent in our older poets, where the reader is apt to suspect some error of the press, so irreconcilable do they seem with grammar or meaning.—HALLAM, HENRY, 1837-39, *Introduction to the Literature of Europe, pt. iii, ch. v, pars.* 36, 37.

"Cooper's Hill" may be considered as belonging in point of composition to the same school with Sir John Davies's "Nosce Teipsum;" and, if it has not all the concentration of that poem, it is equally pointed, correct, and stately, it is, partly owing to the subject, a warmer tone of imagination and feeling, and a fuller swell of verse. The spirit of the same classical style pervades both; and they are the two greatest poems in that style which had been produced down to the date at which we are now arrived.—CRAIK, GEORGE L., *A Compendious History of English Literature and of the English Language, vol.* II, *p.* 33.

Gratification is united with solidity; the author of "Cooper's Hill" knows how to please as well as to impress. His poem is like a king's park, dignified and level without doubt, but arranged for the pleasure of the sight, and full of choice prospects. It leads us by easy digressions across a multitude of varied thoughts.—TAINE, H. A., 1871, *History of English Literature, tr. Van Laun, vol.* I, *bk.* iii, *ch.* i, *p.* 502.

"Cooper's Hill" remains his only really noteworthy production.—MASTERMAN, J. HOWARD B., 1897, *The Age of Milton, p.* 128.

GENERAL

. . . I confess, 'tis somewhat to do well
In our high art, although we can't excel
Like thee, or dare the buskins to unloose
Of thy brave, bold, and sweet Maronian muse.
But since I'm call'd, rare Denham, to be gone,
Take from thy Herrick this conclusion:
'Tis dignity in others, if they be
Crown'd poets, yet live princes under thee;
The while their wreaths and purple robes do shine
Less by their own gems than those beams of thine.
—HERRICK, ROBERT, 1642? *To M. Denham on his Prospective Poem.*

Denham is deservedly considered as one of the fathers of English poetry. . . . He appears to have had, in common with almost all mankind, the ambition of being upon proper occasions *a merry fellow,* and, in common with most of them, to have been by nature, or by early habits, debarred from it. Nothing less exhilarating than the ludicrousness of Denham: he does not fail for want of efforts; he is

familiar, he is gross, but he is never merry, unless the "Speech against Peace in the close Committee" be excepted. For grave burlesque, however, his imitation of Davenant shows him to have been well qualified. . . . He is one of the writers that improved our taste, and advanced our language, and whom we ought therefore to read with gratitude, though, having done much, he left much to do.—JOHNSON, SAMUEL, 1779, *Sir John Denham, Lives of the English Poets.*

Denham was the first writer to adopt the precise manner of versification introduced by Waller. His relation to that poet resembles that taken a century later by Mason with respect to Gray, but Denham is a more original writer than Mason. The names of Waller and Denham were first associated by Dryden, and the critics of the next sixty years were unanimous in eulogizing the sweetness of the one, and the strength of the other. It is quite true that the versification of Denham is vigorous; it proceeds with greater volume than that of Waller, and produces a stronger impression. But he is a very unequal and irregular writer, and not unfrequently descends to doggerel, and very dull doggerel too. His literary taste was superior to his genius; he knew what effect he desired to produce, and strove to conquer the difficulties of antithesis, but the result of his effort was rarely classic. He takes the same place in English poetry as is taken in French by Chapelain and other hard versifiers of the beginning of the seventeenth century, who had lost the romantic fervour and had not yet gained the classic grace. But, like those poets, he has his fine flashes of style.—GOSSE, EDMUND, 1880, *English Poets, ed. Ward, vol.* II, *p.* 279.

Denham's satires are crude doggerel, and show more bad taste than ability.—MASTERMAN, J. HOWARD B., 1897, *The Age of Milton, p.* 128.

Henry King

1592–1669

Eldest son of Bishop John King, a native of Wornall, Buckinghamshire, educated at Christ Church, Oxford, became Archdeacon of Colchester, Residentiary of St. Paul's, Canon of Christ Church, and Chaplain to James I.; Dean of Rochester, 1638; Bishop of Chichester, 1641. He published a number of "Sermons," 1621–65; an "Exposition of the Lord's Prayer," 1628, '34, 4to; the "Psalms in Meter," 1651,

'71, 12mo; and some Latin, Greek, and English Poems. His "Poems, Elegies, Para-doxes, and Sonnets" were published in 1657, sm 4to; with a new title-page, 1664, 8vo; again—with the name of Ben Jonson as the author—1700, 8vo. A new edition of his "Psalms and Poems—edited, with Biographical Notices, Notes, &c., by Dr. John Hannah"—was published by Pickering in 1843., 12mo.—ALLIBONE, S. AUSTIN, 1854–58, *Dictionary of English Literature, vol.* I, *p.* 1031.

PERSONAL

A man generally known by the Clergy of this nation, and as generally noted for his obliging nature.—WALTON, ISAAC, 1640, *Life of Donne.*

The epitome of all honours, virtues and generous nobleness, and a person never to be forgotten by his tenants, and by the poor.—WOOD, ANTHONY, 1691–1721, *Athenæ Oxonienses, vol.* II, *f.* 432.

King's amiability endeared him to his friends. Among these were Ben Jonson, George Sandys, Sir Henry Blount, and James Howell. His friendship with Izaak Walton began about 1624, and continued till death. He was on terms of closest intimacy with John Donne, who appointed him one of his executors, and bequeathed to him the gold medal struck in commemo-ration of the synod of Dort. An elegy by King is prefixed to the 1633 edition of Donne's poems.—BULLEN, A. H., 1892, *Dictionary of National Biography, vol.* XXXI, *p.* 133.

GENERAL

But that which afforded me most enter-tainment in those Miscellanies, was Doctor *Henry King's* Poems, wherein I find not only heat and strength, but also an exact concinnity and evenness of fancy.—HOW-ELL, JAMES, 1637, *Familiar Letters, ed. Jacobs, bk.* ii, *p.* 406.

The greater part of his poetry (which was either written at an early age, or as a relaxation from severer studies) is neat, and uncommonly elegant. —HEADLEY, HENRY, 1787, *Select Beauties of Ancient English Poetry.*

His monody on his wife, who died before her twenty-fifth year, is beautiful and tender, containing the germ of some famous passages by modern poets.—SARGENT, EPES, 1881, *ed., Harper's Cyclopæ-dia of British and American Poetry, p.* 58.

William Prynne

1600–1669

William Prynne, a lawyer and political writer, was b. in 1600, at Swanswick; was educated at Bath grammar school, and Oriel college, Oxford; studied the law at Lincoln's Inn; and was successively made barrister, bencher, and reader. His "Histrio-Mastix," a violent attack on the stage, and his "News from Ipswich," twice brought on him, in 1633 and 1637, the vengeance of the infamous star-chamber. He was branded, deprived of his ears, pilloried, fined ten thousand pounds, and doomed to perpetual imprisonment. He obtained his liberty in 1640, was elected member for Newport, and bore a prominent part in the trial of Laud, his persecutor. After the overthrow of Charles, however, Prynne endeavored to effect an accommodation between him and his subjects; and he opposed Cromwell with such boldness that the protector imprisoned him. He joined in the restoration of Charles II.; was appointed keeper of the records in the Tower; and died 1669.—GODWIN, PARKE, 1851, *Hand-Book of Universal Biography, p.* 703.

PERSONAL

To my Lord Treasurer's . . . to have met my Lord Bellasses and Commissioners of Excise, but they did not meet me, he being abroad. However, Mr. Finch, one of the Commissioners, I met there, and he and I walked two houres together in the garden, talking of many things. . . . He told me Mr. Prin's character; that he is a man of mighty labour and reading and memory, but the worst judge of matters, or layer together of what he hath read, in the world; which I do not, however, believe him in; that he believes him very true to the King in his heart, but can never be reconciled to episcopacy; that the House do not lay much weight upon him, or anything he says.—PEPYS, SAMUEL, 1666, *Diary, July* 3rd.

He was a learned man, of immense

reading, but is much blamed for his un-
faithfull quotations. His manner of studie
was thus: he wore a long quilt cap, which
came, 2 or 3, at least, inches, over his
eies, which served him as an umbrella to
defend his eies from the light.   About
every 3 houres his man was to bring him
a roll and a pott of ale to refocillate his
wasted spirits. So he studied and dranke,
and munched some bread; and this maintained him till night; and then he made a
good supper.   Now he did well not to
dine, which breakes of one's fancy, which
will not presently be regained: and it's
with invention as a flux—when once it
is flowing, it runnes amaine; if it is
checked, flowes but *guttim:* and the like
for perspiration—check it, and 'tis
spoyled. . . .   He was of a strange
Saturnine complexion. Sir C. W. sayd
once, that he had the countenance of a
witch. —AUBREY, JOHN, 1669–96, *Brief
Lives, ed. Clark, vol. II, pp.* 174, 175.

The books and little pamphlets that
he wrote, were theological, historical,
political, controversial, &c., but very
few of his own profession: all which are
in number near 200, . . . bound
up in about 40 volumes in fol. and
qu. in Linc. Inn Library: To which an
eminent sage of the law, [William Noy,]
who had little respect for those published
in his time, promised to give the works of
John Taylor the water poet to accompany
them. 'Twas not only he, but many others afterwards, especially royalists, that
judged his books to be worth little or
nothing, his proofs for no arguments, and
affirmations for no testimonies, having
several forgeries made in them for his and
the ends of his brethren. They are all in
the English tongue, and by the generality
of scholars are looked upon to be rather
rhapsodical and confused, than any way
polite or concise, yet for antiquaries,
critics, and sometimes for divines, they
are useful. In most of them he shews
great industry, but little judgment,
especially in his large folios against the
pope's usurpations. He may be well intituled Voluminous Prynne, as Tostatus
Albulensis was 200 years before his time
called Voluminous Tostatus: for I verily
believe, that if rightly computed, he
wrote a sheet for every day of his life,
reckoning from the time when he came to
the use of reason and the state of man.

His custom when he studied was to put on
a long quilted cap which came an inch
over his eyes, serving as an umbrella to
defend them from too much light, and
seldom eating a dinner, would every 3
hours or more be maunching a roll of
bread, and now and then refresh his exhausted spirits with ale brought to him by
his   servant.—WOOD, ANTHONY, 1691–
1721, *Athenæ Oxonienses, vol.* II, *f.* 439.

His activity, and the firmness and intrepidity of his character in public life,
were as ardent as they were in his study—
his soul was Roman; and Eachard says,
that Charles II., who could not but admire
his earnest honesty, his copious learning,
and the public persecutions he suffered,
and the ten imprisonments he endured, inflicted by all parties, dignified him with
the title of "the Cato of the Age;" and
one of his own party facetiously described
him as "William the Conqueror," a title
he had most hardly earned by his inflexible
and invincible nature. . . .   Such is
the history of a man whose greatness of
character was clouded over and lost in a
fatal passion for scribbling; such is the
history of a voluminous author whose
genius was such that he could write a
folio much easier than a page; and
"seldom dined" that he might quote
"squadrons of authorities."—DISRAELI,
ISAAC, 1812–13, *Voluminous Author Without Judgment, Calamities of Authors.*

HISTRIOMASTIX

Histrio-Mastix: The Player's Scourge,
or Actor's Tragœdie, divided into two
Parts: wherein it is largely evidenced by
divers Arguments; by the concurring
Authorities and Resolutions of sundry
Texts of Scripture, of the whole Primitive
Church both under the Law and the Gospel,
of 55 Synods and Councils, of 71 Fathers
and Christian writers before the year of
our Lord 1200, of above 150 foreign and
domestic Protestant and Popish authors
since, of 40 heathen Philosophers, Historians, and Poets, of many heathen, many
Christian Nations, Republics, Emperors,
Princes, Magistrates; of sundry apostolical, canonical, imperial Constitutions;
and of our own English Statutes, Magistrates, Universities, Writers, Preachers—
That Popular Stage Plays (the very pomps
of the Divell, which we renounce in
Baptism, if we believe the Fathers) are

sinful, heathenish, lewd, ungodly spectacles, and most pernicious corruptions, condemned in all ages as intolerable mischiefs to Churches, to Republics, to the manners, minds, and souls of men; and that the profession of Play-poets, of Stage-Players, together with the penning, acting, and frequenting of stage-plays, are unlawful, infamous, and misbeseeming Christians. All pretences to the contrary are here likewise fully answered, and the unlawfulness of acting or beholding academical Interludes briefly discussed; besides sundry other particulars concerning Dancing, Dicing, Health-drinking, etc., of which the Table will inform you. By William Prynne, an Utter Barrister of Lincoln's Inn.—TITLE PAGE TO FIRST EDITION, 1633.

Prynne's literary character may be illustrated by his singular book, "Histriomastix," where we observe how an author's exuberant learning, like corn heaped in a granary, grows rank and musty, by a want of power to ventilate and stir about the heavy mass.—DISRAELI, ISAAC, 1812–13, *Voluminous Author Without Judgment, Calamities of Authors.*

Heylin, a bigoted enemy of everything puritanical, and not scrupulous as to veracity, may be suspected of having aggravated, if not misrepresented, the tendency of a book much more tiresome than seditious.—HALLAM, HENRY, 1827–41, *The Constitutional History of England, ch.* viii.

This block of a book, on which Prynne had been busy for seven years, was to produce various consequences. Not only were dramatists, players, and all in any way connected with the theatrical interest to be roused in its behalf for personal reasons, but—on the plea that the character of the Queen had been attacked in the book for her patronage of stage-plays, and her performances personally in court-masques—there was to be a sudden rush of other classes of the community to the defence of the tottering institution. The courtiers were to get up masques and plays out of loyalty; the members of the Inns of Court were to do the same with all the more alacrity that it was one of their number that had struck the disloyal blow; the scholars in colleges were to catch the same enthusiasm; and those who had gone to the theatres for mere amusement before, were to go twice as

often to spite Prynne and the Puritans.—MASSON, DAVID, 1858, *The Life of John Milton, vol.* I, *ch.* vi.

The tone of the work is in general dry and calm; but the author is capable of rising to eloquence, as in the final exhortation in act v of the Second Part. In the choice of the arguments themselves, as will be seen from the brief sketch of the book appended below the text, there is nothing new; but they are nowhere else developed with anything like the same fulness; and for the historian of the drama Prynne's treatise furnishes an ample repository of much useful learning. It is to be observed that his acquaintance with the stage-plays of his own times was obviously of the most limited description.—WARD, ADOLPHUS WILLIAM, 1875–99, *A History of English Dramatic Literature, vol.* III, *p.* 241.

He was the author, in the course of his life, of no less than one hundred and eighty distinct works; many of them, it is true, were pamphlets, but others terribly bulky—an inextinguishable man; that onslaught on the drama and dramatic people, and play-goers, including people of the Court, called "Histriomastix," was a foul-mouthed, close-printed, big quarto of a thousand pages. One would think such a book could do little harm; but he was tried for it, was heavily fined, and sentenced to stand in the pillory and lose his ears.—MITCHELL, DONALD G., 1890, *English Lands Letters and Kings, Elizabeth to Anne, p.* 143.

GENERAL

A late hot querist for tythes, whom ye may know, by his wits lying ever beside him in the margin, to be ever beside his wits in the text. A fierce reformer once; now rankled with a contrary heat.—MILTON, JOHN, 1659, *Considerations on the Likeliest Means to Remove Hirelings out of the Church.*

Mr. Prynn's books, having been made use of for wast paper, begin now to be scarce, and to be got into curious hands, purely for this reason, because he commonly cites his vouchers for what he delivers, and thereby gives his reader an opportunity of examining the truth of them. Mr. Baker, of Cambridge, believes his study hath more of Mr. Prynne's books than any one of that university, and he well remembers, that he sent up his "Anti-Arminianism" to Mr. Strype, which he could not meet with at London, when he was writing one of his books, and yet it has two editions.—HEARNE, THOMAS, 1719, *Reliquiæ Hearnianæ, ed. Bliss, Aug. 25, vol.* II, *p.* 105.

The most terrible phenomenon as a Puritan pamphleteer was the lawyer, William Prynne.—MASSON, DAVID, 1858, *The Life of John Milton, vol.* I, *ch.* vi.

They are without style; they speak like business men; at most, here and there, a pamphlet of Prynne possesses a little vigour.—TAINE, H. A., 1871, *History of English Literatue, tr. Van Laun, vol.* I, *bk.* ii, *ch.* v, *p.* 398.

In 1627 Prynne's first book appeared· "The Perpetuity of a Regenerate Man's Estate." Under the forms of theological argument, Prynne's contention is, in the main, a contention for the central idea of Calvinism, the immediate dependence of the individual soul upon God without the intervention of human or material agencies. But in Prynne's hands the theme was stripped of all the imaginative grandeur with which it has been so often clothed. His pages, with their margins crowded with references, afforded a palpable evidence how much he owed to his reading and his memory. He had no formative genius, no broad culture, no sense of humour. He had no perception of the relative importance of things distasteful to him. "Health's Sickness," a violent diatribe on the supreme wickedness of drinking healths, was followed by "The Unloveliness of Lovelocks," an equally violent diatribe on the supreme wickedness

of the long lock of hair floating over the shoulder, which was the latest fashion amongst courtiers. The folly of the day was chastised with a torrent of learned objurgation which would not have been out of place in a harangue directed against the seven deadly sins. He had nothing worse to say when he sat down to prepare "A Brief Survey and Censure of Mr. Cosin's Cozening Devotions."—GARDINER, SAMUEL R., 1883, *History of England from the Accession of James I. to The Outbreak of the Civil War, vol.* VII, *p.* 13.

A number of writers took part in the Puritan and Church controversies, among whom for graphic force William Prynne stands out clearly.—BROOKE, STOPFORD A., 1896, *English Literature, p.* 155.

In point of style Prynne's historical works possess no merits. He apologises to his readers in the epistle to vol. ii. of his "Exact Chronological Vindication" for the absence of "elegant, lofty, eloquent language, embellishments, and transitions," and he understates their defects. The arrangement of his works is equally careless. Yet, in spite of these deficiencies, the amount of historical material they contain and the number of records printed for the first time in his pages give his historical writings a lasting value.—FIRTH, C. H., 1896, *Dictionary of National Biography, vol.* XLVI, *p.* 436.

In their strong convictions, ponderous learning, and stupendous dulness, Prynne's two hundred pamphlets, representing thirty-five years of unintermitted labour, are unique in the literature of the period.—MASTERMAN, J. HOWARD B., 1897, *The Age of Milton, p.* 181.

John Wilkins
1614-1672

John Wilkins was born at Oxford in 1614, and educated in his early years under the care of a well-known dissenter, Mr. John Dod, who was his grandfather on the mother's side. He afterwards entered at Magdalen Hall, Oxford, and after taking his degree went abroad and became Chaplain to the Count Palatine. Joining the Parliamentary side when the Rebellion broke out, he was made Warden of Wadham in 1648, and Master of Trinity, Cambridge, in 1659, having in 1656 married Robina, sister of Oliver Cromwell, and widow of Peter French, Canon of Christ Church. On the Restoration, he was ejected from Trinity, but became Rector of St. Lawrence Jewry; and subsequently, through the help of a somewhat compromising patron, the Duke of Buckingham, he was promoted first to the Deanery of Ripon, and then to the Bishopric of Chester, in 1668. He died in 1672. His works were numerous. In 1638, there appeared "The Discovery of a New World: a Discourse to prove that there may be another habitable world in the Moon." A second part of this treats of "The Possibility of a Passage to the Moon." In 1640, appeared "A Discourse Concerning a new Planet: tending to prove that the Earth may be a Planet." Others of his works were "Mercury, or the Secret Messenger" (1641); "Mathematical Magic" (1684); "The Principles of Natural Religion" (printed after his death); and an "Essay towards a Real Character and Philosophical Language." This last is a scheme for a universal language, and was written for, and published under the auspices of, the Royal Society, of which Wilkins was a devoted member.—CRAIK, HENRY, 1893, *ed., English Prose, vol.* II, *p.* 543.

PERSONAL

Mr. Francis Potter knew him very well, and was wont to say that he was a very ingeniose man, and had a very mechanicall head. He was much for trying experiments, and his head ran much upon the *perpetuall motion.* . . . He was no great read man; but one of much and deepe thinking, and of a working head; and a prudent man as well as ingeniose. He was one of Seth, lord bishop of Sarum's most intimate friends. He was a lustie, strong growne, well sett, broad shouldered person, cheerfull, and hospitable.—AUBREY, JOHN, 1669–96, *Brief Lives, ed. Clark, vol.* II, *pp.* 299, 301.

Almost all that was preserved and kept up, of ingenuity and good learning, of good order and government, in the University of Oxford, was chiefly owing to his prudent conduct and encouragement.—TILLOTSON, JOHN, 1675, *Sermons Preached upon Several Occasions, Preface.*

This Dr. Wilkins was a person endowed with rare gifts, he was a noted theologist and preacher, a curious critic in several matters, an excellent mathematician and experimentist, and one as well seen in mechanisms and new philosophy (of which he was a great promoter) as any of his time.—WOOD, ANTHONY, 1691–1721, *Athenæ Oxonienses, vol.* II, *f.* 506.

He was naturally ambitious, but was the wisest clergyman I ever knew. He was a lover of mankind, and had a delight in doing good.—BURNET, GILBERT, 1715–34, *History of My Own Time.*

GENERAL

Dr. Wilkins, a man of a penetrating genius and enlarged understanding, seems to have been born for the improvement of every kind of knowledge to which he applied himself. He was a very able naturalist and mathematician, and an excellent divine. He disdained to tread in the beaten track of philosophy, as his forefathers had done; but struck into the new road pointed out by the great Lord Bacon.—GRANGER, JAMES, 1769–1824, *Biographical History of England, vol.* V, *p.* 15.

I discovered an alliance between Bishop Wilkins's art of flying, and his plan of universal language; the latter of which he no doubt calculated to prevent the want of an interpreter when he should arrive at the moon.—WALPOLE, HORACE, 1784, *Letters, Oct.* 15, *ed. Cunningham, vol.* VIII, *p.* 511.

One of the most ingenious men of his age.—HALLAM, HENRY, 1837–39, *Introduction to the Literature of Europe, pt.* iv, *ch.* iii, *par.* 104.

The subjects on which the bishop wrote do not attract us, and his knowledge is trebly superannuated. But his style deserves great praise. His sentences are short, pointed, and exact. He has little or nothing of the redundant languor of his contemporaries; and justice has never yet been done to him as a pioneer in English prose. The praise given to Tillotson belongs properly to Wilkins, for Tillotson lived a generation later, and learned to write English from his study of the Bishop of Chester, whom he enthusiastically admired. The curious reader will find much in the style of Wilkins to remind him of that of Bishop Berkeley.—GOSSE, EDMUND, 1888, *A History of Eighteenth Century Literature, 1660–1780, p.* 76.

His great learning and high position made him a connecting link between the new scientific movement that centered in the Royal Society and the Broad Church party that was growing up under the leadership of his friend and son-in-law, Tillotson. . . . He deserves a place among the minor prose writers of the period chiefly as the pioneer of that more concise, exact and pointed literary style, which is especially associated with the literary history of the Restoration period.— MASTERMAN, J. HOWARD B., 1897, *The Age of Milton, pp.* 235, 236.

Anne Bradstreet

1612-1672

The first American woman of letters, and called by her contemporaries "The Tenth Muse." Her prose work includes a brief autobiographic sketch, "Religious Experiences;" "Meditations Divine and Moral," a series of shrewd, strong aphorisms. In her lifetime she was known only as a poet, and her verse, the bulk of which is considerable, comprises elegies, epitaphs; "The Four Monarchies," a rhymed chronicle of ancient history; "The Four Elements;" "The Four Humours of Man;" "The Four Ages of Man;" "The Four Seasons of the Year;" "Dialogue between Old England and New;" "Contemplations." She followed artificial models, and her lines reflect the grotesque conceits of the time, but here and there are gleams of real poetic vigour, while in the poem "Contemplations;" the least laboured of them all, she exhibits true poetic inspiration.—ADAMS, OSCAR FAY, 1897, *A Dictionary of American Authors, p.* 35.

PERSONAL

Having had from her birth a very delicate constitution, prostrated when only sixteen years old by the small-pox, troubled at one time with lameness, subject to frequent attacks of sickness, to fevers, and to fits of fainting, she bore these numerous inflictions with meekness and resignation. Recognizing the inestimable blessing of health, she regarded it as the reward of virtue, and looked upon her various maladies as tokens of the divine displeasure at her thoughtlessness or wrong-doing. She says that her religious belief was at times shaken; but her doubts and fears were soon banished, if, indeed, they were not exaggerated in number and importance by her tender conscience. Her children were constantly in her mind. It was for them that she committed to writing her own religious experiences, her own feelings of joy or sorrow at the various changes which brightened or darkened her life. Her most pointed similes are drawn from the familiar incidents of domestic life, especially the bringing-up of children.—ELLIS, JOHN HARVARD, 1867, *ed., The Works of Anne Bradstreet in Prose and Verse, Introduction, p.* lvii.

Whatever work this writer wrought, whether good or bad, she wrought in the midst of circumstances that did not altogether help her, but hindered her rather. She was the laborious wife of a New England farmer, the mother of eight children, and herself from childhood of a delicate constitution. The most of her poems were produced between 1630 and 1642, that is, before she was thirty years old; and during these years, she had neither leisure, nor elegant surroundings, nor freedom from anxious thoughts, nor even abounding health. Somehow, during her busy life-time, she contrived to put upon record compositions numerous enough to fill a royal octavo volume of four hundred pages,—compositions which entice and reward our reading of them, two hundred years after she lived.—TYLER, MOSES COIT, 1878, *A History of American Literature, 1607-1676, vol.* I, *p.* 280.

Whose Augustan features, if some Smybert only had preserved them for us, assuredly should distinguish the entrance to the Harvard Annex.—STEDMAN, EDMUND CLARENCE, 1885, *Poets of America, p.* 277.

From Anne Bradstreet has descended a sturdy literary progeny. Holmes, Channing, R. H. Dana, Buckminster, and many other New England authors trace a lineal descent from this earliest singer of the new world.—PATTEE, FRED LEWIS, 1896, *A History of American Literature, p.* 36.

GENERAL

The Tenth Muse Lately sprung up in America. Or Severall Poems, compiled with great variety of Wit and Learning, full of delight. Wherein especially is contained a compleat discourse and description of The Four *Elements; Constitutions, Ages of Man, Seasons of the Year.* Together with an Exact Epitomie of the Four Monarchies, *viz.* The *Assyrian, Persian, Grecian, Roman.* Also a Dialogue between Old *England* and New, concerning the late troubles. With divers other pleasant and serious Poems. By a Gentlewoman in those parts. Printed at *London* for *Stephen Bowtell* at the signe of the Bible in Popes Head-Alley. 1650. THE TENTH MUSE, 1650 *Title Page of First Edition.*

Mercury shew'd *Apollo, Bartas* Book,
Minerva this, and wish't him well to look,
And tell uprightly which did which excell,
He view'd and view'd, and vow'd he could
　　not tel
They bid him hemisphear his mouldy nose,
With's crackt leering glasses, for it would
　　pose
The best brains he had in's old pudding-pan,
Sex weigh'd, which best, the Woman or the
　　Man?
He peer'd, and por'd, & glar'd, & said for
　　wore,
I'm even as wise now, as I was before:
They both 'gan laugh, and said it was no
　　mar'l
The Auth'ress was a right *Du Bartas* Girle.
Good sooth quoth the old *Don*, tell ye me so,
I muse whither at length these Girls will go.
It half revives my chil frost-bitten blood,
To see a Woman once do ought that's good;
And chode by *Chaucers* Boots and *Homers*
　　Furrs,
Let Men look to't, least Women wear the
　　Spurrs.
—WARD, NATHANIEL, 1650, *Prefatory
Lines to the Tenth Muse.*

Anne Bradstreet, a New-England poetess, no less in title, viz. before her Poems,
printed in Old-England anno 1650; then
The tenth Muse sprung up in America; the
memory of which poems, consisting chiefly
of Descriptions of the Four Elements, the
Four Humours; the Four Ages, the Four
Seasons, and the Four Monarchies, is not
yet wholly extinct.—PHILLIPS, EDWARD,
1675, *Theatrum Poetarum Anglicanorum.*

Reader, America justly admires the
learned women of the other hemisphere.
She has heard of those that were witnesses
to the old professors of all philosophy:
she hath heard of Hippatia, who formerly
taught the liberal arts; and of Sarocchia,
who, more lately, was very often the
moderatrix in the disputations of the
learned men of Rome: she has been told
of the three Corinnas, which equalled, if
not excelled, the most celebrated poets of
their time: she has been told of the Empress Eudocia, who composed poetical
paraphrases on various parts of the Bible;
and of Rosnida, who wrote the lives of
holy men; and of Pamphilia, who wrote
other histories unto the life: the writings
of the most renowned Anna Maria Schur-
man, have come over unto her. But she
now prays that into such catalogues of
authoresses as Beverovicius, Hottinger,
and Voetius, have given unto the world,
there may be a room now given unto

Madam Ann Bradstreet, the daughter of
our Governor Dudley, and the consort of
our Governor Bradstreet, whose poems,
divers times printed, have afforded a
grateful entertainment unto the ingenious,
and a monument for her memory beyond
the stateliest marbles.—MATHER, COTTON,
1702, *Magnalia Christi Americana.*

In the height of enthusiasm, good John
Norton goes so far as to declare, that if
Virgil could hear her works, he would
condemn his own to the flames. As the
Mantuan Bard is not likely to be gratified
by hearing Mrs. Bradstreet's effusions, it
is idle to discuss the position assumed by
Norton, and argue whether Virgil would
or would not be capable of such an act of
philanthropic abnegation, or ebullition of
disappointed rivalry, as the combustion of
his verses would display to the eyes of an
astonished and mourning world. Miserable
as Virgil's effusions may be, when compared with the verses of Mrs. Bradstreet,
yet somehow we have become accustomed
to him, and could better spare a better
poet,—even the famed "Tenth Muse"
herself.—ALLIBONE, S. AUSTIN, 1854-58,
Dictionary of English Literature, vol. I.

The formal natural history and historical topics, which compose the greater
part of her writings, are treated with
doughty resolution, but without much regard to poetical equality. . . . It is
not to be denied, that, if there is not
much poetry in these productions, there
is considerable information. For the
readers of those times they contained a
very respectable digest of the old historians, and a fair proportion of medical
and scientific knowledge.—DUYCKINCK,
EVERT A. AND GEORGE L., 1855-65-75,
*Cyclopædia of American Literature, ed.
Simons, p. 53.*

Independently of what may be said of
their poetical merits, her poems do honour
to her as a well educated and accomplished
woman, from their frequent and accurate
allusions to ancient literature and to facts
in history; and from the amiable light in
which they present her as a daughter, a
wife, a parent, and a Christian, it cannot
be doubted that she was a bright example
in her whole deportment of whatsoever
things are true, and honest, and just, and
pure, and lovely, and of good report.
—ANDERSON, JAMES, 1861, *Memorable
Women of Puritan Times, vol. I, p. 174.*

She was well read in the literature of the time, poetical, theological, and other, and without possessing genius, was a young woman of talents. It was the fashion to admire Sidney's "Arcadia," so she admired it, and wrote an elegy upon its chivalrous author, whom his contemporaries insisted on idolizing. She also admired Spenser's "Faerie Queene," which was more read in the first half of the seventeenth century than it ever has been since; and she may be said to have doted upon Du Bartas, whom every body was reading then, through the lumbering version of Sylvester, though nobody can be persuaded to read him now. Her master was Du Bartas, whose "sugared lines" she read over and over, grudging that the Muses did not part their overflowing store betwixt him and her:

"A Bartas can do what a Bartas will,
But simple I according to my skill."

—STODDARD, RICHARD HENRY, 1879, *Richard Henry Dana, Harper's Magazine, vol.* 58, *p.* 769.

Though it was only as a poet that Anne Bradstreet was known to her own time, her real strength was in prose, and the "Meditations, Divine and Morall," written at the request of her second son, the Rev. Simon Bradstreet, to whom she dedicated them, March 20, 1664, show that life had taught her much, and in the ripened thought and shrewd observation of men and manners are the best testimony to her real ability. For the reader of to-day they are of incomparably more interest than anything to be found in the poems. There is often the most condensed and telling expression; a swift turn that shows what power of description lay under all the fantastic turns of the style Du Bartas had created for her. That he underrated them was natural.—CAMPBELL, HELEN, 1891, *Anne Bradstreet and Her Time, p.* 288.

While our earliest woman poet was not a genius, her character and abilities excite both admiration and interest. . . . To judge her fairly we must realize how distant she was from the great centers of civilization, and remember the many obstacles she had to overcome. Born when Shakespeare's career was just ending and Milton was still in his infancy, the strictness of her religion as well as the remoteness of her situation shut her out from much that was noblest and most inspiring in the literature of that golden time. . . . Her works show industry, careful reading, and a religious, thoughtful, and appreciative mind. . . . On the whole, we should honor and remember Anne Bradstreet, not so much for the intrinsic worth of what she wrote, as for her place in the progress of our history and culture. We must honor her because she was one of the first among us to seriously devote herself to poetry for its own sake, and because her writings and example exerted a salutary and refining influence on others.—PANCOAST, HENRY S., 1898, *An Introduction to American Literature, pp.* 57, 58, 59.

Margaret Cavendish

Duchess of Newcastle

1624–1673

Margaret Cavendish, Duchess of Newcastle, died 1673, was as fond of authorship as her noble lord proved himself to be. Lord Orford speaks disparagingly of her ladyship's talents, but it is well known that Horace Walpole spared no man (or woman) in his humour. "Philosophical Fancies," Lon., 1653, 12mo. "Poems and Fancies," 1653, fol. "The World's Olio," 1655, fol. "Nature's Picture drawn by Fancie's Pencil, to the Life," 1656, fol. "Philosophical and Physical Opinions," 1655, fol. "Orations," 1662, fol. "Playes," 1662, fol. She wrote 26 Plays, and a number of Scenes. "Sociable Letters," 1664, fol. "Observations upon Experimental Philosophy," 1666, fol. "Life of William Cavendish, Duke of Newcastle," 1667, fol. The same in Latin, 1668, fol:—The Crown of her Labours. "Grounds of Natural Philosophy," 1668, fol. "Letters and Poems," 1676, fol. "Select Poems," edited by Sir E. Brydges, 1813, 8vo. Her "Autobiography," edited by Brydges, 1814, r. 8vo.—ALLIBONE, S. AUSTIN, 1854–58, *Dictionary of English Literature, vol.* I, *p.* 357.

PERSONAL

Why hath this lady writ her own life? since none cares to know whose daughter she was, or whose wife she is, or how she was bred, or what fortunes she had, or how she lived, or what humour or disposition she was of? I answer that it is true that 'tis to no purpose to the reader, but it is to the Authoress, because I write it for my own sake, not theirs; neither did I intend this piece for to delight, but to divulge; not to please the fancy, but to tell the truth, lest after-ages should mistake, in not knowing I was daughter to one Master Lucas of St. John's near Colchester in Essex, and second wife to the Lord Marquis of Newcastle; for my lord having had two Wives, I might easily have been mistaken, especially if I should die and my Lord Marry again.—CAVENDISH, MARGARET (DUTCHESS OF NEWCASTLE), 1667, *Lives of the Duke and Dutchess of Newcastle, ed. Lower, p.* 309.

They received me with great kindnesse, and I was much pleased with the extraordinary fanciful habit, garb, and discourse of the Dutchess. . . . In the afternoone I went againe with my Wife to the Dutchess of Newcastle, who received her in a kind of transport, suitable to her extravagant humour and dresse, which was very singular.—EVELYN, JOHN, 1667, *Diary, April,* 18, 27.

After dinner I walked to Arundell House, the way very dusty, . . . where I find much company, indeed very much company, in expectation of the Duchesse of Newcastle, who had desired to be invited to the Society; and was, after much debate *pro* and *con.*, it seems many being against it; and we do believe the town will be full of ballads of it. Anon comes the Duchesse with her women attending her; among others, the Ferabosco, of whom so much talk is that her lady would bid her show her face and kill the gallants. She is indeed black, and hath good black little eyes, but otherwise but a very ordinary woman, I do think, but they say sings well. The Duchesse hath been a good, comely woman; but her dress so antick, and her deportment so ordinary, that I do not like her at all, nor did I hear her say anything that was worth hearing, but that she was full of admiration, all admiration. Several fine experiments were shown her of colours, loadstones, microscopes, and of liquors. . . . After they had shown her many experiments, and she cried still she was full of admiration, she departed, being led out and in by several Lords that were there.—PEPYS, SAMUEL, 1667, *Diary, May* 30.

She talks like a Nell Gwynne, and looks like her too, though all within bounds.—HUNT, LEIGH, 1847, *Men, Women and Books, vol.* II, *p.* 101.

"The whole story of this lady is a romance, and all she does is romantic," wrote Pepys of the subject of this paper, whom some of her contemporaries irreverently styled "Mad Madge of Newcastle," while later critics thought so highly of her that, in "A Vision of Female Poets," Shakespeare and Milton are represented as respectfully helping her to alight from her Pegasus. The imputation of insanity probably troubled the Duchess but little; she would console herself with the reflection that "great wits are sure to madness near allied;" and if, as some of her biographers assert, her devoted loyalty to her husband, in the extremely disloyal Court of Charles II., earned her the nickname of "Mad Madge," it becomes a title of honour.—MAYER, GERTRUDE TOWNSHEND, 1894, *Women of Letters, vol.* I, *p.* 1.

GENERAL

A Lady worthy of Mention and Esteem of all Lovers of Poetry and Learning. One, who was a fit Consort for so Great a Wit, as the Duke of *Newcastle.* Her Soul sympathising with his in all things, especially in Dramatick Poetry; to which she had a more than ordinary propensity. She has publisht six and twenty Plays, besides several loose Scenes. . . . I know there are some that have but a mean Opinion of her Plays; but if it be consider'd that both the Language and Plots of them are all her own: I think she ought with Justice to be preferr'd to others of her Sex, which have built their Fame on other People's Foundations: sure I am, that whoever will consider well the several Epistles before her Books, and the General Prologue to all her Plays, if he have any spark of Generosity, or Good Breeding, will be favourable in his Censure. LANGBAINE, GERARD, 1691, *An Account of the English Dramatick Poets, pp.* 390, 391.

Her Grace's literary labours have drawn down less applause than her domestic virtues: nor can it be denied that she wrote too much to be expected to write well, had her taste or judgment been greatly superior to what we find them. That she displayed poetical talent, however, when it was not clouded by obscure conceits, or warped by a witless effort to engraft the massy trunk of philosophy on the slender wilding of poesy, will be seen . . . from "The Pastime and Recreation of the Queen of Fairies, in Fairy-land, the Centre of the Earth."—WALPOLE, HORACE, 1758, *A Catalogue of the Royal and Noble Authors of England, Scotland, and Ireland.*

If her merit as an author were to be estimated from the *quantity* of her works, she would have the precedence of all female writers, ancient or modern. There are no less than thirteen folios of her writing; ten of which are in print: They consist chiefly of poems and plays. The life of the duke, her husband, is the most estimable of her productions. This has been translated into Latin. . . . We are greatly surprised that a lady of her quality should have written so much; and are little less surprised that one who loved writing so well, has writ no better. —GRANGER, JAMES, 1769–1824, *Biographical History of England, vol.* V, *p.* 263.

A dear favourite of mine, of the last century but one—the thrice noble, chaste, and virtuous,—but again somewhat fantastical, and original-brained, generous Margaret Newcastle. —LAMB, CHARLES, 1821, *Mackery End in Hertfordshire.*

The labors of no modern authoress can be compared, as to quantity, with those of our indefatigable duchess, who has filled nearly twelve volumes, folio, with plays, poems, orations, philosophical discourses, &c. Her writings show that she possessed a mind of considerable power and activity, with much imagination, but not one particle of judgment or taste.—DYCE, ALEXANDER, 1827, *ed., Specimens of British Poetesses.*

Indisputable evidence of a genius as high-born in the realms of intellect as its possessor was exalted in the ranks of society; a genius strong-winged and swift, fertile and comprehensive, but ruined by deficient culture, by literary dissipation, and the absence of concatenation and the sense of proportion.—JENKINS, EDWARD, 1872, *ed., The Cavalier and His Lady.*

Heroic romance proved as ephemeral in England as the cloaks and feathers with which it had crossed the Channel, and we may pass over such trivial literary attempts as those of the Duchess of Newcastle to the writings of Mrs. Manley and Mrs. Behn.—TUCKERMAN, BAYARD, 1882, *A History of English Prose Fiction, p.* 122.

She had a conceit that rose to an amazing and amusing serenity; yet the artless candour of its utterances disarms criticism of contempt, and positively creates out of her self-esteem a pleasantry of character that half resembles a virtue. She possesses abundance of sense, but very little of it common sense. Humour and wit are native in her; even genius can be claimed for portions of her best work; but so woefully did she lack consistency of taste and that species of literary judgment which has been termed the power of selecting the significant, that her works are the oddest medleys ever hurried through a printing press. Each of her volumes reminds one of a lady's overturned work-basket, into which had crept all kinds of consequent and inconsequent things, with even a jewel or two among the mass. She possessed a perfect frenzy for writing. At twelve she was fond of scribbling on philosophical subjects; and in the deepest distress of her chequered life, as in its brighest moments, the sight of mere wet ink on the page seems to have solaced her beyond anything else. She never revised what she had thus once committed to paper, being of the opinion that the work of revision would have hindered her productive powers, as, indeed, it often would, had she duly considered the quality of the matter thrown off so hastily. There is no method either in her arrangement of subjects or in her style. One of the sentences in her autobiography is twelve pages long. Yet the *bizarrerie* of her modes of working frequently produces powerful effects, and at times you will come on smooth passages of her works in which the diction is almost as perfect as that which the most fastidious artifice could have devised.—ROBERTSON, ERIC S., 1883, *English Poetesses, p* 14.

She wrote a great deal; and not without feeling a somewhat deep and naïvely expressed admiration for her own performances. The epithet "restless" which she applies to her ambition, well fits her whole mind; there is restlessness about everything she did and wrote. She is never satisfied with one epistle to the reader; she must have ten or twelve prefaces and under-prefaces, which forcibly remind us of her contemporary, Oronte, in his famous sonnet scenes with Alceste. . . . Ideas are scattered here and there which were destined to live, and through which she anticipated men of true and real genius. —JUSSERAND, J. J., 1890, *The English Novel in the Time of Shakespeare, pp.* 374, 378.

Robert Herrick
1591–1674

Born, in London, July [?] 1591; baptized, 24 Aug. Probably educated at Westminster School and at St. John's Coll., Camb. Removed to Trinity Hall, 1616; B. A., 1617; M. A., 1620. Rector of Dean Prior, Devonshire, 2 Oct. 1629 to 1647. Deprived of living, 1647; returned to London. Restored to living, 24 Aug. 1662. Died, at Dean Prior, Oct. 1674; buried in Dean Prior church, 15 Oct. *Works:* "King Obron's Feast" (anon., in "A Description of the King and Queene of Fayries"), 1635; "His Mistris Shade" (anon.; in Shakespeare's "Poems"), 1640; "Hesperides" (with "Noble Numbers"), 1648; Poems in "Lacrymæ Musarum," 1649; Poems in "Witt's Recreations," 1650. *Collected Works:* ed. by Lord Dundrennan (2 vols.), 1823; by Grosart (3 vols.), 1876; by A. W. Pollard, 1891; by Saintsbury (2 vols.), 1893.— SHARP, R. FARQUHARSON, 1897, *A Dictionary of English Authors, p.* 132.

PERSONAL

Being in Devonshire during the last summer, we took an opportunity of visiting Dean Prior, for the purpose of making some inquiries concerning Herrick, who, from the circumstance of having been vicar of that parish (where he is still talked of as a poet, a wit, and a hater of the county), for twenty years, might be supposed to have left some unrecorded memorials of his existence behind him. We found many persons in the village who could repeat some of his lines. . . . The person, however, who knows more of Herrick than all the rest of the neighbourhood, we found to be a poor woman in the ninety-ninth year of her age, named Dorothy King. She repeated to us, with great exactness, five of his "Noble Numbers," among which was the beautiful Litany. These she had learned from her mother, who was apprenticed to Herrick's successor in the vicarage. She called them her prayers, which, she said, she was in the habit of putting up in bed, whenever she could not sleep: and she therefore began the Litany at the second stanza,

"When I lie within my bed," &c.

Another of her midnight orisons was the poem beginning

"Every night thou dost me fright,
And keep mine eyes from sleeping," &c.

She had no idea that these poems had ever been printed, and could not have read them if she had seen them. She is in possession of few traditions as to the person, manners, and habits of life of the poet; but in return, she has a whole budget of anecdotes respecting his ghost; and these she details with a careless but serene gravity, which one would not willingly discompose by any hints at a remote possibility of their not being exactly true. Herrick, she says, was a bachelor, and kept a maid-servant, as his poems, indeed, discover; but she adds, what they do not discover, that he also kept a pet-pig, which he taught to drink out of a tankard. And this important circumstance, together with a tradition that he one day threw his sermon at the congregation, with a curse for their inattention, forms almost the sum total of what we could collect of the poet's life.—FIELD, BARRON, 1810, *Select Poems from Herrick, Carew, etc., The Quarterly Review, vol.* IV, *pp.* 171, 172.

This fine old fellow, this joyous heart, who lived to be eighty-three, in spite of "dull Devonshire" and the bad times, wrote almost as much as Carew, Lovelace, and Suckling united, and now much there is in his weed-choked garden, which is comparable with their best compositions! How little we know of him! how scantily he has been realized to us! Could we but raise up for a summer afternoon the Devonshire which he lived in, and the people with whom he mixed or summon the ghost of faithful Prudence Baldwin, we might be furnished with inspiration to do something better than the bare sketch which follows. — HAZLITT, WILLIAM CAREW, 1869, *ed. Hesperides, Preface, vol.* I, *p.* viii.

Rare old Herrick, the Cavalier Vicar
Of pleasant Dean Prior by Totnes Town—
Rather too wont in foaming liquor
 The cares of those troublous times to drown
Of wicked wit by no means chary—
 Of ruddy lips not at all afraid;
If you gave him milk in a Devonshire dairy,
 He'd probably kiss the dairymaid.
—COLLINS, MORTIMER, 1876? *Herrick*.

Being ejected by Cromwell from his church living in 1648, he dropped his title of "Reverend" to assume that of "Esquire," and published a volume to which he gave the title of "Hesperides; or, the Works both Humane and Divine, of Robert Herrick, Esq." Doubtless the "Esquire" was accepted by the public, as well as by himself, as more appropriate than "Reverend" would have been to the character of the lyrics, some part of which he yet seems rather arrogantly to call "Divine."—MORRILL, JUSTIN S., 1887, *Self-Consciousness of Noted Persons, p.* 90.

This Robert Herrick was a ponderous, earthy-looking man, with huge double chin, drooping cheeks, a great Roman nose, prominent glassy eyes, that showed around them the red lines begotten of strong potions of Canary, and the whole set upon a massive neck which might have been that of Heliogabalus. It was such a figure as the artist would make typical of a man who loves the grossest pleasures. —MITCHELL, DONALD G., 1890, *English Lands Letters and Kings, Elizabeth to Anne, p.* 124.

Mr. Gosse, for example, assures us that Julia really walked the earth, and even gives us some details of her mundane pilgrimage; other critics smile, and shake their heads, and doubt. It matters not; she lives, and she will continue to live when we who dispute the matter lie voiceless in our graves. The essence of her personality lingers on every page where Herrick sings of her. His verse is heavy with her spicy perfumes, glittering with her many-colored jewels, lustrous with the shimmer of her silken petticoats. Her very shadow, her sighs, distills sweet odors on the air, and draws him after her, faint with their amorous languor. How lavish she is with her charms, this woman who neither thinks nor suffers; who prays, indeed, sometimes, with great serenity, and dips her snowy finger in the font of blessed water, but whose spiritual humors pale before the calm vigor of her earthly nature! How kindly, how tranquil, how unmoved, she is; listening with the same slow smile to her lover's fantastic wordplay, to the fervid conceits with which he beguiles the summer idleness, and to the frank and sudden passion with which he conjures her, "dearest of thousands," to close his eyes when death shall summon him, to shed some true tears above the sod, to clasp forever the book in which he writes her name! How gently she would have fulfilled these last sad duties had the discriminating fates called her to his bier; how fragrant the sighs she would have wafted in that darkened chamber; how sincere the temperate sorrow for a remediable loss! And then, out into the glowing sunlight, where life is sweet, and the world exults, and the warm blood tingles in our veins, and, underneath the scattered primrose blossoms, the frozen dead lie forgotten in their graves.—REPPLIER, AGNES, 1891, *English Love-Songs, Points of View, p.* 33.

The same sensuous feeling which made him invest his friends with the perfume of Juno or Isis, sing of their complexions as roses overspread with lawn, compare their lips to cherries, and praise their silver feet, had also its other side. The unlucky wights who incurred the poet's wrath were treated in a fashion equally offensive to good taste and good manners. Nor are these gruesome epigrams the only apples in the garden of Herrick's "Hesperides" which have affronted the taste of modern readers. The epigrams indeed, if apples at all, are rather the dusty apples of the Dead Sea than the pleasant fruit of the Western Isles; but Herrick's "Epithalamia," odes whose sustained splendour gives them a high rank among his poems, because they sing of other marriage-rites than those of rice and slipper, have also tended to restrict the circle of his readers in an age which prides itself on its modesty. Hence it has come about that while the names of the lovely ladies of the poet's imagination,—Julia, Dianeme, Electra, Perilla—are widely known, those of the men and women whom Herrick treasured as his friends are all but forgotten.—POLLARD, ALFRED W., 1892, *Herrick and his Friends, Macmillan's Magazine, vol.* 67, *p.* 142.

It seems likely that Perilla and her fair companions were actually known to Herrick in London, and were then made the topic of many a gallant verse; and that after he sailed away to the West he continued to write to their memory as though they were actually present; that, in fact, the goddesses he was never weary of worshipping were, to a large extent, abstractions and ideals. And when in the quiet of his little parsonage, or in a sunny Devonshire meadow bright with wild flowers, his fancy coined some musical verse in honour of his ideal love, his memory would glide quickly back and dwell longingly on her prototype of flesh and blood whom he had known and loved in former years; and, cut off from all the noises and all the rivalries of the town, it must have seemed to him that he was thinking of another Robert Herrick who had lived long ago.—SANDERS, H. M., 1896, *Robert Herrick, The Gentleman's Magazine, vol.* 280, *p.* 604.

Whether or not the bovine features in Marshall's engraving are a libel on the poet, it is to be regretted that oblivion has not laid its erasing finger on that singularly unpleasant counterfeit presentment. . . . The aggressive face bestowed upon him by the artist lends an air of veracity to the tradition that the vicar occasionally hurled the manuscript of his sermon at the heads of his drowsy parishioners, accompanying the missive with pregnant remarks. He has the aspect of one meditating assault and battery. To offset the picture there is much indirect testimony to the amiability of the man, aside from the evidence furnished by his own writings. . . . I picture him as a sort of Samuel Pepys, with perhaps less quaintness, and the poetical temperament added. Like the prince of gossips, too, he somehow gets at your affections.— ALDRICH, THOMAS BAILEY, 1900, *Poems of Robert Herrick, Introduction, pp.* xxvii, xxviii, xxx.

HESPERIDES

1648

I sing of brooks, of blossoms, birds and bowers,
Of April, May, of June and July-flowers;
I sing of may-poles, hock-carts, wassails, wakes,
Of bridegrooms, brides, and of their bridal-cakes;
I write of youth, of love, and have access
By these to sing of cleanly wantonness;
I sing of dews, of rains, and piece by piece,
Of balm, of oil, of spice, and ambergris;
I sing of times trans-shifting; and I write
How roses first came red and lilies white.
I write of groves, of twilights, and I sing
The Court of Mab and of the Fairie King;
I write of Hell; I sing, and ever shall,
Of Heaven, and hope to have it after all.
—HERRICK, ROBERT, 1648, *The Argument of His Book, Hesperides, p.* 3.

Ships lately from the islands came,
With wines, thou never heard'st by name.
Montefiasco, Frontiniac,
Vernaccio, and that old sack
Young Herric took to entertaine
The muses in a sprightly vein.
—ANON, 1656, *To Parson Weeks, an Invitation to London, Musarum Deliciæ.*

An then *Flaccus Horace*,
He was but a sowr-ass,
And good for nothing but *Lyricks*,
There's but One to be found
In all English ground
Writes as well;—who is hight Robert Herick.
—ANON, 1658, *Naps upon Parnassus.*

Herrick published his poems at an age when youth and inexperience could not be urged in extenuation of the blemishes which they presented. The author was fifty-seven years old when the "Hesperides" issued from the press, replete with beauties and excellencies, and at the same time abounding in passages of outrageous grossness. The title was perhaps rather apt to mislead, for besides golden apples, this garden assuredly contained many rank tares and poisonous roots. It would scarcely suffice to plead the freedom and breadth of speech customary among all classes and with both sexes at that period. Some share of the blame must, beyond question, be laid to Herrick's voluptuousness of temperament, and not very cleanly ardour of imagination; yet, after all deductions which it is possible to make, what a noble salvage remains! Enough beauty, wit, nay piety, to convert even the prudish to an admiration of the genius

which shines transparent through all.—
HAZLITT, WILLIAM CAREW, 1869, *ed. Hesperides, Preface, vol.* I, *p.* viii.

The "Hesperides" is so rich in jewelry, that the most careless selection can hardly be unsatisfactory. Yet being so rich, there might have been more independent taste. One is led to ask how much of popular favouritism even in literature is, like fashion in clothes, due to dictation of the purveyors.—LINTON, W. J., 1882, *ed., Rare Poems of the Sixteenth and Seventeenth Centuries, p.* 242, *note.*

Herrick alone, with imperturbable serenity, continued to pipe out his pastoral ditties, and crown his head with daffodils, when England was torn to pieces with the most momentous struggle for liberty in her annals. To the poetic student he is, therefore, of especial interest, as a genuine specimen of an artist, pure and simple. Herrick brought out the "Hesperides" a few months before the King was beheaded, and people were invited to listen to little madrigals upon Julia's stomacher at the singularly inopportune. moment when the eyes of the whole nation were bent on the unprecedented phenomenon of the proclamation of an English republic. To find a parallel to such unconsciousness we must come down to our own time, and recollect that Théophile Gautier took occasion of the seige of Paris to revise and republish his *Emaux et Camées.*—GOSSE, EDMUND, 1883, *Seventeenth-Century Studies, p.* 114.

In the quiet of his parsonage, the music of his life found utterance in every mood. His whole mind expressed itself, animal and spiritual. In the texture of his book he evidently meant to show the warp and woof of life. He aimed at effects of contrast that belonged to the true nature of man, in whom, as in the world at large, "the strawberry grows underneath the nettle," and side by side with promptings of the flesh, spring up the aspirations of the spirit. Even the dainty fairy pieces written under influence of the same fashion that caused Shakespeare to describe Queen Mab and Drayton to write his Nymphidia, even such pieces of his, written in earlier days, Herrick sprinkled about his volume in fragments. He would not make his nosegay with the flowers of each sort bunched together in so many lumps. There is truth in the

close contact of a playful sense of ugliness with the most delicate perception of all forms of beauty. Herrick's "epigrams" on running eyes and rotten teeth, and the like, are such exaggerations as may often have tumbled out spontaneously, in the course of playful talk, and if they pleased him well enough were duly entered in his book. In a healthy mind, this whimsical sense of deformity may be but the other side of a fine sense of beauty.—MORLEY, HENRY, 1884, *ed. Hesperides* (*Morley's Universal Library*), *p.* 7.

That the "Hesperides" is the most typical single book of the class and kind there can be little doubt, though there may be higher and rarer touches in others. Its bulk, its general excellence in its own kind, make it exhibit the combined influences of Donne and Jonson (which, as was pointed out earlier, tell upon, and to some extent account for, this lyrical outburst) better than any other single volume. And long as Herrick had to wait for his public (it must be confessed that, though the times do not seem to have in the least chained the poet's tongue, they did much to block his hearers' ears), there is now not much difference of opinion in general points, however much there may be in particulars, about the poetical value of "The Mad Maid's Song" and "To Daffodils," of the "Night Piece to Julia" and "To the Virgins," of the "Litany" and "The White Island." Yet this book is only the most popular and coherent collection among an immense mass of verse, all informed by the most singular and attractive quality.—SAINTSBURY, GEORGE, 1895, *Social England, ed. Traill, vol.* IV, *p.* 300.

Yellow and frayed and torn; but mark within,
　　The sparkling rhyme
That, like a dimple in an old dame's chin,
　　Laughs out at Time!
—WELCH, ROBERT GILBERT, 1896, *In an Ancient Copy of Herrick's "Hesperides," The Century Magazine, vol.* 51, *p.* 477.

NOBLE NUMBERS
1648

Herrick's sacred poems . . . have often much merit. We cannot doubt their sincerity. But they are mostly strained, and show Herrick ill at ease. They are strangely disfigured with conceits, and the best of them are half secular.—ASHE, T., 1883, *Robert Herrick, Temple Bar, vol.* 68, *p.* 132.

Of the religious poems the already-mentioned "Litany," while much the most familiar, is also far the best. There is nothing in English verse to equal it as an expression of religious fear; while there is also nothing in English verse to equal the "Thanksgiving," also well known, as an expression of religious trust.—SAINTSBURY, GEORGE, 1887, *History of Elizabethan Literature, p.* 356.

The religious pieces grouped under the title of "Noble Numbers" distinctly associate themselves with Dean Prior, and have little other interest. Very few of them are "born of the royal blood." They lack the inspiration and magic of his secular poetry, and are frequently so fantastical and grotesque as to stir a suspicion touching the absolute soundness of Herrick's mind at all times. The lines in which the Supreme Being is assured that he may read Herrick's poems without taking any tincture from their sinfulness might have been written in a retreat for the unbalanced. — ALDRICH, THOMAS BAILEY, 1900, *Poems of Robert Herrick, Introduction, p.* xxv.

GENERAL

One of the Scholars of Apollo of the middle Form, yet something above *George Withers*, in a pretty Flowry and Pastoral Gale of Fancy, in a vernal Prospect of some Hill, Cave, Rock, or Fountain; which but for the interruption of other trivial Passages, might have made up none of the worst Poetick Landskips.—WINSTANLEY, WILLIAM, 1668, *The Lives of the Most Famous English Poets.*

These two books of poetry made him much admired in the time when they were published, especially by the generous and boon loyalists, among whom he was numbred as a sufferer.—WOOD, ANTHONY, 1691–1721, *Athenæ Oxonienses, vol.* II, *f.* 122.

It appears from the effects of her inspiration, that Prue was but indifferently qualified for a tenth muse.—GRANGER, JAMES, 1769–1824, *Biographical History of England, vol.* III, *p.* 136.

Had Herrick adopted any arrangement or classification for his poetry, it would probably have experienced a kinder fate. The reader would then have had the opportunity of choosing the department most congenial to his taste, and without incurring the risk of being seduced into the perusal of matter offensive to his feelings. At present, so injudiciously are the contents of his volume disposed, and so totally divested of order and propriety, that it would almost seem the poet wished to pollute and bury his best effusions in a mass of nonsense and obscenity. Nine persons out of ten who should casually dip into the collection, would, in all probability, after glancing over a few trifling epigrams, throw it down with indignation, little apprehending it contained many pieces of a truly moral and pathetic, and of an exquisitely rural and descriptive, strain.—DRAKE, NATHAN, 1798, *Literary Hours, vol.* III, *No.* xliv.

Herrick is a writer who does not answer the expectations I had formed of him. He is in a manner a modern discovery, and so far has the freshness of antiquity about him. He is not trite and thread bare. But neither is he likely to become so. He is a writer of epigrams, not of lyrics. He has point and ingenuity, but I think little of the spirit of love or wine. From his frequent allusion to pearls and rubies, one might take him for a lapidary instead of a poet.—HAZLITT, WILLIAM, 1820, *Lectures on the Literature of the Age of Elizabeth.*

A coarse-minded and beastly writer, whose dunghill, when the few flowers that grew therein had been transplanted, ought never to have been disturbed. Those flowers indeed are beautiful and perennial; but they should have been removed from the filth and ordure in which they are embedded.—SOUTHEY, ROBERT, 1831, *Lives of Uneducated Poets, p.* 85.

Without the exuberant gayety of Suckling, or perhaps the delicacy of Carew, he is sportive, fanciful, and generally of polished language. The faults of his age are sometimes apparent: though he is not often obscure, he runs, more perhaps for the sake of variety than any other cause, into occasional pedantry. He has his conceits and false thoughts; but these are more than redeemed by the numerous very little poems (for those of Herrick are frequently not longer than epigrams), which may be praised without much more qualification than belongs to such poetry. —HALLAM, HENRY, 1837–39, *Introduction to the Literature of Europe, pt.* iii, *ch.* v.

The Ariel of poets, sucking "where the bee sucks" from the roseheart of nature, and reproducing the fragrance idealized.—BROWNING, ELIZABETH BARRETT, 1842–63, *The Book of the Poets.*

As a loyalist and sufferer in the cause, there can be no doubt that Herrick was popular with the Cavalier party, and that his poems were received with the favour they deserved by his contemporaries, for that they were popular must be inferred from the number of them which were set to music by Henry Lawes, Laniere, Wilson, and Ramsay; it is somewhat difficult to account for the seeming neglect which they experienced in after times.—SINGER, S. W., 1846, *ed. Hesperides, Biographical Notice, vol.* I, *p.* xxv.

More than any eminent writer of that day, Herrick's collection requires careful sifting; but there is so much fancy, so much delicacy, so much grace, that a good selection would well repay the publisher. Bits there are that are exquisite. . . . But his real delight was among flowers and bees, and nymphs and cupids; and certainly these graceful subjects were never handled more gracefully.—MITFORD, MARY RUSSELL, 1851, *Recollections of a Literary Life, pp.* 143, 144.

He was an Anacreon or Catullus in holy orders, whiling away, at the ripe age of forty, the dulness of his Devonshire parsonage in such ditties as these:

"Much I know, of time is spent," &c., &c.

. . . And so, in every other poem, he sings or sips his wine, with his arm round a Julia! What eyes, what lips, what a neck! and so on amorously, beyond all clerical limits. Like Anacreon, he is sweet, too, in light sensuous descriptions of physical nature. . . . There was, moreover, a tinge of amiable melancholy in his genius—the melancholy on which the Epicurean philosophy itself rests.—MASSON, DAVID, 1858, *The Life of John Milton, vol.* I, *ch.* vi.

It is an especial pleasure to write the name of Robert Herrick amongst the poets of religion, for the very act records that the jolly, careless Anacreon of the church, with his head and heart crowded with pleasures, threw down at length his wine-cup, tore the roses from his head, and knelt in the dust.—MACDONALD, GEORGE, 1868, *England's Antiphon, p.* 163.

Making due allowance of the time when Herrick's verses were written, his temptation to suit the taste of courtiers and kings, his volumes contain much admirable poetry, tempered with religious devotion. He wrote sweet and virtuous verse, with lines here and there that should not have been written. But he is an antedote to the vice in his lines, and may well have place in the scholar's library with Donne, Daniel, Cowley, Shakespeare, and contemporaries.—ALCOTT, A. BRONSON, 1869, *Concord Days, p.* 136.

Many of his compositions are, in the fullest sense of the term, trifles; others are at least exquisite trifles; some are not trifles, and are exquisite. After more than a century of neglect, ensuing upon their first ample popularity, Herrick's writings have for years been kept freshened with a steady current of literary laudation—certainly not unjustified, so far as their finer qualities go, but tending a little to the indiscriminate.—ROSSETTI, WILLIAM MICHAEL, 1872–78, *ed. Humorous Poems, p.* 98.

Beyond all dispute, the best of the early lyric poets is Robert Herrick, whose verses are flushed with a joyous and tender spirit. He may be styled the Burns of his time, and was imbued with something of the reckless soul of the great north-countryman. . . . Flowers, music, woman, all these had their intense and several charms for him, and, strangely enough for a middle-aged clergyman, he was clearly an amorous and erotic poet.—SMITH, GEORGE BARNETT, 1875, *English Fugitive Poets, Poets and Novelists, pp.* 381, 382.

Like the holy river of Virgil, to the souls who drink of him, Herrick offers "securos latices." He is conspicuously free from many of the maladies incident to his art. Here is no overstrain, no spasmodic cry, no wire-drawn analysis or sensational rhetoric, no music without sense, no mere second-hand literary inspiration, no mannered archaism:—above all, no sickly sweetness, no subtle, unhealthy affectation. Throughout his work, whether when it is strong, or in the less worthy portions, sanity, sincerity, simplicity, lucidity, are everywhere the characteristics of Herrick: in these, not in his pretty Pagan masquerade, he

shows the note,—the only genuine note,
—of Hellenic descent. Hence, through
whatever changes and fashions poetry
may pass, her true lovers he is likely to
"please now, and please for long."—
PALGRAVE, FRANCIS TURNER, 1877, *Robert
Herrick, Macmillan's Magazine, vol.* 35.

Among the English pastoral poets,
Herrick takes an undisputed precedence,
and as a lyrist generally he is scarcely
excelled, except by Shelley. No other
writer of the seventeenth century approached him in abundance of song, in
sustained exercise of the purely musical
and intuitive gifts of poetry. Shakspeare, Milton, and perhaps Fletcher, surpassed him in the passion and elevated
harmony of their best lyrical pieces, as
they easily excelled him in the wider range
of their genius and the breadth of their accomplishment. But while these men exercised their art in all its branches, Herrick confined himself very narrowly to one
or two, and the unflagging freshness of
his inspiration, flowing through a long life
in so straitened a channel, enabled him to
amass such a wealth of purely lyrical poetry as no other Englishman has produced.
His level of performance was very high;
he seems to have preserved all that he
wrote, and the result is that we possess
more than twelve hundred of his little
poems, in at least one out of every three
of which we may find something charming
or characteristic. Of all the Cavalier
lyrists Herrick is the only one that followed the bent of his genius undisturbed,
and lived a genuine artist's life.—GOSSE,
EDMUND, 1880, *English Poets, ed. Ward,
vol.* II, *p.* 124.

By a strange irony of fortune the only
letters we possess from the genial and
glowing pen of the great poet of the
"Hesperides" are a series of plaintive
notes to his rich uncle, Sir William Herrick; and we may gather from them that
this amiable relative's money paid for the
piping of some of the most graceful lyrics
in the English language.—SCOONES, W.
BAPTISTE, 1880, *Four Centuries of English
Letters, p.* 67.

He sings well chiefly when he sings of
love, but this love is not of the kind which
inspires our greatest poets. He is
enamoured with the accessories of a
woman's beauty—the colour of a ribbon,
the flaunting of a ringlet, with "a careless

shoe-string," or the wave of a petticoat. The charms he sees in his mistress
are likened to precious stones, and all the
treasures of the lapidary are represented
in his verse. There are few traces of
tenderness in Herrick and none of passion; it is probable that every pretty girl
he saw suggested a pretty fancy. To
judge from his own saying, "no man at
one time can be wise and love." Herrick
was not wise. If we may trust his verses,
the poet was perennially in love, chiefly
with Julia, "prime of all," but warmly
too with Anthea, Lucia, Corinna, and
Perilla. Making love is in Herrick's eyes
a charming amusement, and the more
love-making the more poetry. If Julia
prove unkind, he can solace himself
with Sappho; and if Sappho be perverse,
some other mistress will charm him with
her "pretty witchcrafts."—DENNIS, JOHN,
1883, *Heroes of Literature, p.* 97.

None of our English lyric poets has
shown a more perfect sense of words and
of their musical efficiency, none has united
so exquisitely a classic sense of form to
that impulsive tunefulness which we have
come to consider as essentially English.
In his earlier lyrics Herrick has perhaps
more of this impulse, but it served him
with the same youthful freshness to the
last. . . . It is the way in which
Herrick adds to and completes this natural
lyrical impulse by the further grace of
verse taught by the Latin verse-writers
and their English disciples, that makes
him so consummate an artist within his
range. . . . There is magic in these
lyrics, that indefinable quality, born of
the spirit, which can alone avail in the
end to make poetry live.—RHYS, ERNEST,
1887, *Hesperides: Poems by Robert Herrick, Introduction, pp.* xxxi, xxxii, xxxiii.

Many suns have set and shone,
Many springs have come and gone,
Herrick, since thou sang'st of Wake,
Morris-dance, and Barley-break;
Many men have ceased from care,
Many maidens have been fair,
Since thou sang'st of *Julia's* eyes,
Julia's lawns and tiffanies;
Many things are past—but thou,
Golden-Mouth, art singing now,
Singing clearly as of old,
And thy numbers are of gold.

—DOBSON, AUSTIN, 1887, *In a Copy of the
Lyrical Poems of Robert Herrick, Scribner's
Magazine, vol.* 1, *p.* 66.

Divided, in the published form, into two classes: they may be divided, for purposes of poetical criticism, into three. The "Hesperides" (they are dated 1648, and the "Noble Numbers" or sacred poems 1647; but both appeared together) consist in the first place of occasional poems, sometimes amatory, sometimes not; in the second, of personal epigrams. Of this second class no human being who has any faculty of criticism can say any good. They are supposed by tradition to have been composed on parishioners: they may be hoped by charity (which has in this case the support of literary criticism) to be merely literary exercises—bad imitations of Martial, through Ben Jonson. They are nastier than the nastiest work of Swift; they are stupider than the stupidest attempts of Davies of Hereford; they are farther from the author's best than the worst parts of Young's "Odes" are from the best part of the "Night Thoughts." It is impossible without producing specimens (which God forbid that any one who has a respect for Herrick, for literature, and for decency, should do) to show how bad they are. Let it only be said that if the worst epigram of Martial were stripped of Martial's wit, sense, and literary form, it would be a kind of example of Herrick in this vein. In his two other veins, but for certain tricks of speech, it is almost impossible to recognise him for the same man. The secular vigour of the "Hesperides," the spiritual vigour of the "Noble Numbers," has rarely been equalled and never surpassed by any other writer.—SAINTSBURY, GEORGE, 1887, *History of Elizabethan Literature*, p. 355.

Herrick the inexhaustible in dainties; Herrick, that parson-pagan, with the soul of a Greek of the Anthology, and a cure of souls (Heaven help them!) in Devonshire. His Julia is the least mortal of these "daughters of dreams and of stories," whom poets celebrate; she has a certain opulence of flesh and blood, a cheek like a damask rose, and "rich eyes," like Keat's lady; no vaporous Beatrice, she; but a handsome English wench, with

"A cuff neglectful and thereby
Ribbons to flow confusedly;
A winning wave, deserving note
In the tempestuous petticoat."

—LANG, ANDREW, 1889, *Letters on Literature*, p. 149.

There were those critics and admirers who saw in Herrick an allegiance to the methods of Catullus; others who smacked in his epigrams the verbal felicities of Martial; but surely there is no need, in that fresh spontaneity of the Devon poet, to hunt for classic parallels; nature made him one of her own singers, and by instincts born with him he fashioned words and fancies into jewelled shapes. The "more's the pity" for those gross indelicacies which smirch so many pages; things unreadable, things which should have been unthinkable and unwritable by a clergyman of the Church of England. — MITCHELL, DONALD G., 1890, *English Lands Letters and Kings, From Elizabeth to Anne*, p. 125.

In Herrick the air is fragrant with new-mown hay; there is a morning light upon all things; long shadows streak the grass, and on the eglantine swinging in the hedge the dew lies white and brilliant. Out of the happy distance comes a shrill and silvery sound of whetting scythes; and from the near brook-side rings the laughter of merry maids in circle to make cowslipballs and babble of their bachelors. —HENLEY, WILLIAM ERNEST, 1890, *Views and Reviews*, p. 112.

Herrick was practically forgotten until Nichols in 1796-7 drew attention to his poetry in the "Gentleman's Magazine." Nichols was followed by Dr. Nathan Drake, who devoted some papers to Herrick in "Literary Hours;" and in 1810 Dr. Nott published "Select Poems from the 'Hesperides,' " which was reviewed by Barron Field in the "Quarterly Review," August 1810. In 1823 a complete edition, in two volumes, worthily edited by Thomas Maitland, lord Dundrennan, was published at Edinburgh, the "remainder" copies being issued (with a fresh title-page) by William Pickering in 1825. Pickering's edition of 1846 contains a memoir by S. W. Singer; an edition by Mr. Edward Walford was published in 1859; Mr. W. Carew Hazlitt's edition, 1869, 2 vols., has additional information of interest; and there is a valuable edition by Dr. Grosart, 3 vols., 1876. Selections from Herrick have been edited by Professor F. T. Palgrave and others.—BULLEN, A. H., 1891, *Dictionary of National Biography*, vol. XXVI, p. 254.

The passing of the glory of the world

is continually filling his eyes with tears, which overflow in pearls that drop within his book. There are people—surely they must have lived in a monastery or a vacuum—who are always puzzled that the men who do these exquisite things in poetry should be sensuous, let us say sensual, in their lives; but apart from the many-sidedness of man, it is surely the sensuous man alone who is capable of these rich tearful moments. One must have lived to have lost, and Herrick lived as generously as Solomon, and his poems are a sort of Restoration Ecclesiastes, with less of the whine and a kinder heart. Yet his "Noble Numbers," or his "Pious Pieces," though at first they strike one somewhat ludicrously as coming from him, are no mere "making it right" with the powers above—they are the result of the real religious devotion which was at the bottom of Herrick's, as of every other poet's heart.—LE GALLIENNE, RICHARD, 1891–95, *Retrospective Reviews, vol.* I, *p.* 3.

Herrick is distinctively a poet from whom to receive pleasure. He is not necessarily to be studied; he is to be enjoyed. Doubtless many who love his verses will be led on by an honorable curiosity to desire to know this and that concerning the man and his work. But the poetic enjoyment is the main thing. Herrick is a very individual poet. He has something about him which lifts him out of the crowd of Jacobean and Caroline lyrists, such as Carew and Suckling, nor do we think of him as on precisely the same level as his predecessors the Elizabethans. His poems have a certain air of distinction. Many of them are trivial enough, doubtless, but they are never quite commonplace.—HALE, JR., EDWARD EVERETT, 1895, *Selections from the Poetry of Robert Herrick, p.* lxiii.

Herrick is indeed the last expression of the pagan Renaissance, prolonged into the quiddities of the metaphysics, the self-reproaches of the mystics and the devotees, and the darkness of Puritanism. Herrick rises to no spiritual heights nor does he sink into spiritual glooms. He is frankly for this world while it lasts, piously content with its good gifts. His naïveté is partly art, partly nature, or rather it is nature refined by art; for he is out and out an artist—the most perfect

specimen of the minor poet that England has ever known. He is purely a lyrist, and in his own vein he is really unsurpassed, whether in the English lyric or any other.—CARPENTER, FREDERIC IVES, 1897, *English Lyric Poetry,* 1500–1700, *Introduction, p.* liii.

Our own age has awarded the foremost place among Caroline lyrical poets to Robert Herrick, whose verses, after having been unaccountably neglected throughout the eighteenth century, are now represented in all selections of English poetry. . . . "Corinna going a-Maying," perhaps the best known of all Herrick's country poems, is one of the most perfect studies of idealized village life in the language. —MASTERMAN, J. HOWARD B., 1897, *The Age of Milton, pp.* 101, 102, 105.

Indeed within his own sphere, as laureate of pastoral England, and master of the lighter lyric, he has nothing to fear from comparison with the poets of any period of the literature.—PANCOAST, HENRY S., 1899, *Standard English Poems, Spenser to Tennyson, p.* 607.

A little over three hundred years ago England had given to her a poet of the very rarest lyrical quality, but she did not discover the fact for more than a hundred and fifty years afterward. The poet himself was aware of the fact at once, and stated it, perhaps not too modestly, in countless quatrains and couplets, which were not read, or, if read, were not much regarded at the moment. It has always been an incredulous world in this matter. So many poets have announced their arrival, and not arrived. . . . Robert Herrick is a great little poet. The brevity of his poems—for he wrote nothing *de longue haleine*—would place him among the minor singers; his workmanship places him among the masters. The Herricks were not a family of goldsmiths and lapidaries for nothing. The accurate touch of the artificer in jewels and costly metals was one of the gifts transmitted to Robert Herrick. Much of his work is as exquisite and precise as the chasing on a dagger-hilt by Cellini; the line has nearly always that vine-like fluency which seems impromptu, and is never the result of anything but austere labor.—ALDRICH, THOMAS BAILEY, 1900, *Poems of Robert Herrick, Introduction, pp.* xv, xl.

John Milton

1608–1674

John Milton, 1608–1674. Born, in London, 9 Dec. 1608. At St. Paul's School, 1620 (?)–25. Pensioner of Christ's Coll. Camb., 12 Feb. 1625; matric. 9 April 1625; B. A., 26 March 1629; M. A., 3 July 1632. Lived with his father at Horton, Bucks., July 1632 to April 1638. Travelled on continent, April 1638 to July 1639. On his return, settled in London and took pupils. Took active part in ecclesiastical controversy, 1641–42. Married (i.) Mary Powell, May (?) 1643; separated from her shortly afterwards; reconciled, 1645. Latin Secretary to Council of State, March 1649. Became blind, 1650. Wife died, 1652. Married (ii.) Catharine Woodcock, 12 Nov. 1656; she died, Feb. 1658. At Restoration, was arrested for treasonable publications, summer 1660; released soon afterwards. Married (iii.) Elizabeth Minshull, 24 Feb. 1663. Died, in London, 8 Nov. 1674. Buried in St. Giles's, Cripplegate. *Works:* "A Masque ('Comus') presented at Ludlow Castle" (anon.), "Lycidas" in "Justa Edouardo King Naufrago," 1638; "Of Reformation touching Church Discipline in England" (anon.), 1644; "Of Prelatical Episcopacy" (anon.), 1641; "Animadversions upon the Remonstrat's Defence against Smectymnuus" (anon.), 1641; "The Archbishop of Canterburie's Dream" (anon.), 1641; "The Reason of Church Government urged against Prelaty," 1641; Tyrannicall Government anatomized" (anon.), 1642; "An Apology against. . . . 'A Modest Confutation of the Animadversions' " (anon.), 1642; "News From Hell" (anon.), 1642; "The Doctrine and Discipline of Divorce" (anon.), 1643; "Of Education" (anon.), (1644); "Areopagitica," 1644; "Tetrachordon," 1645; "Colasterion" (anon.), 1645; "Poems," 1645; "The Tenure of Kings and Magistrates" (under initials: J. M.), 1649; "Observations on the Articles of Peace," 1649; " 'Εικονοκλαστης" (anon.), 1649; "The Grand Case of Conscience. . . . stated" (anon.), 1650; "Pro Populo Anglicano Defensio," 1650; "The Life and Reign of King Charles "(anon.), 1651; "A Letter written to a Gentleman in the Country," 1653; "Pro Populo Anglicano Defensio Secunda," 1654; "Prose Defensio contra Alexandrum Morum," 1655; "Scriptum Domini Protectoris. . . . contra Hispanos," 1655; "A Treatise of Civil Power in Ecclesiastical Causes," 1659; "Considerations touching the likeliest means to remove Hirelings out of the Church," 1659; "The Ready and Easy Way to Establish a Free Commonwealth" (anon.), 1659; "Brief Notes upon a late Sermon . . . by Mathew Griffith," 1660; "Paradise Lost," 1667; "Accidence commenc't Grammar" (anon.), 1669; "The History of Britain," 1670; "Artis Logicæ Plenior Institutio," 1670; "Paradise Regained . . . To which is added 'Samson Agonistes,' " 1671; "Poems, etc., upon several Occasions," 1673; "Of True Religion, etc." (under initials: J. M.), 1673; "Epistolarum Familiarum liber unus," 1674. *Posthumous:* "Literæ Pseudo-Senatus Anglicani," 1676; "Character of the Long Parliament" (possibly spurious), 1681; "A Brief History of Moscovia," 1682; "De Doctrina Christiana libri duo posthumi," 1825. He *translated:* Martin Bucer's "judgment concerning Divorce," 1644; "A Declaration or Letters Patent of the Election of this present King of Poland" (anon.), 1674; and edited: Raleigh's "Cabinet Council," 1658.—SHARP, R. FARQUHARSON, 1897, *A Dictionary of English Authors*, p. 199.

PERSONAL

I was born at London, of an honest family; my father was distinguished by the undeviating integrity of his life; my mother, by the esteem in which she was held, and the alms which she bestowed. My father destined me from a child to the pursuits of literature; and my appetite for knowledge was so voracious, that, from twelve years of age, I hardly ever left my studies, or went to bed before midnight. This primarily led to my loss of sight. My eyes were naturally weak, and I was subject to frequent head-aches; which, however, could not chill the ardour of my curiosity, or retard the progress of my improvement. My father had me daily instructed in the grammar-school, and by other masters at home. He then, after I had acquired a proficiency in various languages, and had made a considerable progress in philosophy, sent me to the University of Cambridge. Here I passed seven years in the usual course of instruction

JOHN MILTON

From a Miniature of the same size by
Faithorne, Anno 1667. Engraving
by T. Woolnoth.

and study, with the approbation of the good, and without any stain upon my character, till I took the degree of Master of Arts. After this I did not, as this miscreant feigns, run away into Italy, but of my own accord retired to my father's house, whither I was accompanied by the regrets of most of the fellows of the college, who shewed me no common marks of friendship and esteem. On my father's estate, where he had determined to pass the remainder of his days, I enjoyed an interval of uninterrupted leisure, which I entirely devoted to the perusal of the Greek and Latin classics; though I occasionally visited the metropolis, either for the sake of purchasing books, or of learning something new in mathematics or in music, in which I, at that time, found a source of pleasure and amusement. In this manner I spent five years till my mother's death. I then became anxious to visit foreign parts, and particularly Italy. My father gave me his permission, and I left home with one servant. —MILTON, JOHN, 1654, *Second Defence of the People of England.*

He married his first wife (Mary) Powell, of Fosthill, at Shotover, in Oxonshire. . . . Two opinions doe not well on the same boulster. She was a . . . royalist, and went to her mother to the king's quarters, neer Oxford. I have perhaps so much charity to her that she might not wrong his bed: but what man, especially contemplative, would like to have a young wife environ'd and storm'd by the sons of Mars, and those of the enemi partie? . . . He was a spare man. He was scarce so tall as I am— quaere, quot feet I am high: resp., of middle stature. He had abroun hayre. His complexion exceeding faire—he was so faire that they called him *the lady of Christ's College.* Ovall face. His eie a darke gray. He had a delicate tuneable voice, and had good skill. His father instructed him. He had an organ in his howse: he played on that most. Of a very cheerfull humour.—He would be chearfull even in his gowte-fitts, and sing. He was very healthy and free from all diseases: seldome tooke any physique (only sometimes he tooke manna): only towards his latter end he was visited with the gowte, spring and fall. He had a very good memorie; but I beleeve that his excellent

method of thinking and disposing did much to helpe his memorie.—AUBREY, JOHN, 1669–96, *Brief Lives,* ed. Clark, vol. II, pp. 64, 65, 67.

An Author that liv'd in the Reign of King *Charles* the Martyr. Had his Principles been as good as his Parts, he had been an Excellent Person; but his demerits towards his Sovereign, has very much sullied his Reputation.—LANGBAINE, GERARD, 1691, *An Account of the English Dramatick Poets, p. 375.*

He was frequenty visited in his house [in Petty France] by persons of quality, particularly my lady Ranelagh, whose son for some time he instructed; all learned foreigners of note, who could not pass out of the city without giving a visit to a person so eminent; and, lastly, by particular friends that had a high esteem for him— viz. Mr. Andrew Marvel; young Lawrence (the son of him that was president of Oliver's council), to whom there is a sonnet among the rest in his printed poems; Mr. Marchamont Needham, the writer of "Politicus;" but, above all, Mr. Cyriack Skinner, whom he honoured with two sonnets. . . . Those [daughters] he had by his first [wife] he made serviceable to him in that very particular in which he most wanted their service, and supplied his want of eyesight by their eyes and tongue; for, though he had daily about him one or other to read to him—some, persons of man's estate, who of their own accord greedily catched at the opportunity of being his readers, that they might as well reap the benefit of what they read to him as oblige him by the benefit of their reading; others, of younger years, sent by their parents to the same end—yet, excusing only the eldest daughter by reason of her bodily infirmity and difficult utterance of speech (which, to say truth, I doubt, was the principal cause of excusing her), the other two were condemned to the performance of reading and exactly pronouncing of all the languages of whatever book he should at one time or other think fit to peruse—viz. the Hebrew (and, I think, the Syriac), the Greek, the Latin, the Italian, Spanish, and French. All which sorts of books to be confined to read without understanding one word must needs be a trial of patience almost beyond endurance; yet it was endured by both for a time. , , , There [in

Jewin-street] he lived when he married his third wife, recommended to him by his old friend, Dr. Paget in Coleman Street.— PHILLIPS, EDWARD, 1694, *Memoir of Milton, prefixed to the English Edition of Letters of State.*

Understanding that the mediation used for my admittance to John Milton had succeeded so well_that I might come when I would, I hastened to London, and in the first place went to wait upon him. He received me courteously, as well for the sake of Dr. Paget, who introduced me, as of Isaac Penington, who recommended me; to both of whom he bore a good respect. And having inquired divers things of me, with respect to my former progression in learning, he dismissed me, to provide myself such accommodation as might be most suitable to my future studies. I went therefore and took myself a lodging as near his house, which was then in Jewin Street, as conveniently I could; and from thenceforward went every day in the afternoon, except on the first days of the week, and sitting by him in his dining-room, read to him in such books in the Latin tongue as he pleased to hear me read. At my first sitting to read to him, observing that I used the English pronunciation, he told me if I would have the benefit of the Latin tongue, not only to read and understand Latin authors, but to converse with foreigners, either abroad or at home, I must learn the foreign pronunciation. To this I consenting, he instructed me how to sound the vowels. . . . But this change of pronunciation proved a new difficulty to me. . . . He, on the other hand, perceiving with what earnest desire I pursued learning, gave me not only all the encouragement, but all the help he could. For, having a curious ear, he understood by my tone when I understood what I read, and when I did not; and accordingly would stop me, examine me, and open the most difficult passages to me. Thus went I on, for about six weeks' time, reading to him in the afternoons.—ELLWOOD, THOMAS, 1714, *The History of the Life of, Written by His own Hand, ed. Howells, pp.* 275, 276, 277.

An ancient clergyman of Dorsetshire, Dr. Wright, found John Milton in a small chamber hung with rusty green, sitting in an elbow-chair, and dressed neatly in black; pale but not cadaverous; his hands and fingers gouty and with chalk-stones. He used also to sit in a gray, coarse cloth coat, at the door of his house in Bunhill Fields, in warm sunny weather, to enjoy the fresh air; and so, as well as in his room, received the visits of people of distinguished parts as well as quality.— RICHARDSON, JONATHAN, 1734, *Explanatory Notes and Remarks on Milton's Paradise Lost.*

In his youth he is said to have been extremely handsome, and while he was a student at Cambridge, he was called "the Lady of Christ's-College," and he took notice of this himself in one of his Public Prolusions before that university; *"A quibusdam audivi nuper domina."* The colour of his hair was a light brown; the symmetry of his features exact; enlivened with an agreeable air, and a beautiful mixture of fair and ruddy. . . . Mr. Wood observes, that "his eyes were none of the quickest." His stature, as we find it measured by himself, did not exceed the middle-size; he was neither too lean, nor too corpulent; his limbs well proportioned, nervous, and active, serviceable in all respects to his exercising the sword, in which he much delighted, and wanted neither skill, nor courage, to resent an affront from men of the most athletic constitutions. In his diet he was abstemious; not delicate in the choice of his dishes; and strong liquors of all kinds were his aversion. Being too sadly convinced how much his health had suffered by night-studies in his younger years, he used to go early (seldom later than nine) to rest; and rose commonly in the summer at four, and in the winter at five in the morning; but when he was not disposed to rise at his usual hours, he always had one to read to him by his bed-side. At his first rising he had usually a chapter read to him out of the Hebrew bible; and he commonly studied all the morning till twelve, then used some exercise for an hour, afterwards dined, and after dinner played on the organ, and either sung himself, or made his wife sing, who, he said, had a good voice, but no ear, and then he went up to study again till six, when his friends came to visit him, and sat with him till eight. Then he went down to supper, which was usually olives and some light thing; and after supper he smoked his pipe, and drank a glass of water, and went to bed. When his blindness restrained him from other exercises, he had a machine to swing in for the preservation of his health; and diverted himself in his chamber with playing on an organ. He had a delicate ear and excellent voice, and great skill in vocal and instrumental music. His deportment was erect, open and affable; and his conversation easy, cheerful, and instructive. — Birch, Thomas, 1738–53, *An Historical and Critical Account of the Life and Writings of Mr. John Milton, vol.* i, *p.* lxxiii.

In his way of living he was an example of sobriety and temperance. He was very sparing in the use of wine or strong liquors of any kind. . . . He was likewise very abstemious in his diet, not fastidiously nice or delicate in his choice of dishes, but content with anything that was most in season, or easiest to be procured; eating and drinking (according to the distinction of the philosopher) that he might live, and not living that he might eat or drink. So that probably his gout descended by inheritance from one or other of his parents; or, if it was of his own acquiring, it must have been owing to his studious and sedentary life.—Newton, Thomas, 1749–51, *ed., Milton's Poetical Works, Life.*

I am ashamed to relate what I fear is true, that Milton was one of the last students in either university that suffered the public indignity of corporal correction. . . . Milton has the reputation of having been in his youth eminently beautiful, so as to have been called the Lady of his college. His hair, which was of light brown, parted at the foretop, and hung down upon his shoulders, according to the picture which he has given of Adam. He was, however, not of the heroic stature, but rather below the middle size, according to Mr. Richardson, who mentions him as having narrowly escaped from being *short and thick*. He was vigorous and active, and delighted in the exercise of the sword, in which he is related to have been eminently skilful. . . . His eyes are said never to have been bright; but if he was a dexterous fencer, they must have been once quick. His domestick habits, so far as they are known, were those of a severe student. He drank little strong drink of any kind, and fed

without excess in quantity, and in his earlier years without delicacy of choice. . . . Milton, who appears to have had a full conviction of the truth of Christianity, and to have regarded the Holy Scriptures with the profoundest veneration, to have been untainted by any heretical peculiarity of opinion, and to have lived in a confirmed belief of the immediate and occasional agency of Providence, yet grew old without any visible worship. In the distribution of his hours there was no hour of prayer, either solitary or with his household; omitting publick prayers, he omitted all.—Johnson, Samuel, 1779, *John Milton, Lives of the English Poets.*

Yea, our blind Poet, who in his later day,
Stood almost single; uttering odious truth—
Darkness before, and danger's voice behind,
Soul awful—if the earth has ever lodged
An awful soul—I seemed to see him here
Familiarly, and in his scholar's dress
Bounding before me, yet a stripling youth—
A boy, no better, with his rosy cheeks
Angelical, keen eye, courageous look,
And conscious step of purity and pride.
—Wordsworth, William, 1799–1805,
The Prelude, bk. iii.

His literature was immense. . . . With the Hebrew, and its two dialects, he was well acquainted; and of the Greek, Latin, Italian, French, and Spanish languages, he was a master. In Latin, Dr. Johnson observes, his skill was such as places him in the first rank of writers and criticks. In the Italian he was also particularly skilled. His "Sonnets" in that language have received the highest commendation from Italian criticks, both of his own and of modern times. If he had written generally in Italian, it has been supposed, by the late lord Orford, that he would have been the most perfect poet in modern language; for his own strength of thought would have condensed and hardened that speech to a proper degree. The Academy Della Crusca consulted him on the critical niceties of their language. In his early days indeed he had become deeply enamoured of "the two famous renowners of *Beatrice* and *Laura.*" It has been rightly remarked, that he read almost all authors, and improved by all: He himself relates, that his "round of study and reading was ceaseless."—Todd, Henry John, 1801–26, *Some Account of the Life and Writings of John Milton, p.* 346.

We have now completed the history of John Milton;—a man in whom were illustriously combined all the qualities that could adorn, or elevate the nature to which he belonged; a man, who at once possessed beauty of countenance, symmetry of form, elegance of manners, benevolence of temper, magnanimity and loftiness of soul, the brightest illumination of intellect, knowledge the most various and extended, virtue that never loitered in her career nor deviated from her course;—a man, who, if he had been delegated as the representative of his species to one of the superior worlds, would have suggested a grand idea of the human race, as of beings affluent with moral and intellectual treasure, who were raised and distinguished in the universe as the favourites and heirs of Heaven.—SYMMONS, CHARLES, 1809-10, *The Life of John Milton, p.* 593.

. . . Milton stood before him,
Gazing with reverent awe — Milton, his
   guest . . .
. . . Little then, did Galileo think whom he
   received;
That in his hand he held the hand of one
Who could requite him—who would spread
   his name
O'er lands and seas—great as himself, nay,
   greater.
—ROGERS, SAMUEL, 1822-30, *Italy, The Campagna of Florence.*

John Milton, the poet, the statesman, the philosopher, the glory of English literature, the champion and the martyr of English liberty. . . . Neither blindness, nor gout, nor age, nor penury, nor domestic afflictions, nor political disappointments, nor abuse, nor proscription, nor neglect, had power to disturb his sedate and majestic patience. His spirits do not seem to have been high, but they were singularly equable. His temper was serious, perhaps stern; but it was a temper which no sufferings could render sullen or fretful. Such as it was, when, on the eve of great events, he returned from his travels, in the prime of health and manly beauty, loaded with literary distinction and glowing with patriotic hopes, such it continued to be—when, after having experienced every calamity which is incident to our nature, old, poor, sightless, and disgraced, he retired to his hovel to die!—MACAULAY, THOMAS BABINGTON, 1825, *Milton, Edinburgh Review.*

Milton alone remained faithful to the memory of Cromwell. While minor authors, vile, perjured, bought by restored power, insulted the ashes of a great man at whose feet they had grovelled, Milton gave him an asylum in his genius, as in an inviolable temple. Milton might have been reinstated in office. His third wife (for he espoused two after the death of Mary Powell) beseeching him to accept his former place as Secretary, he replied, "You are a woman, and would like to keep your carriage; but I will die an honest man." Remaining a Republican, he wrapped himself in his principles, with his Muse and his poverty. He said to those who reproached him with having served a tyrant, "He delivered us from kings." Milton affirmed that he had only fought for the cause of God and of his country. One day, walking in St. James's Park, he suddenly heard repeated near him, "The king! the king!" "Let us withdraw," he said to his guide, "I never loved kings." Charles II. accosted the blind man. "Thus, Sir, has Heaven punished you for having conspired against my father." "Sire," he replied, "if the ills that afflict us in this world be the chastisements for our faults, your father must have been very guilty."—CHATEAUBRIAND, FRANÇOIS RENÉ, VICOMTE DE, 1837, *Sketches of English Literature, vol.* II, *p.* 80.

We have offered no apology for expanding to such length our commentary on the character of John Milton; who, in old age, in solitude, in neglect, and blind, wrote the "Paradise Lost"; a man whom labor or danger never deterred from whatever efforts a love of the supreme interests of man prompted. For are we not the better; are not all men fortified by the remembrance of the bravery, the purity, the temperance, the toil, the independence and the angelic devotion of this man, who, in a revolutionary age, taking counsel only of himself, endeavored, in his writings and in his life, to carry out the life of man to new heights of spiritual grace and dignity, without any abatement of its strength?—EMERSON, RALPH WALDO, 1838, *Milton.*

Indignant at every effort to crush the spirit, and to cheat it, in his own words, "of that liberty which rarefies and enlightens it like the influence of heaven," he proclaimed the rights of man as a rational immortal being, undismayed by menace and obloquy, amid a generation of servile and unprincipled sycophants. The blindness which excluded him from the things of earth opened to him more glorious and spiritualized conceptions of heaven, and aided him in exhibiting the full influence of those sublime truths which the privilege of free inquiry in religious matters had poured upon the mind. —PRESCOTT, WILLIAM HINCKLING, 1845–55, *Biographical and Critical Miscellanies.*

Perhaps no man ever inhabited more houses than our great epic poet, yet scarcely one of these now remains. . . . We come now to Milton's last house, the narrow house appointed for all living, in which he laid his bones beside those of his father. This was in the church of St. Giles, Cripplegate. He died on Sunday, the 8th of November, 1674, and was buried on the 12th. His funeral is stated to have been very splendidly and numerously attended. By the parish registry we find that he was buried in the chancel: "John Milton, gentleman. Consumption. Chancell. 12. Nov., 1674." Dr. Johnson supposed that he had no inscription, but Aubrey distinctly states that "when the two steppes to the communion-table were raysed in 1690, his stone was removed." Milton's grave remained a whole century without a mark to point out where the great poet lay, till in 1793 Mr. Whitbread erected a bust and an inscription to his memory. What is more, there is every reason to believe that his remains were, on this occasion of raising the chancel and removing the stone, disturbed. The coffin was disinterred and opened, and numbers of relic-hunters were eager to seize and convey off fragments of his bones. The matter at the time occasioned a sharp controversy, and the public were at length persuaded to believe that they were not the remains of Milton, but of a female, that by mistake had been thus treated. But when the workmen had the inscribed stone before them, and dug down directly below it, what doubt can there be that the remains were those of the poet? By an alteration in the church when it was repaired in 1682, that which was the old chancel ceased to be the present one, and the remains of Milton thus came to lie in the great central aisle.

The monument erected by Whitbread marks, as near as possible, the place. The bust is by Bacon. It is attached to a pillar, and beneath it is this inscription:

JOHN MILTON,
AUTHOR OF PARADISE LOST,
BORN DEC$^{R.}$ 1608
DIED NOV$^{R.}$ 1674.

His father, John Milton, died March, 1646. They were both interred in this church.

Samuel Whitbread posuit, 1793.
—HOWITT, WILLIAM, 1847, *Homes and Haunts of the Most Eminent British Poets, vol.* I, *pp.* 75, 115.

No one can read Milton's writings, or contemplate his life, without being persuaded that his first desire was the freedom, and through that, the happiness of his country.—MITFORD, JOHN, 1851–63, ed., *Works of John Milton, Life, vol.* I, *p.* cxxxii.

The best portraits of Milton represent him seated at the foot of an oak at sunset, his face turned towards the beams of the departing luminary, and dictating his verses to his well-beloved Deborah, listening attentively to the voice of her father; while his wife Elizabeth looks on him as Eve regarded her husband after her fault and punishment. His two younger daughters meanwhile gather flowers from the meadows, that he may inhale some of the odors of Eden which perfumed his dreams. Our thoughts turn involuntarily to the lot of that wife and daughters, after the death of the illustrious old man on whom they were attending; and the poet, thus brought back to our eyes again, becomes more interesting than the poem. Happy are they whose glory is watered with tears! Such reputation penetrates to the heart, and in the heart alone the poet's name becomes immortal.—LAMARTINE, ALPHONSE DE, 1854, *Memoirs of Celebrated Characters.*

With respect to the worldly circumstances of this great man, little is known with certainty. It is evident that during his travels, and after his return, the allowance made him by his father was liberal. It was adequate, we may see, to the support of himself and his two nephews, for it is not likely that his sister paid him anything for them. He must also have considered himself able to support a family, without keeping school, when he married Miss Powell. He of course inherited the bulk of his father's property, but of the amount of it we are ignorant; all we know is that it included the interest in his house in Bread-street. His losses were not inconsiderable. A sum of £2000, which he had invested in the Excise Office, was lost at the Restoration, as the Government refused to recognize the obligations of the Commonwealth; according to the account of his granddaughter, he lost another sum of £2000, by placing it in the hands of a money-scrivener; and he also lost at the Restoration a property of £60 a year out of the lands of the Dean and Chapter of Westminster, which he very probably had purchased. His house in Bread-street was destroyed by the Great Fire. The whole property which he left behind him, exclusive of his claim on the Powell family for his wife's fortune, and of his household goods, did not exceed £1500, including the produce of his library, a great part of which he is said to have disposed of before his death.—KEIGHTLEY, THOMAS, 1855, *An Account of the Life, Opinions and Writings of John Milton, p. 75.*

He stands before us as perhaps the grandest and mightiest individual man in literature,—a man who transmuted all thoughts, passions, acquisitions, and aspirations into the indestructible substance of personal character.—WHIPPLE, EDWIN P., 1857–66, *The English Mind, Character and Characteristic Men, p. 194.*

He attends no church, belongs to no communion, and has no form of worship in his family; notable circumstances, which we may refer, in part at least, to his blindness, but significant of more than that. His religion was of the spirit, and did not take kindly to any form. Though the most Puritan of the Puritans, he had never stopped long in the ranks of any Puritan party, or given satisfaction to Puritan ecclesiastics and theologians. In his youth he had loved the night; in his old age he loves the pure sunlight of early morning as it glimmers on his sightless eyes. The music which had been his delight since childhood has still its charm, and he either sings or plays on the organ or bass violin every day. In his grey coat, at the door of his house in Bunhill Fields, he sits on clear afternoons; a proud, ruggedly genial old man, with sharp satiric touches in his talk, the untunable fibre in him to the last. Eminent foreigners come to see him; friends approach reverently, drawn by the splendour of his discourse. It would range, one can well imagine, in glittering freedom, like "arabesques of lightning," over all ages and all literatures. He was the prince of scholars; a memory of superlative power waiting as handmaid on the queenliest imagination. The whole spectacle of ancient civilisation, its cities, its camps, its landscapes, was before him. There he sat in his grey coat, like a statue cut in granite. He recanted nothing, repented of nothing. England had made a sordid failure, but he had not failed. His soul's fellowship was with the great Republicans of Greece and Rome, and with the Psalmist and Isaiah and Oliver Cromwell.—BAYNE, PETER, 1878, *The Chief Actors in the Puritan Revolution, p. 345.*

I do not find that Milton, though he wrote against paid ministers as hirelings, ever expressly formulated an opinion against ministers as such. But as has already been hinted, there grew up in him, in the last period of his life, a secret sympathy with the mode of thinking which came to characterise the Quaker sect. Not that Milton adopted any of their peculiar fancies. He affirms categorically the permissibility of oaths, of military service, and requires that women should keep silence in the congregation. But in negativing all means of arriving at truth except the letter of Scripture interpreted by the inner light, he stood upon the same platform as the followers of George Fox. —PATTISON, MARK, 1879, *Milton (English Men of Letters), p. 148.*

As a man, too, not less than as a poet, Milton has a side of unsurpassable grandeur. A master's touch is the gift of nature. Moral qualities, it is commonly thought, are in our own power. Perhaps the germs of such qualities are in their greater or less strength as much a part of our natural constitution as the sense for style. The range open to our own will and power, however, in developing and establishing them, is evidently much larger. Certain high moral dispositions Milton had from nature, and he sedulously trained and developed them until they became habits of great power.—ARNOLD, MATTHEW, 1879, *Mixed Essays, p. 269.*

On the 4th of August, 1790, according to a small volume written by Philip Neve, Esq. (of which two editions were published in the same year), Milton's coffin was removed and his remains exhibited to the public on the 4th and 5th of that month. Mr. George Stevens, the great editor of Shakspere, who justly denounced the indignity intended, not offered, to the great Puritan poet's remains by Royalist Landsharks, satisfied himself that the corpse was that of a woman of fewer years than Milton. . . . Mr. Stevens's assurance gives us good reason for believing that Mr. Philip Neve's indignant protest is only good in general, and that Milton's hallowed reliques still rest undisturbed within their peaceful shrine.—INGLEBY, C. M., 1883, *Shakspere's Bones.*

Although the "Prince of Poets" was born and died in London, received part of his education in London, was married frequently in London, and lived in many houses in the metropolis, there is left today hardly a trace of anything that he has touched, or that is in any way associated with him. Even his grave was desecrated, and the precise spot in which his bones lie cannot now be discovered.—HUTTON, LAURENCE, 1885, *Literary Landmarks of London, p. 210.*

On the whole, Milton's character was not an amiable one, nor even wholly estimable. It is probable that he never in the course of his whole life did anything that he considered wrong; but unfortunately, examples are not far to seek of the facility with which desire can be made to confound itself with deliberate approval. That he was an exacting, if not a tyrannical husband and father, that he held in the most peremptory and exaggerated fashion the doctrine of the superiority of man to woman, that his egotism in a man who had actually accomplished less would be held ludicrous and half disgusting, that his faculty of appreciation beyond his own immediate tastes and interests was small, that his intolerance surpassed that of an inquisitor, and that his controversial habits and manners outdid the license even of that period of controversial abuse,—these are propositions which I cannot conceive to be disputed by any competent critic aware of the facts. If they have ever been denied, it is merely from the amiable but uncritical point of view which blinks all a man's personal defects in consideration of his literary genius. That we cannot afford to do here, especially as Milton's personal defects had no small influence on his literary character.—SAINTSBURY, GEORGE, 1887, *History of Elizabethan Literature, p. 317.*

There is something very fascinating in the records we have of Milton's one visit to the Continent. A more impressive Englishman never left our shores. Sir Philip Sidney perhaps approaches him nearest. Beautiful beyond praise, and just sufficiently conscious of it to be careful never to appear at a disadvantage, dignified in manners, versed in foreign tongues, yet full of the ancient learning, —a gentleman, a scholar, a poet, a musician, and a Christian,—he moved about in a leisurely manner from city to city, writing Latin verses for his hosts and Italian sonnets in their ladies' albums, buying books and music, and creating, one cannot doubt, an all too flattering impression of an English Protestant.—BIRRELL, AUGUSTINE, 1887, *Obiter Dicta, Second Series, p. 14.*

The new world honors him whose lofty plea
  For England's freedom made her own more sure,
Whose song, immortal as its theme, shall be
  Their common freehold while both worlds endure.
—WHITTIER, JOHN GREENLEAF, 1888, *Milton, Inscription on the Memorial Window in St. Margaret's Church, Westminster, the gift of George W. Childs, of America.*

The vision we have of him is that of a blind, fresh-complexioned, and lightish-haired man, of middle stature or somewhat less, and of slender figure, dressed still usually in a grey suit, and with a small silver-hilted sword by his side, piloted about by some boy or more mature companion, partly for exercise and partly for calls at favourite book-shops. Blind though he was, it was only by his gait that you knew it, for his eyes were clear and without speck or blemish. Nor, though the face was sad and careworn, did it tell the age at which he had arrived. From the still lightish hair and a tinge of colour still in the fair complexion, you would have judged him younger than he was.—MASSON, DAVID, 1893, *In the Footsteps of the Poets, p. 98.*

Milton was nicknamed the "lady" at college, from his delicate complexion and slight make. He was, however, a good fencer, and thought himself a "match for any one." Although respected by the authorities, his proud and austere character probably kept him aloof from much of the coarser society of the place. He shared the growing aversion to the scholasticism against which one of his exercises is directed. Like Henry More, who entered Christ's in Milton's last year, he was strongly attracted by Plato, although he was never so much a philosopher as a poet. He already considered himself as dedicated to the utterance of great thoughts, and to the strictest chastity and self-respect, on the ground that he who would "write well hereafter in laudable things ought himself to be a true poem." —STEPHEN, LESLIE, 1894, *Dictionary of National Biography, vol.* XXXVIII, *p.* 25.

In Milton's life, as in Milton's prose writings, occur passages which are not admirable, which are indeed the reverse of admirable. The student of literature, we may presume, is a lover of beauty, and the temptation with him to shirk the ugly passages of a life is a temptation easily understood. Here he may say, as Mr. Matthew Arnold has said of Shelley, here, in "Comus" and "Samson," here in the Council Chamber sheltering Davenant from dangers incurred through his Royalist ardours, here, in company with Lawrence, listening to the lute well touched, is the Milton we desire to know, the Milton who delights. Let us, at least as long as we are able, avert our eyes from the Milton who disgusts, from the unamiable Milton, the Milton who calls his opponent "an idiot by breeding and a solicitor by presumption," the Milton who helped to embitter his daughters' lives, and remembered them as "unkind children" in his will. What is gained by forcing this disgusting Milton on our attention? We choose, if we can, to retain a charming picture of the great poet. The delightful Milton is the true Milton after all. Ah, give us back the delightful Milton!—DOWDEN, EDWARD, 1895, *New Studies in Literature, p.* 442.

But he is more than idealist or artist— he was a superlatively noble, brave, truly conscientious man, who could never have intentionally done a mean thing; who was pure and clean in thought, speech, and action; who was patriotic to the point of sublime self-sacrifice; who loved his neighbor to the point of risking his life for republican principles of liberty; who, finally, spent his every moment as in the sight of the God he both worshiped and loved. Possessed of sublime powers, his thought was to make the best use of them to the glory of God and the good of his fellow-man. We may not think that he always succeeded; but who among the men of our race save Washington is such an exemplar of high and holy and effective purpose? Beside his white and splendid flame nearly all the other great spirits of earth burn yellow, if not low. Truly, as Wordsworth said, his soul was like a star; and, if it dwelt apart, should we therefore love it the less? It is more difficult to love the sublime than to love the approximately human, but the necessity for such love is the essence of the first and greatest commandment.—TRENT, WILLIAM P., 1899, *John Milton, A Short Study of his Life and Works, p.* 55.

It was fortunate for the harmonious development of Milton's genius that during the critical years between youth and manhood, years which in most men's lives are fullest of turmoil and dubiety, he was enabled to live a life of quiet contemplation. His nature was fiercely polemical, and without this period of calm set between his college life and his life as a public disputant, the sweeter saps of his mind would never have come to flower and fruitage. It was particularly fortunate, too, that this interim should be passed in the country, where the lyric influences were softest, where all that was pastoral and genial in his imagination was provoked. The special danger of men of his stamp, in whom will and doctrine are constantly president over impulse, is the loss of plasticity, the stiffening of imagination in its bonds.—MOODY, WILLIAM VAUGHN, 1899, *ed., Poetical Works of Milton, Life, Cambridge ed., p.* xiii.

COMUS

1634–37

MY LORD: This poem, which received its first occasion of birth from your self and others of your noble family, and much honour from your own person in the performance, now returns again to make a finall dedication of itself to you. Although not openly acknowledged by the author, yet it is a legitimate offspring, so lovely, and so much desired, that the often copying of it hath tired my pen to give my severall friends satisfaction, and brought me to a necessity of producing it to the publike view, and now to offer it up in all rightful devotion to those fair hopes and rare endowments of your much-promising youth, which gave a full assurance, to all that knew you, of a future excellence.—LAWES, HENRY, 1637, *To Lord-Viscount Bracly, First ed.*

Since your going, you have charged me with new obligations, both for a very kinde letter from you, dated the sixth of this month, and for a charity piece of entertainment which came therewith,—wherein I should much commend the tragical part if the lyrical did not ravish me with a certain Dorique delicacy in your songs and odes; whereunto I must plainly confess to have seen nothing parallel in our language.—WOTTON, SIR HENRY, 1638, *Letter to John Milton, April* 13.

On the whole, whether "Comus" be or be not deficient as a drama, whether it is considered as an epic drama, a series of lines, a mask, or a poem, I am of opinion that Milton is here only inferior to his own "Paradise Lost."—WARTON, THOMAS, 1785, *ed., Milton's Poems on Several Occasions, p.* 263.

A work more truly poetical is rarely found; allusions, images, and descriptive epithets, embellish almost every period with lavish decoration. As a series of lines, therefore, it may be considered as worthy of all the admiration with which the votaries have received it.—JOHNSON, SAMUEL, 1779, *John Milton, Lives of the English Poets.*

Even Milton deigned to contribute one of his most fascinating poems to the service of the drama; and, notwithstanding the severity of his puritanic tenets, "Comus" could only have been composed by one who felt the full enchantment of the theatre.—SCOTT, SIR WALTER, 1805, *The Life of John Dryden.*

Can there be a test of merit more indisputable than this?—for "Comus," though by no means faultless as a Masque, has to boast of a poetry more rich and imaginative than is to be found in any

other composition save "The Tempest" of Shakspeare.—DRAKE, NATHAN, 1817, *Shakspeare and his Times, vol.* II, *p.* 579.

It is, certainly, the noblest performance of the kind which exists in any language.—MACAULAY, THOMAS BABINGTON, 1825, *Milton, Edinburgh Review; Critical and Miscellaneous Essays.*

What sensibility breathes in the descriptions of the benighted Lady's singing, by Comus and the Spirit.—CHANNING, WILLIAM ELLERY, 1826, *Remarks on the Character and Writings of John Milton.*

A young girl and her brothers are benighted and separated as they pass through a forest in Herefordshire. How meagre is this solitary fact! how barren a paragraph would it have made for the Herefordshire journal,—had such a journal been then in existence! Submit it to Milton, and beautiful is the form which it assumes. Then rings that wood with the jocund revelry of Comus and his company; and the maiden draws near, in the strength of unblemished chastity, and her courage waxes strong as she sees

"A sable cloud
Turn forth her silver lining on the night"—
and she calls upon Echo to tell her of the flowery cave which hides her brothers, and Echo betrays her to the enchanter. Then comes the spirit from the "starry threshold of Jove's court," and in shepherd-weeds leads on the brothers to her rescue; and the necromancer is put to flight, but not till he has bound up the lady in fetters of stone; and Sabrina hastens from under her "translucent wave" to dissolve the spell—and again they all three bend their happy steps back to the roof of their fathers. This is not extravagant rhapsody—the tale is still actually preserved; but it is preserved like a fly in amber. The image is a mere thing of wood, but Milton enshrines it, and it becomes an object of worship. —SOUTHEY, ROBERT, 1827, *Todd's Edition of Milton, Quarterly Review, vol.* 36, *p.* 45.

One of the last and loveliest radiations of the dramatic spirit, which seemed almost to live its life out in about half a century of English literature, beginning in the times of Queen Elizabeth, and ending in those of Charles the First. . . . Of "Comus," I think, it might be said, as truly as of any poem in the language, that it is admirably adapted to inspire a real feeling for poetry. It abounds with so much of true imagination, such attractiveness of fancy, such grace of language and of metre, and withal contains so much thought and wisdom wherewith to win a mind unused to the poetic processes, that were I asked what poem might best be chosen to awaken the imagination to a healthful activity, I would point to Milton's "Comus," as better fitted than almost any other for the purpose.—REED, HENRY, 1855, *Lectures on English Literature, from Chaucer to Tennyson, pp.* 189, 190.

With these sounds left on the ear, and a final glow of angelic light on the eye, the performance ends, and the audience rises and disperses through the castle. The castle is now a crumbling ruin, along the ivy-clad walls and through the dark passages of which the visitor clambers or gropes his way, disturbing the crows and the martlets in their recesses; but one can stand yet in the doorway through which the parting guests of that night descended into the inner court; and one can see where the stage was, on which the sister was lost by her brothers, and Comus revelled with his crew, and the lady was fixed as marble by enchantment, and Sabrina arose with her water-nymphs, and the swains danced in welcome of the earl, and the Spirit gloriously ascended to its native heaven. More mystic it is to leave the ruins, and, descending one of the winding streets that lead from the castle into the valley of the Teme, to look upwards to castle and town seen as one picture, and, marking more expressly the three long pointed windows that gracefully slit the chief face of the wall towards the north, to realize that it was from that ruin, and from those windows in the ruin, that the verse of "Comus" was first shook into the air of England. Much as Milton wrote afterwards, he never wrote anything more beautiful, more perfect than "Comus."—MASSON, DAVID, 1858, *The Life of John Milton, vol.* I, *ch.* vii.

The sublimity of Milton's genius—the quality which, in the literature of his own country at all events, so pre-eminently distinguishes him as a poet—shines forth with marvellous fulness in this glorious work of his youth. The execution falls but little short of the conception. The lyric portions, although perhaps Macaulay goes too far in describing them as completely overshadowing the dramatic, are among the poet's noblest verse; and the dialogue, though its versification is less stately and its diction less ample than that of *Paradise Lost,* which indeed almost precludes dramatic declamation, rises at the climax of the moral interest—in the argument between Comus and the Lady—to almost matchless beauty. Indeed there may be those who cannot suppress a wish that Milton had always adhered to this earlier and easier treatment of his favourite metre—easier I mean to hands under which language passed into combinations "musical, as is Apollo's lute."—WARD, ADOLPHUS WILLIAM, 1875-99, *A History of English Dramatic Literature, vol.* III, *p.* 200.

The tale is told beautifully, simply; without plot or any artifice; and with no regard to superficial probabilities. Frankly discarding everything of the drama, except its form, the poet does not stoop, as, within certain limits, the successful dramatist must, to be a literary mocking-bird. Aloft on his perch, like a nightingale, he fills the grove with his music, varying his note as the subject varies, but always with the same volume of sound and the same rich and mellow tone. None of the masters of English poetry, Milton's predecessors, not Chaucer, not Spenser, not Shakespeare even, had done much to detract from the originality, or to herald the perfection of Comus. Chaucer's blank verse is not to be mentioned with that of Milton.—BAYNE, PETER, 1878, *The Chief Actors in the Puritan Revolution, p.* 309.

It is moreover raised above an ethical poem by its imaginative form and power; and its literary worth enables us to consider it, if we choose, apart from its dramatic form. Its imagination, however, sinks at times, and one can scarcely explain this otherwise than by saying that the Elizabethan habit of fantastic metaphor clung to Milton at this time. When he does fall, the fall is made more remarkable by the soaring strength of his loftier flight and by the majesty of the verse. Nothing can be worse in conception than the comparison of night to a thief who shuts up, for the sake of his felony, the stars whose lamps burn everlasting oil in his dark lantern. The better it is carried out and the finer the verse, the worse it is. And yet it is instantly followed by the great passage about the fears of night, the fantasies and airy tongues that syllable men's names, and by the glorious appeal to conscience, faith, and God, followed in its turn by the fantastic conceit of the cloud that turns out its silver lining on the night. This is the Elizabethan weakness and strength, the mixture of gold and clay, the want of that art-sensitiveness which feels the absurd: and Milton, even in "Paradise Lost," when he had got further from his originals, falls into it not unfrequently. It is a fault which runs through a good deal of his earlier work, it is more seen in "Comus" than elsewhere; but it was the fault of that poetic age.—BROOKE, STOPFORD, 1879, *Milton (Classical Writers), p.* 24.

The beautiful soul makes beautiful the outward form; the base act debases the soul of him who commits it. This was Milton's highest message to the world. This was the witness of Puritanism at its best. This was "the sage and serious doctrine of virginity," of that singleness of heart and spirit which is the safeguard of purity in marriage or out of marriage. Between the ideal of womanhood formed by Milton in his youth and that of even such a man as Massinger there is a great gulf. To Milton the world is a place in which the lady can break the spells of Comus by the very force of innocence. To Massinger it is a place to be shunned and avoided as altogether evil. His Camiola can only find rest by its renunciation.— GARDINER, SAMUEL R., 1883, *History of England from the Accession of James I. to The Outbreak of the Civil War, vol.* VII, *p.* 337.

His greatest work, if scale and merit are considered. . . . The versification, as even Johnson saw, is the versification of "Paradise Lost," and to my fancy at any rate it has a spring, a variety, a sweep and rush of genius, which are but rarely present later. As for its beauty in parts, *quis vituperavit?* It is impossible to single out passages, for the whole is golden. The entering address of Comus, the song "Sweet Echo," the descriptive speech of the Spirit, and the magnificent eulogy of the "sun-clad power of chastity," would be the most beautiful things where all is beautiful, if the unapproachable "Sabrina fair" did not come later, and were not sustained before and after, for nearly two hundred lines of pure nectar. If poetry could be taught by the reading of it, then indeed the critic's advice to a poet might be limited to this: "Give your days and nights to the reading of Comus."—SAINTSBURY, GEORGE, 1887, *History of Elizabethan Literature, pp.* 318, 321.

Judged simply as a masque, "Comus" is perhaps inferior to some of Ben Jonson's. It is overweighted with moral teaching and lacks the lightening influence of humour. But Milton's genius overflowed the limits of its appointed task, and "Comus" remains a splendid protest, at an hour when such a protest was needed the most, on behalf of a reasonable life. For if "Comus" is the expression of the distaste with which Milton regarded the growing licence of Cavalier society, its production is no less clearly a repudiation of the doctrines of Prynne and the moroser Puritans, to whom the drama was an unholy thing.—MASTERMAN, J. HOWARD B., 1897, *The Age of Milton, p.* 16.

Many years ago, on a summer evening, I wandered through the ruins of Ludlow Castle, in the West of England, where in 1634 the great Earl of Bridgewater, Lord President of Wales, celebrated his entrance into office. The castle has its own wall separate from the wall of Ludlow town, from which town the visitor passes to the castle over moat and drawbridge. The immense thickness of the walls, and the strength of the position on a rocky promontory at the confluence of two beautiful streams, were enough of themselves to attract interest. But the goal to which every foot now tends is the great banquet-hall, now dismantled, where, as a part of the pomp and pageantry of the earl's inauguration, Milton's Masque, entitled "Comus," was first represented. I could imagine the end of the hall turned into a stage; a mimic forest; the young daughter of the house playing the part of the lady, lost in the thickets of the wood; the necromancer and his rout of monsters with heads of beasts and bodies of men; the "barbarous dissonance of Bacchus and his revelers;" the temptation of innocence; the invocation of help; the triumph of virtue. When that Masque was first acted, Milton was a youth unknown, and the castle honored him. Two hundred and fifty years have passed since then, and now it is Milton who gives to Ludlow Castle all its honor. To the pure ambition which that early poem breathed, the poet was true through all his life, and, in spite of French critics, who make a mock at sin and cannot understand how art and faith can ever dwell together, the words of the Attendant Spirit in "Comus" still express, to those who have ears to hear, the mission of his poetry:

Before the starry threshold of Jove's court
My mansion is.

—STRONG, AUGUSTUS HOPKINS, 1897, *The Great Poets and Their Theology, p.* 276.

LYCIDAS
1638

One of the poems on which much praise has been bestowed, is "Lycidas;" of which the diction is harsh, the rhymes uncertain, and the numbers unpleasing. What beauty there is we must, therefore, seek in the sentiments and images. It is not to be considered as the effusion of real passion; for passion runs not after remote allusions and obscure opinions. . . . In this poem there is no nature, for there is nothing new. Its form is that of a pastoral,—easy, vulgar, and therefore disgusting: whatever images it can supply are long ago exhausted, and its inherent improbability always forces dissatisfaction on the mind. . . . This poem has yet a grosser fault. With these trifling fictions are mingled the most awful and sacred truths, such as ought never to be polluted with such irreverend combinations. The shepherd, likewise, is now a feeder of sheep, and afterwards an ecclesiastical pastor, a superintendent of a Christian flock. Such equivocations are always unskilful: but here they are indecent, and at least approach to impiety, —of which, however, I believe the writer not to have been conscious. Such is the power of reputation justly acquired, that its blaze drives away the eye from nice examination. Surely no man could have fancied that he read "Lycidas" with pleasure had he not known its author.— JOHNSON, SAMUEL, 1779, *John Milton, Lives of the English Poets.*

"Lycidas,"—though highly poetical,—I agree, with Jonson, breathes little sincere

sorrow, and is therefore essentially defective as a Monody.—GREEN, THOMAS, 1779–1810, *Diary of a Lover of Literature.*

In "Lycidas" there is perhaps more poetry than sorrow. But let us read it for its poetry. It is true that passion plucks no berries from the myrtle and ivy, nor calls upon Arethus and Mincius, nor tells of rough satyrs with cloven heel. But poetry does this; and in the hands of Milton does it with a peculiar and irresistible charm. —WARTON, THOMAS, 1785, *ed., Milton's Poems on Several Occasions, p.* 36.

Of all Milton's smaller poems, "Lycidas" is the greatest favourite with me. I cannot agree to the charge which Dr. Johnson has brought against it of pedantry and want of feeling. It is the first emanation of classical sentiment in a youthful scholar,—"most musical, most melancholy!" A certain tender gloom overspreads it, a wayward abstraction, a forgetfulness of his subject in the serious reflections that arise out of it. The gusts of passion come and go like the sounds of music borne on the wind. The loss of the friend whose death he laments seem to have recalled, with double force, the reality of those speculations which they had indulged together; we are transported to classic ground, and a mysterious strain steals responsive on the ear while we listen to the poet

"with eager thought warbling his Doric lay."
—HAZLITT, WILLIAM, 1818, *Lectures on the English Poets, Appendix.*

It has been said that this is not the natural mode of expressing passion—that where it is real, its language is less figurative—and that "where there is leisure for fiction there is little grief." In general this may be true; in the case of Milton its truth may be doubted. . . . The mind of Milton was perfect fairy-land; and every thought which entered it, whether grave or gay, magnificent or mean, quickly partook of a fairy form.— SOUTHEY, ROBERT, 1827, *Todd's Edition of Milton, Quarterly Review, vol.* 36, *p.* 46.

The common *metre* of six accents, which spread so widely during the sixteenth century, seldom tolerated a verse with a compound section. The reluctance to admit these verses was strengthened by the example of Drayton, who rigidly excluded them from the "Polyolbion." There are, however, a few poems, in which they are admitted freely enough to give a peculiar character to the rhythm. One of these poems is the "Elegy" written by Brysket, (though generally ascribed to Spenser), on the death of Sir Philip Sidney. It has very little poetical merit, but deserves attention, as having undoubtedly been in Milton's eye, when he wrote his "Lycidas." From it Milton borrowed his irregular rhimes, and that strange mixture of Christianity and Heathenism, which shocked the feelings and roused the indignation of Johnson. It may be questioned, if the peculiarity in the meter can fairly be considered as a blemish. Like endings, recurring at uncertain distances, impart a wildness and an appearance of negligence to the verse, which suits well with the character of elegy. But to bring in St. Peter hand in hand with a pagan deity is merely ludicrous; it was the taste of the age, and that is all that can be urged in its excuse. Still, however, the beauties of this singular poem may well make us tolerant of even greater absurdity. No work of Milton has excited warmer admiration, or called forth more strongly the zeal of the partizan.—GUEST, EDWIN, 1838, *A History of English Rhythms, vol.* I, *p.* 274.

For stately discrimination of language, "Lycidas" is a model unsuperseded to the present day.—ROSSETTI, WILLIAM MICHAEL, 1878, *Lives of Famous Poets, p* 67.

"Lycidas" appeals not only to the imagination, but to the educated imagination. There is no ebb and flow of poetical power as in "Comus"; it is an advance on all his previous work, and it fitly closes the poetic labour of his youth. It is needless to analyse it, and all criticism is weaker than the poem itself. Yet we may say that one of its strange charms is its solemn undertone rising like a religious chaunt through the elegiac musick; the sense of a stern national crisis in the midst of its pastoral mourning; the sense of Milton's grave force of character among the flowers and fancies of the poem; the sense of the Christian religion pervading the classical imagery. We might say that these things are ill-fitted to each other. So they would be, were not the art so fine and the poetry so over-mastering; were they not fused together by genius into a whole so that

the unfitness itself becomes fascination.— BROOKE, STOPFORD, 1879, *Milton* (*Classical Writers*), *p.* 26.

In "Lycidas" (1637) we have reached the high-water mark of English poesy and of Milton's own production. A period of a century and a half was to elapse before poetry in England seemed, in Wordsworth's "Ode on Immortality" (1807), to be rising again toward the level of inspiration which it had once attained in "Lycidas." . . . "Lycidas" opens up a deeper vein of feeling, a patriot passion so vehement and dangerous that, like that which stirred the Hebrew prophet, it is compelled to veil itself from power, or from sympathy, in utterance made purposely enigmatical.—PATTISON, MARK, 1879, *Milton* (*English Men of Letters*), *pp.* 27, 28.

Mr. Arnold, like everyone else who speaks with authority on such matters, is horrified when Dr. Johnson bluntly condemns "Lycidas." Now I could read over the "Allegro" and "Penseroso" a thousand times without tiring of them. "Comus," "Paradise Regained," the other secondary poems, all of them, give me great pleasure, though in different degrees; but as for "Lycidas," well, I say ditto to old Sam. In the first place the kind of idyll is not to my taste. If a poet really sorrows over the death of a friend to that degree that he cannot, as a relief to the soul, refrain from pouring out his sorrow in song, I think his utterance should be natural and straightforward; he should not speak in a falsetto tone, or overlay his theme with classical affectations. On the other hand, if the grief is only a half grief, conjured up by the imagination to play with like a toy, then, in my opinion, the bard had better hold his tongue. In the second place, the jumbling together of Christian and heathen traditions jars upon me just as it jarred upon the tough old dictionary-maker. Nay, besides all this, "Lycidas" appears to me not so much a spontaneous outburst as a self-appointed task. One of Milton's editors tells us that Mr. King's friends— Milton being one of those friends—agreed to write, and bind up together, a lot of verses on his death, but that when "Lycidas" made its appearance, it proved so much more important than all the other poems put together, that it was withdrawn from the book, to be afterwards separately published; and even now, I think, traces of the original business-like arrangement are to be found in the elegy as we have it.—DOYLE, SIR FRANCIS HASTINGS, 1887, *Reminiscences and Opinions, p.* 184.

There are indeed blotches in it. The speech of Peter, magnificently as it is introduced, and strangely as it has captivated some critics, who seem to think that anything attacking the Church of England must be poetry, is out of place, and in itself is obscure, pedantic, and grotesque. There is some over-classicism, and the scale of the piece does not admit the display of quite such sustained and varied power as in "Comus." But what there is, is so exquisite that hardly can we find fault with Mr. Pattison's hyperbole when he called "Lycidas" the "highwater-mark of English poetry." Highwater mark even in the physical world is a variable limit. Shakespere constantly, and some other poets here and there in short passages go beyond Milton. But in the same space we shall nowhere find anything that can outgo the passage beginning "Alas what boots it," down to "head of thine," and the whole conclusion from "Return Alpheus." For melody of versification, for richness of images, for curious felicity of expression, these cannot be surpassed.—SAINTSBURY, GEORGE, 1887, *History of Elizabethan Literature, p.* 322.

A perfect poem.—PATER, WALTER, 1888, *Appreciations, p.* 14.

The flowers that we lay upon a tomb
Are withered by the morrow,—ere the crowd
Which for a moment ceased its hum, and bowed
Its head, as Death flew by and made a gloom,
Resumes its whirl.　And scarcely longer bloom
The sculptured wreathes with which a tomb more proud,
In some pale minster, may have been endowed;
For marble petals share the common doom.
But thou canst twine the wreaths that never die;
And something tells me thou wilt stay behind
When I am gone; I know it, I know not why.
The sea-gull's scream, the wailing of the wind,
The ocean's roar, sound like Death's prophecy:
I fain would have a garland thou hadst twined.
—LEE-HAMILTON, EUGENE, 1888, *Lycidas to Milton* (1637), *Imaginary Sonnets.*

"Lycidas" can only just be drawn within a very liberal definition of lyrical verse, but fortunately the best definition is a wide one, and the poem can be quoted of which Tennyson said that the appreciation of it was a touchstone of poetic taste. —CRAWFURD, OSWALD, 1896, *ed., Lyrical Verse from Elizabeth to Victoria, Note, p.* 428.

"Lycidas" is the elegy of much more than Edward King; it is the last note of the inspiration of an age that was passing away. It is redolent of the "sweet mournfulness of the Spenserian time, upon whose joys Death is the only intruder." No such elegy was to adorn our English literature until "two hundred years after." Shelley and Matthew Arnold produced the two elegiac poems which alone in our language deserve to rank with Milton's—for the wider scope of "In Memoriam" removes it from this category. "Thyrsis" excels "Lycidas" in the expression of chastened sorrow and tender recollection, but Matthew Arnold loved Clough and Oxford as Milton never loved King of Cambridge. "Adonaïs" is charged with deeper thought and more harmonious passion; but both owe to "Lycidas" a debt which "Lycidas" owes to no other poem.—MASTERMAN, J. HOWARD B., 1897, *The Age of Milton, p.* 24.

"Lycidas" has a beauty and passion unknown to its Alexandrian predecessors, and it has not a touch of their oriental effeminacy and licentiousness. . . . The rhythm is varied, and flows now in leaping waves, now in long rolling billows that carry all before them, like the surging periods of "Paradise Lost." There is probably no short poem in the language the rhythm of which has been more deservedly praised and studied, or more despaired of by other poets. Milton's mastery of rhythm, remarkable from the first, almost culminated in "Lycidas," in spite of the fact that he was there subjected (practically for the last time) to what he afterward called "the troublesome and modern boundage of riming."—TRENT, WILLIAM P., 1899, *John Milton, A Short Study of His Life and Works, p.* 140.

Of the language of "Lycidas" perhaps the less said the better, for no analysis can hope to capture its secret.—MOODY, WILLIAM VAUGHN, 1899, *ed., Poetical Works of Milton, Cambridge ed., p.* 60.

PARADISE LOST
1667

Paradise lost. | A | Poem | written in | Ten Books | By John Milton. | Licensed and Entred according | to Order. | London | Printed, and are to be sold by Peter Parker | under Creed Church neer Aldgate; And by | Robert Boulter at the Turks Head in Bishopsgate-street; | And Matthias Walker, under St. Dunstons Church | in Fleet-street, 1667.— TITLE PAGE OF FIRST EDITION.

Mr. Sam. Symons entered for his copie, under the hands of Mr. Thomas Tomkyns and Mr. Warden Royston, a Booke or Copie Intituled Paradise Lost, a Poem in Tenne bookes, by J. M. 6d.— ENTRY AT STATIONERS' HALL, 1667, *August* 20.

Thou hast not miss'd one thought that could be fit,
And all that was improper dost omit;
So that no room is here for writers left,
But to detect their ignorance or theft.
That majesty which thro' thy work doth reign
Draws the devout, deterring the profane.
And things divine thou treat'st of in such state
As them preserves, and thee, inviolate.
At once delight and horror on us seize,
Thou sing'st with so much gravity and ease;
And above human flight dost soar aloft,
With plume so strong, so equal, and so soft:
The bird named from that paradise you sing
So never flags, but always keeps on wing.
Where could'st thou words of such a compass find?
Whence furnish such a vast expense of mind?
Just heaven thee, like Tiresias, to requite,
Rewards with prophecy thy loss of sight.
—MARVELL, ANDREW, 1674, *On Milton's Paradise Lost.*

That "Paradise Lost" of Milton, which some are pleased to call a poem.— RYMER, THOMAS, 1678–92, *On the Tragedies of the Last Age.*

Milton, whose Muse with such a daring Flight,
Led out the warring Saraphims to fight.
—OLDHAM, JOHN, 1680, *A Pastoral on the Death of the Earl of Rochester.*

Imitation is a nice point, and there are few poets who deserve to be models in all they write. Milton's "Paradise Lost" is admirable; but am I therefore bound to maintain, that there are no flats amongst his elevations, when it is evident he creeps along sometimes for above an hundred lines together? Cannot I admire the height of his invention, and the strength of his expression, without defending his antiquated words, and the perpetual harshness of their sound? It is as much commendation as a man can bear, to own him excellent; all beyond it is idolatry.— DRYDEN, JOHN, 1685, *Preface to Second Miscellany, Works, ed. Scott and Saintsbury, vol.* XII, *p.* 300.

As for Mr. Milton, whom we all admire with so much justice, his subject is not that of an heroic poem, properly so called. His design is the losing of our happiness; his event is not prosperous, like that of all other epic works; his heavenly machines are many, and his human persons are but two. But I will not take Mr. Rymer's work out of his hands: he has promised the world a critique on that author; wherein though he will not allow his poem for heroic, I hope he will grant us, that his thoughts are elevated, his words sounding, and that no man has so happily copied the manner of Homer, or so copiously translated his Grecisms, and the Latin elegances of Virgil. It is true, he runs into a flat of thought, sometimes for a hundred lines together, but it is when he is got into a track of Scripture. His antiquated words were his choice, not his necessity; for therein he imitated Spenser, as Spenser did Chaucer. . . . Neither will I justify Milton for his blank verse, though I may excuse him, by the example of Hannibal Caro, and other Italians, who have used it; for whatever causes he alleges for the abolishing of rhyme, (which I have not now the leisure to examine), his own particular reason is plainly this, that rhyme was not his talent; he had neither the ease of doing it, nor the graces of it; which is manifest in his *Juvenilia*, or verses written in his youth, where his rhyme is always constrained and forced, and comes hardly from him, at an age when the soul is most pliant, and the passion of love makes almost every man a rhymer, though not a poet.— DRYDEN, JOHN, 1692, *Essay on Satire, Works, ed. Scott and Saintsbury, vol.* XIII, *pp.* 18, 20.

As the first place among our English poets is due to Milton, and as I have drawn more quotations out of him than from any other, I shall enter into a regular criticism upon his "Paradise Lost," which I shall publish every Saturday till I have given my thoughts upon that poem. . . . I must likewise take notice, that there are in Milton several words of his own coining, as *Cerberean, miscreated, hell-doom'd, embryon* atoms, and many others. If the reader is offended at this liberty in our English poet, I would recommend him to a discourse in Plutarch, which shows us how frequently Homer has made use of the same liberty. Milton, by the above-mentioned helps, and by the choice of the noblest words and phrases which our tongue would afford him, has carried our language to a greater height than any of the English poets have ever done before or after him, and made the sublimity of his style equal to that of his sentiments. . . . This redundancy of those several ways of speech, which Aristotle calls "foreign language," and with which Milton has so very much enriched, and in some places darkened, the language of his poem, was the more proper for his use because his poem is written in blank verse.—ADDISON, JOSEPH, 1711–12, *The Spectator, Nos.* 262, 285.

It must be acknowledged that till about forty years ago Great Britain was barren of critical learning, though fertile in excellent writers; and in particular had so little taste for epic poetry, and was so unacquainted with the essential properties and peculiar beauties of it, that "Paradise Lost," an admirable work of that kind, published by Mr. Milton, the great ornament of his age and country, lay many years unspoken of and entirely disregarded, till at length it happened that some persons of great delicacy and judgment found out the merit of that excellent poem, and, by communicating their sentiments to their friends, propagated the esteem of the author, who soon acquired universal applause. —BLACKMORE, SIR RICHARD, 1716, *Essays.*

"Paradise Lost" had been printed forty years before it was known to the greatest part of England that there barely was such a book.—DENNIS, JOHN, 1721, *Letters.*

When Milton first published his famous poem, the first edition was long of going off; few either read, liked, or understood it; and it gained ground merely by its merit.—SWIFT, JONATHAN, 1732, *Letter to Sir Charles Wogan.*

Milton's style, in his "Paradise Lost," is not natural; 'tis an exotic style.—As his subject lies a good deal out of our world, it has a particular propriety in those

parts of the poem: and, when he is on earth, wherever he is describing our parents in Paradise, you see he uses a more easy and natural way of writing.— Though his formal style may fit the higher parts of his own poem, it does very ill for others who write on natural and pastoral subjects.—POPE, ALEXANDER, 1734–36, *Spence's Anecdotes, ed. Singer, p.* 131.

The British nation, which has produced the greatest men in every profession, before the appearance of Milton could not enter into any competition with antiquity, with regard to the sublime excellencies of poetry. Greece could boast an Euripides, Eschylus, Sophocles and Sappho; England was proud of her Shakespeare, Spenser, Johnson and Fletcher; but their then ancients had still a poet in reserve superior to the rest, who stood unrivalled by all succeeding times, and in epic poetry, which is justly esteemed the highest effort of genius, Homer had no rival. When Milton appeared, the pride of Greece was humbled, the competition became more equal, and since "Paradise Lost" is ours; it would, perhaps, be an injury to our national fame to yield the palm to any state, whether ancient or modern.— CIBBER, THEOPHILUS, 1753, *Lives of the Poets, vol.* II, *p.* 108.

For second He, that rode sublime
Upon the seraph-wings of Extasy,
The secrets of the abyss to spy.
He pass'd the flaming bounds of place and
    time:
The living throne, the sapphire blaze,
Where angels tremble while they gaze,
He saw; but blasted with excess of light,
Closed his eyes in endless night.
—GRAY, THOMAS, 1757, *The Progress of Poesy.*

"What? the barbarian who constructed a long commentary on the first chapter of Genesis in ten books of harsh verse? The clumsy imitator of the Greeks who caricatures creation and who, while Moses represents the Eternal Being as creating the world by his word, makes the Messiah take a big compass out of a cupboard in heaven to trace out the work? What? I admire the man who has spoilt Tasso's hell and Tasso's devil; who makes Lucifer masquerade, now as a toad, now as a pigmy; who puts the same speech in his mouth a hundred times over; who represents him as arguing on divinity; who, in attempting a serious imitation of Ariosto's comic invention of fire-arms, makes the devils fire cannon in heaven? Neither I, nor anybody in Italy, has ever been able to take pleasure in all these dismal extravagances. His marriage of Sin and Death, and the snakes of which Sin is delivered, make any man of tolerably delicate taste sick, and his long description of a hospital is only good for a grave-digger. This obscure, eccentric, and disgusting poem was despised at its birth: and I treat it to-day as it was treated in its own country by its own contemporaries. Anyhow, I say what I think, and I really care very little whether others agree with me or not."—VOLTAIRE, FRANÇOIS MARIE AROUET, 1758–9, *Signor Pococurante, Candide, ch.* xxv.

His "Paradise Lost" was overlooked in the reign of Charles II., an age as destitute of the noble ideas of taste, as it was of those of virtue. Some of the small poets who lived in the sunshine of the court, and now and then produced a madrigal or a song, were much more regarded than Milton.—GRANGER, JAMES, 1769–1824, *Biographical History of England, vol.* v, *p.* 238.

Adam and Eve, in the state of innocence, are well imagined, and admirably supported; and the different sentiments arising from difference of sex, are traced out with inimitable delicacy, and philosophical propriety. After the fall, he makes them retain the same characters, without any other change than what the transition from innocence to guilt might be supposed to produce: Adam has still that preeminence in dignity, and Eve in loveliness, which we should naturally look for in the father and mother of mankind. —Of the blessed spirits, Raphael and Michael are well distinguished; the one for affability, and peculiar good-will to the human race; the other for majesty, but such as commands veneration, rather than fear.—We are sorry to add, that Milton's attempt to soar still higher, only shows, that he had already soared as high, as, without being "blasted with excess of light," it is possible for the human imagination to rise.—BEATTIE, JAMES, 1776–79, *An Essay on Poetry and Music, p.* 85.

I am now to examine "Paradise Lost," a poem which, considered with respect to design, may claim the first place, and with respect to performance, the second, among

the productions of the human mind. . . . There is perhaps no poem, of the same length, from which so little can be taken without apparent mutilation. . . . The thoughts which are occasionally called forth in the progress, are such as could only be produced by an imagination in the highest degree fervid and active, to which materials were supplied by incessant study and ultimate curiosity. The heat of Milton's mind may be said to sublimate his learning, to throw off into his work the spirit of science, unmingled with its grosser parts. . . . He can please when pleasure is required; but it is his peculiar power to astonish. . . . The want of human interest is always felt. "Paradise Lost" is one of the books which the reader admires and lays down, and forgets to take up again. None ever wished it longer than it is. Its perusal is a duty rather than a pleasure. We read Milton for instruction, retire harassed and overburdened, and look elsewhere for recreation; we desert our master and seek for companions. —JOHNSON, SAMUEL, 1779, *John Milton, Lives of the English Poets.*

Was there ever anything so delightful as the music of the "Paradise Lost." It is like that of a fine organ; has the fullest and deepest tones of majesty, with all the softness and elegance of the Dorian flute. Variety without end, and never equalled unless perhaps by Virgil. Yet the Doctor has little or nothing to say upon this copious theme, but talks something about the unfitness of the English language for blank verse, and how apt it is, in the mouth of some readers, to degenerate into declamation. Oh! I could thrash his old jacket, till I made his pension jingle in his pocket.—COWPER, WILLIAM, 1779, *Letter to Unwin, Oct.* 31.

The boldness, freedom, and variety of our blank verse is infinitely more favourable than rhyme; to all kinds of sublime poetry. The fullest proof of this is afforded by Milton; an author whose genius led him eminently to the sublime The whole first and second books of "Paradise Lost," are continued instances of it.—BLAIR, HUGH, 1783, *Lectures on Rhetoric and Belles-Lettres, ed. Mills, Lecture* iv, *p.* 44.

Is not Milton a sublimer poet than Homer or Virgil? Are not his personages more sublimely clothed, and do you not know that there is not perhaps *one page* in *Milton's* "Paradise Lost" in which he has not borrowed his imagery from the *Scriptures?* I allow and rejoice that *Christ* appealed only to the understanding and the affections; but I affirm that after reading Isaiah, or St. Paul's "Epistle to the Hebrews," Homer and Virgil are disgustingly *tame* to me, and Milton himself barely tolerable.—COLERIDGE, SAMUEL TAYLOR, 1796, *Letters, ed. E. H. Coleridge, vol.* I, *p.* 199.

Milton has written a sublime poem upon a ridiculous story of eating an apple, and of the eternal vengeance decreed by the Almighty against the whole human race, because their progenitor was guilty of this black and detestable offence.—GODWIN, WILLIAM, 1797, *Of Choice in Reading, The Enquirer, p.* 135. ·

Nothing can be farther from my intention than to insinuate that Milton was a plagiarist, or servile imitator; but I conceive, that, having read these sacred poems of very high merit, at the immediate age when his own mind was just beginning to teem with poetry, he retained numberless thoughts, passages, and expressions therein, so deeply in his mind, that they hung inherently on his imagination, and became, as it were, naturalized there.—DUNSTER, CHARLES, 1800, *Considerations on Milton's Early Reading, p.* 11.

The merits of his epic do not, accordingly, consist in regularity of plan so much as in scattered passages of independent beauty, and in the perfection of his poetic diction. The universal admiration of Milton in the eighteenth century is based on his isolated descriptions of paradisaic innocence and beauty, his awful picture of Hell, with the character of its inhabitants, whom he sketched, after the antique, as giants of the Abyss. It is questionable if any real benefit accrued to the language of English poetry from its increased leaning to the Latinism of Milton rather than to the Germanism of Spenser: but this tendency being a fact, Milton must be regarded as the greatest master of style, and in many respects the standard of dignified poetic expression.—SCHLEGEL, FREDERICK, 1815, *Lectures on the History of Literature,* XII.

The Genius of Milton, more particularly in respect to its span in immensity,

calculated him, by a sort of birth-right, for such an "argument" as the "Paradise Lost:" he had an exquisite passion for what is properly, in the sense of ease and pleasure, poetical Luxury; and with that, it appears to me, he would fain have been content, if he could, so doing, have preserved his self-respect and feel[ing] of duty performed; but there was working in him, as it were, that same sort of thing as operates in the great world to the end of a Prophecy's being accomplish'd: therefore he devoted himself rather to the ardours than the pleasures of song, solacing himself at intervals with cups of old wine; and those are, with some exceptions the finest parts of the poem.—KEATS, JOHN, 1818, *Notes on Milton's Paradise Lost, Works, ed. Forman, vol.* III, *p.* 19.

He stood alone and aloof above his times, the bard of immortal subjects, and, as far as there is perpetuity in language, of immortal fame. The very choice of those subjects bespoke a contempt for any species of excellence that was attainable by other men. There is something that overawes the mind in conceiving his long deliberated selection of that theme—his attempting it when his eyes were shut upon the face of nature—his dependence, we might almost say, on supernatural inspiration, and in the calm air of strength with which he opens "Paradise Lost," beginning a mighty performance without the appearance of an effort. Taking the subject all in all, his powers could nowhere else have enjoyed the same scope. It was only from the height of this great argument that he could look back upon eternity past, and forward upon eternity to come; that he could survey the abyss of infernal darkness, open visions of Paradise, or ascend to heaven and breathe empyreal air. —CAMPBELL, THOMAS, 1819, *An Essay on English Poetry.*

I am not persuaded that the "Paradise Lost" would not have been more nobly conveyed to posterity, not perhaps in heroic couplets, although even *they* could sustain the subject if well balanced, but in the stanza of Spenser or of Tasso, or in the terza rima of Dante, which the powers of Milton could easily have grafted on our language.—BYRON, LORD, 1820, *Observations upon an Article in Blackwood's Magazine.*

Called at Pickering's in Chancery Lane,

who showed us the original agreement between Milton and Symonds for the payment of five pounds for "Paradise Lost." The contrast of this sum with the £2000 given for [the unexpired term of the copyright of] Mrs. Rundell's "Cookery," comprises a history in itself. Pickering, too, gave forty-five guineas for this agreement, three times as much as the whole sum given for the poem. It was part payment, I think?—MOORE, THOMAS, 1826, *Diary, Oct.* 21.

The Second great name in the annals of English Poetry is Milton: which is the First, of course, I need not say. Many other Poets have excelled him in variety and versatility; but none ever approached him in intensity of style and thought, in unity of purpose and in the power and grandeur with which he piles up the single monument of Genius, to which his mind is for the time devoted. His Harp may have but one string, but that is such an one, as none but his own finger knows how to touch. "Paradise Lost" has few inequalities; few feeblenesses. It seems not like a work taken up and continued at intervals; but one continuing effort; lasting, perhaps, for years, yet never remitted: elaborated with the highest polish, yet all the marks of ease and simplicity in it's composition.—NEELE, HENRY, 1827–29, *Lectures on English Poetry, Lecture* ii.

In the "Paradise Lost"—indeed in everyone of his poems—it is Milton himself whom you see; his Satan, his Adam, his Raphael, almost his Eve—are all John Milton; and it is a sense of this intense egotism that gives me the greatest pleasure in reading Milton's works. The egotism of such a man is a revelation of spirit. — COLERIDGE, SAMUEL TAYLOR, 1833, *Table Talk, Aug.* 18.

"The Paradise Lost" is totally unlike all the poetry that has followed it. Even in the controversial metaphysics of his poetry Milton has found no rival; and although Byron, in his "Cain," has combined tenderness the most touching with a lofty sublimity, still it may be said, with truth, of the Bard of our Republic, that he has nerve been imitated.—ELLIOTT, EBENEZER, 1833, *Spirits and Men, Preface, p.* 213.

If the poet sometimes betrays fatigue, if the lyre drops from his wearied hand, he rests, and I rest along with him. . . . Who ever wrote like this? What poet ever spoke such langauge? How miserable seem all modern compositions beside these strong and magnificent conceptions.—CHATEAUBRIAND, FRANÇOIS RENÉ, VICOMTE DE 1837, *Sketches of English Literature, vol.* II, *pp.* 118, 130.

The slowness of Milton's advance to glory is now generally owned to have been much exaggerated: we might say that the reverse was nearer the truth. . . . It would hardly, however, be said, even in this age, of a poem 3,000 copies of which had been sold in eleven years, that its success had been small; and some, perhaps, might doubt whether "Paradise Lost," published eleven years since, would have met with a greater demand. There is sometimes a want of congeniality in public taste which no power of genius will overcome. For Milton it must be said by every one conversant with the literature of the age that preceded Addison's famous criticism, from which some have dated the reputation of "Paradise Lost," that he took his place among great poets from the beginning.—HALLAM, HENRY, 1837–39, *Literature of Europe, pt.* iv, *ch.* v, *par.* 34.

Adam and Eve are beautiful, graceful objects, but no one has breathed the Pygmalion life into them; they remain cold statues. Milton's sympathies were with things rather than with men, the scenery and phenomena of nature, the trim gardens, the burning lake; but as for the phenomena of the mind, he was not able to see them. He has no delineations of mind except Satan, of which we may say that Satan was his own character, the black side of it. I wish however, to be understood not to speak at all in disparagement of Milton; far from that.—CARLYLE, THOMAS, 1838, *Lectures on the History of Literature, p.* 166.

I, if abruptly called upon in that summary fashion to convey a *commensurate* idea of Milton, one which might at once correspond to his pretensions, and yet be readily intelligible to the savage, should answer perhaps thus:—Milton is not an author amongst authors, not a poet amongst poems, but a power amongst powers; and the "Paradise Lost" is not a book amongst books, not a poem amongst poems, but a central force amongst forces. —DE QUINCEY, THOMAS, 1839–57, *On Milton, Writings, ed. Masson, vol.* X, *p.* 399.

Its sale was no evidence that its merits were comprehended, and may be referred to the general reputation of its author; for we find so accomplished a critic as Sir William Temple, some years later, omitting the name of Milton in his roll of writers who have done honour to modern literature, a circumstance which may, perhaps, be imputed to that reverence for the ancients which blinded Sir William to the merits of their successors. How could Milton be understood in his own generation, in the grovelling, sensual court of Charles the Second? How could the dull eyes, so long fastened on the earth, endure the blaze of his inspired genius? It was not till time had removed him to a distance that he could be calmly gazed on and his merits fairly contemplated. Addison, as is well known, was the first to bring them into popular view, by a beautiful specimen of criticism that has permanently connected his name with that of his illustrious subject. More than half a century later, another great name in English criticism, perhaps the greatest in general reputation, Johnson, passed sentence of a very different kind on the pretensions of the poet. A production more discreditable to the author is not to be found in the whole of his voluminous works; equally discreditable, whether regarded in an historical light or as a sample of literary criticism.—PRESCOTT, WILLIAM HICKLING, 1839–55, *Biographical and Critical Miscellanies, p.* 276.

To the judgment of each individual, among his readers, it must be left, to determine for himself, how far, in the course of his "adventurous song," the poet's prayer for divine illumination has been answered in the sequel. The theology of the poem, in various passages of the deepest interest, may be seriously questioned, but shall here be left with one remark only (not effecting its doctrinal points), namely, that he would be a bold critic who, as a believer in the Christian faith, should venture to justify the extent to which the author has employed the doubtful, though, hitherto, undisputed license of fiction in the supernatural agency of his poem. At the same time, far be it from the present writer to arraign the poet, either of wilful or negligent impiety. It need not be mooted here, whether he considered himself fully authorized to exercise such perilous freedom, but, assuredly, he was mistaken. Tasso, Marini, Camoens, and other epic poets, have likewise intermeddled with "things that were too high for them," and these have all egregiously miscarried, their spiritual agents having been uniformly the most indifferent, and the least effective personages in their stories. Milton far transcends all his predecessors in the use of such preternatural machinery, while none, that have come after, have been able to approach the power and ability with which he has wielded it.— MONTGOMERY, JAMES, 1843–61, *The Poetical Works of John Milton, Memoir, vol.* I, *p.* xxxiii.

"Paradise Lost" is a study for imagination and elaborate musical structure. Take almost any passage, and a lecture might be read from it on contrasts and pauses, and other parts of metrical harmony; while almost every word has its higher poetical meaning and intensity; but all is accompanied with a certain oppressiveness of ambitious and conscious power.—HUNT, LEIGH, 1844, *Imagination and Fancy, p.* 212.

In "Paradise Lost" we feel as if we were admitted to the outer courts of the Infinite. In that all-glorious temple of genius inspired by truth, we catch the full diapason of the heavenly organ. With its first choral swell the soul is lifted from the earth. In the "Divina Commedia" the man, the Florentine, the exiled Ghibelline, stands out, from first to last, breathing defiance and revenge. Milton, in some of his prose works, betrays the partisan also; but in his poetry we see him in the white robes of the minstrel, with upturned though sightless eyes, rapt in meditation at the feet of the heavenly muse. Dante, in his dark vision, descends to the depths of the world of perdition, and, homeless fugitive as he is, drags his proud and prosperous enemies down with him, and buries them, doubly destroyed, in the flaming sepulchres of the lowest hell. Milton, on the other hand, seems almost to have purged off the dross of humanity. Blind, poor, friendless, in solitude and sorrow, with quite as much reason as his Italian rival to repine at his fortune and war against mankind, how calm and unimpassioned is he in all that concerns his own personality! He deemed too highly of his divine gift, to make it the instrument of immortalizing his hatreds. One cry, alone, of sorrow at his blindness, one pathetic lamentation over the evil days on which he had fallen, bursts from his full heart. There is not a flash of human wrath in all his pictures of woe. Hating nothing but evil spirits, in the childlike simplicity of his heart, his pure hands undefiled with the pitch of the political intrigues in which he had lived, he breathes forth his inexpressibly majestic strains,— the poetry not so much of earth as of heaven.—EVERETT, EDWARD, 1853, *Orations and Speeches, vol.* II, *p.* 222.

Milton is one of the three great Christian poets who were to the theogony of the Middle Ages what Homer was to the Olympus of paganism. The triumvirate consists of Dante, Tasso, and Milton. The "Divine Comedy" of Dante, the "Jerusalem Delivered" of Tasso, the "Paradise Lost" of Milton, are the Iliads and Odysseys of our theological system. . . . Milton is the least original of the three great Christian poets. At first he imitates Homer, then Virgil, and lastly Dante and Tasso; but his real model is Dante. He impresses the same supernatural subject on the Christian theogony; he sings to England what Italy has already heard—the strife of created angels in revolt against their Maker—the blissful loves of Eden—the seduction of woman— the fall of man—the intercession of the Son of God with the Father—the mercy obtained by his own sacrifice, and the redemption partially gleaming through the distance, as the *dénouement* of this sublime tragedy. Finally, he embraces the entire series of mysteries which the philosopher penetrates with his conjectures, the theologian explains, and the poet describes, without demanding of them other components than miracles, images, and emotions. Why, then, did Milton select this overpowering theological subject, and transplant it to England, so rich in Saxon and Celtic traditions, already popular, and admirably adapted for the text of a grand national and original northern epic? The answer is to be found in his character and his life. By nature he was theological, and the youngest half of his existence had been passed in Italy. The first voyage of a youth is a second birth; from it he imbibes new sensations and ideas, which

produce a species of personal transformation. The phenomenon of petrification is not confined to the effect of water upon a plant; it operates upon man through the air that he breathes.—LAMARTINE, ALPHONSE DE, 1854, *Memoirs of Celebrated Characters*.

Sublime as Milton's immemorial theme. —DOBELL, SYDNEY, 1855, *America*.

Make a man of Milton's force and affluence of imagination half-intoxicated and half-crazy, and any enterprising bookseller might draw from the lees of his mind a "Festus" once a week, and each monstrosity would doubtless be hailed by some readers, who think they have a taste for poetry, as a greater miracle of genius than "Paradise Lost."—WHIPPLE, EDWIN P., 1857-66, *Character and Characteristic Men, p.* 19.

How noble this metre is in Milton's hands, how completely it shows itself capable of the grand, nay of the grandest, style, I need not say. To this metre, as used in the "Paradise Lost," our country owes the glory of having produced one of the only two poetical works in the grand style which are to be found in the modern languages; the Divine Comedy of Dante is the other. England and Italy here stand alone; Spain, France and Germany have produced great poets, but neither Calderon, nor Corneille, nor Schiller, nor even Goethe, has produced a body of poetry in the true grand style, in the sense in which the style of the body of Homer's poetry, or Pindar's, or Sophocles's, is grand. But Dante has, and so has Milton; and in this respect Milton possesses a distinction which even Shakespeare, undoubtedly the supreme poetical power in our literature, does not share with him. Not a tragedy of Shakespeare but contains passages in the worst of all styles; and the grand style, although it may be harsh, or obscure, or cumbrous, or over-laboured, is never affected. In spite, therefore, of objections which may justly be urged against the plan and treatment of the "Paradise Lost," in spite of its possessing, certainly, a far less enthralling force of interest to attract and to carry forward the reader than the Iliad or the Divine Comedy, it fully deserves, it can never lose, its immense reputation; for, like the Iliad and the Divine Comedy, nay in some respects to a higher degree than either of them, it is in the grand style.— ARNOLD, MATTHEW, 1861, *Lectures On Translating Homer.*

In short Milton is a great poet, doubled with a Saumaise, or a Grotius; a genius, nourished on the marrow of lions, on Homer, Isaiah, Virgil, Dante, but also, like the serpent in Eden, chewing the dust of dull polemic. He is a doctor, a preacher, a pedagogue, and when the day comes for him to be able at last to realize the dreams of his youth, and endow his country with an epic, he will construct it of two matters, of gold and of clay, of sublimity and of scholasticism, and will leave us a poem which is at once the most extraordinary and at the same time the most intolerable in existence. . . . "Paradise Lost" is an unreal poem, a grotesque poem, a tiresome poem. There is not one reader in a hundred who can read Books Nine and Ten without a smile, or Books Eleven and Twelve without a yawn. The thing does not hold toegther: it is a pyramid balanced on its apex, the most terrible problems solved by the most childish of means. And yet "Paradise Lost" is immortal. It lives by virtue of some episodes which will be for ever famous. In contrast with Dante, who must be read as a whole if we wish really to grasp his beauties, Milton ought not to be read except in fragments; but these fragments form a part of the poetic patri- mony of the human race. The invocation to Light, the character of Eve, the de- scription of the earthly Paradise, of the morning of the world, of its first love, are all masterpieces. The discourses of the Prince of Hell are incomparably elo- quent.—SCHERER, EDMOND, 1868–91, *Essays on English Literature, tr. Saints- bury, pp.* 132, 146.

In "Samson" he finds a cold and lofty tragedy, in "Paradise Regained" a cold and noble epic; he composes an imperfect and sublime poem in "Paradise Lost." . . . Adam and Eve, the first pair! I approach, and it seems as though I discov- ered the Adam and Eve of Raphael Sanzio, imitated by Milton, so his biographers tell us, glorious, strong, voluptuous children, naked in the light of heaven, motionless and absorbed before grand landscapes, with bright vacant eyes, with no more thought than the bull or the horse on the

grass beside them. I listen, and I hear an English household, two reasoners of the period—Colonel Hutchinson and his wife. Heavens! dress them at once. Folk so cultivated should have invented before all a pair of trousers and modesty. What dialogues! Dissertations capped by politeness, mutual sermons concluded by bows. . . . This Adam entered Paradise *via* England. There he learned respecta- bility, and there he studied moral speech- ifying.—TAINE, H. A., 1871, *History of English Literature, tr. Van Laun, vol.* I, *bk.* ii, *ch.* vi, *pp.* 441, 443, 444.

This connection with Dryden, which lasted till the poet's death, was of only less importance to the furtherance of Ton- son's fortune than a bargain concluded four years later with Brabazon Aylmer for one half of his interest in the "Paradise Lost," which Dryden told him was one of the greatest poems England had ever pro- duced. Still he waited four years before he ventured to publish, and then only by the safe method of subscription, and in 1788 the folio edition came out, and by the sale of this and future editions Ton- son was, according to Disraeli, enabled to keep his carriage.—CURWEN, HENRY, 1873, *A History of Booksellers, p.* 25.

Let "Paradise Lost," then, be called a *Vorstellung.* But what a *Vorstellung* it is! That World of Man, the world of all our stars and starry transparencies, hung but drop-like after all from an Empyrean; the great Empyrean itself, "undetermined square or round," so that, though we do diagram it for form's sake, it is beyond all power of diagram; A Hell, far beneath, but still measurably far, with its outcast infernal Powers tending disastrously up- wards or tugging all downwards; finally, between the Empyrean and Hell, a blus- tering blackness of unimaginable Chaos, roaring around the Mundane Sphere and assaulting everlastingly its outermost bosses, but unable to break through, or to disturb the serenity of the golden poise that steadies it from the zenith—what phantasmagory more truly all-significant than this has the imagination of poet ever conceived? What expense of space com- parable to this for vastness has any other poet presumed to fill with visual symbol- isms, or to occupy with a coherent story? The physical universe of Dante's great poem would go into a nutshell as compared with that to which the imagination must stretch itself out in "Paradise Lost." In this respect—in respect of the extent of physical immensity through which the poem ranges, and which it orbs forth with soul-dilating clearness and maps out with never-to-be-obliterated accuracy before the eye—no possible poem can ever overpass it. And then the story itself! What story mightier or more full of meaning can there ever be than that of the Archangel rebelling in Heaven, degraded from Heaven into Hell, reascending from Hell to the Human Universe, winging through the starry spaces of that Universe, and at last possessing himself of our central Earth, and impregnating its incipient history with the spirit of Evil? Vastness of scene and power of story together, little wonder that the poem should have so impressed the world. Little wonder that it should now be Milton's Satan, and Milton's narrative of the Creation in its various transcendental connexions, that are in possession of the British imagination, rather than the strict Biblical accounts from which Milton so scrupulously derived the hints to which he gave such marvellous expansion.— MASSON, DAVID, 1874, *ed., The Poetical Works of John Milton, vol.* I, *p.* 101.

I don't think I've read him these forty years; the whole Scheme of the Poem, and certain Parts of it, looming as grand as anything in my Memory; but I never could read ten lines together without stumbling at some Pedantry that tipped me at once out of Paradise, or even Hell, into the Schoolroom, worse than either. —FITZGERALD, EDWARD, 1876, *Letters, vol.* I, *p.* 380.

The description of the garden of Eden, in the fourth book of "Paradise Lost," is magnificent, but vague. The pomp of language and profusion of images leaves on the imagination no definite picture. You have, it is true, "in narrow room Nature's whole wealth," but it does not satisfy, as many a humbler but real scene described with a few strokes satisfies. Such landscapes in poetry, entirely projected by the imagination and answering to no scene on earth, are, like the composition pictures, which some painters delight in, only splendid failures.—SHAIRP, JOHN CAMPBELL, 1877, *On Poetic Interpretation of Nature, p.* 191.

The cosmogony of the universe as conceived by Milton in "Paradise Lost," though very simple, is very little understood. Nobody confesses to not reading the poem. Many do read it; many more to their own loss, begin and do not finish it; all attempt it. And yet how few know the simple plan of creation which it presupposes, and without a just conception of which it is totally impossible to understand the poem. Indeed, it is no doubt in large part the want of this conception which induces many readers to forego the further perusal of the work after having reached the third book. They are wearied by the very peculiar and incomprehensible movements of Satan on his journey earthward. In what kind of a world is it that Satan, Raphael, Michael, Uriel, and the rest move about? How does it happen that Satan, in going from Hell to Earth, flies downward? and how is it that in the journey he is compelled to pass by the gate of Heaven? Where is the Paradise of Fools through which the poet, in one of the most scornful and extraordinary passages in the book, makes him wander? Where is the throne of Chaos and old Night? There is little use in attempting to read the poem without understanding these things. They are very simple. A diagram or two will be sufficient to explain them.—NADEL, E. S., 1877, *The Cosmogony of "Paradise Lost," Harper's Magazine, vol.* 56, *p.* 137.

The triumph of the Puritan poet was as signal as the triumph of the Puritan king. No Anglican minstrel is nearly equal to Milton; neither the Temple nor the Christian Year will compare with "Paradise Lost." We naturally place it side by side with the poem in which Dante enshrined Catholicism. Dante excels Milton in tenderness; in intimate knowledge of the human heart; in the delineation of all passions, except revenge and ambition, pride and hatred. Dante has the infallible Shakespearian touch whenever his theme is love; Milton in the like case paints with great literary dexterity and with a frank audacity of sensuous colour which would fain be passionate and tender; but he never gets beyond painted love. . . . For Eve's face he has not a word; not one syllable for the crimson of the lip, for the ravishment of the smile. Conventional golden tresses, slender waist, and ringlets "wanton," which surely they had no call to be in Eden;—this is what we find in Milton's first woman, whom Charlotte Brontë says he never saw. Against Dante, on the other hand, and in favour of Milton, we have to put the traces of Middle-age childishness, the nursery goblinism, grotesquerie, and allegorical wire-drawing, which are present in the "Divine Comedy," The sustained grandeur which has made "Miltonic" a convertible term with "sublime" is far above all that.—BAYNE, PETER, 1878, *The Chief Actors in the Puritan Revolution, pp.* 335, 36.

How resplendent and superb was the poetry that lay at the heart of Puritanism, was seen by the sightless eyes of John Milton, whose great epic is indeed the epic of Puritanism.—TYLER, MOSES COIT, 1878, *A History of American Literature,* 1607–1676, *vol.* I, *p.* 266.

Whatever conclusion may be the true one from the amount of the public demand, we cannot be wrong in asserting that from the first, and now as then, "Paradise Lost" has been more admired than read. The poet's wish and expectation that he should find "fit audience, though few," has been fulfilled. Partly this has been due to his limitation, his unsympathetic disposition, the deficiency of the human element in his imagination, and his presentation of mythical instead of real beings. But it is also in part a tribute to his excellence, and is to be ascribed to the lofty strain, which requires more effort to accompany than an average reader is able to make, a majestic demeanour which no parodist has been able to degrade, and a wealth of allusion demanding more literature than is possessed by any but the few whose life is lived with the poets. An appreciation of Milton is the last reward of consummated scholarship; and we may apply to him what Quintilian has said of Cicero, "Ille se profecisse sciat, cui Cicero valde placebit."—PATTISON, MARK, 1879, *Milton,* (*English Men of Letters*), *p.* 210.

The Style is always great. On the whole it is the greatest in the whole range of English poetry, so great that when once we have come to know and honour and love it, it so subdues the judgment that the judgment can with difficulty do its work with temperance. It lifts the low, gives life to the commonplace, dignifies even the vulgar, and makes us endure that which is heavy and dull. We catch ourselves admiring things not altogether worthy of admiration, because the robe they wear is so royal. No style, when one has lived in it, is so spacious and so majestic a place to walk in. . . . Fulness of sound, weight of march, compactness of finish, fitness of words to things, fitness of pauses to thought, a strong grasp of the main idea while other ideas play round it, power of digression without loss of the power to return, equality of power over vast spaces of imagination, sustained splendour when he soars "With plume so strong, so equal and so soft," a majesty in the conduct of thought, and a music in the majesty which fills it with solemn beauty, belong one and all to the style; and it gains its highest influence on us, and fulfils the ultimate need of a grand style in being the easy and necessary expression of the very character and nature of the man. It reveals Milton, as much, sometimes even more than his thought.—BROOKE, STOPFORD, 1879, *Milton,* (*Classical Writers*), *p.* 83.

Who now reads the ancient writers? Who systematically reads the great writers, be they ancient or modern, whom the consent of ages has marked out as classics: typical, immortal, peculiar teachers of our race? Alas! the "Paradise Lost" is lost again to us beneath an inundation of graceful academic verse, sugary stanzas of ladylike prettiness, and ceaseless explanations in more or less readable prose of what John Milton meant or did not mean, or what he saw or did not see, who married his great aunt, and why Adam or Satan is like that, or unlike the other. We read a perfect library about the "Paradise Lost," but the "Paradise Lost" itself we do not read.—HARRISON, FREDERIC, 1879, *The Choice of Books and Other Literary Pieces, p.* 13.

Klopstock made up his mind to fulfil the prophecy in himself. When he left school in 1745, he had already conceived the plan of the "Messias," and in his farewell speech on the nature and office of the epic poet, he distinctly alludes to the great work which he contemplated. . . . It was the most popular subject that he could choose, and as yet no poet had exhausted it or brought it once and for all into definite shape, as Milton had the history of the Fall, to the exclusion of all possible rivals on the same ground. It was the vision of Milton that floated before the poet's eyes, and indeed he could not have had a better model, for Milton had achieved the highest that could be done for the Biblical tradition. Milton's "Paradise Lost" stood unrivalled in grandeur of conception and effective development of the theme. Amid Klopstock's many debts to Milton, the following may be mentioned: the detailed description of hell, the council of the devils, the differences of opinion amongst them, their punishment by metamorphosis, the paths through the universe along which devils and angels wander and fly, and the vision of the Last Judgment at the close of the poem. But Klopstock did not profit half enough by Milton's example. While Milton leads us from hell into paradise, and thus relieves a gloomy scene by a bright one, Klopstock, on the contrary, begins with the glories of heaven, and then keeps us in his irksome limbo of disembodied spirits till we long for a change out of very weariness. Milton exerts himself to the utmost not to let the interest flag, and pays particular attention to unity of composition, steady unfolding of the plot, and graphic narration; Klopstock, on the other hand lets the thread of his narrative decidedly drag, and accompanies each step of the gradual *dénouement* with the sentiments of all the spectators. . . . His poetry is full of the very faults which Milton condemned, and, however much Milton may have been his model, yet his "Messias" is more closely related to the religious oratorios than to "Paradise Lost."—SCHERER, WILHELM, 1883–86, *A History of German Literature*, tr. Conybeare, vol. II, *pp.* 31, 32, 33.

The imagination of Cædmon may, in some respects, vie even with that of Milton; but the harsh crudities of the Anglo-Saxon language would have overpowered the genius of Milton himself. Long ages of refinement and philosophy were wanted to prepare for the glories of "Paradise Lost." — COURTHOPE, WILLIAM JOHN, 1885, *The Liberal Movement in English Literature*, p. 28.

The dust of the conflict had fallen; and the mountain heights shone out once more from the serene distance: once more he confronted the mighty works of ancient genius. They pleased him still, from their severity and their simplicity; but they did not satisfy him—because they wanted elevation. In his "Paradise Lost" he raised and endeavoured to spiritualise the antique epic. There are many who will always regard St. Peter's temple in the air as the first of architectural monuments. The admirers of the classic will, however, feel that the amplitude and height of the wondrous dome are no sufficient substitute for that massive simplicity and breadth of effect which belong to the Parthenon; while those who revere our cathedrals will maintain that it lacks the variety, the mystery, the aspiration, and the infinitude which characterise the Christian architecture of the North. On analogous grounds the more devoted admirers of Homer and of Shakespeare will ever be dissatisfied with Milton's work, however they may venerate his genius. It is obviously composite in its character—the necessary result of its uniting a Hebraic spirit with a classic form. Dante, like Milton, uses the Greek mythology freely; considering it, no doubt, as part of that "inheritance of the Heathen," into possession of which Christendom had a right to enter; but he uses it as a subordinate ornament, and in matters of mere detail. His poem is a Vision, not an Epic, that vision of supernatural truth, of Hell, Purgatory, and Paradise, which passed before the eyes of the mediæval Church as she looked up in nocturnal vigil; not the mundane circle of life and experience, of action and of passion, exhibited in its completeness, and contemplated with calm satisfaction by a Muse that looks down from heaven.—DE VERE, AUBREY, 1887, *Essays, Chiefly on Poetry*, vol. II, *p.* 112.

How to speak of "Paradise Lost" I know not. To call it a master-work is superfluous. To say that it stands absolutely alone and supreme is both true and false. Parts of it are like other poems, and yet there is no poem in the world like it. The theme is old; had been treated by the author of Genesis in brief, by Du Bartas and other rhymers at length. The manner is old, inherited from Virgil and Dante. And yet, beyond all question, "Paradise Lost" is one of the most unique, individual, unmistakable poems in the world's literature. Imitations of it have been attempted by Montgomery, Pollok, Bickersteth, and other pious versifiers, but they are no more like the original than St. Peter's in Montreal is like St. Peter's in Rome, or than the pile of coarse-grained limestone on New York's Fifth Avenue is like the Cathedral of Milan.— VAN DYKE, HENRY, 1889-91, *The Poetry of Tennyson, p.* 92.

I cannot stay to characterize his great poem; nor is there need; immortal in more senses than one; humanity counts for little in it; one pair of human creatures only, and these looked at, as it were, through the big end of the telescope; with gigantic, Godlike figures around one, or colossal demons prone on fiery floods. It is not a child's book; to place it in schools as a parsing-book is an atrocity that I hope is ended. Not, I think, till we have had some fifty years to view the everlasting fight between good and evil in this world, can we see in proper perspective the vaster battle which, under Milton's imagination, was pictured in Paradise between the same foes. Years only can so widen one's horizon as to give room for the reverberations of that mighty combat of the powers of light and darkness.—MITCHELL, DONALD G., 1890, *English Lands Letters and Kings, From Elizabeth to Anne, p.* 171.

Much of the perfection of the verse of the "Paradise Lost," both in respect to its music and its rhythmical movements, its pause-melody, and the melodious distribution of emphasis was due, no doubt, to some extent, to Milton's blindness, which, in the first place, must have rendered his ear more delicate than it would otherwise have been (it was naturally fine and had been highly cultivated in early life, through a study of music), and which, in the second place, by its obliging him to dictate his poem instead of writing it silently with his own hand, must have been one cause why the movement of the verse so admirably conforms to its proper elocution.—CORSON, HIRAM, 1892, *A Primer of English Verse, p.* 46.

I have said that the grandest of English supernatural creations is Milton's Satan. No other personage has at once such magnitude and definiteness of outline as that sublime, defiant archangel, whether in action or in repose. Milton, like Dante, has to do with the unknown world. The Florentine bard soars at last within the effulgence of "the eternal, coeternal beam." Milton's imagination broods "in the wide womb of uncreated night." We enter that "palpable obscure," where there is "no light, but rather darkness visible," and where lurk many a "grisly terror" and execrable shape."—STEDMAN, EDMUND CLARENCE, 1892, *The Nature and Elements of Poetry, p.* 245.

Milton's description of hell and its inhabitants is as detailed and conscientious as that of a land-surveyor or a natural philosopher.—NORDAU, MAX, 1895, *Degeneration, p.* 78.

Long after I had thought never to read it—in fact when I was *nel mezzo del cammin di nostra vita*—I read Milton's "Paradise Lost," and found in it a splendor and majestic beauty that justified to me the fame it wears, and eclipsed the worth of those lesser poems which I had stupidly and ignorantly accounted his worthiest. —HOWELLS, WILLIAM DEAN, 1895, *My Literary Passions, p,* 239.

What a magnificent opportunity for describing the gradual dawn of living beauty was in the hands of the man who did not hesitate to write poetry about the creation! Does he avail himself of it? Oh no! Does he give us any suggestion of the tender grace of the young, wondering world, the slow awakening and unfolding of all fair things till they reach the perfection of their loveliness? Oh no! There is chaos, void, abyss, emptiness. We wait and watch. Suddenly—hey! presto! The world is made. There it whirls,—round, smooth, neatly finished. There are the oceans with the fishes, the mountains, the trees, yes, and the flowers and beasts.— SCUDDER, VIDA D., 1895, *The Life of the Spirit in the Modern English Poets, p.* 19.

In reading Milton one rarely forgets that the hand which wrote "Paradise Lost" knew the secrets of the organ and could turn them into sound at will.— MABIE, HAMILTON WRIGHT, 1897, *My Study Fire, First Series, p.* 113.

"Paradise Lost" is the product of two great movements—Puritanism and the Renaissance. Or, to put the same thought in another way, the conception of the poem is Hebraic, its form and imagery are classical. Within the limits of the sacred narrative, from which Milton would not allow himself to deviate, his luxuriant imagination found ample scope for all its stored wealth of learning; and the issue is something far different from the Hebrew original. Few of us, probably, realize how often we unconsciously read into the Scriptural narrative of the Creation and the Fall ideas instilled by Milton's splendid poem.—MASTERMAN, J. HOWARD B., 1897, *The Age of Milton, p.* 54.

Milton never forgets himself so as to contradict what he has written, though he is often charged with forgetfulness. Nothing is put down which has not its most intricate relations diligently considered and adjusted. Nothing is left isolated, inarticulated, disproportionate, or unsymmetrical. Things easily overlooked by the reader often have far-reaching effects. There is a sort of vitality and growth in the ideas, and every part is essential to the life and vigor of the whole. Herein lies the reason why changes or omissions can seldom be made without serious loss. Landor's proposed emended edition of "Paradise Lost" would be an intolerable mutilation.—HIMES, JOHN A., 1898, *ed., Paradise Lost, A General Survey, p.* xxxi.

The first editions of Milton's works have greatly increased in price. Not many years ago a copy of the first edition of the "Paradise Lost" could be obtained for about five pounds, but now a good copy is worth at least four times as much. The prices vary considerably with the date of the title-page, of which there are several issues. G. Daniel's fine copy sold in 1864 for £28, 10s.—WHEATLEY, HENRY B., 1898, *Prices of Books, p.* 219.

PARADISE REGAINED

1671

After I had, with the best attention, read it ["Paradise Lost"] through, I made him another visit, and returned him his book, with due acknowledgement of the favour he had done me in communicating it to me. He asked how I liked it, and what I thought of it; which I modestly, but freely, told him: and, after some further discourse about it, I pleasantly said to him, "Thou hast said much here of Paradise *Lost;* but what hast thou to say of Paradise *Found?*" He made me no answer, but sate some time in a muse, then brake off that discourse and fell upon another subject. After the sickness

was over, and the city well cleansed and become safely habitable again, he returned thither. And when, afterwards, I went to wait on him there (which I seldom failed of doing, whenever my occasions drew me to London), he showed me his second poem, called "Paradise Regained," and in a pleasant tone said to me, "This is owing to you; for you put it into my head by the question you put to me at Chalfont, which before I had not thought of."—ELLWOOD, THOMAS, 1714, *The History of the Life of, Written by his own Hand.*

Had this poem been written not by Milton, but by some imitator, it would have claimed and received universal praise.—JOHNSON, SAMUEL, 1779, *John Milton, Lives of the English Poets.*

Readers would not be disappointed in this latter poem, if they proceeded to a perusal of it with a proper preconception of the kind of interest intended to be excited in that admirable work. In its kind it is the most perfect poem extant, though its kind may be inferior in interest—being in its essence didactic—to that other sort, in which instruction is conveyed more effectively, because less directly, in connection with stronger and more pleasurable emotions, and thereby in a closer affinity with acton. But might we not as rationally object to an accomplished woman's conversing, however agreeably, because it has happened that we have received a keener pleasure from her singing to the harp?—COLERIDGE, SAMUEL TAYLOR, 1807-18, *Lectures and Notes on Shakspeare.*

That Milton was mistaken in preferring this work, excellent as it is, to the "Paradise Lost," we readily admit. But we are sure that the superiority of the "Paradise Lost" to the "Paradise Regained" is not more decided, than the superiority of the "Paradise Regained" to every poem which has since made its appearance. But our limits prevent us from discussing the point at length. We hasten on to that extraordinary production, which the general suffrage of critics has placed in the highest class of human compositions. —MACAULAY, THOMAS BABINGTON, 1825, *Milton, Edinburgh Review; Critical and Miscellaneous Essays.*

The neglect which "Paradise Lost" never experienced seems to have been long the lot of "Paradise Regained." It was not popular with the world: it was long believed to manifest a decay of the poet's genius; and, in spite of all that the critics have written, it is still but the favorite of some whose predilections for the Miltonic style are very strong. The subject is so much less capable of calling forth the vast powers of his mind, that we should be unfair in comparing it throughout with the greater poem: it has been called a model of the shorter epic, an action comprehending few characters and a brief space of time. The love of Milton for dramatic dialogue, imbibed from Greece, is still more apparent than in "Paradise Lost:" the whole poem, in fact, may almost be accounted a drama of primal simplicity; the narrative and descriptive part serving rather to diversify and relieve the speeches of the actors, than their speeches, as in the legitimate epic, to enliven the narration. "Paradise Regained" abounds with passages equal to any of the same nature in "Paradise Lost;" but the argumentative tone is kept up till it produces some tediousness; and perhaps, on the whole, less pains have been exerted to adorn and elevate that which appeals to the imagination.—HALLAM, HENRY, 1837–39, *Introduction to the Literature of Europe*, pt. iv, ch. v, par. 35.

"Paradise Regained" is tedious, though calm and beautiful.—CHATEAUBRIAND, FRANÇOIS RENÉ, VICOMTE DE 1837, *Sketches of English Literature*.

Milton has no idealism,—not even in the "Paradise Regained," where there was most scope for it. His poetry is for the most part quite literal; and the objects he describes have all a certain definiteness and individuality which separates them from the infinite. He has often endeavoured to present images where everything should have been lost in sentiment.—WILSON, JOHN, 1854? *Essays, Critical and Imaginary*.

One of the most unread epics in the English language.—HOWELLS, WILLIAM DEAN, 1877, *Lives of Lord Herbert of Cherbury and Thomas Ellwood, with Essays*, p. 169.

In this poem he has not only curbed his imagination, but has almost suppressed it. He has amplified, but has hardly introduced any circumstance which is not in the original. "Paradise Regained" is little more than a paraphrase of the Temptation as found in the synoptical gospels. It is

a marvel of ingenuity that more than two thousand lines of blank verse can have been constructed out of some twenty lines of prose, without the addition of any invented incident, or the insertion of any irrelevant digression. In the first three books of "Paradise Regained" there is not a single simile. Nor yet can it be said that the version of the gospel narrative has the fault of most paraphrases, viz., that of weakening the effect, and obliterating the chiselled features of the original.—PATTISON, MARK, 1879, *Milton* (*English Men of Letters*), p. 187.

Of necessity the poem is rather a splendid fragment than a complete epic. Satan and his angels are not cast out, nor is man restored to the forfeited delights of Paradise. One blow is struck in the great contest: the obedience of Christ baffles and overcomes the tempter, who had seduced our first parents into disobedience. Then the poem closes with Christ's return to his mother's house, brought on his way with joy by attendant choirs of angels.—MASTERMAN, J. HOWARD B., 1897, *The Age of Milton*, p. 69.

As he grew older the taste of Milton grew more austere. The change in the character of his ornament is deeply marked when we ascend from the alpine meadows of "Paradise Lost" to the peaks of "Paradise Regained," where the imaginative air is so highly rarefied that many readers find it difficult to breathe.—GOSSE, EDMUND, 1897, *Short History of Modern English Literature*, p. 167.

The latter epic indubitably shows some falling off in the poet's powers; the supernatural vein has already yielded the best of its ore; earth must now be the main scene of the drama; the piercing splendors of the poet's earlier verse give place to something more like grand and sonorous prose. Yet now and then the old inspiration seems to sieze him.—STRONG, AUGUSTUS HOPKINS, 1897, *The Great Poets and Their Theology*, p. 252.

In this poem there is noticeable a distinct change from Milton's earlier manner,—a sudden purging away of ornament, a falling back on the naked concept, a preference for language as slightly as possible tinctured with metaphoric suggestion. A portion of this change may be due to failing vividness of imagination; certainly the abandonment of rapid narrative for tedious argumentation marks the increasing garrulity of age. Christ and Satan in the wilderness dispute with studied casuistry, until the sense of the spiritual drama in which they are protagonists is almost lost. As this same weakness is apparent also in the later books of "Paradise Lost," we must lay it largely to the score of flagging creative energy. But in still greater measure the change seems to be a deliberate experiment in style, or perhaps more truly a conscious reproduction, in language, of that rarefied mental atmosphere to which the author had climbed from the rich valley mists of his youth.—MOODY, WILLIAM VAUGHN, 1899, *ed., Poetical Works of Milton, Cambridge ed., Life, p.* xxxi.

SAMSON AGONISTES
1671

In this tragedy are however many particular beauties, many just sentiments and striking lines; but it wants that power of attracting the attention which a well-connected plan produces.—JOHNSON, SAMUEL, 1779, *John Milton, Lives of the English Poets.*

We are by no means insensible to the merits of this celebrated piece, to the severe dignity of the style, the graceful and pathetic solemnity of the opening speech, or the wild and barbaric melody which gives so striking an effect to the choral passages. But we think it, we confess, the least successful effort of the genius of Milton.—MACAULAY, THOMAS BABINGTON, 1825, *Milton, Edinburgh Review, Critical and Miscellaneous Essays.*

I have lately read his "Samson," which has more of the antique spirit than any production of any other modern poet. He is very great, and his own blindness enabled him to describe with so much truth the situation of Samson. Milton was really a poet; one to whom we owe all possible respect.—GOETHE, JOHANN WOLFGANG, 1830, *Conversations with Eckermann, tr. Oxenford, vol.* II, *p.* 220.

The tragedy of "Samson" breathes all the energy and simplicity of the antique. The poet himself is depicted in the person of the Israelite, blind, a prisoner, and unfortunate. A noble way of revenging himself on his age.—CHATEAUBRIAND, FRANÇOIS RENÉ, VICOMTE DE 1837, *Sketches of English Literature, vol.* II, *p.* 106.

Johnson considered the versification of these choruses "so harsh and dissonant, as scarce to preserve (whether the lines end with or without rhime) any appearance of metrical regularity;" and it must be confessed there are lines which almost seem to merit a censure thus severe. But modern pronunciation is *not* the pronunciation of Milton. Many verses, as they are now read by some of Milton's admirers, would disgust the poet, full as much as his critic.—GUEST, EDWIN, 1838, *A History of English Rhythms, vol.* II, *p.* 259.

"Samson Agonistes," a tragedy, most elaborately composed, and on the severest Greek model, is uninviting both in its theme and the treatment of it; yet the dialogues abound with sublime and pious sentiments; while, though much of the versification is harsh, and scarcely reducible to metre, the diction throughout exemplifies the full strength and affluence of the English Language.—MONTGOMERY, JAMES, 1843, *ed., The Poetical Works of John Milton, Memoir, vol.* I, *p.* xlviii.

The most successful attempt at reproducing the Greek tragedy, both in theme and treatment, is the "Samson Agonistes," as it is also the most masterly piece of English versification. Goethe admits that it alone, among modern works, has caught life from the breath of the antique spirit.—LOWELL, JAMES RUSSELL, 1871, *Swinburne's Tragedies, My Study Windows, p.* 220.

From a purely literary point of view the tragedy of "Samson Agonistes," which, as the Preface needlessly states, was "never intended to the stage," cannot be said to possess merits commensurate with its historical and biographical value. That it has escaped representation under conditions wholly uncongenial to it, may be due not only to the sacred character of the source of the subject, but also to the circumstance that by composing music to it as an oratorio Handel has removed it for ever from possible contact with the play-house.—WARD, ADOLPHUS WILLIAM, 1875–99, *A History of English Dramatic Literature, vol.* III, *p.* 204.

We have now shown that the two most noticeable characteristics of the "Samson Agonistes," the personal element which runs through it and its dramatic form, modelled upon that of the ancient Greek tragedy; are even more markedly the special features of the "Samson" of Vondel. We know, further, that the Dutch play preceded the English one by at least five years. It only remains for us to show from internal evidence that Milton was acquainted with the language of Vondel's play in order to complete the chain of evidence, and make it more than probable that the one is the direct descendant of the other.—EDMUNDSON, GEORGE, 1885, *Milton and Vondel, p.*170.

The opinions which critics have ventured on the versification of the choruses in "Samson Agonistes" would be sufficient proof that they had met with something not well understood, even if they had never misinterpreted the rhythm. It is not less than an absurdity to suppose that Milton's carefully-made verse could be unmusical: on the other hand it is easy to see how the farsought effects of the greatest master in any art may lie beyond the general taste.—BRIDGES, ROBERT, 1889–93, *Milton Prosody, p.* 32.

The "Samson Agonistes," the most Greek-like drama ever written since the death of Euripides, gives us some insight into the passion-seething abysses of his soul, whose swelling turbulence was only kept down by a sovereign faith. Professor Seeley finely calls it "the thundering reverberation of a mighty spirit struck by the plectrum of disappointment;" but though that plectrum struck the reverberant chords into thunder, it was the last sob of the retiring storm beyond which we already see the gleam of blue.—FARRAR, FREDERICK WILLIAM, 1891, *Three Portraits of Milton, The English Illustrated Magazine, vol.* 9, *p.* 120.

As an autobiographical fragment, the tragedy is invested with a pecular pathos. We almost forget at times that it is Samson who is speaking, so unmistakably does the personality of the poet break through the conventional setting of the drama.—MASTERMAN, J. HOWARD B., 1897, *The Age of Milton, p.* 70.

SONNETS

They deserve not any particular criticism; for of the best it can only be said, that they are not bad; and perhaps only the eighth and twenty-first are truly entitled to this slender commendation.—JOHNSON, SAMUEL, 1779, *John Milton, Lives of the English Poets.*

The sonnets of Milton, like those of Danté, are frequently deficient in sweetness of diction and harmony of versification, yet they possess, what seldom is discernible in compositions of this kind, energy and sublimity of sentiment. The sonnets to Cyriac Skinner, to Fairfax, Cromwell, and Vane, are remarkable for these qualities, and for vigour of expression, whilst those addressed to the Nightingale and to Mr. Laurence, can boast, I may venture to assert, both of melody in language and elegance in thought. It should also be observed, that Milton has altogether avoided the quaint and metaphysic concetti of Petrarch.—DRAKE, NATHAN, 1798–1820, *Literary Hours, vol.* I, *p.* 80.

The sonnets are more or less striking, according as the occasions which gave birth to them are more or less interesting. But they are, almost without exception, dignified by a sobriety and greatness of mind to which we know not where to look for a parallel.—MACAULAY, THOMAS BABINGTON, 1825, *Milton, Edinburgh Review, Critical and Miscellaneous Essays.*

Scorn not the Sonnet; . . .
     . . . when a damp
Fell round the path of Milton, in his hand
The thing became a trumpet; whence he blew
Soul-animating strains—alas, too few !
—WORDSWORTH, WILLIAM, 1827, *Sonnet.*

Our author's Sonnets are of very unequal, and some of very indifferent merit, though the principal fault of the least excellent is the uncouth intertexture of the lines, the ruggedness of the rhythm, and, in some instances, the barbarity of the rhymes.—MONTGOMERY, JAMES, 1843, *ed., The Poetical Works of John Milton, Memoir, vol.* I, *p.* xxviii.

Few his words, but strong,
And sounding through all ages and all climes.
He caught the Sonnet from the dainty hand
Of Love, who cried to lose it; and he gave
The notes to Glory.
—LANDOR, WALTER SAVAGE, 1853, *To Lamartine, Last Fruit off an Old Tree.*

Milton's English Sonnets are only seventeen in all:

"Soul-animating strains, alas! too few."

They are so far beyond all question the noblest in the language that it is a matter of curious interest to note the utter incapacity of Johnson to recognize any greatness in them at all. The utmost which he will allow is that "three of them are not bad;" and he and Hannah More once set themselves to investigate the causes of their badness, the badness itself being taken for granted. Johnson's explanation of this contains a lively illustration: "Why, Madam," he said, "Milton's was a genius that could hew a Colossus out of a rock, but could not carve heads on cherrystones."—TRENCH, RICHARD CHENEVIL, 1868, *A Household Book of English Poetry.*

Even when Milton's matter repels or fails to interest, there is always something in his manner which compels an attentive and fascinated hearing. The personal quality, which was of pure and high self-containedness all compact, informs the language and gives it a magical power. He on his mountain-top had learned from the silent stars and voiceful winds a speech which was not the dialect of the crowd, and, whatever be the burden of the saying, there is a spell in the mere intonation. We feel the spell sometimes almost humorously, as in the rough-hewn sonnet with its harsh, unpoetic, bald, monosyllabic rhymes—"clogs," "dogs," "frogs," "hogs,"—which leaves almost the same sense of weight and mass that we derive from his nobler and more delightful utterances. Among these, it is needless to say, one stands apart in unapproached and unapproachable majesty. The great sonnet "On the late Massacres in Piedmont" is one of those achievements in which matter of the noblest order moulds for itself a form of the highest excellence, matter and form being, as in music and in all supreme art, so bound up and interfused that, though we know both of them to be there, we cannot know them or think of them apart. Much has been said in eulogy of this sonnet, and said worthily and well; but there is a perfection which mocks praise, and it is this perfection that is here attained; not the perfection which consists in this quality or in that, but which comes when all qualities which may be displayed, all potentialities which can be exerted, meet in triumphant, satisfying, utter accomplishment.—NOBLE, JAMES ASHCROFT, 1880-92, *The Sonnet in England, p.* 33.

They differ from all the sonnets of the time, in that they are simple in thought and unstudied in expression, and that they convince us of the entire sincerity of the singer. We feel that they were not written because other poets had made a reputation by such compositions, but because their writer had something to say, and knew that the best way for him to say it was in this form. If he had read Shakspere and Drummond, or Drayton and Daniel, he forgot them in his remembrance of Petrarch, whose form he mastered, at the age of twenty-three, as no English poet since Sidney had done. They do not read like the productions of a young man, for they are mature in conception and severe in execution—demanding our deepest respect as well as our highest admiration. The credentials of a strong intellect, which knows itself and the work it has to do, their gravity is Shaksperean. They bear a weight of thought which had never before laid upon the English sonnet, and they bear it lightly as a flower.—STODDARD, RICHARD HENRY, 1881, *The Sonnet in English Poetry, Scribner's Monthly, vol.* 22, *p.* 915.

Hallam and certain other writers have declared themselves unable to reconcile their judgment to the frequent violation of the legitimate structure in Milton's sonnets. It is true that the pause between the major and minor portions of the sonnet (so uniformly observed in the best Italian examples) is not to be found in Milton, but the rhyme-scheme is always faultlessly in conformity with the most rigid rule, and the sonnets, even where they link themselves together—as in the cases of the two divorce sonnets and the two sonnets on his blindness—stand alone in self-centered unity, and never become sonnet stanzas. The serious divergence favoured by Milton in his practice of running octave into sestet was clearly the result of a deliberate conviction that the sonnet in his hands was too short a poem to be broken into halves, and hence his sonnets, each done in a breath as to metrical flow, possess the intellectual unity of oneness of conception, at the same time that they are devoid of the twofold metrical and intellectual unity which comes of the rounded perfectness of linked and contrasted parts. Much may be said for the beauty of the sonnet structure adopted by Milton, and indeed the model has been so much in requisition in recent years, that it appears to merit the distinct nomenclature which, in the index of metrical groups, I have ventured to give it.—CAINE, HALL, 1882, *ed., Sonnets of Three Centuries, p.* 280.

Some of Milton's most famous sonnets were never published in his lifetime. They were not even printed until 1694, and then from copies which had been circulating from hand to hand in manuscript. It was not until 1753 that the text was published from the originals. These at once made it plain that the variations which had crept in were, with one possible exception, variations for the worse, and, in some instances, grossly for the worse.—LOUNSBURY, THOMAS R., 1892, *Studies in Chaucer, vol.* I, *p.* 232.

His sonnets were no chamber exercises: each owed its inspiration to a real occasion, and that inspiration of reality lifted it high above mere simulation of the Horatian mode.—QUILLER-COUCH, A. T., 1897, *English Sonnets, Introduction, p.* xvi.

ON THE MORNING OF CHRIST'S NATIVITY
1629

The "Ode on the Nativity," far less popular than most of the poetry of Milton, is perhaps the finest in the English language. A grandeur, a simplicity, a breadth of manner, an imagination at once elevated and restrained by the subject, reign throughout it. If Pindar is a model of lyric poetry, it would be hard to name any other ode so truly Pindaric; but more has naturally been derived from the Scriptures. Of the other short poems, that on the death of the Marchioness of Westminister deserves particular mention.—HALLAM, HENRY, 1837–39, *Introduction to the Literature of Europe, pt.* iii, *ch.* V, *par.* 63.

The most distinct foreshadowing of Milton's great epic poem, and of his own independent genius, is an earlier poem—"The Hymn of the Nativity"—which gives the poet the fame of having composed almost in his youth the earliest of the great English odes, the like of which had not, I believe, been heard, since Pindar, two thousand years before, had struck the lyre for assembled Greece. It is a lyric that might have burst from that religious bard of paganism, could he have had prophetic vision of the Advent. It is a poem that revealed a new mastery of English versificaton, disciplined afterward to such power in the blank verse of "Paradise

Lost." Nothing in the way of meter can be grander than some of the transitions from the gentle music of the quiet passages to the passionate parts, and their deep reverberating lines that seem to go echoing on, spiritually sounding, long after they are heard no more.—REED, HENRY, 1855, *Lectures on English Literature, from Chaucer to Tennyson, p.* 193.

Show me one who delights in the "Hymn on the Nativity," and I will show you one who may never indeed be a singer in this world, but who is already a listener to the best.—MACDONALD, GEORGE, 1868, *England's Antiphon, p.* 200.

When, at the close of 1629, Milton began his "Ode on the Morning of Christ's Nativity," he was still closely imitating the form of these favourites of his, the Fletchers, until the fifth stanza was reached, and then he burst away in a magnificent measure of his own, pouring forth that hymn which carried elaborate lyrical writing higher than it had ever been taken before in England.—GOSSE, EDMUND, 1897, *Short History of Modern English Literature, p.* 143.

The "Hymn" may be reckoned the first fully opened flower of Milton's poetic springtime. . . . It would be difficult to find a poem that would better exemplify certain of the characteristics of a lyric poem than does the "Hymn on the Nativity." The religious fervor of the young poet informs every stanza of the poem; the pictures are painted for their dynamic emotional value only; the language is adorned with "rich and various gems" of expression; the sentiment is elevated; the metrical form is graceful and harmonious with the thought.—WALKER, ALBERT PERRY, 1900, *ed. Selections from the Poetical Works of John Milton, p.* 257.

L'ALLEGRO AND IL PENSEROSO
1633

I have heard a very judicious critic say, that he had an higher idea of Milton's style in poetry from the two following poems, than from his "Paradise Lost." It is certain the imagination shewn in them is correct and strong. The introduction to both in irregular measure is borrowed from the Italians, and hurts an English ear.—GOLDSMITH, OLIVER, 1767, *The Beauties of English Poetry.*

Of all the English poems in the

descriptive stlye, the richest and most remarkable are, Milton's "Allegro" and "Penseroso." The collection of gay images on the one hand, and of melancholy ones on the other, exhibited in these to small, but inimitably fine poems, are as exquisite as can be conceived. They are, indeed, the storehouse whence many succeeding poets have enriched their descriptions of similar subjects; and they alone are sufficient for illustrating the observations which I made, concerning the proper selection of circumstances in descriptive writing. —BLAIR, HUGH, 1783, *Lectures on Rhetoric and Belles-Lettres, ed. Mills, Lecture* xl, *p.* 454.

We find nowhere in his writings that whining sensibility and exaggeration of morbid feeling, which makes so much of modern poetry effeminating. If he is not gay, he is not spirit-broken. His "L'Allegro" proves, that he understood thoroughly the bright and joyous aspects of nature; and in his "Penseroso," where he was tempted to accumulate images of gloom, we learn, that the saddest views which he took of creation, are such as inspire only pensive musing or lofty contemplation.—CHANNING, WILLIAM ELLERY, 1826, *Remarks on the Character and Writings of John Milton.*

There can be little doubt as to which of the two characters he portrays was after Milton's own heart. He portrays "L'Allegro" with much skill and excellence; but he cannot feign with him the sympathy he genuinely feels with the other; into his portrait of "Il Penseroso" he throws himself, so as to speak, with all his soul.— HALES, JOHN W., 1872, *Longer English Poems, p.* 231.

He strictly meditated the Muse, and she was not thankless, for she crystallized the morning dew of his genius into those exquisite jewels in the ears of antiquity, "L'Allegro" and "Il Penseroso." —STODDARD, RICHARD HENRY, 1883, *English Verse: Chaucer to Burns, Introduction, p.* xxxvii.

As for "L'Allegro" and "Il Penseroso," who shall praise them fitly? They are among the few things about which there is no difference of opinion, which are as delightful to childhood as to criticism, to youth as to age. To dwell on their technical excellences (the chief of which is the unerring precision with which the catalectic and acatalectic lines are arranged and interchanged) has a certain air of impertinence about it. Even a critical King Alfonso El Sabio could hardly think it possible that Milton might have taken a hint here, although some persons have, it seems, been disturbed because skylarks do not come to the window, just as others are troubled because the flowers in "Lycidas" do not grow at the same time, and because they think they could see stars through the "star-proof" trees of the "Arcades."—SAINTSBURY, GEORGE, 1887, *History of Elizabethan Literature, p.* 320.

Of course Milton's "Il Penseroso" and "L'Allegro" have far more value even as country poems than hundreds of more literal transcripts. From a literary point of view indeed the juxtapositions of half a dozen epithets alone would prove the genius of the writer. But there are no sharp outlines; the scholar pauses in his walk to peer across the watered flat, or raises his eyes from his book to see the quiver of leaves upon the sunlit wall; he notes an effect it may be; but his images do not come like treasures lavished from a secret storehouse of memory.—BENSON, ARTHUR CHRISTOPHER, 1896, *Essays, p.* 71.

At the time these two poems were written, they stood at the high-water mark of English poetry. In their sphere they have never been excelled. In spite of little inaccuracies of description (for Milton was too much in love with books to be a close observer of nature), we find nowhere else such an exquisite delineation of country life and country scenes. These idyls are the more remarkable because their light, joyous spirit stands in strong contrast with the elevation, dignity, and austerity of his other poems.—PAINTER, F. V. N., 1899, *A History of English Literature, p.* 170.

The language of these two little masterpieces has been the despair of poets. It is not that it is so beautiful, for others have equaled or excelled it in the mere conjuring power of suggestion; but that it is, as a French critic has finely said, so *just* in its beauty. The means are exquisitely proportioned to the end. The speech incarnates the thought as easily, as satisfyingly, as the muscles of a Phidian youth incarnate the motor-impulse

of his brain. Always fruition is just
gently touched. To the connoisseur in
language there is a sensation of almost
physical soothing in its perfect poise and
play.—MOODY, WILLIAM VAUGHN, 1899,
ed., *Poetical Works of Milton, Cambridge
ed., p. 26.*

LATIN POEMS

I know not where the scholars of the
continent could have gone for more beautiful specimens of modern poetry than
his "First Elegy," and the "Address to
his Father."—MITFORD, JOHN, 1851–63,
ed., *Works of John Milton, Life, vol. I, p.*
cxxiii.

Milton, like most of the learned men of
the age, wrote in Latin both in prose and
verse. The former will, we believe, bear
a comparison with any Latin prose of the
time, unless we should think that of the
natives of the countries which speak languages derived from the Latin to be
excepted; as a modern Latin poet, critics
are disposed to assign him a place in the
first rank. It is not unworthy of notice,
that while in English prose he delighted
in long and involving sentences, his Latin
periods are not very long nor much involved.—KEIGHTLEY, THOMAS, 1855, *An
Account of the Life, Opinions, and Writings of John Milton, p. 388.*

It is perhaps sufficient to say that
critics of such different times, tempers,
and attitude towards their subject as Johnson and the late Rector of Lincoln,—
critics who agree in nothing except
literary competence,—are practically at
one as to the remarkable excellence of
Milton's Latin verse at its best. It is
little read now, but it is a pity that any
one who can read Latin should allow himself to be ignorant of at least the beautiful "Epitaphium Damonis" on the poet's
friend, Charles Diodati. —SAINTSBURY,
GEORGE, 1887, *History of Elizabethan
Literature, p. 318.*

The "Epitaphium Damonis" is the best,
and—except for a few fragments—the
last of Milton's Latin poems. His Latin
verse surpassed that of his contemporaries,
not so much in scholarly elegance as in
force of expression. To him Latin is
almost a living language.—MASTERMAN,
J. HOWARD B., 1897, *The Age of Milton,
p. 28.*

As to the artistic qualities of this
poetry, it would not be profitable to speak

here at length. In the main they are
qualities of delicacy and felicitousness
rather than of strength. They bear a relation to Milton's later English poetry
roughly analogous to that which Tennyson's early lyrical experiments bear to his
adult work. In them Milton learned his
trade of poet, at least on its technical and
imitative side. The habit of assimilation,
the power to freight his lines with the
accumulated riches of past thought, we
see here in the making, and we see also
how the habit of conveying commonplace
thought in a sonorous and magniloquent
medium fostered that large Miltonic diction, which was so noble in Milton's own
hands, and so intolerably hollow in the
hands of his eighteenth century imitators.
It would be wrong, however, to think of
these poems as consciously disciplinary.
When they were written, the chances
seemed even that Milton's main work as a
poet would be in Latin rather than in English; they represent sincere creative
effort, and offer many rare intrinsic beauties in spite of their immaturity.—MOODY,
WILLIAM VAUGHN, 1899, ed., *Poetical
Works of Milton, Cambridge ed., p. 320.*

PROSE WRITINGS

His prose writings disagreeable, though
not altogether defective in genius.—HUME,
DAVID, 1762, *History of England, The Commonwealth.*

"Our language," says Addison, "sunk
under him." But the truth is, that, both
in prose and verse, he had formed his style
by a perverse and pedantick principle. He
was desirous to use English words with
foreign idiom. This in all his prose is discovered and condemned; for there judgement operates freely, neither softened by
the beauty nor awed by the dignity of his
thoughts; but such is the power of his
poetry, that his call is obeyed without resistance, the reader feels himself in captivity to a higher and nobler mind, and
criticism sinks in admiration.—JOHNSON,
SAMUEL, 1779, *Milton, Lives of the English Poets.*

Dr. Johnson endeavoured to give an air
of dignity and novelty to his diction by
affecting the order of words usual in
poetry. Milton's prose has not only this
drawback, but it has also the disadvantage
of being formed on a classical model. It
is like a fine translation from the Latin;

and, indeed, he wrote originally in Latin. . . . Milton's prose-style savours too much of poetry, and, as I have already hinted, of an imitation of the Latin.— HAZLITT, WILLIAM, 1821-2, *On the Prose Style of Poets, Table-Talk.*

It is to be regretted that the prose writings of Milton should, in our time, be so little read. As compositions, they deserve the attention of every man who wishes to become acquainted with the full power of the English language. They abound with passages, compared with which the finest declamations of Burke sink into insignificance. They are a perfect field of cloth of gold. The style is stiff, with gorgeous embroidery. Not even in the earlier books of the "Paradise Lost" has he ever risen higher than in those parts of his controversial works, in which his feelings, excited by conflict, find a vent in bursts of devotional and lyric rapture. It is, to borrow his own majestic language, "a sevenfold chorus of hallelujahs and harping symphonies."—MACAULAY, THOMAS BABINGTON, 1825, *Milton, Edinburgh Review; Critical and Miscellaneous Essays.*

In many passages of his polemics there is an intensity of eloquence that seems to fuse the multitude of his thoughts, and send them glowing white, from the crucible of his mind into the mind of the reader, scarcely able to contain them in the mould of his narrower conception. We find also an impetuosity and impatience in Milton's prose which never occurs in his verse. The vehemence of his argument, whether as an advocate or an accuser, carries him out of himself, in acrimonious invective or rapturous panegyric.—MONTGOMERY, JAMES, 1843, *ed., The Poetical Works of John Milton, Memoir, vol.* I. *p.* xv.

His prose was no "cool element:" most often it sparkles and scathes like liquid metal, yet softens here and there, and spreads out into calmer, milder passages, stamped with an inexpressible poetic loveliness.—ARNOLD, THOMAS, 1862-87, *A Manual of English Literature, p.* 180.

The Prose Writings of Milton, inspired by stirring events amid which they were written, form his contribution to the literature of freedom. To them were given the matured powers of a mind enriched by varied studies, and ripened by meditation. They form the labors of his life, grand in thought and expression, as the poetic recreations of his earlier and later years are sublime and beautiful. In them his opinions, character, motives and conduct are portrayed with singular fidelity.—HURD, FAYETTE, 1865, *ed., The Milton Anthology, Preface, p.* i.

The expression is not too strong. There are moments when, shaking from him the dust of his arguments, the poet bursts suddenly forth, and bears us away in a torrent of incomparable eloquence. We get, not the phrase of the orator, but the glow of the poet, a flood of images poured around his arid theme, a rushing flight carrying us above his paltry controversies. The polemical writings of Milton are filled with such beauties. The prayer which concludes the treatise on Reformation in England, the praise of zeal in the "Apology for Smectymnus," the portrait of Cromwell in the "Second Defense of the English People," and, finally, the whole tract on the "Liberty of Unlicensed Printing" from beginning to end, are some of the most memorable pages in English literature, and some of the most characteristic products of the genius of Milton. —SCHERER, EDMOND, 1868, *Milton, Essays on English Literature, tr. Matthew Arnold.*

Marvellous as are Milton's prose works, they are, especially the treatise on Divorce, lacking in lofty rationality and consistency of argument. The poet is revealed in the splendour of occasional thoughts and in passages of noble eloquence; but the imagination has not blended with the understanding so as to give insight, comprehension, and light to the general train of reasoning.—TULLOCH, JOHN, 1872, *Rational Theology and Christian Philosophy in England in the Seventeenth Century, vol.* I, *p.* 350, *note.*

Concerning Milton's style the most diverse opinions have been pronounced. Everything depends upon the point of view. Rich and powerful it is undeniably, coming from such a master of words, and yields in the highest degree the pleasure of luxurious expression. But the student need hardly be warned that Milton's prose is to be enjoyed without being imitated: for modern purposes the language and idiom are too stiffly Latinised, and the imagery too fantastic. Further, for a work of controversy the style is too ornate, too unmethodical, and too coarsely vituperative to have much convincing or converting power. In Milton still more than in Taylor the application is lost in the gorgeous splendour of words and imagery, and all but decided adherents are repelled by the unmeasured discharge of abuse and ridicule.—MINTO, WILLIAM, 1872-80, *Manual of English Prose Literature, p.* 308.

Jeremy Taylor's prose is poetical prose. Milton's prose is not poetical prose, but a different thing, the prose of a poet; not like Taylor's, loaded with imagery on the outside; but coloured by imagination from within. Milton is the first English writer who, possessing in the ancient models a standard of the effect which could be produced by choice of words, set himself to the conscious study of our native tongue with a firm faith in its as yet undeveloped powers as an instrument of thought.—PATTISON, MARK, 1879, *Milton, (English Men of Letters), p.* 68.

Looking upon the life of Milton the politician merely as a disastrous and humiliating episode in the life of Milton the poet, Mr. Pattison cannot be expected to entertain the idea that the poem is in any sense the work of the politician. Yet we cannot help thinking that the tension and elevation which Milton's nature had undergone in the mighty struggle, together with the heroic dedication of his faculties to the most serious objects, must have had not a little to do both with the final choice of his subject and with the tone of his poem. "The great Puritan epic" could hardly have been written by any one but a militant Puritan.—SMITH, GOLDWIN, 1880, *Pattison's Milton, New York Nation, vol.* 30, *p.* 31.

Milton, when, as he said, he wished "to soar a little," had a magnificent abundance of words at his command, and at times he broke out into rich poetical prose. But when he had to write some plain description, his prose lumbered as clumsily as a heavy cart over rough paving-stones.—PERRY, THOMAS SERGEANT, 1883, *English Literature in the Eighteenth Century, p.* 7.

The passages which diversify and relieve his prose works are far more beautiful in their kind than anything to be found elsewere in English prose. . . . There

is no English prose author whose prose is so constantly racy with such a distinct and varied savour as Milton's. It is hardly possible to open him anywhere after the fashion of the *Sortes Virgilianæ* without lighting on a line or a couple of lines, which for the special purpose it is impossible to improve. And it might be contended with some plausibility that this abundance of jewels, or purple patches, brings into rather unfair prominence the slips of grammar and taste, the inequalities of thought, the deplorable attempts to be funny, the rude outbursts of bargee invective, which also occur so numerously. One other peculiarity, or rather one result of these peculiarities, remains to be noticed; and that is that Milton's prose is essentially inimitable. It would be difficult even to caricature or to parody it; and to imitate it as his verse, at least his later verse, has been so often imitated, is simply impossible.—SAINTSBURY, GEORGE, 1887, *History of Elizabethan Literature, p.* 325.

Were Milton, in his diction, more like Bunyan and less like Browne and Burton, the inherent worth of his prose would at once give it power and currency. Instead of this we note harsh inversions and cumbrous constructions. Our attention is called, at every point, rather to the earlier and cruder forms of English than to its more modern improvements. It is thus that Pattison properly speaks of "the absence of construction" by which he means—of clear construction. He adds, "Milton does not seem to have any notion of what a period means. He leaves off, not when the sense closes but when he is out of breath." There is truth in this. Not a few of those passages so often quoted by critics as examples of clear and elegant English, are hopelessly involved and must be annotated and explained in order to be readable. Milton would have presented a clear diction and structure had he known "small Latin" and given full expression to his English speech.—HUNT, THEODORE W., 1887, *Representative English Prose and Prose Writers, p.* 252.

The incoherence and awkwardness of humanistic prose in England reach their climax in some of Milton's cumbrous periods. Sentence, sub-sentence, parenthesis, qualifying clause, are only kept together by a liberal expenditure of what may be described as verbal hooks and eyes.—SYMONDS, JOHN ADDINGTON, 1890, *Essays Speculative and Suggestive, vol.* I, *p.* 324.

No writings are more unequal, but few will deny that they contain some of the grandest and stateliest passages in the English language.—FARRAR, FREDERICK WILLIAM, 1890, *Formative Influences, The Forum, vol.* 10, *p.* 381.

To Milton prose was an unnatural medium, which he never subdued to his purposes. As a prose writer he commands admiration only where he enlists sympathy. He used the weapon provided for him by his age with consummate power; but it was a weapon which he seized as he found it, which owed its force to the arm that wielded it, and which he left with no sharpness added to its temper, no new polish to its surface, no new facility in its contrivance.—CRAIK, HENRY, 1893, *English Prose, Introduction, vol.* II, *p.* 6.

Milton's colloquial sallies are at times such as might be expected from an excessive familiarity with epistolary Latin, at other times they are the efforts of a forced sportiveness too grim to be altogether agreeable. But even in these, and how infinitely more in the wealth of illustrations, images, and ideas lavished upon any subject which he is fain to treat, do we recognise the wealth of an imagination which seems at times, within the limits of a single sentence, to master diction and syntax and all the conditions of written speech! To decry such a style as composite is to revive the short-sighted captiousness of an obsolete method of criticism, which was capable of analysing materials, but not of apprehending the power which transfuses what it has appropriated. Milton's prose, all exceptions taken, and all cavils allowed their force, remains the most extraordinary literary prose, and the most wonderful poet's prose, embodied in English literature.—WARD, ADOLPHUS WILLIAM, 1893, *English Prose, ed. Craik*, II, *p.* 462.

In truth, the influence of Milton's English prose writings seems to have been very slight. In his attacks upon prelacy he went with the stream, and his voice mingled with the universal shout. When he took an independent line, when he pleaded for liberty of divorce, or, with a heroism of which even he might not have been capable if his infirmity had not severed him from the world, launched pamphlets against monarchy on the very vigil of the Restoration, he produced absolutely no effect whatever. Nor can we perceive that his "Areopagitica" hastened the liberty of the press by a day, though, when this had come about by wholly different agencies, it was rightly adopted as the gospel of the new dispensation: as the newly-discovered Venus of Milo might be made the goddess of a classical revival inaugurated while she yet slept under the sod. The only prose production of Milton to which a considerable contemporary effect can be justly ascribed is not an English but a Latin one, his defence of the English people against Salmasius.— GARNETT, RICHARD, 1894, *ed., Prose of Milton, Introduction, p.* viii.

His political essays, sometimes coarse in expression, sometimes harsh with passion, always suggesting the partisan and the advocate, and seldom the philosopher, were nevertheless powerful additions to the discussions of the times.—CHURCH, SAMUEL HARDEN, 1894, *Oliver Cromwell, p.* 326.

Milton's prose works are perhaps not read, at the present day, to the extent demanded by their great and varied merits, among which may be named their uncompromising advocacy of whatsoever things are true, honest, just, pure, lovely, and of good report; their eloquent assertion of the inalienable rights of men to a wholesome exercise of their intellectual faculties, the right to determine for themselves, with all the aids they can command, what is truth and what is error; the right freely to communicate their honest thoughts from one to another,— rights which constitute the only sure and lasting foundation of individual, civil, political, and religious liberty; the ever-conscious sentiment which they exhibit, on the part of the poet, of an entire dependence upon "that Eternal Spirit, who can enrich with all utterance and knowledge, and sends out his Seraphim with the hallowed fire of his altar, to touch and purify the lips of whom he pleases;" the ever-present consciousness they exhibit of that stewardship which every man as a probationer of immortality must render an account, according to the full measure of the talents with which he has been intrusted—of the sacred obligation, incumbent upon every one, of acting throughout the details of life, private or public, trivial or momentous, "as ever in his great Task-Master's eye."—CORSON, HIRAM, 1899, *An Introduction to the Prose and Poetical Works of John Milton, p.* xiii.

DOCTRINE AND DISCIPLINE OF DIVORCE
1643

It is a great deal easier to pass by Milton, or to sneer at him, for his great work on "The Doctrine and Discipline of Divorce," than to answer the arguments therein contained. — HELPS, ARTHUR, 1851, *Companions of My Solitude, p.* 147.

If the early date of the pamphlet be the true date; if the "Doctrine and Discipline" was in the hands of the public on August 1; if Milton was brooding over this seething agony of passion all through July, with the young bride, to whom he had been barely wedded a month, in the house where he was writing, then the only apology for this outrage upon the charities, not to say decencies, of home is that which is suggested by the passage referred to. Then the pamphlet, however imprudent, becomes pardonable. It is a passionate cry from the depths of a great despair; another evidence of the noble purity of a nature which refused to console itself as other men would have consoled themselves; a nature which, instead of an egotistical whine for its own deliverance, sets itself to plead the common cause of man and of society. He gives no intimation of any individual interest, but his argument throughout glows with a white heat of concealed emotion, such as could only be stirred by the sting of some personal and present misery.—PATTISON, MARK, 1879, *Milton (English Men of Letters), p.* 55.

Of Milton's pamphlet it is everyone's duty to speak with profound respect. It is a noble and passionate cry for a high ideal of married life, which, so he argued, had by inflexible laws been changed into a drooping and disconsolate household captivity, without refuge or redemption. . . . This pamphlet on divorce marks the beginning of Milton's mental isolation. Nobody had a word to say for it. Episcopalian, Presbyterian, and Independent held his doctrine in as much abhorrence

as did the Catholic, and all alike regarded its author as either an impracticable dreamer or worse.—BIRRELL, AUGUSTINE, 1887, *Obiter Dicta, Second Series, pp.* 22, 23.

What gross injustice the world has done him on this point! Married at an age when a man who has preserved the lofty ideals and personal purity of youth is peculiary liable to deception, to a woman far below him in character and intellect, a pretty fool utterly unfitted to take a sincere and earnest view of life or to sympathize with him in his studies; deserted by her a few weeks after the wedding-day; met by stubborn refusal and unjust reproaches in every attempt to reclaim and reconcile her; accused by her family of disloyalty in politics, and treated as if he were unworthy of honourable consideration; what wonder that his heart experienced a great revulsion, that he began to doubt the reality of such womanhood as he had described and immortalized in "Comus," that he sought relief in elaborating a doctrine of divorce which should free him from the unworthy and irksome tie of a marriage which was in truth but an empty mockery? That divorce doctrine which he propounded in the heat of personal indignation, disguised even from himself beneath a mask of professedly calm philosophy, was surely false, and we cannot but condemn it. But can we condemn his actual conduct, so nobly inconsistent with his own theory?—VAN DYKE, HENRY, 1889–98, *The Poetry of Tennyson, p.* 80.

OF EDUCATION
1644

Milton was then a reformer "for his own hand;" and notwithstanding his moral and intellectual elevation and his superb power of rhetoric, he seems to me a less useful writer on education than the humble Puritans whom he probably would not deign to read. In his haughty self-reliance, he, like Carlyle with whom Seeley has well compared him, addressed his contemporaries *de haut en bas*, and though ready to teach could learn only among the old renowned authors with whom he associated himself and we associate him. Judged from our present standpoint the Tractate is found with many weaknesses to be strong in this, that it co-ordinates physical, moral, mental and æsthetic training.—QUICK, ROBERT H., 1868-90, *Essays on Educational Reformers, p.* 218.

There was in Milton's time in London a well-known gentleman by the name of Samuel Hartlib. He was the son of a Polish merchant, who had married an English lady and settled himself in England. He seems to have had a fresh, bright, kindly mind. Everybody knew him; he interested himself in everything that was live and good; he talked with everybody who had anything to say. Every great city has just such men—we know such men in ours. This gentleman had often talked with the great schoolmaster about education, and was very much interested in what Milton said; and he had begged Milton often, as they sat together talking, to write down what he was saying, so that it might not be lost. The busy Milton at last complied, and the result is that we have a dozen pages of his stately prose, in which he pictures his ideal of school-teaching and gives us, it is safe to say, a prospectus of philosophic education within which almost all the progress of our modern schools has been included, and which it is very far yet from outgrowing. Surely it will be interesting to look at his ideas in the light of modern developments. I know how often practical teachers are impatient of new theories. They do not love to listen to a mere philosopher who sits in his study and tells them what a school ought to be. But remember, Milton's ideas were not wholly theories. He had seen some practice. And remember, too, that if the teacher's art be in any high sense an art at all, it must have a philosophy behind it. If we would not allow it to sink into a mere set of rules, and depend for its success on certain mere tricks or knacks, it must forever refresh itself out of the fountain of first principles and inspire itself with the contemplation of even unattainable ideals. This leads us to a brief sketch of the main thoughts which this essay of the great Englishman contains. I am surprised, when I enumerate them, to see how thoroughly they are the thoughts which all our modern education has tried to realize. Here they are fully conceived in the rich mind of the representative man of two centuries ago.—BROOKS, PHILLIPS, 1874-94, *Essays and Addresses, p.* 308.

This tract, often reproduced and regarded, along with one of Locke's, as a substantial contribution to the subject, must often have grievously disappointed those who have eagerly consulted it for practical hints or guidance of any kind. Its interest is wholly biographical. It cannot be regarded as a valuable contribution to educational theory, but it is strongly marked with the Miltonic individuality. We find in it the same lofty conception of the aim which Milton carried into everything he attempted; the same disdain of the beaten routine, and proud reliance upon his own resources.—PATTISON, MARK, 1879, *Milton (English Men of Letters), p.* 44.

AREOPAGITICA
1644

It would not be easy to discover, in the whole stream and succession of literary productions any thing more cogent and forcible than this tract.—GODWIN, WILLIAM, 1824, *History of the Commonwealth of England, vol.* I, *p.* 352.

He attacked the licensing system in that sublime treatise which every statesman should wear as a sign upon his hand, and as frontlets between his eyes.—MACAULAY, THOMAS BABINGTON, 1825, *Milton, Edinburgh Review; Critical and Miscellaneous Essays.*

Many passages in this famous tract are admirably eloquent; an intense love of liberty and truth flows through it; the majestic soul of Milton breathes such high thoughts as had not been uttered before. —HALLAM, HENRY, 1837-39, *Introduction to the Literature of Europe, pt.* iii, *ch.* vii, *par.* 35.

The most splendid argument perhaps the world had then witnessed on behalf of intellectual liberty.—PRESCOTT, WILLIAM HICKLING, 1845, *History of Ferdinand and Isabella, vol.* III, *p.* 391.

The "Paradise Lost" is, indeed, scarcely a more glorious monument of the genius of Milton than that "Areopagitica." If, even at the present day, when the cause for which it was written has long since triumphed, it is impossible to read it without emotion, we can hardly doubt that when it first appeared it exercised a mighty influence over the awakening movement of liberty.—LECKY, WILLIAM EDWARD HARTPOLE, 1865, *Spirit of Rationalism in Europe, vol.* II.

All who care for English literature have read the "Areopagitica." It is the most literary of Milton's pamphlets, eloquent, to the point, and full of noble images splendidly wrought and fitted to their place. Its defence of books and the freedom of books will last as long as there are writers and readers of books. Its scorn of the censorship of writing is only excelled by its uplifted praise of true writing.—BROOKE, STOPFORD, 1879, *Milton (Classical Writers)*, p. 45.

Milton's one enduringly popular prose work.—WARD, ADOLPHUS WILLIAM, 1893, *English Prose, ed. Craik, vol. II, p. 451.*

The right of the "Areopagitica" to rank as best, as it is clearly the most popular, of Milton's prose works, has been disputed by the jealous admirers of others. The popularity, no doubt due in part to the subject, is also to be ascribed to the greater equability and clearness of style. If he does not soar to quite such heights, there are fewer descents and contortions, and it remains at a high level of lofty eloquence.—STEPHEN, LESLIE, 1894, *Dictionary of National Biography, vol. XXXVIII, p. 29.*

The "Areopagitica" is the high-water mark of Milton's prose writings. Never again in the years that follow could he write with the same strong assurance of the ultimate triumph of freedom, the same dominant and invincible trust in the divinely appointed destiny of England.—MASTERMAN, J. HOWARD B., 1897, *The Age of Milton, p. 40.*

EIKONOKLASTES
1649

Milton's ready pen completed the answer, Eikonoklastes, a quarto of 242 pages, before October, 1649. It is, like all answers, worthless as a book. Eikonoklastes, the Image-breaker, takes the Image, Eikon, paragraph by paragraph, turning it round, and asserting the negative. To the Royalist view of the points in dispute Milton opposes the Independent view. A refutation, which follows each step of an adverse book, is necessarily devoid of originality. But Milton is worse than tedious; his reply is in a tone of rude railing and insolent swagger, which would have been always unbecoming, but which at this moment was grossly indecent. Milton must, however, be acquitted of one

charge which has been made against him, viz., that he taunts the King with his familiarity with Shakspeare. The charge rests on a misunderstanding. In quoting "Richard III." in illustration of his own meaning, Milton says, "I shall not instance an abstruse author, wherein the King might be less conversant, but one whom we well know was the closet companion of these his solitudes, William Shakspeare." Though not an overt gibe, there certainly lurks an insinuation to Milton's Puritan readers, to whom stage plays were an abomination—an unworthy device of rhetoric, as appealing to a superstition in others which the writer himself does not share. In Milton's contemptuous reference to Sidney's "Arcadia" as a vain amatorious poem, we feel that the finer sense of the author of "L'Allegro" has suffered from immersion in the slough of religious and political faction.—PATTISON, MARK, 1879, *Milton (English Men of Letters), p. 98.*

It was of no use to retort point by point against the piteous meditations of the imprisoned King; pathos is not answered by invective, and the vulgar railing of the great poet was forgotten, as it deserved to be.—HUTTON, WILLIAM HOLDEN, 1895, *Social England, ed. Traill, vol. IV, p. 288.*

DEFENCES OF THE ENGLISH PEOPLE
1651-55

That Mr. Milton doe prepare something in answer to the book of Salmasius, and when he hath done itt bring itt to the Councill.—ORDER-BOOK OF THE COUNCIL OF STATE, 1649–50, *Jan. 8.*

When I consider how equally it teems and rises with so many figures, it seems to me a Trojan's column, in whose winding ascent we see embossed the several monuments of your learned victories.—MARVELL, ANDREW, 1654, *To Cromwell, p. 99.*

Perhaps the King could have wrote better, but I think no man else in the three Kingdoms. What a venomous spirit is in that serpent Milton, that blackmouthed Zoilus, that blows his viper's breath upon those immortal devotions, from the beginning to the end! This is he that wrote with all irreverence against the Fathers of our Church, and showed as little duty to his father that begat him. The same that wrote for the Pharisees, that it was lawful for a man to put away his wife for every cause; and against Christ, for not allowing divorces. The same, O horrid! that defended the lawfulness of the greatest crime that was ever committed, to put our thrice-excellent King to death. A pretty schoolboy scribbler, that durst grapple in such a cause with the prince of the learned men of his age—Salmasius—"the delight, the musick of all knowledge," who would have scorned to drop a pen full of ink against so base an adversary, but to maintain the honour of so good a King, whose merits he adorns with this praise—*De quo si quis dixerit omnia bona, vix pro suis meritis satis illum ornaret* (Contr. Milton, p. 237). Get thee behind me, Milton, thou savourest not the things that be of truth and loyalty, but of pride, bitterness and falsehood.—HACKET, JOHN, 1693, *The Life of Archbishop Williams.*

The celebrated controversy of *Salmasius,* continued by Morus with *Milton*—the first the pleader of King Charles, the latter the advocate of the people—was of that magnitude, that all Europe took a part in the paper-war of these two great men. The answer of Milton, who perfectly massacred Salmasius, is now read but by the few. Whatever is addressed to the times, however great may be its merits, is doomed to perish with the times; yet on these pages the philosopher will not contemplate in vain.—DISRAELI, ISAAC, 1791–1824, *Milton, Curiosities of Literature.*

The "Defence of the People of England," on which his contemporary fame was founded, is, when divested of its pure Latinity, the worst of his works. Only its general aim, and a few elevated passages, can save it. We could be well content, if the flames to which it was condemned at Paris, at Toulouse, and at London, had utterly consumed it. The lover of his genius will always regret that he should not have taken counsel of his own lofty heart at this, as at other times, and have written from the deep convictions of love and right, which are the foundations of civil liberty. There is little poetry or prophecy in this mean and ribald scolding. To insult Salmasius, not to acquit England, is the main design. What under heaven had Madame de Saumaise, or the manner of living of Saumaise, or Salmasius, or

his blunders of grammar, or his niceties of diction, to do with the solemn question whether Charles Stuart had been rightly slain? Though it evinces learning and critical skill, yet, as an historical argument, it cannot be valued with similar disquisitions of Robertson and Hallam, and even less celebrated scholars. But, when he comes to speak of the reason of the thing, then he always recovers himself. The voice of the mob is silent, and Milton speaks. And the peroration, in which he implores his countrymen to refute this adversary by their great deeds, is in a just spirit.—EMERSON, RALPH WALDO, 1838, *Milton, p.* 147.

Controversies like these are pitiful sights. It is sad to see a magnificent genius like Milton stooping to fling those paving-stones of abuse—"rogue, puppy, foul-mouthed wretch"—which come ready to the hand of every sot and shrew in England.—COLLIER, WILLIAM FRANCIS, 1861, *A History of English Literature, p.* 201.

We fancy we are listening to the bellowing of two bulls.—TAINE, H. A., 1871, *History of English Literature, tr. Van Laun, vol.* I, *bk.* ii, *ch.* vi, *p.* 423.

Milton's "Defences of the English People" are rendered provoking by his extraordinary language concerning his opponents. "Numskull," "beast," "fool," "puppy," "knave," "ass," "mongrelcur," are but a few of the epithets that may be selected for this dscriptive catalogue. This is doubtless mere matter of pleading, a rule of the forum where controversies between scholars are conducted; but for that very reason it makes the pamphlets as provoking to an ordinary reader as an old bill of complaint in Chancery must have been to an impatient suitor who wanted his money.—BIRRELL, AUGUSTINE, 1887, *Obiter Dicta, Second Series, p.* 34.

The "Defence" is not wanting in powerful expression, as indeed, being Milton's, it could hardly be; but it bears on the face of it the obvious signs of a work written to order. It has no complete study of government or scheme of political philosophy. It is a robust, but not profound or convincing, answer to a powerful attack. Politics were merged in personalities, and most men must needs admit that it was an ill cause that was driven to accuse

Charles I. of poisoning his father, and to twit Salmasius with being governed by his wife.—HUTTON, WILLIAM HOLDEN, 1895, *Social England, ed. Traill, vol. IV, p.* 289.

THE HISTORY OF BRITAIN
1670

"The historie of Great Britannie, declaring the successe of times and affaires in that Iland, from the Romans first entrance until the reign of Egbert &c." London, printed by Valentine Simmes 1606, 4to. was wrote by John Clapham, no very noted author. John Milton (who takes in that period) I believe is more read; and yet even Milton was infinitely better at poetry than history.—HEARNE, THOMAS, 1731, *Reliquiæ Hearnianæ, ed. Bliss, Nov.* 16, *vol. III, p.* 77.

It would be impossible to preserve the charm of the original in a translation. The narrator renders his style as antique as those of the chronicles whence he draws the recital. — CHATEAUBRIAND, FRANÇOIS RENÉ, VICOMTE DE, 1837, *Sketches of English Literature, vol. II, p.* 89.

In truth the style of this "History" is dry and uninteresting, and conveys to my mind the impression that, though "revised" by the author in his old age, its effectiveness would have been enhanced, had opportunity so served, by further touches from his younger hand.—WARD, ADOLPHUS WILLIAM, 1893, *English Prose, ed. Craik, vol. II, p.* 454.

GENERAL

It is not any private respect of gain, Gentle Reader (for the slightest Pamphlet is nowadays more vendible than the works of learnedest men), but it is the love I have to our own Language that hath made me diligent to collect and set forth such Pieces, both in Prose and Verse, as may renew the wonted honour and esteem of our English tongue; and it's the worth of these both English and Latin Poems, not the flourish of any prefixed encomions, that can invite thee to buy them—though these are not without the highest commendations and applause of the learnedest Academicks, both domestic and foreign, and, amongst those of our own country, the unparalleled attestation of that renowned Provost of Eton, Sir Henry Wootton. . . . The Author's more peculiar excellency in those studies was too well known to conceal his Papers, or to keep me from attempting to solicit them from him. Let the event guide itself which way it will, I shall deserve of the age by bringing into the light as true a birth as the Muses have brought forth since our famous Spenser wrote; whose Poems in these English ones are as rarely imitated as sweetly excelled. Reader, if thou art eagle-eyed to censure their worth, I am not fearful to expose them to thy exactest perusal. — MOSELEY, HUMPH., 1645, *Milton's Poems, The Stationer to the Reader.*

John Milton was one whose natural parts might deservedly give him a place amongst the principal of our English Poets, having written two Heroick Poems and a Tragedy, namely "Paradice Lost," "Paradice Regain'd," and "Sampson Agonista." But his Fame is gone out like a Candle in a Snuff, and his Memory will always stink, which might have ever lived in honourable Repute, had not he been a notorious Traytor, and most impiously and villanously bely'd that blessed Martyr, King *Charles* the First.—WINSTANLEY, WILLIAM, 1668, *The Lives of the Most Famous English Poets.*

A rough, unhewn fellow, that a man must sweat to read him.
—PRIOR, MATTHEW, 1687, *The Hind and the Panther Transversed.*

Three Poets, in three distant ages born,
Greece, Italy, and England did adorn.
The first in loftiness of thought surpass'd;
The next in majesty ; in both the last.
The force of Nature could no further go;
To make a third she join'd the former two.
—DRYDEN, JOHN, 1688, *Under Mr. Milton's Picture Before his Paradise Lost.*

But Milton next, with high and haughty stalks,
Unfetter'd in majestic numbers walks:
No vulgar hero can his muse engage;
Nor earth's wide scene confine his hallow'd rage.
See! see! he upward springs, and towering high
Spurns the dull province of mortality,
Shakes heaven's eternal throne with dire alarms,
And sets the Almighty thunderer in arms.
Whate'er his pen describes I more than see,
Whilst every verse, array'd in majesty,
Bold and sublime, my whole attention draws,
And seems above the critic's nicer laws.
—ADDISON, JOSEPH, 1694, *An Account of the Greatest English Poets.*

Had his education, and first display'd his Parts in *Christ-Colledge* in *Cambridge*, which he improv'd by his Travels and his indefatigable Industry to that Degree, that he became the Wonder of the Age, tho' always affecting uncommon and heterodoxical Opinions. He was made *Lutine* Secretary to the long Parliament, and afterwards to *Cromwell* Himself; in which Stations he shew'd himself a most inveterate and unexampled Enemy to the Memory of the Murder'd and Martyr'd King; insomuch that at the Restoration some of his Books were order'd to be burnt, and he himself was in great Danger. He was certainly a Man of prodigious Parts, and wrot many Books; but what did most, and most justly distinguish him was his Poetry, particularly his "Paradise lost," in which he manifested such a wonderful sublime Genius, as perhaps was never exceeded in any Age or Nation in the World.—ECHARD, LAURENCE, 1718, *The History of England, vol.* III, *p.* 369.

Is not each great, each amiable Muse
Of classic ages in thy Milton met?
A genius universal as his theme,
Astonishing as Chaos, as the bloom
Of blowing Eden fair, as Heaven sublime!
—THOMSON, JAMES, 1727, *The Seasons, Summer.*

Verse without rhyme I never could endure,
Uncouth in numbers, and in sense obscure.
To him as nature, when he ceased to see,
Milton's an universal blank to me.
—BRAMSTON, JAMES, 1731, *The Man of Taste.*

I have nothing to say for rhyme, but that I doubt whether a poem can support itself without it, in our language; unless it be stiffened with such strange words, as are likely to destroy our language itself. The high style, that is affected so much in blank verse, would not have been borne, even in Milton, had not his subject turned so much on such strange out-of-the-world things as it does.—POPE, ALEXANDER, 1737–39, *Spence's Anecdotes, ed. Singer, p.* 151.

He was both a perfect master of rime and could also express something by it which nobody else ever thought of.—PECK, FRANCIS, 1740, *New Memoirs of the Life and Poetical Works of Mr. John Milton.*

I have dwelt chiefly on this ode as much less celebrated than "L'Allegro" and "Il Penseroso," which are now universally known; but which, by a strange fatality, lay in a sort of obscurity, the private enjoyment of a few curious readers, till they were set to admirable music by Mr. Handel. And indeed this volume of Milton's miscellaneous poems has not till very lately met with suitable regard. Shall I offend any rational admirer of Pope, by remarking that these juvenile descriptive poems of Milton, as well as his Latin elegies, are of a strain far more exalted than any the former author can boast?—WARTON, JOSEPH, 1756, *Essay on Pope.*

Milton was forced to wait till the world had done admiring Quarles.—WALPOLE, HORACE, 1757, *Letters, ed. Cunningham, Aug.* 25, *vol.* III, *p.* 99.

The best example of an exquisite ear that I can produce. . . . The more we attend to the composition of Milton's harmony, the more we shall be sensible how he loved to vary his pauses, his measures, and his feet, which gives that enchanting air of freedom and wildness to his versification, unconfined by any rules but those which his own feeling and the nature of his subject demanded. Thus he mixes the line of eight syllables with that of seven, the Trochee and the Spondee with the Iambic foot, and the single rhyme with the double.—GRAY, THOMAS, 1761? *Observations on English Metre, Essays, Works, vol.* I, *p.* 332.

It is, however, remarkable, that the greatest genius by far that shone out in England during this period was deeply engaged with these fanatics, and even prostituted his pen in theological controversy in factious disputes, and in justifying the most violent measures of the party. This was John Milton, whose poems are admirable, though liable to some objections; his prose writings disagreeable, though not altogether defective in genius. Nor are all his poems equal; his "Paradise Lost," his "Comus," and a few others, shine out amidst some flat and insipid compositions; even in the "Paradise Lost," his capital performance, there are very long passages, amounting to near a third of the work, almost wholly destitute of harmony and elegance, nay of all vigour of imagination. This natural inequality in Milton's genius was much increased by the inequalities in his subject; of which some parts are of themselves the most lofty that can enter into human conception, others would have required the most laboured elegance of composition to support them. It is certain, that this author, when in a happy mood, and employed on a noble subject, is the most wonderfully sublime of any poet in any language, Homer and Lucretius and Tasso not excepted. More concise than Homer, more simple than Tasso, more nervous than Lucretius; had he lived in a later age, and learned to polish some rudeness in his verses; had he enjoyed better fortune, and possessed leisure to watch the returns of genius in himself, he had attained the pinnacle of perfection, and borne away the palm of epic poetry.—HUME, DAVID, 1762, *The History of England, The Commonwealth.*

Milton,—the most perfect scholar, as well as the sublimest poet, that our country has ever produced.—JONES, SIR WILLIAM, 1769, *Letter to Lady Spencer. Sept. 7.*

Through all his greater work there prevails an uniform peculiarity of *Diction*, a mode and cast of expression which bears little resemblance to that of any former writer; and which is so far removed from common use, that an unlearned reader, when he first opens his book, finds himself surprised by a new language.—JOHNSON, SAMUEL, 1779, *John Milton, Lives of the English Poets.*

Milton had such superior merit, that I will only say, that if his angels, his Satan, and his Adam have as much dignity as the Apollo Belvidere, his Eve has all the delicacy and graces of the Venus of Medicis; as his description of Eden has the colouring of Albano. Milton's tenderness imprints ideas as graceful as Guido's Madonnas: and the "Allegro," "Penseroso," and "Comus" might be denominated from the three Graces; as the Italians gave similar titles to two or three of Petrarch's best sonnets.—WALPOLE, HORACE, 1785, *Letters, ed. Cunningham, vol.* VIII, *p.* 564.

Of all English poets that ever lived, had certainly the finest ear.—COWPER, WILLIAM, 1786, *Letter to Lady Hesketh, March 6.*

In Homer's craft Jock Milton thrives.
—BURNS, ROBERT, 1796? *Poem on Pastoral Poetry.*

The reader of Milton must be always on his duty: he is surrounded with sense;

it rises in every line; every word is to the purpose. There are no lazy intervals; all has been considered, and demands and merits observation. If this be called obscurity, let it be remembered that it is such an obscurity as is a compliment to the reader; not that vicious obscurity, which proceeds from a muddled head.—COLERIDGE, SAMUEL TAYLOR, 1796, *Common-Place Book.*

The fact seems to be, that Milton was dissatisfied with the shapeless chaos in which our language appeared in former writers and set himself, with that ardour which always distinguished him, to reform it. His success indeed is not entitled to unlimited encomium. The gigantic structure of his genius perhaps somewhat misled him. He endeavoured to form a language of too lofty and uniform a port. The exuberance of his mind led him to pour out his thoughts with an impetuosity, that often swept away with it the laws of simplicity and even the rules of grammatical propriety. His attempt however to give system to the lawless dialect of our ancestors, was the mark of a generous spirit, and entitles him to our applause. If we compare the style of Milton to that of later writers, and particularly to that of our own days, undoubtedly nothing but a very corrupt taste can commend it. But the case is altered, if we compare it with the writings of his predecessors. An impartial critic would perhaps find no language in any writer that went before Milton, of so much merit as that of Milton himself.—GODWIN, WILLIAM, 1797, *Milton and Clarendon, The Enquirer, p.* 405.

Milton! thou shouldst be living at this hour:
England hath need of thee: she is a fen
Of stagnant waters: altar, sword and pen,
Fireside, the heroic wealth of hall and bower,
Have forfeited their ancient English dower
Of inward happiness. We are selfish men;
Oh! raise us up, return to us again;
And give us manners, virtue, freedom, power.
Thy soul was like a Star, and dwelt apart:
Thou hadst a voice whose sound was like the sea:
Pure as the naked heavens, majestic, free,
So didst thou travel on life's common way,
In cheerful godliness; and yet thy heart
The lowliest duties on herself did lay.
—WORDSWORTH, WILLIAM, 1802, *Milton.*

What an extraordinary being was this man, whether we view him in his moral, religious, or poetical character! It is almost impossible for an unprejudiced, good, and susceptible mind, which is powerfully actuated with the love of poetry and virtue; it is almost impossible for *such* a mind to recollect the full memory of Milton, without paying to that memory an enthusiastic homage; a kind of inferior adoration.—STOCKDALE, PERCIVAL, 1807, *Lectures on the Truly Eminent English Poets, p. 222.*

> Chief of organic numbers!
> Old Scholar of the Spheres!
> Thy spirit never slumbers,
> But rolls about our ears,
> For ever, and for ever!
> O what a mad endeavour
>   Worketh he,
> Who to thy sacred and ennobled hearse
> Would offer a burnt sacrifice of verse
>   And melody

—KEATS, JOHN, 1818, *On a Lock of Milton's Hair.*

Milton's works are a perpetual invocation to the Muses; a hymn to Fame. . . . Milton has borrowed more than any other writer, and exhausted every source of imitation, sacred and profane; yet he is perfectly distinct from every other writer. He is a writer of centos, and yet in originality scarce inferior to Homer. The power of his mind is stamped on every line. The fervour of his imagination melts down and renders malleable, as in a furnace, the most contradictory materials. In reading his works, we feel ourselves under the influence of a mighty intellect, that the nearer it approaches to others, becomes more distinct from them. The quantity of art in him shows the strength of his genius; the weight of his intellectual obligations would have oppressed any other writer. Milton's learning has all the effect of intuition. He describes objects, of which he could only have read in books, with the vividness of actual observation. His imagination has the force of nature. He makes words tell as pictures. . . . It has been, indeed, objected to Milton, by a common perversity of criticism, that his ideas were musical rather than picturesque, as if, because they were in the highest degree musical, they must be (to keep the sage critical balance even, and to allow no one man to possess two qualities at the same time) proportionably deficient in other respects. But Milton's poetry is not cast in any such narrow, commonplace mould; it is not so barren of resources. His worship of the Muse was not so simple or confined. A sound arises

"Like a steam of rich distilled perfumes;"

we hear the pealing organ; but the incense on the altars is also there, and the statues of the gods are ranged around. The ear, indeed, predominates over the eye, because it is more immediately affected, and because the language of music blends more immediately with, and forms a more natural accompaniment to, the variable and indefinite associations of ideas conveyed by words. But where the associations of the imagination are not the principal thing, the individual object is given by Milton with equal force and beauty.—HAZLITT, WILLIAM, 1818, *Lectures on the English Poets, Lecture* iii.

> If, fallen in evil days on evil tongues,
> Milton appeal'd to the Avenger, Time,
> If Time, the Avenger, execrates his wrongs,
> And makes the word "Miltonic" mean *sublime,*
> *He* deign'd not to belie his soul in songs,
> Nor turn his very talent to a crime;
> *He* did not loathe the Sire to laud the Son,
> But closed the tyrant-hater he begun.

—BYRON, LORD, 1818, *Don Juan, Dedication.*

> With other emotion
> Milton's severer shade I saw, and, in reverence humbled,
> Gazed on that soul sublime; of passion now as of blindness
> Healed, and no longer here to Kings and to Hierarchs hostile,
> He was assoiled from taint of the fatal fruit; and in Eden
> Not again to be lost, consorted an equal with angels.

—SOUTHEY, ROBERT, 1821, *A Vision of Judgment,* ix.

> He died,
> Who was the Sire of an immortal strain,
> Blind, old, and lonely, when his country's pride
> The priest, the slave, and the liberticide,
> Trampled and mocked with many a loathèd rite
> Of lust and blood. He went, unterrified,
> Into the gulf of death; but his clear sprite
> Yet reigns o'er earth, the third among the Sons of Light.

—SHELLEY, PERCY BYSSHE, 1821, *Adonais; An Elegy on the death of John Keats,* iv.

The works of Milton cannot be comprehended or enjoyed, unless the mind of the reader co-operate with that of the writer.

He does not paint a finished picture, or play for a mere passive listener. He sketches, and leaves others to fill up the outline. He strikes the key-note, and expects his hearer to make out the melody.—MACAULAY, THOMAS, BABINGTON, 1825, *Milton, Edinburgh Review; Critical and Miscellaneous Essays.*

This character of power runs through all Milton's works. His descriptions of nature show a free and bold hand. He has no need of the minute, graphic skill which we prize in Cowper or Crabbe. With a few strong or delicate touches, he impresses, as it were, his own mind on the scenes which he would describe, and kindles the imagination of the gifted reader to clothe them with the same radiant hues under which they appeared to his own. This attribute of power is universally felt to characterize Milton. His sublimity is in every man's mouth. Is it felt that his poetry breathes a sensibility and tenderness hardly surpassed by its sublimity? We apprehend that the grandeur of Milton's mind has thrown some shade over his milder beauties; and this it has done, not only by being more striking and imposing, but by the tendency of vast mental energy to give a certain calmness to the expression of tenderness and deep feeling.—CHANNING, WILLIAM ELLERY, 1826, *Remarks on the Character and Writings of John Milton.*

Of Milton's mind the leading characteristic is its unity. He has the thoughts of all ages at his command; but he has made them his own. He sits "high on a throne of royal state, adorned With all the wealth of Ormus and of Ind, And where the gorgeous East with richest hand Has showered barbaric pearl and gold." There are no false gems in him, no tinsel. It seems as if nothing could dwell in his mind, but what was grand and sterling.—HARE, A. W. AND J. C., 1827-48, *Guesses at Truth.*

In Milton, again, the harmony of the verse is but the echo of the inward music which the thoughts of the poet breathe.—NEWMAN, JOHN HENRY, 1829-71, *Poetry with Reference to Aristotle's Poetics; Essays Critical and Historical, vol.* I, *p.* 26.

Milton was abundantly skilled in the dialectic art; he had a divine intuition into the logic of poetry; but he was not particularly remarkable, among men of genius, for penetrating and comprehensive intellect. This is very clear from his political and theological writings. His scheme of Government is that of a purely ideal commonwealth, and has the fault common to the greater number of such conceptions, that it never could be practised, except among beings for whom no government at all would be necessary. His opinions as to a Church Establishment are of an exactly similar description; and no imagination less powerful than his could have realized such visions to any mind. Nor could these phantom plans have obtained, in the thoughts of a nation, the living force necessary to their action, unless every man had been able to breathe into them from himself a breath of existence as powerful as that with which they were imbued by their creator.—STERLING, JOHN, 1829, *Shades of the Dead, Essays and Tales, ed. Hare, vol.* I, *p.* 76.

Perhaps the subtle genius of Greece was in part withheld from indulging itself in ethical controversy by the influence of Socrates, who was much more a teacher of virtue than even a searcher after truth.

Whom well inspired, the oracle pronounced Wisest of men.

It was doubtless because he chose that better part that he was thus spoken of by the man whose commendation was glory, and who, from the loftiest eminence of moral genius ever reached by a mortal, was perhaps alone worthy to place a new crown on the brow of the Martyr of virtue.—MACKINTOSH, SIR JAMES, 1830, *A General View of the Progress of Ethical Philosophy, sec.* ii.

Milton frequently innovates upon the high harmonies of his *accented* verse with the substitution of *quantities;* sometimes difficult at first sight to master, but generally admirable in effect, and heightening, —even when harshest, the majesty of his strains like a momentary crash of discord, thrown by the skilful organist, into the full tide of instrumental music, which gives intenser sweetness to what follows. —MONTGOMERY, JAMES, 1833, *Lectures on General Literature, p.* 92.

Milton was not an extensive or discursive thinker, as Shakspeare was; for the motions of his mind were slow, solemn, sequacious, like those of the planets; not agile and assimilative; not attracting all things within its own sphere; not multiform: repulsion was the law of his intellect—he moved in solitary grandeur. Yet, merely from this quality of grandeur, unapproachable grandeur, his intellect demanded a larger infusion of Latinity into his diction. For the same reason (and without such aids he would have had no proper element in which to move his wings) he enriched his diction with Hellenisms and with Hebraisms; but never, as could be easy to show, without a full justification in the result. Two things may be asserted of all his exotic idioms—1st, That they express what could not have been expressed by any native idiom; 2nd, That they harmonize with the English language, and give a colouring of the antique, but not any sense of strangeness, to the diction.—DE QUINCEY, THOMAS, 1835, *Autobiography from 1803 to 1808, Collected Writings, ed. Masson, vol.* II, *p.* 69.

It will not be easy to acquit Milton, altogether, of injustice towards his countryman; but if he disdained to mention Surrey, he also disdained to copy from him—both the merits and the faults of Milton's versification are *his own!* . . . Perhaps no man ever paid the same attention to the quality of his rhythm as Milton. What other poets affect, as it were, by chance, Milton, achieved by the aid of science and of art; he *studied* the aptness of his numbers, and diligently tutored an ear, which nature had gifted with the most delicate sensibility. In the flow of his rhythm, in the quality of his letter-sounds, in the disposition of his pauses, his verse almost ever *fits* the subject; and so insensibly does poetry blend with this—the last beauty of exquisite versification, that the reader may sometimes doubt whether it be the thought itself, or merely the happiness of its expression, which is the source of a gratification so deeply felt.—GUEST, EDWIN, 1838, *A History of English Rhythms, vol.* II, *pp.* 240, 242.

He must not be ranked with Shakespeare. He stands relative to Shakespeare as Tasso or Ariosto does to Dante, as Virgil to Homer. He is conscious of writing an epic, and of being the great man he is. No great man ever felt so great a consciousness as Milton. That consciousness was the measure of his greatness; he was not one of those who reach into actual contact with the deep fountain of greatness. His "Paradise Lost" is not an epic in its composition as Shakespeare's utterances are epic. It does not come out of the heart of things; he hadn't it lying there to pour it out in one gush; it seems rather to have been welded together afterward. His sympathies with things are much narrower than Shakespeare's—too sectarian. In universality of mind there is no hatred; it doubtless rejects what is displeasing, but not in hatred for it. Everything has a right to exist. Shakespeare was not polemical: Milton was polemical altogether.—CARLYLE, THOMAS, 1838, *Lectures on the History of Literature, p.* 165.

There is no name in English literature between his age and ours that rises into any approach to his own. . . . Leaving out of view the pretensions of our contemporaries (always an incalculable influence), we think no man can be named whose mind still acts on the cultivated intellect of England and America with an energy comparable to that of Milton. As a poet, Shakspeare undoubtedly transcends, and far surpasses him in his popularity with foreign nations; but Shakspeare is a voice merely; who and what he was that sang, that sings, we know not. Milton stands erect, commanding, still visible as a man among men, and reads the laws of the moral sentiment to the new-born race. There is something pleasing in the affection with which we can regard a man who died a hundred and sixty years ago in the other hemisphere, who, in respect to personal relations, is to us as the wind, yet by an influence purely spiritual makes us jealous for his fame as for that of a near friend. He is identified in the mind with all select and holy images, with the supreme interests of the human race.—EMERSON, RALPH WALDO, 1838, *Milton.*

Milton's immortal verse never flowed between the autumnal and vernal equinox, but, mute in winter, his song was awakened by the temperature that made the groves, too, vocal.—BROUGHAM, HENRY LORD, 1839–56, *Contributions to the Edinburgh Review, vol.* I, *p.* 251

The invectives of this great poet against prelates and Presbyterians will perfectly astonish those, who as yet are conversant only with his immortal work, his descriptions of the Garden of Eden, and the piety and innocence of our first parents.—SMYTH, WILLIAM, 1840, *Lectures on Modern History, Lecture* xvi.

His verse is the most difficult to read properly of all verse in the language (obsolete or modern).—HORNE, R. H., 1841, *Chaucer's Poems Modernized, Introduction, p.* lix.

The consideration occurs to us that a person of historical ignorance in respect to this divine poet, would hesitate and be at a loss to which era of our poetry to attach him through the internal evidence of his works. He has not the tread of a contemporary of Dryden; and Rochester's nothingness is a strange accompaniment to the voice of his greatness. Neither can it be quite predicated of him that he walks an Elizabethan man; there is a certain fine bloom or farina, rather felt than seen, upon the old poems, unrecognized upon his. But the love of his genius leant backward to those olden oracles; and it is pleasant to think that he was actually born before Shakespeare's death; that they too looked upwardly to the same daylight and stars; and that he might have stretched his baby arms ("animosus infans") to the faint hazel eyes of the poet of poets. Let us think in anywise that he drew in some living subtle Shaksperian benediction, providing for greatness.—BROWNING, ELIZABETH BARRETT, 1842–63, *The Book of the Poets.*

Glorious John Milton, upon whom rested an after-glow of the Holy Inspiration of the sacred writers, like the twilight bequeathed by a midsummer sun.—HOOD, THOMAS, 1843, *Memorials, vol.* II, *p.* 280.

Milton was a very great poet, second only (if second) to the very greatest, such as Dante and Shakspeare; and, like all great poets, equal to them in particular instances. He had no pretensions to Shakspeare's universality; his wit is dreary; and (in general) he had not the faith in things that Homer and Dante had, apart from the intervention of words. He could not let them speak for themselves without helping them with his learning. In all he did, after a certain period of youth (not to speak it irreverently), something of the schoolmaster is visible; and a gloomy religious creed removes him still farther from the universal gratitude and delight of mankind. He is understood,

however, as I have just intimated, to have given this up before he died. He had then run the circle of his knowledge, and probably come round to the wiser, more cheerful, and more poetical beliefs of his childhood.—HUNT, LEIGH, 1844, *Imagination and Fancy, p.* 211.

Those who sit at his feet obtain every hour glimpses in all directions. The constant perception of principles, richness in illustrations and fullness of knowledge, make him the greatest Master we have in the way of giving clues and impulses. His plan tempts even very timid students to hope they may thread the mighty maze of the Past.—OSSOLI, MARGARET FULLER, 1846, *Papers on Literature and Art.*

No one can fitly reverence Milton who has not studied the character of the age of Charles II., in which his later fortunes were cast. He was Dryden's contemporary in time, but not his master or disciple in slavishness. He was under the anathema of power; a republican, in days of abject servility; a Christian, among men whom it would be charity to call infidels; a man of pure life and high principle, among sensualists and renegades. On nothing external could he lean for support. In his own domain of imagination perhaps the greatest poet that ever lived, he was still doomed to see such pitiful and stupid poetasters as Shadwell and Settle bear away the shining rewards of letters. Well might he declare that he had fallen on evil times! . . . The genius of Milton is indeed worthy all the admiration we award marvellous intellectual endowment; but how much more do we venerate the whole man, when we find it riveted to that high and hardy moral courage which makes his name thunder rebuke to all power that betrays freedom, to all genius that is false to virtue!—WHIPPLE, EDWIN P., 1846, *Authors in Their Relations to Life, Literature and Life, pp.* 24, 25.

No species of literature, no language, no book, no art or science seems to have escaped his curiosity, or resisted the combined ardour and patience of his industry. His works may be considered as a vast arsenal of ideas drawn from every region of human speculation, and either themselves the condensed quintessence of knowledge and wisdom, or dressing and adoring the fairest and most majestic conceptions.—SHAW, THOMAS B., 1847, *Outlines of English Literature, p.* 162.

Like to some deep-chested organ whose grand
　inspiration,
Serenely majestic in utterance, lofty and
　calm,
Interprets to mortals with melody great as its
　burthen,
The mystical harmonies chiming for ever
　throughout the bright spheres.

—MEREDITH, GEORGE, 1851, *Works, vol.* XXXI, *p.* 139.

Was the stair or high table-land to let down the English genius from the summits of Shakspeare.—EMERSON, RALPH WALDO, 1856–84, *English Traits; Works, Riverside ed., vol.* V, *p.* 232.

He was the most learned of all our poets, the one who from his childhood upwards was a devourer of Greek and Latin books, of the romances of the Middle Ages, of French and Italian poetry, above all of the Hebrew Scriptures. All these became his friends; for all of them connected themselves with the thoughts that occupied men in his own time, with the deep religious and political controversies which were about to bring on a civil war. Many persons think that the side which he took in that war must hinder us from making his books our friends; that we may esteem him as a great poet, but that we cannot meet him cordially as a man. No one is more likely to entertain that opinion than an English clergyman, for Milton dealt his blows unsparingly enough, and we come in for at least our full share of them. I know all that, and yet I must confess that I have found him a friend, and a very valuable friend, even when I have differed from him most and he has made me smart most.—MAURICE, FREDERICK DENISON, 1856–74, *The Friendship of Books and Other Lectures, ed. Hughes, p.* 14.

Graced with every intellectual gift, he was personally so comely that the romantic woods of Vallambrosa are lovelier from their association with his youthful figure sleeping in their shade. He had all the technical excellences of the scholar. At eighteen he wrote better Latin verses than have been written in England. He replied to the Italian poets who complimented him in Italian pure as their own. He was profoundly skilled in theology, in science, and in the literature of all languages. These were his accomplishments,

but his genius was vast and vigorous. While yet a youth he wrote those minor poems which have the simple perfection of productions of nature; and in the ripeness of his wisdom and power he turned his blind eyes to heaven, and sang the lofty song which has given him a twin glory with Shakespeare in English renown. It is much for one man to have exhausted the literature of other nations and to have enriched his own. But other men have done this in various degrees. Milton went beyond it to complete the circle of his character as the scholar. You know the culmination of his life. The first scholar in England and in the world at that time fulfilled his office. His vocation making him especially the representative of liberty, he accepted the part to which he was naturally called, and, turning away from all the blandishments of ease and fame, he gave himself to liberty and immortality. —CURTIS, GEORGE WILLIAM, 1856–93, *The Duty of the American Scholar, Orations and Addresses, vol.* I, *p.* 12.

These are the two contrasts which puzzle us at first in Milton, and which distinguish him from other poets in our remembrance afterwards. We have a superficial complexity in illustration and imagery and metaphor; and in contrast with it we observe a latent simplicity of idea, an almost rude strength of conception. The underlying thoughts are few, though the flowers on the surface are so many. We have likewise the perpetual contrast of the soft poetry of the memory, and the firm—as it were, fused—and glowing poetry of the imagination. His words, we may half fancifully say, are like his character: there is the same austerity in the real essence, the same exquisiteness of sense, the same delicacy of form which we know that he had, the same music which we imagine there was in his voice. In both his character and his poetry there was an ascetic nature in a sheath of beauty.—BAGEHOT, WALTER, 1859, *John Milton, Works, ed. Morgan, vol.* I, *p.* 336.

Take any,—the most hackneyed passage of "Comus," the "L'Allegro," the "Penseroso," the "Paradise Lost," and see the freshness, the sweetness, and the simplicity, which is strangely combined with the pomp, the self-restraint, the earnestness of every word; take him even, as an *experimentum crucis*, when he trenches upon ground heathen and questionable, and tries the court poets at their own weapons, —

"Or whether (as some sages sing),
The frolic wind that breathes the spring,
Zephyr with Aurora playing,
As he met her once a-maying,
There on beds of violets blue,
And fresh-blown roses washed in dew."

but why quote what all the world knows? —Where shall we find such real mirth, ease, sweetness, dance and song of words in any thing written for five-and-twenty years before him? True, he was no great dramatist. He never tried to be one : but there was no one in his generation who could have written either "Comus" or "Samson Agonistes." And if, as is commonly believed, and as his countenance seems to indicate, he was deficient in humour, so were his contemporaries, with the sole exception of Cartwright. Witty he would be, and bitter : but he did not live in a really humorous age ; and if he has none of the rollicking fun of the fox-hound puppy, at least he has none of the obscene gibber of the ape.—KINGSLEY, CHARLES, 1859, *Plays and Puritans, Miscellanies, p.* 111.

Milton does not appear to have derived any pecuniary advantage from his labours as a Poet. His juvenile productions, and a few other minor pieces, were published for the first time in 1645. His Poems were evidently at that period not more esteemed than many of the contemporaneous poetical volumes of similar character. If we may judge from the fact of those poems being issued without any of those commendatory verses,—the tribute of praise so generally accorded by way of introduction to the effusions of a brother poet,—we may fairly come to the conclusion that Milton was, at that period, comparatively little known in the poetical world. Unlike also the works of other poets of the day, those of Milton are not inscribed to any patron, but are merely introduced to the public by an address from Humphrey Moseley the publisher. The volume bears no indication that it had been even published under the superintendence of the author. The Poems are arranged without much attention to their chronological order ; and some of the Sonnets are without the headings that occur in the originals in the Trinity College Manuscript. Besides this, several of the Sonnets written before 1645, are omitted, as also other of his early poetical productions.—SOTHEBY, SAMUEL LEIGH, 1861, *Ramblings in the Elucidation of the Autograph of Milton, p.* 12.

O mighty-mouth'd inventor of harmonies,
O skill'd to sing of Time or Eternity,
    God-gifted organ-voice of England,
    Milton, a name to resound for ages;
Whose Titan angels, Gabriel, Abdiel,
Starr'd from Jehovah's gorgeous armouries,
    Tower, as the deep-domed empyrëan
    Rings to the roar of an angel onset—
Me rather all that bowery loneliness,
The brooks of Eden mazily murmuring,
    And bloom profuse and cedar arches
    Charm, as a wanderer out in ocean,
Where some refulgent sunset of India
Streams o'er a rich ambrosial ocean isle,
    And crimson-hued the stately palm-woods
    Whisper in odorous heights of even.
—TENNYSON, ALFRED LORD, 1863, *Alcaics.*

The finest and the most complex poetic genius of England. — SAINTE - BEUVE, CHARLES-AUGUSTIN, 1864, *English Portraits, p.* 271.

Milton put off his singing robes to labour for the State, and between the springtime of his genius and the glorious harvest of its autumn, gave the summer of his life to direct service of the country. He was then the pen of the Commonwealth, the voice of England to the outer world. And in his earlier and later verse, not less than in the middle period of his prose writing, Milton's genius was rich with the life of his own time, although he thought apart from the crowd, and spoke for himself, royally, with independent power. No poet is for all time who is not also for his age, reflecting little or much of its outward manner, but a part of its best mind. —MORLEY, HENRY, 1868, *ed., The King and the Commons, Introduction, p.* xx.

If George Herbert's utterance is like the sword-play of one skilful with the rapier, that of Milton is like the sword-play of an old knight, flashing his huge but keen-cutting blade in lightnings about his head. Compared with Herbert, Milton was a man in health. He never *shows*, at least, any diseased regard of himself. His eye is fixed on the truth, and he knows of no illfaring. While a man looks thitherward, all the movements of his spirit reveal themselves only in peace. . . . The unity of his being is the strength of Milton. He is harmony, sweet and bold, throughout. Not Philip Sidney, not George Herbert loved words and their melodies more than he; while in their use he is more serious than either, and harder to please, uttering a music they have rarely approached.—MACDON-ALD, GEORGE, 1868, *England's Antiphon,* pp. 194, 195.

Milton was a pamphleteer, only a pamphleteer of original genius. Had he less originality, with the same power of language, he would probably have figured more in the history of the time, because he would have become more distinctly the mouthpiece of a party. But because the weight of his mind always carries him below the surface of the subject, because in these pamphlets he appeals constantly to first principles, opens the largest questions, propounds the most general maxims, we are not therefore unfairly to compare them with complete treatises on politics, or to forget that they are essentially pamphlets still.—SEELEY, JOHN ROBERT, 1868, *Milton's Political Opinions, Macmillan's Magazine, vol.* 17, *p.* 302.

John Milton was not one of those fevered souls, void of self-command, whose rapture takes them by fits, whom a sickly sensibility drives for ever to the extreme of sorrow or joy, whose pliability prepares them to produce a variety of characters, whose inquietude condemns them to paint the insanity and contradictions of passion. Vast knowledge, close logic, and grand passion: these were his marks. His mind was lucid, his imagination limited. He was incapable of disturbed emotion or of transformation. He conceived the loftiest of ideal beauties, but he conceived only one. He was not born for the drama, but for the ode. He does not create souls, but constructs arguments and experiences emotions. Emotions and arguments, all the forces and actions of his soul, assemble and are arranged beneath a unique sentiment, that of the sublime; and the broad river of lyric poetry streams from him, impetuous, with even flow, splendid as a cloth of gold. . . . He was speculative and chimerical. Locked up in his own ideas, he sees but them, is attracted but by them. . . . He lived complete and untainted to the end, without loss of heart or weakness; experience could not instruct nor misfortune depress him; he

endured all, and repented of nothing. . . . When Milton wishes to joke, he looks like one of Cromwell's pikemen, who, entering a room to dance, should fall upon the floor, and that with the extra momentum of his armour.—TAINE, H. A., 1871, *History of English Literature, tr. Van Laun, vol.* I, *bk.* ii, *ch.* vi, *pp.* 409, 417, 418, 422.

I pace the sounding sea-beach and behold,
  How the voluminous billows roll and run,
  Upheaving and subsiding, while the sun
Shines through their sheeted emerald far un-
    rolled,
And the ninth wave, slow gathering fold by
    fold
  All its loose-folding garments into one,
  Plunges upon the shore, and floods the dun
Pale reach of sands, and changes them to
    gold.
So in majestic cadence rise and fall
  The mighty undulations of thy song,
  O sightless bard, England's Mæonides!
And ever and anon, high over all
  Uplifted, a ninth wave superb and strong,
  Floods all the soul with its melodious seas.
—LONGFELLOW, HENRY WADSWORTH, 1873, *A Book of Sonnets.*

Milton was the poet of revealed religion under its Puritanic type. The style and thought of Milton are native to this earnest and extended insight of his mind. From the beginning he manifested the same scope and majesty. He always spread a broad wing, and floated serenely; moving at ease from peak to peak.—BASCOM, JOHN, 1874, *Philosophy of English Literature, p.* 129.

  . . . Milton fills, supreme, alone,
  The Poet-patriot's shrine and throne,
  With renown each year increased. . . .
—DOMETT, ALFRED, 1877? *Cripplegate.*

With Milton, Nature was not his first love, but held only a secondary place in his affections. He was in the first place a scholar, a man of letters, with the theologian and polemic latent in him. A lover of all artistic beauty he was, no doubt, and of Nature mainly as it lends itself to this preception. And as is his mode of apprehending Nature, such is the language in which he describes her.—SHAIRP, JOHN CAMPBELL, 1877, *On Poetic Interpretation of Nature, p.* 186.

He left the upland lawns and serene air
Wherefrom his soul her noble nurture drew,
And reared his helm among the unquiet crew
Battling beneath; the morning radiance rare
Of his young brow amid the tumult there

Grew grim with sulphurous dust and san-
    guine dew;
Yet through all soilure they who marked him
    knew
The signs of his life's dayspring, calm and
    fair.
But when peace came, peace fouler far than
    war,
And mirth more dissonant than battle's tone,
He, with a scornful sigh of his clear soul,
Back to his mountain clomb, now bleak and
    frore,
And with the awful Night he dwelt alone,
In darkness, listening to the thunder's roll
—MYERS, ERNEST, 1877, *Milton, Poems.*

An ordinary mind contemplating Milton
can realize to itself the feeling of the
Athenian who resented hearing Aristides
for ever styled "the Just." Such a mind
feels a little and excusably provoked at
the serene and severe loftiness of a Milton,
and casts about to find him blame-worthy
in his very superiority—an exacting husband and father, an over-learned writer,
cumbrous or stilted in prose and scholas-
tically accoutred in verse, a political and
religious extremist. There may be something in these objections, or the smaller
kind of souls will please themselves by
supposing there is something in them.
Honour is the predominant emotion naturally felt towards Milton—hardly enthusiasm—certainly not sympathy. Perhaps
a decided feeling of unsympathy would
affect many of us, were it not for the one
great misfortune of the poet. Nature
has forbidden him to be infirm in himself,
but gave him a crown of accidental or
physical infirmity, and bowed him somewhat—a little lower than the angels—
towards sympathy.—ROSSETTI, WILLIAM
MICHAEL, 1878, *Lives of Famous Poets*, p.
76.

Admire as we may "Paradise Lost;"
try as we may to admire "Paradise Regained;" acknowledge as we must the
splendour of the imagery and the stately
march of the verse—there comes upon us
irresistibly a sense of the unfitness of the
subject for Milton's treatment of it. If
the story which he tells us is true, it is
too momentous to be played with in
poetry. We prefer to hear it in plain
prose, with a minimum of ornament and
the utmost possible precision of statement.
Milton himself had not arrived at thinking
it to be a legend, a picture, like a Greek
Mythology. His poem falls between two
modes of treatment and two conceptions

of truth; we wonder, we recite, we applaud, but something comes in between
our minds and a full enjoyment, and it
will not satisfy us better as time goes on.
—FROUDE, JAMES ANTHONY, 1880, *Bunyan (English Men of Letters)*, p. 116.

In the treasure-house of that great
poet's mind were gathered memories and
associations innumerable, though the sublimest flights of his genius soared aloft
into regions whither the imagination of
none of our earlier poets had preceded
them.—WARD, ADOLPHUS WILLIAM, 1880,
Chaucer, (English Men of Letters), p. 196.

Milton is the most sublime of our poets,
and next to Wordsworth, he is perhaps
the most intense. I mean that every line
he utters, every scene he describes, is
felt and seen by the writer; that his
poetry is the expression of his innermost
life, and that his individuality pervades it.
Unlike Spenser and Shakespeare, Milton
can seldom escape from himself, but his
egotism is of the noblest order. We see
this egotism in the earliest poems, in the
sonnets written in middle age, and again
in his latest work, the "Samson Agonistes," in which, as in a mirror, may be
witnessed the struggles of his soul and
the sorrows of his life.—DENNIS, JOHN,
1883, *Heroes of Literature*, p. 127.

The greatness of the man was conspicuous in his blindness, for though he was
fallen on evil days and evil tongues, he
was unchanged, and though he was in solitude he was not alone. Urania visited
his slumbers nightly, and governed his
song, and found an audience—fit audience
though few. The Spirit of Heavenly Song
attained its greatest height with "Paradise Lost" in 1667, and, slowly wheeling
through the firmament of English Verse,
began to descend in 1671 with "Paradise
Regained" and "Samson Agonistes." It
reached the lowest deep in the next half
century in the Psalms and Hymns of
Watts.—STODDARD, RICHARD HENRY,
1883, *English Verse, Chaucer to Burns*,
Introduction, p. xxxviii.

When he talked of the "grand style"
of poetic diction he would emphasize his
opinion that he considered that of Milton
even finer than that of Virgil, "the lord
of language."—TENNYSON, ALFRED LORD,
1883, *Some Criticisms on Poets, Memoir by
His Son*, vol. II, p. 284.

The essence of the Greek pastoral elegy

is the contrast of man's individual life with Nature's apparent eternity—a melancholy sentiment becoming the lisp of a modern materialist, but in the author of "Lycidas," the poetical champion of a faith before which the material universe is but dust and ashes compared with the soul of the veriest wretch who wears the form of man, almost grotesquely out of place. Why should Nature lament the escape of a divinity greater than herself from its clay prison? The Greek chorus in the social life of the Hebrews speaking the Puritanism of England in "Samson Agonistes" is not a stranger union of incongruities than the poet of individual immortality repeating the materialism of the Greek in lamentations for Edward King. Plainly the individualism of the sixteenth and seventeenth centuries did not know whether it was of earth or the infinite ; and this confused judgment made it willing to look on Nature partially as a beautiful machine, its exquisite mechanism worthy of such word-pictures as "L'Allegro" and "Il Penseroso" contain, partially as a pagan god to be duly invoked only in good old pagan fashion, and partially as a perishable nullity destined to be "rolled together as a scroll"—in any case connected by no profoundly real links with man's social and individual life.—POSNETT, HUTCHESON MACAULAY, 1886, *Comparative Literature*, p. 384.

The first great English poet who is above all things musical is Milton. The distinction of musical from picturesque qualities has indeed been used as a means of defending Milton's claim to be placed in the first order of poets against those critics who have complained that he does not suggest many subjects for pictures. And we must place Milton among poets whose genius is of the lyrical kind, though most of his work is not technically lyrical —especially if we accept as universal among the greater poets the distinction of lyric from dramatic genius.—WHITTAKER, THOMAS, 1886, *The Musical and the Picturesque Elements in Poetry, Essays and Notices*, p. 102.

Oh, Milton, singing thy great hymn
And quiring with the cherubim,
Thou art not blind, or sad, or old,
Thou hast no part in dark grave-mould,
Forever fair and blithe and young
And deathless as thy golden tongue!
The nightingale upon thy bough

Sang never half so sweet as thou,
And could'st thou only sing to me
I would be blind that thou might'st see !
—SPOFFORD, HARRIET PRESCOTT, 1887, *Blind Milton, Ballads about Authors.*

In calling up Milton's memory we call up, let me say, a memory upon which, in prospect of the Anglo-Saxon contagion and of its dangers supposed and real, it may be well to lay stress even more than upon Shakespere's. If to our English race an inadequate sense for perfection of work is a real danger, if the discipline of respect for a high and flawless excellence is peculiarly needed by us, Milton is of all our gifted men the best lesson, the most salutary influence. In the sure and flawless perfection of his rhythm and diction he is as admirable as Virgil or Dante, and in this respect he is unique amongst us. No one else in English Literature and art possesses the like distinction.—ARNOLD, MATTHEW, 1888, *Milton, The Century, vol.* 36, *p.* 54.

O Milton, thou hast only half thy praise
In having lowered the heavens within man's ken;
Thine other, equal labor was to raise
The human spirit up to heaven again;
So, underneath thy forehead's aureole blaze,
Thine awful eyes are mild with love to men.
—KOOPMAN, HARRY LYMAN, 1888, *Milton, Orestes and Other Poems*, p. 148.

If we were to discuss the influence of Milton in the English poetry of the nineteenth century, we should have to analyse large portions of the works of recent and living English poets. Wordsworth's blank verse, when it is truly verse, is at times almost an echo of Milton ; and Lord Tennyson, far too exquisite an artist to be ever a mere imitator, has in his perfection of form been a true follower of Milton's spirit. Neither has Milton's prose been fruitless in the latter days ; for something of its majestic reverberations may be heard in Landor, a master of English prose if ever there was one, from whom Milton received most loyal and yet unconstrained homage. Johnson's rooted loyalty to letters had constrained him, too, to do homage ; the last paragraph of his life of Milton redeems all the rest, effacing mistakes and prejudices in the fellow-feeling of a true scholar. He must be an exceedingly bold or an exceedingly fastidious Englishman who does not worship where Johnson and Landor have alike bowed the knee.—POLLOCK, FREDERICK, 1890, *John Milton, The Fortnightly Review, vol. 54, p.* 519.

Our amiable Dr. Channing, with excellent data before him, demonstrated his good Unitarian faith; but though Milton might have approved his nice reasonings, I doubt if he would have gone to church with him. He loved liberty; he could not travel well in double harness, not even in his household or with the elders. His exalted range of vision made light of the little aids and lorgnettes which the conventional teachers held out to him. Creeds and dogmas and vestments and canons, and all humanly consecrated helps, were but Jack-o'-lanterns to him, who was swathed all about with the glowing clouds of glory that rolled in upon his soul from the infinite depths.—MITCHELL, DONALD G., 1890, *English Lands Letters and Kings, From Elizabeth to Anne, p.* 179.

Where Milton's style is fine it is *very* fine, but it is always liable to the danger of degenerating into mannerism. Nay, where the imagination is absent and the artifice remains, as in some of the theological discussions in "Paradise Lost," it becomes mannerism of the most wearisome kind. Accordingly, he is easily parodied and easily imitated. Philips, in his "Splendid Shilling," has caught the trick exactly. . . . Philips has caught, I say, Milton's trick; his real secret he could never divine, for where Milton is best, he is incomparable. But all authors in whom imagination is a secondary quality, and whose merit lies less in what they say than in the way they say it, are apt to become mannerists, and to have imitators, because manner can be easily imitated. Milton has more or less colored all blank verse since his time, and, as those who imitate never fail to exaggerate, his influence has in some respects been mischievous. Thomson was well-nigh ruined by him. In him a leaf cannot fall without a Latinism, and there is circumlocution in the crow of a cock. Cowper was only saved by mixing equal proportions of Dryden in his verse, thus hitting upon a kind of cross between prose and poetry. In judging Milton, however, we should not forget that in verse the music makes a part of the meaning, and that no one before or since has been able to give to simple pentameters the majesty and compass of the organ. He was as much composer as poet.—LOWELL, JAMES RUSSELL, 1891, *Fragments, The Century, vol.* 48, *pp.* 24, 25.

No other blank verse in the language exhibits such a masterly skill in the variation of its pauses—pauses, I mean, where periodic groups, or logical sections of groups, terminate, after, or within, it may be, the first, second, third, or fourth foot of a verse. There are five cases where the termination is within the fifth foot.—CORSON, HIRAM, 1892, *A Primer of English Verse, p.* 193.

It might at first sight seem strange enough that even in such a cursory account of those times as this is, the name of Milton should have hardly occured at all. And when it is further remembered that Dryden revered and admired the great epic poet of England at a time when very few were found to do so, it might have been expected that something should be said of him beyond the mere reference to Dryden's rather dubious adaptation from the "Paradise Lost," and to a few scattered Miltonian expressions of his, which it would of course be possible to make. The truth is, that in our literary history both Shakespeare and Milton stand apart by themselves, too inimitable and too spontaneous either to found a critical school or to carry with them any long train of followers. And as regards Milton, he may be viewed as a gigantic survival of the Elizabethan period, more Italianised than Spenser, more of the Puritan Englishman than was Shakespeare. "His soul was like a star, and dwelt apart."—EVANS, JOHN AMPHLETT, 1892, *Dryden and Ben Jonson, Temple Bar, vol.* 95, *p.* 109.

Milton is a sublime Gothic genius in most respects, though tethered to the heavy learning of his century. In his larger aspects he is no classic poet, in his smaller, as in form and perspective, he falls far short of Dante's standard. He was as full of Gothic inspiration as the twelfth-century cathedral architects, and in his great poem strove like them to imprison grandeur. He chose to be vague that he might be vast,—to surround his celestial battlements with fog that the mind of his reader might infer still loftier proportions.—SHERMAN, L. A., 1893, *Analytics of Literature, p.* 143.

Admittedly and indisputably our highest summit in Style. . . . He best proves the truth that in poetry Style is the paramount and invincible force. What else is the secret of his supremacy among our poets—a supremacy which no poet can doubt, and no true critic of poetry? For pure poetic endowment he sits unapproached on England's Helicon; yet, in comparison with Shakespeare, it cannot be said that his is a very rich or large nature uttering itself through literature. He has no geniality, he has no humour; he is often pedantic, sometimes pedagogic. Although his Invention was stupendous, in the quite distinct and finer quality of Imagination, or contagious spiritual vision, he has superiors; his human sympathies were neither warm nor broad; Shakespeare's contempt for the mass of mankind may be hesitatingly inferred from casual evidences, but Milton's is everywhere manifest.—WATSON, WILLIAM, 1893, *Excursions in Criticism, pp.* 105, 110.

> So fair thy vision that the night
> Abided with thee, lest the light,
> A flaming sword before thine eyes,
> Had shut thee out from Paradise.

—TABB, JOHN B., 1894, *Milton, Poems.*

In one respect Milton stands alone in his management of a great poetic medium. Shakespeare, because of the vast license of the English stage and its mixture of verse and prose, here stands out of the comparison, and we know nothing of Homer's predecessors. But no one, not Sophocles with the iambic trimeter, not even Virgil with the Latin hexameter, hardly even Dante with the Italian hendecasyllabic, has achieved such marvellous variety of harmony independent of meaning as Milton has with the English blank verse. All three, perhaps, had a better lexicon—it is permissible to think Milton's choice of words anything but infallible. But no one with his lexicon did such astonishing feats.—SAINTSBURY, GEORGE, 1895, *Social England, ed. Traill, vol.* IV, *p.* 425.

"L'Allegro" and "Il Penseroso," the earliest great lyrics of the landscape in our language, despite all later competition still remain supreme for range, variety, lucidity, and melodious charm within their style. And this style is essentially that of the Greek and the earlier English poets, but enlarged to the conception of whole scenes from Nature; occasionally even panoramic. . . . What we gain from Milton, as these specimens in his very purest vein—his essence of landscape—illustrate, is the immense enlargement, the finer proportions, the greater scope, of his scenes from Nature. And with this we have that exquisite style, always noble, always music itself—Mozart without notes —in which Milton is one of the few very greatest masters in all literature: in company—at least it pleases me to fancy— with Homer and Sophocles, with Vergil, with Dante, with Tennyson.—PALGRAVE, FRANCIS TURNER, 1896, *Landscape in Poetry, pp.* 158, 159.

It attests the native power and superiority of Milton's genius that he was able almost entirely to liberate himself from fetters which still so largely trammelled alike the poetry and the prose literature of his age. Of this his "Lycidas" supplies a striking illustration—a strain of exquisite pathos and beauty rising up amid the forced and jejune conceits which characterize the verses of his fellow mourners, much like the voice of the lady in his "Comus" amid the cries of the wanton revellers around her. In his "Areopagitica" Milton seems himself carried away by this native spirit of independence; and his utterances, noble as is the spirit by which they are dictated, cannot be vindicated from the reproach of neglecting both the historical evidence and the general principles necessary to an adequate conduct of the argument.—MULLINGER, J. BASS, 1897, *The Age of Milton, Introduction, p.* xviii.

It is certain that Milton deals with the invisible more than any other poet that ever lived. . . . Milton has not the spontaneity of imagination that distinguishes Shakespeare, nor has he so large a nature, but his sense of form is more unfailing, and in loftiness of character he towers far above the bard of Avon. Puritan as he is, he is more of an aristocrat, and more of a man, than is Shakespeare. His nobility of poetic form is but the expression of a lofty soul, thrilled to the center of its being with the greatest of possible themes—the struggle of good and evil, of God and Satan, and the triumph of the Almighty in the redemption of man. When this theme grows old, then will "Paradise Lost" and "Paradise

Regained" grow old. But so long as man recognizes and values his own immortality, so long will the poetry of Milton vindicate its claim to be immortal.—STRONG, AUGUSTUS HOPKINS, 1897, *The Great Poets and Their Theology, pp.* 246, 256.

Milton's lyric style is not so purely lyrical and personal; it is rather idyllic and objective. In this he is in a measure the poetic son of Spenser; and he, too, last of the Elizabethans, has a certain turn of lyric rhythm and phrase never afterwards recaptured. "L'Allegro" and "Il Penseroso" are the objective and idyllic presentations of the two fundamental subjective states of the human soul. In these poems all the rhythmical witchery and the subtle beauty of symbolism developed or suggested in the lyrics of Spenser, Shakespeare, Campion, Fletcher, Drummond, and Browne, is taken up and carried into the last perfection of English idyllic metre and fancy. And the "Lycidas" carries on the vein of earlier Ode and Elegy to a like perfection. Through all the concrete symbolism of these poems, however, we read the suggestion of the new ethical and subjective mood of the time, saturated with and subdued to the genius of the man Milton.—CARPENTER, FREDERIC IVES, 1897, *English Lyric Poetry,* 1500–1700, *Introduction, p.* liv.

Every page of the works of that great exemplar of diction, Milton, is crowded with examples of felicitous and exquisite meaning given to the infallible word. Sometimes he accepts the secondary and more usual meaning of a word only to enrich it by the interweaving of the primary and etymological meaning.—RALEIGH, WALTER, 1897, *Style, p.* 35.

Milton is a solitary peak that caught the last gleams of the Renaissance and flashed them across a century.—GEORGE, ANDREW J., 1898, *From Chaucer to Arnold, Types of Literary Art, p.* 633.

That the influence of Milton, in the romantic revival of the eighteenth century, should have been hardly second in importance to Spenser's is a confirmation of our remark that Augustan literature was "classical" in a way of its own. . . . Milton is the most truly classical of English poets; and yet, from the angle of observation at which the eighteenth century viewed him, he appeared a romantic. It was upon his romantic side, at all events, that the new school of poets apprehended and appropriated him.—BEERS, HENRY A., 1898, *A History of English Romanticism, p.* 146.

In Milton, the glorious plea for religious and political freedom is of a haughty antique strain compatible with entire disregard of the welfare of the masses.—SCUDDER, VIDA D., 1898, *Social Ideals in English Letters, p.* 87.

Milton is one of the world's great minds. It is elevating to have intercourse with him and to follow his thought. Even in his partisanship—if to such independent and positive convictions as his that term can be applied—he is great. In carefulness and self-consistency he can give lessons to every living writer. He appears to best advantage when compared with other men of admitted power. Alongside of Homer he seems a kindred spirit. Bacon's interpretation of the ancient myths are puerile in comparison with his. His insight into the Sacred Scriptures often shames trained theologians. That his celebrated epic, the "Paradise Lost," is even now but poorly understood is evidence of his superiority. —HIMES, JOHN A., 1898, *ed., Paradise Lost, Preface, p.* iii.

Milton is the great idealist of our Anglo-Saxon race. In him there was no shadow of turning from the lines of thought and action marked out for him by his presiding genius. His lines may not be our lines; but if we cannot admire to the full his ideal steadfastness of purpose and his masterful accomplishment, it is because our own capacity for the comprehension and pursuit of the ideal is in so far weak and vacillating. And it is this pure idealism of his that makes him by far the most important figure, from a moral point of view, among all Anglo-Saxons.—TRENT, WILLIAM P., 1899, *John Milton, A Short Study of His Life and Works, p.* 53.

His fame is now old-established and settled, so there is no place left for the eloquence of the memorialist, or the studied praises of the pleader. I have tried to understand Milton; and have already praised him as well as I know how, with no stinted admiration, I trust, and certainly with no merely superstitious reverance. — RALEIGH, WALTER, 1900, *Milton, p.* 278.

Edward Hyde

Earl of Clarendon

1609-1674

Edward Hyde, first Earl of Clarendon. Born at Dinton, Wiltshire, Feb. 18, 1608 (O.S.): died at Rouen, France, Dec. 9, 1674. An English statesman and historian. He entered Parliament in 1640; became chancellor of the exchequer in 1643; was the chief adviser of Charles I. during the civil war, and of Prince Charles during his exile; and was lord chancellor of England 1660-67, when he was impeached and banished by Parliament. His chief works are a "True Historical Narrative of the Rebellion and Civil Wars in England" generally termed "History of the Rebellion," 1702-04) and "The Life of Edward, Earl of Clarendon, . . . Written by Himself" (1759).—SMITH, BENJAMIN E., 1894,-97, *ed. The Century Cyclopedia of Names,p.*521.

PERSONAL

He had without doubt great infirmities, which, by providential mercy, were reasonably restrained from growing into vices, at least into any that were habitual. He had ambition enough to keep him from being satisfied with his own condition, and to raise his spirit to great designs of raising himself; but not to transport him to endeavour it, by any crooked and indirect means. He was never suspected to flatter the greatest men, or in the least degree to dissemble his own opinions or thoughts, how ingrateful soever it often proved; and even an affected defect in, and contempt of those two useful qualities cost him dear afterwards. He indulged his palate very much, and took even some delight in eating and drinking well, but without any approach to luxury; and, in truth, rather discoursed like an epicure, than was one. . . . He had a fancy, sharp and luxuriant, but so carefully cultivated and strictly guarded, that he never was heard to speak a loose or profane word, which he imputed to the chastity of the persons where his conversation usually was, where that rank sort of wit was religiously detested; and a little discountenance would quickly root those unsavoury weeds out all discourses where persons of honour are present. He was in his nature inclined to pride and passion, and to a humour between wrangling and disputing very troublesome, which good company in a short time so much reformed and mastered, that no man was more affable and courteous to all kind of persons, and they who knew the great infirmity of his whole family, which abounded in passion, used to say, he had much extinguished the unruliness of that fire. That which supported and rendered him generally accept-

able was his generosity (for he had too much a contempt of money), and the opinion men had of the goodness and justice of his nature, which was transcendent in him, in a wonderful tenderness, and delight in obliging. His integrity was ever without blemish, and believed to be above temptation. He was firm and unshaken in his friendships, and, though he had great candour towards others in the differences of religion, he was zealously and deliberately fixed in the principles, both of the doctrine and discipline of the church. —CLARENDON, LORD (EDWARD HYDE), 1674? *Life.*

His chief failing seems to have been too entire devotion to a prince who did not deserve his generous attachment. Yet could he never subdue his mind to the pliant principles or supple manners of a court; and as he expressed his sentiments without regard to rank, he incurred the imputation of that haughty and uncomplying demeanour, which is so often united with the possession of power. The pride of office, however, seems little consistent with the soundness of his judgment; and, in that eventful age, he could not look around him without seeing examples of the instability of greatness, which would chastise the most flattering suggestions of human presumption.—MACDIARMID, JOHN, 1807, *Lives of British Statesmen, vol.* II.

It is certain that he fell a victim to the hostility of party. The charges against him were not supported by any lawful proof, and most, if not all, were satisfactorily refuted in his answer. Yet he must not be considered an immaculate character. His dread of republicanism taught him to advocate every claim of the prerogative, however unreasonable, and his zeal for orthodoxy led him to persecute all who dissented from the establishment. He was haughty and overbearing; his writings betray in many instances his contempt for veracity: and his desire of amassing wealth provoked Evelyn to remark of him, that "the lord chancellor never did, nor would do, any thing but for money." He bore with impatience the tedium of exile; but his frequent solicitations for permission to return were treated with neglect by Charles, who felt no inclination to engage in a new contest for the sake of a man, whom he had long before ceased to esteem.—LINGARD, JOHN, 1819-30, *A History of England, third ed., vol.* XII.

To the general baseness and profligacy of the times, Clarendon is principally indebted for his high reputation. He was, in every respect, a man unfit for his age, at once too good for it and too bad for it. He seemed to be one of the statesmen of Elizabeth, transplanted at once to a state of society widely different from that in which the abilities of such statesmen had been serviceable.—MACAULAY, THOMAS BABINGTON, 1827, *Hallam's Constitutional History, Critical and Miscellaneous Essays.*

He had a competent estate, and was not obliged to regard his profession solely as a means of immediate profit. It is probable that he then entertained hopes of future political or literary distinction; for, amidst his application to law, he was careful not to neglect such means as might lead to advancement in a different career. Every day he devoted some hours to general literature; and he cultivated the society of many distinguished and valuable friends. With members of his own profession he lived little: but he had been careful to form such connections as were alike honourable and advantageous; and, ere he had attained the age of twenty-seven, could enumerate among his intimate associates many of the most eminent persons in the kingdom—persons distinguished not merely by rank and power, but by their characters, abilities, and acquirements. Among his early literary friends were Ben Jonson—Selden, whose society he felt to have been inestimably valuable to him, and for whose talents and learning he retained a veneration unimpaired by subsequent difference of political opinion; Charles Cotton, a man of taste and letters, now remembered chiefly

as the literary associate of Isaac Walton; May, the able and candid historian of the parliament; Carew, whose graceful poetry still holds its place in public estimation; his more celebrated contemporary, Edmund Waller; the accomplished and versatile Sir Kenelm Digby; Hales, distinguished by his classical acquirements; Chillingworth, the profound theologian and acute controversialist; these were the literary men whose society was cultivated by Hyde; and to these may be added the names of Sheldon, Morley, and Earles, ecclesiastics, then enjoying a high and deserved reputation.—LISTER, T. H., 1838, *Life and Administration of Edward, First Earl of Clarendon, vol.* I, *p.* 14.

Wherever Buckingham presented himself, wit, frolic, and buffoonery, were sure to have the ascendent. The more exalted the personage, the more serious the subject, and the more solemn the occasion, the more certain was it to provoke his merriment and ridicule. The King himself was as much exposed to his jests as was his humblest courtier; and the fortunes of his enemy, Clarendon, were apparently ruined by the systematic ribaldry, with which he persecuted the grave Lord Chancellor. Buckingham's mimicry was irresistible, and when he imitated the stately walk of that solemn personage,—a pair of bellows hanging before him for the purse, and Colonel Titus preceding him with a fire-shovel on his shoulders, by way of mace—the King and his courtiers are described as convulsed with laughter. Buckingham's example was of course followed by others, and when the Chancellor passed by, the ladies of the Court used to touch the King:—"There," said they, "goes your schoolmaster." Clarendon himself alludes with bitterness to this unlicensed buffoonery.—JESSE, JOHN HENEAGE, 1839-57, *Memoirs of The Court of England during the Reign of the Stuarts, including The Protectorate, vol.* III. *p.* 78.

Hyde is a firm-built, eupeptic Barrister, whose usual air is florid-hopeful still; a massive man; unknown depth of impetuosity kept down under mountain rock-strata of discretion, which yearly pile themselves higher and higher and are already very high for his years.—CARLYLE, THOMAS, 1844-49-98, *Historical Sketches of Noble Persons and Events in the Reigns of James I. and Charles I., p.* 329.

And yet Clarendon was not beaten. Amid exile, obloquy, bodily pain, old age, —with the edifice of his ambition lying shattered round him,—denied a hole in his dear England wherein to die,—he held the fortress of his soul invincible, and showed that a man true to himself can smile at fate. In a fine form, without vanity or arrogance, he exhibited in those years that humour which is the habitual mood of reason, the very bloom and aroma of practical philosophy—a humour which has little or no connection with fun, or wit, or audible laughter; but consists in an unsubduable capacity to make the best of things; a clearness and azure serenity of the soul's atmosphere which *cannot* be clouded over; a steadfast realisation, against optimists and pessimists alike, that life on earth is neither celestial nor diabolic, but, under all conditions possible for a wise man, is worth having. Ready to welcome any enlargement, any dawn of royal favour, he did not pine for the want of it, nor did he court the delusive but subtly seductive opiate of egotistic brooding over his virtues and his wrongs. He addressed himself to wholesome labour, wrote his autobiography, studied the languages and literatures of Italy and France, carried on his commentary on the Psalms, and, looking up his controversial harpoon, attempted to fix it in the nose of leviathan Hobbes. He felt and wrote of his dear Falkland with a poetic tenderness which almost makes one love him. In his loyalty to the laws of the universe which had not been for him a garden of roses, and his filial reverence for a Divine Father who had, he believed, afflicted him, he presents a notable illustration of the tendency of sincere religion to promote mental health.—BAYNE, PETER, 1878, *The Chief Actors in the Puritan Revolution, p.* 499.

Of his habits and tastes during his early years, and of his pursuits during his exile, Clarendon gives full details in his autobiography, but says nothing of his private life during the time of his greatness. We learn from others that he was fond of state and magnificence, verging on ostentation. Nothing stirred the spleen of satirists more than the great house which he built for himself in St. James's, and his own opinion was that it contributed more than any alleged misdemeanours to "that gust of envy" which overthrew him. Designed to cost £20,000, it finally cost £50,000, and involved him in endless difficulties. Evelyn describes it as "without hyperbole the best contrived, most useful, graceful, magnificent house in England." In the end it was sold to the Duke of Albemarle for £25,000, and pulled down to make room for new buildings.—FIRTH, C. H., 1891, *Dictionary of National Biography, vol.* XXVIII, *p.* 385.

The worst part of his whole character —and the fault is illustrated in endless ways—is his frequent insincerity. No doubt the events of his life afforded much excuse for it, but it shows itself continually, and almost always in the same form. He keeps continually saying, almost in so many words, but at all events indirectly, "I am a rough, honest, passionate, plain-spoken man, proud of my sincerity, perhaps too secure in my good conscience. My frank harshness of manner was the cause of all my misfortunes." The slyness which lurks under this sort of roughness is the slyest thing in the whole world. —STEPHEN, SIR JAMES FITZJAMES, 1892, *Horae Sabbaticae, First Series, p.* 342.

HISTORY OF THE REBELLION
1702–4

I thinke I told you that this earl of Clarendon told me his father was writing the history of our late times. He beginns with king Charles 1st and brought it to the restauration of king Charles II, when, as he was writing, the, penne fell out of his hand: he took it up again to write: it fell out again. So then he percieved he was attacqued by death, scilicet, the dead palsey.—They say 'tis very well donne: but his sonne will not print it.— AUBRE., JOHN, 1669–96, *Brief Lives, ed. Clark, vol.* I, *p.* 426.

I cannot but let you know the incredible satisfaction I have taken in reading my late Lord Clarendon's "History of the Rebellion," so well and so unexpectedly well written—the preliminary so like that of the noble Polybius, leading us by the courts, avenues, and porches, into the fabric; the style masculine; the characters so just, and tempered without the least impediment of passion or tincture of revenge, yet with such natural and lively touches as show his lordship well knew not only the persons' outsides, but their very interiors.—EVELYN, JOHN, 1702–3, *Letter to Samuel Pepys, Jan.* 20.

I have met, with none that may compare with him in the Weight of Solemnity of his Style, in the Strength and Clearness of Diction, in the Beauty and Majesty of Expression, and that noble Negligence of Phrase, which maketh his Words wait everywhere upon his Subject, with a Readiness and Propriety, that Art and Study are almost Strangers to.—FELTON, HENRY, 1711, *Dessertation on Reading the Classics.*

Had Clarendon sought nothing but power, his power had never ceased. A corrupted court and a blinded populace were less the causes of the chancellor's fall, than an ungrateful king, who could not pardon his lordship's having refused to accept for him the slavery of his country. . . . Buckingham, Shaftsbury, Lauderdale, Arlington, and such abominable men, were the exchange which the nation made for my lord Clarendon! . . . As an historian he seems more exceptionable. His majesty and eloquence, his power of painting characters, his knowledge of his subject, rank him in the first class of writers—yet he has both great and little faults.—WALPOLE, HORACE, 1758, *A Catalogue of the Royal and Noble Authors of England, Scotland, and Ireland,* ed. Park, vol. III, *pp.* 162, 163, 164.

This age affords great materials for history, but did not produce any accomplished historian. Clarendon, however, will always be esteemed an entertaining writer, even independent of our curiosity to know the facts which he relates. His style is prolix and redundant, and suffocates us by the length of its periods; but it discovers imagination and sentiment, and pleases us at the same time that we disapprove of it. He is more partial in appearance than in reality; for he seems perpetually anxious to apologize for the king; but his apologies are often well grounded. He is less partial in his relation of facts, than in his account of characters: he was too honest a man to falsify the former; his affections were easily capable, unknown to himself, of disguising the latter. An air of probity and goodness runs through the whole work, as these qualities did, in reality, embellish the whole life of the author.—HUME, DAVID, 1762, *The History of England, The Commonwealth.*

We see, in the instance of the celebrated person before us, as well as in many others, that the exertion of genius depends more upon chance or opportunity, than upon nature itself. The divisions and distractions of his country called forth the talents of this excellent man. He had a principle share as a speaker, a writer, and an actor, in the transactions of this reign; and was thereby qualified to enrich the world with one of the best histories it ever saw.—GRANGER, JAMES, 1769-1824, *Biographical History of England,* vol. III, *p.* 4.

Though he writes as the professed apologist of one side, yet there appears more impartiality in his relation of facts, than might at first be expected. A great spirit of virtue and probity runs through his work. He maintains all the dignity of an historian. His sentences, indeed, are often too long, and his general manner is prolix; but his style, on the whole, is manly; and his merit, as an historian, is much beyond mediocrity.—BLAIR, HUGH, 1783, *Lecture on Rhetoric and Belles-Lettres,* ed. *Mills, p.* 407

Nothing can be more disgustful to a discerning observer of styles, than the prolixity and perplexity of Clarendon's composition. Yet he will probably be found to have written well for his time. The absurdity is in those persons who would hold up such writing as a model to after time; as if one should show a schoolboy's theme, and maintain that a man of the most approved talents, and the ripest years, could not surpass it. The English language, as well as the English annals, is indebted to the labours of Clarendon.—GODWIN, WILLIAM, 1797, *Milton and Clarendon, The Enquirer, p.* 415.

A work, of which the impressions and profits have increased in an equal ratio—and of which the popularity is built upon an imperishable basis. A statesman, a lawyer, and a philosopher in its most practical, and perhaps rational, sense, there is hardly any name which has reached us, encircled by purer rays of renown, than that of Hyde, Earl of Clarendon; or any which is likely to go down to posterity in a more unsullied state of purity. When one considers the times in which this celebrated Lord Chancellor lived, the station which he filled, the characters with whom he came in competition—(as able as they were intrepid, daring, and corrupt) his family connections, his career of glory; brightest in its wane—and, above all, the legacy, which, in his "History," he has bequeathed to posterity, . . . I hardly know how to call upon both "the Young," and "the Old," lover of good books, sufficiently to reverence those invaluable volumes known by the title of the "History of the Rebellion and Civil Wars in England, begun in the year 1641," by the great author in question.— DIBDIN, THOMAS FROGNALL, 1824, *The Library Companion, p.* 209.

For an Englishman there is no single historical work with which it can be so necessary for him to be well and thoroughly acquainted as with Clarendon. I feel at this time perfectly assured, that if that book had been put into my hands in youth, it would have preserved me from all the political errors which I have outgrown. It may be taken for granted that —— knows this book well. The more he reads concerning the history of these times, the more highly he will appreciate the wisdom and the integrity of Clarendon.—SOUTHEY, ROBERT, 1825, *Letter to Henry Taylor, Dec.* 31.

Is not only ably written and full of valuable information, but has also an air of dignity and sincerity which makes even the prejudices and errors with which it abounds respectable.—MACAULAY, THOMAS BABINGTON, 1825, *Milton, Edinburgh Review; Critical and Miscellaneous Essays.*

The "History of the Rebellion" is a work in which the indications of talent disappear under the impress of virtue. Some portraits are vividly coloured; but the character of these portraits is easy of imitation; it is within the reach of the commonest minds; Clarendon himself is reflected in his pictures; his image is portrayed in every page.—CHATEAUBRIAND, FRANÇOIS RENÉ, VICOMTE DE, 1837, *Sketches of English Literature, vol.* II, *p.* 196.

He is excellent in every thing that he has performed with care; his characters are beautifully delineated; his sentiments have often a noble gravity, which the length of his periods, far too great in itself, seems to befit; but, in the general course of his narration, he is negligent of grammar and perspicuity, with little choice of words, and therefore sometimes idiomatic without ease or elegance. The official papers on the royal side, which are generally attributed to him, are written

in a masculine and majestic tone, far superior to those of the parliament.— HALLAM, HENRY, 1837–39, *Introduction to the Literature of Europe, pt.* iii, *ch.* vii, *par.* 36.

I cannot quit the present subject without a remark on these great party "Histories" of Clarendon and Burnet. Both have passed through the fiery ordeal of national opinion; and both, with some of their pages singed, remain unconsumed: the one criticised for its solemn eloquence, the other ridiculed for its homely simplicity; the one depreciated for its partiality, the other for its inaccuracy; both alike, as we have seen, by their opposite parties, once considered as works utterly rejected from the historical shelf. But Posterity reverences Genius; for Posterity only can decide on its true worth. Time, potent over criticism, has avenged our two great writers of the history of their own days. The awful genius of Clarendon is still paramount, and the vehement spirit of Burnet has often its secret revelations confirmed. Such shall ever be the fate of those precious writings, which, though they have to contend with the passions of their own age, yet, originating in the personal intercourse of the writers with the subject of their narratives, possess an endearing charm which no criticism can dissolve, a reality which outlasts fiction, and a truth which diffuses its vitality over pages which cannot die.—DISRAELI, ISAAC, 1841, *Difficulties of Publishers of Contemporary Memoirs, Amenities of Literature.*

It is easy to point out faults in his "History of the Rebellion,"—its redundances, its omissions, its inaccuracies, its misrepresentations, its careless style, and its immethodical arrangement. But of all history contemporary history is the most valuable; of contemporary histories that is to be preferred which is written by one who took a part in the events related; and of all such contemporary histories, in our own or any other language, this great work is the most to be admired, for graphic narration of facts, for just exposition of motives, and for true and striking delineation of character. We find in it a freshness, a spirit, a raciness, which induce us, in spite of all its imperfections, to lay it down with regret, and to resume it with new pleasure. With regard to its *sincerity,* which has been so much contested, perhaps the author may be acquitted of wilfully asserting what is false; but he seems to have considered himself fully justified in suppressing what is true, when he thought he could do so for the advantage of his party.—CAMPBELL, JOHN LORD, 1845–56, *The Lives of The Lord Chancellors and Keepers of the Great Seal of England.*

His style cannot be commended for its correctness; the manner in which he constructs his sentences, indeed, often sets at defiance all the rules of syntax; but yet he is never unintelligible or obscure —with such admirable expository skill is the matter arranged and spread out, even where the mere verbal sentence-making is the most negligent and entangled. The style, in fact, is that proper to speaking rather than to writing, and had, no doubt, been acquired by Clarendon, not so much from books as from his practice in speaking at the bar and in parliament; for, with great natural abilities, he does not seem to have had much acquaintance with literature, or much acquired knowledge of any kind resulting from study. But his writing possesses the quality that interests above all the graces or artifices of rhetoric—the impress of a mind informed by its subject, and having a complete mastery over it; while the broad full stream in which it flows makes the reader feel as if it were borne along on its tide. The abundance, in particular, with which he pours out his stores of language and illustration in his characters of the eminent persons engaged on both sides of the great contest seems inexhaustible. The historical value of his history, however, is not very considerable: it has not preserved very many facts which are not to be found elsewhere; and, whatever may be thought of its general bias, the inaccuracy of its details is so great throughout, as demonstrated by the authentic evidences of the time, that there is scarcely any other contemporary history which is so little trustworthy as an authority with regard to minute particulars. — CRAIK, GEORGE L., 1861, *A Compendious History of English Literature and of the English Language, vol.* II, *p.* 121.

A work which everybody must read who desires to understand the personal feelings which were elicited, and the men who occupied prominent positions, in that stormy period; and the student, if possible, should endeavour to obtain an edition of it later than the year 1825, as all editions published previous to that date are more or less corrupt.—FRISWELL, JAMES HAIN, 1869, *Essays on English Writers, p.* 32.

The effect which an historical work can have is, perhaps, nowhere seen more strongly than in the "History of the Rebellion." The view of the event in England itself and in the educated world generally, has been determined by the book. The best authors have repeated it, and even those who combat it do not get beyond the point of view given by him; they refute him in details, but leave his views in the main unshaken. Clarendon belongs to those who have essentially fixed the circle of ideas for the English nation. —RANKE, LEOPOLD, VON, 1875, *A History of England, vol.* VI, *p.* 29.

Clarendon's authority, totally worthless as it is, has without question been accepted, as Herr von Ranke says, by a great multitude of persons. It is a question of some interest how this has occurred. Something must be attributed to his style—to that "eloquence of the heart and imagination" which Hallam acknowledges, to that stateliness and felicity of phrase over which Professor Masson walks as if "stepping on velvet;" but perhaps not very much. Hume, who owed Clarendon a good word—for his account of the Puritan Revolution is simply that of Clarendon told by a skilful and unscrupulous literary artist—says plainly that his style is "prolix and redundant, and suffocates by the length of its periods." So it is, and so it does. More is accounted for by his anecdotic talent, his skill at an after-dinner story, his occasional chuckle of dry fun, his grave irony, his strenuous hatreds, his love of scandal.—BAYNE, PETER, 1876, *Clarendon, The Contemporary Review, vol.* 28, *p.* 426.

A history which remains, whatever its faults, the model of such writing, to this day.—WASHBURN, EMELYN W., 1884, *Studies in Early English Literature, p.* 156.

In some of the greatest characteristics of the historian, has been equalled by no Englishman, and surpassed by few foreigners. . . . No one has put together, or, to adopt a more expressive phrase, heaped together such enormous paragraphs; no one has linked clause on clause, parenthesis on parenthesis, epexegesis on exegesis, in such a bewildering concatenation of inextricable entanglement. Sometimes, of course, the difficulty is more apparent than real, and by simply substituting full stops and capitals for his colons and conjunctions, one may, to some extent, simplify the chaos. But it is seldom that this is really effective: it never produces really well balanced sentences and really well constructed paragraphs; and there are constant instances in which it is not applicable at all. It is not that the jostling and confused relatives are as a rule grammatically wrong, like the common blunder of putting an "and which" where there is no previous "which" expressed or implied. They, simply, put as they are, bewilder and muddle the reader because the writer has not taken the trouble to break up his sentence into two or three. —SAINTSBURY, GEORGE, 1887, *History of Elizabethan Literature,.pp.* 315, 347.

To such an experience as Clarendon's, the making of history was far more than the writing of it; and the habits bred of action in a great scene and in a great crisis, the varied tasks which had been thrust upon him, the tragic significance of the long struggle that constituted his life, have, in combination with those literary interests that from first to last sweetened his toil, given to his style its special and inimitable characteristics. It is often cumbrous and prolix; its construction is frequently irregular; the arrangement is sometimes confusing, and the sense of proportion seems to be lost. But its chief note is one of almost tragic

dignity. His "History of the Rebellion" —be it noted, the first history which our literature possesses from the hand of a great actor in the struggle it portrays— has something of the burden of an epic. But it is enlivened by those inimitable characters which his careful study of human nature, his intense desire to know those who were worthy to be known, enabled him to draw; portraits in which every feature is given in its due proportion, and in which no trait, however homely, is omitted which can add to their dramatic force.—CRAIK, HENRY, 1893, *English Prose, vol.* II, *p.* 391.

Clarendon was by a few months Milton's senior, yet in reading him we seem to have descended to a later age. That he owed not a little to the Theophrastian fashion of his youth is certain; but the real portraits which he draws with such picturesque precision are vastly superior to any fantastical abstractions of Overbury or Earle. Clarendon writes, in Wordsworth's phrase, with his eye upon the object, and the graces of his style are the result of the necessity he finds of describing what he wishes to communicate in the simplest and most convincing manner. . . . It is his great distinction that, living in an age of pedants, he had the courage to write history— a species of literature which, until his salutary example, was specially overweighted with ornamental learning—in a spirit of complete simplicity. The diction of Clarendon is curiously modern; we may read pages of his great book without lighting upon a single word now no longer in use.—GOSSE, EDMUND, 1897, *A Short History of Modern English Literature, pp.* 150, 151.

Sir Matthew Hale

1609-1676

Sir Matthew Hale, 1609-1676, though celebrated mainly as a jurist, has also an honorable record as a man of letters. Sir Matthew studied at Oxford, and in Lincoln's Inn. He was made Sergeant-at-Law in 1652, Chief Baron of the Exchequer in 1660, and Lord Chief Justice of England in 1671; and was one of the most renowned and upright judges that ever graced the English bench; equally honored for his general knowledge, legal attainments, and purity of character. A complete collection of his Moral and Religious Works was published in 2 vols., 8vo, 1805, London. The best known of his legal writings are " The History of the Pleas of the Crown;" "The History of the Common Law of England;" and the tract on "The Trial of Witches." —HART, JOHN S., 1872, *A Manual of English Literature, p.* 159.

PERSONAL

He was a man of no quick utterance, but often hesitant; but spoke with great reason. He was most precisely just; insomuch as I believe he would have lost all that he had in the world rather than do an unjust act: patient in hearing the tediousest speech which any man had to make for himself. The pillar of justice, the refuge of the subject who feared oppression, and one of the greatest honours of his majesty's government. — BAXTER, RICHARD, 1682, *Notes on the Life and Death of Sir Matthew Hale.*

This excellent person, whose learning in the law was scarce equalled, and never exceeded; was, in many respects, one of the most perfect characters of his age. Nor was his knowledge limited to his own profession: he was far from inconsiderable as a philosopher and a divine. He was as good and amiable in his private, as he was great and venerable in his public, capacity. His decisions upon the bench were frequently a learned lecture upon the point of law; and such was his reputation for integrity, that the interested parties were generally satisfied with them, though they happened to be against themselves. No man more abhorred the chicane of lawyers, or more discountenanced the evil arts of pleading. He was so very conscientious, that the jealousy of being misled by his affections made him perhaps rather partial to that side to which he was least inclined. Though he was a man of true humility, he was not insensible of that honest praise which was bestowed on him by the general voice of mankind, and which must have been attended with that *self-applause* which is the natural result of good and worthy actions. —GRANGER, JAMES, 1769–1824, *Biographical History of England, vol.* v, *p.* 120.

Gentlemen, in the place where we now sit to administer the justice of this great country, above a century ago the never-to-be-forgotten Sir Matthew Hale presided; whose faith in Christianity is an exalted commentary upon its truth and reason, and whose life was a glorious example of its fruits in man, administering human justice with a wisdom and purity drawn from the pure fountain of the Christian dispensation, which has been, and will be in all ages, a subject of the highest reverence and admiration.—ERSKINE, THOMAS

LORD, 1797, *Speech in the Court of the King's Bench.*

His authority coming at last to be regarded as all but infallible, it would by no means be surprising if he became, as North alleges, exceedingly vain and intolerant of opposition; but of this, beyond North's word, we have no evidence. Hale remained throughout life attached to his early puritanism. He was a regular attendant at church, morning and evening, on Sunday, and also gave up a portion of the day to prayer and meditation, besides expounding the sermon to his children. He was an extreme anti-ritualist, having apparently no ear for music, and objecting even to singing, and in particular to the practice of intoning. Though strictly orthodox in essentials, he was impatient of the subtleties of theology. . . . He carried puritan plainness of dress to such a point as to move even Baxter to remonstrate with him.— RIGG, J. M., 1890, *Dictionary of National Biography, vol.* XXIV, *p.* 20.

GENERAL

The following Treatise, ["Pleas of the Crown"] being the genuine off-spring of that truly learned and worthy Judge, Sir Matthew Hale, stands in need of no other recommendation than what that great and good name will always carry along with it. Whoever is in the least acquainted with the extensive learning, the solid judgment, the indefatiagble labours, and, above all, the unshaken integrity, of the author, cannot but highly esteem whatever comes from so valuable a hand.—EMLYN, S., 1736–39, *ed., Pleas of the Crown, Preface.*

His writings have raised him a character equal to his greatest predecessors, and will always be esteemed as containing the best rationale of the grounds of the law of England. Nor was he an inconsiderable master of polite, philosophical, and especially theological, learning.—BIRCH, THOMAS, 1752, *Life of Archbishop Tillotson.*

In whom
Our British Themis gloried with just cause,
Immortal Hale! for deep discernment praised
And sound integrity not more, than famed
For sanctity of manners undefiled.
—COWPER, WILLIAM, 1785, *The Task, bk.* iii.

So authoritative an "History of the Common Law of England," written by so learned an author, requires neither preface nor commendation. It has ever been justly held in the highest estimation, and, like the virtues of its author, been universally admired and venerated. Here the student will find a valuable guide, the barrister a learned assistant, the court an indisputable authority. — RUNNINGTON, CHARLES, 1820, ed., The History of the

Common Law of England, and an Analysis of the Civil Part of the Law.

Amidst the immorality of Charles II.'s reign, Sir Matthew Hale stands out with peculiar lustre as an impartial, incorruptible, and determined administrator of justice. — CHAMBERS, ROBERT, 1876, Chambers's Cyclopædia of English Literature, ed. Carruthers.

James Harrington

1611–1677

James Harrington, (1611–77), born at Upton, Northants, the son of Sir S. Harrington of Exton, Ruthlandshire, studied at Trinity, Oxford. He travelled to Rome, and though a republican, became in 1646 a personal attendant of Charles I., and attended him to the scaffold. His semi-romance "Oceana" (1656), setting forth the best form of commonwealth, maintains that the real basis of power is property, especially landed property, from which no one person should derive more than £3000 a-year; and that the rulers should be changed every three years, their successors being elected by ballot. In 1661 he was arrested for attempting to change the constitution, and in prison went temporarily insane.—PATRICK AND GROOME, eds., 1897, Chambers's Biographical Dictionary, p. 464.

Harrington published also several other political treatises, an essay on Virgil, and a metrical translation of four books of the Æneid.—HART JOHN S., 1872, A Manual of English Literature, p. 160.

PERSONAL

Anno Domini 1660, he was committed prisoner to the Tower, where he was kept . . . ; then to Portsey castle. His durance in these prisons (he being a gentleman of a high spirit and hot head) was the procatractique cause of his deliration or madnesse; which was not outragious, for he would discourse rationally enough and be very facetious company, but he grew to have a phancy that his perspiration turned to flies, and sometimes to bees —ad cætera sobvius. . . . 'Twas the strangest sort of madnes that ever I found in any one · talke of any thing els, his discourse would be very ingeniose and pleasant. . . . He was of a middling statue, well-trussed man, strong and thick, well-sett, sanguine, quick-hott-fiery hazell eie, thick moyst curled haire, as you may see by his picture. In his conversation very friendly, and facetious, and hospitable.—AUBREY, JOHN, 1669–96, Brief Lives ed. Clark, vol. I, pp. 292, 293.

OCEANA
1656

He made severall essayes in Poetry, viz. love-verses, &c., and translated . . . booke of Virgill's Æn.; but his muse was rough, and Mr. Henry Nevill, an ingeniose and well-bred gentleman, a member of the House of Commons, and an excellent (but concealed) poet, was his great familiar and confident friend, and disswaded him from tampering in poetrie which he did invitâ Minervâ, and to improve his proper talent, viz. Politicall Reflections. Whereupon has writ his "Oceana," printed London (1656). Mr. T. Hobbes was wont to say that Henry Nevill had a finger in that pye; and 'tis like enough. That ingeniose tractat, together with his and H. Nevill's smart discourses and inculcations, dayly at coffee-houses, made many proselytes.—AUBREY, JOHN, 1669–96, Brief Lives, ed. Clark, vol. I, p. 289.

It is strange that Harrington (so short a time ago) should be the first man to find out so evident and demonstrable a truth, as that of property being the true basis and measure of power. His "Oceana," allowing for the different situation of things (as the less number of lords then, those lords having no share in the parliament and the like), is certainly one of the best founded political pieces that ever was writ.—LOCKIER, DR. DEAN OF PETERBOROUGH, 1730–32, Spence's Anecdotes, ed. Singer, p. 57.

The style of this author wants ease and fluency; but the good matter which his work contains makes compensation.— HUME, DAVID, 1762, *The History of England, The Commonwealth.*

The author, who was a great visionary, was sanguine enough to expect to see it put in execution. Baxter's "Holy Commonwealth" was avowedly levelled at this political romance. But Harrington, who expressed a great contempt for that performance, did not vouchsafe to write a serious answer to it; but affected to treat the author in a very cavalier manner, in a half sheet full of cant and ridicule.— GRANGER, JAMES, 1769–1824, *Biographical History of England, vol.* IV, *p.* 60.

Harrington, whose "Oceana" is justly regarded as one of the boasts of English literature.—STEWART, DUGALD, 1815–21, *First Preliminary Dissertation, Encyclopædia Britannica.*

In general, it may be said of Harrington, that he is prolix, dull, pedantic, and seldom profound; but sometimes redeems himself by just observations. Like most theoretical politicians of that age, he had an excessive admiration for the republic of Venice. His other political writings are in the same spirit as the "Oceana," but still less interesting.—HALLAM, HENRY, 1837–39, *Introduction to the Literature of Europe, pt.* iv, *ch.* iv, *par.* 83.

As an early supporter of political liberty in England, the name of Harrington will always be entitled to the respect of posterity, whatever may be thought of the practicability of some of his speculations. —ALLIBONE, S. AUSTIN, 1854–58, *Dictionary of English Literature, vol.* I, *p.* 788.

If he has not the merit of absolute originality in his main propositions, they had at least never been so clearly expounded and demonstrated by any preceding writer. —CRAIK, GEORGE L., 1861, *A Compendious History of English Literature and of the English Language, vol.* II, *p.* 83.

The political influence of the Italian republics upon English public opinion was very powerful in the seventeenth century, when the habit of travelling became general among the upper class of Englishmen, and when a large proportion of the highest intellects acquired in Italy a knowledge of the Italian writers on government, and an admiration for the Italian constitutions, and especially for that of Venice. The highest representative of this action of the Italian upon the English intellect was Harrington. His "Oceana," though published under the Commonwealth and dedicated to Cromwell, was altogether uninfluenced by the inspiration of Puritanism; and it was only by the intercession of Cromwell's favourite daughter, Lady Claypole, that its publication was permitted. (Toland, "Life of Harrington.") It is remarkable that while Harrington's writings were avowedly based in a very great degree upon those of Italians, they also represent more faithfully than any others of the seventeenth century what are regarded as the distinctive merits of English liberty. That a good government is an organism, not a mechanism—in other words, that it must grow naturally out of the condition of society, and cannot be imposed by theorists—that representative assemblies with full powers are the sole efficient guardians of liberty— that liberty of conscience must be allied with political liberty—that a certain balance should be preserved between the different powers of the State, and that property produces empire, are among the main propositions on which Harrington insists; and most of them are even now the main points of difference between English liberty and that which emanates from a French source. Harrington was also a warm advocate of the ballot.—LECKY, WILLIAM HARTPOLE, 1865, *Spirit of Rationalism in Europe, vol.* II, *note.*

Harrington is full of ability, he has studied theoretical politics with immense care, he has observed certain sides of actual politics not without acuteness: he has just censures of "Leviathan" to which his own work is in a manner a counterblast: he is extraordinarily ingenious in the arrangement of the Tribes and the Troops, of the ballot machinery and the "Provincial Orb." But in all this and in the relish with which he draws up accounts for the ballot boxes and the balls of metal and the pavilions, devises elaborate and rather poetical titles for his tribes and their officers, intersperses comic speeches by the "Lord Epimonus" (a genial fanatic of reaction), and adjusts rejoinders to them by Lord Archon (Cromwell), which are in some respects almost startlingly like Cromwell's own speeches: in all this I say it is almost impossible not to detect what is familiarly called the bee in the bonnet.—SAINTSBURY, GEORGE, 1893, *English Prose, ed. Craik, vol.* II, *p.* 504.

The style of the treatise has little to commend it, but some of the views propounded are ingenious and suggestive.—MASTERMAN, J. HOWARD B., 1897, *The Age of Milton, p.* 238.

Owen Feltham

1602?–1677?

Owen Feltham was born about 1610, and but few particulars of his life have been preserved. He is supposed to have acted as secretary to the Earl of Thomond, with whom he resided many years. His celebrity rests upon his "Resolves," of which the first part appeared in 1627. He published "A Brief Character of the Low Countries" in 1659, and is believed to have died about 1678. A life by James Cumming was published in 1806.—TOWNSEND, GEORGE H., 1870, *ed. The Every-Day Book of Modern Literature, vol.* I, *p.* 237.

RESOLVES

Thou hast not one bad line so lustful bred,
As to dye maid or matron's cheek in red.
Thy modest wit, and witty honest letter
Make both at once my wit and me the better.
Thy Book a Garden is, and help us most
To regain that which we in Adam lost.
—RANDOLPH, THOMAS, C 1627, *To Mr. Feltham on his Book of "Resolves," Poems.*

Of this book, the first part of which was published in 1627, the second not till after the middle of the century, it is not uncommon to meet with high praises in those modern writers who profess a faithful allegiance to our older literature. For myself, I can only say that Feltham appears not only a labored and artificial, but a shallow writer. Among his many faults, none strikes me more than a want of depth, which his pointed and sententious manner renders more ridiculous. There are certainly exceptions to this vacuity of original meaning in Feltham: it would be possible to fill a few pages with extracts not undeserving of being read, with thoughts just and judicious, though never deriving much lustre from his diction. He is one of the worst writers in point of style; with little vigor, he has less elegance; his English is impure to an excessive degree, and full of words unauthorized by any usage. Pedantry, and the novel phrases which Greek and Latin etymology was supposed to warrant, appear in most productions of this period; but Feltham attempted to bend the English idiom to his own affectations. The moral reflections of a serious and thoughtful mind are generally pleasing; and to this, perhaps, is partly owing the kind of popularity which the "Resolves" of Feltham have obtained; but they may be had more agreeably and profitably in other books.—HALLAM, HENRY, 1837–39, *Introduction to the Literature of Europe, pt.* iii, *ch.* iv, *par.* 35.

The style of Feltham is not always equal; but is generally strong, harmonious, and well adapted to the subjects of which he treats. He is prodigal of metaphor and quotation, and on that account has been accused of pedantry; but his figures are always beautifully illustrative of his subject, and his quotations generally appropriate. As to his sentiments, they are remarkable for their sound, good sense, as well as for their great purity of moral and religious principle.—CLEVELAND, CHARLES D., 1848, *A Compendium of English Literature, p.* 288.

The thoughts are commonplace, the method bad, being the disjointed method of Bacon's essays without the natural clearness; and there is a constant straining after imagery. Their popularity in Queen Anne's reign is accounted for by their high moral tone, and their occasionally felicitous application of Baconian imagery to common themes, such as moderation in grief, evil-speaking, industry and meditation.—MINTO, WILLIAM, 1872–80, *A Manual of English Prose Literature, p.* 303.

Besides the "Resolves" he wrote some verse, of which the most notable piece is a reply to Ben Jonson's famous ode to himself ("Come Leave the Loathed Stage")—a reply which even such a sworn partisan as Gifford admits to be at least just if not very kind. Felltham seems also to have engaged in controversy with another Johnson, a Jesuit, on theological subjects. But save for the "Resolves" he would be totally forgotten. The estimate of their value will differ very much, as the liking for not very original discussion of ethical subjects and sound if not very subtle judgment on them overpowers or not in the reader a distaste for style that has no particular distinction, and ideas which, though often wholesome, are seldom other than obvious. Wordsworth's well-known description of one of his own poems, as being "a chain of extremely valuable thoughts," applies no doubt to the "Resolves," which, except in elegance, rather resemble the better-known of Cicero's philosophical works. Moreover, though possessing no great elegance, they are not inelegant; though it is difficult to forget how differently Bacon and Browne treated not dissimilar subjects at much the same time.—SAINTSBURY, GEORGE, 1887, *History of Elizabethan Literature, p.* 442.

Feltham's poems are few in number, but varied in style; some have considerable merit, and none are contemptible. His prose, after enjoying much popularity, was almost totally neglected till Cumming's edition of 1806.—BAYNE, REV. RONALD, 1889, *Dictionary of National Biography, vol.* XVIII, *p.* 304.

Isaac Barrow
1630–1677

Born at London, 1630: died at London, April, 1677. A noted English theologian, classical scholar, and mathematician. He was educated at Cambridge (scholar of Trinity 1647, and fellow 1649), traveled on the Continent (1655–59), was appointed professor of geometry at Gresham College, and in 1663 first Lucasian professor of mathematics at Cambridge (resigned 1669 in favor of Newton); was chaplain to Charles II.; and became master of Trinity College in 1672. Among his works are "Lectiones Opticæ et Geometricæ" (1669–1670–74), "Treatise on the Pope's Supremacy" (1680). The best edition of his theological works is that of Rev. A. Napier (1859).—SMITH, BENJAMIN E., 1894–97, *The Century Cyclopedia of Names, p.* 124.

PERSONAL

His humour when a boy and after:—merry and cheerfull and beloved where ever he came. His grandfather kept him till he was 7 years old: his father was faine to force him away, for there he would have been good for nothing there. A good poet, English and Latin. He spake 8 severall languages. . . . He was a strong and a stowt man and feared not any man. He would fight with the butchers' boyes in St. Nicholas' shambles, and be hard enough for any of them. . . . At Constantinople, being in company with the English merchants, there was a Rhadamontade that would fight with any man and bragged of his valour, and dared any man there to try him. So no man accepting his challenge, said Isaac (not then a divine), "Why, if none els will try you I will;" and fell upon him and chastised him handsomely that he vaunted no more mongst them. . . . I have heard Mr. Wilson say that when he was at study, was so intent at it that when the bed was made, or so, he heeded it not nor perceived it, was so *totus in hoc;* and would sometimes be goeing out without his hatt on. He was by no meanes a spruce man, but most negligent in his dresse. As he was walking one day in St. James's parke, looking . . . his hatt up, his cloake halfe on and halfe off, a gent. came behind him and clapt him on the shoulder and sayd "Well, goe thy wayes for the veriest scholar that ever I mett with." He was a strong man but pale as the candle he studyed by.—AUBREY, JOHN, 1669–96, *Brief Lives, ed. Clark, vol.* I, *pp.* 88, 90, 91.

All I have said, or can say, is far short of the idea which Dr. Barrow's friends have formed of him, and that character which he ought to appear to them who knew him not. Besides all the defects on my part, he had in himself this disadvantage, of wanting foils to augment his lustre, and low places to give eminence to his heights, such virtues as his, contentment in all conditions, candour in doubtful cases, moderation among differing parties, knowledge without ostentation, are subjects fitter for praise than narrative.—HILL, ABRAHAM, 1683, *Letter to Archbishop Tillotson, April* 10.

When it is remembered that Barrow was only forty-seven years of age when he died, it seems almost incredible that in so short a life he could have gained so vast and multifarious a store of knowledge. Scholar, mathematician, man of science, preacher, controversialist, he gained enough credit in every one of these departments to make the reputation of an ordinary man; while his blameless, unselfish, christian life would be worth studying if he had gained no intellectual reputation at all. . . . As a mathematician he was considered by his contemporaries as second only to Newton, whose towering genius a little overshadowed that of his master; but on the other hand, his credit as a mathematician is enhanced by the fact that he was the first to recognise and develop the extraordinary talents of Newton, one of whose most famous discoveries he was on the verge of making.—OVERTON, J. H., 1885, *Dictionary of National Biography, vol.* III, *p.* 302.

SERMONS

In Dr. Barrow, one admires more the prodigious fecundity of his invention, and the uncommon strength and force of his conceptions, than the felicity of his execution, or his talent in composition. We see a genius far surpassing the common, peculiar indeed almost to himself; but that genius often shooting wild, and unchastised by any discipline or study of eloquence.—BLAIR, HUGH, 1783, *Lectures on Rhetoric and Belles-Letters, ed. Mills, p.* 325.

Barrow's sermons cannot but strike every one as being the works of a great thinker: they are, in truth, less properly orations, than trains of argumentative thought. His reasoning is prosecuted with an admirable union of comprehensiveness, sagacity, and clearness: and it is expressed in a style which, at once strong and regular, combines many of the virtues of the older writers with not a few of those that were appearing in the new.—SPALDING, WILLIAM, 1852–82, *A History of English Literature, p.* 290.

He had a geometrical method and clearness, an inexhaustible fertility, extraordinary impetuosity and tenacity of logic, writing the same sermon three or four times over, insatiable in his craving to explain and prove, obstinately confined to

his already overflowing thoughts, with a minuteness of division, an exactness of connection, a superfluity of explanation, so astonishing that the hearer at last gives in; and yet the mind turns with the vast machine, carried away and doubled up as by the rolling weight of a flattening machine.—TAINE, H. A., 1871, *History of English Literature, tr. Van Laun, vol.* II, *bk.* iii, *ch.* iii, *p.* 63.

The most celebrated sermons are instruments of edification rather than models of elegance. Barrow is geometrical, revises and re-revises, then revises again, dividing and subdividing, having only one desire—to explain and fully prove what he has to say.—WELSH, ALFRED H., 1883, *Development of English Literature and Language, vol.* II, *p.* 24.

Great as he was in learning of every kind, he was greatest as a preacher. The extraordinary length of his discourses, at which even his own generation protested, gives them the character of treatises rather than sermons, and it is clear that he was nothing if not complete in his treatment of the subjects he took up. But they cannot be considered dull. The style is strong, nervous, and impressive. and there is a force and directness about the argument which compels attention and sustains interest to the end. It is impossible to read his works without the feeling of being in the presence of a commanding personality.—HUTTON, WILLIAM HOLDEN, 1895, *Social England, ed. Traill, vol.* IV, *p.* 419.

GENERAL

The name of Dr. Barrow will ever be illustrious for a strength of mind and a compass of knowledge that did honour to his country. He was unrivalled in mathematical learning, and especially in the sublime geometry; in which he has been excelled only by one man, and that man was his pupil. The same genius that seemed to be born only to bring hidden truths to light, to rise to the heights, or descend to the depths of science, could sometimes amuse itself in the flowery paths of poetry. He at length gave himself up entirely to divinity; and particularly to the most useful part of it, that which has a tendency to make men wiser and better. He has, in his excellent sermons on the Creed, solved every difficulty, and removed every obstacle that opposed itself to our faith, and made divine revelation as clear as the demonstrations in his own "Euclid."—GRANGER, JAMES, 1769-1824, *Biographical History of England, vol.* v, *p.* 42.

Justification by Faith. On this subject I know of nothing so precise and accurate (though numberless and vast volumes have been written upon it from the Reformation downwards), as what is contained in Dr. Barrow's "Discourses on Faith." His notion on the whole is that Justification, as used by the sacred writers, and St. Paul in particular, means remission of sins, and admission into a state of favour with God, as if we were righteous, and not the infusion of inherent holiness by the Spirit; that this justification was primarily made on our entrance into the Christian covenant by baptism, and is afterwards renewed and regranted, as it were, on our repentance and return from such transgressions as we may have fallen into after baptism.—HURD, RICHARD, 1808? *Commonplace Book, ed. Kilvert.*

I mentioned that Mr. Fox always spoke of Barrow with enthusiasm, and that, upon the strength of this opinion, I bought his sermons, but found him insufferably dry; at least as far as I read, which was not very far. It is certain however, I belive, that besides containing the amplest stores of theological learning, he has also bursts of eloquence, which though not so poetical as Jeremy Taylor's, are, from their variety and force, far more striking.—MOORE, THOMAS, 1819, *Diary, Memoirs, ed. Russell, vol.* II, *p.* 286.

The school of Chillingworth, Mede, and Barrow—is the school of acute perception and close reasoning. Yet Barrow was perhaps the most able of the three: not in power of conception or of language— but in the systematic division, and masterly elucidation, of the various subjects of which he treats. He pushes his enquiries to the very verge, or confines, of which they are capable of being pushed; and his works afford a sort of logical Encyclopædia. He had the clearest head with which mathematics ever endowed an individual, and one of the purest and most unsophisticated hearts that ever beat in the human breast. He is to be studied with profit, rather than read with delight. —DIBDIN, THOMAS FROGNALL, 1824, *The Library Companion, p.* 51.

The sermons of Barrow display a strength of mind, a comprehensiveness and fertility, which have rarely been equalled. . . . In his style, notwithstanding its richness and occasional vivacity, we may censure a redundancy, and excess of apposition. . . . The Latin verse of Barrow is forcible and full of mind, but not sufficiently redolent of antiquity.—HALLAM, HENRY, 1837-39, *Introduction to the Literature of Europe, pt.* iv, *ch.* ii, *par.* 55, *ch.* v, *par.* 56.

He once uttered a most memorable observation, which characterizes both the intellectual and moral constitution of his mind,—would that it could be engraven on the mind of every youth, as his guide through life,—"A straight line is the shortest in Morals as well as in geometry." —CLEVELAND, CHARLES D., 1848, *A Compendium of English Literature, p.* 278.

In point of genius, was probably superior to Taylor.—BUCKLE, HENRY THOMAS, 1857, *History of Civilization in England, vol.* I.

The most striking things in his sermons are the extraordinary copiousness and vigour of the language, and the exhaustiveness and subtlety of the thought. He is a perfect mine of varied and vigorous expression. His sentences are thrown up with a rough careless vigour; and extreme antithesis to the polished flow of language and ideas in Addison. In his love of scrupulous definitions and qualifications we discover the mathematician; he divides and subdivides with Baconian minuteness, and in drawing parallels adjusts the compared particulars with acute exactness.—MINTO, WILLIAM, 1872-80, *Manual of English Prose Literature, p.* 332.

By the side of Tillotson, Isaac Barrow appears ponderous and even long-winded. He belongs to the new school more by what he avoids than by what he attains. He was a man of great intellectual force, who, born into an age which was beginning to stigmatise certain faults in its predecessor, was able to escape those particular errors of false ornament and studied quaintness, but could not train his somewhat elephantine feet to dance on the tight-rope of delicate ease. The matter of Barrow is always solid and virile, and he has phrases of a delightful potency. —GOSSE, EDMUND, 1897, *Short History of Modern English Literature, p.* 181.

THOMAS HOBBES

ANDREW MARVELL

Andrew Marvell

1621-1678

Born, at Winestead-in-Holderness, Yorks, 31 March 1621. Educated at Hull Grammar School, of which his father was master. Matric. Trin. Coll., Camb., as Sizar, 14 Dec. 1633; Scholar, 13 April 1638; B. A., 1638. Left Cambridge, 1641. Travelled abroad. Tutor to daughter of Lord Fairfax, 1650 [?]–53. Tutor to William Dutton (a ward of Oliver Cromwell), 1653–57; lived at Eton. Assistant to Milton (as Sec. of Foreign Tongues), 1657. M. P. for Hull, in Cromwell's Parliament, 1660; re-elected, Dec. 1660 and April 1661. On Embassy to Russia, Sweden, and Denmark with Earl of Carlisle, July 1663 to Jan. 1665. Prolific political and ecclesiastical controversial writer. Died, suddenly, in London, 18 Aug. 1678; buried in the church of St. Giles-in-the-Fields. Probably married. *Works:* "The First Anniversary of the Government," 1655; "The Character of Holland," 1665; "Clarendon's House-Warming," 1667; "The Rehearsal Transpos'd," pt. i. (anon.), 1672; pt. ii., 1673; "An Apology and Advice for some of the Clergy," 1674; "Dialogue between two Horses," 1675; "Plain Dealing" (under initials: A. M.), 1675; "A Letter from a Parliament Man to his Friend" (anon.; attrib. to Marvell), 1675; "Mr. Smirke" (under pseud.: "Andreas Rivetus, Junior"), 1686; "A Seasonable Question and a Useful Answer" (anon.; attrib. to Marvell), 1676; "An Account of the Growth of Popery . . . in England" (anon.), 1677; "A Seasonable Argument to persuade all the Grand Juries in England to petition for a new Parliament" (anon.; attrib. to Marvell), 1677; "Advice to a Painter" (anon.), 1678; "Remarks upon a disengenuous Discourse writ by one T. D." (anon.), 1678. *Posthumous:* "A Short Historical Essay touching General Councils," 1680; "Miscellaneous Poems," 1681; "Characters of Popery," 1689; "Poems on Affairs of State," 1689; "The Royal Manual," 1751. He contributed poems to "Musa Cantabrigiensis," 1637; "Lacrymæ Musarum," 1639; Lovelace's "Poems," 1649; Primerose's "Popular Errors," 1651; "Paradise Lost," 2nd edn., 1674; and probably *translated:* Suetonius, 1672. *Collected Works:* ed. by T. Cooke (2 vols.), 1726; ed by E. Thompson (3 vols.), 1776; ed. by Grosart, 1872–75; "Poems and Satires," ed. by G. A. Aitken (2 vols.), 1892. *Life:* by J. Dove, 1832. —SHARP, R. FARQUHARSON, 1897, *A Dictionary of English Authors*, p. 189.

PERSONAL

Near this place lyeth the body of Andrew Marvell, Esq., a man so endowed by Nature, so improved by Education, Study and Travel, so consummated by Experience, that, joining the peculiar graces of Wit and Learning, with a singular penetration and strength of judgment; and exercising all these in the whole course of his life, with an unutterable steadiness in the ways of Virtue, he became the ornament and example of his age, beloved by good men, feared by bad, admired by all, though imitated by few; and scarce paralled by any. But a Tombstone can neither contain his character, nor is Marble necessary to transmit it to posterity; it is engraved in the minds of this generation, and will be always legible in his inimitable writings, nevertheless. He having served twenty years successively in Parliament, and that with such Wisdom, Dexterity, and Courage, as becomes a true Patriot, the town of Kingston-upon-Hull, from whence he was deputed to that Assembly, lamenting in his death the public loss, have erected this Monument of their Grief and their Gratitude, 1688. —INSCRIPTON ON MONUMENT, 1688.

There will be with you to-morrow, upon some occasion of business, a gentleman whose name is Mr. Marvile; a man whom, both by report, and the converse I have had with him, of singular desert for the state to make use of; who alsoe offers himselfe, if there be any imployment for him. His father was the Minister of Hull; and he hath spent four years abroad, in Holland, France, Italy, and Spaine, to very good purpose, as I believe, and the gaineing of those four languages; besides, he is a scholler, and well read in the Latin and Greek authors; and no doubt of an approved conversation, for he comes now lately out of the house of the Lord Fairfax, who was Generall, where he was intrusted to give some instructions in the languages to the Lady his daughter.— MILTON, JOHN, 1652, *Letter to Lord Bradshaw, Feb.* 21.

He was of a middling stature, pretty strong sett, roundish faced, cherry cheek't, hazell eie, browne haire. He was in his conversation very modest, and of very few words · and though he loved wine he would never drinke hard in company, and was wont to say that, *he would not play the good-fellow in any man's company in whose hands he would not trust his life*. . . . He lies interred under the pewes in the south side of Saint Giles' church in-the-fields, under the window wherein is painted in glasse a red lyon, (it was given by the inneholder of the Red Lyon Inne in Holborne) and is the . . . window from the east. This account I had from the sexton that made his grave.—AUBREY, JOHN, 1669-96, *Brief Lives, ed. Clark, vol,* II, *pp.* 53, 54.

As neither wits nor poets have been always remarkable for moral firmness, and are as vulnerable in their vanity and fears as politicians in their avarice and ambition, no means were omitted to win over Marvell. He was threatened, he was flattered, he was thwarted, he was caressed, he was beset with spies, and, if all tales be true, he was way-laid by ruffians, and courted by beauties. But no Dalilah could discover the secret of his strength: his integrity was proof alike against danger and against corruption; nor was it enervated by that flattery, which, more frequently than either, seduces those weak, amiable creatures, whom, for lack of better, we are fain to call good. Against threats and bribes, pride is the ally of principle; but how often has virtue pined away to a shadow, by too fondly contemplating its own image, reflected by insidious praise; as Narcissus, in the fable, consumed his beauty by gazing on its watery shade. In a Court which held no man to be honest, and no woman chaste, this soft sorcery was cultivated to perfection; but Marvell, revering and respecting himself, was proof against its charms. There is a story told of his refusing a bribe, which has been heard and repeated by many, who perhaps did not know in what king's reign he lived, and which has been so often paralleled with the turnips of Curius, and the like common places, that some sceptical persons have held that there is as little truth in the one as in the other. However, we believe it to have been founded in fact, and that the mistake has been in the dulness of those who took a piece of dry English humour for a stoical exhibition of virtue.—COLERIDGE, HARTLEY, 1833? *Biographia Borealis, p.* 57.

The strong views which Marvell took on public affairs—the severe, satirical things which he had said and written from time to time—and the conviction of his enemies, that it was impossible to silence him by the usual methods of a place or a bribe, must have rendered a wary and circumspect conduct very necessary. In fact, we are informed that on more than one occasion he was menaced with assassination. But, though hated by the Court party generally, he was as generally feared, and in some few instances respected. Prince Rupert continued to honour him with his friendship long after the rest of his party had honoured him by their hatred, and occasionally visited the patriot at his lodgings. When he voted on the side of Marvell, which was not infrequently the case, it used to be said that "he had been with his tutor." . . . But admirable as were Marvell's intellectual endowments, it is his moral worth, after all, which constitutes his principal claim on the admiration of posterity, and which sheds a redeeming lustre on one of the darkest pages of the English annals. Inflexible integrity was the basis of it—integrity by which he has not unworthily earned the glorious name of the "British Aristides." With talents and acquirements which might have justified him in aspiring to almost any office, if he could have disburdened himself of his conscience; with wit which, in that frivolous age, was a surer passport to fame than any amount either of intellect or virtue, and which, as we have seen, mollified even the monarch himself in spite of his prejudices; Marvell preferred poverty and independence to riches and servility.—ROGERS, HENRY, 1844, *Andrew Marvell, Edinburgh Review, vol.* 79, *pp.* 80, 102.

He was a genial, warm-hearted man, an elegant scholar, a finished gentleman, at home, and the life of every circle which he entered, whether that of the gay court of Charles II., amidst such men as Rochester and L'Estrange, or that of the republican philosophers who assembled at Miles's Coffee House, where he discussed plans of a free representative government with the author of "Oceana," and Cyriack

Skinner, that friend of Milton, whom the bard has immortalized in the sonnet which so pathetically, yet heroically, alludes to his own blindness. Men of all parties enjoyed his wit and graceful conversation. His personal appearance was altogether in his favor. A clear, dark, Spanish complexion, long hair of jetty blackness falling in graceful wreaths to his shoulders, dark eyes, full of expression and fire, a finely chiseled chin, and a mouth whose soft voluptuousness scarcely gave token of the steady purpose and firm will of the inflexible statesman; these, added to the *prestige* of his genius, and the respect which a lofty, self-sacrificing patriotism extorts even from those who would fain corrupt and bribe it, gave him a ready passport to the fashionable society of the metropolis. He was one of the few who mingled in that society, and escaped its contamination, and who,

> "Amidst the wavering days of sin
> Kept himself icy chaste and pure."

—Whittier, John Greenleaf, 1849, *Old Portraits and Modern Sketches, p.* 111.

ON THE DEATH OF THE LORD PROTECTOR

There is a splendid Ode to Cromwell—a worthy companion of Milton's glorious sonnet—which is not generally known, and which we transfer entire to our pages. Its simple dignity, and the melodious flow of its versification, commend themselves more to our feelings than its eulogy of war. It is energetic and impassioned, and probably affords a better idea of the author, as an actor in the stirring drama of his time, than the "soft Lydian airs" of the poems that we have quoted.—Whittier, John Greenleaf, 1849, *Old Portraits and Modern Sketches, p.* 105.

Marvell showed how well he understood what he was giving to the world in this ode—one of the least known but among the grandest which the English language possesses—when he called it "Horation." In its whole treatment it reminds us of the highest to which the greatest Latin Artist in lyrical poetry did, when at his best, attain. To one unacquainted with Horace, this ode, not perhaps so perfect as his are in form, and with occasional obscurities of expression which Horace would not have left, will give a truer notion of the

kind of greatness which he achieved than, so far as I know, could from any other poem in the language be obtained.—Trench, Richard Chenevix, 1868, *Household Book of English Poetry.*

Marvell's "Horatian Ode," the most truly classic in our language, is worthy of its theme. The same poet's Elegy, in parts noble, and everywhere humanly tender, is worth more than all Carlyle's biography as a witness to the gentler qualities of the hero, and of the deep affection that stalwart nature could inspire in hearts of truly masculine temper.—Lowell, James Russell, 1870, *Dryden, Among My Books, p.* 19.

The "Horatian Ode on Cromwell's Return from Ireland" cannot be positively proved to be the work of Marvell. Yet we can hardly doubt that he was its author. The point of view and the sentiment, combining admiration of Cromwell with respect and pity for Charles, are exactly his: the classical form would be natural to him; and so would the philosophical conceit which disfigures the eleventh stanza. The epithet "indefatigable" applied to Cromwell recurs in a poem which is undoubtedly his; and so does the emphatic expression of belief that the hero could have been happier in private life, and that he sacrificed himself to the State in taking the supreme command. The compression and severity of style are not characteristic of Marvell; but they would be imposed on him in this case by his model. If the ode is really his, to take it from him would do him great wrong. It is one of the noblest in the English language, and worthily presents the figures and events of the great tragedy as they would impress themselves on the mind of an ideal spectator, at once feeling and dispassionate.—Smith, Goldwin, 1880, *English Poets, ed. Ward, vol.* ii, *p.* 383.

The pre-eminent quality of the poem is its art; and its singular charm is the fact that it succeeds, in spite of being artificial, in moving and touching the springs of feeling in an extraordinary degree. It is a unique piece in the collection, the one instance where Marvell's undoubted genius burned steadily through a whole poem. Here he flied *penna metuente solvi.* It is in completeness more than in quality that it is superior to all his other work, but in quality too it has that lurking divinity that cannot be analysed or imitated.—BENSON, ARTHUR CHRISTOPHER, 1896, *Essays, p.* 84.

GENERAL

We still read Marvell's answer to Parker with pleasure, though the book it answers be sunk long ago.—SWIFT, JONATHAN, 1709, *Apology for a Tale of a Tub.*

. . . in those worst of times,
The hardy poet raised his honest rhymes
To dread rebuke, and bade Controlment speak
In guilty blushes on the villain's cheek;
Bade Power turn pale, kept mighty rogues in awe,
And made them fear the Muse, who fear'd not law.
—CHURCHILL, CHARLES, 1764, *The Author.*

His pen was always properly directed, and had some effect upon such as were under no check or restraint from any laws human or divine. He hated corruption more than he dreaded poverty; and was so far from being venal, that he could not be bribed by the king into silence, when he scarce knew how to procure a dinner. His satires give us a higher idea of his patriotism, parts, and learning, than of his skill as a poet.—GRANGER, JAMES, 1769–1824, *Biographical History of England, vol.* v, *p.* 252.

Charles II. was a more polished judge than these uncouth critics; and, to the credit of his impartiality,—for that witty monarch and his dissolute court was never spared by Marvell, who remained inflexible to his seduction—he deemed Marvell the best prose satirist of the age. But Marvell had other qualities than the freest humour and the finest wit in this "newly-refined art," which seems to have escaped these grave critics—a vehemence of solemn reproof, and an eloquence of invective, that awes one with the spirit of the modern Junius, and may give some notion of that more ancient satirist, whose writings are said to have so completely answered their design, that, after perusal, their victim hanged himself on the first tree; and in the present case, though the delinquent did not lay violent hands on himself, he did what, for an author, may be considered as desperate a course, "withdraw from the town, and cease writing for some years."—DISRAELI, ISAAC, 1812–13, *Parker and Marvell, Quarrels of Authors.*

The humour and eloquence of Marvell's prose tracts were admired and probably imitated by Swift. In playful exuberance of figure he sometimes resembles Burke. For consistency of principles, it is not so easy to find his parallel. His few poetical pieces betray some adherence to the school of conceit, but there is much in it that comes from the heart warm, pure, and affectionate.—CAMPBELL, THOMAS, 1819, *Specimens of the British Poets.*

The poems of Marvell are, for the most part, productions of his early youth. They have much of that over-activity of fancy, that remoteness of allusion, which distinguishes the school of Cowley; but they have also a heartfelt tenderness, a childish simplicity of feeling, among all their complication of thought, which would atone for all their conceits, if conceit were indeed as great an offence against poetic nature as Addison and other critics of the French school pretend.—COLERIDGE, HARTLEY, 1833? *Biographia Borealis, p.* 63.

Marvell wrote sometimes with more taste and feeling than was usual; but his satires are gross and stupid.—HALLAM, HENRY, 1837–39, *Introduction to the Literature of Europe, pt.* iv, *ch.* v. *par.* 47.

The characteristic of Marvell's genius was unquestionably wit. . . . Though Marvell was so great a master of wit, and especially of that caustic species which is appropriate to satirists, we will venture to say that he was singularly free from many of the faults which distinguish that irritable brotherhood. Unsparing and merciless as his ridicule is, contemptuous and ludicrous as are the lights in which he exhibits his opponent; nay, further, though his invectives are not only often terribly severe, but (in compliance with the spirit of the age) often grossly coarse and personal, it is still impossible to detect a single particle of malignity. His general tone is that of broad laughing banter, or of the most cutting invective; but he appears equally devoid of malevolence in both. . . . His Latin poems are amongst his best. The composition often shows no contemptible skill in that language; and here and there the diction and versification are such as would not have absolutely disgraced his great coadjutor, Milton. In all the higher poetic qualities there can of course be no comparison between them. . . . The style of Marvell is very unequal. Though often rude and unpolished, it abounds in negligent felicities, presents us with frequent specimens of vigorous idiomatic English, and now and then attains no mean degree of elegance. It bears the stamp of the revolution which was then passing on the language; it is a medium between the involved and periodic structure so common during the former half of the century, and which is ill adapted to a language possessing so few inflections as ours, and that simplicity and harmony which were not fully attained till the age of Addison. —ROGERS, HENRY, 1844, *Andrew Marvell, Edinburgh Review, vol.* 79, *pp.* 92, 99, 100.

To read the noble ode on "Cromwell," in which such a generous compliment is paid to Charles the First,—the devout and beautiful one entitled "Bermuda," and the sweet overflowing fancies put into the mouth of the "Nymph lamenting the loss of her Faun,"—and then to follow up their perusal with some, nay most of the lampoons that were so formidable to Charles and his brother, you would hardly think it possible for the same man to have written both, if examples were not too numerous to the contrary. Fortunately for the reputation of Marvel's wit, with those who chose to become acquainted with it, he wrote a great deal better in prose than verse, and the prose does not take the license of the verse.—HUNT, LEIGH, 1846, *Wit and Humour, p.* 234.

His poems possess many of the finest elements of popularity; a rich profusion of fancy which almost dazzles the mind as bright colours dazzle the eye; an earnestness and heartiness which do not always, —do not often belong to these flowery fancies, but which when found in their company add to them inexpressible vitality and savor; and a frequent felicity of phrase, which, when once read, fixes itself in the memory, and *will* not be forgotten. . . . His mind was a bright garden, such a garden as he has described so finely, and that a few gaudy weeds should mingle with the healthier plants does but serve to prove the fertility of the soil.—MITFORD, MARY RUSSELL, 1851, *Recollections of a Literary Life, pp.* 532, 533.

The genius of Andrew Marvel was as varied as it was remarkable;—not only

was he a tender and exquisite poet, but entitled to stand *facile princeps* as an incorruptible patriot, the best of controversialists, and the leading prose wit of England. We have always considered his as the first of the "sprightly runnings" of that brilliant stream of wit, which will carry with it to the latest posterity the names of Swift, Steele, and Addison. Before Marvel's time, to be witty was to be strained, forced, and conceited; from him—whose memory consecrates that cottage—wit came sparkling forth, untouched by baser matter. It was worthy of him; its main feature was an open clearness. Detraction or jealousy cast no stain upon it; he turned aside, in the midst of an exalted panegyric to Oliver Cromwell, to say the finest things that ever were said of Charles I.—HALL, MRS. S. C., 1851, *Pilgrimages to English Shrines.*

Who has not heard of the political wit of Andrew Marvell,—that stout "Old Roman" member for Hull?—HANNAY, JAMES, 1857-61, *Essays for "The Quarterly Review," p.* 95.

Marvell appears, in biographic and political record, as a thoroughly manly person; and the same is the prevailing character of his poetic work. We observe vigorous strenuous lines, a bluff and sometimes boisterous humour, keen fencing-play of wit, a strong temper, as ready to overstate a prejudice as to pile a panegyric; often too a sharp thrill of tenderness, and a full sense and full power of expressing beauty.—ROSSETTI, WILLIAM MICHAEL, 1872-78, *ed., Humorous Poems, p.* 140.

The Poetry of Marvell can afford the largest deductions from it. It is ludicrous to argue that he was incapable of writing what Addision and Watts did. He had more genius and poetic afflatus in one cell of his compact brain than the pair of them altogether, regarded as Poets. Wherever you turn, you are struck with the spontaneity, the melody, the subtle suggestiveness, the underlying wealth, of these Poems. I am not prepared to defend all that is in the Satires. There is coarseness, there is fierceness, there is mercilessness, . . . there is disregard of others in the vehement resolve to smite crashingly down high-seated offenders. . . . Fundamentally, the

Poetry of Marvell is genuine as a bird's singing, or the singing of the brook on its gleaming way under the leafage.— GROSART, ALEXANDER B., 1872, *The Complete Poems of Andrew Marvell, Memorial, Introduction, pp.* lxiv, lxvi.

Andrew Marvel was not only a public man of mark and the first pamphleteer of his day, but a lyric and satiric poet. As a lyric poet he still ranks high. His range of subjects and styles is wide. He touches at different points Herbert, Cowley, Waller, Dryden, and the group of Lovelace and Suckling. But his most interesting connection is with Milton. Of that intellectual lustre which was produced by the union of classical culture and ancient love of liberty with Puritan enthusiasm, Milton was the central orb, Marvell a satellite, paler yet bright. . . . As a poet Marvell is very unequal. He has depth of feeling, descriptive power, melody; his study of the classics could not fail to teach him form; sometimes we find in him an airy and tender grace which reminds us of the lighter manner of Milton: but art with him was only an occasional recreation, not a regular pursuit; he is often slovenly, sometimes intolerably diffuse, especially when he is seduced by the facility of the octosyllabic couplet. He was also eminently afflicted with the gift of "wit" or ingenuity, much prized in his day. His conceits vie with those of Donne or Cowley. . . . The Satires in their day were much admired and feared: they are now for the most part unreadable.—SMITH, GOLDWIN, 1880, *English Poets, ed. Ward, vol.* II, *pp.* 380, 382, 383.

Is, no doubt, as Hazlitt says, a true poet, but who as a poet is not worthy to untie the shoe strings of the authors of "The Litany," "The Rapture," and "The Flaming Heart."—SAINTSBURY, GEORGE, 1887, *History of Elizabethan Literature, p.* 360.

His exquisite garden-poems, distinguished for their rich imagery and their loyal study of nature. . . . Marvell had learned the secret of the distich.— GOSSE, EDMUND, 1888, *A History of Eighteenth Century Literature, 1660–1780, pp.* 28, 29.

He used a sharp pen in controversy and wrote many pamphlets, some of which even now might serve as models for incisive speech; he was witty with the wittiest; was caustic, humorous; his pages adrip with classicisms; and he had a delicacy of raillery that amused, and a power of logic that smote heavily, where blows were in order.—MITCHELL, DONALD G., 1890, *English Lands Letters and Kings, From Elizabeth to Anne, p.* 190.

Marvell holds a unique place in the seventeenth century. He stands at the parting of the ways, between the extravagancies of the lyrical Jacobeans on the one hand, and the new formalism initiated by Waller on the other. He is not unaffected by either influence. The modish handling of the decasyllable couplet is very marked here and there. . . . Marvell is a Puritan; but his spirit has not entered the prison-house, nor has the key turned on it there. He is a poet still, such as there has been few in any age. The lyric gift of Herrick he has not, nor Donne's incomparable subtlety and intensity of emotion; but for imaginative power, for decent melody, for that self-restraint of phrase which is the fair half of art, he must certainly hold high rank among his fellows. The clear sign of this self-restraint is his mastery over the octosyllable couplet. . . . I must needs see in Marvell something of a naturephilosophy strangely anticipative of George Meredith. For the one, as for the other, complete absorption in nature, the unreserved abandonment of self to the skyey influences, is the really true and sanative wisdom.—CHAMBERS, EDMUND K., 1892, *The Academy, vol.* 42, *p.* 230.

Marvell's literary work is remarkable for its variety. In his own age his reputation rested mainly on his pamphlets, which have ceased to be read since the controversies which gave rise to them have been forgotten. . . . To the generation which immediately succeeded Marvell he seems to have been best known as a political satirist; and the number of pieces ascribed to him in "Poems on State Affairs" and similar collections is evidence of his celebrity. But his satires, like the pamphlets, are essentially of temporary interest, and are mainly of historical value. They are full of allusions unintelligible without a commentary, and so personal that they frequently become mere lampoons. The vice he attacks loses none of its grossness in the verses.

Moreover, his lines are hasty and rough-hewn, and in employing the heroic couplet Marvell is never completely master of his instrument. Yet despite these defects there is much both in his satires and pamphlets which still amuses; a gift of humorous exaggeration which suggests Sydney Smith, and an irony which occasionally recalls Swift.—FIRTH, C. H., 1893, *Dictionary of National Biography, vol.* XXXVI, *p.* 330.

Deserves much more regard for his poetry than is generally allotted him. . . . His poetry shows two very different aspects. Prior to the Restoration it is mostly lyrical, and reveals a fine feeling for Nature with Wordsworthian touches; after that event it is satirical on the subject of vice and tyranny in Church and State, and occasionally as fierce, and even as coarse, as the invectives of Juvenal. It was Marvell's style of satire, the regular heroic couplet, that Dryden adopted, in preference to Donne's or Butler's. His ablest satires are "Last Instructions to a Painter," and "The Character of Holland;" of his lyrical pieces, "The Emigrants in the Bermudas," "Thoughts in a Garden," and the girl's lament for her dead fawn are exquisite examples.—ROBERTSON, J. LOGIE, 1894, *A History of English Literature, p.* 190.

In the style of Marvell's prose, as in the style of his satiric couplets, there are the marks of hesitation between two different manners. He is sometimes clear, quick, and succinct, sometimes he falls back into the heavier manner of the older writers. ◆ His vocabulary is various. His practice on "Bayes" involved a good deal of slang; his satiric medley is dashed with a number of spices from different languages, even from the Malay. He uses, without distress, the heavier Latin armoury.—KER, W. P., 1894, *English Prose, ed. Craik, vol.* III, *p.* 34.

Marvell was a party man, and the estimate formed of his political writings and their justification will always differ according to the private opinions of the critic.—BUXTON, TRAVERS, 1896, *Marvell, The Gentleman's Magazine, vol.* 281, *p.* 570.

One of the most original poets of the Stuart period, the new tentative features of the age in poetry, again, are clearly marked. The lyrical work belonging to his early life has often passages of imaginative quality, equally strong and delicate. If we exclude Milton, no one of that time touches sweeter or nobler lyrical notes; but he is singularly unequal; he flies high, but is not long on the wing. The characteristic Elizabethan smoothness of unbroken melody was now failing; the fanciful style of Donne, the seventeenth century *concetti*, seized on Marvell too strongly, and replaced in him the earlier mythological landscape characteristic of the Renaissance.—PALGRAVE, FRANCIS TURNER, 1896, *Landscape in Poetry, p.* 154.

The poet of spicy gardens and sequestered fields seen through the haze of dawn is gone, not like the Scholar Gipsy to the high lonely wood or the deserted lasher, but has stepped down to jostle with the foulest and most venal of mankind. He becomes a satirist, and a satirist of the coarsest kind. His pages are crowded with filthy pictures and revolting images; the leaves cannot be turned over so quickly but some lewd epithet or vile realism prints itself on the eye. His apologists have said that it is nothing but the overflowing indignation of a noble mind when confronted with the hideous vices of a corrupt court and nation; that this deep-seated wrath is but an indication of the fervid idealistic nature of the man; that the generous fire that warmed in the poems, consumed in the satires; that the true moralist does not condone but condemn. To this we would answer that it is just conceivable that a satirist may be primarily occupied by an immense moral indignation, and no doubt that indignation must bear a certain part in all satires; but it is not the attitude of a hopeful or generous soul. . . . We cannot but grieve when we see a poet over whose feet the stream has flowed, turn back from the brink and make the great denial; whether from the secret consciousness of aridity, the drying of the fount of song, or from the imperious temptations of the busy, ordinary world we cannot say. Somehow we have lost our poet. It seems that,

Just for a handful of silver he left us
Just for a ribbon to stick in his coat.

And the singer of an April mood, who might have bloomed year after year in young and ardent hearts, is buried in the dust of politics, in the valley of dead bones.—BENSON, ARTHUR CHRISTOPHER, 1896, *Essays, pp.* 87, 95.

Thomas Hobbes

1588-1679

Born, at Westport, Wilts, 5 April 1588. At school at Westport, 1592–96; thence to Malmesbury, 1596, and afterwards at another school at Westport. To Magdalen Hall, Oxford, 1603; B.A., 5 Feb. 1608. Tutor and secretary to William Cavendish, son of first Earl of Devonshire, 1608–28; travelled abroad with him, 1610. Travelling tutor to son of Sir Gervase Clifton, 1629–31. Tutor to third Earl of Devonshire, 1631–40. Travelled abroad with him, 1634–37. Fled to Paris at meeting of Long Parliament, Nov. 1640. Remained there till 1651, when he retreated to England in consequence of complications caused by publication of "Leviathan." Resumed post of secretary to Earl of Devonshire, 1663. Pension of £100 from Charles II. at Restoration. Lived in London till 1675; remainder of life spent at country seats of Earl of Devonshire. Died, at Hardwick, Derbyshire, 4 Dec. 1679. Buried in Hault Hucknall Church. *Works:* "De Mirabilibus Pecci" [1636?]; "Elementorum Philosophiæ sectio tertia de Cive" (under initials: T. H.), 1642; "Tractatus Opticus" (in Mersenne's "Cogitata Physico-Mathematica"), 1644; "Humane Nature," 1650; "De Corpore Politico," 1650; "Epistle to Davenant," 1651; "Leviathan," 1651; "Of Liberty and Necessity," 1654; "Elementorum Philosophiæ sectio prima de Corpore," 1655; "A Briefe of the Art of Rhetorique" (anon.), [1655?]; "Questions concerning Liberty, Necessity and Chance," 1656; "Στιγμαι ’Αγεωμετριας" 1657; "Elementorum Philosophiæ sectio secunda de Homine," 1658; "Examinatio et Emendatio Mathematicæ Hodiernæ," 1660; "Dialogus Physicus," 1661; "Problemata Physica," 1662; "Mr. Hobbes considered," 1662; "De Principiis et Ratiocinatione Geometrarum," 1666; "Quadratura Circuli," 1669; "Rosetum Geometricum," 1671; Three Papers presented to the Royal Society attacking Dr. Wallis, 1671; "Lux Mathematica" (under initials: R. R.), 1672; "Principa et Problemata aliquot Geometrica" (under initials: T. H.), 1674; "Decameron Physiologicum," 1678; "Behemoth" (written, and suppressed, 1668), privately published, 1679; publicly (under initials: T. H.), 1680; "Vita, authore seipso," 1679. *Posthumous:* "An Historical Narration concerning Heresie," 1680; "T. H. Malmesb. Vita" (in "Vitæ Hobbianæ Auctarium"), 1681; "Dialogue between a Philosopher and a Student of the Common Law," 1681; "An Answer to . . . "The Catching of the Leviathan," 1682; "Hobbes's Tripos," 1684; "Historia Ecclesiastica," 1688. He *translated:* "Thucydides," 1629; Homer's "Iliad and Odyssey," 1675. *Collected Works:* "Opera Philosophica," 1668; "Moral and Political Works," ed. by J. Campbell, 1750; Complete Works, ed. by Sir W. Molesworth (16 vols), 1839–45. *Life:* by G. C. Robertson, 1886.—SHARP, R. FARQUHARSON, 1897, *A Dictionary of English Authors, p.* 133.

PERSONAL

In his youth unhealthy; of an ill yellowish complexion: wett in his feet, and trod both his shoes the same way. . . . From forty, or better, he grew healthier, and then he had a fresh, ruddy, complexion. He was *sanguineo-melancholicus;* which the physiologers say is the most ingeniose complexion. He would say that "There might be good witts of all complexions; but good-natured, impossible." *Head.* In his old age he was very bald (which claymed a veneration); yet within dore, he used to study, and sitt, bareheaded, and sayd he never tooke cold in his head, but that the greatest trouble was to keepe-off the flies from pitching on the baldness. . . . His skin was soft and of that kind which my Lord Chancellor Bacon in his "History of Life and Death" calles a goose-skin, i. e. of a wide texture. . . . *Face* not very great; ample forehead; whiskers yellowish-reddish, which naturally turned up—which is a signe of a brisque witt. . . . He had a good eie, and that of a hazell colour, which was full of life and spirit, even to the last. When he was earnest in discourse, there shone (as it were) a bright live-coale within it. He had two kind of looks:—when he laugh't, was witty, and in a merry humour, one could scarce see his eies; by and by, when he was serious and positive, he ope'nd his eies round. . . . He was six foote high, and something better (quaere James [Wheldon]), and went indifferently erect, or rather, considering his great age, **very** erect.—AUBREY, JOHN, 1669-96, *Brief Lives*, ed. Clark, vol. I, pp. 347, 348, 349.

He fell sick about the middle of October last. His disease was the strangury, and the physitians judged it incurable by reason of his great age and naturall decay. About the 20th of November, my Lord being to remove from Chatsworth to Hardwick, Mr. Hobbes would not be left behind; and therefore with a fether bed laid into the coach, upon which he lay warme clade, he was conveyed safely, and was in appearance as well after that little journey as before it. But seven or eight days after, his whole right side was taken with the dead palsy, and at the same time he was made speechlesse. He lived after this seven days, taking very little nourishment, slept well, and by intervalls endeavoured to speake, but could not. In the whole time of his sicknesse he was free from fever. He seemed therefore to dye rather for want of the fuell of life (which was spent in him) and meer weaknesse and decay, then by the power of his disease, which was thought to be onely an effect of his age and weaknesse. He was born the 5th of Aprill, in the year 1588, and died the 4th of December, 1679. He was put into a wollen shroud and coffin, which was covered with a white sheet, and upon that a black herse cloth, and so carryed upon men's shoulders, a little mile to church. The company, consisting of the family and neighbours that came to his funerall, and attended him to his grave, were very handsomely entertained with wine, burned and raw, cake, biscuit, etc. He was buried in the parish church of Hault Hucknall, close adjoining to the raile of the monument of the grandmother of the present earle of Devonshire, with the service of the Church of England by the minister of the parish. It is intended to cover his grave with a stone of black marble as soon as it can be got ready, with a plain inscription of his name, the place of his birth, and the time of that and of his death.—WHELDON, JAMES, 1679, *Letter to John Aubrey, Jan. 16, Aubrey's Brief Lives*, ed. Clark, vol. I, p. 382.

I have cursorily looked over Mr. Hobbs his life in Latine which I beleeve will be a very vendible booke both here and beyond sea, for ther is noe lover of learning but will have the curiosity to be particularly informed of the life of soe eminent a person. And truly the reading of it wase very satisfactory to me, for in my apprehension it is very well writ, but I cou'd have wish'd the author had more dilated upon some particulars; and because you intimate a designe to publish it in English I shall hint to you that the author of the life in Latine hath either not taken notice of at all, or too slightingly, some things very remarkeable, relating to the temper of Mr. Hobbs his mind or to the infirmity of his body, as his extraordinary timorusness which he himself in his Latine poem doth very ingeniously confess and attributes it to the influence of his mother's dread of the Spanish invasion in 88, she being then with child of him. And I have been informed, I think by yourself, that Mr. Hobbs wase for severall yeares before he died soe paralyticall that he was scarce able to write his name, and that in the absence of his amenuensis not being able to write anything he made scrawls on a piece of paper to remind him of the conceptions of his mind he design'd to have committed to writing. But the author of his life in Latine only sa(i)th that about 60 yearse of age he wase taken with a trembling in his hands, the forerunner of the palsy; which in my apprehension deserves to be enlarg'd upon, for it is very prodigious that neither the timorousness of his nature from his infancy, nor the decay of his vital heat in the extremity of old age, accompagnied with the palsy to that violence, should not have chill'd the briske fervour and vigour of his mind, which did wonderfully continue to him to his last.—HATTON, HON. CHARLES, c 1681-2, *Letter to William Crooke, Aubrey's Brief Lives*, ed. Clark, vol. I, p. 390.

Mr. Joyner says that Mr. Hobbs used to say, that Mr. Selden understood nothing of mathematicks; which Mr. Selden being informed of, he replyed, that if Mr. Hobbs understood no more mathematicks than he did law, he understood nothing at all of them. And indeed Mr. Selden had such a mean opinion of that Malmsbury philosopher, that he used to say, *All comers were welcome to his table, but Tho. Hobbes and one Rossingham.*—HEARNE, THOMAS, 1705, *Reliquiæ Hearnianæ*, ed. Bliss, Nov. 17, vol. I, p. 58.

Hobbs seems not to have been very amiable in his life; he was certainly incapable of true friendship, for the same cowardice, or false principle, which could instigate him to abandon truth, would likewise teach him to sacrifice his friend to his own safety. When young, he was voluptuous, when old, peevish, destitute alike of resolution and honour. However high his powers, his character is mean, he flattered the prevailing follies, he gave up virtue to fashion, and if he can be produced as a miracle of learning, he can never be ranked with those venerable names, who have added virtue to erudition, and honour to genius; who have illuminated the world by their knowledge, and reformed it by example.—CIBBER, THEOPHILUS, 1753, *Lives of the Poets, vol.* II, *p.* 215.

His greatest imperfection was a monstrous egotism—the fate of those who concentrate all their observations in their own individual feelings. There are minds which may think too much, by conversing too little with books and men. Hobbes exulted he had read little; he had not more than half-a-dozen books about him; hence he always saw things in his own way, and doubtless this was the cause of his mania for disputation. . . . His little qualities were the errors of his own selfish philosophy; his great ones were those of nature. He was a votary to his studies: he avoided marriage, to which he was inclined; and refused place and wealth, which he might have enjoyed, for literary leisure. He treated with philosophic pleasantry his real contempt of money. His health and his studies were the sole objects of his thoughts; and notwithstanding that panic which so often disturbed them, he wrote and published beyond his ninetieth year. He closes the metrical history of his life with more dignity than he did his life itself; for his mind seems always to have been greater than his actions.—DISRAELI, ISAAC, 1812-13, *Hobbes, Quarrels of Authors.*

After the Restoration Charles II treated the philosopher with personal friendship, and gave him a pension. But the publication of the "Behemoth," an historic dialogue in which Hobbes represented the occurrences of the last ten years from his own point of view, was forbidden by the King. For Hobbes stood in open antagonism to the religious ideas as they had taken form after the Restoration. As formerly the Presybterian Parliament under Cromwell, so now also the Anglican Parliament threatened him with religious censure. From the two universities, which he had wished fundamentally to reform, he met with bitter hostility. Into the Royal Society, of which he approved, he still could not gain admittance; amongst its members also his paradoxes and violence had made him enemies. The King once remarked, Hobbes' hand is against every man, and every man's hand against him. Hobbes found a refuge in the family of Cavendish, Earl of Devonshire, to which he had for many years been attached. His books are for the most part dedicated to one or other of its members; he accompanied them to their country houses, for instance to Chatsworth; there in the morning he took long walks over the neighbouring hills, in the afternoon he buried himself in his studies; he was supplied with all that he wanted, tobacco and lights, and then left alone. Hobbes attained the greatest age that nature grants to man; still every year he published something. But even in the Cavendish family he was looked upon as an eccentric character whose opinions no one shared.—RANKE, LEOPOLD VON, 1875, *A History of England, vol.* III, *p.* 575.

The infinite complexity of human life is stretched on the Procrustean bed of simplicity, and truth is thereby sacrificed to system. Beginning from inadequate premmises, unable or unwilling to credit human nature with social as well as with self-regarding instincts, he is forced by the very self-consistency of his logical intellect into conclusions that prove to be irreconcilable with the facts of a more universal experience. In these respects Hobbes resembles Bentham, as in his cynical pessimism he resembles La Rochefoucauld. His genius and tone of feeling have been compared with Swift, but there appears to us to be more point in the contrast than in the comparison, for Swift's temperament was passionate, and his blood red-hot, while Hobbes is always phlegmatic and cold. The one despises, the other hates. Hobbes' adversaries are cut asunder as with a steel edge, Swift's are burnt up as with a consuming fire. Nowhere in the former's life do we come across a Stella or a Vanessa, nor, even if all Hobbes' private papers had come down to us, should we have been likely to discover such an entry as this of Swift's: "Only a woman's hair." It would be difficult to quote any trait from his biographies more characteristic of him than his selection of his own monumental inscription: "This is the true philosopher's stone."—HOARE, H. W., 1884, *Thomas Hobbes, Fortnightly Review, vol.* 42, *p.* 236.

LEVIATHAN
1751

To my booksellers for "Hobb's Leviathan," which is now mightily called for; and what was heretofore sold for 8s., I now give 24s. at the second hand, and is sold for 30s., it being a book the bishops will not let be printed again.—PEPYS, SAMUEL, 1668, *Diary, Sept. 3rd.*

The manner of writing which booke (he told me) was thus. He walked much and contemplated, and he had in the head of his staffe a pen and inke-horne, carried alwayes a note-booke in ,his pocket, and as soon as a thought darted, he presently entred it into his booke, or otherwise he might perhaps have lost it. He had drawne the designe of the booke into chapters, etc., so he knew whereabout it would come in.—AUBREY, JOHN, 1669–96, *Brief Lives, ed. Clark, vol.* I, *p.* 334.

Few books have occasioned more or fiercer controversy than this production of the philosopher of Malmsbury. It is an able, learned, but most paradoxical and irreligious performance. Its principles would justify all social disorder and all impiety. But the scales of the Leviathan are very hard to penetrate, and have injured most of the weapons which have been tried upon it. Lord Clarendon *"surveyed"* it, and Bishop Bramhall endeavoured to *"catch"* it; but the monster still lived, exercising the ingenuity and courage of many a successive combatant. The most formidable of his antagonists were—Cumberland, in his work "De Legibus Naturæ," and Cudworth, in the "Intellectual System."—ORME, WILLIAM, 1830, *The Life and Times of Richard Baxter, p.* 704., *note.*

One corner of his library was filled with a strange company of antiquated books of orthodox type; this he called "the condemned cell." When looking at the "strange bedfellows" that slept on the shelves, the writer asked Huxley what author had most influenced a style whose clearness and vigour, nevertheless, seems unborrowed; and he at once named the masculine and pellucid "Leviathan" of Hobbes.—CLODD, EDWARD, 1897, *Pioneers of Evolution. p.* 241.

POETRY

Hobbes could construe a Greek author; but his skill in words must have been all derived from the dictionary: for he seems not to have known, that any one articulate sound could be more agreeable, or any one phrase more dignified, than any other. In his Iliad and Odyssey, even when he hits the author's sense (which is not always the case), he proves, by his choice of words, that of harmony, elegance, or energy of style, he had no manner of conception. And hence that work, though called a Translation of Homer, does not even deserve the name of *poem;* because it is in every respect *unpleasing,* being nothing more than a fictitious narrative delivered in mean prose, with the additional meanness of harsh rhyme and untuneable measure. — BEATTIE, JAMES, 1776–9, *Essays on Poetry and Music, p.* 239.

Hobbes's clearness and aptness of expression, the effect of which is like that of reading a book with a good light, never forsake him—not even in that most singular performance, his version of Homer, where there is scarcely a trace of ability of any other kind. There are said to be only two lines in that work in which he is positively poetical. . . . For the most part, indeed, Hobbes's Iliad and Odyssey are no better than travesties of Homer's, the more ludicrous as being undesigned and unconscious. Never was there a more signal revenge than that which Hobbes afforded to imagination and poetry over his own unbelieving and scoffing philosophism by the publication of this work. It was almost as if the man born blind, who had all his lifetime been attempting to prove that the sense which he himself wanted was no sense at all, and that that thing, color, which it professed peculiarly to discern, was a mere delusion, should have himself at last taken the painter's brush and pallet in hand, and attempted, in confirmation of his theory, to produce a picture by the mere senses of touch, taste, smell, and hearing.—CRAIK, GEORGE L., 1861, *A Compendious History of English Literature and of the English Language, vol.* II, *pp.* 123, 124.

His verse is a mere curiosity, though a considerable curiosity. The chief of it (the translation of Homer written in the quartrain, which his friend Davenant's "Gondibert" had made popular) is completely lacking in poetical quality, of which, perhaps, no man ever had less than Hobbes; and it is written on a bad model. But it has so much of the nervous bull-dog strength which, in literature if not in life, was Hobbes's main characteristic, that it is sometimes both a truer and a better representative of the original than some very mellifluous and elegant renderings. —SAINTSBURY, GEORGE, 1887, *History of Elizabethan Literature, p.* 350.

GENERAL

He thought interest and fear were the chief principles of society; and he put all morality in the following that which was our own private will or advantage. He thought religion had no other foundation than the laws of the land. And he put all the law in the will of the prince, or of the people: for he writ his book at first in favour of absolute monarchy, but turned it afterwards to gratify the republican party. These were his true principles, though he had disguised them for deceiving unwary readers. And this set of notions came to spread much. The novelty and boldness of them set many on reading them. The impiety of them was acceptable to men of corrupt minds, which were but too much prepared to receive them by the extravagances of the late times.—BURNET, GILBERT, 1715–34, *History of My Own Times, vol.* I

No English author in that age was more celebrated both abroad and at home than Hobbes; in our time he is much neglected: a lively instance how precarious all reputations founded on reasoning and philosophy! . . . Hobbes's politics are fitted only to promote tyranny, and his ethics to encourage licentiousness. Though an enemy to religion he partakes nothing of the spirit of scepticism; but is as positive and dogmatical as if human reason, and his reason in particular, could attain a thorough conviction in these subjects. Clearness and propriety of style

are the chief excellencies of Hobbes's writings.—HUME, DAVID, 1762, *The History of England, The Commonwealth*

His style is incomparably better than that of any other writer in the reign of Charles I. and was, for its uncommon strength and purity, scarcely equalled in the succeeding reign. He has, in translation, done Thucydides as much justice as he has done injury to Homer: but he looked upon himself as born for much greater things than treading in the footsteps of his predecessors. He was for striking out new paths in science, government, and religion; and for removing the landmarks of former ages. His ethics have a strong tendency to corrupt our morals, and his politics to destroy that liberty which is the birthright of every human creature. He is commonly represented as a sceptic in religion, and a dogmatist in philosophy; but he was a dogmatist in both. The main principles of his "Leviathan" are as little founded in moral or evangelical truth, as the rules he laid down for squaring the circle are in mathematical demonstration. His book on human nature is esteemed the best of his works.—GRANGER, JAMES, 1769–1824, *Biographical History of England, vol.* V, *p.* 290.

His success was not great, and the little which he had was principally among foreigners. Of the number of his impartial judges, was the Dutchman *Lambert Velthuysen:* and of his adversaries, *Richard Cumberland* and *Robert Scharrock.*—TENNEMANN, WILHELM GOTTLIEB, 1812, *A Manual of the History of Philosophy, tr. Johnson, ed. Morell, p.* 299.

The genius of Hobbes was of the first order; his works abound with the most impressive truths, in all the simplicity of thought and language, yet he never elevates nor delights. Too faithful an observer of the miserable human nature before him, he submits to expedients; he acts on the defensive; and because he is in terror, he would consider security to be the happiness of man.—DISRAELI, ISAAC, 1812–13, *Hobbes, Quarrels of Authors.*

Philosophy, on the whole, gradually deteriorated during the latter half of the seventeenth century. The example of Hobbes testifies to the facility of transition from Bacon's new method of philosophising—without reflecting any blame on that great man—to the most decided in-fidelity and materialism. — SCHLEGEL, FREDERICK, 1815–59, *Lectures on the History of Literature, Lecture* xiii.

Before dismissing the system of Hobbes, may be worth while to remark that all his leading principles are traced by Cudworth to the remains of the ancient sceptics, by some of whom, as well as by Hobbes, they seem to have been adopted from a wish to flatter the uncontrolled passions of sovereigns.—STEWART, DUGALD, 1815–21, *First Preliminary Dissertation, Encyclopædia Britannica.*

Hobbes having thus struck the affections out of his map of human nature, and having totally misunderstood the nature even of the appetites, it is no wonder that we should find in it not a trace of the moral sentiments. Moral good he considers merely as consisting in the signs of a power to produce pleasure; and repentance is no more than regret at having missed the way; so that, according to this system, a disinterested approbation of and reverence for virtue are no more possible than disinterested affections towards our fellow-creatures.—MACKINTOSH, SIR JAMES, 1830, *Second Preliminary Dissertation, Encyclopædia Brittannica.*

In his magnificent grounds he* erected, at a cost of ten thousand pounds, a retreat to which he repaired when he wished to avoid all visitors, and to devote himself wholly to study. On such occasions, a few young men of distinguished talents were sometimes the companions of his retirement. And among them his quick eye soon discerned the superior abilities of Thomas Hobbes. It is not probable, however, that he fully appreciated the powers of his disciple, or foresaw the vast influence, both for good and for evil, which that most vigorous and acute of human intellects was destined to exercise on the two succeeding generations.—MACAULAY, THOMAS BABINGTON, 1834, *Lord Bacon, Edinburgh Review, Critical and Miscellaneous Essays.*

Hobbes seems to have been one of the first who had any thing like a distinct perception of the real source of wealth.—McCULLOCH, JOHN RAMSAY, 1845, *Literature of Political Economy.*

With Hobbes, shall we say that all our

*Bacon.

thoughts are begotten by, and are the representatives of, objects exterior to us; that our conceptions arise in material motions pressing on our organs, producing motion in them, and so affecting the mind; that our sensations do not correspond with outward qualities; that sound and noise belong to the bell and the air, and not to the mind, and, like color, are only agitations occasioned by the object in the brain; that imagination is a conception gradually dying away after the act of sense, and is nothing more than a decaying sensation; that memory is the vestige of former impressions, enduring for a time; that forgetfulness is the obliteration of such vestiges; that the succession of thought is not indifferent, at random, or voluntary, but that thought follows thought in a determinate and predestined sequence; that whatever we imagine is finite, and hence we can not conceive of the infinite, nor think of any thing not subject to sense?—DRAPER, JOHN WILLIAM, 1862–75, *History of the Intellectual Development of Europe, p.* 171.

The amount of thought contributed by him to deism was small; for his influence on his successors was unimportant. The religious instincts of the heart were too strong to be permanently influenced by the cold materialist tone which reduced religion to state craft. With the exception of Coward, a materialist who doubted immortality about the end of the century, the succeeding deists more generally followed Herbert in wishing to elevate religion to a spiritual sphere, than Hobbes, who degraded it to political expedience. A slight additional interest however belongs to his speculations, from the circumstance that his ideas, together with those of Herbert, most probably suggested some parts of the system of Spinoza.— FARRAR, ADAM STOREY, 1862, *A Critical History of Free Thought in Reference to the Christian Religion, p.* 122.

At the very period when the principle of toleration was first established in England by the union of the spirit of scepticism with the spirit of Christianity, the greatest living anti-christian writer was Hobbes, who was perhaps the most unflinching of all the supporters of persecution. It was his leading doctrine that the civil power, and the civil power alone, has an absolute right to determine the religion of the nation, and that, therefore, any refusal to acquiesce in that religion is essentially an act of rebellion.—LECKY, WILLIAM EDWARD HARTPOLE, 1865, *Spirit of Rationalism in Europe, vol.* II.

All ornament, all emotions, are excluded from the style of Hobbes; it is a mere aggregate of arguments and concise facts, united together by deduction, as by iron bands. There are no tints, no fine or unusual word. He makes use only of words most familiar to common and lasting usage; there are not a dozen employed by him which, during two hundred years, have grown obsolete; he pierces to the root of all sensation, removes the transient and brilliant externals, compresses the solid portion which is the permanent subject-matter of all thought, and the proper object of common intelligence. He curtails throughout in order to strengthen; he attains solidity by expression. Of all the bonds which connect ideas, he retains but one, and that the most stable; his style is only a continuous chain of the most stubborn description, wholly made up of additions and subtractions, reduced to a combination of certain simple processes, which, added on to or diminishing from one another, make up, under various names, the totals or differences, for which we are for ever either studying the formation or unravelling the elements.—TAINE, H. A., 1871, *History of English Literature, tr.* Van Laun, *vol.* I, *bk.* iii, *ch.* i, *p.* 472.

Undoubtedly Hobbes took great pains to be simple and precise. He makes an effort to express himself in familiar words, explains his general positions by examples, and his order of exposition is such as can be easily followed. Having a deep sense of the evils of ambiguous language, he is careful to define his terms. Further, he has great powers of terse and vigorous statement, his figures are studied and apt, and his didactic strain is enlivened by ingenious and occasionally sarcastic point. Yet he is far from being a perfect expositor, as he is by no means always a consistent thinker. When he enters upon details, he is often perplexed, does not keep his main subject prominent, and introduces statements out of their proper order.—MINTO, WILLIAM, 1872–80, *Manual of English Prose Literature, p.* 310.

Hobbes was a genuine child of his age

in everything save the conclusions of his philosophy. He was a radical in the service of reaction. His mind was revolutionary in its vigour and directness, its hardihood and self-assertion, its freedom from pedantry, and contempt for the wisdom of the ancients. There is no one of all the thinkers of the century who has dealt to the old scholasticism such hearty and fatal blows. His clear and subtle, if sometimes coarse analysis, may be said to have laid the foundation of psychological science which has been so fruitful since his day; and to his organising conception political philosophy owes its creation, whatever we may think of the character of the creation in his hands. But behind all his great gifts there was no spiritual insight—no eye for any truths deeper than those of the sense or the intellect. Not only had he no appreciation of such truths, but apparently he had no perception of their existence. He was honestly ignorant of them. In the compass of his own keen and powerful mind he found no trace of them. Accordingly he judged human nature and human society as if they were not. All that he saw, he saw with a rare clearness; but there was a side of human life which he did not see at all—to which he turned an eye wholly blind.—TULLOCH, JOHN, 1872, *Rational Theology and Christian Philosophy in England in the Seventeenth Century, vol.* II, *p.* 26.

Hobbes was the first great English writer who dealt with the science of government from the ground, not of tradition, but of reason. It was in his treatment of man in the stage of human development which he supposed to precede that of society that he came most roughly into conflict with the accepted beliefs. Men, in his theory, were by nature equal, and their only natural relation was a state of war. It was no innate virtue of man himself which created human society out of this chaos of warring strengths. Hobbes, in fact, denied the existence of the more spiritual sides of man's nature. His hard and narrow logic dissected every human custom and desire, and reduced even the most sacred to demonstrations of a prudent selfishness. Friendship was simply a sense of social utility to one another. The so-called laws of nature, such as gratitude or the love of our neighbor, were in fact contrary to the natural passions of man, and powerless to restrain them. Nor had religion rescued man by the interposition of a divine will.—GREEN, JOHN RICHARD, 1874, *A Short History of The English People, ch. ix, sec. i.*

"As God is incomprehensible, it follows that we can have no conception or image of the Deity; and consequently all his attributes signify our inability or defect of power to conceive anything concerning his nature, and not any conception of the same excepting only this, that there is a God." In spite of statements of this kind, which are obviously capable of being taken in a good sense, it has been customary to regard Hobbes as an atheist. The cause is found in the complete inadequacy of his system of morals to make good what might be wanting in his speculative tenets. It is not the omissions and one-sidedness of his metaphysics alone, but it is these, coupled with the perversions in his moral philosophy, which have affixed to his name a reputation for atheism. The doctrine of the existence of God, even attenuated to the form which we have seen above, might have been sufficiently integrated by a sound doctrine respecting the human conscience, the best witness for God, according to the general belief, that it is in man's power to appeal to. But when we examine Hobbes's teaching on moral matters, we find it full of paradox and absurdity.—ARNOLD, THOMAS, 1878, *English Literature, Encyclopædia Britannica.*

Called "the Atheist Hobbes" as long ago as 1646, . . . had become more and more "the atheist Hobbes," with all who found advantage in that style of epithet, by his "Human Nature" and "De Corpore Politico" of 1650, his all-comprehensive "Leviathan" of 1651, and some subsequent writings, while this dreadful fame of his for general Atheism had been fringed latterly by a special reputation for mathematical heterodoxy.—MASSON, DAVID, 1880, *Life of John Milton, vol. VI, p. 280.*

Hobbes was not a great philosopher, and yet he occupies an important place in the history of modern, and especially English, thought. His reduction of all phenomena, including those of mind in their physical relations, to modes of motion, was a rather remarkable declaration of a scientific view, now, at least, universally accredited.—MORRIS, GEORGE S., 1880, *British Thought and Thinkers, p. 165.*

Hobbes had, in early life, been Bacon's secretary, but, though he wrote a work expressly on "Computation or Logic," there is no mention in it of Induction, of the Baconian method, or of Bacon himself. It is, perhaps, still more singular that there is no mention of Bacon in the Epistle Dedicatory to the "Elements of Philosophy," where he refers to Galileo, Kepler, Harvey, Gassendi, Mersenne, &c. Bacon's name, in fact, so far as I am aware, occurs only twice in the whole of Hobbes' works, and there without any epithet of praise or blame. From the extent of Hobbes' writings and the intimate personal relations which had formerly existed between him and Bacon, I can hardly refer this silence to mere accident. It may have been due to some personal pique, or the abstract character of Hobbes' mind may have rebelled against the concrete and inductive spirit of Bacon's philosophy. For, it may be noticed that there are few writers on moral and political questions, in whose works the historical spirit is more conspicuously absent than in Hobbes.—FOWLER, THOMAS, 1881, *Bacon (English Philosophers), p. 194.*

Hobbes stands in sharp contrast to Bacon both in disposition and in doctrine. Bacon was a man of a wide outlook, a rich, stimulating, impulsive nature, filled with great plans, but too mobile and desultory to allow them to ripen to perfection; Hobbes is slow, tenacious, persistent, unyielding, his thought strenuous and narrow. To this corresponds a profound difference in their systems, which is by no means adequately characterized by saying that Hobbes brings into the foreground the mathematical elements neglected by his predecessor, and turns his attention chiefly to politics. The dependence of Hobbes on Bacon is, in spite of their personal acquaintance, not so great as formerly was universally assumed. His guiding stars are rather the great mathematicians of the Continent, Kepler and Galileo, while Cartesian influences are not to be denied. He finds his mission in the construction of a strictly mechanical view of the world.—FALCKENBERG, RICHARD, 1885–93, *History of Modern Philosophy, tr. Armstrong, p. 71.*

Hobbes stands with Bacon and Berkeley at the head of English-speaking philosophers, and is, if not in general grasp, in range of ideas, or in literary polish, yet in acuteness of thought and originality of expression, perhaps the superior of both his companions. . . . Hobbes never "pays himself with words," never evades a difficulty by becoming obscure, never meanders on in the graceful allusive fashion of many philosophers,—a fashion for which the prevalent faults of style were singularly convenient in his time. He has no ornament, he does not seem to aim at anything more than the simplest and most straightforward presentation of his views. But this very aim, assisted by his practice in writing the terse and clear, if not very elegant, Latin which was the universal language of the literary Europe of his time, suffices to preserve him from most of the current sins.—SAINTSBURY, GEORGE, 1887, *History of Elizabethan Literature, pp.* 315, 350.

Hobbes produced a fermentation in English thought not surpassed until the advent of Darwinism. While, however, the opponents of Hobbes were countless, his biographer could discover only a single supporter. "Hobbism" was an occasional name of reproach until the middle of the eighteenth century (he is mentioned on the title-page of "Deism Revealed," 1751), although his philosophy had long been eclipsed by Locke's "Essay." He is one of Kortholt's "three imposters" (1680) along with Spinoza and Herbert of Cherbury. In Farquhar's "Constant Couple," 1699, the hypocritical debauchee carries Hobbes in his pocket; and among "Twelve Ingenious Characters," 1686, is a dissolute town-fop who takes about "two leaves of Leviathan." . . . Atterbury holds him up as a warning in a sermon "on the terrors of conscience." . . . He was reviled on all sides as the typical atheist, materialist, political absolutist, and preacher of ethical selfishness. Hobbes was in truth a product of the great intellectual movement distinguished by such names as Bacon (1561–1629), Galileo (1564–1642) Kepler (1571–1630), Harvey (1578–1657) and Descartes (1596–1650).—STEPHEN, LESLIE, 1891, *Dictionary of National Biography, vol.* XXVII, *p.* 42.

Hobbes's fame as a political writer and moralist has somewhat obscured his merit as an ontologist and psychologist. And unjustly so; for he is the forerunner of materialism, criticism, and modern positivism. . . . Hobbes occupies a position between pure empiricism and Cartesian rationalism—WEBER, ALFRED, 1892–96, *History of Philosophy, tr. Thilly, pp.* 301, 305.

Hobbes's political system is based, as has been said, on his view of human nature. Men are by nature, according to Hobbes, in a state of war—that is, of anarchy, being impelled by their egoistic impulses to contend against each other for all kinds of advantages. To the natural reason of men the advantage there would be to each if certain rules of justice were observed is, indeed, evident; but it is also evident that these can only be observed in a state of peace. The dictate of natural reason accordingly is to escape from the state of war and establish articles of peace. This can only be done by the institution of a Commonwealth or body politic, having a sovereign power entitled to exercise coercive authority over its members. To this sovereign power men give up their natural rights of self-defence in return for protection. They thus contract with one another to obey the sovereign power. This may be either one man, or a few, or the whole people assembled at stated times, the form of government being called monarchy, aristocracy, or democracy as the case may be. The sovereign power in the Commonwealth, wherever it may be situated, is absolute. The dictate at once of natural law and of self-interest is that the sovereign should aim at the safety and good government of the people: under the term "safety" being understood all that distinguishes civilised life from the savagery of the state of nature. Of the possible forms of government, monarchy, according to Hobbes, is to be preferred as being the most efficient in action, the most constant, and, on the whole, the most just. His theory, however, he maintains, is applicable to all forms of government.—WHITTAKER, T., 1895, *Social England, ed. Traill, vol.* IV, *p.* 280.

Hobbes' style has deservedly received high praise. . . . He writes as a man whose one object was to be clearly understood.—MASTERMAN, J. HOWARD B., 1897, *The Age of Milton, p.* 216.

Samuel Butler

1612–1680

Samuel Butler, grievously miscalled "the Hogarth of Poetry," seems to have been mainly a self-taught man. After leaving Worcester Cathedral School he started in life as justice's clerk to a Mr. Jeffries, at Earl's Croome. He was next at Wrest in Bedfordshire, in the service of the Countess of Kent, and here he met and worked for John Selden. Finally he formed part of the household of Sir Samuel Luke, a Presbyterian Colonel, "scout-master for Bedfordshire and governor of Newport Pagnell." At the Restoration he was made Secretary to the President of Wales and steward of Ludlow Castle, and in 1662, at full fifty years old, he published the first part of the immense lampoon whose authorship has given him his place in English letters. The second part of "Hudibras" was issued in 1663; the third in 1678. Two years afterwards Butler died. . . . During his lifetime Butler published but the three parts of "Hudibras," a couple of pamphlets, and an ode on the exploits and renown of the illustrious Claude Duval, which last, in its grave extravagance of irony, is, by anticipation, not unsuggestive of Fielding's "Jonathan Wild." Three volumes of "Remains," mostly spurious, were published in 1715; but in 1759 Thyer of Manchester put forth a couple of volumes of prose and verse selected from Butler's manuscripts, and these, with some scraps printed later on, are all that is known to exist of him.— HENLEY, WILLIAM ERNEST, 1880, *English Poets, ed. Ward, vol.* II, *pp.* 396, 397.

PERSONAL

ℳ. ℮.
𝔖amuelis 𝔅utler
𝔔ui 𝔖trensℌamiae in agro 𝔚igorn.natus 1612,
𝔒biit 𝔏ond. 1680.
𝔙ir doctus imprimis, acer, integer,
𝔒periℬus ingenii non item praemiis felix.
𝔖atyrici apud nos craminis artifer egregius,
𝔔ui simulatae religionis larvam detraxit
𝔈t perduellium scelera liℬerrime exagitavit,
𝔖criptorum in suo genere primus et postremus.
𝔑e cui vivo deerant fere omnia
𝔇eesset etiam mortuo tumulus
ℌoc tandem posito marmore curavit
𝔍oℌannes 𝔅arℬer civis 𝔏ondinensis 1721.
—INSCRIPTION ON MONUMENT, WESTMINSTER ABBEY, 1721.

This little monument was erected in the year 1786, by some of the parishioners of Covent Garden, in memory of the celebrated Samuel Butler, who was buried in this church, A.D. 1680.

A few plain men, to pomp and state unknown,
O'er a poor bard have rais'd this humble stone,
Whose wants alone his genius could surpass,
Victim of zeal! the matchless Hudibras!
What though fair freedom suffer'd in his page,
Reader, forgive the author for the age!
How few, alas! disdain to cringe and cant,
When 'tis the mode to play the sycophant.
But, oh! let all be taught, from Butler's fate,
Who hope to make their fortunes by the great,
That wit and pride are always dangerous things,
And little faith is due to courts and kings.
— INSCRIPTION ON MONUMENT, SAINT PAUL'S CHURCH, COVENT GARDEN, 1786.

He is of a middle stature, strong sett, high coloured, a head of sorrell haire, a severe and sound judgement: a good fellowe. He haz often sayd that way (e.g. Mr. Edmund Waller's) of quibling with sence will hereafter growe as much out of fashion and be as ridicule as quibling with words—quod N. B. He haz been much troubled with the gowt, and particularly 1679, he stirred not out of his chamber from October till Easter.

Obiit Anno $\begin{cases} \text{Domini 1680} \\ \text{circiter 70.} \end{cases}$

He dyed of a consumption September 25; and buried 27, according to his appointment, in the churchyard of Convent Garden; scil. in the north part next the church at the east end. His feet touch the wall. His grave, 2 yards distant from the pillaster of the dore, (by his desire) 6 foot deepe. About 25 of his old acquaintance at his funerall. I myself being one [of the eldest, helped to carry the pall with Tom Shadwell, at the foot, Sir Robert Thomas and Mr. Saunders, esq., at the head; Dr. Cole and Dr. Davenant, middle].—AUBREY, JOHN, 1669–96, *Brief Lives, ed. Clark, vol.* I, *p.* 136.

On *Butler* who can think without just Rage,
The Glory and the Scandal of the Age?
Fair stood his hopes, when first he came to Town,
Met every where with welcome of Renown,
Courted, and lov'd by all, with wonder read,
And promises of Princely Favour fed:
But what Reward for all had he at last,
After a Life in dull expectance pass'd?

The Wretch at summing up his mis-spent
days
Found nothing left, but Poverty and Praise:
Of all his Gains by Verse he could not save
Enough to purchase Flannel, and a Grave:
Reduc'd to want, he in due time fell sick,
Was fain to die, and be interr'd on tick:
And well might bless the Fever that was sent,
To rid him hence, and his worse Fate prevent.
—OLDHAM, JOHN, 1681, *A Satyr Dissuading from Poetry*.

This Samuel Butler, who was a boon
and witty companion, especially among
the company he knew well, died of a consumption, September 25th, 1680, and was,
according to his desire, buried six foot
deep in the yard belonging to the Church
of S. Paul in Covent-Garden within the
liberty of Westminster, viz. at the west
end of the said yard, on the north side,
and under the wall, of the church; and
under that wall which parts the yard from
the common high-way.—WOOD, ANTHONY,
1691–1721, *Athenæ Oxonienses, vol.* II.

Did not the celebrated author of "Hudibras" bring the King's enemies into lower
contempt with the sharpness of his wit
than all the terrors of his administration
could reduce them to? Was not his book
always in the pocket of the prince? And
what did the mighty prowess of this
knight-errant amount to? Why, he died,
with the highest esteem of the court, in a
garret.—CIBBER, COLLEY, 1719, *Ximenes,
Dedication to Sir Richard Steele*.

In this mist of obscurity passed the life
of Butler, a man whose name can only
perish with his language. The mode and
place of his education are unknown; the
events of his life are variously related;
and all that can be told with certainty is,
that he was poor.—JOHNSON, SAMUEL,
1779, *Samuel Butler, Lives of the English
Poets*.

The house of his birth was standing till
very recently; but in 1873 was pulled
down, as no longer tenantable.—ROSSETTI,
WILLIAM MICHAEL, 1878, *Lives of Famous
Poets, p.* 81.

Butler was buried in the yard of St.
Paul's Church, Covent Garden; but contemporary authorities differ as to the exact position of his grave. . . . A
tablet to the memory of Butler was placed
on the south side of the church "by the
inhabitants of the parish" in 1786, nine
years before the old edifice was destroyed

by fire. It was not renewed when the
church was rebuilt; and the clerk of the
vestry in 1885 had no knowledge of it, or
of the position of Butler's grave. The
churchyard has been levelled and covered
with grass, where it is not paved with
fragments of the old tombstones it used
to contain, and few memorials to its illustrious dead are now to be found.—HUTTON, LAWRENCE, 1885, *Literary Landmarks of London, p.* 29.

HUDIBRAS

To St. Paul's Church Yard to my booksellers . . . choose . . . "Hudibras," both parts, the book now in greatest fashion for drollery, though I cannot,
I confess, see enough where the wit lies.
—PEPYS, SAMUEL, 1663, *Diary, Dec.* 10.

CHARLES R. Our will and pleasure is
and we do hereby strictly charge and
command, that no printer, bookseller,
stationer, or other person whatsoever
within our kindgom of England or Ireland,
do print, reprint, utter or sell, or cause
to be printed, reprinted, uttered or sold,
a book or poem called "Hudibras," or any
part thereof, without the consent and approbation of Samuel Boteler, Esq. or his
assignees, as they and every of them will
answer the contrary at their perils.
Given at our Court at Whitehall, the tenth
day of September, in the year of our Lord
God 1677, and in the 29th year of our
reign. By his Majesty's command.—
BERKENHEAD, Jo., 1677, *Miscellaneous
Papers, Mus. Brit. Bibl. Birch, No.* 4293.

The worth of his poem is too well
known to need my commendation, and he
is above my censure. His satire is of the
Varronian kind, though unmixed with
prose. The choice of his numbers is suitable enough to his design, as he has managed it; but in any other hand, the shortness of his verse, and the quick returns of
rhyme, had debased the dignity of style.
—DRYDEN, JOHN, 1692, *Essays on Satire,
Works, ed.* Scott and Saintsbury, *vol.* XIII.

If "Hudibras" had been set out with as
much wit and humour in heroic verse as
he is in doggerel he would have made a
much more agreeable figure than he does;
though the generality of his readers are
so wonderfully pleased with the double
rhymes, that I do not expect many will be
of my opinion in this particular.—ADDISON, JOSEPH, 1711, *The Spectator, Dec.* 15.

Butler set out on too narrow a plan, and even that design is not kept up. He sinks into little true particulars about the Widow, &c.—The enthusiastic Knight, and the ignorant Squire, over-religious in two different ways, and always quarrelling together, is the chief point of view in it. —POPE, ALEXANDER, 1737–39, *Spence's Anecdotes, ed. Singer, p.* 157.

Burlesque may perhaps be divided into such as turns chiefly on the thought and such as depends more on the expression, or we may add a third kind, consisting in thoughts ridiculously dressed, in language much above or below their dignity. "The Splendid Shilling" of Phillips, and the "Hudibras" of Butler are the most obvious instances. Butler, however, depended much on the ludicrous effect of his double rhymes; in other respects, to declare your sentiments, he is rather a witty writer, than a humorous one.—SHENSTONE, WILLIAM, 1763? *Works, 3rd ed., vol.* II, *p.* 182.

Butler stands without a rival in burlesque poetry. His "Hudibras" is, in its kind, almost as great an effort of genius as the "Paradise Lost" itself. It abounds with uncommon learning, new rhymes, and original thoughts. Its images are truly and naturally ridiculous: we are never shocked with excessive distortion nor grimace; nor is human nature degraded to that of monkeys and yahoos. There are in it many strokes of temporary satire, and some characters and allusions which cannot be discovered at this distance of time.—GRANGER, JAMES, 1769–1824, *Biographical History of England, vol.* V, *p.* 243.

The poem of "Hudibras" is one of those compositions of which a nation may justly boast, as the images which it exhibits are domestick, the sentiments unborrowed and unexpected, and the strain of diction original and peculiar.—JOHNSON, SAMUEL, 1779, *Samuel Butler, Lives of the English Poets.*

Unrivall'd Butler! Blest with happy skill
To heal by comic verse each serious ill,
By Wit's strong lashes Reason's light dispense,
And laugh a frantic nation into sense!
—HAYLEY, WILLIAM, 1782, *An Essay on Epic Poetry, Ep.* iii.

Concerning "Hudibras" there is but one sentiment—it is universally allowed to be the first and last poem of its kind: the learning, wit, and humour, certainly stand unrivalled: various have been the attempts to describe and define the two last. . . . If any one wishes to know what wit and humour are, let him read "Hudibras" with attention; he will there see them displayed in the brightest colours: there is lustre resulting from the quick elucidation of an object by a just and unexpected arrangement of it with another subject: propriety of words, and thoughts elegantly adapted to the occasion: objects which possess an affinity and congruity, or sometimes a contrast to each other, assembled with quickness and variety; in short, every ingredient of wit, or of humour, which critics have discovered on dissecting them, may be found in this poem.—NASH, TREADWAY RUSSEL, 1793, *ed. Hudibras, Preface.*

The perpetual scintillation of Butler's wit is too dazzling to be delightful; and we can seldom read far in "Hudibras" without feeling more fatigue than pleasure. His fancy is employed with the profusion of a spendthrift, by whose eternal round of banqueting his guests are at length rather wearied out than regaled. —SCOTT, SIR WALTER, 1805, *The Life of John Dryden.*

There are some excellent moral and even serious lines in "Hudibras;" but what if a clergyman should adorn his sermon with a quotation from that poem! Would the abstract propriety of the verse leave him "honourably acquitted?"—COLERIDGE, SAMUEL TAYLOR, 1807, *Notes on Books and Authors; Miscellanies, Æsthetic and Literary, ed. Ashe, p.* 330.

Matchless Hudibras.—BYRON, LORD, 1811, *Hints from Horace.*

The "Hudibras" of Butler, like the fabled Arabian bird, is in itself a species: it had no precursor, and its imitators are forgotten. With all the disadvantages of a temporary subject, obsolete characters, and "a conclusion in which nothing is concluded," it continues to be the delight of the few, and the text-book of the many: its couplets have passed into proverbs— the names of its heroes are "familiar in our mouths as household words." With the exception of Shakspeare, there is, perhaps, no author whose expressions are so inextricably intertwined with our everyday discourse, and whose writings afford such an inexhaustible variety of apothegms of universal and apposite application; yet there is no author, enjoying any considerable share of popularity, who is so imperfectly understood and appreciated. —BALDWIN, H., 1820, *Butler's Genuine and Spurious Remains, Retrospective Review*, vol. II, p. 256.

The construction of the story, and the delineation of the characters, have been praised far beyond their merits. In these particulars it has very slender claims to originality.—NEELE, HENRY, 1827–29, *Lectures on English Poetry*, p. 171.

The defect of Butler's poem undoubtedly consists in . . . the poverty of the incidents, and the incompleteness and irregularity of the design. The slender strain of narrative which is just visible in the commencement, soon dwindles away and is lost. It is true that the poem abounds with curious and uncommon learning, with original thoughts, happy images, quaint and comic turns of expression, and new and fanciful rhymes. But the humour, instead of being diffused quietly and unostentatiously over the whole poem, in rich harmonious colouring, is collected into short epigrammatic sentences, pointed apothegms, and unexpected allusions. It has the same merits and defects as a poem of a very different kind—Young's "Night Thoughts,"—copious invention, new and pleasing images, and brilliant thoughts; with a want of sufficient connexion in the subject, and progress in the story.—MITFORD, JOHN, 1835, *ed. Hudibras, Life of Butler.*

His reading and illustration are all out of the way; and his manner, dry and crabbed at one time, flowing and free and popular at another. I should call him, therefore, a humorist, not only in the literary sense, but in the sense in which we apply the word to one who has some strong peculiarity of character, which he indulges, ·in whims, in oddities, in comic extravagances, according to the bent of his inclination. There is a kind of likeness between Butler and old Burton the "Anatomy of Melancholy." Both men had various and unusual reading; both were at once comic and grave; and both, amidst wild and homely pleasantry, shoot out flashes of thought and fancy which are equal to the efforts of anybody . . . . Among humorous writers he must always

occupy a very high place. He is a thinker, old Butler, as you see through all his odd comic poem; while as a man of wit, it would be perhaps impossible to name one in whom wit is so absolutely redundant.— HANNAY, JAMES, 1854, *Satire and Satirists, pp.* 114, 115.

It is rather curious to remember that the two best burlesque poems in the English language, "Hudibras" and "Don Juan," are both fragments; and that, in reference to the first of these, at least, we have not the most distant data to guide us in conjecturing what was the ultimate plan or purpose of the poet, beyond, at least, the very probable conjecture that his vigorous and unsparing satire would have swept at least into the ranks of the ungrateful cavaliers. As it is, "Hudibras" now stands before us— not a sublime, unfinished temple consecrated to deities, whose worship was never to be celebrated therein—but a great, grotesque, nameless structure, reared half in sport and half in earnest, which excites in the mind of those who walk in it rather laughter than love, rather wonder than satisfaction, and which, after all the explanations given is far more a problem than a poem.—GILFILLAN, GEORGE, 1854, *ed., Poetical Works of Samuel Butler, Life*, p. xxv.

I love all beauty : I can go
At times from Gainsborough to Watteau;
Even after Milton's thorough-bass
I hear the rhymes of Hudibras,
And find more solid wisdom there
Than pads professor's easy chair.

—LANDOR, WALTER SAVAGE, 1858, *Apology for Gebir.*

An old affection for "Hudibras," acquired nearly half a century ago, at a time when its piquant couplets were still familiarly quoted, had long impressed him [me] with the desire to publish a really popular edition.—BOHN, HENRY G., 1859, *ed. Hudibras, Preface, p.* vi.

Butler's power of arguing in verse, in his own way, may almost be put on a par with Dryden's in his; and, perseveringly as he devotes himself upon system to the exhibition of the ludicrous and grotesque, he sometimes surprises us with a sudden gleam of the truest beauty of thought and expression breaking out from the midst of the usual rattling fire of smartnesses and conundrums,—as when in one place he exclaims of a thin cloud drawn over the moon—

Misterious veil; of brightness made,
At once her lustre and her shade!

He must also be allowed to tell his story and to draw his characters well, independently of his criticisms.—CRAIK, GEORGE L., 1861, *A Compendious History of English Literature and of the English Language*, vol. II, p. 100.

There is hardly another poem in the language which carries so essentially distinct a style of its own. It is at once comic, pointed, and precise, continually surprising the reader with its vivacity and freshness, to the success of which its doggrel verse and odd rhymes no doubt contribute.—FRISWELL, JAMES HAIN, 1869, *Essays on English Writers*, p. 87.

How mean is the wit, with what awkwardness and dulness he dilutes his splenetic satire! Here and there lurks a happy picture, the remnant of a poetry which has just perished; but the whole material of the work reminds one of a Scarron, as unworthy as the other, and more malignant. . . . No action, no nature, all is would-be satire and gross caricature; neither art, nor harmony, nor good taste: the Puritan style is converted into a harsh gibberish; and the engalled rancour, missing its aim by its mere excess, spoils the portrait it wishes to draw. Would you believe that such a writer gives himself airs, wishes to enliven us, pretends to be funny?—TAINE, H. A., 1871, *History of English Literature*, tr. *Van Laun*, vol. I, bk. iii, ch. i, pp. 463, 464.

A poem which the finest wits of his own age, and the finest wits of every age and country to the present time, have concurred in pronouncing the wittiest composition, integrally, that was ever penned. If the story or substructure of this remarkable work had been of more fanciful character, with variety and surprises in the development, and the subject of it more general, and applicable to universal humanity—its causes and effects of action —I believe I may state without fear of contradiction, that it would have stood pre-eminent and unrivalled. . . . Nothing can exceed the slashing style in which this great writer rips open and exposes to view the hypocritcal pretensions of the objects of his ridicule, and the proof of it is, that the book has furnished texts and mottoes to the opponents of bigotry and fanaticisms of all descriptions—whether ecclesiastical or civil—to the present day.—CLARKE, CHARLES COWDEN, 1871, *On the Comic Writers of England, The Gentleman's Magazine*, n. s., vol. 7, pp. 176, 183.

Butler, in his "Hudibras," poured insult on the past with a pedantic buffoonery for which the general hatred, far more than its humor, secured a hearing. —GREEN, JOHN RICHARD, 1874, *A Short History of the English People*, ch. ix, sec. i.

Although the merits of "Hudibras" have, in our opinion, been exaggerated, because largely taken on trust, yet no one can question the power and merit of the poem. It is a rough, strong, grotesque satire, full of point and force, and did more to put the defects of Puritanism in a ridiculous and glaring light and give popular currency to their faults, real and supposed, than anything which has ever been written. The terse and stinging sentences of the mock epic were in every one's mouth; but their author lived and died a neglected and morose man, bequeathing a volume of posthumous papers, full of bitter flings against mankind.—LODGE, HENRY CABOT, 1880, *Masson's Life of Milton, International Review*, vol, 9, p. 129.

"Hudibras" is none the less as notable in these days as it was at the epoch of its birth. It has been more largely read and quoted than almost any book in the language. It contains the best and brightest of Butler, and is a perfect reflex of his mind and temper.—HENLEY, WILLIAM ERNEST, 1880, *English Poets ed. Ward*, vol. II, p. 397.

Every good cause has its Hudibras. Butler wrote, no doubt, as a partisan, but his whole war was against hypocrisy. Against that in every form he waged his war, though putting into the central place what he regarded as the worst hypocrisy of all. But he aimed also his shafts of wit against false show of courage; pedantry of learning; the false conventions of love poetry; the worldliness of love; pretensions of false science; delusive aids of law. Had he completed the book, he would have left few of the shams of life untouched. To the weak side of Law and Divinity he would, no doubt, have added the weak side of Physic, when time came for summoning the Doctor to despatch his knight. An attentive reader of "Hudribas" will not be more impressed by its wit, than by the breadth of its plan. —MORLEY, HENRY, 1885, *ed. Hudibras* (*Universal Library*), *p.* viii.

The poem is a curio of letters—a specimen of literary bric-à-brac—an old, ingeniously enamelled snuff-box, with dirty pictures within the lid.—MITCHELL, DONALD G., 1890, *English Lands, Letters and Kings, From Elizabeth to Anne, p.* 197.

The book is a very great book. Its wonderful skill of doggerel verse and acrobatic rhyme, the inexhaustible abundance of its fantastic imagery, its learning, its fancy, its pictorial skill—great as they all are—yield, perhaps, to the fashion in which the persons, things, systems ridiculed are made to render themselves ridiculous—to the pitiless mastery with which the puppets work out their own failure and contempt. There are many more lovely books of English literature than "Hudibras;" there are, perhaps, not so many of which it can be said that they are intellectually greater.— SAINTSBURY, GEORGE, 1895, *Social England, ed. Traill, vol.* IV, *p.* 427.

It was greatly relished, and though it is a barbarous and ribald production of small literary value, it is still praised, and perhaps occasionally read. It affords rare opportunities for quotation, every few pages containing a line or couplet of considerable facetiousness. "Hudibras" was incessantly imitated, and the generic term Hudibrastics was invented for this kind of daring doggerel. Butler, however, is a mere episode.—GOSSE, EDMUND, 1897, *Short History of Modern English Literature, p.* 188.

GENERAL

Butler was suffered to die in a garret, Otway in an alehouse, Nat Lee in the street. And yet Butler was a whole species of poets in one; admirable in a manner in which no one else has been tolerable; a manner which began and ended in him, in which he knew no guide and has found no followers.—DENNIS, JOHN, 1717, *Remarks on Pope's Homer, p.* 6.

He, consummate master, knew
When to recede, and where pursue;
His noble negligences teach
What others' toils despair to reach.

He, perfect dancer, climbs the rope,
And balances your fear and hope :
If, after some distinguish'd leap,
He drops his pole, and seems to slip,
Straight gathering all his active strength,
He rises higher half his length.
With wonder you approve his sleight;
And owe your pleasure to your fright.
—PRIOR, MATTHEW, 1718, *Alma, Canto* ii.

There was something singular in this same Butler. Besides an infinite deal of wit, he had great sense and penetration, both in the sciences and the world. Yet with all this, he could never plan a work, nor tell a story well. The first appears from his "Hudibras," the other from his "Elephant in the Moon." He evidently appears to have been dissatisfied with it, by turning it into *long* verse : from whence, you perceive, he thought the fault lay in the doggerel verse, but that was his *forte;* the fault lay in the *manner of telling.* . . . Butler's heroics are poor stuff; indeed only doggerel, made languid by heavy expletives. This attempt in the change of his measure was the sillier, not only as he had acquired a mastery in the short measure, but as that measure, somehow or other, suits best with his sort of wit. His characters are full of cold puerilities, though intermixed with abundance of wit, and with a great deal of good sense. He is sometimes wonderfully fine both in his sentiment and expression.—WARBURTON, WILLIAM, 1759, *Letters from a Late Eminent Prelate, July* 8, *p.* 287.

Butler's treasures of knowledge appear proportioned to his expence : whatever topick employs his mind, he shews himself qualified to expand and illustrate it with all the accessaries that books can furnish ; he is found not only to have travelled the beaten road, but the bye-paths of literature ; not only to have taken general surveys, but to have examined particulars with minute inspection.—JOHNSON, SAMUEL, 1779, *Samuel Butler, Lives of the English Poets.*

Butler, who had as much wit and learning as Cowley, and who knew, what Cowley never knew, how to use them. A great command of good homely English distinguishes him still more from the other writers of the time.—MACAULAY, THOMAS BABINGTON, 1827, *Dryden, Edinburgh Review, Critical and Miscellaneous Essays.*

Butler's business was the business of

desecration, the exact reverse of a poet's. When Prior attempted afterwards the same line of composition with his peculiar grace and airiness of diction,—when Swift ground society into jests with a rougher turning of the wheel,—still, then and since, has this Butler stood alone. He is the genius of his class; a natural enemy to poetry under the form of a poet: not a great man, but a powerful man.—BROWNING, ELIZABETH BARRETT, 1842-63, *The Book of the Poets.*

Butler is the wittiest of English poets, and at the same time he is one of the most learned, and what is more, one of the wisest. His "Hudibras," though naturally the most popular of his works from its size, subject, and witty excess, was an accident of birth and party compared with his Miscellaneous Poems; yet both abound in thoughts as great and deep as the surface is sparkling; and his genius altogether, having the additional recommendation of verse, might have given him a fame greater than Rabelais, had his animal spirits been equal to the rest of his qualifications for a universalist. At the same time, though not abounding in poetic sensibility, he was not without it.—HUNT, LEIGH, 1846, *Wit and Humour,* p. 242.

Butler must ever retain his own plot of ground on the English Parnassus: it is a plot however which the other denizens regard as rather an excrescence and perceptibly malodorous, and, in their loftier moods, Apollo and the Muses turn a resolutely blind eye to that particular compartment.—ROSSETTI, WILLIAM MICHAEL, 1878, *Lives of Famous Poets, p.* 89.

Taking them in this order, we will commence with a short notice of the miscellaneous verse. (I) We see Butler here, as in all his writings, a disappointed man, whose hand was raised against every man. He had a keen eye for the ridiculous side of things, but he did not care to draw attention to the better side. This may be said of all satirists, but it is a specially marked characteristic of Butler. One would have thought that there was enough folly on all sides of him to occupy his pen, and it is to be regretted that the new-born love for science and antiquity, which distinguished the Restoration era, should have had so persistent an enemy in this man of genius.—WHEATLEY, HENRY B., 1881, *Butler's Unpublished Remains, The Antiquary, vol.* IV, *p.* 252.

A consummate master of caustic humour.—COLLINS, JOHN CHURTON, 1895, *Essays and Studies, p.* 33.

John Wilmot
Earl of Rochester
1647-1680

John Wilmot, Earl of Rochester, was born at Ditchley, Oxfordshire, 10th April 1647, and was educated at Burford school and Wadham College, Oxford. He travelled in France and Italy, and then repaired to court, where his handsome person and lively wit made him a prominent figure. In 1665 he showed conspicuous courage against the Dutch. With his friend Windham he had engaged that, "if either of them died, he should appear and give the other notice of the future state, if there was any." Windham was killed, but did not disturb the rest of his friend, who now plunged into a life of the grossest debauchery and buffoonery, yet wrote excellent letters, personal satires, bacchanalian and amatory songs, and verses too often obscene and licentious. At the last he was moved to repentance by Bishop Burnet, and died 26 July 1680. His verses show more wit than poetry, but he possessed a rich gift of satire. Among the best of his poems are an imitation of Horace on Lucilius, Verses to Lord Mulgrave, a Satire against Man, and Verses upon Nothing.—PATRICK AND GROOME, *eds.,* 1897, *Chambers's Biographical Dictionary, p.* 797.

PERSONAL

A very prophane wit.—EVELYN, JOHN, 1670, *Diary, Nov.* 24.

To the King's everlasting shame, to have so idle a rogue his companion.—PEPYS, SAMUEL, 1668-69, *Diary, Feb.* 17.

For the benefit of all those whom I have drawn into sin by my example and encouragement, I leave to the world this my last declaration, (which I deliver in the presence of the great God, who knows the secrets of all hearts, and before whom I am now appearing to be judged;) that, from the bottom of my soul, I detest and abhor the whole course of my former wicked life; that I think I can never sufficiently admire the goodness of God, who has given me a true sense of my pernicious opinions and vile practices, by which I have hitherto lived, without hope and without God in the world; have been an open enemy to Jesus Christ, doing the utmost despite to the Holy Spirit of Grace. And that the greatest testimony of my charity to such is, to warn them, in the name of God, and as they regard the welfare of their immortal souls, no more to deny his being or his providence, or despise his goodness; no more to make a mock of sin, or contemn the pure and excellent religion of my ever blessed Redeemer; through whose merits alone, I, one of the greatest of sinners, do yet hope for mercy and forgiveness. Amen.

Declared and signed in the presence of
{ Anne Rochester,
{ Robert Parsons.
—ROCHESTER, JOHN WILMOT, EARL, 1680, *Declaration, June* 19.

Mourn all ye Groves, in darker Shades be
    seen,
Let groans be heard where gentle Winds
    have been:
Ye *Albion* Rivers, weep your Fountains dry,
And all ye Plants your moisture spend, and
    die:
Ye melancholy Flowers, which once were
    Men,
Lament, until you be transform'd agen:
Let every Rose pale as the Lilly be,
And Winter Frost seize the Anemone:
But thou, O *Hyacinth*, more vigorous grow,
In mournful Letters thy sad Glory show,
Enlarge thy Grief, and flourish in thy Woe:
For *Bion*, the beloved *Bion's* dead,
His Voice is gone, his tuneful Breath is fled.
Come, all ye Muses, *come, adorn the Shep-*
    herd's Herse,
With never-fading Garlands, never-dying
    Verse.
—OLDHAM, JOHN, 1680, *A Pastoral on the Death of the Earl of Rochester.*

As on his death-bed gasping, Strephon lay,
    Strephon! the wonder of the plains,
    The noblest of th' Arcadian swains,
Strephon! the bold, the witty, and the gay,
    With many a sigh and many a tear he said—
    Remember me, ye shepherds, when I'm
    dead!
Ye trifling glories of the world, adieu!
    And vain applauses of the age;
    For when we quit this earthly stage,

Believe me shepherds, for I tell you true,
    The pleasures which from virtuous deeds
    we have,
Procure the sweetest slumbers in the grave.
—FLATMAN, THOMAS, 1686, *Poems, p.* 174.

Wilmot, earl of Rochester, was naturally modest till the court corrupted him. His wit had in it a peculiar brightness, to which none could ever arrive. He gave himself up to all sorts of extravagance, and to the wildest frolics that a wanton wit could devise. He would have gone about the street as a beggar, and made love as a porter. He set up a stage as an Italian mountebank. He was for some years always drunk, and was ever doing some mischief. The king loved his company for the diversion it afforded, better than his person; and there was no love lost between them. He took his revenges in many libels. He found out a footman that knew all the court, and he furnished him with a red coat and a musket as a centinel, and kept him all the winter long every night at the doors of such ladies as he believed might be in intrigues. In the court a centinel is little minded, and is believed to be posted by a captain of the guards to hinder a combat: so this man saw who walked about and visited at forbidden hours. . . . In the last year of his life I was much with him, and have writ a book of what pass'd between him and me. I do verily believe he was then so entirely changed, that, if he had recovered, he would have made good all his resolutions.—BURNET, GILBERT, 1715–34, *History of My Own Time.*

Lord Rochester was of a very bad turn of mind as well as debauched. [From the Duke of Buckingham and others that knew him.]—POPE, ALEXANDER, 1728–30, *Spence's Anecdotes, ed. Singer, p.* 4.

He had very early an inclination to intemperance, which he totally subdued in his travels; but, when he became a courtier he unhappily addicted himself to dissolute and vitious company, by which his principles were corrupted, and his manners depraved. He lost all sense of religious restraint; and, finding it not convenient to admit the authority of laws which he was resolved not to obey, sheltered his wickedness behind infidelity. . . . He confessed to Dr. Burnet, he was for five years together continually drunk, or so much inflamed by frequent ebriety, as in no interval to be master of himself. . . . Having an active and inquisitive mind, he never, except in his paroxysms of intemperance, was wholly negligent of study, he read what is considered as polite learning so much, that he is mentioned by Wood as the greatest scholar of all the nobility. . . . Thus in a course of a drunken gaiety and gross sensuality, with intervals of study perhaps yet more criminal, with an avowed contempt of all decency and order, a total disregard to every moral, and a resolute denial of every religious obligation, he lived worthless and useless, and blazed out his youth and his health in lavish voluptuousness: till, at the age of one-and-thirty, he had exhausted the fund of life, and reduced himself to a state of weakness and decay.—JOHNSON, SAMUEL, 1779, *Earl of Rochester, Lives of the English Poets.*

It is not now meant to deny many of the charges made against the character of Rochester, though some of them rest on very slender foundation; and when his memory has, for a century and a half, been loaded with unalloyed obloquy, it might seem the height of folly to offer any thing in its vindication; but if we can shew his character in a more amiable or less odious light, justice demands that his memory should have the benefit of it: and if we can prove that, notwithstanding all his dissipation, and "lavish voluptuousness," he was an affectionate husband, and a fond father, we shall at least exhibit him in a light in which he has not hitherto been regarded. Happily, the evidence on which this will rest, is indisputable: it is drawn from his own domestic letters.— COLLET, STEPHEN, 1823, *Relics of Literature*, p. 44.

His reputation as a wit must rest, in the present day, chiefly upon productions which have long since been condemned as unreadable. Strange to say, when not under the influence of wine, he was a constant student of classical authors, perhaps the worst reading for a man of his tendencies: all that was satirical and impure attracting him most. Boileau, among French writers, and Cowley among the English, were his favorite authors. He also read many books of physic; for long before thirty his constitution was so broken by his life, that he turned his

attention to remedies, and to medical treatment; and it is remarkable how many men of dissolute lives take up the same sort of reading, in the vain hope of repairing a course of dissolute living. As a writer, his style was at once forcible and lively; as a companion, he was wildly vivacious: madly, perilously, did he outrage decency, insult virtue, profane religion.—THOMPSON, KATHERINE AND J. C. (GRACE AND PHILIP WHARTON), 1860, *The Wits and Beaux of Society*, p. 67.

His manners were those of a lawless and wretched mountebank; his delight was to haunt the stews, to debauch women, to write filthy songs and lewd pamphlets; he spent his time between scandal with the maids of honour, broils with men of letters, the receiving of insults, the giving of blows. By way of playing the gallant, he eloped with his wife before he married her. To make a display of scepticism, he ended by declining a duel, and gained the name of a coward. For five years together he was said to be drunk. The spirit within him failing of a worthy outlet, plunged him into adventures more befitting a clown. Once with the Duke of Buckingham he rented an inn on the Newmarket road, and turned innkeeper, supplying the husbands with drink and defiling their wives. He introduced himself, disguised as an old woman, into the house of a miser, robbed him of his wife, and passed her on to Buckingham. The husband hanged himself; they made very merry over the affair. At another time he disguised himself as a chairman, then as a beggar, and paid court to the guttergirls. He ended by turning charlatan, astrologer, and vendor of drugs for procuring abortion, in the suburbs. . . . One cannot copy even the titles of his poems; they were written only for the haunts of vice.—TAINE, H. A., 1871, *History of English Literature, tr. Van Laun, vol.* I, *bk.* iii, *ch.* i, *p.* 469.

Dorimant, the witty aristocratic rake in Etherege's play of "The Man of Mode," represents the Earl of Rochester.—FREY, ALBERT R., 1888, *Sobriquets and Nicknames*, p. 94.

To the same court* belonged Rochester, his great, fine wig covering a great, fine brain; he writing harmonious verses about

*Court of Charles II.

—"Nothing"—or worse than nothing; and at the last wheedling Bishop Burnet into the belief that he had changed his courses, and that if he might rise from that ugly deathbed where the good-natured, pompous bishop sought him, he would be enrolled among the moralists. I think it was lucky that he died with such good impulse flashing at the top of his badnesses.—MITCHELL, DONALD G., 1890, *English Lands Letters and Kings, From Elizabeth to Anne, p.* 185.

GENERAL

Sometimes he has some humour, never wit,
And if it rarely, very rarely, hit,
'Tis under so much nasty rubbish laid
To find it out's the cinder-woman's trade.
—SHEFFIELD, DUKE OF BUCKINGHAM, 1679, *An Essay on Satire.*

He was . . thoroughly acquainted with the classic authors, both Greek and Latin; a thing very rare (if not peculiar to him) among those of his quality.—WOOD, ANTHONY, 1691–1721, *Athenæ Oxonienses.*

Oldham is a very indelicate writer: he has strong rage, but it is too much like Billingsgate. Lord Rochester had much more delicacy, and more knowledge of mankind. —POPE, ALEXANDER, 1728–30, *Spence's Anecdotes, ed. Singer, p.* 14.

Lord Rochester's poems have much more obscenity than wit, more wit than poetry, more poetry than politeness.—WALPOLE, HORACE, 1758, *A Catalogue of the Royal and Noble Authors of England, Scotland and Ireland.*

The very name of Rochester is offensive to modest ears; yet does his poetry discover such energy of style and such poignancy, as give ground to imagine what so fine a genius, had he fallen in a more happy age and had followed better models, was capable of producing. The ancient satirists often use great liberties in their expressions; but their freedom no more resembles the licentiousness of Rochester, than the nakedness of an Indian does that of a common prostitute.—HUME, DAVID, 1762, *History of England, James II.*

There is an immense strength and pregnancy of expression in some of the best of his compositions, careless and unfinished as they are.—CRAIK, GEORGE L., 1861, *A Compendious History of English Literature, vol.* II, *p.* 113.

The volumes which continued to be reprinted for nearly a century under the title of Rochester's Poems form a kind of "Parnasse Satyrique" into which a modern reader can scarcely venture to dip. Of this notorious collection a large part was spurious; the offensive matter that had to be removed from the writings of Dorset, Buckinghamshire, Butler, and other less famous profligate poets, found an asylum under the infamy of the name of Rochester. But readers who are fortunate enough to secure the volume edited by the dead poet's friends in 1691 will find no more indiscretions than are familiar in all poetry of the Restoration, and will discover, what they will not find elsewhere, the exquisite lyrics on which the fame of Rochester should rest. His satires, as trenchant and vigorous as they are foul, are not included in this edition; he uses the English language in them as Poggio and Filelfo had used Latin. . . . With Rochester the power of writing songs died in England until the age of Blake and Burns. He was the last of the cavalier lyrists, and in some respects the best. In the qualities that a song demands, simplicity, brevity, pathos and tenderness, he arrives nearer to pure excellence than any one between Carew and Burns. His style is without adornment, and, save in this one matter of song-writing, he is weighed down by the dryness and inefficiency of his age.—GOSSE, EDMUND, 1880, *English Poets, ed. Ward, vol.* II, *pp.* 424, 425.

Victims of vanity and lechery are seldom worth regret: but this hapless pupil of the Puritans, hounded as he was by false shame and foolish emulation into such inconceivable eccentricities of literary and personal debauchery, was born for so different a fate and so different a record, had not his evil star intervened to thwart it, that no one who realizes what he might and should have been can ever think of the poet or the man without a thrill or a pang of pity. The gallant young volunteer who distinguished himself even among English sailors and soldiers as the hero of a sea fight drank himself into cowardice, and 'truckled to a challenger as a Russo-Radical of our own day would tuckle to any enemy who might assist him in the degradation of this country: the noble and thoughtful poet who might have beaten all competitors out of the field became such a rhymester as Plato might have excepted from the sentence of expulsion—surely in other cases a superfluous sentence—pronounced against poets who might find themselves within the limits of a republic from which Platonic love had excluded the superfluous and obsolete influence of woman.—Swinburne, Algernon Charles, 1891, *Social Verse, The Forum. vol.* 12, *p.* 177

Rochester had as sprightly a lyric gift as any writer of the Restoration. As a satirist he showed much insight and vigour, and, according to Aubrey, Marvell regarded him as the best satirist of his time. But he was something of a plagiarist. His "Satire against Mankind" owes much to Boileau, and to Cowley his lyrics were often deeply indebted.—Lee, Sidney, 1900, *Dictionary of National Biography, vol.* LXII, *p.* 66.

Sir Thomas Browne

1605–1682

Born, in London, 19 Oct. 1605. Educated at Winchester Coll., as Scholar, 1616–23. To Broadgate Hall (now Pembroke Coll.), Oxford, 1623; B. A., 31 June 1626; M. A., 11 June 1629. Practised medicine for a short time. Tour in Ireland, France Italy, Holland. Returned to practice near Halifax, "Religio Medici" probably written 1635. To Norwich, 1637. M. D., Oxford, 10 July 1637. Married Dorothy Mileham, 1641. "Religio Medici" privately published, 1642. Sided with Royalists in Civil Wars. Hon. Fellow of Coll. of Physicians, 6 July 1665. Knighted, on State visit of Charles II. to Norwich, 28 Sept. 1671. Died, 19 Oct. 1682; buried at Norwich. *Works:* "Religio Medici," privately printed, 1642; authorized version, 1643; "Pseudodoxia Epidemica," 1646; "Hydriotaphia," 1658. *Posthumous:* "Certain Miscellany Tracts," 1684; "Works," 1686; "Posthumous Works," 1712; "Christian Morals," 1716. *Collected Works:* including *Life* and Correspondence, ed. by S. Wilkin (4 vols.), 1835–36.—Sharp, R. Farquharson, 1897, *A Dictionary of English Authors, p.* 33.

PERSONAL

M. S.
Hic Situs Est
THOMAS BROWNE, M. D.
Et Miles.
A° 1605. Londoni Natus
Generosa Familia Apud Upton In Agro
Cestriensi Oriundus.
Schola Primum Wintoniensi, Postea
In Coll. Pembr.
Apud Oxonienses Bonis Literis
Haud Leviter Imbutus.
In Urbe Hac Nordovicensi Medicinam
Arte Egregi Et Fœlici Successu Professus,
Scriptis, Quibus Tituli, Religio Medici
Et Pseudodoxia Epidemica Aliisque
Per Orbem Notissimus
Vir Pientissimus, Integerrimus, Doctissimus;
Obiit Octobr. 19, 1682.
Pie Posuit Mœstissima Conjux
Dᵃ Doroth. Br.
—Inscription on Monument, Church of St. Peter, Mancroft, Norwich.

For a character of his person, his complexion and hair was answerable to his name, his stature was moderate, and habit of body neither fat nor lean but εὐσάρκος. In his habit of clothing, he had an aversion to all finery, and affected plainness, both in the fashion and ornaments. He ever wore a cloke, or boots, when few others did. He kept himself always very warm, and thought it most safe so to do, though he never loaded himself with such a multitude of garments, as Suetonius reports of Augustus, enough to clothe a good family. . . . His memory, though not so eminent as that of Seneca or Scaliger, was capacious and tenacious, insomuch as he remembered all that was remarkable in any book that he had read; and not only knew all persons again that he had ever seen at any distance of time, but remembered the circumstances of their bodies, and their particular discourses and speeches. . . . He was never seen to be transported with mirth, or dejected with sadness; always cheerful, but rarely merry, at any sensible rate, seldom heard to break a jest; and when he did, he would be apt to blush at the levity of it: his gravity was natural without affectation. His modesty was visible in a natural habitual blush, which was increased upon the least occasion, and oft discovered without any observable cause. They that knew no more of him than by the briskness of his writings, found themselves deceived in their expectation when they came in his company, noting the gravity and sobriety of his aspect and conversation; so free from loquacity, or much talkativeness, that he was something difficult to be engaged in any discourse; though when he was so, it was always singular and never trite or vulgar. . . . Sir Thomas understood most of the European languages, viz. all that are in Hutter's bible, which he made use of. The Latin and Greek he understood critically. —WHITEFOOT, REV. JOHN, 1699, *Minutes of a Life of Sir Thomas Browne.*

His own character was a fine mixture of humourist, genius, and pedant. A library was a living world to him, and every book a man, absolute flesh and blood! and the gravity with which he records contradictory opinions is exquisite.—COLERIDGE, SAMUEL TAYLOR, 1802, *Notes on Books and Authors; Miscellanies, Æsthetic and Literary, ed. Ashe, p. 300.*

It is very remarkable, that although Sir Thomas Browne had forty children and grand-children (including those who were so by marriage), yet, in the second generation, within thirty years after his decease, the male line became extinct; and of the third generation, none survived their infancy, excepting in the family of his eldest daughter, Anne; of whose eight children, none left any descendants but the third daughter, Frances Fairfax, married to the Earl of Buchan; whose daughter, Lady Frances Erskine, married the celebrated Colonel Gardener, killed at Preston-pans in 1745;—whose grandson was the late Lord Erskine, one of the most splendid ornaments of the English bar, created Lord Chancellor in 1806; and from whom are thus lineally descended Henry David, the present and 12th Earl of Buchan, and David Montagu, the present and 2nd Lord Erskine of Restormel Castle.—WILKIN, SIMON, 1836, *ed., The Works of Sir Thomas Browne, Memoir.*

Of a mild and kindly temperament, fond of his books and his curiosities, and spinning out his subtle and aerial thoughts from materials which the crowded world casts out of its bustling way into nooks and corners—moderate as a politician, averse to all disputes in theology, inclined in both to leave things in their beaten course, beneath the shelter of unexamining veneration—there did not exist for Sir Thomas Browne those great and exciting interests which gird up the loins of a man's mind, and make him in earnest in all that he undertakes.—BULWER-LYTTON, LORD EDWARD GEORGE LYTTON, 1836, *Sir Thomas Browne, Edinburgh Review.*

It is not difficult, from the fragmentary notices that have been left to us, to put together some picture of his personal appearance. He was a man of dignified appearance, with a striking resemblance, as Southey has remarked, to Charles I., "always cheerful, but never merry," given to unseasonable blushing, little inclined to talk, but strikingly original when once launched in conversation; sedate in his dress, and obeying some queer medical crochets as to its proper arrangement; always at work in the intervals of his "drudging practice;" and generally a sober and dignified physician.—STEPHEN, LESLIE 1876, *Hours in a Library, Second Series.*

RELIGIO MEDICI
1642

But to come back to our Physician; truly, my lord, I must needs pay him, as a due, the acknowledging his pious discourses to be excellent and pathetical ones, containing worthy motives to incite one to virtue, and to deter one from vice; thereby to gain heaven, and to avoid hell. Assuredly he is the owner of a solid head, and of a strong, generous heart.—DIGBY, SIR KENELM, 1642, *Letter to the Earl of Dorset.*

The book entitled "Religio Medici" is in high credit here. The author has wit; there are abundance of fine things in that book; he is a humorist, whose thoughts are very agreeable, but who, in my opinion, is to seek for a master in religion—as many others are—and, in the end, perhaps, may find none. One may say of him, as Philip de Comines did the founder of the Minimes, a hermit of Calabria,

Francis de Paula, "he is still alive, and may grow worse as well as better."—PATIN, GUY, 1645, *Letter, from Paris, April* 7.

The "Religio Medici" was no sooner published than it excited the attention of the publick by the novelty of paradoxes, the dignity of sentiment, the quick succession of images, the multitude of abstruse allusions, the subtlety of disquisition, and the strength of language.—JOHNSON, SAMUEL, 1756, *Life of Sir Thomas Browne.*

The "Religio Medici" is one of the most beautiful prose poems in the language; its power of diction, its subtlety and largeness of thought, exquisite conceits and images, have no parallel out of the writers of that brilliant age, when Poetry and Prose had not yet divided their domain, and the Lyceum of Philosophy was watered by the Ilissus of the Nine.—BULWER-LYTTON, LORD EDWARD GEORGE LYTTON, 1836, *Sir Thomas Browne, Edinburgh Review.*

This little book made a remarkable impression: it was soon translated into several languages, and is highly extolled by Conringius and others, who could only judge through these versions. Patin, though he rather slights it himself, tells us in one of his letters that it was very popular at Paris. The character which Johnson has given of the "Religio Medici" is well known; and, though perhaps rather too favorable, appears, in general, just. The mind of Browne was fertile, and, according to the current use of the word, ingenious; his analogies are original, and sometimes brilliant; and, as his learning is also in things out of the beaten path, this gives a peculiar and uncommon air to all his writings, and especially to the "Religio Medici." He was, however, far removed from real philosophy, both by his turn of mind and by the nature of his erudition: he seldoms reasons; his thoughts are desultory; sometimes he appears sceptical or paradoxical; but credulity, and deference to authority, prevail.—HALLAM, HENRY, 1837–39, *Introduction to the Literature of Europe, pt.* iii, *ch.* iv, *par.* 36.

It is not their intrinsic merit that keeps the "Religio Medici" and the "Urn-Burial" alive; it is because they were written by Sir Thomas Browne. The perennial charm of his quaint and engaging

personality is impressed upon every line. Hence their vitality.—SKELTON, SIR JOHN, 1895, *Mainly about The Story-Tellers, Table-Talk of Shirley, p.* 262.

It is a book to be read slowly, with frequent pauses to allow the quaint thoughts to mature, and with full resolve to be led whither the writer's fancy suggests. So read, it is a perpetual refreshment and delight. Though full of allusions, it is free from that overloading of quotation and reference which was a prevailing fault of the age, and which makes Burton's "Anatomy of Melancholy" so hard to enjoy.—MASTERMAN, J. HOWARD B., 1897, *The Age of Milton, p.* 151.

Sir Thomas Browne directed a free play of mind upon the old dogmas, and the result was the "Religio Medici," a work which each generation treasures and rereads, not because of the dogma, but because of the literature; it is a rare specimen of vital, flexible, imaginative writing. —BURROUGHS, JOHN, 1897, *On the Re-reading of Books, The Century, vol.* LV, *p.* 150.

PSEUDOXIA EPIDEMICA
1646

It is, indeed, to be wished, that he had longer delayed the publication, and added what the remaining part of his life might have furnished: the thirty-six years which he spent afterwards in study and experience, would doubtless have made large additions to an Inquiry into Vulgar Errors.—JOHNSON, SAMUEL, 1756, *Life of Sir Thomas Browne.*

Browne was where the learned in Europe had been seventy years before, and seems to have been one of those who saturate their minds with bad books till they have little room for any thing new that is better. A man of so much credulity and such an irregular imagination as Browne was almost sure to believe in witchcraft and all sorts of spiritual agencies. In no respect did he go in advance of his age, unless we make an exception of his declaration against persecution. He seems to have been fond of those trifling questions which the bad taste of the schoolmen and their contemporaries introduced; as whether a man has fewer ribs than a woman, whether Adam and Eve had navels, whether Methusaleh was the oldest man; the problems of children put to adults. With a strong curiosity and a real love of truth, Browne is a striking instance of a merely empirical mind: he is at sea with sails and a rudder, but without a compass or log-book; and has so little notion of any laws of nature, or of any inductive reasoning either as to efficient or final causes, that he never seems to judge anything to be true or false except by experiment.—HALLAM, HENRY, 1837–39, *Introduction to the Literature of Europe, pt.* iii, *ch.* ix, *par.* 47,

No wonder, then, that Browne, who certainly was inferior to several of his contemporaries, should have been affected by a movement which they were unable to resist.—BUCKLE, HENRY THOMAS, 1857, *History of Civilization in England, vol.* I, p. 265.

To modern readers "Vulgar Errors" presents an inexhaustible store of entertainment. The attainment of scientific truth was not for Browne the sole object; it is in the discussion itself that he delights, and the more marvellous a fable is, the more sedulously he applies himself to the investigation of its truth. Though he professed his anxiety to dispel popular superstitions, Browne was himself not a little imbued with the spirit of credulity. He believed in astrology, alchemy, witchcraft, and magic, and he never abandoned the Ptolemaic system of astronomy.—BULLEN, A. H., 1886, *Dictionary of National Biography, vol.* VII, *p.* 67.

Shows Browne's insatiable love of what is strange, grotesque and mysterious. The book is, in truth, a museum of curiosities—the sweepings of an antiquarian's note-book. Here you may read of the phœnix, the·pelican, and the dolphin, of the flowering thorn and of the shrieking mandrake, of strange errors on Scripture or geography. On the whole, Browne seems more anxious to record than to refute; the benefit of the doubt generally falls on the side of credulity, for in a world so full of mystery how many things may be true that cannot be demonstrated. —MASTERMAN, J. HOWARD B., 1897, *The Age of Milton, p.* 151.

HYDRIOTAPHIA
1658

There is, perhaps, none of his works which better exemplifies his reading or memory. It is scarcely to be imagined, how many particulars he has amassed together in a treatise which seems to have been occasionally written; and for which, therefore, no materials could have been previously collected.—JOHNSON, SAMUEL, 1756, *Life of Sir Thomas Browne.*

The slight vacuum in the left-hand case—two shelves from the ceiling—scarcely distinguishable but by the quick eye of a loser—was whilom the commodious resting-place of Brown on Urn Burial. C. will hardly allege that he knows more about that treatise than I do, who introduced it to him, and was indeed the first (of the moderns) to discover its beauties—but so have I known a foolish lover to praise his mistress in the presence of a rival more qualified to carry her off than himself.—LAMB, CHARLES, 1820, *The Two Races of Men.*

GENERAL

The true classical style of Hooker and his fellows was easily open to corruption; and Sir Thomas Browne it was, who, though a writer of great genius, first effectually injured the literary taste of the nation by his introduction of learned words, merely because they were learned. It would be difficult to describe Browne adequately; exuberant in conception and conceit, dignified, hyper-latinistic, a quiet and sublime enthusiast; yet a fantast, a humourist, a brain with a twist; egotistic like Montaigne, yet with a feeling heart and an active curiosity, which, however, too often degenerates into a hunting after oddities. In his "Hydriotaphia" and, indeed, almost all his works, the entireness of his mental action is very observable; he metamorphoses every thing, be it what it may, into the subject under consideration. But Sir Thomas Browne with all his faults had a genuine idiom.—COLERIDGE, SAMUEL TAYLOR, 1818, *Style, Miscellanies Æsthetic and Literary, ed. Ashe,* p. 179.

Sir Thomas Browne seemed to be of opinion that the only business of life was to think, and that the proper object of speculation was, by darkening knowledge, to breed more speculation, and "find no end in wandering mazes lost." He chose the incomprehensible and impracticable as almost the only subjects fit for a lofty and lasting contemplation, or for the exercise of a solid faith. He cried out for an *oh altitudo* beyond the heights of revelation, and posed himself with apocryphal mysteries, as the pastime of his leisure hours. He pushes a question to the utmost verge of conjecture, that he may repose on the certainty of doubt; and he removes an object to the greatest distance from him, that he may take a high and abstracted interest in it, consider it in its relation to the sum of things, not to himself, and bewilder his understanding in the universality of its nature and the inscrutableness of its origin. His is the sublime of indifference; a passion for the abstruse and imaginary. He turns the world round for his amusement, as if it was a globe of pasteboard. He looks down on sublunary affairs as if he had taken his station in one of the planets. The antipodes are next-door neighbours to him, and Doomsday is not far off. With a thought he embraces both the poles; the march of his pen is over the great divisions of geography and chronology. Nothing touches him nearer than humanity. He feels that he is mortal only in the decay of nature, and the dust of long-forgotten tombs. The finite is lost in the infinite. The orbits of the heavenly bodies or the history of empires are to him but a point in time or a speck in the universe. The great Platonic year revolves in one of his periods. Nature is too little for the grasp of his style. He scoops an antithesis out of fabulous antiquity, and rakes up an epithet from the sweepings of Chaos. It is as if his books had dropped from the clouds, or as if Friar Bacon's head could speak. He stands on the edge of the world of sense and reason, and gains a vertigo by looking down at impossibilities and chimeras. Or he busies himself with the mysteries of the Cabala, or the enclosed secrets of the heavenly quincunxes, as children are amused with tales of the nursery. The passion of curiosity (the only passion of childhood) had in him survived to old age, and had superannuated his other faculties. He moralizes and grows pathetic on a mere idle fancy of his own, as if thought and being were the same, or as if "all this world were one glorious lie."—HAZLITT, WILLIAM, 1820, *Lectures on the Literature of the Age of Elizabeth, Lecture* vii.

A writer of this school in the age of Charles I., and incomparably superior to any of the churchmen belonging to it, in the brightness and originality of his genius, sir Thomas Browne, whose varied talents wanted nothing but the controlling supremacy of good sense to place him in the highest rank of our literature, will furnish a better instance of the prevailing bias than merely theological writings. He united a most acute and skeptical understanding with strong devotional sensibility, the temperament so conspicuous in Pascal and Johnson, and which has a peculiar tendency to seek the repose of implicit faith.—HALLAM, HENRY, 1827–46, *The Constitutional History of England, ch.* viii.

Sir Thomas Browne, like most other men of genius, is but an author of great imagination and original habits of thought and study, reflecting back upon us the fantastic light that he received from the influences that gathered and played around him. . . . A scholar by habit, a philosopher by boast, and a poet by nature.—BULWER-LYTTON LORD EDWARD GEORGE LYTTON, 1836, *Sir Thomas Browne, Edinburgh Review.*

One of the most interesting specimens of the genuine philosopher in the annals of literature, is Sir Thomas Browne. His candour, scope, and kindliness, united with bravery of thought and originality of expression, make his works attractive beyond any other of the old English prose writers. The bulk of the writings of Sir Thomas Browne are curious rather than of practical value; but their indirect utility is greater than a casual view of their ostensible design would suggest. A vast amount of quaint knowledge, a vein of original speculation, and a loftiness of conception as well as waywardness of fancy, fix the mind to the page whither the quaint title attracts it.—TUCKERMAN, HENRY T., 1849, *Characteristics of Literature, p.* 14.

Sir Thomas Browne, deep, tranquil, and majestic as Milton, silently premeditating and "disclosing his golden couplets," as under some genial instinct of incubation.—DE QUINCEY, THOMAS, 1859, *Rhetoric, Collected Writings, ed. Masson, vol.* x, *p.* 105.

The thoughtful melancholy, the singular mixture of skepticism and credulity, and the brilliancy of imaginative illustration, give his essays a peculiarity of character

that renders them exceedingly fascinating.
—BOTTA, ANNE C. LYNCH, 1860, *Hand-Book of Universal Literature, p.* 493.

By no means free from blemishes, nor exempt from vain conceits and fancies, Sir Thomas Browne may yet be ranked as one of the foremost philosophical religious writers, of whom our language can boast. —PERRY, GEORGE G., 1861, *History of the Church of England, vol.* I, *p.* 644.

Out of such a writer the rightly attuned and sympathizing mind will draw many things more precious than any mere facts.—CRAIK, GEORGE L., 1861, *A Compendious History of English Literature and of the English Language, vol.* II, *p.* 82.

His mixed devotion to science and credulity, his love of a comprehensive and liberal Christianity, his quaint enthusiasm and love of pleasantry, his vivacious and garrulous mysticism, which peopled the world around him with spiritual agencies, and saw in it everywhere the "picture of the Invisible," closely ally him with such writers as More and Glanvill. Unconnected by any external bonds, he represents with them the same combination of inquiry and faith—the same yearning towards higher forms of truth, and the same love and fondness for the Past—the same eclecticism in thought—and must we not also say the same dreamy religious imaginativeness, more beautiful than strong, more picturesque and ideal than practically earnest, self-denying, and victorious?—TULLOCH, JOHN, 1872, *Rational Theology and Christian Philosophy in England in the Seventeenth Century, vol.* II, *p.* 454.

Browne had not the passionate fervour of Milton; grave, solemn, meditative, without fire or freshness of sentiment, he would have shrunk from Milton's vituperative scorn, and could never have conceived the tender and graceful fancies of Milton's smaller poems. The prevailing characteristic of his style is tranquil elaboration. He abounds in carefully-constructed periods, intermixed with short pointed sentences that have a singularly Johnsonian sound, from the fulness of the rhythm. His sentence-structure is more "formed" than in any previous writer, perhaps more so than in any writer anterior to Johnson. His figures are original, ingenious and peculiarly apt; he does not err in excess of similitudes.

Felicitous and complete expression, comparatively free from tautology, inspires a general feeling of vigour; and here and there we are carried away by flights of high and solemn elevation. The great drawback for the modern reader is his excessive use of words coined from the Latin. Even Johnson condemns him on this score. His Latinised diction is all the more remarkable because he expressly condemns Latin quotations.—MINTO, WILLIAM, 1872–80, *Manual of English Prose Literature, p.* 305

Did any mirror, even of French plate glass, ever reflect any man's outer configuration more vividly and distinctly than the strange inner nature of Sir Thomas Browne is mirrored in his periods? What a revelation we have of his inmost self,—what a picture of his wit, imagination, portentous memory, insatiable curiosity, "humorous sadness," pedantry, and love of crotchets and hobbies, even "a whole stable-full,"—in the quaint analogies, the grotesque fancies, the airy paradoxes, the fine and dainty fretwork, the subtle and stately music, the amazing Latinisms, and the riotous paradoxes and eloquent epigrams of the old knight's style!— MATHEWS, WILLIAM. 1881, *Literary Style, p.* 22.

Paradox though it be, we may venture to say, that even in Sir Thomas Browne there is more of rich, strong, nervous English than in Steele or Tillotson.— WASHBURN, EMELYN W., 1884, *Studies in Early English Literature, p.* 151.

To most persons of mind sensitive as his, his chosen studies would have seemed full of melancholy, turning always, as they did, upon death and decay. It is well, perhaps, that life should be something of a "meditation upon death;" but to many, certainly, Browne's would have seemed too like a lifelong following of one's own funeral. A museum is seldom a cheerful place—oftenest induces the feeling that nothing could ever have been young; and to Browne the whole world is a museum; all the grace and beauty it has being of a somewhat mortified kind. Only, for him (poetic dream, or philosophic apprehension, it was this which never failed to evoke his wonderful genius for exquisitely impassioned speech) over all those ugly anatomical preparations, as though over miraculous saintly relics, there was the perpetual flicker of a surviving spiritual ardency, one day to reassert itself—stranger far than any fancied odylic gravelights!—PATER, WALTER, 1886, *Appreciations, p.* 137.

As an artist, or rather architect, of words in the composite and florid style, it is vain to look anywhere for his superior. . . . The work of this country doctor is, for personal savour, for strangeness, and for delight, one of the most notable things in English literature. . . . In character and interest it yields to the work of no other English prose writer.— SAINTSBURY, GEORGE, 1887, *History of Elizabethan Literature, pp.* 316, 338.

If there were no other reason for our love of the best writings of Sir Thomas Browne, it would be for this—that in some scarce distinguishable way he has inoculated our "Elia" of a later day with something very like his own quaint egoisms and as quaint garniture of speech.— MITCHELL, DONALD G., 1890, *English Lands Letters and Kings, From Elizabeth to Anne, p.* 223.

He was one of those rare prose-writers whom we meet at intervals in the history of literature, who leave nothing to improvisation, but balance and burnish their sentences until they reach a perfection analogous to that of very fine verse. Supported by his exquisite ear, Browne permits himself audacities, neologism, abrupt transitions, which positively take away our breath. But while we watch him thus dancing on the tight-rope of style, we never see him fall; if he lets go his footing in one place, it is but to amaze us by his agility in leaping to another. His scheme has been supposed to be founded on that of Burton, and certainly Browne is no less captivated by the humours of melancholy. But if Burton is the greater favourite among students, Browne is the better artist and the more imaginative writer.—GOSSE, EDMUND, 1897, *Short History of Modern English Literature, p.* 153.

The phrasing of Sir Thomas Browne, Milton's contemporary, is characterized by literary ingenuity and a certain quaint affectation that has an original flavor and a charm of its own, though his great attraction lies in the rhythm of his sentences and the fine quality of his thought. He, too, is disfigured by writing in an artificial language which, however, like the stiff ruff and long waist of the period, could not altogether hide natural grace and symmetry.—JOHNSON, CHARLES F., 1898, *Elements of Literary Criticism, p.* 206.

Isaac Walton
1593–1683

Izaak Walton was born at Stafford in August 1593. He came early up to London, and took a shop in Cornhill. In 1617–18 he was made one of the Ironmonger's Company. In 1624 we find him a linen-draper in Fleet Street, near Chancery Lane, and in 1630 he bought a house in the latter thoroughfare. He possessed many noble and clerical friends, whose acquaintance he sedulously cultivated. To the "LXXX, Sermons" of Dr. Donne he prefixed in 1640 his "Life" of that worthy. His "Life of Sir Henry Wotton" appeared in the same year. During the Civil War he retired to Stafford. His "Complete Angler" made its first appearance in 1653. He published the "Life of Hooker" in 1662; the "Life of George Herbert" in 1670 in a first complete edition of the four "Lives;" the "Life of Sanderson" followed in 1678; and, possibly, a work called "Love and Truth" in 1680. He spent the close of his career in the house of his son-in-law, Prebendary Hawkins, in Winchester, where he died in his ninety-first year on the 15th day of December 1683, and was buried in Winchester Cathedral.—CRAIK, HENRY, 1893, *ed., English Prose, vol.* II, *p.* 338.

PERSONAL

Here resteth the body of
MR. ISAAK WALTON,
Who dyed the 15th of Decr.
    1683.

Alas! He's gone before,
Gone to return no more.
Our panting breasts aspire
After their aged sire,

Whose well-spent life did last
Full ninety years and past.
But now he hath begun
That which will ne'er be done,
Crowned with eternal bliss,
We wish our souls with his.

VOTIS MODESTIS SIC FLERUNT LIBERI!
—INSCRIPTION ON MONUMENT, CATHEDRAL OF WINCHESTER.

Sweet and fresh
As the flower-skirted streams of Staffordshire,
Where, under aged trees, the southwest wind
Of soft June mornings fanned the thin, white
    hair
Of the sage fisher.
    —WHITTIER, JOHN GREENLEAF, 1848, *The
Bridal of Pennacook.*

One of the most interesting memorials
of Walton left us is the monogram "I W."
and the date "1658" scratched by Walton
himself on the mural table to Isaac Casaubon in the south transept of Westminster
Abbey. Dean Stanley was very fond of
pointing this out to his personal friends
as he escorted them to the Poets' Corner;
and it is the only desecration ever committed in the Abbey that he heartily for-
gave.—HUTTON, LAURENCE, 1885, *Literary Landmarks of London, p.* 315.

Without ambition, save to be in the society of good men, he passed through turmoil, ever companioned by content. For
him existence had its trials: he saw all
that he held most sacred overthrown;
laws broken up; his king publicly murdered; his friends outcasts; his worship
proscribed; he himself suffered in property from the raid of the Kirk into England. He underwent many bereavements:
child after child he lost, but content he
did not lose, nor sweetness of heart, nor
belief. He was one of those happy characters which are never found disassociated
from unquestioning faith. Of old he
might have been the ancient religious
Athenian in the opening of Plato's *Republic,* or Virgil's aged gardener. The happiness of such natures would be incomplete
without religion, but only by such tranquil and blessed souls can religion be accepted with no doubt or scruple, no dread,
and no misgiving.—LANG, ANDREW, 1896,
ed., The Compleat Angler, Introduction, p.
xxxi.

COMPLETE ANGLER
1653

And I wish the Reader also to take notice, that in writing of it I have made
myself a recreation of a recreation; and
that it might prove so to him, and not
read dull and tediously, I have in several
places mixed, not any scurrility, but some
innocent, harmless mirth, of which, if
thou be severe, sour-complexioned man,
then I here disallow thee to be a competent judge; for divines say, there are

offences given, and offences not given but
taken.—WALTON, IZAAK, 1653, *The Compleat Angler, The Epistle to the Reader.*

Lays the stress of his arguments upon
other men's observations, wherewith he
stuffs his indigested octavo; so brings
himself under the angler's censure and the
common calamity of a plagiary, to be pitied
(poor man) for his loss of time, in scribbling and transcribing other men's notions.
. . I remember in Stafford, I urged
his own argument upon him, that pickerel
weed of itself breeds pickerel (pike).—
FRANCK, RICHARD, 1658-94, *Northern
Memoirs.*

I have just been reading a book which
I may be too partial to, as it was the delight of my childhood; but I will recommend it to you: it is Izaak Walton's
"Complete Angler." All the scientific
part you may omit in reading. The dialogue is very simple, full of pastoral
beauties, and will charm you.—LAMB,
CHARLES, 1796, *Letter to Coleridge; Letters,
ed. Ainger, vol.* I, *p.* 20.

Let me take this opportunity of recommending the amiable and venerable Isaac
Walton's "Complete Angler;" a work the
most singular of its kind, breathing the
very spirit of contentment, of quiet, and of
unaffected philanthropy, and interspersed
with some beautiful relics of poetry, old
songs, and ballads.—BOWLES, WILLIAM
LISLE, 1807, *ed. Pope's Works. vol.* I, *p.*
135.

That well-known work has an extreme
simplicity, and an extreme interest, arising out of its very simplicity. In the
description of a fishing-tackle you perceive the piety and humanity of the author's mind. This is the best pastoral in
the language, not excepting Pope's or
Philips's. We doubt whether Sannaza-
rius' "Piscatory Eclogues" are equal to
the scenes described by Walton on the
banks of the River Lea. He gives the
feeling of the open air. We walk with
him along the dusty road-side, or repose
on the banks of the river under a shady
tree, and, in watching for the finny prey,
imbibe what he beautifully calls "the patience and simplicity of poor, honest fishermen." We accompany them to their
inn at night, and partake of their simple,
but delicious fare, while Maud, the pretty
milk-maid, at her mother's desire, sings
the classical ditties of Sir Walter Raleigh.

Good cheer is not neglected in this work, any more than in "John Buncle," or any other history which sets a proper value on the good things of life. The prints in the "Complete Angler" give an additional reality and interest to the scenes it describes. While Tottenham Cross shall stand, and longer, thy work, amiable and happy old man, shall last.—HAZLITT, WILLIAM, 1817, The Round Table.

Indeed the "Complete Angler," whether considered as a treatise on the art of angling, or a beautiful pastoral, abounding in exquisite descriptions of rural scenery, in sentiments of the purest morality, and in unaffected love of the Creator and his works, has long been ranked among the most popular compositions in our language.—NICOLAS, SIR N. HARRIS, 1832-36-60, ed., Walton's Complete Angler.

Its simplicity, its sweetness, its natural grace, and happy intermixture of graver strains with the precepts of angling, have rendered this book deservedly popular, and a model which one of the most famous among our late philosophers, and a successful disciple of Isaac Walton in his favorite art, has condescended to imitate. —HALLAM, HENRY, 1837-39, Introduction to the Literature of Europe, pt. iv, ch. vii.

Will be recognized by every student of English literature as one of the most precious gems in the language.—BETHUNE, GEORGE W., 1848, ed., Walton's Complete Angler, Advertisement.

A London linen-draper writes a treatise on Angling, with no other thought, perhaps, than to teach an angler's subtle craft, but infusing into his art so much of Christian meekness, so deep a feeling for the beauties of earth and sky, such rational loyalty to womanhood, and such simple, child-like love of song, the songs of bird, of milk-maid, and of minstrel, that this little book on fishing has earned its life of two hundred years already, outliving many a more ambitious book, and Izaak Walton has a place of honour amid British authors.—REED, HENRY, 1855, Lectures on English Literature, p. 31.

I am glad to remember that there is such a book in our libraries, even if I understand very little of it, because it is one of the links between the life of the woods and streams and the life of the study, which it would be a great misfortune for us to lose.—MAURICE, FREDERICK

DENISON, 1856-74, The Friendship of Books and Other Lectures, ed. Hughes, p. 18.

When I would be quiet and go angling it is my custom to carry in my wallet thy pretty book, "The Compleat Angler." Here, methinks, if I find not trout I shall find content, and good company, and sweet songs, fair milkmaids, and country mirth. —LANG, ANDREW, 1886, Letters to Dead Authors, p. 86.

There are two books which have a place by themselves and side by side in our literature,—Walton's "Complete Angler" and White's "Natural History of Selborne;" and they are books, too, which have secured immortality without showing any tincture of imagination or of constructive faculty, in the gift of one or the other of which that distinction commonly lies. They neither stimulate thought nor stir any passionate emotion. If they make us wiser it is indirectly and without attempting it, by making us more cheerful. The purely literary charm of neither of them will alone authorize the place they hold so securely, though, as respects the "Angler," this charm must be taken more largely into account. They cannot be called popular, because they attract only a limited number of readers, but that number is kept full by new recruits in every generation; and they have survived every peril to which editing could expose them, even the crowning one of illustration. They have this in common, that those who love them find themselves growing more and more to love the authors of them, too. Theirs is an immortality of affection, perhaps the most desirable, as it is the rarest, of all.— LOWELL, JAMES RUSSELL, 1889, ·Walton's Complete Angler, Introduction.

His book holds spicy place among ranks of books, as lavender keeps fresh odor among stores of linen. It is worth any man's dalliance with the fishing-craft to make him receptive to the simplicities and limpidities of Walton's "Angler." I am tempted to say of him again, what I have said of him before in other connection:— very few fine writers of our time could make a better book on such a subject today, with all the added information and all the practice of the newspaper columns.— MITCHELL, DONALD G., 1890, English Lands Letters and Kings, From Elizabeth to Anne, p. 112.

Unquestionably, "Old Izaak," 'as his followers delight to call him, has won the regard and reverence of many generations of anglers throughout the world, not so much because of the literary merit of his book, though that is great, as because of the influence of that rare, restful, humanizing spirit which so largely pervades it. It is for this that the "Complete Angler" occupies, and will, in all likelihood, continue to do so for many and many a day to come, a unique place among the best of our English literature. To all lovers of angling, at any rate, it will never cease to be a classic or to body forth the delightfully unalloyed personality of the writer. Of course, few learners have consulted the book for practical guidance. —CARGILL, ALEXANDER, 1893, *Izaak Walton, Scribner's Magazine, vol.* 14, *p.* 275.

And thou, homely little brown thing with worn leaves, yet more precious to me than all jewels of the earth—come, let me take thee from thy self and hold thee lovingly in my hands and press thee tenderly to this aged and slow-pulsing heart of mine! Dost thou remember how I found thee half a century ago all tumbled in a lot of paltry trash? Did I not joyously possess thee for a sixpence, and have I not cherished thee full sweetly all these years? My Walton, soon must we part forever; when I am gone say unto him who next shall have thee to his own that with his latest breath an old man blessed thee!—FIELD, EUGENE, 1895, *The Love Affairs of a Bibliomaniac, p.* 89.

Walton's "Angler," 1653, first edition. Rev. J. Brand (1807), £3, 3s. (fine copy). Hunter (1813), £7, 10s. Utterson (1852), £11, 15s. Beckford (1883), fine copy, in green morocco, £87—Bain. Gibson-Craig (1887), £195 (morocco). Gibson-Craig (1888), £23 (imperfect, sold with all faults). G. Wood (Sotheby, 1891), £310 (clean, in original sheepskin). Sotheby (December 1895), £415.— WHEATLEY, HENRY B., 1898, *Prices of Books, p.* 247.

LIVES

He talked of Isaac Walton's "Lives," which was one of his most favourite books. Dr. Donne's Life, he said, was the most perfect of them.—BOSWELL, JAMES, 1790, *Life of Dr. Samuel Johnson.*

Izaac Walton, adorned with a guileless simplicity of manners, claims from every good man the tribute of applause. It was his ambition to commend to the reverence of posterity the merits of those excellent persons, whose comprehensive learning and exalted piety will ever endear them in our memories.—ZOUCH, THOMAS, 1796, *Some Account of the Life and Writings of Izaak Walton.*

There are no colours in the fairest sky,
So fair as these. The feather, whence the pen
Was shaped that traced the lives of these good men,
Dropped from an Angel's wing. With moistened eye
We read of faith and purest charity
In Statesman, Priest, and humble Citizen:
Oh could we copy their mild virtues, then
What joy to live, what blessedness to die!
Methinks their very names shine still and bright;
Apart—like glow-worms on a summer night;
Or lonely tapers when from far they fling
A guiding ray; or seen—like stars on high,
Satellites burning in a lucid ring
Around meek Walton's heavenly memory.
—WORDSWORTH, WILLIAM, 1821–22, *Ecclesiastical Sonnets, Part* iii, v.

His life of Dr. Donne, the satirist and theologian, contains an account of a vision (the apparition of a beloved wife in England passing before the waking eyes of her husband in Paris) which both for the clearness of the narration and the undoubted authenticity of the event, is among the most interesting that is to be found in the long catalogue of supernatural visitations. — MITFORD, MARY RUSSELL, 1851, *Recollections of a Literary Life, p.* 203.

The life of the "learned and judicious" Mr. Richard Hooker, by Izaak Walton, is one of the most perfect biographies of its kind in literature. But it is biography on its knees; and though it contains some exquisite touches of characterization, it does not, perhaps, convey an adequate impression of the energy and enlargement of the soul whose meekness it so tenderly and reverentially portrays. The individuality of the writer is blended with that of his subject, and much of his representation of Hooker is an unconscious idealization of himself. The intellectual limitations of Walton are felt even while we are most charmed by the sweetness of his spirit, and the mind of the greatest thinker the Church of England has produced is not reflected on the page which celebrates his virtues.—WHIPPLE, EDWIN P., 1859-68, *The Literature of the Age of Elizabeth*, p. 340.

As a biographer, again, Walton was an innovator. The five short lives which he published, though pale by the side of such work in biography as the end of the eighteenth century introduced, are yet notable as among the earliest which aim at giving us a vivid portrait of the man, instead of a discreet and conventional testimonial. It is to Walton, too, that we owe the idea of illustrating and developing biography by means of correspondence. Without doubt his incorrigible optimism entered into his study of the character of his friends, and it is no part of his inexperience as a portrait-painter that he mixes his colours with so much rosewater. He saw his distinguished acquaintances in that light; he saw them pure, radiant, and stately beyond a mortal guise, and he could not be true to himself unless he gave them the superhuman graces at which we may now smile a little. We sometimes feel that the stiffness of the biographical portrait is irksome to him. But here, as elsewhere, the artist is true to himself.—GOSSE, EDMUND, 1893, *English Prose, ed. Craik, vol. II, p. 341.*

GENERAL

Izaak Walton hallows any page in which his reverend name appears. — LAMB, CHARLES, 1816, *Letter to Wordsworth, Letters, ed. Ainger, vol. I, p. 304.*

Not many English authors have possessed a more attractive or strictly idiomatic style, not many have exhibited a wider variety of expression, than Izaak Walton, but Walton had no classical learning.—MARSH, GEORGE P., 1859, *Lectures on the English Language, First Series,* p. 83.

Few English prose writers again are better known than Izaak Walton, though it might be difficult to prove that in a matter of pure literature he stands very high. The engaging character of his subjects, and the still more engaging display of his own temper and mode of thought which he makes in almost every sentence, both of his "Complete Angler" and of his hardly less known "Lives," account for the survival and constant popularity of books which are neither above nor below the better work of their time in literary form. —SAINTSBURY, GEORGE, 1887, *History of Elizabethan Literature, p. 441.*

He had the purest and the most innocent of minds, he was the master of a style as bright, as sweet, as refreshing and delightful, as fine clean home-spun some time in lavender; he called himself an angler, and he believed in the description with a cordial simplicity whose appeal is more persuasive now than ever. But he was nothing if not the citizen afield—the cockney aweary of Bow Bells and rejoicing in "the sights and sounds of the open landscape."—HENLEY, WILLIAM ERNEST, 1890, *Essays and Reviews, p. 110.*

While thought of thee to men is yet
A sylvan playfellow,
Ne'er by thy marble they forget
In pious cheer to go.
As air falls, the prayer falls
O'er kingly Winchester:
O hush thee, O hush thee! heart innocent
   and dear.

—GUINEY, LOUISE IMOGEN, 1893, *For Izaak Walton, A Roadside Harp, p. 28.*

John Oldham

1653-1683

Born in England; educated at Oxford, where he won distinction by his proficiency in Latin and Greek, and by his English poetry. Want of means forced him to leave the university in 1674, and he soon secured employment as an usher at the free school in Croydon, Surrey. The first of his published poems was a Pindaric ode, on the death of his friend, Richard Morwent; it is rich in comparisons, and shows a tenderness in strong contrast with the fierce satire of his later works. He continued to cultivate poetry as a relief from the drudgery of "beating Greek and Latin for his life," as he describes it; and some of his MS. poems attracted the notice of the reigning London wits, sir Charles Sedley, the earl of Dorset, and the earl of Rochester, who paid him a visit at Croydon. By their influence he was made tutor to the sons of sir Edward Thurlow, with whom he lived till 1680. At this time he was engaged upon his "Satires upon the Jesuits," which appeared in 1679, when the excitement in regard to the so-called "Popish plot" was at its height. They are full of bitterness and Protestant rancor, and gained for Oldham a high reputation. —PECK, HARRY THURSTON, 1898. ed., *The International Cyclopædia, vol.* x, *p.* 756.

PERSONAL

His person was tall and thin, which was much owing to a consumptive complaint, but was greatly increased by study; his face was long, his nose prominent, his aspect unpromising, but satire was in his eye.—THOMPSON, EDWARD, 1770, *The Compositions in Prose and Verse of Mr. John Oldham, to which are added Memoirs of his Life.*

GENERAL

Farewell, too little and too lately known,
Whom I began to think and call my own;
For sure our Souls were near ally'd; and thine
Cast in the same Poetick mould with mine.
One common Note on either Lyre did strike,
And Knaves and Fools we both abhorr'd alike;
. . . .
Thy generous fruits, though gather'd e're their prime
Still shew'd a quickness; and maturing time
But mellows what we write to the dull sweets of Rhime.
Once more, hail and farewel; farewel you young,
But ah! too short, *Marcellus* of our Tongue;
Thy Brows with Ivy, and with Laurels bound;
But Fate and gloomy Night encompass thee around.
—DRYDEN, JOHN, 1684, *To the Memory of Mr. Oldham.*

Inspir'd above, and could command each Passion,
Had all the Wit without the Affectation.
A Calm of Nature still possest his Soul,
No canker'd envy did his Breast controul:
Modest as Virgins that have never known
The jilting Breeding of the nauseous Town;
And easie as his Numbers that sublime
His lofty Strains, and beautifie his Rhime.
—D'URFEY, THOMAS, 1684, *On Mr. John Oldham.*

Oldham is a very indelicate writer: he has strong rage, but it is too much like Billingsgate.—POPE, ALEXANDER, 1728–30, *Spence's Anecdotes, ed. Singer, p.* 14.

He appears to have been no enemy to the fashionable vices of this reign; and as he was of a very different turn from his father, the character of the old parson, at the end of his works, is supposed to have been designed for him. It is perhaps the most extravagant caricature that ever was drawn, and is incomparably more *outré* than the Menalcas of Bruyere.—GRANGER, JAMES, 1769–1824, *Biographical History of England, vol.* v, *p.* 251.

He is spirited and pointed; but his versification is too negligent, and his subjects temporary.—HALLAM, HENRY, 1837–39, *Introduction to the Literature of Europe, pt.* iv, *ch.* v, *par.* 47.

I have been looking over the poems of Oldham, which are now little read. I have never seen the book in any private library in this country; and yet a poet whom Dryden warmly commended, and from whom Pope and Swift and Johnson did not disdain to borrow, cannot be entirely unworthy of attention in an age which has produced so many eminent poets as that in which we live. . . . Although Oldham in his lifetime achieved his fame by what he wrote as a satirist, his principal talent as a poet was not for satire. His odes show that he possessed a genuine poetic enthusiasm, which appears through all his negligence of versification and diction, and often finds expression in majestic imagery and flowing numbers. He is no artist in his vocation. Dryden is our witness that he had not well learned "the numbers of his native tongue." He has none of those happy turns of thought and expression which the practiced and expert author attains by skilful search or resolute waiting: what he has, came to him in the glow of rapid composition; and these so often that few poets can boast of so illustrious a train of imitators. His rhymes are marvellously bad: indeed, it is often amusing to see what distant resemblances of sound he is content to accept as substitutes for rhymes.—BRYANT, WILLIAM CULLEN, 1872, *Oldham's Poems, Prose Writings, vol.* I, *pp.* 115, 127.

The satires of Oldham are distressing to read; the author has no belief in the better part of human nature; he is cynical and bitter to the extreme, and he strikes, not for a party, like Marvell, but wildly, against the world. Oldham is the Ajax among our satirists, and his own contemporaries, not easily moved by personal characteristics, were touched by his strange cold frenzy, his honourable isolation, and his early death. Dryden seems to have been genuinely distressed at the fate of a young man whose personal acquaintance he had but lately formed, and whose work had a character particularly attractive to him. Oldham's versification is better than that of Marvell, in his satires, but still rugged; as Dryden observed, his prosody needed mellowing.— GOSSE, EDMUND, 1888, *A History of Eighteenth Century Literature*, 1660–1780, *p.* 30.

The contemporary of Dryden who approached him most nearly in satiric force, and, generally speaking, in the borderland between poetry and prose, was John Oldham. . . . Oldham's talent, depending upon masculine sense and vigour of expression rather than upon the more ethereal graces of poetry, was of the kind to expand and mellow by age and practice. Had he lived longer he would undoubtedly have left a name conspicuous in English literature. As it is, he can only be regarded as a bright satellite revolving at a respectful distance around the all-illumining orb of Dryden. — GARNETT, RICHARD, 1895, *The Age of Dryden, pp.* 42, 46.

Oldham's productions deserve more notice than they have received. Their own-original power is notable. Pope, and perhaps other of our chief eighteenth-century poets, were under important literary obligations to their author. . . . Whether or no the Pindaric dedicated by Oldham "to the memory of my dear friend, Mr. Charles Morwent," in date of composition preceded his most celebrated "Satires," it must be described as the most finished product of his genius, and as entitled to no mean place in English "In Memoriam" poetry. Cowley is evidently the master followed in this ode. . . . While in "original" satire Oldham cannot be said to have reached the length to which he was desirous of climbing, he is memorable in our poetic literature as one of the predecessors of Pope in the "imitative" or adapting species of satirical and didactic verse. — WARD, ADOLPHUS WILLIAM, 1895, *Dictionary of National Biography, vol.* XLII, *p.* 109.

John Owen
1616–1683

John Owen, Puritan, born at Stadhampton vicarage, Oxfordshire, in 1616, took his B. A. in 1631 from Queen's College, Oxford, and in 1637 was driven from Oxford by dislike to Laud's statues. Some years he spent as private chaplain; then in 1642 he removed to London, and published "The Display of Arminianism," a work for which he was rewarded with the living of Fordham in Essex. In 1646 he removed to Coggeshall, and showed his preference for Independency over Presbyterianism. Cromwell carried him in 1649 as his chaplain to Ireland, where he regulated the affairs of Trinity College. Next year (1650) he went with Cromwell to Scotland. In 1651–52 he became dean of Christ Church and vice-chancellor of Oxford University. Here he wrote his "Diatriba de Divina Justita," his "Doctrine of the Saints' Perseverance," his "Vindiciæ Evangelicæ," and his "Mortification of Sin in Believers." He was one of the Friers appointed to purge the church of scandalous ministers. He opposed the giving the crown to the Protector, and the year after Cromwell's death he was ejected from his deanery. He purchased an estate at Stadham, and formed a congregation. The writings of this period are "Communion with God," "On the Divine Original of the Scriptures," "Theologoumena," and a diatribe against Walton's "Polyglot." These were followed by works on "Indwelling Sin," on the 130th Psalm, and on the Epistle to the Hebrews, the last his greatest work. In 1673 he became pastor in Leadenhall Street. Late publications were "Concerning the Holy Spirit" (1674), "Justification by Faith" (1677), and "Christologia." He wrote replies to a Franciscan and to Bishop Parker, sustained controversies with Sherlock and Stillingfleet, and to the end preached and wrote incessantly. He died 24th August 1683. See Orme's "Memoirs" (1820), and "Life" by Thomson, prefixed to Goold's edition of Owen's works (1850-55).—PATRICK AND GROOME, *eds.*, 1897, *Chambers's Biographical Dictionary, p.* 712.

PERSONAL

Was a person well skill'd in the tongues, rabinical learning, Jewish rites and customs; that he had a great command of his English pen, and was one of the most genteel and fairest writers, who have appeared against the Church of England, as handling his adversaries with far more civil, decent and temperate language than many of his fiery brethren, and by confining himself wholly to the cause without the unbecoming mixture of personal slanders and reflection.—WOOD, ANTHONY, 1691–1721, *Athenæ Oxonienses, vol.* II, *f.* 740.

On the 4th September a vast funeral procession, including the carriages of sixty-seven noblemen and gentlemen, with long trains of mourning coaches and horsemen, took the road to Finsbury; and there in a new burying-ground, within a few paces of Goodwin's grave, and near the spot where, five years later, John Bunyan was interred, they laid the dust of Dr. Owen.—HAMILTON, JAMES, 1857–59, *ed., Our Christian Classics, vol.* II, *p.* 9.

GENERAL

This book ["Exposition"] bears the same rank, and has the same relation to the study of divinity, which the "Principia" of Sir Isaac Newton bears to the true system of the world in the study of natural philosophy; and it is of equal importance to all young divines which that great man's work is to young philosophers. . . . I am ashamed of my countrymen for their ignorance of this incomparable work,—perhaps the very *greatest* of the *kind* that ever was written by a British divine; and it now lies buried in dust amidst the lumber of a bookseller's garret, whilst a thousand volumes of wretched trash in divinity, with their pompous bindings, stand as monuments of human folly in our bookcases and libraries.—RYLAND, JOHN, 1781, *ed. Cotton Mather's Student and Preacher, Select Library for a Student of Divinity.*

If the theological student should part with his coat or his bed to procure the works of Howe, he that would not sell his shirt to procure those of John Owen, and especially his "Exposition," of which every sentence is precious, shews too much regard to his body, and too little for his immortal mind.—BOGUE AND BENNETT, 1809–12, *History of Dissenters, from the Revolution in* 1688 *to the year* 1808.

Spiritual life is the vital energy which pervades the morality and the practice recommended by Owen. It is not the abstraction of a mystical devotion, like that of Fenelon or Law; nor is it the enthusiastic raptures of a Zinzendorf; but the evangelical piety of Paul and the heavenly affection of John. For every practice, mortification, and feeling, Owen assigns a satisfactory, because a scriptural, reason. The service which he recommends is uniformly a reasonable service; and to every required exertion he brings an adequate and constraining motive. In examining the practical writings of such men as Hall and Taylor and Tillotson, we miss the rich vein of evangelical sentiment and that constant reference to the living principle of Christianity which are never lost sight of in Owen. They abound in excellent directions, in rich materials for self-examination and self-goverment; but they do not state with sufficient accuracy the connexion between gracious influence and its practical results, from which all that is excellent in human conduct must proceed. They appear as the anatomists of the skin and the extremities: Owen is the anatomist of the heart. He dissects it with remarkable sagacity, tracing out its course and turnings in every path that leads from integrity, and marking the almost imperceptible steps which conduct to atrocious sins.—ORME, WILLIAM, 1820, *Memoirs of the Life, Writings and Religious Connections of John Owen.*

His devotional, and practical, and expository works are an invaluable treasure of divinity. . . . His writings are eminently spiritual, devotional, and edifying. He is full of Biblical learning, sound exposition of doctrine, acuteness, and information. His controversial writings against the Socinians and Papists, on the question of Justification, on the Jewish Questions, Sabbath, &c., are valuable and important. There is hardly any modern controversy that he has not well digested and furnished matter for the defence of the truth. He gives expanded and rich views of the fulness of the gospel.—BICKERSTETH, EDWARD, 1844, *The Christian Student, pp.* 268, 269.

The publication and sale of two complete editions of his works in upwards of twenty volumes, and during one generation, attests the estimate in which his writings are held by general readers. It may be added that theologically Owen is more Calvinistic than Calvin, and that he was one of the first in England to teach the doctrine of a restricted Atonement.— ANGUS, JOSEPH, 1865, *The Handbook of English Literature, p.* 431.

Owen was a man of great learning, and his industry was prodigious. His works fill twenty-four volumes large octavo. The two of most enduring character are the Commentary on the Hebrews, and the work on the Holy Spirit. . . . Owen did not cultivate the graces of style, but there is always robustness and strength in his argument. He discussed whatever subject he undertook as if he intended to have nothing to be said by those who should come after him. With all the progress made since his time in the science of criticism and exegesis, no prudent commentator, even now, would undertake

to expound the Epistle to the Hebrews without a constant reference to the work of Owen. In his writings of a practical character, he had a peculiarity, beyond all the other great writers of his school, of making his pious emotion dependent in all cases upon some solid scriptural basis. —HART, JOHN S., 1872, *A Manual of English Literature, p.* 178.

Owen ranks with Baxter and Howe among the most eminent of puritan divines. A trenchant controversialist, he distinguished himself no less by temperateness of tone than by vigour of polemic. His learning was vast, various, and profound, and his mastery of calvinistic theology complete. On the other hand, his style is somewhat tortuous and his method unduly discursive, so that his works are often tedious reading.—RIGG, J. M., 1895, *Dictionary of National Biography, vol.* XLII, *p.* 427.

Algernon Sidney

1622–1682

Born at Penshurst, Kent, England, about 1622: beheaded at London, Dec. 7, 1683. An English politician and patriot, younger son of the second Earl of Leicester. He served in the Parliamentary army, being wounded at Marston in 1644; was in 1645 elected to Parliament, where he took rank as one of the leaders of the Independents; became governor of Dublin and lieutenant-general of horse in Ireland 1646; became councilor of state in 1659; was peace commissioner between Denmark and Sweden 1659–60; lived on the Continent after the Restoration until 1677; and, being known to be a supporter of Monmouth, was arrested on the discovery of the Rye House Plot (with which he had no connection) in June, 1683, and condemned to death for high treason. He wrote "Discourses Concerning Government" (1698), etc.—SMITH, BENJAMIN E., 1894–97, *The Century Cyclopedia of Names, p.* 930.

PERSONAL

All who come from Paris commend Algernon for a huge deal of wit and much sweetness of nature.—LEICESTER, COUNTESS OF, 1636, *Letter, Nov.* 10.

When he came on the scaffold, instead of a speech, he told them onely that he had made his peace with God, that he came not thither to talk, but to die; put a paper into the sheriff's hand, and another into a friend's, sayd one prayer as short as a grace, laid down his neck, and bid the executioner do his office.—EVELYN, JOHN, 1683, *Diary, Dec.* 5.

A man of the most extraordinary courage—a steady man even to obstinacy— sincere, but of a rough and boisterous temper that could not bear contradiction. He seemed to be a Christian, but in a

peculiar form of his own; he thought it was to be like a divine philosophy in the mind; but he was against all public worship and everything that looked like a church. He was stiff to all republican principles, and such an enemy to everything that looked like monarchy, that he set himself in a high opposition against Cromwell when he was made protector. He had studied the history of government in all its branches beyond any man I ever knew. . . . Sidney had a particular way of insinuating himself into people that would hearken to his notions, and not contradict him.—BURNET, GILBERT, 1715– 34, *History of My Own Time.*

The production of papers, containing speculative opinions upon government and liberty, written long before, and perhaps never even intended to be published, together with the use made of those papers, in considering them as a substitute for the second witness to the overt act, exhibited such a compound of wickedness and nonsense as is hardly to be paralleled in the history of juridical tyranny. But the validity of pretences was little attended to at that time, in the case of a person whom the court had devoted to destruction, and upon evidence such as has been stated was this great and excellent man condemned to die.—Fox, Charles James, 1806? *A History of the Early Part of the Reign of James II.*

The manifest iniquity of this sentence upon Algernon Sidney, as well as the high courage he displayed throughout these last scenes of his life, have inspired a sort of enthusiasm for his name, which neither what we know of his story, nor the opinion of his contemporaries, seems altogether to warrant. The crown of martyrdom should be suffered perhaps to exalt every virtue, and efface every defect, in patriots, as it has often done in saints. In the faithful mirror of history Sidney may lose something of this lustre. He possessed no doubt a powerful, active, and undaunted mind, stored with extensive reading on the topics in which he delighted. But having proposed one only object for his political conduct, the establishment of a republic in England, his pride and inflexibility, though they gave a dignity to his character, rendered his views narrower and his temper unaccommodating.—Hallam, Henry, 1827–41, *The Constitutional History of England,* vol, ii, ch. xii.

Errors may well be passed over in silence and his faults forgotten, where so much remains to be admired and venerated. One of the noblest martyrs of that liberty which the progress of civilization and the developments of time seem to point out as the heritage of the Anglo-Saxon race. His were virtues which deserve immortality, and his a name which will go down with honor to remote generations of men. The man dies, the principles he cherished are immortal. That cause for which Sidney suffered, proscribed in his day, has been gloriously vindicated in ours. The doctrines of resistance to oppression — of popular sovereignty—of the inalienable right of

mankind to intellectual and moral, to civil and religious freedom—of which he was the champion in life, and in death the martyr, have become the foundation and corner stone of those democratic institutions which since his day have sprung up in the New World. No nobler cenotaph than the free institutions of America can be reared to the memory of the dust which sleeps in its ancestral vault at Penshurst. No more glorious epitaph can be written for the patriot martyr than that which so eloquently speaks in the silent workings of those institutions. Surely while they endure, and while the doctrines which Sidney taught shall continue to be regarded as the elementary truths of our political creed, it may with truth be said that the noble blood shed in their defence on Tower Hill, has not been spilled in vain.—Van Santvoord, G., 1851, *Life of Algernon Sidney, p.* 333.

He lived through most critical times. He was an actor in events which affected the whole of Europe. He was a keen and shrewd observer of men and characters. He was a student and an author. He had a remarkable individuality. His friends and his enemies—he had most of the latter—alike bear witness to the power he exercised over the minds of all with whom he was brought into contact. There is, however, always something strange in the way they speak of him. The affection of his friends is but loving admiration; the opposition of his enemies is always admiring fear. He is a noble-minded, hard-working patriot, and a pure-souled and thoroughly honourable man of the world. He died under an unjust sentence, at perhaps the darkest period of our English history; but what gives him a claim on our interest and sympathy to a far greater extent is the fact of his suffering injustice throughout an almost blameless life. —Blackburne, Gertrude M. Ireland, 1884, *Algernon Sidney, a Review, p.* 1.

GENERAL

They ["Discourses"] are admirably written, and contain great historical knowledge and a remarkable propriety of diction; so that his name, in my opinion, ought to be much higher established in the temple of literature than I have hitherto found it placed.—Boyle, John (Lord Orrery), 1751, *Remarks on the Life and Writings of Dr. Jonathan Swift.*

Algernon Sidney created the language of politics; his "Discourses upon Government" have grown obsolete. . . . The revolution of 1688 arose from the scaffold of Sidney, with the steam of the blood of the holocaust! This bloody dew is now falling, and the England of 1688 is disappearing.—CHATEAUBRIAND, FRANÇOIS RENÉ, VICOMTE DE, 1837, *Sketches of English Literature, vol.* II, *pp.* 197, 198.

In all the discourse of Algernon Sidney upon Government we see constant indications of a rooted dislike to monarchy and ardent love of Democracy; but not a sentence can we find that shows the illustrious author to have regarded the manner in which the people were represented as of any importance.—BROUGHAM, HENRY LORD, 1840-44, *Political Philosophy, pt.* iii, *chap.* xii.

Both in his diplomatic mission, and in his labours on the legislative council, he soon became enrolled among the intellectual minority who lead instead of follow, and organize instead of assent. When he placed pen to paper and logically thought out his speculations, his style, though somewhat heavy, was clear, solid, and vigorous—all he wrote bore the impress of a well-read mind, a mind that was as much accustomed to profound reflection as to practical action.—EWALD, ALEXANDER CHARLES, 1873, *The Life and Times of Hon. Algernon Sydney, vol.* II, *pp.* 334, 335.

More than any other among the distinguished historical personages of the seventeenth century, Algernon Sidney, in point of character and conduct, will continue to have his detractors and admirers. The published letters in the different editions of the Sidney papers serve only to confirm his partisans in their admiration of his consistency of principle as an enemy of monarchical government—even to the extent of deprecating the personal rule of Cromwell—and his enemies in their reprehension of the factious leader who could waste his splendid energies in caballing with France and Holland for the establishment of a republic in England. The most able and eminent of the knot of revolutionary patriots to which he belonged, he was also the most uncompromising and most provokingly obstinate.— SCOONES, W. BAPTISTE, 1880, *Four Centuries of English Letters, p.* 118.

His writings are "Discourses concerning Government," written at Frascati in 1663, but first published in 1698, and letters and memoirs respectively printed in 1742 and 1751. In 1884 a treatise on "Love" was first published from Algernon Sydney's manuscript. Sydney is very diffuse; but the alteration which had come over prose may well be noted by comparing his republican discourses with the totally unreadable reams on the same subject which Harrington had produced in the preceding generation. —GOSSE, EDMUND, 1888, *A History of Eighteenth Century Literature,* 1660-1780, *p.* 81.

The style precisely corresponds to the author's character, haughty, fiery, and arrogant; but thrilling with conviction, and meriting the highest praise as a specimen of masculine, nervous, and at the same time polished English. Much additional zest is imparted to the author's argument by his continual strokes at the political abuses and the unworthy characters of his own day, from Charles II. downwards. He had the advantage of writing under the stimulus of fiery indignation kindled and maintained by the actual existence of a tyranny. He is thus never tame, and depicts himself as one of that remarkable class of men of whom Alfieri is perhaps the most characteristic type—aristocrats by temperament, champions of democracy by intellectual conviction. Although the controversy in which he engaged now belongs entirely to the past, he is often modern in sentiment as well as in style; sometimes we are reminded of Shelley, at other times, and more frequently, of Landor.—GARNETT, RICHARD, 1895, *The Age of Dryden, p.* 171.

Sidney's chief work, the "Discourses concerning Government," was first printed by Toland or Littlebury in 1698. This is an answer to Filmer's "Patriarcha," which was first published in 1680; and the few allusions to contemporary politics in Sidney's book show that a great part of it was written about that year. Though tedious from its extreme length and from following too closely in Filmer's footsteps, it contains much vigorous writing, and shows wide reading.—FIRTH, C. H., 1899, *Dictionary of National Biography, vol.* LII, *p.* 209.

Roger Williams

1604?-1683

A famous clergyman, minister at Salem, Massachusetts, but banished from the Massachusetts Bay colony in 1635 on account of his views upon religious liberty. In 1636 he founded the city of Providence, and was the chief citizen of the Rhode Island colony until his death. He was the first upholder of the doctrine of liberty of conscience in its entirety, and actively sustained his theories in many controversial works. "Key Into the Languages of America;" "The Bloudy Tenent of Persecution for Cause of Conscience;" "The Bloudy Tenent Yet More Bloudy by Mr. Cotton's Endeavour to wash it white in the Bloud of the Lambe;" "Mr. Cotton's Letter Lately Printed, Examined and Answered;" "George Fox Digg'd Out of his Burrowes," include his principal works.—ADAMS, OSCAR FAY, 1897, *A Dictionary of American Authors, p.* 426.

PERSONAL

His history belongs to America rather than England; but we must not even thus casually mention his name, without an expression of respect and reverence, for he was one of the best men who ever set foot upon the new world,—a man of genius and of virtue, in whom enthusiasm took the happiest direction, and produced the best fruits. . . . If ever a Welsh Fuller should write the Worthies of Wales, Roger Williams will deserve, if not the first place, a place among the first, for he began the first civil government upon earth that gave equal liberty of conscience —SOUTHEY, ROBERT, 1813, *Quarterly Review, vol.* 10, *pp.* 107, 113.

Roger Williams asserted the great doctrine of intellectual liberty. . . . It became his glory to found a State upon that principle, and to stamp himself upon its rising institutions, in characters so deep that the impres has remained to the present day, and can never be erased without the total destruction of the work. . . . He was the first person in modern Christendom to establish civil government on the doctrine of the liberty of conscience, the equality of opinions before the law; and in its defence he was the harbinger of Milton, the precursor and the superior of Jeremy Taylor.—BANCROFT, GEORGE, 1834–74, *History of the United States, vol.* I.

We must not rehearse in detail the sequel of the story;—how, instead of a strict enforcement of the sentence, he was permitted in consideration of his health to remain in Salem through the winter, under an injunction "not to go about to draw others to his opinions;"—how, as soon as he was well enough, he renewed his work of agitation;—how the court of magistrates, finding their authority defied and their clemency (or what they thought was clemency) abused, attempted to put him on shipboard, that he might try what liberty there was for such agitation in England; how he escaped out of their hands, and went beyond their jurisdiction into the land of Narragansett, where he builded a city and devoutly named it Providence; how, notwithstanding the contempt with which Puritan statesmen in the other colonies regarded his experiment in the science of government, or as they thought no-government, the relations between him and them were always friendly;—how he grew wiser and gentler, though hardly less crotchetty, as he grew older;—how he kept company with the wild men of the woods, winning their confidence and love;—how his old age was honored;—how he died and was buried, leaving a name not unworthy the grateful and perpetual remembrance wherever there is perfect liberty for men to think, to speak their thoughts, and to worship in spirit and in truth.—BACON, LEONARD, 1877, *As to Roger Williams, The New Englander, vol.* 36, *p.* 23.

Rodger Williams, never in anything addicted to concealments, has put himself without reserve into his writings. There he still remains. There if anywhere we may get well acquainted with him. Searching for him along the two thousand printed pages upon which he has stamped his own portrait, we seem to see a very human and fallible man, with a large head, a warm heart, a healthy body, an eloquent and imprudent tongue; not a symmetrical person, poised, cool, accurate, circumspect; a man very anxious to be genuine and to get at the truth, but impatient of slow methods, trusting gallantly to his own institutions, easily deluded by his own hopes; an imaginative, sympathetic, affluent, impulsive man; an optimist; his master-passion benevolence; his mind clarifying itself slowly; never quite settled on all subjects in the universe; at almost every moment on the watch for some new idea about that time expected to heave in sight; never able by the ordinary means of intellectual stagnation to win for himself in his life-time the bastard glory of doctrinal consistency; professing many things by turn and nothing long, until at last, even in mid-life, he reached the moral altitude of being able to call himself only a Seeker—in which not ignoble creed he continued for the remainder of his days on earth. It must be confessed that there is even yet in the fame of Rodger Williams a singular vitality. While living in this world, it was his fate to be much talked about, as well as to disturb much the serenity of many excellent people; and the rumour of him still agitates and divides men. There are, in fact, some signs that his fame is now about to take out a new lease, and to build for itself a larger habitation. At any rate, the world, having at last nearly caught up with him, seems ready to vote—though with a peculiarly respectable minority in opposition —that Rodger Williams was after all a great man, one of the true heroes, seers, world-movers, of these latter ages.— TYLER, MOSES COIT, 1878, *A History of American Literature, vol.* I, *p.* 241.

GENERAL

His industry in every enterprise which he undertook was indefatigable. . . . He placed the highest estimate upon the value of time. "One grain of its inestimable sand," says he, "is worth a golden mountain." . . . His knowledge, especially in history and theology, appears to have been extensive, and his scholarship in the classic languages unusually varied and exact. As a writer, he had little time, and, it may be, little taste for the elegances of language.—GAMMELL, WILLIAM, 1844, *Life of Roger Williams, ch.* xv.

The "Bloody Tenent" is a noble work, full of brave heart and tenderness; a book of learning and piety,—the composition of a true, gentle nature.—DUYCKINCK, EVERT A. AND GEORGE L., 1855– 65–75, *Cyclopædia of American Literature*, ed. Simons, *vol.* I, *p.* 39.

Of his mental powers we have no means

of judging, except the respect and interest he awakened in those with whom he dwelt, and the writings he left. These are chiefly of a controversial nature, and on questions which have, in a great measure, lost their significance. The style, too, is involved, quaint, and often pedantic. The views, however, advocated even in his polemic discussions, are often in advance of his time, and the sentiments he professes are noble and progressive. Thus, "The Bloody Tenent" is an earnest plea with the clergy for toleration; and "A Hireling Ministry" presents bold and just arguments in support of free churches, and against an arbitrary system of tithes. In the Redwood Library, at Newport, is a copy of "George Fox digged out of his Burrows," a characteristic specimen of the theological hardihood of Williams, as exhibited in his controversy with the Quakers. But it is from his original force of character, and his loyalty to a great principle, that Roger Williams derives his claim to our admiration. His shades of opinion are comparatively unimportant; but the spirit in which he worked, suffered, and triumphed, enrols his name among the moral heroes and benefactors of the world.—TUCKERMAN, HENRY T., 1857, *Essays, Biographical and Critical, p.* 189.

Williams was an able, earnest, and successful pioneer in that great movement towards religious freedom which has characterized the history of the United States. But in justice to the Puritans it should be said that he was sometimes hasty, indiscreet, sensational; and that he lacked the self-control which should be shown by a great reformer, as well as the solid learning of the Puritan leaders.—RICHARDSON, CHARLES F., 1887, *American Literature*, 1607–1885, *vol.* I, *p.* 122.

Milton spoke of Williams as an extraordinary man and a noble confessor of religious liberty, who sought and found a safe refuge for the sacred ark of conscience. His associates in the new world described him in terms less exalted. Bradford calls him a man godly and zealous, having many precious parts, but very unsettled in judgment. Cotton Mather spoke of his having a windmill in his head; Sir William Martin and Hubbard both praised his zeal, but thought it overheated. Southey held his memory in "veneration," which seems hardly the word to apply to a man so profoundly contentious as Williams was. Lowell is substantially just to him when he writes, "He does not show himself a strong or a very wise man," though "charity and tolerance flow so noticeably from his pen that it is plain they were in his heart." Williams's place as a religious leader has perhaps been exaggerated by his eulogists. His views were not in advance of those of many of his contemporaries, his cardinal doctrine that "there is no other prudent Christian way of preserving peace in the world but by permission of different consciences" being scarcely more than a reaffirmation of John Smith's dictum of 1611 to the effect that Christ being the lawgiver of the conscience, the magistrates were not entitled to meddle with religious opinions. His mind had none of the roominess of Fuller's, or of the elevation of Milton's; but he certainly had a firm grip of the necessity of a principle of toleration, and he was one of the very first to make a serious effort to put that principle into practice. —SECCOMBE, THOMAS, 1900, *Dictionary of National Biography, vol.* XLI, *p.* 449.

Robert Leighton
1611–1684

Leighton (Robert), D.D., son of Alexander, b. in Edinburgh in 1611; grad. at the univ. of that city (1631), of which he became prin. in 1653; appointed bp. of Dunblane in 1661, in pursuit of the plan of Charles II. to Anglicize the Ch. of Scot.; appealed twice to the king to adopt milder measures in the attempted reform (1665 and 1669); accepted the archbishopric of Glasgow in 1670 upon conditions which were not fulfilled, and he resigned in 1673. Wrote "Sermons," "Prelectiones Theologicæ," "Commentary on the First Epistle of Peter," and "Posthumous Tracts," etc. D. June 26, 1684.—BARNARD AND GUYOT, eds., 1885, *Johnson's New General Cyclopaedia, vol.* I, *p.* 765.

PERSONAL

He had great quickness of parts, a lively apprehension, with a charming vivacity of thought and expression. He had the greatest command of the purest Latin that ever I knew in any man. He was a master both of Greek and Hebrew, and of the whole compass of theological learning, chiefly in the study of the Scriptures. But that which excelled all the rest was, he was possessed with the highest and noblest sense of divine things that I ever saw in any man. . . . He had so subdued the natural heat of his temper, that in a great variety of accidents, and in the course of twenty-two years' intimate conversation with him, I never observed the least sign of passion but upon one single occasion. . . . There was a visible tendency in all he said to raise his own mind, and those he conversed with, to serious reflections. He seemed to be in a perpetual meditation. . . . His preaching had a sublimity both of thought and expression in it. The grace and gravity of his pronunciation was such, that few heard him without a very sensible emotion: I am sure I never did.—BURNET, GILBERT, 1715–34, *History of my Own Time*

This excellent person is represented by Bishop Burnet as one of the most perfect characters of his own, or any other age. He was learned, eloquent, and devout; but his piety was the most unaffected in the world. His charity was comprehensive with respect to speculative opinions; but he could never overlook flagrant vices and corruptions in the professors of any religion. He was, for his singular merit, preferred to the bishopric of Dumblain, and afterward to the archbishopric of Glasgow. He had many enemies among the rigid Episcopalians, as he was strongly inclined to make some concessions to the Presbyterians, in order to an *accommodation.*—GRANGER, JAMES, 1769–1824, *Biographical History of England, vol.* III, *p.* 346.

He was, indeed, a man whom either church might be glad to claim. But the peculiarity of his position was, that he combined a sanctity equal to that of the strictest Covenanter or the strictest Episcopalian, with a liberality in his innermost thoughts equal to that of the widest Latitudinarian of the school of Jeremy Taylor or of Hoadley. Let us look at both these points more minutely. They both appear far more strongly in the records of his life and conversation than could be inferred from his published writings. There are few men whose character gives the impression of a more complete elevation both above the cares and the prejudice of the world—of a more entire detachment from earth.—STANLEY, ARTHUR PENRHYN, 1872, *Lectures on the History of the Church of Scotland, p. 121.*

As saint, author, and peacemaker, Leighton presents a combination of qualities which has called forth almost unrivalled tributes of admiration. Thomas à Kempis was one of his favourite books, and the "imitation of Christ," whose darling virtues he said were humility, meekness, and charity, was the business of his life. He shrank from every approach to ostentation, and so far from courting the riches and honours of the world he looked upon them with something of holy contempt. On accepting the bishopric he said, "One benefit at least will rise from it. I shall break that little idol of estimation my friends have for me, and which I have been so long sick of." Burnet never saw his temper ruffled but once during twenty-two years of close intimacy, and could not recollect having heard him say one idle word. When reminded of his former zeal for the national covenant, he replied, "When I was a child I spoke as a child," and when charged with apostatising from his father's principles, he meekly answered that a man was not bound to be of his father's opinions. He was habitually abstemious, kept frequent fasts, and often shut himself up in his room for prolonged periods of private devotion. Everything that he could spare was given to pious purposes, and he employed others as the agents of his charity that he might not get the credit of it.—SPROTT, THE REV. G. W., 1893, *Dictionary of National Biography, vol. XXXIII, p. 6.*

GENERAL

All his works are admirable, . . . full of holy simplicity, humility, and benevolent zeal.—WILLIAMS, EDWARD, 1800, *The Christian Preacher.*

Next to the inspired Scriptures,—yea, and as the vibration of that once struck hour remaining on the air, stands Leighton's Commentary on the first Epistle of Peter.—COLERIDGE, SAMUEL TAYLOR, 1809-16, *Omniana, ed. Ashe, p. 400.*

Perhaps there is no expository work in the English language equal altogether to the exposition of Peter. It is rich in evangelical sentiment and exalted devotion. The meaning is seldom missed, and often admirably illustrated. There is learning without its parade, theology divested of systematic stiffness, and eloquence in a beautiful flow of unaffected language and appropriate imagery. To say more would be unbecoming, and less could not be said with justice.—ORME, WILLIAM, 1824, *Bibliotheca Biblica.*

Leighton's praise is in all the churches. . . . He is one of the very first divines of the British Church; and his writings breathe throughout the spirit of devotion: they are distinguished by a noble strain of deep piety, a most humble, heavenly, and loving spirit, an elegant mind, and a scriptural standard of evangelical doctrine.—BICKERSTETH, EDWARD, 1844, *The Christian Student.*

That very remarkable work [on First Peter] teaches a singularly pure and complete theology—a theology thoroughly evangelical, in the true sense of that often abused epithet, being equally free from Legalism on the one hand and Antinomianism on the other; in a spirit of enlightened and affectionate devotion, love to the brotherhood, and charity to all men, and in a style which, though very unequal, indicates in its general structure a familiarity with the classic models of antiquity; and in occasional expressions is in the highest degree felicitous and beautiful. As a Biblical expositor, Leighton was above his own age, and as a theologian and practical writer few have equalled, still fewer surpassed him, either before or since his time. . . . Laboring under more than the ordinary disadvantages of posthumous publications, through the extreme slovenliness with which they, with few exceptions, were in the first instance edited, his works are eminently fitted to form the student of theology to sound views and a right spirit, and to minister to the instruction and delight of the private Christian—possessing in large measure and rare union those qualities which must endear them to every Christian mind, however uncultured, and those which are fitted to afford high gratification to them in whom the knowledge and love of evangelical truth are connected with literary attainment and polished taste.—BROWN, JOHN, 1849, *Expository Discourses on the First Epistle of Peter.*

A man whose apostolic gentleness of conduct endeared him deeply to his contemporaries, and whose devoutly meditative eloquence made him, in our own day, the bosom-oracle of Coleridge.—SPALDING, WILLIAM, 1852–82, *A History of English Literature, p.* 290.

It would not be good, perhaps, to read nothing but Leighton, for he lacks manliness, and would not fit us for the sterner side of Christian duty; but in an age like ours, when all is stir and bustle and push, his books furnish a first-rate alterative, and help to restore the devotional to its true place in the life of the soul.—TAYLOR, WILLIAM M., 1887, *The Scottish Pulpit, p.* 132.

Robert Leighton is as a March swallow among Protestant theologians. . . . Above all things a spiritual divine, he has yet the gift of tongues to put his wisdom before the world in decent and profitable shape. It is but a lax prose, not ordered into periods and paragraphs, but ebbing and flowing comment-wise, as the exigencies of a text require it. The phrase is strong and sweet, a little careless perhaps, as of one disregarding the conventions of deliberate art. But at its best it rises into passages of extraordinary height, glowing with the rich fire of jewels, ringing with the harmonies of restrained music. Nor do such passages affect one as conscious rhetoric; they are not merely purple patches; every elevation of style corresponds directly to some moment of intensity or ecstasy in the course of the preacher's thought. Only Leighton lived in an age when sermons might still be literature; before the eighteenth century had ruled that colour and imagination were out of place in the pulpit. In him, as in Jeremy Taylor or in Donne, dignity of speech is not the first consideration; they are not so far removed, Latinised though they be, from the nervous homespun of Latimer.—CHAMBERS, EDMUND K., 1893, *English Prose, ed. Craik, vol.* II, *p.* 489.

Wentworth Dillon

Earl of Roscommon

1633?–1684

Wentworth Dillon, Earl of Roscommon, born about 1633, nephew and godson to the Earl of Strafford. He was at the Protestant College at Caen when, by the death of his father, he became Earl of Roscommon, at the age of ten. He remained abroad, travelled in Italy till the Restoration, when he came in with the king, became captain of the band of Pensioners, took for a time to gambling, married, indulged his taste in literature, strongly under the French influence, and had a project for an English academy like that of France. He translated into verse Horace's "Art of Poetry," translated into verse Virgil's sixth Eclogue, one or two Odes of Horace, and a passage from Guarini's "Pastor Fido." Of his original writing the most important piece is "An Essay on Translated Verse," carefully polished in the manner of Boileau, sensible, and often very happy in expression. . . . He died in 1684.—MORLEY, HENRY, 1879, *A Manual of English Literature, ed. Tyler, p.* 421.

GENERAL

It was my Lord Roscommon's "Essay on Translated Verse:" which made me uneasy till I tried whether or no I was capable of following his rules, and of reducing the speculation into practice.—DRYDEN, JOHN, 1685, *Second Miscellany, Preface.*

Nor must Roscommon pass neglected by,
That makes even rules a noble poetry;
Rules whose deep sense and heavenly numbers show
The best of critics, and of poets too.
—ADDISON, JOSEPH, 1694, *An Account of the Greatest English Poets.*

In all Charles' days
Roscommon only boasts unspotted bays.
—POPE, ALEXANDER, 1733, *The First Epistle of the Second Book of Horace.*

We must allow of Roscommon, what Fenton has not mentioned so distinctly as he ought, and what is yet very much to his honour, that he is perhaps the only correct writer in verse before Addison; and that, if there are not so many or so great beauties in his compositions as in those of some contemporaries, there are at least fewer faults. . . . Of Roscommon's works, the judgement of the publick seems to be right. He is elegant, but not great; he never labours after exquisite beauties, and he seldom falls into gross faults. His versification is smooth, but rarely vigorous; and his rhymes are remarkably exact. He improved taste, if he did not enlarge knowledge, and may be numbered among the benefactors to English literature.—JOHNSON, SAMUEL, 1779, *Roscommon, Lives of the English Poets.*

> Roscommon fills with elegant remark
> His verse as elegant; unspotted lines
> Flow from a mind unspotted as themslves.

—HURDIS, JAMES, 1788, *The Village Curate.*

Roscommon, one of the best for harmony and correctness of language, has little vigor, but he never offends; and Pope has justly praised his "unspotted bays."—HALLAM, HENRY, 1837–39, *Introduction to the Literature of Europe, pt.* iv, *ch.* v, *par.* 47.

"Dies Iræ," one of the best of this poet's few works; for much greater credit is due to Roscommon for his endeavours to purify our language, than for his poems taken individually. Severe in judgment, he shone chiefly in the didactic style. He was considered as the most correct writer in verse before Addison's time; but the almost total indifference of our own and of recently past times, both to Addison's poems and to those of Lord Roscommon, proves that correctness is one of the merits least appreciated by lovers of poetry. He had, however, a far higher merit; his verses were free from the licentiousness of his times.—THOMPSON, KATHERINE (GRACE WHARTON), 1862, *The Literature of Society, vol.* I, *p.* 262.

Roscommon stands on the same ground with Denham—elegant and sensible, but cold and unimpassioned. — CHAMBERS, ROBERT, 1876, *Cyclopædia of English Literature, ed. Carruthers.*

Roscommon is remarkable as the only writer between Milton and the end of the century who discarded rhyme in serious nondramatic verse. — GOSSE, EDMUND, 1888, *A History of Eighteenth Century Literature, p.* 32.

He has nothing of the salt and savour of Rochester's more serious poetry, and is at best an elegant versifier, who, in his only considerable original poem, the "Essay on Translated Verse," thinks justly, reasons clearly, and expresses himself with considerable spirit when the subject requires. The most original feature of his literary character is his preference in a rhyming age for blank verse, which he enforces in theory, but is far from recommending by his practice. In his rhymed pieces he is a better versifier than poet, and in his blank verse the contrary.— GARNETT, RICHARD, 1895, *The Age of Dryden, p.* 48.

Thomas Otway

1652–1685

Born, at Trotton, Sussex, 3 March 1652. Educated at Winchester College, till 1669. Matriculated, Christ Church, Oxford, 27 May 1669; left in 1672, without degree. To London; devoted himself to writing plays. Produced, at Dorset Gardens Theatre, "Alcibiades," 1675; "Don Carlos," 1676; "Titus and Berenice," 1677; "The Cheats of Scapin," 1677; "Friendship in Fashion," 1678. Enlisted, to serve in army in Holland, 1678. Ensign in Duke of Monmouth's regiment, Feb. 1678; Lieutenant, Nov. 1678. Returned to England, 1679. Produced, at Dorset Gardens Theatre, "The Orphan," Feb. 1680; "History and Fall of Caius Marius," 1680; "The Souldier's Fortune," 1681; "Venice Preserved," Feb. 1682; "The Atheist," 1684. Died, in London, April 1685. Buried in St. Clement Danes Churchyard. *Works:* "Alcibiades," 1675; "Don Carlos," 1676; "Titus and Berenice . . . With a farce called The Cheats of Scapin" (adapted from Racine and Molière), 1677; "Friendship in Fashion," 1678; "The Orphan," 1680; "History and Fall of Caius Marius," 1680; "The Poet's Complaint of his Muse," 1680; "The Souldier's Fortune," 1681; "Venice Preserv'd," 1682; "The Atheist," 1684. Posthumous: "Windsor Castle," 1685; "The History of the Triumvirates" (trans. from the French), 1686. *Collected Works:* in 2 vols., 1713; in 3 vols., ed. by W. T. Thornton, 1813.—SHARP, R. FARQUHARSON, 1897, *A Dictionary of English Authors, p.* 218.

PERSONAL

An Author who was well known to most Persons of this Age, who are famous for Wit and Breeding.—LANGBAINE, GERARD, 1691, *An Account of the English Dramatick Poets, p.* 395.

In this play ["The Jealous Bridegroom"] Mr. Otway, the poet, having an inclination to turn actor, Mr Behn gave him the *King* in the play for a probation part; but he, being not used to the stage, the full house put him to such a sweat and tremendous agony, that being dash't spoilt him for an actor.—DOWNES, JOHN, 1708, *Roscius Anglicanus; or, an Historical View of the Stage, p.* 34.

Otway had an intimate friend (one Blackstone), who was shot; the murderer fled toward Dover; and Otway pursued him. In his return, he drank water when violently heated, and so got a fever which was the death of him.—DENNIS, JOHN, 1728-30, *Spence's Anecdotes, ed. Singer, p.* 33.

> But wherefore need I wander wide
> To old Ilissus' distant side,
>   Deserted stream, and mute?
> Wild Arun, too, has heard thy strains,
> And echo, 'midst my native plains,
>   Been soothed by pity's lute.
> There first the wren thy myrtles shed
> On gentlest Otway's infant head,
>   To him thy cell was shown;
> And while he sung the female heart,
> With youth's soft notes unspoiled by art,
>   Thy turtles mixed their own.

—COLLINS, WILLIAM, 1747, *Ode to Pity.*

His person was of the middle size, about, 5 ft. 7 in. in height, inclinable to fatness. He had a thoughtful speaking eye.—OLDYS, WILLIAM, c 1761, *MS. note to Langbaine's Account of the English Dramatic Poets.*

He died April 14, 1685, in a manner which I am unwilling to mention. Having been compelled by his necessities to contract debts, and hunted, as is supposed, by the tarriers of the law, he retired to a publick-house on Tower-hill, where he is said to have died of want; or, as it is related by one of his biographers, by swallowing, after a long fast, a piece of bread which charity had supplied. He went out, as is reported, almost naked in the rage of hunger, and, finding a gentleman in a neighbouring coffee-house, asked him for a shilling. The gentleman gave him a guinea; and Otway going away bought a roll, and was choaked with the

first mouthful. All this, I hope, is not true; and there is this ground of better hope, that Pope, who lived near enough to be well informed, relates in Spence's Memorials, that he died of a fever caught by violent pursuit of a thief that had robbed one of his friends. But that indigence, and its concomitants, sorrow and despondency, pressed hard upon him, has never been denied, whatever immediate cause might bring him to the grave.—JOHNSON, SAMUEL, 1779, *Otway, Lives of the English Poets.*

If Lee died tipsy outside a public house, Otway died half-starved within one, at the Bull on Tower Hill.—DORAN, JOHN, 1863, *Annals of the English Stage.*

Dryden and Otway were contemporaries, and lived, it is said, for some time opposite to each other in Fetter Lane. One morning the latter happened to call upon his brother bard about breakfast-time, but was told by his servant that his master was gone to breakfast with the Earl of Pembroke. "Very well," said Otway, "tell your master that I will call to-morrow morning." Accordingly he called about the same hour. "Well, is your master at home now?" "No, sir, he is just gone to breakfast with the Duke of Buckingham." "The d— he is!" said Otway; and, actuated either by envy, pride, or disappointment in a kind of involuntary manner he took up a piece of chalk which lay on a table . . . and wrote over the door,—

"Here lives Dryden, a poet and a wit."

The next morning Dryden recognized the handwriting, and told the servant to go to Otway and desire his company to breakfast with him; in the mean time to Otway's line of

"Here lives Dryden, a poet and a wit,"

he added,—

"This was written by Otway, opposit."

When Otway arrived he saw that his line was linked with a rhyme, and, being a man of rather petulant disposition, he took it in dudgeon, and, turning upon his heel, told Dryden he was welcome to keep his wit and his breakfast to himself.—THORNBURY, WALTER, 1872, *Old and New London, vol.* I, *ch.* viii.

Except that Otway's life in London was generally disreputable, little is recorded of it. The low ale-house in which he perished miserably is the only spot mentioned as being in any way positively associated with him, and only the name of that is known now. . . . He was buried in the churchyard of St. Clement Danes, April 16, 1685. No stone marks the spot.—HUTTON, LAURENCE, 1885, *Literary Landmarks of London, pp.* 229, 231.

Weak rather than vicious, ill-used and luckless, Otway's unhappy end makes a pitiful story. There are few sadder pictures in literary history than that of the sensitive soul, famished and despairing, making known his misery in a public place, and for lack of bread startling the careless stranger with the words, "I am the poet Otway." "Alas! poor Castalio!"—SANDERS, H. M., 1899, *Thomas Otway, Temple Bar, vol.* 118, *p.* 386.

DON CARLOS
1676

Tom Otway came next, Tom Shadwell's dear zany,
And swears for heroicks he writes best of any;
Don Carlos his pockets so amply had fill'd,
That his mange was quite cured, and his lice were all kill'd
But Apollo had seen his face on the stage,
And prudently did not think fit to engage
The scum of a play-house, for the prop of an age.
—ROCHESTER, JOHN WILMOT, EARL, 1680? *Session of the Poets.*

Although "Alcibiades" had been a partial failure, Betterton accepted another tragedy from the young author in the following year. "Don Carlos" is as great an advance on its predecessor as it could possibly be. It is difficult to believe that they were written by the same hand. The rhyming tragedies were on their last legs, but "Don Carlos" was a crutch that might have supported the falling fashion for years. The supple, strong verse, un-English in character but worthy of Corneille or at least of Rotrou, assists instead of hampering the dramatic action: the plot is well-considered, tragical, and moving; the characters, stagey though they be, are vigorously designed and sustained. I think we should be justified in calling "Don Carlos" the best English tragedy in rhyme; by one leap the young Oxonian sprang ahead of the veteran Dryden, who thereupon began to "weary of his long-loved mistress, rhyme."—GOSSE, EDMUND, 1883, *Seventeenth-Century Studies, p.* 279.

Might have been a good play if it had not been written in rhyme. The action is highly dramatic, and the characters, though artless, are not ineffective; but the pathos in which the poet excelled is continually disturbed by the bombastic couplets, ever trembling on the brink of the ridiculous. The remorse of Philip after the murder of his wife and son is as grotesque an instance of the forcible feeble as could easily be found, and is a melancholy instance indeed of the declension of the English drama, when contrasted with the demeanour of Othello in similar circumstances. Otway, however, was yet to show that his faults were rather his age's than his own.—GARNETT, RICHARD, 1895, *The Age of Dryden, p.* 103.

THE ORPHAN
1680

Notwithstanding its real beauties, could hardly have taken so prodigiously, as it hath done, on our stage, if there were not somewhere a defect of *good taste* as well as of *good morals.*—HURD, RICHARD, 1757, *Notes on the Art of Poetry, vol.* I, *p.* 42.

This is one of the few plays that keep possession of the stage, and has pleased for almost a century, through all the vicissitudes of dramatick fashion. Of this play nothing new can easily be said. It is a domestick tragedy drawn from middle life. Its whole power is upon the affections; for it is not written with much comprehension of thought, or elegance of expression. But if the heart is interested, many other beauties may be wanting, yet not be missed.—JOHNSON, SAMUEL, 1779, *Otway, Lives of the English Poets.*

But the reputation of Otway for pathetic powers was, by the success of his "Orphan," justly exalted above all the dramatists of his own and succeeding times. The characters, by being brought nearer to the condition of the audience, more deeply interest their passions than the fate and fortune of persons who are eminently placed above them.—DAVIES, THOMAS, 1784, *Dramatic Miscellanies, p.* 183.

In the 'Orphan' there is little else but this voluptuous effeminacy of sentiment and mawkish distress, which strikes directly at the root of that mental fortitude and heroic cast of thought which alone makes tragedy endurable—that renders its sufferings pathetic, or its struggles sublime. Yet there are lines and passages in it of extreme tenderness and beauty; and few persons, I conceive (judging from my own experience) will read it at a certain time of life without shedding tears over it as fast as the "Arabian trees their medicinal gums." Otway always touched the reader, for he had himself a heart. We may be sure that he blotted his page often with his tears, on which so many drops have since fallen from glistening eyes, "that sacred pity had engendered there." He had suceptibility of feeling and warmth of genius; but he had not equal depth of thought or loftiness of imagination, and indulged his mere sensibility too much, yielding to the immediate impression or emotion excited in his own mind, and not placing himself enough in the minds and situations of others, or following the workings of nature sufficiently with keenness of eye and strength of will into its heights and depths, its strongholds as well as its weaksides.—HAZLITT, WILLIAM, 1820, *Lectures on the Literature of the Age of Elizabeth, Lecture* viii.

The plot of the "Orphan" is as clumsy as it is indelicate.—NEELE, HENRY, 1827, *Lectures on English Poetry, Lecture* iv.

The story of the "Orphan" is domestic, and borrowed, as I believe, from some French novel, though I do not at present remember where I have read it: it was once popular on the stage, and gave scope for good acting, but is unpleasing to the delicacy of our own age.—HALLAM, HENRY, 1837-39, *Introduction to the Literature of Europe, pt.* iv, *ch.* vi, *par.* 45.

Has drawn more tears from female eyes than almost any other play. The nature of its central incident has kept it from the stage for the last eighty years, but from the time that Mistress Barry first played Monimia the character has been a favourite one with many of our best actresses, down to Miss O'Neill; while Betterton's part, Castalio, has given opportunities for pathos to an equally long list of his successors. "The Orphan" was the best work that Otway had yet given to the stage. . . . It shows at its highest Otway's power of moving compassion, the continued tension of its unhappiness—when once the earlier scenes are disposed of—being absolutely painful.

In Monimia he has created a victim of love ill-fated, worthy for sadness to rank with Penthea in "The Broken Heart," though she is altogether more lovable and life-like than that somewhat shadowy personage. Indeed, Otway might be called a belated Ford, with tempered horrors and mitigated gloom, yet with fully as intense a sympathy for ill-starred love and the sickness of a heart broken with griefs as he who drew the wretched Annabella; but while Ford in all probability found his sadness in the hearts of others, his own strong and silent nature enabling him to draw coolly with lines not blurred with passion, Otway had in his own breast all too faithful a realisation of the sorrows he portrayed.—SANDERS, H. M., 1899, *Thomas Otway, Temple Bar, vol.* 118, *p.* 378.

CAIUS MARIUS
1680

How little Otway understood the true rules of composition may be inferred from this, that he has taken the half of the scenes of his "Caius Marius" verbally, or with disfiguring changes, from the "Romeo and Juliet" of Shakspeare. Nothing more incongruous can well be conceived than such an episode in Roman manners and in a historical drama. This impudent plagiarism is in no manner justified by his confessing it.—SCHLEGEL, AUGUSTUS WILLIAM, 1809, *Lectures on Dramatic Art and Literature, tr. Black, Lecture* xii, *p.* 396.

VENICE PRESERVED
1682

I will not defend every thing in his "Venice Preserved;" but I must bear this testimony to his memory,—that the passions are truly touched in it, though perhaps there is somewhat to be desired both in the grounds of them and in the height and elegance of expression. But nature is there,—which is the greatest beauty.—DRYDEN, JOHN, 1695, *Du Fresnoy's Art of Painting, Preface.*

His last and greatest dramatick work, "Venice Preserved," a tragedy, which still continues to be one of the favourites of the publick, notwithstanding the want of morality in the original design, and the despicable scenes of vile comedy with which he has diversified his tragick action. By comparing this with his "Orphan," it will appear that his images were by time become stronger, and his language more energetick. The striking passages are in every mouth; and the publick seems to judge rightly of the faults and excellencies of this play, that it is the work of a man not attentive to decency, nor zealous for virtue; but of one who conceived forcibly, and drew originally, by consulting nature in his own breast.—JOHNSON, SAMUEL, 1779, *Otway, Lives of the English Poets.*

Instead of those monsters, he brought forward, early in the month of January 1748, Otway's tragedy of "Venice Preserved." He had studied the character of *Jaffier* in the preceding season, with intent to perform it, with the advantage of having Quin in the part of *Pierre;* but a fever, that lasted three or four weeks, obliged him to postpone that design. He now prevailed on Barry to undertake the part, and, with that great coadjutor, he presented *Jaffier* to the public. The critics have objected to this play, that the title of "Venice Preserved, or a Plot dis covered," is by no means proper, as, instead of keeping the audience in a state of suspence, it announces the catastrophe. This undoubtedly is an error *in limine;* and in the body of the work, we have a gross violation of all decorum, in the low buffoonery of *Antonio* with *Aquilina.* The scene, were it written with true comic humour, would be still exceptionable, as it is detached from the context of the fable, and is merely episodical. It is judiciously omitted in the representation, and the play as acted, is perhaps the best since the days of Shakespeare. *Pierre* is painted in the most striking colours; his zeal for liberty and abhorrence of oppression would be real virtues, had they not been converted, by the violent temper of the man, into the most furious passions. . . . *Jaffier* is a very different character, perhaps the fittest for the stage in the whole circle of the drama.—MURPHY, ARTHUR, 1801, *The Life of David Garrick.*

He is a *legitimate* English classic, and as his "Venice Preserved" is yet among the most justly applauded of our dramatic performances, I should be censurable if I did not allow him a foremost place in the foremost rank of the DRAMATIC WORTHIES of his Country.—DIBDIN, THOMAS FROGNALL, 1824, *The Library Companion, p.* 822.

"Venice Preserved" is more frequently represented than any tragedy after those of Shakspeare; the plot is highly dramatic in conception and conduct: even what seems, when we read it, a defect,—the shifting of our wishes, or perhaps rather of our ill wishes, between two parties, the senate and the conspirators, who are redeemed by no virtue,—does not, as is shown by experience, interfere with the spectator's interest. Pierre, indeed, is one of those villains for whom it is easy to excite the sympathy of the half-principled and the inconsiderate. But the great attraction is in the character of Belvidera; and, when that part is represented by such as we remember to have seen, no tragedy is honored by such a tribute, not of tears alone, but of more agony than many would seek to endure. The versification of Otway, like that of most in this period, runs, almost to an excess, into the line of eleven syllables; sometimes also into the *sdrucciolo* form, or twelve syllables with a dactylic close. These give a considerable animation to tragic verse.—HALLAM, HENRY, 1837–39, *Introduction to the Literature of Europe, pt.* iv, *ch.* vi, *par.* 45.

Undoubtedly a work of genius, far superior to any dramatic composition of this period; it will remain for ever one of the classical tragedies of English literature.—SCHERR, J., 1874–82, *A History of English Literature, p.* 124.

I remember one circumstance connected with my first performance of it which proved how painfully the unredeemed horror and wretchedness of the piece acted upon my nerves and imagination. In the last scene, where poor Belvidera's brain gives way under her despair, and she fancies herself digging for her husband in the earth, and that she at last recovers and seizes him, I intended to utter a piercing scream; this I had not of course rehearsed, not being able to scream deliberately in cold blood, so that I hardly knew, myself, what manner of utterance I should find for my madness. But when the evening came, I uttered shriek after shriek without stopping, and rushing off the stage ran all round the back of the scenes, and was pursuing my way, perfectly unconscious of what I was doing, down the stairs that led out into the street, when I was captured and brought

back to my dressing-room and my senses.
—KEMBLE, FRANCES ANN, 1878, *Records
of a Girlhood, p.* 236.

The best tragedy of the Restoration.
. . . The author of this play, in fact,
seems a sort of prose Shakespeare, a
Shakespeare with the romantic charm
precipitated. The verse, indeed, is
strong and good, but the spirit of the
drama is domestic and mundane; there
are no flights into the spiritual heavens.
The imagination of the dramatist is lucid,
rapid, and direct; there is the utmost
clearness of statement and reflection; but
although this masterpiece of genius is not
obscured, it is certainly toned down by a
universal tinge or haze of the commonplace.—GOSSE, EDMUND, 1888, *A History of
Eighteenth Century Literature, pp.* 55, 56.

Otway's most memorable work, though
inferior in mere poetry and unstudied
simplicity to "The Orphan," surpasses it in
tragic grandeur, in variety of action, and
in intensity of interest. It has the further great advantage that the interest
does not entirely arise from the situation,
but that at least one of the characters is
a skillful piece of painting from the life,
and very probably from the author. In
Jaffier we have a vivid portrait of the man
who is entirely governed by the affections,
and who sways from the ardent resolution
to a weakness hardly distinguishable from
treachery, as friendship and love alternately incline him. The little we know of
Otway warrants the impression that he
was such a man, and assuredly he could
not have excited such warm interest in a
character so feeble in his offence, so abject in his repentance, and in general so
perilously verging on the despicable,
without a keen sympathy with the subject
of his portrait. *Tout comprendre c'est
tout pardonner.*—GARNETT, RICHARD, 1895,
The Age of Dryden; p. 105.

GENERAL

There was a time when Otway charm'd the
    stage;
Otway, the hope, the sorrow of our age;
When the full pitt with pleas'd attention
    hung
Wrap'd with each accent from *Castalio's*
    tongue;
With what a laughter was his *Soldier* read,
How mourned they when his *Jaffier* struck
    and bled!
—ANON, 1698, *Satyr on the Poets, Poems
on Affairs of State, pt.* iii, *p.* 55.

Otway fail'd to polish or refine.
—POPE, ALEXANDER, 1733, *The First
Epistle of the Second Book of Horace.*

Otway has written but two tragedies,
out of six, that are pathetic.—I believe
he did it without much design; as Lillo
has done in his Barnwell.—'Tis a talent
of nature, rather than an effect of judgment, to write so movingly.—POPE, AL-
EXANDER, 1737–39, *Spence's Anecdotes, ed.
Singer, p.* 162.

The English language owes very little
to Otway, though, next to Shakespeare,
the greatest genius England ever produced in tragedy. His excellencies lay in
painting directly from nature, in catching
every emotion just as it rises from the
soul, and in all the powers of the moving
and pathetic. He appears to have had no
learning, no critical knowledge, and to
have lived in great distress. When he
died (which he did in an obscure house
near the Minories), he had about him the
copy of a tragedy, which it seems he had
sold for a trifle to Bentley the bookseller.
—GOLDSMITH, OLIVER, 1759, *The Bee,
No.* 8, *Nov.* 24.

No poet has touched the passions with
a more masterly hand than Otway. He
was acquainted with all the avenues to the
human heart, and knew and felt all its
emotions. He could rouse us into rage,
and melt us into pity and tenderness.
His language is that of nature, and consequently the simplest imaginable. He has
equally avoided the rant of Lee, and the
pomp of Dryden. Hence it was that his
tragedies were received, not with loud applause, but with tears of approbation.—
GRANGER, JAMES, 1769–1824, *Biographical History of England, vol.* v, *p.* 247.

And every charm of Otway's melting page.
—MORE, HANNAH, 1773, *The Search After
Happiness.*

. . . gentle Otway's magic name.
—WHITE, HENRY KIRKE, 1806? *Genius.*

The cannons of Otway in his scenes of
passionate affection rival at least, and
sometimes excel, those of Shakespeare.
More tears have been shed, probably, for
the sorrows of Belvidera and Monimia
than for those of Juliet and Desdemona.
—SCOTT, SIR WALTER, *Miscellaneous
Prose Works.*

Otway was cut off in the spring-tide of
his genius, and his early death was, according to every appearance, a heavy loss

to our drama. It has been alleged, indeed, in the present day, that Otway's imagination showed no prognostics of great future achievements; but when I remember "Venice Preserved," and "The Orphan," as the works of a man of thirty, I can treat this opinion no otherwise than to dismiss it as an idle assertion.—CAMPBELL, THOMAS, 1819, *An Essay on English Poetry.*

With the sweet and mellow diction of the former age, had none of its force, variety, or invention.—JEFFREY, FRANCIS, 1822–44, *Contributions to the Edinburgh Review, vol.* II, *p.* 334.

Otway is the poet of sensual pathos; for, affecting as he sometimes is, he knows no way to the heart but through the senses. His very friendship, though enthusiastic, is violent, and has a smack of bullying. He was a man of generous temperament, spoilt by a profligate age. He seems to dress up a beauty in tears, only for the purpose of stimulating her wrongers.—HUNT, LEIGH, 1851, *Table-Talk, p.* 137.

Through the pompous cloak of the new rhetoric, Thomas Otway now and then reached the passions of the other age. It is plain that the times he lived in marred him; that the oratorical style, the literary phrases, the classical declamation, the well-poised antitheses, buzzed about him, and drowned his note in their sustained and monotonous hum. Had he but been born a hundred years earlier! In his "Orphan" and "Venice Preserved" we encounter the sombre imaginations of Webster, Ford, and Shakspeare, their gloomy idea of life, their atrocities, murders, pictures of irresistible passions, which riot blindly like a herd of savage beasts, and make, a chaos of the battle-field, with their yells and tumult, leaving behind them but devastation and heaps of dead. Like Shakspeare, his events are human transports and furies—a brother violating his brother's wife, a husband perjuring himself for his wife; Polydore, Chamont, Jaffier, weak and violent souls, the sport of chance, the prey of temptation, with whom transport or crime, like poison poured into the veins, gradually ascends, envenoms the whole man, is spread on all whom he touches, and contorts and casts them down together in a convulsive delirium. Like Shakspeare,

he has found poignant and living words, which lay bare the depths of humanity, the strange noise of a machine which is getting out of order, the tension of the will stretched to breaking-point, the simplicity of real sacrifice, the humility of exasperated and craving passion, which longs to the end and against all hope for its fuel and its gratification. Like Shakspeare, he has conceived genuine women, —Monimia, above all Belvidera, who, like Imogen, has given herself wholly, and is lost as in an abyss of adoration for him whom she has chosen, who can but love, obey, weep, suffer, and who dies like a flower plucked from the stalk, when her arms are torn from the neck around which she has locked them. Like Shakspeare again, he has found, at least once, the large bitter buffoonery, the crude sentiment of human baseness; and he has introduced into his most painful tragedy, an obscene caricature, an old senator, who unbends from his official gravity in order to play at his mistress' house the clown or the valet.—TAINE, H. A., 1871, *History of English Literature, tr. Van Laun, vol.* II, *bk.* iii, *ch.* ii, *p.* 24.

In addition to a keen insight into the dramatic excellence of themes, he possessed a real gift of tragic pathos; but he lacked the self-restraint which genius itself can rarely forego, and his efforts were as incomplete as his end was premature.—WARD, ADOLPHUS WILLIAM, 1875–99, *A History of English Dramatic Literature, vol.* III, *p.* 502.

The first writer of any prominence who chose any one for his subject outside of a royal family was Otway, whose "Orphan" (1680) and "Venice Preserved" (1682) long held the stage. The language of these plays is entirely different from that of Dryden's, and, as we shall see, is of itself worthy of attention; but what I wish to mention, first of all, is the introduction of this new hero, and the abandonment of the king. This change was an indication of what was going to take place in the next century, and is but one of the instances which we shall find of the growth of democracy in literature. At this time, however, nothing of the sort was conjectured, and Otway, doubtless, wrote about private people from no desire to revolutionize letters. The poor man had but little chance to think of anything but the day before him, or, more probably, the night that was before him, and he manufactured gross comedies, and wrote two of the most memorable plays of the time.—PERRY, THOMAS SERGEANT, 1883, *English Literature in the Eighteenth Century, p.* 113.

Thomson the poet ranked the parts of Monimia and Belvidera with those of Hamlet and Othello, and many of the greatest actresses owed to these rôles the leading triumphs in their careers. As Belvidera, Mrs. Barry was succeeded in turn by Mrs. Porter, Mrs. Seymour, Mrs. Cibber, Mrs. Siddons, and Miss O'Neill; while Garrick and J. P. Kemble played both Pierre and Jaffier with notable success. Mills, Quin, and Mossop were also popular exponents of Pierre's part, and Macready filled it for many years. As Monimia, Mrs. Oldfield, Mrs. Porter, and Mrs. Cibber all excelled. Miss O'Neill was the last eminent actress to essay the part. Garrick often played Chamont, Monimia's brother. "The Orphan" and "Venice

Preserved" both remained stock pieces until the present century. Twenty revivals of "Venice Preserved" are noticed by Genest, the latest at Drury Lane on 6 April 1829, with Young as Pierre and Miss Phillips as Belvidera. Sixteen performances of "The Orphan" are described by Genest between 1707 and 1815, on 2 Dec. of which year it was played at Covent Garden, with Charles Kemble as Chamont and Miss O'Neill as Monimia. Many modifications were introduced into the text of both pieces. J. P. Kemble printed an acting version of "Venice Preserved," from which the scenes with Antonio were omitted; this was thrice published, in 1795, 1811, and 1814 respectively. A performance of "Venice Preserved," by the boys of Otway's school (Winchester), took place in 1755, when a prologue was written by Robert Lowth, afterwards Bishop of London.—LEE, SIDNEY, 1895, *Dictionary of National Biography, vol.* XLII, *p.* 352.

John Pearson
1613–1686

John Pearson, divine, was born 28th February 1613, at Great Snoring, Norfolk, son of the Archdeacon of Suffolk. He was educated at Eton and at Queen's and King's Colleges, Cambridge, and in 1640, appointed chaplain to the lordkeeper Finch, was presented to the rectory of Thorington in Suffolk. In 1659 he published his learned "Exposition of the Creed," and edited the remains of John Hales of Eton. In 1660 he was presented to the rectory of St. Christopher's in London, and made prebendary of Ely, Archdeacon of Surrey, and Master of Jesus College, Cambridge. In 1661 he was the principal antagonist of Baxter in the Savoy Conference, and became Margaret professor of Divinity; in 1662 he was made Master of Trinity College, Cambridge, and in 1673 Bishop of Chester. He defended the genuineness of the Ignatian epistles (1672), and in 1684 published his "Annales Cyprianici." He died July 16, 1686. Admirable editions of the "Exposition of the Creed" are by Burton (1833) and Chevallier (1849; revised by Sinker, 1882); of the "Minor Theological Works," with Life, by Churton (1844).—PATRICK AND GROOME, *eds.*, 1897, *Chambers's Biographical Dictionary, p.* 726.

PERSONAL

In all respects the greatest divine of the age: a man of great learning, strong reason, and of a clear judgment. He was a judicious and grave preacher, more instructive than affective; and a man of a spotless life, and of an excellent temper. His book on the creed is among the best that our church has produced. He was not active in his diocese, but too remiss and easy in his episcopal function; and was a much better divine than a bishop. He was a speaking instance of what a great man could fall to: for his

memory went from him so entirely, that he became a child some years before he died.—BURNET, GILBERT, 1715–34, *History of My Own Time, vol.* III, *p.* 142.

Pearson was a man of spotless life and of an excellent temper. His equanimity perplexed his nonconformist opponents. This absence of passion, while it proved a most valuable quality in controversy, rendered him "more instructive than affective" as a preacher. Pearson strongly supported the Restoration settlement of the church, and would give no support to any schemes of comprehension which did not insist on uniformity. Among Englishmen of the seventeenth century, Pearson was probably the ablest scholar and systematic theologian.—SANDERS, REV. FRANCIS, 1895, *Dictionary of National Biography, vol.* XLIV, *p.* 170.

EXPOSITION OF THE CREED
1659

This is a work of great learning and merit. It contains a system of theology, a good deal of controversy, and a large portion of biblical exposition. On the last account it is entitled to a place in this work, and will repay an attentive perusal.—ORME, WILLIAM, 1824, *Bibliotheca Biblica.*

The "Exposition of the Creed" . . . has nothing superior to it in any language. Metaphysics, logic, classical and theological erudition, are all brought to bear upon that momentous subject, in a manner so happy and so natural—that the depth of research and variety of knowledge are most concealed by the felicitous manner of their adaptation. Well might the great Bentley say of this yet greater man— that his "very dust was Gold."—DIBDIN, THOMAS FROGNALL, 1824, *The Library Companion, p.* 51.

A standard book in English divinity. It expands, beyond the literal purport of the creed itself, to most articles of orthodox belief, and is a valuable summary of arguments and authorities on that side. The closeness of Pearson, and his judicious selections of proofs, distinguished him from many, especially the earlier theologians. Some might surmise that his undeviating adherence to what he calls the church is hardly consistent with independence of thinking; but, considered as an advocate, he is one of much judgment and skill.—HALLAM, HENRY, 1837–39, *Introduction to the Literature of Europe, pt.* iv, *ch.* ii, *par.* 59.

The respect and popularity which this excellent treatise has so long and so widely obtained are owing in a great extent to the strong good sense and the skill in arrangement of his topics which its author has exhibited.—CREASY, SIR EDWARD, 1850–75, *Memoirs of Eminent Etonians, p.* 171.

The work is laborious, calm, and acute, written in simple and clear language; it follows the easy arrangement of taking each word in order. He was profoundly versed in patristic literature; and in that department criticised with such acuteness that Bentley said "his very dross was gold."—MINTO, WILLIAM, 1872–80, *Manual of English Prose Literature, p.* 296.

Has always been esteemed as a standard work in English divinity, remarkable equally for argument, methodical arrangement, and clearness and beauty of style.—CHAMBERS, ROBERT, 1876, *Cyclopædia of English Literature, ed. Carruthers.*

GENERAL

The most excellent Bishop Pearson, the very dust of whose writings is gold.—BENTLEY, RICHARD, 1699, *Dissertation upon the Letters of Phalaris, p.* 424.

He applied himself to every kind of learning that he thought essential to his profession; and was in every kind a master. His works are not numerous, but they are all excellent; and some of the least of them shew that he was one of the completest divines of his age. The chief are, his "Exposition of the Creed," in English, and his "Vindication of St. Ignatius's Epistles," in Latin. The former, which has gone through twelve or thirteen editions, is one of the most finished pieces of theology in our language. It is itself *a body of divinity*, but not *a body without a spirit*. The style of it is just; the periods are, for the most part, well turned; the method is very exact; and it is in general free from those errors which are too often found in theological systems. —GRANGER, JAMES, 1769–1824, *Biographical History of England, vol.* V, *p.* 18.

He was a man of vast learning, fitter, according to Burnet, to be a divine than a bishop. His vindication of the authenticity of the Epistles of Ignatius is a very masterly production. Lightfoot's "Hora Hebraicæ" and "Harmony of the Four Gospels" are works of a different kind. In these, the writer's profound acquaintance with rabbinical literature enables him to throw a flood of light on the various Jewish usages and rites current in Palestine at the time of the Christian era, and referred to in the New Testament, as well as upon obscure points in the topography.—ARNOLD, THOMAS, 1862–87, *A Manual of English Literature, p.* 212.

It ["Vindiciæ Epistolarum S. Ignatti access. To. Vossii Epistolæ adv. D.

Blondellum"] was incomparably the most valuable contribution to the subject which had hitherto appeared, with the exception of Ussher's work. Pearson's learning, critical ability, clearness of statement, and moderation of tone, nowhere appear to greater advantage than in this work. If here and there an argument is over-strained, this was the almost inevitable consequence of the writer's position as the champion of a cause which had been recklessly and violently assailed on all sides. . . . Compared with Daillé's attack, Pearson's reply was as light to darkness.—LIGHTFOOT, JOSEPH BARBER, 1885, *The Apostolic Fathers, pt.* ii, *vol.* I, *p.* 333.

Pearson's style is clear and uniform, rising on rare occasions to positive felicity.—GOSSE, EDMUND, 1888, *A History of Eighteenth Century Literature, p.* 76.

If in a company of well-informed persons the question were asked, "Who were the three greatest among the masters of theology in the Church of England?"

the answers made might probably vary either as to the selected names, or as to the order in which they were placed; but it would be strange indeed if any of the replies did not include among the three the name of Bishop Pearson. And, beyond all doubt, John Pearson possessed in a high degree a rare combination of great natural gifts, trained and disciplined, with great attainments in learning. In him we find erudition, not only wide but minutely exact, and a critical faculty keen and penetrating. In him we find sound reasoning which never builds, as in the case of some who have great reputations, a huge superstructure of top-heavy inference upon an insufficient or rickety base. In him we find a judicial capacity that seems never swayed by prepossessions, that looks at the evidence, all the evidence, and only the evidence, before pronouncing judgment.—DOWDEN, JOHN, 1897, *Outlines of the History of the Theological Literature of The Church of England, p.* 171.

Charles Cotton

1630–1687

Born at Beresford, Staffordshire, England, April 28, 1630: died at Westminster, Feb., 1687. An English poet, best known as the translator of Montaigne's "Essays" (1685). He published anonymously "Scarronides, or the First Book of Virgil Travestie" (1664 reprinted with the fourth book in 1670), a translation of Corneille's "Horace" (1671), "A Voyage to Ireland in Burlesque," a poem (1670), a translation of Gerard's "Life of the Duke of Espernon" (1670) and of the "Commentaries of De Montluc, Marshal of France" (1674), a "second part" (on fly-fishing) to the fifth edition of Walton's "Complete Angler" (1676), etc. A collection of his poems was published in 1689.—SMITH, BENJAMIN E., ed. 1894-97, *The Century Cyclopedia of Names, p.* 284.

PERSONAL

The noblest of our youth and best of friends, Charles Cotton, Esquire.—LOVELACE, RICHARD, c 1649, *The Triumphs of Philamore and Amoret, Dedication.*

Charles Cotton was a gentleman born to a competent fortune, and so qualified in his person and education, that for many years he continued the greatest ornament of the town, in the esteem of those who had been best bred. His natural parts were very great, his wit flowing in all the parts of conversation: the superstructure of learning not raised to a considerable height; but having passed some years in Cambridge, and then in France, and conversing always with learned men, his expressions were ever proper and significant,

and gave great lustre to his discourse upon any argument; so that he was thought by those who were not intimate with him, to have been much better acquainted with books than he was. He had all those qualities which in youth raise men to the reputation of being fine gentlemen; such a pleasantness and gaiety of humour, such a sweetness and gentleness of nature, and such a civility and delightfulness in conversation, that no man in the court or out of it, appeared a more accomplished person; all these extraordinary qualifications being supported by as extraordinary a clearness of courage and fearlessness of spirit, of which he gave too often manifestation. Some unhappy suits in law, and waste of his fortune in those suits, made some impression upon his mind; which being improved by domestic afflictions, and those indulgences to himself which naturally attend those afflictions, rendered his age less reverenced than his youth had been; and gave his best friends cause to have wished that he had not lived so long.—CLARENDON, LORD (HENRY HYDE), 1674? *Life.*

Though his pecuniary difficulties, which were doubtless largely due to his own improvidence, caused him constant anxiety, his cheerfulness was unfailing. He was loyal to his friends, and generous to the poor; he loved good company and good liquor; he was an excellent angler, a devoted husband, and a man of unaffected piety. The portrait painted by his friend Lely shows him to have been handsome in person, with an engaging, frank countenance.—BULLEN, A. H., 1887, *Dictionary of National Biography, vol.* XII, *p.* 301.

GENERAL

The most celebrated of his works is his "Virgil Travestie," in which he so far succeeded, as to be deemed next to Butler in burlesque; but the reader, upon comparing these two authors, will find a very great disparity in their characters. He was sociable, hospitable, and generous; but as he was far from being an economist, he, in the latter part of his life, was much involved in debt, and perpetually harrassed with duns, attornies, and bailiffs.—GRANGER, JAMES, 1769–1824, *Biographical History of England, vol.* V, *p.* 253.

Finally, I will refer to Cotton's "Ode upon Winter," an admirable composition, though stained with some peculiarities of the age in which he lived, for a general illustration of the characteristics of Fancy.—WORDSWORTH, WILLIAM, 1815, *Lyrical Ballads, Preface.*

Waller's song, "Go, Lovely Rose," is doubtless familiar to most of my readers; but if I had happened to have had by me the Poems of Cotton, more but far less deservedly celebrated as the author of the ''Virgil Travestied,'' I should have indulged myself, and I think have gratified many, who are not acquainted with his serious works, by selecting some admirable specimens of this style. There are not a few poems in that volume, replete with every excellence of thought, image,

and passion, which we expect or desire in the poetry of the milder muse; and yet so worded, that the reader sees no reason either in the selection or the order of the words, why he might not have said the very same in an appropriate conversation, and can not conceive how indeed he could have expressed such thoughts otherwise, without loss or injury to his meaning.—COLERIDGE, SAMUEL TAYLOR, 1817, *Biographia Literaria, ch.* XIX.

There is a careless and happy humour in this poet's "Voyage to Ireland," which seems to anticipate the manner of Anstey, in the "Bath Guide." The tasteless indelicacy of his parody of the Aeneid has found but too many admirers. His imitations of Lucian betray the grossest misconception of humorous effect when he attempts to burlesque that which is ludicrous already. He was acquainted with French and Italian; and, among several works from the former language, translated The "Horace" of Corneille, and Montaigne's "Essays."—CAMPBELL, THOMAS, 1819, *Specimens of the British Poets*

Thy New Years' Days are past. I survive, a jolly candidate for 1821. Another cup of wine—and while that turncoat bell, that just now mournfully chanted the obsequies of 1820 departed, with changed notes lustily rings in a successor, let us attune to its peal the song made on a like occasion, by hearty, cheerful Mr. Cotton. . . . How say you, reader—do not these verses* smack of the rough magnanimity of the old English vein? Do they not fortify like a cordial; enlarging the heart, and productive of sweet blood, and generous spirits, in the concoction? Where be those puling fears of death, just now expressed or affected?—Passed like a cloud —absorbed in the purging sunlight of clear poetry—clean washed away by a wave of genuine Helicon, you only Spa for these hypochondries.—And now another cup of the generous! and a merry New Year, and many of them, to you all, my masters!—LAMB, CHARLES, 1821, *New Year's Eve, London Magazine, January.*

The poems of Cotton have the same moral stain as Herrick's, with not less fancy but a less Arcadian air—more of the world that *is* about them. The spirit of poetry was indeed on the *way downward*

* "The New Year."

from "great Eliza's golden time" till its reascent into the region of the pure and elevated towards the end of the last century, and a declension may even be observed, I think, from Herrick to Cotton, who came into the world about thirty-nine years later. His poetry, indeed, has more of Charles II's time and less of the Elizabethan period in its manner and spirit than that of Waller, who was but twenty-five years his senior. Cotton writes like a man of this world, who has glimpses now and then of the other; not as if he lived utterly out of sight of it, like the dramatists characterized by C. Lamb. There are more detailed corporeal descriptions in his poetry than in any that I know, of not more than equal extent; descriptions of the youthful body more vividly real than is to be desired, and of the body in age, when it "demands the translucency of mind not to be worse than indifferent," so full of mortality, or, what it grieves us more to contemplate than ashes and the grave, the partial perishing of the natural man while he is yet alive, that they excite an indignant disgust on behalf of our common humanity. —COLERIDGE, SARA, 1847, ed., Biographia Literaria, by Samuel Taylor Coleridge, ch. xix, note.

As for Charles Cotton, his "Virgil Travesty" is deader than Scarron's, and deserves to be so. The famous lines which Lamb has made known to every one in the essay on "New Year's Day" are the best thing he did. But there are many excellent things scattered about his work, despite a strong taint of the mere coarseness and nastiness which have been spoken of. And though he was also much tainted with the hopeless indifference to prosody which distinguished all these belated cavaliers, it is noteworthy that he was one of the few Englishmen for centuries to adopt the strict French forms and write rondeaux and the like. On the whole his poetical power has been a little undervalued, while he was also dexterous in prose.—SAINTSBURY, GEORGE, 1887, History of Elizabethan Literature, p. 385.

Cotton was a man of brilliant and versatile genius. His "Ode to Winter," a favourite poem with Wordsworth and Lamb, is a triumph of jubilant and exuberant fancy; and the fresh-coloured, fragrant stanzas entitled "The Retirement" are of rare beauty. . . . His prose style is always easy and perspicuous, instinct with energy and life.—BULLEN, A. H., 1887, Dictionary of National Biography, vol. XII, pp. 300, 301.

Henry More

1614–1687

Henry More was born at Grantham in 1614. His parents were gentlefolk, of small estate and Calvinist principles. He went to Eton, and to Christ's College, Cambridge. He took his degree in 1635, and became a Fellow of his College in 1639. He lived a life of study, refusing all preferment, even the Headship of Christ's. His time was divided between Cambridge and Ragley, in Warwickshire, the home of his friend Lady Conway. Here he found a congenial circle of mystics and wonder-workers. He died in 1687. His writings, controversial and speculative, are very numerous. The most important of them will be found in his "Philosophical Works" (1662), "Divine Dialogues" (1668), "Theological Works" (1675). He published a Latin version of his "Opera Omnia" in 1679. He also wrote poems, which were edited by Dr. Grosart in 1878. There is no modern edition of his prose works. R. Ward's "Life of Henry More" (1710), and the chapter on More in Principal Tulloch's "Rational Theology," vol. ii., are worth consulting.—CRAIK, HENRY, 1893, ed. English Prose, vol. II, p. 553.

PERSONAL

Walking abroad after his studies, his sallies towards Nature would be often inexpressibly ravishing, beyond what he could convey to others. . . . His very chamber-door was a hospital to the needy. . . . When the winds were ruffling about him, he made it his utmost endeavour to keep low and humble, that he might not be driven from that anchor. . . . He seemed to be full of introversions of light, joy, benignity, and devotion at once—as if his face had been overcast with a golden shower of love and purity. . . . There was such a life and spirit in him as loved the exercises

ISAAC WALTON

HENRY MORE

of reason, wit, and divine speculation at once. . . . He could study abroad with less weariness by far to himself than within doors.—WARD, RICHARD, 1710, *Life of Henry More, pp.* 54, 85, 89, 105, 120, 145.

Dr. More, the most rational of our modern Platonists, abounds, however, with the most extravagant reveries, and was inflated with egotism and enthusiasm, as much as any of his mystic predecessors. He conceived that he communed with the Divinity itself! that he had been shot as a fiery dart into the world, and he hoped he had hit the mark. He carried his self-conceit to such extravagance, that he thought his urine smelt like violets, and his body in the spring season had a sweet odor; a perfection peculiar to himself. These visionaries indulge the most fanciful vanity.—DISRAELI, ISAAC, 1791–1824, *Modern Platonism, Curiosities of Literature.*

Dr. More's religion was calm and gentle. He looked out mildly upon the beautiful providence of God, and adored profoundly that wisdom which displayed itself everywhere. He lived the "divine life" with his fellow-men, laboring in their behalf with assiduous diligence, till his mortal course was ended. Few men have attained so great a degree of tranquillity as he. His faith cast out fear. His own character proved the words of the old sage; "It is the quiet and still mind that is wise and prudent."—PARKER, T., 1839, *Dr. Henry More, The Christian Examiner, vol.* 26, *p.* 15.

As the Cambridge movement reached its highest, or at least its most elaborate, intellectual elevation in Cudworth, so it ripened into its finest personal and religious development in Henry More. Cudworth is much less interesting than his writings; More is far more interesting than any of his. He was a voluminous author. His writings fill several folio volumes; they are in verse as well as prose; they were much read and admired in their day; but they are now wellnigh forgotten. Some of them are hardly any longer readable. Yet More himself is at once the most typical and the most vital and interesting of all the Cambridge school. He is the most platonical of the Platonic sect, and at the same time the most genial, natural, and perfect man of

them all. We get nearer to him than any of them, and can read more intimately his temper, character and manners—the lofty and serene beauty of his personality —one of the most exquisite and charming portraits which the whole history of religion and philosophy presents.—TULLOCH, JOHN, 1872, *Rational Theology and Christian Philosophy in England in the Seventeenth Century, vol.* II, *p.* 303.

His portrait represents him in his later years as much such a man as we should have imagined: he wears his hair, which was light and long, over his shoulders, and a faint streak of moustache upon his upper lip; the face is grave but not displeasing; it has the broad arched forehead, strongly indented, that is characteristic of masculine intellect; very high and prominent cheekbones, big firm lips, and a massive chin; the cheek is healthy and not attenuated; the eyes clear and steady, the right eyelid being somewhat drooped, thus conveying a humorous look to the face; he wears the black gown, with girded cassock, and a great silk scarf—the *amussis dignitatis*—over his shoulders; the gown is tied at the neck by strings; and the broad white bands give a precise and quiet air to the whole. —BENSON, ARTHUR CHRISTOPHER, 1896, *Essays, p.* 62.

GENERAL

More was an open-hearted and sincere Christian philosopher, who studied to establish men in the great principles of religion against atheism, that was then beginning to gain ground, chiefly by reason of the hypocrisy of some, and the fantastical conceits of the more sincere enthusiasts.—BURNET, GILBERT, 1715–34, *History of My Own Time.*

One of the most remarkable in the English language, is a writer of the last age, Dr. Henry More. . . . Though his style be now in some measure obsolete, and his speakers be marked with the academic stiffness of those times, yet the dialogue is animated by a variety of character, and a sprightliness of conversation, beyond what are commonly met with in writings of this kind.—BLAIR, HUGH, 1783, *Lectures on Rhetoric and Belles-Lettres, Lecture* XXXVII.

As a poet he has woven together a singular texture of Gothic fancy and Greek philosophy, and made the Christiano-Platonic system of metaphysics a groundwork for the fables of the nursery. His versification, though he tells us that he was won to the Muses in his childhood by the melody of Spenser, is but a faint echo of the Spenserian tune. In fancy he is dark and lethargic. Yet his Psychozoia is not a common-place production: a certain solemnity and earnestness in his tone leaves an impression that he "believed the magic wonders which he sung." His poetry is not, indeed, like a beautiful landscape on which the eye can repose, but may be compared to some curious grotto, whose gloomy labyrinths we might be curious to explore for the strange and mystic associations they excite.—CAMPBELL, THOMAS, 1819, *Specimens of the British Poets.*

Henry More, though by no means less eminent than Cudworth in his own age, ought not to be placed on the same level. More fell not only into the mystical notions of the later Platonists, but even of the Cabalistic writers. His metaphysical philosophy was borrowed in great measure from them; and though he was in correspondence with Descartes, and enchanted with the new views that opened upon him, yet we find that he was reckoned much less of a Cartesian afterwards, and even wrote against parts of the theory. The most peculiar tenet of More was the extension of spirit: acknowledging and even striving for the soul's immateriality, he still could not conceive it to be unextended.—HALLAM, HENRY, 1837–39, *Introduction to the Literature of Europe, pt.* iv, *ch.* iii, *par.* 14

In England it is not just to place Cudworth among the mystics: he is a Platonist of a firm and profound mind, who bends somewhat under the weight of his erudition, and with whom method is wanting; but H. More is decidedly mystic.—COUSIN, M. VICTOR, 1841, *Course of the History of Modern Philosophy, tr. Wight,* Lecture xii.

He is less philosopher or theologian than prophet and gnostic—with his mind brimful of divine ideas, in the delighted contemplation of which he lives, and moves, and writes. All his works are inspired by a desire to make known something that he himself has felt of the Divine. The invisible or celestial, so far

from being hard for him to apprehend, is his familiar haunt. He has difficulty in letting himself down from the higher region of supernal realities to the things of earth. This celestial elevation is the most marked feature at once of his character and his mind. It is the key to his beautiful serenity and singular spiritual complacency—a complacency never offensive, yet raising him somewhat above common sympathy. It is the source of the dreamy imaginings and vague aerial conjectures which fill his books. These may seem to us now poor and unreal, and some of them absurd, but they were to him living and substantial. Nay, they were the life and substance of all his thought. He felt himself at home moving in the heavenly places, and discoursing of things which it hath not entered into the ordinary mind to conceive or utter. He was a spiritual realist.—TULLOCH, JOHN, 1872, *Rational Theology and Christian Philosophy in England in the Seventeenth Century, vol.* II, *p.* 406.

In More we get for the most part rather bad verse, and doubtfully explained philosophy. Even Coleridge, strongly as More's subject, and in part his method of treatment, appealed to him, has left some rather severe criticisms on the "Song of the Soul." It is quite true that More has, as Southey says, "lines and passages of sublime beauty." A man of his time, actuated by its noble thought, trained as we know More to have been in the severest school of Spenser, and thus habituated to the heavenly harmonies of that perfect poet, could hardly fail to produce such. But his muse is a chaotic not a cosmic one.—SAINTSBURY, GEORGE, 1887, *History of Elizabethan Literature, p.* 379.

He was a man of great and extensive learning, but in his writings are found deep tinctures of mysticism. After finishing some of his works, which had occasioned much fatigue, he would say: "Now for three months I will not think a wise thought nor speak a wise word." He was subject to fits of ecstasy, during which he gave himself up to joy and happiness, which obtained for him the nickname of THE INTELLECTUAL EPICURE. His writings have no particular interest for the present generation, but were very popular in his day, as they established great principles of religion, and fixed men's minds against the fantastical conceits of the time, which was fast running towards atheism.—FREY, ALBERT R., 1888, *Sobriquets and Nicknames, p.* 231.

He writes excellent English, easy, leisurely, scholarly, with an abundance of learning, which is yet not ponderous, and occasionally gleams of humour. He is no pedant; good racy, homespun, coarse words diversify pleasantly his philosophic terminology. Yet in the selection of his language he has the nicety of the exact refined man of letters. Pedantry, indeed would have been impossible to him, for, in spite of his airy mysticisms, he is, like Plato himself, well in touch with earth. His love of nature, of outdoor life, is intense, and colours many a passage of his prose. His chief defect as a writer is a tendency to long-windedness in his periods: none the less he rarely fails to be lucid, often succeeds in being vivid, in the expression of his thought.—CHAMBERS, E. K., 1893, *English Prose, ed. Craik, vol.* II, *p.* 554.

Like many others he began as a poet and ended as a prose writer. . . . The mere fact of the continued reproduction, in whole or in part, of More's works is a proof that they were not neglected; and, considering how utterly the refined, dreamy, and poetical sipirt of More was out of sympathy with the practical and prosaic mind of the eighteenth century, it is wonderful that his fame should have been so great as it was during that period. John Wesley, for instance, a man of an entirely different type of mind, strongly recommended More's writings to his brother-clergy. William Law, though he called More "a Babylonish philosopher," and is particularly severe upon the "Divine Dialogues," was deeply impressed with the piety and general interest of his character; and the edition of 1708 was issued through the exertions, and partly at the expense, of a gentleman the description of whom points very distinctly to Dr. Bray, who, except in the matters of piety and goodness, seems to have had little in common with More.— OVERTON, J. H., 1894, *Dictionary of National Biography, vol.* XXXVIII, *pp.* 421, 423.

But More cannot be said to have been a Christian in the sense that Thomas-à-Kempis or Francis of Assisi were Christians; he did not hunger for the personal relation with Christ which is so profoundly essential to the true conception of the Christian ideal. He was a devout, a passionate Deist; he realised the indwelling of God's spirit in the heart, and the divine excellence of the Son of Man. But it was as a pattern, and not as a friend, that he gazed upon Him; the light that he followed was the uncovenanted radiance. For it is necessary to bear in mind that More and the Cambridge Platonists taught that the Jewish knowledge of the mysteries of God had passed through some undiscovered channel into the hands of Pythagoras and Plato; and that the divinity of their teaching was directly traceable to their connection with Revelation. They looked upon Plato and Pythagoras as predestined vehicles of God's spirit, appointed to prepare the heathen world for the reception of the true mysteries, though not admitted themselves to full participation in the same.—BENSON, ARTHUR CHRISTOPHER, 1896, *Essays, p.* 56.

George Villiers

Second Duke of Buckingham

1628–1687

George Villiers, Duke of Buckingham, (b. 1627, d. 1688), wrote "The Rehearsal," and the "Battle of Sedgemoor;" and adapted from Beaumont and Fletcher the comedy of "The Chances." He also produced several religious tracts. A complete edition of his Works was published in 1775. He was the original of the famous character of Zimri in Dryden's "Absalom and Achitophel.—ADAMS, W. DAVENPORT, 1877, *Dictionary of English Literature, p.* 117.

PERSONAL

He was extremely handsome, and still thought himself much more so than he really was: although he had a great deal of discernment, yet his vanity made him mistake some civilities as intended for his person, which were only bestowed on his wit and drollery.—GRAMMONT, COUNT, 1663?–1713, *Memoirs, by Anthony Hamilton.*

A man so various, that he seem'd to be
Not one, but all Mankind's Epitome.
Stiff in Opinions, always in the wrong;
Was everything by starts, and nothing long;
But, in the course of one revolving Moon
Was Chymist, Fiddler, Statesman, and Buffoon.
—DRYDEN, JOHN, 1681, *Absalom and Achitophel, First pt.*

For his person, he was the glory of the age and any court wherever he came. Of a most graceful and charming mien and behaviour; a strong, tall and active body, all of which gave a lustre to the ornaments of his mind; of an admirable wit and excellent judgment; and had all other qualities of a gentleman. He was courteous and affable to all; of a compassionate nature; ready to forgive and forget injuries. What was said of a great man in the court of queen Elizabeth, that he used to vent his discontents at court by writing from company, and writing sonnetts, may be said of him; but when he was provoked by the malice of some and ingratitude of others, he might shew that a good natured man might have an ill natured muse. . . . His amours were too notorious to be concealed, and too scandalous to be justified, by saying he was bred in the latitude, of foreign climates, and now lived in a vicious age and court; where his accusers of this crime were as guilty as himself. He lay under so ill a name for this, that whenever he was shut up in his chamber, as he loved to be, *nescio quid*, or in his laboratory, *meditans purgarum*, over the fumes of charcoal, it was said to be with women. When a dirty chymist, a foxhunter, a pretender to poetry or politicks, a rehearsal should entertain him, when a messenger to summon him to council could not be admitted. . . . We are now come to the last scene of the tragi-comedy of his life. At the death of king Charles he went into the country to his own manor of Helmesly, the seat of the earls of Rutland in Yorkshire. King Charles was his best friend, he loved him and excused his faults. He was not so well assured of his successor. In the country he passed his time in hunting, and entertaining his friends; which he did a fortnight before his death as pleasantly and hospitably as ever he did in his life. He took cold one day after fox-hunting, by sitting on the cold ground, which cast him into an ague

and fever, of which he died, after three days sickness, at a tenant's house, Kirby more side, a lordship of his own, near Helmesly, Ap. 16, 1688; ætat. 60.—FAIRFAX, BRIAN, 1690? *Memoirs of the Life of George Villiers, Second Duke of Buckingham.*

The man was of no religion, but notoriously and professedly lustful, and yet of greater wit and parts, and sounder principles as to the interest of humanity and the common good than most lords in the court. Wherefore he countenanced fanatics and sectaries, among others, without any great suspicion, because he was known to be so far from them himself.—BAXTER, RICHARD, 1691–96, *Reliquiæ Baxterianæ, vol.* III.

He had a great liveliness of wit, and a peculiar faculty of turning all things into ridicule with bold figures and natural descriptions. He had no sort of literature: only he was drawn into chymistry: and for some years he thought he was very near the finding the philosopher's stone; which had the effect that attends on all such men as he was, when they are drawn in, to lay out for it. He had no principles of religion, virtue, or friendship. Pleasure, frolick, or extravagant diversion was all that he laid to heart. He was true to nothing, for he was not true to himself. He had no steadiness nor conduct. He could keep no secret, nor execute any design without spoiling it. He could never fix his thoughts, nor govern his estate, tho' then the greatest in England. He was bred about the King: and for many years he had a great ascendent over him: but he spake of him to all persons with that contempt, that at last he drew a lasting disgrace upon himself. And he at length ruined both body and mind, fortune and reputation equally. The madness of vice appeared in his person in very eminent instances; since at last he became contemptible and poor, sickly, and sunk in his parts, as well as in all other respects, so that his conversation was as much avoided as ever it had been courted.—BURNET, GILBERT, 1715–34, *History of My Own Time.*

The finest gentleman, both for person and wit, I think I ever saw.—RERESBY, SIR JOHN, 1734, *Memoirs.*

He lived an unprincipled statesman, a fickle projector, a wavering friend, a steady enemy; and died a bankrupt, an outcast, and a proverb.—SCOTT, SIR WALTER, 1805, *The Life of John Dryden.*

As a statesman Buckingham's only claim to respect is his consistent advocacy of religious toleration, a cause that lost more than it gained by his support. Vanity, and a restless desire for power, which he was incapable of using when obtained, were the governing motives of his political career. His servant, Brian Fairfax, who complains that the world, severe in censuring his foibles, forgot to notice his good qualities, praises his charity, courtesy, good nature, and willingness to forgive injuries. If he was extravagant, he was not covetous. While "his amours were too notorious to be concealed and too scandalous to be justified," much was imputed to him of which he was guiltless. —FIRTH, C. H., 1899, *Dictionary of National Biography, vol.* LVIII, *p.* 344.

THE REHEARSAL
1671

The | REHEARSAL, | As it was Acted at the | THEATRE-ROYAL. | LONDON, | Printed for *Thomas Dring*, at the *White-Lyon*, | next *Chancery-lane* end in *Fleet-street.* 1672.—TITLE PAGE OF FIRST EDITION.

Went to see the Duke of Buckingham's ridiculous farce and rhapsody, called "The Recital," buffooning all plays, yet prophane enough.—EVELYN, JOHN, 1671, *Diary, Dec.* 14.

The "Rehearsal" (one of the best pieces of criticism that ever was) and Butler's inimitable poem of Hudibras, must be quite lost to the readers in a century more, if not soon well comented. Tonson has a good key to the former, but refuses to print it, because he had been so much obliged to Dryden.—LOCKIER, DEAN, 1730-32, *Spence's Anecdotes, ed. Singer, p.* 48

His poems, which indeed are not very numerous, are capital in their kind; but what will immortalize his memory while our language shall be understood, or true wit relished, is his celebrated play of "The Rehearsal;" . . . a comedy which is so perfect a master-piece in its way, and so truly an original, that notwithstanding its prodigious success, even the task of imitation, which most kinds of excellence have excited inferior geniuses to undertake, has appeared as too arduous to be attempted with regard to this, which through a century and half still stands alone, notwithstanding that the very plays it was written expressly to ridicule are forgotten, and the taste it was meant to expose totally exploded.—REED, ISAAC, 1782, *Biographia Dramatica, vol.* I, *pt.* ii, *p.* 730.

Five editions of "The Rehearsal" appeared in the Author's life time. Of the second and third I cannot learn even the dates. There is a copy of the fourth, 1683, in the Bodleian. An examination of the fifth, 1687, would seem to show a general permanence of the text, but that, probably in each edition, there were here and there additions and alterations *en bloc,* instigated by the appearance of fresh heroic plays: some of these additions increase, with the multiplying corruption of the times, in personality and moral offensiveness. For our literary history, the first edition is sufficient.—ARBER, EDWARD, 1869, *ed., The Rehearsal, Introduction.*

In describing George Villiers, second Duke of Buckingham, as one standing apart, we refer to the character of his solitary work, and not to his share in it; for, though passing solely under his name, there can be little doubt that it was the production of a junto of wits, of whom he was not the wittiest. Butler, Sprat, and Martin Clifford are named as his coadjutors. Buckingham, who must be credited with a keen sense of the ridiculous, had already resolved to satirize rhyming heroic plays in the person of Sir Robert Howard, when the latter's retirement diverted the blow to Dryden, whom Butler, as we shall see, did not greatly relish, and against whose device of rhyme, Sprat, as we have seen, had committed himself by anticipation. The play chiefly selected for parody is "The Conquest of Granada," which certainly invited it. Dryden appears as Bayes, in allusion to his laureateship; and, although his perpetual use of "egad" seems derived from the usage by one of his *dramatis personae* rather than his own, we cannot doubt that his peculiarities of speech and gesture were mostly copied to the life. Within a week the town were unanimously laughing at what they had been unanimously applauding; and, scurrilous and ill-bred as the mockery of "The Rehearsal" was, it must be allowed to have been neither uncalled for nor unuseful.—GARNETT, RICHARD, 1895, *The Age of Dryden, p.* 119.

GENERAL

He had so vitiated a taste, and so vulgar a style, that, except his Pindaric on Lord Fairfax, the following ["To His Mistress"] is, perhaps, the only effort of his

muse which can be selected, without conferring blame on the selector.—WALPOLE, HORACE, 1758, *A Catalogue of the Royal and Noble Authors.*

There is no power in them, [Poems] though there is sometimes a facile execution.—SMITH, GEORGE BARNETT, 1875, *English Fugitive Poets, Poets and Novelists, p.* 386.

Edmund Waller

1606–1687

Born, at Coleshill, Herts, 3 March 1605. Educated at Eton, and at King's Coll., Camb. M. P. for Amersham, 1621; for Chipping Wycombe, 1626; for Amersham, 1628–29, 1640; for Hastings, 1661–78; for Saltash, 1685–87. Married (i) Anna Banks, 15 July 1631; (ii) Mary Bresse [or Breaux?]. Imprisoned for a year, and fined, for high treason, 1643–44; exiled, in France, 1644–53. Died, at Beaconsfield, 21 Oct. 1687. Buried there. *Works:* Four Speeches in the House of Commons, pubd. separately, 1641; "Speech . . . 4 July, 1643," 1643; "Workes," 1645; "A Panegyrick to my Lord Protector" (under initials: E. W.), 1655; "Upon the late Storme and Death of his Highness ensuing the same" [1658]; "To the King, upon his Majestie's Happy Return" [1660]; "Poem on St. James's Park," 1661; "To my Lady Morton" (anon.) 1661; "To the Queen" [1663]; "Pompey the Great" (with others; anon.), 1664; "Upon her Majesties new buildings at Somerset House," 1665; "Instructions to a Painter," 1666. *Posthumous:* "The Maids Tragedy altered, etc.," 1690. *Collected Works:* "Poems," ed. by G. T. Drury 1893. *Life:* by P. Stockdale, 1772.—SHARP, R. FARQUHARSON, 1897, *A Dictionary of English Authors, p.* 291.

PERSONAL

He is of somewhat above a middle stature, thin body, not at all robust: fine thin skin, his face somewhat of an olivaster; his hayre frizzd, of a brownish colour; full eye, popping out and working: ovall faced, his forehead high and full of wrinckles. His head but small, braine very hott and apt to be cholerique— *Quanto doctior, eo iracundior.*—Cicero. He is something magisteriall, and haz a great mastership of the English language. He is of admirable and gracefull elocution and exceeding ready. . . . He haz but a tender weake body, but was always very temperate . . . (quaere Samuel Butler) made him damnable drunke at Somerset-house, where, at the water-stayres he fell downe and had a cruell fall. 'Twas pitty to use such a sweet swan so inhumanely. He hath a great memory and remembers a history etc. etc. best when read to him: he uses to make his daughters read to him. Yet, notwithstanding his great witt and mastership in rhetorique etc. he will oftentimes be guilty of mispelling in English. He writes a lamentably (bad) hand as bad (as)

the scratching of a hen.—AUBREY, JOHN, 1669–96, *Brief Lives, ed.* Clark, vol. II, *pp.* 276, 277.

When he had lost all hopes of Sacharissa, he looked round him for an easier conquest, and gained a Lady of the family of Bresse, or Breaux. The time of his marriage is not exactly known. It has not been discovered that his wife was won by his poetry; nor is anything told of her, but that she brought him many children. He doubtless praised some whom he would have been afraid to marry, and perhaps married one whom he would have been ashamed to praise. Many qualities contribute to domestick happiness, upon which poetry has no colours to bestow; and many airs and sallies may delight imagination, which he who flatters them never can approve. There are charms made only for distant admiration. No spectacle is nobler than a blaze.—JOHNSON, SAMUEL, 1779, *Waller, Lives of the English Poets.*

The courtly Waller, like the lady in the "Maids' Tragedy," loved with his ambition,—not with his eyes; still less with his heart. A critic, in designating the poets of that time, says truly that "Waller still lives in Sacharissa:" he lives in her name more than she does in his poetry; he gave that name a charm and a celebrity which has survived the admiration his verses inspired, and which has assisted to preserve them and himself from oblivion. . . . Waller's Sacharissa was the Lady Dorothea Sydney, the eldest daughter of the Earl of Leicester, and born in 1620. At the time he thought fit to make her the object of his homage, she was about eighteen, beautiful, accomplished, and admired. Waller was handsome, rich, a wit, and five-and-twenty. He had ever an excellent opinion of himself, and a prudent care of his worldly interests. He was a great poet, in days when Spenser was forgotten, Milton neglected, and Pope unborn. . . . The lady was content to be the theme of a fashionable poet: but when he presumed farther, she crushed all hopes with the most undisguised aversion and disdain.—JAMESON, ANNA BROWNELL, 1829, *The Loves of the Poets, vol. II, pp.* 15, 16, 17.

The wife and the mother may be said, however, to have survived, in the popular memory, the gallant husband, and the clever but unstable son. Sacharissa is a name more universally known than the name and title of either Lady Spencer or Countess of Sunderland. Waller formed the name "pleasantly," as he was wont to say, from *saccharum*, sugar. Whether Waller were ever more than her poetical suitor may be doubted; though Dorothy is said to have once rejected his suit.—MANCHESTER, DUKE OF, 1864, *Court and Society from Elizabeth to Anne, vol.* I, *p.* 354.

With all his brilliant poetic gifts and social accomplishments, Waller's seems to have been a mean and poor nature—selfish and pleasure-loving in prosperity, and abject and servile in adversity.—TULLOCH, JOHN, 1872, *Rational Theology and Christian Philosophy in England in the Seventeenth Century, vol.* I, *p.* 110.

As Beatrice and Laura represent the ideal lady of Dante and of Petrarch's age, so Waller's Sacharissa is the type of all that was fair and excellent in the womanhood of the seventeenth century. But Sacharissa, unlike *ces belles dames du tems jadis,* is more for us than a mere dream of beauty and goodness. She

has a very attractive and interesting personality of her own. The pictures of her which Vandyke painted, as she appeared to Waller in the bloom of her youthful loveliness, adorn the walls of more than one ancient and stately house. At Penshurst, at Althrop, at Petworth, we see her under many forms and in many different costumes, and always, as Horace Walpole said, "charmingly handsome."—CARTWRIGHT, JULIA (MRS. HENRY ADY,) 1893, *Sacharissa; Some Account of Dorothy Sidney, Countess of Sunderland, Preface, p.* v.

GENERAL

The best of poets.—DENHAM, SIR JOHN, 1642, *Cooper's Hill.*

The | Workes | of | Edmond Waller | Esquire, | Lately a Member of the Hon | ourable House of | Commons, | in this Present Parliament. | London. | Printed for Thomas Walkley. | 1645.—TITLE PAGE OF FIRST EDITION.

Waller not wants the glory of his verse;
And meets a noble praise, in every Line.
—DANIEL, GEORGE, 1647, *A Vindication of Poesy.*

I cannot but bewail the transitoriness of their fame, as well as other men's, when I hear Mr. Waller is turned to burlesque among them, while he is alive, which never happened to old poets till many years after their death; and though I never knew him enough to adore him as many have done, and easily believe he may be, as your Lordship says, enough out of fashion, yet I am apt to think some of the old cut-work bands were of as fine thread, and as well wrought, as any of our new points; and, at least, that all the wit he and his company spent, in heightening love and friendship, was better employed, than what is laid out so prodigally by the modern wits, in the mockery of all sorts of religion and government.—TEMPLE, SIR WILLIAM, 1667, *Letter to Lord Lisle, August.*

Waller, by Nature for the Bays design'd,
With Force and Fire, and Fancy unconfin'd
In Panegyric, does excel Mankind.
—ROCHESTER, EARL OF, 1678, *An Allusion to the tenth Satire of the first book of Horace.*

Chaucer threw in Latin, French, Provençal, and other languages, like new stum to raise a fermentation; in Queen Elizabeth's time, it grew fine, but came not to an head and spirit, did not shine and sparkle, till Mr. Waller set it a running.—RYMER, THOMAS, 1678-92, *A Short View of the Tragedy of the Last Age.*

Waller came last, but was the first whose art
Just weight and measure did to verse impart;
That of a well-placed word could teach the force,
And show'd for poetry a nobler course;
His happy genius did our tongue refine,
And easy words with pleasing numbers join:
His verses to good method did apply,
And changed hard discord to soft harmony.
All own'd his laws; which long approved and tried,
To present authors now may be a guide
Tread boldly in his steps, secure from fear,
And be, like him, in your expressions clear.
—SOAME, SIR WALTER, 1683, *The Art of Poetry, rev. Dryden.*

Long did the untun'd world in ignorance stray,
Producing nothing that was great and gay,
Till taught by thee the true poetic way;
Rough were the tracks before, dull and obscure,
Nor pleasure nor instruction could procure;
Their thoughtless labours could no passion move
Sure, in that age, the poets knew not love.
That charming god, like apparitions, then,
Was only talked on, but ne'er seen by men.
Darkness was o'er the Muses' land displayed,
And even the chosen tribe unguided strayed,
Till, by thee rescued from the Egyptian night,
They now look up and view the god of light,
That taught them how to love, and how to write.
—BEHN, APHRA, 1687, *On the Death of Waller.*

While tender airs and lovely dames inspire
Soft melting thoughts, and propagate desire;
So long shall Waller's strains our passion move,
And Sacharissa's beauty kindle love.
—ADDISON, JOSEPH, 1694, *An Account of the Greatest English Poets.*

Waller in Granville lives: when Mira sings
With Waller's hand he strikes the sounding strings,
With sprightly turns his noble genius shines,
And manly sense adorns his easy lines.
—GAY, JOHN, 1714, *On a Miscellany of Poems.*

Britain to soft refinement less a foe,
Wit grew polite, and numbers learn'd to flow,
Waller was smooth.
—POPE, ALEXANDER, 1733, *The First Epistle of the second book of Horace.*

Parent of harmony in English verse,
Whose tuneful Muse in sweetest accents flows,
In couplets first taught straggling sense to close.
—CHURCHILL, CHARLES, 1761, *The Apology.*

Waller was the first refiner of English poetry, at least of English rhyme; but his performances still abound with many faults, and what is more material, they contain but feeble and superficial beauties. Gaitey, wit, and ingenuity, are their ruling character: they aspire not to the sublime; still less to the pathetic. They treat of love, without making us feel any tenderness; and abound in panegyric, without exciting admiration. The panegyric, however, on Cromwell, contains more force than we should expect from the other compositions of this poet.—HUME, DAVID, 1762, *The History of England, The Commonwealth.*

Our poetry was not quite harmonized in Waller's time; so that this, ["On the Death of the Lord Protector."] which would be now looked upon as a slovenly sort of versification, was, with respect to the times in which it was written, almost a prodigy of harmony. A modern reader will chiefly be struck with the strength of thinking and the turn of the compliments bestowed upon the Usurper. Every body has heard the answer our poet made Charles II. who asked him how his poem upon Cromwell came to be finer than his panegyric upon himself. Your majesty, replies Waller, knows, that poets always succeed best in fiction.—GOLDSMITH, OLIVER, 1767, *The Beauties of English Poetry.*

Edmund Waller, sometimes styled "the English Tibullus," excelled all his predecessors, in harmonious versification. His love verses have all the tenderness and politeness of the Roman poet; and his panegyric on Cromwell has been ever esteemed a masterpiece in its kind. His vein is never redundant, like that of Cowley; we frequently wish he had said more, but never that he had said less.—GRANGER, JAMES, 1769-1824, *Biographical History of England, vol.* III, *p.* 125.

His works gave a new era to English poetry.—STOCKDALE, PERCIVAL, 1772 *Life of Waller.*

The delicacy, which he cultivated,

restrains him to a certain nicety and caution, even when he writes upon the slightest matter. He has, therefore, in his whole volume, nothing burlesque, and seldom any thing ludicrous or familiar. He seems always to do his best; though his subjects are often unworthy of his care. . . . The amorous verses have this to recommend them, that they are less hyperbolical than those of some other poets. Waller is not always at the last gasp; he does not die of a frown, nor live upon a smile. There is, however, too much love, and too many trifles. Little things are made too important; and the Empire of Beauty is represented as exerting its influence further than can be allowed by the multiplicity of human passions, and the variety of human wants. . . . He certainly very much excelled in smoothness most of the writers who were living when his poetry commenced. . . . The general character of his poetry is elegance and gaiety. He is never pathetick, and very rarely sublime. He seems neither to have a mind much elevated by nature, nor amplified by learning. His thoughts are such as a liberal conversation and large acquaintance with life would easily supply. . . . Of the praise of Waller, though much may be taken away, much will remain; for it cannot be denied that he added something to our elegance of diction, and something to our propriety of thought.—JOHNSON, SAMUEL, 1779, *Waller, Lives of the English Poets.*

Waller, whom you proscribe, Sir, owed his reputation to the graces of his manner, though he frequently stumbled, and even fell flat; but a few of his smaller pieces are as graceful as possible: one might say that he excelled in painting ladies in enamel, but could not succeed in portraits in oil, large as life.—WALPOLE, HORACE, 1785, *Letters (To J. Pinkerton)*, ed. Cunningham, vol. VIII, p. 564.

To say of Carew that he is superior to Waller, is saying nothing; for if every line of Waller were lost, I know not that poetry would have much to lament. The works of both however should be preserved, and I hope ever will be, as necessary to mark the progress of our language toward refinement.—DRAKE, NATHAN, 1798-1820, *Literary Hours, No.* xxviii.

If Waller differed from the Cowleian sect of writers, he differed for the worse. He had as little poetry as they, and much less wit: nor is the langour of his verses less offensive than the ruggedness of theirs.— MACAULAY, THOMAS BABINGTON, 1828, *Dryden, Edinburgh Review, Critical and Miscellaneous Essays.*

His reputation was great, and somewhat more durable than that of similar poets has generally been: he did not witness its decay in his own protracted life, nor was it much diminished at the beginning of the next century. Nor was this wholly undeserved. Waller has a more uniform elegance, a more sure facility and happiness of expression, and, above all, a greater exemption from glaring faults, such as pedantry, extravagance, conceit, quaintness, obscurity, ungrammatical and unmeaning constructions, than any of the Caroline era with whom he would naturally be compared. We have only to open Carew or Lovelace to perceive the difference; not that Waller is wholly without some of these faults, but that they are much less frequent. . . . If he rarely sinks, he never rises very high; and we find much good sense and selection, much skill in the mechanism of language and metre, without ardor and without imagination. In his amorous poetry he has little passion or sensibility; but he is never free and petulant, never tedious, and never absurd. His praise consists much in negations; but, in a comparative estimate, perhaps negations ought to count for a good deal.—HALLAM, HENRY, 1837-39, *Introduction to the Literature of Europe, pt.* iv, *ch.* v, *par.* 22.

The crying truth is louder than Mr. Hallam, and cries, in spite of Fame, with whom poor Waller was an "enfant trouvé," an heir by chance, rather than merit,—that he is feeble poetically quite as surely as morally and politically, and that, so far from being an equal and sustained poet, he has not strength for unity even in his images, nor for continuity in his thoughts, nor for adequacy in his expression, nor for harmony in his versification.—BROWNING, ELIZABETH BARRETT, 1842-63, *The Book of the Poets.*

Edmund Waller hardly deserves a place among the best names in English literature, either as a poet or as a man; and in giving him a small space here, I yield my own judgement to that of Dryden and Pope. . . . As a poet, Waller is certainly "smooth," as Pope styles him, and comparatively destitute of that affectation which characterizes most of his contemporaries.—CLEVELAND, CHARLES D., 1848, *A Compendium of English Literature*, p. 314.

Waller's poems were universally read and admired in the age in which they were published: nor was their general popularity much diminished during the early portion of the last century. The greater part of them now seldom find a reader; and the large majority of educated Englishmen are familiar with only a few lines of Waller; yet these few lines are such standard favourites, that their author's poetical reputation is safely preserved by them.—CREASY, SIR EDWARD, 1850-76, *Memoirs of Eminent Etonians*, p. 132.

Pope said of Waller, that he would have been a better poet had he entertained less admiration of people in power. But surely it was the excess of that propensity which inspired him. He was naturally timid and servile; and poetry is the flower of a man's real nature, whatever it be, provided there be intellect and music enough to bring it to bear. Waller's very best pieces are those in praise of sovereign authority and of a disdainful mistress. He would not have sung Saccharissa so well had she favored him.—HUNT, LEIGH, 1851, *Table-Talk*, p. 136.

. . . Waller of the silvery tongue, . . . —LYTTON, EDWARD LORD, 1860, *St. Stephen's*, pt. i.

There are not, perhaps, two hundred really good lines in all Waller's poetry. Extravagant conceits, feeble verses, and defective rhymes are constantly recurring, although the poems, being mostly short, are not tedious. Of elevated imagination, profound thought, or passion, he was utterly destitute; and it is only in detached passages, single stanzas, or small pieces, finished with great care and elegance, as the lines on a lady's girdle, those on the dwarfs, and a few of the lyrics, that we can discern that play of fancy, verbal sweetness, and harmony which gave so great a name to Waller for more than a hundred years.—CARRUTHERS, ROBERT, 1860, *Waller, Encyclopædia Britannica*, 8th ed., *vol.* XXI, p. 691.

The passages of merit in Waller's writings that elevate him from "the mob of gentlemen who wrote with ease," prove that he had the intellect to be a far greater poet than he was, but he had not the heart. He was a brilliant wit, an elegant verse-writer, but he was as destitute of deep feeling as he was of high principle. It was only when trembling on the borders of the grave that he manifested anything like a noble and generous emotion. . . . He was unfaithful to the trust reposed in him, and, with full and brilliant capacity, fell immeasurably below the high office of the bard.—RICE, G. E., 1860, *Edmund Waller, North American Review, vol.* 91, *pp.* 383, 384.

One thing must be admitted in regard to Waller's poetry: it is free from all mere verbiage and empty sound; if he rarely or never strikes a very powerful note, there is at least always something for the fancy or the understanding, as well as for the ear, in what he writes. He abounds also in ingenious thoughts, which he dresses to the best advantage, and exhibits with great transparency of style. Eminent, however, as he is in his class, he must be reckoned among that subordinate class of poets who think and express themselves chiefly in similitudes, not among those who conceive and write passionately and metaphorically. He had a decorative and illuminating, but not a transforming imagination.—CRAIK, GEORGE L., 1861, *A Compendious History of English Literature and of the English Language, vol.* II, *p.* 102

No man better understood the art of flattery and how to administer it with grace.—SCOONES, W. BAPTISTE, 1880, *Four Centuries of English Letters*, p. 95.

He seizes anything frivolous, new, or convenient, on the wing; and his poetry is only a written conversation,—I mean the conversation which goes on at a ball, when people speak for the sake of speaking, lifting a lock of one's wig, or twisting about a glove. Gallantry, as he confesses, holds the chief place here, and one may be pretty certain that the love is not over-sincere. In fact, Waller sighs on purpose (Sacharissa had a fine dowry), or at least for the sake of good manners; that which is most evident in his tender poems is, that he aims at a flowing style and good rhymes. He is affected, he exaggerates, he strains after wit, he is always an author. . . . Nevertheless Waller is usually amiable; a sort of brilliant light floats like a halo round his verses;

he is always elegant, often graceful. His gracefulness is like the perfume exhaled from the world; fresh toilettes, ornamented drawing-rooms, the abundance and all those refined and delicate comforts give to the soul a sort of sweetness which is breathed forth in obliging compliments and smiles. Waller has such, and that most flattering, apropos of a bud, a girdle, a rose. . . . All his verses flow with a continuous harmony, clearness, facility, though his voice is never raised, or out of tune, or rough, nor loses its true accent, except by the worldling's affectation, which regularly varies all tones in order to soften them. His poetry resembles one of those pretty, affected, bedizened women, busy in inclining their head on one side, and murmuring with a soft voice commonplace things which they cannot be said to think, yet agreeable in their beribboned dress, and who would please altogether if they did not dream of always pleasing.—TAINE, H. A., 1871, *History of English Literature, tr. Van Laun, vol.* I, *bk.* iii, *ch.* i, *pp.* 498, 500.

As a poet he is nothing but a rhetorician.—SCHERR, J., 1874-82, *A History of English Literature, p.* 114.

Had he owned a larger and more sincere nature we might have had in him a great poet.—SMITH, GEORGE BARNETT, 1875, *English Fugitive Poets, Poets and Novelists, p.* 389.

With the poems of Denham he ["Voltaire"] was greatly pleased; and of Waller, whose "Elegy on the Death of Cromwell," he has translated into French verse, he speaks in terms of enthusiastic admiration, ranking him above Voiture, and observing that, "his serious compositions exhibit a strength and vigour which could not have been expected from the softness and fluency of his other pieces."—COLLINS, JOHN CHURTON, 1886, *Voltaire in England, p.* 283.

Waller has come to a casual literary importance in these days under the deft talking and writing of those dilettante critics who would make this author the pivot (as it were) on which British poesy swung away from the "hysterical riot of the Jacobeans" into measured and orderly classic cadence. It is a large influence to attribute to a single writer, though his grace and felicities go far to justify it. And it is further to be remembered that such critics are largely given to the discussion of *technique* only; they write as distinct art-masters; while we, who are taking our paths along English Letters for many other things besides art and rhythm, will, I trust, be pardoned for thinking that there is very little pith or weighty matter in this great master of the juggleries of sound.—MITCHELL, DONALD G., 1890, *English Lands Letters and Kings, From Elizabeth to Anne, p.* 149.

When all claims and candidates have been considered, it is really to Edmund Waller that is due the "negative inspiration" (the phrase is borrowed from Sainte-Beuve) of closing up within bands of smoothness and neatness the wild locks of the British muse. He was the English Malherbe, and wrote with the same constitutional contempt for his predecessors.—GOSSE, EDMUND, 1897, *A Short History of Modern English Literature, p.* 157.

No poetical reputation has suffered such vicissitudes as that of Edmund Waller: described, in the inscription upon his tomb, as "inter poetas sui temporis facile princeps," it was still possible, in 1766, to introduce him to the readers of the Biographia Britannica as "the most celebrated Lyric Poet that ever England produced." . . . The revolt against classicism extinguished the reputation of Waller, as it impaired that of men in every way greater than he. . . . He is credited with having polished his poetry like marble, but his execution is frequently careless, and his ear was by no means exceptionally acute. He uses the feeble expletive "so" upwards of twenty times as a rhyme, and occasionally he is satisfied with an assonance. Of the "essence of poetry, invention," he was practically destitute, but it would be difficult to find in the whole range of English Poetry any one more uniformly successful in improving an occasion. To many people his verses on this or that public occasion must have come as a relief, after the "conceited" obscurities of Donne. He makes no great demand on the understanding, he is singularly free from conceits, and his classical allusions are the most trite and ordinary. . . . The general level of Waller's lyrical work is distinctly high.—DRURY, G. THORN, 1893, *ed., The Poems of Edmund Waller, pp.* lxix, lxxi, lxxiii.

Waller's powers would certainly be in higher repute, but for the trivial or transitory interests to which he gave them. The court poet pays dearly for his courtliness at last. He bestows the best of his experience upon perishable or unprofitable matter, and we are surprised rather than pleased to find not the fly in amber, but amber in the fly.—TOVEY, REV. DUNCAN C., 1897, *Reviews and Essays in English Literature, p.* 101.

Most of his poems are occasional, and many of them trivial in their immediate subject, but they are polished with the utmost care and good taste. His panegyrics and complimentary verses are graceful and often dignified.—MASTERMAN, J. HOWARD B., 1887, *The Age of Milton, p.* 124.

Ralph Cudworth

1617-1688

Ralph Cudworth was born at Aller in Somersetshire in 1617. His father, also a learned man, died in 1624, and his mother then married Dr. Stoughton, who took the greatest pains with his stepson's education. In 1630 he went to Emmanuel College, Cambridge. In 1640, after a brilliant university career, he was presented to the Rectory of North Cadbury, Somersetshire. He was not long a parish priest, for in 1644 he was appointed Master of Clare and stopped at Cambridge, almost without break, for the remaining forty-four years of his life. He was, in 1645, appointed Regius Professor of Hebrew; in 1654, Master of Christ's; and in 1678 Prebendary of Gloucester Cathedral. He died in 1688. Cudworth is best known by his "True Intellectual System of the Universe" (1678), and his "Treatise on Eternal and Immutable Morality" (not published till 1731). He also wrote a "Discourse concerning the true Notion of the Lord's Supper," a "Treatise of Free Will," a couple of sermons, and a **work** on Daniel's prophecy of the LXX weeks.—CRAIK, HENRY, 1893, *ed., English Prose, vol.* II, *p.* 581.

PERSONAL

He was a man of great conduct and prudence; upon which his enemies did **very** falsely accuse him of craft and dissimulation.—BURNET, GILBERT, 1715–34, *History of My Own Time.*

Of his personal character and manners we have no description; nor is it easy to discern the familiar lineaments of the man, as he lived and moved among his friends, through all the meagre and desultory vagueness of Birch's "Account," or any other notices of his life which have come down to us. In his correspondence with Worthington, we have seen some trace of a slight narrowness and jealousy of temper; but this is a mere transitory ebullition, which after all may mean very little. More's more agile and discursive spirit had outstripped him in his favourite intellectual ambition of writing a book on "Natural Ethics," and some soreness of feeling was excusable in the circumstances. Such indications as we can gather point upon the whole to an elevated and noble character—a spirit not only free from the vulgar sectarianisms of the time, but intent upon high objects, and generous as it was lofty. His portrait conveys the same impression. If somewhat heavily lined, like that of Whichcote, and even touched with austerity in its massive and long-drawn features, it is also full of sweetness. The face is that of a severe and powerful, but also a gentle-minded and tolerantly meditative, student.—TULLOCH, JOHN, 1872, *Rational Theology and Christian Philosophy in England in the Seventeenth Century, vol.* II, *p.* 225.

INTELLECTUAL SYSTEM OF THE UNIVERSE

1678

Raised such strong objections against the being of God, and Providence, that many think he has not answered them.—DRYDEN, JOHN, 1697, *The Æneid, Dedication.*

You know the common fate of those who dare to appear fair authors. What was that pious and learned man's case, who wrote the intellectual system of the universe? I confess it was pleasant enough to consider, that though the whole world were no less satisfied with his capacity and learning, than with his sincerity in the cause of Deity; yet was he accused of giving the upperhand to the

Atheists, for having only stated their reasons, and those of their adversaries, fairly together.—COOPER, ANTHONY ASHLEY (LORD SHAFTESBURY), 1709, *The Moralist, pt.* ii, *sec.* iii, *p.* 196.

The very slowest were able to unravel his secret purpose—to tell the world that he was an atheist in his heart and an Arian in his book! Would the reader know the consequence?—why the zealots inflamed the bigots?—

"'Twas the time's plague, when madmen
   led the blind."

The silly calumny was believed; the much-injured author grew disgusted; his ardour slackened; and the rest, and far greatest part, of the defence never appeared.— WARBURTON, WILLIAM, 1741, *Divine Legation of Moses, Preface, vol.* II.

Cudworth never went out of his way for the sake of paradox, never degenerated into affectations for the purpose of displaying originality, was content to be full of his subject, instead of making his subject full of himself; it was not his aim to wrap himself in the clouds of conceitedness, and to make himself obscure to the multitude, but to render himself as intelligible as the subject would admit. His object was to seek for the truth wherever it might be found, and to communicate truth to whomsoever it was desirable.— SEARGILL, W. P., 1822, *Cudworth's Intellectual System of the Universe, Retrospective Review, vol.* 6, *p.* 53.

It contains the greatest mass of learning and argument that ever was brought to bear on atheism. A thousand folio pages, full of learned quotations, and references to all heathen and sacred antiquity, demonstrate the fertility and laborious diligence of the author. And whoever wishes to know all that can be said respecting liberty and necessity, fate and free-will, eternal reason and justice, and arbitrary omnipotence, has only to digest the "Intellectual System."—ORME, WILLIAM, 1824, *Bibliotheca Biblica.*

It is this mine of recondite quotations in their original languages, most accurately translated, which has imparted such an enduring value to this treasure of the ancient theology, philosophy, and literature: for however subtle and logical was the mastermind which carried on his trains of reasoning, its abstract and abstruse nature could not fail to prove repulsive to the superficial; for few could follow the genius who led them into "the very darkest recesses of antiquity," while his passionless sincerity was often repugnant to the narrow creed of the orthodox. . . . "The Intellectual System" has furnished many writers with their secondary erudition, and possibly may have given rise to that portion of "the Divine Legation" of Warburton whose ancient learning we admire for its ingenuity, while we retreat from its paradoxes; for there is this difference between this solid and that fanciful erudition,—that Warburton has proudly made his subject full of himself, while Cudworth was earnest only to be full of his subject —DISRAELI, ISAAC, 1841, *The Intellectual System, Amenities of Literature*

As a vast storehouse of learning, and also as a display of wonderful powers of subtle and far-reaching speculation, this celebrated work is almost unrivalled in our literature; and it is also written in a style of elastic strength and compass which places its author in a high rank among our prose classics. — CRAIK, GEORGE L., 1861, *A Compendious History of English Literature and of the English Language, vol.* II, *p.* 132.

Cudworth, who was much superior to Hume in learning, and much inferior to him in genius, displayed, in his great work on the "Intellectual System of the Universe," a prodigious erudition, to prove that, in the ancient world, the belief in one God was a prevailing doctrine. Hume, who never refers to Cudworth, arrives at a precisely opposite conclusion. Both quoted ancient writers; but while Cudworth drew his inferences from what he found in those writers, Hume drew his from what he found in his own mind. Cudworth, being more learned, relied on his reading; Hume, having more genius, relied on his intellect. Cudworth, trained in the school of Bacon, first collected the evidence, and then passed the judgment. Hume, formed in a school entirely different, believed that the acuteness of the judge was more important than the quantity of the evidence; that witnesses were likely to prevaricate; and that he possessed, in his own mind, the surest materials for arriving at an accurate conclusion. It is not, therefore, strange, that Cudworth and Hume, pursuing opposite methods, should have obtained opposite results, since such a discrepancy is, as I have already pointed out, unavoidable, when men investigate, according to different plans, a subject which, in the existing state of knowledge, is not amenable to scientific treatment.—BUCKLE, HENRY THOMAS, 1862, *History of Civilization in England, vol.* III, *p.* 348.

Cudworth, even with Mosheim's help, must have left the impression upon foreign scholars that our scholarship was somewhat unwieldy. The admirers of Descartes must have thought that one who was in a certain sense his English disciple, had not caught much of this lucid method. Yet to us Cudworth can never be an unimportant person. In the days of Hobbes, in the days when the notion of Hobbes respecting the Divine Being as a mere power, was creeping into the minds of divines of various schools, was finding props in Puritanism and in anti-Puritanism, he stood forth bravely and nobly as the asserter of a moral Divinity, as the witness that wherever the idea of morality is wanting, there is potential, there will be actual, atheism.— MAURICE, FREDERICK DENISON, 1862–73, *Moral and Metaphysical Philosophy, vol.* II, *p.* 347.

The series of emancipations of morality begins with the Intellectual System of Ralph Cudworth.—FALCKENBERG, RICHARD, 1885–93, *History of Modern Philosophy, tr. Armstrong, p.* 196.

GENERAL

An excellent and learned divine, of highest authority at home, and fame abroad.—COOPER, ANTHONY ASHLEY (LORD SHAFTESBURY), 1711–23, *Miscellaneous Reflections, Characteristics, pt.* ii, *ch.* ii.

He was a good antiquary, mathematician, and philosopher; and was superior to all his contemporaries in metaphsyics. —GRANGER, JAMES, 1769–1824, *Biographical History of England, vol.* V, *p.* 43.

A much more eminent and enlightened man than Gale, Ralph Cudworth, by his "Intellectual System of the Universe," published in 1678, but written several years before, placed himself in a middle point between the declining and rising schools of philosophy: more independent of authority, and more close perhaps in argument, than the former; but more prodigal

of learning, more technical in language, and less conversant with analytical and inductive processes of reasoning, than the latter. Upon the whole, however, he belongs to the school of antiquity; and probably his wish was to be classed with it. Cudworth was one of those whom Hobbes had roused by the atheistic and immoral theories of the Leviathan; nor did any antagonist perhaps of that philosopher bring a more vigorous understanding to the combat. This understanding was not so much obstructed in its own exercise by a vast erudition, as it is sometimes concealed by it from the reader. Cudworth has passed more for a recorder of ancient philosophy, than for one who might stand in a respectable class among philosophers; and his work, though long, being unfinished, as well as full of digression, its object has not been fully apprehended.—HALLAM, HENRY, 1837–39, *Introduction to the Literature of Europe, pt.* iv, *ch.* iii, *par.* 6.

If an ordinary sensible Englishman takes up even such a book as Cudworth's "Immutable Morality," it is nearly inevitable that he should put it down as mystical fancy. True as a considerable portion of the conclusions of that treatise are or may be, nevertheless the truth is commonly so put as to puzzle an Englishman, and the error so as particularly to offend him. . . . We do not mean that Cudworth's style is not as good [as] or better than the style of Butler: but that the language and illustrations of the latter belong to the same world as that we live in, have a relation to practice, and recall sentiments we remember to have felt and sensations which are familiar to us; while those of Cudworth, on the contrary, seem difficult, and are strange in the ears of the common people.—BAGEHOT, WALTER, 1850, *Bishop Butler, Works, ed. Morgan, vol.* II, *pp.* 125, 128.

At a time when the history of philosophy was still unknown as a science, he cast his glance over all the systems of antiquity, and brought their results together, if not critically, yet with an appreciation of their difference and relations which would be in vain sought for in any other writer of the century. Immersed in Platonic and pseudo-Platonic conceptions which frequently distort his view of the opinions of others, he seldom allowed them to dominate or corrupt his own rational vision. He kept the eye of his own reason single; and it was a large, open, and discerning eye. On the one hand, he sought to purify the conceptions of the popular theology; and, on the other hand, to vindicate for man a genuine sphere of religious and moral idea, in which he could move freely yet feel securely. The rights of reason and of conscience are alike dear to him.—TULLOCH, JOHN, 1872, *Rational Theology and Christian Philosophy in England in the Seventeenth Century, vol.* II, *p.* 299.

He seems to have been a shy, retiring man, with something of Hooker's disposition; like Hooker, also, an industrious and profound scholar. He was not of a controversial turn, but was pressed by his friends to take the field against Hobbes, Atheism, and every form of heterodoxy. He stated the opinions of his opponents at such length and with such candour that his sincerity was suspected; and he was so alarmed at the outcry raised by his honourable and ingenuous fashion of polemic, that he refrained from farther publication.—MINTO, WILLIAM, 1872–80, *Manual of English Prose Literature, p.* 337.

In combating the atheists, he displays a prodigious amount of erudition, and that rare degree of candour which prompts a controversialist to give a full statement of the opinions and arguments which he means to refute.—CHAMBERS, ROBERT, 1876, *Cyclopædia of English Literature, ed. Carruthers.*

His writings might have been produced in a lonely and silent monastery, instead of amid the rage of factions and the reverberation of the Naseby guns. The hurry and passion of their age are wholly absent from them: with infinite leisure they conduct the reader to the Schools of Athens and Alexandria, and beguile him there with spacious arguments, interrupted often by a series of concentric episodes, till he forgets where he is, and is lost, except to the world of theosophic abstractions.—MARTINEAU, JAMES, 1885, *Types of Ethical Theory, p.* 396.

Cudworth is probably the most learned, able, and sensible of his school. The book is in form as much historical as argumentative. The fourth chapter, which is more than half the book, is intended to show that a primitive montheistic creed

was implied in the ancient paganism. The rest of the book is devoted to a consideration of the various forms of atheism held by the ancient philosophers, with an elaborate reply to their arguments. Cudworth was undoubtedly aiming at Hobbes, the great contemporary advocate of materialist philosophy, but his discussion generally takes the shape of an attack upon Democritus, Strabo, and Lucretius, and a defence of Plato and Aristotle. Though abandoning the old scholasticism, he scarcely appreciates the modern theories of Bacon, Descartes, and Spinoza, . . . and thus appears rather antiquated for his time. His profound learning in the ancient philosophy did not lead him, like his friend Henry More, into the mysticism of the later platonists.—STEPHEN, LESLIE, 1888, *Dictionary of National Biography, vol.* XIII, *p.* 272.

Cudworth's works deserve to be studied by the modern student of English literature, not only for the excellence of their style but for the value of their contents. Many of his strictures upon the materialistic philosophies of his own and of a bygone day still bear on latter-day controversies, while his exhortations to live the Christ-like life rather than wrangle over doctrinal niceties would not come amiss in these times of party shibboleths.—FITZROY, A. I., 1893, *English Prose, ed. Craik, vol.* II, *p.* 582.

His life was mainly spent in his study, in the production of vast folios, where the ignots of philosophy lay stored while Locke's current coin passed nimbly from hand to hand. The contrast between the men and the systems is complete at every point; and it is assuredly one of the strangest ironies of fate that Cudworth's daughter should have become the good angel of Locke's old age. Cudworth is no doubt by much the more attractive figure to imaginative minds; but it must be conceded as an indisputable truth that his way of thinking could not possibly have produced nearly so much good, have so profoundly leavened men's ideas on legislation and education, or have so contributed to build up the national character for sound common sense. This admitted, Cudworth may be heartily praised as a sublime and refined thinker, epithets inappropriate to Locke.—GARNETT, RICHARD, 1895, *The Age of Dryden, p.* 165.

John Bunyan

1628–1688

Born, at Elstow, Bedfordshire, Nov. 1628. Educated at parish school, and brought up to father's trade of tinker. Served as soldier, 1644-46. Married, 1648 (?) or 1649(?). Lived at Elstow. Joined Nonconformists, 1653. Removed to Bedford, 1655(?); wife died there. Elected Deacon, 1655; Preacher, 1657. Married again, 1659. At Restoration was arrested, 12 Nov. 1660, for preaching. Imprisoned in Bedford Gaol, 1660-72. Released for a few weeks in 1666. Chosen Minister to Bedford Nonconformists, Jan. 1672; received license to preach, 9 May 1672. Received formal pardon from Crown, 13 Sept. 1672. Perhaps imprisoned for six months in 1675, during which time "Pilgrim's Progress" was written. Active life—preaching in neighbourhood of Bedford and in London. Chaplain to Lord Mayor of London, 1688. Died in London, 31 Aug. 1688; buried in Bunhill Fields, Finsbury. *Works:* "Some Gospel Truths Opened," 1656; "Vindication" of same, 1657; "A Few Sighs from Hell," 1658; "The Doctrine of the Law," 1659; "Profitable Meditations," (1661); "I will pray with the Spirit," 1663; "Christian Behaviour," 1663; "The Four Last Things, etc." (1664?); "The Holy City," 1665; "The Resurrection," 1665; "Grace Abounding," 1666; "Defence of the Doctrine of Justification," 1672; "Confession of Faith," 1672; "Difference of Judgment about Water Baptism," 1673; "Peaceable Principles," 1674; "Reprobation Asserted" (1675?); "Light for them that sit in Darkness," 1675; "Instruction for the Ignorant," 1675; "Saved by Grace," 1675; "The Strait Gate," 1676; "Pilgrim's Progress," pt. i., 1678 (2nd. edn. same year); pt. ii., 1684; "Come, and Welcome, to Jesus Christ," 1678; "Treatise of the Fear of God," 1679; "Life and Death of Mr. Badman," 1680; "Holy War," 1682; "Barren Fig Tree," 1682; "Greatness of the Soul," 1683; "Case of Conscience Resolved," 1683; "Seasonable Counsel," 1684; "Holy Life the Beauty of Christianity," 1684; "A Caution to stir up to Watch against Sin," 1684; "Questions about the Nature . . . of the . . . Sabbath," 1685; "The Pharisee and the Publican," 1685; "Book for Boys and Girls" (in later edns. called "Divine Emblems") 1686; "Jerusalem Sinner Saved" (anon.), 1688; "Advocateship of Jesus Christ," 1688 (another edn. under title: "Work of Jesus Christ as an Advocate," 1688); "Discourse of the . . . House of God," 1688; "Water of Life," 1688; "Solomon's Temple Spiritualized," 1688. *Posthumous:* "Acceptable Sacrifice," 1689; "Last Sermon," 1688; "Works" (including ten posthumous works), 1692; "Heavenly Footman," ed. by C. Doe, 1698 "Pilgrim's Progress," pt. i. and ii. together, 1728; "Relation of the Imprisonemnt of Mr. J. Bunyan" (written in Bedford Gaol), 1765. *Collected Works:* ed. by S. Wilson (2 vols.), 1736; ed. by H. Stebbing (4 vols.), 1859.—SHARP, R. FARQUHARSON, 1897, *A Dictionary of English Authors, p.* 38.

PERSONAL

To the Constables of Bedford and to every of them

J. Napier

W. Beecher

G. Blundell

Hum : Monoux

Whereas information and complaint is made unto us that (notwithstanding the King's Majties late Act of most gracious generall and free pardon to all his subjects for past misdemeanors that by his said clemencie and indulgent grace and favor they might bee moved and induced for the time to come more carefully to observe his Highness' lawes and Statutes and to continue in theire loyall and due obedience to his Majtie) Yett one John Bunnyon of youre said Towne Tynker hath divers times within one month last past in contempt of his Majties Good Lawes preached or teached at a Conventicle Meeting, or Assembly under color or ptence of exercise of Religion in other manner than according to the Liturgie or practiss of the Church of England. These are therefore in his Majties name to command you forthwith to apprehend and bring the Body of the said

Will ffranklin John Bunnion before us or any of us or other his Majties Justice of Peace within the said County to answer the premisses and further to doo and receave as to
John Ventris Lawe and Justice shall appertaine and hereof you are not to faile. Given under our handes and seales this fforth day of March in the seven and twentieth yeare of the Raigne of our most gracious Soveraigne Lord King Charles the Second. A° que Dñi juxta &c 1674

Will Spencer

Will Gery	St Jo Chervocke	Wm Daniels
	T Browne	W ffoster
	Gaius Squire.	

—ORDER FOR ARREST, 1674.

What hath the devil, or his agents, gotten by putting our great gospel minister Bunyan, in prison? For in prison he wrote many excellent books, that have published to the world his great grace, and great truth, and great judgment, and great ingenuity; and to instance in one, the "Pilgrim's Progress," he hath suited to the life of a traveller so exactly and pleasantly, and to the life of a Christian, that this very book, besides the rest, hath done the superstitious sort of men more good than if he had been let alone at his meeting at Bedford, to preach the gospel to his own auditory.—DOE, CHARLES, 1692, *The Struggler; Life and Actions of John Bunyan.*

He was not only well furnished with the helps and endowments of nature beyond ordinary, but eminent in the graces and gifts of the Spirit and fruits of holiness. He was a true lover of all that love our Lord Jesus and did often bewail the different and distinguishing appellations that are among the godly, saying, he did believe a time would come when they should be all buried. His carriage was condescending, affable and meek to all; yet bold and couragious for Christ's and the gospel's sake. He was much struck at in the late times of persecution and his sufferings were great, under all which he behaved himself like Christ's soldier, being far from any sinful compliance to save himself, but did chearfully bear the cross of Christ. As a minister of Christ he was laborious in his work of preaching, diligent in his preparation for it and faithful in dispensing the word, not sparing reproof for outward circumstances whether in the pulpit or no, yet ready to succour the tempted; a son of consolation to the broken-hearted, yet a son of thunder to secure and dead sinners. . . . His remembrance is sweet and refreshing to many and so will continue: For the righteous shall be had in everlasting remembrance.—WILSON, JOHN, 1692, *Bunyan's Works, Epistle to the Reader.*

I heard Mr. Bagford (some time before he dyed) say, that he walked once into the country on purpose to see the study of John Bunyan. When he came, John received him very civilly and courteously, but his study consisted only of a Bible and a parcell of books, (the "Pilgrim's Progress" chiefly,) written by himself, all lying on a shelf or shelves.—HEARNE, THOMAS, 1723, *Reliquiæ Hearnianæ, ed. Bliss, April 7, vol. II, p. 157.*

Of gipsey descent or otherwise, Bunyan was bred up with, and speedily forgot, the slender proportion of schooling then accessible to the children of the poor in England. He was by nature of enthusiastic feelings, and so soon as the subject of religion began to fix his attention, his mind appears to have been agonized with the retrospect of a misspent youth. A quick and powerful imagination was at work on a tender conscience; for it would appear that his worst excesses fell far short of that utter reprobation to which he conceived them entitled.—SCOTT, SIR WALTER, 1830, *Southey's Life of John Bunyan, Quarterly Review, vol. 43, p. 470.*

John Bunyan was a decided Baptist; and in his days, the most incredible falsehoods were invented, and actively circulated, to bias the minds of all classes against this proscribed sect, or any of their writings. Although he had carefully come to a decision upon this subject, he never obtruded it upon public notice; so that, in nearly all his works, water baptism is swallowed up in his earnest desire to win souls to Christ. All his effort is, to fix attention upon that spiritual baptism, or regeneration, which is essential to salvation, and by which the soul passeth from death unto life. He appeared, in one respect, as an Ishmaelite, and differed with all the numerous sects by which he was surrounded. In his early days, the sectarian spirit was very exclusive; Episcopalians, Presbyterians, Independents, and Baptists, rarely permitted any but members of their own community to partake with them at the Lord's table. Bunyan was the leader in publicly breaking through this practice. He considered that water baptism was not a church ordinance, but a personal duty, upon which, as to the outward form of ceremony, every one should be left to his own judgment; and he firmly believed that all, who, by the baptism of the Spirit, called God their father, were entitled to a seat at his table, notwithstanding any peculiar or sectarian bias about days, meats, and ceremonies. This drew upon him the severest censures of his brethren in the ministry, particularly of the Baptist denomination. — OFFOR, GEORGE, 1850, *ed., The Works of John Bunyan, Preface, vol.* I, *p.* iv.

"As I walked through the wilderness of this world I lighted upon a certain place where was a den." These words have been translated into hundreds of languages, and hundreds and thousands in all parts of the world and all classes of mankind have asked, "Where was that place, and where was that den?" and the answer has been given that the name of the "place" was Bedford, and that the "den" was Bedford gaol. This it is which has given to the town of Bedford its chief—may I say, without offence, its only—title to universal and everlasting fame. It is now two hundred years ago since Bunyan must have resolved on the great venture—so it seemed to him—of publishing the work which has given to Bedford this immortal renown; and Bedford is this day endeavouring to pay back some part of the debt which it owes to him.—STANLEY, ARTHUR PENRHYN, 1874, *John Bunyan, An Address Delivered at Bedford June* 10, *Macmillan's Magazine, vol.* 30, *p.* 273.

It has been the fashion to dwell on the disadvantages of his education, and to regret the carelessness of nature which brought into existence a man of genius in a tinker's hut at Elstow. Nature is less partial than she appears, and all situations in life have their compensations along with them. Circumstances, I should

say, qualified Bunyan perfectly well for the work which he had to do. If he had gone to school, as he said, with Aristotle and Plato; if he had been broken in at a university and been turned into a bishop; if he had been in any one of the learned professions, he might easily have lost, or might have never known, the secret of his powers. He was born to be the Poet-apostle of the English middle classes, imperfectly educated like himself; and, being one of themselves, he had the key of their thoughts and feelings in his own heart. Like nine out of ten of his countrymen, he came into the world with no fortune but his industry. He had to work with his hands for his bread, and to advance by the side of his neighbours along the road of common business. His knowledge was scanty, though of rare quality. He knew his Bible probably by heart. He had studied history in Foxe's "Martyrs," but nowhere else that we can trace. The rest of his mental furniture was gathered at first hand from his conscience, his life, and his occupations. Thus, every idea which he received falling into a soil naturally fertile, sprouted up fresh, vigorous, and original.—FROUDE, JAMES ANTHONY, 1880, *Bunyan* (*English Men of Letters*), *p.* 172.

The County Gaol in which Bunyan spent the twelve years of his life, from 1660 to 1672, was taken down in 1801. It stood on what is now the vacant piece of land at the corner of the High Street and Silver Street, used as a market-place. Silver Street, so named because it was the quarter where the Jews in early times trafficked in the precious metals, was afterwards known as Gaol Lane, but, since the disappearance of the gaol, has become Silver Street again. The only trace of the gaol itself still left on the spot is the rough stone wall on the north side of the market-place, which was the wall of the small courtyard used by the prisoners. From the interior of the prison, a massive door made of three transverse layers of oak fastened through with iron bolts, and having bars across an open centre, is preserved in the vestry of Bunyan Meeting, Bedford, as a relic of Bunyan's imprisonment; but no sketch of the building itself of any kind has come down to us. There were iron-grated windows on the Gaol Lane, or

Silver Street side, and the older people of the last generation used to tell how the prisoners hung purses out of these windows on Sunday mornings, asking the pitiful help of such passers by as were on their way to church or chapel.—BROWN, JOHN, 1885, *John Bunyan, His Life, Times and Work,* p. 162.

Bunyan's personal appearance is thus described by a contemporary: "He was tall of stature, strong-boned though not corpulent, somewhat of a ruddy face with sparkling eyes, wearing his hair on his upper lip after the old British fashion; his hair reddish, but in his latter days had sprinkled with grey; his nose well-set, but not declining or bending, and his mouth moderately large, his fore-head something high, and his habit always plain and modest." Another contemporary writes: "His countenance was grave and sedate, and did so to the life discover the inward frame of his heart, that it was convincing to the beholders, and did strike something of awe into them that had nothing of the fear of God." A third thus describes his manner and bearing: "He appears in countenance to be of a stern and rough temper, but in his conversation mild and affable, not given to loquacity or much discourse in company, unless some urgent occasion required it, observing never to boast of himself in his parts, but rather seem low in his own eyes, and submit himself to the judgment of others."—VENABLES, EDMUND, 1886, *Dictionary of National Biography, vol.* VII, *p.* 282.

Buckingham, who courted almost all orders of men, would not have honored him with a nod of recognition; nor would Bishop Burnet. I think even the amiable Dr. Tillotson, or the very liberal Dr. South, would have jostled away from him in a crowd, rather than toward him. Yet he was more pious than they; had more humor than Buckingham; and for imaginative power would outrank every man living in that day, unless we except the blind old poet Milton.—MITCHELL, DONALD G., 1890, *English Lands Letters and Kings, From Elizabeth to Anne,* p. 209.

Our result can be briefly stated. This is unquestionably a fairly typical case of a now often described mental disorder. The peculiarities of this special case lie largely in the powers of the genius who here suffered from the malady. A man of sensitive and probably somewhat burdened nervous constitution, whose family history, however, so far as it is known to us, gives no positive evidence of serious hereditary weakness, is beset in childhood with frequent nocturnal and even diurnal terrors of a well-known sort. In youth, after an early marriage, under the strain of a life of poverty and of many religious anxieties, he develops elementary insistent dreads of a conscientious sort, and later a collection of habits of questioning and of doubt which erelong reach and obviously pass the limits of the normal. His general physical condition meanwhile failing, in a fashion that, in the light of our very imperfect information concerning this aspect of the case, still appears to be of some neurasthenic type, there now appears a highly systematized mass of insistent motor speech-functions of the most painful sort, accompanied with still more of the same fears, doubts, and questions. After enduring for a pretty extended period, after one remission, and also after a decided change in the contents of the insistent elements, the malady then more rapidly approaches a dramatic crisis, which leaves the sufferer for a long period in a condition of secondary melancholic depression, of a somewhat benign type—a depression from which, owing to a deep change of his mental habits, and to an improvement of his physical condition, he finally emerges cured, although with defect, of his greatest enemy—the systematized insistent impulses. This entire morbid experience has lasted some four years. Henceforth, under a skilful self-imposed mental regimen, this man, although always a prey to elementary insistent temptations and to fits of deep depression of mood, has no return of his more systematized disorders, and endures heavy burdens of work and of fortune with excellent success. Such is the psychological aspect of a story whose human and spiritual interest is and remains of the very highest.—ROYCE, JOSIAH, 1898, *Studies of Good and Evil,* p. 74.

GRACE ABOUNDING
1666

What genuine superstition is exemplified in that bandying of texts and half-texts, and demi-semi-texts, just as memory happened to suggest them, or chance brought them before Bunyan's mind! His tract, entitled, "Grace abounding to the Chief of Sinners," is a study for a philosopher.—COLERIDGE, SAMUEL TAYLOR, 1830, *Table-Talk, June* 10.

The author of the "Pilgrim's Progress" has also left an autobiography, under the title of "Grace Abounding," which is as remarkable from a psychological as from an historical point of view. This book is the best study for the origin and essence of Puritanism. It is a work which, in spite of its being specifically English, has the significance for the seventeenth century that the "Confessiones" of St. Augustin have for the fifth, and the "Confessions" of Rousseau for the eighteenth. In these three books beats the full and living pulse of the times in which they were composed.—SCHERR, J., 1874–82, *A History of English Literature, p.* 126, *note.*

This proved to be one of his most memorable compositions, and associates itself in one's mind with Augustine's confessions and the heart-utterances of Luther. . . . This book, which in parts is weird and terrible as his own picture of the valley of the shadow of death, is yet in its alternations a faithful transcript of the writer's soul, and must be read in order to a right understanding of the man as he was, both in strength and weakness.—BROWN, JOHN, 1885, *John Bunyan, His Life, Times and Work, pp.* 179, 186.

The value of the "Grace Abounding," however, as a work of experimental religion may be easily overestimated. It is not many who can study Bunyan's minute history of the various stages of his spiritual life with real profit. To some temperaments, especially among the young, the book is more likley to prove injurious than beneficial; it is calculated rather to nourish morbid imaginations, and a dangerous habit of introspection, than to foster the quiet growth of the inner life. —VENABLES, EDMUND, 1888, *Life of John Bunyan* (*Great Writers*), *p.* 130.

"Grace Abounding"resembles thousands of similar narratives in essentials, differing principally in the vigour with which a terrifying religious experience is portrayed. It .does not, as some seem to have taken for granted, terminate with what would be technically considered as Bunyan's conversion; on the contrary, a large portion is employed in recording his agonies of apprehension long after he had become a recognized religious instructor, even so late as the beginning of his imprisonment, when he was so little acquainted with the law as to suppose himself in jeopardy of the gallows. Much might be said in censure or compassion of his lamentably distorted views of divine things; but one thing cannot be said, there is not from first to last the slightest symptom of cant. The book is more sincere than Rousseau's "Confessions," but could not, like that book, have helped a Carlyle or a George Eliot to learn that there was something in them. As Pilgrim's Progress may be termed a prosaic Divine Comedy, so might the Bunyan of "Grace Abounding" rank as a prosaic Augustine, but an Augustine without a Monica.—GARNETT, RICHARD, 1895, *The Age of Dryden, p.* 243.

PILGRIM'S PROGRESS
1678–84

> Well, when I had thus put mine ends together,
> I shew'd them others, that I might see whether
> They would condemn them, or them justify:
> And some said, let them live; some, let them die.
> Some said, *John,* print it; others said, Not so:
> Some said, It might do good; others said, No.
> Now was I in a strait, and did not see
> Which was the best thing to be done by me:
> At last I thought, Since you are thus divided,
> I print it will; and so the case decided.

—BUNYAN, JOHN, 1678, *Pilgrim's Progress, The Author's Apology for His Book.*

I have been better entertained, and more informed, by a few pages in the "Pilgrim's Progress," than by a long discourse upon the will and the intellect, and simple or complex ideas.—SWIFT, JONATHAN, 1719–20, *A Letter to a Young Clergyman.*

My life and opinions . . . will . . . be no less read than the "Pilgrim's Progress" itself.—STERNE, LAURENCE, 1759, *The Life and Opinions of Tristram Shandy, vol.* I, *ch.* iv.

His "Pilgrim's Progress" has great merit, both for invention, imagination, and the conduct of the story; and it has had the best evidence of its merit, the general and continued approbation of mankind Few books, I believe, have had a more extensive sale. It is remarkable, that it begins very much like the poem of Dante; yet there was no translation of Dante when Bunyan wrote. There is reason to think that he had read Spenser.—JOHNSON, SAMUEL, 1773, *Life by Boswell, April 30.*

Ingenious dreamer, in whose well-told tale
Sweet fiction and sweet truth alike prevail;
Whose humorous vein, strong sense, and simple style,
May teach the gayest, make the gravest smile;
Witty, and well employ'd, and, like thy Lord,
Speaking in parables his slighted word;
I name thee not, lest so despised a name
Should move a sneer at thy deserved fame;
Yet e'en in transitory life's late day,
That mingles all my brown with sober gray,
Revere the man, whose pilgrim marks the road,
And guides the progress of the soul to God.
—COWPER, WILLIAM, 1784, *Tirocinium.*

The plan of this work is admirable, being drawn from the circumstances of his own life, as a stranger and pilgrim, who had left the "City of Destruction" upon a journey towards the "Celestial Country." The difficulties he met with in his determination to serve Jesus Christ, suggested the many circumstances of danger through which this pilgrim passed. The versatile conduct of some professors of religion, suggested the different characters which Christian met with in his way; these, most probably, were persons whom he well knew, and who, perhaps, would be individually read at the time.—IVIMEY, JOSEPH, 1809, *A Life of John Bunyan.*

A splendid edition of "Bunyan's Pilgrim!" Why, the thought is enough to turn one's moral stomach. His cockle-hat and staff transformed to a smart cock'd beaver and a jemmy cane; his amice gray, to the last Regent Street cut; and his painful palmer's pace to the modern swagger. Stop thy friend's sacreligious hand. Nothing can be done for B. but to reprint the old cuts in as homely but good a style as possible. The Vanity Fair, and the Pilgrims there—the silly-soothness in his setting-out countenance —the Christian Idiocy (in a good sense) of his admiration of the shepherds on the Delectable Mountains; the lions, so truly allegorical, and remote from any similitude to Pidcock's; the great head (the author's), capacious of dreams and similitudes, dreaming in the dungeon. Perhaps

you don't know my edition, what I had when a child. If you do, can you bear new designs from Martin, enamelled into copper or silver plate by Heath, accompanied with verses from Mrs. Hemans's pen, O · how unlike his own!—LAMB, CHARLES, 1828, *Letter to Bernard Barton, Oct. 11, Letters, ed. Ainger, vol. II, p. 203.*

His is a homespun style, not a manufactured one; and what a difference is there between its homeliness and the flippant vulgarity of the Roger L'Estrange and Tom Brown school! If it is not a well of English undefiled, to which the poet as well as the philologer must repair if they would drink of the living waters, it is a clear stream of current English, the vernacular speech of his age; sometimes, indeed, in its rusticity and coarseness, but always in its plainness and its strength. To this natural style Bunyan is in some degree beholden for his general popularity; his language is everywhere level to the most ignorant reader and to the meanest capacity; there is a homely reality about it; a nursery tale is not more intelligible, in its manner of narration, to a child.— SOUTHEY, ROBERT, 1830, *ed., Pilgrim's Progress, Preface.*

The parable of the Pilgrim's Progress is, of course, tinged with the tenets of the author, who might be called a Calvinist in every respect, save his aversion to the institution of a regular and ordained clergy. To these tenets he has, of course, adapted the pilgrimage of Christian, in the incidents which occur, and opinions which are expressed. The final condemnation of Ignorance, for instance, who is consigned to the infernal regions when asking admittance to the celestial city, because unable to produce a certificate of his calling, conveys the same severe doctrine of fatalism which had well nigh overturned the reason of Bunyan himself. But the work is not of a controversial character,—it might be perused without offence by sober-minded Christians of all persuasions; and we all know that it is read universally, and has been translated into many languages. It, indeed, appears from many passages in Bunyan's writings, that there was nothing which he dreaded so much as divisions amongst sincere Christians.—SCOTT, SIR WALTER, 1830, *Southey's Life of John Bunyan, Quarterly Review, vol. 43, p. 488.*

Bunyan's imagination was powerful enough, in connection with his belief in God's superintending Providence, to array his inward trials with a sensible shape, and external events with a light reflected from his own experience; hopes and fears were friends and enemies; acting in concert with these, all things he met with in the world were friends or enemies likewise, according as they aided or opposed his spiritual life. He acted always under one character, the Christian Soldier, realizing, in his own conflicts and conquests, the Progress of his own Pilgrim. Therefore his book is a perfect Reality in oneness as a whole, and in every page a book not of imaginations and shadows, but of Realities experienced. To those who have never set out on this pilgrimage, nor encountered its dangers, it is interesting, as would be a book powerfully written of travels in an unknown, romantic land. Regarded as a work of original genius simply, without taking into view its spiritual meaning, it is a wonder to all, and cannot cease to be.—CHEEVER, GEORGE BARRELL, 1833, *Southey's Life of Bunyan, North American Review, vol.* 36, *p.* 453.

There is no long allegory in our literature at all comparable to Bunyan's "Pilgrim's Progress;" and one principal reason why this is the most delightful thing of the kind in the world is, that, though "written under the similitude of a dream," there is very little of pure allegory in it, and few abstract qualities or passions are personified. From the very constitution of the latter, the reader almost certainly foresees what such typical beings will say, suffer, or do, according to the circumstances in which they are placed. The issue of every trial, of every contest, is known as soon as the action is commenced.—MONTGOMERY, JAMES, 1833, *Lectures on General Literature, Poetry, etc., p.* 147.

I wish I could sympathize with you in what you say of our old Divines. I quite agree as to their language; it is delightful to my taste; but I cannot find in any of them a really great man. . . . I never yet found one of them who was above mediocrity. . . . But if I could find a great man amongst them, I would read him thankfully and earnestly. As it is, I hold John Bunyan to have been a man of incomparably greater genius than

any of them, and to have given a far truer and more edifying picture of Christianity. His "Pilgrim's Progress" seems to be a complete reflection of Scripture, with none of the rubbish of the theologians mixed up with it.—ARNOLD, THOMAS, 1836, *Letter to Mr. Justice Coleridge, Nov.* 30, *ed. Stanley, vol.* II, *p.* 67.

John Bunyan may pass for the father of our novelists. His success in a line of composition like the spiritual romance or allegory, which seems to have been frigid and unreadable in the few instances where it had been attempted, is doubtless enhanced by his want of all learning, and his low station in life. He was therefore rarely, if ever, an imitator: he was never enchained by rules. Bunyan possessed, in a remarkable degree, the power of representation: his inventive faculty was considerable; but the other is his distinguishing excellence. He saw, and makes us see, what he describes: he is circumstantial without prolixity, and, in the variety and frequent change of his incidents, never loses sight of the unity of his allegorical fable. His invention was enriched, and rather his choice determined, by one rule he had laid down to himself, —the adaptation of all the incidental language of Scripture to his own use. There is scarce a circumstance or metaphor in the Old Testament which does not find a place, bodily and literally, in the story of the "Pilgrim's Progress"; and this peculiar artifice has made his own imagination appear more creative than it really is.—HALLAM, HENRY, 1837–39, *Introduction to the Literature of Europe, pt.* iv, *ch.* vii, *par.* 57.

In childhood, we sit, as it were, on Christian's knee, listening to the tale of his
"Hair-breadth escapes
By flood and field."
In youth we join him upon his perilous journey, to obtain directions for our own intended pilgrimage in the narrow way. Before manhood is matured, we know experimentally that the Slough of Despond, and Doubting Castle, are no fictions. And even in old age, Christians are more than ever convinced of the heights, and depths, and breadths, and lengths of Bunyan's spiritual wisdom.—PHILIP, ROBERT, 1839, *Life, Times and Characteristics of John Bunyan, p.* 592.

The "Pilgrim's Progress" is an Allegory,

and a beautiful, just and serious one.—
CARLYLE, THOMAS, 1840, *The Hero as Divinity, Heroes and Hero-Worship.*

It is a significant circumstance that, till
a recent period, all the numerous editions
of the "Pilgrim's Progress" were evidently meant for the cottage and the servant's hall. The paper, the printing, the
plates, were all of the meanest description. In general, when the educated
minority and the common people differ
about the merit of a book, the opinion of
the educated minority finally prevails.
The "Pilgrim's Progress" is perhaps the
only book about which, after the lapse of
a hundred years, the educated minority
has come over to the opinion of the common people.—MACAULAY, THOMAS BABINGTON, 1843, *John Bunyan, Critical and
Historical Essays.*

What were bars and bolts and prison
walls to him, whose eyes were anointed
to see, and whose ears opened to hear,
the glory and the rejoicing of the City of
God, when the pilgrims were conducted
to its golden gates, from the black and
bitter river, with the sounding trumpeters, the transfigured harpers with their
crowns of gold, the sweet voices of
angels, the welcoming peal of bells in the
holy city, and the songs of the redeemed
ones? In reading the concluding pages
of the first part of "Pilgrim's Progress,"
we feel as if the mysterious glory of the
Beatific Vision was unveiled before us.
We are dazzled with the excess of light.
We are entranced with the mighty melody; overwhelmed by the great anthem
of rejoicing spirits. It can only be adequately described in the language of Milton in respect to the Apocalypse, as "a
seven-fold chorus of hallelujahs and harping symphonies." — WHITTIER, JOHN
GREENLEAF, 1849, *John Bunyan, Old Portraits and Modern Sketches,* p. 29.

Out of that old notion of the Christian
life as a pilgrimage, which had existed in
hundreds of minds before till it had become a commonplace, there grew and
grew in Bunyan's mind the whole visual
allegory of his book—from the Wicketgate seen afar over the fields under the
Shining Light, on, by the straight undeviating road itself, with all its sights and
perils, and through the Enchanted Ground
and the pleasant land of Beulah, to the
black and bridgeless river by whose

waters is the passage to the glimmering
realms, and the brightness of the Heavenly City.—MASSON, DAVID, 1859, *British
Novelists and Their Styles,* p. 74.

But what can we say of the Prison
Book of John Bunyan? Dear to all people,
the favourite of every nation, it is
scarcely possible to add one word to what
has been long ago said in its glory. The
simple fact that from the day of its publication to the present time, it has been
the delight and instructor of thousands,
is its greatest eulogy. Translated into
every known tongue, all sects and all religions have done honour to its wonderful
powers. With one little curtailment, our
Roman Catholic friends have a "Pilgrim's
Progress;" and though Giant Pope be
taken out, we are sure that thousands of
them must have been made a little more
catholic by reading the work of the sectarian tinker of Elstow. All men alike,
learned and ignorant, gentle and simple,
bear their testimony to the genius of the
great Baptist.—LANGFORD, JOHN ALFRED,
1861, *Prison Books and Their Authors,* p.
230.

After the Bible, the book most widely
read in England is the "Pilgrim's Progress," by John Bunyan. . . . Poor
in ideas, full of images, given up to a
fixed and single thought, plunged into this
thought by his mechanical pursuit, by his
prison and his readings, by his knowledge
and his ignorance, circumstances, like
nature, make him a visionary and an artist,
furnish him with supernatural impressions, and sensible images, teaching him
the history of grace and the means of expressing it. . . . As children, countrymen, and all uncultivated minds, he transforms arguments into parables; he only
grasps truth when it is made simple by
images; abstract terms elude him; he
must touch forms and contemplate colours.
—TAINE, H. A., 1871, *History of English
Literature, tr. Van Laun, vol.* I, *bk.* ii,
ch. v, *pp.* 398, 402, 404.

It is in this amazing reality of impersonation that Bunyan's imaginative genius
specially displays itself. But this is far
from being his only excellence. In its
range, in its directness, in its simple
grace, in the ease with which it changes
from living dialogue to dramatic action,
from simple pathos to passionate earnestness, in the subtle and delicate fancy

which often suffuses its childlike words, in its playful humor, its bold character-painting, in the even and balanced power which passes without effort from the Valley of the Shadow of Death to the land "where the Shining Ones commonly walked, because it was on the borders of Heaven," in its sunny kindliness, unbroken by one bitter word, the "Pilgrim's Progress" is among the noblest of English poems.—GREEN, JOHN RICHARD, 1874, *A Short History of the English People, ch.* ix. *sec.* ii.

There are many little defects in the "Pilgrim's Progress," yet for two centuries it has been, and it seems likely to continue, the most popular of allegories. This is due to its vivid painting; its stiring action; its all-important theme; its quiet humor, whose lambent flames light many a dark page; its tenderness for the weak; its perfectly intelligible language, whole pages of which contain no word which any child of eight years may not understand; and, above all, its strong human interest, which makes every Christian feel that he is reading the story of his own inner life, while he recognizes the portrait of many a neighbor in those representative characters, which Bunyan delineates with a pen hardly less felicitious than Shakespeare's.—SPRAGUE, HOMER B., 1874–77, *Masterpieces in English Literature, p.* 288.

It might, perhaps, have been thought that Bunyan, with his rough and imperfect education, must have erred—as it may be he has sometimes erred—in defective appreciation of virtues and weaknesses not his own; but one prevailing characteristic of his work is the breadth and depth of his intellectual insight. For the sincere tremors of poor Mrs. Much-afraid he has as good a word of consolation as he has for the ardent aspirations of Faithful and Hopeful. For the dogmatic nonsense of Talkative he has a word of rebuke as strong as he has for the gloomy dungeons of Doubting Castle; and for the treasures of the past he has a feeling as tender and as pervasive as if he had been brought up in the cloisters of Oxford or Westminster Abbey.—STANLEY, ARTHUR PENRHYN, 1874, *John Bunyan, An Address Delivered at Bedford June* 10, *Macmillan's Magazine, vol.* 30, *p.* 277.

Bunyan then achieved one of the greatest

marvels of human fancy. But in order to appreciate its full worth we must understand the difficulties in the face of which he produced such an effect, difficulties of which some were quite peculiar to him, while others have not been present in the same degree to other poets. . . . No poet, I suppose, ever lived in so limited a circle of ideas and emotions as Bunyan. . . . "The Pilgrim's Progress," if comparable to the greatest poems of all time for other artistic excellences, is not so in respect of the expression of the passions. Its personages have in the highest degree the qualities of objectivity, and, if I may say so, visibility, but their action upon the mind of the spectator is not equally great, indeed it is much more subdued than is usually the case with the personages of other great poems. Speaking generally it may be said that Bunyan's story masters the whole of our imagination and our faith, but barely half our emotion. His characters let us see all that they are, but they do not let us see the growth, the outburst, the shock, of their passions. Even those amongst them who are continually upon the scene, who perform before our eyes the whole of their journey to the celestial city, brief, rapid, and true as are the actions in which their personality unfolds itself, yet never give us any great development of emotion, anything to suggest the hidden tragedy that is going on within them.—ZUMBINI, BONAVENTURA, 1876, *Saggi Critici, tr. Nettleship.*

The Pilgrim, though in a Puritan dress, is a genuine man. His experience is so truly human experience, that Christians of every persuasion can identify themselves with him; and even those who regard Christianity itself as but a natural outgrowth of the conscience and intellect, and yet desire to live nobly and make the best of themselves, can recognise familiar footprints in every step of Christian's journey. Thus "The Pilgrim's Progress" is a book which, when once read, can never be forgotten. We too, every one of us, are pilgrims on the same road, and images and illustrations come back upon us from so faithful an itineray, as we encounter·similar trials, and learn for ourselves the accuracy with which Bunyan has described them.—FROUDE, JAMES ANTHONY, 1880, *Bunyan (English Men of Letters), p.* 152.

Bunyan's writings have formed the subject of commentaries and essays immensely exceeding themselves in aggregate bulk, and all the fine things which could be said about them have been said. There are two things, however, with which, in reading them once more in connection with Mr. Brown's biography, we are specially struck. One is the entire absence of fanaticism. Bunyan believes that the world is evil, and that the Christian must separate himself from it; but in this he was like the other Christians of his time, and indeed of all times down to the present. He believes that there is a wrath to come, and that we must flee from it; but so do the Pope and the Archbishop of Canterbury. Not only is there no fanaticism, but there is hardly even anything sectarian in his writings; saving one or two passages about the Pope, they might almost have been used by Francis of Assisi, to whose spiritual character that of Bunyan has a certain affinity. The "Pilgrim's Progress" is simple Christianity of primitive type, and almost as unadulterated and unsophisticated by secular learning or science, as it was in its Galilean birthplace.—SMITH, GOLDWIN, 1886, *John Bunyan, The Contemporary Review,* vol. 50, p. 464.

Lastly, I must name the "Pilgrim's Progress," a book that breathes of every beautiful and valuable emotion.—STEVENSON, ROBERT LOUIS, 1887, *Books Which Have Influenced Me,* p. 5.

Among this heterogeneous mass of reading two or three books stand out in my memory towering above all the rest. Unquestionably the book which most seized my imagination was the immortal "Pilgrim's Progress." It still seems to me the book which has influenced the minds of Englishmen more than any other outside the covers of the Bible. While it survives, and is read by our boys and girls, two or three great truths will remain deeply burned into the English soul. The first is the personal responsibility of each man; the next is that Christianity does not want, and cannot have, a priest. I confess that the discovery, by later reading, that the so-called Christian priest is a personage borrowed from surrounding superstition, and that the great ecclesiastical structure is entirely built by human hands, filled me with only a deeper grati-

tude to John Bunyan.—BESANT, WALTER, 1887, *Books Which Have Influenced Me,* p. 20.

The "Pilgrim's Progress" has been translated into the following languages and dialects:—*Aneityumese,* 1880; *Arabic,* 1834; *Modern Arminian,* 1882; *Armeno-Turkish,* 1881; *Assamese,* 1856; *Bengali,* 1821, 1854, 1877; *Bohemian,* 1871; *Bulgarian,* 1866; *Burmese,* 1841; *Canarese,* 1861, 1867; *Chinese*—(*Wenli* or *Classical Style,* 1874; *Mandarin* or *Court Dialect,* 1872; *Canton Vernacular,* 1870–1; *Amoy Dialect,* 1865); *Dakota,* 1858; *Danish,* 1862; *Dutch,* 1682, etc.; *Dyak,* 1879; *Efik* (*Old Calabar*), Part 1, 1868, Part 2, 1882; *Esthonian,* 1870; *Fanti,* 1887; *Fijian,* 1867; *Finnish,*—; *French,* 1685, etc.; *Gaelic,* 1812, 1869; *German,* 1703, etc.; *Modern Greek,* 1824, 1831, 1854; *Greco-Turkish,* 1879; *Gujarati,*—; *Hawaiian,* 1842; *Hebrew,* 1844, 1851; *Hindi,*—; *Hungarian,* 1867; *Icelandic,* 1876; *Irish,* 1837; *Italian,* 1851? 1855, 1863; *Japanese,*—; *Kafir,* 1868; *Khasi,*—; *Lettish,*—; *Lithuanian,* 1878; *Malagasy,* 1838, etc.; *Malay,* 1854; *Malayalim,* 1847; *Maori,* 1854; *Marathi-Balbodh,*—; *Mexican,* 1880; *Norwegian,* 1868, 1874; *Otyiheroro,* 1873; *Panjabi* or *Sikh,* 1843; *Pashtu* or *Afghani,* 1877; *Persian,*—; *Polish,* 1728; *Portuguese,* 1782; *Raratongan,* 1846; *Romaic,* 1824, 1831, 1854; *Russian,* 1881; *Sechuana,* 1848; *Servian,* 1879; *Sesuto,* 1877; *Sgau-Karen,* 1863; *Sindi,*—; *Singhalese,* 1826, 1867; *Spanish,* 1851; *Swedish,* 1743; *Modern Syriac,* 1848; *Tahitian,* 1847; *Tamil,* 1793, 1882; *Telugu,* 1882; *Tshi* or *Ashanti,* 1885; *Urdu* or *Hindostani,* 1841, 1847; *Persian Urdu,*—; *Roman Urdu,*—; *Uriya* or *Orissa,* 1873; *Welsh,* 1688, etc.; *Yoruba,*—.—ANDERSON, JOHN P., 1888, *Life of John Bunyan, by Edmund Venables, Bibliography,* p. xxii.

A few years ago I witnessed, in a London suburb, a stage performance of "The Pilgrim's Progress," by George Macdonald and his family. The audience consisted mainly of young people from the surrounding churches, interested in Macdonald's religious romances, but they were unable to restrain laughter at Christiana's lamentations about her soul, or their contempt for Christian when he abandoned his family to the City of Destruction. It occurred to me that the newer generation has, happily, known too little of the catechetical cavern in which their fathers were affectionately prisoned, to realize the splendor of Bunyan's many-colored torch for imaginations which but for it had been eyeless. I had got hold of "Don Quixote," and was scandalized that the noblest enthusiasms should be mocked; from that cynical Slough the Pilgrim rescued me.—CONWAY, MONCURE D., 1888, *Books That Have Helped Me*, p. 91.

It is worth remembering that out of Puritanism, which is regarded as a narrow creed and life, came the only book since the Reformation which has been acceptable to the whole of Christendom, and is still regardéd as the substantial truth of the Christian life in all the churches that preach it under any creed of orthodoxy. —WOODBERRY, GEORGE EDWARD, 1890, *Studies in Letters and Life*, p. 218.

The "Pilgrim's Progress" was doubtless not written in any special sense for young readers; but successive generations of children have so fastened upon it and made it their own, that we cannot exclude the book from their literature. . . . The intense earnestness of the Elstow tinker appeals to that stratum of seriousness which is the foundation of the English character, and expresses itself in a directness and simplicity of diction which goes straight to the heart of a child.—FIELD, MRS. E. M., 1891, *The Child and his Book*, p. 202.

The people are living now—all the people: the noisy bullying judges, as of the French Revolutionary Courts, or the Hanging Courts after Monmouth's war; the demure, grave Puritan girls; and Matthew, who had the gripes; and lazy, feckless Ignorance, who came to so ill an end, poor fellow; and sturdy Old Honest, and timid Mr. Fearing; not single persons, but dozens arise on the memory. They come, as fresh, as vivid, as if they were out of Scott or Molière; the Tinker is as great a master of character and fiction as the greatest, almost; his style is pure, and plain, and sound, full of old idioms, and even of something like old slang. But even his slang is classical. Bunyan is everybody's author. The very Catholics have their own edition of the Pilgrim: they have cut out Giant Pope, but have been too good-natured to insert Giant

Protestant in his place. Unheralded, un-announced, though not uncriticised (they accused the Tinker of being a plagiarist, of course), Bunyan outshone the Court wits, the learned, the poets of the Restoration, and even the great theologians. —LANG, ANDREW, 1891, *Essays in Little*, p. 188.

We get in the Pilgrim's Progress an inimitable picture of social life in the lower middle class of England, and in this second part a very vivid glimpse of a Puritan household. The glimpse is corrective of a too stern and formal apprehension of social Puritanism, and in the story are exhibited the natural charms and graces which not only could not be expelled by a stern creed, but were essentially connected with the lofty ideals which made Puritanism a mighty force in history. Bunyan had a genius for story-telling, and his allegory is very frank; but what he showed as well as what he did not show in his picture of Christiana and the children indicates the constraint which rested upon the whole Puritan conception of childhood. It is seen at its best in Bunyan, and this great Puritan poet of common life found a place for it in his survey of man's estate; nature asserted itself in spite of and through Puritanism.—SCUDDER, HORACE E., 1894, *Childhood in Literature and Art*, p. 132.

We find at last in the "Pilgrim's Progress" a sentence which belongs to the essential paragraph structure. Bunyan has mastered the short sentence. He can vary it with longer ones—not very periodic ones—and produce effects of severe variety and of sober rhythm. The most important outcome of the age that ends with Bunyan is this short sentence. The vernacular stream that has found its way through the obstacles of the age emerges bright and strong in Bunyan. When the next period of development sets in the writers gradually bring this short sentence into the service of the longer thought-integer, and so the new unit of style is evolved.—LEWIS, EDWIN HERBERT, 1894, *The History of the English Paragraph*, p. 103.

John Bunyan, rough vagrant tinker that he had been, unlearned but for the homely wisdom of the Scriptures and that inborn genius for the comprehending of humanity that Chaucer and Shakespeare had before him,—John Bunyan, reprobate but converted, dreamed in the little room at Bedford Jail a dream that made his prison a classic place, and gave England of the seventeenth century its one true picture of human life and human victory. We cannot doubt that many a devout Puritan of Bunyan's day, with head bent over the record of Christian's falls and Christian's triumphs, whispered softly to himself, as tears rolled down his cheeks, "It is I, it is I!" One step more, and but one step, and to paint men and women in the relations familiar to us and amid the surroundings of the world wherein we live.—SIMONDS, WILLIAM EDWARD, 1894, *Study of English Fiction, p. 38.*

About my favorite copy of the "Pilgrim's Progress" many a pleasant reminiscence lingers, for it was one of the books my grandmother gave my father when he left home to engage in the great battle of life; when my father died this thick, dumpy little volume, with its rude cuts and poorly printed pages, came into my possession. I do not know what part this book played in my father's life, but I can say for myself that it has brought me solace and cheer a many times.—FIELD, EUGENE, 1895, *The Love Affairs of a Bibliomaniac, p. 194.*

Its language, the language of the Bible, and its allegorical form, initiated a plentiful prose literature of a similar kind. But none have equalled it. Its form is almost epic: its dramatic dialogue, its clear types of character, its vivid descriptions, as of Vanity Fair, and of places, such as the Valley of the Shadow of Death and the Delectable Mountains, which represent states of the human soul, have given an equal but a different pleasure to children and men, to the villager and the scholar.—BROOKE, STOPFORD A., 1896, *English Literature, p. 169.*

Its origin and its history combine to make it one of the most interesting of literary masterpieces which the world possesses. In graphic characterization, in breadth of sympathy, in richness of imagination, in clearness and force of homely Saxon speech, it is the greatest of all the monuments created by the English Bible. As a product of the influences of the Reformation, it stands beside the works of Milton, with which it is spiritually akin.—GEORGE, ANDREW J., 1898,

From Chaucer to Arnold, Types of Literary Art, p. 635.

Next to the Bible, the "Pilgrim's Progress" is probably the book which has exercised more influence over the Religion of England than any other. It did for Protestantism what Dante did for Roman Catholicism—whilst exposing sometimes naïvely its weak points, it affirmed its doctrines, and popularized their application to current life. It supplied what Milton's "Paradise Lost" failed to give—some account of the ethics of the soul. From Milton we get our plan of salvation, but from Bunyan we get our conceptions of morality and our theory of spiritual development. Perhaps few of those many who believe that the Bible is their sole spiritual guide realize the extent to which they see the Old Testament through Milton's eyes, and believe in the Gospel according to Bunyan. There is yet another parallel. Bunyan supplied that imaginative touch and that glow of pictorial sentiment without which no religious message seems to win the masses. He did with his "Pilgrim's Progress"—for a somewhat arid and stern Evangelicalism which repudiated the saintly legends and the material splendors of Rome—what Keble, with his "Christian Year," did for the dry bones of Anglicanism. Keble made Anglicanism poetical. Bunyan made Evangelicalism romantic. A greater than Bunyan or Keble adopted a similar method, when, as we read, "Without a parable He taught not the people." The extraordinary popularity of Bunyan's great book, one hundred thousand copies of which were circulated in his own lifetime, is not far to seek. He embodied his age—not its secular, but its religious side. No man could have been less influenced by the decapitation of Charles I, the accession of Cromwell, the restoration of that mundane merry monarch, Charles II. He lived through all these, in and out of prison, married and single, with his finger ever on the religious pulse of England; he was as little disturbed by wars and rumors of wars, political cabals and commercial bubbles, as were the great violin-makers of Brescia and Cremona by the political disturbances and bloody squabbles of the small Italian princelets of their day.—HAWEIS, H. R., 1898, *The Pilgrim's Progress, Introduction, p. vii.*

In Bunyan's beautiful book, we have a social document of the highest value, witnessing to the habits and modes of life of the new burgher-class with a vivid simplicity unsurpassed. Christian's house and the Town of Destruction, Vanity Fair with its chaffer and gossip, the talk of the pilgrims by the way, are the best pictures we possess of middleclass life in seventeenth century England.—SCUDDER, VIDA D., 1898, *Social Ideals in English Letters, p.* 87.

To John Bunyan the English novel owes a very great debt. What fiction needed, if it was ever to come near a portrayal of real life, was first of all to rid itself of the extravagances of the romancer and the cynicism of the picaresque story-teller. Though Bunyan was despised by his contemporary men of letters, it surely could be but a little time before the precision of his imagination and the force and charm of his simple and idiomatic English would be felt and then imitated. As no writer preceding him, Bunyan knew the artistic effect of minute detail in giving reasonableness to an impossible story. In the "Pilgrim's Progress" (1678–84) he so mingled with those imaginative scenes of his own familiar Scripture imagery and the still more familiar incidents of English village life, that the illusion of reality must have been to the readers for whom he wrote well-nigh perfect. The allegories of Barclay and Scudéri could not be understood without keys; Bunyan's "Palace Beautiful" needed none.—CROSS, WILBUR L., 1899, *The Development of the English Novel, p.* 21.

In the last chapters of "Pilgrim's Progress," where the company wait in the land of Beulah by the side of the great river for the summons to cross to the eternal city, Bunyan reaches a dignified pathos unexampled in all literature. If this book were in an unknown tongue, the scholars of the world would sound its praises, but as it is folk literature and perfectly intelligible, it is neglected for matter entirely inferior. It remains one of the greatest books in the English language, and no other nation has anything of the same kind to compare with it. In devotion to what he considered his religious duty, Bunyan was not less heroic than Milton.—JOHNSON, C.F., 1900, *History of English and American Literature, p.* 242.

HOLY WAR
1682

If the Pilgrim's Progress did not exist, would be the best allegory that ever was written.—MACAULAY, THOMAS BABINGTON, 1843, *John Bunyan, Critical and Historical Essays.*

Though far less varied and fascinating than the "Pilgrim's Progress," is a more perfect allegory, full of passages of exquisite symbolism and tenderness. As a piece of metaphysical writing, it seems to me wonderful, from its profound, thoroughly uncalvinistic recognition of the *native powers* of the soul. . . . It is the most useful book I ever met with to lecture on to poor *men*, or an intelligent class of boys.—GREENWELL, DORA, 1863, *Memoirs, p.* 76.

I cannot agree with Macaulay in thinking that, if there had been no "Pilgrim's Progress," "The Holy War" would have been the first of religious allegories. . . . "The Holy War" would have entitled Bunyan to a place among the masters of English Literature. It would never have made his name a household word in every English-speaking family on the globe.—FROUDE, JAMES ANTHONY, 1880, *Bunyan (English Men of Letters), p.* 118.

There was not much literature in that early home of ours, and what little there was by no means attracted me. Boston's "Fourfold State" and Hervey's "Meditations" were not lively reading. Happily, they were relieved by "The Pilgrim's Progress" and "The Holy War;" and in those years I had the bad taste to prefer the latter; to boys pilgrims are by no means so interesting as soldiers.—SMITH, REV. WALTER C., 1887, *Books Which Have Influenced Me, p.* 91.

The style of "Pilgrim's Progress" is the very perfection of what the style of such a book should be—homely and yet distinguished, exquisitely simple, yet tuned to music at all its finer moments. The allegory is successful above all other allegories in literature. The abstractions which people it, even when they are mentioned only in one or two lines, never fail to live and stand out vividly as human beings. Admirers of "The Holy War" have tried to assert as much for that longer and more laborious work. But popular taste has rightly determined that there should be a thousand readers of the first story to ten of the second. There are very fine passages in "The Holy War;" the opening, especially all the first siege of Mansoul, is superbly conceived and executed. But the personages which are introduced are too incongruous, the intrigues of Shaddei and the resistance of Diabolus are too incredible, the contest is too one-sided from the first, to interest us as we are interested in the human adventures of Christian. Bunyan seems powerless to close "The Holy War," and before he is able to persuade himself to drop the threads, the whole skein of the allegory is hopelessly entangled.—GOSSE, EDMUND, 1888, *A History of Eighteenth Century Literature*, p. 85.

There can, in fact, be little doubt that the idea is consciously derived from "Paradise Lost." In both the banished fiends cast about for some means of retaliating upon their omnipotent foe; in Milton their attack is levelled against the Garden of Eden, in Bunyan against the soul of man. All human attributes, virtuous or vicious, are allegorized with graphic liveliness, but at length one wearies of the crowd of abstractions; and where strength was most necessary, Bunyan is weak. Emanuel is not godlike, and Diabolus is not terrible. The book is perhaps chiefly interesting as an index to the great progress effected since Bunyan's time in spirituality as regards men's religious conceptions, and in freedom and enlightenment as concerns the things of earth. No one would now depict the offended majesty of Heaven as so like the offended majesty of the Stuarts; or deem that the revolters' offence could be mitigated by the abjectness of their submission; or try criminals with such unfairness; or lecture them upon conviction with such lack of judicial decorum. Bunyan's own spirit seems narrower than of old; among the traitors upon whom Emanuel's ministers execute justice he includes not only Notruth and Pitiless, but also Electiondoubter and Vocation-doubter, who represent the majority of the members of the Church of England. The whole tone, in truth, is such as might be expected from one nurtured upon the Old rather than the New Testament, and who had never conceived any doubts of the justice of the Israelites' dealings with the Canaanites. The literary power, nevertheless, is unabated; much ingenuity is shown in keeping up the interest of the story; and there is the old gift of vitalizing abstractions by uncompromising realism of treatment.—GARNETT, RICHARD, 1895, *The Age of Dryden*, p. 239.

The singular similarity both in the drama and in the spirit of the history and of the allegory cannot be explained, so far as I can see, except by supposing that Bunyan had heard and assimilated the story of the Anabaptist Kingdom of Münster, and had heard it, not through distorted histories, but by the living voice of tradition. And if it be admitted that the struggle of which Münster became the centre was the archetype of Bunyan's "Holy War," then we not only get an interesting literary fact, but, what is more important, a vivid light on the mind of the religious common people of England during a period when this country was as virile in its character as at any period in its history.—HEATH, RICHARD, 1897, *The Archetype of "The Holy War," The Contemporary Review*, vol. 72, p. 118.

POEMS

Bunyan's muse is clad in russet, wears shoes and stockings, has a country accent, and walks along the level Bedfordshire roads. If as a poet he is homely and idiomatic, he is always natural, straightforward, and sincere. His lines are unpolished, but they have pith and sinew, like the talk of a shrewd peasant. In the "Emblems" there are many touches of pure poetry, shewing that in his mind there was a vein of silver which, under favourable circumstances, might have been worked to rich issues; and everywhere there is an admirable homely pregnancy and fulness of meaning. He has the strong thought, and the knack of the skilled workman to drive, by a single blow, the nail home to the head.—SMITH, ALEXANDER, 1867? ed., *Divine Emblems, by John Bunyan*, p. x.

It has been the fashion to call Bunyan's verse doggerel; but no verse is doggerel which has a sincere and rational meaning in it. Goethe, who understood his own trade, says that the test of poetry is the substance which remains when the poetry is reduced to prose. Bunyan had infinite invention. His mind was full of objects which he had gathered at first-hand, from observation and reflection. He had excellent command of the English language, and could express what he wished with sharp, defined outlines, and without the waste of a word. The rhythmical structure of his prose is carefully correct. Scarcely a syllable is ever out of place. His ear for verse, though less true, is seldom wholly at fault, and, whether in prose or verse, he had the superlative merit that he could never write nonsense. If one of the motives of poetical form be to clothe thought and feeling in the dress in which it can be most easily remembered, Bunyan's lines are often as successful as the best lines of Quarles or George Herbert.—FROUDE, JAMES ANTHONY, 1880, *Bunyan (English Men of Letters), p.* 91.

The more we read of these poems, not given to the world till twelve years after Bunyan's death, and that by a publisher who was "a repeated offender against the laws of honest dealing," the more we are inclined to agree with Dr. Brown, that the internal evidence of their style renders their genuineness at the least questionable. In the dull prosaic level of these compositions there is certainly no trace of the "force and power" always present in Bunyan's rudest rhymes, still less of the "dash of genius" and the "sparkle of soul" which occasionally discover the hand of a master. Of the authenticity of Bunyan's "Divine Emblems," originally published three years after his death under the title of "Country Rhymes for Children," there is no question. The internal evidence confirms the external. The book is thoroughly in Bunyan's vein, and in its homely naturalness of imagery recalls the similitudes of the "Interpreter's House," especially those expounded to Christiana and her boys.—VENABLES, EDMUND, 1888, *Life of John Bunyan (Great Writers), p.* 122.

GENERAL

His masterpiece is his "Pilgrim's Progress," one of the most popular, and, I may add, one of the most ingenious books in the English language. The works of Bunyan, which had been long printed on tobacco-paper, by Nicholas Boddington and others, were, in 1736 and 1737, reprinted in two decent volumes folio. They are now come forth in a fairer edition than ever, with the recommendation of Mr. George Whitfield.—GRANGER, JAMES, 1769–1824, *Biographical History of England, vol.* V, *p.* 99.

Bunyan is the Spenser of the people. The fire burned towards Heaven, although the altar was rude and rustic.—DISRAELI, ISAAC, 1796–1818, *Self-Education, The Literary Character.*

The style of Bunyan is delightful to every reader, and invaluable as a study to every person who wishes to obtain a wide command over the English language. The vocabulary is the vocabulary of the common people. There is not an expression, if we except a few technical terms of theology, which would puzzle the rudest peasant. We have observed several pages which do not contain a single word of more than two syllables. Yet no writer has said more exactly what he meant to say. For magnificence, for pathos, for vehement exhortation, for subtle disquisition, for every purpose of the poet, the orator, and the divine, this homely dialect —the dialect of plain working men—was perfectly sufficient.—MACAULAY, THOMAS BABINGTON, 1831, *Southey's Edition of the Pilgrim's Progress, Edinburgh Review, vol.* 54, *p.* 460.

One of the greatest poets that ever lived—we mean John Bunyan, homely as may be the associations connected with the inspired tinker's name—has left some most pertinent instances in his writings of the sway exercised by the imagination over the external senses. In describing the dark internal conflicts which convulsed him, during one stage of his religious experience, he says:—"I lifted up my head, and methought I saw as if the sun that shineth in the heavens did *grudge* to give me light; as if the very stones in the street, and tiles upon the houses, did band themselves against me." This is as perfect poetry as ever was written.—WHIPPLE, EDWIN P., 1844, *Wordsworth, Essays and Reviews.*

The impressiveness of Bunyan resembles that of the old woodcuts executed in the infancy of the art of engraving: there is in both cases a rude vigour and homeliness of outline, a strange ignorance of costume, and a powerful tendency to realise even the most abstract things by connecting them with the ordinary details of every day life; there is also the same earnest intensity of purpose, and incessant struggle to bring the objects within the comprehension of the uncultivated minds to which the work was addressed. Above all there is visible, in the rude woodcut of the old German artist, as in the hardly less rude narrative morality of the English tinker, the unmistakable and inimitable originality of genius.—SHAW, THOMAS B., 1847, *Outlines of English Literature, p.* 194.

The more we study the "Pilgrim's Progress" and the "Holy War," in connection with his own history and times, the more will we see reason to believe that their numerous characters directly and broadly reflect both the outer and inner characteristics of the religious world familiar to him. . . . There is also everywhere, in his allegories, the evidence of a rare power of actual observation,—of sharp insight into the living characteristics around him,—and great fulness of artistic skill in drawing these from the life as he knew and saw them. . . . It is, above all, this realistic element that gives to Bunyan's great allegory its special interest. It is because he draws so much from outward fact that we find his pages so living—and linger over them—and return to them—and find them not only instructive, but entertaining. Spenser in his great allegory is richer, . . . but he has nowhere caught life and mirrored it, as Bunyan has done. . . . Puritanism lives in his pages—spiritually and socially—in forms and in colouring which must ever command the sympathy and enlist the love of all good Christians. —TULLOCH, JOHN, 1861, *English Puritanism and Its Leaders, pp.* 478, 480, 487.

He is the prince of dreamers, as Homer is the prince of poets. The scenery of his vision has become familiar as the scenery which surrounds our homes. We know the whole course of the journey—from the City of Destruction to the Slough of Despond; past the House of the Interpreter; up Hill Difficulty; the meeting of Christian with the Maidens, Piety, Prudence, and Charity; Christian's rest in the "large upper chamber whose window opened towards the sun-rising," the name of which chamber was Peace; the journey down into the Valley of the Shadow of Death: the combat which took place there; Vanity Fair and the burning of Faithful; the imprisonment of Hopeful

and Christian by the Giant, and their escape; the Delectable Mountains, with the Golden City seen in the distance shining like a star; the Land of Beulah; the passage across the dark river, with troops of angels, and melody of hymns and trumpets, waiting the pilgrims on the further bank;—all this every boy knows as he knows the way to school—with this every man is familiar as with his personal experience—and the curious thing is, that the incidents and the scenery which we accept with such belief are but the dark conceits and shadows of things; in all there is more than meets the eye. Under everything lies the most solemn meanings. "The Pilgrim's Progress" is not only the most enchanting story in the world, it is one of the best manuals of theology.—SMITH, ALEXANDER, 1867? *ed., Divine Emblems by John Bunyan, p.* v.

These two men were living together at the same time. There are no such men living now as they were; no such religious genius as Bunyan; no spirit so deeply absorbed in philosophy as Spinoza. They had probably never heard of one another's names; but if they had, one would have devoted the other to eternal flames, and that other would have regarded him as an ignorant fellow and a madman. Such awful misunderstandings there have been in this world. If we could imagine them knowing one another intimately (for all persons think differently of those whom they know), then perhaps a feeling of surprise might have arisen at so much good being united with so much evil. They might have wondered to see how by different roads they had arrived, if not quite, yet nearly, at a common end. They might have learned partly to understand one another, and the calmness and wisdom of the one might have tempered the fire and enthusiasm of the other.— JOWETT, BENJAMIN, 1871, *Bunyan and Spinoza, Sermons, ed. Fremantle, p.* 55.

We are apt to view him too exclusively as the author of the "Pilgrim's Progress," and to search there, and there only, for the signs of his intellectual power. . . . Imaginative power and knowledge of men (which may be said to be different aspects of the constructive faculty) are the main secrets of his success as a writer. Perhaps too much has been made of his style, viewed merely as written composition. His language is simple and often forcible, and, particularly in "Grace Abounding," has a soft melodious flow. The most pleasing element is the graphic force of the similitudes. And this is almost all that can be said. . . . As for the "old unpolluted English language," it needs no microscopical eye to detect in the "Pilgrim's Progress" a considerable sprinkling of vulgar provincialisms, and even of such Latin idioms as are to be found in his favourite old martyrologist Fox.—MINTO, WILLIAM, 1872-80, *A Manual of English Prose Literature, pp.* 300, 301.

The immortal "Dreamer" of Bedford had a miniature successor in the dreamer of Salem; and there was not a wide divergence, in some respects, in the character of the genius of the two men.—SMITH, GEORGE BARNETT, 1875, *Nathaniel Hawthorne, Poets and Novelists, p.* 159.

The very homeliness of Bunyan's names and the every dayness of his scenery, too, put us off our guard, and we soon find ourselves on as easy a footing with his allegorical beings as we might be with Adam or Socrates in a dream. Indeed, he has prepared us for such incongruities by telling us at setting out that the story was of a dream. The long nights of Bedford jail had so intensified his imaginaiton, and made the figures with which it peopled his solitude so real to him, that the creatures of his mind become *things*, as clear to the memory as if we had seen them.—LOWELL, JAMES RUSSELL, 1875, *Spenser, Prose Works, Riverside ed., vol.* IV, *p.* 322.

John Bunyan dipped his pen in the catholicism of Catholicity. He had no sympathy with any ism, however novel or specious or popular, which corrupted or darkened the simplicity of the Gospel. With him charity was not a mere claptrap sentiment for the platform, but a deep conviction, a strong principle, a fruit of the Holy Spirit.—ANDERSON. W., 1879, *Selfmade Men.*

His service to humanity was not that of massively grouping great truths into systematic form and opening the way to new realms of light. What he did, and did powerfully, was to make vital with the warm life-blood of his own strong heart truths and systems already in existence around him. With the wealth of his own opulent imagination he places these in vivid and striking light, and in such fervid shape that at once they lay hold of the popular mind and heart. Beautiful images, vivid expressions, forcible arguments all aglow with passion, tender pleadings, solemn warnings, these, all through his writings as through his preaching, make those to whom he speaks all eye, all ear, all soul. To use a phrase which has come to have an equivocal significance, he was a popular preacher and writer, but only in a high and noble sense. He never panders to the mere love of excitement and novelty. His errand is much too serious, and men's need and peril much too urgent, for him to waste time and power in merely playing before them on a pleasant instrument. He would beseech them with tears, as Paul did, and like him, too, speak with authority as a messenger from heaven. To him the burning pit was a reality, from which he had himself barely escaped, and heaven a substantial verity he could all but see.—BROWN, JOHN, 1885, *John Bunyan, His Life, Times and Work, p.* 451.

Read not Addison nor Johnson, read Bunyan, who employed direct and true English. . . . The man who would speak good English should take for his company the authorized version of the Bible and Bunyan's "Pilgrim's Progress." Bunyan's is chapel English, man's English, woman's English, the English spoken anywhere by the native sons and daughters of the soil.—DAWSON, GEORGE, 1886, *Biograhical Lectures.*

If by a "Great Writer" we understand one who combines the power of expressing thoughts of universal acceptability in a style of the most perfect clearness, with a high degree of imaginative genius, and a vivid descriptive faculty; whose works are equally attractive to readers of all ages and every variety of mental culture, which are among the first to be taken up in the nursery and among the last to be laid down when life is closing in on us, which have filled the memory with pictures and peopled it with characters of the most unforgetable reality, which have been probably translated into more languages, and attained popularity in more lands, than any books ever written—then the claim of the author of "The Pilgrim's

Progress," "The Holy War," and "Grace Abounding" to a place, and that a very high one, in the catalogue of "Great Writers," is undeniable.—VENABLES, EDMUND, 1888, *Life of John Bunyan (Great Writers), p. 5.*

The work of John Bunyan hardly finds its proper place in a history of prose fiction; he regarded it as anything but fictitious. Moreover, in form and outline it bears something the same relation to the novel proper that the "Morality" bears to the drama proper. Yet how rich are his works, not only the "Pilgrim's Progress" (1678), but the "Holy War" (1682), and the "Life and Death of Mr. Badman" (1680), in literary, as well as practical and moral lessons, in demonstrations whereby the novelists might profit to learn character-painting, admirable narrative, and the attainment of the illusion of reality. Where was the professed writer of fiction in the seventeenth century who could enthral the reader's imagination by his two opening sentences, and hold him spell-bound to the end?—RALEIGH, WALTER, 1894, *The English Novel, p. 115.*

While in all his writing there is abundant evidence of brain-power, and his skill in marshalling texts to defend his dogmatic positions is admirable, yet this general cleverness would not have raised him above the rank of the popular preacher whose performances in the next generation cumber the book-stalls, had it not been for that drop of precious elixir which nature infused into his eyes at birth, as into those of such different people as Geoffrey Chaucer and Jane Austen. It is this which divides Bunyan from one in other respects so like him as George Fox. Both were children of the people, both were intensely religious, both were given to hearing voices in their ears speaking the words of God or of Satan, both for their faith were "in prisons oft;" but the discriminating eye, and the sense of humour which accompanies it, were lacking to Fox, as his "Journal" makes abundantly conspicuous.—BEECHING, H. C., 1894, *English Prose, ed. Craik, vol. III, p. 73.*

The Bunyan literature now constitutes a library by itself, while every year new editions appear in still more elaborate forms. The book has been criticised and

sneered at as few writings ever were, but it has steadily risen to the highest level in the world of letters. Bunyan's place is beside Shakespeare, Milton, and Dante. His allegory is a worthy companion for the immortal work of Dante, with the difference that while the Englishman endeavors to delineate the growth of a soul on the earth, the Florentine seeks to follow its upward movement beyond death. —BRADFORD, ARMORY H., 1898, *The Pilgrim's Progress, Outlook, vol. 60, p. 622.*

The sermons of Bunyan, a number of which have been preserved, are in keeping with the general style of preaching then in vogue. Compared with sermons of the present day, they are tediously long. They are designed to be comprehensive in treatment; and therefore, instead of leaving something to the intelligence of the hearer, they abound in the most obvious commonplaces. There is scarcely any end to the divisions and subdivisions. They are more concerned with thought than style; and instead of rhetorical grace, we find only simplicity and directness. Their remarkable effectiveness was due to the intellectual vigor and moving earnestness of the speaker—a fact that emphasizes for us the importance of the personal element in public discourse.—PAINTER, F. V. N., 1899, *A History of English Literature, p. 185.*

In the first place, his style is simple. Secondly, rare earnestness is coupled with this simplicity. He had something to say, and in his inmost soul he felt that this something was of supreme importance for all time. Only a great man can tell such truths without a flourish of language, or without straining after effect. . . . Thirdly, Bunyan has a rare combination of imagination and dramatic power. His abstractions become living persons. . . . It would be difficult to find English prose more simple, earnest, strong, imaginative, and dramatic than this. Bunyan's style felt the shaping influence of the *Bible* more than of all other works combined. He knew the *Scriptures* almost by heart.— HALLECK, REUBEN POST, 1900, *History of English Literature, pp. 227, 228, 229.*

Cromwell, Milton, Bunyan—what can non-Puritan England, of their day, show to match these three names?—ROOSEVELT, THEODORE, 1900, *Oliver Cromwell, p. 232, note.*

William Chamberlayne

1619–1689

Physician and poet, was born in 1619. He practised as a physician at Shaftesbury in Dorsetshire. During the civil wars he was distinguished for his loyalty to Charles I.; and it appears from a passage at the close of the second book of "Pharonnida" that he was present at the second battle at Newbury. He died in January 1689, and was buried at Shaftesbury in the churchyard of the Holy Trinity, where a monument was erected to him by his son Valentine Chamberlayne. In 1658 he published "Love's Victory a Tragi-Comedy," 4to, dedicated to Sir William Portman, bart. There are some fine passages in the play, and plenty of loyal sentiment.—BULLEN, A. H., 1887, *Dictionary of National Biography, vol. x, p.* 10.

PHARONNIDA

This Poem tho' it hath nothing extraordinary to recommend it, yet appear'd abroad in Prose 1683, under the Title of a Novel called "Eromena, or The Noble Stranger."—LANGBAINE, GERALD, 1691, *An Account of the English Dramatick Poets, p.* 57.

A poet to whom I am indebted for many hours of delight. . . . A poet who has told an interesting story in uncouth rhymes, and mingles sublimity of thought and beauty of expression with the quaintest conceits and most awkward inversions.—SOUTHEY, ROBERT, 1796, *Joan of Arc, note.*

His "Pharonnida," an heroic poem, in five books, which Langbaine says has nothing to recommend it, is one of the most interesting stories that was ever told in verse, and contained so much amusing matter as to be made into a prose novel in the reign of Charles II. What Dr. Johnson said unjustly of Milton's "Comus," that it was like gold hid under a rock, may unfortunately be applied with too much propriety to "Pharonnida." Never perhaps was so much beautiful design in poetry marred by infelicity of execution: his ruggedness of versification, abrupt transitions, and a style that is at once slovenly and quaint, perpetually interrupted in enjoying the splendid figures and spirited passions of this romantic tablet, and make us catch them only by glimpses.—CAMPBELL, THOMAS, 1819, *Specimens of the British Poets.*

Chamberlain's "Pharonnida" is a very noble work. The characters are drawn and supported with great truth and force; the action of the Poem is eventful and interesting, and the images bold, natural, and original.—NEELE, HENRY, 1827–29, *Lectures on English Poetry, p.* 56.

The imagery is often very beautiful, and the emotions excited and described strong and passionate, but the style is slovenly and the whole piece wearisome. Among his excellences may be mentioned his keen perception of natural beauty. Indeed he has given several descriptions of the glories of the morning, in a manner not unworthy of Milton.—ANGUS, JOSEPH, 1865, *The Handbook of English Literature, p.* 178.

The poem is in rhymed heroics; there are five books and four cantos to each book. As the fourth book commences with fresh pagination and in different type, it has been conjectured that the printing was interrupted by the author's employment in the wars. In spite of its diffuseness and intricacy, the story is interesting; and much of the poetry is remarkable for happy imagery and rich expressions. Both in its faults and in its beauties "Pharonnida" bears considerable resemblance to "Endymion."—BULLEN, A. H., 1887, *Dictionary of National Biography, vol. x, p.* 10.

Though hardly deserving the high praise of Campbell, who styles it "one of the most interesting stories that ever was told in verse," the poem is seldom dull, and the metre is free from the monotony of the regular heroic couplet. . . . Mr. Gosse has pointed out the close resemblance, in metrical form, between Chamberlayne's poem and Keats' "Endymion," and is inclined to regard the debt that Keats owed to the author of "Pharonnida" as larger than has generally been recognized.—MASTERMAN, J. HOWARD B., 1897, *The Age of Milton, pp.* 144, 145.

GENERAL

The play ["Love's Victory"] bears a very strong resemblance, both in the tone of feeling and in the sentiments, to his more matured production—there is the same dignity of action and of thought in the higher scenes, mixed, however, with much more that is mean, and some that is utterly contemptible. There is frequently an admirable propriety in his thoughts, but he wanted judgement in the selection, and taste in the disposition of them. He is fond of illustrating the grand and the beautiful in nature and in feeling, by allusions to objects of art and of science, more especially in his own profession, which sometimes lead him into conceit and sometimes into meanness. . . . His poem is written in blank verse, tagged with a rhyme which the reader finds it impossible to rest upon, and difficult to pass over; and which is moreover in itself awkward and constrained. . . . He is no ordinary poet—he had the living elements of poetry within him, though he wanted a better judgement to manage them.—ROBINSON, G., 1820, *Chamberlayne's Love's Victory, Retrospective Review, vol. I, pp.* 258, 259.

With no court connection, no light or witty copies of verses to float him into popularity, relying solely on his two long and comparatively unattractive works— to appreciate which, through all the windings of romantic love, plots, escapes, and adventures, more time is required than the author's busy age could afford—we need hardly wonder that Chamberlayne was an unsuccessful poet. . . . We cannot, however, suppose that the works of this poet can ever be popular; his beauties are marred by infelicity of execution; though not deficient in the genius of a poet, he had little of the skill of the artist. —CHAMBERS, ROBERT, 1876, *Cyclopædia of English Literature,* ed. *Carruthers.*

Aphra Behn
1640-1689

Born [Aphra Johnson], at Wye, Kent, 10 July 1640. Taken to West Indies early in life. Returned to England, 1658. Married to —— Behn, 1660[?]. In favour with Charles II. ; sent by him on secret service to Antwerp, 1665. On return to England took to playwriting. First play produced at Duke's Theatre, 1671. Various plays produced, 1671-78, 1681-87. Died, in London, 16 April, 1689. Buried in Westminster Abbey. *Works:* "The Forc'd Marriage," 1671; "The Amorous Prince," 1671; "The Dutch Lover," 1673; "Abdelazar," 1677; "The Rover," pt. i. (anon.), 1677; pt. ii., 1681; "The Debauchee" (anon.), 1677; "The Town Fop," 1677; "Sir Patient Fancy," 1678; "The Feign'd Curtizana," 1679; "The Roundheads," 1682; "The City Heiress," 1682; "The False Count," 1682; "The Young King," 1683; "Poems upon several occasions," 1684; "The Adventures of the Black Lady," 1684; two "Pindarick Poems" and a poem to the Queen Dowager, 1685; "La Montre," 1686; "Emperor of the Moon," 1687; "The Lucky Chance," 1687; "Lycidus," 1688;" "A Poem to Sir Roger L'Estrange," 1688; Three "Congratulatory Poems" to the Queen, 1688; "The Lucky Mistake," 1689; "Congratulatory Poem" to the Queen 1689. *Posthumous:* "The Widow Ranter," ed. by "G. J.," 1690; "The Younger Brother," ed. by Gildon, 1696; "The Lady's Looking Glass," 1697. She *translated:* (with others) Ovid's "Heroical Epistles," 1683; Fontenelle's "Discovery of New Worlds," 1688; Van Dale's "History of Oracles," 1699; and *edited* "Miscellany," 1685. *Collected Works:* "Poetical Remains," ed. by Gildon, 1698; "Histories and Novels," 1698; "Plays," 1702; "Plays, Histories and Novels . . . with Life" (6 vols.), 1871.—SHARP, R. FARQUHARSON, 1897, *A Dictionary of English Authors, p.* 22.

PERSONAL

Poetry, the supreme pleasure of the mind, is begot, and born in pleasure, but oppressed and killed with pain. This reflexion ought to raise our admiration of Mrs. Behn, whose genius was of that force, to maintain its gaiety in the midst of disappointments, which a woman of her sense and merit ought never to have met with. But she had a great strength of mind, and command of thought, being able to write in the midst of company, and yet have the share of the conversation : which I saw her do in writing "Oroonoko," and other parts of her works, in every part of which you'll find an easy stile and a peculiar happiness of thinking. The passions, that of love especially, she was mistress of, and gave us such nice and tender touches of them, that without her name we might discover the author. —GILDON, CHARLES, 1698, *Mrs. Behn's Histories and Novels, Epistle Dedicatory.*

Aphra Behn was a graceful, comely woman, with brown hair and bright eyes, and was painted so in an existing portrait of her by John Ripley. She is said to have introduced milk punch into England. She deserves our sympathy as a warmhearted, gifted, and industrious woman, who was forced by circumstance and temperament to win her livelihood in a profession where scandalous writing was at that time obligatory. It is impossible, with what we know regarding her life, to defend her manners as correct or her attitude to the world as delicate. But we may be sure that a woman so witty, so active, and so versatile, was not degraded, though she might be lamentably unconventional. She was the George Sand of the Restoration, the "chère maître" to such men as Dryden, Otway, and Southerne, who all honoured her with their friendship. Her genius and vivacity were undoubted; her plays are very coarse, but very lively and humorous, while she possessed an indisputable touch of lyric genius. Her prose works are decidedly less meritorious than her dramas and the best of her poems.—GOSSE, EDMUND, 1885, *Dictionary of National Biography*, vol. IV, p. 130.

Despite the offensiveness of her writings, . . . is personally a sympathetic figure. . . . Her eighteen plays, have, with few exceptions, sufficient merit to entitle her to a respectable place among the dramatists of her age, and sufficient indelicacy to be unreadable in this. It may well be believed, on the authority of a female friend, that the authoress "had wit, humour, good-nature, and judgment; was mistress of all the pleasing arts of conversation; was a woman of sense, and *consequently* a woman of pleasure." She was buried in Westminster Abbey, but not in Poets' Corner.—GARNETT, RICHARD, 1895, *The Age of Dryden*, p. 146, 147.

OROONOKO

She had a great command of the stage, and I have often wondered that she would bury her favourite hero in a novel, when she might have revived him in the scene.

She thought either, that no actor could represent him, or she could not bear him represented; and I believed the last, when I remember what I have heard from a friend of her's, that she always told a story more feelingly than she writ.—SOUTHERNE, THOMAS, 1696, *Oroonoko, Dedication.*

I have said that "Oroonoko" is the best known of Mrs. Behn's novels, but I doubt whether more than a very few of the present generation have read or even seen it, and I had some difficulty in procuring a copy.—FORSYTH, WILLIAM, 1871, *The Novels and Novelists of the Eighteenth Century*, p. 181.

The tragic and pathetic story of "Oroonoko" does only less credit to her excellent literary ability than to the noble impulse of womanly compassion and womanly horror which informs the whole narrative and makes of it one ardent and continuous appeal for sympathy and pity, one fervent and impassioned protest against cruelty and tyranny.—SWINBURNE, ALGERNON CHARLES, 1891, *Social Verse, Studies in Prose and Poetry*, p. 95.

Posterity is content to know that Astræa trod the stage loosely, and so she gets no credit for the merits of her novels. Yet these merits are real, for Mrs. Aphra Behn had passed her childhood in Surinam, where her father was governor; for some years after the Restoration she had lived at Antwerp as a Government agent; and it was on sundry experiences in these two places that she based her two best-known novels, published in 1698, after her death,—"Oroonoko" and "The Fair Jilt." For making use of incidents of real life in the service of fiction at a time when the heroic romance was at the height of its vogue, she deserves all credit. And yet it was no literary reform that she effected. . . . The story of "Oroonoko," the love-lorn and magnanimous negro, of "very little religion" but "admirable morals," who meets a tragic death, belongs to a class of romance that flourished almost a century later, when Rousseau had given popularity to the philosophical ideas that underlie it. In this novel Mrs. Behn is one of the early precursors of the romantic revival, and finds her logical place in that movement. But her bold conduct of a simple story and her popularity with her contemporaries entitle her also to claim a share in the attempt, faint and ineffective, that the later seventeenth century witnessed, to bring romance into closer relation with contemporary life.—RALEIGH, WALTER, 1894, *The English Novel, pp.* 107, 108.

"Oroonoko" is the first humanitarian novel in English. Though its spirit cannot for a moment be compared, in moral earnestness, with "Uncle Tom's Cabin," yet its purpose was to awaken Christendom to the horrors of slavery. The time being not yet ripe for it, the romance was for the public merely an interesting story to be dramatized.—CROSS, WILBUR L., 1899, *The Development of the English Novel, p.* 20.

GENERAL

I was desired to say that the author, who is of the fair sex, understood not Latin; but if she do not, I am afraid she has given us occasion to be ashamed who do.—DRYDEN, JOHN, 1680, *Ovid's Epistles, Preface.*

But when you write of Love, Astrea, then
Love dips his Arrows, where you wet your pen
Such charming Lines did never Paper grace;
Soft as your Sex; and smooth as Beauty's Face.
—COTTON, CHARLES, C 1687, *Verses Prefixed to Mrs. Behn's translation of Bonnecorse's La Montre.*

A Person lately deceased, but whose Memory will be long fresh amongst the Lovers of Dramatick Poetry, as having been sufficiently Eminent not only for her Theatrical Performances, but several other Pieces both in Verse and Prose; which gain'd her an Esteem among the Wits, almost equal to that of the incomparable *Orinda,* Madam *Katharine Phillips.* . . . Most of her Comedies have had the good fortune to please: and tho' it must be confest that she has borrow'd very much, not only from her own Country Men, but likewise from the French Poets: yet it may be said in her behalf, that she has often been forc'd to it through hast: and has borrow'd from others Stores, rather of Choice than for want of a fond of Wit of her own: it having been formerly her unhappiness to be necessitated to write for Bread, as she has publisht to the world. 'Tis also to her Commendation, that whatever she borrows she improves for the better: a Plea which our late Laureat has not been asham'd to make use of. If to this, her *Sex* may plead in her behalf, I doubt not but she will be allowed equal with several of our Poets her Contemporaries.—LANGBAINE, GERARD, 1691, *An Account of the English Dramatick Poets, p.* 17.

The stage how loosely does Astræa tread,
Who fairly puts all characters to bed!
—POPE, ALEXANDER, 1733, *The First Epistle of the Second book of Horace.*

This young fellow lay in bed, reading one of Mrs. Behn's novels, for he had been instructed by a friend that he could not find a more effectual method of recommending himself to ladies, than by improving his understanding, and filling his mind with good literature.—FIELDING, HENRY, 1749, *The History of Tom Jones.*

Mrs. Behn perhaps, as much as any one, condemned loose scenes, and too warm descriptions; but something must be allowed to human frailty. She herself was of an amorous complexion, she felt the passions intimately which she describes, and this circumstance added to necessity, might be the occasion of her plays being of that cast.—CIBBER, THEOPHILUS, 1753, *Lives of the Poets, vol.* III, *p.* 26.

Her plays, which are numerous, abound with obscenity; and her novels are little better. Mr. Pope speaks thus of her:
"The stage how loosely does Astræa tread,
Who fairly puts all characters to bed!"
The poet means behind the scenes. There is no doubt but she would have literally put them to bed before the spectators; but here she was restrained by the laws of the drama, not by her own delicacy, or the manners of the age. Sir Richard Steele tells us, that she "understood the practic part of love better than the speculative."—GRANGER, JAMES, 1769-1824, *Biographical History of England, vol.* V, *p.* 261.

A grand-aunt of my own, Mrs. Keith of Ravelstone, who was a person of some condition, being a daughter of Sir John Swinton of Swinton—lived with unabated vigour of intellect to a very advanced age. She was very fond of reading, and enjoyed it to the last of her long life. One day she asked me, when we happened to be alone together, whether I had ever seen Mrs. Behn's novels?—I confessed the charge.—Whether I could get her a sight of them?—I said, with some hesitation, I believed I could; but that I did not think she would like either the manners, or the language, which approached too near that of Charles II.'s time to be quite proper reading. "Nevertheless," said the good old lady, "I remember them being so much admired, and being so much interested in them myself, that I wish to look at them again." To hear was to obey. So I sent Mrs. Aphra Behn, curiously sealed up, with "private and confidential" on the packet, to my gay old grand-aunt. The next time I saw her afterwards, she gave me back Aphra, properly wrapped up, with nearly these words:—"Take back your bonny Mrs. Behn; and, if you will take my advice, put her in the fire, for I found it impossible to get through the very first novel. But is it not," she said, "a very odd thing, that I, an old woman of eighty and upwards, sitting alone, feel myself ashamed to read a book which, sixty years ago, I have heard read aloud for the amusement of large circles, consisting of the first and most creditable society in London?"—SCOTT, SIR WALTER, c 1821, *Letter to Lady Louisa Stuart, Lockhart's Life, ch.* liv.

Her verses are natural and cordial, written in a masculine style, and yet womanly withal. If she had given us nothing but such poetry as this ["Love Armed"], she would have been as much admired, and known among us all, to this day, as she consented to be among the rakes of her time. Her comedies indeed are alarming and justly incurred the censure of Pope: though it is probable, that a thoughtless good-humor made her pen run over, rather than real licentiousness; and that, although free enough in her life, she was not so "extravagant and erring" as persons with less mind.—HUNT, LEIGH, 1847, *Specimens of British Poetesses; Men, Women and Books.*

Her name would have been excluded from all mention in these pages, had it not been necessary to mark the true state of female literature at this period. Aphara Behn is the first English authoress upon record whose life was openly wrong, and whose writings were obscene.—WILLIAMS, JANE, 1861, *The Literary Women of England, p.* 128.

In eighteen years she saw nineteen of her dramas applauded or hissed by the debauched and idle groundlings of the Duke's Theatre; and forced to write what would please, she wrote in a style that has put a later generation very justly to the blush. But in power of sustained production she surpassed all her contemporaries expect Dryden, since beside this ample list of plays, she published eight novels, some collections of poetry, and various miscellaneous volumes. The bulk of her writings, and the sustained force so considerable a body of literature displays, are more marked than the quality of her style, which is very irregular, uncertain and untutored. She possessed none of that command over her pen which a university training had secured to the best male poets of her time. But she has moments of extraordinary fire and audacity, when her verse throws off its languor, and progresses with harmony and passion. Her one long poem, "The Voyage to the Isle of Love," which extends to more than two thousand lines, is a sentimental allegory, in a vague and tawdry style, almost wholly without value; her best pieces occur here and there in her plays and among her miscellaneous poems. It is very unfortunate that one who is certainly to be numbered, as far as intellectual capacity goes, in the first rank of English female writers, should have done her best to remove her name from the recollection of posterity by the indelicacy and indiscretion of her language.—GOSSE, EDMUND, 1880, *English Poets, ed. Ward, vol.* II, *p.* 419.

It is a pity, almost, that the next name must have a place accorded to it; certainly a pity that beside any records of what the more exalted spirit of woman has achieved, mention should be made of so unsexed a writer as Mrs. Aphra Behn. Yet she was a woman, writing much that was vigorous and a little that was poetical, and so must needs be catalogued among the verse writers with whom it is the business of these pages to deal.—ROBERTSON, ERIC S., 1883, *English Poetesses, p.* 9.

She was an undoubted wit, and was never dull, but so wicked and coarse that she forfeited all right to fame.—SANBORN, KATE, 1885, *The Wit of Women, p.* 195.

Her plays have in relation to those of her contemporaries a rather unfair reputation for license, but are of small literary worth. Her prose has much merit, and she ranks early and high in the list of

English novelists.—SAINTSBURY, GEORGE, 1886, *Specimens of English Prose Style*, p. 117.

Dryden, the greatest and most various representative of his age at its best and at its worst, is not for a moment comparable as a song-writer to Lord Rochester or to Mrs. Behn. . . . Like Marcus Cato's or Joseph Addison's Marcia "the virtuous Aphra towers above her sex" in the passionate grace and splendid elegance of that melodious and magnificent song ("Love in fantastic triumph sat") to which Leigh Hunt alone among critics has ever done justice—and has done no more than justice in the fervour of his impassioned panegyric.—SWINBURNE, ALGERNON CHARLES, 1891, *Social Verse, Studies in Prose and Poetry*, pp. 93, 94.

Mrs. Behn wrote foully; and this for most of us, and very properly, is an end of the whole discussion.—HUDSON, WILLIAM HENRY, 1897, *Idle Hours in a Library*, p. 161.

Robert Barclay

1648–1690

Robert Barclay, the apologist of the Quakers, was born at Gordonstown near Elgin, December 23, 1648. His father, Col. David Barclay (1610–86), had served under Gustavus Adolphus, and in 1666 became a convert to Quakerism. Robert was educated at the Scots College at Paris, of which his uncle was rector; and here he withstood every temptation to embrace Catholicism. He returned to Scotland in 1664, and in 1667 joined the Society of Friends. He prosecuted his studies ardently, married a Quakeress in 1670, and became involved in controversies in which he showed himself the superior in logic and learning, no less than in tolerance. In 1672 he startled Aberdeen by walking through its streets in sackcloth and ashes. He suffered much persecution and was frequently imprisoned, but at last found a protector in the Duke of York, afterwards James II. He made several journeys into Holland and Germany, the last in company with William Penn and George Fox. He was one of the twelve Quakers who acquired East New Jersey in 1682, and was appointed its nominal governor. He visited London, but continued to live at his estate of Urie, near Stonehaven, where he died October 3, 1690. Barclay's works were collected in 1692 in a folio entitled "Truth Triumphant," republished in 3 vols. in 1717–18. Of these the greatest is "An Apology for the True Christian Divinity held by the Quakers" (1678). —PATRICK AND GROOME, *eds.*, 1897, *Chambers's Biographical Dictionary*, p. 68.

GENERAL

Memorandum:—this John Barclay haz a sonne, now (1688) an old man, and a learned quaker, who wrote a Systeme of the Quakers' Doctrine in Latine, dedicated to King Charles II, now (to) King James II; now translated by him into English, in . . . The Quakers mightily value him. The booke is common.—AUBREY, JOHN, 1669–96, *Brief Lives, ed. Clark, vol. I, p.* 86.

An Apology for the true Christian Divinity, as the same is held forth and preached by the People called in Scorn, Quakers; being a full Explanation and Vindication of their Principles and Doctrines, by many Arguments deduced from Scripture and Right Reason, and the Testimonies of famous Authors, both Ancient and Modern, with a full Answer to the strongest Objections usually made against them: Presented to the King. Written and published in London, for the Information of Strangers, by Robert Barclay, and now put into our Language for the Benefit of his Countrymen.—TITLE PAGE OF FIRST EDITION, 1678.

A man of eminent gifts and great endowments, expert not only in the languages of the learned, but also well versed in the writings of the ancient Fathers, and other ecclesiastical writers, and furnished with a great understanding, being not only of a sound judgment, but also strong in arguments.—SEWEL, WILLIAM, 1722, *History of the Quakers.*

Robert Barclay was no common character, either as respects natural capacity, extensive learning, indomitable energy, or persevering zeal.—ALLIBONE, S. AUSTIN, 1854–58, *Dictionary of English Literature, vol. I, p.* 118.

The "Apology" of Barclay is a learned and methodical treatise, very different from what the world expected on such a subject, and it was therefore read with avidity both in Britain and on the continent. . . . It would be erroneous, however, to regard this work of Barclay as an exposition of all the doctrines which have been or are prevalent among the Quakers, or, indeed, to consider it as anything more than the vehicle of such of his own views as, in his character of an apologist, he thought it desirable to state. The dedication of Barclay's "Apology" to King Charles II. has always been particularly admired for its respectful yet manly freedom of style, and for the pathos of its allusion to his majesty's own early troubles, as a reason for his extending mercy and favour to the persecuted Quakers.—CHAMBERS, ROBERT, 1876, *Chambers's Cyclopædia of English Literature*, ed. *Carruthers*.

Barclay's great book, "The Apology," is remarkable as the standard exposition of the principles of his sect, and is not only the first defence of those principles by a man of trained intelligence, but in many respects one of the most impressive theological writings of the century. In form it is a careful defence of each of the fifteen theses previously published. It is impressive in style; grave, logical, and often marked by the eloquence of lofty moral convictions.—STEPHEN, LESLIE, 1885, *Dictionary of National Biography*, *vol.* III, *p.* 169.

This remarkable book, which has been recommended by bishops to theological students as the best available for many purposes, is the standard exposition of Quakerism, and undoubtedly ranks among the classics of its period. Mr. Leslie Stephen describes it as "one of the most impressive theological writings of the century: grave, logical, and often marked by the eloquence of lofty moral convictions." "The St. Paul of the Quakers," says Coleridge of the author.—GARNETT, RICHARD, 1895, *The Age of Dryden, p.* 226.

John Eliot

1604–1690

John Eliot, 1604–1690. A Puritan minister of Roxbury who came to America in 1631, and is famous in history as the "Indian Apostle." He is chiefly remembered for his famous translation of the Bible into the Indian language, but he was the author of other works, among which are the "Communion of Churches;" "The Harmony of the Gospels;" "Dying Speeches of Several Indians;" "The Indian Primer;" "Indian Logic Primer."—ADAMS, OSCAR FAY, 1897, *A Dictionary of American Authors, p.* 116.

GENERAL

The Indian Apostle.—THOROWGOOD, T., 1660, *Jews in America, p.* 24.

Mamusse Wunneetupanatamwe Up-Biblum God naneeswe Nukkone Testament kah wonk Wusku Testament. Ne quoshkinnumuk nashpe Wuttinneumoh Christ noh asooweesit John Eliot.—TITLE PAGE OF FIRST EDITION, 1661–63.

Since the death of the apostle Paul, a nobler, truer, and warmer spirit than John Eliot never lived.—EVERETT, EDWARD, 1835, *Address at Bloody Brook*, *Orations and Speeches*.

I have sometimes doubted whether there was more than a single man among our forefathers who realized that an Indian possesses a mind, and a heart, and an immortal soul. That single man was John Eliot. . . . Eliot was full of love for them; and therefore so full of faith and hope that he spent the labor of a lifetime in their behalf. . . . To learn a language utterly unlike all other tongues—a language which hitherto had never been learned, except by the Indians themselves from their mothers' lips—a language never written, and the strange words of which seemed inexpressible by letters if the task were, first to learn this new variety of speech, and then to translate the Bible into it, and to do it so carefully that not one idea throughout the holy book should be changed . . . this was what the Apostle Eliot did. . . . There is no impiety in believing that, when his long life was over, the apostle of the Indians was welcomed to the celestial abodes by the prophets of ancient days and by those earliest apostles and evangelists who had drawn their inspiration from the immediate presence of the Saviour. They first had preached truth and salvation to the world. And Eliot, separated from them by many centuries, yet full of the same spirit, has borne the like message to the new world of the west. Since the first days of Christianity there has been no man more worthy to be numbered in the brotherhood of the apostles than Eliot.—HAWTHORNE, NATHANIEL, 1841, *Grandfather's Chair.*

In his intercourse with his parishioners, and in his private life, Eliot was remarkable for mildness, meekness, and generosity. He combined with the latter virtue a total forgetfulness of self, and his household affairs would often have been in sorry plight, had he not had a good wife who shared his old age as she had his youth, to look after them. She one day, by way of a joke, pointing out their cows before the door, asked him whose they were, and found that he did not know. The treasurer of his church paying him a portion of his salary on one occasion, tied the coin in the pastor's pocket-handkerchief with an abundance of knots, as a check to his freedom of disbursement in charity. On his way home, the good man stopped to visit a destitute family, and was soon tugging at the knots to get at his money. Quickly growing impatient he gave the whole to the mother of the family, saying, "Here, my dear, take it; I believe the Lord designs it all for you."—DUYCKINCK, EVERT A. AND GEORGE L., 1855-65-75, *Cyclopædia of American Literature, ed. Simons, vol.* I, *p.* 46.

He was the first to carry the gospel to the red man, and perhaps the earliest who championed the negro. Strangers with whom he came in contact spoke of the peculiar charm of his manners. He united fervent piety and love of learning to burning· enthusiasm for evangelisation, these qualities being tempered with worldly wisdom and shrewd common sense. Taking into consideration the nature of his life, his literary activity is remarkable. No name in the early history of New England is more revered than his. Eliot was truly a saintly type, without fanaticism, spiritual pride, or ambition.—TEDDER, H. R., *Dictionary of National Biography, vol.* XVII, *p.* 192.

Although producing little that can be accounted as literature. John Eliot deserves prominent mention in the history of American letters. . . . Eliot's Bible is now the most valuable relic of a vanished race. Aside from its great interest to the ethnologer and the antiquarian, it has the added interest of being the first Bible printed in America. Copies of it are exceedingly rare and costly.—PATTEE, FRED LEWIS, 1896, *History of American Literature, pp.* 33, 34.

Sir George Etheredge

1635?-1691?

Sir George Etherege, 1635(?)-1691. Born, 1635(?). Perhaps educated at Cambridge, and subsequently at one of the Inns of Court. Comedy, "The Comical Revenge," produced at Lincoln's Inn Fields Theatre, 1664; other plays, 1667-76. Knighted, about 1680(?). Married about same time. To Hague on diplomatic mission, 1684 (?); at Ratisbon, 1685-88. To Paris; died there, 1691. *Works:* "The Comical Revenge," 1664; "She Wou'd if She Cou'd," 1667; "The Man of Mode," 1676. *Collected Works:* 1704; ed. by A. W. Verity, 1888.—SHARP, R. FARQUHARSON, 1897, *A Dictionary of English Authors, p.* 94.

PERSONAL

Nature, you know, intended me for an idle fellow, and gave me passions and qualities fit for that blessed calling, but fortune has made a changeling of me, and necessity now forces me to set up for a fop of business.—ETHEREDGE, SIR GEORGE, 1687, *The Letterbook, ; Gosse, Seventeenth-Century Studies, p.* 264

Sir George Etherege was as thorough a fop as ever I saw; he was exactly his own Sir Fopling Flutter. And yet he designed Dorimant, the genteel rake of wit, for his own picture.—LOCKIER, DR. DEAN OF PETERBOROUGH, 1730-32, *Spence's Anecdotes, ed. Singer, p.* 47.

In the words of Oldys, Sir George Etherege was "a man of much courtesy and delicate address." Profligacy, sprightliness, and good humour, seem to have been his principal characteristics. In person he is described as a "fair, slender, and genteel man," and his face is said to have been handsome. In later times, however, his comeliness is reported to have been spoiled by the effect of intemperance and the exceeding irregularity of his career. —JESSE, JOHN HENEAGE, 1839–57, *Memoirs of the Court of England during the Reign of the Stuarts, Including the Protectorate, vol.* III, *p.* 324.

There seems no clue whatever to the date of his death, except that in an anonymous pamphlet, written by John Dennis, and printed in 1722, Etheredge is spoken of as having been dead "nearly thirty years." Dennis was over thirty at the Revolution, and is as trustworthy an authority as we could wish for. By this it would seem that Etheredge died about 1693, nearer the age of sixty than fifty. But Colonel Chester found the record of administration to the estate of a Dame Mary Etheredge, widow, dated Feb. 1, 1692. As we know of no other knight of the name, except Sir James Etheredge, who died in 1736, this was probably the poet's relict; and it may yet appear that he died in 1691. He was a short, brisk man, with a quantity of fair hair, and a fine complexion, which he spoiled by drinking. He left no children, but his brother, who long survived him, left a daughter, who is said to have married Aaron Hill. — GOSSE, EDMUND, 1883, *Seventeenth-Century Studies, p.* 265.

GENERAL

George Etheridge a Comical writer of the present age, whose two Comedies, "Love in a Tub," and "She would if she could," for pleasant wit and no bad Oeconomy are judged not unworthy the applause they have met with.—PHILLIPS, EDWARD, 1675, *Theatrum Poetarum Anglicanorum, ed. Brydges, p.* 130.

Shakespear and Jonson . . .
Whom refin'd Etherege copies not at all,
But is himself a sheer Original.

—ROCHESTER, JOHN WILMOT, EARL, 1678, *An Allusion to the Tenth Satire of the First Book of Horace.*

A Gentleman sufficiently eminent in the Town for his Wit and Parts, and One whose tallent in sound Sence, and the Knowledge of true Wit and Humour, are sufficiently conspicuous. . . . "Comical Revenge." . . . This Comedy tho' of a mixt nature, part of it being serious,

and writ in Heroick Verse; yet has succeeded admirably on the Stage, it having always been acted with general approbation. "Man of Mode, or Sir Fopling Flutter." . . . This Play is written with great Art and Judgment, and is acknowledg'd by all, to be as true Comedy, and the Characters as well drawn to the Life, as any Play that has been Acted since the Restauration of the *English* Stage. . . . "She wou'd if she cou'd." . . . This Comedy is likewise accounted one of the first Rank, by several who are known to be good Judges of Dramatick Poesy. Nay our present Laureat says, 'Tis the best Comedy written since the Restauration of the Stage. I heartily wish for the publick satisfaction, that this great Master would oblidge the World with more of his Performances, which would put a stop to the crude and indigested Plays, which for want of better, cumber the Stage.—LANGBAINE, GERARD, 1691, *An Account of the English Dramatick Poets, pp.* 186, 187

The standard of thy style let Etheredge be.—DRYDEN, JOHN, 1692, *To Mr. Southern.*

This expedient to supply the deficiencies of wit, has been used more or less by most of the authors who have succeeded on the stage; though I know but one who has professedly writ a play upon the basis of the desire of multiplying our species, and that is the polite Sir George Etheridge; if I understand what the lady would be at, in the play called "She would if She could." Other poets have, here and there, given an intimation that there is this design, under all the disguises and affectations which a lady may put on: but no author except this, has made sure work of it, and put the imaginations of the audience upon this one purpose, from the beginning to the end of the comedy. It has always fared accordingly; for whether it be that all who go to this piece would if they could, or that the innocents go to it, to guess only what *she would if she could*, the play has always been well received.—ADDISON, JOSEPH, 1711, *Indecency Proceeds From Dulness, The Spectator, No.* 51, *Apr.* 28.

He seems to have possessed a sprightly genius, to have had an excellent turn for comedy, and very happy in a courtly dialogue. We have no proof of his being a scholar, and was rather born, than made a poet. He has not escaped the censure of the critics; for his works are so extremely loose and licentious, as to render them dangerous to young, unguarded minds: and on this account our witty author is, indeed, justly liable to the severest censure of the virtuous, and sober part of mankind.—CIBBER, THEOPHILUS, 1753, *Lives of the Poets, vol. III, p. 39.*

Lastly, that I may leave the reader in better humour with the name at the head of this article, I shall quote one scene from Etherege's "Love in a Tub," which for exquisite, genuine, original humour, is worth all the rest of his plays, though two or three of his witty contemporaries were thrown in among them, as a make weight.—COLERIDGE, SAMUEL TAYLOR, 1812, *Omniana, ed. Ashe, p. 388.*

I have only to add a few words respecting the dramatic writers about this time, before we arrive at the golden period of our comedy. Those of Etherege are good for nothing, except "The Man of Mode, or Sir Fopling Flutter," which is, I think, a more exquisite and airy picture of the manners of that age than any other extant. Sir Fopling himself is an inimitable coxcomb, but pleasant withal. He is a suit of clothes personified. Doriman (supposed to be Lord Rochester) is the genius of grace, gallantry and gaiety. The women in this courtly play have very much the look and air (but something more demure and significant) of Sir Peter Lely's beauties. Harriet, the mistress of Dorimant, who "tames his wild heart to her loving hand," is the flower of the piece. Her natural, untutored grace and spirit, her meeting with Dorimant in the Park, bowing and mimicking him, and the luxuriant description which is given of her fine person, altogether form one of the *chefs-d'œuvre* of dramatic painting. I should think this comedy would bear reviving; and if Mr. Liston were to play Sir Fopling, the part would shine out with double lustre, "like the morn risen on mid-noon."—HAZLITT, WILLIAM, 1818, *Lectures on the English Comic Writers, p.* 78.

George Etheredge first distinguished himself among the libertine wits of the age by his "Comical Revenge, or Love in a Tub." He afterwards gained a more deserved distinction in the comic drama

by his "Man of Mode, or Sir Fopling Flutter," a character which has been the model of all succeeding stage petits-maîtres.—CAMPBELL, THOMAS, 1819, *Specimens of the British Poets.*

Etheredge is the first to set the example of imitative comedy in his "Man of Fashion."—TAINE, H. A., 1871, *History of English Literature, tr. Van Laun, vol.* I, *bk.* iii, *ch.* i, *p.* 479.

Etheredge's comedies possess, in their chronological progression, both importance and interest, as furnishing early—probably the earliest—examples of a style of comic dialogue which was of natural growth and which owed much less than might at first be supposed to French examples. . . . He wrote as a man of the world for men and women of the world, who flocked to his plays to see themselves in his comic mirror, and pointed the way to the style of English comedy, of which Congreve afterwards shone as the acknowledged master. Of characterisation few traces are perceptible in Etheredge's comedies; and in this respect too he anticipated Congreve.—WARD, ADOLPHUS WILLIAM, 1875-99, *A History of English Dramatic Literature, vol.* III, *pp.* 443, 444.

According to all the bibliographers, old and new, Etheredge's first play was "She Would if She Could," 1668, immediately followed by "The Comical Revenge," first printed in 1669. If this were the case, the claim of Etheredge to critical attention would be comparatively small. Oldys, however, mentions that he had heard of, but never seen, an edition of this latter play of 1664. Neither Langbaine, Gildon, or any of their successors believe in the existence of such a quarto, nor is a copy to be found in the British Museum. However, I have been so fortunate as to pick up two copies of this mythical quarto of 1664, the main issue of which I suppose to have been destroyed by some one of the many accidents that befell London in that decade, and Etheredge's precedence of all his more eminent comic contemporaries is thus secured. The importance of this date, 1664, is rendered still more evident when we consider that it constitutes a claim for its author for originality in two distinct kinds. "The Comical Revenge, or Love in a Tub," which was acted at the Duke of York's

Theatre in Lincoln's Inn Fields, in the summer of 1664, is a tragi-comedy, of which the serious portions are entirely written in rhymed heroics, and the comic portions in prose. . . . The serious portion of "The Comical Revenge" is not worth considering in comparison with the value of the prose part. In the under-plot, the gay, realistic scenes which give the play its sub-title of the "Tale of a Tub," Etheredge virtually founded English comedy, as it was successively understood by Congreve, Goldsmith, and Sheridan.—GOSSE, EDMUND, 1883, *Seventeenth-Century Studies, pp.* 235, 239.

Etheredge was clever in catching the fashions of the day; but the vivacity which won popularity for his plays has long evaporated.—STEPHEN, LESLIE, 1889, *Dictionary of National Biography, vol.* XVIII, *p.* 44.

Sir George Etheredge is neither an edifying nor an attractive writer of comedy, but his plays are of considerable historical importance as prototypes of the comedy of manners afterwards so brilliantly developed by Congreve. They are "Love in a Tub" (1664), "She Would if She Could" (1668), and "The Man of Mode" (1676). The last is celebrated for the character of Sir Fopling Flutter, who is said to have been the image of the author, though it is added on the same authority that his intention had been to depict himself in the character of the heartless rake Dorimant, whom others took for Rochester. All the plays suffer from a deficiency of plot, a deficiency of wit, and a superfluity of naughtiness, but cannot be denied to possess a light airy grace, and to have imbibed something of the manner, though little of the humour, of Molière.—GARNETT, RICHARD, 1895, *The Age of Dryden, p.* 121.

Robert Boyle

1627–1691

The Hon. Robert Boyle, (1627–91), physicist, fourteenth child of the first Earl of Cork, was born at Lismore Castle in Munster, and after studying at Eton, and under the rector of Stalbridge, Dorset, went to the Continent for six years. On his return in 1644, he found himself in possession, by his father's death, of the manor of Stalbridge, where he devoted himself to chemistry and natural philosophy. He was one of the first members of the association (1645) which became the Royal Society. Settling at Oxford in 1654, he experimented in pneumatics, and improved the air-pump. As a director of the East India Company (for which he had procured the Charter) he worked for the propagation of Christianity in the East, circulated at his own expense translations of the Scriptures, and by bequest founded the "Boyle Lectures" in defence of Christianity. In 1668 he took up residence in London with his sister, Lady Ranelagh, and gave much of his time to the Royal Society. In 1688 he shut himself up, in order to repair the loss caused by the accidental destruction of his MSS. He believed in the possibility of some of the alchemistic transmutations; but has justly been termed the true precursor of the modern chemist. He discovered "Mariotte's law" seven years before Mariotte. His complete works (with his correspondence and a Life by Dr. Birch) were published in 5 vols. fol. (1744).—PATRICK AND GROOME, *eds.* 1897, *Chambers's Biographical Dictionary, p.* 125.

PERSONAL

He is very tall (about six foot high) and streight, very temperate, and vertuouse, and frugall: a batcheler; keepes a coach; sojournes with his sister, the lady Ranulagh. His greatest delight is chymistrey. He haz at his sister's a noble laboratory, and severall servants (prentices to him) to looke to it. He is charitable to ingeniose men that are in want, and foreigne chymists have had large proofe of his bountie, for he will not spare for cost to gett any rare secret. At his owne costs and chardges he gott translated and printed the New Testament in Arabique, to send into the Mahometan countreys. He has not only a high renowne in England, but abroad; and when foreigners come to hither, 'tis one of their curiosities to make him a visit.—AUBREY, JOHN, 1669–96, *Brief Lives, ed. Clark, vol.* I. *p.* 121.

At the funeral of Mr. Boyle at St. Martin's, Dr. Burnet, Bp. of Salisbury, preach'd on 2 Eccles. v. 26. He concluded with an eulogy due to the deceas'd, who made God and Religion the scope of all his excellent tallents in the knowledge of nature, and who had arriv'd to so high a degree in it, accompanied with such zeale and extraordinary piety, wch he shoew'd in the whole course of his life, particularly in his exemplary charity on all occasions. . . . He dilated on his learning in Hebrew and Greek, his reading of the Fathers, and solid knowledge in theology, once deliberating about taking holy orders, and that at the time of the restoration of K. Cha. 2, when he might have made a greate figure in the nation as to secular honour and titles, his fear of not being able to discharge so weighty a duty as the first, made him decline that, and his humility the other. He spake of his civility to strangers, the greate good which he did by his experience in medicine and chemistry, and to what noble ends he applied himself to his darling studies; the works both pious and useful, which he publish'd; the exact life he led, and the happy end he made.—EVELYN, JOHN, 1691–92, *Diary, Jan.* 6.

He was looked upon by all who knew him as a very perfect pattern. He was a very devout Christian; humble and modest, almost to a fault; of a most spotless and exemplary life in all respects. He was highly charitable, and was a mortified and self-denied man that delighted in nóthing so much as doing good.—BURNET, GILBERT, 1715–34, *History of My Own Time.*

Mr. Boyle, was tall of stature, but slender, and his countenance pale and emaciated. His constitution was so tender and delicate that he had divers sorts of cloaks to put on when he went abroad, according to the temperature of the air, and in this he governed himself by his thermometer. He escaped, indeed, the small-pox, during his life, but for almost forty years he laboured under such a feebleness of body and lowness of strength and spirits that it was astonishing how he could read meditate, try experiments, and write as he did. He had likewise a weakness in his eyes, which made him very tender of them, and extremely apprehensive of such distempers as might affect them.—BIRCH, THOMAS, 1741–44, *Life of the Hon. Robert Boyle,* p. 86.

We are at a loss which to admire most, his extensive knowledge, or his exalted piety. These excellences kept pace with each other: but the former never carried him to vanity, nor the latter to enthusiasm. He was himself *The Christian virtuoso* which he has described. Religion never sat more easy upon a man, nor added greater dignity to a character. He particularly applied himself to chymistry; and made such discoveries in that branch of science, as can scarce be credited upon less authority than his own.—GRANGER, JAMES, 1769–1824, *Biographical History of England, vol.* V, *p.* 283.

Mr. Boyle, the glory of his age and nation. . . . To the accomplishments of a scholar and a gentleman, he added the most exalted piety, the purest sanctity of manners. His unbounded munificence was extended to the noblest, and most honourable purposes, . . . the advancement of true religion, in almost all parts of the world. A firm friend to the church of England, he was one of her brightest ornaments. So long as goodness, learning, and charity, are held in estimation, the name of BOYLE will be revered.—ZOUCH, THOMAS, 1796, *ed., Walton's Lives, vol.* II, *p.* 265.

Eton can point to Robert Boyle as one of the purest and the best, as well as one of the most renowned of her sons.—CREASY, SIR EDWARD, 1850–76, *Memoirs of Eminent Etonians, p.* 139.

There are many other philosophers, ancient and modern, with whom we have taken similar pains; but Boyle is the most admirable character we have met with in the whole range of philosophy, science, and literature; and if instead of being born in Ireland he had been a Hindoo, a Laplander, or an African, we would have sought to do him equal justice, and to prove that wherever his ancestors were born, whether they were persons who threw down mass-houses or "transplanted multitudes of barbarous septs" from their own soil into "the wilds and deserts," he was not a degenerate son, but far nobler than any of his ancestors—vastly superior to any "great Earl" that ever oppressed a generous people.—SEARS, EDWARD I., 1866, *Robert Boyle, National Quarterly Review, vol.* 14, *p.* 84.

His services to science were unique. The condition of his birth, the elevation of his character, the unflagging enthusiasm of his researches, combined to lend dignity and currency to their results. These were coextensive with the whole range, then accessible, of experimented investigation. He personified, it might be said, in a manner at once impressive and conciliatory, the victorious revolt against scientific dogmatism then in progress. Hence his unrivalled popularity and privileged position, which even the most rancorous felt compelled to respect. No stranger of note visited England without seeking an interview, which he regarded it as an obligation of christian charity to grant. Three successive kings of England conversed familiarly with him, and he was considered to have inherited, nay outshone, the fame of the great Verulam. —CLERKE, MISS A. M., 1886, *Dictionary of National Biography, vol.* VI, *p.* 121.

GENERAL

The excellent Mr. Boyle was the person who seems to have been designed by nature to succeed to the labours and inquiries of that extraordinary genius I have just mentioned (Bacon). By innumerable experiments, he in a great measure filled up those plans and outlines of science, which his predecessor had sketched out. His life was spent in the pursuit of nature through a great variety of forms and changes, and in the most rational as well as devout adoration of its Divine Author. —HUGHES, JOHN, 1712, *On Men of Genius in the Arts and Sciences, The Spectator, No.* 554. *Dec.* 5.

Here was a noble soul; a true philosophical mind, well seasoned with humanity, beneficence, and goodnesss. After he had led us through all the regions of nature, considered her various productions, showed us their uses and the manner of converting them to our several purposes, convinced us that we live in a world most wisely contrived wherein numberless good designs are at once carried on with unceasing variety and manifested that all the beings and all the bodies we know jointly conspire, as one whole, in bringing about the great ends of nature. —SHAW, PETER, 1725, *Robert Boyle's Philosophical Works, Abridgment.*

Perhaps Mr. Boyle may be considered as the first person, neither connected with pharmacy nor mining, who devoted a considerable degree of attention to chemical pursuits. Mr. Boyle, though, in common with the literary men of his age, he may be accused of credulity, was both very laborious and intelligent; and his chemical pursuits, which were various and extensive, and intended solely to develop the truth without any regard to previously conceived opinions, contributed essentially to set chemistry free from the trammels of absurdity and superstition in which it had been hitherto enveloped, and to recommend it to philosophers as a science deserving to be studied on account of the important information which it was qualified to convey. His refutation of the alchemistical opinions respecting the constituents of bodies, his observations on cold, on the air, on phosphorus, and on ether, deserve particularly to be mentioned as doing him much honor. We have no regular account of any one substance or of any class of bodies in Mr. Boyle, similar to those which at present are considered as belonging exclusively to the science of chemistry. Neither did he attempt to systematize the phenomena, nor to subject them to any hypothetical explanation.— THOMSON, THOMAS, 1812, *History of the Royal Society.*

To Boyle the world is indebted, besides some very acute remarks and many fine illustrations of his own upon metaphysical questions of the highest moment, for the philosophical arguments in defence of religion, which have added so much lustre to the names of Derham and Bentley; and, far above both, to that of Clarke. . . . I do not recollect to have seen it anywhere noticed, that some of the most striking and beautiful instances of design in the order of the material world, which occur in the sermons preached at Boyle's Lecture, are borrowed from the works of the founder.—STEWART, DUGALD, 1815–21, *First Preliminary Dissertation, Encyclopædia Britannica.*

The peculiar merits of Robert Boyle, have, in later times, been more praised, than known: canonized, rather, by the discerning few, than justly estimated, by the unreflecting many. His works, indeed, still occupy a space, though seldom frequented, in the collections of the learned.—JEBB, JOHN, 1833, *ed., Burnet's Lives, Characters, and An Address to Posterity, Introduction, p.* i.

The metaphysical treatises, to use

that word in a large sense, of Boyle, or rather those concerning Natural Theology, are very prespicuous, very free from system, and such as bespeak an independent lover of truth. His "Disquisition on Final Causes" was a well-timed vindication of that palmary argument against the paradox of the Cartesians, who had denied the validity of an inference from the manifest adaptation of means to ends in the universe to an intelligent Providence. Boyle takes a more philosophical view of the principle of final causes than had been found in many theologians, who weakened the argument itself by the presumptuous hypothesis, that man was the sole object of Providence in the creation. His greater knowledge of physiology led him to perceive, that there are both animal and what he calls cosmical ends, in which man has no concern.—HALLAM, HENRY, 1837–39, *Introduction to the Literature of Europe, pt.* iv, *ch.* viii, *par.* 8.

The value of his contributions to the cause of science, to the province of Natural Philosophy especially, cannot be too highly esteemed. More than two-thirds of his works are composed of the results of his investigations in Pneumatics, Chemistry, Medicine, and kindred subjects. The philosophers of the day and of succeeding times acknowledge their obligations to Boyle in the strongest terms. What a splendid eulogy is that of the great Boerhaave! "Mr. Boyle, the ornament of his age and country, succeeded to the genius and enquiries of the great Chancellor Verulam. Which of all Mr. Boyle's writings shall I recommend? All of them! To him we owe the secrets of fire, air, water, animals, vegetables, fossils: so that from his works may be deduced the whole system of natural knowledge."—ALLIBONE, S. AUSTIN, 1854–58, *Dictionary of English Literature, vol.* I, *p.* 233.

After the death of Bacon, one of the most distinguished Englishmen was certainly Boyle, who, if compared with his contemporaries, may be said to rank immediately below Newton, though, of course, very inferior to him as an original thinker. With the additions he made to our knowledge we are not immediately concerned; but it may be mentioned that he was the first who instituted exact experiments into the relation between colour and heat. . . . It is also to Boyle, more than to any other Englishman, that we owe the science of hydrostatics, in the state in which we now possess it. He is the original discoverer of that beautiful law, so fertile in valuable results, according to which the elasticity of air varies as its density. And, in the opinion of the most eminent modern naturalists, (Cuvier) it was Boyle who opened up those chemical inquiries, which went on accumulating until, a century later, they supplied the means by which Lavoisier and his contemporaries fixed the real basis of chemistry, and enabled it for the first time to take its proper stand among those sciences that deal with the external world.—BUCKLE, HENRY THOMAS, 1857, *History of Civilization in England, vol.* I.

In Robert Boyle the fresh study of nature quickened love of God; his scientific thought was blended with simple and deep religious feeling.—MORLEY, HENRY, 1879, *A Manual of English Literature, ed. Tyler, p.* 464.

Enjoyed in the reign of Charles II. the same European reputation which Bacon had posssesed in that of James I. He wrote on so many subjects, and some of them so trifling, that Swift made fun of him in his "Meditation on a Broomstick;" and his "New Philosophy," his trimming system of natural religion, has gone the way of all intellectual makeshifts. But in the field of physics he was on safer ground, and some of his chemical and pneumatical discoveries have proved of lasting value. His style is wearisome and without elevation. Cudworth, who urged him to translate his voluminous treatises into Latin and destroy the originals, may possibly have been ironical as well as pedantic in so advising.—GOSSE, EDMUND, 1888, *A History of Eighteenth Century Literature, p.* 81.

We find in them still the note of impatience of form: he had not time to be brief. There is scarce a trace in him of the first quality of an artist in prose, rejection. Now and again a well-turned phrase strikes the reader, but, given a certain condition of language, the phrase is found to be that which would have occurred at once to a certain order of intellect. Happily for Boyle the English of his time was comparatively free from the more vulgar sort of stereotyped phrase; but still a full and sonorous tone. But from the greater masters of sonorous English, Boyle was as far removed as from the clear-cut simplicity and directness of Swift. His style is not involved, and is not affected; it is merely rarified and verbose. In his religious writings the same thing is noticeable as in his scientific. Here again he was deeply interested in his subject, a sincerely pious man applying his best powers, or trying so to do, to the subject he deemed of first importance. And here again he is essentially impatient of form; his sincerity gave him an infrequent warmth of phrase, the general and vague nature of his reflections an occasional rotundity, but again the average is jejune. . . . His attainments as a scholar, while they impelled him to attempt a literary form for his thoughts and discoveries, were not strong enough in the balance of his mind to compel the sacrifices necessary to an artistic result.—STREET, G. S., 1894, *English Prose, ed. Craik, vol. III, pp.* 64, 65.

An admirable natural philosopher, but feeble and diffuse as a natural theologian.—GARNETT, RICHARD, 1895, *The Age of Dryden, p.* 229.

George Fox
1624–1691

Born at Fenny Drayton (Drayton-in-the-Clay), Leicestershire, July, 1624: died Jan. 13, 1691. The founder of the Society of Friends. He was the son of Christopher Fox, a Puritan weaver, and in his youth was apprenticed to a shoemaker at Nottingham. About the age of twenty-five he began to disseminate as an itinerant lay preacher the doctrines peculiar to the Society of Friends, the organization of which he completed about 1669. He made missionary journeys to Scotland in 1657, to Ireland in 1669, to the West Indies and North America 1671–72, and to Holland in 1677 and 1684, and was frequently imprisoned for infraction of the laws against conventicles as at Lancaster and Scarborough 1663–66 and at Worcester 1673–74. He married in 1669, Margaret Fell, a widow, who was a woman of superior intellect and gave him much assistance in the founding of his sect. An edition of his "Works" was published at Philadelphia in 1831.—SMITH, BENJAMIN E., 1894–97, *The Century Cyclopedia of Names, p.* 405.

PERSONAL

"Perhaps the most remarkable incident in Modern History," says Teufelsdrockh, "is not the Diet of Worms, still less the Battle of Austerlitz, Waterloo, Peterloo, or any other Battle; but an incident passed carelessly over by most Historians, and treated with some degree of ridicule by others: namely, George Fox's making to himself a suit of Leather. This man, the first of the Quakers, and by trade a Shoemaker, was one of those, to whom, under ruder or purer form, the Divine Idea of the Universe is pleased to manifest itself; and, across all the hulls of Ignorance and earthly Degradation, shine through, in unspeakable Awfulness, unspeakable Beauty, on their souls: who therefore are rightly accounted Prophets, God-possessed; or even Gods, as in some periods it has chanced. Sitting in his stall; working on tanned hides, amid pincers, paste-horns, rosin, swine-bristles, and a nameless flood of rubbish, this youth had, nevertheless, a Living Spirit belonging to him; also an antique Inspired Volume, through which, as through a window, it could look upwards, and discern its celestial Home. The task of a daily pair of shoes, coupled even with some prospect of victuals, and an honourable Mastership in Cordwainery, and perhaps the post of Thirdborough in his hundred, as the crown of long faithful sewing,—was nowise satisfaction enough to such a mind: but ever amid the boring and hammering came tones from that far country, came Splendours and Terrors; for this poor Cordwainer, as we said, was a Man; and the Temple of Immensity, wherein as Man he had been sent to minister, was full of holy mystery to him."—CARLYLE, THOMAS, 1831, *Sartor Resartus, bk.* iii, *ch.* i, *p.* 202.

He exhibits, in his own example, that the attainment of sincere and spiritual piety, is far more profitable than the learning and knowledge required to maintain the controverted points of religious practices; and proves, in his own case, that the study of the holy writings, assisted by divine grace, is of itself sufficient to produce newness of the heart, without any reliance upon the observances of outward forms and ceremonies.—JANNEY, SAMUEL N. (JOSIAH MARSH), 1853, *Life of George Fox, p.* 38.

I think it will be admitted that we have here the portrait not only of a strong, but of a lovable man. That keen and piercing eye of his was not always sparkling with indignation against hypocritical "professors"—it could also shed tears of sympathy with the sorrowful, and there was something in his face which little children loved. To sum up in fewest possible words the impression made by his words and works upon one who studies them across the level of two centuries: he was a man of lion-like courage and adamantine strength of will, absolutely truthful, devoted to the fulfilment of what he believed to be his God-appointed mission, and without any of those side-long looks at worldly promotion and aggrandizement which many sincere leaders of Church parties have cast at intervals of their journey. The chief defect in Fox's character will perhaps be best described in the words of Carlyle—"Cromwell found George Fox's enormous sacred self-confidence none of the least of his attainments."—HODGKIN, THOMAS, 1896, *George Fox* (*Leaders of Religion*), *p.* 278.

GENERAL

One assertion I will venture to make, as suggested by my own experience, that there exist folios on the human understanding, and the nature of man, which would have a far juster claim to their high rank and celebrity, if, in the whole huge volume, there could be found as much fulness of heart and intellect, as bursts forth in many a simple page of George Fox.—COLERIDGE, SAMUEL TAYLOR, 1817, *Biographia Literaria.*

I have read quite through the ponderous folio of George Fox. . . . Pray how may I return it to Mr. Shewell, at Ipswich? I fear to send such a treasure by a stagecoach; not that I am afraid of the coachman or the guard's *reading it,* but it might be lost. Can you put me in a way of sending it in safty? The kind-hearted owner trusted it to me for six months; I think I was about as many days in getting through it, and I do not think that I skipped a word of it.—LAMB, CHARLES, 1823, *Letter to*

Bernard Barton, Feb. 17, *Letters, ed. Ainger, vol.* II, *pp.* 64, 65.

For my part, born and educated in this Society, I have seen enough to induce me to confess, that for its peculiarities I have little respect; for its great leading principles, the highest veneration. Amongst all the various society I have mingled in, I have nowhere seen a greater purity of life and sentiment; a more enviable preservation of a youth-like tenderness of conscience; a deeper sense of the obligations of justice; of the beauty of punctuality; or so sweet a maintenance of the domesticities of life. A thousand memories of youth, and youthful actions now past—a thousand happy and tender associations—bind me in affection to it. I look with a grateful complacency on the luminous views of truth which George Fox drew from the great archives of Christianity, as a glorious legacy to the world; which has already received mighty benefits therefrom, and is now prepared to reap still greater.—HOWITT, WILLIAM, 1834, *George Fox, Tait's Edinburgh Magazine, n. s., vol.* I, *p.* 585.

John Sterling is interesting himself much about George Fox, whose life he means to write. He sadly misses his earnest, prophetic spirit in the present day, and thinks Carlyle the only one who at all represents it. . . . Sterling has finished George Fox's Journal, which has interested him much, though he does not find it as remarkable as he had expected,—less originality and outflashing of the man's peculiar nature.—FOX, CAROLINE, 1842, *Memories of Old Friends.*

He was so far from knowing many languages, that he knew none; nor can the most corrupt passage in Hebrew be more unintelligible to the unlearned, than his English often is to the most acute and attentive reader.—MACAULAY, T. B., 1843, *George Fox, Critical and Historical Essays.*

The influence of the career of George Fox is best appreciated by considering the subsequent character and action of the Society of Friends, of which he was the organiser. For few religious sects have been more thoroughly molded by their early leaders, and, so to speak, stereotyped as to their future constitution, than that Christian body.—TALLACK, WILLIAM, 1868, *George Fox, The Friends, and the Early Baptists, p.* 1.

An illegitimate son of the Church in a time of religious excitement, one of the most extraordinary men of genius in this eccentric generation. He was a grave, sober, reflective man, with no outgoings of volatile imagination, buoyant egotism, or healthy energy in any shape; as passive, unexcited, vacuous, as Bunyan was active, excitable, teeming with creative energy, —not pouring out force, but letting the world flow in upon him, judging and measuring the traditions and opinions floating about him, and striving in a calm way to reduce the bewildering mass to consistent clearness. Probably the more he pondered, the more he entangled himself in perplexing mazes, and he finally ceased to ponder, and took refuge in a set of arbitrary dogmas. . . . His style is more compact, and has greater graphic felicity of plain language, than Bunyan's, but it has none of the Pilgrim's figurative richness.—MINTO, WILLIAM, 1872–80, *Manual of English Prose Literature*, p. 298.

The most enthusiastic admirer of Fox need feel no sensitiveness at the exposure of his greatest defects, for after all deductions there will still remain in any fair characterization enough to fill the candid observer with highest respect.—FOX, NORMAN, 1877, *George Fox and the Early Friends, Baptist Quarterly*, vol. 11, p. 452.

The bibliography of Fox's writings fill fifty-three pages of Smith's Catalogue. . . . There can be no question of the healthiness and strength of his moral fibre. It is remarkable that Wesley, who was acquainted with Barclay's "Apology," never mentions Fox. Yet the early quakerism anticipated methodism in many important points, as well as in the curious detail of conducting the business of meetings by means of answers to queries. The literary skill of the "Apology" has drawn readers to it rather than to Fox's amorphous writings; but for pure quakerism, not yet fixed (1676) in scholastic forms, it is necessary to go to Fox.—GORDON, REV. ALEXANDER, 1889, *Dictionary of National Biography*, vol. XX, p. 121.

He is deficient in imagination and poetry. Stern, bare facts are his province, and he lays them before the reader with absolute impartiality. Of much the same religious opinions as John Bunyan, he differs widely from him, looking upon life with the eye of a moralist, and not of a poet. There are no flowers of imagination in his writings. He is no genius, no great writer. A plain earnest man, thinking only of his mission and never of himself, he tells us the story of his life in plain earnest words, without self-consciousness and without effort. He is a man of sound common sense, great readiness of wit and undaunted courage. He, here and there, displays a certain grim humour and occasionally a touch of pathos. The main charms of his journal seem to consist in its sincerity and truthfulness. George Fox's style is emphatically the right sort for his matter. The interest of the reader is sustained but never inflamed. He carries conviction and arouses our sympathies by his unaffectedness and simplicity.—FITZROY, A. I., 1894, *English Prose, ed. Craik, vol.* III, p. 54.

Fox was in prison oft in days when prisons were sickening receptacles of indescribable filth. His teaching, directed as it was against the intellectual formalities of Puritanism, was as effective as had been the Puritan attack upon the ceremonial formalities of Laud. Moreover, Fox's uncomplaining acceptance of every evil that befell him, and, above all, the sincerity exhibited by his refusal to strive with the ruffians who struck him gained him many a disciple who would not have been won over by the most attractive preaching. His sobriety of judgment—within certain limits—was as remarkable as his spiritual exaltation, and after thousands of excitable converts had swelled the numbers of the society it was George Fox who was the restraining influence in their midst.—GARDINER, SAMUEL RAWSON, 1897, *History of the Commonwealth and Protectorate, vol.* II, p. 24.

In spite of his extraordinary interpretations of Scripture, he had in all practical matters great shrewdness and common sense. . . . Nor is it fair to judge him by his ungrammatical English, which had to be corrected for publication by better-educated Quakers. . . . Even to this day one cannot read Fox's "Journal" without feeling the wonderful power and spirit of the man, and at times the homely beauty of his words.—FISHER, SYDNEY GEORGE, 1900, *The True William Penn*, p. 75.

Richard Baxter

1615-1691

Born at Eaton-Constantine, near Shrewsbury, 12 [?] Nov. 1615. At Free School, Wroxeter, 1630-33; then for a short time under tuition of Richard Wickstead at Ludlow Castle. To Court of Whitehall with introduction to Master of the Revels, 1633. Return home owing to mother's death, 1634. In charge of Wroxeter School for three months. Began theological studies. Ordained, and appointed Headmaster of new school at Dudley, 1638. Assistant minister at Bridgnorth, 1639-41. Appointed preacher at Kidderminster, 5 April 1641. Espoused cause of Parliament in Civil War. To Coventry, 1643 [?]. Chaplain to Captain Whalley's regiment, 1645. In retirement, owing to ill-health, 1647-50. "Aphorisms of Justification" published, 1649; "The Saint's Everlasting Rest," 1650. Returned to Kidderminster. To London, 1660. Preached before House of Commons at St. Margaret's, 30 April 1660; before Lord Mayor and Alderman at St. Paul's, 10 May 1660. Appointed Chaplain to Charles II. Finally left Church of England, 16 May 1662, and retired to Acton. Married Margaret Charlton, 10 Sept. 1662. Visit to Richard Hampden in Buckinghamshire, 1665. "A Call to the Unconverted" published, 1665. Wife died, 1681. Wrote "Breviate" of her Life, 1681. Arrested, 28 Feb. 1685, for libel on the Church in his "Paraphrase of the New Testament." Trial, 30 May. Sentenced to fine of 500 marks and imprisonment till paid. Discharged from prison, 24 Nov. 1686, fine being remitted. Active in coalition of dissenters with conforming clergy, 1688. Died, 8 Dec. 1691. Buried in Christ Church, London. *Works:* Between 1649 and 1691 Baxter published 148 works. Nine were published posthumously between 1692 and 1701. A complete list is given in Orme's "Life of Baxter," 1830, and A. B. Grosart's "Annotated List" of Baxter's Writings, 1868. Baxter's "Practical Works" were published in 4 vols. 1707; again, in 23 vols., with life, by W. Orme, 1830. "Reliquiæ Baxterianæ" (autobiography), edited by M. Sylvester, 1696.—SHARP, R. FARQUHARSON, 1897, *A Dictionary of English Authors, p. 19.*

PERSONAL

Between the years 1641 and 1660 this town was the scene of the labours of
RICHARD BAXTER,
renowned equally for his Christian learning
and his pastoral fidelity.
In a stormy and divided age
he advocated unity and comprehension,
pointing the way to the Everlasting Rest.
Churchmen and Nonconformists united to raise this memorial, A. D. 1875.
—INSCRIPTION ON MONUMENT, KIDDERMINSTER, 1875.

Richard, Richard, dost thou think we'll hear thee poison the court? Richard, thou art an old fellow, an old knave; thou hast written books enough to load a cart, every one is full of sedition, I might say treason, as an egg is full of meat. Hadst thou been whipped out of thy writing trade forty years ago, it had been happy. Thou pretendest to be a preacher of the Gospel of peace, and thou hast one foot in the grave: it is time for thee to begin to think what account thou intendest to give. But leave thee to thyself, and I see thou'lt go on as thou hast begun; but, by the grace of God, I'll look after thee. I know thou hast a mighty party, and I see a great many of the brotherhood in corners, waiting to see what will become of their mighty Don, and a Doctor of the party (looking to Dr. Bates) at your elbow; but, by the grace of Almighty God, I'll crush you all. Come, what do you say for yourself, you old knave; come, speak up. What doth he say? I am not afraid of you, for all the snivelling calves you have got about you.—JEFFREYS, GEORGE LORD, 1685, *Speech at Trial of Richard Baxter, ed. Orme, vol.* I, *p.* 368.

Concerning almost all my writings, I must confess that my own judgment is, that fewer, well studied and polished, had been better; but the reader who can safely censure the books, is not fit to censure the author, unless he had been upon the place, and acquainted with all the occasions and circumstances. Indeed, for the "Saint's Rest," I had four months' vacancy to write it, but in the midst of continual languishing and medicine; but, for the rest, I wrote them in the crowd of all my other employments, which would allow me no great leisure for polishing and exactness, or any ornament; so that I scarce ever wrote one sheet twice over, nor stayed to make any blots or interlinings, but was fain to let it go as it was first conceived; and when my own desire was rather to stay upon one thing long than run over many, some sudden occasions or other extorted almost all my writings from me. —BAXTER, RICHARD, 1691? *Memorable Passages of My Life and Times.*

Mr. Baxter, an eminent school-master, (who put out Horace and Anacreon, and was the chief mourner at the famous Mr. Rich. Baxter's funeral, who was his near relation,) did assure Mr. Halley, that old Baxter, when he was opened after his death, had a gaul in him as large as that of an horse.—HEARNE, THOMAS, 1706, *Reliquiæ Hearnianæ, ed. Bliss, Oct. 9, vol.* I, *p.* 116.

His zeal for religion was extraordinary, but it seems never to have prompted him to faction, or carried him to enthusiasm. This champion of the Presbyterians was the common butt of men of every other religion, and of those who were of no religion at all. But this had very little effect upon him: his presence and his firmness of mind on no occasion forsook him. He was just the same man before he went into prison, while he was in it, and when he came out of it; and he maintained a uniformity of character to the last gasp of his life. His enemies have placed him in hell; but every man who has not ten times the bigotry that Mr. Baxter himself had, must conclude that he is in a better place. This is a very faint and imperfect sketch of Mr. Baxter's character: men of his size are not to be drawn in miniature.—GRANGER, JAMES, 1769–1824, *Biographical History of England, vol.* V, *p.* 81.

The natural temper of Baxter was quick and irritable, impatient of contradiction, and prone to severity. This was partly owing to the diseased state of body, from which he endured constant and incredible pain. It appears that he was deeply sensible of this infirmity, and that he laboured hard to subdue it. It led him frequently to use harsh and irritating language towards his opponents, which created increased hostility, and gave them an idea that he was an unamiable man, who might be feared or esteemed, but who could not be loved. But if Baxter was easily

provoked, he was ever ready to forgive. He was warm, but not irascible. He cherished no resentments, was always happy to accept an explanation or apology, and was as prompt to pardon, as he had been to take offence. In the expression of all his feelings, he was open and undisguised. He always spoke from the heart, whether it was filled with indignation, or overflowed with love.—ORME, WILLIAM, 1830, *Life of Richard Baxter, p.* 792.

One of the warmest admirers and ablest commentators of Baxter designates the leading and peculiar trait of his character as *unearthliness.* In our view, this was its radical defect. He had too little of humanity, he felt too little of the attraction of this world, and lived too exclusively in the spiritual and the unearthly, for a full and healthful development of his nature as a man, or of the graces, charities, and loves of the Christian.—WHITTIER, JOHN GREENLEAF, 1849, *Richard Baxter, Old Portraits and Modern Sketches, p.* 207.

His character is wanting in hearty vigour—in emotional healthiness. There is a poverty of the merely natural life—a lack of genial interest—and of the appreciation of any mere earthly beauty or art —that takes from it the richness of a full manhood. He was a Puritan, and little more. . . . He rose but slightly above his time. As its systems confined his intellect, its moral narrowness bound his character. He was strong in its strength; he was weak in its deficiencies. The very intensity of his spiritual earnestness was in some degree born of this one-sidedness. Had he possessed a broader feeling, and sympathies more widely responsive to nature and life, he could not have lived so entirely as he did above the world, and given himself with such an unresting vigilance to the love and ministry of souls. If we look at him as a man, this want of breadth and variety of interest diminishes his greatness; if we look at him as the Puritan pastor and divine, it was the very singleness of his spiritual energy that made his excellence and crown.—TULLOCH, JOHN, 1861, *English Puritanism and Its Leaders, p.* 389.

Even in his outward life he exemplified as few men else have ever done the confluence of all Christian influences. He was born of Puritan parents, yet converted by a book of Jesuit devotions. He was ordained in Anglican orders, offered an Anglican Bishopric, the pastor of an Anglican parish, even a candidate, though an unsuccessful candidate, for a place in Convocation; yet the oracle and patriarch of Evangelical Nonconformity, the friend of Calamy and Howe, of Hampden, and of Pym. Immersed as he was in the controversial theology of the Puritans, he was yet the zealous admirer of Richard Hooker, the most majestic of our divines, of George Herbert, the most saintly of our sacred poets—Herbert in whose "temple" he took refuge with the "sound of Aaron's bells from the jingling of scholastic philosophy;"—and he delighted in the converse of Tillotson and Tillotson's disciples and companions, whom the fanatics of his own and of later times have so severely condemned as almost unworthy of the name of Christian. He is claimed as the first parent of the Society for the Propagation of the Gospel, the most venerable of the Missionary Societies of the Church; he is claimed also as the first parent of the extreme school of Nonconformity which in Kidderminster possesses his pulpit, and which, in a wider sense, dating its spiritual lineage from his large and liberal spirit, has often, with whatever departure from his theology, lifted up before the churches the banner of tolerance and freedom that Baxter was among the first to unfurl.—STANLEY, ARTHUR PENRHYN, 1875, *Richard Baxter, Macmillan's Magazine, vol.* 32, *p.* 393.

His strong sense of the reality of the spiritual world and his tenderness in dealing with individual cases endeared him to his congregation. Yet Baxter was above all things a controversialist, one who loved to set forth the gospel as addressed indeed to the hearts of men, but as guarded by all the minute distinctions of Puritan theology. For forms of church government he did not care much. He did not altogether approve of the system which Parliament and Assembly were attempting to set up, and he would probably at any time of his life have been content with a compromise, if such could be found, between Presbyterianism and Episcopacy. His mind, in fact, was essentially unpolitical. He could comprehend ideas, but he could not comprehend men, and even in 1645 the common-place about fighting for

King and Parliament was still for him a stern reality, which every man in England was bound to do his best to carry into effect.—GARDINER, SAMUEL RAWSON, 1886–91, *History of the Great Civil War, vol.* II, *p.* 327.

He was a voracious reader and an acute critic; but he was, most of all, successful as a preacher and a parish priest. At Kidderminster, during the crisis of the Civil War, and at Coventry, he ministered with assiduous eagerness, and he had the firmness to maintain his opinions in the face of both parties. He was of the Parliament side, but he could not reconcile himself to a republic. He opposed both the Covenant and the Engagement, and the abolition of bishops, yet he was much more of a Presbyterian than a Churchman. A strong Parliament man, after the Restoration he refused a bishopric, and by his nonconformity laid himself open to the persecuting violence of the state laws. He was, in fact, so honest, so firm, and, it must be admitted, so narrow in his own opinions, that he could find no party in the state, and but few in religion, who would agree with or even tolerate them. In literature he was a master, but in practical life he was unfit for the rubs of daily existence. Though Cromwell's theology was inadequate in his eyes, he was just as little willing as the great Protector to tolerate religious teaching beyond certain fixed limits. He, more than any single man, stood in the way of toleration of Roman Catholics at the Restoration. His political tracts were burnt by the University of Oxford with those of Buchanan and Milton, in the fervour of the Royalist reaction. The fierce persecuting ardour of the secular power, the squires and the lawyers who could never forgive the Commonwealth, broke over his head. He would not conform to the laws, and he was committed to prison by two justices of the peace.—HUTTON, W. H., 1895, *Social England*, ed. Traill, *vol.* IV, *p.* 294.

THE SAINT'S EVERLASTING REST
1650

Let me mention here, before entering into deeper matters, one formal merit which the Saint's "Everlasting Rest" eminently possesses. I refer to that without which, I suppose, no book ever won permanent place in the literature of a nation, and which I have no scruple in ascribing to it—I mean its style. A great admirer of Baxter has recently suggested a doubt whether he ever recast a sentence or bestowed a thought on its rhythm and the balance of its several parts; statements of his own make it tolerably certain that he did not. As a consequence he has none of those bravura passages which must have cost Jeremy Taylor, in his "Holy Living and Dying" and elsewhere, so much of thought and pains, for such do not come of themselves and unbidden to the most accomplished masters of language. But for all this there reigns in Baxter's writings, and not least in "The Saint's Rest," a robust and masculine eloquence; nor do these want from time to time rare and unsought felicity of language, which once heard can scarcely be forgotten. In regard, indeed, of the choice of words, the book might have been written yesterday. There is hardly one which has become obsolete, hardly one which has drifted away from the meaning which it has in his writings. This may not be a great matter, but it argues a rare insight, conscious or unconscious, into all which was truest, into all which was furthest removed from affectation and untruthfulness in the language, that after more than two hundred years so it should be; and one may recognise here an element, not to be overlooked, of the abiding popularity of the book.—TRENCH, RICHARD CHENEVIX, 1877, *Baxter and the Saint's Rest, Companions for the Devout Life, p.* 89.

Its deep piety, its clear and beautiful style, the dignity and enthusiasm and modernness of its language, have made it an English classic. Narrow as Baxter's system may seem, we feel that he is more tolerant than his creed, and at the root of all his stubborn individuality lies a true and tender conscience. If the Nonconformity of the Stuart age laid heavy burdens on men's shoulders, it suffered from the consequences of its actions. In its provision for men of religion it brought upon itself the severity of secular opinion. But it left two priceless gifts to English literature and English religion in the "Pilgrim's Progress" and the "Saints' Rest."—HUTTON, WILLIAM HOLDEN, 1895, *Social England, ed. Traill, vol.* IV, *p.* 295.

GENERAL

Baxter wrote as in the view of eternity; but generally judicious, nervous, spiritual, and evangelical, though often charged with the contrary. He discovers a manly eloquence, and the most evident proofs of an amazing genius, with respect to which he may not improperly be called the *English Demosthenes.*—DODDRIDGE, PHILIP, 1763? *Lectures on Preaching.*

I would recommend you to read some practical divinity every day; especially the works of Howe, Henry, Watts, Doddridge, and writers of that strain and spirit, whom God eminently honoured as instruments of great usefulness in his church. Above all, Baxter, who was, with regard to the success of his labours and writings, superior to them all.—ORTON, JOB, 1783–1806, *Letters to Dissenting Ministers.*

There is a living energy and spirit in the practical writings of Baxter, which the reader seldom meets with in any other author. His appeals to the conscience are often mighty and irresistible.—WILLIAMS, EDWARD, 1800, *The Christian Preacher.*

Among the chief, if not the very chief, of those writers of "an opposition persuasion," was Richard Baxter; a divine of a most capricious, yet powerful and original mind. What Prynne was in law and history, Baxter was in theology: as the similarity, in point of quaintness, of the titles of their respective works, testifies. . . . Baxter was a man of great gravity of demeanor and great piety of soul. He was acute and learned withal, and an air of originality pervades most of his writings.—DIBDIN, THOMAS FROGNALL, 1824, *The Library Companion, note, p.* 50.

Pray read with great attention Baxter's Life of himself. It is an inestimable work. I may not unfrequently doubt Baxter's memory, or even his competence, in consequence of his particular modes of thinking; but I could almost as soon doubt the Gospel verity as his veracity.—COLERIDGE, SAMUEL TAYLOR, 1827, *Table Talk, ed. Ashe, July* 12.

The style of Baxter is considerably diversified. It is often incorrect, rugged, and inharmonious, abounding in parentheses and digressions, and enfeebled by expansion. It is happiest when it is divested entirely of a controversial character, and the subject relates to the great interests of salvation and charity. It then flows with a copiousness and purity to which there is nothing superior in the language in which he wrote. The vigorous conceptions of his mind are then conveyed in a corresponding energy of expression; so that the reader is carried along with a breathless impetuosity, which he finds it impossible to resist. . . . Truth in all its majesty and infinite importance alone occupied the throne of his spirit, and dictated the forms in which its voice should be uttered. And when it spoke, it was in language divinely suited to its nature, never distracting by its turgidness, or disgusting by its regularity. He could be awful or gentle, pathetic or pungent, at pleasure; always suiting his words to his thoughts, and dissolving his audience in tenderness, or overwhelming them with terror, as heaven or hell, the mercies of the Lord, or the wrath to come, was the topic of discourse. It may confidently be affirmed, that from no author of the period could a greater selection of beautiful passages of didactic, hortatory, and a consolatory writings, be made.—ORME, WILLIAM, 1830, *Life of Richard Baxter, p.* 788.

To substitute for this self-portraiture, any other analysis of Baxter's intellectual and moral character would indeed be a vain attempt. If there be any defect or error of which he was unconscious, and which he therefore has not avowed, it was the combination of an undue reliance on his own powers of investigating truth, with an undue distrust in the result of his enquiries. He proposed to himself, and executed, the task of exploring the whole circle of the moral sciences, logic, ethics, divinity, politics, and metaphysics, and this toil he accomplished amidst public employments of ceaseless importunity, and bodily pains almost unintermitted. Intemperance never assumed a more venial form; but that this insatiate thirst for knowledge was indulged to a faulty excess, no reader of his life, or of his works, can doubt.—STEPHEN, SIR J., 1839, *Life and Times of Richard Baxter, Edinburgh Review, vol.* 70, *p.* 219.

His theological writings, though too moderate to be pleasing to the bigots of any party, had an immense reputation. Zealous Churchmen called him a Roundhead; and many Nonconformists accused him of Erastianism and Arminianism. But the integrity of his heart, the purity of his life, the vigour of his faculties, and the extent of his attainments, were acknowledged by the best and wisest men of every persuasion. His political opinions, in spite of the oppression which he and his brethren had suffered, were moderate. He was partial to that small party which was hated by both Whigs and Tories.— MACAULAY, THOMAS BABINGTON, 1843, *Richard Baxter, Critical and Historical Essays.*

The author of works so elaborate and profound as to frighten by their very titles and ponderous folios the modern ecclesiastical student from their perusal, his hold upon the present generation is limited to a few practical treatises, which, from their very nature, can never become obsolete. The "Call to the Unconverted," and "The Saint's Everlasting Rest," belong to no time or sect. They speak the universal language of the wants and desires of the human soul. They take hold of the awful verities of life and death, righteousness and judgment to come. Through them the suffering and hunted minister of Kidderminster has spoken in warning, entreaty, and rebuke, or in tones of tenderest love and pity, to the hearts of the generations which have succeeded him. His controversial works, his confessions of faith, his learned disputations, and his profound doctrinal treatises, are no longer read.—WHITTIER, JOHN GREENLEAF, 1849, *Richard Baxter, Old Portraits and Modern Sketches, p.* 165.

Differing as Baxter did from Owen and others; involved as he was in constant controversy with the extreme Calvinists of his generation; and disposed as some would be to deny him the name of a Calvinist altogether,—there is yet no divine of his age bears, in deeper and broader impress, the spirit of its religious and theological belief. He rose above a mere formal Calvinism; but the very processes of reasoning, and peculiarities of intellectual apprehension, by which he did so, were Calvinistic. He waged a ceaseless fight with the Sectarian exaggerations, both of doctrine and ecclesiastical practice, that surrounded him; but the weapons by which he did so were the very same which had cut out for the sects a more lawless and independent way on the great high-road of Protestantism. Certainly, of all the men who express and represent the spiritual thought of the Puritan age, none does so more completely, and to the very center of his intelligence, than Richard Baxter.—TULLOCH, JOHN, 1861, *English Puritanism and Its Leaders, p.* 377.

Grasping his fecundity of publication with the engrossing ministry which occupied his chief energies, it must be manifest that Richard Baxter was an extraordinary man. In his *physique* naturally weak, and tainted from the outset with consumptive tendencies, and later worn and valetudinarian, he so conquered the body, that he did the work of a score of ordinary men as an author alone. Baxter had beyond all dispute a penetrative, almost morbidly acute brain. He was the creator of our popular christian literature. Regarded intrinsically and as literature, his books need fear no comparison with contemporaries.—GROSART, ALEXANDER B., 1885, *Dictionary of National Biography, vol.* III, *p.* 434.

The autobiography of this pious, useful, boisterous heresiarch, which appeared posthumously in 1696, is pleasant reading. —GOSSE, EDMUND, 1888, *A History of Eighteenth Century Literature, p.* 77.

One of the greatest of Englishmen, not only of his own, but of any time. . . . Considering his character and popularity, the extent of his writings, his genius and learning, he may be said to be the greatest of English theologians (or one of the greatest), as he has certainly been one of

the most lasting influences on popular theology. He was not without faults, of which, we gather from his writings and also from the narrative to which I referred at first, too great pugnacity and contentiousness were the most serious. In the days of his youth he was too fervid and vehement and inconsiderate.—JOWETT, BENJAMIN, 1891, *Richard Baxter, Sermons, ed.* Fremantle, pp. 66, 72.

Considering the defects of his education, and the incessant whirl in which his life was passed, his literary fecundity is perfectly marvellous. He is said to have taken no pains with his style, and to have written straight from the heart; "he never recast a sentence or bestowed a thought on its rhythm, and the balance of its several parts;" but in spite—or shall we say, in consequence?—of this, his style is in its way remarkably good; there is a freedom and naturalness about it which perhaps would have been lost if he had elaborated his compositions more carefully. Earnestness and robust eloquence breathe through every page. . . . That, in spite of his independent position, his works were admired, is partly due to the obvious earnestness and sincerity of the man, but partly to the excellence of his matter and style. He was to a great extent a self-taught man, and his writings bear traces of this; he was not a trained theologian, and can hardly be ranked with the giants of that golden age of theology; but his works are read where theirs are not.—OVERTON, J. H., 1893, *English Prose, ed. Craik, vol.* II, *pp.* 568, 569.

Sir George Mackenzie

1636–1691

George Mackenzie, nephew to the Earl of Seaforth, and grandson to Dr. Bruce, principal of St. Leonard's College, St. Andrews, was born at Dundee in 1636. He studied at Scottish and French Universities, and was called to the bar in 1656. He published "Arètina," an original "heroic" romance, in 1660, and in the following year was engaged in his first famous pleading, the defence of the Marquis of Argyll. Knighted and made King's advocate in 1674, he became notorious with the Covenanters as "the bloodthirsty advocate and persecutor of the saints of God," a reputation which still clings to his name in Scotland although his conduct in his hated office was upright and even humane. He spent the leisure snatched from his legal duties in writing sundry moral essays on religion, solitude, moral gallantry, and the like; wherein, it may be said, the lawyer pleads for his clients the scholar, the gentleman, and the pedant. On the accession of James II. and the abrogation of the penal laws against the Catholics, he resigned his office, and was induced to re-accept it only to resign it for good when the Revolution, which he opposed, became an accomplished fact. He retired to the scholarly solitude that he loved at Oxford, and died on a visit to London in 1691. He was buried in the churchyard of the Greyfriars, Edinburgh, where his tomb is still noted by the populace, although De Quincey's is forgotten. Almost all his works, except "Aretina," are included in the two vol. folio edition, Edinburgh, 1722.—CRAIK, HENRY, ed., 1893, *English Prose, vol.* III, *p.* 261.

PERSONAL

The memory of that "noble wit of Scotland" is far from being honoured— nay, it is execrated by his countrymen— by the common people we mean—and, in the long run, they are no bad judges of merit. He was, we believe, no great shakes as a lawyer, either within or without the bar; and, like many other well-born, weak-minded men, had a taste for elegant literature and vulgar blood. Of his "voluminous works, historical and juridical," we know less than nothing; but his "Essays on several moral subjects," have more than once fallen out of our hands.—WILSON, JOHN, 1845, *Dryden and Pope, Blackwood's Magazine.*

Sir George Mackenzie's tomb in the Greyfriars churchyard of Edinburgh is a gloomy structure of stone, erected by him in his lifetime, surmounted by a ponderous cupola, and shut in by a massive door, locked and barred. At the present day, as for generations back, the boys of the old town of Edinburgh (those of them especially whose parents are connected with the moorland districts of Scotland), hold it a feat of daring to go to the persecutor's tomb as the gloaming darkens into night, and with trembling lips and feet prepared for instant flight, to shout through the key-hole the quaint and horrible adjuration—

"Lift the sneck and draw the bar,
Bluidy Mackenyie, come out an ye daur!"

Now who was this man, buried for centuries under the execration of a whole people? He was, as a political adversary, but a wise judge and a most candid contemporary observer, confessed, "the brightest Scotsman of his time." Even Dryden, at the summit of his fame, avowed that his poetic efforts and successes were originated by the conversation of "that noble wit of Scotland, Sir George Mackenzie." He was an eminent lawyer, in the great age of the lawyers of a nation which has always been governed by its lawyers; and his institutional works are to this day of high authority in the jurisprudence of Scotland. He was not only a lawyer, but a reformer of the law, and he claims, with justice, that the changes in its administration which he procured were in the direction of protecting the rights of the subject and of the accused against the influence of the Crown and the Bench. Lastly, we shall be able to prove that this alleged persecutor was anything but a bigot; that he was imbued with large and latitudinarian principles in all matters relating to religion; that these principles had the strongest influence over himself personally, and were the rule and guide of his whole public course; and, in particular, that they had the closest connection with those political measures against the Presbyterians which he originated as a minister of the Crown, or carried into execution as public prosecutor.—INNES, ALEXANDER TAYLOR, 1871, "*The Bloody Mackenzie*," *Contemporary Review, vol.* 18, *p.* 249.

All through life he manifested a continuous devotion to literary pursuits, but these were not permitted to interfere with his professional duties. His rise to eminence at the bar was exceptionally rapid. If in solid legal accomplishments he had several superiors, few excelled him in ready eloquence, or the adroit use of legal technicalities. . . . Mackenzie's career as public prosecutor can only be defended on the supposition that in law, as well as in love and war, "all things are fair." His eager interest in constitutional history, and his overbearing temper, are partly accountable for his misuse of legal forms to obtain convictions; and his hatred of religious fanaticism seems also to have itself verged on fanaticism. The one redeeming feature of his character was his devotion to literature and learning.—HENDERSON, T. F., 1893, *Dictionary of National Biography, vol.* XXXV, *pp.* 142, 144.

GENERAL

He has published many books, some of law, and all full of faults; for he was a slight and superficial man.—BURNET, GILBERT, 1715-34, *History of My Own Time.*

Mackenzie may be regarded as the first successor of his countryman Drummond of Hawthornden in the cultivation of an English style; he was the correspondent of Dryden and other distinguished English writers of his day; but he has no pretensions of his own to any high rank either for the graces of his expression or the value of his matter. Whatever may have been his professional learning, too, his historical disquisitions are as jejune and uncritical as his attempts at fine writing are, with all their elaboration, at once pedantic and clownish. He has nothing either of the poetry or the elegance of Drummond.—CRAIK, GEORGE L., 1861, *A Compendious History of English Literature and of the English Language, vol. II, p. 189.*

His conceits are the offspring of a powerful poetic fancy; some of them would have pleased Donne, others, no doubt, delighted Dryden. Mackenzie stands between the two ages, belonging to the earlier by sympathy, and yet coming sometimes very close to the later when he indulges his satirical foible. The last of the old wits, belated in the North, he holds out his hand to the first of the new.—RALEIGH, W. A., 1893, *English Prose, ed. Craik, vol. III, p. 263.*

Nathaniel Lee

1653–1692

Nathaniel Lee (d. 1692), the son of Dr. Lee, Incumbent of Hatfield, was educated at Westminster School and at Trinity College, Cambridge; but, left to his own resources, he took to the stage, and, in 1672, played at the Duke's Theatre the part of Duncan in "Macbeth." Although an admirable reader, he was unable to get his living as an actor. He then produced, at the age of twenty-five, the first of his eleven plays, "Nero;" and between 1675 and 1684, this was followed by eight other plays of his own, including his two most popular, "The Rival Queens; or, Alexander the Great" (1677), and "Theodosius; or, the Force of Love" (1680). He also joined Dryden in the plays of "Œdipus" (1679) and "The Duke of Guise" (1683). There was a wildfire of imagination in Lee, and he drank too freely. In November, 1684, he was received into Bedlam, where he remained four years. . . . Between his recovery and his death, at the age of about forty, Lee wrote, in 1689 and 1690, two more plays, "The Princess of Cleve" and "The Massacre of Paris;" but he was chiefly dependent upon ten shillings a week from the Theatre Royal.—MORLEY, HENRY, 1879, *A Manual of English Literature, ed. Tyler, p. 426.*

PERSONAL

6 April, 1692, Nathaniel Lee a man bur.—BURIAL REGISTER, ST. CLEMENT'S DANES.

I remember, poor Nat. Lee, who was then upon the very verge of madness, yet made a sober and a witty answer to a bad poet, who told him, "It was an easie thing to write like a madman:" "No," said he, "it is very difficult to write like a madman, but it is a very easie matter to write like a fool."—DRYDEN, JOHN, 1694? *Letter to Dennis, Malone's Dryden, vol. II.*

Nathaniel Lee was fellow of Trinity College in Cambridge. The Duke of Buckingham (Villiers) brought him up to town; where he never did anything for him: and that, I verily believe, was one occasion of his running mad. He was rather before my time; but I saw him in Bedlam.—LOCKIER, DR., DEAN OF PETERBOROUGH, 1730–32, *Spence's Anecdotes, ed. Singer, p. 47.*

Was so pathetic a reader of his own scenes, that I have been informed by an actor who was present, that while Lee was reading to major Mohun at a rehearsal, Mohun in the warmth of his admiration threw down his part and said—"Unless I were able to play it as well as you read it, to what purpose should I undertake it?" And yet this very author, whose elocution raised such admiration in so capital an actor, when he attempted to be an actor himself, soon quitted the stage in an honest despair of ever making any profitable figure there.—CIBBER, COLLEY, 1739, *An Apology for His Life, p. 71.*

Educated at Westminster school, and Trinity Hall, Cambridge. He was very handsome as well as ingenious man; but given to debauchery which necessitated milk-diet, when some of his university comrades visiting him, he fell to drinking with them out of all measure, which flying up into his head, caused his face to break out into those carbuncles which were afterwards observed there; and also touched his brain, occasioning that madness so much lamented in so rare a genius. Tom Brown says he wrote while he was in Bedlam a play of twenty-five acts; and Mr. Bowman tells me that going once to visit him there, Lee shewed him a scene, "in which," says he, "I have done a miracle for you." "What's that?" said Bowman "I have made you a good priest."—OLDYS, WILLIAM C., 1761, *MS., Note to Langbaine's Account of the English Dramatick Poets.*

As he is known to have entered college in 1668, he must have been older than thirty-five when he died twenty-four years later. No trace of his grave remains in St. Clement Danes; and Butcher Row, afterwards called Pickett Street, in which stood the Bear and Harrow, was wiped out of existence some years ago, and the New Law Courts stand on its site. It was a very narrow street, running from Ship Yard to Holywell Street, by the side of St. Clement's Church.—HUTTON, LAURENCE, 1885, *Literary Landmarks of London, p. 196.*

GENERAL

Your beauteous images must be allowed
By all but some vile poets of the crowd.
But how should any sign-post dauber know
The worth of Titian or of Angelo?
Hard features every bungler can command;
To draw true beauty shows a master's hand.
—DRYDEN, JOHN, 1677, *To Nathaniel Lee.*

Nat Lee stepp'd in next, in hopes of a prize.
Apollo rememb'ring he had not once in thrice.
By the rubies in's face, he could not deny
But he had as much wit as wine would supply;
Confess'd that indeed he had a musical note,
But sometimes strained so hard that it rattled in the throat;
Yet own'd he had sense and 't encourage him for 't
He made him his Ovid in Augustus's court.
—ROCHESTER, JOHN WILMOT, EARL, 1680?
Session of the Poets.

It has often been observed against me, that I abound in ungoverned fancy; but I hope the world will pardon the sallies of youth. Age, despondence, and dullness come too fast of themselves. I discommend no man for keeping the beaten road; but I am sure the noble hunters that follow the game must leap hedges and ditches sometimes, and run at all, or never come into the fall of the quarry. My comfort is, I cannot be so ridiculous a creature to any man as I am to myself: for who should know the house so well as the good man at home?—who, when his neighbours come to see him, still sets the best rooms to view; and, if he be not a wilful ass, keeps rubbish and lumber in some dark hole, where nobody comes but himself, to mortifie at melancholy hours.—LEE, NATHANIEL, 1680, *Theodosius, or the Force of Love, Dedication.*

An Author whose Plays have made him sufficiently remarkable to those who call themselves *The Witts;* and One whose Muse deserv'd a better Fate than Bedlam. . . . However, before this misfortune befel him, he writ several Dramatical Pieces, which gave him Title to the first Rank of Poets; there being several of his Tragedies, as "Mithridates," "Theodosius," &c., which have forc'd Tears from the fairest Eyes in the World: his Muse indeed seem'd destin'd for the Diversion of the Fair Sex; so soft and passionately moving, are his Scenes of Love written.—LAGBAINNE, GERARD, 1691, *An Account of the English Dramatick Poets, pp. 320, 321.*

Among our modern English poets, there was none who was better turned for tragedy than Lee; if instead of favouring the impetuosity of his genius, he had restrained it, and kept it within its proper bounds. His thoughts are wonderfully suited to tragedy, but frequently lost in such a cloud of words, that it is hard to see the beauty of them. There is an infinite fire in his works, but so involved in smoke, that it does not appear in half its lustre. He frequently succeeds in the passionate parts of the tragedy, but more particularly where he slackens his efforts, and eases the stile of those epithets and metaphors, in which he so much abounds.—ADDISON, JOSEPH, 1711, *On Tragedy, The Spectator, No. 39, April 14.*

There cannot be a stronger proof of the charms of harmonious elocution, than the many, even unnatural, scenes and flights of the false sublime it has lifted into applause. In what raptures have I seen an audience at the furious fustian and turgid rants in Nat. Lee's "Alexander the Great!" For though I can allow this play a few great beauties, yet it is not without its extravagant blemishes. Every play of the same author has more or less of them.—CIBBER, COLLEY, 1739, *An Apology for His Life, p.* 66.

He seems to have been born to write for the Ladies; none ever felt the passion of love more intimately, none ever knew to describe it more gracefully, and no poet ever moved the breasts of his audience with stronger palpitations, than Lee.—CIBBER, THEOPHILUS, 1753, *Lives of the Poets, vol.* II, *p.* 227.

Lee's "Theodosius, or the Force of Love," is the best of his pieces, and, in some of the scenes, does not want tenderness and warmth, though romantic in the plan, and extravagant in the sentiments. —BLAIR, HUGH, 1783, *Lectures on Rhetoric and Belles-Lettres, ed. Mills, p.* 531.

Many of the Bedlam witticisms of this unfortunate man have been recorded by those who can derive mirth from the most humiliating shape of human calamity. His rant and turgidity as a writer are proverbial; but those who have witnessed justice done to the acting of his "Theodosius" must have felt that he had some powers in the pathetic.—CAMPBELL, THOMAS, 1819, *Specimens of the British Poets.*

Of Lee nothing need be said, but that he is, in spite of his proverbial extravagance, a man of poetical mind and some dramatic skill. But he has violated historic truth in "Theodosius," without gaining much by invention.—HALLAM, HENRY, 1837–39, *Introduction to the Literature of Europe, pt.* iv, *ch.* vi, *par.* 46.

The tragedies of Lee discover noble if not rare gifts; his choice of subjects exhibits a soaring delight in magnificent and imposing historic themes, and is in general felicitous as well as ambitious. In execution he displays an impetuosity in which it is easy to discover the traces of incipient insanity; Dryden, who cooperated with him, speaks of him as one "who had a great genius for tragedy," but who, following the fury of his natural temper, made every man, and woman too, in his plays stark raging mad; there was not a sober person to be had for love or money." But, as one of his critics has observed, there is "method in his madness" and his "frenzy is the frenzy of a poet." In bombast he may almost be said to be without an equal—but a real passion

often burns beneath the heap of words superimposed upon it. . . . Nor is it possible to part from this author without pointing out that, as typically characteristic of him, the constant extravagance of his diction is even less noticeable than is the uniform extravagance of his imagination; it might be said of his personages that they are mad even before they go mad (as they often do); and none of our later tragic poets has dealt so persistently on images of lust and wantonness. Lee had in him some genuine fire of passion, but it burnt with an impure flame.— WARD, ADOLPHUS WILLIAM, 1875–99, *A History of English Dramatic Literature, vol.* III, *pp.* 408, 412.

In spite of his undoubted ability and his increasing experience, he did not contrive to write one really good play, except, perhaps, "Lucius Junius Brutus." . . . Lee came very near being a master of sounding blank verse. He was solitary among the dramatists of the age in taking Milton for his model, and even when he is most turgid and most unnatural, there is often a Miltonic swell in his verse which preserves it from complete absurdity. He has often been compared to the early Elizabethans, and he may be called a vulgar Marlowe. His heroic language is often spoiled in its most gorgeous passages by an incidental meanness of expression, as in the famous line where Brutus says to his son—
"I'll *tug* with Teraminta for thy heart."
Lee marks a certain crisis in tragedy. He shrieked so loud that succeeding playwrights gave up the idea of out-screaming so bombastic a writer, and the tendency of tragedy in future was to become sentimental and reflective.—GOSSE, EDMUND, 1888, *A History of Eighteenth Century Literature, p.* 58.

Throughout his tragedies Lee borrows phrases and turns of thought from Shakespeare. But it is in their barbaric extravagances rather than their rich vein of poetry that Lee resembles Shakespeare's contemporaries, and hardly any Elizabethan was quite so bombastic in expression and incident as Lee proved himself in his "Cæsar Borgia."—LEE, SIDNEY, 1892, *Dictionary of National Biography, vol.* XXXII, *p.* 367.

The only tragic dramatist of the age, after Dryden and Otway, who had any pretension to rank as a poet, was Nathaniel Lee, and his claims are not very high. Notwithstanding his absurd rants, however, there are fire and passion in his verse which lift him out of the class of mere playwrights. . . . He is mainly glare and gewgaw, and seldom succeeds but in those scenes of passion and frenzy where extravagant declamation seems a natural language. There is little to remark on his dramatic economy, which is that of the French classical drama. His characters are boldly outlined and strongly coloured, but transferred direct from history to the stage, or wholly conventional. His merit is to have been really a poet.—GARNETT, RICHARD, 1895, *The Age of Dryden, pp.* 109, 112.

Thomas Shadwell

1642?–1692

Born, at Broomhill House, Norfolk, 1640. At school at Bury St. Edmunds, 1645–46. Matric., Caius Coll., Cambridge, as Pensioner, 17 Dec. 1656; took no degree. Studied Law at Middle Temple. First play, "The Sullen Lovers," produced at Lincoln's Inn Fields, 5 May 1668. Devoted himself mainly to drama, 1668–82. Poet-Laureate and Historiographer Royal, 1688. Died suddenly, in London, 19 Nov. 1692. *Works:* "The Sullen Lovers," 1668; "The Royal Shepherdess," 1669; "The Humourists," 1671; "The Miser," 1672; "Epsom Wells," 1673; "Notes and Observations on the Empress of Morocco" (anon.; with Dryden and John Crown), 1674; "Psyche," 1675; "The Libertine," 1676; "The Virtuoso," 1676; "The History of Timon of Athens," 1678; "A True Widow," 1679; "The Woman-Captain," 1680; "The Medal of John Bayes" (anon.), 1682; "Satyr to his Muse" (anon.; attrib. to Shadwell), 1682; "The Lancashire Witches, and Teague O'Divelly," 1682; "A Lenten Prologue" [1683?]; "The Squire of Alsatia," 1688; "Bury Fair," 1689; "A Congratulatory Poem on his Highness the Prince of Orange" (under initials: T. S.), 1689; "A Congratulatory Poem to . . . Queen Mary," 1689; "The Amorous Bigotte," 1690; "Ode on the Anniversary of the King's Birth," 1690; "Ode to the King on his Return from Ireland," [1690]; "The Scowrers," 1691; "Votum Perenne," 1692. *Posthumous:* "The Volunteers," 1693. He *translated:* Juvenal's Tenth Satire, 1687. *Collected Works:* "Dramatic Works" (4 vols.), 1720.—SHARP, R. FARQUHARSON, 1897, *A Dictionary of English Authors, p.* 252.

PERSONAL

That our author was a man of great honesty and integrity, an inviolable fidelity and strictness in his word, an unalterable friendship wherever he professed it, and however the world may be mistaken in him, he had a much deeper sense of religion than many who pretended more to it. His natural and acquired abilities made him very amiable to all who knew and conversed with him, a very few being equal in the becoming qualities, which adorn, and set off a complete gentleman; his very enemies, if he have now any left, will give him this character, at least if they knew him so thoroughly as I did.—His death seized him suddenly, but he could not be unprepared, since to my certain knowledge he never took a dose of opium, but he solemnly recommended himself to God by prayer.—BRADY, NICHOLAS, 1692, *Funeral Sermon.*

Notwithstanding that Lord Rochester has said,

None seem to touch upon true comedy,

But hasty Shadwell and slow Wycherley;

yet that Lord had a better opinion of his conversation than his writings, when he said, that if Shadwell had burned all he wrote, and printed all he spoke, he would have shewn more wit and humour than any other poet. But the wit of his conversation was often very immoral, obscene, and profane. By which course having meanness of spirit and servility to render himself ridiculous and contemptible to men of fortune, title, and wit, he got their favour and assistance, under the pretence of being a useful instrument of the Revolution. Lord Lansdowne has a short discourse on these two lines above, against the remark of Wycherley's being a slow writer.—OLDYS, WILLIAM C., 1761, *MS., Note to Langbaine's Account of the English Dramatick Poets.*

GENERAL

Is counted the best comoedian we have now.—AUBREY, JOHN, 1669-96, *Brief Lives, ed. Clark, vol.* II, *p.* 226.

Of all our modern wits, none seem to me
Once to have touched upon true comedy,
But hasty Shadwell, and slow Wycherly.
Shadwell's unfinished works do yet impart
Great proofs of force of nature, none of art.
With just, bold strokes he dashes here and there,
Showing great mastery with little care,
Scorning to varnish his good touches o'er,
To make fools and women praise them more.
—ROCHESTER, JOHN WILMOT, EARL 1680?
A Session of Poets.

> Shadwell alone my perfect image bears,
> Mature in dulness from his tender years;
> Shadwell alone of all my sons is he
> Who stands confirmed in full stupidity.
> The rest to some faint meaning make pretence,
> But Shadwell never deviates into sense.
> Some beams of wit on other souls may fall,
> Strike through and make a lucid interval;
> But Shadwell's genuine night admits no ray,
> His rising fogs prevail upon the day.

—DRYDEN, JOHN, 1682, *Mac Flecknoe,* v. 15-24.

I am willing to say the less of Mr. *Shadwell,* because I have publickly profess'd a Friendship for him: and tho' it be not of so long date, as some former Intimacy with others; so neither is it blemished with some unhandsome Dealings, I have met with from Persons, where I least expected it. I shall therefore speak of him with the Impartiality that becomes a Critick; and own I like *His* Comedies better than Mr. *Dryden's;* as having more Variety of Characters, and those drawn from the Life; I mean Men's Converse and Manners, and not from other Mens Ideas, copied out of their publick Writings: tho' indeed I cannot wholly acquit our *Present Laureat* from borrowing; his Plagiaries being in some places too bold and open to be disguised, of which I shall take Notice, as I go along; tho' with this Remark, That several of them are observed to my Hand, and in a great measure excused by himself, in the publick Acknowledgment he makes in his several Prefaces, to the Persons to whom he was obliged for what he borrowed.—LANGBAINE, GERARD, 1691, *An Account of the English Dramatick Poets, p.* 443.

Shadwell, the great support o' the comic stage,
Born to expose the follies of the age.
To whip prevailing vices, and unite
Mirth with Instruction, Profit with Delight.
For large ideas and a flowing pen,
First of our times, and second but to Ben.
Shadwell, who all his lines from Nature drew,
Copied her out, and kept her still in view.
Who ne'er was bribed by title or estate,
To fawn and flatter with the rich and great.
To let a gilded vice or folly pass,
But always lashed the villain and the ass.
—ANON, 1693, *The Volunteers; or, The Stock-Jobbers, Epilogue.*

Shadwell's "Squire of Alsatia" took exceedingly at first, as an occasional play: it discovered the cant terms that were before not generally known, except to the cheats themselves; and was a good deal instrumental in causing that nest of villains to be regulated by public authority. The story it was built on was a true fact.—DENNIS, JOHN, 1728-30, *Spence's Anecdotes, ed. Singer, p.* 33.

The "Virtuoso" of Shadwell does not maintain his character with equal strength to the end: and this was that writer's general fault. Wycherly used to say of him: "That he knew how to start a fool very well; but that he was never able to run him down."—POPE, ALEXANDER, 1728-30, *Spence's Anecdotes, ed. Singer, p.* 10.

An acute observer of nature.—SCOTT, SIR WALTER, 1805-21, *The Life of John Dryden.*

His "Libertine" (taken from the celebrated Spanish story) is full of spirit; but it is the spirit of licentiousness and impiety.—HAZLITT, WILLIAM, 1818, *Lectures on the English Comic Writers, Lecture* iii.

Nahum Tate, of all my predecessors, must have ranked the lowest of the laureates, if he had not succeeded Shadwell.
—SOUTHEY, ROBERT, 1835, *Life of Cowper.*

Shadwell's plays abound in songs, but the bulk of them are too slovenly, frivolous, or licentious, to deserve preservation in a separate form. His comedies, admirable as pictures of contemporary meanness, supplied an appropriate setting for his coarse and reckless verses; but such pieces will not bear to be exhibited apart from the scenes for which they were designed.—BELL, ROBERT, 1867, *ed., Songs from the Dramatists, p.* 248.

Posterity is not obliged to imitate Shadwell's disappointed adversaries in grudging him the recognition earned by his consistent and useful support of a cause which commended itself to many fine minds and clear intelligences, although its popularity in the world of letters and on the stage was naturally enough of tardy growth. No very close scrutiny need even be applied to the substance of his boast, that he should not be afraid of these adversaries—

"till they have shown you more Variety
Of natural, unstol'n Comedy than he."

As a matter of fact, he so well fitted to himself much that he had taken over from previous writers as to be fairly entitled to claim it as part of his own equipment; and in the invention of comic characters he was often original. With Ben Jonson, whom he manifestly thought that he followed at no immeasurable distance, he had in common something of the old dramatist's industry; something of his humour; and more of his healthiness of spirit. If Shadwell is often gross and indecent, it has been observed, I think truly, that he is not profane; and if he altogether lacks elevation of spirit, he is by no means deficient in moral purpose. As a comedian of manners he is obviously often truthful as well as vivid; but his grain is coarse, and brutal though the manners and sentiments of his age most assuredly were in many respects, they can hardly have been so uniformly brutal as he represents them. He did little or nothing to advance his art; but his vigour of comic invention, his hatred of political shams and social abuses, and his healthy antagonism to much that really endangered the national future, contributed to arrest the decay which was overtaking English comedy by reason of its lack both of intellectual breadth and of moral fibre. But the artistic pleasure is scant that is to be derived from the comic pictures in which he faithfully reproduces many of the unattractive features of his age.—WARD, ADOLPHUS WILLIAM, 1875–99, *A History of English Dramatic Literature, vol.* III, *p.* 460.

He is known to us chiefly from Dryden's ludicrous caricature, but under that burly and unwieldy exterior—that "tun of man" —there lurked a rich vein of comic humour, keen power of observation, and much real dramatic power both in vivid portraiture and in the presentation of incident.—COLLINS, JOHN CHURTON, 1878–95. *Dryden, Quarterly Review; Essays and Studies, p.* 46.

Notwithstanding the peculiarities of Shadwell's outspoken muse, there are many scenes in his comedies of great humour and originality; in "The Virtuoso," for instance, the scene in the laboratory, where Sir Nicholas Gimcrack, the Virtuoso, is learning to swim upon a table, by imitating the movements of a frog in a bowl of water, has some exceedingly comical situations and dialogue, quite equal to the celebrated Undertaker's Scene in Steele's "Funeral."—HAMILTON, WALTER, 1879, *The Poets Laureate of England, p.* 121.

Shadwell would have passed without much notice among the second-rate writers of his time, if he had not drawn down upon himself the anger of Dryden. As it is, he lives for all time as a black and ridiculous object seen in relief against the blaze of Dryden's wit. . . . Dull was hardly the true epithet for Shadwell; but he was certainly heavy. He laboured at composition, and procured "The Virtuoso," it is said, after a prolonged agony of five years. Shadwell's ambition to be ever representing "some natural humour not represented before," his coarseness, his total want of distinction and elevation, have justly deprived him of a high place in literature. But, in spite of Dryden, he was no fool; his comedy of "Epsom Wells" (1676), to name no other, may still be read with pleasure and amusement; and his works are particularly full of matter attractive to antiquaries.—GOSSE, EDMUND, 1888, *A History of Eighteenth Century Literature, pp.* 48, 49.

Shadwell's odes to William were poor enough. Had they been better it is doubtful if William would have known it. —WEST, KENYON, 1895, *The Laureates of England, p.* 54.

Shadwell's plays, though poorly written, might still be read for their humour, were it not for their obscenity; his chief merit, however, is to bring the society of his time nearer to us than any other writer. No other records such minute points of manners, or enables us to view the actual daily life of the age with so much clearness.—GARNETT, RICHARD, 1895, *The Age of Dryden, p.* 117.

Shadwell depended, like Jonson—whom

he vainly tried to imitate—for the amusement of his hearers on the "humours" of his characters; he had little wit, though it is not fair to bracket him, as Dryden did, with Settle. His comedies are useful for the vivid account they give of the life of his time. Although no poet, he was, as Scott says, an acute observer of nature, and he showed considerable skill in invention. He seems to have been naturally coarse, and was grossly indecent without designing to corrupt.—AITKEN, G. A., 1897, *Dictionary of National Biography, vol.* LI, *p.* 342.

Elias Ashmole

1617–1692

The founder of the Ashmolean Museum at Oxford, a celebrated philosopher, antiquary, and chemist, was born at Lichfield, in Staffordshire. In 1641 he became attorney of the Common Pleas. In 1644 he entered himself of Brasenose College, Oxford, where he zealously devoted himself to the study of Mathematics, Natural Philosophy, and Astronomy. Upon his return to London, he became an associate of Moore, Lilly, Booker, and other astrologers and Rosicrucianists, the effects of which studies were seen by his publication, in 1650, of Dr. Arthur Dee's Fasciculus Chemicus; together with another tract of the same character, by an unknown author. In 1652 appeared his "Theatrum Chemicum Britannicum," a collection of the works of such English Chemists as had remained in manuscript. In a letter to Mr. (afterwards Sir William Dugdale, whom he accompanied in his Survey of the Fens, he gives an account of the Roman Road called *Bennevanna*, in Antoninus's Itinerary. In 1655 or 1658 he began to collect materials for his "History of the Institutions, Laws, and Ceremonies of the most Noble Order of the Garter," which he published in 1672: upon presenting a copy to King Charles II., he granted him a privy seal for £400. In 1679 he lost, by a fire, a collection of 9,000 coins, a fine library, and many curiosities. In 1682, the University of Oxford having prepared a building for their reception, he sent thither his collection of coins, medals, &c.; and at his death the Ashmolean Museum was still further enriched by the bequest of the books and MSS. of the learned founder. His "History of Berkshire" was published after his death (in 1715) in 3 vols. folio, and is not thought to do the author justice.—ALLIBONE, S. AUSTIN, 1854–58, *Dictionary of English Literature, vol.* I, *p.* 74.

GENERAL

Memorandum—the lives of John Dee, Dr. (Richard) Nepier, Sir William Dugdale, William Lilly, Elias Ashmole, esq., —Mr. Ashmole haz and will doe those himselfe: as he told me formerly but nowe he seemes to faile.—AUBREY, JOHN, 1669–96, *Brief Lives, ed. Clark, vol.* I, *p.* 33.

He was the greatest virtuoso and curioso that ever was known or read of in England before his time. *Uxor Solis* took up its habitation in his breast, and in his bosom the great God did abundantly store up the treasures of all sorts of wisdom and knowledge. Much of his time, when he was in the prime of his years, was spent in chymistry; in which faculty being accounted famous, did worthily deserve the title of Mercuriophilus Anglicus. — WOOD, ANTHONY, 1691–1721, *Athenæ Oxonienses, vol.* II, *f.* 889.

In our return, passing by the house where Mr. Ashmole once lived, we visited the widow, who showed us the remains of Mr. Tradescant's rarities, amongst which some valuable shells and Indian curiosities.—THORESBY, RALPH, 1712, *Diary, June* 1.

Elias Ashmole, whom Mr. Wood styles "the greatest virtuoso and curioso that was ever known or read of in England," had a happy facility in learning every art or science to which he applied himself. He studied astrology, botany, chemistry, heraldry, and antiquities; in all which he was a great proficient.—GRANGER, JAMES, 1769–1824, *Biographical History of England, vol.* IV, *p.* 55.

The Ashmolean Museum, though really formed by Tradescant, has indeed secured its donar a celebrity which he could not have obtained by his writings. Ashmole was nevertheless no ordinary man. His industry was most exemplary, he was disinterestedly attached to the pursuit of knowledge, and his antiquarian researches,

RICHARD BAXTER

JOHN ROBERT TILLOTSON

at all events, were guided by great good sense. His addiction to astrology was no mark of weakness of judgment in that age; he can hardly have been more attached to it than Dryden or Shaftesbury, but he had more leisure and perseverance for its pursuit. Alchemy he seems to have quietly dropped. He appears in his diary as a man by no means unfeeling or ungenerous, constant and affectionate in his friendships, and placable toward his adversaries. He had evidently, however, a very keen eye to his own interests, and acquisitiveness was his master passion. His munificence, nevertheless, speaks for itself, and was frequently exercised on unlooked-for occasions, as when he erected monuments to his astrological friends, Lilly and Booker. He was also a benefactor to his native city.—GARNETT, RICHARD, 1885, *Dictionary of National Biography, vol.* II, *p.* 174.

John Robert Tillotson

1630–1694

Archbishop of Canterbury, born at Sowerby, Yorkshire, was elected a fellow of Clare Hall, Cambridge, in 1651. Ranged among the Presbyterians at the Savoy Conference (1661), he submitted to the Act of Uniformity (1662), and in 1663 became rector of Keddington, S. W. Suffolk, in 1664 preacher at Lincoln's Inn, where his mild, evangelical, but *un*doctrinal morality was at first little relished. That same year he married a niece of Oliver Cromwell. In 1670 he became a prebendary, in 1672 dean, of Canterbury. Along with Burnet he attended Lord Russell on the scaffold (1683). In 1689 he was appointed Clerk of the Closet to King William and Dean of St. Paul's, and in 1691 was raised to the see of Canterbury, vacant by the deposition of the Nonjuror Sancroft. He accepted this elevation with the greatest reluctance, nor could all the insults of the Nonjurors to the end of his life extort either complaint or retaliation. According to Burnet, "he was not only the best preacher of the age, but seemed to have brought preaching to perfection." His "Posthumous Sermons" were edited by his chaplain, Dr. Barker (14 vols. 1694). His complete works appeared in 1707–12, with Life by Dr. Birch, 1752; and an annotated selection of his sermons by Weldon in 1886.—PATRICK AND GROOME, *eds.,* 1897, *Chambers's Biographical Dictionary, p.* 918.

PERSONAL

Tillotson was a man of a clear head, and a sweet temper. He had the brightest thoughts and the most correct style, of all our divines; and was esteemed the best preacher of the age. He was a very prudent man; and had such a management with it, that I never knew any clergyman so universally esteemed and beloved, as he was, for above twenty years. He was eminent for his opposition to popery. He was no friend to persecution, and stood up much against atheism. Nor did any man contribute more to bring the city to love our worship, than he did. But, there was so little superstition, and so much reason and gentleness, in his way of explaining things, that malice was long levelled at him, and, in conclusion, broke out fiercely on him.—BURNET, GILBERT, 1715–34, *History of My Own Time.*

Tillotson taught by his sermons more ministers to preach well, and more people to live well, than any man since the apostles' days. He was the ornament of the last century, and the glory of his function; in the pulpit, another Chrysostom; and in the episcopal chair, a second Cranmer.—WILFORD, JOHN, 1741, *Memorials and Characters.*

As a preacher, I suppose his established fame is chiefly owing to his being the first City-divine who talked rationally and wrote purely. I think the sermons published in his life-time are fine moral discourses. They bear indeed the character of their author, simple, elegant, candid, clear, and rational. No orator in the Greek and Roman sense of the word, like Taylor: nor a discourser in their sense, like Barrow; free from their irregularities, but not able to reach their heights. On which account I prefer them infinitely to him. You cannot sleep with Taylor; you cannot forbear thinking with Barrow. But you may be much at your ease in the midst of a long lecture from Tillotson; clear, and rational, and equable as he is.—WARBURTON, WILLIAM, 1752, *Letters from a Late Eminent Prelate, Dec.* 15, *p.* 127.

He was buried in the church of St. Lawrence Jewry, near Guildhall. It was there that he had won his immense oratorical reputation. He had preached there during the thirty years which preceded his elevation to the throne of Canterbury. . . . His remains were carried now through a mourning population. The hearse was followed by an endless train of splendid equipages from Lambeth through Southwark and over London Bridge. Burnet preached the funeral sermon. His kind and honest heart was overcome by so many tender recollections that, in the midst of his discourse, he paused and burst into tears, while a loud moan of sorrow rose from the whole auditory. The Queen could not speak of her favourite instructor without weeping. Even William was visibly moved. "I have lost," he said, "the best friend that I ever had, and the best man I ever knew." . . . Such was his fame among his contemporaries that those sermons [left in MS.] were purchased by the booksellers for the almost incredible sum of two thousand five hundred guineas, equivalent, in the wretched state in which the silver coin then was, to at least three thousand six hundred pounds. Such a price had never before been given in England for any copyright.—MACAULAY, THOMAS BABINGTON, 1855, *History of England, vol.* IV, *ch.* XX.

A pattern of all the domestic and social virtues; the most admired preacher of his day; liberal, just, active, humble, cheerful; he was yet scarce fitted for the high requirements of the Metropolitan See; neither as a theologian nor as a bishop did he catch the true tone of the English Church.—PERRY, GEORGE G., 1864, *The History of the Church of England, vol.* III, *p.* 84.

The last days of Tillotson were altogether embittered by the stream of calumny, invective, and lampoons of which he was the object. One favourite falsehood, repeated in spite of the clearest disproof, was that he had never been baptised. He was charged, without a shadow of foundation, with infamous conduct during his collegiate life. He was accused of Hobbism. He was accused, like Burnet and Patrick, of being a Socinian, though the plainest passages were cited from his writings, as well as from those of his colleagues, asserting the divinity of Christ. One writer, who was eulogised by Hickes as a person "of great candour and judgment," described the Archbishop as "an atheist as much as a man could be, though the gravest certainly that ever was." Nor was this a mere transient ebullition of scurrility.—LECKY, WILLIAM EDWARD HARTPOLE, 1877, *History of England in the Eighteenth Century, vol.* I, *ch.* i.

A liberal and fair-minded man and a polished though cold preacher.—TOUT, T. F., 1890, *History of England, pt.* iii, *p.* 4.

With the possible exception of Archbishop Herring, he was the most amiable man that ever filled the see of Canterbury, and was pronounced by the discerning and experienced William III. the best friend he had ever had and the best man he had ever known. To the meekness of the pastor Tillotson added the qualities of the statesman, and happy was it for the Church of England that such a man could be found to fill the primacy at such a time. As a master of oratory he is greatly inferior in eloquence to both Barrow and South, but historically is more important than either, for Addison was influenced by him, and his discourses long gave the tone to the English pulpit, affording the almost universally accepted model throughout the greater part of the eighteenth century.—GARNETT, RICHARD, 1895, *The Age of Dryden, p.* 225.

Testimony is unanimous as to Tillotson's sweetness of disposition, good humour, absolute frankness, tender-heartedness, and generosity. A sensitive man, he bore with an unruffled spirit the calumnious insults heaped upon him by opponents. He spent a fifth of his income in charity. . . . He was perhaps the only primate who took first rank in his day as a preacher, and he thoroughly believed in the religious efficacy of the pulpit; "good preaching and good living," he told Beardmore in 1661, "will gain upon people."—GORDON, ALEXANDER, 1898, *Dictionary of National Biography, vol.* LVI, *p.* 398.

GENERAL

The way to obtain this, [perspicuity] is to read such books as are allowed to be writ with the greatest clearness and propriety, in the language that a man uses. An author excellent in this faculty, as well as several others, is Dr. Tillotson, late Archbishop of Canterbury, in all that

is published of his.—LOCKE, JOHN, 1704?
*Some Thoughts concerning Reading and
Study for a Gentleman.*

Art, eloquence, and perspicuity appear
in the utmost perfection in Tillotson's
sermons; and when I would labour to
compose a sermon, I would prepare my
mind, and consequently my style, with
reading some few of those discourses beforehand.—WOTTON, WILLIAM, 1726-34,
*Some Thoughts Concerning a Proper Method
of Studying Divinity.*

His words are frequently ill chosen,
and almost always ill placed; his periods
are both tedious and unharmonious, as
his metaphors are generally mean, and
often ridiculous.—MELMOTH, WILLIAM,
1742, *Letters on Several Subjects by Sir
Thomas Fitzosborne.*

There is nothing peculiar to the language of Archbishop Tillotson, but his
manner of writing is inimitable; for one
who reads him, wonders why he himself did
not think and speak in that very manner.
—GOLDSMITH, OLIVER, 1759, *The Bee,
Nov. 24.*

I should not advise a preacher at this
day to imitate Tillotson's style: though I
don't know; I should be cautious of objecting to what has been applauded by so
many suffrages.—JOHNSON, SAMUEL, 1778,
Life, by Boswell.

Simplicity is the great beauty of Archbishop Tillotson's manner. Tillotson has
long been admired as an eloquent writer,
and a model for preaching. But his eloquence if we can call it such, has been
often misunderstood. For, if we include
in the idea of eloquence, vehemence and
strength, picturesque description, glowing
figures, or correct arrangement of sentences, in all these parts of oratory the
Archbishop is exceedingly deficient. His
style is always pure, indeed, and perspicuous, but careless and remiss; too often
feeble and languid; little beauty in the
construction of his sentences, which are
frequently suffered to drag unharmoni-
ously; seldom any attempt towards
strength or sublimity. But, notwithstanding these defects, such a constant vein of
good sense and piety runs through his
works, such an earnest and serious manner, and so much useful instruction conveyed in a style so pure, natural, and unaffected, as will justly recommend him
to high regard, as long as the English

language remains; not, indeed, as a model
of the highest eloquence, but as a simple and
amiable writer, whose manner is strongly
expressive of great goodness and worth.
—BLAIR, HUGH, 1783, *Lectures on Rhetoric and Belles-Letters, ed. Mills, p.* 208.

Archbishop Tillotson is certainly a
writer of some merit. There are few authors who convey more sound sense in
more perspicuous expression. It is no
mean art of composition, where every
sentence comes to us with the force of a
proverb, and presents us with "what oft
was thought," but never before set down
in so manly a style. Tillotson however
appears to have fallen into disrepute.—
GODWIN, WILLIAM, 1797, *Of English Style,
The Enquirer, p.* 422.

Tillotson's method is clear; his notions
of religion are much in the Arminian
strain; his style is defective both in harmony of numbers and energy of manner.
—WILLIAMS, EDWARD, 1800, *The Christian
Student.*

The Archbishop has long been one of
my most favourite divines; and a complete set of his sermons really *"sets me
up."*—WHITE, HENRY KIRKE, 1804, *Letter,
Oct.* 4; *Remains, ed. Southey, vol.* I, *p.* 137.

Without soaring to the height of eloquence, Tillotson refined the language of
the pulpit.—CHATEAUBRIAND, FRANÇOIS
RENÉ, VICOMTE DE, 1837, *Sketches of English Literature, vol.* II, *p.* 195.

The sermons of Tillotson were for half
a century more read than any in our language. They are now bought almost as
waste paper, and hardly read at all.
Such is the fickleness of religious taste,
as abundantly numerous instances would
prove. Tillotson is reckoned verbose and
languid. He has not the former defect
in nearly so great a degree as some of his
eminent predecessors; but there is certainly little vigor or vivacity in his style.
Full of the Romish controversy, he is perpetually recurring to that "world's debate;" and he is not much less hostile to
all the Calvinistic tenets. What is most
remarkable in the theology of Tillotson,
is his strong assertion, in almost all his
sermons, of the principles of natural religion and morality, not only as the basis of
all revelation, without a dependence on
which it cannot be believed, but as nearly
coincident with Christianity in their extent; a length to which few at present

would be ready to follow him. Tillotson is always of a tolerant and catholic spirit, enforcing right actions rather than orthodox opinions, and obnoxious, for that and other reasons, to all the bigots of his own age.—HALLAM, HENRY, 1837–39, *Introduction to the Literature of Europe, pt.* iv, *ch.* ii, *par.* 57.

His style is not brilliant; but it is pure, transparently clear, and equally free from the levity and from the stiffness which disfigure the sermons of some eminent divines of the seventeenth century. He is always serious: yet there is about his manner a certain graceful ease which marks him as a man who knows the world, who has lived in populous cities and in splendid courts, and who has conversed, not only with books, but with lawyers and merchants, wits and beauties, statesmen and princes. The greatest charm of his compositions, however, is derived from the benignity and candour which appear in every line, and which shone forth not less conspicuously in his life than in his writings.—MACAULAY, THOMAS BABINGTON, 1843, *Critical and Historical Essays.*

Archbishop Tillotson has pronounced an authoritative opinion in favour of Natural Religion as essential to the proof of Revealed. His admirable sermons abound in such statements,—thus, in the 41st. . . . The sermon on Steadfastness in Religion, one of the Archbishop's great masterpieces, and in which he demonstrates as against Rome the right of private judgment, tallies with the 41st in the doctrine on Natural Religion.—BROUGHAM, HENRY LORD, 1856, *Discourse on Natural Theology.*

It is the general withholding of the all-enlivening and vivifying doctrines of the gospel, and frequent statements which tend another way, (statements to which the excesses of former times seem to have given rise), that form our grand objections to the divinity of Tillotson.—BICKERSTETH, EDWARD, 1844, *The Christian Student.*

Tillotson's "Sermons," still familiarly known by reputation, long continued to be the most generally esteemed collection of such compositions in the language; but are probably now very little read. They are substantial performances, such as make the reader feel, when he has got through one of them, that he has accomplished something of a feat; and, being withal as free from pedantry and every other kind of eccentricity or extravagance as from flimsiness, and exceedingly sober in their strain of doctrine, with a certain blunt cordiality in the expression and manner, they were in all respects very happily addressed to the ordinary peculiarities of the national mind and character. But, having once fallen into neglect, Tillotson's writings have no qualities that will ever revive attention to them. — CRAIK, GEORGE L., 1861, *A Compendious History of English Literature, vol.* II, *p.* 195.

Here is Tillotson first, the most authoritative of all, a kind of Father of the Church, so much admired that Dryden tells us that he learned from him the art of writing well, and that his sermons, the only property which he left his widow, were bought by a publisher for two thousand five hundred pounds. This work has, in fact, some weight; there are three folio volumes, each of seven hundred pages. To open them, you must be a critic by profession, or absolutely desire to get saved. . . . What a style! and it is the same throughout. There is nothing lifelike; it is a skeleton, with all its joints coarsely displayed. All the ideas are ticketed and numbered. The schoolmen were not worse. Neither rapture nor vehemence; no wit, no imagination, no original and brilliant idea, no philosophy; nothing but quotations of mere scholarship, and enumerations from a handbook. The dull argumentative reason comes with its pigeon-holed classifications upon a great truth of the heart or an impassioned word from the Bible, examines it "positively and negatively," draws thence "a lesson and an encouragement," arranges each part under its heading, patiently, indefatigably, so that sometimes three whole sermons are needed to complete the division and the proof, and each of them contains in its exordium the methodical abstract of all the points treated and the arguments supplied. . . . But he writes like a perfectly honest man; we can see that he is not aiming in any way at the glory of an orator; he wishes to persuade soundly, nothing more. We enjoy this clearness, this naturalness, this justness, this entire loyalty.—TAINE, H. A., 1871, *History of English Literature, tr. Van Laun, vol.* II, *bk.* iii, *ch.* iii.

A good, easy, clear-headed man, with not a little of the character of Paley. The merits of his style are simplicity, and a happy fluency in the choice and combination of words. He probably had no small influence in forming the style of Addison. The defects are considerable. In his easy way he lingers upon a idea, and gives two or three expressions where one would serve the purpose; passing on, he rambles back again, and presents the idea in several other different aspects. The result is an enfeebling tautology and want of method. Taken individually, the expressions are admirably easy and felicitous; but there are too many of them, and they are ill arranged.—MINTO, WILLIAM, 1872–80, *Manual of English Prose Literature,* p. 333.

The debt which Dryden owed to Tillotson, was exaggerated by his own generosity; but his acknowledgment at least shows that the two were akin in their literary taste and judgment.—CRAIK, HENRY, 1894, *English Prose, Introduction, vol.* III, *p.* 4.

Henry Vaughan

1622–1695

Henry Vaughan was born in Llansaintfread, Brecknockshire, Wales in 1621. He was educated at Oxford, where he suffered a short imprisonment for his too zealous loyalty to the royal cause, left without taking a degree, studied medicine in London, and passed the remainder of his life in his native parish. He published four volumes of poetry: a translation of the tenth satire of Juvenal, with original amatory pieces, 1646; "Silex Scintillans," 1650; "Olor Iscanus" (Swan of the Usk), 1651; and "Thalia Rediviva, the Pastimes and Diversions of a Country Muse," 1678;—and two of prose: "The Mount of Olives," 1652; and "Flores Solitudinis," 1678. All of these, except the first, were devotional. From his living in the country of the ancient Silures, Vaughan was called "the Silurist." He died on the 23d of April, 1695. —JOHNSON, ROSSITER, 1875, *Little Classics, Authors, p.* 238.

PERSONAL

There are two Vaughans, twinnes, both very ingeniose and writers. One writt a poeme called "Olor Iscanus" (Henry Vaughan, the first-borne), and another booke of Divine Meditations. His brother wrote severall treatises, whose names I have now forgott, but names himself *"Eugenius Philalethes."* . . . Henry Vaughan, "Silurist:"—you know Silures contayned Breconockshire, Herefordshire, etc.—AUBREY, JOHN, 1669–96, *Brief Lives, ed. Clark, vol.* II, *pp.* 268, 269.

Henry Vaughan, called the *Silurist* from that part of Wales whose inhabitants were in ancient times called Silures, brother twin (but elder) to Eugenius Philalethes, alias Tho. Vaughan . . . was born at Newton S. Briget, lying on the river Isca, commonly called Uske in Brecknockshire, educated in grammar learning in his own country for six years under one Matthew Herbert a noted schoolmaster of his time, made his first entry into Jesus College in Mich. term 1638, aged 17 years: where spending two years or more in logicals under a noted tutor, was taken thence and designed by his father for the obtaining of some knowledge in the municipal laws at London. But soon after the civil war beginning, to the horror of all good men, he was sent for home, followed the pleasant paths of poetry and philology, became noted for his ingenuity, and published several specimens thereof, of which his "Olor Iscanus" was most valued. Afterwards applying his mind to the study of physic, became at length eminent in his own country for the practice thereof, and was esteemed by scholars an ingenious person, but proud and humorous. . . . He died in the latter end of April (about the 29th day) in sixteen hundred ninety and five, and was buried in the parish church of Llansenfreid about two miles distant from Brecknock in Brecknockshire.—WOOD, ANTHONY, 1691–1721, *Athenæ Oxonienses, vol.* II, *ff.* 926, 927.

If ever Poet had a poet's birth-place it was the Silurist. . . . One marvels how William and Mary Howitt missed such a shrine for their "Homes and Haunts." . . . Dates are sorrowfully lacking:

but having either in London or Edinburgh, or in some continental University taken his diploma of Doctor of Medicine—search and research far and wide, in which I have been generously aided, have failed to come on his name anywhere—he began his "practice" in the town of Brecon. . . . Such is the imperfect Story of the outer Life of Henry Vaughan. None can mourn our scanty materials more than ourselves, fuller though they be relatively to our precursor's. Yet we have done our fruitless best to get more.—GROSART, ALEXANDER B., 1871, *ed., Works in Verse and Prose Complete of Henry Vaughan, Silurist; Memorial Introduction, vol.* I, *pp.* xxxiv, xxxv, xxxix, xlvi.

Constrained by promptings of thy ancient race,
　Thy gown and books thou flungst away,
To meet the sturdy Roundhead face to face
　On many a hard-fought day,
Till thy soft soul grew sick, and thou didst turn
　To our old hills; and there, ere long,
Love for thy Amoret, at times, would burn
　In some too fervid song.
But soon thy wilder pulses stayed, and, life
　Grown equable, thy sweet muse mild,
Sobered by tranquil love of child and wife,
　Flowed pure and undefiled.
A humble healer thro' a life obscure,
　Thou didst expend thy homely days;
Sweet Swan of Usk! few know how clear and pure
　Are thy unheeded lays.
One poet shall become a household name
　Into the nation's heart ingrown;
One more than equal miss the meed of fame,
　And live and die unknown.
—MORRIS, SIR LEWIS, 1874, *To An Unknown Poet, Songs of Two Worlds, Second Series, p.* 72.

He was an affectionate husband and father, by all inference and indication. He was twice married, but we only know that there were two sons and three daughters by the first marriage, and one daughter by the second. No names are left; but the youngest daughter married John Turberville, and "her grand-daughter died single in 1780, aged ninety-two." Otherwise the family of Henry Vaughan has been as modest and retiring as himself. . . . On his tomb, as though he were indeed the pioneer of other poets, journeying palmerwise, humbly and prayerfully to lead them and their singing upward through night to light, was cut this motto:

SERVUS INUTILIS,
PECCATOR MAXIMUS,
HIC JACEO.
Gloria! ✠ Miserere!

It might have been set over the bosom of some patient knight, who had fought his last fight with his face toward Jerusalem, and whose *gloria* and *miserere* were the chariot of fire, and the dropping mantle, of a prophetic rapture. He rests sweetly in that land of his own vision

"Where growes the flower of peace,
　The rose that cannot wither,"

and where he now is

"More and more in love with day."

—DUFFIELD, SAMUEL W., 1880, *Henry Vaughan, the Poet of Light; Presbyterian Review, vol.* 1, *pp.* 302, 303.

In his own person, Henry Vaughan left no trace in society. His life seemed to slip by like the running water on which he was forever gazing and moralizing, and his memory met early with the fate which he hardly foresaw. Descended from the royal chiefs of southern Wales whom Tacitus mentions, and whose abode, in the day of Roman domination, was in the district called Siluria, he called himself the Silurist upon his title-pages; and he keeps the distinctive name in the humblest of epitaphs, close by his home in the glorious valley of the Usk and the little Honddu, under the shadow of Tretower, the ruined castle of his race, and of Peny-Fan and his kindred peaks.—GUINEY, LOUISE IMOGEN, 1894, *A Little English Gallery, p.* 55.

GENERAL

Silex Scintillans: | or | Sacred Poems | and | Private Eiaculations | by | Henry Vaughan Silurist. | London: Printed by T. W. for H. Blunden | at yᵉ Castle in Cornehill, 1650.—TITLE PAGE OF FIRST EDITION, 1650.

"The God of the spirits of all flesh" hath granted me a further use of mine than I did look for in the body; and when I expected, and had by His assistance prepared for a "message of death," then did he answer me with life; I hope to His glory and my great advantage, that I may flourish not with leaf only, but with some fruit also; which hope and earnest desire of His poor creature, I humbly beseech Him to perfect and fulfil for His dear Son's sake, unto Whom, with Him and the most holy and loving Spirit, be ascribed by angels, by men, and by all His works, all glory, and wisdom, and dominion, in this the temporal and in the eternal being. Amen.—VAUGHAN, HENRY, 1654, *Silex, Scintillans, Preface.*

He is one of the harshest even of the inferior order of the school of conceit; but he has some few scattered thoughts that meet our eye amidst his harsh pages, like wild flowers on a barren heath.—CAMPBELL, THOMAS, 1819, *Specimens of the British Poets.*

This little volume has long lain hid in undeserved oblivion. Henry Vaughan, the Silurist, as he loved to be called, appears to have been a very accomplished individual, though given, as we learn from Anthony Wood, to be "singular and humoursome." He has not, indeed, scaled the highest heaven of invention, nor even succeeded in bestowing fame and celebrity on his favourite river of Isca; but if a considerable command of forcible language, and an occasional richness of imagery, be sufficient to arrest a poet fast falling into total oblivion, we think we shall be justified in selecting the "*Olor Iscanus*" as the subject of an article. This little production is moreover peculiarly adapted to our purposes. We could not recommend a reprint of the whole, though the poetry only runs to sixty-four small octavo pages, for there are many parts in which the author falls into dulness or obscurity, or where, following the cold and vapid taste of the times, he spends his strength on frigid and bombastic conceits; but, at the same time, Vaughan possessed both feeling and imagination,—flowers which not unfrequently shew themselves above the weeds which the warped judgment of the age encouraged to grow up in too great luxuriance. Added to this, he is a translator of no little skill; and has succeeded in turning many of the metrical pieces of Boëtius, and some of the odes of Casimir, into free and forcible English. It is very much to be lamented, that he did not give more of his attention to this good service.—SOTHERN, H., 1821, *Vaughan's Olor Iscanus, Retrospective Review, vol. 3, p.* 336.

His poems display much originality of thought, and frequently likewise much felicity of expression. The former is,

indeed, at times condensed into obscurity, and the latter defaced with quaintness. But Vaughan never degenerates into a smooth versifier of commonplaces. One, indeed, of his great faults as a poet, is the attempt to crowd too much of matter into his sentences, so that they read roughly and inharmoniously, the words almost elbowing each other out of the lines. His rhymes, too, are frequently defective; and he delights in making the sense of one line run over into the line following. . . . His faults are in a great measure those of the age he lived in, and the matter he imitated, while his beauties are all his own. . . . Among those who can prize poetic thought, even when clad in a dress somewhat quaint and antiquated, who love to commune with a heart overflowing with religious ardour, and who do not value this the less because it has been lighted at the earlier and purer fires of Christianity, and has caught a portion of their youthful glow, poems like those of Henry Vaughan's will not want their readers, nor will such readers be unthankful to have our author and his works introduced to their acquaintance.—LYTE, H. F., 1847, *ed., Poetical Works of Henry Vaughan, Biographical Sketch.*

He is very often dull and obscure, and spends his strength on frigid and bombastic conceits; but occasionally, and especially in his sacred poems, he exhibits considerable originality and picturesque grace, and breathes forth a high strain of morality and piety.—CLEVELAND, CHARLES D., 1848, *A Compendium of English Literature, p.* 339.

We have said little about the deep godliness, the spiritual Christianity, with which every poem is penetrated and quickened. Those who can detect and relish this best, will not be the worst pleased at our saying little about it. Vaughan's religion is deep, lively, personal, tender, kindly, impassioned, temperate; "it sits i' the centre." His religion grows up, effloresces into the ideas and forms of poetry as naturally, as noiselessly, as beautifully as the life of the unseen seed finds its way up into the "bright consummate flower." — BROWN, JOHN, 1849, *Vaughan's Poems, North British Review, vol. 11, p.* 59.

Let every one who is well-acquainted with Wordsworth's grand ode—that on the Intimations of Immortality—turn his mind to a comparison between that and this: he will find the resemblance remarkable. Whether "The Retreat" suggested the form of the "Ode" is not of much consequence, for the "Ode" is the outcome at once and essence of all Wordsworth's theories; and whatever he may have drawn from "The Retreat" is glorified in the "Ode." . . . Vaughan's poem is the more definite of the two, and gives us in its close, poor as that is compared with the rest of it, just what we feel is wanting in Wordsworth's—the hope of return to the bliss of childhood.—MACDONALD, GEORGE, 1868, *England's Antiphon*.

I thought of dear Henry Vaughan.—LOWELL, JAMES RUSSELL, 1869, *On a Certain Condescension in Foreigners*.

I have another reason for presenting "The Retreate," that will appear immediately: but apart from that and inevitable memories of Wordsworth, surely we have there some very remarkable scrutiny and interrogation of subtleties of our deepest spiritual being, such as were not frequent two hundred and fifty years ago or thereby. I ask the Reader to mark the intense yearning and feeling away back to child-time in the poem: the resolute and almost awesome getting back again in maturity, thinkings and feelings and instinct-aspirations long vanished, as of a lost tune returning in a dream. I don't know that anywhere in our elder Literature (out of "Hamlet" with which comparison were simply idle) you can put your finger on finer utterance of what most would have found un-utterable or utterable alone by music.—GROSART, ALEXANDER B., 1871, *ed., Works in Verse and Prose Complete of Henry Vaughan, Silurist; Essay, vol. II, p.* lv.

He is in various respects diverse from Herbert, and in some even superior to him: he has a larger range, and, in point of thought and of perception, a certain subtlety mingled with intensity which brings him into specially close relation to the modern tone in poetry. . . . Of course a volume of Humorous Poetry is not the place where the deservings of Vaughan can be shown forth in any sufficient measure.—ROSSETTI, WILLIAM MICHAEL, 1872–78, *ed., Humorous Poems, p.* 144.

As a sacred poet, Vaughan has an intensity of feeling only inferior to Crashaw.—CHAMBERS, ROBERT, 1876, *Cyclopædia of English Literature, ed. Carruthers*.

It would, indeed, be difficult to find a true and lofty singer who has been so seriously underrated as Vaughan. It is his glory—as it has been his literary shame—that his entire works are purely and consistently devout. He dared, among Cavaliers and as a Cavalier, to borrow the verse of Herrick, in which to praise the God of the Commonwealth. Hence it has needed the long purgation of these centuries, to eliminate passion and prejudice from the sentence which we can now safely pronounce, upon his contemporaries and himself. Old Longinus said, that he called that alone poetry which permanently pleased and was suitable to any age. By this severest of tests Henry Vaughan is at last vindicated and held in honor.—DUFFIELD, SAMUEL W., 1880, *Henry Vaughan the Poet of Light, Presbyterian Review, vol.* 1, *p.* 292.

A physician living in his native Wales and calling himself "The Silurist." He is remembered under that name yet with peculiar regard by lovers of rare old English poetry, and was esteemed "an ingenious person, but proud and humorous."—MASSON, DAVID, 1880, *The Life of John Milton, vol.* VI, *p.* 312.

Vaughan only began to be a poet when Crashaw's career was over; and he did not continue to be a poet to any purpose long. Everything he wrote before or after the two parts of "Silex Scintillans" might be spared. He is a mystic, as Herbert is an ascetic and Crashaw a devotee. Herbert's temptation is the world, Vaughan's temptation is the flesh; the special service that Herbert does him is to lift his mind from profane love to sacred. He is quite pathetic in the preface to "Silex Scintillans" about his early loose love-poetry. He suppressed the worst of it, and adjures his reader to leave the sufficiently harmless collection which escaped him unread. . . . The sanctity and insight of childhood are more to him than even to Wordsworth. . . . In his own translations Henry Vaughan uses Neoplatonists quite as familiarly as Jesuits. His prose is rich and musical; his few Latin poems mostly insignificant, more pointless than Herbert's and quite without the airy grace of Crashaw's Bubble, of which Mr. Grosart has made a very pretty English poem. His translations from Ovid and Juvenal are rough and cumbrous; he writes decasyllabics very badly compared not only with Sandys but with Crashaw, whose description of a Religious House contains one line, "Obedient slumbers that can wake and weep," worthy of Pope. His translations in octosyllabics from Casimir and Boethius are excellent, especially the poem on the Golden Age from Boethius.—SIMCOX, G. A., 1880, *English Poets, ed. Ward, vol.* II, *pp.* 197, 198.

Henry Vaughan's sacred verse, although, like Herbert's, disfigured with the conceits of his time, is yet eminently spiritual, and replete with rare beauty, both of thought and expression.—SAUNDERS, FREDERICK, 1885, *Evenings with the Sacred Poets, p.* 277.

Among the greatest of childhood's poets.—ROBERTSON, ERIC S., 1886, *The Children of the Poets, Introduction, p.* xxxii.

Like Herbert, and in pretty obvious imitation of him, he set himself to bend the prevailing fancy for quips and quaintnesses into sacred uses, to see that the Devil should not have all the best conceits. But he is not so uniformly successful, though he has greater depth and greater originality of thought. — SAINTSBURY, GEORGE, 1887, *History of Elizabethan Literature, p.* 375.

Eternity has been known to spoil a poet for time, but not in this instance. Never did religion and art interchange a more fortunate service, outside Italian studios. Once he had shaken off secular ambitions, Vaughan's voice grew at once freer and more forceful. In him a marked intellectual gain sprang from an apparently slight spiritual readjustment, even as it did, three centuries later, in one greater than he, John Henry Newman. . . . Vaughan has very little quaintness, as we now understand that word, and none of the cloudiness and incorrigible grotesqueness which dominated his Alexandrian day. He has great temperance; he keeps his eye upon the end, and scarcely falls at all into "the fond adulteries of art," inversions, unscholarly compound words, or hard-driven metaphors. If he be difficult to follow, it is only because he lives, as it were, in

highly oxygenated air; he is remote and peculiar, but not eccentric. — GUINEY, LOUISE IMOGEN, 1894, *A Little English Gallery, pp.* 59, 80.

In Vaughan we also find a sense of the lessons Nature has for man, the harmony of the visible world with the invisible,— not only in its details, but in its larger, its cosmic aspects, what he styles "the great chime and symphony of Nature," —such as hardly reappear before we reach Wordsworth. Yet Vaughan, whose special aim that of rendering religious sentiment, restricted his landscape, and whose language is often obscure or fanciful, we must confess cannot compare with the largeness, the exquisite refinement, of the later poet.—PALGRAVE, FRANCIS T., 1896, *Landscape in Poetry, p.* 161.

One must not, however, exaggerate the extent of Herbert's influence. When we have allowed that Vaughan owed to him his religious life, and so the practice of religious poetry, that he followed him in the employment of certain metres and in the treatment of certain topics, that he was content to adopt certain of his tropes and phrases, and to vie with him in the manufacture of curious conceits, we have perhaps stated the case not unfairly. But there was a radical diversity in the nature of the two men that could not but find expression in their poetry. As Mr. Simcox justly phrases it, Herbert was an ascetic, Vaughan a mystic. And it is undoubtedly the mystical element in Vaughan's writing by which he takes rank as a poet. He may occasionally out-Herbert Herbert in metaphors and emblems, but in spite of them, and even through them, it is easy to see that he has a passion for Nature for her own sake; that he has observed her moods; that indeed the world is to him no less than a veil of the Eternal Spirit, whose presence may be felt in any, even the smallest, part. Such a temper, notwithstanding occasional aberration, is poles apart from one which merely ransacks phenomena for quaint similitudes. . . . Indeed, if truth must be told, Vaughan is very much the poet of fine lines and stanzas, of imaginative intervals. . . . If still more truth must be told (*pace* Dr. Grosart), it must be allowed that there are far too large a number of the religious poems entirely unrelieved by any spark; and some for which there is no epithet but *banal.*—BEECHING, H. C., 1896. *Poems of Henry Vaughan, Silurist, ed. Chambers, Introduction, vol.* I, *pp.* xli, xlviii, xlix.

Unequal as a whole, love nature dearly, and leap sometimes into a higher air of poetry than Herbert could attain.—BROOKE, STOPFORD A., 1896, *English Literature, p.* 159.

Vaughan's verse is highly remarkable and original—that of a genius *manqué* but rising to gleams of inspiration. In form he is careless and unequal, but his lyric is meditative, fresh, and highly subjective, the deep and pregnant reflection of a life and experience of much sorrow. In feeling and in phrase he is often strangely modern.—CARPENTER, FREDERIC IVES, 1897, *English Lyric Poetry, 1500–1700, Introduction, p.* lix.

Henry Vaughan was an Anglican mystic. . . . Delicate, meditative, usually a little humdrum, but every now and then flashing out for a line or two into radiant intuitions admirably worded. In both there is much obscurity to be deplored; but while we cultivate Crashaw for the flame below the smoke, we wait in Vaughan for the light within the cloud. —GOSSE, EDMUND, 1897, *Short History of Modern English Literature, p.* 156.

Vaughan knew neither himself nor his fellow-men as Herbert knew them, and the shrewd counsels of the author of "The Temple" often become in the poetry of his disciple mere querulous platitudes. In two respects, however, Vaughan shows the clearer insight. He has a keener eye for the teaching of nature, and a deeper sense of the mystery of childhood. In several of his poems on children may be found the germ of that idea which Wordsworth developed in his "Ode to Immortality," indeed some admirers of Vaughan have claimed for "The Retreat" the actual parentage of the one.—MASTERMAN, J. HOWARD B., 1897, *The Age of Milton, p.* 114.

Vaughan's position among English poets is not only high, but in some respects unique. The pervading atmosphere of mystic rapture, rather than isolated fine things, constitute the main charm of his poems; yet two, "The Retreat" and "They are all gone into the world of light," rank among the finest in the language, and, except the poems on scripture history and church festivals, there is scarcely one without some memorable thought or expression, though frequently kindling, to use his own simile, like "unanticipated sparks from a flinty ground." He not unfrequently lapses into absurdity, misled by the affectation of wit and ingenuity which beset the poetry of his time; but his taste is on the whole better than Herbert's, and much better than Crashaw's. . . . Herbert is devout according to recognised methods, Vaughan is a devout mystic. Herbert visits the spiritual world as a pious pilgrim, but Vaughan is never out of it.—GARNETT, RICHARD, 1899, *Dictionary of National Biography, vol.* LVIII, *p.* 165.

Anthony Wood
1632–1695

Anthony Wood, called Anthony à Wood. Born at Oxford, England, Dec. 17, 1632: died there, Nov. 28, 1695. An English antiquary. He was educated at Oxford. He wrote "Historia et Antiquitates Universitatis Oxoniensis" (written in English and translated into Latin for the University Press in 1674). He was dissatisfied with the translation, and afterward rewrote his English MS., and it was published after his death in two volumes—the first as "The History and Antiquities of the Colleges and Halls of the University of Oxford, with a Continuation to the Present Time by John Gutch," with "Fasti (Annals) Oxoniensis" (1786–90); the second as "The History and Antiquities of the University of Oxford" (1792–1796). He also wrote "Athenæ Oxonienses: an Exact History of all the Writers and Bishops who have had their Education in the University of Oxford from 1500 to 1690," with "Fasti." Two volumes of this were printed (1691–92) before his death; the third he prepared, and it appeared in the second edition 1721; third enlarged edition by Bliss 1813–20. He also wrote "Modus Salium: a Collection of Pieces of Humour" (1751), and "The Ancient and Present State of the City of Oxford" (1773).—SMITH, BENJAMIN E., 1894–97, *The Century Cyclopedia of Names, p.* 1069.

PERSONAL

Mr. Anthony à Wood, M. A., antiquarius, in his lettre to me, Palm Sunday March 23, 1672, writes thus, viz. "My nativity I cannot yet retrive; but by talking with an ancient servant of my father's I find I was borne on the 17 of Decemb., but the year when I am not certain: 'twas possibly about 1647.—Jonh Selden was borne the 16 of December and Sir Symonds Dews the 17. But of these matters I shall tell you more when my trouble is over."— AUBREY, JOHN, 1669–96, *Brief Lives, ed. Clark, vol.* II, *p.* 311.

Immediately sent to a very good man, his confident, to pray with him, appointing his hours; received the Sacrament the next morning very devoutly; made his Will; went into his study with his two friends, Mr. Bisse and Mr. Tanner, to sort that vast multitude of Papers, Notes, Letters:—about two bushels full he ordered for the fire to be lighted as he was expiring, which was accordingly done, he expressing both his knowledge and his approbation of what was done by throwing out his hands.—CHARLETT, DR. A., 1695, *To Archbishop Tenison, Dec.* 1.

Mr. Powell told me, Ant. à Wood used sometimes to call at his house, on purpose to inquire of him about antiquities. Old Ralph Sheldon, of Beoly, esq. (commonly called *Great Sheldon*), was Ant. à Wood's great friend, and Anthony used sometimes to go and lye at his house. When he was there one time, some young ladies there, having a mind to make sport with Anthony, put some antimony and something else into his liquor, which made him so sick, that it was thought he would have died; at which Mr. Sheldon was confounded angry with the ladies, who did it out of a frolick, Anthony being looked upon by them as a quere fellow.—HEARNE, THOMAS, 1722, *Reliquiæ Hearnianæ, ed. Bliss, June* 9, *vol.* II, *p.* 152.

He was known to all Oxford as a large-boned man, of crabbed temper and surly habits, whose recreations, amid his hard antiquarian labours, were ale and tobacco in moderation and music to any extent. No man had more heartily welcomed the Restoration, with the deliverance it brought from those he called "the Presbyterians and Phanatics." — MASSON, DAVID, 1880, *The Life of John Milton, vol.* VI, *p.* 316.

Of the man himself but little outside testimony exists, and what does, certainly tends to present him in the light of an eccentric, censorious, and sour-minded recluse. Indeed, his own nephew speaks of him as "a wonderful pryer," who "wore his hat over his eyes, seemed to take notice of nothing, and to know nothing, and yet he took notice of everything and knew everything;" while Wood himself more than once complains of having been called "a listener at key-holes," and it is regretable to find him "expelled the comon room, and his company avoyded as an observing person, and not fit to be present where matters of moment were discussed." These characteristics agree but ill with the dignity proper to the carriage of the historian of Oxford University; though they are qualities not altogether unserviceable in the case of a diarist.—CLAY, T. L., 1888, *Anthony à Wood, The Gentleman's Magazine, vol.* 265, *p.* 76.

The disagreeable side of Wood's nature now [1670–74] became predominant. The severity of his studies had given him exaggerated ideas of his own importance; his increasing deafness cut him off from social intercourse, and he became ill-natured, foolishly obstinate in his own opinion, and violently jealous of his own dignity. He quarrelled with his own family; he quarrelled with the fellows of Merton. He quarrelled with his good friend Bathurst, with his patron Fell, with every one who sought either to help him or to shun him. It was said of him, not untruly, that he "never spake well of any man." Of John Aubrey, the chief contributor to his fame, whose biographical notes he annexed page by page, his language is ungenerous and most ungrateful. He shut himself up more and more in his study, very busy but very unhappy, the antitype of the alchemists' dragon, killing itself in its prison by its own venom.—CLARK, REV. ANDREW, 1900, *Dictionary of· National Biography, vol.* LXII, *p.* 351.

GENERAL

The truth is, his books are little more than a medley of notes and such informations as were sent in from his several correspondents; without being digested into any other method than the throwing them under that particular author's name to which they chiefly related. It is no blemish on his memory to observe that he had his share of that peevishness and austerity, both in his style and manners, which is commonly incident to antiquaries; and thus much we ought gratefully to acknowledge, that he has furnished us with a larger stock of useful material than perhaps any one man of this age has collected. If he was too sullen among courtiers, he paid sufficiently for all the liberty he took, [he was expelled from Oxford for some strictures on the late Earl of Clarendon;] and it is illegal to object to a crime for which a suitable penance has been already enjoined and performed.—NICOLSON WILLIAM, 1696–1714, *English Historical Library.*

Hard was the fate of honest Anthony Wood, when Dr. Fell undertook to have his history of Oxford translated into Latin; the translator, a sullen dogged fellow, when he observed that Wood was enraged at seeing the perpetual alterations of his copy made to please Dr. Fell, delighted to alter it the more; while the greater executioner supervising the printed sheets, "by correcting, altering, or dashing out what he pleased," compelled the writer publicly to disavow his own work!—DISRAELI, ISAAC, 1791–1824, *Of Suppressors and Dilapidators of Manuscripts, Curiosities of Literature.*

The dulness of Michael de Marolles and Anthony Wood acquires some value from the faithful representation of men and manners.—GIBBON, EDWARD, 1794–96, *Autobiography.*

The indefatigable though tasteless Anthony Wood. . . . That tasteless though useful drudge.—BRYDGES, SIR

SAMUEL EDGERTON, 1800, *Phillips's Theatrum Poetarum Anglicanorum.*

"The Ostade of Literary History." A name given to Anthony Wood, the English antiquary, on account of his ability to surprise our judgment into admiration, his dry humor of honesty, and the breadth of his knowledge.—FREY, ALBERT R., 1888, *Sobriquets and Nicknames, p. 263.*

He collects a world of "surfaces," impressions that well portray himself. He is a newsletter also. Monstrous births, escapes, blazing stars, scandals among the venerable, hangings, suicides, and all manner of deaths: ballads and all processions royal and funereal—all pageantries and dignified masquerades—are meat and drink to him; nor ever fails he narrowly to scrutinise the hatchments on coffins and tombs, and mete sarcasm to false displays of arms. Meanwhile he is daily dredging and ravaging college archives, with fierce tenacity, for fifty years. The mind had therefore no leisure strongly to react on the vast material amassed, and this failure is reflected in his style. . . . His style has no pretensions to form, and presents few notable features. Throughout it is more or less disjointed by scrappy treatment, and marred by the jerkiness of the habitual notetaker, and lengthy passages of continuous prose seldom occur. He is hampered by a painful accuracy which loads the unpremeditated sentence with parentheses. In the "Athenæ" it is most continuous, and on the whole the best, becoming less full of cumbrous gravity as he approaches the writers of his own generation.—TRENCH, F. H., 1894, *English Prose, ed. Craik, vol.* III, *p.* 169.

George Savile

Marquis of Halifax

1633–1695

George Savile, first Marquis and Earl of Halifax, was born 11th November 1633. He was descended from an ancient Yorkshire family, and succeeded to the paternal baronetcy in 1641. In the year of the Restoration he entered Parliament as member for Pontefract. In 1668 he was raised to the peerage as Baron Savile of Eland and Viscount Halifax, and in the following year he began, as a Commissioner of the Board of Trade, an official career of unusual diversity, including a joint ambassadorship at the Hague. In 1675 his name was struck off the Privy Council, during the ascendancy of Danby, but it was restored in 1679, when he became a member of Shaftesbury's administration and was created Earl of Halifax. He remained in office after Shaftesbury's dismissal, and in 1680 was mainly instrumental in bringing about the rejection of the Exclusion Bill by the House of Lords. In 1682 he was created Marquis of Halifax and appointed Lord Privy Seal. He was, however, out of sympathy with the Court and in favour of the recall of Monmouth; and on the accession of James II., after being removed to the Presidency of the Council, he was in December 1685 dismissed from office. He took an active part in the operations which led to the overthrow of James II., and in the Convention Parliament of 1689 acted as Speaker of the House of Lords. He held office under the new *régime* as Lord Privy Seal from March 1689 to February 1690; but after this he withdrew from public life, and spent the remainder of his days chiefly in his country-seat of Rufford in Nottinghamshire, to which he was deeply attached. He died 5th April 1695, and was buried in Westminster Abbey. Halifax's first wife, Lady Dorothy Spencer, was a daughter of the first Earl of Sunderland and his Countess ("Sacharissa").—CRAIK, HENRY, 1894, *ed., English Prose, vol.* III, *p.* 207.

PERSONAL

Jotham of piercing wit and pregnant thought,
Endued by nature and by learning taught
To move assemblies, who but only tried
The worse a while, then chose the better side,
Nor chose alone, but turned the balance too,
So much the weight of one brave man can do.
—DRYDEN, JOHN, 1681, *Absalom and Achitophel,* v. 882–887.

He passed for a bold and determined atheist, though he often protested to me he was not one, and said he believed there was not one in the world.—BURNET, GILBERT, 1715–34, *History of My Own Time.*

A man more remarkable for his wit than his steadiness.—WALPOLE, HORACE, 1758, *A Catalogue of the Royal and Noble Authors of England, Scotland and Ireland.*

Among the statesmen of that age, Halifax was, in genius, the first. His intellect was fertile, subtle, and capacious. His polished, luminous, and animated eloquence, set off by the silver tones of his voice, was the delight of the House of Lords. His conversation overflowed with thought, fancy, and wit. His political tracts well deserve to be studied for their literary merit, and fully entitle him to a place among English classics. To the weight derived from talents so great and various, he united all the influence which belongs to rank and ample possessions. Yet he was less successful in politics than many who enjoyed smaller advantages. Indeed, those intellectual peculiarities which make his writings valuable, frequently impeded him in the contests of active life; for he always saw passing events, not in the point of view in which they commonly appear to one who bears a part in them, but in the point of view in which, after the lapse of many years, they appear to the philosophic historian.—MACAULAY, THOMAS BABINGTON, 1843, *George Savile, Critical and Historical Essays, vol.* VI, *p.* 111.

He was, to use his own word, a Trimmer, nor was he ashamed to profess its creed. Among the statesmen of our country the name of Halifax will always occupy a conspicuous position. He was more a speculative philosopher than a man of action: he lacked decision; he was so anxious to be neutral, that his views were sometimes colourless and sophistical; but it was to his sound judgment, his finely balanced intellect, his exquisite tact, that we owe much of the freedom and the moderation of the constitution under which we have the happiness to live.—EWALD, ALEXANDER, CHARLES, 1878, *Ministers and Maxims, Temple Bar, vol.* 53, *p.* 232.

In private life Lord Halifax appears to have shown himself both amiable and deserving of respect. Fascinating and witty in conversation, during youth conspicuous among the brilliant dissolute society which surrounded the Duke of Buckingham, his personal morality seems to have been unusually high. For wine and cards, the fashionable excesses of the time, he expressed a lively contempt, while from other yet more fashionable vices he seems to have been singularly exempt. It is, of course, improbable that his austerity was quite unremitting; indeed (as Macaulay reminds us), posterity believed him to have left in Henry Carey, the musician, an illegitimate son; which hypothesis, however, appears somewhat dubious. An affectionate husband to a wife whose virtues and accomplishments were distinguished as her beauty; a careful, if not a very sympathetic father, the statesman was by no means deficient in

the graceful "art d'etre grand-pere."
. . . In one respect alone does the
personal disposition of Lord Halifax appear singularly deficient. Exempt from
the foppery, moral, intellectual, and social,
to which the virile understanding of his
grandson, the celebrated Earl of Chesterfield, too often stooped; superior, by
political and family sympathies, to the
purely individualistic tendencies of Chesterfieldian morality—he yet showed something of Chesterfield's serene, unconscious cynicism.—FOXCROFT, H. C., 1899,
*A Character of "The Trimmer," Fortnightly
Review, vol.* 71, *pp.* 812, 813.

GENERAL

His letters are remarkable for the
calmness and solidity of their impartial
arguments.—RANKE, LEOPOLD VON, 1875,
A History of England, vol. IV, *p.* 456.

He was a politician who had a difficult
path to pursue across an ocean of battling
factions, and who employed his literary
skill usually anonymously, to trim the boat
as well as he might. . . . Halifax is as
simple and as vernacular as Temple, and
he has almost as much grace. His "Character of a Trimmer" . . . is a piece of
brilliant writing which can never become
obsolete. . . . A modern reprint of
the political tracts of Halifax would be
welcome, and would do much to give popularity to one who is at present little but
a name to all except professional students
of history.—GOSSE, EDMUND, 1888, *A
History of Eighteenth Century Literature.*

The effect of this remarkable breadth
of view was not with Halifax, as so frequently the case, to paralyze energy, and
render the comprehensive mind unfit for
practical action. He was not retained in
equilibrium by the difficulty of deciding
between two courses, but was an enthusiast for the *via media,* as great a zealot
for compromise as zealots commonly are
for strong measures; and, though sometimes too yielding or too speculative for
the unquiet times in which his lot was
cast, would have made an almost ideal
prime minister for the nineteenth century.
His praise of trimming, which to more
fiery spirits must have seemed an ignoble
policy, rings with the eloquence and passion of the most genuine conviction.—
GARNETT, RICHARD, 895, *The Age of
Dryden, p.* 251.

They are all exceedingly important
documents, showing first that inclination
to the essay—to the short, forcible, not
inelegant, and yet first of all popular,
treatment of manageably limited subjects,
which was such a feature of the time;
and secondly, the progress which was
being made in the elaboration of a style
suitable to such treatment in the special
department of politics. It may be observed, from a comparison of many instances, that irony is an almost inseparable accompaniment and ornament of the
plainer styles. For it not only does not
require, but is positively repugnant to,
flowing and florid periods, involved constructions, and the like, and it gives the
salt and savour of which the plain style is
in especial need. Accordingly there is
irony in Cowley, and plenty of it in Dryden. But Halifax's variety is different
from that of either of his forerunners—
drier, more antithetic with a quiet antithesis, more suggestive of a "word to the
wise." Not that Halifax by any means
scorns a flight now and then—there is in
the "Character of a Trimmer" a passage
on Truth beyond doubt suggested by the
famous text on that subject in the "Areopagitica" (which Halifax was almost or
quite old enough to have read at the time
of its publication), and very well worth
comparing with it. But these things are
not his staple; that is the statement of
the case to the plain man in a plain way,
yet with such a shrewdness and pungency
as may give satisfaction to those whose
wits, though plain, are not absolutely
sluggish. For political purposes such a
style is the most valuable of all, and Halifax, beyond all doubt, showed the way
to the greater but fiercer and less equable
genius of Swift.—SAINTSBURY, GEORGE,
1898, *A Short History of English Literature, p.* 511.

Halifax had none of Swift's brutality
and none of Burke's magniloquence. He
wrote as a highly cultivated man of his
day would talk—with more correctness,
indeed, but with the same absence of formality and the same dignified ease. He
had not Burke's earnestness. If he hated
anything except the Church of Rome, he
hated a bore. Burke, as we know,
emptied the House of Commons, and his
pamphlets are very like his speeches.
Both are now regarded as standards of

classic oratory and storehouses of political wisdom. In his lifetime he had less influence than Halifax, until he hit the temper of the middle class by his diatribes against the French Revolution. Halifax knew exactly what people would read and what they would not. He always amused them, he never wearied them, he did not leave them for a moment in doubt of his meaning. He had the art, essential to a good advocate, of making readers and jurors think that they have arrived at their conclusions for themselves. Burke lectures and scolds even while he is reasoning with consummate force; Halifax smiles and persuades. . . . If Halifax had a fault as a controversialist, it was that he indulged with too much freedom in the priceless and permanent luxury of intellectual contempt, which money cannot purchase and custom cannot stale. . . . The combination of terseness and fulness, of wit and sense, of logic and fancy, are the principal characteristics of Halifax. . . . As a political philosopher, Halifax stands a head and shoulders above all his contemporaries except Locke.—PAUL, HERBERT, 1899, *The Great Tractarian, The Nineteenth Century, vol.* 45, *pp.* 456, 457, 459.

John Aubrey
1626–1697

John Aubrey, antiquary (b. 1626, d.1700), wrote the "Natural History and Antiquities of the County of Surrey" (1719), "Miscellanies upon Various Subjects" (1696), and "A History of Wiltshire," besides contributing "Minutes of Lives" of eminent men to Wood's "Athenæ Oxonienses," and aiding Dugdale in the preparation of his "Monastican Anglicanum." A biography of Aubrey by Britton was published in 1845 by the Wiltshire Topographical Society, and an edition of the "Lives," &c., was issued in 1813.—ADAMS, W. DAVENPORT, 1877, *Dictionary of English Literature.*

PERSONAL

His life is more remarqueable in an astrologicall respect then for any advancement of learning, having from his birth (till of late yeares) been labouring under a crowd of ill diretions: for his escapes of many dangers, in journeys both by land and water, 40 yeares. . . . I gott not strength till I was 11 or 12 yeares old; but had sicknesse of vomiting, for 12 houres every fortnight for . . . years, then about monethly, then quarterly, and at last once in halfe a yeare. About 12 it ceased. . . . He began to enter into pocket memorandum bookes philosophicall and antiquarian remarques, Anno Domini 1654, at Llantrithid. Anno 16—I began my lawe-suite on the entaile in Brecon, which lasted till . . . and it cost me 1200 *li.* Anno—I was to have married Mris K. Ryves, who died when to be married, 2000 li. +, besides counting care of her brother, 1000 *li.* per annum. . . . A strange fate that I have laboured under never in my life to enjoy one entire monethe or 6 weekes *otium* for contemplation. My studies (geometry) were on horse back, and (in) the house of office: (my father discouraged me). My head was alwaies working; never idle, and even travelling (which from 1649 till 1670 was never off my horseback) did gleane som observations, of which I have a collection in folio of 2 quiers of paper + a dust basket, some whereof are to be valued. His chiefe vertue, gratitude. . . . My fancy lay most to geometrie. If ever I had been good for anything, 'twould have been a painter, I could fancy a thing so strongly and had so cleare an idaea of it. —AUBREY, JOHN, 1669–96, *Brief Lives* ed. Clark, vol. I, *pp.* 35, 39, 42, 43.

He had a stronger tincture of superstition than is commonly found in men of his parts and learning. In his "Miscellanies," among which are some things well worth the reader's notice, is a receipt against an evil tongue, which was formerly thought much worse than an evil eye. *Ob. circ.* 1700. A. Wood, whom he esteemed his friend, speaks of him as a pretender to antiquities, and as vain, credulous, and whimsical; he adds, that he was expensive to such a degree, as to be forced to sell his estate of 700 *l.* a year, and afterward to become a dependant on his friends for subsistence. There seems to be a tincture of gall in this censure of the Oxford antiquary.— GRANGER, JAMES, 1769–1824, *Biographical History of England, vol.* V, *p.* 272.

Aubrey was the very type of the man who is no man's enemy but his own. He possessed every virtue usually associated with an easy careless temper, and an industry in his own pursuits which would have done credit to one of robuster mould. "My head," he says, "was always working, never idle, and even travelling did glean some observations, some whereof are to be valued." They assuredly are, and many, especially those on the alteration of manners in his time, exhibit real shrewdness. He was well aware of his failings, and it is impossible not to sympathise with his regret for the abolition of the monasteries which would have afforded him a congenial refuge; and his verdict that "if ever I had been good for anything, 'twould have been a painter." His buoyant cheerfulness defied calamity, and preserved his self-respect under the hard trial of dependence.—GARNETT, RICHARD, 1885, *Dictionary of National Biography,* vol. II, p. 245

Aubrey was one of those eminently good-natured men, who are very slothful in their own affairs, but spare no pains to work for a friend. He offered his help to Wood; and, when it was decided to include in Wood's book short notices of writers connected with Oxford, that help proved most valuable. Aubrey, through his family and family-connexions, and by reason of his restless goings-to-and-fro, had a wide circle of acquaintance among squires and parsons, lawyers and doctors, merchants and politicians, men of letters and persons of quality, both in town and country. He had been, until his estate was squandered, an extensive and curious buyer of books and MSS. And above all, being a good gossip, he had used to the utmost these opportunities of inquiry about men and things which had been afforded him by societies grave, like the Royal Society, and frivolous, as coffee-house gatherings and tavern clubs. The scanty excerpts, given in these volumes from letters written by him between 1668 and 1673, supply a hint of how deeply Wood's "Historia et Antiquitates Universitatis Oxoniensis," published in 1674, was indebted to the multifarious memory and unwearying inquiries of the enthusiastic Aubrey.—CLARK, ANDREW, 1898, *ed., Brief Lives, chiefly of Contemporaries, by Aubrey, Introduction,* vol. I, p. 1.

GENERAL

Aubrey, the little Boswell of his day. —DISRAELI, ISAAC, 1812–13, *Hobbes, Quarrels of Authors.*

Whoever expects a rational account of any fact, however trite, from Aubrey, will meet with disappointment. . . . Aubrey thought little, believed much, and confused everything.—GIFFORD, WILLIAM, 1816, *ed., The Works of Ben Jonson.*

A very interesting old gentleman he is. Everybody has heard more or less about him as a gossiping old soul of the latter part of the seventeenth century, who went about collecting scraps of information and personal anecdote about notable persons of his own day and of the immediately preceding generations, for some of which scraps we are now much indebted to him. He was one of those useful individuals who, having themselves a passion for knowing what kind of noses and mouths, and what kind of eyes and hair eminent men have, and what dresses they wear, and what they like for dinner, and so on, take the trouble to jot down the information they obtain on these points for the satisfaction of posterity. Something of a taste for these minutiæ, as every one knows, is found in most persons who have any liveliness of fancy, and is almost a necessary ingredient in the character of the historian or the general man of letters; but occasionally we find the taste developed to the dimensions of a constitutional mania, leaving room for little else. In this case we have what is called "a gossip," or perhaps a collector of portraits and autographs. Boswell, on the whole, belonged to this type, but by good luck, and his own enthusiasm for one man, his passion for gossip and anecdote became concentrated, and enabled him to be the author of the best biography in the language. Pepys, the Paul Pry of his day, was another example; less effective, because more diffuse. Aubrey, who was contemporary with Pepys, was, we fear, a lower man in the class than even Pepys.—MASSON, DAVID, 1856, *John Aubrey, British Quarterly Review,* vol. 24, p. 153.

He was a "perambulator," and, in the words of one of his critics, "picked up information on the highway, and scattered it everywhere as authentic." . . . The searcher for authentic material must carefully scrutinize Aubrey's *facts ;* but, with much that is doubtful, valuable information may be obtained from his pages. —COPPÉE, HENRY, 1872, *English Literature, p.* 232.

In matters of religious opinion, Aubrey's judgment is of no more value than that of any social gossip-monger would be in our own day.—TULLOCH, JOHN, 1872, *Rational Theology and Christian Philosophy in England in the Seventeenth Century, vol.* I, *p.* 206, *note.*

His character as an antiquary has been unworthily traduced by Anthony à Wood, but fully vindicated by his recent editors and biographers. He certainly is devoid of literary talent, except as a retailer of anecdotes; his head teems with particulars which he lacks the faculty to reduce to order or combine into a whole. As a gossip, however, he is a kind of immature Boswell; and we are infinitely beholden to him for the minute but vivid traits of Bacon, Milton, Raleigh, Hobbes, and other great men preserved in his "Minutes of Lives." His "Natural History of Wilts" is full of quaint lore, and one need not believe in spirits to enjoy his "Miscellanies." Half the charm is in the simple credulity of the narrator.—GARNETT, RICHARD, 1885, *Dictionary of National Biography, vol.* II, *p.* 245.

The Dictionaries fail to tell us that he was about as credulous an old goose as one could hope to find out of Gotham—an inveterate, good-natured gossip, as fond of a cock and bull story, and as certain to adorn it *(nihil tetigit quod non ornavit)* as the very latest editor of Mr. Joseph Miller or Barnum. He was ready to believe the *ipse dixit* of any one mortal man, woman, or child, that fell in his way, on any subject under the sun, from a cure for the toothache to a discourse with the Angel Gabriel. All this, however, one has to find out for oneself, and the task is an easy and amusing one, by simply wandering pleasantly through one of his most characteristic books just now republished, and rightly named ("Miscellanies upon various subjects ")—JOHNS, B. G., 1891, *John Aubrey of Wilts, The Gentleman's Magazine, vol.* 271, *p.* 279.

Aubrey's lives supply an inviting field for comment, correction, and addition. But, even so treated, they will never be a biographical dictionary. Their value lies not in statement of bibliographical or other facts, but in their remarkably vivid personal touches, in what Aubrey had seen himself and what his friends had told him.—CLARK, ANDREW, 1898, *ed., Brief Lives, Chiefly of Contemporaries, by John Aubrey, Introduction, vol.* I, *p.* 7.

Edward Stillingfleet

1635–1699

Divine, born at Cranborne, 17th April 1635, studied at St John's College, Cambridge, in 1653 obtained a fellowship, and in 1657 became rector of Sutton in Bedfordshire. In 1659 appeared his "Irenicum," a catholic (perhaps latitudinarian) attempt to find a basis of union for the divided church. His "Origines Sacræ" (1662), followed by his "Rational Account of the Grounds of the Protestant Religion" (1664), a defence of the Church of England from the charge of schism, led to rich preferment. He became in 1665 rector of St. Andrews, Holborn, chaplain to Charles II., a canon of St. Paul's (1670), dean (1678), and after the Revolution Bishop of Worcester. He died at Westminster, 27th March 1699. Other works were his "Mischiefs of Separation" (1680); "Origines Britannicæ, or Antiquities of the British Churches" (1685); and a defence of the doctrine of the Trinity (1697). See Life prefixed to works (6 vols 1710).—PATRICK AND GROOME, *eds.,* 1897, *Chambers's Biographical Dictionary, p.* 885.

PERSONAL

Thence to the Chappell and heard the famous young Stillingfleete, whom I knew at Cambridge, and is now newly admitted one of the King's chaplains; and was presented, they say, to my Lord Treasurer for St. Andrew's, Holborn, where he is now minister, with these words . that

they (the Bishops of Canterbury, London, and another) believed he is the ablest young man to preach the Gospel of any since the Apostles. He did make the most plain, honest, good, grave sermon, in the most unconcerned and easy yet substantial manner, that ever I heard in my life, upon the words of Samuel to the people, "Fear the Lord in truth with all your heart, and remember the great things that he hath done for you." It being proper to this day, the day of the King's Coronation. — PEPYS, SAMUEL, 1665, *Diary, April* 23.

Narcissus Marsh, archbishop of Armagh, gave 2,500 libs. for bishop Stillingfleet's library, which, like that of Dr. Isaac Vossius, was suffered to go out of the nation, to the eternal scandal and reproach of it. The said archbishop has built a noble repository for them.—HEARNE, THOMAS, 1705, *Reliquiæ Hearnianæ, ed. Bliss, Nov.* 2, *vol.* I, *p.* 49.

Stillingfleet was a man of much more learning [than Tillotson], but of a more reserved and a haughtier temper. . . . He was a great man in many respects. He knew the world well, and was esteemed a very wise man. . . . He applied himself much to the study of the law and records, and the original of our constitution, and was a very extraordinary man. —BURNET, GILBERT, 1715–34, *History of My Own Time.*

If the clergy of England had been polled for the selection of the most distinguished and profound divine of the day, their choice would probably have fallen on Edward Stillingfleet. The learned Dr. Bentley, his friend and chaplain for fourteen years, scarcely exaggerates when he says of the Dean of St. Paul's, "Even envy itself will allow him to be the glory of our Church and nation; who, by his vast and comprehensive genius, is as great in all parts of learning as the greatest next himself are in any."—PERRY, GEORGE G., 1864, *History of the Church of England, vol.* III, *p.* 82.

GENERAL

The best account of the present state of our tithes . . . is lately given by the most learned Bishop Stillingfleet, who never fails of exhausting whatever subject he pretends to treat on.—NICOLSON, WILLIAM, 1696–1714, *English Historical Library.*

He, in his youth, writ an "Irenicum" for healing our divisions, with so much learning and moderation that it was esteemed a masterpiece. . . . The argument was managed with so much learning and skill, that none of either side

ever undertook to answer it.—BURNET, GILBERT, 1715–34, *History of My Own Time.*

Of Locke he [Coleridge] spoke, as usual, with great contempt, that is, in reference to his metaphysical work. He considered him as having led to the destruction of metaphysical science by encouraging the unlearned public to think that with mere common sense they might dispense with disciplined study. He praised Stillingfleet as Locke's opponent. —ROBINSON, HENRY CRABB, 1810, *Diary, Dec.* 23.

If it be true, as it was reported at the time, that the Reverend Prelate died from vexation at the issue of the contest he had engaged in, his memory as a metaphysician has at least been preserved from oblivion by the celebrity of his antagonist, and by his own signal defeat.—KING, LORD, 1829, *The Life of John Locke, vol.* I, *p.* 359

A man deeply versed in ecclesiastical antiquity, of an argumentative mind, excellently fitted for polemical dispute, but perhaps by those habits of his life rendered too much of an advocate to satisfy an impartial reader. In the critical reign of James II., he may be considered as the leader on the Protestant side.—HALLAM, HENRY, 1837–39, *Introduction to the Literature of Europe, pt.* iv, *ch.* ii, *par.* 15.

Stillingfleet, again, is antiquarian, formal, and controversial. His intellect is acute, hard, and ingenious, ready to cope with any subject and any opponent that may cross his path, or may seem to him inimical to the Church. He is alert alike against the Romanist, the Separatist, and the Rationalist—one of a common type of theologians bred by all Churches, who delight to go forth with weapons of war against all assailants of official orthodoxy and official privilege.—TULLOCH, JOHN, 1872, *Rational Theology and Christian Philosophy in England in the Seventeenth Century, vol.* I, *p.* 347.

He fought against Atheists, Unitarians, Papists, and Dissenters, and rendered distinguished service to his cause. His best known engagements were with Dryden and Locke. Against Dryden, though far inferior in style, he had the best of the argument; but in the encounter with Locke he sustained a defeat so signal and humiliating that it was said to have hastened his death. He wrote with great vigour, but his expressions are neither original nor felicitous. To a modern reader his manner seems too arrogant and personal to be persuasive. Although Clarendon professes himself "exceedingly delighted with the softness, gentleness, and civility of his language," this word-praise is not borne out by facts; there is no evidence that he had Tillotson's power of bringing over opponents.—MINTO, WILLIAM, 1872–80, *Manual of English Prose p.* 333.

His works are chiefly argumentative; but his Sermons, published after his death, deservedly bear a high character for good sense, sound morality, energy of style, and the knowledge of human nature which they display.—CHAMBERS, ROBERT, 1876, *Chambers's Cyclopædia of English Literature, ed. Carruthers.*

As he confined himself closely to the particular aspect of each question as it presented itself in his own day, his controversial writings have now little more than an historical interest. They differ in this respect from those of such writers as Waterland and Butler. Waterland's writings against the Arians and Socinians, and Butler's against the Deists, have a real value at the present day; but Stil-lingfleet's against his various adversaries, though nearly as able, have, from the cause above-mentioned, lost much of their value. He is seen at his best in his sermons, his charges, and his "Origines Sacræ." His style is clear and nervous, and he had a lawyer-like mind, which enabled him to marshall his arguments with great force and precision. As a writer of good English he is still well worth reading; and therefore his name cannot be omitted in any notice of English Prose writers.—OVERTON, JOHN HENRY, 1894, *English Prose, ed. Craik, vol. III, p.* 256.

His learning and acuteness amazed his contemporaries. He appeared as the antagonist of Locke, and the defender of Laud, as a philosopher, theologian, and preacher, and in all with distinguished success. His "Origines Sacræ," an assertion of the Divine authority of the Scriptures, and his "Origines Britannicæ," are still referred to; and it must be admitted that he had no inconsiderable knowledge of antiquity, both literary and historical. But his work was not of a nature to permanently affect posterity. He served his age, and served it well.—HUTTON, W. H., 1895, *Social England, ed. Traill, vol. IV, p.* 418.

Sir William Temple

1628-1699

Sir William Temple, 1628-1699. Born, in Blackfriars, 1628. At schools at Penshurst and Bishop's Stortford, till 1643. Lived at home, 1643–45. Matric. Emmanuel Coll., Camb., 1645(?). Travelled on Continent, 1647–53(?). Married Dorothy Osborne, 1654. Member of Irish Convention at Restoration, 1660. M. P. for Carlow, 1661. Abroad on business of State, 1665–69. In retirement at Sheen, 1669–73. In Holland on State business, 1673–76, 1678–79. Retired from public life, 1685. Died at Moor Park, Surrey, 27 Jan. 1699. *Works:* "Poems" (under initials: Sir W. T.) [1670?]; "Observations upon the United Provinces of the Netherlands," 1672; "Miscellanea" (anon.)1680; "Memoirs of what past in Christendom from. . . . 1672. . . . to . . . . 1679," 1692; "An answer to a scurrilous pamphlet" (anon.; attrib. to Temple), 1693; "An Essay upon Taxes" (anon.), 1693; "An Introduction to the History of England," 1695. *Posthumous:* "Letters written by Sir W. Temple during his being Ambassador at the Hague," ed. by D. Jones, 1699; "Letters written . . . both at home and abroad," ed. by J. Swift (3 vols.), 1700–03; "Miscellanea (2nd ser.), ed. by J. Swift, 1701. *Collected Works:* ed. by J. Swift (2 vols.), 1720.—SHARP, R. FARQUHARSON, 1897, *A Dictionary of English Authors, p.* 277.

PERSONAL

He died at one o'clock this morning, 27th January, 1698-9, and with him all that was good and amiable among men.—SWIFT, JONATHAN, 1699, *Journal.*

A diplomatist and man of the world, prudent, wise, and polite, gifted with tact in conversation and in business, expert in the knowledge of the times, and in not compromising himself, adroit in pressing forward and in standing aside, who knew how to attract to himself the favour and the expectations of England, to obtain the eulogies of men of letters, of savants, of politicians, of the people, to gain a European reputation, to win all the crowns appropriated to science, patriotism, virtue, genius, without having too much of science, patriotism, genius, or virtue.—TAINE, H. A., 1871, *History of English Literature, tr. Van Laun, vol.* I, *bk.* iii, *ch.* i, *p.* 492.

Moor Park, the country home of Sir William Temple, stood not far from London, in a pleasant landscape, surrounded by its trim lawns and productive gardens. The house was plain; its owner was not wealthy; but he was famous for honesty in politics, for his success in cultivating fruits and vegetables, and for some knowledge of the classics. He wrote essays that are scarcely remembered, and produced grapes and peaches that were probably much better appreciated by his friend Charles II. or William III. Moor Park itself, and perhaps its owner, would long since have been forgotten had it not contained within its quiet shelter a dark and turbid genius, slowly struggling upward to renown, and a pale and thoughtful girl, studious at once and beautiful, whose name and fate were never to be separated from that of her modern Abelard.—LAWRENCE, EUGENE, 1872, *The Days of Queen Anne, Harper's Magazine, vol.* 44, *p.* 405.

"Sir William Temple's person," says the nameless writer of "a short character" prefixed to his works, "is best known by his pictures and prints. He was rather tall than low; his shape, when young, very exact; his hair a dark brown, and curled naturally, and, whilst that was esteemed a beauty, nobody had it in greater perfection; his eyes grey, but lively; and his body. lean, but extreme active, so that none acquitted themselves better at all sorts of exercise." What principally strikes us in Temple's intellect is its singular measure, solidity, sagacity. In negotiating he timed his movements with admirable skill; he succeeded in whatever he undertook; he was the author of the most famous alliance in that generation, and nobody has detected a flaw in his plans, or proved that in his diplomacy he should have acted otherwise than he did. The same sagacity appears in his political speculations; he keeps

close to the facts, and does not begin to speculate till he has mastered them. Such he was as a man of practice and a thinker, attempting comparatively little, and doing what he attempted with thoroughness. When we view him on the æsthetic side, we see the same characteristic appearing in the shape of refined taste. He did not attempt works of the imagination, but he studied the beauties of order and finished rhythm, and even in his most didactic compositions the language and the similitudes have a refined elevation.—MINTO, WILLIAM, 1872–80, *Manual of English Prose Literature, p.* 314.

Throughout his whole career, the conduct of Sir William Temple was marked by a cautious regard for his personal comfort and reputation; which strongly disposed him to avoid risks of every kind, and to stand aloof from public business where the exercise of eminent courage and decision was required. His character as a patriot is therefore not one which calls for high admiration; though it ought to be remarked in his favour, that as he seems to have had a lively consciousness that neither his abilities nor dispositions fitted him for vigorous action in stormy times, he probably acted with prudence in withdrawing from a field in which he would have only been mortified by failure, and done harm instead of good to the public. Being subject to frequent attacks of low spirits, he might have been disabled for action by the very emergencies which demanded the greatest mental energy and self-possession. But as an adviser, he was enlightened, safe and sagacious. As a private character, Sir William was respectable and decorous: his temper, naturally haughty and unamiable, was generally kept under good regulation; and among his foibles, vanity was the most prominent.—CHAMBERS, ROBERT, 1876, *Cyclopædia of English Literature, ed. Carruthers.*

He had great dignity; he had wealth; a sort of earlier Edward Everett—as polished and cold and well-meaning and fastidious; looking rather more to the elegance of his speech than to the burden of it; always making show of Classicism— nothing if not correct; cautious; keeping well out of harm's way, and all pugnacious expressions of opinion; courteous to strong Churchmen; courteous to Papists; bowing low to my Lady Castlemaine; very considerate of Cromwellians who had power; moulding his habit and speech so as to show no ugly angles of opinion anywhere, but only such convenient roundness as would roll along life's level easily to the very end.—MITCHELL, DONALD G., 1890, *English Lands Letters and Kings, from Elizabeth to Anne*, p. 225.

Sir William himself, in his youthful days, had been one of Sacharissa's most ardent admirers, and made no secret of the regard he retained for her in later days. His betrothed bride often alludes playfully to his silent adoration of this fair lady, in whom all perfections were supposed to meet. If she praises Lady Ann Wentworth, who she calls the finest lady she knows, she hastens to add, with that arch smile we know so well, *"One always excepted,"* and when she sends her lover her own portrait, at his request, begs that it may not presume to disturb my Lady Sunderland's which always hangs in his closet.—CARTWRIGHT, JULIA (MRS. HENRY ADY), 1893, *Sacharissa, Some Account of Dorothy Sidney, Countess of Sunderland*, p. 64.

GENERAL

In my first setting out, I never read any Art of Logic or Rhetoric. I met with Locke, he was quite insipid to me. I read Sir William Temple's "Essays" too then, but whenever there was anything political in them, I had no manner of feeling for it.—POPE, ALEXANDER, 1737–39, *Spence's Anecdotes, ed. Singer*, p. 151.

Wrote always like a man of sense and a gentleman; and his style is the model by which the best prose writers in the reign of Queen Anne formed theirs.—GOLDSMITH, OLIVER, 1759, *The Bee*, No. 8, *Nov.* 24.

Of all the considerable writers of this age, Sir William Temple is almost the only one that kept himself altogether unpolluted by that inundation of vice and licentiousness which overwhelmed the nation. The style of this author, although extremely negligent, and even infected with foreign idioms, is agreeable and interesting. That mixture of vanity which appears in his works is rather a recommendation to them. By means of it we enter into acquaintance with the character

of the author, full of honour and humanity, and fancy that we are engaged, not in the perusal of a book, but in conversation with a companion.—HUME, DAVID, 1762, *History of England, James II., ch.* lxxi.

Sir William Temple was the first writer who gave cadence to English prose. Before this time they were careless of arrangement, and did not mind whether a sentence ended with an important word or an insignificant word, or with what part of speech it was concluded.—JOHNSON, SAMUEL, 1778, *Life by Boswell*.

Temple is a very sensible writer, and draws more from his own stock of observation and reflection than is usual with the writers of the present day. . . . Temple, whatever topic he treats, always entertains: he has an easy regular stream of good sense, which never overflows, or fails, or stagnates.—GREEN, THOMAS, 1779–1810, *Diary of a Lover of Literature*.

Sir William Temple is another remarkable writer in the style of simplicity. In point of ornament and correctness, he rises a degree above Tillotson; though, for correctness, he is not in the highest rank. All is easy and flowing in him; he is exceedingly harmonious; smoothness, and what may be called amenity, are the distinguishing characters of his manner; relaxing, sometimes, as such a manner will naturally do, into a prolix and remiss style. No writer whatever has stamped upon his style a more lively impression of his own character. In reading his works, we seem engaged in conversation with him; we become thoroughly acquainted with him, not merely as an author, but as a man; and contract a friendship for him. He may be classed as standing in the middle, between a negligent simplicity, and the highest degree of ornament, which this character of style admits.—BLAIR, HUGH, 1783, *Lectures on Rhetoric and Belles-Lettres, ed. Mills, Lecture* xix, p. 208.

I have heard that, among works of prose, Pope was most fond of the second part of Sir William Temple's "Miscellanies."—WARTON, JOSEPH, 1797, *ed., Pope's Works, vol.* I, *Preface*, p. 3.

Swift represents him as having brought English style to perfection. Hume, I think, mentions him; but of late he is not often spoken of as one of the reformers of our style—this, however, he certainly was. The structure of his style is perfectly modern; and I have not marked above half a dozen words that are become obsolete. He has, indeed, several gallicisms, but they are chiefly in letters, written in Flanders and Holland, when he was every day speaking French.—MACKINTOSH, SIR JAMES, 1812, _Diary, Life, ed. Mackintosh, vol._ II, _p._ 204.

The day light of pure taste rose, when Sir William Temple put his pen to paper, and committed his lucubrations to the press. On every account I recommend his Works to a conspicuous place in the library of every youthful and aged person, who has the literary renown of his country at heart. Temple was among the earliest of the polishers of our prose; and bringing to his works liberal principles, a cultivated taste, and a kind heart, it is not to be wondered at that his popularity has been so great, as it is generally allowed to be.—DIBDIN, THOMAS FROGNALL, 1824, _The Library Companion, p._ 602.

It is an ordinary criticism, that my Lord Shaftesbury, and Sir William Temple, are models of the genteel style in writing. We should prefer saying—of the lordly, and the gentlemanly. Nothing can be more unlike than the inflated finical rhapsodies of Shaftesbury, and the plain natural chit-chat of Temple. The man of rank is discernible in both writers; but in the one it is only insinuated gracefully, in the other it stands out offensively. The peer seems to have written with his coronet on, and his Earl's mantle before him; the commoner in his elbow chair and undress.—What can be more pleasant than the way in which the retired statesman peeps out in the essays, penned by the latter in his delightful retreat at Shene? They scent of Nimeguen, and the Hague. Scarce an authority is quoted under an ambassador.—LAMB, CHARLES, 1825? _The Genteel Style in Writing._

The style of his essays is, on the whole, excellent,—almost always pleasing, and now and then stately and splendid. The matter is generally of much less value. . . . He was no profound thinker. He was merely a man of lively parts and quick observation,—a man of the world amongst men of letters,—a man of letters amongst men of the world. Mere scholars were dazzled by the embassador and cabinet councillor; mere politicians by the essayist and historian. But neither as a writer nor as a statesman can we allot to him any very high place. As a man, he seems to us to have been excessively selfish, but very sober, wary, and far-sighted in his selfishness;—to have known better than most people know what he really wanted in life; and to have pursued what he wanted with much more than ordinary steadiness and sagacity;—never suffering himself to be drawn aside either by bad or by good feelings. It was his constitution to dread failure more than he desired success,—to prefer security, comfort, repose, leisure, to the turmoil and anxiety which are inseparable from greatness;—and this natural languor of mind, when contrasted with the malignant energy of the keen and restless spirits among whom his lot was cast, sometimes appears to resemble the moderation of virtue. But we must own, that he seems to us to sink into littleness and meanness when we compare him—we do not say with any high ideal standard of morality,—but with many of those frail men who, aiming at noble ends, but often drawn from the right path by strong passions and strong temptations, have left to posterity a doubtful and checkered fame. —MACAULAY, THOMAS BABINGTON, 1836, _Sir William Temple, Edinburgh Review; Critical and Miscellaneous Essays._

Next to Dryden, the second place among the polite writers of the period from the Restoration to the end of the century has commonly been given to Sir William Temple. His "Miscellanies," to which principally this praise belongs, are not recommended by more erudition than a retired statesman might acquire with no great expense of time, nor by much originality of reflection. But, if Temple has not profound knowledge, he turns all he possesses well to account; if his thoughts are not very striking, they are commonly just. He has less eloquence than Bolingbroke, but is also free from his restlessness and ostentation. Much also, which now appears superficial in Temple's historical surveys, was far less familiar in his age: he has the merit of a comprehensive and a candid mind. His style, to which we should particularly refer, will be found, in comparison with his contemporaries, highly polished, and sustained with more equability than they preserve, remote from any thing either pedantic or humble. The periods are studiously rhythmical; yet they want the variety and peculiar charm that we admire in those of Dryden.—HALLAM, HENRY, 1837-39, *Introduction to the Literature of Europe, pt. iv, ch. vii, par.* 42.

Sir William Temple was the D'Ossat of England; but in the views and the style of his "Observations," his "Miscellaneous Works," and his "Memoirs," he is far inferior to our diplomatist.—CHATEAU-BRIAND, FRANÇOIS RENÉ, VICOMTE DE, 1837, *Sketches of English Literature. vol.* II, *p.* 195.

His mode as an author agrees with his maxims as a politician. His principles and style are homogeneous; a genuine diplomatist, such as one meets in the drawing-rooms, having probed Europe and touched everywhere the bottom of things; tired of everything, especially of enthusiasm, admirable in an arm-chair or at a levee, a good story-teller, waggish if need were, but in moderation, accomplished in the art of maintaining the dignity of his station and of enjoying himself.—TAINE, H. A., 1871, *History of English Literature, tr. Van Laun, vol.* I, *bk.* iii, *ch.* i, *p* 492.

He seems to have been a man of deep tenderness and strong personal feelings, a great favourite with children, a passionate lover, a fond husband, a constant friend. As his likes were strong, so were his dislikes; he had such an aversion for some men as to be impatient of their conversation.—MINTO, WILLIAM, 1872-80, *Manual of English Prose Literature, p.* 314.

When the critical admirers of the prose style of Sir William Temple ask us to believe that the distinguished diplomate "advanced our English tongue to as great a perfection as it well can bear," they ask too much. In marking the progress and development of English prose style from the overcharged rhetoric of the sixteenth century to a more simple and perspicuous arrangement of sentences, Temple was no doubt an important unit; but Cowley, Tillotson, Barrow, Jeremy Taylor, Dryden, and Locke also contributed, in their several degrees of excellence, to create a new standard of refinement and

verpal purity in our language. The elegance and naïveté of Sir William Temple's style are illustrated nowhere better than in his letters. He had a happy knack of suiting his manner and wording to the character of the person addressed.—SCOONES, W. BAPTISTE, 1880, *Four Centuries of English Letters, p.* 122.

As an author he ranks high, not so much because his works show great power of genius, as because he was one of the first to obtain a mastery over the great and difficult art of English prose composition.—NICOLL, HENRY J., 1882, *Landmarks of English Literature, p.* 164.

In a treatise on "Ancient and Modern Learning," written in his most chaste and dignified prose, he supported the cause of the Ancients. Avowedly the essay is rather literary than critical: and here and there remarks are introduced which give a graceful turn to the paragraphs, but could hardly be gravely employed as arguments in the controversy. Legendary resources are drawn upon so as to embellish with something of biographical detail what are little more than names in ancient literature. In many passages Temple has doubtless laid himself open to the ridicule which has been thrown upon him with much skill, but little measure, by Lord Macaulay. But the intention of the essay has been purposely distorted by Macaulay. Appeals made by Temple to the general impressions which are to be drawn from classical legends or literature, are twisted by Macaulay into positive assertions falsely claiming historical basis. . . . The treatise is of little value save for its gracefulness of language and tone, but it served very well to give to English readers an introduction to a topic in the literature of their more polite and facile neighbours. What it wants in criticism, it here and there supplies by a humour which Macaulay leaves out of sight.—CRAIK, HENRY, 1882, *The Life of Jonathan Swift, pp.* 64, 65.

It is the fault of Temple's discourses that they are too much like popular lectures by a very ignorant man who presumes upon his genteel appearance and elegant delivery. There are no productions which must be read more exclusively for their manner and not for their matter. Temple tells us nothing very agreeably, and then, while we are applauding, he dares to assert that there is no more for us to know. He was not a scholar, nor a critic, nor a geographer, nor even a botanist, and yet scholarship, criticism, geography, and botany, are the themes of his four principal essays. His discourse on learning, by a man who could not construe a page of Greek, set Bentley lashing his sides, and woke a din in which the clear falsetto of Temple was entirely drowned. Nevertheless, Temple is eminently readable. We forgive his parental condescension, his patent ignorance, in the delight and surprise of his modern tone. When he babbles of his oranges and his figs, and says he must leave the flowers to the ladies; when he talks of a friend of his who has a gamekeeper who is a Rosicrucian, and a laundress who is firm in the philosophy of Epicurus; when he laughs and sparkles over his runic nonsense and his Phalaris forgeries like some fine blue-stocking in a Congreve comedy —we feel that English prose has come to the birth, and that here is a man at last who can write about Nothing like a gentleman.—GOSSE, EDMUND, 1888, *A History of Eighteenth Century Literature, p.* 87.

If wise as a serpent he was timid as a dove. . . . Temple's memoirs give a lively picture of the mortifications he underwent as he gradually dwindled into a cipher. . . . At length he escaped to his books and gardens, and spent the rest of his life in the enjoyment of a character for consummate statesmanship, which he took care never to bring to the test. Wisdom and virtue he certainly did possess, but both with him were too much of the self-regarding order. His claims to rank as a restorer of English prose are better founded, though these, too, have been exaggerated. Johnson's assertion that Temple was the first writer who attended to cadence in English prose merely evinces how completely the power of appreciating the grand harmonies of the Elizabethan period had died out in the eighteenth century. He must, notwithstanding, be allowed an honourable place among those who have rendered English prose lucid, symmetrical, and adapted for business; and Macaulay has justly pointed out that the apparent length of his sentences is mainly a matter of punctuation. The elegance of the writer, and the egotistic caution of the man, are excellently represented by the concluding passage of his "Memoirs."—GARNETT, RICHARD, 1895, *The Age of Dryden, p.* 191.

His style, at its best extremely engaging, manifests the new form—plain, but carefully balanced and polished. From the agreeable nature of the subjects, and the air of gentlemanly but not too patronising condescension which it displays, it exercised great influence on a generation which thoroughly respected "quality." Once (in the thousand times quoted close of his "Essay on Poetry") Temple went higher than Dryden, higher than any one of his own school, in developing the music of prose; in the context of this and in many other places he goes very high. —SAINTSBURY, GEORGE, 1898, *A Short History of English Literature, p.* 510.

As a writer, apart from a weakness for gallicisms, which he admitted and tried to correct, his prose marked a development in the direction of refinement, rhythmical finish, and emancipation from the pedantry of long parentheses and superfluous quotations. He was also a pioneer in the judicious use of the paragraph. Hallam, ignoring Halifax, would assign him the second place, after Dryden, among the polite authors of his epoch. Swift gave expression to the belief that he had advanced our English tongue to as great a perfection as it could well bear; Chesterfield recommended him to his son; Dr. Johnson spoke of him as the first writer to give cadence to the English language; and Lamb praises him delightfully in his "Essay on the Genteel Style." During the eighteenth century his essays were used as exercises and models. But the progress made during the last half-century in the direction of the sovereign prose quality of limpidity has not been favourable to Temple's literary reputation, and in the future it is probable that his "Letters" and "Memoirs" will be valued chiefly by the historian, while his "Essays" will remain interesting primarily for the picture they afford of the cultured gentleman of the period. A few noble similes, however, and those majestic words of consolation addressed to Lady Essex, deserve and will find a place among the consecrated passages of English prose.—SECCOMBE, THOMAS, 1898, *Dictionary of National Biography, vol.* LVI, *p.* 51.

Joseph Beaumont

1616–1699

Joseph Beaumont, D.D., 1615–1699, a descendant of the ancient family of the name in Leicestershire, was entered at Peterhouse, Cambridge, at the age of 16. He was elected Fellow and tutor, but was ejected in 1643. In 1663 he became master of his college. He attacked Dr. Henry More's work, "The Mystery of Godliness," published in 1665, and for his zeal received the thanks of the university, which elected him Professor of Divinity His Poems in English and Latin were published in 1749, 4to, with an Appendix containing comments on the Epistle to the Colossians. . . . His principal work was "Psyche, or Love's Mystery," in 24 cantos, displaying the Intercourse between Christ and the Soul. This was begun in April, 1647, finished before the end of March, 1648, and published in the same year, folio. This poem was once very popular, but has been long neglected.—ALLIBONE, S. AUSTIN, 1854–58, *Dictionary of English Literature, vol.* I, *p.* 151.

GENERAL

This allegorical poem ("Psyche") was not without its admirers in the last age. Giles Jacob calls it an *invaluable work.*—GRANGER, JAMES, 1769–1824, *Biographical History of England, vol.* V, *p.* 44.

In his capacity as author of "Psyche," Beaumont is a forgotten rather than an "overlooked" poet. The work is said to have been once popular, and went through at least two editions folio; but readers of more recent days seldom have time or patience to grapple with so immoderate a task, and it is perhaps not surprising that even special students and compilers of the sacred poetry of that age have generally ignored it. . . . However much a poet by nature, he was rather a scholar by choice: he cared more for making acquaintance with the children of other men's brains than for begetting or nourishing any of his own: the creative fire in him was smothered under so great a weight of paper and leather. For nearly his last half-century, he wrote no verses (unless a few in Latin), nor seems to have bestowed a thought on those he had written before. When a man is thus careless of his literary fame, he cannot expect others to be more careful; and in some cases the loss may be, and is, the world's as well as his own.—BIRD, F. M., 1870, *An Overlooked Poet, Hours at Home, vol.* 11, *pp.* 561, 564.

In 1644 he was one of the royalist fellows ejected from Cambridge, and he retired to his old home at Hadleigh, where he sat down to write his epic poem of "Psyche." As this is of very great length, extending in its first form to twenty cantos, it is surprising to learn that its composition occupied Beaumont only eleven months.—GOSSE, EDMUND, 1885, *Dictionary of National Biography, vol.* IV, *p.* 61.

Beaumont, a strong cavalier and an orthodox churchman, was a kind of adversary of More's, whose length and quaintness he has exceeded, while he has almost rivalled his learning in "Psyche, or Love's Mystery," a religious poem of huge dimensions, first published in 1648 and later in 1702. Beaumont, as both fragments of this vast thing and his minor poems show, had fancy, taste, and almost genius on opportunity; but the prevailing mistake of his school, the idea that poetry is a fit vehicle for merely prosaic expression, is painfully appparent in him.—SAINTSBURY, GEORGE, 1887, *History of Elizabethan Literature, p.* 379.

To Dr. Beaumont belongs the honour of having written the longest poem in the English language. . . . The poem is marked by much facility of expression, and some power of imagery; but most of all by earnest religious feeling, touched with something of Crashaw's mysticism and much of Herbert's reverence for external symbolism. Alike in style and in subject, it forms a connecting link between the work of these poets and the "essay in verse" of the eighteenth century. Beaumont has nothing of Milton's power of broad characterization; his good and evil spirts must be, as in *Dante,* painted with all the wealth of detail—delightful or repulsive—that a fertile imagination can supply. And this heaping together of imagery becomes wearisome in a poem where the philosophic and didactic predominate over the allegorical and descriptive.—MASTERMAN, J. HOWARD B., 1897, *The Age of Milton, p.* 142.

John Dryden

1631–1700

Born, at Aldwinkle All Saints, Northamptonshire, 9 Aug.[?] 1631. Educated first at a school at Tichmarsh; at Westminster School, as scholar, 1640[?]–1650. Scholarship at Trinity Coll., Cambridge, 11 May 1650; matriculated, 6 July 1650; "discommuned" in July 1652, but allowed to continue residence on apology; B.A., Jan. 1654. To London, possibly as clerk to Judge Sir Gilbert Pickering; afterwards made living by literature. Married Lady Elizabeth Howard, 1 Dec. 1663. Member of Royal Soc., 26 Nov. 1662. Play, "The Wild Gallant," performed at King's Theatre, Feb. 1663; "Rival Ladies," 1663; "The Indian Queen" (with Sir Robert Howard), Jan. 1664; "The Indian Emperor," 1665. At Charlton, Wilts, during plague and fire of London. "Secret Love," King's Theatre, March 1667; "Sir Martin Mar-all" (adapted from Molière), 1667. Position as dramatist established; contract with King's Theatre to provide three plays a year. Degree of M.A. conferred at King's request by Archbp. of Canterbury, 1668. Poet Laureate and Historiographer Royal, 1670–88. Lived in Fetter Lane, 1673–82; in Long-Acre, 1682–86. Collector of Customs in Port of London, 17 Dec. 1683. Religious controversies, 1686–88. Dramatic writing, 1690–92. Poems and translations from classics, 1693–97. Died in Gerrard St., Soho, 1 May 1700. Buried in Westminster Abbey. *Works:* "A Poem upon the Death of his late Highness Oliver" (also known as "Heroic Stanzas"), 1659 (2nd edn., same year); "Astræa Redux," 1660; "To His Sacred Majesty, a Panegyrick on his Coronation," 1661; "The Rival Ladies," 1664; "Annus Mirabilis," 1667; "The Indian Emperor," 1667; "Of Dramatick Poesie," 1668; "Secret Love" 1668; "Sir Martin Mar-all" (anon.), 1668; "The Wild Gallant," 1669; "The Tempest" (with Davenant), 1670; "Tyrannic Love," 1670; "An Evening's Love," 1671; "Conquest of Granada" (2 pt.), 1672; "Marriage à la Mode," 1673; "The Assignation," 1673; "Amboyna," 1673; "Notes and Observations on the Empress of Morocco" (anon.), 1674; "The State of Innocence," 1674; "The Mall" (anon.; attributed to Dryden), 1674; "Aurungzebe," 1676; "All for Love," 1678; "The Kind Keeper," 1678; "Œdipus" (with Lee), 1679; "Troilus and Cressida," 1679; "The Spanish Friar," 1681; "Absolom and Achitophel" (anon.), pt. i., 1681; pt. ii. (with Tate; anon.), 1682; "His Majesty's Declaration Defended" (anon.), 1681; "The Medal" (anon.), 1682; "Mac Flecknoe" (anon.), 1682; "Religio Laici," 1682; "The Duke of Guise" (with Lee), 1683; "Vindication" of same, 1683; "Albion and Albanius," 1685; "Threnodia Augustalis," 1685; "Defence of Papers written by the late King" (anon.), 1686; "The Hind and Panther" (anon.), 1687; "A Song for St. Cecilia's Day," 1687; "Britannia Rediviva," 1688; "Don Sebastian," 1690; "Amphitryon," 1690; "King Arthur," 1691; "Cleomenes," 1692; "Eleonora," 1692; "Love Triumphant," 1694; "Alexander's Feast," 1697; "Fables, Ancient and Modern, translated . . . With Original Poems," 1700. He *translated:* Maimbourg's "History of the League," 1684; Bohour's "Life of Xavier," 1688; "Juvenal and Persius," 1693; Dufresnoy's "Art of Painting," 1695; "Virgil," 1697; preface and two epistles in trans. of Ovid's "Epistles," 1680; most of trans. in vols. i., ii. of "Miscellany Poems," 1684–85; some in vols. iii, iv., 1685–94. He wrote nearly 100 prologues and epilogues; and contrib. verses or prefaces to "Lachrymæ Musarum," 1649; Hoddesdon's "Sion and Parnassus," 1650; Sir R. Howard's Poems, 1660; Charleton's "Chorea Gigantum," 1663; [possibly to "Covent Garden Drollery," 1672; and New Court Songs and Poems," 1672]; Lee's "Alexander," 1677; Roscommon's "Essay on Translated Verse," 1680; a translation of Plutarch, 1683; Anne Killigrew's "Poems," 1686; Walsh's "Dialogue concerning Women," 1691; St. Evremond's "Miscellaneous Essays," 1692; Sir H. Sheere's trans. of Polybius, 1693; Congreve's "Double Dealer," 1694. *Collected Works:* "Poems on Various Occasions," ed. by Tonson, 1701; "Dramatic Works," ed. by Tonson, 1701; ed. by Congreve (6 vols.), 1717; Original Poems and Translations, ed. by Tonson (2 vols.), 1742; "Poems and Fables," 1753; Poems, ed. by Derrick (4 vols.), 1760; "Critical and Miscellaneous Prose Works," ed. by Malone (4 vols.), 1800; "Works," ed. by Scott (18 vols.), 1808;

WILLIAM WYCHERLEY

JOHN DRYDEN

"Aldine" edn., 1854; "Globe" edn., 1870, etc. *Life:* by Johnson in ("Lives of Poets"); by Malone, 1800; by Scott in 1808 edn. of "Works;" by Bell in "Aldine" edn. of Works, 1854; by Christie in "Globe" edn., 1870; by Saintsbury ("English Men of Letters" series), 1881.—SHARP, R. FARQUHARSON, 1897, *A Dictionary of English Authors, p.* 88.

PERSONAL

I confess my chief endeavours are to delight the age in which I live. If the humour of this be for low comedy, small accidents and raillery, I will force my genius to obey it, though with more reputation I could write in verse. I know I am not fitted by nature to write comedy; I want that gaiety of humour which is required to it. My conversation is slow and dull, my humour saturnine and reserved: In short I am none of those who endeavour to break jests in company, or make repartees. So that those, who decry my comedies, do me no injury except it be in point of profit: reputation in them is the last thing to which I shall pretend. —DRYDEN, JOHN, 1668, *A Defence of an Essay of Dramatic Poetry.*

Last night, Mr. Dryden, the famous poet, coming from a coffee-house in Covent Garden, was set upon by three persons unknown to him; and so rudely by them handled, that it is said his life is in no small danger. It is thought to have been the effect of a private grudge rather than upon the too common design of unlawful gain; an unkind trespass by which not only he himself, but the commonwealth of learning may receive injury.— CONTEMPORARY NEWSPAPER, 1679, *Dec.* 19th, Maloniana.

Whereas John Dryden, Esq., was on Monday the 18th instant, at night, barbarously assaulted, and wounded in Rosestreet, in Covent-garden, by divers men unknown; if any person shall make discovery of the said offenders to the said Mr. Dryden, or to any justice of the peace, he shall not only receive fifty pounds, which is deposited in the hands of Mr. Blanchard, goldsmith, next door to Temple-bar, for the said purpose; but if he be a principal, or an accessory, in the said fact, his Majesty is graciously pleased to promise him his pardon for the same.— LONDON GAZETTE, 1679, *December* 18, 22.

It is true, he had somewhat to sink from in matter of wit; but, as for his morals, it is scarcely possible for him to grow a worse man than he was.—BURNET, GILBERT, 1687, *A Defence of the Reflections*

on the Ninth Book of the First Volume of M. Varillas's History of Heresies; being a Reply to his Answer.

A sleepy eye he shows, and no sweet feature,
Yet was indeed a favourite of nature.
Endow'd and graced with an exalted mind,
With store of wit, and that of every kind.
Juvenal's tartness, Horace's sweet air,
With Virgil's force, in him concenter'd were.
But though the painter's art can never show it,
That his exemplar was so great a poet,
Yet are the lines and tints so subtly wrought,
You may perceive he was a man of thought.
Closterman, 'tis confess'd, has drawn him well,
But short of Absalom and Achitophel.
—ANON, 1700, *Epigrams on the Paintings of the Most Eminent Masters.*

John Dryden, Esq., the famous poet, lies a-dying.—POSTBOY, 1700, *April* 30.

I come now from Mr. Dryden's Funeral, where we had an Ode in Horace sung, instead of David's Psalms; whence you may find that we don't think a Poet worth Christian Burial; the Pomp of the Ceremony was a kind of Rhapsody, and fitter, I think, for Hudibras than him; because the Cavalcade was mostly Burlesque; but he was an extraordinary Man, and bury'd after an extraordinary Fashion; for I believe there was never such another Burial seen; the Oration indeed was great and ingenious, worthy the Subject, and like the Author [Dr. Garth], whose Prescriptions can restore the Living, and his Pen embalm the Dead. And so much for Mr. Dryden, whose Burial was the same with his Life,—Variety, and not of a Piece. The Quality and Mob, Farce and Heroicks, the Sublime and Ridicule mixt in a Piece, great Cleopatra in a Hackney Coach.—FARQUHAR, GEORGE, 1700, *Letter.*

Epitaph upon Mr. John Dryden.

Here lyes John Dryden, who had enemies three,
Old Nick, sir Dick, and Jeremy.
The fustian knight was forc'd to yield,
The other two maintain'd the field,
But had our poet's life been holier,
He had knick't both Devil and the Collier.
—HEARNE, THOMAS, 1707, *Reliquiæ Hearnianæ, ed. Bliss, Nov.* 5, *vol.* I, *p.* 137.

He was of a nature exceedingly humane and compassionate; easily forgiving injuries, and capable of a prompt and sincere reconciliation with them who had offended him. . . . His friendship, where he professed it, went much beyond his professions. . . . As his reading had been very extensive, so was he very happy in memory, tenacious of everything that he had read. He was not more possessed of knowledge than he was communicative of it. But then his communication of it was by no means pedantic, or imposed upon the conversation; but just such, and went so far, as, by the natural turns of the discourse in which 'he was engaged, it was necessarily promoted or required. He was extreme ready and gentle in his correction of the errors of any writer, who thought fit to consult him; and full as ready and patient to admit of the reprehension of others, in respect of his own oversight or mistakes. He was of very easy, I may say, of very pleasing access; but something slow, and, as it were, diffident in his advances to others. He had something in his nature, that abhorred intrusion into any society whatsoever. Indeed, it is to be regretted, that he was rather blamable in the other extreme; for, by that means, he was personally less known, and, consequently, his character might become liable both to misapprehensions and misrepresentations.—CONGREVE, WILLIAM, 1717, ed., The Works of John Dryden, Dedication.

Mr. John Dryden, the great poet, was buried in Westminster abbey among the old poets in May 1700, being carried from the college of Physicians, where an oration was pronounced by the famous Dr. Garth, in which he did not mention one word of Jesus Christ, but made an oration as an apostrophe to the great god Apollo, to influence the minds of the auditors with a wise, but, without doubt, poetical understanding, and, as a conclusion, instead of a psalm of David, repeated the 30th ode of the third book of Horace's odes, beginning, "Exegi monumentum," &c. He made a great many blunders in tᴜᴄ pronunciation.—HEARNE, THOMAS, 1726, Reliquiæ Hearnianæ, ed. Bliss, Nov. 6, vol. II, p. 267.

As we have sometimes great composers of music who cannot sing, we have as frequently great writers that cannot read;

and though without the nicest ear no man can be master of poetical numbers, yet the best ear in the world will not always enable him to pronounce them. Of this truth Dryden, our first great master of verse and harmony, was a strong instance. When he brought his play of "Amphytrion" to the stage, I heard him give it his first reading to the actors, in which, though it is true he delivered the plain sense of every period, yet the whole was in so cold, so flat, and unaffecting a manner, that I am afraid of not being believed when I affirm it.—CIBBER, COLLEY, 1739, An Apology for His Life.

Dryden was not a very genteel man, he was intimate with none but poetical men.—He was said to be a very good man, by all that knew him; he was as plump as Mr. Pitt; of a fresh colour, and a down look, and not very conversible.—POPE, ALEXANDER, 1742–43, Spence's Anecdotes, ed. Singer, p. 197.

Dryden was as disgraceful to the office [of laureat], from his character, as the poorest scribbler could have been from his verses.—GRAY, THOMAS, 1757, Letter to Mason, Dec. 19.

Of his petty habits or slight amusements, tradition has retained little. Of the only two men whom I have found to whom he was personally known, one told me, that at the house which he frequented, called Will's Coffee-house, the appeal upon any literary dispute was made to him: and the other related, that his armed chair, which in the winter had a settled and prescriptive place by the fire, was in the summer placed in the balcony, and that he called the two places his winter and his summer seat. This is all the intelligence which his two survivors afforded me.—JOHNSON, SAMUEL, 1779–81, Dryden, Lives of the English Poets.

We are enabled, from the various paintings and engravings of Dryden, as well as from the less flattering delineations of the satirists of his time, to form a tolerable idea of his face and person. In youth, he appears to have been handsome, and of a pleasing countenance; when his age was more advanced, he was corpulent and florid, which procured him the nickname attached to him by Rochester. In his latter days, distress and disappointment probably chilled the fire of his eye, and the advance of age destroyed the animation of his countenance. Still, however, his portraits bespeak the look and features of genius; especially that in which he is drawn with his waving grey hairs.— SCOTT, SIR WALTER, 1808–21, *Life of Dryden, ed. Saintsbury, p.* 371.

Poor Dryden! what with his wife—consort one can not call her, and helpmeet she was not—and with a tribe of tobaconist brothers on one hand, and proud Howards on the other; and a host of titled associates, and his bread to dig with his pen, one pities him from one's heart. Well might he, when his wife once said it would be much better for her to be a book than a woman, for then she should have more of his company, reply, "I wish you were, my dear, an almanac, and then I could change you once a year." It is not well to look much into such a home, except for a warning.—HOWITT, WILLIAM, 1846, *Homes and Haunts of the Most Eminent British Poets, vol.* I, *p.* 129.

Dryden's mixture of simplicity, good-nature, and good opinion of himself is here seen in a very agreeable manner. It must not be omitted that it was to this house [Will's] Pope was taken when a boy, by his own desire, on purpose to get a sight of the great man, which he did. According to Pope, he was plump, with a fresh color, and a down look, and not very conversible. It appears, however, that what he did say was much to the purpose; and a contemporary mentions his conversation on that account as one of the few things for which the town was desirable. He was a temperate man, though he drank with Addison a great deal more than he used to do, probably so far as to hasten his end.—HUNT, LEIGH, 1848, *The Town, ch.* viii.

He was married by license in the Church of St. Swithin, by London Stone (as appears by the register of that Church), on the 1st December, 1663. The entry of the license, which is dated "ultimo Novembis," 1663, and is in the office of the Vicar-General of the Archbishop of Canterbury, describes him as a parishioner of St. Clement Danes of about the age of thirty, and the Lady Elizabeth [Howard] as twenty-five and of the parish of St. Martin-in-the-Fields. The poet's signature to the entry is written "Driden."— CUNNINGHAM, PETER, 1854, *Johnson's Lives of the Poets, note.*

The licentiousness of Dryden's plays admits of no palliation or defence. He wrote for a licentious stage in a profligate age, and supplied, much to his own disgrace, the kind of material the vicious taste of his audiences demanded. Nor will it serve his reputation to contrast his productions in this way with those of others. Shadwell alone transcends him in depravity. But there is some compensation for all his grossness in turning from his plays to his life, and making the contrast. The morality of his life—the practical test of his heart and his understanding—was unimpeachable. The ingenuity of slander was exhausted in assailing his principles, and exposing his person to obloquy—but the morality of his life comes pure out of the furnace. The only kind of personal indiscretion ascribed to him is that of having eaten tarts with Mrs. Reeve the actress, in the Mulberry garden.—BELL, ROBERT, 1854, *ed., Dryden's Poems, Life.*

Such was John Dryden's life. It is a life where neither the heroic constancy of the martyr, nor the imaginative seclusion and loftiness of the idealist, have any place. But it is one not less interesting to those who are not afraid to look closely, yet fairly and temperately, at human nature. For it is the life of a great man who descended into the arena, who mixed with the crowd, who drudged painfully for daily bread, who, in an unpropitious and unhappy age, was forced to keep body and soul together as he best might. That after half a century of ignoble and ill-requited toil he retained a youthful ingenuousness and purity of soul, need not be maintained. But that an evil life had destroyed his manliness, his sincerity, his kindly heart, his natural generosity of temper, and had converted him into a sordid knave and hypocritical adventurer, who sold his birthright for a mess of pottage and his master for thirty pieces of silver, is a view which is refuted by the clearest evidence, internal and external, and which we may safely refuse to entertain.—SKELTON, JOHN, 1865–83, *John Dryden, Fraser's Magazine, Essays in History and Biography, p.* 164.

The Father, as he has been called, of modern English Poetry, was laid almost in the very grave of the Father of Ancient English Poetry, whose gravestone was actually sawn asunder to make room for his monument. That monument was long delayed. But so completely had his grave come to be regarded as the most interesting spot in Poets' Corner, that when Pope wrote the epitaph for Rowe, the highest honour he could pay to him was that his tomb should point the way to Dryden's. . . . The "rude and nameless stone" roused the attention of Sheffield, Duke of Buckingham, who in consequence raised the present monument. For the inscription, Pope and Atterbury were long in earnest correspondence. . . . Pope improved upon these suggestions, and finally wrote—

This Sheffield raised: the sacred dust below Was Dryden's once—the rest who does not know?

This was afterwards altered into the present plain inscription; and the bust erected by the Duke was exchanged for a finer one by Scheemakers, put up by the Duchess, with a pyramid behind it. So the monument remained till our own day, when Dean Buckland, with the permission of the surviving representative of the poet, Sir Henry Dryden, removed all except the simple bust and pedestal.—STANLEY, ARTHUR PENRHYN, 1867, *Historical Memorials of Westminster Abbey.*

Some notion of Dryden's personal appearance may be gathered from contemporary notices. He was of short stature, stout, and ruddy in the face. Rochester christened him Poet Squab, and Tom Brown always calls him "little Bayes." Shadwell in his "Medal of John Bayes" sneers at him as a cherry-cheeked dunce; another lampooner calls him "learned and florid." Pope remembered him as plump and of fresh colour, with a down look. Lady de Longueville, who died in 1763 at the age of 100, told Oldys that she remembered Dryden's dining with her husband, and that the most remarkable part of his appearance was an uncommon distance between his eyes. He had a large mole on his right cheek. The friendly writer of some lines on his portrait by Closterman says:

"A sleepy eye he shows, and no sweet feature."

He appears to have become gray comparatively early, and he let his gray hair grow long. We see him with his long gray locks in the portrait by which through engravings his face is best known to us, painted by Kneller in 1698. The face, as we know it by that picture and the engravings, is handsome; it indicates intellect, and sensual characteristics are not wanting.—CHRISTIE, W. D., 1870, *ed, Poetical Works of John Dryden, Memoir.*

He flung himself, like the men of his day, into the reaction against Puritanism. His life was that of a libertine, and his marriage with a woman of fashion, who was more dissolute than himself, only gave a new spur to his debaucheries. Large as was his income from the stage—and it equalled for many years the income of a country squire—he was always in debt, and forced to squeeze gifts from patrons by fulsome adulation. Like the rest of the fine gentlemen about him, he aired his Hobbism in sneers at the follies of religion and the squabbles of creeds. The grossness of his comedies rivalled that of Wycherley himself. But it is the very extravagance of his coarseness which shows how alien it was to the real temper of the man. . . . Dryden scoffs at priests and creeds, but his greater poetry is colored throughout with religion. He plays the rake, but the two pictures which he has painted with all his heart are the pictures of the honest country squire and the poor country parson. He passes his rivals in the grossness of his comedies; he flings himself recklessly into the evil about him, because it is the fashion and because it pays; but he cannot sport lightly and gayly with what is foul. He is driven, if he is coarse at all, to be brutally coarse. . . . No man denounced the opponents of the crown with more ruthless invective. No man humbled himself before the throne with more fulsome adulation. Some of this no doubt was mere flattery, but not all of it. Dryden, like his age, was conscious that new currents of feeling and opinion were sweeping him from the old moorings of mankind; but he shrank in terror from the wide ocean over whose waters he drifted. In religion he was a rationalist, a sceptic, whether he would or no; but he recoiled from the maze of "anxious thoughts" which spread before him—of thoughts

"That in endless circles roll, Without a centre where to fix the soul."

and clung to the church that would give him, if not peace, at least quiet. In politics he was as much a rationalist as in religion, but he turned horror-struck from the sight of a "State drawn to the dregs of a democracy," and in the crisis of the popish plot he struck blindly for the crown.—GREEN, JOHN RICHARD, 1877–80, *History of the English People.*

In private life a very respectable, a very amiable, and a very generous man. . . . He was, indeed, always going out of his way to do a kindness to his fellow-labourers in literature. He welcomed Wycherley with open arms, though he knew that Wycherley's success must be, to some extent, based on his own depression. Dennis, Shere, Moyle, Motteaux, and Walsh were constantly assisted by him. By his patronage Addison, then a diffident lad at Oxford, and Congreve, a timid aspirant for popular favour, came into prominence. When Southerne was smarting under the failure of his comedy, Dryden was near to cheer and condole with him. He helped Prior, and he was but ill rewarded. He did what he could for young Oldham; and when the poor fellow buried in his premature grave abilities which might have added to the riches of our literature, he dedicated a touching elegy to his memory. Lee and Garth were among his disciples; and, if he was at first blind or unjust to Otway's fine genius, he afterwards made ample amends. He gave Nell Gwynn a helping hand at the time when she sorely needed it. His letters to Mrs. Thomas still testify not only of his willingness to oblige, but the courtesy and kindliness with which he proffered his services. He was, we are told, beloved by his tenants in Northamptonshire for his liberality as a landlord. The few private letters which have been preserved to us clearly indicate that, if he was not happy with his wife, he was a forbearing and kindly husband, and his devotion to his children is touching in the extreme.—COLLINS, JOHN CHURTON 1878–95, *Dryden, Quarterly Review; Essays and Studies, p.* 84.

Several of the Dryden's biographers, in their anxiety to screen the poet, have endeavored to paint him blameless as a man. . . . Surely it is possible to admire the poetry of Dryden, without seeking to justify its licentiousness, or its sickening adulation of the predominant faction. What need to distort facts with a view of proving Dryden to have been a spotless, innocent, and all contemporary writers, liars?—HAMILTON, WALTER, 1879, *The Poets Laureate of England.*

Dryden seems to have borne a fair character in general and family morals; but he is numbered, apparently with reason, among those poets who have found little heartfelt satisfaction in marriage. His wife, it seems, thought him capricious and neglectful, she not making sufficient allowance for his literary pursuits and poetic variability of mood; and recrimination was frequently between them. He wrote an anticipative epitaph for his wife, who, however, survived him; if it is genuine—and I am not aware that this has ever been questioned—it speaks volumes for his disesteem of her, and very little for his own good-feeling or courtesy. It has, at any rate, the merit of terseness:

"Here lies my wife; here let her lie:
Now she's at rest—and so am I."

—ROSSETTI, WILLIAM MICHAEL, 1881. *The Wives of Poets, Atlantic Monthly, vol.* 47, *p.* 389.

We have seen what foundation there is for this gross charge against Lady Elizabeth; now let us see what ground there is for the charge against Dryden. There are the libels of Shadwell and the rest of the crew, to which not even Mr. Christie, a very severe judge of Dryden's moral character, assigns the slightest weight; there is the immorality ascribed to Bayes in the Rehearsal a very pretty piece of evidence indeed, seeing that Bayes is a confused medley of half-a-dozen persons; there is a general association by tradition of Dryden's name with that of Mrs. Reeve, a beautiful actress of the day; and finally there is a tremendous piece of scandal which is the battle-horse of the devil's advocates. A curious letter appeared in the *Gentleman's Magazine* for 1745, the author of which is unknown, though conjectures, as to which there are difficulties, identify him with Dryden's youthful friend Southern. "I remember," says this person "plain John Dryden before he paid his court with success to the great, in one uniform clothing of Norwich drugget. I have ate tarts with him and Madam Reeve at the Mulberry Garden, when our author advanced to a sword, and a Chedreux wig." Perhaps there is no more curious instance of the infinitesimal foundation on which scandal builds than this matter of Dryden's immorality. Putting aside mere vague libellous declamation, the one piece of positive information on the subject that we have is anonymous, was made at least seventy years after date, and avers that John Dryden, a dramatic author, once ate tarts with an actress and a third person. This translated into the language of Mr. Green becomes the dissoluteness of a libertine, spurred up to new debaucheries.—SAINTSBURY, GEORGE, 1881, *Dryden (English Men of Letters), p. 25.*

One of the most famous of these houses of entertainment was "Wills'," rendered celebrated by being the haunt of the great Dryden; and here it was he gathered around him the wits and men of letters and culture of his day. In the principal room of "Wills'," there was a great armchair specially reserved for "the old man venerable," which, during the winter, was placed by the fireside, and, during the summer, in the balcony, and these spots he used to refer to as his winter and summer residences. In the great room at "Wills'," common to all, the old man, grown garrulous in his latter days, would talk to any chance visitor who interested him, and tell anecdotes of blind John Milton, whom he had known, and of all the rare events which had happened during his life. Two men, whose names afterwards became famous, first saw Dryden at "Wills'," one of whom was Alexander Pope, then about twelve years of age, who, at his entreaty, as brought by Sir Charles Wogan from the Forest of Windsor for this purpose; the other being Dean Lockier, who has fortunately left us his first impressions of the poet, whom Colley Cibber used to speak of as "a decent old man."—MOLLOY, J. FITZGERALD, 1882, *Court Life Below Stairs, p. 260.*

The house in Fetter Lane known as Dryden's house, has just been demolished. It was visited by a good many poeple, and I daresay it may have existed in Dryden's time, but there is considerable doubt whether he was ever inside of it. However, it had a good reputation among lovers of antiquity, and I daresay its woodwork, if the woodwork happened to be sound, will be converted into book covers for future editions of Dryden. I understand the balustrades of the staircase

realized a good price, and it will probably reach even a higher figure among relic-lovers.—STERRY, J. ASHBY, 1887, *English Notes, The Book Buyer, vol. 4, p. 191.*

The affection of his contemporaries and literary disciples proves, as well as their direct testimony, that in his private relations Dryden showed a large and generous nature. Congreve dwells especially upon his modesty, and says that he was the "most easily discountenanced" of all men he ever knew. The absence of arrogance was certainly combined with an absence of the loftier qualities of character. Dryden is the least unworldly of all great poets. He therefore reflects most completely the characteristics of the society dominated by the court of Charles II, which in the next generation grew into the town of Addison and Pope.—STEPHEN, LESLIE, 1888, *Dictionary of National Biography, vol.* XVI, *p.* 73.

Asaph.—Bayes.—Glorious John.—Ignoramus.—Matthew Coppinger.—Neander.—Old Squab.—Poet Squab.—Reverend Levi.—Shimei.—FREY, ALBERT R., 1888, *Sobriquets and Nicknames, p. 401.*

On the whole, we may say that he was one whom we would probably have esteemed if we could have known him; but in whom, apart from his writings, we should not have discovered the first literary figure of his generation.—GARNETT, RICHARD. 1895, *The Age of Dryden, p.* 16.

DRAMAS

I don't think Dryden so bad a dramatic writer as you seem to do. There are as many things finely said in his plays, as almost by anybody. Beside his three best, ("All for Love," "Don Sebastian," and the "Spanish Fryar,") there are others that are good: as, "Sir Martin Mar-all," "Limberham," and "The Conquest of Mexico." His "Wild Gallant" was written while he was a boy, and is very bad.—All his plays are printed in the order they were written.—POPE, ALEXANDER, 1734–36, *Spence's Anecdotes, ed. Singer, p.* 128.

Dryden's comedies have all the point that there is in ribaldry, and all the humour that there is in extravagance. I am sorry I can say nothing better of them. He was not at home in this kind of writing, of which he was himself conscious. His play was *horse-play.* His wit (what there is of it) is ingenious and scholar-like, rather than natural and dramatic.—HAZLITT, WILLIAM, 1818, *Lectures on the English Comic Writers, p.* 78.

Dryden had no dramatic genius either in tragedy or comedy. In his plays he mistakes blasphemy for sublimity, and ribaldry for wit.—HAZLITT, WILLIAM, 1820, *Lectures on the Literature of the Age of Elizabeth, Lecture* viii.

The genius of Dryden appears nowhere to so little advantage as in his tragedies; and the contrast is truly humiliating when, in a presumptuous attempt to heighten the colouring, or enrich the simplicity of Shakespeare, he bedaubs with obscenity, or deforms with rant, the genuine passion and profligacy of Antony and Cleopatra—or intrudes on the enchanted solitude of Prospero and his daughter, with the tones of worldly gallantry, or the caricatures of affected simplicity.—JEFFREY, FRANCIS, 1822–44, *Contributions to the Edinburgh Review, vol.* II, *p.* 333.

His plays, his rhyming plays in particular, are admirable subjects for those who wish to study the morbid anatomy of the drama. He was utterly destitute of the power of exhibiting real human beings. Even in the far inferior talent of composing characters out of those elements into which the imperfect process of our reason can resolve them, he was very deficient. His men are not even good personifications; they are not well-assorted assemblages of qualities. Now and then, indeed, he seizes a very coarse and marked distinction; and gives up, not a likeness, but a strong caricature, in which a single peculiarity is protruded, and every thing else neglected.—MACAULAY, THOMAS BABINGTON, 1828, *Dryden, Edinburgh Review, Critical and Miscellaneous Essays.*

Of their rant, their fustian, their bombast, their bad English, of their innumerable sins against Dryden's own better conscience both as poet and critic, I shall excuse myself from giving any instances. I like what is good in Dryden so much, and it *is* so good, that I think Gray was justified in always losing his temper when he heard "his faults criticised."—LOWELL, JAMES RUSSELL, 1868–90, *Dryden, Prose Works, Riverside ed., vol.* III, *p.* 173.

He had, in truth, few of the qualities essential to a comic dramatist. . . . He had indeed little humour: he had no

grace; he had no eye for these subtler improprieties of character and conduct which are the soul of comedy; what wit he had was coarse and boisterous; he had no power of inventing ludicrous incidents, he could not manage the light artillery of colloquial raillery.—COLLINS, JOHN CHURTON, 1878–95, *Dryden, Quarterly Review; Essays and Studies, p.* 24.

We next have to contemplate Dryden in the character of a dramatist; a character which he sustained for many years, with no little acceptance among his contemporaries, although now, and for a century or more past, his dramas barely survive in the quality of literary curiosities, unread save by the fewest, and regarded as marked examples of inflation and artificial inspiration, perversions of a forcible, strenuous, and rich nature. This nature asserts itself notwithstanding, and makes the works the object of active disapproval, rather than negligent unconcern, to those who will still be at the pains to examine them. Energy and capacity abound; the discipline and beauty of proportion, the authentic accent of truth, are deficient. —ROSSETTI, WILLIAM MICHAEL, 1878, *Lives of Famous Poets, p.* 93.

It is but too certain, on the other hand, —and I should be the last to question or dispute the certainty,—that no lover of Dryden's fame could wish to see any addition made to the already too long list of his comedies. Rather might we reasonably desire, were it possible, to strike off several of these from the roll and erase the record of their perpetration for ever. . . . A reader must be very imperfectly imbued with the spirit or skilled in the manner of his work, who imagines that the sole representative and distinctive qualities of his tragic or serious dramatic verse are to be sought or found in the resonant reverberations of amœbæan rant which roll and peal in prolonged and portentous echoes of fulminant epigram through the still dilating dialogue of his yet not undelightful heroic plays.—SWINBURNE, ALGERNON CHARLES, 1880, *A Relic of Dryden, The Gentleman's Magazine, vol.* 249, *pp.* 416, 422.

Of Dryden's comedies, then, it may be sufficient to say that, while they missed success themselves for very cogent reasons, they yet paved the way for the success of others. Of the blank-verse tragedies, which are esteemed the best of his dramatic works, we have nothing particular to say. But the rhymed heroic tragedies, whatever else may be said of them, are very remarkable productions, which maintained their popularity for some time. On the one hand, they have been unmercifully and very cleverly parodied, on the other they were written by a theatrical manager well versed in the business of the stage; they were clearly used as libretti for spectacular melodrama; and lastly, they, along with many successful French tragedies, point to the conclusion that rhyme has more dramatic value than may hitherto have been supposed. If there is room for the display of tragic power in an Italian opera, and if music may even assist the dramatic effect, why should either metre or rhyme be such a hindrance to it?—Evans, John Amphlett, 1892, *Dryden and Ben Jonson*, *Temple Bar*, vol. 95, p. 107.

The tragedies are far more remarkable. He slipped almost at once into, and for many years persevered in, the famous "heroic" tragedy, from which, in 1678, he returned to blank verse, in the splendid though daring variation on "Antony and Cleopatra" called "All for Love;" while in it he later produced what is generally thought his dramatic masterpiece—the fine play of "Don Sebastian." But as a blank-verse dramatist Dryden has the drawback of coming into competition with his betters. We admire his work, but we do not love it; we are always thinking of another music, of a higher strain, as we read him. No one has since written in English a tragedy that will bear comparison with "All for Love" and "Don Sebastian." But when we turn from "Don Sebastian" and "All for Love" to "Hamlet" and "Othello" the result is reversed. In the "heroic" drama, on the other hand, Dryden is king, though the sceptre be too suggestive of pasteboard and the crown patched with, if not wholly composed of tinsel.—Saintsbury, George, 1895, *Social England*, ed. Traill, vol. IV, p. 434.

It cannot be said that Dryden was in any respect a dramatist of a high order. As a writer of comedy he was not only inferior to contemporaries and immediate successors like Wycherley, Congreve, Vanburgh and Farquhar, but in certain ways he was surpassed by Shadwell, the very man whom he himself has consigned to a disagreeable immortality as the hero of the "MacFlecknoe." His comedies are not merely full of obscenity,—which seems to have been a necessary ingredient to suit them to the taste of the age,—but they are full of a peculiar disagreeable obscenity.—Lounsbury, Thomas R., 1897, *Library of the World's Best Literature*, ed. Warner vol. IX, p. 4922.

THE WILD GALLANT
1662–69

Took coach and to Court, and there got good places, and saw "The Wilde Gallant," performed by the King's house, but it was ill acted, and the play so poor a thing as I never saw in my life almost, and so little answering the name, that from beginning to end, I could not, nor can at this time, tell certainly which was the Wild Gallant. The King did not seem pleased at all, the whole play, nor anybody else, though Mr. Clerke whom we met here did commend it to us.—Pepys, Samuel, 1662–63, *Diary*, *Feb.* 23.

His first piece was a comedy called the "Wild Gallant." He began with no happy auguries; for his performance was so much disapproved, that he was compelled to recall it, and change it from its imperfect state to the form in which it now appears, and which is yet sufficiently defective to vindicate the criticks.—Johnson, Samuel, 1779–81, *Dryden*, *Lives of the English Poets*.

In the under characters, some liveliness of dialogue is maintained; and the reader may be amused with particular scenes, though, as a whole, the early fate of the play was justly merited. These passages, in which the plot stands still, while the spectators are entertained with flippant dialogue and repartee, are ridiculed in the scene betwixt Prince Prettyman and Tom Thimble in the "Rehearsal;" the facetious Mr. Bibber being the original of the latter personage. . . . The whole piece seems to have been intended as a sacrifice to popular taste.—Scott, Sir Walter, 1808, ed., *The Works of John Dryden, by Saintsbury*, vol. II, p. 24.

Can by no possibility be called a good play.—Saintsbury, George, 1881, *Dryden (English Men of Letters)*, p. 42.

THE RIVAL LADIES
1664.

A very innocent and most pretty witty play.—PEPYS, SAMUEL, 1664, *Diary, Aug. 4.*

The ease with which the affections of almost every female in the drama are engrossed by Gonsalvo, and afterwards transferred to the lovers, upon whom the winding up of the plot made it necessary to devolve them, will, it is probable, strike every reader as unnatural. In truth, when the depraved appetite of the public requires to be gratified by trick and bustle, instead of nature and sentiment, authors must sacrifice the probable, as well as the simple process of events.—SCOTT, SIR WALTER, 1808, *ed., The Works of John Dryden, by Saintsbury, vol.* II, *p.* 127.

Is chiefly remarkable for containing some heroic scenes in rhyme, for imitating closely the tangled and improbable plot of its Spanish original, for being tolerably decent, and I fear it must be added, for being intolerably dull.—SAINTSBURY, GEORGE, 1881, *Dryden* (*English Men of Letters*), *p.* 42.

THE INDIAN EMPEROR
1667

After dinner with my Lord Bruncker and his mistress to the Knig's playhouse, and there saw "The Indian Emperour;" where I find Nell come again, which I am glad of; but was most infinitely displeased with her being put to act the Emperour's daughter; which is a great and serious part, which she doe most basely. The rest of the play, though pretty good, was not well acted by most of them, me thought; so that I took no great content in it.—PEPYS, SAMUEL, 1667, *Diary, Aug.* 22.

The "Indian Emperor" is the first of Dryden's plays which exhibited, in a marked degree, the peculiarity of his style, and drew upon him the attention of the world. Without equalling the extravagancies of the "Conquest of Granada," and the "Royal Martyr," works produced when our author was emboldened, by public applause, to give full scope to his daring genius, the following may be considered as a model of the heroic drama.—SCOTT, SIR WALTER, 1808-21, *ed., The Works of John Dryden, by Saintsbury, vol.* II, *p.* 317.

The chief attraction of the play doubtless consisted neither in the cleverness and spirit of particular passages in the dialogue, nor even in the effectiveness or strong sensationalism of particular situations, but in the uniformly pleasing flow of the versification, and in the supernatural business introduced. For us, however, the main interest of this production lies in the fact that the form of versification which Dryden desired to establish in the English serious drama was here for the first time fairly on its trial; and that, without proving throughout adequate to the demands imposed upon its new-fledged strength (see *e. g.* the important first scene of act IV), it achieved a success which on the whole cannot be described as other than brilliant, although it manifestly lacked the elements of permanence.—WARD, ADOLPHUS WILLIAM, 1875-99, *A History of English Dramatic Literature, vol.* III, *p.* 349.

A masterpiece in ornate and musical rhetoric.—COLLINS, JOHN CHURTON, 1878-95, *Dryden, Quarterly Review; Essays and Studies, p.* 25.

If the "Indian Emperor" could now be acted under the management of Mr. Imré Karalfy, we should probably be charmed with the sonorous splendour of its couplets and the gorgeous ritual of its scenes.—GOSSE, EDMUND, 1897, *Short History of Modern English Literature, p.* 179.

THE MAIDEN QUEEN
1668

After dinner, with my wife, to the King's house to see "The Maiden Queene," a new play of Dryden's, mightily commended for the regularity of it, and the strain and wit; and, the truth is, there is a comical part done by Nell, which is Florimell, that I never can hope ever to see the like done again, by man or woman. The King and the Duke of York were at the play. But so great performance of a comical part was never, I believe, in the world before as Nell do this, both as a mad girle, then most and best of all when she comes in like a young gallant; and hath the motions and carriage of a spark the most that ever I saw any man have. It makes me, I confess, admire her.—PEPYS, SAMUEL, 1666-67, *Diary, March* 2.

The serious portion though not devoid

of merit, has a blemish of which the author was well aware; but the chief merit of the play lies in the comic between the unstable Celadon and his mistress Florimel —who marry one another with their eyes perfectly open, though the lady was first courted as a "miss in a mask." If a licence in both situation and sentiment which it would not be ready to defend be frankly condoned, the fresh and enjoyable gaiety of these figures will be readily acknowledged; Florimel (to whose mirthful ways full justice was no doubt done by Nell Gwynn) is a lively and delightful type evidently drawn from real life.—WARD, ADOLPHUS WILLIAM, 1875–99, *A History of English Dramatic Literature, vol.* III.

SIR MARTIN MAR-ALL
1668

"Sir Martin Marr-all" was originally a mere translation from the French, made by William, Duke of Newcastle, and by him presented to Dryden, who revised and adapted it to the stage. . . . None of Dryden's pieces appear to have been more successful than this.—MALONE, EDMUND, 1800, *ed., Works of John Dryden.*

The merits of "Sir Martin Mar-All" (which was very successful) lie in the humour, novel as far as I know to the English drama, of the chief character.— WARD, ADOLPHUS WILLIAM, 1875–99, *A History of English Dramatic Literature.*

No one can deny its coarseness, but it is perhaps the most uniformly amusing of Dryden's comic plays, and the humour is by no means all borrowed.—SAINTSBURY, GEORGE, 1883, *ed., The Works of John Dryden, vol.* III, *p.* 2.

THE ENCHANTED ISLAND
1670

The storm, which vanished on the neighbouring shore,
Was taught by Shakespeare's Tempest first to roar.
That innocence and beauty, which did smile
In Fletcher, grew on this enchanted isle.
But Shakespeare's magic could not copied be;
Within that circle none durst walk but he.
I must confess 'twas bold, nor would you now
That liberty to vulgar wits allow,
Which works by magic supernatural things:
But Shakespeare's power is sacred as a king's.
Those legends from old priesthood were received,
And he then writ, as people then believed.
—DRYDEN, JOHN, 1669, *The Tempest; or The Enchanted Island, Prologue.*

Much has been said, and deservedly, in reprobation of the vile mixture which Dryden has thrown into the "Tempest;" doubtless without some such vicious alloy, the impure ears of that age would never have sate out to hear so much innocence of love as is contained in the sweet courtship of Ferdinand and Miranda.—LAMB, CHARLES, 1810, *On the Tragedies of Shakespear.*

In sketching characters drawn from fancy, and not from observation, the palm of genius must rest with the first inventor; others are but copyists, and a copy shows nowhere to such disadvantage as when placed by the original. Besides, although we are delighted with the feminine simplicity of Miranda, it becomes unmanly childishness in Hippolito; and the premature coquetry of Dorinda is disgusting, when contrasted with the maidenly purity that chastens the simplicity of Shakespeare's heroine. The latter seems to display, as it were by instinct, the innate dignity of her sex; the former, to show, even in solitude, the germ of those vices, by which, in a voluptuous age, the female character becomes degraded. The wild and savage character of Caliban is also sunk into low and vulgar buffoonery. Dryden has not informed us of the share he had in this alteration: It was probably little more than the care of adapting it to the stage. The prologue is one of the most masterly tributes ever paid at the shrine of Shakespeare.—SCOTT, SIR WALTER, 1808, *ed., The Works of John Dryden, by Saintsbury, vol.* III, *p.* 102.

His treatment of "The Tempest" shows that he wanted intelligence of highest passions and imagination. One powerful mind must have discernment of another; and he speaks best of Shakspeare when most generally. Then we might believe that he understood him in all the greatness of his might; but our belief cannot support itself among the many outrages offered by him to nature, in a blind or wanton desecration of her holiest revealments to her inspired priest. In the sense stated above, his transformation of "The Tempest," is an implicit criticism of "The Tempest." And, assuredly, there is no great rashness of theorizing in him who finds in this barbarous murder, evidence to a lack of apprehension in Dryden, for some part of the beauty which he swept away. It would be unjustifiable towards the man to believe that, for the lowest legitimate end of a playwright—money—or for the lower, because illegitimate end, the popular breath of a day amongst a public of a day—he voluntarily ruined one of the most delicate amongst the ɔeautiful creations with which the divine muse, his own patroness, had enlarged and adorned the bright world of mind—ruined it down to the depraved, the degraded, the debased, the groveling, the vulgar taste of a corrupt court and town. "The Inchanted Island" is a dolorous document ungainsayable, to the appreciation, in particulars, by that Dryden who could, in generals, laud Shakspeare so well—of that Shakspeare. And, if by Dryden, then by the age which he eminently led and for which he created, and for which he—destroyed.—WILSON, JOHN, 1845, *Dryden and Pope, Blackwood's Magazine.*

TYRANNICK LOVE
1670

But I am strangely mistaken if I have not seen this very *Almanzor* of yours in some disguise about this town, and passing under another name. Pr'ythee tell me true, was not this Huffcap once the *Indian Emperor?* and at another time did he not call himself *Maximin?* Was not *Lyndaraxa* once called *Almeira?* I mean under *Montezuma* the Indian Emperor. I protest and vow they are either the same, or so alike, that I cannot, for my heart, distinguish one from the other. You are therefore a strange unconscionable thief; thou are not content to steal from others, but dost rob thy poor wretched self too.—CLIFFORD, MARTIN, 1672-87, *Notes upon Mr. Dryden's Poems, First Letter.*

I remember some verses of my own, "Maximin and Almanzor," which cry vengeance upon me for their extravagance, and which I wish heartily in the same fire with Statius and Chapman.—DRYDEN, JOHN, 1681, *Spanish Friar, Dedication; Works, ed. Scott and Saintsbury, vol.* VI, *p.* 406.

The "Royal Martyr" is one of Dryden's most characteristic productions. The character of Maximin, in particular, is drawn on his boldest plan. . . . In the Prologue, he has boldly stated and justified his determination to rush forwards, and hazard the disgrace of a fall, rather than the loss of the race. Certainly a genius, which dared so greatly as that of Dryden, cannot always be expected to check its flight upon the verge of propriety; and we are often hurried along with it into extravagant and bombast, when we can seldom discover the error till a second reading of the passage. —SCOTT, SIR WALTER, 1808-21, *ed., The Works of John Dryden, by Saintsbury, vol.* III, *p.* 371.

A compound of exquisite beauties and absurdities of the most frantic description. The part of St. Catherine (very inappropriately allotted to Mrs. Eleanor Gwyn) is beautiful throughout, and that of Maximin is quite captivating in its outrageousness. The Astral spirits who appear gave occasion for some terrible parody in the "Rehearsal," but their verses are in themselves rather attractive.—SAINTSBURY, GEORGE, 1881, *Dryden (English Men of Letters), p.* 44.

AN EVENING'S LOVE
1671

Up and talked with my wife all in good humour, and so the office, where all the morning, and then home to dinner, and so she and I alone to the King's house, and there I saw this new play my wife saw yesterday, and do not like it, it being very smutty, and nothing so good as "The Maiden Queen," or "The Indian Emperour," of his making, that I was troubled at it; and my wife tells me wholly (which he confesses a little in the epilogue) taken out of the "Illustre Bassa."—PEPYS, SAMUEL, 1668, *Diary, June* 20.

The piece is specially noteworthy for the four charming songs it contains. They are of Dryden's best lyric stamp, but unluckily the "smuttiness," of which even Pepys complained, extends to them. —SAINTSBURY, GEORGE, 1883, *ed., The Works of John Dryden, vol.* III, *p.* 238.

THE CONQUEST OF GRANADA
1672

If, however, the reader can abstract his mind from the qualities now deemed essential to a play, and consider the "Conquest of Granada' as a piece of romantic poetry there are few compositions in the English language, which convey a more lively and favourable display of the magnificence of fable, of language, and of action, proper to that style of composition. Amid the splendid ornaments of the structure we lose sight of occasional disproportion and incongruity; and, at an early age particularly, there are few poems which make a more deep impression upon the imagination than the "Conquest of Granada."—SCOTT, SIR WALTER, 1808–21, *ed., The Works of John Dryden, by Saintsbury, vol.* IV, *p.* 6.

Has been generally, and justly, regarded as the most prominent type of the "heroic plays" of this age. . . . If a vast quantity of rant is requisite to give expression to the "over-boiling" courage of Almanzor, and if the conception of his pride and valour are alike hyper-Achillean so that altogether he was a fit model for the caricature of Drawcansir in "The Rehearsal"—yet many of the turns of diction are extraordinarily vigorous, and the force of the impetus which enables the author to sustain the character through ten acts is simply without parallel.—WARD, ADOLPHUS WILLIAM, 1875–99, *A History of English Dramatic Literature, vol.* III, *p.* 360.

MARRIAGE À LA MODE
1673

"Marriage-à-La-Mode" . . . is thoroughly amusing in its comic action, which, though occasionally as Melantha would say *risquée* to a considerable degree, is yet (as the author with some pride points out in the Epilogue) kept within certain bounds. The character of the "fair impertiment" Melantha herself, a fashionable lady and "one of those who run mad in new French words," is excellent; Congreve has hardly surpassed it; and we are already near to the height of the Restoration comedy of manners.—WARD, ADOLPHUS WILLIAM, 1875–99, *A History of English Dramatic Literature, vol.* III, *p.* 366.

It is Dryden's only original excursion into the realms of the higher comedy. For his favourite pair of lovers he here substitutes a quartette. Rhodophil and Doralice are a fashionable married pair, who, without having actually exhausted their mutual affection, are of opinion that their character is quite gone if they continue faithful to each other any longer.

Rhodophil accordingly lays siege to Melantha, a young lady who is intended though he does not know this, to marry his friend Palamede, while Palamede, deeply distressed at the idea of matrimony, devotes himself to Doralice. The cross purposes of this quartette are admirably related, and we are given to understand that no harm comes of it at all. But in Doralice and Melantha Dryden has given studies of womankind quite out of his usual line. Melantha is, of course, far below Millamant, but it is not certain that that delightful creation of Congreve's genius does not owe something to her. Doralice, on the other hand, has ideas as to the philosophy of flirtation which do her no little credit. It is a thousand pities that the play is written in the language of the time, which makes it impossible to revive and difficult to read without disgust.—SAINTSBURY, GEORGE, 1881, *Dryden (English Men of Letters), p.* 54.

THE ASSIGNATION
1673

An Author did to please you, let his Wit run
Of late, much on a Serving-man, *and* Cittern,
And yet you would not like the Serenade,
Nay, and you damn'd his Nuns *in* Masquerade.
You did his Spanish *Sing-song too abhor,*
Ah! que locura con tanto rigor.
In fine, the whole by you so much was blam'd,
To act their parts the Players *were asham'd;*
Ah! how severe your Malice was that Day;
To damn at once the Poet and his Play.
But why, was your Rage just at that time shown,
When what the Poet *writ, was all his own?*
Till then he borrow'd from Romance, and did translate,
And those Plays *found a more indulgent* Fate.
—RAVENSCROFT, EDWARD, 1673, *Careless Lovers, Prologue.*

Bayes. I remember once, in a play of mine, I set off a scene, i'gad, beyond expectation, only with a petticoat and the belly-ache.

Smith. Pray, how was that, sir?

Bayes. Why, sir, I contrived a petticoat to be brought in upon a chair (nobody knew how), into a prince's chamber, whose father was not to see it, that came in by chance.

Johns. God's-my-life, that was a notable contrivance indeed!

Smith. Ay, but, Mr. Bayes, how could you contrive the belly-ache?

Bayes. The easiest i'the world, i'gad: I'll tell you how; I made the prince sit down upon the petticoat, no more than so, and pretended to his father that he had just then got the belly-ache; whereupon his father went out to call a physician, and his man ran away with the petticoat.
—Villiers, George (Duke of Buckingham), 1673, *The Rehearsal.*

This play was unfortunate in the representation. It is needless, at the distance of more than a century, to investigate the grounds of the dislike of an audience, who, perhaps, could at the very time have given no good reason for their capricious condemnation of a play, not worse than many others which they received with applause. . . . The play certainly contains, in the present instance, nothing to justify them. In point of merit, "The Assignation" seems pretty much on a level with Dryden's other comedies; and certainly the spectators, who had received the blunders of Sir Martin Mar-all with such unbounded applause, might have taken some interest in those of poor Benito. Perhaps the absurd and vulgar scene, in which the prince pretends a fit of the colic, had some share in occasioning the fall of the piece.—Scott, Sir Walter, 1808–21, *ed. The Works of John Dryden, by Saintsbury, vol. IV, p. 366.*

"The Assignation," though written with great ease, and containing one rather humorous character (the bungling Benito) is a worthless play.—Ward, Adolphus William, 1875–99, *A History of English Dramatic Literature, vol. III, p. 366.*

It is vulgar, coarse, and dull; it was damned, and deserved it.—Saintsbury, George, 1881, *Dryden (English Men of Letters), p. 55.*

AMBOYNA
1673

This play is beneath criticism; and I can hardly hesitate to term it the worst production Dryden ever wrote.—Scott, Sir Walter, 1808–21, *ed. The Works of John Dryden, by Saintsbury, vol. V, p. 3.*

The play is the one production of Dryden which is utterly worthless except as a curiosity.—Saintsbury, George, 1883, *ed., The Works of John Dryden, vol. V, p. 3.*

THE STATE OF INNOCENCE
1674

I would embrace, but not with flatt'ry stain.
Something I would to your vast virtue raise,
But scorn to daub it with a fulsome praise;
That would but blot the work I would commend,
And show a court-admirer, not a friend.
To the dead bard your fame a little owes,
For Milton did the wealthy mind disclose,
And rudely cast what you could well dispose:
He roughly drew, on an old fashioned ground,
A chaos; for no perfect world was found,
Till through the heap your mighty genius shined:
He was the golden ore, which you refined.
He first beheld the beauteous rustic maid,
And to a place of strength the prize conveyed:
You took her thence; to court this virgin brought,
Drest her with gems, new weaved her hard-spun thought,
And softest language, sweetest manners taught;
Till from a comet she a star doth rise,
Not to affright, but please, our wondering eyes.
—Lee, Nathaniel, 1674, *To Mr. Dryden on his Poem of Paradise*

Altered as this poem was from the original, in order to accommodate it to the state of a frivolous age, it still retained too much fancy to escape the raillery of the men of wit and fashion, more disposed to "laugh at extravagance, than to sympathise with feelings of grandeur."— Scott, Sir Walter, 1808–21, *ed., The Works of John Dryden, by Saintsbury, vol. V, p. 98.*

Of the execution of this performance, I know not what to say, but that all who can estimate the greatness of Milton's images, the simplicity, the majesty, the richness of his language, the exquisite propriety of his thoughts, the fine ideal of his characters, Dryden's distorted reflection of it must appear very grotesque and ridiculous; in many parts puerile and weak; in all, losing sight of the exalted strains of poetry, and the noble conception of the original. That great creation of Milton's genius, the character of Satan, the angel of sorrow is sullied or lost. All his majestic lineaments disappear, the eye of pride, the lurid brow of woe, the greatness of his scorn, the conscious dignity of his demeanour, the feelings of one who had stood before the throne of light, (himself the morning star of heaven) all are destroyed; while only the impish cunning, the wicked, malignant, fiendish joy of the satyr and the demon is left. The simplicity of Eve is impaired, and even her purity and innocence stained; while the behaviour of Adam to his angel guest and his pertinacious arguments on the doctrines of liberty and necessity, which it took two angels, with the assistance of old Hobbes to answer, is in strong and humiliating contrast with the exquisite truth, the delicacy and propriety of Milton's picture.—MITFORD, JOHN, 1834, *ed., Poems of Dryden, Memoir, p. liii.*

How all this might take with a mixed audience, we do not presume to conjecture, yet very great absurdities do sometimes take almost as well on as off the stage. . . . Suppose Booth perfectly sober in Adam, and Nell Gwynne up merely to the proper pitch of vivacity in Eve, we do not see why the opera might not have had a run during the reign of the Merry Monarch. The first sight we have of Adam is, "as newly created, laid on a bed of moss and flowers, by a rock." He rises as he begins to utter his earliest soliloquy; and we believe it as an established rule not to turn your back on, or—in playhouse phrase—not to rump your audience. In such a case, however, considerable latitude would have been conceded by both sexes to our original; and what with shades and shrubs, and, above all, the rock, an adroit actor could have had little difficulty in accommodating to his posterity their progenitor. Of Eve our first glimpse is among "trees cut out on each side, with several fruits upon them; a fountain in the midst; at the far end the prospect terminating in walks." Nelly might have worn her famous felt chapeau, broad as a coachwheel, as appropriately in that as in any other character, and contrived to amble about with sufficient decorum for those fastidious times.—WILSON, JOHN, 1845, *Dryden and Pope, Blackwood's Magazine.*

The conception of such an opera has sometimes been derided as preposterous —a derision which seems to overlook the fact that Milton was himself, in some degree, indebted to an Italian dramatic original. The piece is not wholly in rhyme, but contains some very fine passages.—SAINTSBURY, GEORGE, 1881, *Dryden (English Men of Letters), p. 56.*

AURENGZEBE
1676

Dryden's last and most perfect tragedy in rhyme was "Aurengzebe." In this play, the passions are strongly depicted, the characters well discriminated, and the diction more familiar and dramatic, than in any of his preceding pieces. Hart and Mohun greatly distinguished themselves in the characters of Aurengzebe, and the old Emperor. Mrs. Marshall was admired in Nourmahul; and Kynaston has been much extolled, by Cibber, for his happy expression of the arrogant and savage fierceness in Morat. "Booth, in some part of this character," says the same critical historian, "was too tame, from an apprehension of raising the mirth of the audience improperly."—DAVIES, THOMAS, 1784, *Dramatic Micellanies, vol. III, p. 157.*

This tragedy is written in rhyme, and appears to have had great pains taken with it; parts of it are deservedly celebrated, but whatever are its beauties, its being conveyed through this vehicle is an unsurmountable objection to its keeping a place on the theatre, where otherwise it might perhaps have been deservedly a favourite. —DIBDIN, CHARLES, 1795, *A Complete History of the Stage, vol. IV, p. 169.*

It is perhaps the only one of Dryden's which, with very little alterations, might be acted, at least as a curiosity, at the present day.—SAINTSBURY, GEORGE, 1881, *Dryden (English Men of Letters), p. 57.*

ALL FOR LOVE
1678

It is by universal consent accounted the work in which he has admitted the fewest improprieties of style or character; but it has one fault equal to many, though rather moral than critical, that, by admitting the romantick omnipotence of Love, he has recommended, as laudable and worthy of imitation, that conduct which, through all ages, the good have censured as vicious, and the bad despised as foolish. —JOHNSON, SAMUEL, 1779–81, *Dryden, Lives of the English Poets.*

"Antony and Cleopatra," with instances abundant of those deprivations in the sense, construction, and meter, too often recurring throughout these works, is written in our author's best manner; and though Dryden has dilated and nobly refined some passages, the "All for Love" will, I believe, for interest, animation, and energy, be found far inferior to its original.—SEYMOUR, F. H., 1805, *Remarks on Shakspeare, vol.* II, *p.* 83.

"All for Love" was the author's favourite drama;—he said, he wrote it solely to please himself, and had succeeded in his design. Yet, were it not for the interest which attaches to the names of his hero and heroine, their characters are too feebly drawn to produce those emotions which an audience at a tragedy come prepared to feel. Who can be inattentive to the loves of Marc Antony and Cleopatra? Yet, thus described, their fate in representation seldom draws a tear, or gives rise to one transport of passion in the breast of the most observing auditor. The work is, nevertheless, highly valuable. It is one of the most interesting parts of Roman and Egyptian history; and the historian—Dryden.— INCHBALD, MRS. ELIZABETH, 1806-9, *ed. The British Theatre, All for Love, Remarks, vol.* VI.

Having given Dryden the praise of superior address in managing the story, I fear he must be pronounced in most other respects inferior to his grand prototype. Antony, the principal character in both plays, is incomparably grander in that of Shakespeare. The majesty and generosity of the military hero is happily expressed by both poets; but the awful ruin of grandeur, undermined by passion, and tottering to its fall, is far more striking in the Antony of Shakespeare. . . . In the Cleopatra of Dryden, there is greatly less spirit and originality than in Shakespeare's. The preparation of the latter for death has a grandeur which puts to shame the same scene in Dryden, and serves to support the interest during the whole fifth act, although Antony has died in the conclusion of the fourth. No circumstance can more highly evince the power of Shakespeare's genius, in spite of his irregularities; since the conclusion in Dryden, where both lovers die in the same scene, and after a reconciliation, is infinitely more artful, and better adapted to theatrical effect.—SCOTT, SIR WALTER, 1808-21, *ed., The Works of John Dryden, by Saintsbury, vol.* V, *pp.* 308, 310.

What a wretchedness, to reduce such events to a pastoral, to excuse Antony, to praise Charles II. indirectly, to bleat as in a sheepfold! And such was the taste of his contemporaries.—TAINE, H. A., 1871, *History of English Literature, tr. Van Laun, vol.* II, *bk.* iii, *ch.* ii, *p.* 17.

Dryden's complacency in the result is not wholly unjustified. In a sense, his tragedy is original; the character of Antony is drawn with considerable skill; the dominion which passion is capable of acquiring over a human being is, I think, exhibited quite as effectively as it is in Shakspere—but Dryden's Antony lacks elevation. His Cleopatra is comparatively uninteresting. The writing maintains a high level throughout; and the scene to which, as just noted, the author directs special attention is undoubtedly admirable. The construction of the play is close and effective; and its general tone is sufficiently moderated, without becoming open to the charge of tameness. Within certain limits, there assuredly never was a more flexible genius than Dryden's. The tasks which he set himself, without actually failing in their performance, are many and extraordinary; in the present instance he cannot be said to rival Shakspere on his own ground, and he follows him on it without making himself guilty of servile imitation or breaking down from lack of original force. "All for Love" has been not unjustly designated by an eminent critic as "Dryden's finest play."—WARD, ADOLPHUS WILLIAM, 1875-99, *A History of English Dramatic Literature, vol.* III, *p.* 372.

To compare "All for Love" with "Antony and Cleopatra" would be to compare works which, in all that pertains to the essence of poetry and tragedy, differ not in degree merely but in kind. And yet Dryden's tragedy, even from a dramatic point of view, is, with three or four exceptions, superior to anything produced by his contemporaries. If his Cleopatra is wretched, his Antony is powerfully sketched. The altercation between Antony and Ventidius, though modelled too closely on that between Brutus and Cassius in "Julius Cæsar," is a noble piece of dialectical rhetoric, while the scene between Cleopatra and Octavia is perhaps finer than anything which the stage had seen since Massinger.—COLLINS, JOHN CHURTON, 1878-95, *Dryden, Quarterly Review; Essays and Studies, p.* 36.

Dryden's "All for Love; or, The World

Well Lost," "written in imitation of Shakespeare's style" was its author's favourite production,—"the only play he wrote for himself;" its popularity was great; and the older critics were fond of praising its regularity and poetic harmony, though they generously recognised that it fell short of its first model in fire and originality (cf. Baker's "Bibliographia Dramatica"). It held the stage for a century, and has in all probability been acted ten times oftener than Shakespeare's "Antony and Cleopatra." Campbell evidenced this fact as a proof of England's neglect of Shakespeare, as a disgrace to British taste.—GOLLANCZ, ISRAEL, 1896, *ed. Temple Shakespeare, Preface to Antony and Cleopatra, p.* vii.

LIMBERHAM
1678

In this Play, (which I take to be the best Comedy of his) he so much expos'd the keeping part of the Town, that the Play was stopt, when it had but thrice appear'd on the Stage; but the Author took a becoming Care, that the things that offended him on the Stage were either alter'd or omitted in the Press.—LANGBAINE, GERARD, 1691, *An Account of the English Dramatick Poets, p.* 164.

The reader will probably easily excuse any remarks upon this comedy. It is not absolutely without humour, but is so disgustingly coarse, as entirely to destroy that merit.—SCOTT, SIR WALTER, 1808–21, *ed., The Works of John Dryden, by Saintsbury, vol.* VI, *p.* 2.

The outrageous comedy.—WARD, ADOLPHUS WILLIAM, 1875–99, *A History of English Dramatic Literature, vol.* III, *p.* 373.

There is little doubt that Langbaine is right in describing this play, from the merely dramatic point of view, as the best of Dryden's comedies. The action is well imagined and kept up; the scheme (setting aside a few of the commonplaces of such subjects) original; the dialogue lively; and the characters (especially Pleasance and Brainsick) well marked and life-like. The reason of its damnation is certainly mysterious. For, even supposing it to be a personal attack, of which there is no evidence whatever, the amusement of the majority would probably have overcome the resentment of the victim

and his friends. That the causes which would be sufficient to make its production impossible now should have had any force then is extremely unlikely, and one is driven to believe that the satire did actually touch a prevailing vice too closely to be borne. Of the offensiveness of the language and incidents, there is no need to say anything, except to remark that some of the coarsest language in the play is put in the mouth of Pleasance, the only virtuous character, who is represented as a young and pretty girl. This would not have shocked audiences at the time, but it is disgusting enough to modern ideas of decency.—SAINTSBURY, GEORGE, 1883, *ed., The Works of John Dryden, vol.* VI, *p.* 3.

ŒDIPUS
1679

The language of "Œdipus" is, in general, nervous, pure, and elegant; and the dialogue, though in so high a tone of passion, is natural and affecting. Some of Lee's extravagancies are lamentable exceptions to this observation. . . . These blemishes, however, are entitled to some indulgence from the reader, when they occur in a work of real genius. Those who do not strive at excellence will seldom fall into absurdity; as he who is contented to walk is little liable to stumble.—SCOTT, SIR WALTER, 1808–21, *ed., The Works of John Dryden, by Saintsbury, vol.* VI, *p.* 127.

This tragedy, which should be compared not only with Corneille's but also with Sophocles' and Seneca's treatment of the same theme, is constructed with no ordinary skill, as well written with undeniable power. How, then, is the fact to be explained that its horrors remain as intolerable to the reader, as on an attempted revival of the play they appear to have proved to the spectators?—WARD, ADOLPHUS WILLIAM, 1875–99, *A History of English Dramatic Literature, vol.* III, *p.* 373.

TROILUS AND CRESSIDA
1679

This Play was likewise first written by *Shakespear*, and revis'd by Mr. *Dryden*, to which he added several new Scenes, and even cultivated and improv'd what he borrow'd from the Original. The last Scene in the third Act is a Masterpiece, and whether it be copied from *Shakespear*,

Fletcher, or *Euripides*, or all of them, I think it justly deserves Commendation.— LANGBAINE, GERARD, 1691, *An Account of the English Dramatick Poets, p.* 173.

Mr. Godwin has justly remarked, that the delicacy of Chaucer's ancient tale has suffered even in the hands of Shakespeare; but in those of Dryden it has undergone a far deeper deterioration. Whatever is coarse and naked in Shakespeare, has been dilated into ribaldry by the poet laureate of Charles the Second; and the character of Pandarus, in particular, is so grossly heightened, as to disgrace even the obliging class to whom that unfortunate procurer has bequeathed his name. So far as this play is to be considered as an alteration of Shakespeare, I fear it must be allowed that our author has suppressed some of his finest poetry, and exaggerated some of his worst faults.—SCOTT, SIR WALTER, 1808–21, *ed., The Works of John Dryden, by Saintsbury, vol.* VI, *p.* 245.

THE SPANISH FRIAR

1681

One of the best and most popular of our poet's dramatic efforts. . . . The tragic part of "The Spanish Friar" has uncommon merit. The opening of the drama, and the picture of a besieged town in the last extremity, is deeply impressive, while the description of the noise of the night attack, and the gradual manner in which the intelligence of its success is communicated, arrests the attention, and prepares expectation for the appearance of the hero, with all the splendour which ought to attend the principal character in tragedy.—SCOTT, SIR WALTER, 1808–21, *ed., The Works of John Dryden, by Saintsbury, vol.* VI, *pp.* 395, 398.

Beyond question the most skilfully con structed of all Dryden's plays.—COLLINS, JOHN CHURTON, 1878–95, *Dryden, Quar terly Review; Essays and Studies, p.* 42.

A popular piece, possessed of a good deal of merit, from the technical point of view of the play-wright, but which I think has been somewhat over-rated, as far as literary excellence is concerned. The principal character is no doubt amusing, but he is heavily indebted to Falstaff on the one hand, and to Fletcher's Lopez on the other; and he reminds the reader of both his ancestors in a way which cannot

but be unfavourable to himself. The play is to me most interesting because of the light it throws on Dryden's grand characteristic, the consummate craftsmanship with which he could throw himself into the popular feeling of the hour. This "Protestant play" is perhaps his most notable achievement of the kind in drama, and it may be admitted that some other achievements of the same kind are less creditable.—SAINTSBURY, GEORGE, 1881, *Dryden (English Men of Letters), p.* 60.

THE DUKE OF GUISE

1683

Our author's part of "The Duke of Guise" is important, though not of great extent, as his scenes contain some of the most striking political sketches. The debate of the Council of Sixteen, with which the play opens, was his composition; the whole of the fourth act, which makes him responsible for the alleged parallel betwixt Guise and Monmouth, and the ridicule cast upon the sheriffs and citizens of the popular party, with the first part of the fifth, which implicates him in vindicating the assassination of Guise.—SCOTT, SIR WALTER, 1808–21, *ed., The Works of John Dryden, by Saintsbury, vol.* VII, *p.* 7.

This play is not distinguished for any high strain of poetic feeling, for the loftier flights of genius, or for any elaborate display of dramatic skill. Much of the descriptions and sentiments is taken closely from Davila, and the strong picturesque language of the historian is without difficulty raised into elegant and harmonious verse. In the character of Marmoutiere, an allusion to the Duchess of Buccleuch and Monmouth is probably intended. The story of Malecorn is said to be taken from Rossett's Hist. Tragiques, and one or two striking passages from Pulci. Sir Walter Scott thinks that the last scene between the fiend and the necromance horrribly fine; but I do not feel certain that the parting speech of Malecorn would be considered natural; surely in his situation an agony of terror would overwhelm all reflection and stifle all argument. This part of the play failed in the representation; indeed the whole encountered a stormy, if not an unfavorable reception. Its poetry was but the vehicle for political sentiments; but as the court party increased in strength, its success became more assured.—MIT-FORD, JOHN, 1834, *ed., Poems of Dryden, Memoir.*

ALBION AND ALBANIUS
1685

The reader finds none of these harsh inversions, and awkward constructions, by which ordinary poets are obliged to screw their verses into the fetters of musical time. Notwithstanding the obstacles stated by Dryden himself, every line seems to flow in its natural and most simple order; and where the music required repetition of a line, or a word, the iteration seems to improve the sense and poetical effect. Neither is the piece deficient in the higher requisites of lyric poetry. —SCOTT, SIR WALTER, 1808–21, *ed., The Works of John Dryden, by Saintsbury, vol.* VII, *p.* 224.

DON SEBASTIAN
1690

Is commonly esteemed either the first or second of his dramatick performances. It is too long to be all acted, and has many characters and many incidents; and though it is not without sallies of frantick dignity, and more noise than meaning, yet as it makes approaches to the possibilities of real life, and has some sentiments which leave a strong impression, it continued long to attract attention. Amidst the distresses of princes, and the vicissitudes of empire, are inserted several scenes which the writer intended for comick; but which, I suppose, that age did not much commend, and this would not endure. There are, however, passages of excellence universally acknowledged; the dispute and the reconciliation of Dorax and Sebastian has always been admired. —JOHNSON, SAMUEL, 1779–81, *Dryden, Lives of the English Poets.*

In the poet's very best manner; exhibiting dramatic persons, consisting of such bold and impetuous characters as he delighted to draw, well contrasted, forcibly marked, and engaged in an interesting succession of events.—SCOTT, SIR WALTER, 1808–21, *Life of Dryden, ed. Saintsbury, p.* 407.

Dorax is indeed the *chef-d'œuvre* of Dryden's tragic characters, and perhaps the only one, in which he has applied his great knowledge of human kind to actual delineation. It is highly dramatic, because formed of those complex feelings, which may readily lead either to virtue or vice, and which the poet can manage, so as to surprise the spectator, without transgressing consistency. The Zanga of Young, a part of great theatrical effect, has been compounded of this character and of that of Iago. But "Don Sebastian" is as imperfect as all plays must be, in which a single personage is thrown forward in too strong relief for the rest. The language is full of that rant which characterized Dryden's earlier tragedies, and to which a natural predilection seems, after some interval, to have brought him back.—HALLAM, HENRY, 1808, *Scott's Edition of Dryden, Edinburgh Review, vol.* 13, *p.* 125.

In general, the style of this tragedy, notwithstanding an ingredient of rant in its earlier part, is strong as well as attractive; and in the serious portions of the action Dryden repeatedly rises to an unusual height of dramatic effect.—WARD, ADOLPHUS WILLIAM, 1875–99, *A History of English Dramatic Literature, vol.* III, *p.* 383.

If we except Otway's two tragedies, "Don Sebastian" is beyond comparison the finest tragedy the English stage had seen since Fletcher had passed away. The celebrated scene in the fourth act between Dorax and Sebastian is one of the gems of the English drama.—COLLINS, JOHN CHURTON, 1878–95, *Dryden, Quarterly Review; Essays and Studies, p.* 66.

AMPHITRYON
1690

The modern poets have treated the subject, which they had from Plautus, each according to the fashion of his country; and so far did the correctness of the French stage exceed ours at that period, that the palm of the comic writing must be, at once, awarded to Molière. . . . Yet although inferior to Molière, and accommodated to the gross taste of the seventeenth century, "Amphitryon" is one of the happiest effusions of Dryden's comic muse. He has enriched the plot by the intrigue of Mercury and Phædra; and the petulant interested "Queen of Gipsies," as her lover terms her, is no bad paramour for the God of Thieves.— SCOTT, SIR WALTER, 1808–21, *ed., The Works of John Dryden, by Saintsbury, vol.* VIII, *p.* 2.

The flame of his genius—though fed by impure materials—once more bursts forth with splended brightness. . . . The writing must be acknowledged to be admirable, and in parts nothing less than magnificent.—WARD, ADOLPHUS WILLIAM, 1875–99, *A History of English Dramatic Literature, vol.* III, *p.* 384.

"Amphitryon," which some critics have treated most mistakenly as a mere translation of Molière. The truth is, that the three plays of Plautus, Molière, and Dryden are remarkable examples of the power which great writers have treading in each other's steps without servile imitation. In a certain dry humor Dryden's play is inferior to Plautus, but, as compared with Molière, it has two features which are decided improvements—the introduction of the character of Judge Gripus, and the separation of the part of the Soubrette into two.—SAINTSBURY, GEORGE, 1881, *Dryden* (*English Men of Letters*), *p.* 115.

KING ARTHUR
1691

I went to "King Arthur" on Saturday, and was tired to death, both of the nonsense of the piece and the execrable performance, the singers being still worse than the actors.—WALPOLE, HORACE, 1770, *Letters, ed.* Cunningham, *Dec.* 25.

Of the music in "King Arthur" I shall say but little, as it has been lately revived, well performed, and printed. If ever it could, with truth, be said of a composer that he had *devancé son siecle*, Purcell is entitled to that praise; as there are movements in many of his works which a century has not injured, particularly the duet in "King Arthur," "Two Daughters of this aged stream," and "Fairest isles all Isles excelling," which contain not a single passage that the best composers of the present times, if it presented itself to their imagination, would reject.—BURNEY, CHARLES, 1776–89, *A General History of Music, vol.* III, *p.* 492.

 . . . Dryden, in immortal strain,
Had raised the Table Round again,
But that a ribald King and Court
Bade him toil on, to make them sport; . . .
The world defrauded of the high design,
Profaned the God-given strength, and marred the lofty line.

—SCOTT, SIR WALTER, 1808, *Marmion, Introduction to Canto* i.

The main interest of the piece, such as it is, turns on the rival passions of Arthur and the heathen King of Kent for the blind Emmeline. Her blindness is treated with a mixture of naïveté and something quite the reverse; and this attempt in a direction in which few dramatists have ventured with success, is only noteworthy as a proof that no art in the poet—or, it may be added, in the actor—can render tolerable on the stage the analysis of a physical infirmity. This particular infirmity may indeed occasionally be represented with great and legitimate effect; but an endeavour to analyse it appertains to a sphere different from that of the drama.—WARD, ADOLPHUS WILLIAM, 1875–99, *A History of English Dramatic Literature, vol.* III, *p.* 382.

LOVE TRIUMPHANT
1694

Supp'd at Mr. Edw[d] Sheldon's, where was Mr. Dryden the poet, who now intended to write no more plays, being intent on his translation of "Virgil." He read to us his prologue and epilogue to his valedictory play now shortly to be acted.—EVELYN, JOHN, 1693–4, *Diary, Jan.* 11.

This piece, which concluded our author's labours as a dramatic poet, was unsuccessful when represented, and affords very little pleasure when perused. If we except "Amboyna," our author never produced a play where the tragic part had less interest, or the comic less humour. . . . It is impossible to dismiss the performance of Dryden without some tribute of praise. The verse, where it is employed, possesses, as usual, all the dignity which numbers can give to language; and the Song upon Jealousy, as well as that in the character of a Girl, have superior merit.—SCOTT, SIR WALTER, 1808–21, *ed., The Works of John Dryden, by* Saintsbury, *vol.* VIII, *pp.* 367, 369.

It is only in his last play, the tragicomedy of "Love Triumphant," that we are forced to admit that the natural force of the playwright is wholly abated.—GOSSE, EDMUND, 1888, *A History of Eighteenth Century Literature, p.* 45.

HEROIC STANZAS
1659

That these stanzas should have made him a name as a poet does not appear surprising when we compare them with Waller's verses on the same occasion. Dryden took some time to consider them, and was impossible that they should not give an impression of his intellectual strength. Donne was his model; it is obvious that both his ear and his imagination were saturated with Donne's elegiac strains when he wrote; yet when we look beneath the surface, we find unmistakable traces that the pupil was not without decided theories that ran counter to the practice of the master. It is plainly not by accident that each stanza contains one clear-cut brilliant point. The poem is an academic exercise, and it seems to be animated by an under-current of strong contumacious protest against the irregularities tolerated by the authorities.—MINTO, WILLIAM, 1877, *Encyclopædia Britannica, Ninth edition, vol.* VII.

There were not three poets then living who could have written the best lines of the "Heroic Stanzas," and what is more, those lines were not in the particular manner of either of the poets who, as far as general poetical merit goes, might have written them.—SAINTSBURY, GEORGE, 1881, *Dryden (English Men of Letters)*, p. 28.

ASTRÆA REDUX

1662

Is well versified; the lines are seldom weak; the couplets have that pointed manner which Cowley and Denham had taught the world to require; they are harmonious, but not so varied as the style he afterwards adopted.—HALLAM, HENRY, 1837–39, *Introduction to the Literature of Europe, pt.* iv, *ch.* v, *par.* 38.

ANNUS MIRABILIS

1667

I am very well pleased this night with reading a poem I brought home with me last night from Westminster Hall, of Dryden's upon the present war; a very good poem.—PEPYS, SAMUEL, 1666–67, *Diary, Feb.* 2.

This poem is written with great diligence, yet does not fully answer the expectation raised by such subjects and such a writer. With the stanza of Davenant he has sometimes his vein of parenthesis, and incidental disquisition, and stops his narrative for a wise remark. The general fault is, that he affords more sentiment than description, and does not so much impress scenes upon the fancy, as deduce consequences and make comparisons.—JOHNSON, SAMUEL, 1779–81, *Dryden, Lives of the English Poets.*

Dryden fails in the power of elegant expression, till he ventures upon something which it is impossible to express. The love of conceit and point, that inveterate though decaying disease of the literature of the time, has not failed to infect the "Annus Mirabilis."—SCOTT, SIR WALTER, 1808–21, *The Works of John Dryden, by Saintsbury, vol.* IX, *p.* 83.

The "Annus Mirabilis" is a tedious performance; it is a tissue of far-fetched, heavy, lumbering conceits, and in the worst style of what has been denominated metaphysical poetry.—HAZLITT, WILLIAM, 1818, *Lectures on the English Poets, p.* 96.

The "Annus Mirabilis" shows great command of expression, and a fine ear for heroic rhyme. Here its merits end. Not only has it no claim to be called poetry; but it seems to be the work of a man who could never, by any possibility, write poetry. Its affected similes are the best part of it. Gaudy weeds present a more encouraging spectacle than utter barrenness. There is scarcely a single stanza in this long work, to which the imagination seems to have contributed any thing. It is produced, not by creation, but by construction. It is made up, not of pictures, but of inferences.—MACAULAY, THOMAS BABINGTON, 1828, *Dryden, Edinburgh Review, Critical and Miscellaneous Essays.*

A very good poem, in some sort, it continues to be, in spite of its amazing blemishes.—LOWELL, JAMES RUSSELL, 1868–90, *Dryden, Prose Works, Riverside ed., vol.* III, *p.* 134.

Both in its merits and in its defects it bears a close resemblance to the "Pharsalia" of Lucan. It is enriched with some fine touches of natural description, and, if the moonlight night at sea and the simile of the bees were borrowed from Virgil, the pictures of the dying hare, of the baffled falcon, of the herded beasts lying on the dewy grass, and of the moon "blunting its crescent on the edge of day," show that Dryden had the eye of an artist as he wandered about the park at Charlton. The work is disfigured with many "metaphysical" extravagances, but the King's prayer, as well as the concluding stanzas, must rank among the most majestic passages in English rhetorical poetry. —COLLINS, JOHN CHURTON, 1878–95, *Dryden, Quarterly Review; Essays and Studies, p.* 29.

The fire and spirit of "Annus Mirabilis" are nothing short of amazing, when the difficulties which beset the author (though partly by his own choosing) are remembered. There was, first, the difficulty of his subject, which, as a perusal of the poem cannot fail to reveal the most unsuspecting reader, was by no means made up altogether of materials for congratulation. Yet the "Annus Mirabilis" must really have "done good" to the public; even at the present day it agreeably warms the John Bull sentiment, compounded of patriotism and prejudice, in the corner of an Englishman's heart.— WARD, ADOLPHUS WILLIAM, 1880, *English Poets, ed. Ward, vol.* II, *p.* 440.

Dryden's poem is distinguished by masterly execution and dignity of style, but it has been justly pointed out that the subject lacks variety. Indeed, the feeling with which we read it is not wholly that of pleasure; but some admiration must be given to the viguor of the writer and to his skilful manipulation of a difficult stanza. A curious feature of the poem is the pious prayer which Charles is made to offer up for his afflicted subjects, and the answer it received.—DENNIS, JOHN, 1883, *Heroes of Literature, p.* 161.

There are good lines here and there,— flashes of genius to lighten the way for one who will plod doggedly through. Few read it once; none read it a second time. —WATROUS, GEORGE A., 1898, *ed., Selections from Dryden, Burns, Wordsworth, and Browning, Introduction, p.* 3.

RELIGIO LAICI
1682

Is almost the only work of Dryden which can be considered as a voluntary effusion; in this, therefore, it might be hoped, that the full effulgence of his genius would be found. But unhappily the subject is rather argumentative than poetical; he intended only a specimen of metrical disputation:

And this unpolish'd rugged verse I chose,
As fittest for discourse, and nearest prose.

This, however, is a composition of great excellence in its kind, in which the familiar is very improperly diversified with the solemn, and the grave with the humorous; in which metre has neither weakened the force, nor clouded the perspicuity of argument; nor will it be easy to find another example equally happy in this middle kind of writing, which, though prosaick in some parts, rises to high poetry in others, and neither towers to the skies, nor creeps along the ground.—JOHNSON, SAMUEL, 1779–81, *Dryden, Lives of the English Poets.*

Took a walk, with Wordsworth, under Loughrigg. His conversation has been remarkably agreeable. To-day he talked of Poetry. He held Pope to be a greater poet than Dryden; but Dryden to have most talent, and the strongest understanding. Landor once said to me: "Nothing was ever written in hymn equal to the beginning of Dryden's 'Religio Laici,'—the first eleven lines."—ROBINSON, HENRY CRABB, 1842, *Diary, Jan.* 6.

If in point of style the "Religio Laici" has none of that lightness of touch, and none of that felicitous grace, which throw such charm over the "Epistles" of Horace, on which it was, he says, modelled, it may, short though it be, challenge comparison with any didactic writing in verse since Lucretius vindicated the tenets of Epicurus. The opening verses of this poem are among the most majestic passages in our poetry.—COLLINS, JOHN CHURTON, 1878–95, *Dryden, Quarterly Review; Essays and Studies, p.* 51.

In one respect this takes the highest place among the works of Dryden, for it is the most perfect example he has given of that reasoning in rhyme of which he was so great a master. There is not and could not be any originality in the reasonings themselves, but Pope's famous couplet was never so finely illustrated, except by Pope himself:

"True wit is nature to advantage drest;
What oft was thought, but ne'er so well exprest."

At the same time the poetry hardly rises to the height which the theme might have justified. There is little to captivate or astonish, but perpetual admiration attends upon the masterly conduct of the argument, and the ease with which dry and difficult propositions melt and glide in harmonious verse. — GARNETT, RICHARD, 1895, *The Age of Dryden, p.* 27.

THRENODIA AUGUSTALIS
1685

The pindaric measure, in which the "Threnodia Augustalis" is written, contains nothing pleasing to modern ears. The rhymes are occasionally so far disjoined, that, like a fashionable married couple, they have nothing of union but the name. The inequalities of the verse are also violent, and remind us of ascending a broken and unequal staircase. But the age had been accustomed to this rhythm, which, however improperly, was considered as a genuine imitation of the style of Pindar. It must also be owned that, wherever, for a little way, Dryden uses a more regular measure, he displays all his usual command of harmony.— SCOTT, SIR WALTER, 1808–21, ed., The Works of John Dryden, by Saintsbury, vol. x, p. 61.

Nothing which Dryden wrote with deliberation in his mature years could be wholly worthless, but it would be difficult to name another of his poems which contains fewer beauties, more prolixity, less merit. It is perhaps the best example to be found in our poetry of what the Greeks called parenthyrsus. — COLLINS, JOHN CHURTON, 1878–95, Dryden, Quarterly Review; Essays and Studies, p. 55.

Even the most willing and the most fluent muse must rapidly exhaust such a theme as the virtues of King Charles II., and in his "Threnodia Augustalis," written on the King's death, Dryden found little to add to what he had sung in the "Astræa Redux," composed in honour of the Restoration,—except that his Majesty died hard.—WARD, ADOLPHUS WILLIAM, 1880, English Poets, ed. Ward, vol. II, p. 439.

His "Threnodia Augustalis," or funeral poem on Charles the Second, may be taken as the chief official production of his laureateship. The difficulties of such performances are well known, and the reproaches brought against their faults are pretty well stereotyped. "Threnodia Augustalis" is not exempt from the faults of its kind; but it has merits which for that kind are decidedly unusual. The stanza which so adroitly at once praises and satirizes Charles's patronage of literary men is perhaps the best, and certainly the best known; but the termination is also fine. —SAINTSBURY, GEORGE, 1881, Dryden (English Men of Letters), p. 94.

THE HIND AND THE PANTHER
1687

If he did it well or handsomely, he might deserve some pardon; but alas! how ridiculously doth he appear in print for any religion, who hath made it his business to laugh at all! How can he stand up for any mode of worship, who hath been accustomed to bite, and spit his venom against the very name thereof?— BROWN, TOM, 1687, Four Letters.

Mr. Wynne has sent me "The Hind and the Panther," by which I find John Dryden has a noble ambition to restore poetry to its ancient dignity in wrapping up the mysteries of religion in verse. What a shame it is to me to see him a saint, and remain still the same devil (myself).—ETHEREDGE, SIR GEORGE, 1687, The Letter-book. Gosse, Seventeenth-Century Studies, p. 263.

As if by being Laureat, he were as Infallible as St. Peter's Successor; and had as large a Despotick Power as Pope Stephanus the Sixth to damn his Predecessors; he has assaulted with all the Bitterness imaginable not only the Church of England, but also ridicul'd the several Professions of the Lutherans, Calvinists, Socinians, Presbyterians, Hugonots, Anabaptists, Independents, Quakers, &c., tho' I must observe by the way, that some people among the Perswasions here mention'd might justly have expected better usage from him on Account of old Acquaintance in the Year 1659.—LANGBAINE, GERARD, 1691, An Account of the English Dramatick Poets, p. 139.

The verse in which these doctrines, polemical and political, are delivered, is among the finest specimens of the English heroic stanza. The introductory verses, in particular, are lofty and dignified in the highest degree: as are those in which the splendour and majesty of the Church of Rome are set forth, in all the glowing colours of rich imagery and magnificent language. But the same praise extends to the versification of the whole poem. It never falls, never becomes rugged; rises with the dignified strain of the poetry; sinks into quaint familiarity, where sarcasm and humour are employed; and winds through all the mazes of theological argument without becoming either obscure or prosaic.—SCOTT, SIR WALTER, 1808–21, ed., Works of Dryden, vol. x, p. 101.

Is every way an extraordinary poem. . . . The first lines in the "Hind and Panther" are justly reputed among the most musical in our language; and perhaps we observe their rhythm the better because it does not gain much by the sense. . . . The wit in the "Hind and Panther" is sharp, ready, and pleasant; the reasoning is sometimes admirably close and strong; it is the energy of Bossuet in verse. I do not know that the main argument of the Roman Church could be better stated; all that has been well said for tradition and authority, all that serves to expose the inconsistencies of a vacillating Protestantism, is in the Hind's mouth.—HALLAM, HENRY, 1837–39, *Introduction to the Literature of Europe, pt.* iv, *ch.* v, *par.* 41, 42, 43.

Criticism of this kind, involving, as it does, inquiry into the heart and the conscience, is always attended with a measure of uncertainty. But it appears to me that Dryden's subsequent career attests the sincerity of his change of faith. The internal evidence of "The Hind and Panther" cannot be disregarded. "The Hind and Panther" is the work of an honest Roman Catholic. Whatever might have been the original and exciting cause of the change, there can be no doubt that, while engaged in the composition of that remarkable poem, the writer earnestly believed that he had done his duty. He educated his younger sons in the Catholic faith: spite of solicitation, spite of menace, he never wavered in his allegiance. He had made his choice, and he did not flinch. He was true to his religion and to his king.—SKELTON, JOHN, 1865–83, *John Dryden, Fraser's Magazine; Essays in History and Biography, p.* 150.

Dryden's conversion to Romanism has been commonly taken for granted as insincere, and has therefore left an abiding stain on his character, though the other mud thrown at him by angry opponents or rivals brushed off so soon as it was dry. But I think his change of faith susceptible of several explanations, none of them in any way discreditable to him. Where Church and State are habitually associated, it is natural that minds even of a high order should unconsciously come to regard religion as only a subtler mode of police. Dryden, conservative by nature, had discovered before Joseph de Maistre, that Protestantism, so long as it justified its name by continuing to be an active principle, was the abettor of Republicanism, perhaps the vanguard of Anarchy. I think this is hinted in more than one passage in his preface to "The Hind and Panther." He may very well have preferred Romanism because of its elder claim to authority in all matters of doctrine, but I think he had a deeper reason in the constitution of his own mind. That he was "naturally inclined to scepticism in philosophy," he tells us of himself in the preface to the "Religio Laici;" but he was a sceptic with an imaginative side, and in such characters scepticism and superstition play into each other's hands. . . . Have we forgotten Montaigne's votive offerings at the shrine of Loreto?—LOWELL, JAMES RUSSELL, 1868–90, *Dryden, Prose Works, Riverside ed., vol.* III, *pp.* 186, 187.

The plot is singular, and in the highest degree absurd, but it contains passages of as rich imagery and fancy as, perhaps, any other of his works.—YONGE, CHARLES DUKE, 1882, *ed. Essays of John Dryden, Introduction, p.* xii.

The production of its entirety is remarkable for the skill which its author displayed in carrying on an argument in verse. In this he certainly had no superior among poets, perhaps no equal.—LOUNSBURY, THOMAS R., 1897, *Library of the World's Best Literature, ed. Warner, vol.* IX, *p.* 4929.

BRITANNIA REDIVIVA
1688

The luckless "Britannia Rediviva" written on the birth of the most ill-starred of all princes of Wales, born in the purple. It is in couplets, and as no work of Dryden's written at this time could be worthless, it contains some vigorous verse, but on the whole it is by far the worst of his serious poems; and it was no misfortune for his fame that the Revolution left it out of print for the rest of the author's life.—SAINTSBURY, GEORGE, 1881, *Dryden (English Men of Letters), p.* 98.

ALEXANDER'S FEAST
1697

I am writing a song for St. Cecilia's feast, who, you know, is the patroness of music. This is troublesome, and no way beneficial; but I could not deny the stewards, who came in a body to my house to desire that kindness, one of them being Mr. Bridgeman, whose parents are your mother's friends.—DRYDEN, JOHN, 1697, *Letter to his Son.*

This ode has been more applauded, perhaps, than it has been felt; however, it is a very fine one, and gives its beauties rather at a third or fourth than at a first perusal.—GOLDSMITH, OLIVER, 1767, *The Beauties of English Poetry.*

One composition must however be distinguished. The ode to "St. Cecilia's Day," perhaps the last effort of his poetry, has been always considered as exhibiting the highest flight of fancy, and the exactest nicety of art. This is allowed to stand without a rival. If indeed there is any excellence beyond it in some other of Dryden's works, that excellence must be found.—JOHNSON, SAMUEL, 1779–81, *Dryden, Lives of the English Poets.*

Dryden's wonderful ode; which is of itself worth all that Pindar has written, as a large diamond is worth a vast heap of gold, because that master-piece is a dithyrambic poem, not a lyric one. And that as well for its want of regularity, as for its subject, which, being perfectly convivial as its title speaks, falls with much propriety into that class which the ancients called dithyrambic, and which were most commonly sacred to Bacchus.—PINKERTON, JOHN (ROBERT HERON), 1785, *Letters of Literature, p. 34.*

The language, lofty and striking as the ideas are, is equally simple and harmonious; without far-fetched allusions, or epithets, or metaphors, the story is told as intelligibly as if it had been in the most humble prose.—SCOTT, SIR WALTER, 1808–21, *Life of John Dryden, ed. Saintsbury, vol. I, p. 409.*

Dryden's "Alexander's Feast" is a magnificent composition, and has high poetical beauties; but to a refined judgment there is something intrinsically unpoetical in the end to which it is devoted, the praises of revel and sensuality. It corresponds to a process of clever reasoning erected on an untrue foundation—the one is a fallacy, the other is out of taste.—NEWMAN, JOHN HENRY, 1829–71, *Poetry, with reference to Aristotle's Poetics; Essays Critical and Historical, vol. I, p. 22.*

Dryden's "Alexander's Feast" is undoubtedly the lyric master-piece of English poetry, in respect to versification; exemplifying as it does, all the capabilities of our language in the use of iambics, trochees, anapæsts, dactyls, and spondees.—MONTGOMERY, JAMES, 1833, *Lectures on General Literature, Poetry, etc., p. 175.*

A masterpiece of rapture and of art, which Victor Hugo alone has come up to.—TAINE, H. A., 1871, *History of English Literature, tr. Van Laun, vol. II, bk. iii, ch. ii, p. 42.*

His best lyric composition, "Alexander's Feast" was once thought the finest thing of the kind in English literature, but time has been gradually, and surely and justly, diminishing its reputation. — WHITE, RICHARD GRANT, 1897, *English Literature, rev. Beers, Johnson's Universal Cyclopædia, vol. III, p. 130.*

VIRGIL
1697

I am informed Mr. Dryden is now translating of Virgil; and although I must own it is a fault to forestall or anticipate the praise of a man in his labours, yet, big with the greatness of the work, and the vast capacity of the author, I cannot here forbear saying, that Mr. Dryden, in the translating of Virgil, will of a certain make Maro speak better than ever Maro thought.—HOWARD, EDWARD, 1695, *Essay on Pastoral, and Elegy on Queen Mary, Poem.*

The Works of Virgil; containing his Pastorals, Georgics, and Eneis, translated into English verse, by Mr. Dryden, and adorned with one hundred cuts, will be finished this week, and be ready next week to be delivered, as subscribed for, in quires, upon bringing the receipt for the first payment, and paying the second. Printed for Jacob Tonson, etc.—TONSON, JACOB, 1697, *London Gazette, June 28th, Advertisement.*

Dryden, in a long harangue, soothed up the good ancient; called him father, and, by a large deduction of genealogies, made it plainly appear that they were nearly related. Then he humbly proposed an exchange of armour, as a lasting mark of hospitality between them. Virgil consented, (for the goddess Diffidence came unseen, and cast a mist before his eyes,) though his was of gold, and cost a hundred beeves, the other's but of rusty iron. However, this glittering armour became the modern yet worse than his own. Then they agreed to exchange horses; but, when it came to the trial, Dryden was afraid, and utterly unable to mount.—SWIFT, JONATHAN, 1704, *Battle of the Books.*

Had he translated the whole work, I would no more have attempted Homer after him than Virgil: his version of whom (notwithstanding some human errors) is the most noble and spirited translation I know in any language.—POPE, ALEXANDER, 1715, *Homer's Iliad, Preface.*

His Virgil abounds in lines and couplets of the most perfect beauty; but these are mixed with others of a different stamp: nor can they who judge of the original by this translation, ever receive any tolerable idea of that uniform magnificence of sound and language, that exquisite choice of words and figures, and that sweet pathos of expression and of sentiment, which characterise the Mauntan Poet.—BEATTIE, JAMES, 1776-9, *Essays on Poetry and Music, p.* 16, *note.*

That his cannot be the language of imagination, must have necessarily followed from this,—that there is not a single image from nature in the whole body of his works; and in his translation from Virgil, wherever Virgil can be fairly said to have his *eye* upon his object, Dryden always spoils the passage.—WORDSWORTH, WILLIAM, 1805, *Letter to Scott, Scott's Life, ed. Lockhart, vol.* I, *p.* 218.

He who sits down to Dryden's translation of Virgil, with the original text spread before him, will be at no loss to point out many passages that are faulty, many indifferently understood, many imperfectly translated, some in which dignity is lost, others in which bombast is substituted in its stead. But the unabated vigour and spirit of the version more than overbalance these and all its other deficiencies. A sedulous scholar might often approach more nearly to the dead letter of Virgil, and give an exact, distinct, sober-minded idea of the meaning and scope of particular passages.—SCOTT, SIR WALTER, 1808-21, *Life of John Dryden, by Saintsbury, vol.* I, *p.* 431.

His Virgil is, in my apprehension, the least successful of his chief works. Lines of consummate excellence are frequently shot, like threads of gold, through the web; but the general texture is of an ordinary material. Dryden was little fitted for a translator of Virgil: his mind was more rapid and vehement than that of his original, but by far less elegant and judicious. This translation seems to have been made in haste; it is more negligent than any of his own poetry; and the style is often almost studiously, and, as it were, spitefully vulgar.—HALLAM, HENRY, 1837-39, *Introduction to the Literature of Europe, pt.* iv, *ch.* v, *par.* 46.

Dryden's "Virgil" is, on the whole, a failure; but I am not sure that it does not exhibit the best specimens of his versification: in that work he had not to tax his invention; he had only to think of the expression and versification.—ROGERS, SAMUEL, 1855, *Recollections of the Table-Talk of Samuel Rogers, p.* 29.

He had dashed it off with the utmost freedom and fire, and no work was ever more thoroughly identified with its translator. It is *Dryden's* "*Virgel*," every line of it. A great and almost national interest was felt in the undertaking, such as would be felt now, were it announced that Tennyson was engaged in a translation of Goethe.—GILFILLAN, GEORGE, 1855, *ed., Poetical Works of John Dryden, Life, vol.* I, *p.* xxii.

The verses of the Latin poet have the velvet bloom, the dewy softness, the delicate odour of a flower; the version of the Englishman has the hardness and brilliance of a gem: and, when we find only flowers cut in stone, where we expect to see flowers blooming in sweet reality—no matter how skilful the lapidary, how rich the colouring, or pure the water of the jewel—admiring the triumph of art, we miss the sweetness of nature, and long to exchange the rainbow play of coloured light for the stealing fragrance and tender hues of the living blossom.—COLLIER, WILLIAM FRANCIS, 1861, *A History of English Literature, p.* 239.

Previous to the present century, the extant translations of the Æneid outnumbered those of the Iliad and Odyssey in the proportion of nearly three to one: now, while the press is sending forth version after version of one or both of the Homeric poems, scarcely any one thinks it worth his while to attempt a translation of the Roman epic. But it may be fairly doubted whether Dryden did not close the question a hundred and seventy years ago for any one not, like himself, a poet of commanding original power.—CONINGTON, JOHN, 1867, *tr., The Æneid of Virgil, Preface.*

One need only compare the best known version, Dryden's, with the Latin, to see the lamentable transformations the old Roman bard has suffered (even when piloted by a poet) at the hands of that seductive siren, Rhyme.—CRANCH, CHRISTOPHER PEARSE, 1872, *The Æneid of Virgil, Preface.*

Marred by coarseness, marred by miserable inequalities, marred by errors of ignorance and errors of inadvertancy, it is still a noble achievement. It is a work instinct with genius, but it is instinct not with the placid and majestic genius of the most patient of artists, but with the impetuous energy of the prince of English rhetorical poets. The tender grace, the pathetic cadences, the subtle verbal mechanism of the most exquisite poet of antiquity will be sought in vain in its vehement and facile diction, in the rushing and somewhat turbid torrent of its narrative. It is indeed one of those works which will never cease to offend the taste and never fail to captivate the attention.—COLLINS, JOHN, CHURTON 1878–95, *Dryden, Quarterly Review; Essays and Studies, p.* 70.

Has been extolled with perhaps as great unanimity as any translation in any language.—YONGE, CHARLES DUKE, 1882, *ed., Essays of John Dryden, Introduction, p.* xiii.

Dryden's most extended task, and famous in its time. Though he rarely reproduced the grace of classical writers, he caught their fire; and his scholarship and practised command of verse made him a fluent and usually accurate translator.—GREGORY, WARREN F., 1896, *ed., Dryden's Palamon and Arcite, Literary Productions.*

FABLES

1699

I Doe hereby promise to pay John Dryden, Esquire, or order, on the 25th of March, 1699, the sume of two hundred and fifty guineas, in consideration of ten thousand verses, which the said John Dryden, Esquire, is to deliver to me Jacob Tonson, when finished, whereof seaven

thousand five hundred verses, more or lesse, are already in the said Jacob Tonson's possession. And I do hereby further promise and engage my selfe to make up the said sume of two hundred and fifty guineas, three hundred pounds sterling, to the said John Dryden, Esquire, his executors, administrators, or assigns, att the begining of the second impression of the said ten thousand verses. In witness whereof, I have hereunto sett my hand and seal this twentieth day of March, 1698–9.—TONSON, JACOB, 1698–9, *Agreement Concerning The Fables.*

His alterations from Chaucer and Boccaccio show a greater knowledge of the taste of his readers, and power of pleasing them, than acquaintance with the genius of his authors. He ekes out the lameness of the verse in the former, and breaks the force of the passion in both. The Tancred and Sigismunda is the only general exception, in which, I think, he has fully retained, if not improved upon, the impassioned declamation of the original. The Honoria has none of the bewildered, dreary, preternatural effect of Boccaccio's story. Nor has the Flower and the Leaf any thing of the enchanting simplicity and concentrated feeling of Chaucer's romantic fiction.—HAZLITT, WILLIAM, 1818, *Lectures on the English Poets, Lecture* iv.

The "Fables" of Dryden, or stories modernized from Boccaccio and Chaucer, are at this day probably the most read and the most popular of Dryden's poems. They contain passages of so much more impressive beauty, and are altogether so far more adapted to general sympathy, than those we have mentioned, that I should not hesitate to concur in this judgment. Yet Johnson's accusation of negligence is better supported by these than by the earlier poems. Whether it were that age and misfortune, though they had not impaired the poet's vigor, had rendered its continual exertion more wearisome, or, as is perhaps the better supposition, he reckoned an easy style, sustained above prose, in some places, rather by metre than expression, more fitted to narration, we find much which might appear slovenly to critics of Johnson's temper.—HALLAM, HENRY, 1837–39, *Introduction to the Literature of Europe, pt.* iv, *ch.* v, *par.* 44.

No narrative poems in the language

have been more generally admired or read.
—CHAMBERS, ROBERT, 1876, *Cyclopædia of English Literature*, ed. *Carruthers*.

The last and one of the most singular, but at the same time the most brilliantly successful of all his poetical experiments.
—SAINTSBURY, GEORGE, 1881, *Dryden (English Men of Letters)*, p. 153.

His "Fables" . . . are deservedly placed at the head of his works. It is of course impossible that they should exhibit the same intellectual strength as his argumentative and satirical poems, but this is more than compensated by their superior attractiveness, the additional scope offered for the display of art, and their comparative freedom from everything that can repel.—GARNETT, RICHARD, 1895, *The Age of Dryden*, p. 14.

They sin from coarseness, but in style, in magnificent march of verse, in intellectual but not imaginative fire, in ease but not in grace, they are excellent.—BROOKE, STOPFORD A., 1896, *English Literature*, 177.

SATIRES

How long shall I endure without reply,
To hear this *Bayes*, this hackney-rayler lie?
The fool uncudgell'd for one libel, swells,
Where not his wit, but sauciness excells;
Whilst with foul words and names which he lets flie,
He quite defiles the *satyr's* dignity.
For libel and true satyr different be,
This must have *truth* and *salt*, with modesty.
Sparing the persons, this does tax the crimes,
Galls not great men, but vices of the times,
With witty and sharp, not blunt and bitter rimes.
Methinks the ghost of *Horace* there I see,
Lashing this cherry-cheek'd Dunce of fifty-three;
Who, at that age, so boldly durst profane,
With base hir'd libel, the free satyr's vein.
Thou stil'st it satyr, to call names, rogue, whore,
Traytor and rebel and a thousand more;
An oyster wench is sure thy muse of late,
And all thy *Helicon's* at *Billingsgate*. · ·
As far from satyr does thy talent lye,
As from being cheerful, or good company;
For thou art *Saturnine*, thou dost confess
A civil word thy *dulness* to express. · · ·
Now farewell wretched, mercenary *Bayes*,
Who the king libell'd, and did *Cromwell*, praise;
Farewell, abandon'd rascal, only fit
To be abus'd by thy own scurrilous wit.
—SHADWELL, THOMAS, 1682, *The Medal of John Bayes*.

When I name DRYDEN, I comprehend every varied excellence of *our* poetry. In harmony, strength, modulation, rhythm, energy, he first displayed the full power of the English language. . . . He was the first poet who brought to perfection, what I would term, "The Allegory of Satire." . . . It was the peculiar happiness of Dryden to give an eternal sense and interest to subjects which are transitory. He placed his scene on the ground of actual history.—MATHIAS, THOMAS JAMES, 1798, *Pursuits of Literature, Introductory Letter, pp*, 34, 35.

Dryden occupies the foremost place in the foremost ranks of English Didactic Writers. . . . His Satire is appalling, and tremendous; and not the less so, for its extreme polish and splendour. It excites our indignation against its objects, not only on account of the follies, or faults, which it imputes to them, but also·on account of their writhing beneath the infliction of so splendid a weapon. We forgot the offender in the awfulness and majesty of the power by which he is crushed. Instead of shrinking at the horror of the carnage, we are lost in admiration of the brilliancy of the victory. Like the lightning of heaven, the Satire of Dryden throws a splendour around the objects which it destroys. He has immortalised the persons whom he branded with infamy and contempt; for who would have remembered Shadwell, if he had not been handed down to everlasting fame as Mac Flecnoe?—NEELE, HENRY, 1827-29, *Lectures on English Poetry*.

But there is a difference between a spontaneous effusion of rage and hate, and a cold and malignant preparation of bitterness. The satire which indignation makes will always be the most sympathized with; and the genial man, like Dryden, the most admired. Dryden professes to prefer Juvenal to Horace for his own reading; and this I can quite understand. There are the marks of personal heat in old Dryden's Satires, and generally a blending of humor and passion, a qualification of scorn by fun, which show you that it was natural for him to hold that opinion. In him, as in Juvenal and some others, the personality and the savageness are accompanied by traces of the satirist's other private qualities—his wisdom, fancy homeliness. The rod with which he castigates has the leaves and blossoms still sticking to it. The goodness of his nature shows itself when he is angry, even; consequently you sympathize with him, and do not pity his victims so much.— HANNAY, JAMES, 1854, *Satire and Satirists, p.* 126.

There are passages of Dryden's satires in which every couplet has not only the force but the actual sound of a slap in the face. The rapidity of movement from one couplet to the other is another remarkable characteristic. Even Pope, master as he was of verse, often fell into the fault of isolating his couplets too much, as if he expected applause between each, and wished to give time for it. Dryden's verse, on the other hand, strides along with a careless Olympian motion, as if the writer were looking at his victims rather with a kind of good-humoured scorn than with any elaborate triumph.— SAINTSBURY, GEORGE, 1881, *Dryden (English Men of Letters), p.* 76.

ABSALOM AND ACHITOPHEL
1681–82

The true end of satire is the amendment of vices by correction. And he who writes honestly is no more an enemy to the offender than the physician to the patient, when he prescribes harsh remedies to an inveterate disease; for those are only in order to prevent the chirurgeon's work of an *Ense rescindendum,* which I wish not to my very enemies. To conclude all; if the body politic have any analogy to the natural, in my weak judgment, an act of oblivion were as necessary in a hot distempered state as an opiate would be in a raging fever.—DRYDEN, JOHN, 1681, *Absalom and Achitophel, To the Reader.*

This natural pride and ambition of the soul is very much gratified in the reading of a fable; for, in writings of this kind the reader comes in for half of the performance; every thing appears to him like a discovery of his own. . . . For this reason the "Absalom and Achitophel" was one of the most popular poems that ever appeared in English.—ADDISON, JOSEPH, 1712, *Spectator, No.* 512, *Oct.* 17.

This poem is said to be one of the most perfect allegorical pieces that our language has produced. It is carried on

through the whole with equal strength and propriety. The veil is no where laid aside. There is a just similarity in the characters, which are exactly pourtrayed; the lineaments are well copied; the colouring is lively; the groupings show the hand of a master, and may serve to convince us, that Mr. Dryden knew his own power when he asserted, that he found it easier to write severely than gently.— DERRICK, SAMUEL, 1760, *Miscellaneous Works of John Dryden, with Explanatory Notes and Observations.*

"Absalom and Achitophel" is a work so well known, that particular criticism is superfluous. If it be considered as a poem political and controversial, it will be found to comprise all the excellences of which the subject is susceptible; acrimony of censure, elegance of praise, artful delineation of characters, variety and vigour of sentiment, happy turns of language, and pleasing harmony of numbers; and all these raised to such a height as can scarcely be found in any other English composition.—JOHNSON, SAMUEL, 1779–81, *Dryden, Lives of the English Poets.*

You will find this a good gage or criterion of genius,—whether it progresses and évolves, or only spins upon itself. Take Dryden's Achitophel and Zimri,— Shaftesbury and Buckingham; every line adds to or modifies the character, which is, as it were, a-building up to the very last verse; whereas, in Pope's Timon, &c., the first two or three couplets contain all the pith of the character, and the twenty or thirty lines that follow are so much evidence or proof of overt acts of jealousy, or pride, or whatever it may be that is satirised.—COLERIDGE, SAMUEL TAYLOR, 1832, *Table Talk, ed. Ashe, Aug.* 6, *p.* 177.

The greatest of his satires is "Absalom and Achitophel,"—that work in which his powers become fully known in the world, and which, as many think, he never surpassed. The admirable fitness of the English Couplet for satire had never been shown before; in less skilful hands it had been ineffective. He does not frequently, in his poem, carry the sense beyond the second line, which except when skilfully contrived, as it often is by himself, is apt to enfeeble the emphasis; his triplets are less numerous than usual, but energetic. The spontaneous ease of expression, the rapid transitions, the general elasticity and movement, have never been excelled. It is superfluous to praise the discrimination and vivacity of the chief characters.—HALLAM, HENRY, 1837–39, *Introduction to the Literature of Europe, pt.* iv, *ch.* v, *par.* 39.

Not even in the elegant gallery of the Horatian satire, nor in the darker and more tragic pictures of Juvenal, can we find any delineations, admirable though they be, equal in vigour, life likeness, and intensity of colouring, to the rich and magnificent collection of portraits given in "Absalom and Achitophel."—SHAW, THOMAS B., 1847, *Outlines of English Literature, p.* 182.

Of Dryden's Satires we have already spoken in a general way. "Absalom and Achitophel" is of course the masterpiece, and cannot be too highly praised as a gallery of portraits, and for the daring force and felicity of its style. Why enlarge on a poem, almost every line of which has become a proverb?—GILFILLAN, GEORGE, 1855, *ed., Poetical Works of John Dryden, Critical Estimate, vol.* II, *p.* xvii.

In one respect this poem stands alone in literature. A party pamphlet dedicated to the hour, it is yet immortal. No poem in our language is so interpenetrated with contemporary allusion, with contemporary portraiture, with contemporary point, yet no poem in our language has been more enjoyed by succeeding generations of readers. Scores of intelligent men who know by heart the characters of Zimri and Achitophel are content to remain in ignorance of the political careers of Buckingham and Shaftesbury. The speech in which Achitophel incites his faltering disciple has been admired and recited by hundreds who have been blind to its historical fidelity and to its subtle personalities.—COLLINS, JOHN CHURTON, 1878–95, *Dryden, Quarterly Review; Essays and Studies, p.* 43.

In what other poem of the kind will be found, together with so much versatility of wit, so incisive a directness of poetic eloquence? Dryden is here at his best; and being at his best, he is entirely free from that irrepressible desire to outdo himself.—WARD, ADOLPHUS WILLIAM, 1880, *English Poets, ed. Ward, vol.* II, *p.* 441.

THE MEDAL
1682

The "Medal," written upon the same principles with "Absalom and Achitophel," but upon a narrower plan, gives less pleasure, though it discovers equal abilities in the writer. The superstructure cannot extend beyond the foundation; a single character or incident cannot furnish as many ideas, as a series of events, or multiplicity of agents. This poem therefore, since time has left it to itself, is not much read, nor perhaps generally understood; yet it abounds with touches both of humorous and serious satire.—JOHNSON, SAMUEL, 1779–81, *Dryden, Lives of the English Poets.*

The merits of "The Medal," as a satirical poem, are universally acknowledged; nor does it greatly suffer from being placed as the subject naturally invites, in comparison with "Absalom and Achitophel." . . . The language is as striking as the ideas and subject. The illustrations and images are short and apposite, such as give force to the argument, and flow easily into the diction, without appearing to have been laboured, or brought from a distance. I fear, however some of the scriptural allusions are censurable as too free, if not profane. The verse has all the commanding emphasis with which Dryden, beyond any other poet, knew how to body forth and adorn his poetical arguments. . . . The popularity of "The Medal" did not cease with the crisis that gave it birth.—SCOTT, SIR WALTER, 1808–21, *The Works of John Dryden, by Saintsbury, vol.* IX, *pp.* 417, 418, 419.

In "The Medal" he hurled at Shaftesbury and his party a philippic which, for rancorous abuse, for lofty and uncompromising scorn, for coarse, scathing, ruthless denunciation, couched in diction which now swells to the declamatory grandeur of Juvenal and now sinks to the sordid vulgarity of Swift, has no parallel in our literature. The former attack, indeed, was mercy to this new outburst. To find anything approaching to it in severity and skill we must go back to Claudian's savage onslaught on the Achitophel of the fourth century, or forward to Akenside's diatribe against Pulteney.—COLLINS, JOHN CHURTON, 1878–95, *Dryden, Quarterly Review; Essays and Studies, p.* 45.

MAC FLECKNOE
1682

The severity of this satire, and the excellence of its versification, give it a distinguished rank in this species of composition. At present, an ordinary reader would scarcely suppose that Shadwell, who is here meant by Mac Flecknoe, was worth being chastised; and that Dryden, descending to such game, was like an eagle stooping to catch flies. The truth however is, Shadwell at one time held divided reputation with this great poet. Every age produces its fashionable dunces, who, by following the transient topic or humour of the day, supply talkative ignorance with materials for conversation.—GOLDSMITH, OLIVER, 1767, *The Beauties of English Poetry.*

"Mac-Flecknoe" must be allowed to be one of the keenest satires in the English language. It is what Dryden has elsewhere termed a Varronian satire; that is, as he seems to use the phrase, one in which the author is not contented with general sarcasm upon the object of attack, but where he has woven his piece into a sort of imaginary story, or scene, in which he introduces the person whom he ridicules as a principal actor. The position in which Dryden has placed Shadwell is the most mortifying to literary vanity which can possibly be imagined, and is hardly excelled by the device of Pope in "The Dunciad," who has obviously followed the steps of his predecessor.—SCOTT, SIR WALTER, 1808–21, *ed., The Works of John Dryden, by Saintsbury, vol. x, p.* 431.

Certainly to be numbered among Dryden's masterpieces. The raillery, though neither nice nor graceful, is light, and with one or two exceptions free from that offensive coarseness which mars so many of his satirical compositions.—COLLINS, JOHN CHURTON, 1878–95, *Dryden, Quarterly Review; Essays and Studies p.* 48.

This most happily executed retort upon a by no means despicable antagonist has a double claim to immortality:—its own delightful execution, and the fact that this attempt to extinguish a single Dunce suggested to Pope the heroic idea of annihilating the whole tribe.—WARD, ADOLPHUS WILLIAM, 1880, *English Poets, ed. Ward, vol.* II, *p.* 442.

PROSE

The prefaces of Dryden,
For these our critics much confide in
Though merely writ at first for filling,
To raise the volume's price a shilling.
—SWIFT, JONATHAN, 1733, *The Rhapsody.*

Dryden may be properly considered as the father of English criticism, as the writer who first taught us to determine upon principles the merit of composition. Of our former poets, the greatest dramatist wrote without rules, conducted through life and nature by a genius that rarely misled, and rarely deserted him. Of the rest, those who knew the laws of propriety had neglected to teach them.—JOHNSON, SAMUEL, 1779–81, *Dryden, Lives of the English Poets.*

If a new edition be wanted of Dryden's critical prose works, I know of nothing better worth republishing. The matter is for the most part excellent: the manner incomparable throughout. There cannot be a better antidote against our modern innovations in style than his compositions—perspicuous, graceful, elegant, humorous and easy.—CLAREMONT, LORD, 1794, *Letter to Edmund Malone, ed. Prior, p.* 251.

The prose of Dryden may rank with the best in the English language. It is no less of his own formation than his versification, is equally spirited and equally harmonious. Without the lengthened and pedantic sentences of Clarendon, it is dignified where dignity is becoming, and is lively without the accumulation of strained and absurd allusions and metaphors, which were unfortunately mistaken for wit by many of the author's contemporaries.—SCOTT, SIR WALTER, 1808–21, *Life of John Dryden, ed. Saintsbury, p.* 436.

It would be superfluous to echo the praise of Dryden's prose style, which is in every one's mouth. Perhaps it may not be equally so, to suggest a limitation of it. Its excellence is an ease and apparent negligence of phrase, which shows, as it were, a powerful mind *en deshabille*, and free from the fetters of study. . . . We cannot think the style of Dryden adapted to an historical, much less to a didactic work. We should, indeed, strongly recommend the study of it to those engaged in such compositions, so far as to relieve, in some degree, by its variety and copiousness of English idiom, that stiffness and monotony, which habits of precise and laborious thinking, especially upon abstract subjects, are very apt to engender.—HALLAM, HENRY, 1808, *Scott's Edition of Dryden, Edinburgh Review, vol.* 13, *p.* 133.

He had a large soul for a man, containing sundry Queen Anne's men, one with another, like quartetto tables; but it was not a large soul for a poet, and it entertained the universe by potato-patches. He established finally the reign of the literati for the reign of the poets—and the critics clapped their hands. He established finally the despotism of the final emphasis—and no one dared, in affecting criticism, to speak any more at all against a tinkling cymbal.—BROWNING, ELIZABETH BARRETT, 1842–63, *The Book of the Poets.*

Dryden then has the merit of converting this corruption and dissolution of our old language into a new birth and renovation. And not only must we thank him for making the best of the inevitable circumstances and tendencies of the time, but also praise him absolutely for definitely improving our language. It is true that he sacrificed a great deal of the old beauty of English writing, but that sacrifice was inevitable; he retained all that it was practicable to save, and he added at the same time all the new excellence of which the time was capable. You may call it, if you please, a democratic movement in the language. It was easier henceforth both to write and to read. To understand written English, it was not necessary first to understand Latin; and yet written English was little less instructive than it had been, or if it was less elevating, it was on the other hand more refining.—CLOUGH, ARTHUR HUGH, 1852? *On Dryden's English, Prose Remains, p.* 327.

English prose is indebted to Dryden for having freed it from the cloister of pedantry. He, more than any other single writer, contributed, as well by precept as example, to give it suppleness of movement and the easier air of the modern world. His own style, juicy with proverbial phrases, has that familiar dignity, so hard to attain, perhaps unattainable except by one who, like Dryden, feels that his position is assured. Charles Cotton is as easy, but not so elegant; Walton as familiar, but not so flowing; Swift as

idiomatic, but not so elevated; Burke more splendid, but not so equally luminous.—LOWELL, JAMES RUSSELL, 1868–90, *Dryden, Prose Works, Riverside ed., vol.* III, *p.* 129.

We feel in him the stress of modern society, the shiftings of modern thought, the modern spirit of criticism which tries, in the balance of reasoning opinion and the recognized canons of excellence, himself and his performances in one scale, and all sorts of other writers and their performances in another, not perhaps too equitably poised. . . . In his time criticism was almost a novelty in England. His method was trenchant, decisive, and broad, his perceptions fresh and vigorous, his grasp solid and firm; he said many fine things finely; and his writings of this class had what they merited, a great deal of influence.—ROSSETTI, WILLIAM MICHAEL, 1878, *Lives of Famous Poets, pp.* 91, 96.

The occasional insertion of a harmless colloquialism or trifling touch of pathos betray the hand of the man who is already master both of his thoughts and of his pen. Swift and Thackeray alone excel Dryden in this peculiar excellence. No one can throw in a political allusion with more effect except Swift himself.—FLETCHER, C. R. L., 1881, *The Development of English Prose Style, p.* 15.

He is one of the few English poets of high excellence—they may be counted on the fingers—who deserve almost equal credit for their healthy judgments as critics. Right or wrong, his criticism is always manly, always intelligent, always rich in the suggestiveness which is the fruit of a fine imagination and of a capacious intellect.—DENNIS, JOHN, 1882, *John Dryden, Fraser's Magazine, vol.* 25, *n. s., p.* 191.

Verily, John Dryden perpetuated more rhetorical nonsense than any other literary critic that ever lived.—CORSON, HIRAM, 1892, *A Primer of English Verse, p.* 107.

Respect for Dryden as a critic has been steadily growing during the last two centuries; what he wrote of Chaucer may with a modification be applied to himself—"He is a fountain of good sense." He was so open minded and progressive all through his life that the study of his criticism becomes especially interesting as an illustration of literary development. His mind was vigorous rather than subtle, and his sympathies were with the Restoration school, at whose head he stands; yet he manifests no little catholicity and sensitiveness. He is moreover one of the most agreeable prose authors in our literature, writing "prose such as we would all gladly use if we only knew how"—easy and clear, entirely unostentatious, with the pleasantest touches of familiarity, and yet not lacking in seriousness and a gentleman's dignity.—McLAUGHLIN, EDWARD T., 1893, *Literary Criticism for Students, p.* 16.

To him we owe that perfection of ease, that familiar intercourse between author and reader, that constant reference to the common judgment of educated men, which gave its best note to English prose.— CRAIK, HENRY, 1894, *English Prose, Introduction, vol.* III, *p.* 4.

No later prose writer can approach him in strength, freedom, and harmony of expression. In reading him, when at his best, we are reminded of his own description of Absalom:

"Whate'er he did, was done with so much ease,
In him alone 'twas natural to please."

The most skilful critic finds it sometimes hard to discriminate between the style of Addison and Steele; Johnson's style had many imitators; but no man could imitate the style of Dryden. Of no writer can it be more truly said, *Le style c'est l'homme.* Like the Socrates of Plato he runs before his argument as a ship under sail, and whatever be his subject of the moment, he suffuses it with all the glow and colour of his rich vocabulary. The coarse immorality of Charles II.'s Court, as he paints it, takes an air of grace and refinement. A few strokes of unequalled vigour place before us, with perfect discrimination, the varied characters of Shakespeare, Fletcher, and Jonson. Even in the midst of his servility he seems to be sustained by a sense of inward greatness, which allows him to speak to his readers with self-respect. Nothing can surpass the dignity of his attitude before Collier; his haughty disdain of Buckingham and the authors of the "Rehearsal;" his pathetic reference to his old age in the "Postscript to the Æneis."—COURTHOPE, W. J., 1894, *English Prose, ed. Craik, vol.* III, *p.* 146.

Dryden is master of comparative criticism: he has something of the historical method; he is unrivalled in the art of seizing the distinctive qualities of his author and of setting them before us with the lightest touch. His very style, so pointed yet so easy, is enough in itself to mark the gulf that lies between the age of Elizabeth and the age of the Restoration. All the Elizabethan critics, Sidney himself hardly excepted, bore some trace of the schoolmaster. Dryden was the first to meet his readers entirely as an equal, and talk to them as a friend with friends. It is Dryden, and not Sainte-Beuve, who is the true father of the literary *causerie;* and he still remains its unequalled master.—VAUGHAN, C. E., 1896, *English Literary Criticism, p.* xxvii.

Dryden's position as the first writer of modern English prose has been long recognized, with hardly a dissenting voice. The "Essay of Dramatic Poesy," his first separate publication in prose, is thus a work memorable in the history of English style.—STRUNK, JR., WILLIAM, 1898, *ed. Dryden, Essays on the Drama, Introducton, p.* xxxviii.

The separate, positive sentences of Dryden, are of small account in his work as critic. His virtue is that, in a time when literature was pestered and cramped with formulas, he found it impossible to write otherwise than freely. He is skeptical, tentative, disengaged, where most of his contemporaries, and most of his successors for a hundred years, are pledged to certain dogmas and principles.—KER, W. P., 1900, *ed., Essays of John Dryden, vol.* I, *p.* xv.

Dryden himself had given English prose its most masterly, almost its final form. —WENDELL, BARRETT, 1900, *A Literary History of America, p.* 25.

GENERAL

You do live in as much ignorance and darkness as you did in the womb: your writings are like a Jack-of-all-trade's shop; they have a variety, but nothing of value; and if thou art not the dullest plant-animal that ever the earth produced, all that I have conversed with are strangely mistaken in thee.—CLIFFORD, MARTIN, 1672–87, *Notes upon Mr. Dryden's Poems, First Letter.*

While the Town-Bayes writes all the while
and spells,
And like a pack-horse tires without his bells.
—MARVELL, ANDREW, 1674, *On Milton's
Paradise Lost.*

Well, sir, 'tis granted; I said Dryden's rimes
Were stolen, unequal, nay dull, many times:
What foolish patron is there found of his,
So blindly partial to deny me this?
But that his plays, embroider'd up and down
With wit and learning, justly please the
town,
In the same paper I as freely own.
Yet, having this allow'd, the heavy mass
That stuffs up his loose volumes must not
pass.
. . . .
But to be just, 'twill to his praise be found,
His excellences more than faults abound:
Nor dare I from his sacred temples tear
The laurel, which he best deserves to wear.
—ROCHESTER, JOHN WILMOT, EARL, 1678,
*An Allusion to the Tenth Satire of the
First book of Horace.*

Mr. *Dryden* is the most Voluminous
Dramatick Writer of our Age, he having
already extant above Twenty Plays of his
own writing, as the Title-page of each
would perswade the World; tho' some
people have been so bold as to call the
Truth of this in question, and to propogate
in the world another Opinion. His Genius seems to me to incline to Tragedy and
Satyr, rather than Comedy: and methinks
he writes much better in *Heroicks*, than in
blank Verse.—LANGBAINE, GERARD, 1691,
*An Account of the English Dramatick
Poets, p.* 130.

But see where artful Dryden next appears
Grown old in rhyme, but charming even in
years!
Great Dryden next! whose tuneful Muse
affords
The sweetest numbers, and the fittest words.
Whether in comic sounds or tragic airs
She forms her voice, she moves our smiles or
tears.
—ADDISON, JOSEPH, 1694, *An Account of
the Greatest English Poets.*

'Tis true, that when the coarse and worthless
dross
Is purg'd away, there will be mighty loss;
Ev'n Congreve, Southern, manly Wycherley,
When thus refin'd, will grievous sufferers be;
Into the melting pot when Dryden comes,
What horrid stench will rise, what noisome
fumes!
How will he shrink, when all his lewd allay,
And wicked mixture, shall be purg'd away!
—BLACKMORE, SIR RICHARD, 1700, *A Sat-
ire Against Wit.*

I cannot pass by that admirable English
poet, without endeavouring to make his
country sensible of the obligations they
have to his Muse. Whether they consider the flowing grace of his versification,
the vigorous sallies of his fancy, or the
peculiar delicacy of his periods, they all
discover excellences never to be enough
admired. If they trace him from the first
productions of his youth to the last performances of his age, they will find that
as the tyranny of rhyme never imposed on
the perspicuity of sense, so a languid sense
never wanted to be set off by the harmony
of rhyme. And as his earlier works
wanted no maturity, so his latter wanted
no force or spirit. The falling off of his
hair had no other consequence than to
make his laurels be seen the more.—
GARTH, SIR SAMUEL, 1717, *tr. Ovid's Metamorphoses, Preface.*

No man hath written in our language
so much, and so various matter, and in so
various manners so well. . . . He
was equally excellent in verse and in
prose. His prose had all the clearness
imaginable, together with all the nobleness of expression; all the graces and ornaments proper and peculiar to it, without deviating into the language or diction
of poetry. . . . His versification and
his numbers he could learn of nobody;
for he first possessed those talents in perfection in our tongue. And they, who
have best succeeded in them since his
time, have been indebted to his example.
. . . Take his verses and divest them of
their rhymes, disjoint them in their numbers, transpose their expressions, make
what arrangement and disposition you
please of his words, yet shall there eternally be poetry, and something which will
be found incapable of being resolved into
absolute prose; an incontestable characteristic of a truly poetical genius. I will
say but one word more in general of his
writings, which is, that what he has done
in any one species, or distinct kind, would
have been sufficient to have acquired him a
great name. If he had written nothing but
his prefaces, or nothing but his songs or
his prologues, each of them would have
entitled him to the preference and distinction of excelling in his kind.—CONGREVE,
WILLIAM, 1717, *ed. The Works of John
Dryden, Dedication, ed. Scott and Saintsbury, vol.* II, *pp.* 18, 19.

> . . . Dryden taught to join
> The varying verse, the full resounding line,
> The long majestic march and energy divine
> Though still some traces of our rustic vein
> And splay-foot verse remain'd and will re-
>   main.
>
> . . . .
>
> E'en copious Dryden wanted, or forgot,
> The last and greatest art,—the art to blot.

—POPE, ALEXANDER, 1733, *The First Epistle of the second book of Horace.*

Dryden, though my near relation, is one I have often blamed as well as pitied. He was poor, and in great haste to finish his plays, because by them he chiefly supported his family, and this made him so very incorrect; he likewise brought in the Alexandrine verse at the end of his triplets.—SWIFT, JONATHAN, 1735, *Letter to Mr. Thomas Beach, April* 12.

In this almost general corruption Dryden, whose plays were more famed for their wit than their chastity, led the way, which he fairly confesses and endeavours to excuse in his epilogue to the "Pilgrim," revived in 1700 for his benefit in his declining age and fortune.—CIBBER, COLLEY, 1739, *An Apology for His Life.*

I learned versification wholly from Dryden's works; who had improved it much beyond any of our former poets; and would, probably, have brought it to its perfection, had not he been unhappily obliged to write so often in haste.—POPE, ALEXANDER, 1742–43, *Spence's Anecdotes, ed. Singer, p.* 212.

The critics have remarked, that as to tragedy, he seldom touches the passions, but deals rather in pompous language, poetical flights, and descriptions; and too frequently makes his characters speak better than they have occasion, or ought to do, when their sphere in the drama is considered: And it is peculiar to Dryden (says Mr. Addison) to make his personages, as wise, witty, elegant and polite as himself. That he could not so intimately affect the tender passions, is certain, for we find no play of his, in which we are much disposed to weep; and we are so often inchanted with beautiful descriptions, and noble flights of fancy, that we forget the business of the play, and are only attentive to the poet, while the characters sleep.—CIBBER, THEOPHILUS, 1753, *Lives of the Poets, vol.* III, *p.* 66.

The character of Dryden's poetry is as animated as what it paints.—WALPOLE, HORACE, 1757, *Letters, ed. Cunningham, Aug.* 25, *vol.* III, *p.* 97.

> Behold, where Dryden's less presumptuous
>   car,
> Wide o'er the fields of glory bear
> Two coursers of ethereal race,
> With necks in thunder clothed, and long-
>   resounding pace.

—GRAY, THOMAS, 1757, *The Progress of Poesy, pt.* iii.

The strongest demonstration of his no-taste for the buskin are his tragedies fringed with rhyme; which, in epic poetry is a sore disease, in the tragic absolute death. To Dryden's enormity, Pope's was a slight offence. . . . "Must rhyme," then say you, "be banished?" I wish the nature of our language could bear its entire expulsion; but our lesser poetry stands in need of a toleration for it; it raises that, but sinks the great; as spangles adorn children, but expose men.—YOUNG, EDWARD, 1759, *Conjectures on Original Composition, p.* 574.

Dryden, though a great and undisputed genius, had the same cast as L'Estrange. Even his plays discover him to be a party-man, and the same principle infects his style in subjects of the lightest nature; but the English tongue, as it stands at present, is greatly his debtor. He first gave it regular harmony, and discovered its latent powers. It was his pen that formed the Congreves, the Priors, and the Addisons, who succeeded him; and had it not been for Dryden we never should have known a Pope, at least in the meridian lustre he now displays. But Dryden's excellencies as a writer were not confined to poetry alone. There is in his prose writings an ease and elegance that have never yet been so well united in works of taste or criticism.—GOLDSMITH, OLIVER, 1759, *The Bee, No.* 8, *Nov.* 24.

> Dryden, the great high-priest of all the Nine.

—CHURCHILL, CHARLES, 1763, *An Epistle to William Hogarth.*

Remember Dryden, and be blind to all his faults.—GRAY, THOMAS, 1765, *Letter to James Beattie, Oct.* 2.

Dryden was the father of true English poetry, and the most universal of all poets. This universality has been objected to him as a fault; but it was the unhappy effect of penury and dependance. He was not at liberty to pursue his own inclination; but was frequently obliged to prostitute his pen to such persons and things as a man of his talents must have despised. He was the great improver of our language and versification. The chains of our English bards were formerly heard to rattle only; in the age of Waller and Dryden, they became harmonious. He has failed in most of his dramatic writings, of which the prologues, epilogues, and prefaces, are generally more valuable than the pieces to which they are affixed. But even in this branch of poetry, he has written enough to perpetuate his fame; as his "All for Love," his "Spanish Friar," and "Don Sebastian," can never be forgotten. There was a native fire in this great poet, which poverty could not damp, nor old age extinguish. On the contrary, he was still improving as a writer, while he was declining as a man; and was far advanced in years when he wrote his "Alexander's Feast," which is confessedly at the head of modern lyrics, and in the true spirit of the ancients. Great injury has been done him, in taking an estimate of his character from the meanest of his productions. It would be just as uncandid, to determine the merit of Kneller, from the vilest of his paintings.—GRANGER, JAMES, 1769–1824, *Biographical History of England, vol.* v, *p.* 240.

There is no modern writer, whose style is more distinguishable. . . . His English is pure and simple, nervous and clear, to a degree which Pope has never exceeded, and not always equalled. . . . Dryden's genius did not lead him to the sublime or pathetic. Good strokes of both may be found in him; but they are momentary, and seem to be accidental. He is too witty for the one, and too familiar for the other. . . . Pope excels in solemnity of sound; Dryden, in an easy melody, and boundless variety of rhythm. In this last respect he is perhaps superior to all other English poets, Milton himself not excepted. Till Dryden appeared, none of our writers in rhyme of the last century approached in any measure to the harmony of Fairfax and Spenser.—BEATTIE, JAMES, 1776–9, *Essays on Poetry and Music, pp.* 15, 16, 17, *note.*

His literature, though not always free from ostentation, will be commonly found either obvious, and made his own by the art of dressing it; or superficial, which, by what he gives, shews what he wanted; or erroneous, hastily collected, and negligently scattered. Yet it cannot be said that his genius is ever unprovided of matter, or that his fancy languishes in penury of ideas. His works abound with knowledge, and sparkle with illustrations. There is scarcely any science or faculty that does not supply him with occasional images and lucky similitudes; every page discovers a mind very widely acquainted both with art and nature, and in full possession of great stores of intellectual wealth. Of him that knows much it is natural to suppose that he has read with diligence: yet I rather believe that the knowledge of Dryden was gleaned from accidental intelligence and various conversation, by a quick apprehension, a judicious selection, and a happy memory, a keen appetite of knowledge, and a powerful digestion; by vigilance that permitted nothing to pass without notice, and a habit of reflection that suffered nothing useful to be lost. A mind like Dryden's, always curious, always active, to which every understanding was proud to be associated, and of which every one solicited the regard, by an ambitious display of himself, had a more pleasant, perhaps a nearer way to knowledge than by the silent progress of solitary reading. I do not suppose that he despised books, or intentionally neglected them; but that he was carried out, by the impetuosity of his genius, to more vivid and speedy instructors; and that his studies were rather desultory and fortuitous than constant and systematical.—JOHNSON, SAMUEL, 1779–81, *Dryden, Lives of the English Poets.*

. . . Dryden, with imperial grace,
Gives to th' obedient lyre his rapid laws;
Tones yet unheard, with touch divine, he
    draws,
The melting fall, the rising swell sublime,
And all the magic of melodious rhyme.
—HAYLEY, WILLIAM, 1782, *An Essay on Epic Poetry, Ep.* III.

But I admire Dryden most, [he had been speaking of Pope], who has succeeded by a mere dint of genius, and in spite of a laziness and a carelessness almost peculiar to himself. His faults are numberless, and so are his beauties. His faults are those of a great man, and his beauties are such (at least sometimes) as Pope with all his touching and retouching, could never equal.—COWPER, WILLIAM, 1782, *Letter to Mr. Unwin, Jan.* 5.

Then comes a bard
Worn out and penniless, and poet still,
Though bent with years, and in impetuous
　　rhyme
Pours out his unexhausted song. What muse
So flexible, so generous as thine,
Immortal Dryden! From her copious fount
Large draughts he took, and unbeseeming
　　song
Inebriated sang. Who does not grieve
To hear the foul and insolent rebuke
Of angry satire from a bard so rare,
To trace the lubricous and oily course
Of abject adulation, the lewd line
Of shameless vice from page to page, and
　　find
The judgment bribed, the heart unprincipled,
And only loyal at the expense of truth,
Of justice, and of virtue?
—HURDIS, JAMES, 1788, *The Village Curate.*

Dryden's practical knowledge of English was beyond all others exquisite and wonderful.—TOOKE, JOHN HORNE, 1789–1805, *The Diversions of Purley.*

Dryden has rather paraphrased than translated, and though in the small portion he has favoured us with, his versification be, as usual, spirited and easy, it wants the majesty and solemn colouring of Lucretius; and towards the conclusion of the fourth book he is more licentious, broad and open, than the text, faulty as it undoubtedly is, in this respect, will warrant.—DRAKE, NATHAN, 1798–1820, *Literary Hours, vol.* I, *No.* 1.

I was much pleased to hear of your engagement with Dryden: not that he is, as a poet, any great favourite of mine: I admire his talents and genius highly,—but his is not a poetical genius. The only qualities I can find in Dryden that are *essentially* poetical, are a certain ardour and impetuosity of mind, with an excellent ear. It may seem strange that I do not add to this, great command of language: *That* he certainly has, and of such language, too, as it is most desirable that a poet should possess, or rather that he should not be without. But it is not language that is, in the highest sense of the word, poetical, being neither of the imagination nor of the passions; I mean the amiable, the ennobling, or the intense passions. I do not mean to say that there

is nothing of this in Dryden, but as little, I think, as is possible, considering how much he has written. . . . Dryden had neither a tender heart nor a lofty sense of moral dignity.—WORDSWORTH, WILLIAM, 1805, *Letter to Scott, Scott's Life, ed. Lockhart.*

This man, from his influence in fixing versification and diction, especially in rhyme, has acquired a reputation altogether disproportionate to his true merit. We shall not here inquire whether his translations of the Latin poets are not manneristical paraphrases, whether his political allegories, now that party interest is dead, can be read without the greatest wearisomeness; but his plays are, considered with reference to his great reputation, incredibly bad. Dryden had a flowing and easy versification, the knowledge which he possessed was rather considerable, but undigested, and all this was coupled with the talent of giving a certain appearance of novelty to what he borrowed from every quarter: his serviceable muse was the resource of an irregular life.—SCHLEGEL, AUGUSTUS WILLIAM, 1809, *Dramatic Art and Literature, tr. Black, Lecture* xiii, *p.* 395.

Dryden's slovenly verses written for the trade. — COLERIDGE, SAMUEL TAYLOR, 1817, *Letter to Henry Crabb Robinson, Reminiscences of H. C. Robinson.*

Dryden was a better prose-writer, and a bolder and more varied versifier, than Pope. He was a more vigorous thinker, a more correct and logical declaimer, and had more of what may be called strength of mind than Pope; but he had not the same refinement and delicacy of feeling.—HAZLITT, WILLIAM, 1818, *Lectures on the English Poets, Lecture* iv.

He is a writer of manly and elastic character. His strong judgement gave force as well as direction to a flexible fancy; and his harmony is generally the echo of solid thoughts. But he is not gifted with intense or lofty sensibility; on the contrary, the grosser any idea is the happier he seems to expatiate upon it. The transports of the heart, and the deep and varied delineations of the passions, are strangers to its poetry. He could describe character in the abstract, but could not embody it in the drama, for he entered into character more than clear perception than fervid sympathy. This great high-priest of all the nine was not a confessor to the finer secrets of the human breast. Had the subject of Eloisa fallen into his hands, he would have left but a coarse draught of her passion.— CAMPBELL, THOMAS, 1819, *An Essay on English Poetry.*

Dryden was, beyond all comparison, the greatest poet of his own day; and, endued as he was with a vigorous and discursive imagination, and possessing a mastery over his language which no later writer has attained, if he had known nothing of foreign literature, and been left to form himself on the models of Shakespeare, Spenser, and Milton; or if he had lived in the country, at a distance from the pollutions of courts, factions, and playhouses, there is reason to think that he would have built up the pure and original school of English poetry so firmly, as to have made it impossible for fashion, or caprice, or prejudice of any sort, ever to have rendered any other popular among our own inhabitants. As it is, he has not written one line that is pathetic, and very few that can be considered as sublime.—JEFFREY, FRANCIS, 1819–44, *Contributions to the Edinburgh Review, vol.* II, *p.* 291

The public voice has assigned to Dryden the first place in the second rank of our poets—no mean station in a table of intellectual precedency so rich in illustrious names. It is allowed that, even of the few who were his superiors in genius, none has exercised a more extensive or permanent influence on the national habits of thought and expression. His life was commensurate with the period during which a great revolution in the public taste was effected; and in that revolution he played the part of Cromwell. By unscrupulously taking the lead in its wildest excesses, he obtained the absolute guidance of it. By trampling on laws, he acquired the authority of a legislator. By signalizing himself as the most daring and irreverent of rebels, he raised himself to the dignity of a recognised prince. He commenced his career by the most frantic outrages. He terminated it in the repose of established sovereignty—the author of a new code, the root of a new dynasty. . . . His imagination resembled the wings of an ostrich. It enabled him to run, though not to soar.

When he attempted the highest flights, he became ridiculous; but while he remained in a lower region, he outstripped all competitors. . . . His command of language was immense. With him died the secret of the old poetical diction of England—the art of producing rich effects by familiar words. In the following century, it was as completely lost as the gothic method of painting glass, and was but poorly supplied by the laborious and tesselated imitations of Mason and Gray. On the other hand, he was the first writer under whose skilful management the scientific vocabulary fell into natural and pleasing verse. In this department, he succeeded as completely as his contemporary Gibbons succeeded in the similar enterprise of carving the most delicate flowers from heart of oak. The toughest and most knotty parts of language became ductile at his touch. His versification, in the same manner, while it gave the first model of that neatness and precision which the following generation esteemed so highly, exhibited, at the same time, the last examples of nobleness, freedom, variety of pause and cadence.—MACAULAY, THOMAS BABINGTON, 1828, *Dryden, Edinburgh Review; Essays.*

Of all our really great poets, Dryden is the one least indebted to woman, and to whom, in return, women are least indebted: he is almost devoid of *sentiment* in the true meaning of the word. . . . In his tragedies, his heroines on stilts, and his drawcansir heroes, whine, rant, strut and rage, and tear passion to tatters —to very rags; but love, such as it exists in gentle, pure, unselfish bosoms—love, such as it glows in the pages of Shakespeare and Spenser, Petrarch and Tasso, —such love

As doth become mortality
Glancing at heaven,

He could not imagine or appreciate, far less express or describe. He could pourtray a Cleopatra; but he could not conceive a Juliet. His ideas of our sex seem to have been formed from a profligate actress, and a silly, wayward, provoking wife; and we have avenged ourselves,— for Dryden is not the poet of women; and, of all our English classics, is the least honoured in a lady's library.—JAMESON, ANNA BROWNELL, 1829, *The Loves of the Poets, vol.* II, *pp.* 38, 39.

Dryden's genius was of that sort which catches fire by its own motion; his chariot wheels *get* hot by driving fast.—COLERIDGE, SAMUEL TAYLOR, 1833, *Table Talk, ed. Ashe, Nov.* 1, *p.* 266.

In Dryden, such is the difference in the structure of his dramas, the characters are, from the outset, surrounded with elaborate contrivances of perplexity. Affections are dissembled, perverted, or misplaced; the calls of duty and the feelings of desire are placed in opposition to each other; the difficulties do not grow out of the progress of the plot, or arise from the natural development of individual character, and the conflict or combinations of the varied passions and affections, but are gratuitously formed: and, at length, when ingenuity has been exhausted, and the arts of evasion baffled by the stubbornness of the materials, a conclusion is obtained by an unnatural and rapid removal of part of the characters, or by an unexpected and unaccountable alteration of their sentiments. . . . In the very best of Dryden's plays, there is something of an artificial medium which the poet has interposed between us and nature; we see her features in a glass darkly. It is a style formed after the rules of criticism, from arbitrary opinions and narrow views; its illustrations are tedious, its events improbable, its catastrophes ridiculous. It is wanting in real force, and rapidity of thought and language; it gives no emphatic imitation of real individual character, no strong representation of powerful feeling; the perfume is drawn through a limbec before it reaches us. In Shakespeare, it comes with all the woodland fragrance on its wing, fresh blowing from the violet banks, and breathing the vernal odours. Dryden's composition is like the artificial grotto raised amid level plains, sparkling with imported minerals, and glittering with reflected and unnatural lights. The old drama resembles rather the cavern, hewn from the marble rock by nature's hand, whose lofty portals, winding labyrinths, and gigantic chambers, fill the mind with wonder and delight. The one opens into decorated gardens, trellised bowers, and smooth and shaven lawns; the other lies amid nature's richest and wildest scenes, the glacier, and the granite hills above,—wild flowers, and viny glens and sunlit lakes below.—MITFORD, JOHN, 1834, *ed. Poems of Dryden, Memoir.*

Few of his poems are completely unexceptionable, but what transcendent passages are to be found in almost all!—MACREADY, WILLIAM CHARLES, 1835, *Diary, Reminiscences, ed. Pollock, March* 20.

He never loiters about a single thought or image, never labors about the turn of a phrase. The impression upon our minds, that he wrote with exceeding ease, is irresistible; and I do not know that we have any evidence to repel it. The admiration of Dryden gains upon us, if I may speak from my own experience, with advancing years, as we become more sensible of the difficulty of his style, and of the comparative facility of that which is merely imaginative.—HALLAM, HENRY, 1837–39, *Introduction to the Literature of Europe, pt.* iv, *ch.* v, *par.* 38.

In studying his works you are struck, throughout, with a mind loosely disciplined in its great intellectual powers. In his critical writings, principles hastily proposed from partial consideration, are set up and forgotten. He intends largely, but a thousand causes restrain and lame the execution. Milton, in unsettled times, maintained his inward tranquility of soul —and "dwelt apart." Dryden, in times oscillating indeed and various, yet quieter and safer, discloses private disturbance. His own bark appears to be borne on continually on a restless, violent, whirling and tossing stream. It never sleeps in brightness in its own calm and bright shadow. An unhappy biography weaves itself into the history of the inly dwelling Genius.—WILSON, JOHN, 1845, *Dryden and Pope, Blackwood's Magazine.*

Dryden's wardrobe, we are told, was like that of a Russian noble,—"all filth and diamonds, dirty linen and inestimable sables." To such speculations and fancies as these are we led, when we acknowledge the truth of the maxim, that words are the dress of thought.—WHIPPLE, EDWIN P., 1845, *Words, Essays and Reviews.*

Chatting on deck was Dryden too,
The Bacon of the riming crew;
None ever cross'd our mystic sea
More richly stored with thought than he;
Tho' never tender nor sublime,
He wrestles with, and conquers Time.

—LANDOR, WALTER SAVAGE, 1846, *To Wordsworth.*

If Dryden had been cast in a somewhat finer mould, and added sentiment to his other qualifications, he would have been almost as great a poet in the world of nature, as he was in that of art and the town. He had force, expression, scholarship, geniality, admirable good sense, musical enthusiasm. The rhymed heroic couplet in his hands continues still to be the finest in the language. But his perceptions were more acute than subtle; more sensual, by far, than spiritual. The delicacy of them had no proportion to the strength. He prized the flower, but had little sense of the fragrance; was gross as well as generous in his intellectual diet; and if it had not been genuine and hearty, would have shown an almost impudent delight in doing justice to the least refined of Nature's impressions. His Venus was not the Celestial. He would as soon have described the coarsest flower, as a rose; sooner, if it was large and luxuriant. . . . Agreeably to this character of his genius, Dryden's wit is less airy than masculine; less quick to move than eloquent when roused; less productive of pleasure and love than admiration and a sense of his mastery. His satire, if not so learned and universal as Butler's, is aimed more at the individual and his public standing, and therefore comes more home to us.—HUNT, LEIGH, 1846, *Wit and Humour, pp.* 260, 261.

. . . Dryden came, a mind of giant mould,
Like the north wind, impetuous, keen, and cold;
Born to effect what Waller but essay'd,
In rank and file his numbers he array'd,
Compact as troops exact in battle's trade.
Firm by constraint, and regularly strong,
His vigorous lines resistless march along,
By martial music order'd and inspired,
Like glowing wheels by their own motion fired.
. . . Dryden nobly earn'd the poet's name,
And won new honours from the gift of fame.
—COLERIDGE, HARTLEY, 1849, *Dryden*.

Next to this poet's astonishing ease, spirit, and elastic vigour, may be ranked his clear, sharp intellect. He may be called more a logician than a poet. He reasons often, and always acutely, and his rhyme, instead of shackling, strengthens the movement of his argumentation. Parts of his "Religio Laici" and the "Hind and Panther" resemble portions of Duns Scotus or Aquinas set on fire. Indeed, keen, strong intellect, inflamed with passion, and inspirited by that "ardour and impetuosity of mind" which Wordsworth is compelled to allow to him, rather than creative or original genius, is the differentia of Dryden.—GILFILLAN, GEORGE, 1855, *Poetical Works of John Dryden, Critical Estimate, vol.* II, *p.* ix.

His genius did not raise itself above his times, but dwelling there, a habitation steaming with a thousand vices, his garland and singing-robes were polluted by the contagion.—REED, HENRY, 1855, *Lectures on English Literature, p.* 225.

I do not know that one could make the writings of John Dryden friends; so many of the very cleverest of them are bitter satires, containing a great deal of shrewd observation, sometimes just, as well as severe, but certainly not binding us by any strong ties of affection to their author. Yet there is such a tragedy in the history of a mind so full of power as his, and so unable to guide itself amidst the shoals and quicksands of his time, that I believe we need not, and that we cannot, speak of him merely with the admiration which is due to his gifts; we must feel for him somewhat of the pity that is akin to love.—MAURICE, FREDERICK DENISON, 1856–74, *The Friendship of Books and Other Lectures, ed. Hughes.*

Without either creative imagination or any power of pathos, he is in argument, in satire, and in declamatory magnificence, the greatest of our poets. His poetry, indeed, is not the highest kind of poetry, but in that kind he stands unrivaled and unapproached. Pope, his great disciple, who, in correctness, in neatness, and in the brilliancy of epigrammatic point, has outshone his master, has not come near him in easy flexible vigor, in indignant vehemence, in narrative rapidity, any more than he has in sweep and variety of versification. Dryden never writes coldly, or timidly, or drowsily. The movement of verse always sets him on fire, and whatever he produces is a coinage hot from the brain, not slowly scraped or pinched into shape, but struck out as from a die with a few stout blows or a single wrench of the screw. It is this fervor especially which gives to his personal sketches their wonderful life and force.—CRAIK, GEORGE L., 1861, *A Compendious History of English Literature and of the English Language, vol.* II, *p.* 118.

Within the limited circle that we have described, Dryden was a conscious artist, and exercised dominion with conscious facility. He had attained to perfect mastery over his medium. Poetic diction and facile rhyme were at his command, and the poet exulted in their use, showing neither effort nor exhaustion in his work. His work was mainly intellectual. He scarcely attempted any that aimed at a boundary, beyond that which circumscribed the usual processes of the understanding. His mind, within such limits, moved with logical precision; but to what has been since called the "Vision and the Faculty divine" he was a stranger. It was neither the gift of his age nor of his genius. The former had to wait for a new birth of the creative power, and attained it in due course. . . . Let us recognise in Dryden his mental vigour, his vivid touch, his willing service, his impassioned courage, his detestation of vice and meanness, his fiery eloquence, his subtle rhetoric, his steady pursuit of what appeared to him to be truth, and the progress that he made in the direction that led to the desired goal.—HERAUD, JOHN A., 1863, *Dryden, Temple Bar, vol. 7, p.* 100.

After Milton, the many-sided, fecund, flexible, unequal Dryden, the man of transition and of partition, first in date among the classics, but still broad and powerful.—SAINTE-BEUVE, C. A., 1864, *English Portraits, p.* 277.

John Dryden stands in the foremost rank of English satirists. He is the most forcible and masculine of English poets. For sheer downright intellectual strength we must seek his fellow among the great philosophers and divines,—not among poets. His justice of judgment, variety of faculty, felicity of diction, splendour of invective, have rarely been matched. It is true that the finer and more delicate forms of the imagination did not visit him; his keen observant eye failed to detect their difficult beauty; his ear was deaf to their haunting music. Yet even in his infirmities we have been used to regard him as a not unworthy representative of the English type of character, —unideal, yet manly, sagacious, affectionate, and fairly if not scrupulously honest. —SKELTON, JOHN, 1865-83, *John Dryden, Fraser's Magazine; Essays in History and Biography, p.* 143.

The songs scattered through Dryden's plays are strikingly inferior to the rest of his poetry. The confession he makes in one of his dedications that in writing for the stage he consulted the taste of the audiences and not his own, and that, looking at the results, he was equally ashamed of the public and himself, applies with special force to his songs. They seem for the most part to have been thrown off merely to fill up a situation, or produce a transitory effect, without reference to substance, art, or beauty, in their structure. Like nearly all pieces written expressly for music, the convenience of the composer is consulted in many of them rather than the judgment of the poet, although the world had a right to expect that the genius of Dryden would have vindicated itself by reconciling both. Some of the verses designed on this principle undoubtedly exhibit remarkable skill in accommodating the diction and rhythm to the demands of the air; and, however indifferent they may be in perusal, it can be easily understood how effective their breaks, repetitions, and sonorous words (sometimes without much meaning in them) must have been in the delivery. Dryden descended to the smallest things with as much success as he soared to the highest; and, if he had cared to bestow any pains upon such compositions, two or three of the following specimens are sufficient to show with what a subtle fancy and melody of versification he might have enriched this department of our poetical literature.—BELL, ROBERT, 1867? *ed. Songs from the Dramatists, p.* 237.

In the second class of English poets perhaps no one stands, on the whole, so high as he. . . . Thrice unhappy he who, born to see things as they might be, is schooled by circumstances to see them as people say they are,—to read God in a prose translation. Such was Dryden's lot, and such, for a good part of his days, it was by his own choice. He who was of a stature to snatch the torch of life that flashes from lifted hand to hand along the generations, over the heads of inferior men, chose rather to be a link-boy to the stews. . . . Was he, then, a great poet? Hardly, in the narrowest definition. But he was a strong thinker who sometimes carried common sense to a height where it catches the light of a diviner air, and warmed reason till it had wellnigh the illuminating property of intuition. Certainly he is not, like Spenser, the poets' poet, but other men have also their rights. . . . He had, beyond most, the gift of the right word.—LOWELL, JAMES RUSSELL, 1868–90, *Dryden, Prose Works, Riverside ed., vol.* III, *pp.* 99, 102, 188, 189.

A strong, sharp, subtle and versatile intellect, and a fine ear for numbers, which with practice gave him a matchless power of versification, are Dryden's chief characteristics of excellence as a poet. The self-contained, self-subsisting imagination of the greater Milton is wanting. He has more strength and larger grasp of mind than his more polished and equable successor, Pope, who divides with him suffrages for the superior place among our classic poets of second rank.—CHRISTIE, W. D., 1870, *ed. Poetical Works of John Dryden, Memoir, p.* xv.

Within a limited range he was a true poet; his imagination was far from fertile, nor had he much skill in awakening emotion, but he could treat certain subjects magnificently in verse, and often where his imagination fails him he is sustained by the vigor of his understanding and the largeness of his knowledge.— BRYANT, WILLIAM CULLEN, 1870, *A New Library of Poetry and Song, Introduction, vol.* I, *p.* 41.

Dryden has left undone what he should have done, and has done what he should not have done. . . . His was a singularly solid and judicious mind, an excellent reasoner, accustomed to discriminate his ideas, armed with good long meditated proofs, strong in discussion, asserting principles, establishing his subdivisions, citing authorities, drawing inferences; so that, if we read his prefaces without reading his dramas, we might take him for one of the masters of the dramatic art. He naturally attains a definite prose style; his ideas are unfolded with breadth and clearness; his style is well moulded, exact and simple, free from the affectations and ornaments with which Pope afterwards burdened his own; his expression is, like that of Corneille, ample and periodic, by virtue simply of the internal argumentativeness which unfolds and sustains it. We can see that he thinks, and that on his own behalf; that

he combines and verifies his thoughts; that beyond all this, he naturally has a just perception, and that with his method he has good sense. . . . I have found in him beautiful pieces, but never pleasing ones; he cannot even argue with taste. . . . In spite of several falls and many slips, he shows a mind constantly upright, bending rather from conventionality than from nature, with a dash and afflatus, occupied with grave thoughts, and subjecting his conduct to his convictions.—TAINE, H. A., 1871, *History of English Literature, vol.* II, *bk.* iii, *ch.* ii, *pp.* 9, 27, 30

To the plays of Dryden we must not look for the enduring part of his writings. Versatile, vigorous, and inventive as they are, they nevertheless lack wit and genuine pathos, and they are disfigured by bombast, and a coarseness of the crudest, not satisfactorily explained by the prevailing profligacy of the time, or excused by the tardy regrets of the poet's maturer years. Few of them survived the age of their writer. It is in his satires, translations, fables, and prologues, where he gives full play to his matchless mastery over heroics, that his successes are most signal. As a satirist he was probably unequalled, whether for command of language, management of metre, or the power of reasoning in verse.—DOBSON, AUSTIN, 1874–79, *Handbook of English Literature, p.* 106.

His character led him to conciliation and concession. He was governed by no supreme, elevated impulse, he was a devotee to no theory, but with considerable insight and power of adaptation, adjusted his action to the predominant impressions, the passing circumstances. He undertook literary labor as work, and wrought at it as one apprenticed to the business, rather than as one who felt chiefly the control of inspiration, who built above and beyond the style about him, by impulses transcending it. He bound himself to furnish a certain number of plays each year, and like a shrewd contractor, tried to fill the order in a manner agreeable to the taste of those who gave it.—BASCOM, JOHN, 1874, *Philosophy of English Literature, p.* 150.

Dryden's conversion to Catholicism had a great indirect influence on the preservation of his fame. It was this which gained him the discipleship and loving imitation of Pope. He thus became by accident, as it were, the literary father and chief model of the greatest poet of the next generation. If his fame had stood simply upon his merits as a poet, he would in all likelihood have been a much less imposing figure in literary history than he is now. The splendid force of his satire must always be admired, but there is surprisingly little of the vast mass of his writings that can be considered worthy of lasting remembrance. He showed little inventive genius. He was simply a masterly *littérateur* of immense intellectual energy, whose one lucky hit was the first splendid application of heroic couplets to satire and religious, moral, and political argument. Upon this lucky hit supervened another, the accidental discipleship of Pope. Dryden lent his gift of verse to the service of politics, and his fame profited by the connection. It would be unjust to say that his fame was due to this, but it was helped by this; apart from the attachment of Pope, he owed to party also something of the favor of Johnson and the personal championship and editorial zeal of Scott.—MINTO, WILLIAM, 1877, *Encyclopædia Britannica, Ninth Edition, vol.* VII.

His services had indeed been manifold and splendid. He had determined the bent of a great literature at a great crisis. He had banished for ever the unpruned luxuriance, the licence, the essentially uncritical spirit, which had marked expression in the literature of Elizabeth and James, and he had vindicated the substitution of a style which should proceed on critical principles, which should aim at terseness, precision, and point, should learn to restrain itself, should master the mysteries of selection and suppression. . . . He had given us the true canons of classical translation. He had shown us how our language could adapt itself with precision to the various needs of didactic prose, of lyric poetry, of argumentative exposition, of satirical invective, of easy narrative, of sonorous declamation. He had exhibited for the first time in all their fulness the power, ductility, and compass of the heroic couplet; and he had demonstrated the possibility of reasoning closely and vigorously in verse, without the elliptical obscurity of Fulke

Greville on the one hand or the painful condensation of Davies on the other. Of English classical satire he had practically been the creator. . . . He had reconstructed and popularised the poetry of romance. He had inaugurated a new era in English prose, and a new era in English criticism. . . . He is one of those figures which are constantly before us, and if his writings in their entirety are not as familiar to us as they were to our forefathers, their influence is to be traced in ever-recurring allusion and quotation; they have moulded or leavened much of our prose, more of our verse, and almost all our earlier criticism.—COLLINS, JOHN CHURTON, 1878–95, *Dryden, Quarterly Review; Essays and Studies, pp.* 1, 2, 3, 4.

None of his moral qualities better consorted with his magnificent genius than the real modesty which underlay his buoyant self-assertion.—WARD, ADOLPHUS, WILLIAM, 1880, *English Poets, ed. Ward, vol.* II, *p.* 437.

By the suffrages of his own and succeeding generations, his place is first in the second class of English poets. Perhaps his fame would have suffered little, if he had written not one of his twenty-eight dramas. He could not produce correct representations of human nature, for his was an examining rather than a believing frame of mind; and he wrought literature more as one apprenticed to the business than as one under the control of inspiration: he attained, however, the excellences that lie on the lower grade of the satirical, didactic, and polemic. Not to be numbered with those who have sounded the depths of soul, he is incomparable as a reasoner in verse.—WELSH, ALFRED H., 1883, *Development of English Literature and Language, vol.* II, *p.* 63.

Let us remember the almost universal corruption of the time, and in special defence of Dryden the fact that, a great poet as he was, he wrote mainly as a journalist, so to speak. In the absence of other ways of reaching the public, his poems were written to order for direct, immediate political effect, and with the same unscrupulousness that is sometimes seen in a corrupt press. This by no means frees his conduct from blame, but it may possibly be in part an explanation. —PERRY, THOMAS SERGEANT, 1883, *English Literature in the Eighteenth Century.*

His drama, composed when the drama was most dependent upon the court, was written, rather in spite of his nature, to win bread and to please his patrons. His comedies are a lamentable condescension to the worst tendencies of the time. His tragedies, while influenced by the French precedents, and falling into the mock heroics congenial to the hollow sentiment of the court, in which sensuality is covered by a thin veil of sham romance, gave not infrequent opportunity for a vigorous utterance of a rather cynical view of life. The declamatory passages are often in his best style. Whatever their faults no tragedies comparable to his best work have since been written for the stage. The masculine sense and power of sustained arguments gave a force unrivalled in English literature to his satires, and the same qualities appear in the vigorous versification of the "Fables," which are deformed, however, by the absence of delicate or lofty sentiment. His lyrical poetry, in spite of the vigorous "Alexander's Feast," has hardly held its own, though still admired by some critics. His prose is among the first models of a pure English style.—STEPHEN LESLIE, 1888, *Dictionary of National Biography, vol.* XVI, *p.* 73.

I can conceive nothing more sinister for the future of English literature than that to any great extent, or among any influential circle of reading and writing men, the majesty and sinewy force of the most masculine of all the English poets should be despised and rejected. Something of a temper less hurried than that of the man who runs and reads is no doubt required for the appreciation of that somewhat heavy-footed and sombre giant of tragic and of narrative song, John Dryden, warring with dunces, marching with sunken head—"a down look," as Pope described it—through the unappreciative flat places of our second Charles and James. Prosaic at times he is, slow, fatigued, unstimulating; but, at his best, how full of the true sublime, how uplifted by the wind of tragic passion, how stirred to the depths by the noblest intellectual and moral enthusiasm! For my own part, there are moments and moods in which nothing satisfies my ear and my brain as do the great accents of Dryden, while he marches down the page, with his elephants and his standards and his kettledrums,

"in the full vintage of his flowing honours." There must be something effeminate and feeble in the nervous system of a generation which cannot bear this grandiose music, this virile tramp of Dryden's soldiers and camp-followers; something singularly dull and timid in a spirit that rejects this robust intellectual companion. And, with all his russet suit of homespun, Dryden is imbued to the core with the truest and richest blood of poetry.— GOSSE, EDMUND, 1889, *What is a Great Poet? Questions at Issue, p.* 102.

A writer, who in the matter of verbal and rhythmical construction, has been used as a "Gradus ad Parnassum" by such poets as Pope, Goldsmith, and Tennyson, and who is nothing less than the literary ancestor of Walter Scott, his chief admirer and editor, ought certainly to be more generally appreciated than he seems to be at present. . . If a young lady should express a wish to become acquainted in a harmless way, with the general texture and spirit of Dryden's satire, we should refer her to the imitation of it in Tennyson's "Sea-dreams," with the comment at the end which so well illustrates the difference in the spirit of the time.—EVANS, JOHN AMPHLETT, 1890, *Dryden, The Temple Bar, vol.* 88, *pp.* 380, 381.

No fictitious character of his is a live one to-day; you can hardly recall one if you try. No couplet or verselet of his is so freighted with a serene or hopeful philosophy as to make our march the blither by reason of it down the corridors of time. No blast of all his fanfaron of trumpets sounds the opening of the gates upon any Delectable Mountains. A great, clever, literary worker! I think that is all we can say of him. And when you or I pass under his monument in the corner of Westminster Abbey, we will stand bowed respectfully, but not with any such veneration, I think, as we expect to carry to the tomb of Milton or of Chaucer; and if one falls on Pope—what then? I think we might pause—waver; more polish here —more power there—the humanities not radiant in either; and so we might safely sidle away to warm ourselves before the cenotaph of Goldsmith.—MITCHELL, DONALD G., 1890, *English Lands Letters and Kings, From Elizabeth to Anne, p.* 247.

By him poetry was made subservient to

politics and to religious polemics, and addressing himself with his varied intellectual gifts to the leading topics of the day, literature, under his auspices, became for the first time a great political power.—SWANWICK, ANNA, 1892, *Poets, the Interpreters of Their Age, p.* 245.

His faults were many, both as a man and as a poet, but he belongs to the race of the giants, and the impress of greatness is stamped upon his works. No student of Dryden can fail to mark the force and sweep of an intellect impatient of restraint. His "long-resounding march" reminds us of a turbulent river that overflows its banks, and if order and perfection of art are sometimes wanting in his verse, there is never the lack of power. Unfortunately many of the best years of his life were devoted to a craft in which he was working against the grain.—DENNIS, JOHN, 1894, *The Age of Pope, p.* 1.

On the whole, few poets have been more fortunate in their critics than Dryden.—SYLE, L. DuPONT, 1894, *From Milton to Tennyson, Notes, p.* 26.

The poet makes cunning pivots and spring-boards out of identical words, on which, without any disgusting repetition, the verse circles, from whence it leaps, and on which the reader's eye and ear travel easily and pleasantly to the close. The individual line often attempts, and sometimes gains, that magnificent thunder and roll which, to one who has once discerned it, is the very hallmark of the Drydenian decasyllable. With such facilities he must have made his way at any time—how much more at that time, when the contemporary models we have mentioned were rapidly removed by death (except Waller, who lived longer, but produced nothing), when Milton was out of touch with the audience, and when there was no one else?—SAINTSBURY, GEORGE, 1895, *Social England, ed. Traill, vol.* IV, *p.* 433.

Dryden is an admirable example [of the man of letters]: ready to turn his hand to anything, swift in production, easy in manner, free from pedantry, yet accurate, and careful of pure diction; proud of his profession, not treating it as a plaything, like Byron and Scott, yet a man of the world, with his eyes open to what went on about him.—BRADFORD, GAMALIEL, JR., 1895, *The American Man of Letters, Types of American Character, p.* 119.

The songs in Dryden's plays are cheerful and sprightly. In the higher graces of poetry they are infinitely inferior to Fletcher's, but they are very good of their kind. With all his consummate genius Dryden could not reproduce such strains as "Lay a garland on my hearse" or "God Lyæus ever young."—BULLEN, A. H., 1895, *Musa Proterva, p.* x.

Dryden was a great originator.—BROOKE, STOPFORD A., 1896, *English Literature, p.* 178.

The recognizing and following of popular taste can easily become other than a merit; but it marks the true journalistic mind, which was Dryden's, and at another period he would have written very differently. In our own time we can conceive of his occupying such a position as Charles A. Dana, with his ability for polemic writing and leadership in diction, but with the literary side more emphasized, as in the case of Bryant. He has left much that will stand the test of any age, but his whole work must not be judged save in connection with the ferments in which his lot was cast.—GREGORY, WARREN F., 1896, *ed. Dryden's Palamon and Arcite, Biographical Sketch, p.* 25.

Though Dryden's poetry is not of the highest class, it is of the very highest kind in its class. Wherever the pure intellect comes into play, there he is invariably excellent. There is never any weakness; there is never any vagueness; there is never any deviation from the true path into aimless digression. His words invariably go straight to the mark, and not unfrequently with a directness and force that fully merit the epithet "burning" applied to them by the poet Gray. His thoughts always rise naturally out of the matter in hand; and in the treatment of the meanest subjects he is not only never mean, but often falls without apparent effort into a felicity of phrase which holds the attention and implants itself in the memory.—LOUNSBURY, THOMAS R., 1897, *Library of the World's Best Literature, ed. Warner, vol.* IX, *p.* 4931.

Dryden, a man of supreme talent rather than of great spontaneous genius, was preeminently a man of his age. He reflected its gayety, its brilliance, its wit, its immorality; he reflected, also, those nobler and more serious elements of life which it did not utterly lack. He possessed, moreover, many noble qualities which raised him above the level of his age and made him worthy to rank with the great ones of our literature. Strength and solidity of mind, accuracy and comprehensiveness of scholarship, astonishing fluency and versatility, masterly skill as a literary workman, brilliant wit, keenness of discrimination and insight, an imagination vivid if not original, a poetic sense real if not profound,—these are some of the qualities which made Dryden great. Nothing about him is more impressive than the range of his literary work, unless it be its excellence in every kind. . . . As a poet, he was first without even a near rival. No one was his equal as an original poet; no one was his equal as a translator. In imaginative prose, he must yield the palm to Bunyan; but as a literary critic, and master of a thoroughly modern prose style, he was first in his own time, and still commands the respect of the student of literature. It will thus appear that in each of the great departments of literature in his own age his name must be placed in the first rank. Dryden is more, however, than the greatest figure in a comparatively inferior literary period. He is one of the great poets of English literature. Though not of supreme stature, he is still one of the race of giants.—CRASHAW, W. H., 1898, *ed. Dryden's Palamon and Arcite, pp.* 118, 119.

It was the fault of his age that he was not greater. No man can wholly detach himself from the influences by which he is surrounded; and Dryden came on the stage when a false taste prevailed, and when licentiousness gave moral tone to poetry. Living in the midst of burning religious and political questions, he was drawn into the vortex of controversy. He was always a partisan in some religious or political issue of the day. While this fact has given us some of the best satirical and didactic poems in our language, it did not contribute, perhaps, to the largest development of his poetical powers. . . . Dryden did not attain to the highest regions of poetry. He could not portray what is deepest and finest in human experience. His strong, masculine hands were too clumsy. He has no charm of pathos; he does not touch that part of our nature where "thoughts do often lie too deep for tears." But he was a virile thinker and a master of the English tongue. He had the gift of using the right word.—PAINTER, F. V. N., 1899, *A History of English Literature, pp.* 215, 226.

He wrote a great number of plays, usually in rhyme. . . . Of these "All's for Love," based on the Antony and Cleopatra story, is one of the best, but they all seem to us very tedious, and need be read only by those who wish to make a special study of the theatre of this time. Bits of splendid declamation can be found,—Dryden is always vigorous,—but the plays are artificial structures, and their interest depended on a literary fashion which is past. There is not enough of the stuff of genuine human nature in them to give them vitality. At the same time we cannot fail to be struck with the excellence of the literary workmanship.—JOHNSON, CHARLES F., 1900, *English and American Literature, p.* 229.

We now possess, thanks to Mr. Christie and Mr. Ker, scholarly, if not irreproachable, editions of Dryden's poems and of his chief prose writings. His dramas, which, aside from their historical importance, contain much of his best poetry, have yet to be made generally accessible. But a greater need than this remains to be supplied. Despite the seamy side of his character, which is only too obvious, Dryden had a personality full of grace and charm, which reveals itself to sympathetic readers of his works, and for which illustration might be found in contemporary literature. But he has been unfortunate in his biographers. Even Johnson and Scott, of whom most might have been expected, dwell too exclusively on the literary and political aspects of his career. Hence Dryden, who should be as well loved as Dr. Johnson or Charles Lamb—to choose widely different illustrations—is known to the "average man" only as a political and religious turn-coat, who wrote satires on forgotten men and dead issue. Some true lover may yet produce an imaginative portrait of Dryden such as Carlyle has given us of Burns, showing him as the "high and remarkable man" he really was.—NOYES, G. R., 1900, *Dryden as a Critic, The Nation, vol.* 71, *p.* 232.

Sir Charles Sedley

1639?–1701

Born, at Aylesford, Kent, 1639. Matric., Wadham Coll., Oxford, 22 March 1656. Succeeded to Baronetcy, 1656. M. P. for New Romney, 1668–81, 1690–95, 1696–1701. Married. Died, 20 Aug. 1701. *Works:* "The Earle of Pembroke's Speech in the House of Peeres" (anon.,) 1648; "The Last Will and Testament of the Earl of Pembroke" [1650]; "The Mulberry Garden," 1668; "Antony and Cleopatra," 1677; "Bellamira," 1687. *Posthumous:* "Beauty the Conqueror," 1702; "The Grumbler" (anon.), 1702; "The Tyrant King of Crete," 1702; "The Happy Pair," 1702. *Collected Works:* 1707.—SHARP, R. FARQUHARSON, 1897, *A Dictionary of English Authors, p.* 251.

PERSONAL

Pierce do tell me, among other news, the late frolick and debauchery of Sir Charles Sidley and Buckhurst, running up and down all the night, almost naked through the streets; and at last fighting and being beat by the watch and clapped up all night, and how the king takes their parts; and my Lord Chief Justice Keeling hath laid the constable by the heels to answer it next Session, which is a horrid shame. —PEPYS, SAMUEL, 1668, *Diary, Oct.* 23.

Think, if you please, that this dedication is only an occasion I have taken, to do myself the greatest honour imaginable with posterity; that is, to be recorded in the number of those men whom you have favoured with your friendship and esteem. For I am well assured, that, besides the present satisfaction I have, it will gain me the greatest part of my reputation with after ages, when they shall find me valuing myself on your kindness to me; I may have reason to suspect my own credit with them, but I have none to doubt of yours. And they who, perhaps, would forget me in my poems, would remember me in this epistle.—DRYDEN, JOHN, 1673, *The Assignation, Dedication to Sir Charles Sedley.*

I am glad the town has so good a taste as to give the same just applause to S.' Charles Sidley's writing which his friends have always done to his conversation. Few of our plays can boast of more wit than I have heard him speak at a supper. Some barren sparks have found fault with what he has formerly done, only because the fairness of the soil has produced so big a crop. I daily drink his health my Lord Dorset's, your own, and all our friends'. —ETHEREDGE, SIR GEORGE, 1687, *The Letterbook. Gosse, Seventeenth-Century Studies, p.* 262.

Sedley had a more sudden and copious wit, which furnished a perpetual run of discourse; but he was not so correct as Lord Dorset, nor so sparkling as Lord Rochester.—BURNET, GILBERT, 1715–34, *History of My Own Time.*

When his comedy of "Bellamira" was played, the roof fell in, and he was one of the very few that were hurt by the accident. A flatterer told him that the fire of the play had blown up the poet, house, and all. "No," he replied, "the play was so heavy that it broke down the house, and buried the poet in his own rubbish."—CAMPBELL, THOMAS, 1819, *Specimens of the British Poets.*

Profligate and debauched Sedley certainly was. His disgraceful frolic at the Cock Tavern, in Bow Street, Covent Garden, on which his genius has conferred an unfortunate notoriety, is not only too indecent to bear repetition, but was an insult even to the age in which he lived.—JESSE, JOHN HENEAGE, 1839–40, *Memoirs of the Court of England During the Reign of the Stuarts, Including the Protectorate, p.* 328.

One of the most brilliant and profligate wits of the Restoration. The licentiousness of his writings is not redeemed by much grace or vivacity, but the charms of his conversation were acknowledged even by sober men who had no esteem for his character. To sit near him at the theatre, and to hear his criticisms on a new play, was regarded as a privilege. Dryden had done him the honour to make him a principal interlocutor in the dialogue on dramatic poesy. The morals of Sedley were such as, even in that age, gave great scandal.—MACAULAY, THOMAS BABINGTON, 1843, *Catharine Sedley, Critical and Historical Essays.*

Sir Charles Sedley was a fashionable wit, and the foulness of his words made ever the porters of Covent Garden pelt him from the balcony when he ventured to address them.—GREEN, JOHN RICHARD, 1874, *A Short History of the English People*.

GENERAL

Sedley has that prevailing, gentle art
That can with a resistless charm impart
The loosest wishes to the chastest heart.
—ROCHESTER, JOHN WILMOT, EARL, 1678, *An Allusion to the Tenth Satire of the First Book of Horace*.

Heard him speak more Wit at a Supper, than all his Adversaries, with their Heads joyn'd together, could write in a Year. That his Writings are not unequal to any Man's of this Age, (not to speak of Abundance of Excellent Copies of Verses). That he has in the "Mulberry Garden," shown the true Wit, Humour, and Satyr of a Comedy; and in "Anthony and Cleopatra," the true Spirit of a Tragedy.—SHADWELL, THOMAS, 1679, *A True Widow, Epistle Dedicatory*.

A Gentleman whose Name speaks a greater *Panegyrick*, than I am able to express; and whose Wit is so well known to this Age, that I should but tarnish its Lustre, by my Endeavouring to deliver it over to the next: His Wit is too Noble a Subject to need any Herald to proclaim its Titles and Pedigree; or if it did, my Voice and Skill are too weak, to sound out his Praises in their due measures. I shall therefore only content my self, as the Vallys, that have no Voice of their own, to eccho out his Merits at the Second-hand.—LANGBAINE, GERARD, 1691, *An Account of the English Dramatick Poets*, p. 485.

Sedley is a very insipid writer; except in some few of his little love-verses.—POPE, ALEXANDER, 1734–36, *Spence's Anecdotes, ed. Singer*, p. 103.

Sedley's poems, however amorously tender and delicate, yet have not much strength; nor do they afford great marks of genius. The softness of his verses is denominated by the Duke of Buckingham, Sedley's Witchcraft. It was an art too successful in those days to propagate the immoralities of the times, but it must be owned that in point of chastity he excels Dorset, and Rochester; who as they conceived lewdly, wrote in plain English, and did not give themselves any trouble to wrap up their ribbaldry in a dress tollerably decent. But if Sedley was the more chaste, I know not if he was the less pernicious writer: for that pill which is gilded will be swallowed more readily, and with less reluctance, than if tendered in its own disgustful colours. Sedley insinuates gently into the heart, without giving any alarm, but is no less fraught with poison, than are those whose deformity bespeaks their mischief.—CIBBER, THEOPHILUS, 1753, *Lives of the Poets. vol. III*, p. 99.

Sir Charles Sedley was distinguished for writing poems of considerable impurity of idea and considerable purity of language. His biographer therefore is careful to inform us that though the sentiments of Sir Charles were as foul as those of Rochester, they were not so immodest, because they were arrayed in clean linen.—WHIPPLE, EDWIN P., 1845, *Words, American Review, Feb.; Essays and Reviews*.

As a lyrical writer Sedley's merit was his demerit. There was poison in his love poems; but it was a poison that enchanted the wits of the day, and Buckingham called it Sedley's "Witchcraft."—THOMPSON, KATHERINE (GRACE WHARTON), 1862, *The Literature of Society, vol. I*, p. 275.

Sir Charles Sedley ruins and pollutes himself, but Charles II. calls him "the viceroy of Apollo." Buckingham extols "the magic of his style." He is the most charming, the most sought after of talkers; he makes puns and verses, always agreeable, sometimes refined; he handles dexterously the pretty jargon of mythology; he insinuates into his airy, flowing verses all the dainty and somewhat affected prettinesses of the drawing-room. . . . There is no love whatever in these pretty things; they are received as they are presented, with a smile; they form part of the conventional language, the polite attentions due from gentlemen to ladies. I suppose they would send them in the morning with a nosegay, or a box of preserved fruits.—TAINE, H. A., 1871, *History of English Literature, tr. Van Laun, vol. I*, p. 497.

Sedley, as it is needless to adduce evidence to prove, was commonly accounted one of the most notorious profligates of the most dissolute period of Charles II's reign; but he was a capable politician of moderate views, and gained distinction in more than one branch of literature. His lyrics contain occasional turns of a felicitous and engaging simplicity, such as is not generally observable in his plays; and he wrote a facile and clear style as a prose pamphleteer.—WARD, ADOLPHUS WILLIAM, 1875-99, *A History of English Dramatic Literature*, vol. III, *p.* 447.

Sedley was one of the most graceful and refined of the mob of Restoration noblemen who wrote in prose and verse. For nearly forty years he was recognised as a patron of the art of poetry, and as an amateur of more than usual skill. Three times, at intervals of ten years, he produced a play in the taste of the age, and when his clever comedy of "Bellamira" was refused at the Duke's Theatre, on account of its intolerable indelicacy, he sulked for the remainder of his life, and left to his executors three more plays in manuscript. His songs are bright and lively, but inferior to those of Rochester in lyrical force. A certain sweetness of diction in his verse delighted his contemporaries, who praised his "witchcraft" and his "gentle prevailing art." In his plays he seems to be successively inspired by Etheredge, Shadwell and Crowne. Two lines in his most famous song have preserved his reputation from complete decay.—GOSSE, EDMUND, 1880, *English Poets, ed. Ward*, vol. II, *p.* 415.

A genuine but inferior humourist and poet, only not quite so deeply tainted by the "fat pollutions" of their time.—SWINBURNE, ALGERNON CHARLES, 1891, *Social Verse, Studies in Prose and Poetry, p.* 97.

A still smaller gleaning comes to us from Sir Charles Sedley, who, for two hundred years, has been preserved from oblivion by a little wanton verse about Phillis, full of such good-natured contentment and disbelief that we grow young and cheerful again in contemplating it. Should any long-suffering reader desire to taste the sweets of sudden contrast and of sharp reaction, let him turn from the strenuous, analytic, half-caustic, and wholly discomforting love-poem of the nineteenth century—Mr. Browning's word-picture of "A Pretty Woman," for example—back to those swinging and jocund lines where Phillis,

"Faithless as the winds or seas,"

smiles furtively upon her suitor, whose clear-sightedness avails him nothing, and who plays the game merrily to the end:—

"She deceiving,
I believing,
What need lovers wish for more?"

We who read are very far from wishing for anything more.—REPPLIER, AGNES, 1891, *English Love-Songs, Points of View.*

From Sir Charles Sedley I have drawn very freely. In his own sphere Sedley is unapproachable; such songs as "Love still has something of the sea" or "Phillis is my only joy" easily out-distance all rivals. He does not occupy an exalted place in English literature; but his seat is secure.—BULLEN, A. H., 1895, *Musa Proterva, p.* xiii.

John Pomfret

1667–1702

A native of Luton, Bedfordshire; educated at Queen's College, Cambridge; became Vicar of Malden, and was presented to a living of greater value, institution into which was at first refused by Bishop Compton, in consequence of a misconstruction of a passage in the parson's poem of "The Choice." Pomfret made a satisfactory vindication; but whilst he lingered in London, engaged in this business, he caught the smallpox, the fatal termination of which abruptly ended alike his anxieties and his hopes. A volume of his Poems—"The Choice," and others—was pub. in 1699; and in 1724 appeared his "Remains:" a volume containing two poetical pieces, —"Reason," and "Dies Novissima, or The Last Epiphany; a Pindaric Ode." This volume was published by a friend, under the name of Philalethes. The 4th ed. of "The Choice" was published 1701, folio; the Tenth Edition of his "Poems on Several Occasions, with an Account of his Life and Writings, to which are added his Remains," was issued in 1740, 8vo. Many editions of his Poems have since appeared; and they are republished in Johnson's and Chalmers's collections.—ALLIBONE, S. AUSTIN, 1870, *Dictionary of English Literature*, vol. II, *p.* 1619.

GENERAL

This Gentleman's works are held in very great esteem by the common readers of poetry; it is thought as unfashionable amongst people of inferior life, not to be possessed of the poems of Pomfret, as amongst persons of taste not to have the works of Pope in their libraries. The subjects upon which Pomfret wrote were popular, his versification is far from being unmusical, and as there is little force of thinking in his writings, they are level to the capacities of those who admire them.—CIBBER, THEOPHILUS, 1753, *Lives of the Poets, vol.* III, *p.* 218.

His "Choice" exhibits a system of life adapted to common notions, and equal to common expectations; such a state as affords plenty and tranquility, without exclusion of intellectual pleasures. Perhaps no composition in our language has been oftener perused than Pomfret's "Choice." In his other poems there is an easy volubility; the pleasure of smooth metre is afforded to the ear, and the mind is not oppressed with ponderous or entangled with intricate sentiment. He pleases many, and he who pleases many must have some species of merit.—JOHNSON, SAMUEL, 1779–81, *Pomfret, Lives of the English Poets, p.* 191.

Why is Pomfret the most popular of the English Poets? the fact is certain, and the solution would be useful.—SOUTHEY, ROBERT, 1807, *Specimens of the Later English Poets, vol.* I, *p.* 91.

It is asked, in Mr. Southey's "Specimens of English Poetry," why Pomfret's "Choice" is the most popular poem in the English language: it might have been demanded with equal propriety, why London bridge is built of Parïan marble.—CAMPBELL, THOMAS, 1819, *Specimens of the British Poets.*

William's reign, always excepting Dryden, is our *nadir* in works of imagination. Then came Blackmore with his epic poems of Prince Arthur and King Arthur, and Pomfret with his Choice, both popular in their own age, and both intolerable, by their frigid and tame monotony, in the next.—HALLAM, HENRY, 1837–39, *Introduction to the Literature of Europe, pt.* iv.

The concentrate essence of namby-pambyism.—BROWNING, ELIZABETH BARRETT, 1842–63, *The Book of the Poets.*

It is difficult in the present day . . . to conceive that the "Choice" could ever have been a very popular poem. It is tame and commonplace. The idea, however, of a country retirement, a private seat, with a wood, garden, and stream, a clear and competent estate, and the enjoyment of lettered ease and happiness, is so grateful and agreeable to the mind of man, especially in large cities, that we can hardly forbear liking a poem that recalls so beloved an image to our recollection.—CHAMBERS, ROBERT, 1876, *Cyclopædia of English Literature, ed. Carruthers.*

Our grandfathers or our great-grandfathers might with some fair show of reason have maintained that it was impossible to believe that a poem which had so well stood the test of time would ever sink into forgetfulness. Let me suggest to you that if any one in your hearing foretells immortality for some writer for whom you have no relish, you should ask him at once whether he has read Pomfret's "Choice."—HILL, GEORGE BIRKBECK, 1892, *Writers and Readers, p.* 28.

He dabbled in verse at least as early as 1694, when he wrote an elegy upon the death of Queen Mary. This was published in 1699, with other pieces in heroic couplets, remarkable chiefly for their correctness, under the title of "Poems on Several Occasions." One of the longer poems, called "Cruelty and Lust," commemorates an act of barbarity said to have been perpetrated by Colonel Kirke during the western rebellion. Pomfret's treatment of the situation is prosaically tame. . . . When the scheme for the "Lives of the Poets" was submitted by the booksellers to Dr. Johnson, the name of Pomfret (together with three others) was added by his advice; Johnson remarks that "perhaps no poem in our language has been so often perused" as "The Choice." It is an admirable exposition in neatly turned verse of the everyday epicureanism of a cultivated man. Pomfret is said to have drawn some hints from the study of the character of Sir William Temple. . . . The exclusion of Pomfret from more recent literary manuals and anthologies sufficiently indicates that Johnson's strange verdict finds few supporters at the present day.—SECCOMBE, THOMAS, 1896, *Dictionary of National Biography, vol.* XLVI, *pp.* 74, 75.

Samuel Pepys

1633–1703

Born, in London(?), 23 Feb. 1633. Early education at a school at Huntingdon. At St. Paul's School, London, as Scholar. Matric., Trin. Hall, Camb., 21 June 1650; removed to Magdalene Coll., as Sizar, 5 March 1651; B. A., 1653; M. A., 1660. Married Elizabeth St. Michel, 1 Dec. 1655. Sec. to Sir Edward Montagu, 1656–60. Clerk of the Acts, July 1660. Clerk of Privy Seal, July 1660. Justice of the Peace, Aug. 1660. Younger Brother of the Trinity House, Feb. 1662. Mem. of Tangier Commission, Aug. 1662; Treasurer, March 1665. F. R. S., 15 Feb. 1665. Surveyor-General of Victualling Office, Oct. 1665. Visit to France and Holland, 1669. Sec. for the Affairs of the Navy, 1673. M. P. for Castle Rising, Nov. 1673. Master of Trinity House, 1676 and 1685. Governor of Christ's Hospital, 1676; Treasurer, 1698; Vice-Pres., 1699. Master of Clothworkers Co., 1677. M. P. for Harwich, 1679. Committed to Tower, on charge of Treason, 22 May, 1679; released March 1680. To Tangier with Lord Dartmouth, 1683. Pres., Royal Soc., Nov. 1684. M. P. for Harwich, 1685. Sec. of Admiralty, June 1686. Resigned office, March 1689. Imprisoned in Gate-house on charge of Treason, 25 June to July, 1689. Retired to Clapham, 1690. Died there, 26 May, 1703. Buried in St. Olave's, Hart Street. *Works:* "The Portugal History" (under initials: S. P., Esq.), 1677; "Memoirs relating to the State of the Royal Navy" (anon.), 1690. *Posthumous:* "Diary," ed. by Lord Braybrooke, 1825; ed. by H. B. Wheatley (8 vols.), 1893, etc.—SHARP, R. FARQUHARSON, 1897, *A Dictionary of English Authors*, p. 225.

PERSONAL

Memorandum: that Peapys and Hind were solemnly admonished by myself and Mr. Hill, for having been scandalously over-served with drink ye night before. This was done in the presence of all the Fellows then resident, in Mr. Hill's chamber.—WOOD, JOHN, 1653, *Registrar's Book, Magdalene College, Cambridge*, Oct. 21.

Last night, at 9 a clock, I did the last office for your and my good friend, Mr Pepys, at St Olave's Church, where he was laid in a vault of his own makeing, by his wife and brother. The greatness of his behaviour, in his long and sharp tryall before his death, was in every respect answerable to his great life; and I believe no man ever went out of this world with greater contempt of it, or a more lively faith in every thing that was revealed to the world to come. I administered the Holy Sacrament twice in his illness to him, and had administered it a third time, but for a sudden fit of illness that happened at the appointed time of administering of it. Twice I gave him the absolution of the Church, which he desired, and received with all reverence and comfort; and I never attended any sick or dying person, that dyed with so much Christian greatness of mind, or a more lively sense of immortality, or so much fortitude and patience, in so long and sharp a tryall, or greater resignation to the will, which he most devoutly acknowledged to be the wisdom of God; and I doubt not but he is now a very blessed spirit, according to his motto, MENS CUJUSQUE IS EST QUISQUE.—HICKES, GEORGE, 1703, *Letter to Dr. Charlett.*

This day died Mr. Sam. Pepys, a very worthy, industrious and curious person, none in England exceeding him in knowledge of the navy, in wch he had passed thro' all the most considerable offices, Clerk of the Acts, and Secretary of the Admiralty, all wch he perform'd with great integrity. . . . He liv'd at Clapham, where he enjoy'd the fruite of his labours in greate prosperity. He was universally belov'd, hospitable, generous, learned in many things, skill'd in music, a very greate cherisher of learned men of whom he had the conversation. His library and collection of other curiosities were of the most considerable, the models of ships especially. Besides what he publish'd of an account of the Navy, as he found and left it, he had for divers yeares under his hand the "History of the Navy," or "Navalia" as he call'd it; but how far advanc'd, and what will follow of his, is left, I suppose, to his sister's son Mr. Jackson, a young gentleman whom Mr. Pepys had educated in all sorts of useful learning, sending him to travel abroad, from whence he return'd with extraordinary accomplishments, and worthy to be heir. Mr. Pepys had been for neere 40 yeaers so much my particular friend, that Mr. Jackson sent me complet mourning, desiring me to be one to hold up the pall at his magnificent obsequies, but my indisposition hinder'd me from doing him this last office.—EVELYN, JOHN, 1703, *Diary, May 26.*

The administration of the Admiralty under Pepys is still regarded as a model for order and economy.—HUME, DAVID, 1854–62, *History of England, James II., ch.* lxxi.

It is well known that the naval history of Charles II. is the most shining part of the annals of his reign; and that the business of the navy was conducted with the utmost regularity and prudence, under Charles and James, by this worthy and judicious person. He first reduced the affairs of the admiralty to order and method; and that method was so just, as to have been a standing model to his successors in his important office. His "Memoirs," relating to the navy, is a well written piece; and his copious collection of manuscripts, now remaining, with the rest of his library, at Magdalen College, in Cambridge, is an invaluable treasure of naval knowledge. He was far from being a mere man of business; his conversation and address had been greatly refined by travel. He thoroughly understood and practised music; was a judge of painting, sculpture, and architecture; and had more than a superficial knowledge in history and philosophy. His fáme among the virtuosi was such, that he was thought a very proper person to be placed at the head of the Royal Society, of which he was some time president.—GRANGER, JAMES, 1769–1824, *Biographical History of England, vol.* VI, *p.* 132.

Though we laugh at Pepys with his cockney revels, and his beatitudes of lace and velvet, and his delight at having his head patted by Lord Clarendon, and his honest uproariness, and his not knowing; "what to think," between his transport with the court beauties, and the harm he is afraid they will do the state—we feel that he ends in being a thoroughly honest man, and even a very clever one, and that we could have grown serious in his behalf, had his comfort or good name been put in jeopardy.—HUNT, LEIGH, 1841, *Men, Women and Books.*

The pronunciation of Pepys's name has long been a disputed point, but although the most usual form at the present day is *Peps,* there can be little doubt that in his own time the name was pronounced as if written *Peeps.* The reasons for this opinion are: (1) that the name was sometimes so spelt phonetically by some of his contemporaries, as in the Coffee-house paper quoted in the "Diary" (ed. Mynors Bright, vol. vi. p. 292): "On Tuesday last Mr. Peeps went to Windsor," &c.; (2) that this pronunciation is still the received one at Magdalene College, Cambridge; and (3) that the present bearers of the name so pronounce it.—WHEATLEY, HENRY B., 1880, *Samuel Pepys and the World he Lived in, Preface, p.* vii.

He must always be doing something agreeable, and, by preference, two agreeable things at once. In his house he had a box of carpenter's tools, two dogs, an eagle, a canary, and a blackbird that whistled tunes, lest, even in that full life, he should chance upon an empty moment. If he had to wait for a dish of poached eggs, he must put in the time by playing on the flageolet; if a sermon were dull, he must read in the book of Tobit or divert his mind with sly advances on the nearest women. When he walked, it must be with a book in his pocket to beguile the way in case the nightingales were silent; and even along the streets of London, with so many pretty faces to be spied for and dignitaries to be saluted, his trail was marked by little debts "for wine, pictures, etc.," the true headmark of a life intolerant of any joyless passage. He had a kind of idealism in pleasure; like the princess in the fairy story, he was conscious of a rose-leaf out of place. Dearly as he loved to talk, he could not enjoy nor shine in a conversation when he thought himself unsuitably dressed. Dearly as he loved eating, he "knew not how to eat alone;" pleasure for him must heighten pleasure; and the eye and ear must be flattered like the palate ere he avow himself content.—STEVENSON, ROBERT LOUIS, 1882, *Samuel Pepys, Familiar Studies of Men and Books.*

In truth, Elizabeth had reason for the display of temper. Mr. Pepys, now a great man, in enlarging his scheme of pleasure gradually expands in a forbidden direction. Always sufficiently appreciative of a pretty woman, his interest in a handsome face grows with his opportunities, and there come occasions when the jealousy that arises in Elizabeth's heart is not, like his green-eyed fits, without foundation. His heart is always faithfully hers, but his eyes note beauty in other faces than her own; and the manners of the age could not, in her opinion, excuse his predilection for kissing every pretty woman he might meet. . . . In spite of the remarkable brain, and the even more noteworthy honesty, that made him the important personage of his group, Samuel Pepys was naught but the tailor's son, after all, with his eyes turned wholly toward the goods of the world and the attainment thereof; and Elizabeth, aside from her French cleverness and her beauty, had neither dignity nor nobility to aid her to order her life in a difficult age. She had the power to inspire in her husband the one love of his selfish heart; she had no capacity to control his roving fancy. Like a child in her love of frivolity, she was like a child still in meeting misery.—WHITING, MARGARET CHRISTINE, 1890, *The Wife of Mr. Secretary Pepys, Atlantic Monthly, vol. 66, pp. 750, 751.*

Few men are better known than Samuel Pepys.—FIRTH, C. H., 1894, *The Early Life of Pepys, Macmillan's Magazine, vol. 69, p. 32.*

Amongst the games in which Mr. Secretary Pepys seems to have found special satisfaction, tennis, ninepins, and billiards hold high place; but these, after all, never yielded him a tithe of the pure enjoyment that he derived from his more intellectual pastimes, reading and music. Pepys was a genuine musician; and we get the impression from the journal that his love of music reached the proportions of a real passion—the only passion, indeed, of his life. On the other hand, he was not a systematic scholar, though he devoured books with avidity, keeping in touch with the literary output of his day, and at least tasting all sorts of things, from Cicero, the Hebrew Grammar, and Hooker's "Ecclesiastical Polity," downward to Audley's "Way to be Rich," and the last-published comedy of the popular playwrights of his time. . . . Pepys's passing opinions have not much critical value.—HUDSON, WILLIAM HENRY, 1897, *Pepys and his Diary, Idle Hours in a Library, pp. 100, 101.*

DIARY

Of very great interest and curiosity. . . . Fortunately for the public part of the story, the author was, from the very beginning, in immediate contact with persons in high office and about court—and, still more fortunately for the private part, seems to have been possessed of the most extraordinary activity, and the most indiscriminating, insatiable, and miscellaneous curiosity, that ever prompted the researches, or supplied the pen, of a daily chronicler.—JEFFREY, FRANCIS LORD, 1825, *Pepys's Memoirs, Edinburgh Review, vol. 43, p. 26.*

If quitting the broad path of history we seek for minute information concerning ancient manners and customs, the progress of arts and sciences, and the various branches of antiquity, we have never seen a mine so rich as the volumes before us. The variety of Pepys's tastes and pursuits led him into almost every department of life.—SCOTT, SIR WALTER, 1826, *Pepys's Memoirs, Quarterly Review, vol. 33, p. 308.*

It is an advantage to have the observations of a common mind, strong but coarse. We take a vulgar man's account of his own times, written probably in the same spirit as household expenses are kept—for reference, and for his own eye alone. That eye was keen-sighted to foibles, sins, deceit, worldliness, and to every thing—its own interest more especially. We value our diarist for being of so little taste as to tell *every* thing, and of so slight a moral perception as to give everything the hue not of our age, but of his own. We value him that he tells us things as they were, and calls them by expressive names. He is the photographer of the Court of Charles the Second. His pictures are ugly, but accurate. Welcome, therefore, in his full bottomed wig, his long worked cambric tie, frilled at the end; welcome in his official robes, with his hand on a chart, a pair of compasses beside it,—with his violin in the gloom,—his globe, the implement of his office, at his side; welcome with his marked eyebrows, his long, narrow, shrewd eyes, his vulgar nose, his double chin, and full cheeks; welcome with his large, sensible, but sensual mouth—Samuel Pepys, as Kneller, in vulgarity a kindred spirit, has bequeathed him to a

grateful posterity.—THOMPSON, KATHER-
INE (GRACE WHARTON), 1862, *The Literature of Society,* .vol. I, p. 240.

No history gives us so clear an understanding of the moral condition of average men after the restoration of the
Stuarts as the unconscious blabbings of
the Puritan tailor's son, with his two consciences, as it were,—an inward, still
sensitive in spots, though mostly tough-
ened to India-rubber, and good rather for
rubbing out old scores than retaining
them, and an outward, alert, and ter-
magantly effective in Mrs. Pepys.—LOW-
ELL, JAMES RUSSELL, 1871, *A Great Public Character, My Study Windows,* p. 91.

Milverton. Let us take five or six of
the men who are best known to the world.
Now they shall not be saints or martyrs;
or men especially renowned for goodness
of any kind. I will choose them only from
the fact that they happen to be well
known to us—not their lives particularly,
but themselves. . . . The men I will
choose are Horace, Dante, Montaigne,
Pepys, Dr. Johnson, and Rousseau.

Ellesmere. A queer collection. How
they would have quarrelled!

Milverton. I don't know about that.
All I contend for is, that there is much
to admire and like in each of these men,
however great their faults may have been.

Sir Arthur. Pepys?

Ellesmere. The best chosen of all.
Now, there is a book I have read—his
"Diary"—over and over again. I give
Milverton great credit for choosing him.
He does not pretend to be a mass of virtue, but, after all, how much good and
worth there is in the fellow. I look upon
that "Diary" of his as the truest book
ever written. Even when he condescends
to conformity, you can see that he does
not take in himself, or wish to take in
any reader, if that "Diary" was ever intended to be read. One day he goes in a
barge with the King and the Duke of
York. "Good Lord!" he says, "what
poor stuff they did talk." Then recol-
lecting that, as an official man, he must
not even to himself, run down his official
superiors, he adds, "But, God be praised,
they are both of them princes of marvellous nobleness and spirit."—HELPS, SIR
ARTHUR, 1875, *Social Pressure,* pp. 162,
163.

The importance of Pepy's 'Diary,''

historically speaking, may be summed up
by saying that without it the history of the
court of Charles II. could not have been
written. We do not, it is true, gain from
it any information as to what was going
on in the country. Utterly destitute of
imagination or political knowledge, Pepys
could only record the sights and the gossip
that were evident to all. It is because
he did record these, without hesitation or
concealment, that from his "Diary" we
can understand the brilliancy and wickedness of the court, as well as the social
state and daily life of the bourgeois class.
—AIRY, OSMUND, 1885, *Encyclopædia
Britannica, vol.* XVIII.

It is scarcely literature—that is to say,
there is neither art nor effort at construction; but Pepys has extraordinary picturesqueness and great capacity in describing
what he has seen in the best and briefest
words. Evelyn's diary has a coldness, a
dignity, in its ease, that suggest that he
conceived that the world might force it
into publication. Pepys believed himself
absolutely safe behind the veil of his
cipher, and he made no effort to paint the
lily.—GOSSE, EDMUND, 1888, *A History
of Eighteenth Century Literature,* p. 97.

And it is delightful; it is so true and
honest, and straightforward, and gossipy;
and it throws more light upon the every-
day life in London in those days of the
Restoration than all the other books ever
written.—MITCHELL, DONALD G., 1890,
*English Lands Letters and Kings, From
Elizabeth to Anne,* p. 200.

Honoured Sir: It was the saying of a
wise man, though a young one, that we
do all of us travel through life with a
donkey. You kept your donkey in a
stable very private. The charger dwelt
in that noted "Diary" of yours, a journal
written in cipher, which has now for
many years been transcribed in plain hand,
and given to the world. Mr. Pepys, do
not, I pray you, blush so fiery a red; not
all the "Diary" hath yet been made public, and the world is still a stranger to
many of those most private confidences
between your donkey and yourself. Matters there be which I could mention, an'
I would, but I write for a generation in
which they who read not are very modest,
and will raise a cry against you and me,
if I keep not a bridle on my pen. The
record of a whole day in the sad story of

Deb is omitted, concerning Knip and Pierce, and *a certain other lady* (oh fie, Mr. Pepys!) the world knows no more than the worthy minister, your editor, chose to tell it.—LANG, ANDREW, 1893, *A Letter to Samuel Pepys, Esq., Scribner's Magazine,* vol. 14, *p.* 354.

In spite of all the research which has brought to light so many incidents of interest in the life of Samuel Pepys, we cannot but feel how dry these facts are when placed by the side of the living details of the "Diary." It is in its pages that the true man is displayed, and it has therefore not been thought necessary here to do more than set down in chronological order such facts as are known of the life outside the Diary.—WHEATLEY, HENRY B., 1893, *ed., The Diary of Samuel Pepys, vol.* I, *p.* liii.

There is possible misapprehension of Pepys's character, which may be removed by argument, if it is anywhere entertained. Pepys is so little reticent about his follies, blunders, and misfortunes that he may create in some minds the impression that he was a booby and a ridiculous person. The "Diary" in truth, with all its particularity and sincerity, is unjust to its author. The reader has to remind himself that it is microscopic, and that to get a just view of Pepys one ought not to know all about him. It may be difficult to understand where there was room for all his work, in the perpetual trade of morning draughts and suppers, plays in the afternoon, and the lute and the theorbo in the evening. But the secret of the "Diary," if there be a secret in it, is that it was written by an industrious man of business, who did well for himself, and worked honestly for his office.—KER, W. P., 1894, *English Prose, ed. Craik, vol.* III.

Its piquancy is not due to its expression of uncommon emotions, but precisely to the frankness which reveals emotions, all but universal, which most people conceal from themselves, and nearly all men from others. Boswell not only felt but avowed similar weaknesses. Pepys avowed them, though only to himself. He was not a hypocrite in cipher, though no doubt as reserved as his neighbours in longhand. The "unconscious humour" which Lowell attributes to him lies in the coolness of his confession, with which his readers sympathise, though they would not make similar confessions themselves. It seems to be highly improbable that he ever thought of publicity for his diaries, though he may have kept them as materials for an autobiography which was never executed.—STEPHEN, LESLIE, 1895, *Dictionary of National Biography, vol.* XLIV.

We sympathize with Pepys as we sympathize with Ulysses, and are for the time much more anxious about the liquidation of his tailor's bill, or the adjustment of his misunderstandings with his wife, than "what the Swede intends or what the French." . . . No work of the kind in the world's literature can for a moment be compared to Pepys's "Diary." . . . The "Diary," besides, is no less admirable as a delineation of the macrocosm than of the microcosm. It paints the official and private circles in which the author moved, the course of public affairs, the humours of social life, with no less truth and frankness than it reveals the author himself. It is by far the most valuable document extant for the understanding of the times; better than all the histories and all the comedies. It seems an unequalled piece of irony that the supreme piece of workmanship in its way and the most lucid mirror of its age should be the performance of an ordinary citizen who had not the least idea that he was doing anything remarkable; who expected celebrity, if he expected it at all, from his official tasks and scientific recreations; who shrouded his work in shorthand lest the world should profit by it; and who would have been dismayed beyond measure if he had foreseen that it would be published after his death.—GARNETT, RICHARD, 1895, *The Age of Dryden, pp.* 199, 201, 202.

If ever a man was designed to keep a diary, it was Pepys. He is naïve and communicative to a fault. Seated in his own confessional, he unbosoms his memory and absolves his conscience. . . . This typical *bourgeois* of his day, fussy and pompous, petty and busybodying, regular in his irregularities as in his expenditure, thrifty, vain, and passionately inquisitive, would retire into his sanctum, produce the treasured pages, and find his relief in the truthful industry of his chronicle. For truth and industry are among his redeeming features.—SICHEL, W., 1899, *Men Who Have Kept A Diary, Blackwood's Magazine, vol.* 165, *p.* 71.

John Wallis

1616–1703

Mathematician, born at Ashford, Kent, was trained at Cambridge, and took orders, but in 1648 became Savilian professor of Geometry at Oxford. He sided with the parliament, was secretary to the Westminster Assembly, but strenuously favoured the Restoration. Besides the *Arithmetica Infinitorum*, he wrote on proportion, mechanics, the quadrature of the circle (against Hobbes), grammar, logic, theology, and the teaching of the deaf and dumb, and edited some of the Greek mathematicians. He was a founder of the Royal Society. His collected works appeared in 1791.—PATRICK AND GROOME, eds., 1897, *Chambers's Biographical Dictionary*, p. 952.

PERSONAL

The doctor has less in him of the gallant man than Mr. Hobbes; and, if you should see him with his university cap on his head, as if he had a *porte-feuille* on, covered with black cloth, and sewed to his calot, you would be as much inclined to laugh at this diverting sight as you would be ready to entertain the excellency and civility of my friend [Hobbes] with esteem and affection. . . . What I have said concerning Dr. Wallis is not intended in the least to derogate from the praises due to one of the greatest mathematicians in the world.—SORBIERE, SAMUEL, 1663? *Journey to England*, pp. 39, 41.

Dr. Wallis was a man of most admirable fine parts, and great industry, whereby in some years he became so noted for his profound skill in mathematics that he was deservedly accounted the greatest person in that profession of any in his time. He was withal a good divine, and no mean critic in the Greek and Latin tongues.—HEARNE, THOMAS, 1735? *Collections*.

GENERAL

The book, next to the elements, which was put into his [Isaac Newton's] hands was Wallis's "Arithmetic of Infinities," a work well fitted for suggesting new views in geometry and calling into activity the powers of mathematical invention. Wallis had effected the quadrature of all those curves in which the value of one of the co-ordinates can be expressed in terms of the other without involving either fractional or negative exponents. Beyond this point neither his researches nor those of any other geometer had yet reached, and from this point the discoveries of Newton began. . . . Wallis appears to have been the first writer who, in his "Mechanica," published in 1669, founded an entire system of statics on the principle of Galileo, or the equality of the opposite momenta. — PLAYFAIR, JOHN, 1853, *Fourth Dissertation, Encyclopædia Britannica*.

It ["Treatise of Algebra"] is the first work in which a copious history of the subject was mixed with its theory.— KNIGHT, CHARLES, ed., 1858, *English Cyclopaedia*.

Not ["Institutio Logicæ"] rising above a humble mediocrity, even at the date of its composition.—HAMILTON, SIR WILLIAM, 1860, *Lectures on Logic*, Lecture ii.

The author of many works of great learning, ingenuity, and profoundness on algebra, geometry, and mechanical philosophy. Among the practical subjects to which he devoted himself were the deciphering of secret writing, and the teaching of persons born deaf to speak.—CRAIK, GEORGE L., 1861, *English Literature, vol.* II.

In mathematical history Wallis ranks as the greatest of Newton's English precursors. He was as laborious as he was original; and, by the judicious use of his powers of generalisation, he prepared all the subsequent discoveries of that age. The principles of analogy and continuity were introduced by him into mathematical science. His interpretation of negative exponents and unrestricted employment of fractional exponents greatly widened the range of the higher algebra. Finally, he invented the symbol for infinity, ∞. His memory for figures was prodigious. He often whiled away sleepless nights with exercises in mental arithmetic. On one occasion he extracted the square root of a number expressed by fifty-three figures, and dictated the result to twenty-seven places next morning to a stranger. It proved exact. He made use of no special technique in performing such feats, working merely by common rules on the blackboard of his own tenacious mind.—CLERKE, MISS A. M., 1899, *Dictionary of National Biography, vol.* LIX, *p.* 144.

John Locke

1632–1704

Born, at Wrington, Somerset, 29 Aug. 1632. At Westminster School, 1646[?]–52. Matric. Ch. Ch., Oxford, as Junior Student, 27 Nov. 1652; B.A., 14 Feb. 1656; M.A., 29 June 1658; Greek Lecturer, 1661; Reader in Rhetoric, 1662; Censor of Moral Philosophy, 1663. Student at Gray's Inn, 1656. Incorporated at Cambridge, 1663. Sec. to Sir Walter Vane on embassy to Brandenburg, Dec. 1665 to Feb. 1666. Settled again at Oxford on his return to England. F.R.S., 23 Nov. 1668. Studied medicine, and practised as physician. B. Med., Oxford, 6 Feb. 1675. Resided in house of first Earl of Shaftesbury, as physician, from 1667. Visit to France, Sept. 1672. Sec. of Presentations to Earl of Shaftesbury, when latter became Lord Chancellor, Nov. 1672. Sec. to Council of Trade, Oct. 1673–75. At Montpellier, for health, Dec. 1675 to March 1677. In Paris, as tutor to a son of Sir John Banks, May 1677 to June 1678; at Montpellier, Oct. to Nov. 1678; in Paris, Nov. 1678 to April 1679. Returned to England. Resided chiefly with Earl of Shaftesbury, 1679–81; at Oxford, 1681–83. Being suspected of treason, retired to Holland, autumn of 1683. Expelled from studentship at Ch. Ch., Oxford, Nov. 1684. In Holland, 1683–89. Returned to England, Feb. 1689. Commissioner of Appeals, 1689–1704. Lived at Westminster, 1689–91; removed to Oates, High Laver, Essex, 1691. Mem. of Council of Trade, May 1696 to 1700. Lived at Oates, boarding in household of Sir Francis Masham, 1700–04. Died at Oates, 28 Oct. 1704. Buried in High Laver Churchyard. *Works:* "Methode nouvelle de dresser les Recueils," 1686 (English trans., called: "A New Method of Making Commonplace Books," 1697); "Epistola de Tolerantia," 1689 (English trans. by W. Popple, same year); "A Second Letter concerning Toleration" (signed: "Philanthropus"), 1690; "A Third Letter" (signed: "Philanthropus"), 1690; "An Essay concerning Humane Understanding," 1690; "Two Treatises of Government" (anon.), 1690; "Five Letters concerning the Inspiration of the Holy Scriptures" (anon.; attrib. to Locke), 1690; "Some Considerations of the consequences of the Lowering of Interest" (anon.), 1692; "Some Thoughts concerning Education" (anon.), 1693; "The Reasonableness of Christianity" (anon.), 1695; "Short Observations on a printed paper intituled, 'For encouraging the Coining of Silver Money in England'" (anon.), 1695; "Further Considerations Concerning Raising the Value of Money," 1695; "Letter to the . . . Lord Bishop of Worcester," 1697; "Reply to the Bishop of Worcester's Answer to his Letter," 1697; "Reply to the Bishop's Answer to his Second Letter," 1697; "A Commonplace Book in reference to the Holy Bible" (anon.; attrib. to Locke), 1697. *Posthumous:* "A Paraphrase and Notes on the Epistle of St. Paul to the Galatians" (6 pts.), 1705–1707; "The History of Our Saviour" (anon.; attrib. to Locke), 1705; "Select Moral Books of the Old Testament . . . paraphrased" (anon.; attrib. to Locke), 1706; "A Paraphrase and Notes on the First Epistle . . . to the Corinthians" (anon.), 1706; "Posthumous Works," 1706; "Some Familiar Letters," 1708; "Remains," 1714; "A Collection of several Pieces," 1720; "Elements of Natural Philosophy" [1750?]; "Some thoughts on the conduct of the Understanding," 1762; "Observations upon the Growth and Culture of Vines and Olives," 1766; "Discourses translated from Nicole's 'Essays,'" ed. by T. Hancock, 1828; "Original Letters of Locke, A. Sidney and Lord Shaftesbury," ed. by T. Forster, 1830. He *edited:* Æsop's "Fables," 1703. *Collected Works:* in 3 vols., 1714; in 10 vols., 1823. *Life:* by H. R. Fox Bourne, 1876; by T. Fowler, 1880.—SHARP, R. FARQUHARSON. 1897, *A Dictionary of English Authors, p.* 170.

PERSONAL

If we consider his genius and penetrating and exact judgment, or the strictness of his morals, has scarce any superior, and few equals, now living.—SYDENHAM, THOMAS, 1675, *Observationes Medicæ circa Morborum Acutorum Historium et Curationem.*

John Locke lives very quietly with us, and not a word ever drops from his mouth that discovers anything of his heart within. Now his master is fled, I suppose we shall have him altogether. He seems to be a man of very good converse, and that we have of him with content; as for what else he is he keeps it to himself, and

JOHN LOCKE

ROBERT BOYLE

therefore troubles not us with it nor we him.—PRIDEAUX, HUMPHREY, 1682, *Letter to John Ellis, Oct. 24, Camden Soc. Pub.*

Mr. Locke being, as your Lordship is truly informed, a person who was much trusted by the late Earl of Shaftesbury, and who is suspected to be ill-affected to the Government, I have for divers years had an eye upon him; but so close has his guard been on himself, that after several strict inquiries, I may confidently affirm there is not any one in the college, however familiar with him, who has heard him speak a word either against, or so much as concerning the Government; and although very frequently, both in public and in private, discourses have been purposely introduced, to the disparagement of his master, the Earl of Shaftesbury, his party, and designs, he could never be provoked to take any notice, or discover in word or look the least concern; so that I believe there is not in the world such a master of taciturnity and passion.—FELL, JOHN, 1684, *Letter to Sunderland.*

To the Right Reverend Father in God, John, Lord Bishop of Oxon, Dean of Christ-Church, and our trusty and well-beloved the Chapter there.

Right Reverend Father in God, and trusty and well-beloved, we greet you well. Whereas we have received information of the factious and disloyal behaviour of Locke, one of the students of that our College; we have thought fit hereby to signify our will and pleasure to you, that you forthwith remove him from his said student's place, and deprive him of all the rights and advantages thereunto belonging, for which this shall be your warrant; and so we bid you heartily farewell. Given at our Court at Whitehall, 11th day of November, 1684.—*By His Majesty's Command*—SUNDERLAND.

Sir,—Being of opinion that you endeavoured to embroil me with women and by other means, I was so much affected with it, as that when one told me you were sickly and would not live, I answered 'twere better if you were dead. I desire you to forgive me this uncharitableness. For I am now satisfied that what you have done is just, and I beg your pardon for my having hard thoughts of you for it, and for representing that you struck at the root of morality, in a principle you laid down in your book of ideas, and

designed to pursue in another book, and that I took you for a Hobbist. I beg your pardon also for saying or thinking that there was a design to sell me an office, or to embroil me. I am your most humble and unfortunate servant.—NEWTON, ISAAC, 1693, *Letter to John Lock.*

Feby. By six weeks' lodging to Mrs. R. Pawling during my stay in London, 36s. By a breast of mutton, 1s. 1d. By $3\frac{1}{2}$ yds. grey cloth, 55s. By 5 yds. silk, for a waistcoat, at 6s.=32s. 6d. By one pair worsted hose, 4s. 4d. By $4\frac{1}{2}$ coat buttons, 3s. 4d. One dozen gold breast buttons, 9s. By bread, cheese, oranges, and butter, 2s. 6d. By cherrys and strawberrys, 2s. 6d. By Rhenish wine, one quart, 2s. 6d. By six tarts and three cheesecakes, 3s. 9d. By two papers of patches, bought in London for my Lady Masham, 1s. By a porter for a basket for E. Masham, 8d. By Gooseberrys and strawberrys, 8s. $2\frac{1}{2}$d. By milk, 5s. 9d. By ten weeks' lodging in London, from April 23 to July 3, £3. By three weeks' lodging in London, from September 19 to October 9, 18s. By two weeks' lodging in London, Dec. 7 to 22, 12s. By postages, from Feb. 16 till April 23, 33s. By a pair of worsted stockings, 4s. 8d. By a box of sugar, bought for Mrs. Cudworth, 23s. 10d. By a brasse locke for my Lady Masham, 6s. 6d. By Thomas Baley for a peruke, 60s. Oct. 7. Paid to Awnsham Churchill, bookseller.—By Norris's "Letters," 3s.; Burnett's "Sermons," 6d.; "Assembly's Confession," 2s. 3d.; Gassendi's "Astronomia," for my Lady Masham, 4s. 4d.—LOCKE, JOHN, 1694, *Book of Accounts.*

I began a course of chemistry under the noted chemist and rosicrucian Peter Sthael of Strasburg, a strict Lutheran, and a great hater of women. The club consisted of ten, whereof were Frank Turner, now Bishop of Ely, Benjamin Woodroof, now canon of Christ Church, and John Locke of the same house, now a noted writer. This same John Locke was a man of a turbulent spirit, clamorous, and never contented; while the rest of our club took notes from the mouth of their master, who sat at the upper end of a long table, the said Locke scorned to do this; but was for ever prating and troublesome.—WOOD, ANTHONY, 1695?-1848, *Autobiography.*

You will not, perhaps, dislike to know, that the last scene of Mr. Locke's life was no less admirable than any thing else in him. All the faculties of his mind were perfect to the last; but his weakness, of which only he died, made such gradual and visible advances, that few people, I think, do so sensibly see death approach them as he did. During all which time, no one could observe the least alteration in his humour,—always chearful, civil, conversible, to the last day, thoughtful of all the concerns of his friends, and omitting no fit occasion of giving Christian advice to all about him. In short, his death was like his life,—truly pious, yet natural, easy, and unaffected; nor can time, I think, ever produce a more eminent example of reason and religion than he was, living and dying.—MASHAM, LADY ESTHER, 1704? *Letter to Mr. Laughton.*

He knew something of almost everything which can be useful to mankind, and was thoroughly master of all that he had studied, but he showed his superiority by not appearing to value himself in any way on account of his great attainments. Nobody assumed less the airs of a master, or was less dogmatical, and he was never offended when any one did not agree with his opinions. . . . He considered civility not only as something agreeable and proper to gain people's hearts, but as a duty of Christianity, which ought to be more insisted on than it commonly is. . . . His conversation was very agreeable to all sorts of people, and even to ladies; and nobody was better received than he was among people of the highest rank. . . . Those who courted the acquaintance of Mr. Locke to collect what might be learned from a man of his understanding, and who approached him with respect, were surprised to find in him not only the manners of a well-bred man, but also all the attention which they could expect. . . . He was very charitable to the poor, provided they were not the idle or the profligate, who did not frequent any church, or who spent their Sundays in an alehouse. He felt, above all, compassion for those who, after having worked hard in their youth, sunk into poverty in their old age. He said, that it was not sufficient to keep them from starving, but that they ought to be enabled to live with some comfort. He sought opportunities of doing good to deserving objects; and often in his walks he visited the poor of the neighbourhood, and gave them the wherewithal to relieve their wants, or to buy the medicines which he prescribed for them if they were sick, and had no medical aid. He did not like any thing to be wasted; which was, in his opinion, losing the treasure of which God has made us the economists. He himself was very regular, and kept exact accounts of every thing. . . . He was kind to his servants, and showed them with gentleness how he wished to be served. He not only kept strictly a secret which had been confided to him, but he never mentioned anything which could prove injurious, although he had not been enjoined to secrecy; nor did he ever wrong a friend by any sort of indiscretion or inadvertency.—LE CLERC, JEAN, 1705, *Eloge de M. Locke, Bibliothèque Choisie.*

Mr. Locke had a great knowledge of the world, and of the business of it. Prudent without being cunning; he won people's esteem by his probity, and was always safe from the attacks of a false friend, or a sordid flatterer. Averse to all mean complaisance; his wisdom, his experience, his gentle and obliging manners, gained him the respect of his inferiours, the esteem of his equals, the friendship and confidence of the greatest quality. Without setting up for a teacher, he instructed others by his own conduct. He was at first pretty much disposed to give advice to such of his friends as he thought wanted it; but at length, finding that, "good counsels are very little effectual in making people more prudent," he grew much more reserved in that particular. I have often heard him say, that the first time he heard that maxim, he thought it very strange; but that experience had fully convinced him of the truth of it. . . . But then Mr. Locke was very liberal of his counsels, when they were desired; and no body ever consulted him in vain. An extreme vivacity of mind, one of his reigning qualities, in which perhaps he never had an equal; his great experience, and the sincere desire he had of being serviceable to all mankind; soon furnished him with the expedients, which were most just and least dangerous. I say, the least dangerous; for what he proposed to himself before all things was to lead those, who consulted him, into no trouble. . . . Mr. Locke, above all things, loved order. . . . Never man employed his time better than Mr. Locke. —COSTE, PETER, 1705, *The Character of Mr. Locke, Nouvelles de la Republique des Lettres, Feb.*

In October 1704, his disorder greatly increased: on the 27th of that month, Lady Masham not finding him in his study as usual, went to his bedside, when he told her that the fatigue of getting up the day before had been too much for his strength, and that he never expected to rise again from his bed. He said that he had now finished his career in this world, and that in all probability he should not outlive the night, certainly not to be able to survive beyond the next day or two. After taking some refreshments he said to those present that he wished them all happiness after he was gone. To Lady Masham, who remained with him, he said that he thanked God he had passed a happy life, but that now he found that all was vanity, and exhorted her to consider this world only as a preparation for a better state hereafter. He would not suffer her to sit up with him, saying, that perhaps he might be able to sleep, but if any change should happen, he would send for her. Having no sleep in the night, he was taken out of bed and carried into his study, where he slept for some time in his chair; after waking, he desired to be dressed, and then heard Lady Masham read the Psalms apparently with great attention, until perceiving his end to draw near, he stopped her, and expired a very few minutes afterwards about three o'clock in the afternoon of the 28th October, in his 73d year.—KING, LORD, 1829–30, *The Life of John Locke, vol.* II, *p.* 45.

We consider Locke as one of the best examples of the Christian character. . . . We admire Locke as an example of the manly Christian character; and the union of vast intellectual strength with calm and fervent devotion, so beautifully displayed in his life and writings, shows what our religion is when it resides in a powerful mind and an open heart. In the intercourse of the world, his gentleness was like that of childhood; his object was to make others happy, and while he exerted himself for this purpose, he kept a guard over his manners that he might not give pain by the slightest inattention; for he well knew, that there are many who will do kindnesses to others, but will not regard the little things on which the comfort of life depends. But though nothing could exceed his mildness in familiar conversation, which made friends of all who ever knew him, he was firm as a rock on every point of duty, and no fear of slander or injury, nor even of exile or bondage, could induce him to refrain from expressing his convictions, or retract one word which he had deliberately spoken to the world. In these respects, he was tried, and not found wanting; and the cause of civil and religious freedom numbers him among those noble spirits, who, in every age, have put forth their gigantic strength to break the arm of the oppressor and to set the prisoner free.—PEABODY, W. B. O., 1832, *Locke's Character and Writings, Christian Examiner, vol.* 11, *pp.* 381, 402.

John Locke hated tyranny and persecution as a philosopher; but his intellect and his temper preserved him from the violence of a partisan. He had lived on confidential terms with Shaftesbury, and had thus incurred the displeasure of the court. Locke's prudence had, however, been such that it would have been to little purpose to bring him even before the corrupt and partial tribunals of that age. In one point, however, he was vulnerable. He was a student of Christ Church in the University of Oxford. It was determined to drive him from that celebrated college the greatest man of whom it could ever boast; but this was not easy. Locke had, at Oxford, abstained from expressing any opinion on the politics of the day. Spies had been set about him. Doctors of divinity and masters of arts had not been ashamed to perform the vilest of all offices, that of watching the lips of a companion in order to report his words to his ruin. The conversation in the hall had been purposely turned to irritating topics, to the Exclusion Bill, and to the character of the Earl of Shaftesbury, but in vain. Locke never broke out, never dissembled, but maintained such steady silence and composure as forced the tools of power to own with vexation that never man was so complete a master of his tongue and of his passions. When it was found that treachery could do nothing, arbitrary power was used. After vainly trying to inveigle Locke into a fault, the government resolved to punish him without one. Orders came from Whitehall that he should be ejected, and those orders the dean and canons made haste to obey.— MACAULAY, THOMAS BABINGTON, 1843, *John Locke, Critical and Historical Essays.*

He was pre-eminently a philosopher— that is, a lover of wisdom. Whether, till late in life at any rate, it ever occurred to him that he could teach much to the world may well be doubted. For a long while he was content to do all he could in teaching himself. With that object he studied all that Oxford could provide for him; all that, in his student's quarters at Christ Church, in the society of friends outside of the university, and in the more bustling scenes that he occasionally visited, he could learn of the ways and thoughts of men, and the best means of helping them to lead worthy and happy lives. With that object he read all the books that came in his way, romances and travel-books as well as abstruse treatises of every sort, and applied himself with special eagerness, not only to the medical and kindred researches that were directly connected with the practical work to which he was anxious to devote his life, but also to every other scientific pursuit that he deemed useful in disclosing the secrets of nature and promoting the welfare of mankind. With that object, also he accustomed himself to write down his thoughts on all kinds of subjects, not, it would seem, with the design of giving them to the world, but in order thus to be the better able to test their value, and see how much truth was in them.— BOURNE, H. R. FOX, 1876, *Life of John Locke, vol.* I, *p.* 145.

His epitaph, in Latin, was written by himself, and the reader may be curious to see it in English: "Stay, traveler: near this place lies JOHN LOCKE. If you ask what sort of man he was, the answer is that he was contented with his modest lot. Bred a scholar, he used his studies to contend for truth alone. This you may learn from his writings, which will show you any thing else that may be said about him more faithfully than the doubtful eulogies of an epitaph. His virtues, if he had any, were too slight for

him to offer them to his own credit or as an example to you. Let his vices be buried with him. Of good life you have an example, should you desire it, in the Gospel; of vice, would there were none any where; of mortality, surely (and you may profit by it) you have one here and every where. That he was born on the 29th of August, 1632, and that he died on the 28th of October, in the year of our Lord 1704, this tablet, which itself will quickly perish, is a record.—MURRAY-NAIRNE, CHARLES, JOHN LOCKE, 1876, *Harper's Magazine, vol.* 53, *p.* 924.

An ancestral connection with Locke was not a source of pride to Southey; he respected neither the philosopher's politics nor his metaphysics; still, it is pleasant, he says, to hear of somebody between one's self and Adam who has left a name. —DOWDEN, EDWARD, 1880, *Southey, English Men of Letters, p.* 108.

We are too apt, I think, to dismiss this author from our thoughts as a man full only of dreary metaphysic subtleties; and support the belief with the story that our Jonathan Edwards read his treatise on the "Human Understanding" with great delight at the age of fourteen. Yet Locke, although a man of the keenest and rarest intellect—which almost etherialized his looks—was possessed of a wonderful deal of what he would have called "hard, round-about sense;" indeed it would be quite possible to fill a whole calendar with bits of his printed talk that would be as pitpat and common-sensical as anything in "Poor Richard's Almanac." Moreover, he could, on occasions, tell a neat and droll story, which would set the "table in a roar."—MITCHELL, DONALD G., 1890, *English Lands Letters and Kings, From Elizabeth to Anne, p.* 249.

So ended the prudent, moderate, and tranquil life, pious and inquisitive, which began at Wrington and Beluton in the stormy years of Charles I. On Tuesday, the 31st of October, they buried him on the sunny side of the parish church of High Laver, where, almost two centuries ago, that serene and pensive face, pale and tinged with sadness, which Kneller has made familiar to us all, was often seen. A few chosen friends, including the Masham family, King, Collins, and Coste, and neighbours at Oates, seem to have formed the little company who gathered round his grave, when the aged rector read the beautiful service of the Church of England, on that autumn day in Essex. The lines of the Latin inscription composed by himself, lately traced with difficulty upon the stone, suggest the pensive language of the "Essay" about human memory, in which it is suggested that "the ideas as well as the children of our youth often die before us, and our minds thus represent to us those tombs to which we are approaching, where, though the brass and marble remain, yet the inscriptions are effaced by time, and the imagery moulders away." Especially in that remote rural scene, the tomb of Locke may touch the imagination of the wayfarer. According to tradition, Sir Isaac Newton was one of the first who visited it.—FRASER, ALEXANDER CAMPBELL, 1890, *Locke* (*Philosophical Classics*), *p.* 271.

LETTERS ON TOLERATION
1689-90

How far are we, at this moment, from adopting these admirable principles! and with what absurd confidence do the enemies of religious liberty appeal to the authority of Mr. Locke for continuing those restrictions on conscience which he so deeply lamented!—MACKINTOSH, SIR JAMES, 1821, *Stewart's Introduction to the Encyclopædia, Edinburgh Review, vol.* 36, *p.* 230, *note.*

It is hard to say, whether mankind are more indebted to this illustrious person as a philosopher, or as a politician. The publication of his great work undoubtedly fixed an era in the history of science: But his writings, and his personal exertions in favour of liberty, and more especially of religious Toleration, may be truly said to have had a greater effect than can be ascribed to the efforts of any other individual who bore a part in the transactions of that important period. The true doctrines of Toleration were first promulgated by him, and in their fullest extent; for he maintained the whole stretch of the principle, that opinion is not a matter cognizable by the civil magistrate, and that belief, being the result of reason, is wholly independent of the will, and neither the subject of praise nor of blame, far less the object of punishment or of reward.—BROUGHAM, HENRY LORD, 1829, *Lord King's Life of John Locke, Edinburgh Review, vol.* 50, *p.* 28.

A complete and satisfactory work.—BICKERSTETH, EDWARD, 1844, *The Christian Studen*

Locke's position is given in the "Letters on Toleration," the first of which sufficiently indicates his position. The others, devoted to meeting the cavils of an antagonist, consist chiefly of incessant and wearisome repetitions of the same arguments. As in his other controversies, Locke has no mercy upon the patience of his readers.—STEPHEN, LESLIE, 1876, *History of English Thought in the Eighteenth Century, vol.* II, *p.* 145.

The authorship of the "Letters on Toleration," though it could hardly fail to be pretty generally known, was first distinctly acknowledged by Locke in the codicil to his will. Limborch, on being hard pressed, had divulged it, in the spring of 1690, to Guenellon and Veen, but they appear, contrary to what generally happens in such cases, to have kept the secret to themselves. Locke, however, was much irritated at the indiscretion of Limborch, and for once wrote him an angry letter. "If you had entrusted me with a secret of this kind, I would not have divulged it to relation, or friend, or any mortal being, under any circumstances whatsoever. You do not know the trouble into which you have brought me."—FOWLER, THOMAS, 1880 *Locke* (*English Men of Letters*), *p.* 60.

ON THE HUMAN UNDERSTANDING
1690

Were it fit to trouble thee with the history of this "Essay," I should tell thee that five or six friends meeting at my chamber, and discoursing on a subject very remote from this, found themselves quickly at a stand, by the difficulties that arose on every side. After we had a while puzzled ourselves, without coming any nearer a resolution of those doubts which perplexed us, it came into my thoughts, that we took a wrong course, and that, before we set ourselves upon inquiries of that nature, it was necessary to examine our own abilities, and see what objects our understandings were, or were not, fitted to deal with. This I proposed to the company, who all readily assented; and thereupon it was agreed that this should be our first inquiry. Some hasty and undigested thoughts, on a subject I had never before considered, which I set down against our next meeting, gave the first entrance into this discourse; which, having been begun by chance, was continued by entreaty; written by incoherent parcels, and after long intervals of neglect, returned again as my humour or occasions permitted; and at last, in a retirement, where an attendance on my health gave me leisure, it was brought into that order thou now seest it.—LOCKE, JOHN, 1690, *An Essay Concerning Human Understanding, Epistle to the Reader.*

To none do we owe for a greater advancement in this part of philosophy, [logic] than to the incomparable Mr. Locke, who, in his "Essay of Human Understanding," hath rectified more received mistakes, and delivered more profound truths, established on experience and observation, for the direction of man's mind in the prosecution of knowledge, which I think may be properly termed logic, than are to be met with in all the volumes of the ancients. He has clearly overthrown all those metaphysical whimsies which infected men's brains with a spice of madness, whereby they feigned a knowledge where they had none by making a noise with sounds without clear and distinct significations.—MOLYNEUX, WILLIAM, 1692, *Diopterica Nova, Dedication.*

Which may as well qualify for business and the world as for the sciences and a university. No one has done more towards the recalling of philosophy from barbarity into use and practice of the world, and into the company of the better and politer sort, who might well be ashamed of it in its other dress. No one has opened a better or clearer way to reasoning.—COOPER, ANTHONY ASHLEY (EARL OF SHAFTESBURY), 1707–16, *Letters to a Student at the University.*

After clearing the way by setting aside the whole doctrine of innate notions and principles, both speculative and practical, the author traces all ideas to two sources, sensation and reflection; treats at large of the nature of ideas simple and complex; of the operation of the human understanding in forming, distinguishing, compounding, and associating them; of the manner in which words are applied as representations of ideas; of the difficulties and obstructions, in the search after truth, which arise from the imperfections of these

signs; and of the nature, reality, kinds, degrees, casual hindrances, and necessary limits of human knowledge.—BRUCKER, JOHANN JAKOB, 1742–44, *Historia Critica Philosophiæ, tr. Enfield.*

It may be said that Locke created the science of Metaphysics, in somewhat the same way as Newton created Physics. . . . To understand the soul, its ideas and its affections, he did not study books; they would have misdirected him; he was content to descend within himself, and after having, so to speak, contemplated himself a long while, he presented in his "Essay" the mirror in which he had seen himself. In one word, he reduced Metaphysics to that which it ought to be, viz. the experimental physics of the mind.—D'ALEMBERT, JEAN LE ROND, 1751, *Discours Preliminaire Encyclopedie.*

Perhaps it was for mankind a lucky mistake (for it was a mistake) which Mr. Locke made when he called his book, An Essay on Human *Understanding.* For some part of the inestimable benefit of that book has, merely on account of its title, reached to many thousands more than, I fear, it would have done, had he called it (what it is merely) A *Grammatical* Essay, or a Treatise on *Words,* or on *Language.*—TOOKE, JOHN HORNE, 1789–1815, *The Diversions of Purley, note.*

The endless disputations of the learned led him to suspect that they had their origin in an improper use of words and a defective use of conceptions; which he proposed to rectify by ascertaining the grounds and extent of human knowledge, through investigation of the properties of the human understanding. This was the origin of his renowned work on the Human Understanding, by which he justly acquired the greatest distinction for the modesty and tolerance of his way of thinking, the clearness and rectitude of his understanding, evinced in the course of a correspondence with the most accomplished men of his day, and his penetrating acuteness and manly honesty. He so far adopted Bacon's principles that he pursued the method of experiment and observation, in preference to that of speculation; applying it principally to our inner nature. His method of philosophizing has many advantages, but at the same time some great defects; especially that of avoiding the great obstacles and difficulties in the course of philosophical knowledge instead of directly sounding them by a more radical and a deeper research. . . . Locke's great object and merit, was the investigation of the origin, reality, limits, and uses of knowledge. . . . Locke has also suggested some admirable ideas on Language, and the abuses to which it is liable. . . It was the object of Locke to liberate philosophy from vain disputations and unprofitable niceties; but his work had the effect of discouraging, by the facility and accommodating character of its method, more profound investigation; at the same time that he gave a popular air to such inquiries, diminishing the interest they excited, and affording advantages to Eclecticism and Materialism.—TENNEMANN, WILLIAM GOTTLIEB, 1812, *A Manual of the History of Philosophy, tr. Johnson, ed. Morell, pp.* 325, 326, 327.

Locke met with general acceptance, just because his system was not so inconsistent with the recognized moral principles and feelings of his time; and the exposition of his views, though prolix, was yet easy of comprehension—or, at least, seemed so.—SCHLEGEL, FREDERICK, 1815–59, *Lectures on the History of Literature.*

As the antagonists chiefly contemplated by Mr. Locke were the followers of Descartes, perhaps the only proposition for which he must necessarily be held to contend was, that the mind has no ideas which do not *arise* from impressions on the senses, or from reflections on our own thoughts and feelings. But it is certain that he sometimes appears to contend for much more than this proposition; that he has generally been understood in a larger sense; and that, thus interpreted, his doctrine is not irreconcilable to those philosophical systems with which he has been supposed to be most at variance.—MACKINTOSH, SIR JAMES, 1821, *Stewart's Introduction to the Encyclopædia, Edinburgh Review; vol.* 36, *p.* 233.

No serious work is less read than that of Locke. I very much doubt whether there be a single person in Paris who has perused from beginning to end the "Essay on the Human Understanding." It is much talked of and quoted, but always upon trust. . . . In most other books, even of little value, there are some instructive or amusing passages, but in the Essay there is nothing to console you; it is as dreary as a vast Arabian desert. Not the smallest *oasis,* not a single inch of verdure, to afford the weary traveller a temporary refreshment. . . . The proper title of the work is not "An Essay on the Human Understanding," but "An Essay on the Understanding of John Locke." It is, in fact, a full length portrait of the author, executed to the life. We recognise at the first glance a man of natural good sense and honesty, but completely bewildered and led astray by party spirit, besides being absolutely deficient in power of thinking and in the most ordinary philosophical learning. . . . The icy dulness of his style would have destroyed, in a great measure, the effect of his detestable doctrines; but it was warmed into life in the hot-houses of Paris, and there brought forth the revolutionary monster that has devoured Europe. *Contempt of Locke is the beginning of wisdom.*—MAISTRE, JOSEPH, 1822, *Evenings at St. Petersburgh.*

Locke is also a child of Descartes: he is imbued with his spirit and his method; he rejects every other authority than that of reason, and he sets out from the analysis of consciousness; but, instead of seeing all the elements which it comprehends, without rejecting, entirely, the interior element, liberty and intelligence, he considers more particularly the exterior element, he is above all struck with sensation. The philosophy of Locke is a branch of Cartesianism, but it is a straggling one, like Spinozism.—COUSIN, VICTOR, 1828–29, *History of Modern Philosophy, tr. Wight, vol.* I, *p.* 236.

It is the glory of Newton and Locke, to have directed their labors at once, and with all the necessary zeal and perseverance, to the most important subjects in physical and intellectual science; and the splendor of the results corresponded with, or even surpassed, all that might have been expected from the excellence of the new method, and the extraordinary talent of those who made the application of it. It does not belong to our subject to insist on the value of the astonishing discoveries of Newton. The efforts of Locke in an equally or still more interesting field, were hardly less successful, although the truths he has made known, from their entirely abstract character, are somewhat less fitted to attract the attention and excite the imagination of the world at large. . . . In the "Essay on the Human Understanding," intellectual science appeared for the first time in a clear and intelligible shape, unmingled with the vain and visionary fancies which had previously disfigured it, and accessible to the plain good sense of every cultivated mind. This great work is, and will probably always remain, the text-book of the noblest branch of human learning. What higher honor could mortal ambition attain or aspire to, than that of achieving it? It is not, perhaps, free from errors; for what work of the same extent was ever faultless? But of the exceptions that have been taken to it, the most considerable have been or will be overruled by the great tribunal of public opinion; and those that are better founded, are of too little consequence to affect its general value.—EVERETT, ALEXANDER HILL, 1829, *History of Intellectual Philosophy, North American Review, vol.* 29, *pp.* 78, 79.

It is perhaps the first, and still the most complete, chart of the human mind which has been laid down, the most ample repertory of truths relating to our intellectual being, and the one book which we are still compelled to name as the most important in metaphysical science. Locke had not, it may be said, the luminous perspicuity of language we find in Descartes, and, when he does not soar too high, in Malebranche; but he had more judgment, more caution, more patience, more freedom from paradox, and from the sources of paradox, vanity, and love of system, than either.—HALLAM, HENRY, 1837–39, *Introduction to the Literature of Europe, pt.* iv, *ch.* iii, *par.* 105.

Few among the great names in philosophy have met with a harder measure of justice from the present generation than Locke, the unquestioned founder of the analytic philosophy of mind, but whose doctrines were first caricatured, then, when the reaction arrived, cast off by the prevailing school even with contumely, and who is now regarded by one of the conflicting parties in philosophy as an apostle of heresy and sophistry; while among those who still adhere to the standard which he raised, there has been a disposition in later times to sacrifice his reputation in favor of Hobbes; a great

writer and a great thinker for his time, but inferior to Locke not only in sober judgment but even in profundity and original genius. Locke, the most candid of philosophers, and one whose speculations bear on every subject the strongest mark of having been wrought out from the materials of his own mind, has been mistaken for an unworthy plagiarist, while Hobbes has been extolled as having anticipated many of his leading doctrines.—MILL, JOHN STUART, 1843, *System of Logic.*

Reiterated depreciation had somewhat defaced his image in my mind. The time came however when, for the purposes of this history, I had to read the "Essay on Human Understanding" once more, carefully, pen in hand. The image of John Locke was again revived within me; this time in more than its former splendor. His modesty, honesty, truthfulness, and directness I had never doubted; but now the vigor and originality of his mind, the raciness of his colloquial style, the patient analysis by which he has laid open to us such vast tracts of thought, and above all, the manliness of his truly practical understanding, are so strongly impressed upon me, that I feel satisfied the best answer to his critics is to say, *"Read him."* From communion with such a mind as his, nothing but good can result. He suggests as much as he teaches.—LEWES, GEORGE HENRY, 1845–67, *Biographical History of Philosophy.*

Its empiricism is clear as day. The mind, according to it, is in itself bare, and only a mirror of the outer world,—a dark space which passively receives the images of external objects; its whole content is made by the impressions furnished it by material things. *Nihil est in intellectu, quod non fuerit in sensu*—is the watchword of this standpoint. . . . It is true that Locke was not always logically consistent, and in many points did not thoroughly carry out his empiricism: but we can clearly see that the road which will be taken in the farther development of this direction, will result in a thorough denial of the ideal factor.—SCHWEGLER, ALBERT, 1848? *History of Philosophy in Epitome, tr. Seelye.*

It is impossible to deny that the immortal "Essay" is disfigured by serious blemishes—by some errors, and many inconsistencies and ambiguities. The latter flowed chiefly from that figurative and popular style which is yet one of its most attractive, as well as serviceable features; but partly also from the desultory manner in which the "Essay" was composed, and the length of time (nearly twenty years) occupied in its completion. This allowed, it is true, time for elaboration; but it also allowed time for the "sleepy nods" which proverbially overtake a man in a "long work;" and for those variations which are sure to characterise every large edifice when it is an aggregate of accretions. Hence the apparent, and sometimes real consistencies and ambiguities of expression which are found in Locke's frequent repetitions of the same or similar thoughts, and which have made it possible for critics to fight so long even over the fundamental principles of his philosophy.—ROGERS, HENRY, 1854, *John Locke, Edinburgh Review, vol.* 99, *p.* 402.

Locke himself, by his training and associations, would naturally occupy the ground of mediation. His education as a physician, his sympathy with the new physics which were coming into notice, and his cool and tolerant temper, all contributed to this tendency. The temper of his times was practical rather than speculative, cautious rather than adventurous, critical and analytic rather than bold and dogmatic. The Essay on the human understanding did not attain the form in which we find it, till the sixth edition. The first edition contains not even the rudiment of the celebrated chapter on the Association of Ideas, which subsequently obtained such extensive currency among English psychologists, and so decided an influence over English speculation. This is the more surprising if we consider that Hobbes distinctly recognizes the law of association and attaches to it great importance. In the first edition the distinction between desire and will—of which so much was subsequently made, is not recognized — the necessitarianism of Hobbes is broadly asserted, and liberty is limited to the power of acting. . . . It should be observed also that the essay is more logical or metaphysical than psychological in its aims. Sir Isaac Newton terms it "your book of ideas," in a letter of apology to its author. The criticisms upon it and the replies which they called forth, indicate that its doctrine of ideas was the chief feature which attracted the public attention. If we compare the essay with the Port Royal Logic, then well known in England, and especially if we view attentively Locke's own account of the design of his essay, we shall be satisfied that he did not so much propose to give a complete outline of the powers of man as to analyze the different forms of human knowledge into their ultimate elements. The critics and antagonists of Locke all confirm this view. They criticize and assail his positions on the ground of their supposed inconsistency with important theological, practical, or scientific truths rather than in respect to their psychological validity.—UEBERWEG, FRIEDRICH, 1871, *History of Philosophy, tr. Morris, vol.* II, *pp.* 363, 364.

It was the most renowned treatise of its time. It was the book of its generation. Its fame, as we have already noted, was not confined to Great Britain and Ireland, but extended to France, Germany, and even Italy. Its author was believed to have taken a new departure in the study of mind. His doctrines were accepted as the truth by all parties, believers and skeptics alike. He was the master metaphysician; and we have found that the imperfection of his work lay not in his method, which was the only true one, but in his neglect to observe it steadfastly in his own practice.—MURRAY-NAIRNE, CHARLES, 1876, *John Locke, Harper's Magazine, vol.* 53, *p.* 920.

Probably intended by his father to be a theologian, certainly intending himself to be a physician, and deeply imbued all through his life by a religious spirit while he was persistent in his devotion to medical pursuits, these diverse, though not in his case contrary, influences greatly affected his philosophical studies. It was at no time possible for him to believe that he could find out everything, or even to desire, in this life, to do so; least of all did he desire, or was it possible for him, so to reject all that he could not understand as to lose his belief in God or to take no account of him in his studies; he only thought that he should serve God best by striving to find out what powers of intellect he had endowed men with and how they ought to use them. This may have been to a certain degree a bias, and may to some extent have led him towards dogmatism; but never was an avowed theologian more free from either fault. . . . No man ever strove more, or did more, to bring metaphysics out of the desert of idle speculation or the dream-land of foolish fancy into the domain of common-sense and every-day life; and no metaphysician ever concerned himself more, or more worthily, with the practical business of his own time and country. —BOURNE, H. R. FOX, 1876, *Life of John Locke, vol. II, pp.* 525, 528.

The conditions and surrounding that matured Locke are distinctly opposed to those which produce the great German thinkers. It is, indeed, especially when compared with the German school that Locke's genius appears most striking. Both have travelled on the long and difficult journey after truth. Both have reaped the gratitude of mankind. But their paths diverged. Locke found food for thought in the brilliant yet boisterous age which surrounded him at the courts of kings and the mansions of great noblemen, while the master minds of Germany seem to have been inspired only by the solitude of great universities and the silence of great libraries. Locke developed the "Essay Concerning Human Understanding" in the excitement and turmoil of London life, amidst a marvellous variety of active pursuits. Kant evolved the "Kritik der Reinen Vernunft" in the solitudes of Königsberg. Kant devoted a life to his work, Locke a few leisure hours. Locke was the amateur, Kant the professional. Yet the amateur can scarce be mentioned with less gratitude or respect.—RICE, A. T., 1877, *Contemporary Literature, North American Review, vol.* 124, *p.* 138.

Many of its individual doctrines, doubtless, could not now be defended against the attacks of hostile criticism, and some even of those which are true in the main, are inadequate or one-sided. But its excellence lies in its tone, its language, its method, its general drift, its multiplicity of topics, the direction which it gave to the thoughts and studies of reflecting men for many generations subsequent to its appearance. . . . He may almost be said to have recreated that philosophy. There is hardly a single French or English writer (and we may add Kant) down to the time of Dugald Stewart, or even of Cousin, Hamilton, and J. S. Mill, who

does not profess either to develope Locke's system, or to supplement, or to criticise it. Followers, antagonists, and critics alike seem to assume on the part of the reader a knowledge of the "Essay on the Human Understanding," and to make that the starting-point of their own speculations. The office which Bacon assigns to himself with reference to knowledge generally might well have been claimed by Locke with reference to the science of mind. Both of them did far more than merely play the part of a herald, but of both alike it was emphatically true that they "rang the bell to call the other wits together."—FOWLER, THOMAS, 1880, *Locke (English Men of Letters), pp.* 148,150.

It is an earnest appeal in favour of devotion to the attainment of truth, and an exposure of *all* the various sources of error, moral and intellectual; more especially prejudices and bias. There are not, however, many references to book study; and such as we find are chiefly directed to the one aim of painful and laborious examination, first, of an author's meaning, and next of the goodness of his arguments.—BAIN, ALEXANDER, 1884, *Practical Essays, p.* 209.

He received £30 for the copyright, about the same sum as Kant received, ninety-one years after, for his "Kritik of Pure Reason,"—the philosophical complement to the "Essay." These two great works are the fountains of the philosophy of our epoch, the one dominating philosophical thought in the eighteenth, and the other, partly by reaction, in the nineteenth century.—FRASER, ALEXANDER CAMPBELL, 1890, *Locke (Philosophical Classics), p.* 87.

You will not find this world of Locke an exciting one.—ROYCE, JOSIAH, 1892, *The Spirit of Modern Philosophy, p.* 85.

Became at once the leading philosopher of his time. . . . Locke's authority as a philosopher was unrivalled in England during the first half of the eighteenth century, and retained great weight until the spread of Kantian doctrines. His masculine common sense, his modesty and love of truth have been universally acknowledged; and even his want of thoroughness and of logical consistency enabled him to reflect more fully the spirit of a period of compromise. His spiritual descendant, J. S.

Mill, indicates his main achievement by calling him the "unquestioned founder of the analytic philosophy of mind." By fixing attention upon the problem of the necessary limits of thought and investigating the origin of ideas, his writings led to the characteristic method of his English successors, who substituted a scientific psychology for a transcendental metaphysic. His own position, however, was not consistent, and very different systems have been affiliated upon his teaching. His famous attack upon "innate ideas" expressed his most characteristic tendency, and was generally regarded as victorious; but critics have not agreed as to what is precisely meant by "innate ideas," and Hamilton, for example, maintains that if Locke and Descartes, at whom he chiefly aimed, had both expressed themselves clearly, they would have been consistent with each other and with the truth. Hume's scepticism was the most famous application of Locke's method; but Reid and his follower Dugald Stewart, while holding that the theory of "ideas" accepted by Locke would logically lead to Hume, still hold that a sound philosophy can be constructed upon Locke's method, and regard him as one of the great teachers. In France, Locke's name is said to have been first made popular by Fontenelle. He was enthusiastically admired by Voltaire and by d'Alembert, Diderot, Helvetius, and their contemporaries. Condillac, his most conspicuous disciple in philosophy, gave to his teaching the exclusively sensational turn which Locke would have apparently disavowed. —STEPHEN, LESLIE, 1893, *Dictionary of National Biography, vol.* XXXIV, *pp.* 32, 35.

Notwithstanding its enormous influence, the "Essay" contains very little in the way of definite solution of philosophical problems. The results attained by Hobbes and by Berkeley are as much more definite than Locke's as their literary style is superior to his. The place of Locke in English philosophy is like that of Kant in German philosophy. He takes up the problem of "criticism of knowledge," and determines the questions that his successors shall put to themselves. Berkeley is directly dependent on Locke for his starting-point, as Hume is in turn on Berkeley and Locke.—WHITTAKER, T., 1895, *Social England, ed. Traill, vol.* IV, *p.* 564.

ON EDUCATION

Education in England has been in danger of being hurt by two of its greatest men, Milton and Locke. Milton's plan is impracticable, and I suppose has never been tried. Locke's, I fancy, has been tried often enough, but is very imperfect: it gives too much to one side, and too little to the other; it gives too little to literature.—JOHNSON, SAMUEL, 1778, *Life by Boswell.*

He has uttered, to say the least, more good sense on the subject than will be found in any preceding writer. Locke was not like the pedants of his own or other ages, who think that to pour their wordy book-learning into the memory is the true discipline of childhood. . . . Much has been written, and often well, since the days of Locke: but he is the chief source from which it has been ultimately derived; and, though the "Emile" is more attractive in manner, it may be doubtful whether it is as rational and practicable as the "Treatise on Education." If they have both the same defect, that their authors wanted sufficient observation of children, it is certain that the caution and sound judgment of Locke have rescued him better from error. There are, indeed, from this or from other causes, several passages in the "Treatise on Education" to which we cannot give an unhesitating assent. Locke appears to have somewhat exaggerated the efficacy of education. This is an error on the right side in a work that aims at persuasion in a practical matter; but we are now looking at theoretical truth alone.—HALLAM, HENRY, 1837–39, *Introduction to the Literature of Europe, pt.* iv, *ch.* iv, *pars.* 54, 55.

When an English University established an examination for future teachers, the "special subjects" first set were "Locke and Dr. Arnold." The selection seems to me a very happy one. Arnold greatly affected the spirit and even the organization of our public schools at a time when the old schools were about to have new life infused into them, and when new schools were to be started on the model of the old. He is perhaps the greatest educator of the English type, *i. e.*, the greatest educator who had accepted the system handed down to him and tried to make the best of it. Locke on the other hand, whose reputation is more European than English, belongs rather to the continental type. Like his disciple Rousseau and like Rousseau's disciples the French Revolutionists, Locke refused the traditional system and appealed from tradition and authority to reason. We English revere Arnold, but so long as the history of education continues to be written, as it has been written hitherto, on the Continent, the only Englishman celebrated in it will be as now not the great schoolmaster but the great philosopher.—QUICK, ROBERT HERBERT, 1868–90, *Essays on Educational Reformers, p.* 219.

The great defect of this tractate (but its brevity makes the defect of less importance) is its singular want of method. In fact, it appears never to have undergone revision. The author seems to throw together his remarks and precepts without any attempt at order, and he never misses any opportunity of repeating his attacks on what he evidently regarded as being, in his own time, the main hindrances to the acquisition of a sound understanding —prejudice and pedantry. But in justness of observation, incisiveness of language, and profound acquaintance with the workings of the human mind, there are many passages which will bear comparison with anything he has written. . . . Except for the inveterate and growing custom of confining works employed in education to such as can be easily lectured on and easily examined in, it is difficult to understand why this "student's guide," so brief, and abounding in such valuable cautions and suggestions, should have so nearly fallen into desuetude.—FOWLER, THOMAS, 1880, *Locke (English Men of Letters), pp.* 177, 178.

One of the most attractive traits in Locke's character was his sympathy with children. One feels that, childless though he was, yet in writing these counsels concerning their proper education, he is performing a labor of love. The work is remarkable for the due and catholic regard evinced for every means of education necessary for a perfect manhood, in body as well as in knowledge and character. But there is in it no false sentimentalism. The truest love is the firmest.—MORRIS, GEORGE S., 1880, *British Thought and Thinkers, p.* 199.

Virtue, practical worldly wisdom, goodbreeding, and last, "though this may seem strange in the mouth of a bookish man," learning, as something which may be easily and incidentally had "into the bargain," are the objects of education in the order of their importance. To this extent character is the product of education, as knowledge is of experience, so that here again Locke is most modern and most German.—HALL, GRANVILLE STANLEY, 1881, *Aspects of German Culture, p.* 126.

The ideas on education first mooted in an irregular and jesting manner by Rabelais, then developed and made current in good society by Montaigne, were popularised in England by Locke, and through him exercised a mighty influence over Europe in the Émile of Rousseau. Although Locke's "Thoughts on Education" are probably little read in the present day, they have had a powerful effect on the attitude of English society toward education, and, consciously or unconsciously, they determine the character of our most characteristic educational institution, the English public school. These schools, on their intellectual sides the creation of John Sturm and the Jesuits, have been deeply penetrated by the spirit of naturalism, but we imagine that few of those who defend the fresh air and healthy exercise, the self-government and the *savoir faire* which our public schools provide with such success, have any idea that the principles which they support from prejudice have their origin in the theories of two such philosophers as Locke and Rousseau.—BROWNING, OSCAR, 1881, *An Introduction to the History of Educational Theories, p.* 102.

Of all Locke's works, "Some Thoughts Concerning Education" is perhaps the most universally approved, and it is in truth a golden treatise, the very incarnation of good sense and right feeling; and more useful in its own time than it can be now that the errors which Locke especially assailed have become contrary, instead of congenial, to the general spirit of the age. The prevailing tone, the confidence in human nature rightly treated, the abhorrence of the merely arbitrary and despotic, render the work an epoch in the history of culture, and, compared with the coarse maxims of a Defoe, or even the "Whole Duty of Man's" exclusive reliance upon authority, show how greatly

Locke was beyond his contemporaries in enlightenment and the genuine spirit of humanity. The insight and penetration into children's characters are surprising in a man who had no children of his own, or much direct concern with the education of the children of others. They prove that Locke must have been a most careful and accurate observer. If there is a fault in the treatise, it is that the range of view is not always sufficiently wide, and that the author's precepts are too exclusively propounded with reference to the individual, and too little with a view to the general advantage of society.—GARNETT, RICHARD, 1895, *The Age of Dryden, p.* 163.

ON GOVERNMENT

For my own part, I must confess, that, in these latter chapters of Locke on Government, I see, what sometimes appears in his other writings, that the influence of temporary circumstances on a mind a little too susceptible of passion and resentment, had prevented that calm and patient examination of all the bearings of this extensive subject which true philosophy requires.—HALLAM, HENRY, 1837–39, *Introduction to the Literature of Europe, pt.* iv, *ch.* iv, *par.* 100.

In 1669 a Constitution for the Carolinas was framed by the celebrated John Locke; and so widely different is practical statesmanship from profound philosophy, that it was found altogether unmanageable, grounded on principles extremely illiberal and wholly inconsistent with its author's theoretical love of freedom. It was universally disliked and vehemently opposed; nor did the colony, according to the common tradition, ever enjoy a day of peace or happiness under it, till in 1693 it was abandoned and the old government restored.—BROUGHAM, HENRY LORD, 1840–44, *Political Philosophy, pt.* iii.

Hobbes seems to have been one of the first who had any thing like a distinct perception of the real source of wealth. . . . Locke, however, had a much clearer apprehension of this doctrine. His "Essay on Civil Government," published in 1689, is, in fact, the earliest work in which the true sources of wealth are distinctly pointed out. . . . Locke has here all but completely established the fundamental principle which lies at the bottom of the science of wealth. . . . But though Locke gave, in the passage referred to above, a far more distinct and comprehensive statement of the fundamental principle that labour is the grand source of value, and consequently of wealth, than is to be found even in the "Wealth of Nations," it was but little attended to either by his contemporaries or by subsequent inquirers. Locke was not himself aware of the vast importance of the principle he had developed; and three-quarters of a century elapsed before it began to be generally perceived that an inquiry into the means by which labour might be rendered most efficient was the object of that portion of political economy which treats of the production of wealth. —McCULLOCH, JOHN RAMSAY, 1845, *Literature of Political Economy.*

John Locke hated tyranny and persecution as a philosopher; but his intellect and his temper preserved him from the violence of a partisan.—MACAULAY, THOMAS BABINGTON, 1849–55, *History of England.*

Locke's work on Civil Government contains incidental arguments, subordinate to its philosophical principles, some of which are of great merit. It contains the earliest recognition of the true sources of wealth and value. Locke was among the first to see distinctly that gold and silver are not real wealth; that a State unprovided with either, if well supplied with food and other useful articles, would be wealthy; while it must perish, however abundant its supply of the precious metals, so long as it could not exchange them for the means of subsistence. He enlarges upon the dependence of wealth on labour, and of human labour on individual freedom, and touches principles which are at the root of modern socialism. . . . Locke's appeals to ethical principles in the "Treatise on Government" usually presuppose that they are founded in the reason or nature of things, independently of utilitarian considerations, although he is always ready to reinforce moral rules by considerations of pleasure and pain as the motive to action. In treating of natural law he is some points in advance of Grotius and Puffendorf.—FRASER, ALEXANDER CAMPBELL, 1890, *Locke (Philosophical Classics), pp.* 101, 102.

COMMENTARIES

It contains ["On St. Paul"] much important truth and some very considerable errors. Locke read St. Paul with great attention, and yet missed his meaning on some leading subjects. His ideas of the person of Christ, of the doctrine of justification by faith, and the character and privileges of the Christian Church, are grossly erroneous. But, apart from his theological errors, his work possesses very considerable merit. He set the example, in English, of a style of criticizing the New Testament which was afterwards followed by Pierce and Benson, who, in a series of similar works, completed the epistolary part of the New Covenant.—ORME, WILLIAM, 1824, *Bibliotheca Biblica.*

Locke himself is far from being a scriptural writer. . . . He concurred with the Arminians, and was intimate with their leaders in Holland. . . . Whatever desire of peace and union among Christians may have actuated him, we cannot but consider that his influence has been decidedly prejudicial to the pure gospel of Christ. . . . We cannot acquit him of a tendency to Socinian principles. His works must therefore be read with caution.—BICKERSTETH, EDWARD, 1844, *The Christian Student.*

It is needless to remark that these commentaries are distinguished by sound, clear sense, and by a manifest spirit of candour and fairness. They are often quoted with approbation by commentators of the last century. But in the present more advanced state of grammatical and historical criticism, they are likely to remain, as they now are, the least consulted of all his works.—FOWLER, THOMAS, 1880, *Locke (English Men of Letters), p.* 166.

GENERAL

I will forbear to speak of the valuableness of his works. The general esteem they have attained, and will preserve, as long as good sense and virtue are left in the world; the service they have been of to England in particular, and universally to all that set themselves seriously to the search of truth, and the study of christianity, are their best eulogium. The love of truth is visible in every part of them. This is allowed by all that have read them. For even they, who have not relished some of Mr. Locke's opinions, have done

him the justice to confess, that the manner, in which he defends them, shows he advanced nothing that he was not sincerely convinced of himself.—COSTE, PETER, 1705, *The Character of Mr. Locke, Nouvelles de la Republique des Lettres, Feb.*

After all, we must admit that anybody who has read Locke, or rather who is his own Locke, must find the Platos mere fine talkers, and nothing more. In point of philosophy a chapter of Locke or Clarke is, compared with the babble of antiquity, what Newton's optics are compared with those of Descartes.—VOLTAIRE, FRANCOIS MARIE AROUET, 1736, *Correspondence.*

The clearness of Mr. Locke's head renders his language perspicuous, the learning of Stillingfleet's clouds his. This is an instance of the superiority of good sense over learning, towards the improvement of every language.—GOLDSMITH, OLIVER, 1759, *The Bee, No.* 8, *Nov.* 24.

Every rational admirer of Mr. Locke will acknowledge, that if his learning had been equal to his good sense and manly spirit, his works would have been still more creditable to himself, and more useful to mankind.—BEATTIE, JAMES, 1776–9, *Essay on the Usefulness of Classical Learning, p.* 496.

Perspicuous and pure, but almost without any ornament whatever.—BLAIR, HUGH, 1783, *Lectures on Rhetoric and Belles-Lettres, Lecture* xviii, *p.* 202.

Locke was a man of an uncommonly clear and masculine understanding, and greatly superior to many of his most distinguished contemporaries, who, instead of being contented to trace facts and phenomena as he has done, idly bewildered themselves in the invention of fanciful theories. His work forms too memorable an epoch in the annals of literature, not to render it improper that it should be omitted even in this slight essay towards a history of the English language.—GODWIN, WILLIAM, 1797, *Of English Style, The Enquirer, p.* 429.

Perhaps no writer can be named, of ancient or of modern times, to whom mankind are under more extensive obligations than Mr. Locke. By his "Essay on Human Understanding" he effected what may well be called, a complete revolution of opinion in metaphysics. Metaphysics, which had so long and so justly lain under the reproach of bewildering the understanding in a maze of words, destitute of real meaning—metaphysics, which had so long discoursed in an unintelligible jargon, became in the hands of Mr. Locke a most interesting and important branch of true philosophy. By his Treatises on Government and Toleration, he fixed the civil and religious rights of mankind upon a firm and immovable basis: and in his theological works he exhibited the Reasonableness of Christianity, and the solidity of the evidence on which our holy religion is founded, in a clear, perspicuous, and convincing point of view.—BELSHAM, W., 1799, *Essays, vol.* I, *p.* 17.

The affectation of passing for an original thinker glares strongly and ridiculously in Mr. Locke. Who sees not that a great part of his Essay on Man is taken from Hobbes? and almost everything in his Letters on Toleration from Bayle? Yet he nowhere makes the least acknowledgment of his obligations to either of those writers. They were both of them indeed writers of ill fame. But was that a reason for his taking no notice of them? He might have distinguished between their good and ill deserts.—HURD, RICHARD, 1808? *Commonplace Book, ed. Kilvert, p.* 242.

The studies to which Mr. Stewart has devoted himself have lately fallen out of favour with the English public; and the nation which once placed the name of Locke immediately under those of Shakspeare and of Newton, and has since repaid the metaphysical labours of Berkeley and of Hume with such just celebrity, seems now to be almost without zeal or curiosity as to the progress of the Philosophy of Mind.—JEFFREY, FRANCIS LORD, 1810–44, *Contributions to the Edinburgh Review, vol.* III, *p.* 373.

Locke himself, indeed, was a good Christian; but this is only one instance more that he who first opens a new line of thought very seldom pursues it so far as to perceive even its most inevitable consequences. If we adopt his principles, we must inevitably renounce all other thoughts, and limit ourselves to the feeling, the experience, and the enjoyment of the senses: and those who in later times have openly professed these notions, although they called themselves independent philosophers, were in truth only the

disciples of Locke.—SCHLEGEL, FREDERICK, 1815–59, *Lectures on the History of Literature.*

Few books have contributed more than Mr. Locke's Essay to rectify prejudice; to undermine established errors; to diffuse a just mode of thinking; to excite a fearless spirit of inquiry, and yet to contain it within the boundaries which Nature has prescribed to the human understanding. . . . His writings have diffused throughout the civilized world, the love of civil liberty and the spirit of toleration and charity in religious differences, with the disposition to reject whatever is obscure, fantastic, or hypothetical in speculation, —to reduce verbal disputes to their proper value,—to abandon problems which admit of nosolution,—to distrust whatever cannot clearly be expressed,—to render theory the simple expression of facts,—and to prefer those studies which most directly contribute to human happiness. If Bacon first discovered the rules by which knowledge is improved, Locke has most contributed to make mankind at large observe them. . . . If Locke made few discoveries, Socrates made none: yet both did more for the improvement of the understanding, and not less for the progress of knowledge, than the authors of the most brilliant discoveries. Mr. Locke will ever be regarded as one of the great ornaments of the English nation; and the most distant posterity will speak of him in the language addressed to him by the poet, "O Decus Angliacæ certè, O Lux altera gentis!"—MACKINTOSH, SIR JAMES, 1821, *Stewart's Introduction to the Encyclopædia, Edinburgh Review, vol.* 36, *pp.* 242, 243.

In regard to style, it is generally agreed that the prose of Locke is the best of his times; and it requires no great knowledge of the English to perceive in it the manners of a man who has lived in the best society, and who expresses his thoughts without pedantry, in the most clear, most simple, and most familiar terms. . . . I need not tell you that the eminent characteristic of this style is clearness.— COUSIN, VICTOR, 1826–41, *History of Modern Philosophy, tr. Wight, vol.* II, *p.* 171.

Locke, himself a clear, humble-minded, patient, reverent, nay, religious man, had paved the way for banishing religion from the world. Mind, by being modelled in men's imaginations into a shape, a visibility; and reasoned of as if it had been some composite, divisible and reunitable substance, some finer chemical salt, or curious piece of logical joinery—began to lose its immaterial, mysterious, divine, though invisible character; it was tacitly figured as something that might, were our organs fine enough, be *seen*. Yet, who had ever seen it? Who could ever see it? Thus by degrees it passed into doubt, a relation, some faint possibility; and at last into a highly probable nonentity.—CARLYLE, THOMAS, 1828, *Goethe*.

In his *language* Locke is, of all philosophers, the most figurative, ambiguous, vacillating, various, and even contradictory;—as has been noticed by Reid and Stewart, and Brown himself,—indeed, we believe, by every author, who has had occasion to comment on this philosopher. The opinions of such a writer are not, therefore, to be assumed from isolated and casual expressions, which themselves require to be interpreted on the general analogy of his system.—HAMILTON, SIR WILLIAM, 1830, *Reid and Brown, Edinburgh Review, vol. 52, p.* 189.

From 1792 to 1800 I seldom heard Locke mentioned in England: his system, it was said, had become obsolete, and he was regarded as weak in *ideology*.—CHATEAUBRIAND, FRANÇOIS RENÉ, VICOMTE DE, 1837, *Sketches of English Literature*.

In our own country, in like manner, the immortal Locke, under James II., was a student persecuted and silent: the world received no benefit from the labours of his thoughts. But the lapse of a few years and the renewal of a free form of government saw him cherished and admired; saw him give to mankind his "Treatise on Government," his "Reasonableness of Christianity," his "Essay on Toleration," his "Essay on the Human Mind," and contribute more, perhaps, than any individual who can be mentioned, to the best interests of his fellow-creatures, by contributing to remove obscurity from the mind, servility from the heart, and dogmatism from the understanding.—SMYTH, WILLIAM, 1840, *Lectures on the History of the French Revolution, Lecture* iii.

One of the wisest of Englishmen. . . . That Locke never read Hobbes

may seem incredible, but is, we are convinced, the truth. It is one among many examples of how few were the books he had read. He never alludes to Hobbes in any way that can be interpreted into having read him. Twice only, we believe, does he allude to him, and then so distantly, and with such impropriety, as to be almost convincing with respect to his ignorance. . . . It is strange that any man should have read Locke, and questioned his originality. There is scarcely a writer we could name whose works bear such an indisputable impress of his having "raised himself above the almsbasket, and not content to live lazily on scraps of begged opinions, set his own thoughts to work to find and follow truth." It is still more strange that any man should have read Locke and questioned his power. That patient sagacity which, above all things, distinguishes a philosopher, is more remarkable in Locke than almost any writer. He was also largely endowed with good sense; a quality, Gibbon remarks, which is rarer than genius. In these two qualities, and in his homely racy masculine style, we see the type of the English mind, when at its best.—LEWES, GEORGE HENRY, 1845–47, *Biographical History of Philosophy*.

His reputation has been great, but his wrongs have been as memorable as his celebrity. . . . He was an honest man, and great alike in integrity and power. His moral courage was calm, self-sustained, and of the highest order. It sometimes disposed him almost to rashness. Nevertheless, his wisdom in most things was greater than commonly falls to the lot even of the wise. He was a sincere lover of truth and of humanity. If we except Lord Bacon, no single mind in modern times has exercised so powerful an influence on the progress of philosophy.—VAUGHAN, R., 1847, *Locke and his Critics, British Quarterly Review, vol.* 5, *p.* 337.

His style and language are everywhere clear, simple, and idiomatic to the highest degree; not always quite elegant, it is true, but invariably addressing itself directly to the understanding of a plain, cautious, and intelligent reader. It should be distinctly remembered that Locke is the steady and professed enemy of all scholastic and learned phraseology; and perhaps the very skill with which he has popularised his difficult and important subject may have tended to diminish our sense of the obligations which science owes to his name: he has himself often furnished us with arms which we have become so dextrous in using, that we forget they were not of our own invention—a fate which awaits almost all who have simplified human knowledge—SHAW, THOMAS B., 1847, *Outlines of English Literature, p.* 201.

Though, like the other greater luminaries of philosophy and science, Locke has shone on with tolerably uniform lustre, he has had, like most of them, his periods, if not of waxing and waning, yet of brighter effulgence or transient obscuration. He seems to us labouring under some such partial eclipse at present. In the reaction against the sensational schools of the last century—in itself a happy revolution—he has been in some danger of having his merits underrated from his presumed connexion with the extravagancies of those schools. . . . The principal characteristics of the genius of Locke are visible at once to the reader in almost every page. No author has impressed the image of his own mind more indelibly on his works, or given them a character of more perfect originality. Hence, in part, and in great part, the continued popularity they possess, and the delight and profit with which they are perused; delight and profit, as usual, often greater than can be reaped from writings less marked indeed by defects, and even by errors, but tamer in character, and less stimulating to the mind of the student. . . . As to the *learning* of Locke, it has, like that of Shakspeare, been most variously estimated. While some would make him almost ignorant of what his predecessors had written, and such a very Troglodyte in metaphysics that he was not properly acquainted even with such writers as Descartes or Hobbes,—others are of opinion (with Stillingfleet) that he is under vast but unconscious obligations to them. The truth lies, as usual, between the extreme estimates. To suppose that a mind so inquisitive and powerful as Locke's should not have been tolerably conversant with the principal productions of philosophers, is extravagant; to suppose that a mind so original and independent should

be a servile imitator, is equally so. If any man ever thought for himself, it was Locke. He avows it everywhere, that he had faithfully endeavoured to trace the origin and analyse the composition . of thought in his own mind, totally careless what might or might not be the opinions of others. His whole work bears the marks of this; and if he has erred, it is in not having sufficiently and carefully examined the opinions of others.—ROGERS, HENRY, 1854, *John Locke, Edinburgh Review, vol.* 99, *pp.* 384, 385, 390.

Locke was in religion the avowed disciple of Chillingworth, and in politics the highest representative of the principles of Harrington; and it was on the double ground of the sanctity of an. honest conviction, and of the danger of enlarging the province of the civil magistrate, that he defended toleration against the theologians of Oxford.—LECKY, WILLIAM EDWARD HARTPOLE, 1865, *Spirit of Rationalism in Europe.*

Newton attained at most an incomplete idea of space, and was only a mathematician. Locke, almost as poor, gropes about, hesitates, does little more than guess, doubt, start an opinion to advance and withdraw it by turns, not seeing its far-off consequences, nor, above all, exhausting anything. In short, he forbids himself lofty questions, and is very much inclined to forbid them to us. He has written a book to inquire what objects are within our reach, or above our comprehension. He seeks for our limitations; he soon finds them, and troubles himself no further.—TAINE, H. A., 1871, *History of English Literature, tr. Van Laun, vol.* II, *bk.* iii, *ch.* iii, *p.* 70.

The doubt which Voltaire praised in Locke had nothing to do with that shivering mood which receives overmuch poetic praise in our day, as the honest doubt that has more faith than half your creeds. There was no question of the sentimental juvenilities of children crying for light. It was by no means religious doubt, but philosophic; and it affected only the possibilities of ontological knowledge, leaving the grounds of faith on the one hand, and practical conduct on the other, exactly where they were. His intense feeling for actualities would draw Voltaire irresistibly to the writer who, in his judgment, closed the gates of the dreamland of metaphysics, and banished the vaulting ambition of à priori certainties, which led nowhere and assured nothing.—MORLEY, JOHN, 1872, *Voltaire, p.* 65.

The intellectual ruler of the eighteenth century. . . . Locke's candour breathes in every line of his work. He has an unmistakable right to his place in that roll-call of eminent believers which is to this day thundered from pulpits against the pride of the infidel. No child or clergyman of the present time could accept the plenary inspiration of the Scriptures with a simpler faith than this intellectual progenitor of the whole generation of eighteenth-century iconoclasts— the teacher of Toland and Collins, the legitimate precursor of Hume and of Condillac, the philosopher before whom Voltaire is never tired of prostrating himself with unwonted reverence. There is no sign of a consciousness that biblical criticism may turn out to be a destructive agent, and scarcely of a consciousness that it exists. Like Chillingworth, whose congenial intellect excites his admiration, he accepts the authority at once of reason and of the Bible ; and never suspects that there will be any difficulty in serving the two masters.—STEPHEN, LESLIE, 1876, *History of English Thought in the Eighteenth Century, vol.* I, *pp.* 86, 94.

His style is slovenly but clear : that is to say, there is no possibility of mistaking his meaning. The meaning in his case being the result of important and forcible thought, his directness of expression has gained him credit as a writer which is not strictly deserved.—SAINTSBURY, GEORGE, 1886, *Specimens of English Prose Style, p.* 110.

Setting apart the extraordinary merits of Locke's contributions to thought, as a mere writer he may be said to exhibit the prose of the Restoration in its most humdrum form. We have now progressed too far into the new period to expect to find the faults of the old lumbering and stately prose, nor are these in the slightest degree the faults of Locke. But his style is prolix, dull, and without elevation ; he expresses himself with perfect clearness indeed, but without variety or charm of any kind. He seems to have a contempt for all the arts of literature, and passes on from sentence to sentence, like a man talking aloud in his study, and intent only

on making the matter in hand perfectly clear to himself.—GOSSE, EDMUND, 1888, *A History of Eighteenth Century Literature, p.* 96.

Perhaps no philosopher since Aristotle has represented the spirit and opinions of an age so completely as Locke represents philosophy and all that depends upon philosophic thought, in the eighteenth century—especially in Britain and France. Reaction against his real or supposed opinions, and therefore indirectly due to his influence, is not less marked in the later intellectual history of Europe, wherever the influence of Leibniz, and then of Kant and of Hegel has extended ; in Britain the reaction is marked in Coleridge. . . . what strikes one about Locke and his fortunes, besides the large place which he fills in the history of modern opinion—religious and political as well as metaphysical—is the difficulty of interpreting his philosophy without reading into it the history of the man and his surroundings, and also the abundance of imperfectly used materials for this purpose which exist.—FRASER, ALEXANDER CAMPBELL, 1890, *Locke* (*Philosophical Classics*), *pp.* v, vi.

Can hardly be classed otherwise than as a mercantilist, and must even be written down as a systematic upholder of the errors of that system. Nevertheless, in respect of certain theories in detail,—such as property, which he bases upon work done, and money, the debasing of which he loudly condemned in spite of Lowndes and Barbon,—he has claims to originality and soundness.—COSSA, LUIGI, 1891-93, *An Introduction to the Study of Political Economy, p.* 241.

It would be absurd to say that Locke's style is nervous, or original, or instinct with any impulse of feeling, or stimulated by any current of imagination. But it is almost always correct ; it flows evenly and smoothly, and has dignity and even grace, if it lacks variety and force. . . . If Locke is never original in his style, and never shows the force and vigour of one who speaks straight to the deeper instincts of human nature, we must still accord to him the praise of regularity, of dignity, of scrupulous accuracy in diction, up to the measure of logical accuracy to which his thought attained.—CRAIK, HENRY, 1894, *English Prose, vol.* III, *p.* 179.

Sir Roger L'Estrange

1616–1704

Born, at Hunstanton, 17 Dec. 1616. Probably educated at Cambridge. To Scotland with army of Charles I., 1639. Sentenced, by House of Commons, to death for share in Royalist plot, 28 Dec. 1644. Imprisoned till spring of 1648, when he escaped from Newgate with connivance of Governor. At first went to Kent, carrying on Royalist propaganda; but soon withdrew to Holland. Returned to England, Aug. 1653. Active political pamphleteer. Appointed Surveyor of the Imprimery, 15 Aug. 1663. Married Mary Doleman. Edited "The Kingdom's Intelligencer," and "The News," each weekly, Aug. 1663 to Jan. 1666. Edited (and wrote) "The Observator," April 1681 to March 1687. M. P. for Winchester, March 1685. Arrested on political charge 3 March 1696. Imprisoned till May 1696. Died, in London, 11 Dec. 1704. Buried in the church of St. Giles-in-the-Fields. *Works:* His literary works (exclusive of a large number of controversial pamphlets and such works as "The Gentleman Pothecary," 1678, and "Love Letters between a Nobleman and his Sister," posth., 1734) consist of the following *translations:* F. de Quevedo Villegas' "Visions," 1667; Cardinal Bona's "Guide to Eternity," 1672; M. d' Alcoforado's "Five Love Letters from a Nun to a Cavalier," 1678; "Tully's Offices," 1680; "Twenty Select Colloquies of Erasmus," 1680; "The Spanish Decameron," 1687; "The Fables of Æsop," 1692; Seneca's "Morals," 1693; Terence's "Comedies," 1698; "Tacitus," 1698; Flavius Josephus' Works, 1702.—Sharp, R. Farquharson, 1897, *A Dictionary of English Authors, p.* 167.

In 1663 he published a pamphlet entitled, "Considerations and Proposals in order to the Regulation of the Press; together with Diverse Instances of Treasonous and Seditious Pamphlets, proving the necessity thereof." This got him the post of Licenser, in succession to Sir John Birkenhead, and also "all the sole privilege of printing and publishing all narratives, advertisements, Mercuries, intelligencers, diurnals, and other books of public intelligence." He began business at the end of August, 1663, with "The Public Intelligencer." . . . In November, 1665, when the plague in London had driven the Court to Oxford, appeared No. 1 of "The Oxford Gazette." When the Court returned to London, it appeared, on the 5th of February, 1666, as "The London Gazette," under which name it still exists. It was placed at once under Sir Joseph Williamson, Under-Secretary of State (from whom Addison had his Christian name), and his deputy writer of it was, for the first five years, Charles Perrot, M. A., of Oriel. L'Estrange set up, in November, 1675, the first commercial journal, "The City Mercury," and in 1679 an "Observator," in defence of the king's party. In April, 1680, the first literary journal appeared, as a weekly or fortnightly catalogue of new books, the "Mercurius Librarius."—Morley, Henry, 1879, *A Manual of English Literature, ed. Tyler, pp.* 486, 487.

PERSONAL

A man of fine conversation, I think, but I am sure most courtly and full of compliments.—Pepys, Samuel, 1664, *Diary, Dec.* 17.

A man of a good wit, and a fancy very luxuriant, and of an enterprising nature. —Clarendon, Lord (Edward Hyde), 1674? *History of the Rebellion and Civil Wars in England, vol.* iv.

A gentleman whom I had long known, and a person of excellent parts abating some affectations.—Evelyn, John, 1685, *Diary, May* 7.

Sir Roger was but ill-rewarded by the Tories, for having been their champion; the latter part of his life was clouded with poverty, and though he descended in peace to the grave, free from political turmoils, yet as he was bowed down with age and distress, he cannot be said to have died in comfort. He had seen much of the world, examined many characters, experienced the vicissitudes of fortune, and was as well instructed as any man that ever lived, in the important lesson of human life, viz. That all things are vanity.—Cibber, Theophilus, 1753, *Lives of the Poets, vol.* iv, *p.* 302.

L'Estrange had many domestic difficulties. His wife gambled; he had always suffered pecuniary difficulties. His grandnephew, he admits, did him "many charitable offices," and he received frequent

presents from admirers personally unknown to him in acknowledgement of his
public services. Pope's sneer in a letter
to Swift, that the tory party "never gave
him sixpence to keep him from starving"
dose not seem wholly justifiable. But he
had to depend for his livelihood mainly on
his pen, and the hackwork that he did for
the booksellers as a translator only
brought him a precarious income.—LEE,
SIDNEY, 1893, *Dictionary of National
Biography, vol.* XXXIII, *p.* 126.

GENERAL

He with watchful eye
Observes and shoots their treasons as they fly,
Their weekly frauds his keen replies detect,
He undeceives more fast than they infect.
—TATE, NAHUM, 1682, *Absalom and Achitophel, pt.* ii.

Those who shall consider the number
and greatness of his books, will admire he
should ever write so many; and those
who have read them, considering the skill
and method they are written in, will admire he should write so well. Nor is he
less happy in verse than in prose, which
for elegance of language, and quickness
of invention, deservedly entitles him to
the honour of a poet.—WINSTANLEY,
WILLIAM, 1687, *Lives of the Most Famous
English Poets.*

He was certainly a very great master
of the English tongue.—BOYER, ABEL,
1703–13, *Annals of the Reign of Queen
Anne, vol.* III, *p.* 243.

The chief manager of all those angry
writings was one Sir Roger L'Estrange,
a man who had lived in all the late times,
and was furnished with many passages and
an unexhausted copiousness in writing:
so that for four years he published three
or four sheets a week under the title of
the "Observator," all tending to defame
the contrary party, and to make the
clergy apprehend that their ruin was de-
signed.—BURNET, GILBERT, 1715–34, *History of My Own Time.*

Sir Roger's works indeed are often calculated for the meanest capacities, and
the phrase is consequently low; but a
man must be greatly under the influence
of prejudice, who can discover no genius
in his writings; nor an intimate acquaintance with the state of parties, human life,
and manners.—CIBBER, THEOPHILUS, 1753,
Lives of the Poets, vol. IV, *p.* 302.

L'Estrange, who was by no means so
bad a writer as some have represented
him, was sunk in party faction, and having generally the worst side of the argument, often had recourse to scolding,
pertness, and consequently a vulgarity
that discovers itself even in his more
liberal compositions. He was the first
writer who regularly enlisted himself
under the banners of a party for pay, and
fought for it through right and wrong
for upwards of forty literary campaigns.
This intrepidity gained him the esteem of
Cromwell himself, and the papers he wrote
even just before the revolution, almost
with the rope about his neck, have his
usual characters of impudence and perseverance. That he was a standard-writer
cannot be disowned, because a great many
very eminent authors formed their style
by his. But his standard was far from
being a just one; though, when party considerations are set aside, he certainly
was possessed of elegance, ease, and perspicuity.—GOLDSMITH, OLIVER, 1759, *The
Bee, No.* 8, *Nov.* 24.

His Esop's "Fables" was more a new work
than a translation. The most valuable of
his books is his translation of Josephus,
which, though in a better style than most
of his writings, has been very justly
censured. He was one of the great cor-
rupters of our language, by excluding
vowels and other letters not commonly
pronounced, and introducing pert and
affected phrases.—GRANGER, JAMES, 1769–
1824, *Biographical History of England, vol.*
V, *p.* 270.

Sir Roger L'Estrange among his rivals
was esteemed as the most perfect model
of political writing. He was a strong
party-writer on the government side, for
Charles the Second, and the compositions
of the author seem to us coarse, yet they
contain much idiomatic expression. His
Æsop's Fables are a curious specimen of
familiar style. Queen Mary showed a due
contempt of him after the Revolution, by
this anagram:—

> Roger L'Estrange,
> Lye strange Roger !

—DISRAELI, ISAAC, 1791–1824, *Origin of
Newspapers, Curiosities of Literature, p.*
230.

The pattern of bad writing in this respect was Sir Roger L'Estrange: his
Æsop's Fables will present every thing

that is hostile to good taste; yet, by a certain wit and readiness in raillery, L'Estrange was a popular writer, and may even now be read, perhaps, with some amusement.—HALLAM, HENRY, 1837–39, *Introduction to the Literature of Europe, pt.* iv, *ch.* vii, *par.* 32.

"Eminent writer in the 17th century," who eminently displays the worse characteristics of that period of our literature. —COLERIDGE, SARA, 1847, ed., *Biographia Literaria, by Samuel Taylor Coleridge, ch.* xvii, *note.*

L'Estrange was by no means deficient in readiness and shrewdness; and his diction, though coarse, and disfigured by a mean and flippant jargon which then passed for wit in the green-room and the tavern, was not without keenness and vigour. But his nature, at once ferocious and ignoble, showed itself in every line that he penned.—MACAULAY, THOMAS BABINGTON, 1849, *History of England, vol.* I.

All the translations [Quevedo] I have seen are bad. The best is that of L'Estrange, or at least the most spirited; but still L'Estrange is not always faithful when he knew the meaning, and he is sometimes unfaithful from ignorance. Indeed, the great popularity of his translations was probably owing, in some degree, to the additions he boldly made to his text, and the frequent accommodations he hazarded of its jests to the scandal and tastes of his times by allusions entirely English and local.—TICKNOR, GEORGE, 1849–55, *History of Spanish Literature, vol.* II, *p.* 271, *note.*

He excelled in the coarse derision and invective—the rough give-and-take of the time; so much so, that he has been, absurdly enough, accused of corrupting the English language. He earned the hatred of lovers of freedom by his opposition to the emancipation of the press (which was accomplished in 1694), and by his rude exercise of authority while he was himself censor; but these offences may fairly enough be considered the accidents of his time and his position.—MINTO, WILLIAM 1872–80, *Manual of English Prose Literature, p.* 339.

As a controversialist, L'Estrange was bold, lively, and vigorous, but coarse, impudent, abusive, and by no means a scrupulous regarder of truth.—CHAMBERS, ROBERT, 1876, *Cyclopædia of English Literature, ed. Carruthers.*

L'Estrange has been accused of corrupting the language, and certainly he was not in the habit of inquiring too closely into the parentage or the associations of any term that seemed to him either striking or appropriate. But in literature we are to judge by results, and here the result is plainly a style so idiomatic, so pungent, and so telling as completely to justify his audacity. The flat-nosed, hunch-backed, blubber-lipped, big-bellied, baker-legged Æsop; the wife of Xanthus, horribly bold, meddling and expensive, easily put off the hooks and hard to be pleased again; the kite who comes powdering down on the frogs and mice; the lark who goes out progging for food for little ones; the snake lazing at his length in the gleam of the sun; the weasel who tried what she could do with her wits when she could live no longer upon the square;—these and a thousand other vivid and surprising turns of phrase must delight all but the purist as surely as they demonstrate the possibility of a literary employment of "slang" which, if attempted by any but an artist, would result in nothing save imbecility, vulgarity, and nonsense.—MILLAR, J. H., 1893, *English Prose, ed. Craik, vol.* II, *p.* 589.

He has a permanent place in history as the first "able editor," who not only made his journal the vehicle for political discussions, and availed himself of regular news-letters, but employed a regular staff of assistants to collect news. . . . L'Estrange's prose style is bad, but he was the author of several useful translations. . . . He was a courtly and well-bred man, of considerable culture, and would be mentioned with more respect if he had not exercised a function detestable to the entire republic of letters. Dr. Johnson regarded him as the first writer upon record who regularly enlisted himself under the banners of a party for pay, and fought for it through right and wrong. This is probably correct as a mere statement of fact, but unjust if it was intended to imply any doubt of the purity of L'Estrange's motives in serving the high monarchial party, or of the sincerity of his advocacy of its principles.—GARNETT, RICHARD, 1895, *The Age of Dryden, pp.* 174, 175.

Thomas Brown

1663–1704

Tom Brown, "of facetious memory" in Addison's phrase, was born at Shifnal, Shropshire, in 1663. His studies at Christ Church, Oxford, were most probably cut short by his irregularities, but are remembered by his clever extempore adaptation of Martial's epigram, "Non amo te, Sabidi:" "I do not love thee, Dr. Fell." After a few years of teaching at Kingston-on-Thames, he settled in London, where he made an uncertain living by writing satirical poems and pamphlets, many of them remarkable more for their scurrility than their wit. He is principally interesting now as the assailant of Dryden, Sherlock, Durfey, Sir Richard Blackmore, &c. He lived a shifty and disreputable life, and dying 16th June 1704, was buried in the Westminster cloisters near his friend, Mrs. Afra Behn.—PATRICK AND GROOME, eds., 1897, Chambers's Biographical Dictionary, p. 139.

PERSONAL

THOMAS BROWN,
AUTHOR OF "THE LONDON SPY*,"
BORN 1663, DIED 1704.
—Inscription on Tomb, Westminster Abbey.

Lazy, low-minded, dissolute, and clever.
—MORLEY, HENRY, 1873, First Sketch of English Literature, p. 703.

He was educated at Newport school, in the same county, whence he proceeded in 1678 to Christ Church, Oxford. Here his irregular habits brought him into trouble. The story goes that the dean of Christ Church, Dr. Fell, threatened to expel him, but, on receipt of a submissive letter, promised to forgive him if he would translate extempore the epigram of Martial (i. 32), "Non amo te, Sabidi," &c., which Brown promptly rendered by—

I do not love thee, Dr. Fell,
The reason why I cannot tell;
But this I know, and know full well,
I do not love thee, Dr. Fell.

Brown afterwards made amends by writing the doctor's epitaph. . . . Tom Brown's life was as licentious as his writings. Much of his time was spent in a low tavern in Gower's Row in the Minories. His knowledge of London was certainly "extensive and peculiar," and his humorous sketches of low life are both entertaining and valuable.—BULLEN, A. H., 1886, Dictionary of National Biography, vol. VII, pp. 29, 30.

GENERAL

Some of our authors indeed, when they would be more satirical than ordinary, omit only the vowels of a great man's name, and fall most unmercifully upon all the consonants. This way of writing was first of all introduced by T-m B—wn, of

*?

facetious memory.—ADDISON, JOSEPH, 1714, The Spectator, No. 567, July 14.

Most of the anonymous pieces which happened to please the town, were fathered upon him. This, though in reality an injury to him, is yet a proof of the universality of his reputation, when whatever pleased from an unknown hand was ascribed to him; but by these means he was reputed the writer of many things unworthy of him. In poetry he was not the author of any long piece, for he was quite unambitious of reputation of that kind. They are generally Odes, Satires, and Epigrams, and are certainly not the best part of his works. His Translations in Prose are many, and of various kinds. His stile is strong and masculine; and if he was not so nice in the choice of his authors, as might be expected from a man of his taste, he must be excused; for he performed his translations as a task, prescribed him by the Booksellers, from whom he derived his chief support. It was the misfortune of our author to appear on the stage of the world, when fears, and jealousies had soured the tempers of men, and politics, and polemics, had almost driven mirth and good nature out of the nation: so that the careless gay humour, and negligent cheerful wit, which in former days of tranquility, would have recommended him to the conversation of princes, was, in a gloomy period, lost upon a people incapable of relishing genuine humour.—CIBBER, THEOPHILUS, 1753, Lives of the English Poets, vol. III, p. 207.

Brown was a man not deficient in literature, nor destitute of fancy; but he seems to have thought it the pinnacle of excellence to be a merry fellow; and therefore laid out his powers upon small jests and gross buffoonery, so that his performances have little intrinsic value, and were read only while they were recommended by the novelty of the event that occasioned them.—JOHNSON, SAMUEL, 1779–81, *Dryden, Lives of the English Poets.*

The wits laughed, but did not give him reason to laugh also. His conversation of Mr. Bays, related in dialogue, raised his character with the public, as a man of sense, wit, and humour. This was followed by other dialogues, odes, satires, letters, epigrams, and translations without number; for Tom's tavern bills were long, and he lived solely by his pen, which, as well as his tongue, ever made more enemies than friends: a buffoon in company, his raillery was neither delicate nor decent. He loved low abuse, and scattered it everywhere with a liberal hand: the clergy came in for more than their share of it.—NOBLE, MARK, 1806, *Biographical History of England, vol.* I.

I would fain believe, to speak from a mere glance into these volumes, that the Meridian of London is improved since Mr. Brown's days: and sorry to learn that this "vulgar writer's" works are not likely just yet to visit
"The waters of Oblivion's lake."
The author appears to have possessed, besides an acquaintance with French, Italian, and Spanish, some classical lore, and to have employed it in working up the alloy and baser portions of ancient wit into modern shapes. "And if he was not so nice in the choice of his authors," says Dr. Drake, "as might be expected from a man of his taste, he must be excused; because, doing those things for his subsistence, he did not consult his own liking so much as his booksellers', taking such as they have offered the best price for." Poor man! he had better have tried to dig, and ought to have been less ashamed to beg, than to follow in the track of those who, though they do not call evil good, yet stimulate under pretence of satirizing it.—COLERIDGE, SARA, 1847, *ed. Biographia Literaria, by Samuel Taylor Coleridge, ch.* xvii, *note.*

What, Tom Brown "of facetious memory!" Tom Brown, the witty, the learned, the convivial! Tom Brown, the topmost of topshelfers, the wittiest of witsnappers, the most humoursome of humourists!—he who stood literary sponsor for Tom Moore's "Twopenny Post-Bag," even as older Democritus did for Robert Burton's "Anatomy"—who, I thought, was as well known to the youngest book-luney as to the veteran Dibdinite and Heberian,—to the humblest bookster who displays his ragged wares on a hand-barrow as to the bibliopolic successors of Rodd and Lilly—Tom Brown "an unknown worthy!" . . . Whose writings are not only characterized by a large amount of wit and learning, but are now especially valuable for the vivid picture which they afford of the habits and the customs, the amusements and the pleasures, the morals and the manners of the period at which they were written.—BATES, WILLIAM, 1880, *Notes and Queries, 6th Series, vol.* I, *p.* 316.

Tom Brown hardly deserves a place in my anthology; but I have found room for one copy of verses—a clever imitation of one of Martial's epigrams.—BULLEN, A. H., 1895, *ed. Musa Proterva, p.* xii.

John Ray

1628–1705

John Ray was the chief botanist of the time. He was a blacksmith's son, born in 1628 at Black Notley, near Braintree, Essex. He was sent from Braintree School to Cambridge, where he obtained a fellowship of Trinity; in 1651 was Greek Lecturer of his college, and afterwards Mathematical Reader. In 1660 he published a Latin Catalogue of Plants growing about Cambridge, and then made a botanical tour through Great Britain. His Latin "Catalogue of the Plants of England and the Adjacent Isles" first appeared in 1670. Ray took orders at the Restoration, but refused subscription, and resigned. In 1663 he spent three years with a pupil, Mr. F. Willoughby, on the Continent, and published an account of his travels in 1673, as "Observations made in a Journey through Part of the Low Countries, Germany, Italy, and France, with a Catalogue of Plants not Natives of England." Ray married in 1673, a lady twenty-four years younger than himself; educated the children of his friend Mr. Willoughby, who had died in 1672; and finally, in 1679, he settled in his native place, and lived there till his death, in 1705. Among his chief books was "A Collection of English Proverbs, with Short Annotations," first published in 1670; and in the reign of William III. he produced, in 1691, "The Wisdom of God Manifested in the Creation;" in 1692, "Miscellaneous Discourses concerning the Dissolution and Changes of the World;" in 1693, "Three Physico-Theological Discourses concerning Chaos, the Deluge, and the Dissolution of the World;" and in 1700, "A Persuasive to a Holy Life."—MORLEY, HENRY, 1873, *First Sketch of English Literature, p.* 760.

PERSONAL

Dear Sir,—The best of friends. These are to take a final leave of you as to this world. I look upon myself as a dying man. God requite your kindness expressed any ways towards me an hundredfold,—bless you with a confluence of all good things in this world, and eternal life and happiness hereafter,—grant us an happy meeting in heaven. I am, Sir, eternally yours.—RAY, JOHN, 1704, *Letter to Sir Hans Sloane, Jan.* 7.

Mr. Ray was a man of excellent natural parts, and had a singular vivacity in his style, whether he wrote in English or Latin, which was equally easy to him; all which (notwithstanding his great age, and the debility and infirmities of his body) he retained, even to his dying day; of which he gave good proof in some of his letters, written manifestly with a dying hand. In a word, in his dealings, no man more strictly just; in his conversation, no man more humble, courteous, and affable; towards God, no man more devout; and towards the poor and distressed, no man more compassionate and charitable, according to his abilities.—DERHAM, WILLIAM, 1760, *Select Remains of the Learned John Ray, Life.*

He found the highest wisdom to consist in the cordial reception of the revealed will of God, and in unfeigned subjection to it.—ORME, WILLIAM, 1824, *Bibliotheca Biblica, p.* 368.

In the likeness of Ray the phrenologist will look in vain for indications of those intellectual faculties which are displayed in his writings. The forehead is contracted in all its dimensions; so as to form a direct contrast to that of Cuvier, another naturalist of equal industry and zeal, but perhaps of not more comprehensive mind.—MACGILLIVRAY, W., 1834, *Lives of Eminent Zoölogists, p.* 182.

Ray died rich in honours, but not rich in money, as he had to give up his living

in the Church for conscience's sake and conform as a layman. He was singularly charitable in his opinions to others; and as his work has lasted until the present day, and has influenced the progress of natural history, England may well be proud of the blacksmith's son.—DUNCAN, P. MARTIN, 1882, *Heroes of Science, p.* 46.

GENERAL

Of this inestimable writer, whose works do honour to our nation, as a late disciple of the great Swedish naturalist justly observes, I cannot help saying further, that no writer till his time ever advanced all the branches of natural history so much as that sagacious, diligent, English observer, whose systematical spirit threw a light on everything he undertook, and contributed not a little to those great and wonderful improvements which have since been introduced.—STILLINGFLEET, BENJAMIN, 1755–61, *Calendar of Flora.*

Our countryman, the excellent Mr. Ray, is the only describer that conveys some precise idea in every term or word, maintaining his superiority over his followers and imitators, in spite of the advantage of fresh discoveries, and modern information.—WHITE, GILBERT, 1789, *Natural History of Selborne, pt.* ii, *Letter* x.

Mr. Ray had the singular happiness of devoting fifty years of his life to the cultivation of the sciences he loved. Incited by the most ardent genius, which overcame innumerable difficulties and discouragements, his labours were, in the end, crowned with success before almost unequalled. He totally reformed the studies of botany and zoology; he raised them to the dignity of a science, and placed them in an advantageous point of view; and, by his own investigations, added more real improvement to them in England than any of his predecessors. The extent of his improvements in science procured him the admiration of his contemporaries, and have justly transmitted his name to posterity, among those who have done honour to their age and country.—PULTENEY, RICHARD, 1790, *Historical and Biographical Sketches of the Progress of Botany in England.*

The distinctive character of Ray's works consists in the clearness of his methods, which were not only more rigorous than those of any of his predecessors, but applied with great uniformity and precision. The divisions which he introduced into the classes of quadrupeds and birds have been followed by English naturalists even to the present day; and we find evident traces of Ray's arrangement of birds in Linnæus, Brisson, Buffon, and all authors who have written upon this class of animals. . . . These labours, however, in nearly all branches of natural history, vast as they appear to the imagination, did not distract Ray from his earlier theological studies. In his treatise entitled "The Wisdom of God manifested in the Works of the Creation," he has well shown how these studies could be combined. . . . All his works on natural history are in Latin; they are composed in an unaffected style, and are less cumbered than those of his successors with a multitude of new terms, so burdensome to the memory.—CUVIER, GEORGE, BARON AND THOUARS, AUBERT DUPETIT, 1832? *Biographie Universelle, tr. Busk.*

His merits have been duly appreciated, both by foreigners and his own countrymen; and although, in the last century, they seemed in danger of falling into oblivion, amid the blaze of the numerous discoveries and improvements then made, they are, at the present day, brought more prominently into view, when men have begun to compare systems, and to shake off the influence of party-spirit. An interesting commemoration of him was made in London on the 29th November 1828. A genus of plants was dedicated to his memory by Plumier, under the name of *Jan Raia*, which Linnæus changed into *Rajania*, and Smith into *Raiana.*—MACGILLIVRAY, W., 1834, *Lives of Eminent Zoologists*, p. 179.

Among the original works of Ray, we may select the "Synopsis Methodica Animalium Quadrupedum et Serpentini Generis," published in 1693. This book makes an epoch in zoölogy, not for the additions of new species it contains, since there are few wholly such, but as the first classification of animals that can be reckoned both general and grounded in nature. He divides them into those with blood and without blood. The former are such as breathe through lungs, and such as breathe through gills. Of the former of these, some have a heart with two ventricles; some have one only. And, among the former class of these, some are viviparous, some oviparous. We thus come to the proper distinction of mammalia. But, in compliance with vulgar prejudice, Ray did not include the cetacea in the same class with quadrupeds, though well aware that they properly belonged to it; and left them as an order of fishes. Quadrupeds he was the first to divide into *ungulate* and *unguiculate*, hoofed and clawed; having himself invented the Latin words. . . . Ray was the first zoölogist who made use of comparative anatomy.—HALLAM, HENRY, 1837–39, *Introduction to the Literature of Europe, pt.* iv, *ch.* viii, *pars.* 16, 17.

The extent of the influence of the genius of Ray on the science of natural history is far greater than can be estimated by the number or size of the volumes which he wrote, and is to be traced to his habit of acute observation of facts and the logical accuracy with which he arranged them. He made his knowledge of the structure and physiology of plants subservient to a great plan for their arrangement, and this plan, when carefully examined, will be found to contain the fundamental principles of all the more recent scientific systems in natural history, and to have laid the foundation of the views of a natural classification of the vegetable kingdom put forward in later times.—LANKESTER, EDWIN, 1846, *ed. Memorials of John Ray, Preface*, p. viii.

Ray, who first supplied materials for the argument for natural religion, drawn from final causes.—FARRAR, ADAM STOREY, 1862, *A Critical History of Free Thought, Lecture* viii, *note.*

'Though he was not quite clear as regards the distinction, which we now express by the words dicotyledonous and monocotyledonous embryo, yet he may claim the great merit of having founded the natural system in part upon this difference in the formation of the embryo. He displays more conspicuously than any systematist before Jussieu the power of perceiving the larger groups of relationship in the vegetable kingdom, and of defining them by certain marks; these marks, moreover, he determines not on *a priori* grounds, but from acknowledged affinities; but it is only in the great divisions of his system that he is thus true to the right course; in the details he commits many and grievous offences against his own method.—SACHS, JULIUS VON, 1875-90, *History of Botany, tr. Garnsey, rev. Balfour, p.* 69.

Wrote chiefly in Latin, but composed his treatise on "The Wisdom of God in the Creation" in his mother-tongue. The anthropomorphism of this earnest, lucid, and ingenious book, the prototype of Paley's, is a defect hardly to be avoided in an age when the Deity was almost universally conceived as an artificer; and yet Ray comes very near indeed to the conception of a power imminent in Nature. His style is limpid and persuasive; his reasoning cogent; his good sense is apparent in his discussion of spontaneous generation and the stories related in its support, although the caution and modesty of his temper sometimes incline him to defer too much to authority. He has no mercy, for example, on frogs rained from the sky, but will not, in the face of the testimony of eye-witnesses, carry scepticism to the point of disputing that they may have been occasionally found immured in the middle of stones.—GARNETT, RICHARD, 1895, *The Age of Dryden, p.* 228.

Though the purity of Ray's Latin has formed the topic of many encomia, Ray's English style is perhaps hardly sufficiently distinguished to secure for him any great position in general literature. His merits as a writer on other topics than natural science are those of the man of science who amasses materials with painstaking care and critical capacity. John Locke, speaking of his "Travels" (1673), mentions Ray's brief yet ingenious descriptions of everything that he saw, and his enlargement upon everything that was curious and rare; but it is only at the present day, since the rise of the scientific study of dialect and folklore, that the value of some of his collections, such as those of proverbs and rare words, is fully realised. Contrary to what has been sometimes said of him, Ray was never a mere compiler. He well knew how to adopt and combine the results of others with his own investigations, but he never blindly copied the statements of others, while he always acknowledged his obligations.—BOULGER, G. S., 1896, *Dictionary of National Biography, vol.* XLVII, *p.* 343.

John Howe

1630-1705

John Howe, Puritan divine, was born 17th May 1630 at Loughborough. He studied at Cambridge and Oxford, and, after preaching for some time at Winwick and Great Torrington, he was appointed domestic chaplain to Cromwell in 1656. In 1659 he returned to Torrington, but the Act of Uniformity ejected him in 1662, and he wandered about preaching in secret till 1671. In 1668 he published "The Blessedness of the Righteous," in 1671 became domestic chaplain to Lord Massereene, of Antrim Castle in Ireland. Here he wrote his "Vanity of Man as Mortal," and began his greatest work, "The Good Man the Living Temple of God" (1676-1702). In 1676 he became pastor of the dissenting congregation in Silver Street, London. In 1685 he travelled with Lord Wharton on the Continent, and settled at Utrecht, till in 1687 the Declaration of Indulgence recalled him to England. He died in London, 2d April 1705. He was a profound thinker, and gifted with great practical sagacity. His own convictions were very decided, yet he had large toleration for the opinions of others. His writings are marred by a poor style and innumerable digressions. See Life by Calamy prefixed to his works (1724), and that by Henry Rogers (1836; new ed. 1879).—PATRICK AND GROOME, eds., 1897, *Chambers's Biographical Dictionary, p.* 507.

PERSONAL

He told me it was upon these occasions his common way to begin about nine in the morning, with a prayer for about a **quarter** of an hour, in which he begged a blessing on the work of the day; and afterwards read and expounded a chapter or psalm, in which he spent about three quarters of an hour, then prayed for an hour, preached for another hour, and prayed for half-an-hour. After this he retired and took some little refreshment for about a quarter of an hour or more (the people singing all the while), and then came again into the pulpit, prayed for another hour, and gave them another sermon of about an hour's length, and so concluded the service of the day at about four o'clock in the evening, with about half-an-hour or more in prayer.—CALAMY, EDMUND, 1724, *ed. Works of John Howe, Memoir.*

It is pleasant to contemplate such a man as Howe amid the fierce passions and rude and often petty conflicts of his age. He could not but bear their dint, living, as he did, in the very midst of them; but they touch him as little as possible. His countenance shows the traces of a refined and elevated nature, and of the same largeness and tenderness of soul that mark his writings. It would be difficult to conceive a more noble, spiritual, or gentle set of features. A native dignity of manner and character shine in them. The court of Cromwell may not seem the most fitting nursery of such a nature; but the presence of one who, like Howe, combined earnestness with refinement, and all the glow of the Puritan religious feeling with a chastened taste and a radiancy of imagination, is enough to show that we are not to judge this court according to any mere vulgar estimate. It must have been a pure and high atmosphere in which Howe moved freely and exercised influence. One who lived so much above the world, and on whose spirit dwelt so familiarly the awe and grandeur of the Unseen, would be a constant monitor, both of high principle and duty, in circumstances sufficient to try the one and seduce from the other.— TULLOCH, JOHN, 1861, *English Puritanism and Its Leaders, p.* 285.

Here is a life of true nobility, a simple unostentatious adherence to truth and principle, a brave endurance of the countless troubles into which the lover of truth is led. There is a purity of motive, a directness of aim, a width of understanding, an inclusive charity in the man. The scandal of an unsympathetic age can find nothing to say against him; the reverence and love of the friends who knew him cannot say enough in his praise. If it should be possible to draw the portrait with any

fidelity, and to present the subject of it, not merely as a writer or a theologian, but as a man, a warm and living heart, a large and enterprising brain, the author would incur the benediction of many people in the present day for introducing them to so attractive a person.—HORTON, ROBERT F., 1895, *John Howe (Leaders of Religion), p.* 2.

GENERAL

One of the most learned and polite writers among the dissenters. His reading in divinity was very extensive: he was a good Orientalist, and understood several of the modern languages. . . . His "Blessedness of the Righteous" was the most generally-esteemed of his performances. He was an admired preacher, but was sometimes too profound for ordinary capacities. There is an uncommon depth of thought in several of his works.— GRANGER, JAMES, 1769–1824, *Biographical History of England, vol.* v, *p.* 66.

For depth and originality of thought, John Howe has never been surpassed by any theological writer whatever. His principles were strictly evangelical, and his spirit eminently catholic and devout. His "Living Temple," especially, is a masterpiece of profound argumentation. . . . His best pieces are "The Blessedness of the Righteous," "Delighting in God," "Enmity and Reconciliation," "Redeemer's Tears, and Dominion." Some "Funeral Sermons," and part of his "Living Temple," are most excellent.—WILLIAMS, EDWARD, 1800, *The Christian Preacher.*

"The Blessedness of the Righteous" is a first-rate performance, and contains a vast extent of thought, of learning, but especially of piety. . . His "Delighting in God" is one of the purest treatises of practical theology to be found in the English language. . . . Perhaps it may be considered as no unfair test of intellectual and spiritual excellence that a person can relish the writings of John Howe: if he does not, he may have reason to suspect that something in the head or heart is wrong. A young minister who wishes to attain eminence in his profession, if he has not the works of John Howe, and can procure them in no other way, should sell his coat and buy them; and, if that will not suffice, let him sell his bed and lie on the floor;

and if he spend his days in reading them he will not complain that he lies hard at night.—BOGUE AND BENNETT, 1809, *History of the Dissenters*.

Possessed of the learning of Cudworth, the evangelical piety of Owen, and the fervour of Baxter, with a mind of larger dimensions than what belonged to any of these distinguished individuals, every thing which fell from his pen is worthy of immortality. He delights while he instructs, and impresses while he enlightens. His "Living Temple," "The Blessedness of the Righteous," "Of Delighting in God," "The Redeemer's Tears," are among the finest productions of uninspired genius, and must be read with high gratification by every Christian. His style is occasionally rugged and inharmonious; but the sentiment will richly repay the trifling annoyance of its harsh and involved structure.—ORME, WILLIAM, 1824, *Bibliotheca Biblica*.

None can peruse his writings without feeling that his mind was habitually filled with the contemplation of that peculiar but truly divine character, that comprehensiveness and all-pervading excellence, the ultimate development of which, in those who embrace Christianity, is the design of the mysteries it reveals, and of all the powerful motives by which it prompts to action.—ROGERS, HENRY, 1836, *Life of Howe*.

A very extraordinary, original, sublime, and splendid writer, but sometimes obscure and heavy. Few writers will more strengthen and enlarge the reader's mind; but he is deficient in evangelical statement and simplicity.—BICKERSTETH, EDWARD, 1844, *The Christian Student*.

Few, if any, uninspired men have equalled him in what may be called a *philosophic* knowledge of Christianity, understanding thereby an extensive and harmonized acquaintance with the facts it embraces, derived from a diligent and impartial examination of the divine testimony which reveals it.—URWICK, W., 1846, *The Redeemer's Tears, Life of John Howe*, p. xlviii.

Though excelled by Baxter as a pulpit orator, and by Owen in exegetical ingenuity and in almost every department of theological learning, Howe compares favorably with either as a sagacious and profound thinker, while he was more successful in combining religious earnestness and fervor of conviction with large-hearted tolerance and cultured breadth of view. His style, moreover, though not altogether free from the literary faults which may almost be called characteristic of Puritanism, has often a stately yet graceful flow which the modern reader will look for in vain in most of Howe's theological contemporaries. — BAYNES, THOMAS SPENCER, *ed.*, 1881, *Encyclopædia Britannica, ninth ed., vol.* XII.

His writings show an original mind, contemplative rather than profound, with considerable power of discrimination, and some warmth of fancy. His spirit is superior to his style; his diction rarely rises to the elevation of his thought; his sentences are negligent, and his punctuation seems devised for the ruin of perspicuity. He shines at his best in his consolatory letters . . . which are full of pathos and calm wisdom.—GORDON, ALEXANDER, 1891, *Dictionary of National Biography, vol.* XXVIII, *p.* 88.

He formed his own system of divinity, and wrote many works, practical and polemical, marked by depth, solidity, and eloquent expression. His abilities and character won for him the high esteem of good men in all parties.—SANDERSON, EDGAR, 1893, *History of England and the British Empire, p.* 648.

John Evelyn

1620–1706

Born at Wotton, 31 Oct. 1620. From age of five lived in household of his grandmother, at Lewes. Educated at Southover Free School. Admitted to Middle Temple as student, 13 Feb. 1637. Fellow Commoner of Balliol Coll., Oxford, 10 May, 1638. Took no degree. Took chambers in Temple, 1640. In Holland, July to Oct., 1641. In Civil War joined King's army, Nov. 1642, but was not received, and returned to Wotton. In France, Nov. 1643 to Oct. 1644; in Italy, Oct. 1644 to April 1646; returned through Switzerland to Paris; married Mary Browne there, 27 June, 1647.

Returned to England, Sept. 1647, without his wife. Returned to Paris, 1 Aug. 1649.
Visit to England, 1650. Returned to England to live, Feb. 1652; his wife returned,
June 1652; they settled at Sayes Court, Deptford. Inaugurated scheme of Royal Society; first meeting held, Jan. 1661; elected fellow and member of Council. On
various Metropolitan Commissions, 1662. On commission for care of prisoners and
wounded in Dutch War, 1644. Hon. D.C.L., Oxford, 1669. Member of Council of
foreign plantations, 28 Feb. 1671. Commissioner for Privy Seal, Dec. 1685 to March
1687. Sec. to Royal Soc., Dec. 1772 to Dec. 1773. Left Sayes Court and settled
with brother at Wotton, May 1694. Treasurer of Greenwich Hospital, 1695 to Aug.
1703. Inherited Wotton estate from his bróther, Oct. 1699. Died there, 27 Feb.
1706; buried in Wotton Church. *Works:* "Of Liberty and Servitude," 1649; "The
State of France . . . in the ninth year of . . . Lewis XIII.," (under initials:
J. E.), 1652; "A Character of England" (anon.), 1659; "Apology for the Royal
Party" (anon.), 1659: "The Late Newes from Brussels Unmasked" (anon.),
1660; "A Poem upon His Majesty's Coronation," 1661; "Encounter be-
tween the French and Spanish Ambassadors," 1661; "Fumifugium," 1661;
"Tyrannus" (anon.), 1661; "Sculptura," 1662; "Sylva," 1664; "Kalendarium
Hortense," 1664; "Public Employment, and an Active Life, preferred to Soli-
tude," 1667; "The three late famous Imposters" (under initials: J. E.), 1669;
"Navigation and Commerce," 1674; "A Philosophical Discourse of Earth," 1676;
"The Whole Body of Antient and Modern Architecture," 1680; "Mundus Muliebris"
(anon.), 1690; "Mundus Foppensis" (anon.), 1691; "Numismata," 1697; "Acetaria"
(anon.), 1699. *Posthumous:* "Diary," ed. by W. Bray as "Memoirs . . . of John
Evelyn," 2 vols., 1818; "Life of Mrs. Godolphin," ed. by Bp. Wilberforce, 1847;
"History of Religion," ed. by R. M. Evanson, 1850. He *translated:* Lucretius, Bk. I.,
1656; "The French Gardener," 1658; "The Golden Book" of St. Chrysostom, 1659;
Naudé's "Instructions concerning the erection of a Library," 1661: Pt. II. of "The
Mystery of Jesuitism," 1658; Fréart de Chambray's "Parallel of Ancient Architecture
with Modern," 1664, and "Idea of the Perfection of Painting," 1668; La Quintinie's
"The Compleat Gardener," 1698. He *edited:* translation, by his son John, of René
Rapin's "Of Gardens," 1673. *Life:* by H. B. Wheatley, in 1879 edn. of "Diary."—
SHARP, R. FARQUHARSON, 1897, *A Dictionary of English Authors, p.* 95.

PERSONAL

By water to Deptford, and there made
a visit to Mr. Evelyn, who, among other
things, showed me most excellent painting in little, in distemper, in Indian
incke, water colours, graveing, and, above
all, the whole secret of mezzo-tinto, and
the manner of it, which is very pretty,
and good things done with it. . . .
In fine, a most excellent person he is, and
must be allowed a little for a little conceitedness; but he may well be so, being
a man so much above others.—PEPYS,
SAMUEL, 1665, *Diary, November* 5.

Happy art thou, whom God does bless
With the full Choice of thine own Happiness;
  And happier yet, because thou'rt blest
With Prudence, how to choose the best;
In Books and Gardens thou hast plac'd aright
  (Things which thou well dost understand;
And both dost make with thy laborious Hand)
  Thy noble, innocent Delight:
And in thy virtuous Wife, where thou again
    dost meet
  Both Pleasures more refin'd and sweet;
The fairest Garden in her Looks,

And in her Mind the wisest Books.
Oh, who would change those soft, yet solid
    Joys,
  For empty Shows and senseless Noise;
And all which rank Ambition breeds,
Which seem such beauteous Flow'rs, and are
    such pois'nous Weeds?
—COWLEY, ABRAHAM, 1667? *The Garden,
to J. Evelyn, Esquire.*

If Mr. Evelyn had not been an artist
himself, as I think I can prove he was, I
should yet have found it difficult to deny
myself the pleasure of alloting him a place
among the arts he loved, promoted,
patronised, and it would be but justice to
inscribe his name with due panegyric in
these records, as I have once or twice
taken the liberty to criticize him. But
they are trifling blemishes compared with
his amiable virtues and beneficence; and
it may yet be remarked that the worst I
have said of him is, that he knew more
than he always communicated. It is no
unwelcome satire to say, that a man's intelligence and philosophy is inexhaustible.
I mean not to write his life, which may

be found detailed in the new edition of his "Sculptura," in "Collins's Baronetage," in the "General Dictionary," and in the new "Biographical Dictionary;" but I must observe that his life, which was extended to eighty-six years, was a course of inquiry, study, curiosity, instruction, and benevolence. The works of the Creator, and the mimic labours of the creature, were all objects of his pursuit. He unfolded the perfection of the one, and assisted the imperfection of the other. —WALPOLE, HORACE, 1762–86, *Anecdotes of Painting in England, Catalogue of Engravers.*

His manners we may presume to have been most agreeable: for his company was sought by the greatest men, not merely by inviting him to their own tables, but by their repeated visits to him at his own house; and this was equally the case with regard to the ladies, of many of whom he speaks in the highest style of admiration, affection and respect. He was master of the French, Italian, and Spanish languages. That he had read a great deal is manifest; but at what time he found opportunities for study, it is not easy to say.—BRAY, WILLIAM, 1818, *ed. Diary and Correspondence of John Evelyn, Introduction, vol.* I, *p.* xi.

No change of fashion, no alteration of taste, no revolutions of science, have impaired or can impair his celebrity. Satire, from which nothing is sacred, scarcely attempted to touch him while living; and the acrimony of political and religious hatred, though it spares not even the dead, has never assailed his memory.— SOUTHEY, ROBERT, 1818, *Evelyn's Memoirs, Quarterly Review, vol.* 19, *p.* 53.

Evelyn was at least the Sir Joseph Banks of his times. I have before had occasion to notice his intimacy with the leading families of rank, which appears little, if at all, to have spoilt his natural frankness of manner, and sincerity of character.—DIBDIN, THOMAS FROGNALL, 1824, *The Library Companion.*

I would also, if you have no objection, and without doing injustice to a valuable, but I think hitherto over-estimated character, propose to show Evelyn in a new light, as a regular town and court gossip, going among people (for curiosity's sake) whose society he affected to think a contamination, bowing (for he *must* have bowed) in the levées of the King's mistresses, and getting himself invited to dinner on purpose to meet *Blood,* of whose villainous countenance he has given an admirable description.—HUNT, LEIGH, 1844, *Letter to Macvey Napier, Correspondence, vol.* II, *p.* 34.

Amid all the demoralisation of White-hall, Evelyn appears never to have waived his higher duties for the sake of mere sublunary considerations,—never to have forgotten his responsibility as a Christian. It is difficult to imagine how he could reconcile the nicety of his principles to the impurity of what he saw and heard; but so it was. We know that some men do live in the world, without being *of* the world; and Evelyn may have felt that, to carry out schemes for the public benefit, court favour must be maintained. He seems, also, to have felt for the Stuarts that personal liking with which even the most reprehensible of that family inspired their followers. . . . Evelyn's name is perhaps dearer to England than that of any other of our countrymen who have been engaged in civil employments, if we except Shakspeare. He lived and died among his people, showing how erroneous is the idea that to be religious, or studious, or philosophic, it is necessary to be a recluse. By his social virtues he did as much good as by his works. He first introduced and ennobled the science of making English homes elegant as well as happy.—THOMSON, KATHARINE (GRACE WHARTON), 1861, *Celebrated Friendships, vol.* I, *pp.* 42, 51.

Evelyn is the typical instance of the accomplished and public-spirited country gentleman of the Restoration, a pious and devoted member of the church of England, and a staunch loyalist in spite of his grave disapproval of the manners of the court. His domestic life was pure and his affections strong, and he devoted himself to work of public utility, although prudence or diffidence kept him aloof from the active political life which might have tested his character more severely. His books are for the most part occasional and of little permanent value. The "Sylva," upon which he bestowed his best work, was long a standard authority, and the "Diaries" have great historical value. —STEPHEN, LESLIE, 1889, *Dictionary of National Biography, vol.* XVIII, *p.* 81.

We can imagine no one whom it would have been more delightful to have had for a friend or relation than the all-accomplished Christian gentleman, philanthropist, scholar, artist, author, and scientist who wrote Evelyn's Diary. Living in a corrupt yet bigoted and superstitious age, he is our ideal of all that is pure, liberal, charitable, lovely, and of good report. . . . He entirely escaped depreciation and satire in a day and generation which was in the habit of making a jest of goodness, and was loved and reverenced even by those who were too evil or too weak to follow his example of holy living and dying. The preparation for this noble and vigorous life was a youth of hard and profitable study and travel; of the sowing, not of wild oats, but of good seed which yielded an abundant harvest.—STEELE, MARY DAVIES, 1889, *John Evelyn's Youth, Atlantic Monthly, vol.* 64, *p.* 74.

SYLVA
1664

It may therefore, perhaps, be esteemed a small character of Mr. Evelyn's discourse of forest-trees to say, that it outdoes all that Theophrastus and Pliny have left us on that subject; for it not only does that and a great deal more, but contains more useful precepts, hints, and discoveries, upon that now so necessary a part of our *Res Rustica* than the world had till then known, for all the observations of former ages. To name others after him would be a derogation to his performance.—WOTTON, WILLIAM, 1694, *Reflections on Ancient and Modern Learning.*

Had Evelyn only composed the great work of his "Sylva, or a Discourse of Forest Trees," his name would have excited the gratitude of posterity. The voice of the patriot exults in the dedication to Charles II. prefixed to one of the later editions. "I need not acquaint your majesty, how many millions of timbertrees, besides infinite others, have been propagated and planted throughout your vast dominions, at the instigation and by the sole direction of this work, because your majesty has been pleased to own it publicly for my encouragement." And surely while Britain retains her awful situation among the nations of Europe, the "Sylva" of Evelyn will endure with her triumphant oaks. It was a retired philosopher who aroused the genius of the nation, and who, casting a prophetic eye toward the age in which we live, contributed to secure our sovereignty of the seas. The present navy of Great Britain has been constructed with the oaks which the genius of Evelyn planted!—DISRAELI, ISAAC, 1791–1824, *Introducers of Exotic Flowers, Curiosities of Literature.*

The "Sylva" has no beauties of style to recommend it, and none of those felicities of expression by which the writer stamps upon your memory his meaning in all its force. Without such charms, "A Discourse of Forest Trees, and the Propagation of Timber in his Majesty's Dominions" might appear to promise dry entertainment; but he who opens the volume is led on insensibly from page to page, and catches something of the delight which made the author enter with his whole heart and all his faculties into the subject. . . . It is a great repository of all that was then known concerning the forest trees of Great Britain, their growth and culture, and their uses and qualities real or imaginary; and he has enlivened it with all the pertinent facts and anecdotes which occurred to him in his reading.—SOUTHEY, ROBERT, 1818, *Evelyn's Memoirs, Quarterly Review, vol.* 19, *p.* 47, 48.

Say's Court was afterwards the residence of the celebrated Mr. Evelyn, whose "Silva" is still the manual of British planters, and whose life, manners, and principles, as illustrated in his Memoirs, ought equally to be the manual of English gentlemen.—SCOTT, SIR WALTER, 1821, *Kenilworth, chap.* XIII.

DIARY

The author was a much more important and worthy personage than his friend Pepys, and yet his work is of somewhat less interest, if not of less value. He travelled extensively in different parts of Europe, and he made record of what impressed him most. But those objects which interested Evelyn were the very objects which Pepys cared least about. In this way the works supplement each other, and give us the most perfect view we have of manners and customs in England during the latter part of the seventeenth century.—ADAMS, CHARLES KENDALL, 1882, *A Manual of Historical Literature, p.* 463.

Evelyn's "Diary" was found, among other papers, at his country seat at Wotton, in Surrey. Evelyn has himself told us in what way the book originated:—"In imitation of what I had seen my father do," he remarks, when speaking of himself in his twelfth year, "I began to observe matters more punctually, which I did use to set down in a blank almanack." These fragmentary memoranda were, it seems, transferred from the blank almanacs to the quarto blank book in which they were afterwards found, and from which the work was printed. This quarto volume, still at Wotton, consists of seven hundred pages, written closely by Evelyn, in a very small hand, and comprising the continuous records of fifty-six years,—a period the most romantic and stirring in the English annals. Sir Walter Scott said that "he had never seen a mine so rich." And of Evelyn himself, it may be said that he was one of the noblest and most exemplary of men in an age not remarkable for purity and virtue in its high places of power. The manuscript diary of the celebrated John Evelyn lay among the family papers, at his country seat, from the period of his death, in 1706, until their rare interest and value were discovered in the following singular manner. Mr. Upcott, of the London Institution, was requested to arrange and catalogue the library at Wotton, and one day Lady Evelyn remarked, as he had expressed his great interest in the collection of autographs, the manuscript of Evelyn's "Sylva" would be interesting to him. Replying, as may be imagined, in the affirmative, the servant was directed to bring the papers from a loft in the old mansion, and soon Upcott had the delight of finding among the collection the manuscript "Diary of John Evelyn,"—one of the most finished specimens of autobiography in the whole realm of English literature. The work was published in 1818.—SAUNDERS, FREDERICK, 1887, *The Story of Some Famous Books, p. 45.*

John Evelyn, possessing neither the humour, the *naïveté,* the shrewdness, or the uncompromising frankness of his rival and friend, occupies a much lower place as an autobiographer, though more highly endowed as a scholar and a man of letters. . . . The chief literary merits of the "Diary" are its unassuming simplicity and perfect prespicuity of style and phrase. Infinitely less interesting than Pepys's, it has the advantage of covering a much more extensive period, and faithfully reflecting the feelings of a loyal, pious, sensible Englishman at various important crises of public affairs. Unlike Pepys, whose estimates of men and things are very fluctuating, Evelyn is consistent, and we may feel sure that any modification of sentiment that may be observed in him faithfully represents the inevitable influence of circumstances upon a man of independent judgment.—GARNETT, RICHARD, 1895, *The Age of Dryden, pp.* 195, 196.

Over Evelyn's own diary we shall not linger. It is a most valuable repository of sights and things at home and abroad; but it is photographic, it lacks distinction and temperament. Evelyn himself may be well portrayed by his own account of his younger brother,—"A sober, prudent, worthy gentleman." A country magnate who survived terrible crises, travelled much when travel was a rarity, he always preserved an open heart and an open mind as well as an open house. He maps out rather than paints his stormy, stirring periods. His own individuality does not modify or tinge his theme. One phase of his, however, we feel constrained to rescue: "This day I paid all my debts to a farthing, O blessed day!"—SICHEL, W., 1899, *Men Who Have Kept a Diary, Blackwood's Magazine, vol.* 165, *p.* 73.

GENERAL

That most ingenious and virtuous gentleman, Mr. Evelyn, who is not satisfied to have advanced the knowledge of this age by his own useful and successful labours about planting and divers other ways, but is ready to contribute every thing in his power to perfect other men's endeavours.—BURNET, GILBERT, 1679–1715, *History of the Reformation of the Church of England.*

We might justly have expected whatever could have been desired on this subject, from the excellently-learned pen of Mr. Evelyn; and he bent his thoughts, as was believed, towards the consideration of our British coins, as well as medals. It now appears that his "Numismata" carried him no farther than those larger and more choice pieces that are usually called by this latter name; whereon he has, indeed treated with that accuracy and fineness which become a gentleman and a scholar.—NICOLSON, WILLIAM, 1696-1714, *English Historical Library, ch.* vii.

John Evelyn, the English Peiresc, was a gentleman of as universal knowledge as any of his time; and no man was more open and benevolent in the communication of it. He was particularly skilled in gardening, painting, engraving, architecture, and medals; upon all which he has published treatises.—GRANGER, JAMES, 1769-1824, *Biographical History of England, vol.* V, *p.* 285.

Evelyn wrote in 1651 a little piece, purporting to be an account of England by a Frenchman. It is very severe on our manners, especially in London; his abhorrence of the late revolutions in church and state conspiring with his natural politeness, which he had lately improved by foreign travel. It is worth reading as illustrative of social history; but I chiefly mention it here on account of the polish and gentlemanly elegance of style, which very few had hitherto regarded in such light compositions. . . . The later writings of Evelyn are such as his character and habits would lead us to expect; but I am not aware that they often rise above that respectable level, nor are their subjects such as to require an elevated style.—HALLAM, HENRY, 1837-39, *Introduction to the Literature of Europe,* pt. iv, *ch.* vii, *par.* 35.

Although a very miscellaneous as well as voluminous writer, has hardly left any work that is held in esteem for either style or thought, or for anything save what it may contain of positive information or mere matter of fact.—CRAIK, GEORGE L., 1861, *History of English Literature and of the English Language, vol.* II, *p.* 187.

There are few writers of the XVII century who portray so faithfully the inner life of their era as Evelyn. To the student of history, as well as the student of philology, he is alike rich in suggestion and instruction.—SHEPHERD, H. E., 1883, *John Evelyn's Plan for the Improvement of the English Language, American Journal of Philology, vol.* IV, *p.* 459.

When we come to Evelyn, we have in him one who fitly represents the new spirit in English prose. His style may be cumbrous, artificial, even tedious; but it is impossible to deny its stateliness, its dignity, its consummate calm. It lacked much which the succeeding generation was to bring, and which was fully attained by those who follow him in this volume. The long roll of his sentences was monotonous, and the reader instinctively calls for the relief of variety. But the essential elements of regularity, formal order, and restraint, were distinctly present. He retains much of the pedantic learning and far-fetched allusion which were so rife in the preceding age; but he retains also—and for this we have to thank him—the richness of ornament and metaphor that prevent an impression of dulness and barrenness. Luxuriance of fancy had yet to be pruned: the spirit of the succeeding generation was to bring greater lucidity and exactness of thought and method, and as a result the cumbrous period was to be shortened, and the movement of our prose made more quick and natural. But even what is best in the full ripeness of the later harvest owes something to the luxuriance of such prose as that of Evelyn.—CRAIK, HENRY, 1894, *English Prose, vol.* III, *Introduction, p.* 2.

Among the many candidates for the praise of having reformed our wild and loose methods in prose, John Evelyn seems to be the one who best deserves it. He was much the oldest of the new writers, and he was, perhaps, the very earliest to go deliberately to French models of brevity and grace. Early in the Commonwealth he was as familiar with La Motte le Vayer as with Aristotle; he looked both ways and embraced all culture. Yet Evelyn is not a great writer; he aims at more than he reaches; there is notable in his prose, as in the verse of Cowley, constant irregularity of workmanship, and a score of faults have to be atoned for by one startling beauty. Evelyn, therefore, is a pioneer.—GOSSE, EDMUND, 1897, *Short History of Modern English Literature, p.* 180.

In all his work Evelyn's style is that of a thoroughly cultivated gentleman who, on the one hand, has had the full education of his time, and on the other is familiar with the language of its best society. But he has little idiosyncrasy of composition or expression. He has neither the splendour of the old style nor the precision and telling point of the new.—SAINTSBURY, GEORGE, 1898, *A Short History of English Literature, p.* 519.

Charles Sackville

Earl of Dorset

1638–1706

Charles Sackville, born January 24, 1638, succeeded as sixth Earl of Dorset in 1677, having two years before been made Earl of Middlesex. He was returned by East Grinstead to the first parliament of Charles II., and became an especial favourite of the king, and notorious for his boisterous and indecorous frolics. He served under the Duke of York at sea, was employed on various missions, but could not endure the tyranny of James II., and was one of the most ardent in the cause of William. His later years were honoured by a generous patronage of Prior, Wycherley, Dryden, &c. He died at Bath, Jan. 19, 1706. He wrote lyrical and satirical pieces, but is remembered only for one bright and delightful song, "To all you Ladies now at Land."
—PATRICK AND GROOME, eds., 1897, Chamber's Biographical Dictionary, p. 815.

PERSONAL

The Muse's Darling, Confidant and Friend.—HALIFAX, CHARLES MONTAGU, EARL, c. 1700, An Epistle to Charles, Earl of Dorset.

Dorset, the Grace of the Courts, the Muses' Pride,
Patron of Arts, and Judge of Nature, died.
The scourge of Pride, tho' sanctify'd or great,
Of Fops in Learning, and of Knaves in State:
Yet soft his Nature, tho' severe his Lay;
His Anger moral, and his Wisdom gay.
Blest Satirist! who touch'd the Mean so true,
As show'd, Vice had his hate and pity too.
Blest Courtier! who could King and Country please,
Yet sacred keep his Friendships and his Ease.
Blest Peer! his great Forefathers' ev'ry grace
Reflecting, and reflected in his Race;
Where other Buckhursts, other Dorsets shine,
And Patriots still, or Poets, deck the Line.
—POPE, ALEXANDER, 1706, On Charles Earl of Dorset, Epitaphs.

He was the finest gentleman in the voluptuous court of Charles the second, and in the gloomy one of King William. He had as much wit as his first master, or his contemporaries Buckingham and Rochester, without the royal want of feeling, the duke's want of principles, or the earl's want of thought.—WALPOLE, HORACE, 1758–1806, A Catalogue of the Royal and Noble Authors of England, Scotland and Ireland, vol. IV, p. 15.

A huge stout figure rolls in now to join the toasters in Shire Lane. In the puffy, once handsome face, there are signs of age, for its owner is past sixty; yet he is dressed in superb fashion; and in an hour or so, when the bottle has been diligently circulated, his wit will be brighter and keener than that of any young man present. I do not say it will be repeatable, for the talker belongs to a past age, even coarser than that of the Kitkat. He is Charles Sackville, famous as a companion of the merriest and most disreputable of the Stuarts, famous—or, rather, infamous—for his mistress, Nell Gwynn, famous for his verses, for his patronage of poets, and for his wild frolics in early life, when Lord Buckhurst.—THOMPSON, MRS. KATHERINE AND J. C. (GRACE AND PHILIP WHARTON), 1860, The Wits and Beaux of Society.

A small poet, but a generous patron of poets.—DENNIS, JOHN, 1894, The Age of Pope, p. 65.

GENERAL

To my Lord Brunker's, by appointment, in the Piazza, in Covent-Guarding; where I occasioned much mirth with a ballet I brought with me, made from the seamen at sea to their ladies in town; saying Sir W. Pen, Sir G. Ascue, and Sir J. Lawson made them.—PEPYS, SAMUEL, 1664–65, Jan. 2.

Yet, my Lord, you must suffer me a little to complain of you, that you too soon withdraw from us a contentment, of which we expected the continuance, because you gave it us so early. It is a revolt, without occasion, from your party, where your merits had already raised you to the highest commands, and where you have not the excuse of other men, that you have been ill-used, and therefore laid down arms. I know no other quarrel you can have to verse, than that which Spurina had to his beauty, when he tore and mangled the features of his face, only because they pleased too well the sight. It was an honour which seemed to wait for you, to lead out a new colony of writers from the mother-nation: and, upon the first spreading of your ensigns, there had been many in a readiness to have followed so fortunate a leader.—DRYDEN, JOHN, 1668, *Essay of Dramatic Poesy, Dedication, Works, vol.* XV, *p.* 278.

A person that hath been highly esteemed for his admirable vein in poetry, and other polite learning, as several things of his composition, while Lord Buckhurst, shew. —WOOD, ANTHONY, 1691-1721, *Athenæ Oxonienses, vol.* I, *f.* 348.

Now, my lord, that the muses' commonweal is become your province; what may we not expect? This, I say, not with intent to apply that of Quintilian, or Augustus Cæsar, *parum diis visum est esse eum maximum poetarum;* that were a common topick: but because, when some years ago I tryed the publick with observations concerning the stage; it was principally your countenance that buoy'd me up, and supported a righteous cause against the prejudice and corruption then reigning.—RYMER, THOMAS, 1693, *A Short View of the Tragedy of the Last Age.*

In Dorset's sprightly muse but touch the lyre,
The smiles and graces melt in soft desire,
And little loves confess their am'orous fire.
—GARTH, SIR SAMUEL, 1699, *The Dispensary, canto* iv.

His wit was abundant, noble, bold. Wit, in most writers is like a fountain in a garden, supplied by several streams brought through artful pipes, and playing sometimes agreeably: but the Earl of Dorset's was a source rising from the top of a mountain, which forced its own way, and, with inexhaustible supplies, delighted and enriched the country through which it passed. This extraordinary genius was accompanied with so true a judgment in all parts of fine learning, that whatever subject was before him, he discoursed as properly of it, as if the peculiar bent of his study had been applied that way; and he perfected his judgment by reading and digesting the best authors, though he quoted them very seldom. . . . There is a lustre in his verses, like that of the sun in Claude Loraine's landscapes; it looks natural, and is inimitable.—PRIOR, MATTHEW, 1718, *Poems, Dedication, pp.* 35, 36.

Donne had no imagination, but as much wit, I think, as any writer can possibly have.—Oldham is too rough and coarse. —Rochester is the medium between him and the Earl of Dorset.—Lord Dorset is the best of all those writers.—"What! better than Lord Rochester?"—Yes, Rochester has neither so much delicacy or exactness as Lord Dorset.—POPE, ALEXANDER, 1734-36, *Spence's Anecdotes, ed. Singer, p.* 102.

From the specimens lord Dorset has given us of his poetical talents, we are inclined to wish, that affairs of higher consequence had permitted him to have dedicated more of his time to the Muses. Though some critics may alledge, that what he has given the public is rather pretty than great; and that a few pieces of a light nature do not sufficiently entitle him to the character of a first rate poet; yet, when we consider, that notwithstanding they were merely the amusement of his leisure hours, and mostly the productions of his youth, they contain marks of a genius, and as such, he is celebrated by Dryden, Prior, Congreve, Pope, &c.— CIBBER, THEOPHILUS, 1753, *Lives of the Poets, vol.* III, *p.* 122.

He was a man whose elegance and judgment were universally confessed, and whose bounty to the learned and witty was generally known. To the indulgent affection of the publick, Lord Rochester bore ample testimony in this remark: *I know not how it is, but* Lord Buckhurst *may do what he will, yet is never in the wrong.* If such a man attempted poetry, we cannot wonder that his works were praised. Dryden, whom, if Prior tells truth, he distinguished by his beneficence, and who lavished his blandishments on those who are not known to have so well deserved them, undertaking to produce authors of our own country superior to those of antiquity, says, *I would instance your Lordship in satire, and Shakespeare in tragedy.* Would it be imagined that of this rival to antiquity, all the satires were little personal invectives, and that his longest composition was a song of eleven stanzas? The blame, however, of this exaggerated praise falls on the encomiast, not upon the author; whose performances are, what they pretend to be, the effusions of a man of wit; gay, vigorous, and airy. His verses to Howard shew great fertility of mind, and his "Dorinda" has been imitated by Pope.— JOHNSON, SAMUEL, 1779-81, *Dorset, Lives of the English Poets.*

The point and sprightliness of Dorset's

pieces entitle him to some remembrance, though they leave not a slender apology for the grovelling adulation that was shown to him by Dryden in his dedications.—CAMPBELL, THOMAS, 1819, *Specimens of the British Poets.*

The munificent earl might, if such had been his wish, have been the rival of those of whom he was content to be the benefactor; for the verses which he occasionally composed, unstudied as they are, exhibit the traces of a genius which, assiduously cultivated, would have produced something great. In the small volume of his works may be found songs which have the easy vigour of Suckling, and little satires which sparkle with wit as splendid as that of Butler.—MACAULAY, THOMAS BABINGTON, 1843, *Critical and Historical Essays.*

Plays with poetry without excess or assiduity, with a rapid pen, writing today a verse against "Dorinda," to-morrow a satire against Mr. Howard, always easily and without study, like a true gentleman. He is an earl, a chamberlain, and rich; he pensions and patronises poets as he would flirts—to amuse himself, without binding himself.—TAINE, H. A., 1871, *History of English Literature, vol.* I.

It is recorded of Lord Dorset that he refused all offers of political preferment in early life that he might give his mind more thoroughly to study. He was the friend and patron of almost all the poets from Waller to Pope; Dryden adored him in one generation, and Prior in the next: nor was the courtesy that produced this affection mere idle complaisance, for no one was more fierce than he in denouncing mediocrity and literary pretension. Of all the poetical noblemen of the Restoration, Lord Dorset alone reached old age, yet with all these opportunities and all this bias toward the art, the actual verse he has left behind him is miserably small. A splendid piece of society verse, a few songs, some extremely foul and violent satires, these are all that have survived to justify in the eyes of posterity the boundless reputation of Lord Dorset.—GOSSE, EDMUND, 1880, *English Poets, ed. Ward, vol.* II, *p.* 411.

His munificence to men of letters speaks for itself, and tempts us to accept in the main the favourable estimate of Prior, overcoloured as it is by the writer's propensity to elegant compliment, his confessed obligations to Dorset, and its occurrence in a dedication to his son. . . . Prior's eulogiums on Dorset's native strength of understanding, though it is impossible that they should be entirely confirmed, are in no way contradicted by the few occasional poems which are all that he has left us. Not one of them is destitute of merit, and some are admirable as "the effusions of a man of wit" (in Johnson's words), "gay, vigorous, and airy." "To all you Ladies" is an admitted masterpiece; and the literary application of the Shakespearian phrase "alacrity in sinking" comes from the satirical epistle to the Hon. Edward Howard.—GARNETT, RICHARD, 1897, *Dictionary of National Biography, vol.* L, *p.* 87.

George Farquhar

1678–1707

George Farquhar, 1678–1707. Born, in Londonderry, 1678. Educated at Londonderry. To Trinity Coll., Dublin, as sizar, 17 July 1694. Left college, 1695 [?]; appeared soon after on Dublin stage. To London, 1697 [?]. First play, "Love and a Bottle," produced at Drury Lane, 1699; "The Constant Couple," in 1700; "Sir Harry Wildair," in 1701. Presented by Earl of Orrery with lieutenant's commission, 1700 [?]. In Holland, 1700. Married, 1703 [?]. Visit to Dublin, 1704; continued to produce plays. Sold commission to pay debts. Died, April 1707. *Works:* "Love and a Bottle," 1699; "Sir Harry Wildair," 1701; "The Inconstant," 1702; "The Twin Rivals," 1702; "The Stage-coach" (with Motteux; anon.), 1705; "The Recruiting Officer" [1706]; "The Beaux Stratagem" [1707]; "Love's Catechism" (anon.; compiled by Farquhar from preceding), 1707. *Posthumous:* "The Constant Couple," 1710. *Collected Works:* "Comedies," 1710; "Works" (in 2 vols.), 1718–36; in 2 vols., 1892. *Life:* by Wilkes, in 1775 edn. of "Works;" by A. C. Ewald, in 1892 edn.—SHARP, R. FARQUHARSON, 1897, *A Dictionary of English Authors, p.* 96.

PERSONAL

DEAR BOB, I have not anything to leave thee, to perpetuate my memory, but two helpless girls. Look upon them sometimes, and think of him that was, to the last moment of his life, thine.—FARQUHAR, GEORGE, 1707, *Letter to Wilks.*

Mr. Farquhar had now been about a twelve-month married, and it was at first reported, to a great fortune; which indeed he expected, but was miserably disappointed. The lady had fallen in love with him, and so violent was her passion, that she resolved to have him at any rate; and as she knew Farquhar was too much dissipated in life to fall in love, or to think of matrimony unless advantage was annexed to it, she fell upon the stratagem of giving herself out for a great fortune, and then took an opportunity of letting our poet know that she was in love with him. Vanity and interest both uniting to persuade Farquhar to marry, he did not long delay it, and, to his immortal honour let it be spoken, though he found himself deceived, his circumstances embarrassed, and his family growing upon him, he never once upbraided her for the cheat, but behaved to her with all the delicacy, and tenderness of an indulgent husband. . . . If he was not a man of the highest genius, he seems to have had excellent moral qualities.—CIBBER, THEOPHILUS, 1753, *Lives of the Poets, vol.* III, *p.* 133.

The time is at the close of the seventeenth century; the scene is at the Mitre Tavern, in St. James's Market, kept by one Mrs. Voss. . . . On the threshold of the open door stand a couple of guests. . . . The one is a gay, rollicking young fellow, smartly dressed, a semi-military look about him, good humor rippling on his face, combined with an air of astonishment and delight. . . . His sight and hearing are wholly concentrated on that enchanted and enchanting girl who, unmindful of aught but the "Scornful Lady," continues still reading aloud that rattling comedy by Beaumont and Fletcher. . . . Captain Farquhar, at whatever passage in the play, betrayed his presence by his involuntary applause. The girl looks towards him more pleased than abashed; and when the captain pronounced that there was in her stuff for an exquisite actress, the fluttered thing clasped her hands, glowed at the prophecy, and protested in her turn, that of all conditions it was the one she wished most ardently to fulfil.—DORAN, JOHN, 1863, *Annals of the English Stage, vol.* I, *ch.* xix.

Through his influence, Anne Oldfield became an actress, and was for years one of the queens of the stage. Farquhar seems to have been seriously in love with her; but, perhaps fortunately for them both, she preferred a richer and more illustrious lover. As for Farquhar, he married a woman who, having lost her heart to him, caused the report to be carried to his ears that a lady of great fortune was dying of an unrequited attachment to him. Impelled either by pity or by self-interest, or both together, he married her to discover that she was as penniless as himself. Yet it is told to his credit that he never reproached her for the deceit about her fortune, but made her a kind and devoted husband as long as she lived.—RICHARDSON, ABBY SAGE, 1882, *Old Love-Letters, p.* 9.

We can follow him pretty closely through his day. He is a queer mixture of profanity and piety, of coarseness and loyalty, of cleverness and density; we do not breed this kind of beau nowadays, and yet we might do worse, for this specimen is, with all his faults, a man. He dresses carefully in the morning, in his uniform or else in his black suit. When he wants to be specially smart, as, for instance, when he designs a conquest at a birthday-party, he has to ferret among the pawnbrokers for scraps of finery, or secure on loan a fair, full-bottom wig. But he is not so impoverished that he cannot on these occasions give his valet and his barber plenty of work to do preparing his face with razors, perfumes and washes. He would like to be Sir Fopling Flutter, if he could afford it, and gazes a little enviously at that noble creature in his French clothes, as he lounges luxuriantly past him in his coach with six before and six behind.—GOSSE, EDMUND, 1891, *Gossip in a Library, p.* 150.

LOVE AND A BOTTLE

1699

Is fluent rather than sparkling in its dialogue.—WARD, ADOLPHUS WILLIAM, 1875–99, *A History of English Dramatic Literature, vol.* III, *p.* 482.

THE CONSTANT COUPLE
1700

As I freely submit to the criticisms of the judicious, so I cannot call this an ill play, since the town has allowed it such success. When they have pardoned my faults 'twere very ill manners to condemn their indulgence. Some may think (my acquaintance in town being too slender to make a party for the play) that the success must be derived from the pure merits of the cause. I am of another opinion: I have not been long enough in town to raise enemies against me; and the English are still kind to strangers. I am below the envy of great wits, and above the malice of little ones. I have not displeased the ladies, nor offended the clergy; both which are now pleased to say, that a comedy may be diverting without smut and profaneness.—FARQUHAR, GEORGE, 1700, *The Constant Couple, Preface.*

Sir Harry Wildair, a character in George Farquhar's comedy "The Constant Couple," is supposed to be a portrait of the author himself.—FREY, ALBERT R., 1888, *Sobriquets and Nicknames, p.* 323.

SIR HENRY WILDAIR
1701

The character of Wildair appears to me to be one of the most naturally buoyant pieces of delineation that ever was written—buoyant without inanity; reckless, wanton, careless, irrepressibly vivacious and out-pouring, without being obstreperous and oppressive, and all the while totally free from a tinge of vulgarity in the composition.—CLARKE, CHARLES COWDEN, 1872, *On the Comic Writers of England, Gentleman's Magazine, n. s. vol.* 8, *p.* 50.

THE INCONSTANT
1702

The romantic interest and impressive catastrophe of this play, I thought, had been borrowed from the more poetical and tragedy-practised muse of Beaumont and Fletcher; but I find they are taken from an actual circumstance which took place in the author's knowledge, at Paris.—HAZLITT, WILLIAM, 1818, *Lectures on the English Comic Writers, p.* 102.

Unlike the "Provoked Wife" and nearly all of its contemporaries, "The Inconstant" has survived to the present day,

and was re-produced only a few seasons ago by Augustin Daly, with John Drew and Ada Rehan in the cast.—ROBINS, EDWARD, JR., 1895, *Echoes of the Playhouse, p.* 99.

THE TWIN RIVALS
1702

The most material objection against this play is the importance of the subject, which necessarily leads into sentiments too grave for diversion, and supposes vices too great for comedy to punish. 'Tis said, I must own, that the business of comedy is chiefly to ridicule folly; and that the punishment of vice falls rather into the province of tragedy; but if there be a middle sort of wickedness, too high for the sock, and too low for the buskin, is there any reason that it should go unpunished? What are more obnoxious to human society, than the villainies exposed in this play, the frauds, plots and contrivances upon the fortunes of men, and the virtue of women? But the persons are too mean for the heroic: then what must we do with them? Why, they must of necessity drop into comedy; for it is unreasonable to imagine that the lawgivers in poetry would tie themselves up from executing that justice which is the foundation of their constitution; or to say, that exposing vice is the business of the drama, and yet make rules to screen it from persecution.—FARQUHAR, GEORGE, 1702, *The Twin Rivals, Preface.*

THE RECRUITING OFFICER
1706

In the "Recruiting Officer" Farquhar took his revenge. He threw himself entirely upon his animal spirits, and produced accordingly one of his very best plays. In everything connected with it he was fortunate; for he went only upon grounds of truth and observation, and his own impulses. The humours were drawn from what he had seen while he was on the recruiting party to which we have alluded; his hospitable friends "round the Wrekin," to whom it was dedicated, furnished some of the characters.—HUNT, LEIGH, 1840, *ed. The Works of Wycherley, Congreve, Vanbrugh, and Farquhar, p.* lviii.

THE BEAUX STRATAGEM
1707

The reader may find some faults in this play, which my illness prevented the amending of; but there is great amends made in the representation, which cannot be matched, no more than the friendly and indefatigable care of Mr. Wilks, to whom I chiefly owe the success of the play.— FARQUHAR, GEORGE, 1707, *The Beaux-Stratagem, Advertisement.*

It is an honour to the morality of the present age, that this most entertaining comedy is but seldom performed; and never, except some new pantomime, or other gaudy spectacle, be added, as an afterpiece, for the attraction of an audience. The well-drawn characters, happy incidents, and excellent dialogue, in "The Beaux' Stratagem," are but poor atonement for that unrestrained contempt of principle which pervades every scene. —ICHBALD, MRS. ELIZABETH, 1806–9, *The British Theatre, The Beaux Stratagem, Remarks, vol.* XX, *p.* 3.

"The Beaux' Stratagem" is the best of his plays as a whole; infinitely lively, bustling, and full of point and interest.— HAZLITT, WILLIAM, 1818, *Lectures on the English Comic Writers.*

Its plot is new, simple, and interesting; the characters various, without confusing it; the dialogue sprightly and characteristic; the moral bold, healthy, admirable, and doubly needed in those times, when sottishness was a fashion. *Archer* and *Aimwell* who set out as mere intriguers, prove in the end true gentlemen, candid, conscientious, and generous. *Scrub* and *Boniface*, though but a servant and an innkeeper, are quotable fellows both, and have made themselves prominent in theatrical recollection,—the former especially, for his quaint ignorance and sordid cunning. And *Mrs. Sullen* is the more touching in her distress, from the cheerfulness with which she wipes away her tears. *Sullen* is an awful brute, yet not thoroughly inhuman; for he feels, after all, that he has no right to such a wife.—HUNT, LEIGH, 1840, *ed. The Works of Wycherley, Congreve, Vanbrugh, and Farquhar, p.* lviii.

It was fortunate for his fame, in every view, that his expiring effort should have proved, in all its points, his most successful one; for the "Beaux' Stratagem" has retained possession of the stage to the present day, and it is always attractive when there is a company of performers ready to sustain its delightful variety of characters. That of Archer, the hero of the piece, is the refined version of the author's former gallants. He is gay, without boisterousness, rallying and imprudent without a tinge of coarseness: and, that which is best of all, his lovemaking and his intrigues have no participation in that absorbing indifference to others that distinguish the gallants of his immediate predecessors, and even of his own contemporaries.—CLARKE, CHARLES COWDEN, 1872, *On the Comic Writers of England, Gentleman's Magazine, n. s. vol.* 8, *p.* 56.

In "The Beaux' Stratagem" (1707) Farquhar achieved his masterpiece. This comedy, justly the most celebrated of his plays and destined to an enduring life on the stage, deserved its success in the first instance by the cleverness of the plot, which is ingenious without being improbable. Some of the incidents, indeed, are of dubious import, including one at the close,—a separation by mutual consent, —which throws a glaring light on the view taken by the author and his age of the sanctity of the marriage-tie. But the comedy is also an excellent picture of manners. The inn with its rascally landlord and highwaymen-guests and the country-house into which the Beau is carried in a fainting-fit, stand before us as scenes from real life; and some of the characters are drawn with much humour and spirit. The most successful conception is that of Archer, who pretends to be the valet of his friend the Beau, but carries on adventures on his own account. This became one of Garrick's most famous parts; and indeed the easy volubility of the pretended servant furnishes an admirable opportunity for a fine actor of light comedy. Altogether this play is written in the happiest of veins; and may be regarded as the prototype of Goldsmith's "She Stoops to Conquer," like which it hovers rather doubtfully on the borders —not always easy to determine—of comedy and farce.—WARD, ADOLPHUS WILLIAM, 1875–99, *A History of English Dramatic Literature, vol.* III, *p.* 484.

This is not a review of the dramatists of this era, but the figure of the jovial humorous Farquhar—Captain Farquhar— is conspicuous, and cannot be passed over. His comedy, "The Beaux's Stratagem," is full of the freshest humour, and if acted at all respectably, must entertain. There is nothing more exhilarating, and the characters and incidents come back on us with a perpetual pleasure. We find ourselves thinking with a smile of Scrub, and the presumed London servant whom he so admires. It is extraordinary how Goldsmith later caught the same freshness of handling in "She Stoops to Conquer." Such broad treatment is essential in true comedy, and will be found in all the great writers from Molière downwards. Nowadays a more trifling local treatment is in vogue, and the other style is scarcely appreciated.—FITZGERALD, PERCY, 1882, *A New History of the English Stage, vol.* I, *p.* 184.

That "The Beaux Stratagem" is the best of our author's comedies, there can be no question. Decenter in language, its plot is comparatively inoffensive, and it has given to literature types of character of which universal acceptance proves the truth. The gracious figure of Lady Bountiful has flitted across many a page, whose reader knew not whence she came; and Boniface has baptized half the innkeepers of Christendom with his dishonest name. . . . Archer and Aimwell, Dorinda and Mrs. Sullen, were in London only two years ago.—HUNTINGTON, H. A., 1882, *Captain Farquhar, Atlantic Monthly, vol.* 49, *pp.* 405, 407.

GENERAL

What pert low dialogue has Farquhar writ!
—POPE, ALEXANDER, 1733, *First Epistle of the Second Book of Horace.*

He seems to have been a man of a genius rather sprightly than great, rather flow'ry than solid; his comedies are diverting, because his characters are natural, and such as we frequently meet with; but he has used no art in drawing them, nor does there appear any force of thinking in his performances, or any deep penetration into nature; but rather a superficial view, pleasant enough to the eye, though capable of leaving no great impression on the mind. He drew his observations chiefly from those he conversed with, and has seldom given any additional heightening, or indelible marks to his characters; which was the peculiar excellence of Shakespear, Johnson, and Congreve. . . . He had certainly a lively imagination, but then it was capable of no great compass; he had wit, but it was of so peculiar a sort, as not to gain ground upon consideration; and it is certainly true, that his comedies in general owe their success full as much to the player, as to any thing intrinsically excellent in themselves.—CIBBER, THEOPHILUS, 1753, *Lives of the Poets, vol.* III, *pp.* 136, 137.

Farquhar is a light and gay writer, less correct and less sparkling than Congreve; but he has more ease; and perhaps fully as great a share of the vis comica. The two best and least exceptionable of his plays, are the "Recruiting Officer," and the "Beaux' Stratagem." I say, the least exceptionable; for, in general, the tendency of both Congreve and Farquhar's plays is immoral. Throughout them all, the rake, the loose intrigue, and the life of licentiousness, are the objects continually held up to view; as if the assemblies of a great and polished nation could be amused with none but vicious objects.—BLAIR, HUGH, 1783, *Lectures on Rhetoric and Belles-Letters, ed. Mills, p.* 542.

He makes us laugh from pleasure oftener than from malice. He somewhere prides himself in having introduced on the stage the class of comic heroes here spoken of, which has since become a standard character, and which represents the warm-hearted, rattle-brained, thoughtless, high-spirited young fellow, who floats on the back of his misfortunes without repining, who forfeits appearances, but saves his honour—and he gives us to understand that it was his own. He did not need to be ashamed of it. Indeed there is internal evidence that this sort of character is his own, for it pervades his works generally, and is the moving spirit that informs them. His comedies have on this account probably a greater appearance of truth and nature than almost any others. His incidents succeed one another with rapidity, but without premeditation; his wit is easy and spontaneous; his style animated, unembarrassed, and flowing; his characters full of life and spirit, and never overstrained so as to "o'erstep the modesty of nature," though they sometimes, from haste and carelessness, seem left in a crude, unfinished state. There is a constant ebullition of gay, laughing invention, cordial good humour, and fine animal spirits, in his writings. Of the four writers here classed together, we should perhaps have courted Congreve's acquaintance most, for his wit and the elegance of his manners; Wycherley's, for his sense and observation on human nature; Vanbrugh's, for his power of farcical description and telling a story; Farquhar's, for the pleasure of his society, and the love of good fellowship.—HAZLITT, WILLIAM, 1818, *Lectures on the English Comic Writers*.

The artificial Comedy, or Comedy of manners, is quite extinct on our stage. Congreve and Farquhar show their heads once in seven years only, to be exploded and put down instantly. The times cannot bear them. Is it for a few wild speeches, an occasional licence of dialogue? I think not altogether. The business of their dramatic characters will not stand the moral test.—LAMB, CHARLES, 1824? *On the Artificial Comedy of the Last Century*.

The thoughtless and volatile, but good-natured and generous, character of Farquhar is reflected in his comedies, which, with less sparkle, have more natural life and airiness, and are animated by a finer spirit of whim, than those of either Vanbrugh or Congreve. His morality, like theirs, is abundantly free and easy; but there is much more heart about his profligacy than in theirs, as well as much less grossness or hardness. — CRAIK, GEORGE L., 1861, *A Compendious History of English Literature and of the English Language, vol. II, p. 274.*

He extended the list of the comic dramatic personages of the day, and his Captain Plume, the fine gentleman officer, Boniface, the innkeeper, Cherry, his lively daughter, Scrub, the country servant who guesses they are talking of *him*, "for they laughed consumedly," and above all the inimitable recruiting officer, Sergeant Pike—are all invaluable additions to our stock of comedy characters. His plots are simpler and better than those of his brother playwrights, they have more life and movement, and the episodes succeed each other in an unforced way which must have made his pieces very pleasant to audiences.—CRAWFURD, OSWALD, 1883, *ed. English Comic Dramatists, p. 172.*

Borne down with trouble and debts, he secured his place among the greatest of writers of English comedy in a life which did not reach to thirty years.—AITKEN,

GEORGE A., 1889, *Life of Richard Steele, vol. I, p. 152.*

Without the keen wit or the sardonic force of his rivals, he has more genuine high spirits and good nature.—STEPHEN, LESLIE, 1889, *Dictionary of National Biography, vol. XVIII, p. 222.*

He was a smart, soldier-like Irishman, of "a splenetic and amorous complexion," half an actor, a quarter a poet, and altogether a very honest and gallant gentleman. He had taken to the stage kindly enough, and at twenty, had written "Love and a Bottle." Since then, two other plays, "The Constant Couple" and "Sir Harry Wildair," had proved that he had wit and fancy, and knew how to knit them together into a rattling comedy. But he was poor, always in pursuit of that timid wild-fowl, the occasional guinea, and with no sort of disposition to settle down into a heavy citizen. In order to bring down a few brace of golden game, he shovels into Lintott's hands his stray verses of all kinds, a bundle of letters he wrote from Holland, a dignified essay or discourse upon Comedy, and, with questionable taste perhaps, a set of copies of the love-letters he had addressed to the lady who became his wife. All this is not very praiseworthy, and as a contribution to literature it is slight indeed; but, then, how genuine and sincere, how guileless and picturesque is the self-revelation of it! There is no attempt to make things better than they are, nor any pandering to a cynical taste by making them worse. Why should he conceal or falsify? The town knows what sort of a fellow George Farquhar is. Here are some letters and some verses; the beaux at White's may read them if they will, and then throw them away.—GOSSE, EDMUND, 1891, *Gossip in a Library, p. 148.*

It is fortunate for Farquhar that he could not emulate the exquisitely civilized depravities of Congreve's urban Muse. But his dialogue is not "low" to modern tastes; it has, in general, a simple, natural zest, infinitely preferable to the Persian apparatus of the early eighteenth century. Even he, however, can rant and deviate into rhetoric, as soon as his lovers drop upon one knee. More plainly in Farquhar's work than in that of any contemporary, we mark the glamour of the Caroline literature fading, and the breath of life blowing in. . . . His mind was a Medea's kettle, out of which everything issued cleaner and more wholesome. . . . Though Farquhar did not live, like Vanbrugh and the magnanimous Dryden, to admit the abuse of a gift, and to deplore it, he alone, of the minor dramatists, seems all along to have had a negative sort of conscience better than none. His instincts continually get the better not only of his environment, but of his practice. Some uneasiness, some misgiving, are at the bottom of his homely materialism. He thinks it best, on the whole, to forswear the temptation to be sublime, and to keep to his cakes and ale; and for cakes and ale he had an eminent and inborn talent.—GUINEY, LOUISE IMOGEN, 1894, *A Little English Gallery, pp.* 132, 136, 137.

William Walsh

1663–1708

Poet, critic and scholar, born in Worcestershire in 1663. A member of several parliaments, and a gentleman of the horse under the Duke of Somerset. Chiefly remembered as the friend of Dryden and Pope. *Works:* "The Golden Age Restored;" "Eugenia, a Defence of Women;" "Esculapius: or, the Hospital of Fools;" "A Collection of Letters, Amorous and Gallant." *Life:* in Johnson's "Lives of the English Poets."—MOULTON, CHARLES WELLS, 1901.

PERSONAL

About fifteen, I got acquainted with Mr. Walsh. He used to encourage me much, and used to tell me, that there was one way left of excelling: for though we had several great poets, we never had any one great poet that was correct; and he desired me to make that my study and aim.—POPE, ALEXANDER, 1742–43, *Spence's Anecdotes, ed. Singer, p.* 212.

GENERAL

William Walsh, of Abberley, Esq., who has so long honoured me with his friendship, and who, without flattery, is the best critic of our nation.—DRYDEN, JOHN, 1697, *Postscript to Virgil.*

To him the wit of Greece and Rome was known,
And every author's merit, but his own.
Such late was Walsh—the Muse's judge and friend,
Who justly knew to blame or to commend;
To failings mild, but zealous for desert;
The clearest head and the sincerest heart.
—POPE, ALEXANDER, 1711, *An Essay on Criticism, III,* 727–732.

He is known more by his familiarity with greater men, than by any thing done or written by himself. . . . In his "Golden Age Restored," there was something of humour, while the facts were recent; but it now strikes no longer. In his imitation of Horace, the first stanzas are happily turned; and in all his writings there are pleasing passages. He has, however, more elegance than vigour, and seldom rises higher than to be pretty.—JOHNSON, SAMUEL, 1779–81, *Walsh, Lives of the English Poets.*

Mr. Walsh's other pieces consist chiefly of Elegies, Epitaphs, Odes, and Songs; they are elegant, tho' not great, and he seems to have had a well cultivated, tho' not a very extensive, understanding. Dryden and Pope have given their sanction in his favour, to whom he was personally known, a circumstance greatly to his advantage, for had there been no personal friendship, we have reason to believe, their encomiums would have been less lavish; at least his works do not carry so high an idea of him, as they have done.—CIBBER, THEOPHILUS, 1753, *Lives of the Poets, vol.* III, *p.* 155.

Except his encouragement of the early genius of Pope, he seems to have no claim to remembrance.—CAMPBELL, THOMAS, 1819, *Specimens of the British Poets.*

The qualities which Pope attributes to the person of Walsh are found in his writings, which have certainly been unduly neglected. The Propertius of the Restoration, he alone among the writers of his age understood the passion of love in an honourable and chivalric sense. Dryden, however, was almost the only person who perceived the moral beauty of Walsh's verse, and certainly was alone in praising his very remarkable "Defence of the Fair Sex," in which the young poet, in an age given up to selfish gallantry, recommended the honourable equality of the sexes and the views now understood as the extension of women's rights. He possessed little versatility, but much sweetness in the use of the heroic measure, and a certain delicate insight into emotion. His poem entitled "Jealousy" cannot be quoted here; but it is by far the most powerful of his productions, and a marvellously true picture of a heart tossed in an agony of jealousy and love. In studying the versification of Pope, the influence of Walsh upon the style of the younger and greater man should not be overlooked, and there will be found in Walsh couplets such as this—

"Embalmed in verse, through distant times
    they come,
Preserved, like bees within an amber
    tomb."

which Pope did not disdain to re-work

on his own anvil into brighter shapes. It should be noted that Walsh is the author of the only sonnet written in English between Milton's, in 1658, and Warton's, about 1750*.—GOSSE, EDMUND, 1880, *English Poets, ed. Ward, vol. III, p.* 6.

If we search amongst contemporary authorities to discover who he was, we at last come upon his works described in the "Rambler" as "pages of inanity."— MOULTON, RICHARD G., 1885, *Shakespeare as a Dramatic Artist, p.* 17.

His own writings are insignificant. . . . Walsh's chief title to fame lies in his connection with Pope, and in the tributes from the latter that resulted from it.— WARD, ADOLPHUS WILLIAM, 1899, *Dictionary of National Biography, vol.* LIX, *pp.* 226, 227.

*Gray's on Richard West, in 1742—Dennis.

William Sherlock

1641?–1707

A divine then high in repute, born in 1641, educated at Eton and Peterhouse, Cambridge; in 1669 Rector of St. George's, Botolph Lane, and Prebendary of St. Paul's; then Master of the Temple, an active preacher and writer against the Roman Catholics. At the time of his deprivation, Sherlock published, in 1689, the most popular of his books, "Practical Discourse concerning Death." His deprivation was soon followed by his acceptance of the established authority in 1691, when he was restored to his office of Master of the Temple, and made Dean of St. Paul's. In 1692 appeared his "Practical Discourse concerning a Future Judgment;" and he was involved in a long and bitter controversy upon the Trinity, with Robert South, a learned, zealous, and good-natured divine. Sherlock died in 1707.—MORLEY, HENRY, 1879, *A Manual of English Literature, ed. Tyler, p.* 503.

GENERAL

He was a clear, a polite, and a strong writer; . . . but he was apt to assume too much to himself, and to treat his adversaries with contempt; this created him many enemies, and made him pass for an insolent, haughty man.—BURNET, GILBERT, 1715–34, *History of My Own Time.*

Perhaps no single presbyter of the Church of England has ever possessed a greater authority over his brethren than belonged to Sherlock at the time of the Revolution. He was not of the first rank among his contemporaries as a scholar, as a preacher, as a writer on theology, or as a writer on politics; but in all the four characters he had distinguished himself. The perspicuity and liveliness of his style have been praised by Prior and Addison. The facility and assiduity with which he

wrote are sufficiently proved by the bulk and the dates of his works. There were indeed among the clergymen of brighter genius and men of wider attainments: but during a long period there was none who more completely represented the order, none who, on all subjects, spoke more precisely the sense of the Anglican priesthood.—MACAULAY, THOMAS BABINGTON, 1843, *Dr. William Sherlock, Critical and Historical Essays.*

Sherlock's practical works are better than his controversial.—BICKERSTETH, EDWARD, 1844, *The Christian Student, p.* 455.

His "Discourse concerning Death" is a standing article in second-hand bookstalls. This continued popularity is due more to the matter than to the manner. —MINTO, WILLIAM, 1872–80, *Manual of English Prose Literature, p.* 334.

Of his most popular book, his "Practical Treatise on Death," no less than thirty editions were called for, and Prior expressed the contemporary feeling when he called it "a nation's food." Addison also yielded conspicuous praise to Sherlock, who is nevertheless a writer of no great importance.—GOSSE, EDMUND, 1888, *A History of Eighteenth Century Literature, p.* 101.

He is competent in learning and in ability, well-bred, persuasive, not too enthusiastic, as the age was already beginning to say, and deeply imbued with that not unkindly but somewhat unheroic and intensely commonsense morality which dominated the religion and the literature of the next century. He has not the polish of the younger generation of those who admired him; but, on the other hand, he has still a touch of the older directness and simplicity. Above all, he is completely free from the somewhat arrogant and insulting preponderance of intellect which made his elder contemporary and enemy, South, not exactly loved, and which made his younger contemporary, Bentley, feared and hated. He was too hardened a controversialist to show traces of the almost too abundant milk of human kindness which flowed in Tillotson; but there is nothing savage or overweening about him.—SAINTSBURY, GEORGE, 1894, *English Prose, ed. Craik, vol.* III, *p.* 299.

It ["Discourse"] is a model of clear and forcible writing, but on the lowest plane of unspiritual selfishness. "How unreasonable is it for us to trouble ourselves about this world longer than we are like to continue in it!" exclaims Sherlock, with the air of one apologizing for enunciating a truism.—GARNETT, RICHARD, 1895, *The Age of Dryden, p.* 228.

John Philips

1676–1708

John Philips, or Phillips. Born at Bampton, Oxfordshire, 1676: died 1708. An English writer. He was educated at Winchester and at Oxford (Christ Church). "The Splendid Shilling," a burlesque of Milton's "Paradise Lost," appeared about 1703. In 1705 he published "Blenheim," also in imitation of Milton, and in 1706 "Cyder," his most ambitious work, in imitation of Vergil's "Georgics."—SMITH, BENJAMIN E., 1894–97, *The Century Cyclopedia of Names, p.* 803.

PERSONAL

Somewhat reserved and silent amongst strangers, but free, familiar, and easy with his friends; he was averse to disputes, and thought no time so ill spent, and no wit so ill used, as that which was employed in such debates; his whole life was distinguished by a natural goodness, and well-grounded and unaffected piety, an universal charity, and a steady adherence to his principles; no one observed the natural and civil duties of life with a stricter regard, whether a son, a friend, or a member of society, and he had the happiness to fill every one of these parts, without even the suspicion either of undutifulness, insincerity, or disrespect. Thus he continued to the last, not owing his virtues to the happiness of his constitution, but the frame of his mind, insomuch, that during a long sickness, which is apt to ruffle the smoothest temper, he never betrayed any discontent or uneasiness, the integrity of his life still preserving the cheerfulness of his spirits; and if his friends had measured their hopes of his life, only by his unconcern in his sickness, they could not but conclude, that either his date would be much longer, or that he was at all times prepared for death.—SEWELL, GEORGE, 1763, *Life of Philips.*

Philips has been always praised, without contradiction, as a man modest, blameless, and pious; who bore narrowness of fortune without discontent, and tedious and painful maladies without impatience; beloved by those that knew him, but not ambitious to be known. He was probably not formed for a wide circle. His conversation is commended for its innocent gaiety, which seems to have flowed only among his intimates, for I have been told, that he was in company silent and barren, and employed only upon the pleasures of his pipe. His addiction to tobacco is mentioned by one of his biographers, who remarks that in all his writings, except "Blenheim" he has found an opportunity of celebrating the fragrant fume. In common life he was probably one of those who please by not offending, and whose person was loved because his writings were admired. He died honoured and lamented, before any part of his reputation had withered, and before his patron St. John had disgraced him.—JOHNSON, SAMUEL, 1779–81, *Philips, Lives of the English Poets.*

THE SPLENDID SHILLING
1703

Philips's "Splendid Shilling" may have pleased, because its manner was new, and we often find people of the best sense throw away their admiration on monsters, which are seldom to be seen, and neglect more regular beauty, and juster proportion.—CIBBER, THEOPHILUS, 1753, *Lives of the Poets, vol. III, p. 146.*

This is reckoned the best parody of Milton in our language; it has been an hundred times imitated without success. The truth is, the first thing in this way must preclude all future attempts, for nothing is so easy as to burlesque any man's manner, when we are once shewed the way. —GOLDSMITH, OLIVER, 1767, *The Beauties of English Poetry.*

. . . in thy numbers, Phillips, shines for aye
The solitary Shilling.
—COWPER, WILLIAM, 1785, *The Task, The Garden.*

John Philips was a young and lively writer, who, having succeeded in a burlesque, was unfortunately induced to attempt serious poetry, and devoted himself to it with a scholarly dulness which he would probably have seen the folly of in any one else. His serious imitations of Milton are not worth a penny; but his burlesque of the style of "Paradise Lost," though it no longer possesses the novelty which made it popular, is still welcome to the lover of wit. The low every-day circumstances, and the lofty classic manner with its nomenclatures, are happily interwoven; the more trivial words are brought in with unlooked-for effect; the motto is particularly felicitous; and the comparison of the rent in the small-clothes with the ship that has sprung a leak at sea, and founders, concludes the poem with a tremendous and calamitous grandeur, only to be equalled by the exclamation of the Spaniard; who said he had torn his "breeches, as if heaven and earth had come together."—HUNT, LEIGH, 1846, *Wit and Humour, p. 274.*

In style as in subject it was small coin glorified, perhaps the best piece of burlesque writing in our literature.—MORLEY, HENRY, 1879, *A Manual of English Literature, ed. Tyler, p. 528.*

This parody still retains its humour.— GOSSE, EDMUND, 1888, *A History of Eighteenth Century Literature, p. 108.*

GENERAL

Received then of Jacob Tonson forty guineas in full for the copy of a poem intituled "Cyder," in two books.—PHILIPS, JOHN, 1707, *Agreement, Jan. 24.*

The French are very just to eminent men in this point; not a learned man nor a poet can die, but all Europe must be acquainted with his accomplishments. They give praise and expect it in their turns: they commend their Patrus and Molieres as well as their Condes and Turennes; their Pellisons and Racines have their elegies, as well as the prince whom they celebrate; and their poems, their mercuries, and orations, nay their very gazettes, are filled with the praises of the learned. I am satisfied, had they a Philips among them, and known how to value him; had they one of his learning, his temper, but above all of that particular turn of humour, that altogether new genius, he had been an example to their poets, and a subject of their panegyricks, and perhaps set in competition with the ancients, to whom only he ought to submit.—SMITH, EDMUND, 1708? *A Prefatory Discourse to the Poem of Mr. Philips, with a Character of His Writings.*

Philips, by Phœbus and his Aldrich taught,
Sings with that heat wherewith his Churchill
    fought,
Unfetter'd in great Milton's strain he writes,
Like Milton's angels, whilst his hero fights;
Pursues the bard whilst he with honour can,
Equals the poet and excels the man.
—TICKELL, THOMAS, 1733, *Oxford.*

Philips in his "Cyder" has succeeded extremely well in his imitation of it ("Paradise Lost"), but was quite wrong in endeavouring to imitate it on such a subject.—POPE, ALEXANDER, 1734–36, *Spence's Anecdotes, ed. Singer, p. 131.*

The "Splendid Shilling" has the uncommon merit of an original design, unless it may be thought precluded by the ancient *Centos*. . . . The poem of "Blenheim" was never denied to be tolerable, even by those who do not allow its supreme excellence. It is indeed the poem of a scholar, *all inexpert of war;* of a man who writes books from books, and studies the world in a college. . . . He imitates Milton's numbers indeed, but imitates them very injudiciously. Deformity is easily copied; and whatever there is in Milton which the reader wishes away, all that is obsolete, peculiar, or licentious, is accumulated with great care by Philips. . . . To the poem on "Cider," written in imitation of the *Georgicks*, may be given this peculiar praise, that it is grounded in truth; that the precepts which it contains are exact and just; and that it is therefore, at once, a book of entertainment and of science.—JOHNSON, SAMUEL, 1779–81, *Philips, Lives of the English Poets.*

The fame of this poet (says the grave doctor of the last century), will endure as long as Blenheim is remembered, or cider drunk in England. He might have added, as long as tobacco shall be smoked; for Philips has written more meritoriously about the Indian weed, than about his native apple; and his Muse appears to be more in her element amidst the smoke of the pipe than of the battle. . . . Philips had the merit of studying and admiring Milton, but he never could imitate him without ludicrous effect, either in jest or earnest. His "Splendid Shilling" is the earliest, and one of the best of our parodies; but "Blenheim" is as completely a burlesque upon Milton as the "Splendid Shilling," though it was written and read with gravity. In describing his hero, Marlborough, stepping out of Queen Anne's drawing-room, he unconsciously carries the mock heroic to perfection, when he says,

"His plumy crest
Nods horrible. With more terrific port
He walks, and seems already in the fight."

Yet such are the fluctuations of taste, that contemporary criticism bowed with solemn admiration over his Miltonic cadences.—CAMPBELL, THOMAS, 1819, *Specimens of the British Poets, p. 367.*

His serious poetry is not worth much, at least as poetry.—CRAIK, GEORGE L., 1861, *A Compendious History of English Literature and of the English Language, vol.* II, *p.* 282.

He seems to have been the earliest genuine *literary* admirer of Milton.—ARNOLD, THOMAS, 1868–75, *Chaucer to Wordsworth, p.* 282.

His poems, written in revolt against the heroic couplet, between the death of Dryden and the appearance of Pope, occupy an important position in the history of English literature.—AITKEN, G. A., 1896, *Dictionary of National Biography, vol.* XLV, *p.* 177.

Author of the admirable Miltonic burlesque of the "Splendid Shilling" and of a good poem, or at least verse-essay, on "Cider."—SAINTSBURY, GEORGE, 1898, *A Short History of English Literature.*

George Bull

1634–1710

George Bull, D.D., divine, was born at Wells, 25th March 1634, and studied at Exeter College, Oxford, whence he retired in 1649, having refused to take the commonwealth oath. Ordained in 1655, he took the small parish of St. George's, Bristol, and subsequently obtained the rectory of Siddington, Cirencester (1658), that of Avening, Stroud (1685), the acrhdeaconry of Llandaff (1686), and the bishopric of St. David's (1705). He died at Brecknock, 17th February 1710. His "Harmonia Apostolica" (1670), designed to reconcile Paul and James as to justification, occasioned controversy, and, in answer, Bull published his "Examen Censuræ" and "Apologia pro Harmonia." His greatest work, the "Defensio Fidei Nicenæ" (1685), was directed against Arians and Socinians; for his "Judicium Ecclesiæ Catholicæ" (1694) the thanks of the French clergy were sent to him through Bossuet. These are included in Dr. Burton's edition of his works (8 vols. Oxford, 1827), with a Life by R. Nelson; and they are translated in the "Library of Anglo-Catholic Theology" (Oxford, 1842–55).—PATRICK AND GROOME, eds., 1897, *Chambers's Biographical Dictionary, p.* 149.

GENERAL

One of the soundest and shrewdest of our older Divines.—DIBDIN, THOMAS FROGNALL, 1824, *The Library Companion,* p. 62, *note*.

Notwithstanding the popularity of this defence of the Nicene faith, and the learning it displays, the author was far from ending the controversy, or from satisfying all his readers. It was alleged, that he does not meet the question with which he deals; that the word ὁμοούσιος being almost new at the time of the council, and being obscure and metaphysical in itself, required a precise definition to make the reader see his way before him, or, at least, one better than Bull has given, which the adversary might probably adopt without much scruple.—HALLAM, HENRY, 1837–39, *Introduction to the Literature of Europe,* pt. iv, ch. ii, par. 31.

One of the most learned divines whom our Church has produced, a man equal to Stillingfleet in the depth of his researches, and superior to him as a practical working clergyman.—PERRY, GEORGE C., 1864, *History of the Church of England, vol.* III.

When it ["Defensio"] was printed in 1685, it was most favourably received; its fame extended to foreign lands; it was mentioned with praise by the great Bossuet, bishop of Meaux, who, in his controversy with Jurieu, referred his adversary to "that learned English protestant, Dr. Bull." The "Defensio" was a very seasonable as well as a very valuable work; for not only the antitrinitarians, but also some of the believers in the Trinity—notably Petavius the jesuit, and Episcopius—denied that the ante-Nicene fathers held the same doctrines as those which were established at the council of Nicæa. Bull took upon himself to prove that they did. The "Defensio" was written in excellent Latin. It still remains the "locus classicus" of

that particular branch of the great trinitarian controversy with which it exclusively deals, and the objections which have been raised against it seem, partly at least, to have risen from what really is one of its chief merits. Bull showed great self-restraint in never being tempted to diverge from his proper subject (the opinions of the ante-Nicene fathers) into any of the other numerous questions connected with the doctrine of the Trinity; and consequently those who have looked for a satisfactory reply to any question except that to which Bull confined himself, have not found what they wanted.—OVERTON, J. H., 1886, *Dictionary of National Biography, vol.* VII, *p.* 237.

He received the rare honour of a formal letter of thanks from the great Bossuet and the French bishops for his defence of the Catholic creeds. His most famous works are his "Defensio Fidei Nicenæ," his "Harmonia Apostolica," and his sermons, particularly that treating of the Fall. As an historical and theological vindication of the work of the Nicene Council as the necessary and inevitable consequence of the teaching of the Bible and the Church, Bull's defence has never been superseded. It was recognised at once as a great book, and the judgment of England was confirmed by that of foreign nations and posterity. The "Harmonia Apostolica," an explanation of the doctrine of justification, and of the agreement between St. Paul and St. James in their treatment of faith and works, has been considered to have as great practical value. Scarcely less attention has been bestowed on his discussion of the Fall. It was the fashion to think lightly of his sermons, because they wanted the florid eloquence in which the age delighted. —HUTTON, WILLIAM HOLDEN, 1895, *Social England, ed. Traill, vol.* IV, *p.* 420.

Henry Dodwell
1641-1711

Henry Dodwell; chronologist; born in Dublin, in Oct., 1641; educated at Trinity College, Dublin; elected Camden Professor of History at Oxford in 1688, but deposed from his chair in 1691 because he refused to take the oath of allegiance to William III. Among his noteworthy contributions to Greek and Roman chronology are his "Annales Vellei, Quintil., Station." (1698); "Annales Thucyd. et Xenophont." (1702). Died in Schottesbrook, June 7, 1711. See Dodwell's "Works," abridged, with an account of his life, by Fr. Brokesby (2 vols., London, 1723).—GUDEMAN, ALFRED, 1897, *Johnson's Universal Cyclopædia, vol.* II, *p.* 802.

PERSONAL

On Thursday last, June 7th, died Mr. Henry Dodwell, that great and good man, in the 70th year of his age, at Shottes-brooke, in Berks, where he had lived in a most retired, studious, private condition for several years. He died with the same piety with which he had always lived, and was buried on Saturday, June the 9th, in the church of Shottesbrooke. This extraordinary person might have reached an hundred years, if he had taken but ordinary care of his health. He was of small stature of body, but vigorous and healthy; of a brisk, facetious constitution, always chearful, even in the worst of times. He was humble and modest, to a fault. His learning was above the common reach. . . . I take him to be the greatest scholar in Europe when he died; but, what exceeds that, his piety and sanctity was beyond compare. Had he indulged himself a little, and not abstained so much from even the ordinary refreshments of nature, 'twould certainly have conduced to the lengthening of his life; but a severe, steddy course of life, like the primitive Christians, and the most renowned philosophers, could not comply with those principles. His name will always be mentioned and spoke of with honour as long as there is any regard for true religion, virtue, probity, and learning. . . . As to his person, he was of a small stature of body, yet of a strong, vigorous constitution, chiefly owing to his abstemious and temperate way of living. He was of a sanguine complexion, of a grave, modest, ingenious countenance, of a piercing eye, and of a quick apprehension. He was acute and chearful in his discourse, ready and forward in his advice, and delighted to have difficult questions proposed to him for solution.—HEARNE, THOMAS, 1711, *Reliquiæ Hearnianæ, ed. Bliss, June 15, vol.* I, *pp.* 227, 228, 229.

GENERAL

Dodwell's learning was immense; in this part of history especially (that of the Upper Empire) the most minute fact or passage could not escape him; and his skill in employing them is equal to his learning. The worst of this author is his method and style; the one perplexed beyond imagination, the other negligent to a degree of barbarism.—GIBBON, EDWARD, 1762, *Journal, June* 8.

Its ["De Veteribus"] absurdity is so evident, that only the character of Dodwell, and the seriousness and labour with which he defended it, could persuade us to think that he believed it himself. The work is very curious, as a specimen of the torture to which a corrupted creed or system is capable of putting the Scriptures. It contains some singular remarks on the scriptural distinction between *soul* and *spirit* which is the foundation of his whole hypothesis.—ORME, WILLIAM, 1824, *Bibliotheca Biblica.*

He had perused innumerable volumes in various languages, and had indeed acquired more learning than his slender faculties were able to bear. The small intellectual spark which he possessed was put out by the fuel. Some of his books seem to have been written in a mad-house, and, though filled with proofs of his immense reading, degraded him to the level of James Naylor and Ludowick Muggleton. —MACAULAY, THOMAS BABINGTON, 1843, *Critical and Historical Essays.*

A man of wonderful, though very eccentric, erudition and talents.—PERRY, G. G., 1864, *History of the Church of England.*

Dodwell was a most voluminous writer on an immense variety of subjects, in all of which he showed vast learning, great ingenuity, and, in spite of some eccentricities, great power of reasoning.—OVERTON, J. H., 1888, *Dictionary of National Biography, vol.* XV, *p.* 180.

Thomas Ken

1637–1711

Born, at Berkhampstead, Hertfordshire, July 1637. Scholar of Winchester Coll., Sept. 1651; admitted, Jan. 1652. Fellow of New Coll., Oxford, 1656–66. To Hart Hall, Oxford, 1656; to New Coll., 1657; B.A., 3 May 1661; M.A., 21 Jan. 1665; Tutor of New Coll., 1661. Ordained 1661 [or 1662]. Rector of Little Easton, Essex, 1663–65. Domestic Chaplain to Bishop of Winchester, and Rector of St. John-in-the-Soke, 1665. Fellow of Winchester Coll., 8 Dec. 1666. Rector of Brightstone (or

Brixton), I. of W., 1667–69. Prebendary of Winchester, 1669. Rector of East Woodhay, Hampshire, 1669–72. Lived at Winchester, 1672–79. Travelled on Continent, 1675. D.D., Oxford, 1679. To the Hague, as Chaplain to Mary Princess of Orange, 1679–80. Returned to Winchester, 1680; appointed Chaplain to King. With Lord Dartmouth to Tangier, as Chaplain, Aug. 1683. Returned to England, April 1684. Bishop of Bath and Wells, Nov. 1684; compelled to resign, as a Nonjuror, April 1691. For rest of life under patronage of Lord Weymouth. Crown pension, 1704. Died, at Longleat, 19 March 1711. Buried at Frome Selwood. *Works:* "Manual of Prayers" (anon.), 1674 (another edn., with "Hymns," 1695); Funeral Sermon for Lady Margaret Mainard, 1682; "Sermon preached at Whitehall," 1685; "An Exposition on the Church Catechism; or, Practice of Divine Love" (anon.), 1685 (another edn., with "Directions for Prayers," 1686); "Pastoral Letter," 1688; "Prayers for the use of all persons who come to Bath for cure" (anon.), 1692; "A Letter to the Author of a 'Sermon preached at the Funeral of her late Majesty'" (anon.), 1695 (another edn., called "A Dutifull Letter," 1703); "The Royal Sufferer" (under initials: T. K.; attributed to Ken), 1699; "Expostulatoria," 1711. *Collected Works:* ed. by Hawkins (4 vols.), 1721. *Life:* by Dean Plumptre, revised edn., 1890.—SHARP, R. FARQUHARSON, 1897, *A Dictionary of English Authors, p.* 156.

PERSONAL

Oddsfish! who shall have Bath and Wells, but the little fellow who would not give poor Nelly a lodging?—CHARLES II., 1684.

He had a very edifying way of preaching: but it was more apt to move the passions, than to instruct. So that his sermons were rather beautiful than solid: yet his way in them was very taking.—BURNET, GILBERT, 1715–34, *History of My Own Time.*

When he was afflicted with the colic, to which he was very subject, he frequently amused himself with writing verses. Hence some of his pious poems are entitled "Anodynes, or the Alleviation of Pain." There is a prosaic flatness in his heroic poem called "Edmund;" but some of his Hymns, and other compositions, have more of the spirit of poetry, and give us an idea of that devotion which animated the author.—GRANGER, JAMES, 1769–1824, *Biographical History of England, vol.* VI, *p.* 93.

A name his country once forsook,
    But now with joy inherits,
Confessor in the Church's book,
    And martyr in the Spirit's!
That dared with royal power to cope,
    In peaceful faith persisting,
A braver Becket—who could hope
    To conquer unresisting!

—MILNES, RICHARD MONCKTON, 1876, *On the Grave of Bishop Ken, Poetical Works.*

At the time of his retirement Bishop Ken lived upon the bounty of Lord Weymouth, who allowed him £80 per annum, in lieu of property valued at about £700, and which Ken transferred to his patron, retaining only his books and musical instruments. It is recorded of him that he kept with him, as his immediate personal property, "his lute," and a Greek Testament, together with a favorite but "sorry" horse. The Testament was said to open, of its own accord, at the 15th chapter of 1st Corinthians. His preaching was not that of a Boanerges, but of a Barnabas. He aimed to secure his hearers, rather than to stun them. And Dryden's portrait of a "Good Parson" is enlarged from Chaucer's (supposed) character of Wiclif in the "Canterbury Tales," and is considered by excellent critics to have been Ken's own picture.—DUFFIELD, SAMUEL WILLOUGHBY, 1886, *English Hymns: Their Authors and History, p.* 172.

It seems probable that that memorable day on which Ken read his protest from his throne in the cathedral was his last appearance in the church which he loved so dearly until, many years afterwards, he perhaps appeared there in another character, and with very different feelings. It was followed soon afterwards, we must believe, by his departure from his palace. There must have been partings, of which we have no record, from the cathedral clergy, with whom, though they did not follow his example, he had always been on the friendliest terms; from the poor, who had been his Sunday guests; from the boys, whom he had catechised and confirmed, and to whom he had administered their first Communion. And now all was over. Those six happy years— happy as far as his work in his diocese was concerned—had come to an end; and he left his home, not knowing what the future had in store for him, full of anxious forebodings for himself, for his flock, and for the Church at large.—PLUMPTRE, EDWARD HAYES, 1888, *Life of Thomas Ken.*

In person Ken was short and slender, with dark eyes and hair. His expression was winning. He wore no hair on his face and no wig, allowing his thin hair to grow long at the sides of his head. In manner he was courteous, and in disposition affectionate, tender, and compassionate. Though he was learned, there is no ground for ranking him with the most learned men of the time; he was accomplished, having a knowledge of French, Italian, and Spanish, and was a musician and a poet. He was an eloquent and energetic preacher. In speech and action he was guided by conscience rather than by local reasoning; his conscience was tender and his feelings sensitive. By nature he seemed to have been quick-tempered, but was always ready to ask pardon of any whom he had offended. In the cause of right he was outspoken and courageous. Liberal, unselfish, and unostentatious, he gave largely though his means were small. —HUNT, REV. WILLIAM, 1892, *Dictionary of National Biography, vol.* XXX, *p.* 402.

GENERAL

The simple and touching devoutness of many of Bishop Kenn's lyrical effusions has been unregarded, because of the ungraceful contrivances and heavy movement of his narrative. . . . We shall hardly find, in all ecclesiastical history, a greener spot than the later years of this courageous and affectionate pastor; persecuted alternately by both parties, and driven from his station in his declining age; yet singing on, with unabated cheerfulness, to the last. His poems are not popular, nor, probably, ever will be, for reasons already touched upon; but whoever in earnest loves his three well-known hymns, and knows how to value such unaffected strains of poetical devotion, will find his account, in turning over his four volumes, half narrative, and half lyric, and all avowedly on sacred subjects: the narrative often cumbrous, and the lyric verse not seldom languid and redundant: yet all breathing such an angelic spirit, interspersed with such pure and bright touches of poetry, that such a reader as we have supposed will scarcely find it in his heart to criticise

them.—KEBLE, JOHN, 1825, *Sacred Poetry, Quarterly Review, vol.* 32, *pp.* 217, 230.

Ken's faults in poetry arose from his rejecting his own feelings of simplicity and nature, and proposing to himself a model of false imagery and affected diction. Always intent on this artificial model, he sacrificed his native good sense; turned from what is simple, sublime, and pathetic; shut his eyes to all that is most interesting in rural scenery and external nature; and even in addressing Heaven under the intense feelings of devotion, appears affected and artificial. . . . If he had only followed his own native feelings, he would have been an interesting, if not pathetic or sublime, poet.— BOWLES, WILLIAM LISLE, 1830, *Life of Thomas Ken, vol.* II, *p.* 300.

Bishop Ken's works are still much esteemed, particularly his Manual of Prayers.—LOWNDES, WILLIAM THOMAS, 1839, *British Librarian, p.* 623.

He was a man of parts and learning, of quick sensibility and stainless virtue. His elaborate works have long been forgotten; but his morning and evening hymns are still repeated daily in thousands of dwellings. Though, like most of his order, zealous for monarchy, he was no sycophant.—MACAULAY, THOMAS BABINGTON, 1849, *History of England, vol.* I.

If at any time men of tender consciences, in their aspirations after some ideal perfection, be tempted to swerve from their obedience to the Church of England, let them study the writings of humble, simple-hearted, steadfast Bishop Ken, (steadfast, *because* humble and simple-hearted), and they will find solid arguments to preserve them from "widening her deplorable divisions," and inspire them with his own firm resolves to "continue steadfast in her bosom, and improve all those helps to true piety, all those means of grace, all those incentives to the love of God," which He has mercifully afforded to them in her communion.—ANDERDON, J. L., 1851, *The Life of Thomas Ken, Bishop of Bath and Wells.*

What Christian bosom but warms with a glow of loving veneration at the name of the heavenly-minded author of those sweet lyrics of the Church, the Morning Hymn and the Evening Hymn! They have been for nearly two centuries familiar to the lips of the infants of the flock as to the hoary-headed elders of the congregation, and yet they tire not—they never can tire—for they are in their sublime simplicity suited to the comprehensions and adapted to the wants of all, from the youngest to the most mature, from the highest to the lowest. The hearts of rich and poor, the learned and the ignorant, alike swell for a moment as the successive appeals, so full of the fervour and the poetry of prayer, thrill from the ear to the soul.—STRICKLAND, AGNES, 1866, *The Lives of the Seven Bishops Committed to the Tower in* 1688, *p.* 234.

It has been said that by his three hymns —the Morning, Evening, and the less known Midnight Hymn—he has conferred a greater benefit upon posterity than if he had founded three hospitals. It had always been his devout and earnest wish that the saints of God might praise God in words of his; and that wish has been abundantly granted. His other poems, though they are always beautiful in sentiment and often bright in langugae, are practically dead. They are poems of a saint, but of one who did not possess "the vision and the faculty divine" of the poet. But it was not in vain that he, like another displaced bishop to whom he compares himself—St. Gregory of Nazianzus—devoted to sacred song what he calls "the small dolorous remnant of my days." There is a value in the thoughts which he expressed apart from the too prosaic verse in which he enshrined them, and they brought him the most powerful anodynes for his many sorrows. . . . He is perhaps the loveliest figure in an age full of moral catastrophe, and there is no reward which he could have more desired than the one which God has granted to him—that as for the past two centuries so for many a generation yet to come, it is in *his* words that in many an English home the outgoings of the morning and evening shall praise God.—FARRAR, FREDERIC W., 1888, *Bishop Ken, Good Words, vol.* 29, *p.* 777.

Poetry more absolutely sincere, more high-minded than Bishop Ken's, does not exist. But heaviness of style, prolixity, want of charm and of variety, has sunk most of his work irretrievably.—PALGRAVE, FRANCIS T., 1889, *The Treasury of Sacred Song, p.* 348, *note.*

The last two years have witnessed a remarkable revival of the slumbering interest which has always existed in the story of one who was certainly among the greatest the Church of England has ever produced.—TEAGUE, J. JESSOP, 1890, *A Seventeenth-Century Prelate, Nineteenth Century, vol.* 27, *p.* 424.

As early as 1711 Dryden's description of the poor parson of a town, from Chaucer, was appropriated to Ken (Preface to *Expostularia*), and a panegyric was written on him in English and Latin verse by the laureate, Joshua Perkins. Bowles's "Life" in 1830 revived the reverence felt for him, which was further heightened by the high church movement at Oxford. J. H. Newman, in No. lxxv. of "Tracts for the Times," published in June 1836, drew out a form of service for 21 March, the day of Ken's burial; Isaac Williams celebrated him in his "Lyra Apostolica," No. cxiii., and his "Cathedral," p. 58; and Monckton Milnes (Lord Houghton) wrote verses on his tomb. In 1848 a memorial window was set up in Frome parish church by the Marchioness of Bath; in 1867 his bust was placed in the shire-hall at Taunton; and in 1885 a window was set up to his memory in Wells Cathedral, and a commemorative service was held on the 29 June, the anniversary of the trial of the "Seven Bishops."—HUNT, REV. WILLIAM, 1892, *Dictionary of National Biography, vol.* XXX, *p.* 403.

If this were a hagiology there would be much to be said about the saintly character of Bishop Ken; or if it were a critique on poetry the writer of the most popular hynms in the English language might claim a high place; but as a prose writer Ken holds a very subordinate position. —OVERTON, J. H., 1894, *English Prose, ed.* Craik, *vol.* III, *p.* 278.

Poetry was indeed, in a sense, the *pursuit* of his life. "Hymnotheo," a poem based upon the story of St. John and the Robber, told by Clement of Alexandria, is certainly "an idealised autobiography." The unnamed youth, St. John's catechumen, who after relapsing into a wild lawless life, was won back by the self-devoting love of the aged apostle, is called by Ken "Hymnotheo," a name the significance of which is obvious. The story is a mere thread on which are strung verses and episodes, some of them curiously incongruous. . . . It hardly need be said that Ken's poetry as a whole must be regarded not as an achievement, but as an occupation, an "employment." . . . More than once he alludes to his custom to write "new hymns every day"—*two* a day, if we take him literally. . . . From such a rate of production nothing excellent could be hoped. The mass of his verse is only interesting for what it reveals of the man; his editor, Hawkins, merely exaggerates a truth when he says that "these composures" "contain the full Beams of his God-enamour'd Soul." The portrait they paint is poor and faulty, but it is authentic. . . . In one essential part of the poetic faculty Ken was deficient—the eye, the heart, for Nature. . . . The mass of Ken's verse is entombed in four forgotten volumes; his three hymns live on the lips and in the heart of thousands.—CLARKE, F. A., 1896, *Thomas Ken pp.* 208, 210, 211, 213, 217.

Probably no other verse is so often sung by Christians of all denominations as this brief outburst of praise and gratitude; and yet the glad devotion expressed in any of the numerous adaptations never fails to kindle an audience. Originally written as the closing stanzas of "Awake my soul, and with the sun," the author, Bishop Ken, derived so much benefit from the use of it in his morning devotions that he added it to his now equally famous evening hymn, "Glory to Thee, my God, this night." It was the habit of this saintly sufferer to accompany his ever cheerful voice with the lute which penetrated beyond his prison walls; and the oft-repeated song of praise, which was soon taken up by his religious sympathisers listening without, has gone on singing itself into the hearts of Christians until the fragment has very nearly approached the hymn universal. During revivals it is sometimes the custom to sing it after every conversion. Once at Sheffield, England, under Billy Dawson, they sang it thirty-five times in one evening. It is frequently the last articulate sound that is heard from the lips of the dying, and it is not less frequently the expression of intense gratitude of the living in the moments when life throbs and swells most exultantly in the breast.—STEAD, W. T., 1897, *Hymns That Have Helped, p.* 32.

John Norris

1657–1711

John Norris, theologian and Platonic philosopher (born 1657, died 1711), wrote "The Picture of Love Unveiled" (1682), "The Idea of Happiness" (1688), "The Theory and Regulation of Love" (1688), "Reflections on the Conduct of Human Life" (1690), "Cursory Reflections on a Book called an Essay concerning Human Understanding" (1690),"Practical Discourses on the Beatitudes" (1690), "Account of Reason and Faith in relation to the Mysteries of Christianity" (1697), and "The Theory of the Ideal or Intelligible World" (1701). See Sir R. Waring's "Quid sit Amor."—ADAMS, W. DAVENPORT, 1877, *Dictionary of English Literature, p.* 474.

GENERAL

He search'd Malebranche, and now the Rabbi knows
The secret springs whence truth and error flows.
Directed by his leading light, we pass
Through nature's rooms and tread in ev'ry maze.
—DUNTON, JOHN, 1705, *The Eminent Conformists.*

Norris is more thoroughly Platonic than Malebranche, to whom, however, he pays great deference, and adopts his fundamental hypothesis of seeing all things in God. He is a writer of fine genius and a noble elevation of moral sentiments, such as predisposes men for the Platonic schemes of theosophy. He looked up to Augustin with as much veneration as to Plato, and respected, more perhaps than Malebranche, certainly more than the generality of English writers, the theological metaphysicians of the schools. With these he mingled some visions of a later mysticism. But his reasonings will seldom bear a close scrutiny.—HALLAM, HENRY, 1837–39, *Introduction to the Literature of Europe, pt.* iv, *ch.* iii, *par.* 65.

Yet he is not for a moment to be compared for learning, compass of thought, or power and skill of expression, to either Cudworth or More.—CRAIK, GEORGE L., 1861, *A Compendious History of English Literature and of the English Language, vol.* II, *p.* 188.

Norris was a disciple of Malebranche, and expounds his master's doctrine of the vision of all things in God, in opposition to the philosophy of Locke. He is interesting as the last offshoot from the school of Cambridge Platonists, except so far as the same tendency is represented by Shaftesbury. . . . Norris, though an able writer, is chiefly valuable as a solitary representative of Malebranche's theories in England.—STEPHEN, LESLIE, 1895, *Dictionary of National Biography, vol.* XLI.

Joshua Barnes

1654–1712

Born at London, Jan. 10, 1654: died Aug. 3, 1712. An English classical scholar and antiquarian, appointed professor of Greek at Cambridge in 1695. He was a voluminous writer, but is not in high repute as a scholar. His "Gerania, or the Discovery of a Better Sort of People, anciently discoursed of, called Pygmies," is his best-known work. He published an edition of Homer (1710).—SMITH, BENJAMIN E., 1894–97, *The Century Cyclopedia of Names, p.* 122.

PERSONAL

On the 3d of this month, being Sunday, between 6 and 7 o'clock in the evening, died the famous Mr. Joshua Barnes, S. T. B. and professor of the Greek tongue in the university of Cambridge, as I have been informed, by a letter, dated Aug. 9th, from his wife, Mrs. Mary Barnes. This great man died a very easy death, occasioned by a consumptive cough. He was my great friend and acquaintance, and I look upon him to have been the best Grecian (especially for poetical Greek) in the world. He was withall a man of singular good nature, and never spoke ill of any man, unless provoked to the highest degree.—HEARNE, THOMAS, 1712, *Reliquiæ Hearnianæ, ed. Bliss, vol.* I, *p.* 263, *Aug.* 13.

Let us exhibit one more picture of the calamities of a laborious author, in the character of Joshua Barnes, editor of Homer, Euripides, and Anacreon, and the writer of a vast number of miscellaneous compositions in history and poetry. Besides the works he published, he left behind him nearly fifty unfinished ones; many were epic poems, all intended to be in twelve books, and some had reached their eighth! His folio volume of "The History of Edward III." is a labour of valuable research. He wrote with equal facility in Greek, Latin, and his own language, and he wrote all his days; and, in a word, having little or nothing but his Greek professorship, not exceeding forty pounds a year, Barnes, who had a great memory, a little imagination, and no judgment, saw the close of a life, devoted to the studies of humanity, settle around him in gloom and despair. The great idol of his mind was the edition of his Homer, which seems to have completed his ruin; he was haunted all his days with a notion that he was persecuted by envy, and much undervalued in the world; the sad consolation of the secondary and third-rate authors, who often die persuaded of the existence of ideal enemies. To be enabled to publish his Homer at an enormous charge, he wrote a poem, the design of which is to prove that Solomon was the author of the Iliad; and it has been said that this was done to interest his wife, who had some property, to lend her aid towards the publication of so divine a work. This happy pun was applied for his epitaph:—

Joshua Barnes
Felicis memoriæ, judicium expectans.
Here lieth
Joshua Barnes,
Of happy memory, awaiting judgment!

—DISRAELI, ISAAC, 1812–13, *Laborious Authors, Calamities of Authors.*

GENERAL

Above all, Mr. Joshua Barnes has diligently collected whatever was to be had, far and near, upon the several passages of this great King's [Edw. III.] reign. His quotations are many; and generally, his authors are as well chosen as such a multitude can be supposed to have been. His inferences are not always becoming a statesman; and sometimes his digressions are tedious. His deriving of the famous institution of the Garter from the Phœnicians, is extremely obliging to good Mr. Sammes; but came too late, it seems, to Mr. Ashmole's knowledge, or otherwise would have bid fair for a choice post of honour in his elaborate book. In short, this industrious author seems to have driven his work too fast to the press, before he had provided an index, and some other accoutrements, which might have rendered it more serviceable to his readers.—NICOLSON, WILLIAM, 1696–1714, *English Historical Library.*

Joshua Barnes, from constantly perusing and talking Greek, had the name of Greek Barnes. . . . His memory and facility in writing have been greatly extolled. He would, and he always did, quote many Greek passages in conversation. He wrote incessantly, but seldom well. . . . Absorbed in his studies of Greek authors, he knew nothing of *English* manners; he would have been at "home" in Athens.—NOBLE, MARK, 1806, *A Biographical History of England, vol.* I, *pp.* 109, 110.

His facility in writing and speaking Greek was remarkable. He tells us in the parody of Homer, prefixed to his poem on Esther, that he could compose sixty Greek verses in an hour. He also avows in the preface to Esther that he found it much easier to write his annotations in Greek than in Latin, or even in English, "since the ornaments of poetry are almost peculiar to the Greeks, and since he had for many years been extremely conversant in Homer, the great father and source of the Greek poetry." He could off-hand turn a paragraph in a newspaper, or a hawker's bill, into any kind of Greek meter, and has been often known to do so among his Cambridge friends. Dr. Bentley used to say of Barnes that he "understood as much Greek as a Greek cobbler:" meaning doubtless by this that he had rather the "colloquial readiness of a vulgar mechanic," than the erudition, taste, and judgment of a scholar.—ALLIBONE, S. AUSTIN, 1854–58, *Dictionary of English Literature, vol.* I, *p.* 126.

Bentley, in the famous "Dissertation on Phalaris," describes him as "one of a singular industry and a most diffuse reading." His enthusiasm led him to undertake work for which he was in no degree qualified. Not content with writing a life of Edward III. and editing Homer, he had determined to write the life of Tamerlane, though he had no knowledge of oriental languages (Cole's *Athenæ*). His "Gerania" shows that he had some fancy and could write with ease and fluency. He is said to have been possessed of no little vanity; but this fault can readily be forgiven to one whose charity was such that he gave his only coat to a poor fellow who begged at his door.—BULLEN, A. H., 1885, *Dictionary of National Biography, vol.* III, *p.* 251.

Thomas Sprat

1635–1713

Born in Devonshire in 1636, was a clergyman's son. He studied at Wadham College, Oxford, became M. A. in 1657, and obtained a fellowship. His turn for science meant no more than activity of mind under the influence of Dr. Wilkins, who was Warden of Wadham. His turn for verse seems to have meant no more than activity of mind under the influence of Cowley, who, since 1657, had been, as Dr. Cowley, one of Wilkins's circle of philosophers. Sprat's last poem was upon Cowley's death; one of his earliest poems was on the death of Cromwell, "To the Happy Memory of the late Lord Protector;" and he published also, in 1659, a Cowleian poem, in thirty-one "Pindaric" stanzas, on "The Plague of Athens," suggested by the description of it in Thucydides. Sprat took orders at the Restoration, was chaplain to the Duke of Buckingham, and soon afterwards to the king. Cowley, with whom he was intimate, died in 1667; and Sprat's enthusiastic ode on Cowley's poetry was written in the year of the publishing of his "History of the Royal Society." Cowley had intrusted to his friend Sprat the care of his writings, and in 1668 Sprat published Cowley's Latin works, prefaced with a "Life of Cowley," also in Latin. This was amplified and prefixed, in 1688, to an edition of Cowley's English works. Thomas Sprat's life after the age of thirty-two does not concern literature. In 1688 he had been four years Bishop of Rochester. He complied as passively as he could with the Revolution, and died in 1713.—MORLEY, HENRY, 1879, *A Manual of English Literature, ed. Tyler, p.* 467.

THOMAS SPRAT

SIR WILLIAM TEMPLE

PERSONAL

A man whose convivial wit was equal to his convivial excesses, and these excesses were proverbial among his friends, and long remembered by the good people about Chertsey.—COLLINS, JOHN CHURTON, 1878-95, *Dryden, Quarterly Review, Essays and Studies, p. 33.*

"Maxime semper valuit authoritate," says the inscription on Sprat's monument in the abbey, and that was a leading trait in his character. He also loved ease and good living, and was warped in his views by the advantages of the position which he had acquired. Macaulay calls him "a great master of our language, who possessed at once the eloquence of the preacher, of the controversialist, and of the historian." Dr. Johnson had heard it observed, "and with great justness," that every book by him is of a different kind, "and that each has its distinct and characteristical excellence." His name is connected with a masterpiece in English literature, for he assisted Dean Aldrich in revising for original publication Lord Clarendon's "History of the Civil War." .—COURTNEY, W. P., 1898, *Dictionary of National Biography, vol. LIII, p. 423.*

HISTORY OF THE ROYAL SOCIETY
1667–1702

A nonsensical and illiterate history.—STUBBE, HENRY, 1670, *Legends no History.*

Some account it to be one of the most exact pieces for curiousness and delicacy of language that was ever yet extant in our tongue.—WOOD, ANTHONY, 1691–1721, *Athenæ Oxonienses, f.* 1097.

Their history is writ so well by Doctor Sprat that I will insist no more on them, but go on to other matters.—BURNET, GILBERT, 1715–34, *History of My Own Time.*

This is one of the few books which selection of sentiment and elegance of diction have been able to preserve, though written upon a subject flux and transitory. The history of the Royal Society is now read, not with the wish to know what they were then doing, but how their Translations are exhibited by Sprat.—JOHNSON, SAMUEL, 1779–81, *Sprat, Lives of the English Poets.*

Sprat's name is no longer a magnet; and, in truth, although his enthusiasm for scientific research is highly honourable to him, his style exceedingly lively, and many

of his observations replete with good sense, his work as a whole is discursive and ill-digested, and so little of a history that it hardly ever gives a date. The writer himself confesses that it is only the second of his three books has any proper claim to the title of history. But it is important on grounds of its own, which render it of more real value than the more exact and pragmatical narratives which have superseded it. The glow of youth is upon it. It paints vividly the great scientific awakening which coincided with the accession of Charles II. The mere list of the experiments which the Royal Society had performed, or proposed to perform, attests the devouring scientific curiosity of the age, and shows at once the reaction of men's minds in the direction of the tangibly useful after a long series of fruitless theological and political controversies, and how deep in the long run had been the influence of the great man who had lost his life in performing an experiment. At the same time there is a humorous side to the picture: much of the curiosity of the time was idle, much was founded on credulity. Many of the queries which Sprat catalogues with such complacency would now be thought too trivial to engage the attention of a learned society, and some are not a little absurd. In the main, however, they are most significant of the new spirit that had come into the world. —GARNETT, RICHARD, 1895, *The Age of Dryden, p. 264.*

GENERAL

The correctest writer of the age, and comes nearest to the great original of *Greece* and *Rome*, by a studious imitation of the ancients. . . . His sermons are truly fine.—FELTON, HENRY, 1711, *Dissertation on Reading the Classics.*

But for the wits of either Charles's days,
The mob of gentlemen who write with ease;
Sprat, Carew, Sedley, and a hundred more,
(Like twinkling stars the Miscellanies o'er);
One simile, that solitary shines
In the dry dessert of a thousand lines,
Or lengthen'd thought, that gleams through
many a page,
Has sanctified whole poems for an age.
—POPE, ALEXANDER, 1733, *First Epistle of the Second Book of Horace.*

Upon a review of Sprat's works, his language will sooner give you an idea of one of the insignificant tottering boats upon the Thames, than of the smooth noble current of the river itself.—BOYLE, JOHN (LORD ORRERY), 1751, *Remarks on the Life and Writings of Dr. Jonathan Swift.*

The life of Cowley, by Dr. Sprat has been esteemed one of the most elegant compositions in our language.—CIBBER, THEOPHILUS, 1753, *Lives of the Poets, vol.* III, *p.* 241.

His style in general, which has been greatly applauded, has neither the classic simplicity of Hobbes, nor the grace of Sir William Temple. His poetry is unequal, and sometimes inharmonious. He has, however, been justly ranked with the best writers in the reign of Charles the Second.—GRANGER, JAMES, 1769–1824, *Biographical History of England, vol.* 6, *p.* 94.

He considered Cowley as a model; and supported that, as he was imitated, perfection was approached. Nothing, therefore, but Pindarick liberty was to be expected. There is in his few productions no want of such conceits as he thought excellent; and of those our judgement may be settled by the first that appears in his praise of Cromwell, where he says, that Cromwell's "fame, like man, will grow white as it grows old."—JOHNSON, SAMUEL, 1779–81, *Sprat, Lives of the English Poets.*

They who shall study his pages will find no richness, ardour, or strength in his diction, but, on the contrary, an air of feebleness, and a species of imbecile spruceness, pervading all his productions. They must acknowledge, however, much clearness in his construction, and will probably agree that his cadences are often peculiarly well turned, especially those which terminate his paragraphs, and which sometimes possess a smartness which excites attention.—DRAKE, NATHAN, 1804, *Essays Illustrative of the Tatler, Spectator, and Guardian, vol.* II, *p.* 69.

An author who was finical and nice in his use of words.—DE QUINCEY THOMAS, 1823–4, *English Dictionaries.*

Unhappily for his fame, it has been usual to print his verses in collections of the British poets; and those who judge of him by his verses must consider him as a servile imitator, who, without one spark of Cowley's admirable genius, mimicked whatever was least commendable in Cowley's manner; but those who are acquainted

with Sprat's prose writings will form a very different estimate of his powers. He was, indeed, a great master of our language, and possessed at once the eloquence of the preacher, of the controversialist, and of the historian. His moral character might have passed with little censure had he belonged to a less sacred profession; for the worst that can be said of him is that he was indolent, luxurious, and worldly; but such failings, though not commonly regarded as very heinous in men of secular callings, are scandalous in a prelate.— MACAULAY, THOMAS BABINGTON, 1849, *History of England.*

His style, which was so much admired in his own age. is a Frenchified English, with an air of ease and occasionally of vivacity, but without any true grace or expressiveness.—CRAIK, GEORGE L., 1861, *A Compendious History of English Literature and of the English Language, vol.* II, *p.* 188.

There is indeed a certain flow and rotund finish about his diction. Some of his sentences would pass for Johnson's. Had the matter been more substantial, he might have taken a higher place in our literature; but he was a good genial fellow, rather fond of the bottle, and his lubricated eloquence perished with him. —MINTO, WILLIAM, 1872–80, *Manual of English Prose Literature, p.* 335.

Sprat's theological writings are few and insignificant, and it is hard not to allow that his merits as a prose-writer have been praised with some exaggeration. He is neat, clear, and often dignified, but the epithets "splendid" and "shining" can scarcely be granted to his style without demur.—GOSSE, EDMUND, 1888, *A History of Eighteenth Century Literature, p.* 101.

His chief claim to remembrance lies in his efforts both by precept and example to purge English prose of its rhetorical and decorative encumbrances, and to show that there is as much art "to have only plain conceptions on some arguments as there is in others to have extraordinary flights." It may well be urged that Sprat deserves a share in the credit, so commonly yielded to Dryden alone, of having inaugurated modern English prose.—RALEIGH, W. A., 1894, *English Prose, ed. Craik, vol.* III, *p.* 269.

Thomas Ellwood

1639–1713

Born at Crowell in Oxfordshire, was converted at twenty to Quakerism; in 1662 made Milton's acquaintance; and soon, visiting him almost daily, "read to him in such books in the Latin tongue as he pleased to hear read." In 1665 he hired a cottage at Chalfont St. Giles, where Milton might escape the plague in London. Milton gave him the MS. of "Paradise Lost" to read, and on returning it Ellwood said, "Thou hast said much of 'Paradise Lost,' but what hast thou to say of 'Paradise Found'?" Ellwood was busy in controversy, and had more than his share of persecution as a Quaker almost till his death. Of his many writings, only his Autobiography (1683; new ed. by Prof. H. Morley, 1885) is now interesting for Milton's sake.—PATRICK AND GROOME, *eds.*, 1897, *Chambers's Biographical Dictionary, p.* 337.

PERSONAL

Let no one imagine a prevailing absurdity in Thomas Ellwood's life; he was a man whom every reader must heartily respect and honor. He was incorruptibly true and unimpeachably brave, and he suffered for his faith, outrage and injustice with saintly patience and manly strength. Again and again he was seized and cast into prison without cause; every ruffian and coward felt free to insult the gallant youth who had once been so quick with his sword. If the reader will know how, without striking a blow, a man of courage may make knightly defence of a lady, let him turn to Ellwood's modest account of how he protected the beautiful Guli Pennington, afterwards the wife of William Penn, from the rudeness of some drunken troopers; and if he will learn how a true man is always efficiently a man, let him compare the quiet fearlessness of Ellwood in moments of peril with the valor of Lord Herbert. . . . The Quaker will suffer nothing by contrast with the cavalier.—HOWELLS, WILLIAM DEAN, 1877, *ed., Life of Thomas Ellwood, p.* 171.

HISTORY OF THOMAS ELLWOOD

1683

At about this date [1683] his narrative ceases. We learn, from other sources, that he continued to write and print in defence of his religious views up to the year of his death, which took place in 1713. One of his productions, a poetical version of the "Life of David," may be still met with, in the old Quaker libraries. On the score of poetical merit, it is about on a level with Michael Drayton's verses on the same subject.—WHITTIER, JOHN GREENLEAF, 1849, *Old Portraits and Modern Sketches, p.* 69.

Many of Ellwood's writings have not been printed; but the fact that twenty-four works of all kinds—poems, pamphlets, and controversial treatises—were published and forgotten must be our comfort and stay in this partial deprivation. His autobiography has alone survived to our time, and it will probably keep his memory alive as long as men love to read simple, sincere, and manly books. Its manner has for me a great charm, and from the clearness with which it mirrors the author and the profound religious movement in which he was so largely concerned, it must always be interesting to the student of history; whoever loves a quaint force of style, and many delicate unconscious flavors of character, or values rare pictures of the intimate life of the past, must also enjoy it. No one will like it the less for the harmless vanity which occasionally appears in it. Ellwood came hardly by his religion and his learning, and so much as any man might, had a right to self-satisfaction in them.—HOWELLS, WILLIAM DEAN, 1877, *ed., Life of Thomas Ellwood, p.* 177.

Distinguished for many literary excellences, and entirely free from the fanaticism and intolerance so generally displayed in other writings of the early Friends.—BALDWIN, JAMES, 1883, *English Literature and Literary Criticism, Prose, p.* 435.

"The History of Thomas Ellwood, written by Himself," is interesting for the frankness with which it makes Thomas Ellwood himself known to us; and again, for the same frank simplicity that brings us nearer than books usually bring us to a living knowledge of some features of a bygone time; and yet again, because it helps us a little to come near to Milton in his daily life. He would be a good novelist who could invent as pleasant a book as this unaffected record of a quiet life touched by great influences in eventful times.—MORLEY, HENRY, 1885, *ed., The History of Thomas Ellwood (Universal Library), Introduction, p. 5.*

As regards diction and rhetoric, there is nothing antique or affected in the "History of Thomas Ellwood." He does not seem to have been influenced much by the older generation of English authors; like Bunyan he seems to have adopted naturally a practical style of composition, not overweighted in any way, good at reporting conversations. In Ellwood's case, and from the character of his mind, there was one subject only, the history of his own life, to which this style could be applied with full success. The same conditions that went to make his "History" so good were those that kept him from writing any other work that can be compared with it.—KER, W. P., 1894, *English Prose, ed. Craik, vol. III, p. 287.*

Anthony Ashley Cooper

Third Earl of Shaftesbury

1671–1713

Born, in London, 26 Feb. 1671. Early education under tutorship of John Locke. At a private school, 1682–83; at Winchester, Nov. 1683 to 1686. Travelled on Continent, 1686–89. M. P. for Poole, May 1695; re-elected, Nov. 1695. Retired from Parliament, owing to ill-health, July 1698. Visit to Holland, 1698–99. Succeeded to Earldom, on death of his father, 10 Nov. 1699. Took his seat in House of Lords, 19 Jan. 1700. In Holland, Aug. 1703 to Aug. 1704. Married Jane Ewer, Aug. 1709. To Italy, for health, autumn of 1711. Died, in Naples, 15 Feb. 1713. Buried at St. Giles's. *Works:* "An Inquiry concerning Virtue" (anon.), 1699; "A Letter Concerning Enthusiasm" (anon.), 1708; "Sensus Communis" (anon.), 1709; "The Moralists" (anon.), 1709; "Soliloquy, or Advice to an Author" (anon.), 1710; "Characteristics of Men, Manners, Opinions, Times" (3 vols.), 1711; "A Notion of the Historical Draught . . . of the Judgment of Hercules" (anon.), 1713; "Several Letters written by a Noble Lord to a Young Man at the University" (anon.), 1716. *Posthumous:* "Letters . . . to R. Molesworth," 1721; "Letters, collected," 1746; "Original Letters by Locke, Sidney, and Shaftesbury," ed. by T. Foster, enlarged edn. 1847. He *edited:* B. Whichcot's "Select Sermons," 1689.—SHARP, R. FARQUHARSON, 1897, *A Dictionary of English Authors, p.* 253.

PERSONAL

As regards personal habits, Shaftesbury is reported to have been remarkably abstemious at a time when riotous living was the rule amongst the upper classes of society, and not the exception. . . . As an earnest student, an ardent lover of liberty, an enthusiast in the cause of virtue, and a man of unblemished life and untiring beneficence, Shaftesbury probably had no superior in his generation. His character and pursuits are the more remarkable, considering the rank of life in which he was born and the circumstances under which he was brought up. In many respects, he reminds us of the imperial philosopher, Marcus Aurelius, whose works we know him to have studied with avidity, and whose influence is unmistakably stamped upon his own productions. . . . Though Shaftesbury was one of the earliest of English moralists, and died so long ago as 1712-13, the present Earl is only his great-grandson.—FOWLER, THOMAS, 1882, *Shaftesbury and Hutcheson (English Philosophers), pp.* 39, 40, 41.

Shaftesbury was a man of lofty and ardent character, forced by ill-health to abandon politics for literature. He was liberal, though much fretted by the difficulty of keeping out of debt. He was resolved, as he tells his steward, not to be a slave to his estates, and never again to be "poorly rich." He supported several young men of promise at the university or elsewhere. He allowed a pension of £20 a year to the deist Toland, after Toland's surreptitious publication of his papers, though he appears to have dropped it in his fit of economy in 1704. He gives exceedingly careful directions for regulating his domestic affairs during his absence. His letters to his young friends are full of moral and religious advice, and the "Shaftesbury Papers" show many traces of his practical benevolence to them. He went to church and took the sacrament regularly, respecting religion though he hated the priests. He is a typical example of the whig aristocracy of the time, and with better health might have rivalled his grandfather's fame.— STEPHEN, LESLIE, 1887, *Dictionary of National Biography, vol.* XII, *p.* 132.

There is nothing that demands concealment in his career, whatever his mistakes or shortcomings; the more closely one presses home upon the inner motives and exalted purpose of his life the richer and more ennobling does his character appear. —RAND, BENJAMIN, 1900, *ed., The Life, Unpublished Letters, and Philosophical Regimen of Anthony, Earl of Shaftesbury, Introduction, p.* vi.

GENERAL

The generality of moralists and philosophers have hitherto agreed that there could be no virtue without self-denial; but a late author, who is now much read by men of sense, is of a contrary opinion, and imagines that men, without any trouble or violence upon themselves, may be naturally virtuous. He seems to require and expects goodness in his species, as we do a sweet taste in grapes and China oranges, of which, if any of them are sour, we boldly pronounce that they are not come to that perfection their nature is capable of. This noble writer fancies that, as man is made for society, so he ought to be born with a kind affection to the whole, of which he is a part, and a propensity to seek the welfare of it. In pursuance of this supposition, he calls every action performed with regard to the public good, virtuous; and all selfishness, wholly excluding such a regard, vice. In respect to our species, he looks upon virtue and vice as permanent realities that must ever be the same in all countries and all ages, and imagines that a man of sound understanding, by following the rules of good sense, may not only find out that "Pulchrum et Honestum" both in morality and the works of art and nature, but likewise govern himself, by his reason, with as much ease and readiness as a good rider manages a well-taught horse by the bridle. . . . Two systems cannot be more opposite than his Lordship's and mine.— MANDEVILLE, BERNARD DE, 1723, *A Search into the Nature of Society.*

More surprising that a young nobleman should have published so many tracts, so generally read by men of sense, than that there should be so few errors found in them.—FIDDES, RICHARD, 1724, *A General Treatise of Morality formed upon the Principles of Natural Reason only.*

The rest of his time he employed in ordering his writings for publication, which he placed in the order they now stand. The several prints then first interspersed in the work were all designed by himself, and each device bears an exact affinity to the passage to which it refers. That no mistake might be committed, he did not leave to any other hand, even so much as the drudgery or correcting the press. In the three volumes of the "Characteristics" he completed the whole of his writings which he intended should be made public, though some people have, however, in a very ungenerous manner, without any application to his family, or even their knowledge, published several of his letters, and those too of a private nature, many of which were written in so hasty and careless a manner, that he did not so much as take copies of them.—SHAFTESBURY, FOURTH EARL, C 1734–41, *A Sketch of the Life of the Third Earl of Shaftesbury.*

Had many excellent qualities, both as a man and a writer. He was temperate, chaste, honest, and a lover of his country. In his writings he has shewn how largely he has imbibed the deep sense, and how naturally he could copy the gracious manner, of Plato.—WARBURTON, WILLIAM, 1738, *Divine Legation of Moses, Dedication.*

It hath been the fate of Lord Shaftesbury's "Characteristics," beyond that of most other books, to be idolized by one party, and detested by another. While the first regard it as a work of perfect excellence, as containing everything that can render mankind wise and happy; the latter are disposed to rank it among the most pernicious of writings, and brand it as one continued heap of fustian, scurrility, and falsehood. . . . The noble writer hath mingled beauties and blots, faults and excellencies, with a liberal and unsparing hand.—BROWN, JOHN, 1751, *Essays on the Characteristics.*

You say you cannot conceive how Lord Shaftesbury came to be a philosopher in vogue; I will tell you: First, he was a Lord; secondly, he was as vain as any of his readers; thirdly, men are very prone to believe what they do not understand; fourthly, they will believe anything at all, provided they are under no obligation to believe it; fifthly, they love to take a new road, even when that road leads nowhere; sixthly, he was reckoned a fine writer, and seemed always to mean more than he said. Would you have any more reasons? An interval above forty years has pretty well destroyed the charm. A dead Lord ranks with Commoners; Vanity is no longer interested in the matter, for the new road has become an old one.—GRAY, THOMAS, 1758, *Letters, Aug.* 18.

The writings of the latter breathe the virtues of his mind, for which they are much more estimable than for their style and manner. He delivers his doctrines in ecstatic diction, like one of the Magi inculcating philosophic visions to an eastern auditory.—WALPOLE, HORACE, 1758, *A Catalogue of the Royal and Noble Authors, of England, Scotland and Ireland, ed. Park, vol.* IV, *p.* 55.

The philosophical manner of Lord Shaftesbury's writing is nearer to that of Cicero than any English author has yet arrived at; but perhaps had Cicero written in English, his composition would have greatly exceeded that of our countryman. The diction of the latter is beautiful, but such beauty as, upon nearer inspection, carries with it evident symptoms of affectation. This has been attended with very disagreeable consequences. Nothing is so easy to copy as affectation, and his lordship's rank and fame have procured him more imitators in Britain than any other writer I know; all faithfully preserving his blemishes, but unhappily not one of his beauties.—GOLDSMITH, OLIVER, 1759, *The Bee, No.* 8, *Nov.* 24.

Considerable merit, doubtless, he has. His works might be read with profit for the moral philosophy which they contain, had he not filled them with so many oblique and invidious insinuations against the christian religion; thrown out, too, with so much spleen and satire, as do no honour to his memory, either as an author or a man. His language has many beauties. It is firm, and supported in an uncommon degree; it is rich and musical. No English author, as I formerly showed, has attended so much to the regular construction of his sentences, both with respect to

propriety, and with respect to cadence. All this gives so much elegance and pomp to his language, that there is no wonder it should have been highly admired by some. It is greatly hurt, however, by perpetual stiffness and affectation. This is its capital fault. His lordship can express nothing with simplicity. He seems to have considered it as vulgar, and beneath the dignity of a man of quality, to speak like other men. Hence he is ever in buskins; and dressed out with magnificent elegance. In every sentence, we see the marks of labour and art; nothing of that ease which expresses a sentiment coming natural and warm from the heart. Of figures and ornament of every kind, he is exceedingly fond, sometimes happy in them; but his fondness for them is too visible; and having once laid hold of some metaphor or allusion that pleased him, he knows not how to part with it. . . . Lord Shaftesbury possessed delicacy and refinement of taste, to a degree that we may call excessive and sickly; but he had little warmth of passion; few strong or vigorous feelings, and the coldness of his character, led him to that artificial and stately manner which appears in his writings. He was fonder of nothing than of wit and raillery; but he is far from being happy in it. He attempts it often, but always awkwardly; he is stiff, even in his pleasantry; and laughs in form, like an author, and not like a man.—BLAIR, HUGH, 1783, *Lectures on Rhetoric and Belles-Letters, ed. Mills, pp.* 209, 210.

For a considerable time he stood in high repute as a polite writer, and was regarded by many as a standard of elegant composition: his imitators as well as admirers were numerous, and he was esteemed the head of the school of sentimental philosophy. Of late years he has been as much depreciated as he was before extolled, and in both cases the matter has been carried to an extreme.—PARK, THOMAS, 1806, *ed. Walpole's Royal and Noble Authors, vol.* IV, *p.* 59.

Grace belongs only to natural movements; and Lord Shaftesbury, notwithstanding the frequent beauty of his thoughts and language, has rarely attained it. . . . He had great power of thought and command over words. But he had no talent for inventing character, and bestowing life on it. The Inquiry concerning

Virtue is nearly exempt from the faulty peculiarities of the author; the method is perfect, the reasoning just, the style precise and clear.—MACKINTOSH, SIR JAMES, 1830, *Second Preliminary Dissertation.*

Shaftesbury retains a certain place as one of the few disciples of idealism who resisted the influence of Locke; but his importance is purely historical. His cold and monotonous though exquisitely polished dissertations have fallen into general neglect, and find few readers and exercise no influence. The shadow of the tomb rests upon them all; a deep unbroken silence, the chill of death surrounds them. They have long ceased to wake any interest, or to suggest any enquiries, or to impart any impulse to the intellect of England.—LECKY, WILLIAM EDWARD HARTPOLE, 1865, *Spirit of Rationalism in Europe, vol.* I.

Shaftesbury's relation to Christianity involves some difficult questions. If all we had to settle were simply whether or not he went with the Christianity prevalent in his time, the answer would be easy. He stood apart from the clergy, ridiculed "the heroic passion of *saving souls,*" and the Christian who had "his conversation in heaven." He said, with a sneer, that he dutifully and faithfully embraced the holy mysteries, conforming to the Church by law established, and making no researches into the origin of the rites and symbols. If he were to exercise himself in such speculations, he was quite sure that the further he inquired the less satisfaction he would find; for inquiry was the sure road to heterodoxy. This was a mode of writing common with the Deists. It must have been provoking and offensive, not only to the clergy, against whom it was aimed, but to all right-minded people. It is evident, however, that he was only bantering the clergy, whose ignorance and prejudice may have been equally provoking to all sensible men. He immediately after asserts the right of every man to examine the Scriptures for himself; and not only to examine them, but to know their history, what they profess to be, and what authority they claim. If Scripture be the only religion of Protestants, we ought, surely, as Protestants, to know what Scripture is.—HUNT, JOHN, 1868, *Anthony Earl of Shaftesbury, The Contemporary Review, vol.* 8, *p.* 521.

He may be called the first of the intuitional school, writing without being at all aware of the difficulties of his position. . . . His style is highly elaborated. His first care is to be delicately melodious. He strives also to avoid the very appearance of harshness in the union of ideas. As a consequence, he is rather wanting in vigour, is driven upon affected inversions, and is obliged often to prolong his sentences to a tedious length before his smooth circumlocutions amount to a complete expression. —MINTO, WILLIAM, 1872–80, *The Manual of English Prose Literature, p.* 401.

The third Lord Shaftesbury is one of the many writers who enjoy a kind of suspended vitality. His volumes are allowed to slumber peacefully on the shelves of dusty libraries till some curious student of English literature takes them down for a cursory perusal. Though generally mentioned respectfully, he has been dragged deeper into oblivion by two or three heavy weights. Besides certain intrinsic faults of style to be presently noticed, he has been partly injured by the evil reputation which he shares with the English Deists. Their orthodox opponents succeeded in inflicting upon those writers a fate worse than refutation. The Deists were not only pilloried for their heterodoxy, but indelibly branded with the fatal inscription "dulness." The charge, to say the truth, was not ill-deserved; and though Shaftesbury is in many respects a writer of a higher order than Toland, Tindal, or Collins, he cannot be acquitted of that most heinous of literary offences. . . . A second-rate English author of Queen Anne's time. . . . Whenever he tries to be facetious he is intolerable; he reminds one of that painful jocosity which is sometimes assumed by a grave professor, who fancies, with perfect truth, that his audience is inclined to yawn, and argues, in most unfortunate conflict with the truth, that such heavy gambols as he can manage will rouse them to the smiling point. The result is generally depressing. Yet Shaftesbury is less annoying when he is writhing his grave face into a contorted grimace than when the muse, whom he is in the habit of invoking, permits him to get upon stilts. His rhapsodies then are truly dismal.—STEPHEN, LESLIE, 1873, *Shaftesbury's Characteristics, Fraser's Magazine, vol.* 87, *pp.* 76, 77.

Shaftesbury, it is plain, took great pains in the elaboration of his style, and he succeeded so far as to make his meaning transparent. The thought is always clear. We are spared the trouble of deciding between different interpretations of his doctrines, a process so wearisome in the case of most philosophical authors. But, on the other hand, he did not equally succeed in attaining elegance, an object at which he seems equally to have aimed. There is a curious affectation about his style, a falsetto note, which, notwithstanding all his efforts to please, is often irritating to the reader. The main characteristic of Shaftesbury's style is, perhaps, best hit off by Charles Lamb, when he calls it "genteel." He poses too much as a fine gentleman, and is so anxious not to be taken for a pedant of the vulgar, scholastic kind, that he falls into the hardly more attractive pedantry of the æsthete and *virtuoso.* The *limæ labor* is almost everywhere apparent. The efforts at raillery and humour are sometimes so forced as to lose their effect, and he is too apt to inform his reader beforehand, when he is about to put on his light and airy manner. —Fowler, Thomas, 1882, *Shaftesbury and Hutcheson* (*English Philosophers*), p. 61.

Nor can we permit the mere æsthetic interpreters of life to carry off Shaftesbury into their camp, on the plea that he regarded morals as only one of the fine arts, and virtue as no more than the supreme accomplishment. No doubt, it is easy to quote from him many detached sentences which are open to this construction; as when he bids you pursue the beautiful, and then the good will come of itself; and says, that virtue is moral beauty, and that the knowledge of beauty is the discipline of virtue. And it must be admitted that his own high artistic perception and culture blended too closely in himself the distinct though allied feelings of *approbation* and of *admiration,*— one of the many marks of an ethical commencement from the idea, not of Duty, but of Good. But still, these partial indications must accept the limitations which are clearly imposed upon them by other and more exact statements of his doctrine; and when this is done, he will be found to say, that the right indeed is always beautiful, but not that it is the beautiful which constitutes the right.—Martineau, James, 1885, *Types of Ethical Theory, vol.* II, *p.* 467.

He writes in a style which is consummately easy and lucid. There are none of those obscurities and experimental reaches of thought which in other thinkers one sometimes finds so puzzling and so suggestive; his meaning may not be very profound, but it is at least expressed for the better understanding of the plain man. He brings into English prose an order and a clearness of which it was beginning to stand in some need. The worst that can be said of him is that he is terribly affected—"genteel" was Charles Lamb's epithet. He is not always in buckram; he will unbend to you; but all the same his treatises invariably smack of the superior person, the man of birth, debarred by circumstances from his natural pursuit of politics, and condescending to while away a part of his too abundant leisure in unravelling some niceties of the intellect. Unwilling to appear a pedant, he falls into the opposite vices of desultoriness and superficiality.—Chambers, E. K., 1894, *English Prose, ed. Craik, vol.* III, *p.* 448.

Judged by his influence on the age Shaftesbury's place in the history of literature and of philosophy is an important one. Seed springs up quickly when the soil is prepared for it, and Shaftesbury by his belief in the perfectability of human nature through the aid of culture, appealed as Mandeville also did from a lower and opposite platform, to the views current in polite society. According to Shaftesbury men have a natural instinct for virtue, and the sense of what is beautiful enables the virtuoso to reject what is evil and to cleave to what is good. Let a man once see that to be wicked is to be miserable, and virtue will be dear for its own sake apart from the fear of punishment or the hope of reward. He found salvation for the world in a cultivated taste, but had no gospel for the men whose tastes were not cultivated.—Dennis, John, 1894, *The Age of Pope, p.* 214.

The influence of Shaftesbury's "Characteristics," 1711, was far more literary than metaphysical. He condemned metaphysics, but his philosophy, such as it was, inspired Pope and his cultivated thinking on several subjects made many writers in the next generation care for beauty and grace.—BROOKE, STOPFORD A., 1896, *English Literature, p.* 190.

If philosophy at the opening of the eighteenth century could give a better account of itself, it was mainly because the leading philosopher was a born writer. The third Earl of Shaftesbury has been strangely neglected by the historians of our literature, partly because his scheme of thought has long been rejected, and partly because his style, . . . was presently obliterated by the technical smartness of Addison and Swift. . . . His influence on writing in his own age and down the entire eighteenth century is highly important to us. Commonly as the fact is overlooked, Shaftesbury was one of the literary forces of the time—he was, perhaps, the greatest between Dryden and Swift. . . . Shaftesbury's long residences in Holland gave him the opportunity of becoming thoroughly acquainted with the movement of Continental thought to an extent doubtless beyond any previous writer of English prose. The effect is seen on his style and temper, which are less insular than those of any of the men with whom it is natural to compare him. It is to be noted also that Shaftesbury was the earliest English author whose works in the vernacular were promptly admired abroad, and he deserves remembrance as the first who really broke down the barrier which excluded England from taking her proper place in the civilisation of literary Europe. . . . The style of Shaftesbury glitters and rings, proceeding along in a capricious, almost mincing effort to secure elegance, with a sort of colourless euphuism, which is desultory and a little irritating indeed, yet so curious that one marvels that it should have fallen completely into neglect. He is the father of æstheticism, the first Englishman who developed theories of formal virtue, who attempted to harmonise the beautiful with the true and the good. His delicate, Palladian style, in which a certain external stiffness and frigidity seem to be holding down a spirit eager to express the passion of beauty, is a very interesting feature of the period to which we have now arrived. The modern attitude of mind seems to meet us first in the graceful, cosmopolitan writings of Shaftesbury, and his genius, like a faint perfume, pervades the contemplation of the arts down to our own day. Without a Shaftesbury there would hardly have been a Ruskin or a Pater.—GOSSE, EDMUND, 1897, *Short History of Modern English Literature, pp.* 203, 204.

Although the philosophy of Shaftesbury is thus founded on stoicism, this Philosophical Regimen is a new and brilliant presentation of that moral system. The discourses of Epictetus were uttered, it is believed, extempore. They have a popular form, but often lack in continuity of expression. The thoughts of Marcus Aurelius, on the other hand, were written down merely for personal use. They bear the evidence of private honesty, but are stated in short paragraphs which are often obscure. The merits rather than the defects of these two works are combined in the Philosophical Regimen of Shaftesbury. It is written in a style that can at all times be readily understood, and it likewise possesses all the sincerity of personal writing where the purpose is "only to improve by these, not publish, profess, or teach them." The eloquence of the utterance is frequently such as could only have proceeded from Shaftesbury, whose method of philosophical rhapsody so captivated his contemporary Leibnitz. The permanent strength of this Regimen, however, consists in the fact that it is one of the most consistent and thorough-going attempts ever made to transform a philosophy into a life. Just as Spinoza was "God-intoxicated," so Shaftesbury was "intoxicated with the idea of virtue." He is the greatest Stoic of modern times. Into his own life he wrought the stoical virtue for virtue's sake. This exalted purpose he sought to attain by means of this Regimen. It thus embodies a philosophy which must compel a renewed and critical study from the stoical standpoint of his "Characteristics." Indeed, it may be said, we believe, with perfect truth that there has been no such strong expression of stoicism since the days of Epictetus and Marcus Aurelius as that contained in the Philosophical Regimen of Shaftesbury. The Greek slave, the Roman Emperor, and the English nobleman, must abide the three great exponents of stoical philosophy.— RAND, BENJAMIN, 1900, *ed. The Life, Unpublished Letters, and Philosophical Regimen of Anthony, Earl of Shaftesbury, Introduction, p.* xii.

Thomas Rymer

1641-1713.

Born at Yafforth Hall, Northallerton, the son of a Roundhead gentleman who was hanged at York in 1664, studied at Sidney Sussex, Cambridge, and entered Gray's Inn in 1666. He published translations, critical discussions on poetry, dramas, and works on history, and in 1692 was appointed historiographer royal. Pope considered him "one of the best critics we ever had;" Macaulay, "the worst critic that ever lived." His principal critical work is "The Tragedies of the Last Age Considered" (1678); but he is chiefly remembered as the compiler of the invaluable collection of historical materials known as the "Fœdera," extending from the 11th century to his own time. Vols. i.-xv. were published in 1704-13, vols. xvi, xx, in 1715-35, a third edition (incomplete) of the Record Commission in 1816-30, and Sir Thomas Hardy's "Syllabus" of the whole in 1869-85.—PATRICK AND GROOME, eds., 1897, Chambers's Biographical Dictionary, p. 814.

PERSONAL

Of Rymer's personal character and the circumstances of his life at the time of his appointment to this important post, we know comparatively nothing. That he lived in an honourable intimacy with Hobbes and Waller there is no doubt, and that he addressed Bishop Nicolson as his "old acquaintance" is equally clear. Familiar allusions to various members of several noble families are scattered throughout his writings, and John Dunton styles him the "orthodox and modest Rymer." Dr. Smith thought well of him, and George Stephney numbered him amongst his friends. In Thoresby's Diary he is alluded to, some years later, as "good old Mr. Rymer;" and Bishop Kennett, writing after his death, mentions him with respect.—HARDY, THOMAS DUFFUS, 1869, Syllabus of "Rymer's Fœdera," Preface, vol. I, p. xxv.

FŒDERA

This great work we have from Thomas Rymer, Historiographer Royal, commanded and supported by Her Majesty; and it may justly be reckoned one of the many glories of her reign.—NICOLSON, WILLIAM, 1696-1714, English Historical Library.

No historical student can possibly proceed with his labours, nor is any historical library complete, without this invaluable collection. The Hague edition may be recommended as the most convenient and valuable.—NICOLAS, SIR NICHOLAS HARRIS, 1830, Observation upon the Present State of Historical Literature, etc.

Compiler of Carlyle's favourite butt, Rymer's "Fœdera."—MINTO, WILLIAM, 1872-80, Manual of English Prose Literature, p. 339.

In the year 1693, mainly, it would appear, at the suggestion of the eminent statesmen, Somers and Halifax, Thomas Rymer, in his capacity of historiographer royal, was appointed to transcribe and publish all the leagues, treaties, alliances, capitulations, and confederacies which had, at any time, been made between the Crown of England and other kingdoms. As the result of these instructions there successively appeared, in the early part of the eighteenth century, the volumes of his well-known "Fœdera," the series being continued by his assistant, Robert Sanderson, in the year 1735. The work, as it issued from the press, attracted considerable attention both at home and on the Continent, and, though severly criticised, has generally been admitted to be a collection of the highest value and authority. It commences with the reign of Henry I. (ann. 1134), and extends to 1654. A new edition, published at the Hague, 1737-45, is of greatly superior typographical accuracy; while the utility of the collection to students has been much enhanced by the Syllabus of the work by the late Sir T. D. Hardy.—GARDINER AND MULLINGER, 1881-94, Introduction to the Study of English History, p. 224.

Rymer the Dryasdust, however, cannot quite forget Rymer the Longinus; his work is graced with a Latin address to Queen Anne, more like a dithyrambic than a dedication.—GARNETT, RICHARD, 1895, The Age of Dryden, p. 260.

Though defective at some points, and defaced by errors of date and by many misprints, Rymer's "Fœdera" remains a collection of high value and authority for almost all periods of the middle ages and for the sixteenth century. For the period of the Commonwealth the work is meagre, and Dumont's "Corps Universel Diplomatique" (8 vols. 1726) is for that epoch an indispensable supplement.—LEE, SIDNEY, 1897, *Dictionary of National Biography, vol.* L, *p.* 68.

GENERAL

TO SHAKESPEARE'S CRITIC he bequeathes the curse,—
To *find his faults*, and yet HIMSELF MAKE WORSE.
—DRYDEN, JOHN, 1694, *Love Triumphant, Prologue.*

You see what success this learned critick has found in the world, after his blaspheming Shakspeare. Almost all the faults which he has discovered are truly there; yet who will read Mr. Rymer, or not read Shakspeare? For my own part 1 reverence Mr. Rymer's learning, but I detest his ill-nature and his arrogance. I indeed, and such as I, have reason to be afraid of him, but Shakspeare has not.— DRYDEN, JOHN, 1694? *Letter to Dennis, Works, ed. Scott and Saintsbury, vol.* XVIII, *p.* 117.

"Rymer a learned and strict critic?"— Ay, that's exactly his character. He is generally right, though rather too severe in his opinion of the particular plays he speaks of; and is, on the whole, one of the best critics we ever had.—POPE, ALEXANDER, 1734-36, *Spence's Anecdotes, ed. Singer, p.* 130.

The different manner and effect with which critical knowledge may be conveyed, was perhaps never more clearly exemplified than in the performances of Rymer and Dryden. It was said of a dispute between two mathematicians, "malim cum Scaligero errare, quam cum Clavio recte sapere;" that "it was more eligible to go wrong with one, than right with the other." A tendency of the same kind every mind must feel at the perusal of Dryden's prefaces and Rymer's discourses. With Dryden we are wandering in quest of Truth; whom we find, if we find her at all, drest in the graces of elegance; and, if we miss her, the labour of the pursuit rewards itself; we are led only through fragrance and flowers. Rymer, without taking a nearer, takes a rougher way; every step is to be made through thorns and brambles; and Truth, if we meet her, appears repulsive by her mien, and ungraceful by her habit. Dryden's criticism has

the majesty of a queen; Rymer's has the ferocity of a tyrant.—JOHNSON, SAMUEL, 1779-81, *Dryden, Lives of the English Poets.*

Mr. Rymer has his own stately notions of what is proper for tragedy. He is zealous for poetical justice; and as he thinks that vice cannot be punished too severely, and that the poet ought to leave his victims objects of pity, he protests against the introduction of very wicked characters. . . . Our author understands exactly the balance of power in the affections. He would dispose of all the poet's characters to a hair, according to his own rules of fitness. He would marshal them in array as in a procession, and mark out exactly what each ought to do or suffer. According to him, so much of presage and no more should be given—such a degree of sorrow, and no more ought a character to endure; vengeance should rise precisely to a given height, and be executed by a certain appointed hand. He would regulate the conduct of fictitious heroes as accurately as of real beings, and often reasons very beautifully on his own poetic decalogue. . . . Mr. Rymer is an enthusiastic champion for the poetical prerogatives of kings. No courtier ever contended more strenuously for their divine right in real life, than he for their pre-eminence in tragedy.—TALFOURD, SIR THOMAS NOON, 1820, *Rymer on Tragedy, Retrospective Review, vol.* I, *pp.* 8, 9.

The worst critic that ever lived.—MACAULAY, THOMAS BABINGTON, 1831, *Boswell's Life of Johnson, Edinburgh Review, Critical and Miscellaneous Essays.*

Rymer, however, was a ripe scholar, and the founder, in our literature, of what has been considered as the French or the classical school of criticism; and he has won the unlucky distinction of being designated as "Shakespeare's critic!" —DISRAELI, ISAAC, 1841, *Shakespeare, Amenities of Literature.*

Thomas Rymer and John Dennis may be regarded as the first regular and professional critics, and, apart from the fact that they were contemporaries, resemble one another in many respects. Each was a man of considerable ability, each passed through a University curriculum, each was maddened by a furious zeal for the honour of tragedy, and each, after a chequered career in which poverty, criticism, and ill-temper strongly obtained, died, if not quite "unknelled, uncoffined and unknown," at all events unregretted. The latent "ferocity" of the two men became active and aggressive so soon as they touched upon the subject of Shakespeare's plays, which, indeed, in the nineteenth century as in the eighteenth, have formed the happy hunting-grounds of a few incipient madmen and American "theorizers." Thoroughly recognizing the value of illustrating their precepts by examples, both Rymer and Dennis proved—as the Abbe d'Aubignac had proved—by their own plays the unutterable stupidity and lifeless character of these precepts. Amid all the rubbish and pathos which the last two centuries have to answer for in the shape of dramatic works, it is certain that the *ultima Thule* of absurdity was reached when such men as Banks, Rymer, and Dennis proclaimed themselves heaven-born writers of tragedy.—ROBERTS, WILLIAM, 1889, *Two Eighteenth Century Critics, The Bookworm, vol. 2, p. 146.*

It would be unfair to Rymer to make of him nothing but a shocking example. A little grain of imagination leavens all his criticism. His admiration for the Greeks is not pretence; he knows the difference between Euripides and Seneca, and his description of the character of Phædra, as represented by the Greek and by the Latin tragic poet, is sensible. None of his critical writing is hard to read. His plan of a tragedy of "The Invincible Armado," on the classical model, to compete with the *Persians* of Æschylus, will hold its own, though nothing but an outline, against the more romantic tragedy of "Tilburina." The plan of the fourth act—the old dames of the Court "alarming our gentlemen with new apprehensions"—is not less pleasant to meditate upon than the inventions of Sheridan's *Tragedy Rehearsed.* Dennis, in his remarks on Rymer, took this seriously, but Rymer is not quite free from malice in his commendation of his classical play. —KER, W. P., 1894, *English Prose, ed. Craik, vol. III, p. 292.*

Matthew Henry

1662-1714.

Born at Broad Oak, Flintshire, Wales, Oct. 18, 1662: died at Nantwich, England, June 22, 1714. An English biblical commentator, son of Philip Henry. He became a nonconformist minister at Chester in 1687, and in 1712 removed to Hackney. His chief work is the "Exposition of the Old and New Testament" (1708-10). He also wrote "A Method for Prayer" (1710), etc.—SMITH, BENJAMIN E., 1894–97, *The Century Cyclopædia of Names, p. 495.*

GENERAL

Mr. Henry's admirable "Commentary on the Scriptures," which hath been blessed to the instruction and edification of hundreds of ministers, and thousands of Christians, for more than a century, still maintains its reputation above most, if not all, other commentaries.—BURNHAM, RICHARD, 1753–1820, *Pious Memorials.*

M. Henry's work has long enjoyed a high and deserved reputation. The work is distinguished, not for the depth of its learning or the originality of its views, but for the sound practical piety and large measure of good sense which it discovers. The author was well acquainted with the character and ways of God, and profoundly versant in the science of human nature; so that from his own experience he very often instructs and edifies his readers. He often leaves difficulties unremoved and even unnoticed; and there is a peculiar quaintness in the turn of many of his remarks, which renders his work somewhat repulsive to persons of fastidious taste; but few books of such extent on the Bible contain so much writing to the purpose, or are so well fitted to promote the general good of men.—ORME, WILLIAM, 1824, *Bibliotheca Biblica.*

"I have often read portions of Henry's 'Commentary,' and consulted it; but I have now begun with the first chapter of Genesis, and I mean to read the work through regularly. I have set myself, sir, two chapters every morning, and I anticipate it as a feast. This is the way to read Matthew Henry, sir. I discover new beauties in him every day, that are not obvious when reading detached parts.

I would advise you to adopt the same method, sir; you will be quite delighted with it. I have found that the most pious persons of my acquaintance, in the latter period of their lives, have been great readers of Henry. There must be something next to inspiration in him, sir; for as face answers to face, so does the heart of one Christian to another." I asked his opinion of Scott's Commentary. "Oh, it is a good work, sir, but it is not to be compared to Henry; there is not that unction of spirit that there is in Henry."—HALL, ROBERT, 1831, *Reminiscences, ed. Green.*

This work has now been before the Christian community for more than a hundred years, and has, from its first publication, been so well received, and is so generally approved, that all recommendation of the work seems now superfluous. . . . Many other valuable commentaries, it is true, have been given to the public since this work was first edited, and have deservedly gained for themselves a high estimation and extensive circulation. But it may be safely said that Henry's "Exposition of the Bible" has not been superseded by any of these publications, and, in those points in which its peculiar excellence consists, remains unrivalled. For some particular purposes, and in some particular respects, other commentaries may be preferable; but, taking it as a whole, and as adapted to every class of readers, this "Commentary" may be said to combine more excellences than any work of the kind which was ever written in any language. It may be more necessary for the unlearned to read such works as this, than for the learned; yet I am persuaded that there is no man living, however learned, but might derive much practical instruction from Henry's "Exposition of the Bible"; and if ministers of the gospel would spend much time in perusing this work, it would manifest itself by the richness and spirituality of their sermons and lectures.—ALEXANDER, ARCHIBALD, 1833, *Henry's Commentary on the Old and New Testament, Preface.*

The "Commentary" of Matthew Henry has for above a century been highly prized by Christians of all denominations; nor has any subsequent one rendered it less valuable, or less desirable in every Christian library. With such views of the virtue and excellence of this work, views which the writer has long entertained, and some sense of the benefit which he trusts that he has personally derived from it for many years, he has great pleasure in making these introductory remarks. . . . Very practical and edifying, lively, sound and devotional.—BICKERSTETH, EDWARD, 1844, *The Christian Student.*

Bishop Atterbury's controversial eloquence is forgotten; while, without eloquence, and with no distinguished power of thought, a devout spirit and doctrinal accuracy have preserved the works of Matthew Henry.—SPALDING, WILLIAM, 1852–82, *A History of English Literature, p.* 319.

Whose "Commentary" formed the "daily reading," of Robert Hall and Thomas Chalmers, and is remarkable alike for the copiousness and pious ingenuity of its thoughts, and for the strength and simplicity of its language.—ANGUS, JOSEPH, 1865, *The Handbook of English Literature, p.* 448.

The author [in his "Exposition"] betrays a remarkable fertility of practical suggestion; and, although the work at first sight seems diffuse, it will be found on closer study to contain rich stores of tersely spoken truths, which hold the attention by their quaint freshness and aptness, and feed the spiritual life by their scriptural unction. It has no critical value. —SCHAFF-HERZOG, eds., 1883, *Encyclopædia of Religious Knowledge, vol.* II, *p.* 973.

Henry's "Exposition of the Old and New Testament," which for practical uses has not been superseded, was begun in November 1704. The first volume was published in 1708, fol.; that and four other volumes, bringing his labours to the end of the gospels, appeared in a uniform edition in 1710, fol. Before his death he completed the Acts for an unpublished sixth volume. After his death the Epistles and Revelation were prepared by thirteen nonconformist divines, whose names are given by John Evans (1767–1827) in the "Protestant Dissenters' Magazine," 1797, p. 472, from a memorandum by Isaac Watts. The complete edition of 1811, 4to, 6 vols., edited by George Burder and John Hughes, has additional matter from Henry's manuscripts. Henry's "Exposition" has often been abridged.— GORDON, ALEXANDER, 1891, *Dictionary of National Biography, vol.* XXVI, *p.* 124.

Charles Montagu

Earl of Halifax

1661-1715.

Poet and statesman, a grandson of the Parliamentary general, the Earl of Manchester, was born at Horton, Northamptonshire, 16th April 1661, and from Westminster passed in 1679 to Trinity College, Cambridge. His most notable poetical achievement was a parody on Dryden's "Hind and Panther," entitled "The Town and Country Mouse" (1687), of which he was joint-author with Matthew Prior. M. P. for Maldon (1688) and a lord of the treasury (1692), he in that year proposed to raise a million sterling by way of loan—so the National Debt was established. In 1694 money was again wanted, and Montagu supplied it by originating the Bank of England, as proposed by William Paterson three years earlier. For this service Montagu was appointed Chancellor of the Exchequer. His next work was the recoinage in 1695, appointing his friend Newton warden of the Mint, and raising a tax on windows to pay the expense; and now he first introduced exchequer bills. In 1697 he became premier, but his arrogance and vanity soon made him unpopular, and on the Tories coming into power in 1699 he was obliged to accept the auditorship of the exchequer and withdraw from the Commons as Baron Halifax. He was impeached for breach of trust in 1701, and again in 1703, but the proceedings fell to the ground. He strongly supported the union with Scotland and the Hanoverian succession. On the queen's death he was appointed a member of the council of regency, and on George I.'s arrival became an earl and prime-minister. He died 19th May 1715.—PATRICK AND GROOME, eds., 1897, *Chambers's Biographical Dictionary*, p. 452.

PERSONAL

Last rose *Bathillo*, deck'd with borrow'd bays,
Renown'd for others' projects, others' lays;
A gay, pragmatical, pretending tool,
Opinionately wise, and pertly dull.
A demy-statesman, talkative and loud,
Hot without courage, without merit proud,
A leader fit for the unthinking crowd.
—SHIPPEN, WILLIAM, ? 1704, *Faction Displayed*.

A certain minister, renowned for wit, and called a poet by all the poets (for fathering a copy of verses, by whomever wrote); the Mecenas of the age, an honour acquired with little expense, when few or none are found to contest it with him.—MANLEY, MRS. DE LA RIVIÈRE, 1709, *The New Atalantis, Second ed., vol. I, p. 183.*

I agree with you, Lord Halifax has no other principle but his ambition; so that he would put all in distraction rather than not gain his point.—MARLBOROUGH, DUKE OF, 1709, *Letter to the Duchess of Marlborough, Feb.* 7.

Your patronage had produced those arts, which before shunned the commerce of the world, into the service of life; and it is to you we owe, that the man of wit has turned himself to be a man of business. . . . Your own studies have been diverted from being the highest ornament, to the highest use to mankind; and the

capacities which would have rendered you the greatest poet of your age, have to the advantage of Great Britain been employed in pursuits which have made you the most able and unbiased patriot.—STEELE, RICHARD, 1711, *The Tatler, Dedication, vol.* IV.

Thus Congreve spent in writing plays
And one poor office half his days;
While Montague, who claim'd the station
To be Mæcenas of the nation,
For poets open table kept,
But ne'er consider'd where they slept:
Himself as rich as fifty Jews,
Was easy though they wanted shoes.
—SWIFT, JONATHAN, 1729, *A Libel on the Rev. Dr. Delany, and his Excellency John Lord Carteret.*

Proud as Apollo on his forked hill
Sat full-blown *Bufo*, puff'd by every quill;
Fed with soft Dedication all day long,
Horace and he went hand in hand in song.
—POPE, ALEXANDER, 1735, *Epistle to Dr. Arbuthnot.*

The brilliancy of Montague's genius was such, that his works as a poet had been read, *admired*, and patronised, by Dorset. Cambridge left her accustomed precision to honour him: in the senate he commanded the utmost attention; and in the palace he was trusted, promoted, and ennobled. He was the active principle that moved the council, the exchequer, and the treasury. His mind pervaded every department of the state. The king valued him as his chief support; queen Anne's prejudices gave way to applause; and George I. created him earl of Halifax, and gave him the garter. This nobleman, whom the Commons had recommended as "deserving William's favour," persecuted him afterwards with a virulence that disgraced them;—a strange retribution this for restoring the credit of the national bank; for completing a new coinage of the silver money in two years, which was judged *impossible;* for his first proposing and affecting the union of the British kingdoms; and his earnestly promoting the settlement of the crown in the Brunswick line.—NOBLE, MARK, 1806, *A Biographical History of England, vol.* I, *p.* 251.

Those who have written on the life of Newton have touched with the utmost reserve upon the connexion which existed between his half-niece Catherine Barton, and his friend Charles Montague, who died Earl of Halifax. They seem as if they were afraid that, by going fairly into the matter, they should find something they would rather not tell. The consequence is, that when a writer at home or abroad, Voltaire or another, hints with a sneer that a pretty niece had more to do with Newton's appointment to the Mint than the theory of gravitation, those who would like to know as much as can be known of the whole truth find nothing in any attainable biography except either total silence or a very awkward and hesitating account of half something.—DE MORGAN, AUGUSTUS, 1853, *Lord Halifax and Mrs. Catherine Barton, Notes and Queries, First Series, vol.* 8, *p.* 429.

My own belief is that Mrs. Barton was neither Halifax's mistress nor his wife, and that the *liaison* between them was of the same sort with that between Congreve and Mrs. Bracegirdle, with that between Swift and Stella, and that between Pope and Martha Blount, with that between Cowper and Mrs. Unwin.—MACAULAY, THOMAS BABINGTON, 1853, *Letter to Augustus De Morgan, Newton: His Friend: and His Niece, p.* 70.

GENERAL

The noble Montagu remains unnamed,
For wit, for humour, and for judgment famed;
To Dorset he directs his artful muse,
In numbers such as Dorset's self might use.
How negligently graceful he unreins
His verse, and writes in loose, familiar strains!
—ADDISON, JOSEPH, 1694, *An Account of the Greatest English Poets.*

For ev'ry Grace of every Muse is thine;
In thee their various Fires united shine,
Darling of Phœbus and the tuneful Nine!
—CONGREVE, WILLIAM, 1698, *The Birth of the Muse.*

Considered as a poet his lordship makes a less considerable figure than the earl of Dorset: there is a languor in his verses which seems to indicate that he was not born with a poetical genius. That he was a lover of the Muses there is not the least doubt, as we find him patronizing the poets so warmly; but there is some difference between a propensity to poetry and a power of excelling in it.—CIBBER, THEOPHILUS, 1753, *Lives of the Poets vol.* III.

Many a blandishment was practised upon Halifax, which he would never have known, had he no other attractions than those of his poetry, of which a short time has withered the beauties. It would now be esteemed no honour, by a contributor to the monthly bundles of verses, to be told, that, in strains either familiar or solemn, he sings like Montague.—JOHNSON, SAMUEL, 1779–81, *Halifax, Lives of the English Poets.*

Of him, as of several of his contemporaries, especially of Mulgrave and of Sprat, it may be said that his fame has suffered from the folly of those editors who, down to our own time, have persisted in reprinting his rhymes among the works of the British poets. There is not a year in which hundreds of verses as good as any that he ever wrote, are not sent in for the Newdigate prize at Oxford, and for the Chancellor's medal at Cambridge. His mind had indeed great quickness and vigour, but not that kind of quickness and vigour which produces great dramas or odes: and it is most unjust to him that his "Man of Honour" and his "Epistle on the Battle of the Boyne" should be placed side by side with "Comus" and "Alexander's Feast." Other eminent statesmen and orators, Walpole, Pulteney, Chatham, Fox, wrote poetry not better than his. But fortunately for them, their metrical compositions were never thought worthy to be admitted into any collection of our national classics.—MACAULAY, THOMAS BABINGTON, 1843, *Charles Montague, Critical and Historical Essays.*

Nahum Tate

1652-1715.

Nahum Tate, joint author with Dryden of the Second Part of "Absalom and Achitophel," was born in Dublin, in 1652, the son of Dr. Faithful Tate, and educated at Trinity College there. He came to London, published in 1677 a volume of "Poems," and between that date and 1682 had produced the tragedies of "Brutus and Alba" and "The Loyal General; Richard II.; or, the Sicilian Usurper;" an altered version of Shakespeare's "King Lear;" and an application of "Coriolanus" to court politics of the day, as "The Ingratitude of a Comomnwealth; or, The Fall of Coriolanus." Tate wrote three other plays before the Revolution. It was not till 1696 that he produced, with Dr. Nicholas Brady (born 1659, died 1726), also an Irishman, and then chaplain to William III., a "New Version of the Psalms of David;" and in 1707 one more tragedy of his was acted, "Injured Love; or, The Cruel Husband." In 1692, Tate became poet-laureate, and remained laureate during the rest of Dryden's life, and throughout Queen Anne's reign.—MORLEY, HENRY, 1879, *A Manual of English Literature, ed. Tyler, p.* 453.

PERSONAL

These are to certify that I have sworn and admitted Nahum Tate into ye place and quality of Poet Laureate to Her Majesty in ordinary, to have, hold, and exercise and enjoy the said place, together with all rights, profits, privileges, and advantages thereunto belonging, in as full and ample manner as any Poet Laureate hath formerly held, and of right ought to have held and enjoyed the same. Given under my hand this 24th day of December, in the first year of her Majesty's reign.—JERSEY, 1702, *Letters Patent.*

Tate's morality was so obstrusive that it gave rise to many bitter satires against him. From choice he mingled little with the wits and dramatists of the time, though with a few chosen companions he was free and jovial. In general society he was, however, taciturn and reserved, showing little trace of brilliancy of mind or ease of manner. His portrait is not extant. He is said to have had a somewhat refined face, with a downcast look, and that in many respects he realised in his personal appearance the drowsy characteristics of his muse.—WEST, KENYON, 1895, *The Laureates of England, p.* 63.

KING LEAR

Though Tate's alterations are, in many places, mean and unworthy to be placed so near the composition of the best dramatic author, it must be confessed, that, in the conduct of some scenes, whether contrived by himself or hinted to him by his friend Dryden, he is not unhappy.— DAVIES, THOMAS, 1783, *Dramatic Miscellanies, vol.* II, *p.* 326.

Tate has put his hook in the nostrils of this Leviathan, for Garrick and his followers, the showmen of the scene, to draw the mighty beast about more easily. A happy ending!—as if the living martyrdom that Lear had gone through,—the flaying of his feelings alive, did not make a fair dismissal from the stage of life the only decorous thing for him. If he is to live and be happy after, if he could sustain this world's burden after, why all this pudder and preparation,—why torment us with all this unnecessary sympathy? As if the childish pleasure of getting his gilt robes and sceptre again could tempt him to act over again his misused station,— as if at his years, and with this experience, anything was left but to die.— LAMB, CHARLES, 1810? *On the Tragedies of Shakespeare.*

At the commencement of the eighteenth century the eclipse was total. In 1707, one called Nahum Tate published a "King Lear," warning his readers "that he had borrowed the idea of it from a play which he had read by chance, the work of some nameless author." This "nameless author" was Shakespeare.—HUGO, VICTOR, 1864, *William Shakespeare, tr. Baillot, p.* 25.

GENERAL

There is another, called Nahum Tate, who is ready to make oath, that he has caused many reams of verse to be published, whereof both himself and his bookseller (if lawfully required) can still produce authentic copies; and therefore wonders, why the world is pleased to make such a secret of it.—SWIFT, JONATHAN, 1704, *A Tale of a Tub, Dedication.*

In the year 1680, Mr. Dryden undertook the poem of "Absalom and Achitophel," upon the desire of King Charles II. The performance was applauded by every one; and several persons pressing him to write a second part, he, upon declining it himself, spoke to Mr. Tate to write one, and gave him his advise in the direction of it; and that part beginning,

"Next these, a troop of busy spirits press,"

and ending

"To talk like Doeg, and to write like thee,"

containing near two hundred verses, were entirely Mr. Dryden's composition, besides some touches in other places.—TONSON, JACOB, 1716, *ed., Absalom and Achitophel, Preface.*

The Bard whom pilfer'd Pastorals renown,
Who turns a Persian tale for half-a-crown,
Just writes to make his barrenness appear,
And strains, from hard-bound brains, eight
  lines a year;
He who, still wanting, though he lives on
  theft,
Steals much, spends little, yet has nothing
  left:
And He who, now to sense, now nonsense
  leaning,
Means not, but blunders round about mean-
  ing;
And He, whose fustian's so sublimely bad,
It is not Poetry, but prose run mad.
All these, my modest satire, bade translate,
And own'd that nine such Poets made a *Tate.*
—POPE, ALEXANDER, 1735, *Epistle to Dr. Arbuthnot.*

He was a man of learning, courteous, and candid, but was thought to possess no great genius, as being deficient in what is its first characteristic, namely, invention.—CIBBER, THEOPHILUS, 1753, *Lives of the Poets, vol. III, p. 258.*

One of those second-rate bards, who, by dint of pleonasm and expletive, can find smooth lines if any one will supply them with ideas.—SCOTT, SIR WALTER, 1808–21, *Life of Dryden, p. 288.*

There is an English word-joiner—author we will not call him—who has had the temerity to accomplish two things, either of which would have been enough to have conferred upon him a bad immortality. Nahum Tate has succeeded, to an extent which defies all competition, in degrading the Psalms of David and the Lear of Shakspere to the condition of being tolerated, and perhaps even admired, by the most

dull, gross, and anti-poetical capacity. These were not easy tasks; but Nahum Tate has enjoyed more than a century of honour for his labours; and his new versions of the Psalms are still sung on (like the shepherd in Arcadia piped) as if they would never be old, and his Lear was ever the Lear of the playhouse, until Mr. Macready ventured upon a modern heresy in favour of Shakspere.—KNIGHT, CHARLES, 1849, *Studies of Shakspere.*

This poor grub of literature. . . . Mr. Nahum Tate is not of a class of whom it can be safe to say that they are "well known:" they and their desperate tricks are essentially obscure, and good reason he has to exult in the felicity of such obscurity; for else this same vilest of travesties, Mr. Nahum's "Lear," would consecrate his name to everlasting scorn. For himself, he belonged to the age of Dryden rather than of Pope: he "flourished," if we can use such a phrase of one who was always withering, about the era of the Revolution; and his "Lear," we believe, was arranged in the year 1682. But the family to which he belongs is abundantly recorded in the "Dunciad," and his own name will be found amongst its catalogues of heroes.—DE QUINCEY, THOMAS, 1847? *Biographical Essays, pp.* 6, 7.

The greatest merit of Tate's official odes is their brevity. . . . A Laureate inferior to many of the race, though very far from being the worst poet, and by no means a vicious one.—HAMILTON, WALTER, 1879, *The Poets Laureate of England, pp.* 125, 130.

A personal study of Tate's work results in disappointment. It is wholly lacking in imagination, has no depth of insight or feeling, except as it shows depth in the borrowed thought with which it is pervaded; yet it contains often wit and fancy, and has much beauty of phrase and of versification. His translations from Juvenal and Ovid have many graces of style, and his own poem called "Panacea" has much artistic excellence. The subject is uninteresting to readers now, concerned as it is with the charms of tea, but in Tate's time tea was a luxury which was very much prized. Tate's great defect is that he had not only little originality of thought, but that his metaphors and turns of expression are borrowed right and left. As Pope said:

"He steals much, spends little, yet has nothing left."

Tate's merit is, that, in an age which enjoyed the coarseness of Dryden and Shadwell, he lived a moral and upright life, and reflected that morality in his later poetry. When first he began to write he catered to the taste of the age by the usual coarse allusions in his plays. But as the profligacy of the Restoration gradually grew less, and virtue and religion began once more to be considered of some importance, Tate of course had the good sense to forecast the future and change his methods. And therefore his later poems are not disfigured by the impurity unhappily so prevalent.—WEST, KENYON, 1895, *The Laureates of England*, p. 62.

Several hymns are attributed to him, and some of these are so good that they cover a multitude of shortcomings. For those well-known lines on the lips of almost every boy and girl at Christmastide, "While shepherds watched their flocks by night," we thank him.—WRIGHT, J. C., 1896, *The Poets Laureate*, p. 24.

Gilbert Burnet
1643–1715

Born, in Edinburgh, 18 Sept. 1643. To Marischal Coll., Aberdeen, 1653; M. A., 1657. Studied theology. Probationer for Presbyterian Ministry, 1661. Visited English Universities, 1663. Travelled in Holland and France, 1664; spent some time at Court on return. F.R.S., 1664. Inducted to living of Saltoun, 29 Jan. 1665. Clerk of Presbytery of Haddington, 9 May 1667. Prof. of Divinity, Glasgow Univ., 1669; resigned living of Saltoun. To London, 1671. Returned to Glasgow and married Lady Margaret Kennedy, 1672. To London, 1673. Chaplain to King, 1673–74. Chaplain to Rolls Chapel, 1675–84. In France, Sept. to Oct., 1683. Wife died, 1684. In France, Italy, and Holland, 1685–87. In favour at Court of William of Orange. Married Mary Scott, 25 May 1687. Returned to England with William of Orange, Nov. 1687. Bishop of Salisbury, 1688. Second wife died, 1698; married Mrs. Elizabeth Berkeley same year. Appointed Governor to Duke of Gloucester, 1698. Active part in ecclesiastical politics. Died, in London, 7 March, 1715; buried in St. James's Church, Clerkenwell. *Works:* [A complete list in 1823 edn. of his "History of his Own Times."] Chief Works: "Discourse on Sir Robert Fletcher of Saltoun," 1665; "Conference between a Conformist and a Nonconformist," 1669; "Vindication of the Authority . . . of Church and State of Scotland," 1673; "The Mystery of Iniquity Unveiled," 1673; "Rome's Glory," 1673; "Memories of . . . James and William, Dukes of Hamilton," 1852; "History of the Reformation," vol. i., 1679; vol. ii., 1681; vol. iii., 1714; "Some Passages in the Life and Death of John Wilmot, Earl of Rochester," 1680; "News from France," 1682; "Life and Death of Sir Matthew Hale," 1682; "Life of Bishop Bedell," 1685; "Essay on the Memory of Queen Mary," 1695; "Exposition of the Thirty-nine Articles," 1699; "A Collection of Tracts and Discourses," 1704; "Exposition of the Church Catechism," 1710; "Speech on the Impeachment of Sacheverell," 1710. *Posthumous:* "History of his Own Times," with *life* (2 vols.), 1723–34.—SHARP, R. FARQUHARSON, 1897, *A Dictionary of English Authors*, p. 40.

PERSONAL

A portly prince, and goodly to the sight,
He seemed a son of Anak for his height;
Like those whom stature did to crowns prefer;
Black-browed and bluff, like Homer's Jupiter;
Broad-backed and brawny-built for love's delight,
A prophet formed to make a female proselyte.
A theologue more by need than genial bent;
By breeding sharp, by nature confident,
Interest in all his actions was discerned;
More learned than honest, more a wit than learned;
Or forced by fear or by his profit led,
Or both conjoined, his native clime he fled;
But brought the virtues of his heaven along;
A fair behaviour, and a fluent tongue.
—DRYDEN, JOHN, 1687, *The Hind and the Panther.*

Dr. Burnet is like all men who are above the ordinary level, seldom spoken of in a mean—he must either be railed at or admired. He has a swiftness of imagination that no other comes up to; and, as our nature hardly allows us to have enough of anything without having too much, he cannot at all times so hold in his thoughts but that at some time they may run away with him, as it is hard for a vessel that is brimful when in motion not to run over; and therefore, the variety of matter that he ever carries about him may throw out more than an unkind critic would allow of. His first thoughts may sometimes require more digestion, not from a defect in his judgment, but from the abundance of his fancy, which furnishes too fast for him. His friends love him too well to see small faults, or, if they do, think that his greater talents give him a privilege of straying from the strict rules of caution, and exempt him from the ordinary rules of censure. He produces so fast, that what is well in his writings calls for admiration, and what is incorrect deserves an excuse. He may in some things require grains of allowance which those only can deny him who are unknown or unjust to him. He is not quicker in discerning other men's faults than he is in forgiving them; so ready, or rather glad, to acknowledge his own, that from blemishes they become ornaments.—HALIFAX, MARQUIS OF, c 1710, *Character of Burnet.*

During the five years he remained at Saltoun, he preached twice every Sunday, and once more on one of the weekdays; he catechised three times a week, so as to examine every parishioner, old or young, thrice over in the compass of a year; he went round his parish, from house to house, instructing, reproving, or comforting them, as occasion required; those that were sick, he visited twice a day; he administered the sacrament four times a year, and personally instructed all such as gave notice they intended to receive it; all that remained above his own necessary subsistence (in which he was very frugal), he gave away in charity.—BURNET, THOMAS, 1724–34, *ed., History of My Own Time, by Gilbert Burnet, Life.*

Bishop Burnet was a man of the most extensive knowledge I ever met with; had read and seen a great deal, with a prodigious memory, and a very indifferent judgment: he was extremely partial, and readily took every thing for granted that he heard to the prejudice of those he did not like: which made him pass for a man of less truth than he really was. I do not think he designedly published any thing he believed to be false. He had a boisterous vehement manner of pressing himself, which often made him ridiculous, especially in the house of lords, when what he said would not have been thought so, delivered in a lower voice, and a calmer behaviour. His vast knowledge occasioned his frequent rambling from the point he was speaking to, which ran him into discourses of so universal a nature, that there was no end to be expected but from a failure of his strength and spirits, of both which he had a larger share than most men; which were accompanied with a most invincible assurance.—DARTMOUTH, EARL, 1734? *Burnet's History of My Own Time, note.*

With whose character and conduct we should have been perhaps better acquainted had he spoken less of them himself.—LODGE, EDMUND, 1821–34, *Portraits of Illustrious Personages of Great Britain, vol. VII, p. 37.*

The fame of Burnet has been attacked with singular malice and pertinacity. The attack began early in his life, and is still carried on with undiminished vigour, though he has now been more than a century and a quarter in his grave. He is, indeed, as fair a mark as factious animosity and petulant wit could desire. The faults of his understanding and temper lie on the surface, and cannot be missed. They were not the faults which are ordinarily considered as belonging to his country. Alone among the many Scotchmen who have raised themselves to distinction and prosperity in England, he had that character which satirists, novelists, and dramatists, have agreed to ascribe to Irish adventurers. His high animal spirits, his boastfulness, his undissembled vanity, his propensity to blunder, his provoking indiscretion, his unabashed audacity, afforded inexhaustible subjects of ridicule to the Tories. Nor did his enemies omit to compliment him, sometimes with more pleasantry than delicacy, on the breadth of his shoulders, the thickness of his calves, and his success in matrimonial projects on amorous and opulent widows. Yet Burnet, though open in many respects to ridicule, and even to serious censure, was no contemptible man.—MACAULAY,

THOMAS BABINGTON, 1849 *History of England, ch.* vii.

An able and well-read, but reckless and unscrupulous man, Burnet has been more violently assailed than most men, and his statements as to the history of his times have been often impugned. Certainly he cannot be acquitted of inaccuracy, and probably not of wilful misstatement, but he had many fine traits in his character, and must be allowed to have proved himself useful not only as a politician, but also, and much more markedly, as a bishop.—PERRY, GEORGE G., 1864, *History of the Church of England, vol.* III, *p.* 14.

No English bishop exhibited a greater activity in combating the evil of pluralities; in watching over the character and education of his clergy; in making himself intimately acquainted with the wants and circumstances of the parishes under his care, than this great scholar and active politician.—LECKY, WILLIAM EDWARD HARTPOLE, 1877, *History of England in the Eighteenth Century, vol.* I, *p.* 90.

The historical interest of Burnet's character lies in the fact that from his entrance upon public life as a mere boy he was the consistent representative of broad church views both in politics and doctrine. Except in the two or three instances mentioned, his voice was ever for toleration, and his practice in his diocese was still more emphatically so. He was a man perfectly healthy and robust in body and in mind; a meddler, and yet no intriguer; a lover of secrets, which he was incapable of keeping; a vigorous polemist, but without either spite or guile; whatever the heart conceived the tongue seemed compelled to utter or the pen to write.—AIRY, OSMUND, 1886, *Dictionary of National Biography, vol.* VII, *p.* 404.

HISTORY OF THE REFORMATION
1679–1714

Burnet wrote the "History of the English Reformation" in a partial, caustic, but interesting manner: his greatest honour consists in having been refuted by Bossuet. Burnet was a blunderer and a factious man, of a spirit akin to that of the Frondeurs: neither the revolutionary candour of Whitelocke, nor the republican enthusiasm of Ludlow, is to be found in his memoirs.—CHATEAUBRIAND, FRANÇOIS RENÉ, VICOMTE DE, 1837, *Sketches of English Literature, vol.* II, *p.* 196.

Written in a better style than those, who know Burnet by his later and more negligent work, are apt to conceive, and which has the signal merit of having been the first in English, as far as I remember, which is fortified by a large appendix of documents.—HALLAM, HENRY, 1837–39, *Introduction to the Literature of Europe, pt.* iv, *ch.* viii, *par.* 49.

No cautions need be suggested before the perusal of the laborious work of this impartial and liberal churchman, an ornament to his order, and who deserved the name of Christian.—SMYTH, WILLIAM, 1840, *Lectures on Modern History.*

One of the most thoroughly digested works of the century.—BOTTA, ANNE C. LYNCH, 1860, *Hand-Book of Universal Literature, p.* 500.

HISTORY OF MY OWN TIME

Learning is sunk so very low, that I am most certainly inform'd, that nothing is now hardly read but Burnett's romance or libel, call'd by him "The History of his Own Times." 'Tis read by men, women, and children. Indeed it is the common table-book for ladies as well as gentlemen, especially such as are friends to the revolution scheme. . . . Burnett must have been the greatest of villains, in writing such libells or romances, in order to poison present and future ages. For tho' honest wise men will rightly judge of such performances, and be by no means byass'd by them, yet they bear no proportion to others, who will be sway'd by such books, and will greedily imbibe the principles in them, and instill them in their children and dependents.—HEARNE, THOMAS, 1733–34, *Reliquiæ Hearnianæ ed. Bliss, Mar.* 19, *April* 9, *vol.* III, *pp.* 125, 129.

I would willingly live to give that rascal the lie in half his history.—PETERBOROUGH, LORD, 1734–36, *Spence's Anecdotes, ed. Singer, p.* 117.

This author is, in most particulars, the worst qualified for an historian that ever I met with. His style is rough, full of improprieties, in expressions often Scotch, and often such as are used by the meanest people. He discovers a great scarcity of words and phrases, by repeating the same several hundred times, for want of capacity to vary them. His observations are mean and trite, and very often false. His Secret History is generally made up of coffeehouse scandals, or at best from reports at the third, fourth, or fifth hand. . . . He is the most partial of all writers that ever pretended so much to impartiality; and yet I, who knew him well, am convinced that he is as impartial as he could possibly find in his heart; I am sure more than I ever expected from him; particularly in his accounts of the Papist and fanatic plots. This work may more properly be called A History of Scotland during the Author's Time, with some Digressions relating to England, rather than deserve the title he gives it; for I believe two-thirds of it relates only to that beggarly nation, and their insignificant brangles and factions. . . . After all, he was a man of generosity and good-nature, and very communicative; but, in his ten last years, was absolutely party-mad, and fancied he saw Popery under every bush. He has told me many passages not mentioned in his history, and many that are, but with several circumstances suppressed or altered. He never gives a good character without one essential point, that the person was tender to dissenters, and thought many things in the church ought to be amended.—SWIFT, JONATHAN, 1734? *Short Remarks on Bishop Burnet's History, Works, vol.* XII, *pp.* 187, 188, 189.

Thus piously ends the most partial, malicious heap of scandal and misrepresentation, that was ever collected, for the laudable design of giving a false impression of persons and things to all future ages.—DARTMOUTH, EARL, 1734? *Burnet's History of my Own Time, note.*

Burnet's "History of his Own Times" is very entertaining. The style, indeed, is mere chit-chat. I do not believe that Burnet intentionally lied; but he was so much prejudiced, that he took no pains to find out the truth. He was like a man who resolves to regulate his time by a certain watch; but will not inquire whether the watch is right or not.—JOHNSON, SAMUEL, 1773, *Life by Boswell.*

Did you ever read that garrulous, pleasant history? He tells his story like an old man past political service, bragging to his sons on winter evenings of the part he took in public transactions, when his "old cap was new." Full of scandal, which all true history is. No palliatives; but all the stark wickedness, that actually gives the *momentum* to national actors.

Quite the prattle of age, and outlived importance. Truth and sincerity staring out upon you perpetually in *alto relievo.* Himself a party man—he makes you a party man. None of the cursed philosophical Humeian indifference, so cold, and unnatural, and inhuman! None of the cursed Gibbonian fine writing, so fine and composite! None of Dr. Robertson's periods with three members. None of Mr. Roscoe's sage remarks, all so apposite, and coming in so clever, lest the reader should have had the trouble of drawing an inference. Burnet's good old prattle I can bring present to my mind; I can make the revolution present to me: the French revolution, by a converse perversity in my nature, I fling as far *from* me.—LAMB, CHARLES, 1800, *Letters to Manning, ed. Fitzgerald, March* 1, *vol.* II, *p.* 174.

We are apt to mistake, or dissemble at least, even to ourselves, our true principles of action. Bishop Burnet professes to write his "History of his Own Time" for public ends, *pro bono publico.* This might be one inducement; but who sees not that the main motive for engaging in that work was a love of prate, a busy, meddling humour to pry into State secrets, and the vanity of disclosing the part which he had, or fancied he had, in them? He had sense and honesty; but was warped in his judgment of men and things, as most men are, by strong prejudices, and a heat of temper that sometimes looks fanatical. As a writer, he is not very respectable. A vague, general, indistinct expression, and a slovenly neglect of grammar make the reading of his works uninstructing and unpleasant. He neither informs us clearly and precisely, nor entertains us agreeably. He wrote too much and too hastily to write well.—HURD, RICHARD, 1808? *Commonplace Book, ed. Kilvert, p.* 243.

Arbuthnot, Swift and Pope directed their merciless satire against him; their satire is still read, but so is his history; and the history will continue to increase in estimation when the satire will be perused only by a few curious readers, and by them chiefly because it relates to so eminent a man. The personal faults and weaknesses of the historian were undisguised, he wore them *on his Sleeve, for daws to peck at;* but they were proofs rather of simplicity of character than of worldliness, and both in his life and writings the good predominated greatly.—SOUTHEY, ROBERT, 1823, *Burnet's History of his Own Time, Quarterly Review, vol.* 29, *p.* 170.

Burnet's "History of his own Times" is a truly valuable book. His credulity is great, but his simplicity is equally great; and he never deceives you for a moment. —COLERIDGE, SAMUEL TAYLOR, 1830, *Table Talk, ed. Ashe, June* 15, *p.* 98.

Whatever he reports himself to have heard or seen, the reader may be assured he really did hear or see. But we must receive his representations and conclusions with that caution which must ever be observed when we listen to the relation of a warm and busy partisan, whatever be his natural integrity and good sense. He is often censured, and sometimes corrected; but the fact seems to be, that, without his original, and certainly honest account, we should know little about the wants and affairs he professes to explain. Many of the writers who are not very willing to receive his assistance, would be totally at a loss without it.—SMYTH, WILLIAM, 1840, *Lectures on Modern History.*

Is gossiping and garrulous, but honest. No reader can doubt that the author might easily have been misled by his own prejudices and the misrepresentations of others. As little would it be denied by any one that this history is in the main a faithful picture of the men and scenes which it portrays.—PORTER, NOAH, 1870, *Books and Reading, p.* 184.

His words are generally well chosen, his illustrations appropriate, and his diction copious without being in any way extravagant; but his dry correctness is not made up for by fluent melody or by happy originality of combination. The great charms of his "History of my own Times" lie in the gossip from behind the scenes, and the skilful delineation of character. He had something of Boswell's faculty for noting characteristic incidents, besides the power of showing them briefly in a connected portraiture. None of our historians surpass, if any equal him, in this respect. When we compare his vivid delinations of the men of the Revolution with Macaulay's jumble of characteristic traits and high-flown moral commonplaces, we at once recognise the hand of a natural master of the art.—MINTO, WILLIAM, 1872-80, *Manual of English Prose Literature, p.* 338.

To literary style or to eloquence Burnet has no pretensions, nor is there even the slightest appearance of an attempt at style; his epithets are often clumsy, and his constructions ungainly. From this criticism, however, the most admirable "conclusion" must be excepted. This gives Burnet at his very best; the thoughts are matured and noble, and the diction is elevated and impressive. The whole work has been subject to the acrimonious criticism of Dartmouth and the pungent satire of Swift, to whom he was especially obnoxious, and who is no doubt the author of a satirical epitaph upon him (Hist. MSS. Comm. of the Rep. 468*b*); but while the former of these, who frequently accuses him of deliberate falsehood through party feeling (*e. g.* 6th Rep. 245 note), has now and again hit undoubted blots, the value of the "History of his own Time" as a candid narrative and an invaluable work of reference has continually risen as investigations into original materials have proceeded.—AIRY, OSMUND, 1886, *Dictionary of National Biography, vol.* VII, *p.* 404.

Whatever the subject in hand, a battle or a revolution, the character of a great statesman or the untimely death of a dear friend, Burnet's narrative jogs along at the same slow apathetic pace. The lack of eloquence is not compensated by clearness or method, for the arrangement is careless and the impression left on the reader is one of confusion. Still less is the uncouthness of the form compensated by the profundity of the thought.—MONTAGUE, F. C., 1894, *English Prose, ed. Craik, vol.* III, *p.* 319.

Burnet's "History of his Own Times" actually deserves the character which Clarendon incorrectly gives of his own; it is rather the material for history than history itself. This is not a consequence of crude treatment, for all is well arranged and lively, nor from the encumbrance of original documents, of which it is nearly destitute. It arises rather from the predominance of the autobiographic tone, much more marked than in Clarendon, though Clarendon also relates as an eyewitness, which almost brings the book down to the level of personal memoirs. It must nevertheless be classed with histories, and, if not one of the most dignified, it is undoubtedly one of the most entertaining.—GARNETT, RICHARD, 1895, *The Age of Dryden, p.* 179.

A Whig Clarendon, without the genius and the art.—SAINTSBURY, GEORGE, 1898, *A Short History of English Literature, p.* 523.

GENERAL

This mitred historian, who seems to know more personal secrets than any that ever writ before him.—CIBBER, COLLEY, 1739, *An Apology for His Life.*

When the nation was no longer agitated by domestic faction, literature was again cultivated and restored with unexampled success. During the civil wars, the classical learning for which the Scots were early distinguished, was absorbed and lost in the controversial vortex of religion and liberty; two names ever dear to mankind, with which the world has alternately been guided or deceived. From the restoration down to the union, the only author of eminence whom Scotland produced, was Burnet, the celebrated bishop of Sarum, who, when transplanted into England, was conspicuous as a political writer, an historian, and a divine. As an historian alone he descends to posterity; and his curious research into facts, the unaffected ease and simplicity of his dramatic narrative, his bold and glowing delineations of character, are far superior to every historical production of the period.—LAING, MALCOLM, 1800-4, *History of Scotland, vol.* IV, *p.* 389.

The Spirit of Party has touched with its plague-spot the character of Burnet; it has mildewed the page of a powerful mind, and tainted by its suspicions, its rumours, and its censures, his probity as a man. Can we forbear listening to all the vociferations which faction has thrown out? Do we not fear to trust ourselves amid the multiplicity of his facts? And when we are familiarised with the variety of his historical portraits, are we not startled when it is suggested that "they are tinged with his own passions and his own weaknesses?" Burnet has indeed made "his humble appeal to the Great God of Truth" that he has given it as fully as he could find it; and he has expressed his abhorrence of "a lie in history," so much greater a sin than a lie in common discourse, from its lasting and universal nature. Yet these hallowing protestations have not saved him! A cloud of witnesses, from different motives, have risen up to attaint his veracity and his candour; while all the Tory wits have ridiculed his style, impatiently inaccurate, and uncouthly negligent, and would sink his vigour and ardour, while they expose the meanness and poverty of his genius. Thus the literary and the moral character of no ordinary author have fallen a victim to party-feeling.—DISRAELI, ISAAC, 1814, *Political Criticism, Quarrels of Authors.*

With all his talents and integrity, was sometimes rather hasty than wise.—DIBDIN, THOMAS FROGNALL, 1824, *The Library Companion, p.* 114, *note.*

A writer, whose voluminous works, in several branches of literature, find numerous readers a hundred and thirty years after his death, may have great faults, but must also have had great merits; and Burnet had great merits, a fertile and vigorous mind, and a style far indeed removed from faultless purity, but always clear, often lively, and sometimes rising to solemn and fervid eloquence.—MACAULAY, THOMAS BABINGTON, 1843, *Bishop Burnet, Critical and Historical Essays.*

Burnet's writings are still popular. His "History of the Reformation" is in the hands of every student of religious progress. The lives of Hale and Wilmot are widely read. The "History of his Own Times" is a work of unusual interest. Even its great faults lend it a peculiar charm. The innocent vanity, the earnest sincerity, his fear and hatred of tory principles, his blind approval of those of the whigs, lend to Burnet's narrative a vigor and an artlessness that win the attention of the reader. His learning, upon any single topic, was not great, but his knowledge extended over a wide circle of subjects peculiarly well suited to the designs upon which he entered. His chief works had a political and controversial bearing. They were intended to serve the purposes of his party in the government or the church. They were written hastily, and seem rather to satisfy the understanding than the taste. It is a sufficient test, therefore, of his real ability, that notwithstanding many faults, they have attained a reputation with posterity that has not yet died out. . . . His histories are arranged without art, and with none of those philosophic views which indicate a reflective power. He thought justly but not deeply; he wrote clearly but too hastily; and the only trait that will give vitality to his writings is the constancy with which they defend freedom of thought in politics and religion.—LAWRENCE, EUGENE, 1855, *The Lives of the British Historians, vol.* I, *pp.* 304, 311.

Fox considered Burnet's style to be perfect. We were once talking of our historian's introducing occasionally the words of other writers into his work without marking them as quotations, when Fox said, "that the style of some of the authors so treated might need a little mending, but that Burnet's required none."—ROGERS, SAMUEL, 1855? *Table Talk.*

Bishop Burnet was very strenuous for the passing of the Comprehension Bill. Having been all his life connected with the Church, but able to look at her condition and wants with eyes of one who had looked at her from a distance, and had mingled much with men of other churches, he seemed to have discerned better than any other prelate, at least of his time, wherein her true policy lay. By no means a Puritan himself, in the strict sense of the word—too much a courtier for that—he yet saw the reasonableness of many of the objections of the Puritans, and marvelled at the obstinacy of many of his brethren to retain, simply out of pride, many of those things whose removal would have been every way a gain to the Church. But the good bishop in this matter was a man in advance of his age, and had to pay the penalty of failing to aid those whom he wished to serve, and not failing to incur the odium of his own friends.—CONDER, G. W., 1863, *Bishop Burnet and the English Revolution, Exeter Hall Lectures.*

Bishop Burnet was the greatest name in literature which Scotland produced in the seventeenth century. . . . He had a wide and ready command of language, and his historical method and style are equal, if not superior, to the best English writers of his day. His narrative is always methodical, and runs on naturally with much simplicity and ease. His chief historical works are still valuable as sources of information, and they are also more interesting reading than almost any writings on the same subjects of that generation or the succeeding one.—MACKINTOSH, JOHN, 1878–92, *The History of Civilisation in Scotland, vol.* III, *pp.* 364, 365.

Burnet's prejudices were at least those of a great mind and a benevolent heart, and his narrative is perhaps as fair as it was possible for a man of that generation to pen.—WYON, FREDERICK WILLIAM, 1875, *The History of Great Britain During the Reign of Queen Anne, vol.* II, *p.* 328.

Burnet had talent and merit, but was hot-headed, pragmatical, and injudicious.—SAINTSBURY, GEORGE, 1886, *Specimens of English Prose Style, p.* 119.

The active, fussy, good-natured Whig partisan.—TOUT, T. F., 1890, *History of England, pt.* iii, *p.* 4.

Thomas Burnet
1635 ?–1715

Master of the Charter-house, was born in 1635, and died in 1715. His chief work, originally in Latin, but rendered into English in 1691, was "The Sacred Theory of the Earth." Written in a day when geological science was yet unborn, it is, of course, full of error and wild speculation; but its eloquence and picturesque grandeur of style redeem it from oblivion. Burnet's other principal works were, "Archæologia Philosophica"—"On Christian Faith and Duties"—and "The State of the Dead and Reviving." He held some peculiar religious views, which debarred him from preferment in the Church.—COLLIER, WILLIAM FRANCIS, 1861, *A History of English Literature, p.* 248.

THE SACRED THEORY OF THE EARTH

We know the highest pleasure our minds are capable of enjoying with composure, when we read sublime thoughts communicated to us by men of great genius and eloquence. Such is the entertainment we meet with in the philosophic parts of Cicero's writings. Truth and good sense have there so charming a dress, that they could hardly be more agreeably represented with the addition of poetical fiction, and the power of numbers. This ancient author, and a modern one, have fallen into my hands within these few days; and the impressions they have left upon me, have at the present quite spoiled me for a merry fellow. The modern is that admirable writer the author of "the Theory of the Earth."—STEELE, RICHARD, 1711, *The Spectator, No. 146, Aug. 17.*

The novelty of his ideas, the perspicuity and elegance of his style recommended his works to the attention of the learned.—ENFIELD, WILLIAM, 1791, *History of Philosophy.*

They, who are indifferent to science, will find, in this "Theory of the Earth," a philosophical romance which delights by its admirable contrivances, its vigorous language, its noble descriptions of the stupendous objects of nature, its new views of ages and of scenes, which, though they never rolled over this habitable globe, easily might, and which if they did not, one cannot help wishing they had. All that is grand and awful in mundane commotions, in a deluge, or in a conflagration, of a world, is here described, by a pencil that puts the picture before the eyes. Those blissful ages, when storms and winds, and changes of seasons, were unknown in a globe of perpetual spring, when centuries were as years, and the human frame rejoiced in the purity and pellucidness of the atmosphere, which fed instead of corroding it, are here not only presented to the imagination, but almost proved to the understanding. And with a pen of equal power, are sketched the close of the world, the moment when the foundations of the earth sink, its joints and ligatures burst asunder, the mountains melt, and the sea is evaporated.—SOUTHERN, H., 1822, *Dr. Burnet's Theory of the Earth, Retrospective Review, vol. 6, p.* 133.

Apart from his mistakes, his works contain some things relating to the Scriptures worth reading; while the reader ought to be on his guard against their sophistry and skepticism.—ORME, WILLIAM, 1824, *Bibliotheca Biblica.*

As regards ingenuity of hypothesis and majesty of style, the work is beyond praise; as a philosophical system, it is beneath criticism.—ALLIBONE, S. AUSTIN, 1854–58, *Dictionary of English Literature, vol.* I, *p.* 298.

With his genius and imagination and consummate scholarship, he is a very different species of writer from his garrulous and mitred namesake: his English style is singularly flowing and harmonious, as well as perspicuous and animated, and rises on

fit occasions to much majesty and even splendor.—CRAIK, GEORGE L., 1861, *A Compendious History of English Literature, and of the English Language, vol.* II, *p.* 191.

His pictures of the devastation caused by the unbridled powers of Nature are grand and magnificent, and give him a claim to be placed among the most eloquent and poetical of prose-writers.—BACKUS, TRUMAN J., 1875, *ed., Shaw's New History of English Literature, p.* 195.

The secret of this effect upon his readers was that Burnet was enamoured of his own pre-geological dream. He thought himself inspired with superhuman insight. He believed that it was his divine mission to retrieve the scene of the Golden Age and to chronicle its ruin. He introduces his singular book with no mock-modesty; he confesses that what we are about to read has "more masculine beauty than any poem or romance." This mystical conviction carried away the learned alike and the unlearned, and even Burnet's fiercest opponents admitted, as Keill does, that "never was any book of philosophy written in a more lofty and plausible style." When a vision is presented to us with such gestures of rapture, in accents of such melodious solemnity, it seems almost rude to hint that it is mathematically and geologically absurd. Burnet was like the sorcerer in "Kubla Khan;" the reader had to flee from his enchantment, for "he on honey dew had fed, and drunk the milk of Paradise." He was so positive that he fell into an opposite extreme of danger, and was accused of scepticism because he would insist that things must have been as he dreamed they might have been.—GOSSE, EDMUND, 1894, *English Prose, ed. Craik, vol.* III, *p.* 246.

Burnet's mind was the mind of a poet; he had just enough science to misguide him, and more than enough learning to gloss over the vagaries of his science. He is quite as much at home in expounding the catastrophe of the future, the final conflagration, as the watery catastrophe of which he believes the traces to be visible everywhere around him. At the same time he has a strong affinity to the rationalizing divines, even more visible in his strictly theological writings, and would not for the world propound anything of whose reasonableness he has not first convinced himself. As a writer he stands high, combining the splendour and melody of a former age with the ease and lucidity of his own.—GARNETT, RICHARD, 1895, *The Age of Dryden, p.* 230.

Burnet's book is a fanciful explanation of cosmogony and cosmolysis, in which the Deluge is the great event in the past and the final conflagration the great event of the future. From this point of view it is chiefly interesting as an attempt to combine the nascent interest in physical science with the expiring tendency to imaginative romance. Something of the same mixture appears in the manner, for there are touches of the vernacularity, and even the meanness, which was invading style. But on the whole the older magnificence prevails, and Burnet has a just, though probably rather a vague, repute as commanding real eloquence of description, marred at times by a tawdriness which reminds us that we are in the half-century of Lee, not in that of Shakespeare, but showing in prose not a little of the redeeming splendour which Lee shows in verse. — SAINTSBURY, GEORGE, 1898, *A Short History of English Literature, p.* 518.

George Hickes

1642–1715

George Hickes, D. D., nonjuror and philologist, born at Newsham near Thirsk, June 20, 1642, in 1664 was elected fellow of Lincoln College, Oxford, and in 1666 took orders. In 1676 he became chaplain to the Duke of Lauderdale, in 1682 a royal chaplain, and in 1683 Dean of Worcester. Refusing to take the oaths to William III., he was deprived of his benefices. In 1693 he was sent with a list of the nonjuring clergy to the exiled king at St. Germains, and in 1694 was consecrated Bishop of Thetford. He published works in controversial and practical divinity, a "Thesaurus Linguarum Veterum Septentrionalium" (1705), and a grammar of Anglo-Saxon and Mœso-Gothic (1689). He died December 15, 1715.—PATRICK AND GROOME, *eds.*, 1897, *Chambers's Biographical Dictionary, p.* 489.

GENERAL

The book ["Institutiones"] discovers an accuracy in this language beyond the attainments of any that had gone before him in that study, and will be of most necessary use to such as shall apply themselves to the right understanding of the ancient history and laws of this kingdom. But, as all first draughts of any sort are usually imperfect, so there seem to be some defects in it that might have been supplied. For example: There wanted a chapter of the variety of dialects, which might have been had out of the northern interlineary versions of the gospel, mentioned by Dr. Marshall; one whereof is peremptorily affirmed to have belonged to St. Cuthbert, as the other, in all likelihood, did to venerable Bede.—NICOLSON, WILLIAM, 1696–1714, *English Historical Library.*

A few other nonjurors ought to be particularly noticed. High among them in rank was George Hickes, Dean of Worcester. Of all the Englishmen of his time he was the most versed in the old Teutonic languages; and his knowledge of the early Christian literature was extensive. As to his capacity for political discussions, it may be sufficient to say that his favourite argument for passive obedience was drawn from the story of the Theban legion.—MACAULAY, THOMAS BABINGTON, 1855, *History of England, ch.* xiv.

His learning has been commended by Ingram the Saxon scholar, by Bishops Nicolson, Horne, and Van Mildert, and even by Burnet, Kennett, and others most opposed to him on polemical grounds. Horne and Van Mildert agree in praising his skill and judgment in the controversy with Rome. His many controversial treatises have deservedly sunk into oblivion, but the most ephermeral of them abound in recondite allusions to the Fathers and the classical writers, as well as in the facts and precedents of ecclesiastical history. His fame, however, rests upon his researches into the history of the languages kindred to the mother tongue of the English race.—MASKELL, J., 1885, *George Hickes the Nonjuror, Notes and Queries, Sixth Series, vol.* 12, *p.* 402.

In 1703–5 his best-known work appeared, in one large folio volume, from the university press at Oxford, the "Linguarum veterum septentrionalium thesaurus grammatico-criticus et archæologicus." It is a stupendous monument of learning and industry, and that it should be the product of anxious years of suffering and perpetual turmoil affords wonderful testimony to the author's mental power and energy.—MACRAY, W. D., 1891, *Dictionary of National Biography, vol.* XXVI, *p.* 352.

William Wycherley

1640?–1715

William Wycherley, 1640–1715. Born, in London, 1640. Educated in France, 1655. Became a Roman Catholic. Abjured Church of Rome, and matriculated at Queen's Coll., Oxford. Took no degree. Student of Inner Temple, 1659. Served in Army during war with Holland. Play, "Love in a Wood," produced at Drury Lane, 1671; "The Gentleman Dancing Master," Dorset Gardens Theatre, Jan. 1672; "The Country Wife," Lincoln's Inn Fields Theatre, 1673 [?]; "The Plain Dealer," Lincoln's Inn Fields Theatre, 1674. Married (i.) Countess of Drogheda, 1678[?]. After her death was imprisoned for seven years in the Fleet for debt. Debts paid by James II., who gave him a pension of £200. Friendship with Pope begun, 1704. Married (ii.) Miss Jackson, Nov. 1715. Died, in London, Dec. 1715. Buried in St. Paul's, Covent Garden. *Works:* "Love in a Wood," 1672; "The Gentleman Dancing Master," 1673; "The Country Wife," 1675; "The Plain Dealer," 1677; "Epistles to the King and Duke" (anon.), 1682; "Miscellany Poems," 1704; "Works," 1713. *Posthumous:* "Posthumous Works," ed. by L. Theobald, 1728. *Collected Works:* "Plays, etc." (2 vols.), 1720.—SHARP, R. FARQUHARSON, 1897, *A Dictionary of English Authors, p.* 306.

PERSONAL

My friend the *Plain-Dealer.*—DRYDEN, JOHN, 1692, *Essay on Satire.*

Wycherley died a Romanist, and has owned that religion in my hearing.—It was generally thought by this gentleman's friends, that he lost his memory by old age; it was not by age, but by accident, as he himself told me often. He remembered as well at sixty years old, as he had done ever since forty, when a fever occasioned that loss to him. . . . Wycherley was a very handsome man. His acquaintance with the famous Duchess of Cleveland commenced oddly enough. One day, as he passed that duchess's coach in the ring, she leaned out of the window, and cried out loud enough to be heard distinctly by him; "Sir, you're a rascal: you're a villain!" Wycherley from that instant entertained hopes. He did not fail waiting on her the next morning: and with a very melancholy tone begged to know, how it was possible for him to have so much disobliged her Grace? They were very good friends from that time; yet, after all, what did he get by her? He was to have travelled with the young Duke of Richmond; King Charles gave him, now and then, a hundred pounds, not often. . . . We were pretty well together to the last: only his memory was so totally bad, that he did not remember a kindness done to him, even from minute to minute. He was peevish too latterly; so that sometimes we were out a little, and sometimes in. He never did any unjust thing to me in his whole life; and I went to see him on his death-bed.—POPE, ALEXANDER, 1728–30, *Spence's Anecdotes, ed. Singer, pp.* 2, 13.

Wycherley was in a bookseller's shop at Bath, or Tunbridge, when Lady Drogheda came in and happened to inquire for the "Plain Dealer." A friend of Wycherley's, who stood by him, pushed him toward her, and said, "There's the Plain Dealer, Madam, if you want him?" Wycherley made his excuses; and Lady Drogheda said, "that she loved plain-dealing best." He afterwards visited that lady, and in some time after married her. This proved a great blow to his fortunes; just before the time of his courtship, he was designed for governor to the late Duke of Richmond; and was to have been allowed fifteen hundred pounds a year from the government. His absence from court in the progress of this amour, and his being yet more absent after his marriage, (for Lady Drogheda was very jealous of him), disgusted his friends there so much, that he lost all his interest with them. His lady died; he got but little by her: and his misfortunes were such, that he was thrown into the Fleet, and lay there seven years. —DENNIS, JOHN, 1728-30, *Spence's Anecdotes, ed. Singer, p.* 33.

A man who seems to have had among his contemporaries his full share of reputation, to have been esteemed without virtue, and caressed without good nature. Pope was proud of his notice. Wycherley wrote verses in his praise, which he was charged by Dennis with writing to himself, and they agreed for awhile to flatter one another. It is pleasant to remark how soon Pope learnt the cant of an author, and began to treat critics with contempt, though he had yet suffered nothing from them. But the fondness of Wycherley was too violent to last. His esteem of Pope was such that he submitted some poems to his revision; and when Pope, perhaps proud of such confidence, was sufficiently bold in his criticisms and liberal in his alterations, the old scribbler was angry to see his pages defaced, and felt more pain from the detection than content from the amendment of his faults. They parted; but Pope always considered him with kindness; and visited him a little before he died.—JOHNSON, SAMUEL, 1779-81, *Pope, Lives of the English Poets.*

In reading this author's best works, those which one reads most frequently over, and knows almost by heart, one cannot help thinking of the treatment he received from Pope about his verses. It was hardly excusable in a boy of sixteen to an old man of seventy.—HAZLITT, WILLIAM, 1818, *Lectures on the English Comic Writers.*

So high did Wycherley stand in the royal favour, that once, when he was confined by a fever to his lodgings in Bow-street, Charles, who, with all his faults, was certainly a man of a social and affable disposition, called on him, sat by his bed, advised him to try change of air, and gave him a handsome sum of money to defray the expense of the journey. Buckingham, then master of the horse, and one of that infamous ministry shown by the name of the Cabal, had been one of the duchess's innumerable paramours. He at first showed some symptoms of jealousy, but soon, after his fashion, veered round from anger to fondness, and gave Wycherley a commission in his own regiment, and a place in the royal household.—MACAULAY,

THOMAS BABINGTON, 1841, *Comic Dramatists of the Restoration, Edinburgh Review; Critical and Miscellaneous Essays.*

He ended as he had begun, by unskilfulness and misconduct, having succeeded neither in becoming happy nor honest, having used his vigorous intelligence and real talent only to his own injury and the injury of others.—TAINE, H. A., 1871, *History of English Literature, tr. Van Laun, vol.* I, *bk.* iii, *ch.* i., *p.* 480.

LOVE IN A WOOD
1672

The comedy itself is poor and feeble, and does not contain a single passage from which the wit that Wycherley afterwards displayed in his writings could be reasonably predicated.—DUNHAM, S. ASTLEY, 1838, *Literary and Scientific Men of Great Britain and Ireland, vol.* III, *p.* 167.

Is worth little in style or plot; yet we think, upon the whole, it has been undervalued. It is not unamusing. It gives early evidence of that dislike of backbiting and false friendship, which honourably distinguished Wycherley through life.—HUNT, LEIGH, 1840, *ed., The Dramatic Works of Wycherley, Congreve, Vanbrugh, and Farquhar.*

The comedy of "Love in a Wood" is, indeed, an extraordinary piece of invention, and of writing, too, for a youth of nineteen. His knowledge of the arcana of town life, with its interminable intrigues and love-treasons—if it be not profanation to use the term "love" in this description of social commerce—is certainly remarkable. The disguises and blunders and perplexities are conducted with all the display of a young ambition to build up a dramatic plot: they are spun out to wearisomeness, and mostly improbable in design. One must keep one's mental eyes closed while reading it, and, like children, play at "make-believe." Moreover, we feel little or no sympathy with even the better class of the characters; one cares nothing whether they "marry and live happy afterwards," or not; for their whole course of conduct shows that their jealousy arises from sensual vanity, and not from a worthy pride of exclusiveness; and, moreover, we feel that if in the end they had all been jilted, they would have quickly righted themselves by some other toy object. Nevertheless, it must be confessed that, gross as many of the scenes are, the "mirror held up to nature" is not a distorted one.—CLARKE, CHARLES COWDEN, 1871, *On the Comic Writers of England, The Gentleman's Magazine, n. s., vol.* 7, *p.* 824.

Is in the style of Etheredge and Sedley, —indeed "The Mulberry Garden" of the latter (1668) has been justly held to have suggested this play. Its satire on manners is, however, perhaps more incisive and contemptuous than theirs; and, in contrast to the fantastic figures of Sedley's production, it already exhibits signs of a realistic vigour capable of taking us back from the Restoration writers to Elisabethans like Middleton.—WARD, ADOLPHUS WILLIAM, 1875–99, *A History of English Dramatic Literature, vol.* III, *p.* 463.

THE GENTLEMAN DANCING-MASTER
1672

This play sparkles with wit; but, being founded for the most part in fugitive manners, and being deficient in the more durable elements of nature, its popularity ceased with the age in which its points and allusions were familiar to the audience. —DUNHAM, S. ASTLEY, 1838, *Literary and Scientific Men of Great Britain and Ireland, vol.* III. *p.* 170.

Preposterously improbable in plot; overcharged, and yet feeble in character; and the dialogue, not merely "flat, stale, and improbable;" but, what is the greatest of all defects in a play, there is frequent repetition in it.—CLARKE, CHARLES COWDEN, 1871, *On the Comic Writers of England, The Gentleman's Magazine, n. s., vol.* 7, *p.* 825.

"The Gentleman's Dancing-Master" resembles Molière in manner more than any other of Wycherley's plays; indeed its intrigue has been compared to that of "L'Ecole des Femmes," but, in accordance with this author's general method of working, the resemblance is by no means close. The English work may be described as a capital farce, written with genuine vigour and freshness of humour; and to my mind this is by far the most agreeable of Wycherley's plays. —WARD, ADOLPHUS WILLIAM, 1875–99, *A History of English Dramatic Literature, vol.* III, *p.* 463.

THE COUNTRY WIFE
1673

This evening the comedy called the Country Wife was acted in Drury-lane, for the benefit of Mrs. Bignell. . . . The poet, on many occasions, where the propriety of the character will admit of it, insinuates, that there is no defence against vice but the contempt of it; and has, in the natural ideas of an untainted innocent, shown the gradual steps to ruin and destruction which persons of condition run into, without the help of a good education to form their conduct. The torment of a jealous coxcomb, which arises from his own false maxims, and the aggravation of his pain by the very words in which he sees her innocence, makes a very pleasant and instructive satire. The character of Horner, and the design of it, is a good representation of the age in which that comedy was written; at which time love and wenching were the business of life, and the gallant manner of pursuing women was the best recommendation at Court. To this only it is to be imputed, that a gentleman of Mr. Wycherley's character and sense condescends to represent the insults done to the honour of the bed, without just reproof; but to have drawn a man of probity with regard to such considerations had been a monster, and a poet had at that time discovered his want of knowing the manners of the Court he lived in, by a virtuous character in his fine gentleman, as he would shew his ignorance by drawing a vicious one to please the present audience.—STEELE, RICHARD, 1709, *The Tatler, No.* 3, *Apr.* 16, *pp.* 96, 97.

Wycherley was before Congreve; and his "Country Wife" will last longer than anything of Congreve's as a popular acting play. It is only a pity that it is not entirely his own; but it is enough so to do him never-ceasing honour, for the best things are his own. His humour is, in general, broader, his characters more natural, and his incidents more striking than Congreve's. It may be said of Congreve, that the workmanship overlays the materials: in Wycherley, the casting of the parts and the fable are alone sufficient to ensure success. We forget Congreve's characters, and only remember what they say: we remember Wycherley's characters, and the incidents they meet with, just as if they were real, and forget what they say, comparatively speaking.—HAZLITT, WILLIAM, 1818, *Lectures on the English Comic Writers.*

It was evidently suggested by L'Ecole des Femmes: the character of Arnolphe has been copied; but even here the whole conduct of the piece of Wycherley is his own. It is more artificial than that of Molière, wherein too much passes in description; the part of Agnes is rendered still more poignant; and, among the comedies of Charles's reign, I am not sure that it is surpassed by any.—HALLAM, HENRY, 1837–39, *Introduction to the Literature of Europe, pt. iv, ch. vi, par. 48.*

In the "Country Wife" there are no such scenes and dialogue of continued excellence as those of Olivia and her visitors in the second act of the "Plain Dealer;" but the principal female character hits a point of more lasting nature, and is an exquisite meeting of the extremes of simplicity and cunning; so that with some alterations, especially of the impudent project of Horner, which would have been an affront in any other age to a decent audience, this comedy outlasted the performances of the graver one.— HUNT, LEIGH, 1840, *ed., The Dramatic Works of Wycherley, Congreve, Vanbrugh, and Farquhar.*

Though one of the most profligate and heartless of human compositions, it is the elaborate production of a mind, not indeed rich, original, or imaginative, but ingenious, observant, quick to seize hints, and patient of the toil of polishing.—MACAULAY, THOMAS BABINGTON, 1841, *Comic Dramatists of the Restoration, Edinburgh Review; Critical and Miscellaneous Essays.*

The play itself, with all its extravagant coarseness, is not without its home-speaking moral: for the unrestricted woman of society, Alithea, vindicates her own self-respect by a steadiness and constancy towards the man to whom she had pledged her truth, till he himself, by wanton absurdity and self-seeking, forces her to marry the man she preferred, but had resolutely refused, because of her previous engagement; while the "cribbed and cabined" country wife, mewed up before marriage, and jealously watched, and mistrusted, and locked up afterwards, is ready to rush into any eccentricity of conduct from pure ignorance, with resentment at

the injustice exercised towards her. Bad education, and want of confidence, from first to last, was the cause of all the evil; for her nature is frank and generous, and even lovable. She is a wild weed brought suddenly into the hothouse of artificial and licentious society. Another unfavourable feature in the play is the hollowness and utter absence of all confidence in the men towards each other: there is no resting-place for the heart—all are "dear friends," and all would be traitors at the first glance of an inducement. They certainly are not hypocrites to each other, for no one is deceived in his estimate of his companion's friendship.—CLARKE, CHARLES COWDEN, 1871, *On the Comic Writers of England, The Gentleman's Magazine, n. s., vol. 7, p. 827.*

Of all comedies I have witnessed none appeared more amusing, more genuine, or more original.—FITZGERALD, PERCY, 1882, *A New History of the English Stage, vol. I, p. 182, note.*

There can be no question that the men and women who sat through the acting of Wycherley's "Country Wife" were past blushing.—MEREDITH, GEORGE, 1897, *An Essay on Comedy and the Uses of the Comic Spirit, p. 6.*

It is the most brilliant but the most indecent of Wycherley's works. When it was revived in 1709, after an interval of six years, for Mrs. Bicknell's benefit, Steele, in a criticism in the "Tatler" (16 April 1709), said that the character of the profligate Horner was a good representation of the age in which the comedy was written, when gallantry in the pursuit of women was the best recommendation at court. A man of probity in such manners would have been a monster. In 1766 Garrick brought out an adaptation of the play, under the title of "The Country Girl," which is still acted occasionally; but, as Genest says (v. 116), in making it decent he made it insipid. Another adaptation, by John Lee, was published in 1765.— AITKEN, GEORGE A., 1900, *Dictionary of National Biography, vol. LXIII, p. 197.*

THE PLAIN-DEALER
1674

Since the Plain Dealer's scenes of manly rage
Not one has dared to lash this crying age.
—CONGREVE, WILLIAM, 1695, *Love for Love, Prologue.*

There is a heaviness about it, indeed, an extravagance, an overdoing both in the style, the plot, and characters, but the truth of feeling and the force of interest prevail over every objection. The character of Manly, the Plain Dealer, is violent, repulsive, and uncouth, which is a fault, though one that seems to have been intended for the sake of contrast; for the portrait of consummate, artful hypocrisy in Olivia, is, perhaps, rendered more striking by it. The indignation excited against this odious and pernicious quality by the masterly exposure to which it is here subjected, is "a discipline of humanity." No one can read this play attentively without being the better for it as long as he lives. It penetrates to the core; it shows the immorality and hateful effects of duplicity, by showing it fixing its harpy fangs in the heart of an honest and worthy man. It is worth ten volumes of sermons.—HAZLITT, WILLIAM, 1818, *Lectures on the English Comic Writers.*

The feelings of the public saw better than the court-wits, and instinctively revolted against this play in spite of the exquisite scenes of the scandal-mongering fine ladies and gentlemen.—HUNT, LEIGH, 1840, *ed., The Dramatic Works of Wycherley, Congreve, Vanbrugh, and Farquhar.*

In "The Plain-Dealer" (1674) the cynicism of Wycherley has reached its acme. . . . As for the plot of this famous comedy, it is not less horrible than the chief character, Manly the "Plain-Dealer," is revolting. The repulsiveness of the story, and of its *dénouement,* is such as to make description irksome; but the character of the hero may be judged by contrasting it with the original—if it can be so called—which suggested it, viz. the noble hero of Molière's immortal "Misanthrope." . . . Wycherley must in this play be allowed to have given proofs of genuine force and of essential originality, and to have produced what is indisputably one of the most powerful dramas of its age.—WARD, ADOLPHUS WILLIAM, 1875–99, *A History of English Dramatic Literature, vol. III, pp.* 464, 465, 466.

One of the most brutally cynical, but none the less one of the best-constructed pieces which have ever held the stage. With his magnificent gaiety and buoyancy, Wycherley exaggerated and disfigured the qualities which should rule the comic

stage, but they were there; he was a ruffian, but a ruffian of genius.—GOSSE, EDMUND, 1897, *Short History of Modern English Literature, p.* 191.

The coarseness of Wycherley's touch is nowhere more obvious than when we compare the picture of Fidelia, the girl who loves Manly and follows him to sea in man's clothes, with Shakespeare's Viola in "Twelfth Night." Fidelia, with whom we are expected to be in sympathy, aids Manly in his revolting plot against Olivia. But much may be forgiven on account of the underplot of the litigious widow Blackacre, and her son Jerry, a raw squire. They are the forerunners of Goldsmith's Mrs. Hardcastle and Tony Lumpkin, and of Steele's Humphry Gubbin, and the scenes in which they appear enabled Wycherley to make use of such knowledge of the law as he had picked up at the Temple, and supply a much-needed lighter element to the play.—AITKEN, G. A., 1900, *Dictionary of National Biography, vol.* LXIII, *p.* 197.

GENERAL

. . . Wycherley earns hard whate'er he gains;
He wants no Judgment, and he spares no Pains:
He frequently excels; and at the least,
Makes fewer Faults than any of the rest.
—ROCHESTER, JOHN WILMOT EARL, 1678, *An Allusion to the Tenth Satire of the First Book of Horace.*

A Gentleman, whom I may boldly reckon amongst the Poets of the First Rank: no Man that I know, except the Excellent *Johnson,* having outdone him in Comedy; in which alone he has imploy'd his Pen, but with that Success, that few have before, or will hereafter match him.—LANGBAINE, GERARD, 1691, *An Account of the English Dramatick Poets, p.* 514.

The satire, wit, and strength of manly Wycherly.
—DRYDEN, JOHN, 1693, *Epistle to my dear friend, Mr. Congreve, on his Comedy called the Double Dealer.*

In sense and numbers if you would excel,
Read Wycherley, consider Dryden well.
In one, what vig'rous turns of fancy shine!
In th' other, sirens warble in each line.
—GARTH, SIR SAMUEL, 1696, *The Dispensary, Canto* iv.

Methinks Mr. *de Muralt* should have mention'd an excellent comic writer, (living when he was in *England*) I mean Mr.

Wycherley, who was a long time known publickly to be happy in the good graces of the most celebrated mistress of King *Charles* the second. This gentleman, who pass'd his life among persons of the highest distinction, was perfectly well acquainted with their lives and their follies, and painted them with the strongest pencil, and in the truest colours. He has drawn a *Misanthrope* or man-hater, in imitation of that of *Moliere*. All *Wycherley's* strokes are stronger and bolder than those of our *Misanthrope*, but then they are less delicate, and the rules of decorum are not so well observ'd in this play. The *English* writer has corrected the only defect that is in *Moliere's* Comedy, the thinness of the plot, which also is so dispos'd, that the characters in it do not enough raise our concern. The *English* Comedy affects us, and the contrivance of the plot is very ingenious, but at the same time it is too bold for the *French* manners.—VOLTAIRE, FRANCOIS MARIE AROUET, 1732? *Letters on the English Nation, p.* 143.

Wycherley was really angry with me for correcting his verses so much. I was extremely plagued, up and down, for almost two years with them. However, it went off pretty well at last; and it appears, by the edition of Wycherley's Posthumous Works, that he had followed the advice I so often gave him; and that he had gone so far as to make some hundreds of prose maxims out of his verses.—Those verses that are published, are a mixture of Wycherley's own original lines, with a great many of mine inserted here and there, (but not difficult to be distinguished), and some of Wycherley's softened a little in the running, probably by Theobald, who had the chief care of that edition.—POPE, ALEXANDER, 1734–36, *Spence's Anecdotes, ed. Singer, p.* 113.

Wycherley was ambitious of the reputation of wit and libertinism; and he attained it: he was probably capable of reaching the fame of true comedy and instructive ridicule.—HUME, DAVID, 1762, *The History of England, James II.*

If he had composed nothing but his poems, he would have been one of the most neglected writers in the English language.—GRANGER, JAMES, 1769–1824, *Biographical History of England, vol.* v, *p.* 248.

Wycherley was formed for his times, and the times for him; indeed his works were too voluptuous for any but the gay "Charles' golden days;" besides they are wanting in most requisites of fine writing; yet he laboured much to form the manners of the times, which procured him the appellation of slow Wycherley, from Rochester.—NOBLE, MARK, 1806, *A Biographical History of England, vol.* I, *p.* 239.

Translated into real life, the characters of . . . Wycherley's dramas, are profligates and strumpets,—the business of their brief existence, the undivided pursuit of lawless gallantry. No other spring of action, or possible motive of conduct, is recognized; principles which, universally acted upon, must reduce this frame of things to a chaos. But we do them wrong in so translating them. No such effects are produced in *their* world. When we are among them, we are amongst a chaotic people. We are not to judge them by our usages. No reverend institutions are insulted by their proceedings, —for they have none among them. No peace of families is violated,—for no family ties exist among them. No purity of the marriage bed is stained,—for none is supposed to have a being. No deep affections are disquieted,—no holy wedlock bands are snapped asunder,—for affection's depth and wedded faith are not of the growth of that soil. There is neither right or wrong,—gratitude or its opposite,—claim or duty,—paternity or sonship. Of what consequence is it to virtue, or how is she at all concerned about it, whether Sir Simon, or Dapperwit, steal away Miss Martha; or who is the father of Lord Froth's, or Sir Paul Pliant's children?—LAMB, CHARLES, 1824? *On the Artificial Comedy of the Last Century.*

Wycherley has justly been considered as the earliest of our comic prose dramatists, who forsook the fleeting shapes of custom and manners that were brought to their gayest head in Etherege, for the more lasting wit and humour natural to the prevailing qualities of mankind. Etherege was the "dandy" of the prose drama, and Wycherley the first man. . . . He is somewhat heavy as well as "brawny" in his step; and when he moves faster, it is seldom from gayety. He has "wit at will" also, but then the will to be witty is frequently too obvious. It has too artificial an air of thought and antithesis.

His best scenes are those of cross purposes, mutual exposure, or the contrast of natural with acquired cunning; those, in short, in which reflection and design have much more to do than animal spirits. His style is pure and unaffected, and clearness and force are his characteristics, in preference to what is either engaging or laughable. We can easily believe him to have been a "slow" writer; not from dullness, but from care and consideration. —HUNT, LEIGH, 1840, *ed.*, *The Dramatic Works of Wycherley, Congreve, Vanbrugh, and Farquhar.*

Wycherley's plays are said to have been the produce of long and patient labour. The epithet of "slow" was early given to him by Rochester, and was frequently repeated. In truth, his mind, unless we are greatly mistaken, was naturally a very meager soil, and was forced only by great labour and outlay to bear fruit, which, after all, was not of the highest flavour. He has scarcely more claim to originality than Terence. It is not too much to say, that there is hardly anything of the least value in his plays, of which the hint is not to be found elsewhere. The best scenes in the "Gentleman Dancing-Master," were suggested by Calderon's *Maestro de Danzar*, not by any means one of the happiest comedies of the great Castilian poet. The "Country Wife" is borrowed from the *Ecole des Maris* and the *Ecole des Femmes*. The groundwork of the "Plain Dealer" is taken from the *Misanthrope* of Molière. One whole scene is almost translated from the *Critique de l'Ecole des Femmes;* Fidelia is Shakspeare's Viola stolen, and marred in the stealing; and the Widow Blackacre, beyond comparison Wycherley's best comic character, is the Countess in Racine's *Plaideurs,* talking the jargon of English instead of that of French chicane.— MACAULAY, THOMAS BABINGTON, 1841, *Comic Dramatists of the Restoration, Edinburgh Review; Critical and Miscellaneous Essays.*

Wycherley, the coarsest writer who has polluted the stage. . . . His style is laboured, and troublesome to read. His tone is virulent and bitter. He frequently forces his comedy in order to get at spiteful satire. Effort and animosity mark all that he says or puts into the mouths of others. . . . We find in him no poetry of expression, no glimpse of the ideal, no system of morality which could console, raise, or purify men. . . . If Wycherley borrows a character anywhere, it is only to do it violence, or degrade it to the level of his own characters. If he imitates the Agnes of Molière, as he does in the "Country Wife," he marries her in order to profane marriage, deprives her of honour, still more of shame, still more of grace, and changes her artless tenderness into shameless instincts and scandalous confessions. If he takes Shakspeare's Viola, as in the "Plain Dealer," it is to drag her through the vileness of infamy, amidst brutalities and surprises. If he translates the part of Célimène, he wipes out at one stroke the manners of a great lady, the woman's delicacy, the tact of the lady of the house, the politeness, the refined air, the superiority of wit and knowledge of the world, in order to substitute the impudence and cheats of a foulmouthed courtesan. If he invents an almost innocent girl, Hippolita, he begins by putting into her mouth words that will not bear transcribing. Whatever he does or says, whether he copies or originates, blames or praises, his stage is a defamation of mankind, which repels even when it attracts, and which sickens one while it corrupts. A certain gift hovers over all —namely, vigour—which is never absent in England, and gives a peculiar character to their virtues as to their vices.—TAINE, H. A., 1871, *History of English Literature, tr. Van Laun, vol.* I, *bk.* iii, *ch.* i, *pp.* 480, 481, 483.

Wycherley, the first dramatist of the time, remains the most brutal among all writers for the stage; and nothing gives so damning an expression of his day as the fact that he found actors to repeat his words and audiences to applaud him. In men such as Wycherley Milton found types for the Belial of his great poem, "than whom a spirit more lewd fell not from Heaven, or more gross to love vice for itself." He piques himself on the frankness and "plain dealing" which painted the world as he saw it, a world of brawls and assignations, of orgies at Vauxhall and fights with the watch, of lies and double entendres, of knaves and dupes, of men who sold their daughters and women who cheated their husbands. But the cynicism of Wycherley was no greater than that of the men about him;

and in mere love of what was vile, in contempt of virtue and disbelief in purity and honesty, the King himself stood ahead of any of his subjects.—GREEN, JOHN RICHARD, 1874, *A Short History of the English People, ch.* ix, *sec.* i.

His merits lie in the vigour with which his characters are drawn, the clearness with which they stand out from one another, and the naturalness with which he both constructs his plots and chooses his language. As for his plots, they are rarely original, and in the main based upon Molière; but Wycherley neither borrows without reflexion, nor combines without care. The wit of his dialogue is less sparkling and spontaneous than that of Congreve's or of Vanbrugh's; he is, as Leigh Hunt says, somewhat heavy as well as brawny in his step, and he lacks in general the gaiety of spirit which is the most charming phase of comic humour. On the other hand, he excels in satire of an intenser kind; his sarcasms are as keen as they are cruel; and the cynicism of his wit cannot prevent us from acknowledging its power. But while he ruthlessly uncloaks the vices of his age, his own moral tone is affected by their influence to as deplorable a degree as is that of the most light-hearted and unthinking of the dramatists contemporary with him.—WARD, ADOLPHUS WILLIAM, 1875–99, *A History of English Dramatic Literature, vol.* III, *p.* 462.

Wycherley has this merit, that he was first in the field of our best school of comedy-writers. He virtually began the school of the Restoration comic dramatists,

the so-called comedy of manners. True it is that had Molière not written comedies Wycherley would not have written as he did, and it must be admitted that Sir George Etheredge wrote plays as unconventionally natural so far as dialogue is concerned as Wycherley's; but Etheredge's comedies are altogether beneath notice as literature, while Wycherley is, and ever will be, a true English classic. If he transferred to our stage whole scenes from Molière, he did them into strong, nervous English, racy with mother wit.—CRAWFURD, OSWALD, 1883, *ed., English Comic Dramatists, p.* 66.

Whatever the cause, he was lost to the stage at thirty, and his occasional poetical productions, the most important of which have been already noticed, were far from qualifying him to sit in the seat of Dryden. He enjoyed, nevertheless, supremacy of another kind. Regarded as an extinct volcano, he gave umbrage to no rivals; his urbane and undemonstrative temper kept him out of literary feuds; all agreed to adore so benign and inoffensive a deity, and the general respect of the lettered world fitly culminated in Pope's dedication of his "Homer" to him, the most splendid literary tribute the age could bestow.—GARNETT, RICHARD, 1895, *The Age of Dryden, p.* 126.

In Wycherley's plays the immorality is more realistic, and therefore more harmful, than in other Restoration dramas; but his vigour and clearness of delineation are his greatest merits.—AITKEN, G. A., 1900, *Dictionary of National Biography, vol.* LXIII, *p.* 201.

Robert South
1634–1716

Robert South, born at Hackney in 1633, from Westminster passed as a student to Christ Church in 1651. In 1658 he received orders from a deprived bishop, and in 1660 was appointed public orator. His vigorous sermons, full of mockery of the Puritans, delighted the restored royalists. He became domestic chaplain to Clarendon, prebendary of Westminster in 1663, canon of Christ Church in 1670, rector of Islip in Oxfordshire in 1678, and chaplain to Clarendon's son on his embassy to the Polish court of John Sobieski (1676). He suppressed his disapproval of James II.'s Declaration of Indulgence, "acquiesced in" the Revolution, but blazed out with anger against the proposed scheme of Comprehension. In 1693 began his great controversy with Sherlock, Dean of St. Paul's, who had defended the Trinity against the Socinians. South flung his "Animadversions" anonymously into the fray, but the bitter irony and fierce sarcasms quickly betrayed his hand. Sherlock published a "Defence," to which South rejoined in his "Tritheism charged upon Dr. Sherlock." The controversy became the talk of the town, and the king himself interposed. South made interest for

Sacheverell, and is said to have refused the see of Rochester and deanery of Westminster (1713). He died 8th July 1716. . . . His sermons fill 11 vols. (1692-1744); in 1717 appeared his "Posthumous Works," with Memoir; also his "Opera Posthuma Latina" (all republished by the Clarendon Press in 1823). See his "Sermons on Several Occasions" (new ed. 1878), *Quarterly Review* (1868), and Dean Lake in "Classic Preachers" (1877).—PATRICK AND GROOME, *eds.*, 1897, *Chambers's Biographical Dictionary, p.* 868.

PERSONAL

Odd's fish, Lory, your chaplain must be a bishop; therefore put me in mind of him at the next death.—CHARLES II., 1677? *To Lord Rochester.*

Pray, my lord, desire Dr. South to die about the fall of the leaf; for he has a prebend of Westminster . . . and a sinecure in the country . . . which my friends have often told me would fit me extremely.—SWIFT, JONATHAN, 1709, *Letter to Earl of Halifax, Jan.* 13.

Dr. South holds out still; but he cannot be immortal.—HALIFAX, EARL OF, 1709, *Letter to Jonathan Swift, Oct.* 6.

Robert South stands hardly in the first rank, but he has never been surpassed, and not often imitated, in his own style as a preacher. He was a stout defender of orthodoxy, and a very hard hitter of his opponents. Men admired him, as they have admired some modern preachers, for the sharp things he said; but they admired him more for his irrepressible and inimitable humour. A sermon of South's is a perpetual succession of jocularities; and the churches in which he preached resounded with the laughter of the congregations. But his ridicule was always directed against pretence, or falseness, or self-assertion, or pride—never against anything high or noble. He was an earnest, self-denying ecclesiastic, and entirely without aims for his own advancement. He remained content with preferment which was considered slight in comparison to his genius, and died a poor man, having spent his income on good works. —HUTTON, WILLIAM HOLDEN, 1895, *Social England, ed. Traill, vol.* IV, *p.* 418.

On the whole perhaps the greatest preacher of his age.—GARNETT, RICHARD, 1895, *The Age of Dryden, p.* 223.

South, a man of strong prejudices and warm attachments, was never a self-seeker, and, when he changed his attitude, followed what appeared to be the dictates of common sense. His use of humour in the pulpit suggested to Tillotson a want of seriousness in his character. Yet no preacher was more direct in his dealing with the vices of the age, no court preacher more homely in his appeals. His humour has a native breadth and freshness. Like Fuller's pleasant turns, it always illuminates his subject; but, unlike Fuller's conceits, it does not cloy. Baxter says that South was "a fluent, extemporate speaker," yet tells a story of his breaking down, which shows that in early life his sermons were learnt by heart. Kennett tells of his attention to delivery, and how he "worked up his body" as he approached his points. Wood's harsh judgment on South is said to have been inspired by a jest with which South received Wood's mention of a bodily ailment from which he suffered.—GORDON, ALEXANDER, 1898, *Dictionary of National Biography, vol.* LIII, *p.* 276.

SERMONS

South had great qualifications for that popularity which attends the pulpit; and his manner was at that time original. Not diffuse, not learned, not formal in argument like Barrow, with a more natural structure of sentences; a more pointed, though by no means a more fair and satisfactory, turn of reasoning; with a style clear and English, free from all pedantry, but abounding with those colloquial novelties of idiom, which, though now become vulgar and offensive, the age of Charles II. affected; sparing no personal or temporary sarcasm, but, if he seems for a moment to tread on the verge of buffoonery, recovering himself by some stroke of vigorous sense and language,—such was the witty Dr. South, whom the courtiers delighted to hear. His sermons want all that is called unction, and sometimes even earnestness, which is owing, in a great measure, to a perpetual tone of gibing at rebels and fanatics; but there is a masculine spirit about them, which combined with their peculiar characteristics, would naturally fill the churches where he might be heard.—HALLAM, HENRY, 1837-39,

Introduction to the Literature of Europe, pt. iv, *ch.* ii, *par.* 56.

Of all the English preachers, South seems to us to furnish, in point of *style*, the truest specimens of the most effective species of pulpit eloquence. We are speaking, it must be remembered, simply of his style: we offer no opinion on the degree of truth or error in the system of doctrines he embraced; and for his un-christian bitterness and often unseemly wit, would be the last to offer any apology. But his robust intellect—his shrewd common sense—his vehement feelings—and a fancy ever more distinguished by force than by elegance, admirably qualified him for a powerful public speaker. His style is accordingly marked by all the characteristics which might naturally be expected from the possession of such qualities. It is everywhere direct, condensed, pungent. His sermons are well worthy of frequent and diligent perusal by every young preacher.—ROGERS, HENRY, 1840, *The British Pulpit, Edinburgh Review, vol.* 72, *p.* 82.

No explorer of the thorny tracts of theology can ever forget his exhilaration of spirit on first reading the sermons of Dr. South, the shrewdest, sharpest, bitterest, and wittiest of English divines. His character, formed by a curious interpenetration of strong prejudices and great powers, and colored by the circumstances of his age and position, is one of the most peculiar in English literature, and, as displayed in his works, repays the most assiduous study. In some points he reminds us of Sydney Smith, though distinguished from him by many striking individualities, and utterly opposed to him in political sentiment and principle. He is a grand specimen of the old Tory; and he enforced his Toryism with a courage, heartiness, and wealth of intellectual resources, to which the warmest radical could hardly refuse admiration and respect.—WHIPPLE, EDWIN P., 1846, *Essays and Reviews, vol.* II, *p.* 74.

The English language affords no higher specimen of its richness and strength than is to be found in this beautiful discourse. . . . Every student for the Pulpit or the Bar should read this eloquent Sermon.—MONTAGU, BASIL, 1860, *ed. Adam in Paradise, Preface.*

I have been re-reading South's sermons, and like the handsome way he has of taking everything for granted while he seems to be arguing its probability. But you can hear as good at St. Paul's—I was going to say.—LOWELL, JAMES RUSSELL, 1890, *Letters, ed. Norton, Dec.* 18, *vol.* II, *p.* 428.

Robert South stands midway between the older and the newer generation. He preached good sense and good morals with masculine force, but he was not a reconciler, rather he was an unflinching combatant, and a too truculent victor; among his gifts the grace of charity can hardly be reckoned; he sets forth his gospel of good morals with great intellectual clearness and energy, but rarely with what we understand by unction. . . . South's preaching was not dry or cold; through the vigour and perspicacity of his intellect, aided by the power of a strong rhetoric, he rises at times to a kind of rational enthusiasm.—DOWDEN, EDWARD, 1900, *Puritan and Anglican, pp.* 325, 326.

GENERAL

South's sentences are gems, hard and shining: Voltaire's look like them, but are only French paste.—HARE, A. W. AND J. C., 1827–48, *Guesses at Truth, First Series.*

Thro' listening palaces did rhymeless South
Pour sparkling waters from his golden mouth.
—LANDOR, WALTER SAVAGE, 1846, *Satirists.*

As a writer, Dr. South is conspicuous for good practical sense, for a deep insight into human character, for liveliness of imagination, and exuberant invention, and for a wit that knew not always the limit of propriety. In perspicuity, copiousness, and force of expression, he has few superiors among English writers.—CLEVELAND, CHARLES D., 1848, *A Compendium of English Literature, p.* 363.

Nor can the ingenuity, the subtlety, the brilliancy of South, though too exuberant in point, and drawing away the attention from the subject to the epigrammatic diction, be regarded otherwise than as proofs of the highest order of intellect.—BROUGHAM, HENRY LORD, 1856, *Contributions to Edinburgh Review, vol.* I, *p.* 128.

South astonishes us by his wit, while he instructs us with his wisdom.—PORTER, NOAH, 1870, *Books and Reading, p.* 20.

He who was called the wittiest of ecclesiastics, Robert South, as different from Barrow in his character and life as in his works and his mind; armed for war, an impassioned royalist, a partisan of divine right and passive obedience, an acrimonious controversialist, a defamer of the dissenters, a foe to the Act of Toleration, who never refused to use in his enmities the licence of an insult or a foul word. . . . His style is anecdotic, striking, abrupt, with change of tone, forcible and clownish gestures, with every species of originality, vehemence, and boldness. He sneers in the pulpit, he rails, he plays the mimic and comedian. He paints his characters as if he had them before his eyes. The audience will recognise the originals again in the streets; they could put the names to the portraits.—TAINE, H. A., 1871, *History of English Literature, tr. Van Laun, vol.* II, *bk.* iii, *ch.* iii, *pp.* 65, 66.

A quick and powerful intellect, soliderudition, a superlative command of homely racy English, and wit of unsurpassed brilliancy, make a combination that, in a literary point of view, places the possessor at least on a level with Taylor and Barrow. Doubtless his fame would have been equal to his powers had he not mistaken his vocation. He shows little religious earnestness, and without *that*, devotional, and even controversial, religious works can hardly pretend to the first rank. He was an earnest Churchman, but not an earnest Christian. — MINTO, WILLIAM, 1872–80, *Manual of English Prose Literature, p.* 334.

No person who is wont to slake his intellectual thirst at "the wells of English undefiled," will soon forget the tingling delight, the exhilaration of mind and spirit, with which he first read the sermons of Robert South, the shrewdest, most caustic, most firey, and, with the exception of Thomas Fuller, the wittiest of the old English divines. Among the giants of English theology he stands alone. . . . He was a kind of Tory Sydney Smith, yet lacking the genial, sunny disposition, and the humor, of that divine wit and witty divine; and in reading his works, it is difficult to say which is most to be admired, the thorough grasp and exhaustive treatment of the subject, the masterly arrangement of the thoughts, or the vitality, energy and freshness of expression, which have given his sermons a higher place in

the library of the scholar than even in that of the theologian or the pulpit orator. . . . South's writings are a storehouse of vehement expression, such as can be found in no other English writer. He had at his command the whole vocabulary of abuse, satire, and scorn, and, when his ire was aroused, he was never niggard of the treasures of his indignant rhetoric. Against everything, especially, which militated with the doctrines or ceremonies of the English church, he hurled his anathemas and shot his sarcasms. Radical editors should study his writings day and night; nowhere else (except in Milton) will they find such biting words and stinging phrases with which to denounce wicked men, wicked institutions, and wicked practices. The intensity of thought and feeling which burns through his writings has hardly any parallel in English literature. It has been compared to the unwearied fire of the epic poet. There are times when he seems to wrestle with his subject, as if he would grind it into powder; and when he seems to say all that he does say to us, only that we may conjecture how much more he could say if he were able to wreak his thoughts upon expression. It has been truly said that many sentences in his works appear torn from his brain by main strength, expressing not only the thought he intended to convey, but a kind of impatient rage that it did not come with less labor. With all his command of language, he seems often to struggle with it in order to wrestle from it words enough for his wealth of thought.—MATHEWS, WILLIAM, 1877, *Hours With Men and Books, pp.* 58, 71.

His style is voluble and nervous; he runs while he talks, and without pausing he snatches, now from one side and now from the other, missiles, ornaments, objects of every description, all of which find their proper places in his motley discourse. He never hesitates to invite virulence, buffoonery, or even downright hateful faslehood to adorn his attacks upon a brother divine, and, as Stillingfleet said, waits in figurative lanes and argumentative narrow passages ready to bespatter his opponents with dirt amid fits of roguish laughter. There is something impish about Dr. South.—GOSSE, EDMUND, 1888, *A History of Eighteenth Century Literature, p.* 100.

"The Scourge of Fanaticism." An epithet conferred on Robert South, a noted English preacher. He had sharp wit, keen satire, and was a man to be admired and not imitated. He was embittered against Dissenters. He was not diffuse, not learned, but he had ingenuity, subtlety, and brilliancy, and in his sermons often approached buffoonery, which made him popular with the courtiers.—FREY, ALBERT R., 1888, *Sobriquets and Nicknames, p.* 315.

Was as witty in rhetoric as he was fierce in controversy.—BROOKE, STOPFORD A., 1896, *English Literature, p.* 179.

The most masculine of English seventeenth-century writers except Hobbes, and indeed a sort of orthodox pair to that writer. . . . His literary reputation rests upon his numerous and very remarkable sermons. . . . South has still something of Elizabethan conceit and word-play, and a great deal of Jacobean scholasticism. . . . While he never has the beauty of Taylor, while he lacks the easy lambent light of Fuller's wit, he is in better fighting trim, better balanced, less unequal and disquieting than either, and provides in almost all his work quite admirable examples of the more scholastic prose.—SAINTSBURY, GEORGE, 1898, *A Short History of English Literature, pp.* 443, 444.

Andrew Fletcher

1655–1716

Andrew Fletcher, of Saltoun, was educated by Bishop Burnet, then minister of Saltoun. He first appears as Commissioner for East Lothian in the Scotch Parliament; but his opposition to the court occasioned his outlawry and the confiscation of his estates. In 1685 he engaged in Monmouth's rebellion, but quarrelled with a fellow-officer named Dare, and shot him. Monmouth was obliged to dismiss Fletcher, who withdrew to the Continent, and entered the Austrian service against the Turks. In 1688 he joined William of Orange at the Hague, and after the Revolution his estates were restored to him. He soon joined the "Club," a body of politicians who were dissatisfied with the Revolution Settlement in Scotland. Proud of his good family and theoretical Liberalism, Fletcher hated monarchy and democracy: and desired to make Scotland an oligarchical republic, of the Venetian or Bernese type. At this time he published two "Discourses" concerning the affairs of Scotland, in one of which he recommended predial slavery as a remedy for pauperism. He formed a friendship with Paterson, the originator of the Bank of England, and supported his Darien scheme. In Anne's reign he led the "Patriots" in their opposition to the Union. In 1703 he introduced his "Limitations" for Queen Anne's successor, some of which strangely anticipate modern Liberalism, and was a prime mover of the "Bill of Security," which passed in 1704, while the "Limitations" were accepted in 1705. But, finding he could not withstand the Union, he exerted his influence more practically to secure freedom of trade. This attitude, rather than any real connection with the Jacobite conspiracies, led to his arrest in 1708.—LOW AND PULLING, *eds.,* 1884, *Dictionary of English History, p.* 464.

PERSONAL

Here is one Fletcher, Laird of Saltoun, lately come from Scotland. He is an ingenious but a violent fanatic, and doubtless hath some commission, for I hear he is very busy and very virulent.—PRESTON, LORD, 1683, *Letter to Lord Halifax from Paris, Oct.* 5.

A Scotch gentleman of great parts, and many virtues, but a most violent republican, and extravagantly passionate.—BURNET, GILBERT, 1715–34, *History of My Own Time.*

One of the brightest of our gentry, remarkable for his fine taste in all manner of polite learning, his curious library, his indefatigable diligence in every thing he thought might benefit and improve his country.—WODROW, ROBERT, 1721–22, *History of the Sufferings of the Church of Scotland, vol.* IV, *p.* 227.

A low, thin man, brown complexion, full of fire, with a stern, sour look.—MACKY, JOHN, 1733, *Memoirs of his Secret Services, p.* 223.

A most arrogant, conceited pedant in politics; cannot endure the least contradiction in any of his visions or paradoxes.

—SWIFT, JONATHAN, 1745? *Remarks on the Characters of The Court of Queen Anne, note.*

A man distinguished by learning and eloquence, distinguished also by courage, disinterestedness, and public spirit, but of an irritable and impracticable temper. Like many of his most illustrious contemporaries, Milton for example, Harrington, Marvel, and Sidney, Fletcher had, from the misgovernment of several successive princes, conceived a strong aversion to hereditary monarchy. Yet he was no democrat. He was the head of an ancient Norman house, and was proud of his descent. He was a fine speaker and a fine writer, and was proud of his intellectual superiority. Both in his character of gentleman, and in his character of scholar, he looked down with disdain on the common people, and was so little disposed to entrust them with political power that he thought them unfit even to enjoy personal freedom. It is a curious circumstance that this man, the most honest, fearless, and uncompromising republican of his time, should have been the author of a plan for reducing a large part of the working classes of Scotland to slavery. He bore, in truth, a lively resemblance to those Roman Senators who, while they hated the name of King, guarded the privileges of their order with inflexible pride against the encroachments of the multitude, and governed their bondmen and bondwomen by means of the stocks and the scourge.—MACAULAY, THOMAS BABINGTON, 1849, *History of England, ch.* v.

There are books, like "Robert Elsmere," written to illustrate passing interest, or to picture transitory events. They are received with much enthusiasm, provoke much discussion, and monopolise public attention for a time, and then are forgotten as others serving the same purpose in constantly changing conditions take their place. And there are men like these books—Sordellos who are born in times when activity must be spent on interests and events soon to be forgotten, who adopt attitudes which do not make history, and who, though they play a large part in their own day, have little influence on, because they have little sympathy with, the future. Their ability cannot save them; the storms and passions they raise or quell cannot make them live; their proportions in their own time are not their proportions in history. Contemporaries who were weak in comparison with them often become of great magnitude and live, whilst they pass away and are hidden amongst the majority of men. One of these, to whom posterity has done but scant justice, is Andrew Fletcher of Saltoun. On the one hand, as a parliamentary representative, he supported a party which was routed and which has left no trace in history; on the other, as a political philosopher, he was at once before and behind his time. Yet of no man could it be more truly said that he erred on the side of uprightness, that he ordered his life too much in accordance with principle, that his honesty deprived his country of the brilliance of his talents. As a politician, he stood head and shoulders over his contemporaries; he played a leading part in every revolutionary project of his troubled times; as a writer and man of letters he was one of the most cultured and erudite of his day; and as a patriot he rose supreme in a crisis when patriotism was never so strong, and when no greater temptations were ever held out to public men to abandon it.—MACDONALD, J. R., 1893, *Andrew Fletcher, The Scottish Review, vol.* 22, *p.* 61.

Whose personality is embalmed by his saying or quotation about the ballads of a nation; and by his not quite senseless crotchet about enslaving beggars.—SAINTSBURY, GEORGE, 1898, *A Short History of English Literature, p.* 523.

GENERAL

His countryman, Andrew Fletcher, is a better master of English style: he writes with purity, clearness, and spirit; but the substance is so much before his eyes, that he is little solicitous about language.—HALLAM, HENRY, 1837–39, *Introduction to the Literature of Europe, pt.* iv, *ch.* vii, *par.* 44.

As an accurate descriptive writer of the manners of his time he ranks high. His pictures are generally sad, though his hopes were ever bright. They are full of gloom, with the shades dull and dark and full of awe; but, vivid with picturesque terseness, they lift his writings above the fleeting reputation of an essayist into the position of valuable historical materials. Sir Walter Scott was among the first to recognize this value of his being a limner of national life; and in the novelist's pages we come across quotations from Fletcher, which give us glimpses into the cavalier-like manners of the time and the deplorable state of the country. His accuracy is undoubted, and a page of his description is like a table of statistics clothed in realization.—PURVES, JAMES, 1882, *Fletcher of Saltoun's Writings, The Antiquary, vol.* 6, *p.* 151.

As a writer he is superior to any Scotchman of his age, and his oratory, nervous and incisive, is made eloquent by his sincerity and earnestness.—ESPINASSE, FRANCIS, 1889, *Dictionary of National Biography, vol.* XIX, *p.* 296.

Fletcher wrote as he must have spoken, clearly and simply. Always full of his subjects, he strung his arguments in a plain sequence, using little or no rhetoric, and seeking no illustration except in history, from which he had extracted a marvellously sound philosophy. Comparison with his pedantic Scottish contemporaries lifts him high above them all in style, his distinguishing qualities being a just choice of words, neatness of construction, and a certain elegance, which is in itself evidence of the breadth of his culture. He has recourse to no passion as an aid to persuasion, except that of patriotism, and though he continually works upon the self-interest of his audience, the largeness and dignity of that interest at once save his theme from debasement and elevate the tone of his eloquence. He may be classed as a strenuous debater, rather than as an orator.—WALLACE, W., 1894, *English Prose, ed. Craik, vol.* III, *p.* 346.

In point of style Fletcher is unique. He had no models. If he had written ten or fifteen years later, it might have been supposed that he had imitated Addison; for, especially in the "Account of a Conversation," the style of Fletcher resembles the style of Addison. But he had ceased to write long before the "*Spectator*" appeared. To Burnet he doubtless owed a sound classical education, and a knowledge of political history. The clearness and elegance of his style, however, were certainly not learned from Burnet, but were evidently the result of studying, very closely, the literature of Greece and Rome, from which he loves to draw illustrations for the purpose of enforcing his own theories of government, and his peculiar political schemes.—OMOND, G. W. T., 1897, *Fletcher of Saltoun* (*Famous Scots Series*), *p.* 150.

John Lord Somers

1651–1716

Somers studied at Oxford, was admitted to the bar, and was one of the counsel for the famous seven bishops, in 1681. In 1692 he became Attorney-General, and in 1697 was made Lord Chancellor, and raised to the peerage. He was afterwards deprived of his Chancellorship and impeached, but was acquitted. Somers was chairman of the committee that drafted the celebrated Declaration of Right, in 1689. *Works:*—The works that Somers has left are scarcely proportionate to his great fame as a jurist. His speeches were never preserved. The most important of his published works are "A Brief History of the Succession of the Crown," and "The Security of Englishmen's Lives," a treatise on grand juries. Besides his graver works, Somers is the author of the translation of Dido's "Epistle to Æneas," and of Plutarch's "Alcibiades," in Tonson's English versions of Ovid and Plutarch. The "Declaration of Right" is conjectured to have emanated wholly from him, and also King William's last Speech to Parliament. —HART, JOHN S., 1872, *A Manual of English Literature, p.* 238.

PERSONAL

The life, the soul, and the spirit of his party.—SUNDERLAND, ROBERT SPENCER, EARL, 1701, *To King William, Sept.* 11; *Miscellaneous State Papers, vol.* III, *p.* 446.

A shallow statesman, though of mighty fame:
An unjust judge, and blemish of the mace,
Witness the bankers' long-depending case,

—SHIPPEN, WILLIAM?, 1704, *Faction Displayed.*

He was very learned in his own profession, with a great deal more learning in other professions, in divinity, philosophy, and history. He had a great capacity for business, with an extraordinary temper; for he was fair and gentle, perhaps to a fault, considering his post. So that he had all the patience and softness, as well as the justice and equity, becoming a great magistrate.—BURNET, GILBERT, 1715–34, *History of My Own Time.*

His life was, in every part of it, set off with that graceful modesty and reserve, which made his virtues more beautiful, the more they were cast in such agreeable shades. . . . His greatest humanity appeared in the minutest circumstances of his conversation. You found it in the benevolence of his aspect, the complacency of his behaviour, and the tone of his voice. His great application to the severer studies of the law, had not infected his temper with anything positive or litigious. He did not know what it was to wrangle on indifferent points, to triumph in the superiority of his understanding, or to be supercilious on the side of truth. He joined the greatest delicacy of good breeding to the greatest strength of reason. . . . His principles were founded in reason, and supported by virtue; and, therefore, did not lie at the mercy of ambition, avarice, or resentment. His notions were no less steady and unshaken, than just and upright.—ADDISON, JOSEPH, 1716, *The Freeholder, No.* 39.

Somers, whose timorous nature, joined with the trade of a common lawyer, and the consciousness of a mean extraction, had taught him the regularity of an alderman, or a gentleman usher.—SWIFT, JONATHAN, 1719, *Letter to Lord Bolingbroke, Dec.* 19.

One of those divine men, who, like a chapel in a palace, remain unprofaned, while all the rest is tyranny, corruption, and folly. All the traditional accounts of him, the historians of the last age, and its best authors, represent him as the most incorrupt lawyer, and the honestest statesman; as a masterly orator, a genius of the finest taste, and as a patriot of the noblest and most extensive views; as a man, who dispensed blessings by his life, and planned them for posterity. He was at once the model of Addison, and the touchstone of Swift: the one wrote from him, the other for him.—WALPOLE, HORACE, 1758, *A Catalogue of the Royal and Noble Authors of England, Scotland and Ireland, vol.* IV, *p.* 76.

In truth, he united all the qualities of a great judge, an intellect comprehensive, quick and acute, diligence, integrity,

patience, suavity. In council, the calm wisdom, which he possessed in a measure rarely found among men of parts so quick and of opinions so decided as his, acquired for him the authority of an oracle. The superiority of his powers appeared not less clearly in private circles. The charm of his conversation was heightened by the frankness with which he poured out his thoughts. His good temper and his good breeding never failed. His gesture, his look, his tones were expressive of benevolence. His humanity was the more remarkable; because he had received from nature a body such as is generally found united with a peevish and irritable mind. His life was one long malady: his nerves were weak: his complexion was livid: his face was prematurely wrinkled. Yet his enemies could not pretend that he had ever once, during a long and troubled public life, been goaded, even by sudden provocation, into vehemence inconsistent with the mild dignity of his character. All that was left to them was to assert that his disposition was very far from being so gentle as the world believed, that he was really prone to the angry passions, and that sometimes, while his voice was soft, and his words kind and courteous, his delicate frame was almost convulsed by suppressed emotion. It will perhaps be thought that this reproach is the highest of all eulogies. The most accomplished men of those times have told us that there was scarcely any subject on which Somers was not competent to instruct and to delight.—MACAULAY, THOMAS BABINGTON, 1855, *History of England, ch.* XX.

Somers's learning and judgment, his honesty, his eloquence, his modesty, mildness, candour, and taste, together with his sweetness of temper, have been acknowledged by all modern authors of whose writings he has been the subject.—FOSS, EDWARD, 1864, *The Judges of England, vol.* VII, *p.* 362.

Learning, patience, industry, instinctive equitableness of judgment, comprehensiveness of view, subtlety of discernment, and command of apt and perspicuous language; in short, all the qualities best fitted to adorn the woolsack, are ascribed to Somers by his contemporaries. Yet, partly by the fault of his reporters, partly in consequence of the dearth of *causes célèbres*, partly by reason of his early surrender of the great seal, his recorded achievement is by no means commensurate with his reputation. . . . Courtly and reserved by nature or habit, Somers carried into the relations of ordinary life a certain formality of demeanour, but in his hours of relaxation could be an agreeable companion. It does not appear that he was a brilliant talker, but his vast erudition and knowledge of affairs placed him at his ease with men of the most diverse interests and occupations. His religious opinions appear to have been latitudinarian. His domestic life did not escape the breath of scandal. His oratory, which cannot be judged by the meagre reports which alone are extant, is said to have united close reasoning with a masculine eloquence, the charm of which was enhanced by a musical voice. To Burke, Somers was the type of "the old whigs" to whom was addressed the famous "Appeal;" to Macaulay he was no less a symbol of awe and veneration. Yet as a statesman he does not merit all the praise which has been lavished upon him by whig panegyrists.—RIGG, J. M., 1898, *Dictionary of National Biography, vol.* LIII, *pp.* 224, 227.

GENERAL

His style in writing was chaste and pure, but, at the same time, full of spirit and politeness; and fit to convey the most intricate business to the understanding of the reader, with the utmost clearness and prespicuity. And here it is to be lamented, that this extraordinary person, out of his natural aversion to vain-glory, wrote several pieces, as well as performed several actions, which he did not assume the honour of: though, at the same time, so many works of this nature have appeared, which every one has ascribed to him, that, I believe, no author of the greatest eminence would deny my Lord Somers to have been the best writer of the age in which he lived.—ADDISON, JOSEPH, 1716, *The Freeholder, No.* 39.

The world will do that justice to the collection, as not to suppose that these specimens from it, *immitis ignis reliquiœ*, will afford an adequate idea of its merits. It filled upwards of sixty volumes in quarto, and did not contain a paper from Lord Somers's pen which the most intimate friend would have wished to secrete, or the bitterest enemy could have fairly turned to his prejudice.—HARDWICKE, LORD, 1778, *ed., Miscellaneous State Papers.*

This great lawyer, to whom every Englishman who feels the blessings of that constitution of government under which he has the happiness to live, owes the highest obligations for the excellent and spirited defences he made of the two great bulwarks of it, the limited succession to the crown, and the trial by jury.—SEWARD, WILLIAM, 1795–97, *Anecdotes of Some Distinguished Persons, vol.* II, *p.* 272.

Political studies alone did not occupy the active mind of Mr. Somers. He had devoted himself with much ardour to classical pursuits; and of the progress which he had made in these, and of his general attachment to literature, he afforded an instance in 1681, by the publication of a translation, into English, of the Epistles of Dido to Æneas, and of Ariadne to Theseus, from Ovid. It would be unreasonable to institute a comparison between the versions of Mr. Somers and those of Dryden and Pope; but may be asserted that in Mr. Somers's attempt there is considerable power of diction, and some ease of versification. — ROSCOE, HENRY, 1830, *Lives of Eminent British Lawyers, p.* 145.

But the greatest man among the members of the Junto, and in some respects, the greatest man of that age, was the Lord Keeper Somers. He was equally eminent as a jurist and as a politician, as an orator and as a writer. His speeches have perished; but his State papers remain, and are models of terse, luminous, and dignified eloquence. — MACAULAY, THOMAS BABINGTON, 1855, *History of England, ch.* XX.

Thomas Parnell

1679–1718

Thomas Parnell, born in Dublin in 1679, and M. A. of Trinity College there, took deacon's orders in 1700, and in 1705 was made Archdeacon of Clogher. He married, was intimate with the wits of Queen Anne's time, and towards the end of her reign went over to the Tories. The queen's death destroyed his hope of advancement by the change. Parnell obtained a prebend through the influence of Swift, and in 1716 was vicar of Finglass. He died in 1718, aged thirty-nine, and his friend Pope published, in 1722, a collected edition of his poems. The best of them was "The Hermit," modernized from an old moral tale.—MORLEY, HENRY, 1879, *A Manual of English Literature, ed. Tyler, p.* 533.

PERSONAL

Such were the notes thy once-loved poet sung,
Till death untimely stopp'd his tuneful tongue.

O, just beheld and lost, admired and mourn'd!
With softest manners, gentlest arts adorn'd!
Bless'd in each science! bless'd in every strain!

Dear to the Muse! to Harley dear—in vain!
—POPE, ALEXANDER, 1721, *To the Right Honourable Robert, Earl of Oxford.*

Dr. Thomas Parnell was archdeacon of Clogher in Ireland. He was a very ingenious man. His poems were published by Mr. Pope. He took at last to immoderate drinking of mild ale, which kill'd him when he was hardly 40. 'Tis said he translated Homer's Iliad into English in excellent prose, and that Mr. Pope afterwards put it into verse, and that this is what goes for Mr. Pope's translation of the Iliad, that he (Mr. Pope) understands little or nothing of the original.—HEARNE, THOMAS, 1734, *Reliquiæ Hearnianæ, ed. Bliss, May 26, vol.* III, *p.* 139.

Parnell, by what I have been able to collect from my father and uncle, who knew him, was the most capable man in the world to make the happiness of those he conversed with, and the least able to secure his own. He wanted that evenness of disposition which bears disappointment with phlegm, and joy with indifference. He was ever much elated or depressed; and his whole life spent in agony or rapture. But the turbulence of these passions only affected himself, and never those about him: he knew the ridicule of his own character, and very effectually raised the mirth of his companions, as well at his vexations as at his triumphs. How much his company was desired, appears from the extensiveness of his connections, and the number of his friends. Even before he made any figure in the literary world, his friendship was sought by persons of every rank and party.—GOLD-SMITH, OLIVER, 1770, *The Life of Dr. Parnell.*

Parnell, who did not want ambition or vanity, was desirous to make himself conspicuous, and to shew how worthy he was of high preferment. As he thought himself qualified to become a popular preacher, he displayed his elocution with great success in the pulpits of London; but the queen's death putting an end to his expectations, abated his diligence; and Pope represents him as falling from that time into intemperance of wine. That in his latter life he was too much a lover of the bottle, is not denied; but I have heard it imputed to a cause more likely to obtain forgiveness from mankind, the untimely death of a darling son; or, as others tell, the loss of his wife, who died (1712) in the midst of his expectations.—JOHNSON, SAMUEL, 1779–81, *Parnell, Lives of the English Poets.*

The whole tenor of Parnell's history convinces us that he was an easy-tempered, kind-hearted, yet querulous and self-indulgent man, who had no higher motive or object than to gratify himself. His very ambition aspired not to very lofty altitudes. His utmost wish was to attain a metropolitan pulpit, where he could have added the reputation of a popular preacher to that of being the *protégé* of Swift, and the pet of the Scriblerus Club.—GILFILLAN, GEORGE, 1855, *ed., The Poetical Works of Johnson, Parnell, Gray, and Smollett, Memoir, p.* 89.

He was always in a state either of elation or depression. His company was much sought by men of both parties, for he was agreeable, generous, and sincere. When he had a fit of spleen he withdrew to a remote part of the country, that he might not annoy others. He shared Swift's dislike of Ireland, and was consequently not popular with his neighbours. In spite of his considerable fortune, he seemed to have often exceeded his income; but his chief weakness, according to Pope, was his inability to resist the general habit of heavy drinking. Pope ascribes the intemperance to dejection occasioned by the death of Parnell's wife. But the vice was apparently neither gross nor notorious. Parnell was fond of popular preaching, and was often heard in public places in Southwark and London in Queen Anne's time.—AITKEN, GEORGE

A., 1895, *Dictionary of National Biography, vol.* XLIII, *p.* 350.

GENERAL

The agreeable Parnell.—SMOLLETT, TOBIAS GEORGE, 1757–58, *History of England, George I., notes.*

It is sufficient, to run over Cowley once: But Parnel, after the fiftieth reading, is as fresh as at the first.—HUME, DAVID, 1753–77, *Of Simplicity and Refinement in Writing.*

The universal esteem in which his poems are held, and the reiterated pleasure they give in the perusal, are a sufficient test of their merit. He appears to me to be the last of that great school that had modelled itself upon the ancients, and taught English poetry to resemble what the generality of mankind have allowed to excel. . . . Parnell is ever happy in the selection of his images, and scrupulously careful in the choice of his subjects. His productions bear no resemblance to those tawdry things, which it has for some time been the fashion to admire; in writing which the poet sits down without any plan, and heaps up splendid images without any selection; where the reader grows dizzy with praise and admiration, and yet soon grows weary, he can scarcely tell why. Our poet, on the contrary, gives out his beauties with a more sparing hand; he is still carrying his reader forward, and just gives him refreshment sufficient to support him to his journey's end.—GOLDSMITH, OLIVER, 1770, *The Life of Dr. Parnell.*

The general character of Parnell is not great extent of comprehension, or fertility of mind. Of the little that appears still less is his own. His praise must be derived from the easy sweetness of his diction: in his verses there is more happiness than pains; he is sprightly without effort, and always delights, though he never ravishes; every thing is proper, yet every thing seems casual. If there is some appearance of elaboration in the "Hermit," the narrative, as it is less airy, is less pleasing. Of his other compositions it is impossible to say whether they are the productions of Nature, so excellent as not to want the help of Art, or of Art so refined as to resemble Nature.—JOHNSON, SAMUEL, 1779–81, *Parnell, Lives of the English Poets.*

Mr. Parnell's tale of the "Hermit" is conspicuous throughout the whole of it, for beautiful descriptive narration. The manner of the Hermit's setting forth to visit the world; his meeting with a companion, and the houses in which they are successively entertained, of the vain man, the covetous man, and the good man, are pieces of very fine painting, touched with a light and delicate pencil, overcharged with no superfluous colouring, and conveying to us a lively idea of the objects.—BLAIR, HUGH, 1783, *Lectures on Rhetoric and Belles-Lettres, ed. Mills, Lecture* xl, *p.* 454.

The compass of Parnell's poetry is not extensive, but its tone is peculiarly delightful: not from mere correctness of expression, to which some critics have stinted its praises, but from the graceful and reserved sensibility that accompanied his polished phraseology. The *curiosa felicitas,* the studied happiness of his diction, does not spoil its simplicity. His poetry is like a flower that has been trained and planted by the skill of the gardener, but which preserves, in its cultured state, the natural fragrance of its wilder air.—CAMPBELL, THOMAS, 1819, *Specimens of the British Poets.*

A gentle wit was pure, polite Parnell,
By many praised, for many loved him well.
His muse glides on "with gentle swimming walk,"
And e'en while singing only seems to talk.
In fact she is an English gentlewoman,
Whom no one would believe a thing uncommon,
Till, by experience taught, we find how rare
Such truly English gentlewomen are.
—COLERIDGE, HARTLEY, 1849, *Sketches of English Poets, Poems, vol.* II.

We know not how it is with others, but we never think of Parnell's "Hermit" without tranquilizing and grateful feelings. Parnell was a true poet of a minor order; he saw nature for himself, though he wrote a book style; and this, and one or two other poems of his, such as the eclogue on "Health," and the "Fairy Tale," have inclined us to believe that there is something in the very name of "Parnell" peculiarly gentle and agreeable. —HUNT, LEIGH, 1849, *A Book for a Corner.*

The character of his poetry is in keeping with the temperament of the man. It is slipshod, easy, and pleasing. If the distinguishing quality of poetry be to give pleasure, then Parnell is a poet. You never thrill under his power, but you read him with a quiet, constant, subdued gratification. If never eminently original, he has the art of enunciating commonplaces with felicity and grace. The stories he relates are almost all old, but his manner of telling them is new. His thoughts and images are mostly selected from his common-place book; but he utters them with such a natural ease of manner, that you are tempted to think them his own. He knows the compass of his poetical powers, and never attempts anything very lofty or arduous.—GILFILLAN, GEORGE, 1855, *ed.*, *The Poetical Works of Johnson, Parnell, Gray, and Smollett, Memoir*, p. 89.

Parnell is always an inoffensive and agreeable writer; and sometimes, as, for example, in his Nightpiece on Death, which probably suggested Gray's more celebrated Elegy, he rises to considerable impressiveness and solemn pathos. But, although his poetry is uniformly fluent and transparent, and its general spirit refined and delicate, it has little warmth or richness, and can only be called a sort of water-color poetry.—CRAIK, GEORGE L., 1861, *A Compendious History of English Literature and of the English Language*, *vol.* II, *p.* 264.

The great drawback to Parnell, notwithstanding the simplicity and charm of his style, is the want of the popular element in his subjects, and the absence of anything of passion or enthusiasm in his manner. The periodical contributions of Parnell were in the style of visions and allegories, which Addison so successfully employed, without the coldness and tediousness which usually characterised them in other hands. Those of Parnell possess considerable merit, but none of his prose was equal to his verse.—MONTGOMERY, HENRY R., 1862, *Memoirs of the Life and Writings of Sir Richard Steele, vol.* I, *p.* 261.

In contemplating the Lampadephoria of poetical history we sometimes meet with a figure whose torch was well charged with the resin of genius and ready to be enflamed, but whom accidental circumstances removed from the line of light so long and so far that its destiny was never properly fulfilled. Such a figure is Parnell, who, having spent his youth as a thoroughly insignificant amateur in verse,

was roused during the last five years of his life, under the influence of Pope, a much younger man than he, to strike a few magnificent chords on the lyre of a true poet. . . . This sententious and sonorous writer, whose verse in its deeper harmonies surpasses even Pope's in melody, fancied himself a satirist, a society-singer, and emulated in his false ambition the successes of Oldham and Prior. But while he was vainly attempting to subdue for himself a province in Acrostic-land, there lay unvisited a romantic island of poesy, which was his by birthright, and it was Pope who opened his eyes to this fact. . . . "The Hermit" may be considered as forming the apex and *chef d'auvre* of Augustan poetry in England. It is more exactly in the French taste than any work that preceded it, and after it English poetry swiftly passed into the degeneracy of classicism. Parnell's poem is the model of a moral *conte;* the movement is dingified and rapid, the action and reflection are balanced with exquisite skill, the surprise is admirably prepared, and the treatment never flags from beginning to end.—GOSSE, EDMUND, 1880, *English Poets, ed. Ward, vol.* III, *pp.* 133, 134.

Besides Parnell's significance as the first of the churchyard poets, there is in his poetry a genuine feeling for Nature, which is very unlike the Augustan spirit, and which even suggests Wordsworth. It seems as if the latter might have named Parnell along with Lady Winchelsea in his famous utterance in 1815.—PHELPS, WILLIAM LYON, 1893, *The Beginnings of the English Romantic Movement, p.* 26.

Who possessed the soul of a poet, but gave limited expression to it, for it was only during the later years of a short life that he discovered where his genius lay.—DENNIS, JOHN, 1894, *The Age of Pope, p.* 107.

We quite agree with Blair that Parnell would stand much higher in popular estimation had his merits not been so preposterously overrated by Hume.—COLLINS, JOHN CHURTON, 1895, *Essays and Studies, p.* 110.

As a poet, Parnell's work is marked with sweetness, refined sensibility, musical and fluent versification, and high moral tone. There are many faulty lines and awkward expressions, and there would have been more had not Pope revised the more important pieces. Pope, his junior by nine years, gave him much good advice, and the twenty poems which Pope published contain all by which his friend will be remembered. The best are "The Hermit," "The Fairy Tale," "The Night Piece on Death," "The Hymn to Contentment," and "Hesiod, or the Rise of Woman." Parnell was a careful student of Milton, and his writings influenced Young and Blair in one direction and Goldsmith, Gay, and Collins in another.—AITKEN, GEORGE A., 1895, *Dictionary of National Biography, vol.* XLIII, *p.* 351.

It is curious that, out of the small bulk of Parnell's poetical work, poetical criticism of the most various times and tastes has been able to pick quite different things to sustain its reputation. The famous "Hermit" has kept its place in all anthologies; Goldsmith extolled the translations, and Johnson endorsed his views, though he himself liked the "Allegory on Man"

best. And later censorship, which finds the "Hermit" not much more than a smooth and ingenious exercise in verse, and the translations and imitations unimportant, has lavished praise on two small pieces, "The Night-Piece on Death" and the "Hymn to Contentment," the former of which certainly displays nature-painting of a kind unknown in the work of any but one contemporary, while the return of the second to the "Comus" alternation of trochaic and iambic cadence is an almost equally important, though doubtless unintended, protest against the ceaseless iambs of the couplet. It is not possible to call Parnell a great poet as he stands; but the quality and the variety of his accomplishment show that in slightly different circumstances and in other times he would probably have been one.—SAINTSBURY, GEORGE, 1898, *A Short History of English Literature, p.* 562.

Nicholas Rowe

1674–1718.

Born at Little Barford, Bedfordshire, 1674; baptized, 30 June. Early education at a school at Highgate. To Westminster School as King's Scholar, 1638. Called to Bar at Middle Temple. Abandoned legal profession after death of his father in 1692. Married (i.) Antonia Parsons, 1700 [?]. Play, "The Ambitious Stepmother," produced at Lincoln's Inn Fields, 1700; "Tamerlane," 1702; "The Fair Penitent," 1703; "The Biter," 1704; "Ulysses," 1706. "The Royal Convert," Haymarket, 25 Nov. 1707; "Jane Shore," Drury Lane, 2 Feb. 1714; "Lady Jane Grey," Drury Lane, 20 April 1715. Wife died, 1706. Under-Secretary to Sec. of State for Scotland, 1709-11. Poet Laureate, Aug. 1715. Surveyor of Customs, Oct. 1715. Married (ii.) Anne Devenish, 1717. Clerk of Council to Prince of Wales. Clerk of Presentations, 1718. Died, in London, 6 Dec. 1718. Buried in Westminster Abbey. *Works:* "The Ambitious Stepmother," 1701; "Tamerlane," 1702; "The Fair Penitent," 1703; "Britannia's Charge to the Sons of Freedom," 1703; "The Biter," 1705; "Ulysses," 1706; "Ode on the late Glorious successes of Her Majesty's Arms," 1707; "The Royal Convert," 1708; "The Tragedy of Jane Shore," [1714]; "Poems on Several Occasions," 1714; "Mæcenas," 1714; "The Tragedy of Lady Jane Grey," 1715; "Ode for the New Year 1716," 1716. He *translated:* Boileau's "Lutrin," 1708; De La Bruyère's "Characters," 1708; Quillet's "Callipædiæ," 1710; Lucan's "Pharsalia," 1718; and *edited:* Shakespeare's Works, 1709. *Collected Works:* in 3 vols., 1727; in 2 vols., ed. by Dr. Johnson, 1792.—SHARP, R. FARQUHARSON, 1897, *A Dictionary of English Authors, p.* 241.

PERSONAL

Mr. Rowe accompanied me, and passed a week in the forest. I need not tell you how much a man of his turn entertained me; but I must acquaint you there is a vivacity and gaiety of disposition, almost peculiar to him, which make it impossible to part from him without that uneasiness which generally succeeds all our pleasures. —POPE, ALEXANDER, 1715–16, *Letter to Edward Blount, Feb.* 10.

Mr. Nic. Rowe is made poet laureat in the room of Mr. Tate, deceased. This Rowe is a great whig, and but a mean poet.—HEARNE, THOMAS, 1715, *Reliquiæ Hearnianæ, ed. Bliss, Aug.* 26, *vol.* II, *p.* 16.

Mr. Rowe, as to his person, was graceful and well made, his face regular and of a manly beauty; he had a quick, and fruitful invention, a deep penetration, and a large compass of thought, with a singular dexterity, and easiness in communicating his opinions. He was master of most parts of polite learning, especially the Classic Authors, both Greek and Latin; he understood the French, Italian and Spanish languages. He had likewise read most of the Greek and Roman histories in their original languages; and most that are written in English, French, Italian and Spanish: He had a good taste in philosophy, and having a firm impression of religion upon his mind, he took delight in divinity, and ecclesiastical history, in both which he made great advances in the times he retired to the country, which were frequent. He expressed upon all occasions, his full perswasion of the truth of revealed religion; and being a sincere member of the established church himself, he pitied, but condemned not, those who departed from him; he abhorred the principle of persecuting men on account of religious opinions, and being strict in his own, he took it not upon him to censure those of another persuasion. His conversation was pleasant, witty, and learned, without the least tincture of affectation or pedantry; and his inimitable manner of diverting, or enlivening the company, made it impossilbe for any one to be out of humour when he was in it: Envy and detraction, seemed to be entirely foreign to his constitution; and whatever provocation he met with at any time, he passed them over, without the least thought of resentment or revenge. There were not wanting some malevolent people, and some pretenders to poetry too, that would some times bark at his best performances; but he was too much conscious of his own genius, and had so much good-nature as to forgive them, nor could however be tempted to return them an answer.—WELWOOD, JAMES, 1716–18, ed., Rowe's Lucan's Pharsalia, Preface.

Mr. Rowe's Plays were written from the heart. He practised the virtue he admired, and he never, in his gayest moments, suffered himself to talk loosely or lightly upon religious or moral subjects; or to turn any thing sacred, or which good men reverenced as such, into ridicule.—

CIBBER, THEOPHILUS, 1753, Lives of the Poets, vol. III, p. 279.

Rowe, in the opinion of Mr. Pope, maintained a decent character, but had no heart. Mr. Addison was justly offended with him for some behaviour which arose from that want, and estranged himself from him; which Rowe felt very severely. Mr. Pope, their common friend, knowing this, took an opportunity, at some juncture of Mr. Addison's advancement, to tell him poor Rowe was grieved at his displeasure, and what satisfaction he expressed at his good fortune; which he expressed so naturally, that he could not but think him sincere. Addison replied, I do not suspect that he feigned; but the levity of his heart is such, that he is struck with any new adventure, and it would affect him just in the same manner if he heard I was going to be hanged. —Mr. Pope said, he could not deny but that Mr. Addison understood Rowe well. —RUFFHEAD, OWEN, 1769, Life of Alexander Pope.

Deserves to be remembered as a tragic dramatist on grounds more solid than those which entitle him to an "esteem" such as too many of his contemporaries have failed to secure. The success of his literary career, which may be held to have culminated in his appointment (just after the close of our period) to the Poet-Laureateship, was due in part to his personal presence, breeding, and training,—in part to his assiduous service in the interest of the dominant political party to which he remained consistently attached,—and very largely to the versatility of his talents and to the modesty with which he bore the successes of a singularly prosperous career.—WARD, ADOLPHUS WILLIAM, 1875–99, A History of English Dramatic Literature, vol. III, p. 433.

Rowe died on the 6th December, 1718, and was buried in Westminster Abbey, where there is a handsome monument to his memory in Poet's Corner. On the front of the pedestal is the inscription:— "To the memory of Nicholas Rowe, Esq., who died in 1718, aged forty-five; and of Charlotte, his only daughter, wife of Henry Fane, Esq., who, inheriting her father's spirit, and amiable in her own innocence and beauty, died in the twenty-second year of her age, 1739." Then follows a poetical epitaph:—

"Thy reliques, Rowe, to this sad shrine we trust,
And near thy Shakespeare place thy honour'd
bust.
Oh! next him skilled to draw the tender tear,
For never heart felt passion more sincere;
To nobler sentiments to fire the brave,
For never Briton more disdain'd a slave.
Peace to thy gentle shade, and endless rest;
Blest in thy genius, in thy love too blest!
And blest, that timely from our scene removed,
Thy soul enjoys the liberty it loved.
To thee so mourn'd in death, so loved in life,
The childless parent, and the widow'd wife
With tears inscribes this monumental stone
That holds their ashes, and expects her own."
—HAMILTON, WALTER, 1879, *The Poets Laureate of England, p.* 137.

TAMERLANE
1702

This was the tragedy which Rowe valued most, and that which probably, by the help of political auxiliaries, excited most applause; but occasional poetry must often content itself with occasional praise. "Tamerlane" has for a long time been acted only once a year, on the night when king William landed. Our quarrel with Lewis has been long over; and it now gratifies neither zeal nor malice to see him painted with aggravated features, like a Saracen upon a sign.—JOHNSON, SAMUEL, 1779–81, *Rowe, Lives of the English Poets.*

The play upon which its author is said to have "valued himself most," chiefly interests us as treating one of the most famous themes of the Elisabethan drama. But most assuredly this Tamerlane would have caused supreme astonishment to Marlowe. In the place of the truculent hero of the old tragedy, with his "high astounding terms," we are here met by a calm, tolerant, nay philosophic prince, who discusses the common merits of varying forms of religion in a tone resembling that of Nathan the Wise, and whom the severest of personal trials hardly suffice to move from his temperate calm. . . . The plot is altogether without dramatic probability; everything as usual resolves itself into a love-story; but even here the poet fails to rise to the height of his own situations; his efforts indeed are perceptible, but to borrow a phrase which he appears to affect, "it wo' not be."—WARD, ADOLPHUS WILLIAM, 1875–99, *A History of English Dramatic Literature, vol.* III, *pp.* 434, 435.

THE FAIR PENITENT
1703

One of the most pleasing tragedies on the stage, where it still keeps its turns of appearing, and probably will long keep them, for there is scarcely any work of any poet at once so interesting by the fable, and so delightful by the language. The story is domestick, and therefore easily received by the imagination, and assimilated to common life; the diction is exquisitely harmonious, and soft or sprightly as occasion requires.—JOHNSON, SAMUEL, 1779–81, *Rowe, Lives of the English Poets.*

It is a remarkable instance of the decay of dramatic art at this period, that several of the principal authors of the time felt themselves at liberty to write imitations of old plays belonging to the original school, by way of adapting them to the taste of their own age. "The Fair Penitent" of Rowe is well known as a poor imitation of Massinger's "Fatal Dowry." It does not greatly excel the original in the management and conduct of the piece; and, in everything else, falls as far beneath it as the baldest translation can sink below the most spirited original.—SCOTT, SIR WALTER, 1814–23, *Essay on the Drama.*

In my opinion "The Fair Penitent" while sharing the general features that are so attractive in the works of Rowe, is not indebted for its extraordinary success to any special merit. It is to be feared that this success was not unconnected with the ghastly device of the first scene of the last act, where the unhappy heroine is discovered "in a room hung with Black; on one side Lothario" (her seducer)'s "Body on a Bier; on the other, a Table, with a Skull and other Bones, a Book and a Lamp on it." It would be an error to suppose that this play, the idea of which is borrowed from Massinger and Field's "The Fatal Dowry," shows any sustained endeavour to trace the purifying power of penitence, or to rival the tender pathos of such an Elisabethan tragedy as Heywood's "A Woman Killed with Kindness."—WARD, ADOLPHUS WILLIAM, 1875–99, *A History of English Dramatic Literature, vol.* III, *p.* 435.

SHAKESPEARE'S WORKS
1709

I believe, those who compare it with former copies will find that he has done more than he promised; and that, without the pomp of notes or boasts of criticisms, many passages are happily restored. . . . He at least contributed to the popularity of his author.—JOHNSON, SAMUEL, 1779-81, *Rowe, Lives of the English Poets.*

Rowe's edition of Shakspere, we doubt not, supplied a general want. Its critical merits were but small.—KNIGHT, CHARLES, 1849, *Studies of Shakspere.*

In 1709 Nicholas Rowe published a life of the poet, the materials for which were contributed chiefly by Betterton, the celebrated Restoration actor. "I must own," says Rowe, "a particular obligation to him for the most considerable part of the passage relating to his life which I have here transmitted to the public, his veneration for the memory of Shakspere having engaged him to gather up what remains he could of a name for which he had so great value." Thus Rowe's account claims to be based on special inquiry, and though the accuracy of many of its statements has often been questioned, it bears upon it intrinsic evidence of good faith, and in several points it has been strikingly verified by modern research. In the acceptance of tradition scepticism may be pushed to a point where it is little less of a historical vice than uncritical credulity, and because some of Rowe's anecdotes are picturesque they are not therefore necessarily untrue.—BOAS, FREDERICK S., 1896, *Shakspere and his Predecessors, p. 92.*

One of Rowe's chief achievements was an edition of Shakespeare's works. . . . This is reckoned the first attempt to edit Shakespeare in the modern sense. In the prefatory life Rowe embodies a series of traditions which he had commissioned the actor Betterton to collect for him while on a visit to Stratford-on-Avon; many of them were in danger of perishing without a record. Rowe displayed much sagacity in the choice and treatment of his biographic materials, and the memoir is consequently of permanent value. As a textual editor his services were less notable, but they deserve commendations as the labours of a pioneer.—LEE, SIDNEY, 1897, *Dictionary of National Biography, vol.* XLIX, *p.* 343.

JANE SHORE
1714

It was mighty simple in Rowe, to write a play now, professedly in Shakespeare's style, that is, professedly in the style of a bad age.—POPE, ALEXANDER, 1734-36, *Spence's Anecdotes, ed. Singer, p.* 131.

In what he thought himself an imitator of Shakspeare, it is not easy to conceive. The numbers, the diction, the sentiments, and the conduct, every thing in which imitation can consist, are remote in the utmost degree from the manner of Shakspeare; whose dramas it resembles only as it is an English story, and as some of the persons have their names in history. This play, consisting chiefly of domestick scenes and private distress, lays hold upon the heart. The wife is forgiven because she repents, and the husband is honoured because he forgives. This, therefore, is one of those pieces which we still welcome on the stage.—JOHNSON, SAMUEL, 1779-81, *Rowe, Lives of the English Poets.*

Perhaps you never saw Mrs. Siddons act it; but, even read, it is most touching poetry. You must allow Jane Shore her rank among the heroines of the English stage. . . . Rowe's Jane Shore I maintain to be perfectly moral; he paints her only in her penitence—in all the horror of remorse—in abject poverty: she is brought before you as the victim of her own guilt, and, if you will compare with Shakespeare, I must say that Cleopatra is immoral, and Jane Shore is not.—MACKINTOSH, SIR JAMES, 1846, *Portfolio of a Man of the World, Gentleman's Magazine, vol.* 117, *pp.* 587, 588.

GENERAL

Rowe writ a foolish farce, called "The Biter," which was damned.—CONGREVE, WILLIAM, 1704, *Letter to Keally, Dec.* 9.

The pomp of verse and golden lines of Rowe.—THOMSON, JAMES, 1745, *Tancred and Sigismunda, Prologue.*

We deem it unnecessary to give any specimen of Mr. Rowe's poetry; the most celebrated speeches in his plays, which are beautifully harmonious; are repeated by every body who reads poetry, or attends plays; and to suppose the reader ignorant of them, would be to degrade him from that rank of intelligence, without which he can be little illuminated by perusing the "Lives of the Poets."—CIBBER, THEOPHILUS, 1753, *Lives of the Poets, vol.* III, *p.* 284.

Rowe's genius was rather delicate and soft than strong and pathetic; his compositions soothe us with a tranquil and tender sort of complacency, rather than cleave the heart with pangs of commiseration. His distresses are entirely founded on the passion of love. His diction is extremely elegant and chaste, and his versification highly melodious. His plays are declamations rather than dialogues, and his characters are general and undistinguished from each other.—WARTON, JOSEPH, 1756–82, *Essay on Pope.*

Rowe, solemn, florid, and declamatory. —SMOLLETT, TOBIAS GEORGE, 1757–58, *History of England.*

The version of "Lucan" is one of the greatest productions of English poetry; for there is perhaps none that so completely exhibits the genius and spirit of the original. "Lucan" is distinguished by a kind of dictatorial or philosophick dignity, rather, as Quintilian observes, declamatory than poetical; full of ambitious morality and pointed sentences, comprised in vigorous and animated lines. This character Rowe has very diligently and successfully preserved. His versification which is such as his contemporaries practised, without any attempt at innovation or improvement, seldom wants either melody or force. His author's sense is sometimes a little diluted by additional infusions, and some times weakened by too much expansion. But such faults are to be expected in all translations, from the constraint of measures and dissimilitude of languages. The "Pharsalia" of Rowe deserves more notice than it obtains, and as it is more read will be more esteemed.—JOHNSON, SAMUEL, 1779–81, *Rowe, Lives of the English Poets.*

He is full of elevated and moral sentiments. The poetry is often good, and the language always pure and elegant; but in most of his plays, he is too cold and uninteresting; and flowery rather than tragic. Two, however, he has produced, which deserve to be exempted from this censure, "Jane Shore" and the "Fair Penitent;" in both of which there are so many tender and truly pathetic scenes, as to render them justly favourites of the public.— BLAIR, HUGH, 1783, *Lectures on Rhetoric and Belles-Letters, ed. Mills, Lecture* xlvi, *p.* 532.

Rowe's "Despairing Shepherd" is the sweetest poem of the kind we have in England.—DRAKE, NATHAN, 1798–1820, *Literary Hours, vol.* I, *No.* xvi, *p.* 258.

Rowe was an honest admirer of Shakspeare, and his modest reverence for this superior genius was rewarded by a return to nature and truth. The traces of imitation are not to be mistaken: the part of Gloster in "Jane Shore" is even directly borrowed from "Richard the Third." Rowe did not possess boldness and vigour, but sweetness and feeling; he could excite the softer emotions, and hence, in his "Fair Penitent," "Jane Shore," and "Lady Jane Gray," he has successfully chosen female heroines and their weaknesses for his subject.—SCHLEGEL, AUGUSTUS WILLIAM, 1809, *Dramatic Art and Literature, Lecture* xiii, *tr. Black.*

If he did not bring back the full fire of the drama, at least preserved its vestal spark from being wholly extinguished.— CAMPBELL, THOMAS, 1819, *An Essay on English Poetry.*

The ashes, and scarcely glowing embers, of Rowe. — JEFFREY, FRANCIS LORD, 1822–44, *Contributions to the Edinburgh Review, vol.* II, *p.* 334.

Rowe, though deeply infected with the false French taste which was then fashionable, was not unacquainted with the early English writers, and some beneficial effects from this acquaintance are visible in all his Dramas. Perhaps his versification is the best part about him; and his blank verse has a flow and an easy sweetness, which are advantageously contrasted to the tumidity of Dryden, and the feebleness of Otway.—NEELE, HENRY, 1827–29, *Lectures on English Poetry.*

Was esteemed in his own day a great master of the pathetic, but is now regarded as little more than a smooth and occasionally sounding versifier.—CRAIK, GEORGE L., 1861, *A Compendious History of English Literature and of the English Language, vol.* II, *p.* 275.

Rowe's general characteristics as a man of letters reflect themselves with sufficient distinctness in his tragic dramas, which in a single respect only—but that a very important one—surpass the endeavours of the foremost among his predecessors. In dramatic power, as exhibiting itself in characterisation, he cannot be said to have excelled. Of a genuinely poetic touch he shows few signs. His plays are still occupied almost entirely with themes of "heroic love;" on this pivot everything is made to turn, whatever other passions may be nominally brought into play. In the invention of situations exciting terror or pity Rowe is fertile and skilful; he is fond of night-scenes, and of all the outward machinery of awe and gloom. But he rarely exhibits any natural force even in his most effective passages, and is wanting in impetus or in aspiring ardour, where some exceptional movement of the kind seems to be demanded by his theme. His most distinctive and most praiseworthy feature lies in the greater degree of refinement to which in expression if not in sentiment he has attained. Rowe is indeed far from being an English Racine; his style is too tame to rise to the dignified beauty and exquisite grace proper to the great French tragedian; but he is at least subject to none of those grosser influences which depressed the higher impulses of so many dramatists whose creative genius was not inferior to his own.—WARD, ADOLPHUS WILLIAM, 1875–99, *A History of English Dramatic Literature, vol. III, p.* 433.

His English verse may be taken to represent what Lord Macaulay calls the critical poetry of his age, the poetry by courtesy,—the poetry to which the memory, the judgment, and the wit contribute far more than the imagination. During the short time he held office as Laureate he appears to have escaped the fate of most of his predecessors; his amiability of temper preserved him from the dislike or envy of his contemporaries, whilst his cleverness protected him from ridicule.—HAMILTON, WALTER, 1879, *The Poets Laureate of England, p.* 136.

Rowe's dramatic work is not yet absolutely forgotten by the world. We still hear of the "gallant gay Lothario," although many of those who are glib with the words do not know that they come from the "Fair Penitent," and would not care even if they did know.—McCARTHY, JUSTIN, 1884, *A History of the Four Georges, ch.* ii.

Measured by his contemporary dramatists he is a distinguished playwright. His characters do not live, but he could invent effective scenes, though in some cases the poet's taste may be questioned. —DENNIS, JOHN, 1894, *The Age of Pope, p.* 103.

To Rowe's devotion to tragedy alone we owe "Jane Shore" and "Lady Jane Grey." The tenderness, the grace, the pathos of these plays show how thorough and affectionate had been Rowe's study of the great Elizabethan drama. The proof of Rowe's power is in the fact that they held the stage so long and were so popular even in the age other than his own. *Jane Shore* was one of the great Sarah Siddons's favourite characters. Sir James Mackintosh spoke with great feeling of the way she acted it, but he added that even were the play never seen upon the stage, but simply read, it would prove itself to be most thrilling poetry, dealing as it does with some of the most touching phases of remorse and pain. But with all the genuine power of these two great tragedies, Rowe's chief distinction in the history of English literature lies in the fact that he was the first to bring out an edition of Shakespeare, and to inaugurate that revival of the legitimate Shakespearean drama which gave Shakespeare his rightful place in the hearts of the people. His admiration of Shakespeare was honest and sincere, and the effect of that admiration is seen in the excellence of his own work. —WEST, KENYON, 1895, *The Laureates of England, p.* 75.

Is dull, but never gross.—BROOKE, STOPFORD A., 1896, *English Literature, p.* 195.

Richard Cumberland

1631–1718.

Richard Cumberland, D. D., bishop of Peterborough, a learned divine and archæologist, was born in London in 1632, and was educated at St. Paul's School, and Magdalen College, Cambridge. He was made rector of Brampton, and in 1667 vicar of All Hallows, Stamford. In 1691 he was raised to the see of Peterborough without any solicitation on his part. He was previously known by his treatise "De Legibus Naturæ," (London, 1672, 4to), in answer to Hobbes, and by his "Essay on Jewish Weights and Measures," (London, 1686, 8vo). He was indefatigable in performing his episcopal duties. Being advised, on account of his age and infirm state, to relax a little, he replied, "It is better to wear out than rust out." After his death appeared his "Origines Gentium" (London 1724, 8vo); and his translation of "Sanchoniatho's Phœnician History" (London, 1720, 8vo). At the age of eighty-three, Dr. Cumberland, having been presented by Dr. Wilkins with a copy of his Coptic Testament, then just published, commenced, like another Cato, the study of Coptic. "At this age," says Mr. Payne, "He mastered the language, and went through great part of this version, and would often give me excellent hints and remarks as he proceeded in reading of it." He died Oct. 9, 1718. Cumberland's theory of morals is set forth in his treatise "De Legibus Naturæ."—M'CLINTOCK AND STRONG, eds., 1868, *Cyclopædia of Biblical, Theological and Ecclesiastical Literature, vol.* II, *p.* 602.

PERSONAL

The pastoral industry, affectionate zeal, and fervent piety of Bishop Cumberland, were as conspicuous as his learning and theological acumen.—ALLIBONE, S. AUSTIN, 1854–58, *Dictionary of English Literature, vol.* I, *p.* 459.

From Payne's account he appears to have been a man of great simplicity and entire absence of vanity. He was slow and phlegmatic, and preferred the accumulation to the diffusion of knowledge. He received a copy of Wilkins's Coptic Testament at the age of eighty-three, and learned the language in order to examine the book. At the same age he was forced to give up the visitation of his diocese. He had previously discharged his duties conscientiously, saying often that "a man had better wear out than rust out." He was liberal, and at the end of every year gave all surplus revenue to the poor, reserving only 25*l.* to pay for his funeral. —STEPHEN, LESLIE, 1888, *Dictionary of National Biography, vol.* XIII, *p.* 290.

GENERAL

It ["Recovery of Jewish Weights and Measures"] discovers great sagacity, learning, and research. The subject is attended with many difficulties, which the Bishop of Peterborough combats, perhaps as successfully as could reasonably be expected. The work was attacked by Bernard in a Latin work on the same subject, published two years after; but it is highly spoken of by Le Clerc.—ORME, WILLIAM, 1824, *Bibliotheca Biblica.*

His manner of reasoning is diffuse, abounding in repetitions, and often excursive: we cannot avoid perceiving that he labors long on propositions which no adversary would dispute, or on which the dispute could be little else than one of verbal definition. . . . As Taylor's "Ductor Dubitantium" is nearly the last of

a declining school, Cumberland's "Law of Nature" may be justly considered as the herald, especially in England, of a new ethical philosophy, of which the main characteristics were, first, that it stood complete in itself without the aid of revelation; secondly, that it appealed to no authority of earlier writers whatever, though it sometimes used them in illustration; thirdly, that it availed itself of observation and experience, alleging them generally, but abstaining from particular instances of either, and making, above all, no display of erudition; and, fourthly, that it entered very little upon casuistry, leaving the application of principles to the reader.—HALLAM, HENRY, 1837–39, *Introduction to the Literature of Europe, pt.* iv, *ch.* iv, *pars.* 22, 36.

Cumberland stands by himself, . . . is important as a distinctly philosophical disquisition, but its extraordinarily discursive character renders impossible anything like analysis.—BAIN, ALEXANDER, 1869, *Moral Science, p.* 142.

His doctrines have an independent place in the history of philosophy; but as he wrote in Latin, he has but a quasi-legitimate standing in the history of English literature.—MINTO, WILLIAM, 1872–80, *Manual of English Prose Literature, p.* 337.

Bishop Cumberland was the first of English-speaking moralists to teach that virtue or rectitude consists in general or universal benevolence. For this, his name is worthy of perpetual remembrance among philosophers.—MAGOUN, GEORGE F., 1887, *A Fountain-Head of English Ethics, Bibliotheca Sacra, vol.* 44, *p.* 92.

His book on the laws of nature was one of the innumerable treatises called out by opposition to Hobbes. It is rather cumbrous and discursive, but is ably written, and remarkable as laying down distinctly a utilitarian criterion of morality. The public good is the end of morality, and "universal benevolence" the source of all virtues. Cumberland occupies an important place in English ethical speculation, and his influence seems to be traceable in the writings of Shaftesbury and Hutcheson.—STEPHEN, LESLIE, 1888, *Dictionary of National Biography, vol.* XIII, *p.* 290.

The bishop wrote an excessively bad style, alike in Latin and in English. He is often quite unintelligible and always dull. Long, involved sentences, and tedious, almost irrelevant, digressions, mar his pages. That he was a man of deep learning, careful judgment, and acute reasoning power is evident enough, but that he either could not or would not put his doubtless valuable matter into an attractive form, is also only too painfully evident. There is neither humour, poetry, nor any embellishment in his writings. Clumsy, long-winded disquisitions on themes that have years ago lost any interest they may ever have had, constantly recur as we turn over page after page of his treatises. To serve as a warning that, however valuable the matter, badness of manner will inevitably damn a book in the eyes of posterity is the only lasting good poor old Bishop Cumberland can claim to have accomplished.—FITZROY, A. I., 1894, *English Prose, ed. Craik, vol.* III, *p.* 201.

Culverwell and Cumberland scarcely rank in a literary history.—GARNETT, RICHARD, 1895, *The Age of Dryden, p.* 164.

While the doctrine of Universalistic Hedonism has played a most conspicuous part in English Ethics since the time of Paley and Bentham, it is not commonly realized that the essential features of the system were stated and developed by a contemporary of the Cambridge Platonists. It is true that Cumberland's treatise, *De legibus naturae,* like most ethical works of the time, were largely controversial in character, being written to refute Hobbes. Moreover, the jural aspect of the system, implied by the very title of the treatise, tends to obscure what for us is by far its most important feature. And even this is not all. The "common good" which Cumberland regarded as the end of all truly moral action, includes "perfection" as well as "happiness," which leads to serious confusion in the working out of the system. But, making all allowances for what was incidental in the external form of the work, and the confusion of two principles which have long since become clearly differentiated, it is well worth while to examine with some care the ablest, or at any rate the most successful, opponent of Hobbes and the true founder of English Utilitarianism. . . . While the thinker of an ordinary ability, and standing for a principle which has become clearly differentiated in the later development of English Ethics, Cumberland is so utterly lacking in a talent for exposition that the adequate presentation of his views is a matter of peculiar difficulty. Indeed, even apart from its singular lack of method, the fact that the work is so largely controversial in character, increases the difficulty of extracting from it the author's own system.—ALBEE, ERNEST, 1895, *The Ethitical System of Richard Cumberland, The Philosophical Review, vol.* 4, *pp.* 264, 277.

William Penn

1644–1718.

He was born in 1644, the son of Admiral Sir William Penn, educated at Christ church, Oxford, and, having turned Quaker, was twice turned out of doors by his father. Then he was tolerated, but not helped, at home, and no effort was made to release him when he was imprisoned for attendance at religious meetings. He began at the age of twenty-four (in 1668) to preach and write. For his second paper, "The Sandy Foundation Shaken," he was imprisoned seven months in the Tower, and he wrote in prison, at the age of twenty-five, his most popular book, "No Cross, no Crown." He obtained release by a vindication called "Innocency with her Open Face." In 1670 his father died, reconciled to him. Penn inherited his estate; then wrote, travelled, supported his religious faith; and in 1681, for his father's services and debts to him from the Crown, obtained a grant of New Netherlands, thenceforward called Pennsylvania. In 1682, having published his scheme in "A Brief Account of the Province of Pennsylvania," he embarked for America, and founded Philadelphia. In 1684, the last year of Charles II., Penn revisited England. He published, in 1694, "A Brief Account of the Rise and Progress of the People called Quakers," and an "Account of his Travels in Holland and Germany in 1677, and for the Service of the Gospel of Christ, by way of Journal." He died in 1718; and his collected writings, published in 1726, fill two folio volumes.—MORLEY, HENRY, 1879, *A Manual of English Literature, ed. Tyler, p.* 498.

PERSONAL

Mr. Pen, Sir William's son, is come back from France and come to visit my wife. A most modish person, grown, she says, a fine gentleman. . . . After dinner comes Mr. Pen to visit me, and staid an houre talking with me. I perceive something of learning he hath got, but a great deale if not too much, of the vanity of the French garbe and affected manner of speech and gait. I fear all real profit he hath made of his travel will signify little.—PEPYS, SAMUEL, 1664, *Diary, Aug.* 26–30.

Went to schoole in London, a private schole on that hill, and his father kept a tutor in the house: but first he went to school at Chigwell in Essex. (He was) mighty lively, but with innocence; and extremely tender under rebuke; and very early delighted in retirement; much given to reading and meditating of the scriptures, and at 14 had marked over the Bible. Oftentimes at 13 and 14 in his meditations ravisht with joy, and dissolved into teares. The first sense he had of God was when he was 11 yeares old at Chigwell, being retired in a chamber alone. He was so suddenly suprized with an inward comfort and (as he thought) an externall glory in the roome that he has many times sayd that from thence he had the seale of divinity and immortality, that there was a God and that the soule of man was capable of enjoying his divine communications.—His schoolmaster was not of his perswasion. . . . He speaks well the Latin and the French tongues, and his owne with great mastership. He often declares in the assemblies of his Friends, and that with much eloquence and fervency of spirit—by which, and his perpetuall attendances on K(ing) and P(rince) for the reliefe of his Friends, he often exposes his health to hazard.—AUBREY, JOHN, 1669–96, *Brief Lives, ed. Clark, vol.* II, *pp.* 132, 133.

William Penn was greatly in favor with the king—the Quaker's sole patron at court—on whom the hateful eyes of his enemies were intent. The king loved him as a singular and entire friend, and imparted to him many of his secrets and counsels. He often honored him with his company in private, discoursing with him of various affairs, and that, not for one, but many hours together, and delaying to hear the best of his peers who at the same time were waiting for an audience. One of these being envious, and impatient of delay, and taking it as an affront to see the other more regarded than himself, adventured to take the freedom to tell his majesty, that when he met with Penn he thought little of his nobility. The king made no other reply, than that Penn always talked ingeniously, and he heard him willingly.—CROESE, GERARD, 1696, *General History of the Quakers, p.* 106.

My friend Penn came there, Will Penn the Quaker, at the head of his brethren, to thank the Duke for his kindness to their people in Ireland. To see a dozen scoundrels with their hats on, and the Duke complimenting with his off, was a good sight enough.—SWIFT, JONATHAN, 1712, *Journal to Stella, Jan.* 15.

He was a vain talking man. . . . He had such an opinion of his own faculty of persuading, that he thought none could stand before it: though he was singular in that opinion: for he had a tedious, luscious way, that was not apt to overcome a man's reason, though it might tire his patience.—BURNET, GILBERT, 1715–34, *History of My Own Time.*

It appears that he was tall in stature and of an athletic make. He delighted when young, as has been before observed, in manly sports. In maturer years he was inclined to corpulency, but using a great deal of exercise he was very active with it. His appearance at this time was that of a fine portly man. . . . William Penn was very neat, though plain, in his dress. He walked generally with a cane.

This cane he was accustomed to take with him in the latter part of his life into his study, where, when he dictated to an amanuensis, as was frequently his practice, he would take it in his hand, and walking up and down the room, would mark, by striking it against the floor, the emphasis on points he wished particularly to be noticed. . . . He was very neat also as to his person, and had a great aversion to the use of tobacco. However, when he was in America he was often annoyed by it, but he bore it with good humour. . . . Having a great variety of business to go through, he was obliged to be an œconomist of his time. He was therefore regular and methodical in his movements. . . . He is handed down, by those who knew him, to have been very pleasant and strikingly animated in conversation. He had rather a disposition to facetiousness, clothed, however in the purest habit of decorum.—CLARKSON, THOMAS, 1813, *Memoirs of the Private and Public Life of William Penn, vol. II, pp.* 266, 267, 268, 271.

William Penn and Robert Barclay are the names of the two most eminent members of the Society of Friends. They may be entitled to an equal measure of pure and desirable fame, the former as the practical, the latter as the theoretical, champion of their principles. But if services are to be weighed and measured by actual sum and cost, Penn, both in the labors of his life and of his pen, will receive the higher estimate. Barclay's father approved and favored the devotion of his son to a despised sect; but Penn, as we have seen, found his first foe in his best friend. Through the whole of his subsequent life, his principles cost him a large amount of suffering of body and of mind; a loss of friends, and honors, and property; a subjection to insults and reproaches. They weighed with such a burden of care upon his active career, and were attended with such a disappointment of his most cherished wishes at his death, that we pronounce upon him the highest but well deserved encomium in saying, that, had he foreseen the course and issue of his life, he would not have shrunk from it.—ELLIS, GEORGE E., 1844, *William Penn, Library of American Biography, ed. Sparks, vol. XXII, p.* 212.

To speak the whole truth concerning Penn is a task which requires some courage; for he is rather a mythical than a historical person. Rival nations and hostile sects have agreed in canonising him. England is proud of his name. A great commonwealth beyond the Atlantic regards him with a reverence similar to that which the Athenians felt for Theseus, and the Romans for Quirinus. The respectable society of which he was a member honours him as an apostle. By pious men of other persuasions, he is generally regarded as a bright pattern of Christian virtue. Meanwhile admirers of a very different sort have sounded his praises. The French philosophers of the eighteenth century pardoned what they regarded as his superstitious fancies in consideration for his contempt for priests, and of his cosmopolitan benevolence, impartially extended to all races and to all creeds. His name has thus become, throughout all civilised countries, a synonyme for probity and philanthropy. Nor is this high reputation altogether unmerited. Penn was without doubt a man of eminent virtues. He had a strong sense of religious duty and a fervent desire to promote the happiness of mankind. . . . His writings and his life furnished abundant proofs that he was not a man of strong sense. He had no skill in reading the characters of others. His confidence in persons less virtuous than himself led him into great errors and misfortunes. His enthusiasm for one great principle sometimes impelled him to violate other great principles which he ought to have held sacred. Nor was his rectitude altogether proof against the temptations to which it was exposed in that splendid and polite, but deeply corrupted society, with which he now mingled. . . . Unhappily it cannot be concealed that he bore a chief part in some transactions condemned, not merely by the rigid code of the society to which he belonged, but by the general sense of all honest men. He afterwards solemnly protested that his hands were pure from illicit gain, and that he had never received any gratuity from those whom he had obliged, though he might easily, while his influence at court lasted, have made a hundred and twenty thousand pounds. To this assertion full credit is due. But bribes may be offered to vanity as well as to cupidity, and it is impossible to deny that Penn was cajoled into bearing a part in some unjustifiable transactions of which others enjoyed the profits.—MACAULAY, THOMAS BABINGTON, 1849, *History of England*, ch. v.

Lord Shelburne, Charles Austin, and Milman to breakfast. A pleasant meal. Then the Quakers, five in number. Never was there such a rout. They had absolutely nothing to say. Every charge against Penn came out as clear as any case at the Old Bailey. They had nothing to urge but what was true enough, that he looked worse in my History than he would have looked on a general survey of his whole life. But that is not my fault. I wrote the History of four years during which he was exposed to great temptations; during which he was the favourite of a bad king, and an active solicitor in a most corrupt court. His character was injured by his associations. Ten years before, or ten years later, he would have made a much better figure. But was I to begin my work ten years earlier or ten years later for William Penn's sake? The Quakers were extremely civil. So was I. * —MACAULAY, THOMAS BABINGTON, 1849, *Diary, Feb. 5, Life by Trevelyan*.

My hope was that Macaulay would in time withdraw his charges as disproved. I had some reason for this hope. His mind was racked by doubts, and he was often busy with this portion of his book. It is within my knowledge that his latest thoughts on earth were given to Penn and that which he had said of Penn. Some part of what he might have done, the world can guess from what he did. He ceased the work of calumny. In what he wrote after 1857, there is not a single sneer at Penn. His indexes were greatly changed. He struck out much that was false, and more that was abusive. Penn's Jacobitism was no longer "scandalous," his word was no longer a "falsehood." Penn was no longer charged with "treasonable conduct," with "flight to France," and with "renewing his plots." What else Macaulay might have done can only be surmised; but it is fair to think that changes in his index would have been followed by

<hr>

*If Macaulay's History was not a Life of William Penn, this book is still less so. Those who are honorably jealous for Penn's reputation will forgive me if I do not express an opinion of my own with regard to the controversy; an opinion which, after all, would be valueless. In my uncle's papers there can be found no trace of his ever having changed his mind on the merits of the question.—TREVELYAN, GEORGE OTTO, 1876, *Life and Letters of Lord Macaulay*.

amendments in his text. I know that he was far from satisfied with his "Notes" of 1857, and that he was engaged in reconsidering the defence of Penn when he leaned back in his chair and died.—DIXON, WILLIAM HEPWORTH, 1851–72, *History of William Penn, Note*.

A pleasant walk of about two miles from Chalfont St. Giles brings us to Jordans meeting-house. . . . In front of the meeting-house, and divided from it by a low fence and wicket, is the "dead garth." . . . The grave farthest from the wicket in the first row of graves on the right is that of Penn and his second wife. It bears the inscription: "William Penn, 1718, and Hannah Penn, 1726." The grave next this is that of Gulielma Maria Penn, his first wife, who died in 1689, while the next two are occupied by the remains of her mother and step-father respectively. In the second row are the graves of two other of Penn's children, those of Letitia and Springett Penn. In the third row is that of Thomas Ellwood, the simple-hearted man who read to Milton when blindness had befallen him; also that of his wife. For periods of from one to two centuries all these graves were without memorials, as are still many others in this out-of-the-way burial-ground. A few years ago it might have been said with entire truth, in the words of Wordsworth:

"In our church-yard
Is neither epitaph nor monument,
Tombstone nor grave; only the turf we tread,
And a few natural graves."

A few graves and flower-grown hillocks within a narrow inclosure fronting a plain cottage-like structure over which the trees swayed and the birds sang in their season: that was all there was to mark the last earthly resting-place of one of the world's noblest heroes, surrounded by those he loved. The simple headstones they now bear were erected some seventeen or eighteen years ago by those who have the custody of the little meeting-house and its attached burial-ground. The records of the district meeting contain the minute that in July, 1862, a committee was appointed "to place gravestones over such of the graves at Jordans the identity of which had been ascertained." The committee reported in June, 1863, that this had been done. The grave, of the Penns, Peningtons, and Ellwoods, are fitly placed close together: all formed one community when living, rejoicing and suffering in common.—STORY, ALFRED T., 1881, *The Grave of William Penn, Harper's Magazine, vol.* 64, *pp.* 84, 85.

He was not born with his hat on, but this is the only time he was ever seen in his bare head.—BURDETTE, ROBERT J., 1882, *William Penn (Lives of American Worthies), p.* 1.

William Penn is now usually thought of as a pious, contemplative man, a peace-loving Quaker in a broad brim hat and plain drab clothes, who founded Pennsylvania in the most successful manner, on beautiful, benevolent principles, and kindness to the Indians. But the real Penn, though of a very religious turn of mind, was essentially a man of action, restless and enterprising, at times a courtier and a politician, who loved handsome dress, lived well and lavishly, and, although he undoubtedly kept his faith with the redmen, Pennslyvania was the torment of his life. He came, moreover, of fighting ancestry, and was himself a soldier for a short time. His life was full of contests, imprisonments, disasters, and suffering, if not of actual fighting, and he lived during the most critical periods of English history. Few, if any, Quakers have shown so much energy as he. Indeed, there have been few men who have attempted to accomplish so much.—FISHER, SYDNEY GEORGE, 1900, *The True William Penn, p.* 11.

PENNSYLVANIA

This day my country was confirmed to me under the great seal of England, with large powers and privileges, by the name of Pennsylvania; a name the king would give it in honor of my father. I chose New Wales, being, as this, a pretty hilly country, but Penn being Welsh for a head, as Pennanmoire in Wales, and Penrith in Cumberland, and Penn in Buckinghamshire, the highest land in England, called this Pennsylvania, which is the high or head woodlands; for I proposed when the secretary, a Welshman, refused to have it called New Wales, Sylvania, and they added Penn to it; and though I much opposed it and went to the king to have it struck out and altered, he said it was past and would take it upon him; nor could twenty guineas move the under secretary

to vary the name; for I feared lest it should be looked on as a vanity in me, and not as a réspect in the king, as it truly was, to my father, whom he often mentions with praise.—PENN, WILLIAM, 1681, *Letter to Robert Turner, Hazard's Annals of Pennsylvania, p.* 500.

William Pen might glory in having brought down upon earth the so much boasted golden age, which in all probability never excited but in *Pensilvania.*—VOLTAIRE, FRANCOIS MARIE AROULET, 1732? *Letters Concerning the English Nation, p.* 25.

Of all great reputations, Penn's is that which has been most the effect of accident. The great action of his life was his turning Quaker: the conspicuous one, his behaviour upon his trial. In all that regards Pennsylvania, he has no other merit than that of having followed the principles of the religious community to which he belonged, when his property *happened* to be vested in colonial speculations.—SOUTHEY, ROBERT, 1814, *Letter to Bernard Barton, Dec.* 19.

The immortal memory of Penn, who subdued the ferocity of savages by his virtues, and enlightened the civilized world by his institutions.—MADISON, JAMES, 1830, *Toast, Oct.* 13, *Works, vol.* IV, *p.* 118.

This admirable person had employed his great abilities in support of civil as well as religious liberty, and hath both acted and suffered for them under Charles II. Even if he had not founded the Commonwealth of Pennsylvania as an everlasting memorial of his love of freedom, his actions and writings in England would have been enough to absolve him from the charge of intending to betray the rights of his countrymen.—MACKINTOSH, SIR JAMES, 1832?-34, *History of the Revolution in England in* 1688.

Beneath a large elm tree at Shakamaxon, on the northern edge of Philadelphia, William Penn, surrounded by a few friends, in the habiliments of peace, met the numerous delegation of the Lenni Lenape tribes. The great treaty was not for the purchase of lands, but, confirming what Penn had written, and Markham covenanted, its sublime purpose was the recognition of the equal rights of humanity. Under the shelter of the forest, now leafless by the frosts of autumn, Penn proclaimed to the men of the Algonquin race, from both banks of the Delaware, from the borders of the Schuylkill, and, it may have been, even from the Susquehannah, the same simple message of peace and love which George Fox had professed before Cromwell, and Mary Fisher had borne to the Grand Turk. The English and the Indian should respect the same moral law, should be alike secure in their pursuits and their possessions, and adjust every difference by a peaceful tribunal, composed of an equal number of men from each race. "We meet," such were the words of William Penn, "on the broad pathway of good faith and good will; no advantage shall be taken on either side, but all shall be openness and love. I will not call you children; for parents sometimes chide their children too severely; nor brothers only; for brothers differ. The friendship between me and you I will not compare to a chain; for that the rains might rust, or the falling tree might break. We are the same as if one man's body were to be divided into two parts; we are all one flesh and blood." The children of the forest were touched by the sacred doctrine, and renounced their guile and their revenge. They received the presents of Penn in sincerity; and with hearty friendship they gave the belt of wampum.— Bancroft, George, 1834–38, *History of the United States, ch.* xvi.

To William Penn belongs the distinction, destined to brighten as men advance in virtue, of first in human history establishing the *Law* of *Love* as a rule of conduct in the intercourse of nations.—Sumner, Charles, 1850, *The True Grandeur of Nations, Orations and Speeches, vol.* i, *p.* 114.

Controversy has now quite ceased to busy itself about his noble character, and his life of splendid unostentatious beneficence. His name, which without his consent and against his wishes was made part of the name of the State which he founded, will be remembered in connection with its history while the Delaware and the Schuylkill flow. Of his famous treaty with the Indians nothing perhaps was ever better said than the comment of Voltaire, that it was the only league between savages and white men which was never sworn to and never broken.—McCarthy, Justin, 1884, *A History of the Four Georges, vol.* i, *p.* 235.

GENERAL

Especially of late some of them (the Quakers) have made nearer advances towards Christianity than ever before; and among them the ingenious Mr. Penn has of late refined some of their gross notions, and brought them into some form, and has made them speak sense and English, of both which George Fox, their first and great apostle, was totally ignorant.— Leslie, Charles, 1698, *The Snake in the Grass, Introduction to Third ed.*

The Life of William Penn, the settler of Pennsylvania, the founder of Philadelphia, and one of the first lawgivers in the Colonies, now United States, in 1682, containing also his celebrated Treaty with the Indians, his purchase of their country; valuable anecdotes of Admiral Penn, also King Charles II., James II., King William and Queen Anne, in whose reigns William Penn lived; curious circumstances that led him to become a Quaker, with a view of the admirable traits in the character of the people called Friends or Quakers, who have done so much to meliorate the condition of suffering humanity. — Weems, Mason L., 1829, *Title Page.*

Penn however is worthy of a place in every theological collection.— Dibdin, Thomas Frognall, 1824, *The Library Companion, p.* 56.

It is doubtful whether any other work ["Reflections"] of the size can be found, containing so much sound, practical wisdom.—Cleveland, Charles D., 1848, *A Compendium of English Literature, p.* 370.

"No Cross, no Crown is a serious cross to me," said Admiral Penn on reading this unworldly book. "No Cross, no Crown" arose out of the writer's own position. He was suffering for opinion: he was suffering at the hands of men who professed to be the servants of God. He wished to present clearly to his own mind and to impress upon others the great Christian doctrine that every man must bear the cross who hopes to wear the crown. To this end he reviewed the character of the age. He showed how corrupt was the laity, how proud and self-willed were the priests.—Dixon, William Hepworth, 1851–72, *History of William Penn, p.* 81.

Neither Penn nor Barclay has any special grace or vigour of style. Penn is lively and pointed, Barclay grave and argumentative.—MINTO, WILLIAM, 1872–80, *Manual of English Prose Literature, p.* 335.

William Penn possessed in full measure the culture of his century, and was himself a zealous writer, always full of his object. His abstractions remind one sometimes of Hobbes: his arguments of Sidney and Sidney's historical learning; like Harrington he loves to analyse and weigh the interests on which states appear to rest. But all requires a special character and vigour from the special end which he pursues, namely, the emancipation of his sect from all oppression.—RANKE, LEOPOLD VON, 1875, *A History of England, vol.* IV, *p.* 316.

The plain recital of his doings is his best eulogy. — BRUCHHAUSEN, CASPAR 1877, *Cyclopaedia of Biblical, Theological and Ecclesiastical Literature, ed. M'Clintock and Strong, vol.* VII, *p.* 898.

His character is a curious mingling of dissimilar qualities. He was at once a saint and a courtier, a religious fanatic and a shrewd man of affairs and of the world. With the controversies awakened by Macaulay's sweeping charges we have here nothing to do. Penn appears in American history simply as the wise founder of a state, the prudent and just magistrate, the liberal-minded law-giver and ruler.—LODGE, HENRY CABOT, 1881, *A Short History of the English Colonies in America, p.* 211.

As an author, Penn appears as a defender of the views of Fox and Barclay, a writer of sententious ethical precepts, an opponent of judicial oaths, an advocate of a Congress of Nations for the settlement of international disputes, and a champion of complete and universal religious liberty. Many of his books and pamphlets were translated into German, French, Dutch and Welsh.—MANN, W. J., 1883, *Schaff-Herzog Encyclopædia of Religious Knowledge, vol.* III, *p.* 1789.

It ["No Cross, No Crown"] is an earnest, sometimes eloquent, exposition of the duty of self-denial as the chief requisite for salvation, denouncing all lip service and ceremonialism. The style is grave and uniform. It is perhaps somewhat ponderously earnest, and lacks the refreshing humour and imagery of some of his contemporary theologians. It is always clear, though the effect is sometimes spoilt by too much amplification. A fair amount of learning and culture is shown without pedantry.—FITZROY, A. I., 1894, *English Prose, ed. Craik, vol.* III, *p.* 333.

His piety was profound; and though he had little or no interest in humane learning for its own sake, his knowledge of the Christian and prechristian mystics was considerable, and enabled him to give to the doctrine of the "light within" a certain philosophical breadth. . . . His style is clear and nervous, and his theological polemics, though for the most part occupied with questions of ephemeral importance, evince no small controversial power.—RIGG, J. M., 1895, *Dictionary of National Biography, vol.* XLIV, *p.* 317.

Penn himself during his residence in the colony wrote nothing except letters; these, however, are pleasant reading, something of the large, calm beauty of his spirit passing into his style. The long letter written in 1683 to the Free Society of Traders contains an interesting description of the Indians, whose friendship Penn so well knew how to win.—BRONSON, WALTER C., 1900. *A Short History of American Literature, p.* 40.

Penn had done what George Fox could also so effectually do. He had not merely endured his imprisonment with a spirit that won the respect both of his followers and his enemies, but he had made the imprisonment a means of advancing the cause he had at heart, of making it known to the world in a way that would arouse enthusiasm. He had stated more fully and completely than had yet been done the fundamental doctrines of his faith in his two pamphlets, "The Sandy Foundation" and "Innocency with her Open Face;" and these two pamphlets, the one that imprisoned him and the one that released him, are to this day the authorities used to prove the original doctrines of the Quakers. When we add to these two pamphlets his book, "No Cross, No Crown," which has also a permanent value, we have Penn's three most important works; and it was a good deal to be accomplished within a twelvemonth by a young man of only twenty-four, who had spent most of that time locked up in the Tower.—FISHER, SYDNEY GEORGE, 1900, *The True William Penn, p.* 136.

Joseph Addison

1672–1719

Joseph Addison, 1672–1719. Born, at Milston, Wilts, 1 May 1672. Educated at private schools at Amesbury and Salisbury; at Lichfield School, 1683; at Charterhouse [1685–87?]; to Queen's Coll., Oxford, 1687. Demyship at Magdalen Coll., 1689; B.A., 6 May 1691; M.A., 14 Feb. 1693; Fellowship, 1697–1711. Crown Pension of £300 a year, 1697. To France, autumn of 1699; lived in Blois and Paris (1700). Tour in Italy, winter of 1700–01. At Geneva, 1701; Vienna, 1702. In Germany, Holland, and return to England, 1703. Member of Kitcat Club. Commissioned to write poem to celebrate Battle of Blenheim, 1704; appointed to Under-Secretaryship of State, 1706. With Halifax on Mission to Hanover, 1707. M.P. for Lostwithiel, Nov. 1708; election quashed, Dec. 1709. Sec. to Lord Lieut. of Ireland, and Keeper of Records, 1709. Contributed to Steele's "Tatler," 1709–10. M.P. for Malmesbury, 1710. Published "Whig Examiner," (5 nos.) Sept.–Oct., 1710. Bought estate of Bilton in Warwickshire, 1711. "Spectator" published daily, 1 March 1711 to Dec. 1712. "Cato" produced at Drury Lane, 14 April 1713. Contrib. to "The Guardian," May–Sept. 1713; to Steele's "Lover," and to a revived "Spectator," June–Sept. 1714. Comedy "The Drummer" anonymously produced, 1715. Resumed political appointments, 1715–16. "The Freeholder" (55 nos.), published anonymously, Dec. 1715–June 1716. Married Countess of Warwick, 3 Aug. 1716. Retired from appointments, March 1718, owing to ill-health. Daughter born in Jan. 1718. Controversy with Steele in "Old Whig" (2 nos., 19 March and 2 April 1719). Died, in London, 17 June 1719. *Works:* "Dissertatio de insignioribus Romanis poetis," 1692; "A Poem to His Majesty," 1695; Latin Poem on the Peace of Ryswick, 1697; Lat. poems in "Examen Poeticum Duplex," 1698, and "Musarum Anglicanarum Analecta," vol. ii., 1699; "Letters from Italy to the Rt. Hon. Charles, Lord Halifax," 1703; "Remarks on several Parts of Italy," 1705; "The Campaign," 1705; "Fair Rosamond" (anon.), 1707; "The Present State of the War" (anon.), 1708; Papers in "Tatler," 1709–10; "Whig Examiner," 1710; 274 nos. in "Spectator," 1711–12; "The Late Tryal and Conviction of Count Tariff" (anon.), 1713; "Cato," 1713; Papers in "Guardian," 1713; in "Lover" and new "Spectator," 1714; "Essay concerning the Error in distributing modern Medals," 1715; "The Drummer" (anon.), 1716; [Poetical addresses to Princess of Wales and Sir G. Kneller, 1716]; "The Freeholder" (anon.), 1715–16; Translations of Ovid's "Metamorphoses" with Dryden and others, 1717; "Two Poems; viz., I. On the Deluge. . . . An ode to Dr. Burnett; II. In praise of Physic and Poetry. An ode to Dr. Hannes" (Lat. and Eng.), 1718; "The Resurrection: a poem," 1718: "The Old Whig" (anon.), 1719; "The Patrician" (anon.), 1719. *Posthumous:* "Notes upon the twelve books of Paradise Lost" (from "Spectator"), 1719; "Skating: a poem" (Lat. and Eng.), 1720; "Evidences of the Christian Religion," 1730; "Discourse on Ancient and Modern Learning," 1739. "Collected Works:" first published by T. Tickell in 1721. *Life:* by Miss Aikin, 1843; by W. J. Courthope, 1884.—SHARP, R. FARQUHARSON, 1897, *A Dictionary of English Authors, p.* 2.

PERSONAL

I dined to-day with Dr. Garth and Mr. Addison at the Devil Tavern, by Temple Bar; and Garth treated. And it is well I dine every day, else I should be longer making out my letters. . . . Mr. Addison's election has passed easy and undisputed, and I believe if he had a mind to be chosen King he would not be refused.
—SWIFT, JONATHAN, 1710, *Journal to Stella, Oct.* 12.

Were there One whose fires
True Genius kindles, and fair Fame inspires;

Blest with each talent and each art to please,
And born to write, converse, and live with ease:
Should such a man, too fond to rule alone,
Bear, like the Turk, no brother near the throne.
View him with scornful, yet with jealous eyes,
And hate for arts that caus'd himself to rise;
Damn with faint praise, assent with civil leer,
And without sneering, teach the rest to sneer;
Willing to wound, and yet afraid to strike,
Just hint a fault, and hesitate dislike;
Alike reserv'd to blame, or to commend,
A tim'rous foe, and a suspicious friend;

JOSEPH ADDISON

WILLIAM CONGREVE

Dreading ev'n fools, by Flatterers besieg'd,
And so obliging, that he ne'er oblig'd;
Like *Cato*, give his little Senate laws,
And sit attentive to his own applause;
While Wits and Templars ev'ry sentence
    raise,
And wonder with a foolish face of praise:—
Who but must laugh, if such a man there be?
Who would not weep, if ATTICUS were he?
—POPE, ALEXANDER, 1715-23-27-35,
Epistle to Dr. Arbuthnot.

Mr. Jo. Addison, who was made, about
Easter last, secretary of state, is *turned
out of office*, and made one of the tellers of
the exchequer. His under-secretary was
Mr. Tho. Tickell, that pretender to poetry,
of Queen's college. Mr. Addison was by
no means qualified for the office of secretary, being not skilled in business, and
not knowing how to speak. This is what
is commonly said.—HEARNE, THOMAS,
1717, *Reliquiæ Hearnianæ, ed. Bliss, Nov.
9, vol.* II, *p.* 54.

It could not be imagined that to diminish a worthy man, as soon as he was no
more to be seen, could add to him who had
always raised, and almost worshipped,
him when living. There never was a more
strict friendship than between those
gentlemen; nor had they ever any difference but what proceeded from their different way of pursuing the same thing. The
one with patience, foresight, and temperate address always waited and stemmed
the torrent; while the other often plunged
himself into it, and was as often taken out
by the temper of him who stood weeping
on the brink for his safety, whom he
could not dissuade from leaping into it.—
STEELE, RICHARD, 1720, *The Theatre, No.*
12.

Can I forget the dismal night, that gave
My soul's best part for-ever to the grave!
How silent did his old companions tread,
By mid-night lamps, the mansions of the
    dead,
Through breathing statues, then unheeded
    things,
Through rowes of warriors, and through
    walks of kings!
What awe did the slow solemn knell inspire;
The pealing organ, and the pausing choir;
The duties by the lawn-robe'd prelate pay'd;
And the last words, that dust to dust con-
    vey'd!
While speechless o'er thy closing grave we
    bend,
Accept these tears, thou dear departed friend!
Oh, gone for-ever, take this long adieu;
And sleep in peace, next thy lov'd Montagu!
. . . .

That awful form (which, so ye heavens de-
    cree,
Must still be lov'd and still deplor'd by me)
In nightly visions seldom fails to rise,
Or, rous'd by fancy, meets my waking eyes.
If business calls, or crowded courts invite,
Th' unblemish'd statesman seems to strike
    my sight;
If in the stage I seek to soothe my care,
I meet his soul, which breathes in Cato there;
If pensive to the rural shades I rove,
His shape o'ertakes me in the lovely grove:
'Twas there of Just and Good he reason'd
    strong,
Clear'd some great truth, or rais'd some seri-
    ous song;
There patient show'd us the wise course to
    steere.
A candid censor, and a friend sincere;
There taught us how to live; and (oh! too
    high
The price for knowledge) taught us how to
    die.
—TICKELL, THOMAS, 1721, *To the Right
Honourable the Earl of Warwick.*

Mr. Addison wrote very fluently; but he
was sometimes very slow and scrupulous
in correcting. He would show his verses
to several friends; and would alter almost
everything that any of them hinted at as
wrong. He seemed to be too diffident of
himself; and too much concerned about
his character as a poet: or (as he worded
it) too solicitous for that kind of praise,
which, God knows, is but a very little
matter after all! . . . Many of his
Spectators he wrote very fast; and sent
them to the press as soon as they were
written. It seems to have been best for
him not to have had too much time to correct. . . . Addison was perfect good
company with intimates; and had something more charming in his conversation
than I ever knew in any other man: but
with any mixture of strangers, and sometimes only with one, he seemed to preserve
his dignity much; with a stiff sort of
slience. — POPE, ALEXANDER, 1728-30,
Spence's Anecdotes, ed. Singer, pp. 37, 38.

To this great man I am the nearest male
relation now living; I owe part of my education to him.—BUDGELL, EUSTACE, 1732,
Liberty and Property, p. 143.

Mr. Addison stayed above a year at
Blois.—He would rise as early as between
two and three in the height of summer,
and lie a bed till between eleven and twelve
in the depth of winter.—He was untalka-
tive whilst here, and often thoughtful:

sometimes so lost in thought, that I have come into his room and stayed five minutes there, before he has known anything of it. —He has his masters, generally, at supper with him; kept very little company beside; and had no amour whilst here, that I know of; and I think I should have known it, if he had had any.—PHILIPPEAUX, ABBÉ OF BLOIS, 1737–39, *Spence's Anecdotes, ed. Singer, p.* 139.

Addison was the best company in the world.—MONTAGUE, LADY MARY WORTLEY, 1740–41, *Spence's Anecdotes, ed. Singer, p.* 175.

In a word, one may justly apply to him what Plato, in his allegorical language, says of Aristophanes, that the Graces, having searched all the world for a temple wherein they might for ever dwell, settled at last in the breast of Mr. Addison.—MELMOTH, WILLIAM, 1742, *Letters on Several Subjects by Sir Thomas Fitzosborne.*

Mr. Addison was stedfast to his principles, faithful to his friends, a zealous patriot, honourable in public stations, amiable in private life, and as he lived, he died, a good man, and a pious Christian. —CIBBER, THEOPHILUS, 1753, *Lives of the Poets, vol.* III, *p.* 320.

Atticus could be a friend to men, without awaking their resentment, and be satisfied with his own virtue without seeking popular fame: he had the reward of his wisdom in his transquality, and will ever stand among the few examples of true philosophy, either ancient or modern. . . . You will think I have been too long on the character of Atticus. I own I took pleasure in explaining it. Pope thought himself covertly very severe on Addison, by giving him that name; and I feel indignation whenever he is abused, both from his own merit, and because he was ever your father's friend; besides that it is naturally disgusting to see him lampooned after his death by the same man who paid him the most servile court while he lived, and was besides highly obliged by him.—MONTAGU, LADY MARY WORTLEY, 1755, *Letter to the Countess of Bute, July* 20.

Dr. Young has published a new book, on purpose, he says himself, to have an opportunity of telling a story that he has known these forty years. Mr. Addison sent for the young Lord Warwick, as he was dying, to show him in what peace a Christian could die—unluckily he died of brandy—nothing makes a Christian die in peace like being maudlin! but don't say this in Gath, where you are.—WALPOLE, HORACE, 1759, *Letters, May* 16, *ed. Cunningham, vol.* III, *p.* 227.

Addison, a crawling sycophant, full of envy and spleen; frantic when a friend prospered; happy only when misfortune lighted on his associates; a hypocrite who would take you by the hand, and if he heard you utter a sentiment which in his heart he knew to be erroneous, would labour to confirm you in it with all his zeal, rejoicing in your inexperience, as Satan might exult over the fall of a young novice.—MONTAGU, EDWARD WORTLEY, 1776? *An Autobiography, vol.* I, *p.* 57.

Of this memorable friendship the greater praise must be given to Steele. It is not hard to love those from whom nothing can be feared; and Addison never considered Steele as a rival; but Steele lived, as he confesses, under an habitual subjection to the predominating genius of Addison, whom he always mentioned with reverence, and treated with obsequiousness. Addison, who knew his own dignity, could not always forbear to shew it, by playing a little upon his admirer; but he was in no danger of retort: his jests were endured without resistance or resentment. But the sneer of jocularity was not the worst. Steele, whose imprudence of generosity, or vanity of profusion, kept him always incurably necessitous, upon some pressing exigence, in an evil hour, borrowed an hundred pounds of his friend, probably without much purpose of repayment; but Addison, who seems to have had other notions of a hundred pounds, grew impatient of delay, and reclaimed his loan by an execution. Steele felt with great sensibility the obduracy of his creditor; but with emotions of sorrow rather than of anger.—JOHNSON, SAMUEL, 1779–81, *Addison, Lives of the English Poets.*

Many persons having doubts concerning this fact, I applied to Dr. Johnson to learn on what authority he asserted it. He told me he had it from Savage, who lived in intimacy with Steele, and who mentioned that Steele told him the story with tears in his eyes. Ben Victor, Johnson said, likewise informed him on this remarkable transaction, from the relation of Mr. Wilks the comedian, who was also an intimate of Steele's. Some, in defence of Addison, here said, that "the act was done with the good-natured view of rousing Steele and correcting that profusion which always made him necessitous." "If that were the case," said Johnson, "and that he only wanted to alarm Steele, he would afterwards have *returned* the money to his friend, which it is not pretended he did.— MALONE, EDMUND, 1781, *March* 15, *Boswell by Croker, p.* 671.

Among the Literary Quarrels of Pope one acquires dignity and interest from the characters of both parties. It closed by producing the severest, but the most masterly portrait of one man of genius, composed by another, which has ever been hung on the satiric Parnassus for the contemplaticn of ages. Addison must descend to posterity with the dark spots of Atticus staining a purity of character which had nearly proven immaculate.— DISRAELI, ISAAC, 1814, *Pope and Addison, Quarrels of Authors.*

Addison, according to the traditions of Holland House, used, when composing, to walk up and down the long gallery there, with a bottle of wine at each end of it, which he finished during the operation. There is a little white house, too, near the turnpike, to which he used to retire when the Countess was particularly troublesome.— MOORE, THOMAS, 1818, *Diary, Oct.* 23.

Addison, I know not why, is personally no such favorite of mine as Sir Roger de Coverley should make him.—SCOTT, SIR WALTER, 1819, *Familiar Letters, June* 15, *vol.* II, *p.* 44.

Addison. Dick! I am come to remonstrate with you on those unlucky habits which have been so detrimental to your health and fortune.

Steele. Many thanks, Mr. Addison; but really my fortune is not much improved by your arresting me for the hundred pounds; nor is my health, if spirits are an indication of it, on seeing my furniture sold by auction to raise the money.

Addison. Pooh, pooh, Dick! what furniture had you about the house.

Steele. At least I had the arm-chair, of which you never before had dispossessed me longer than the evening; and happy should I have been to enjoy your company in it again and again, if you had left it me.

Addison. We will contrive to hire another. I do assure you, my dear Dick, I have really felt for you.

Steele. I only wish, my kind friend, you had not put out your feelers quite so far, nor exactly in this direction; and that my poor wife had received an hour's notice; she might have carried a few trinkets to some neighbour. She wanted her salts; and the bailiff thanked her for the bottle that contained them, telling her the gold head of it was worth pretty nearly half-a-guinea.
—LANDOR, WALTER SAVAGE, 1828, *Imaginary Conversations, Third Series, Works, vol.* V, *p.* 50.

Some blemishes may undoubtedly be detected in his character; but the more carefully it is examined, the more will it appear, to use the phrase of the old anatomists, sound in the noble parts—free from all taint of perfidy, of cowardice, of cruelty, of ingratitude, of envy. Men may easily be named in whom some particular good disposition has been more conspicuous than in Addison. But the just harmony of qualities, the exact temper between the stern and the humane virtues, the habitual observance of every law, not only of moral rectitude, but of moral grace and dignity, distinguished him from all men who have been tried by equally full information.—MACAULAY, THOMAS, BABINGTON, 1843, *Life and Writings of Addison, Critical and Miscellaneous Essays.*

Addison espoused a countess; and spent the rest of his life in taverns, clubs, and repentance.—WHIPPLE, EDWIN P., 1846–71, *Authors, Literature and Life, p.* 31.

Of Holland House, the last residence of Addison, it would require a long article to give a fitting idea. . . . The general form is that of a half H. The projection in the center, forming at once porch and tower, and the two wings supported on pillars, give great decision of effect to it. . . . There is a fine entrance hall, a library behind it, and another library extending the whole length of one of the wings and the house upstairs, one hundred and five feet in length. The drawing-room over the entrance hall, called the Gilt Room, extends from front to back of the house, and commands views of the gardens both way; those to the back are very beautiful. In the house, are, of course, many interesting and valuable works of art; a great portion of them memorials of the distinguished men who have been accustomed to resort thither. . . . In the gardens are various memorials of distinguished men. . . . The traditions regarding Addison here are very slight. They are, simply, that he used to walk, when composing his "Spectators," in the long library, then a picture gallery, with a bottle of wine at each end, which he visited as he alternately arrived at them; and that the room in which he died, though not positively known, is supposed to be the present dining-room, being then the state bed-room. The young Earl of Warwick, to whom he there addressed the emphatic words, "See in what peace a Christian can die!" died also, himself, in 1721, but two years afterward. The estate then devolved to Lord Kensington, descended from Robert Rich, earl of Warwick, who sold it, about 1762, to the Right Honorable Henry Fox, afterwards Lord Holland. Here the early days of the great statesman, Charles James, were passed; and here lived the late patriotic translator of Lope de Vega, amid the society of the first spirits of the age.—HOWITT, WILLIAM, 1846, *Homes and Haunts of the Most Eminent British Poets*, pp. 153, 154, 155, 156.

To us it seems clear, that the great failing in Addison's character was his fastidiousness; excellent as his heart was, this difficulty prevented his sympathies from extending as widely as religion would have them. It made him shrink from near approach to mankind in general, though warm-hearted to his friends and companions; and thus it often happens, that literary habits and a sensitive nature, though they have their own ways of manifestation, do something to unfit men for active usefulness; as the marble, though excellent for sculpture, is less adapted for works of public improvement than coarser varieties of stone. But after making all possible abatement, enough will remain to establish the character of Addison on the highest ground. As a writer, we look through the history of letters, and we find very few before him; as a man and a Christian, we know of none.—PEABODY, W. B. O., 1847, *Aikin's Life of Addison, North American Review*, vol. 64, p. 372.

When this man looks from the world whose weaknesses he describes so benevolently, up to the Heaven which shines over us all, I can hardly fancy a human face lighted up with a more serene rapture; a human intellect thrilling with a purer love and adoration than Joseph Addison's. Listen to him: from your childhood you have known the verses; but who can hear their sacred music without love and awe?
"Soon as the evening shades prevail,
The moon takes up the wondrous tale," etc.
It seems to me those verses shine like the stars. They shine out of a great deep calm. When he turns to heaven, a Sabbath comes over that man's mind: and his face lights up from it with a glory of thanks and prayer. . . . If Swift's life was the most wretched, I think Addison's was one of the most enviable. A life prosperous and beautiful—a calm death—an immense fame and affection afterwards for his happy and spotless name.—THACKERAY, WILLIAM MAKEPEACE, 1853, *English Humourists of the Eighteenth Century.*

It seems to have been in Holland House (for he died shortly afterwards) that Addison was visited by Milton's daughter, when he requested her to bring him some evidences of her birth. The moment he beheld her he exclaimed: "Madam, you need no other voucher; your face is a sufficient testimonial whose daughter you are." It must have been very pleasing to Addison to befriend Milton's daughter, for he had been the first to popularize the great poet by his critiques on "Paradise Lost," in the "Spectator." — HUNT, LEIGH, 1855, *The Old Court Suburb*, ch. xv.

There is not a name in the annals of English literature more widely associated with pleasant recollections than that of Addison. His beautiful hymns trembled on our lips in childhood; his cheerful essays first lured us, in youth, to a sense of the minor philosophy of life; we tread his walk at Oxford with loving steps; gaze on his portrait, at Holland House or the Bodleian Gallery, as on the lineaments of a revered friend; recall his journey into Italy, his ineffectual maiden speech, his successful tragedy, his morning studies, his evenings at Button's, his unfortunate marriage, and his holy death-bed, as if they were the experiences of one personally known, as well as fondly admired; and we muse beside the marble that designates his sepulchre in Westminster Abbey, between those of his first patron and his most cherished friend, with an interest such as is rarely awakened by the memory of one familiar to us only through books. The harmony of his character sanctions his writings; the tone of the "Spectator" breathes friendliness as well as instruction; and the tributes of contemporaries to his private worth, and of generations to his literary excellence, combine with our knowledge of the vicissitudes of his life, to render his mind and person as near to our sympathies as they are high in our esteem. Over his faults we throw the veil of charity, and cherish the remembrance of his benevolence and piety, his refinement and wisdom, as the sacred legacy of an intellectual benefactor.—TUCKERMAN, HENRY T., 1857, *Essays, Biographical and Critical, p.* 394.

He was an amiable and highly gifted, rather than a strong or great man. His shrinking timidity of temperament, his singular modesty of manners, his quiet, sly power of humorous yet kindly observation, his minute style of criticism, even the peculiar cast of his piety, all served to stamp the lady-man. In taciturnity alone he bore the sex no resemblance. And hence it is that Campbell in poetry, and Addison in prose, are, or were, the great favourites of female readers. He had many weaknesses, but, as in the character of woman, they appeared beautiful, and cognate to his gentle nature. His fear of giving offence was one of the most prominent of these. In his writings and in his life, he seems always treading on thin ice. —GILFILLAN, GEORGE, 1859, *ed., Poetical Works of Joseph Addison, etc., Life, p.* xxx.

Thus died one to whom the English nation owes the formation of mind and character in its youth of modern times. A gentler monitor never wrote for the delight of ages; a truer friend never existed; a more religious man—his faith being as pure from Calvinism as it was from superstition,—never combated with this world's sins and temptations than Addison. We would willingly draw a veil over his reported habits of intemperance; but if that cannot be done, we may plead that they were the effect rather of unhappiness than of criminal self-indulgence.

—THOMSON, KATHARINE, 1861 (GRACE WHARTON), *Celebrated Friendships, vol.* I, *p.* 291.

Next came the age of the "Tatler" and "Spectator." Steele, editor of the first, is buried at his seat near Carmarthen. His second wife, "his dearest Prue," is laid amongst the poets. But the great funeral of this circle is that of Addison. The last serene moments of his life were at Warwick House. "See how a Christian can die." . . . The spot selected was the vault in the north aisle of that Chapel, in the eastern recess of which already lay the coffins of Monk and his wife, Montague Earl of Sandwich, and the two Halifaxes. Craggs was to follow within a year. Into that recess, doubtless in order to rest by the side of his patron, Montague Earl of Halifax, the coffin of Addison was lowered. At the head of the vault, Atterbury officiated as Dean, in his prelate's robes. Round him stood the Westminster scholars, with their white tapers, dimly lighting up the fretted aisle. One of them has left on record the deep impression left on them by the unusual energy and solemnity of Atterbury's sonorous voice. Close by was the faithful friend of the departed—Tickell, who has described the scene in poetry yet more touching than Macaulay's prose.—STANLEY, ARTHUR PENRHYN, 1867-96, *Historical Memorials of Westminster Abbey.*

His politeness received from his character a singular bent and charm. It was not external, simply voluntary and official; it came from the heart. He was gentle and kind, of a refined sensibility, so timid even as to remain quiet and seem dull in a numerous company or before strangers, only recovering his spirits before intimate friends, and confessing that he could not talk well to more than one. He could not endure a sharp discussion; when the opponent was intractable, he pretended to approve, and for punishment, plunged himself discreetly into his own folly. . . . Picture now this mind, so characteristically mediocre, limited to the discovery of good motives of action. What a reflective man, always equal and dignified! What a store he has of resolutions and maxims! All rapture, instinct, inspiration, and caprice, are abolished or disciplined. No case surprises or carries him away. He is always ready and protected;

so much so, that he is like an automaton. Argument has frozen and invaded him.—TAINE, H. A., 1871, *History of English Literature, tr. Van Laun, vol.* II, *bk.* iii, *ch.* iv, *pp.* 93, 99.

He was possessed of qualities which in a smaller man must have been held up to ridicule and contempt. Those who call him proud forget that he was sometimes obsequious; those who call him modest forget that he was an egotist; those who call him noble as a man forget that he was treacherous as a friend and cowardly as an enemy. He was certainly selfish; he was certainly mean. He was cautiously solicitous to serve his own ends, and cautiously solicitous to defeat the ends of others. As a writer he was the purest that ever took pen in hand; as a man he was the most insidious that ever sapped the hopes of those whom he seemed to caress.—RUSSELL, WILLIAM CLARK, 1871, *Book of Authors, p.* 153, *note.*

Swift, looking with a slight touch at Addison's easy stride onward, remarks to Stella his belief that he could become a king if he chose. His wife, the Countess of Warwick, might be said to have been given to him as a reward. It was a mistake, and gave satisfaction to neither of the parties, though perhaps it was of service in teaching to the world the lesson that if, in wedded life, community of taste is desirable, the natural rise of the indissoluble union out of a community of social conditions is still more desirable.—BURTON, JOHN HILL, 1880, *A History of the Reign of Queen Anne, vol.* III, *p.* 243.

The "Dunciad" is the imperishable monument of his animosities. In all the literature of that age "no whiter page than Addison's remains;" yet even Addison he cruelly maltreated. It may be doubted whether a subsequent generation will recognise the great humane humorist, except as he appears in Pope's cruelly skilful lines. Already the "Spectator's" mild features begin to grow indistinct, and the formidable shade of Atticus usurps his place. The copy, of course, bears a likeness to the original; and though the wrinkles and crows'-feet obtain malicious prominence, yet are they drawn with exquisite delicacy, and a touch of surprising lightness and dextrous reserve. Nor need we wonder that Pope and Addison could not continue friends. The temperance of Addison's character would not exercise a soothing influence over Pope's vehement temper. We can fancy that the exquisite urbanity which no provocation could disturb must have often exasperated the "formidable cripple" past endurance.—SKELTON, JOHN, 1883, *The Great Lord Bolingbroke, Essays in History and Biography, p.* 198.

Without taint of perfidy, of cowardice, of cruelty, of ingratitude, or of envy; satirical without abuse, tempering ridicule with a tender compassion for all that is frail, and a profound reverence for all that is sublime. The greatest and most salutary reform of public morals and tastes ever affected by any satirists, he accomplished without a personal lampoon. Himself a Whig, he was described by the bitterest Tories as a gentleman of wit and virtue, in whose friendship many persons of both parties were happy, and whose name ought not to be mixed up with factious squabbles. In the heat of controversy, no outrage could provoke him to a retaliation unworthy of a Christian and a gentleman. With a boundless power of abusing men, he never used it. His modesty amounted to bashfulness.—WELSH, ALFRED H., 1883, *Development of English Literature and Language, vol.* II, *p.* 86.

He had political friends who loved him, and he went with them into politics as he might have travelled in company with them, and for the sake of their company, although caring nothing for travel himself. No man was better aware of his incapacity for the real business of public life. Addison had himself pointed out all the objections to his political advancement before that advancement was pressed upon him. He was not a statesman; he was not an administrator; he could not do any genuine service as head of a department; he was not even a good clerk: he was a wretched speaker; he was consumed by a morbid shyness, almost as oppressive as that of the poet Cowper in a later day, or of Nathaniel Hawthorne, the American novelist, later still. His whole public career was at best but a harmless mistake. It has done no harm to his literary fame. The world has almost forgotten it. Even lovers of Addison might have to be reminded now that the creator of Sir Roger de Coverley was once a diplomatic agent, and a secretary of State, and a member of the House of Commons. Some of the essays which Addison contributed to the "Spectator" are like enough to outlive the system of government by party, and perhaps even the whole system of representative government. Sir Roger de Coverley will not be forgotten until men forget Parson Adams, and Robinson Crusoe, and Gil Blas, and for that matter Sir John Falstaff and Don Quixote.—McCarthy, Justin, 1884, *A History of the Four Georges, vol.* I, *ch.* x.

This absence of dramatic incident in Addison's life would lead us naturally to conclude that he was deficient in the energy and passion which cause a powerful nature to leave a mark upon its age. Yet such a judgment would certainly be erroneous. Shy and reserved as he was, the unanimous verdict of his most illustrious contemporaries is decisive as to the respect and admiration which he excited among them. The man who could exert so potent an influence over the mercurial Steele, who could fascinate the haughty and cynical intellect of Swift, whose conversation, by the admission of his satirist Pope, had in it something more charming than that of any other man; of whom it was said that he might have been chosen king if he wished it; such a man, though to the coarse perception of Mandeville he might have seemed no more than "a parson in a tye-wig," can hardly have been deficient in force of character.—Courthope, W. J., 1884, *Addison (English Men of Letters)*, *p.* 2.

Addison lies under more obligations to happy fortune than any other literary Englishman of high rank. Halifax saved him from the Church and the probable oblivion of a seat on the bench of bishops, and sent him to cultivate his genius by foreign travel. When, on his return, he seemed sinking into poverty, the same warm patron introduced him to Godolphin's notice and procured for him the inspiration of "The Campaign" in the shape of a promise of office. Throughout life, as thus in its opening, friends, admirers, employments, themes, and applause were found for him; and if in his death he had not the crowning favor of a good biographer, the defect was more than made up in later years by the luck of having Macaulay for his eulogist. . . . At the time, Macaulay's rhetoric, force, and fame

bore down the feeble protests that strove here and there against the injustice and untruthfulness of the funeral oration he had pronounced over his predecessor in the Great-Mogulship of the middle classes. He had not, however, erased the name of "Atticus"—ah, if Addison had only escaped Pope's satire as nobly as Swift's jests! "Atticus" is a perpetual interrogation mark affixed to Addison's repute; it cannot be passed by, it tempts curiosity, it leads on to investigation.—Woodberry, George E., 1884, *Addison, The Nation, vol.* 38, *p.* 127.

It is generally said that Addison gave in too much to the ordinary drinking habits of the time; and indications in his letters and elsewhere confirm this solitary imputation upon his moral propriety. The annotator to the "Tatler" (vol. iv. p., 300, ed. 1797) gives a report that Addison shortened his life by an excessive use of "Canary wine and Barbadoes water," and says that Tonson boasted of paying his court to the great man by giving him excuses for such indulgence. Steele seems to suggest the truth in the "Tatler" (No. 252). Speaking obviously of Addison, he says that "you can seldom get him to the tavern; but when once he is arrived to his pint and begins to look about and like his company, you admire a thousand things in him which before lay buried." Addison, in fact, though not intemperate according to the standard of his time, sometimes resorted to stimulants to overcome bashfulness or depression of spirits. The charm of his conversation when once the ice was broken is attested by observers less partial than Steele. Swift, who never mentions him without praise, declares that, often as they spent their evenings together, they never wished for a third person (Delany, *Observations*, p. 32). Lady Mary Wortley Montagu declared that Addison was the best company in the world; Dr. Young speaks of his "noble stream of thought and language" when once he had overcome his diffidence; and even Pope admitted the unequalled charm of his conversation.—Stephen, Leslie, 1885, *Dictionary of National Biography, vol.* I, *p.* 125.

Addison Road, Kensington, runs from the Kensington Road, west of Holland House, to the Uxbridge Road, opposite Royal Crescent, named after Joseph

Addison, who lived at Holland House after his marriage with the Countess of Warwick.—WHEATLEY, HENRY B. AND CUNNINGHAM, PETER, 1891, *London Past and Present, vol.* I, *p.* 3.

The harmony and symmetry of this winning personality has, in a sense, told against it; for men are prone to call the well-balanced nature cold and the well-regulated life Pharisaic. Addison did not escape charges of this kind from the wild livers of his own time, who could not dissociate genius from profligacy nor generosity of nature from prodigality. It was one of the greatest services of Addison to his generation and to all generations, that in an age of violent passions, he showed how a strong man could govern himself. In a time of reckless living, he illustrated the power which flows from subordination of pleasure to duty. In a day when wit was identified with malice, he brought out its power to entertain, surprise, and delight, without taking on the irreverent levity of Voltaire, the bitterness of Swift, or the malice of Pope.—MABIE, HAMILTON WRIGHT, 1896, *Library of the World's Best Literature, ed. Warner, vol.* I, *p.* 153.

Addison's individuality stands in striking contrast with that of his friend, Steele. He was a man of pure and noble character, of lofty ideals, and genuine piety; but we miss in him the fervour and spontaneity that make Steele, with all his errors and infirmities, so delightful and engaging a figure. He was proud, shy, reserved, intensely self-conscious, and thus often left with those about him an impression of coldness and austerity. But he was, in reality, one of the kindest and most sympathetic of men. In the annals of literature he may well bear "without abuse the grand old name of gentleman," for along with exquisite breeding and urbanity he possessed masculine courage and feminine sensibility and grace.—HUDSON, WILLIAM HENRY, 1899, *ed., The Sir Roger De Coverley Papers, Introduction, p.* xiii.

AN ACCOUNT OF THE GREATEST ENGLISH POETS
1694

His "Account of the Principal English Poets" is just but tame; he probably wrote it in metre merely because Roscommon had done something of the same kind before him; at any rate, by the side of

the animated judgments of Pope in his "Epistle to Augustus," his historical survey of English poetry seems flat and languid.—COURTHOPE, W. J., 1880, *English Poets, ed. Ward, vol.* III, *p.* 1.

It would be a great mistake to confound these verses, which are scarcely more than an exercise in penmanship, with Addison's real work.—PERRY, THOMAS SERGEANT, 1883, *English Literature in the Eighteenth Century, p.* 133, *note.*

LETTERS FROM ITALY
1703

Few poems have done more honour to English genius than this. There is in it a strain of political thinking that was, at that time, new in our poetry. Had the harmony of this been equal to that of Pope's versification, it would be incontestably the finest poem in our language; but there is a dryness in the numbers, which greatly lessens the pleasure excited both by the poet's judgment and imagination.—GOLDSMITH, OLIVER, 1767, *The Beauties of English Poetry.*

REMARKS ON SEVERAL PARTS OF ITALY
1705

Mr. Addison's "Travells" is a book very trite, being made up of nothing but scraps of verses, and things which have been observed over and over, without any additions of things not discovered before; and even some of those which he has inserted, that have been already taken notice of, are ridiculous; though it must be acknowledged, that the book is written in a clean style, and for that reason will please novices and superficial readers.—HEARNE, THOMAS, 1705, *Reliquiæ Hearnianæ, ed. Bliss, Nov.* 28, *vol.* I, *p.* 73.

At his return he published his "Travels," with a dedication to lord Somers. As his stay in foreign countries was short, his observations are such as might be supplied by a hasty view, and consist chiefly in comparisons of the present face of the country with the descriptions left us by the Roman poets, from whom he made preparatory collections, though he might have spared the trouble, had he known that such collections had been made twice before by Italian authors. The most amusing passage of his book is his account of the minute republick of San Marino; of many parts it is not a very severe censure to say, that they might have been written at home. His elegance of language, and variegation of prose and verse, however, gains upon the reader; and the book, though a while neglected, became in time so much the favourite of the public, that before it was reprinted it rose to five times its price.—JOHNSON, SAMUEL, 1779-81, *Addison, Lives of the English Poets.*

Many parts of this work exhibit Addison as a vulgar bigot.—JENKINS, O. L., 1876, *The Student's Handbook of British and American Literature, p.* 183.

From one end of Italy to the other, this ingenious young gentleman of Oxford, with difficulty snatched from Anglican orders, is sternly Protestant. The legends of Rome are all "imposture" and "bungling tricks;" at Siena the stories about St. Catherine seem to him nothing but "Gross and absurd." Nor is he more or less opposed to the Gothic forms of architecture than were his contemporaries. He is passionately in favour of the Palladian style, and all others seem to him savage. With Milan Cathedral he is extremely disappointed, and he dismisses Siena as a "barbarous Building." Palladio's church of Santa Justina in Padua, on the other hand, lifts him to an ecstasy; it is "the most handsome, luminous, disencumber'd Building" Addison ever saw. In this the young traveller was of his time. . . . On the whole, Addison's lively description of Swiss places and conditions is better calculated than are his stiffer and more pedantic Italian chapters to make us realize what he visited, and the changes 'twixt now and then. For one thing, his inevitable Commonplace-book from the Classics gave out as soon as he crossed the Alps, and he had no Lucan or Silius Italicus to tell him beforehand what his sensations ought to be by the Lake of Geneva or in the crocus meadows of the valley of the Aar.—GOSSE, EDMUND, 1897, *Addison's Travels, Literature, vol.* I, *pp.* 241, 242.

THE CAMPAIGN
1705

On Addison's sweet lays attention waits,
And silence guards the place while he repeats;
His Muse alike on ev'ry subject charms,
Whether she paints the God of love, or arms:
In him, pathetick Ovid sings again,
And Homer's "Iliad" shines in his "Campaign."
—GAY, JOHN, 1714, *To Bernard Lintot, Miscellaneous Poems.*

That gazette in rhyme.—WARTON, JOSEPH, 1756-72, *Essay on Pope, vol.* I, *p.* 30.

The next composition is the far-famed "Campaign," which Dr. Warton has termed a "Gazette in Rhyme," with harshness not often used by the good-nature of his criticism. Before a censure so severe is admitted, let us consider that War is a frequent subject of Poetry, and then enquire who has described it with more justness and force. Many of our own writers tried their powers upon this year of victory: yet Addison's is confessedly the best performance; his poem is the work of a man not blinded by the dust of learning; his images are not borrowed merely from books. The superiority which he confers upon his hero is not personal prowess, and "mighty bone," but deliberate intrepidity, a calm command of his passions, and the power of consulting his own mind in the midst of danger. The rejection and contempt of fiction is rational and manly.—JOHNSON, SAMUEL, 1779-81, *Addison, Lives of the English Poets.*

Mr. Harte related to me that Pope, in one of their usual walks together, desired him to go with him to a house in Haymarket, where he would show him a curiosity. On being admitted by an old woman who kept a little shop, and going up three pair of stairs into a small room: "In this garret," said Pope, "Addison wrote his 'Campaign'."—WARTON, JOSEPH, 1797, ed., *Pope's Works, vol.* VII, *p.* 347.

A *commanded* poem, "The Campaign" has experienced the constant fate of performances of its own class—works of skill, of talent, and of elegance, which, confounded often at their first appearance with the diviner inspirations of the muse, fall afterwards not only into neglect, which might perhaps be excusable, but into contempt, which is certainly unjust. Of this poem it may be said with confidence that it set an example of good sense and good taste before undreamed of in similar productions. There is no exaggeration, no bombast, no extravagance of flattery, no insipid parade of classical allusions and Homeric machinery. . . The poem is, however, far from faultless; for even if it could with truth be said that the plan and conduct of the piece were free from objection, it must be admitted that in frequent examples of feebleness and tautology it betrays at least a hasty and careless execution, if not some barrenness of fancy. But these blemishes are well redeemed by passages of indisputable and varied merit. The celebrated simile of the angel, though defective as a comparison from too great resemblances to the object compared, may justly claim the character of grandeur, if not of absolute sublimity.—AIKIN, LUCY, 1843, *The Life of Joseph Addison.*

Addison's "Blenheim" is poor enough; one might think it a translation from some German original of those times. Gottsched's aunt, or Bodmer's wet-nurse, might have written it.—DE QUINCEY, THOMAS, 1847–58, *Schlosser's Literary History, Works, ed. Masson, vol.* XI, *p.* 27.

Addison left off at a good moment. That simile was pronounced to be of the greatest ever produced in poetry. That angel, that good angel, flew off with Mr. Addison, and landed him in the place of Commissioner of Appeals—vice Mr. Locke providentially promoted. In the following year, Mr. Addison went to Hanover with Lord Halifax, and the year after was made Under-Secretary of State. O angel visits? you come "few and far between" to literary gentlemen's lodgings! Your wings seldom quiver at second-floor windows now! . . . How many fourth-form boys at Mr. Addison's school of Charter-house could write as well as that now? The "Campaign" has blunders, triumphant as it was; and weak points like all campaigns.—THACKERAY, WILLIAM MAKEPEACE, 1853, *The English Humourists of the Eighteenth Century.*

Marlborough, though a first-rate marshal, was not a great man, not by any means so great as Wellington, far less as Napoleon; and how can a heroic poem be written without a hero? Yet the poem fell in with the humour of the times, and was cried up as though it had been another book of the Iliad.—GILFILLAN, GEORGE, 1859, *ed., Poetical Works of Joseph Addison, etc., Life, p.* xxiii.

His principal piece, "The Campaign," is an excellent model of becoming and classical style. Each verse is full, perfect in itself, with a clever antithesis, or a good epithet, or a figure of abbreviation. —TAINE, H. A., 1871, *History of English Literature, tr. Van Laun, vol.* II, *bk.* iii, *ch.* iv, *p.* 92.

As a poem, "The Campaign" shows neither loftiness of invention nor enthusiasm of personal feeling, and it cannot therefore be ranked with such an ode as Horace's "Qualem ministrum," or with Pope's very fine "Epistle" to the Earl of Oxford after his disgrace. Its methodical narrative style is scarcely misrepresented by Warton's sarcastic description of it; but it should be remembered that this style was adopted by Addison with deliberate intention. . . . The design here avowed is certainly not poetical, but it is eminently business-like and extremely well adapted to the end in view. What Godolphin wanted was a set of complimentary verses on Marlborough. Addison, with infinite tact, declares that the highest compliment that can be paid to the hero is to recite his actions in their unadorned grandeur. This happy turn of flattery shows how far he had advanced in literary skill since he wrote his address "To the King."—COURTHOPE, W. J., 1884, *Addison (English Men of Letters), pp.* 61, 62.

The poem, like all Addison's performances of the kind, shows facility and poetic sensibility, stopping short of poetic genius. It is better than a similar poem of Halifax's on the battle of the Boyne, but does not stand out at any great elevation above the work of the time; and Macaulay's remark that it is not absurdly mythological is praise which might equally be applied to Halifax and others. Macaulay notes that the simile of the angel owed its great effect to its allusion to the famous storm of 1703; and Johnson quotes the remark of Dr. Madden that if he had proposed the same topic to ten schoolboys, he should not have been surprised if eight had brought him the angel. Warton unkindly calls the poem a "Gazette in rhyme." We may be content to say that it was on the higher level of official poetry, and helped Addison's rise in literature and politics.—STEPHEN, LESLIE, 1885, *Dictionary of National Biography, vol.* I, *p.* 124.

FAIR ROSAMOND
1707

A criticism on this most wretched performance is more than it deserves, but, to account for the bad reception it met with, it is necessary to mention that the music preponderating against the elegance and humour of the poetry, and the reputation of its author, bore it down the third night of representation. To begin with the overture; it is in three parts, and in the key of D with the greater third; the first movement pretends to a great deal of spirit, but is mere noise. The two violin parts are simple counterpoint, and move in thirds almost throughout; and the last movement intended for an air is the most insipid ever heard. As to the songs, they have neither air nor expression. There is one that sings thus:—

O the pleasing, pleasing, pleasing, pleasing, pleasing anguish.

An ingenious and sensible writer, mentioned in a preceding note, who was present at the performance, says of "Rosamond" that it is a confused chaos of music, and that its only merit is its shortness.—HAWKINS, SIR JOHN, 1776, *A General History of the Science and Practice of Music, ch.* clxxi.

The whole drama is airy and elegant; engaging in its process, and pleasing in its conclusion. If Addison had cultivated the lighter parts of poetry, he would probably have excelled.—JOHNSON, SAMUEL, 1779–81, *Addison, Lives of the English Poets.*

One of the most pleasing of his compositions.—DRAKE, NATHAN, 1804, *Essays Illustrative of the Tatler, Spectator, and Guardian, vol.* I, *p.* 328.

It is in the highest and easiest style of Dryden,—that in which he wrote "Alexander's Feast," and some other of his lyrics,—but is sustained for some fifteen hundred lines with an energy and a grace which we doubt if even Dryden could have equalled. Its verses not only move but dance. The spirit is genial and sunny, and above the mazy motions shines the light of genuine poetry.—GILFILLAN, GEORGE, 1859, *ed., Poetical Works of Joseph Addison, etc., Life, p.* xxiv.

Critics melted to the foreign syren. Addison himself condescended to write a musical piece on the story of Fair Rosamond; and when he had written his text, announced his wonderful taste in music by abusing the strange musician who had lately come to London—one "Mynheer Handel," as he called him in contempt—and setting Clayton to write the score! "Rosamond," as an opera, had but a poor success—and critics laughed at the anachronism of a reference to French artillery in the reign of Henry II!

Crushed by the thunder of the Gaul

was perhaps a lost line from "The Campaign."—MANCHESTER, DUKE OF, 1864, *Court and Society from Elizabeth to Anne, vol.* II, *p.* 288.

Addison lacked the qualities of a successful libretto writer. He was too serious, and despite the lightness of his touch, there was a certain rigidity in him which made him unapt at versification which required quickness, agility, and variety. When he attempted to give his verse gayety of manner, he did not get beyond awkward simulation of an ease which nature had denied him.—MABIE, HAMILTON WRIGHT, 1896, *Library of the World's Best Literature, ed. Warner, vol.* I, *p.* 152.

The opera of "Rosamond" is, indeed, clearly modelled on Dryden in its serious parts, but is no great success there. The lighter and more whimsical quality of Addison's humour enabled him to do better in the farcical passages, which, especially the speeches of Sir Trusty, sometimes have a singularly modern and almost Gilbertian quality about them.—SAINTSBURY, GEORGE, 1898, *A Short History of English Literature, p.* 537.

THE TATLER
1709–10

A finer piece of humour was never written, than Addison's Journal of the Court of honour in the "Tatler;" in which every reader perceives the opposition of dignity and meanness: the latter arising from the insignificance of the causes; the former from the serious air of the narrative, from the accuracy of detail and minuteness of enquiry in the several examinations, and from the grave deportment of the judge and jury. Indeed, through the whole work, the personage of Isaac Bickerstaff is supported with inimitable pleasantry. The conjurer, the politician, the man of humour, the critic; the seriousness of the moralist, and the mock dignity of the astrologer; the vivacities and the infirmities peculiar to old age, are all so blended and contrasted in the censor of Great Britain, as to form a character equally complex and natural, equally laughable and respectable.—BEATTIE, JAMES, 1776–9, *Essays, p.* 356.

It has been too much the fashion to depreciate the *Tatler,* and to contrast it with its more elaborate and finished successor the *Spectator*. The attempt, however, is not just; they are built upon very different plans; and if it be allowed, as it probably must upon comparison, that there is more unity, regularity, and polish in the conduct and plan of the *Spectator*, it may, I think, with equal truth be asserted of the *Tatler*, that it possesses more vivacity, wit, and variety, than any periodical paper extant.—DRAKE, NATHAN, 1804, *Essays Illustrative of the Tatler, Spectator and Guardian, vol.* I, *p.* 342.

We now enter on those parts of Mr. Addison's prose works, which have done him the greatest honour, and have placed him at the head of those whom we call our polite writers. I know that many readers prefer Dr. Swift's prose to his:—but, whatever other merit the Dean's writings may have, (and they have, certainly, a great deal,) I affirm it with confidence, (because I have examined them both with care,) that they are not comparable to Mr. Addison's, in the correctness, propriety, and elegance of expression. Mr. Addison possessed two talents, both of them very uncommon, which singularly qualified him to excel. . . . I mean an exquisite knowledge of the English tongue in all its purity and delicacy; and a vien of humour, which flowed naturally and abundantly from him on every subject; and which experience hath shown to be inimitable. But it is in the *former* respect only that I shall criticise these papers; and I shall do it with severity, lest time, and the authority of his name, (which, of course, must become sacred,) should give a sanction even to his defects. If any man of genius should be so happy, as to equal all the excellencies of his prose, and to avoid the few blemishes which may, haply, be found in it, he would be a perfect model of style, in this way of writing: but of such an one, it is enough to say at present, (and I shall, surely, offend no good writer in saying it,)
"—hunc nequeo monstrare, et sentio tantùm."
—HURD, RICHARD, 1808–10, *ed., Works of Joseph Addison, The Tatler.*

Apart from the fortunate popularity attaching to the central figure, and the advantage arising from a narrower field of operation, it can scarcely be affirmed

that the "Spectator" greatly excelled the "Tatler," especially when attention is confined to its more enduring characteristics. If we withdraw the critical work of Addison, part of which, according to Tickell, was not prepared expressly for its pages, and to-day has lost much of its value,—if we withdraw the moral essays of Steele, now grown tedious by frequent imitation, what remains is neither better nor worse than the staple material of the "Tatler." In the social paper neither writer surpassed what he had done before. As already stated, Addison's best work in the "Spectator," though perhaps more sustained, is not superior to his best work in its predecessor; while Steele in that predecessor is distinctly stronger.—DOBSON, AUSTIN, 1886, *Richard Steele* (*English Worthies*), *p.* 141.

THE SPECTATOR
1711–12

It would have been impossible for Mr. Addison, who made little or no use of letters sent in by the numerous correspondents of the "Spectator," to have executed his large share of this task, in so exquisite a manner, if he had not ingrafted into it many pieces, that had lain by him in little hints and minutes, which he from time to time collected, and ranged in order, and moulded into the form in which they now appear.—TICKELL, THOMAS, 1721, *ed., The Works of Joseph Addison, Preface, vol.* I, *p.* xiii.

Many of his "Spectators" he wrote very fast; and sent them to the press as soon as they were written. It seems to have been best for him not to have had too much time to correct.—POPE, ALEXANDER, 1728–30, *Spence's Anecdotes, ed. Singer, p.* 38.

When panting Virtue her last efforts made,
You brought your Clio to the virgin's aid
—SOMERVILLE, WILLIAM, 1711, *To Addison.*

Rare as the intercourse was between the capital and the Highlands of Scotland, yet did the "Spectator" find its way regularly to that part of the kingdom. Mr. Steuart of Dalguise, a gentleman of Perthshire, of very great respectability, who died, near ninety, about twelve or fourteen years ago, has informed us, that when, as usual in that country, the gentlemen met after church on Sunday, to discuss the news of the week, the "Spectators" were read as regularly as the journal. He informed us also, that he knew the perusal of them to be general through the country.—Bisset, Robert, 1793, *ed., The Spectator, Life of Joseph Addison, vol.* I, *p.* 36.

It is in the "Spectator" that the genius of our author beams with unclouded lustre. The essays most valuable for their humour, invention, and precept, are the product of his pen; and it soon became, in consequence of his large contributions, the most popular work this country has produced.—Drake, Nathan, 1804, *Essays Illustrative of the Tatler, Spectator, and Guardian, vol.* I, *p.* 345.

I have lately studied "The Spectator," and with increasing pleasure and admiration. Yet it must be evident to you that there is a class of thoughts and feelings, and these, too, the most important, even practically, which it would be impossible to convey in the manner of Addison, and which, if Addison had possessed, he would not have been Addison. . . . "The Spectator" itself has innocently contributed to the general taste for unconnected writing, just as if "Reading made easy" should act to give men an aversion to words of more than two syllables, instead of drawing them *through* those words into the power of reading books in general.—Coleridge, Samuel Taylor, 1810, *Letters, ed., E. H. Coleridge, vol.* II, *p.* 557.

Not many years ago, it was very generally the custom, I remember, for every young person, male and female, to go through a course of reading of the papers of the "Spectator." This has fallen quite into disuse now-a-days, and I do not know that it is much to be regretted. The "Spectator" contains, undoubtedly, much sensible and sound morality; but it is not a very high order of Christian ethics. It contains much judicious criticism, but certainly not comparable to the deeper philosophy of criticism which has entered into English literature in the present century. Those papers will always have a semi-historical interest, as picturing the habits and manners of the times—a moral value, as a kindly, good-natured censorship of those manners. In one respect, the "Spectator" stands unrivalled to this day: I allude to the exquisite humour in those numbers in which Sir Roger de Coverley figures. If any one desire to form a just notion of what is meant by that

very indefinable quality called "humour," he cannot more agreeably inform himself than by selecting the Sir Roger de Coverley papers, and reading them in series.—Reed, Henry, 1855, *Lectures on English Literature, From Chaucer to Tennyson, p.* 231.

He has, in his imaginary Club, created a number of characters which will be recognized and loved wherever English is read. The prose of these exquisite Essays is perfect, as a specimen of the very best work of the era. To the young student it will, of course, have something of an old-world flavour, but its quaintness and pleasantness will amply repay him for any unfamiliarity with the terms of the expression of the day. It is always clear and easy, free from pomposity, pedantry, and verbosity, deeply religious in feeling, and tenderly humorous in expression.—Knox, Kathleen, 1882, *English Lessons, p.* 61.

It civilized England more, perhaps, than any one book.—Perry, Thomas Sergeant, 1883, *English Literature in the Eighteenth Century, p.* 179.

Addison was certainly at his best in the "Spectator." . . . Addison had, indeed, been little more than an occasional contributor to the "Tatler," and although some of his articles in that periodical take rank among his finest work, yet it was only in the "Spectator" that he found opportunity to show fully all his powers.—Aitken, George A., 1889, *The Life of Richard Steele, vol.* I, *p.* 312.

Finished in style, but genuinely human in feeling, betraying the nicest choice of words and the most studied care for elegant and effective arrangement, and yet penetrated by geniality, enlivened by humor, elevated by high moral aims, often using the dangerous weapons of irony and satire, and yet always well-mannered and kindly,—these papers reveal the sensitive nature of Addison and the delicate but thoroughly tempered art which he had at his command. Rarely has literature of so high an order had such instant success; for the popularity of the "Spectator" has been rivaled in English literature only by that of the Waverley novels or of the novels of Dickens. Its influence was felt not only in the sentiment of the day, and in the crowd of imitators which followed in its wake, but also across the Channel.

In Germany, especially, the genius and methods of Addison made a deep and lasting impression.—MABIE, HAMILTON WRIGHT, 1896, *Library of the World's Best Literature, ed. Warner, vol.* I, *p.* 156.

The treatment of the character-sketch by Steele and Addison in the "Spectator" (1711–12) was highly original. They drew portraits of representative Englishmen, and brought them together in conversation in a London club. They conducted Sir Roger de Coverley through Westminster Abbey, to the playhouse, to Vauxhall, into the country to Coverley church and assizes; they incidentally took a retrospective view of his life, and finally told the story of his death. When they had done this they had not only created one of the best defined characters in our prose literature, but they had almost transformed the character-sketch into a novel of London and provincial life. From the "Spectator" the character-sketch, with its types and minute observation and urbane ridicule passed into the novel, and became a part of it.—CROSS, WILBUR L., 1899, *Development of the English Novel, p.* 24.

SIR ROGER DE COVERLEY

It is recorded by Budgell, that of the characters feigned or exhibited in the "Spectator," the favourite of Addison was Sir Roger de Coverley, of whom he had formed a very delicate and discriminate idea, which he would not suffer to be violated; and therefore, when Steele had shewn him innocently picking up a girl in the Temple, and taking her to a tavern, he drew upon himself so much of his friend's indignation, that he was forced to appease him by a promise of forbearing Sir Roger for the time to come. The reason which induced Cervantes to bring his hero to the grave, *para mi sola nacio Don Quixote, y yo para el*, made Addison declare, with undue vehemence of expression, that he would kill Sir Roger; being of opinion that they were born for one another, and that any other hand would do him wrong.—JOHNSON, SAMUEL, 1779 –81, *Addison, Lives of the English Poets*.

Sir Roger de Coverley is one of those truthful types of character, which, though created by the mind of man, yet, by the ordination of Nature herself (for Nature includes art among her works), outlasts the successive generations of flesh and blood which it represents. The individuals perish, and leave no memorial; nay, we hardly care to know them while living. We might find them tiresome. We feel that Nature has done well in making them; we are grateful for the race; especially on behalf of others, and of the poor; but we do not particularly see the value of their society; when, lo! in steps one of Nature's imitators—called men of genius—and, by the mere fact of producing a likeness of the species to the mind's eye, enchants us forever both with it and himself. A little philosophy may easily explain this; but perhaps a little more may still leave it among the most interesting of mysteries.—HUNT, LEIGH, 1849, *A Book for a Corner*.

No truer or more winning picture of worthy old English knighthood can you find anywhere in literature; nowhere such a tender twilight color falling through brooks upon old English country homes. Those papers made the scaffolding by which our own Irving built up his best stories about English country homesteads, and English revels of Christmas; and the De Coverley echoes sound sweetly and surely all up and down the pages of "Bracebridge Hall."—MITCHELL, DONALD G., 1890, *English Lands Letters and Kings, From Elizabeth to Anne, p.* 291.

Of all things else that Addison has done there remains one preëminent figure which is his chief claim to immortality. "The Campaign" has disappeared out of literature; "Cato" is known only by a few well-known lines; the "Spectator" itself, though a work which no gentleman's library can be without, dwells generally in dignified retirement there, and is seldom seen on any table but the student's, though we are all supposed to be familiar with it: but Sir Roger de Coverley is the familiar friend of most people who have read anything at all, and the acquaintance by sight, if we may so speak, of everybody. There is no form better known in all literature. His simple rustic state, his modest sense of his own importance, his kind and genial patronage of the younger world, which would laugh at him if it were not overawed by his modesty and goodness, and which still sniggers in its sleeve at all those kind, ridiculous ways of his as he walks about in London, taken in on all sides, with his hand always in his purse, and his heart in its right place, are always familiar and delightful. We learn with a kind of shock that it was Steele who first introduced this perfect gentleman to the world, and can only hope that it was Addison's idea from the first, and that he did not merely snatch out of his friend's hands and appropriate a conception so entirely according to his own heart.— OLIPHANT, MRS. M. O. W., 1894, *Historical Characters of the Reign of Queen Anne, p.* 193.

It is a rather singular circumstance that we have in our literature one well-drawn character—fulfilling all the requirements of a "study" from the life, one of our important and most classic characters indeed—existing entirely outside the pages of a novel, a drama, or of any formal fiction. This is genial, worthy old Sir Roger de Coverley, who in the year 1711 strolled into England quietly and unannounced, introduced and hospitably entertained by Joseph Addison and Richard Steele. Addison, it is true, produced no novel; he did as great a thing, for he drew a character so strongly individualized, so amiable in its attributes, that it has lived from that day to ours one of the best beloved in English fiction. Thus Joseph Addison may be regarded as at the very beginning of the century suggesting if not inventing the novel form, and as setting a pattern in the portrayal of real character which has rarely been surpassed.—SIMONDS, WILLIAM EDWARD, 1894, *Introduction to the Study of English Fiction, p.* 39.

While "The Spectator" contains ample material for a fully developed novel, it only just falls short of making a fully developed novel out of it. Had the various detached episodes in which the essayist and his companions figure been more closely related to one another—had they been gathered up and carfully woven into the definite pattern of a plot—then the "Sir Roger de Coverley Papers" here reprinted would have been to all intents and purposes a serial novel running through a periodical. As it is, we can never properly neglect them in any historical survey of English prose fiction.— HUDSON, WILLIAM HENRY, 1899, *ed., The Sir Roger de Coverley Papers, Introduction, p.* xxiii.

CATO
1713

"Cato," a most noble play of Mr. Addison, and the only one he writ, is to be acted in Easter week. The town is full of expectation of it, the Boxes being already bespoke, and he designing to give all the Benefit away among the Actors in proportion to their performing.—BERKELEY, GEORGE, 1712–13, *Letter to Sir John Perceval.*

I was this morning, at ten, at the rehearsal of Mr. Addison's play called "Cato," which is to be acted on Friday. There was not above a score of us to see it. We stood on the stage, and it was foolish enough to see the actors prompted every moment, and the poet directing them; and the drab, that acts Cato's daughter, out in the midst of a passionate part, and then calling out, "What's next?" The Bishop of Clogher was there too, but he stood privately in a gallery.—SWIFT, JONATHAN, 1713, *Letter to Miss Johnson, April* 6.

Cato was not so much the wonder of Rome in his days as he is of Britain in ours; and though all the foolish industry possible has been used to make it thought a party play, yet what the author once said of another may the most properly in the world he applied to him on this occasion:

Envy itself is dumb, in wonder lost,
And factions strive who shall applaud him most.

The numerous and violent claps of the Whig-party on the one side of the theatre were echoed back by the Tories on the other, while the author sweated behind the scenes with concern to find their applause proceeding more from the hand than the head. This was the case, too, of the prologue-writer, who was clapped into a stanch Whig at almost every two lines. I believe you have heard, that after all the applauses of the opposite faction, my Lord Bolingbroke sent for Booth, who played Cato, into the box between one of the acts, and presented him with fifty guineas in acknowledgment (as he expressed it) for defending the cause of liberty so well against a perpetual dictator. The Whigs are unwilling to be distanced this way, as it is said, and therefore design a present to the same Cato very speedily; in the meantime they are getting ready as good a sentence as the former on their side, so betwixt them it is probable that Cato (as Dr. Garth expressed it) may have something to live upon after he dies.—POPE, ALEXANDER, 1713, *Letter to Sir William Trumbull, April* 30.

While you the fierce divided Britons awe,
And Cato with an equal virtue, draw;
While Envy is itself in Wonder lost,
And Factions strive who shall applaud you most;
Forgive the fond ambition of a friend,
Who hopes himself, not you, to recommend,
And join th' applause which all the Learn'd bestow
On one, to whom a perfect work they owe.
To my light Scenes I once inscrib'd your name,
And impotently strove to borrow fame:
Soon will that die, which adds thy name to mine;
Let me, then, live, join'd to a work of thine.
—STEELE, RICHARD, 1713, *To the Author of Cato.*

Illustrious deeds in distant nations wrought,
And virtues by departed heroes taught,
Raise in your soul a pure immortal flame,
Adorn your life, and consecrate your fame;
To your renown all ages you subdue,
And Cæsar fought, and Cato bled for you.
—YOUNG, EDWARD, 1713, *To the Author of Cato.*

But now let us sum up all these absurdities together. Sempronius goes at noonday, in Juba's guards, to Cato's palace, in order to pass for Juba, in a place where they were both so very well known: he meets Juba there, and resolves to murder him with his own guards. Upon the guards appearing a little bashful, he threatens them:

Hah! Dastards, do you tremble!
Or act like men; or, by yon azure heav'n!

But the guards still remaining restive, Sempronius himself attacks Juba, while each of the guards is representing Mr. Spectator's sign of the Gaper, awed, it seems, and terrified by Sempronius's threats. Juba kills Sempronius, and takes his own army prisoners, and carries them in triumph away to Cato. Now, I would fain know, if any parts of Mr. Bayes's tragedy is so full of absurdity as this?—DENNIS, JOHN, 1713, *Criticism on Cato.*

It is in every body's memory, with what applause it was received by the public; that the first run of it lasted for a month; and then stopped, only because one of the performers became incapable of acting a principle part. The Author received a message, that the Queen would be pleased to have it dedicated to her: but as he had designed that compliment elsewhere, he found himself obliged by his duty on the one side, and his honour on the other, to send it into the world without any dedication. The fame of this Tragedy soon spread through *Europe*, and it has not only been translated, but acted in most of the languages of Christendom. The translation of it into *Italian*, by Signor *Salvini*, is very well known; but I have not been able to learn, whether that of Signor *Valetta*, a young *Neapolitan* nobleman, has ever been made public.—TICKELL, THOMAS, 1721, *ed., The Works of Joseph Addison, Preface, vol.* I, *p.* xiv.

The first *English* writer who compos'd a regular Tragedy, and infus'd a spirit of elegance thro' every part of it, was the illustrious Mr. *Addison*. His CATO is a master-piece both with regard to the diction, and to the beauty and harmony of the numbers. The character of *Cato* is, in my opinion, vastly superior to that of *Cornelia* in the POMPEY of *Corneille:* For *Cato* is great without any thing like fustian, and *Cornelia*, who besides is not a necessary character, tends sometimes to bombast. Mr. *Addison's Cato* appears to me the greatest character that ever was brought upon any Stage, but then the rest of them do not correspond to the dignity of it: And this dramatic piece so excellently well writ, is disfigur'd by a dull love-plot, which spreads a certain languor over the whole, that quite murders it. . . . The judicious Mr. *Addison* had the effeminate complaisance to soften the severity of his dramatic character so as to adapt it to the manners of the age; and from an endeavour to please quite ruin'd a master-piece in its kind.—VOLTAIRE, FRANCOIS MARIE AROUET, 1732? *Letters Concerning the English Nation, pp.* 141, 142.

In 1703, nine years before it was acted, I had the pleasure of reading the first four acts (which was all of it then written) privately with Sir Richard Steele: it may be needless to say it was impossible to lay them out of my hand until I had gone through them; or to dwell upon the delight his friendship to the author received, upon my being so warmly pleased with them; but my satisfaction was as highly disappointed when he told me, whatever spirit Mr. Addison had shown in his writing it, he doubted he would never have courage enough to let his "Cato" stand the censure of an English audience; that it had only been the amusement of his leisure hours in Italy, and was never intended for the stage. The poetical diffidence sir Richard himself spoke of with some concern, and in the transport of his imagination could not help saying, "Good God! what a part would Betterton make of Cato!" But this was seven years before Betterton died, and when Booth (who afterwards made his fortune by acting it) was in his theatrical minority. In the latter end of queen Anne's reign, when our national politics had changed hands, the friends of Mr. Addison then thought it a proper time to animate the public with the sentiments of Cato. In a word, their importunities were too warm to be resisted; and it was no sooner finished than hurried to the stage, in April 1712. —CIBBER, COLLEY, 1739, *An Apology for His Life.*

Is a glaring instance of the force of party; so sententious and declamatory a drama would never have met with such rapid and amazing success, if every line and sentiment had not been particularly tortured and applied to recent events, and the reigning disputes of the times. The purity and energy of the diction, the loftiness of the sentiments, copied in a great measure from Lucan, Tacitus, and Seneca the philosopher, merit approbation. But I have always thought, that those pompous Roman sentiments are not so difficult to be produced, as is vulgarly imagined; and which, indeed, dazzle only the vulgar. A stroke of nature is, in my opinion, worth a hundred such thoughts as
When vice prevails, and impious men bear sway,
The post of honour is a private station.

"Cato" is a fine dialogue on liberty, and the love of one's country; but considered as a dramatic performance, nay, as a model of a just tragedy, as some have affectedly represented it, it must be owned to want action and pathos; the two hinges, I presume, on which a just tragedy ought necessarily to turn, and without which it cannot subsist. It wants also character. —WARTON, JOSEPH, 1756, *Essay on the*

Genius and Writings of Pope, vol. I, *p.* 270.

Of a work so much read, it is difficult to say any thing new. About things on which the publick thinks long, it commonly attains to think right; and of "Cato" it has been not unjustly determined, that it is rather a poem in dialogue than a drama, rather a succession of just sentiments in elegant language, than a representation of natural affections, or of any state probable or possible in human life. —JOHNSON, SAMUEL, 1779–81, *Addison, Lives of the English Poets.*

Addison possesses an elegant mind, but he was by no means a poet. He undertook to purify the English tragedy, by a compliance with the supposed rules of good taste. We might have expected from a judge of the ancients, that he would have endeavoured to approach the Greek models. Whether he had any such intention I know not, but certain it is, that he has produced nothing but a tragedy after the French cut. "Cato" is a feeble and frigid piece, almost destitute of action, without one truly overpowering moment. Addison has so narrowed a great and heroic picture by his timid manner of treating it, that he could not even fill up the frame without foreign intermixtures. . . . Addison took his measures well; he brought all the great and small critics, with Pope at their head, the whole militia of good taste under arms, that he might excite a high expectation of the piece which he had produced with so much labour. "Cato" was universally praised, as a work without an equal. And on what foundation do these boundless claims rest? On regularity of form? This had been already observed by the French poets for nearly a century, and notwithstanding the constraint, they had often attained a much stronger pathetic effect. Or on the political sentiments? But in a single dialogue between Brutus and Cassius, in Shakspeare, there is more of a Roman way of thinking, and republican energy, than in all "Cato."—SCHLEGEL, AUGUSTUS WILLIAM, 1809, *Dramatic Art and Literature, Lecture* xiii, *tr. Black.*

Addison's "Cato," in spite of Dennis's criticism, still retains possession of the stage with all its unities. My love and admiration for Addison is as great as any person's, let that other person be who he will; but it is not founded on his "Cato," in extolling which Whigs and Tories contended in loud applause. The interest of this play (bating that shadowy regret that always clings to and flickers round the form of free antiquity) is confined to the declamation, which is feeble in itself, and not heard on the stage. I have seen Mr. Kemble in this part repeat the Soliloquy on Death without a line being distinctly heard; nothing was observable but the thoughtful motion of his lips, and the occasional extension of his hand in sign of doubts suggested or resolved; yet this beautiful and expressive dumb-show, with the propriety of his costume, and the elegance of his attitude and figure, excited the most lively interest, and kept attention even more on the stretch, to catch every imperfect syllable or speaking gesture. There is nothing, however, in the play to excite ridicule, or shock by absurdity, except the love scenes, which are passed over as what the spectator has no proper concern with; and however feeble or languid the interest produced by a dramatic exhibition, unless there is some positive stumbling-block thrown in the way, or gross offence given to an audience, it is generally suffered to linger on to a *euthanasia*, instead of dying a violent and premature death.—HAZLITT, WILLIAM, 1820, *Lectures on the Dramatic Literature of the Age of Elizabeth, Lecture* viii.

The exquisite taste and fine observation of Addison, produced only the solemn mawkishness of Cato.—JEFFREY, FRANCIS LORD, 1822–44, *Contributions to the Edinburgh Review, vol.* II, *p.* 334.

A tragedy, which, whatever merit it may possess, notwithstanding Pope's deprecation of "French translation" and his panegyric on "native rage," is as completely *un-English* in its whole conception and conduct, as Aaron Hill's Merope, or Alzire, or any other avowed translation from the French theatre.—PRESCOTT, WILLIAM HICKLING, 1832, *English Literature of the Nineteenth Century, North American Review, vol.* 35, *p.* 168.

A play, the whole merit of which consists in its stately rhetoric,—a rhetoric sometimes not unworthy of Lucan,—about hating tyrants and dying for freedom, is brought on the stage in a time of great political excitement. Both parties crowd to the theatre. Each affects to consider every line as a compliment to itself, and an attack on its opponents. The curtain falls amidst an unanimous roar of applause. The Whigs of the "Kit Cat" embrace the author, and assure him that he has rendered an inestimable service to liberty. The Tory Secretary of State represents a purse to the chief actor for defending the cause of liberty so well. The history of that night was, in miniature, the history of two generations.—MACAULAY, THOMAS BABINGTON, 1834, *Mackintosh's History, Critical and Miscellaneous Essays.*

"Cato" was really and afflictingly a *rational* play.—WILSON, JOHN, 1845, *Dryden and Pope, Blackwood's Magazine.*

"Cato" was not popular for a moment, nor tolerated for a moment, upon any literary ground, or as a work of art. It was an apple of temptation and strife thrown by the goddess of faction between two infuriated parties. "Cato," coming from a man without parliamentary connections, would have dropped lifeless to the ground.—DE QUINCEY, THOMAS, 1847–58, *Schlosser's Literary History, Works, ed. Masson, vol.* XI, *p.* 28.

Time is a great iconoclast—reverses all sort of verdicts. What has become of "Cato"? as a poem? as a play? In his day it did much to raise Addison's fame: it does little to support it now. Johnson calls it the noblest production of Addison's genius. Macaulay places it long after the masterpieces of the Attic stage, after the Elizabethan dramatists, after Schiller, Alfieri, Voltaire, Corneille, Racine. In truth, Addison, in spite of his refinedly sensitive organisation and his great knowledge and appreciation of human nature, produced a play without feeling and without nature—a literary bas-relief, carven out of cold and colourless stone—its only recommendations, that it was right according to rule, and fashioned accurately after classical patterns. It gave London a month's excitement, and has since supplied the world with some trite quotations—that is all. It is melancholy to think that Mr. John Dennis's coarse criticisms were probably just.—COOK, DUTTON, 1861, *"Cato" on the Boards, Once a Week, vol.* 5, *p.* 76.

Addison designed his "Cato" (1713) as a great contribution to the task of reforming English tragedy in several important respects. Licentious language was to be banished as a matter of course; but also the British lawlessness in regard to technical rules was to be abjured; and an English tragedy, written in the language and metre of Shakspeare, was to have as much classical correctness, and observe the unities as scrupulously, as the master-pieces of Racine. The play was success-ful at the time, and it may be pronounced to be still worth reading; several lines from it are familiar to all ears; never-theless it was not written with sufficient power to found a new school, or form an era in style; it is better than any of its imitations, but not good enough for immortality.—ARNOLD, THOMAS, 1868–75, *Chaucer to Wordsworth, p.* 312.

It is difficult to consider the success of "Cato" in the first instance, and its sub-sequent protracted popularity, to have resulted from any other influence than that of extravagant puffery, aided in its effect by the elevated station of the author.—CLARKE, CHARLES COWDEN, 1871, *On the Comic Writers of England, Gentle-man's Magazine, n. s., vol.* 7, *p.* 329.

Addison's poetry in general is rhetor-ical prose in verse; a striking proof of this is his tragedy "Cato." It was per-formed at Drury Lane in 1713, and the immense applause it called forth bore witness to the deterioration of dramatic taste in the native country of Shakespeare.—SCHERR, J., 1874–82, *A History of English Literature, p.* 147.

"Cato" is full of effective common-places, many of which are to this day current as familiar quotations; but other-wise it would be difficult to find in it any distinguishing feature. Voltaire extolled it as the first English *tragedie raisonnable, i. e.* as the first in which the Rules had been observed with perfect obedience to them as based upon reason; but Dennis had some grounds for his remark, that by observing the Unity of Place the author had only contrived to render the action impossible. For, in order to accommodate his incidents to the Rules, Addison was obliged to exclude much that was essential to the action, while he included much that is not only non-essential but disturbing. It would be difficult to mention a drama in which the amatory episodes are more decidedly tedious and intrusive. Not less than six lovers appear in the piece, and at the close, as Schlegel points out, Cato, before dying, feels himself called upon like a good father in a comedy to arrange a brace of marriages. Moreover, with the exception of these arrangements, the hero of the tragedy is given nothing to do; and where an original feature is added, its introduction is inopportune—thus, the apprehension expressed by Cato that he has been too hasty in commiting suicide, seems quite out of harmony with his Stoic opinions. Macaulay with his usual courage defends "Cato," but can-not say more on its behalf than that it "contains excellent dialogue and decla-mation, and that among plays fashioned on the French model, it must be allowed to rank high." But even to this praise certain exceptions might with justice be taken. The language, like every page that came from Addison's pen, is trans-parently pure; but where can it be said to approach the grandeur of "Cinna," or to sparkle like that pure stream from the Castalian fount which permeates the dramas of Racine, even when they fall short of the highest excellence within his reach? And if excellent dialogue means a lifelike interchange of speech—is even so much as this to be found in "Cato?"—WARD, ADOLPHUS WILLIAM, 1875–99, *A History of English Dramatic Liter-ature, vol.* III, *p.* 441.

Its dramatic weakness has never been denied. The love scenes are incongruous. It consists in the great part of declama-tion which Addison's taste restrained within limits, and polished into many still familiar quotations, but which remains commonplace.—STEPHEN, LESLIE, 1885, *Dictionary of National Biography, vol.* I, *p.* 128.

It had its day of prosperity upon the stage; indeed, it supplied the model for many a later example of less scholarly writers, and now it enjoys the somewhat dubious honor of being bound as part of Addison's Works—and frequently skipped in the reading thereof. Viewed from the present standpoint it seems prosy and lacking in situation.—ROBINS, EDWARD, JR., 1895, *Echoes of the Playhouse, p.* 102.

THE DRUMMER
1716

It had been some years in the hands of the author, and falling under my perusal, I thought so well of it, that I persuaded him to make some additions and alterations to it, and let it appear upon the stage. I own I was very highly pleased with it, and liked it the better, for the want of those studied similies and repartees, which we, who have writ before him, have thrown into our plays, to indulge and gain upon a false taste that has prevailed for many years in the British theatre. I believe the author would have condescended to fall into this way a little more than he has, had he, before the writing of it, been often present at theatrical representations. . . . As it is not in the common way of writing, the approbation was at first doubtful, but has risen every time it has been acted, and has given an opportunity in several of its parts for as just and good action as ever I saw on the stage.—STEELE, SIR RICHARD, 1721, *The Drummer, Preface.*

Is a pleasant farce enough, but adds nothing to our idea of the author of the "Spectator."—HAZLITT, WILLIAM, 1818, *Lectures on the English Comic Writers, Lecture* VIII.

It is one of the wonders of literature that Addison with a wit so keen, a literary touch so delicate, and a fertility of fancy so great, should have failed as a comedy-writer. Macaulay, noting how the "Roger de Coverley" papers work into a charming narrative, regrets that a writer so capable of invaluable character-fiction should never have attempted a true novel. Addison's comedy, "The Drummer," written with probably some help from Steele, goes some way, though not the whole way, to induce us to think that this regret was groundless. The "Drummer" has in places a humour of its own, but were its authorship unknown few critics probably would detect in its scenes the masterly touch and refined taste of Addison. It was perhaps the moralizing tendency of the author and the age that make this comedy wanting in the right comedy flavour.—CRAWFURD, OSWALD, 1883, *ed., English Comic Dramatists, p.* 162.

CRITICISMS

It gives one pain to refuse to such a writer as Mr. *Addison,* any *kind* of merit, to which he appears to have laid claim, and which the generality [of his readers] have seemed willing to allow him. Yet it must not be dissembled, that *criticism* was, by no means, his talent. His taste was truly elegant; but he had neither that vigour of understanding, nor chastised, philosophical spirit, which are so essential to this character, and which we find in hardly any of the antients, besides Aristotle, and but in a very few of the moderns. For what concerns his *criticism on Milton* in particular, there was this accidental benefit arising from it, that it occasioned an admirable poet to be read, and his excellencies to be observed. But for the merit of the work itself, if there be anything just in the *plan,* it was, because Aristotle and Bossu had taken the same route before him. And as to his *own* proper observations, they are for the most part, so general and indeterminate, as to afford but little instruction to the reader, and are, not unfrequently, altogether frivolous.—HURD, RICHARD, 1751, *Comments on Horace's Epistola ad Augustum.*

It is already well known, that Addison had no very intimate acquaintance with the literature of his own country. It is known, also, that he did not think such an acquaintance any ways essential to the character of an elegant scholar and *littérateur.* Quite enough he found it, and more than enough for the time he had to spare, if he could maintain a tolerable familiarity with the foremost Latin poets, and a very slender one indeed with the Grecian. *How* slender, we can see in his "Travels." Of modern authors, none as yet had been published with notes, commentaries, or critical collations of the text; and, accordingly, Addison looked upon all of them, except those few who professed themselves followers in the retinue and equipage of the ancients, as creatures of a lower race. Boileau, as a mere imitator and propagator of Horace, he read, and probably little else amongst the French classics. Hence it arose that he took upon himself to speak sneeringly of Tasso. To this, which was a bold act for his timid mind, he was emboldened by the countenance of Boileau. Of the elder Italian authors, such as Ariosto, and, *a fortiori,* Dante, he knew absolutely nothing. Passing to our own literature, it is certain that Addison was profoundly ignorant of Chaucer and of Spenser. Milton only, —and why? simply because he was a brilliant scholar, and stands like a bridge between the Christian literature and the

Pagan,—Addison had read and esteemed. —DE QUINCEY, THOMAS, 1847? *Shakspeare, Works, ed. Masson, vol.* IV, *p.* 22.

We must remember that, however narrow, and prejudiced, and exclusive may seem to us the dogmas of Addison's literary criticisms, yet that these were the first *popular* essays in English towards the investigation of the grounds and axioms of æsthetic science, and that even here, in innumerable instances (as, for example, in the celebrated reviews of "Paradise Lost," and of the old national ballad of "Chevy Chase"), we find the author's natural and delicate sense of the beautiful and sublime triumphing over the accumulated errors and false judgment of his own artificial age, and the author of "Cato" doing unconscious homage to the nature and pathos of the rude old Border balladmaker.—SHAW, THOMAS B., 1847, *Outlines of English Literature, p.* 241.

These papers constitute a Primer to "Paradise Lost." Most skilfully constructed both to interest and instruct, but still a Primer. As the excellent setting may the better display the gem of incalculable value: so may Addison's thought help us to understand Milton's "greatness of Soul, which furnished him with such glorious Conceptions." Let us not stop at the Primer, but pass on to a personal apprehension of the great English Epic.—ARBER, EDWARD, 1868, *ed., Joseph Addison, Criticism on Milton's Paradise Lost, Introduction, p.* 7.

His celebrated commentary on "Paradise Lost" is little better than the dissertations of Batteux and Bossu. —TAINE, H. A., 1871, *History of English Literature, tr. Van Laun, vol.* II, *bk.* iii, *ch.* iv, *p.* 106.

Addison's sensitive nature gave refinement to his humour, and delicacy to his sense of the charm of style. He was the best critic of his day, and the more readily accepted because he shared to some extent, conventional opinions of his time. He enjoyed "Chevy Chase" and "the Babes in the Wood," and did so for good human reasons. But when he tried in Spectator papers to show cause for his enjoyment, it was by suggesting resemblances to Horace and Vergil. There are passages in Addison's criticisms of "Paradise Lost" by which he made Spectator papers a means of rescuing Milton from the prejudices of

the day, in which the prejudices themselves govern his argument; and what we might now look upon as the weak part of his criticism, was in his own time a safeguard to his reputation. But there was nothing conventional in Addison's tastes. The sympathetic insight of genius and the religious depths of character caused him to fasten only on that which was good; all that could be affected by convention was his manner of accounting critically for his right impressions.—MORLEY, HENRY, 1881, *Of English Literature in the Reign of Victoria with a Glance at the Past.*

In his own day Addison was held in higher esteem as a critic than later generations have deemed him to deserve. His formal critical studies show no especial force or insight. That refined taste and correctness which always marked him, certainly appears in his judgments of literature, but frequently his thoughts are too mild to be stimulating, and we turn from the papers on Milton, as well as from the various ethical reflections, to his delicate social satire, or those genial charactersketches which never lose their charm. Yet all his writing is agreeable, if for nothing more than its exquisite expression —clear, quiet, unobtrusive, finished yet always easy; every essay shows, too, the thought and spirit as well as the language of a cultivated gentleman.—McLAUGHLIN, EDWARD T., 1893, *Literary Criticism for Students, p.* 33.

Addison brought to the study of literature a mind which was open to receive impressions from every side. He commenced, as he was bound to do, with an application of the rules of Aristotle, but he acquired confidence in his own judgment as he proceeded in his researches, and finally availed himself freely of new elements of human knowledge which were unknown to Aristotle. His application of the Aristotelian canons to "Paradise Lost" was undertaken in deference to the spirit of the age, but in his essay on "The Pleasures of the Imagination," he discovers a new principle to which the charm and power of poetic literature is to be referred: a principle which, unlike the appeal to "fear and pity," is applicable not to one but to every form of poetry and fiction. And in so doing he introduces fresh considerations, which affect all manifestations of art, but of which the rules of Aristotle take no account, and notices new effects for which these rules provide no tests; and in supplying these omissions he has permanently widened the scope of criticism, whether the object of its inquiry be a picture or a poem, form or thought. . . . By the work of Addison criticism was brought into line with modern thought; and the critic was provided with a test which he could apply with equal success to every fresh form which literature had developed.—WORSFOLD, W. BASIL, 1897, *The Principles of Criticism, pp.* 59, 107.

GENERAL

The ingenious Mr. Addison, of Oxford. —DRYDEN, JOHN, 1697, *Virgil's Æneas, Postscript.*

His wit, natural good sense, generous sentiments, and enterprising genius, with a peculiar delicacy and easiness of writing, seem those qualities which distinguished Mr. Steele. Mr. Addison has the same talents in a high degree, and is likewise a great philosopher, having applied himself to the speculative studies more than any of the wits that I know.—BERKELEY, GEORGE, 1712–13, *Letter to Sir John Perceval.*

With graceful step see Addison advance,
The sweetest child of Attic elegance.

—WARTON, THOMAS, 1749, *The Triumph of Isis.*

Mr. Addison, for a happy and natural style, will be always an honour to British literature. His diction indeed wants strength, but it is equal to all the subjects he undertakes to handle, as he never (at least in his finished works) attempts anything in the argumentative or demonstrative way.—GOLDSMITH, OLIVER, 1759, *The Bee, No.* 8, *Nov.* 24.

Addison wrote little in verse, much in sweet, elegant, Virgilian prose; so let me call it, since Longinus calls Herodotus most Homeric; and Thucydides is said to have formed his style on Pindar. Addison's compositions are built with the finest materials, in the taste of the ancients. I never read him, but I am struck with such a disheartening idea of perfection, that I drop my pen. And, indeed, far superior writers should forget his compositions, if they would be greatly pleased with their own.—YOUNG, EDWARD, 1759, *Conjectures on Original Composition.*

The cold and well-discipline merit of Addison.—WALPOLE, HORACE, 1765, *Letters, ed. Cunningham, March* 18, *vol.* III, *p.* 333.

His own powers were such as might have satisfied him with conscious excellence. Of very extensive learning he has indeed given no proofs. He seems to have had small acquaintance with the sciences, and have read little except Latin and French; but of the Latin poets his "Dialogues on Medals" shew that he had perused the works with great diligence and skill. The abundance of his own mind left him little indeed of adventitious sentiments; his wit always could suggest what the occasion demanded. He had read with critical eyes the important volume of human life, and knew the heart of man from the depths of stratagem to the surface of affectation. . . . His poetry is first to be considered; of which it must be confessed that it has not often those felicities of diction which gave lustre to sentiments, or that vigour of sentiment that animates diction: there is little of ardour, vehemence, or transport; there is very rarely the awfulness of grandeur, and not very often the splendour of elegance. He thinks justly; but he thinks faintly. This is his general character; to which, doubtless, many single passages will furnish exception. Yet, if he seldom reaches supreme excellence, he rarely sinks into dulness, and is still more rarely entangled in absurdity. He did not trust his powers enough to be negligent. There is in most of his compositions a calmness and equability, deliberate and cautious, sometimes with little that delights, but seldom with anything that offends. . . . As a describer of life and manners, he must be allowed to stand perhaps the first of the first rank. . . . As a teacher of wisdom, he may be confidently followed. His religion has nothing in it enthusiastick or superstitious: he appears neither weakly credulous, nor wantonly sceptical; his morality is neither dangerously lax, nor impracticably rigid. . . . His prose is the model of the middle style; on grave subjects not formal, on light occasions not groveling; pure without scrupulosity, and exact without apparent elaboration; always equable, and always easy, without glowing words or pointed sentences. . . . Whoever wishes to attain an English style, familiar but not coarse, and elegant but not ostentatious, must give his days and nights to the volumes of Addison.—JOHNSON, SAMUEL, 1779–81, *Addison, Lives of the English Poets.*

> In front of these came Addison. In him
> Humour in holiday and slightly trim,
> Sublimity and Attic taste combined,
> To polish, furnish, and delight the mind.

—COWPER, WILLIAM, 1782, *Table Talk.*

Of the latter of these, the highest, most correct, and ornamented degree of the simple manner, Mr. Addison, is, beyond doubt, in the English language, the most perfect example: and, therefore, though not without some faults, he is, on the whole, the safest model for unitation, and the freest from considerable defects, which the language affords. Perspicuous and pure, he is in the highest degree; his precision, indeed, not very great, yet nearly as great as the subjects which he treats of require; the construction of his sentences easy, agreeable, and commonly very musical; carrying a character of smoothness more than of strength. In figurative language, he is rich particularly in similes and metaphors; which are so employed, as to render his style splendid, without being gaudy. There is not the least affectation in his manner; we see no marks of labour, nothing forced or constrained; but great elegance, joined with great ease and simplicity. He is, in particular, distinguished by a character of modesty, and of politeness, which appears in all his writings. No author has a more popular and insinuating manner; and the great regard which he every where shows for virtue and religion, recommends him highly. If he fails in anything it is in want of strength and precision, which renders his manner, though perfectly suited to such essays as he writes in the "Spectator," not altogether a proper model for any of the higher and more elaborate kinds of composition. Though the public have ever done much justice to his merit, yet the nature of his merit has not always been seen in its true light; for, though his poetry be elegant, he certainly bears a higher rank among the prose writers, than he is entitled to among the poets, and, in prose, his humour is of a much higher, and more original

strain, than his philosophy. The character of Sir Roger de Coverly discovers more genius than the critique on Milton.—BLAIR, HUGH, 1783, *Lectures on Rhetoric and Belles-Letters, ed. Mills Lecture* xix, *p.* 208.

Addison is a writer eminently enervated; and few authors, distinguished in the *belles-lettres* and of so recent a date, will be found more strikingly loose and unsystematical in their diction.—GODWIN, WILLIAM, 1797, *Of English Style, The Enquirer, p.* 438.

To the keenest preception of the beautiful and sublime in composition, he added a taste pre-eminently delicate and correct, and the most engaging and fascinating style that this country had ever witnessed; with these were combined the most unrivalled humour, a morality lovely and interesting as it was pure and philanthrophic, and a fancy whose effusions were peculiarly sweet, rich, and varied. . . . The great object which Addison ever steadily held in view, and to which his style, his criticism, his humour and imagination are alike subservient, was the increase of religious, moral, and social virtue. Perhaps to the writings of no individual, of any age or nation, if we except the result of inspiration, have morality and rational piety been more indebted than to those which form the periodical labours of our author.—DRAKE, NATHAN, 1804, *Essays Illustrative of the Tatler, Spectator and Guardian, vol.* II, *pp.* 141, 319.

The style of Addison is pure and clear, rather diffuse than concentrated, and ornamental to the highest degree consistent with good taste. But this ornament consists, not in the splendor of imagery, not in the ordonnance of words; his readers will seek in vain for those sonorous cadences with which the public ear has been familiarized since the writings of Dr. Johnson. They will find no stately magnificence of phrase, no trials of sentences artfully balanced, so as to form a sweep of harmony, at the close of a period. His words are genuine English; he deals little in inversions, and often allows himself to conclude negligently with a trivial word. The fastidious ear may occasionally be offended with some colloquial phrases, and some expressions which would not now, perhaps, be deemed perfectly accurate—the remains of barbarisms which he, more than any one, had labored to banish from good writing—but the best judges have doubted whether our language has not lost more than it has gained since his time. An idiomatic style gives a truth and spirit to a composition that is but ill compensated by an elaborate pomp, which sets written composition at too great a distance from speech, for which it is only the substitute.—BARBAULD, ANNA LETITIA, 1804, *ed., Selections from the Spectator, Tatler, Guardian and Freeholder.*

The extreme caution, timidity, and flatness of this author in his poetical compositions—the narrowness of his range in poetical sentiment and diction, and the utter want either of passion or of brilliancy, render it difficult to believe that he was born under the same sun with Shakespeare, and wrote but a century after him. His fame, at this day, stands solely upon the delicacy, the modest gaiety, and ingenious purity of his prose style;—for the occasional elegance and small ingenuity of his poems can never redeem the poverty of their diction, and the tameness of their conception.—JEFFREY, FRANCIS LORD, 1819–44, *Contributions to the Edinburgh Review, vol.* II, *p.* 291.

The very name of Addison inspires delight. That charming writer was not only, in himself, one of the most perfect of prose authors, but, in the *Spectator,* (of which he might be called at once the patron and promoter) he set an example of instructing the intellectual public, at certain short periods, with essays, tales, allegories, and criticisms, such as had never before met their eyes. He not only brought a good philological taste into fashion, and placed Milton upon a pedestal from which he can never be pulled down, but gave a pleasing and popular turn to religious studies and duties. In this latter department there is, occasionally, a sort of easy and natural sublimity about Addison, which belongs peculiarly to himself. Confidence, hope, comfort, love, gratitude, and adoration, are what he infuses into a christian spirit; and his two celebrated pieces of poetry, or short hymns, illustrative of what he has inculcated in prose, are perfect master-pieces of their kind. But the reader, I apprehend, is beginning to be fearful lest I

should omit the mention of that peculiar feature in the compositions of Addison, which stamps him as an undoubted original. It is his Humour, then, wherein he is unrivalled. But this is a theme, almost inexhaustible in itself, and familiar to us from boyhood; and so I draw back from expatiating.—DIBDIN, THOMAS FROGNALL, 1824, *The Library Companion, p.* 603, *note.*

I have sometimes thought that Addison wanted profundity, though he was always elegant and always just. I prefer Cowley's prose style to Addison's.—BRYDGES, SIR EGERTON, 1834, *Autobiography, p.* 166.

Addison was a mere lay preacher, completely bound up in formalism, but he did get to say many a true thing in his generation; an instance of one formal man doing great things. Steele had infinitely more *naïveté*, but he was only a fellow-soldier of Addison, to whom he subordinated himself more than was necessary. It is a cold vote in Addison's favor that one gives.—CARLYLE, THOMAS, 1838, *Lectures on the History of Literature, p.* 176.

As a moral satirist, he stands unrivalled. If ever the best "Tatlers" and "Spectators" were equalled in their own kind, we should be inclined to guess that it must have been by the lost comedies of Menander. In wit, properly so called, Addison was not inferior to Cowley or Butler. No single ode of Cowley contains so many happy analogies as are crowded into the lines to Sir Godfrey Kneller; and we would undertake to collect from the "Spectators" as great a number of ingenious illustrations as can be found in "Hudibras." The still higher faculty of invention Addison possessed in still larger measure. The numerous fictions, generally original, often wild and grotesque, but always singularly graceful and happy, which are found in his essays, fully entitle him to the rank of a great poet—a rank to which his metrical compositions give him no claim. As an observer of life, of manners, of all the shades of human character, he stands in the first class. And what he observed he had the art of communicating in two widely different ways. He could describe virtues, vices, habits, whims, as well as Clarendon. But he could do something better. He could call human beings into existence, and make them exhibit themselves. If we wish to find anything more vivid than Addison's best portraits, we must go either to Shakspeare or to Cervantes. . . . We own that the humour of Addison is, in our opinion, of a more delicious flavour than the humour of either Swift or Voltaire. . . . Of Addison it may be confidently affirmed that he has blackened no man's character, nay, that it would be difficult, if not impossible, to find in all the volumes which he has left us a single taunt which can be called ungenerous or unkind. . . . We have not the least doubt, that, if Addison had written a novel, on an extensive plan, it would have been superior to any that we possess. As it is, he is entitled to be considered, not only as the greatest of the English essayists, but as the forerunner of the great English novelists. — MACAULAY, THOMAS BABINGTON, 1843, *Life and Writings of Addison, Critical and Miscellaneous Essays.*

In refined and delicate humour Addison has no superior, if he has any equal, in English prose literature. . . Who can set limits to the influence which such a mind has exerted? And what a lesson should it read to the conductors of our periodic press, from the stately quarterly to the daily newspaper! What untold gain would it be to the world if they would think less of party, and more of TRUTH: if they would ever be found the firm advocates of every thing that tends to elevate and bless man, and the steadfast, outspoken opponents of all that tends to degrade, debase, and brutalize him.— CLEVELAND, CHARLES D., 1848, *A Compendium of English Literature, pp.* 377, 391.

He amuses himself with people, not because he dislikes them, but because he likes them, and is not discomposed by their absurdities. He does not go very far down into the hearts of them; he never discovers any of the deeper necessities which there are in human beings. But everything that is upon the surface of their lives, and all the little cross-currents which disturb them, no one sees so accurately, or describes so gracefully. In certain moods of our mind, therefore, we have here a most agreeable friend, one who takes us to no great effort, who does not set us on encountering any terrible evils, or carrying forward any high purpose, but whom one must always admire for his

quietness and composure; who can teach us to observe a multitude of things that we should else pass by, and reminds us that in man's life, as in nature, there are days of calm and sunshine as well as of storm.—MAURICE, FREDERICK DENISON, 1856-74, *The Friendship of Books and Other Lectures, ed. Hughes.*

Exquisite Genius, to whose chisell'd line
The ivory's polish lends the ivory's shine—
—LYTTON, EDWARD LORD, 1860, *St. Stephen's.*

The distinctive characteristic of Addison may perhaps be compared to what is said to give the peculiar charm to Circassian beauty—a certain luxurious air of dreamy repose in the half-closed eyelids. —MONTGOMERY, HENRY R., 1862, *Memoirs of the Life and Writings of Sir Richard Steele, vol.* I, *p.* 178.

Well, but Addison's prose is Attic prose. Where, then, it may be asked, is the note of provinciality in Addison? I answer, in the commonplace of his ideas. This is a matter worth remarking. Addison claims to take leading rank as a moralist. To do that, you must have ideas of the first order on your subject,—the best ideas, at any rate, attainable in your time,—as well as be able to express them in a perfectly sound and sure style. . . . Now Addison has not, on his subject of morals, the force of ideas of the moralists of the first class,—the classical moralists; he has not the best ideas attainable in or about his time, and which were, so to speak, in the air then, to be seized by the finest spirits; he is not to be compared for power, searchingness, or delicacy of thought to Pascal, or La Bruyère, or Vauvenargues; he is rather on a level, in this respect, with a man like Marmontel; therefore, I say, he has the note of provinciality as a moralist; he is provincial by his matter, though not by his style.— ARNOLD, MATTHEW, 1865, *The Literary Influence of Academies, Essays in Criticism, pp.* 58, 59.

Addison's style is indeed simple, beautiful, clear, and expressive: It has the greatest ease possible. Even when the matter is small and insignificant, one reads on and on with pleasure, because a master holds the pen.—FRISWELL, JAMES HAIN, 1869, *Essays on English Writers, p.* 112.

For graceful style, for polished satire, for delicate delineation of character,

Addison has never been surpassed; but on the stage of active politics he was scarce a match for the passionate ardour, the withering irony, of Swift.—STANHOPE, EARL, 1870, *History of England, Comprising the Reign of Queen Anne Until the Peace of Utrecht*, p. 565.

His writings are conversations, masterpieces of English urbanity and reason; nearly all the details of his character and life have contributed to nourish this urbanity and this reasonableness. . . . His writings are the pure source of classical style; men never spoke in England better. Ornaments abound, and rhetoric has no part in them. Throughout we have just contrasts, which serve only for clearness, and are not too much prolonged; happy expressions, easily discovered, which give things a new and ingenious turn; harmonious periods, in which the sounds flow into one another with the diversity and sweetness of a quiet stream; a fertile vein of inventions and images, through which runs the most amiable irony.—TAINE, H. A., 1871, *History of English Literature, tr. Van Laun, vol.* II, *bk.* iii, *ch.* iv, *pp.* 90, 104.

He made all that he wrote luminous with piety and fragrant with virtue. Writing in a day when blasphemy was accounted a high kind of wit, and obscenity a high kind of humour, he has transmitted almost nothing to which the most rigid female purist of our own most moral epoch could take the smallest exception. You will appreciate the amazing vigour of his mind which enabled him to leap so effectually and so far from the gutter in which the turgid and noisome dialect of that era flowed into the sewers, by comparing him with his contemporaries. Swift, who was exceptionally bad, may be omitted; but compare him with Wycherley, Congreve, Gay, Garth, Prior, Dryden (who was still recent), and the noble rhymesters, such as Buckingham, Halifax, and Granville.—RUSSELL, WILLIAM CLARK, 1871, *Book of Authors*, p. 153, *note*.

The clouded fame of Marlborough has sensibly decayed; few now care to pursue the devious intrigues of Bolingbroke and Oxford; but from the successful reign of Queen Anne still gaze down upon us a cluster of thoughtful faces whose lineaments the world will never cease to trace with interest, and to whom mankind must ever turn with grateful regard. One fair, soft countenance alone is always serene. No lines of fierce struggles or of bitter discontent, of brooding madness or of envious rage, disturb that gentle aspect. A delicate taste, a tranquil disposition, a clear sense of the vanity of human passions and of all earthly aims, have softened and subdued the mental supremacy of Addison. To some he has seemed feeble; for many he wants the fire of genius. But multitudes in every age have been held willing captives by the lively play of his unwearied fancy, his melodious periods, his tenderness and truth; have yielded to a power that is never asserted, and to an art that is hidden in the simplicity of a master.—LAWRENCE, EUGENE, 1872, *The Days of Queen Anne, Harper's Magazine, vol.* 44.

The crowning quality of these papers, as work of literature, is their elegance. This made of prose a fine art, and ranked its best productions, with those of poetry, among the permanent products of taste. This excellence was fully achieved, for the first time in our literature, by Addison; and since his day elegant culture has found constant expression in prose. The art of Addison is far less cold and critical than that of Pope. It preserves its freedom, and moves with a simplicity and ease, that are open indeed to error, but are also able to make that error seem slight and unimportant. There is in his style no opposition between nature and art; the substance and form remain inseparable, the thought lifting itself into light and being at once, rising in a single creative act out of the chaos of material.—BASCOM, JOHN, 1874, *Philosophy of English Literature*, p. 175.

Greater energy of character, or a more determined hatred of vice and tyranny, would have curtailed his usefulness as a public censor. He led the nation gently and insensibly to a love of virtue and constitutional freedom, to a purer taste in morals and literature, and to the importance of those everlasting truths which so warmly engaged his heart and imagination. The national taste and circumstances have so much changed during the last century and a half, that these essays, inimitable as they are, have become antiquated, and are little read.—CHAMBERS, ROBERT, 1876, *Cyclopædia of English Literature, ed. Carruthers* . 281.

Little as the people had previously read English books, there is no evidence that Addison's numerous papers on "Paradise Lost," in which he taught the readers of the "Spectator" how to enjoy and appreciate a poem which few newspaper readers of the present day are capable of enjoying, were less popular than those on higher subjects. Steele made his subscribers acquainted with Pope, Dryden, Swift, and other writers who had previously been read by few but schoolmen; while it is not improbable, even, that Addison did more than the clergy to persuade men to read the Bible for other purposes than that of quieting conscience.—HABBERTON, JOHN, 1876, *ed., The Spectator, Selected Papers, p.* xxiii.

His style, with its free, unaffected movement, its clear distinctness, its graceful transitions, its delicate harmonies, its appropriateness of tone; the temperance and moderation of his treatment, the effortless self-mastery, the sense of quiet power, the absence of exaggeration or extravagance, the perfect keeping with which he deals with his subjects; or again the exquisite reserve, the subtle tenderness, the geniality, the pathos of his humour—what are these but the literary reflection of Addison himself, of that temper so pure and lofty yet so sympathetic, so strong yet so lovable.—GREEN, JOHN RICHARD, 1880, *ed., Essays of Joseph Addison, Introduction, p.* xxiv.

Accustomed as we are to the pungent and the drastic, we yawn over the stingless, self-effacing irony of the gentle Addison; the colors seem pale, the *bouquet* imperceptible. Is it possible that time has bleached the page of Addison, until it has become like a faded fresco by some old master who worked in inferior colors? Can it be that there are now scores of writers his equals in point of style, his superiors in intellectual resources? Must then this stylist, whose primacy no contemporary dared question, who made the term "Addisonian" signify for prose what "Virgilian" singifies for verse, of whom Thackeray so lately said, "We owe as much pleasure to him as to any human being that ever wrote,"—must he who has charmed, consoled, instructed, formed, so many generations, now become an *emeritus?* It is safe to assume that those who would answer these questions affirmatively have

never lived with Addison; that they have, at best, but a bowing acquaintance with him. . . . Perhaps there has never been a time since the immediate objects of the "Spectator" were accomplished when its satire and instruction were more applicable than here and now.—ANDERSON, MELVILLE B., 1884, *The Dial, vol.* 4, *p.* 283.

Addison was welcome for the same reason for which Butler and Swift were unwelcome. He knew as they did not the more sympathetic side of human nature and how to address himself to it. He was in this respect the Washington Irving of English Prose. . . . So particular was he in composition, that, according to Warton, he would often stop the press to insert a new preposition or conjunction. He was as fastidious in prose as Pope and Dryden were in poetry. . . . Verbal precision overreaches itself in Addison. It was, indeed, the error of the age.— HUNT, THEODORE W., 1887, *Representative English Prose and Prose Writers, pp.* 294, 296, 297.

It is difficult in a short summary of facts to give any impression of the influence exercised on the mind and feelings of his country by Addison. It was out of proposition with the mere outcome of his literary genius. It was the result of character almost more than of intellect, of goodness and reasonableness almost more than of wit. His qualities of mind, however, if not of the very loftiest order, were relatively harmonised to an astonishing degree, so that the general impression of Addison is of a larger man than the close contemplation of any one side of his genius reveals him as being. He has all the moral ornaments of the literary character; as a writer he is urbane, cheerful, charming, and well-mannered to a degree which has scarcely been surpassed in the history of the world. His wit is as penetrating as a perfume; his irony presupposes a little circle of the best and most cultivated listeners; his fancy is so well tempered by judgment and observation that it passes with us for imagination. We delight in his company so greatly that we do not pause to reflect that the inventor of Sir Roger de Coverley and Will Honeycomb had not half of the real comic force of Farquhar or Vanbrugh, nor so much as that of the flashing wit of Congreve.

Human nature, however, is superior to the rules, and Addison stands higher than those more original writers by merit of the reasonableness, the good sense, the wholesome humanity that animates his work. He is classic, while they are always a little way over on the barbaric side of perfection. The style of Addison is superior to his matter, and holds a good many flies in its exquisite amber. It did not reach its highest quality until Addison had become acquainted with "A Tale of a Tub," but it grew to be a finer thing, though not a greater, than the style of Swift.—GOSSE, EDMUND, 1888, *A History of Eighteenth Century Literature, p.* 193.

Nobody nowadays reads his verse, which was so loudly applauded by his contemporaries; and only those among us who are curious in tracing the history of English prose affect to find any pleasure in his contributions to the "Tatler" and the "Spectator."—STODDARD, RICHARD HENRY, 1891, *A Box of Autographs, Scribner's Magazine, vol.* 9, *p.* 215.

The finest critic, the finest gentleman, the most tender humorist of his age. . . . Of the humorists we may venture to say that Addison is the first, as well as the most refined and complete. Swift draws a heavier shaft, which lacerates and kills, and Pope sends his needle-pointed arrows, all touched with poisonous venom, to the most vulnerable points; but Addison has no heart to slay. He transfixes the veil of folly with light, shining, irresistible darts, and pins it aloft in triumph, but he lets the fool go free—perhaps lets you see even, by some reflection from his swift-flying polished spear, a gleam of human meaning in the poor wretch's face which touches your heart.—OLIPHANT, MRS. M. O.W., 1894, *Historical Characters of the Reign of Queen Anne, pp.* 167, 169.

The alliance between Addison and Steele was so intimate, that to judge of one apart from the other, would be fair to neither. . . . That while Steele might, under very inferior conditions, have produced the "Tatler" and "Spectator" without Addison, it is highly improbable that Addison, as an essayist, would have existed without Steele.—DENNIS, JOHN, 1894, *The Age of Pope, p.* 125.

It is the supreme distinction of Addison, as the chief founder of English essay-writing, to have created in England a school of literary taste which, without sacrificing any of the advantages derived from liberty, has raised our language almost to a level with the French in elegance and precision. . . . These characteristics of Addison's thought are reproduced in his style, which reflects in the most refined and beautiful form the conversational idiom of his period. He is, indeed, far from attaining that faultless accuracy which has been sometimes ascribed to him. It was his aim to make philosophy popular, and always to discourse with his readers in familiar language; but it is observable that, when writing on abstract subjects, he frequently becomes involved and obscure. . . . In a word, it may be said that the essay in the hands of Addison acquired that perfection of well-bred ease which arises from a complete understanding between an author and his audience.—COURTHOPE, W. J., 1894, *English Prose, ed. Craik, vol.* III, *pp.* 491, 493, 496.

Addison's unity is usually faultless. His coherence depends largely upon word-order and sentence-structure; of 300 sentences only 13 begin with *and*, 16 with *but*. His massing, when compared with Swift's, is defective. In brief, the paragraph structure is easy and flowing, correct in unity, defective in emphasis. Addison's favorite paragraph is loose, with one or two introductory sentences. Deductive specimens are not infrequent. The topic is often developed by repetition from changing points of view,—what Scott and Denney have termed the alternating method. The method is frequently overdone. Addison had little sense of the value of the short sentence, either as a means of emphasis, or as a way of varying paragraph rhythm. His rhythm remained a somewhat monotonous sentence-rhythm.—LEWIS, EDWIN HERBERT, 1894, *The History of the English Paragraph, p.* 111.

He [Landor] was interesting about Addison: he said that an engaging simplicity shone through all that he wrote; that there was coyness in his style, the archness and shyness of a graceful and beautiful girl. — LAMPSON, FREDERICK LOCKER, 1896, *My Confidences, p.* 162.

Style without "preciosity;" natural style; fitness of phrase: clearness and "netteté:" a style without mannerism:

yet wholly individual: this seems to be more likely to be attained by the reading of Addison than by that of Stevenson.—BESANT, WALTER, 1898, *The Pen and the Book, p.* 45.

In graphic portraiture and genial humor, in sweet temper and moral purity, combined with a courtly grace and tender sympathy, Addison stands surpassingly great. He is a great poet using the form of prose. His imagination is associative, penetrative, and reflective. — GEORGE, ANDREW J.,1898, *From Chaucer to Arnold.*

Of his English verse nothing has survived, except his really beautiful hymns, where the combination of sincere religious feelings (of the sincerity of Addison's religion there is absolutely no doubt, though it was of a kind now out of fashion) and of critical restraint produced things of real, though modest and quiet, excellence. "The Lord my pasture shall prepare," "The spacious firmament on high," and "How are Thy servants blest! O Lord," may lack the mystical inspiration of the greatest hymns, but their cheerful piety, their graceful use of images, which, though common, are never mean, their finish and even, for the time, their fervour make them singularly pleasant. The man who wrote them may have had foibles and shortcomings, but he can have had no very grave faults, as the authors of more hysterical and glowing compositions easily might. The two principal prose works are little read now, but they are worth reading. . . . They exhibit, in the opening of the "Medals" and in all the descriptive passages of the "Italy," the curious insensibility of the time to natural beauty, or else its almost more curious inability to express what it felt, save in the merest generalities and commonplaces.—SAINTSBURY, GEORGE, 1898, *A Short History of English Literature.*

As a rule his epistolary style has the defect of his essays: it is too finished, formal, and self-conscious. He is so desperately afraid of betraying the least emotion, that he appears more frigid than he really was. *Suaviter subridens* he dares not break into a hearty laugh. "Elegant" to the point of exasperation, he conveys an unfortunate, and indeed erroneous, impression of insincerity.—POOLE, STANLEY LANE-1898, *Eighteenth Century Letters,* ed. *Johnson, Introduction, p.* xxvii.

Occasionally a writer may even gain deserved eminence chiefly by the excellence of his style. Joseph Addison was regarded for nearly a century as our first master of English prose. And not unjustly. Few writers ever have been able to render themselves with greater nicety. His style is flexible, graceful, urbane; it is Mr. Addison in speech. As we read it we see the very man as he was. As far as style goes, our grandfathers were right in their praise. But Addison never added much to the stock of human thought, never stirs our feelings very deeply. We see that there is not much in the man after all—no profound or original ideas, no deep passions.—WINCHESTER, C. T., 1899, *Some Principles of Literary Criticism.*

Excellent and devout spirit as Addison was, he escaped the dangers of zeal, and to him party-spirit appeared to be a deplorable form of madness. He could not understand why multitudes of honest gentlemen, who entirely agree in their lives, should take it in their heads to differ in their religion.—DOWDEN, EDWARD, 1900, *Puritan and Anglican, p.* 337.

We read his writings with a refined and soothing pleasure. They possess a genial humor and unvarying cheerfulness that are contagious and delightful. There is no other writer who has greater power to dispel gloominess. As seen through his pages, the world appears wrapped in a mellow light. We learn to think more kindly of men, to smile at human foibles, to entertain ennobling sentiments, to trust in an overruling providence. He does not indeed usually treat of the deeper interests of human life; he is never profound; he does not try to exhaust a subject—to write it to the dregs. His sphere is rather that of minor morals, social foibles, and small philosophy. But if he is not deep, he is not trifling; and if he is not exhaustive, he is always interesting.—PAINTER, F. V. N., 1899, *A History of English Literature, p.* 229.

Addison's prose is simple and intelligible, and, although he undoubtedly took great pains to make it finished, and was about the first to regard prose writing as an art, it always appears natural and unaffected.—JOHNSON, CHARLES F., 1900, *Outline History of English and American Literature, p.* 253.

John Flamsteed
1646-1719

John Flamsteed, the first astronomer-royal of England, was born at Denby near Derby, 19th August 1646. His success in mathematics and astronomy procured him the appointment of astronomer to the king in 1675. Next year Greenwich Observatory was built, and Flamsteed began the observations that commenced modern practical astronomy. He formed the first trustworthy catalogue of the fixed stars, and furnished those observations by which Newton verified his luna theory. His great work is "Historia Caelestis Britannica," an account of astronomical observation (3 vols. 1723). Flamsteed took holy orders, and from 1684 till his death, 31st December 1719, held the Surrey living of Burstow.—PATRICK AND GROOME, eds., 1897, Chambers's Biographical Dictionary, p. 367.

PERSONAL

Mr. John Flamsteed, the King's astronomer at Greenwich, was formerly my constant correspondent for many years, but upon publication of my "Dioptrics," he took such offence at my placing a solution of his, of the 16, 17, and 18 propositions thereof, after, and not before, the solution I myself gave of the said proposition, that he broke his friendship with me, and that, too, with so much inveteracy, that I could never bring him to a reconciliation, though I have often endeavoured it, so that at last I slighted the friendship of a man of so much ill nature and irreligion, how ingenious and learned soever.—MOLYNEUX, WILLIAM, 1694, Life: An Account of the Family and Descendants of Sir Thomas Molyneux, Bart.

Mr. John Flamsteed, the astronomer, was born at Darby. His father was a wealthy maltster, and this gentleman being deformed, and therefore the outcast of the family, was imployed by his father to carry out maly with the brewing pan; but finding this way of carrying very tiresome, he invented and made with his own hands a wheel-barrow, by which he thought to have eased the trouble and pains of carrying it on his back; but instead of ease, he found greater trouble, the burthen now being more considerable than before, by reason he had a much larger quantity to convey away at a time. This inconvenience made him repent that ever he had made a wheel-barrow, the thought of which he could never afterwards endure. At leisure times he studied the art of astronomy, and became eminent in it, insomuch that at last he sent to Mr. William Lilly, the famous figure-flinger, and took occasion to correct many of his errors and mistakes. Upon which Lilly, sir Jonas More, and sir George Wharton agreed to give him a meeting, appointing the place for the conference to be the middle way between London and Derby. Upon this conference the said gentlemen were so well satisfied with Flamsteed's skill in the art of astronomy, that at their return to London they recommended him to king Charles the IId. as a man of great abilities in the foresaid profession. Whereupon the king erected him an observatory at Greenwich, upon the hill, where he hath continued ever since to make observations, and hath promised to publish a very large book in folio, containing the remarks he hath made in astronomy from the first beginning of his observations at Greenwich: which book is all, or at least most of it, already printed by the encouragement of prince George of Denmark. It hath been revised by Dr. Halley, and many mistakes found in it; but I do not hear that 'tis to come out as yet, Mr. Flamsteed endeavouring as much as he can to hinder it's publication, being not thoroughly pleased that Dr. Halley should discover his errours; and withall he thinks that he ought to have more and better rewards than he hath yet met with, before his works appear, tho' 'tis very certain that the encouragement he hath already found is much beyond his merits, if we may credit divers ingenious persons that know the man, and his principles, (which are republican), and his sniveling, covetous temper.—HEARNE, THOMAS, 1715, Reliquiæ Hearnianæ, ed. Bliss, Oct. 31, vol. II, p. 26.

Attainments in science have certainly nothing to do with the present question; but after Flamsteed has charged Newton with illegal, unjust, and immoral acts, upon no evidence but his own, and has sullied that venerable name with vulgar and offensive abuse,—it is a strange position to maintain, that we are not to inquire into the temper and character of the accuser. In the revolting correspondence which Flamsteed has bequeathed to posterity, he has delineated his own character in sharp outline and glaring tints; and Newton requires no other Ægis to defend him than one whose compartments are emblazoned with the scurrilous invectives against himself, and garnished with pious appeals to God and to Providence. We have hesitated, however, to associate the sacred character of the accuser with systematic calumny; and we hasten to forget that there may be an astronomer without principle, and a divine without charity.—BREWSTER, SIR DAVID, 1855, *Memoirs of the Life and Writings of Sir Isaac Newton, vol. II, p. 241.*

Flamsteed was in many respects an excellent man—pious and conscientious, patient in suffering, of unimpeachable morality, and rigidly abstemious habits. His wife and servants were devoted to him, living and dead; but his naturally irritable temper, aggravated by disease, could not brook rivalry. He was keenly jealous of his professional reputation. His early reverence for Newton was recorded in the stray note among his observations: "I study not for present applause; Mr. Newton's approbation is more to me than the cry of all the ignorant in the world." Later he was not ashamed to call him "our great pretender," and to affect scorn for his "speculations about gravity," "crotchets," and "conceptions." The theory of gravitation he described in 1710 as "Kepler's doctrine of magnetical fibres, improved by Sir C. Wren, and prosecuted by Sir I. Newton" adding, "I think I can lay some claim to a part of it." He had certainly, in 1681, spoken of the attraction of the sun as determining the fall towards him of the great comet, but attributed the curve of its path to the resistance of the planetary vortex.—CLERKE, MISS A. M., 1889, *Dictionary of National Biography, vol. XIX, p.* 247.

GENERAL

Galileo Galilei was the first who discovered four planets moving constantly round Jupiter, from thence usually called his satellites, which afterwards were observed to have a constant, regular, and periodical motion. This motion is now so exactly known, that Mr. Flamsteed, who

is one of the most accurate observers that ever was, has been able to calculate tables of the eclipses of the several satellites, according to which, Astronomers in different quarters of the world, having notion of the precise time when to look for them, have found them to answer to his predictions, and published their observations accordingly.—WOTTON, WILLIAM, 1694–1705, *Reflections upon Ancient and Modern Learning.*

Mr. Flamsteed, with indefatigable pains, for more than forty years, watched the motions of the stars, and has given us innumerable observations of the sun, moon, and planets, which he made with very large instruments exactly divided by most exquisite art, and fitted with telescopical sights.—KEILL, JOHN, 1701–36, *Introduction to the True Philosophy, Preface.*

One of the greatest astronomers that Europe produced in the seventeenth century. . . . It is greatly to Flamsteed's credit, that he brought into disrepute the silly study of astrology, which the wisest men, as well as the most ignorant, had pursued with a strange partiality, for more than two centuries.—NOBLE, MARK, 1806, *A Biographical History of England, vol. II, pp.* 132, 134.

It is a matter of astonishment that he accomplished so much, considering his slender means, and the vexations which he continually experienced.—BAILY, FRANCIS, 1835, *An Account of the Rev. John Flamsteed, the first Astronomer Royal.*

He made no improvements in theory; but he is entitled to the merit of having been the first who brought into common use the method of simultaneously observing the right ascension of the sun and a star.—PROCTOR, R. A., 1878, *Encyclopœdia Britannica, vol. II.*

His ingenuity in the improvement of instruments, his scrupulous accuracy, his indomitable perseverance under difficulties, place him beside Tycho Brahé as an observer of the first order; but he differed from the Danish astronomer, both in the greater advantage of possessing telescopes and in the greater misfortunes of poverty and ill health. He was presented to a small living, and his salary as Astronomer Royal was £100 a year; out of this he had to buy and keep in repair all his instruments, and to pay his assistant.—MORTON, E. J. C., 1882, *Heroes of Science, p.* 219.

Sir Samuel Garth

1661–1719

Sir Samuel Garth, 1661-1719. Born, in Yorkshire, 1661. At School at Ingleton. To Peterhouse, Camb., 1676; B. A. 1679; M. A., 1684. To Leyden to study medicine, 1687. M. D., Camb., 7 July 1691. Fellow of Coll. of Physicians, 26 June 1693; Gulstonian Lecturer, 1694; Harvey Orator, 1697. Censor, Oct. 1702. Mem. of Kit-Cat Club, 1703. Married Martha Beaufoy. Knighted, 1714. Physician in Ordinary to King, and Physician General to army. Died, in London, 18 Jan. 1719. Buried at Harrow. *Works:* "Oratio Laudatoria" (Harveian Oration), 1697; "The Dispensary: a poem" (anon.), 1699 (2nd and 3rd edns. same year); "A Prologue for the 4th of November," 1711; "A Complete Key to the seventh edition of 'The Dispensary,'" 1714; "Claremont" (anon.), 1715. He *translated:* Demosthenes' "First Philippick," 1702; Ovid's "Metamorphoses," 1717. *Collected Works:* "Works," 1769; "Poetical Works," 1771; . . . *Life:* in 1769 edn. of Works; by Dr. Johnson, in 1822 edn. of Poems.—SHARP, R. FARQUHARSON, 1897, *A Dictionary of English Authors*, p. 109.

PERSONAL

Garth, generous as his muse.—DRYDEN, JOHN, 1699, *To My Honoured Kinsman.*

As soon as I thought of making the "Lover" a present to one of my friends, I resolved, without further distracting my choice, to send it to the Best Natured-Man. You are so universally known for this character, that an epistle so directed would find its way to you without your name; and I believe nobody but you yourself would deliver such a superscription to any other person.—STEELE, SIR RICHARD, 1715, *The Lover, Dedication to Sir Samuel Garth.*

The best-natured of men, Sir Samuel Garth, has left me in the truest concern for his loss. His death was very heroical, and yet unaffected enough to have made a saint or a philosopher famous. But ill tongues and worse hearts have branded even his last moments, as wrongfully as they did his life, with irreligion. You must have heard many tales on this subject; but if ever there was a good Christian without knowing himself to be so, it was Dr. Garth.—POPE, ALEXANDER, 1718, *Letter to Jervas.*

When Doctor Garth had been for a good while in a bad state of health, he sent one day for a physician with whom he was particularly intimate, and conjured him by their friendship, and by everything that was most sacred (if there was anything more sacred), to tell him sincerely, whether he thought he should be ever able to get rid of his illness or not. His friend, thus conjured, told him; "that he thought he might struggle on with it,

perhaps for some years; but that he much feared he could never get the better of it entirely." Dr. Garth thanked him for dealing so fairly with him, turned the discourse to other things, and talked very cheerfully all the rest of the time he stayed with them.—As soon as he was gone, he called for his servant, said he was a good deal out of order, and would go to bed: he then sent him for a surgeon to bleed him. Soon after, he sent for a second surgeon, by a different servant, and was bled in the other arm. He then said he wanted rest, and when everybody had quitted the room he took off the bandages, and lay down with the design of bleeding to death. His loss of blood made him faint away, and that stopped the bleeding: he afterwards sunk into a sound sleep, slept all the night, waked in the morning without his usual pains, and said, "if it would continue so, he could be content to live on."—In his last illness, he did not use any remedies, but let his distemper take its course. He was the most agreeable companion I ever knew.—TOWNLEY, MR., OF TOWNLEY IN LANCASHIRE, 1732-33, *Spence's Anecdotes, ed. Singer*, p. 85.

Garth, we have reason to believe, was as universally liked as any private person of his day. He was mild and complacent, though a zealous party-man; and kind, though a wit. Pope, who certainly did not resemble him in those respects, always speaks of him with the most decided affection.—NOBLE, MARK, 1806, *A Biographical History of England*, vol. I, p. 248.

We never cast our eyes toward "Harrow on the Hill" (let us keep these picturesque

JOHN EVELYN

SIR SAMUEL GARTH

denominations of places as long as we can) without thinking of an amiable man and most pleasant wit and physician of Queen Anne's time, who lies buried there,—Garth, the author of the "Dispensary." He was the Whig physician of the men of letters of that day, as Arbuthnot was the Tory: and never were two better men sent to console the ailments of two witty parties, or show them what a nothing party is, compared with the humanity remaining under the quarrels of both.—HUNT, LEIGH, 1847, *Men, Women and Books, vol.* II.

Garth is perhaps the most cherished by the present generation of all the physicians of Pope's time. He was a whig without rancor, and a *bon-vivant* without selfishness. Full of jest and amiability, he did more to create merriment at the Kit-Kat club than either Swift or Arbuthnot. He loved wine to excess; but then wine loved him too, ripening and warming his wit, and leaving no sluggish humour behind. His practice was a good one, but his numerous patients prized his bon-mots more than his prescriptions. His enemies averred that he was not only an epicure, but a profligate voluptuary and an infidel. Pope, however, wrote of him after his death, "If ever there was a good Christian, without knowing himself to be so, it was Dr. Garth."—JEAFFRESON, JOHN CORDY, 1860, *A Book About Doctors.*

The Kit-kat Poet. A nickname given to Samuel Garth, an English poet. He was a member of the Kit-kat Club, and extemporized most of the verses which were inscribed on the toasting-glasses of that society.—FREY, ALBERT R., 1888, *Sobriquets and Nicknames, p.* 178.

His portrait, of kit-cat size, by Kneller, hangs to the left of the fire-place in the censor's room at the College of Physicians, and gives him a fresh complexion and a cheerful expression, in a flowing wig. A drawing by Hogarth represents him at Buttons' coffee-house standing by a table at which Pope is sitting.—MOORE, NORMAN, M. D., 1890, *Dictionary of National Biography, vol.* XXI, *p.* 32.

THE DISPENSARY
1699

This sixth canto of the "Dispensary," by Dr. Garth, has more merit than the whole preceeding part of the poem; and, as I am told, in the first edition of this work, it is more correct than as here exhibited; but that edition I have not been able to find. The praises bestowed on this poem are more than have been given to any other; but our approbation at present is cooler, for it owed part of its fame to party.—GOLDSMITH, OLIVER, 1767, *The Beauties of English Poetry.*

His poetry has been praised at least equally to its merit. In the "Dispensary" there is a strain of smooth and free versification; but few lines are eminently elegant. No passages fall below mediocrity, and few rise much above it. The plan seems formed without just proportion to the subject; the means and end have no necessary connection. *Resnel*, in his Preface to *Pope's* Essay, remarks, that Garth exhibits no discrimination of characters; and that what any one says might, with equal propriety, have been said by another. The general design is, perhaps, open to criticism; but the composition can seldom be charged with inaccuracy or negligence. The author never slumbers in self-indulgence; his full vigour is always exerted, scarcely a line is left unfinished; nor is it easy to find an expression used by constraint, or a thought imperfectly expressed. It was remarked by Pope, that the "Dispensary" had been corrected in every edition, and that every change was an improvement. It appears, however, to want something of poetical ardour, and something of general delectation; and therefore, since it has been no longer supported by accidental and intrinsick popularity, it has been scarcely able to support itself.—JOHNSON, SAMUEL, 1779–81, *Garth, Lives of the English Poets.*

Is only inferior in humour, discrimination of character, and poetical ardour to the "Rape of the Lock."—ANDERSON, ROBERT, 1799, *ed., The Works of the British Poets.*

It is an obvious imitation of the Lutrin. Warton blames the poet for making the fury, Disease, talk like a critic. It is certain however, that criticism is often a disease, and can sometimes talk like a fury.—CAMPBELL, THOMAS, 1819, *Specimens of the British Poets.*

The versification of this once-famous mock-heroic poem is smooth and regular, but not forcible; the language clear and neat; the parodies and allusions happy. Many lines are excellent in the way of pointed application; and some are remembered and quoted, where few call to mind the author. It has been remarked, that Garth enlarged and altered the "Dispensary" in almost every edition; and, what is more uncommon, that every alteration was for the better. This poem may be called an imitation of the Lutrin, inasmuch as, but for the Lutrin, it might probably not have been written; and there are even particular resemblances. The subject, which is a quarrel between the physicians and apothecaries of London, may vie with that of Boileau in want of general interest; yet it seems to afford more diversity to the satirical poet. Garth, as has been observed, is a link of transition between the style and turn of poetry under Charles and William, and that we find in Addison, Prior, Tickell, and Pope, during the reign of Anne.—HALLAM, HENRY, 1837–39, *Introduction to the Literature of Europe, pt.* iv, *ch.* v, *par.* 48.

The wit of this slight performance may have somewhat evaporated with age, but it cannot have been at any time very pungent.—CRAIK, GEORGE L., 1861, *A Compendious History of English Literature and of the English Language, vol.* II, *p.* 269.

Garth is mainly interesting at the present day because he was the first writer who took the couplet, as Dryden had fashioned it, from Dryden's hands, and displayed it in the form it maintained throughout the eighteenth century. In some respects it may be said that no advance in this peculiar model was ever made on "The Dispensary." Its best lines are equal to any of Pope's in mere fashion, and in it appear clearly enough the inherent defects of the form when once Dryden's "energy divine" and his cunning admixture of what looked like roughness had been lost or rejected. . . . Except for its versification, which not only long preceded Pope, but also anticipated Addison's happiest effort by some years, "The Dispensary" is not now an interesting poem. The dispute on which it is based is long forgotten, its mock heroic plan looks threadbare to our eyes, and the machinery and imagery have lost all the charm that they may at one time have had. But as a versifier Garth must always deserve a place in the story of English Literature.—SAINTSBURY,

GEORGE, 1880, *English Poets, ed. Ward, vol.* III, *p.* 13.

In 1699 Garth published "The Dispensary, a Poem," which is a record of the first attempt to establish those out-patient rooms now universal in the large towns of England. "The Dispensary" ridicules the apothecaries and their allies among the fellows. It was circulated in manuscript, and in a few weeks was printed and sold by John Nutt, near Stationers' Hall. A second and a third edition appeared in the same year, to which were added a dedication to Anthony Henley, an introduction explaining the controversy in the College of Physicians, and copies of commendatory verses. A fourth edition appeared in 1700, a sixth in 1706, a seventh in 1714, and a tenth in 1741. The poem continued to be generally read for fifty years, and some of its phrases are still quoted. —MOORE, NORMAN, M. D., 1890, *Dictionary of National Biography, vol.* XXI, *p.* 31.

GENERAL

Whenever Garth shall raise his sprightly song,
Sense flows in easie numbers from his tongue;
Great Phœbus in his learned son we see
Alike in physick as in poetry.
—GAY, JOHN, 1714, *To Bernard Lintot, Poems.*

His works will scarce make a moderate volume, and though they contain many things excellent, judicious, and humorous, yet they will not justify the writer, who dwells upon them in the same rapturous strain of admiration, with which we speak of a Horace, a Milton, or a Pope. He had the happiness of an early acquaintance with some of the most powerful, wisest, and wittiest men of the age in which he lived; he attached himself to a party, which at last obtained the ascendant, and he was equally successful in his fortune as his friends: Persons in these circumstances are seldom praised, or censured with moderation.—CIBBER, THEOPHILUS, 1753, *Lives of the Poets, vol.* III, *p.* 270.

The fun has all faded out of "The Dispensary," and Garth is no longer in the least degree attractive. But his didactic verse is the best between Dryden and Pope, though we see beginning in it the degradation of the overmannered style of the eighteenth century.—GOSSE, EDMUND, 1888, *A History of Eighteenth Century Literature, p.* 34.

John Hughes

1677–1720

John Hughes (born 1677, died 1720) was educated at a Dissenter's College in London; wrote a poem in 1697 on "The Triumph of Peace, occasioned by the Peace of Ryswick," and afterwards several odes, papers in the "Tatler" and in the "Spectator," translations from Fontenelle, and several plays. He had a situation in the Ordnance Office; was made afterwards, by Lord-Chancellor Cowper, Secretary to the Commissions of the Peace; and died of consumption on the first night of his most successful play, "The Seige of Damascus."—MORLEY, HENRY, 1879, *A Manual of English Literature*, ed. *Tyler, p.* 532.

GENERAL

His head, hand, or heart was always employ'd in something worthy imitation; his pencil, his bow-string, or his pen, each of which he us'd in a masterly manner, were always directed to raise and entertain his own mind, or that of others, to a more cheerful prosecution of what was noble and virtuous.—STEELE, SIR RICHARD, 1720, *The Theatre, No.* 15.

He is too grave a poet for me, and I think among the *mediocribus* in prose as well as verse.—SWIFT, JONATHAN, 1735, *Letter to Alexander Pope, Sept.* 3.

To answer your question as to Mr. Hughes, what he wanted as to genius he made up as an honest man; but he was of the class you think him.—POPE, ALEXANDER, 1735, *Letter to Jonathan Swift, Nov.*

His last work was his tragedy, "The Siege of Damascus," after which *a Siege* became a popular title. This play, which still continues on the stage, and of which it is unnecessary to add a private voice to such continuance of approbation, is not acted or printed according to the author's original draught, or his settled intention. He had made *Phocyas* apostatize from his religion; after which the abhorrence of *Eudocia* would have been reasonable, his misery would have been just, and the horrors of his repentance exemplary. The players, however, required that the guilt of *Phocyas* should terminate in desertion to the enemy; and Hughes, unwilling that his relations should lose the benefit of his work, complied with the alteration.—JOHNSON, SAMUEL, 1779–81, *Hughes, Lives of the English Poets.*

Hughes was a man of good sense, and well versed in some branches of learning. He had applied himself to the study of the classics, especially the Greek and Roman poets, with diligence and success. He perceived and felt the beauties with which they abound. . . . Hughes was ambitious to distinguish himself in heroic odes and tragedy. As he neither excelled in sublimity or in pathos, he did not succeed in either. As an essayist, his observations are just and judicious, and expressed in suitable language. . . . On the whole, Hughes was a man better qualified to excel in the lower than in the higher kinds of composition. In operas, songs, and translations, he succeeded very well; in attempting heroic odes and tragedy, he seems not to have remembered, or not to have applied his favourite Horace's advice to poets, to consider *quid ferre recusant; quid valeant bumori;* "what weight their talents can bear, or what exceeds their strength."—Though not entitled to the character of a very great poet, he deserved a still high praise, he was an upright, benevolent, religious man.—BISSET, ROBERT, 1793, *ed., The Spectator, vol.* I, *pp.* 237, 238, 239.

The only piece, however, which can with any propriety claim for Hughes the appellation of a poet, is "The Siege of Damascus." Of this Drama, which is still occasionally acted, the sentiments and morality are pure and correct, the imagery frequently beautiful, and the diction and versification for the most part clear and melodious. It is defective, notwithstanding, in the most essential quality of dramatic composition, the power of affecting the passions; and is, therefore, more likely to afford pleasure in the closet than on the stage. . . . On the prose of Hughes I am inclined to bestow more praise than on his poetry. . . . Hughes has more merit as a translator of poetry, than as an original poet. . . . All the periodical essays of Hughes are written in a style which is, in general, easy, correct, and elegant: they occasionally exhibit wit and humour; and they uniformly tend to inculcate the best precepts, moral, prudential, and religious.—DRAKE, NATHAN, 1804, *Essays Illustrative of the Tatler, Spectator and Guardian, vol.* III, *pp.* 29, 30, 31, 50.

Hughes was a ready and smooth versifier; but nothing that he wrote rose above mediocrity, if it ever reached it.—ARNOLD, THOMAS, 1868-75, *Chaucer to Wordsworth, p.* 282.

Anne Finch
Countess of Winchilsea
1660?-1720

Anne Finch, Countess of Winchilsea, was born about 1660, at Sidmonton, Hants, the residence of her father, Sir William Kingsmill. She married Heneage Finch, fourth Earl of Winchilsea, who survived her six years. She died on the 5th of August, 1720, leaving no issue. Her works consist of "The Spleen," a pindaric ode, 1701; "The Prodigy," 1706; "Miscellany Poems," 1713; and "Aristomenes," a tragedy.—WARD, THOMAS HUMPHRY, 1880, *ed., English Poets, vol.* III, *p.* 27.

GENERAL

There is one poetess to whose writings I am especially partial, the Countess of Winchelsea. I have perused her poems frequently, and should be happy to name such passages as I think most characteristic of her genius, and most fit to be selected. . . . Her style in rhyme is often admirable, chaste, tender, and vigorous, and entirely free from sparkle, antithesis, and that overculture, which reminds one, by its broad glare, its stiffness, and heaviness, of the double daisies of the garden, compared with their modest and sensitive kindred of the fields. Perhaps I am mistaken, but I think there is a good deal of resemblance in her style and versification to that of Tickell, to whom Dr. Johnson justly assigns a high place among the minor poets, and of whom Goldsmith rightly observes, that there is a strain of ballad thinking through all his poetry, and it is very attractive.—WORDSWORTH, WILLIAM, 1829-30, *Letter to Mr. Dyce, Memoirs by C. Wordsworth, ed. Reed, Oct.* 16, *May* 10, *vol.* II, *pp.* 220, 222.

She was a poetess of singular originality and excellence; her lines "To the Nightingale" have lyrical qualities which were scarcely approached in her own age, and would do credit to the best, while her odes and more weighty pieces have a strength and accomplishment of style which make the least interesting of them worth reading. Lady Winchilsea was one of the last pindaric writers of the school of Cowley. Her odes display that species of writing in the final dissolution out of which it was redeemed by Gray and Collins. Such a poem as her "All is Vanity," full as it is of ingenious thought, and studded

with noble and harmonious lines, fails to impress the attention as a vertebrate composition. Her "Ode to the Spleen," from which Pope borrowed his famous "aromatic pain," is still more loose and fragmentary in structure. On the other hand, her less ambitious studies have a singular perfection of form and picturesqueness of manner. She lights upon the right epithet and employs it with precision, and gives a brilliant turn, even to a triviality, by some bright and natural touch. Her "Nocturnal Reverie" is worthy of Wordsworth's commendation; it is simply phenomenal as the creation of a friend of Prior and of Pope, and some of the couplets, especially those which describe the straying horse, and the cries of the birds, are worthy of the closest observers of nature in a naturalistic age.—GOSSE, EDMUND, 1880, *English Poets, ed. Ward, vol.* III, *p.* 27.

In general feeling an Augustan, with an under-currant of real love for nature. It is in her fondness for country life, her love of out-door beauty, and her accurate descriptions of nature, that she differs from her contemporaries. In these important points, she may certainly be classed as reactionary in tendency. Her octosyllabic ode, "To the Nightingale," has true lyric quality, and her short poems, "The Tree" and "A Nocturnal Reverie," are notable expressions of nature-worship.—PHELPS, WILLIAM LYON, 1893, *The Beginnings of the English Romantic Movement, p.* 28.

It is a pity that her poems have not been reprinted and are difficult of access, for it is desirable to read the whole in order to appreciate the unconscious clash of style and taste in them. . . .

Fortunately for Lady Winchelsea, natural taste and the opportunities of life seem to have inclined her to take natural objects as the source of her imagery. What place suggested the "Nocturnal Reverie" we cannot say, but it is clearly a corrected impression and not merely conventional. It is all *seen :* the waving moon on the river, the sleepy cowslip, the foxglove, paler than by day, but chequering still with red the dusky brakes, and the wonderful image of the horse, take us almost a century away from the drawing-rooms and the sham shepherdesses of her contemporaries.

And she could manage the shortened octosyllable even better than Parnell, could adjust the special epithet (Pope borrowed or stole "aromatic pain" from her, though probably she took it from Dryden's "aromatic splinters"). Altogether she is a most remarkable phenomenon, too isolated to point much of a moral, but adoring the lull of early eighteenth-century poetry with images even more correct than Thomson's and put in language far less artificial.—SAINTSBURY, GEORGE, 1898, *A Short History of English Literature, pp.* 562, 563.

Simon Ockley

1678-1720

A native of Exeter, educated at Queen's College, Cambridge; Vicar of Swavesey, 1705; Arabic Professor at Cambridge, 1711, until his death. He published two occasional sermons, 1710-13, and several works, the most important of which are: 1. "Introductio ad Linguis Orientales," Cantabury, 1706, 12mo. 2. "History of the Present Jews throughout the World," 1707, 12mo. 3. "History of the Conquest of Egypt, Persia, Syria, &c., by the Saracens, &c., 632-705," London, 2 vols. 8vo: vol. i., 1708; ii., 1718. . . . 4. "The Improvement of Human Reason; from the Arabic," 1708, 8vo. 5. "An Account of South West Barbary, 1713, 8vo."—ALLIBONE, S. AUSTIN, 1870, *Dictionary of English Literature, vol.* II, *p.* 1447.

PERSONAL

At a time when oriental studies were in their infancy in this country, Simon Ockley, animated by the illustrious example of Pococke and the laborious diligence of Prideaux, devoted his life and his fortune to these novel researches, which necessarily involved both. With that enthusiasm which the ancient votary experienced, and with that patient suffering the modern martyr has endured, he pursued, till he accomplished, the useful object of his labours. He, perhaps, was the first who exhibited to us other heroes than those of Rome and Greece; sages as contemplative, and a people more magnificent even than the iron masters of the world. Among other oriental productions, his most considerable is "The History of the Saracens." The first volume appeared in 1708, and the second ten years afterwards. In the preface to the last volume, the oriental student pathetically counts over his sorrows, and triumphs over his disappointments; the most remarkable part is the date of the place from whence this preface was written—he triumphly closes his labours in the confinement of Cambridge Castle for debt!—DISRAELI, ISAAC, 1812-

13, *The Rewards of Oriental Students, Calamities of Authors.*

GENERAL

Ockley had the culture of oriental learning very much at heart, and the several publications which he made were intended solely to promote it.—HEATHCOTE, RALPH, 1761-1815, *Chalmer's General Biographical Dictionary, vol.* XXIII, *p.* 294.

The very curious history of the Saracens, given by Ockley, should be consulted, and is somewhat necessary to enable the studen more exactly to comprehend the character of the Arabians, which is there displayed, by their own writers, in all its singularities.—SMYTH, WILLIAM, 1840, *Lectures on Modern History, Lecture* iii.

Although many of its details require correction, the importance of Ockley's work in relation to the progress of oriental studies cannot be overestimated. Following in the steps of Pocock's famous "Specimen Historiæ Arabum," but adopting a popular method, and recommending it by an admirable English style, Ockley for the the first time made the history of the early Saracen conquests attractive to the general reader, and stimulated the student to further research. With all its inaccuracies, Ockley's "History of the Saracens" became a secondary classic, and formed for generations the main source of the average notions of early Mohammedan history.—POOLE, STANLEY LANE–1895, *Dictionary of National Biography, vol.* XLI, *p.* 364.

John Sheffield
Third Earl of Mulgrave
1648–1721

John Sheffield, Duke of Buckinghamshire (1648–1721), succeeded his father as third Earl of Mulgrave in 1658, served in both navy and army, and was Lord Chamberlain to James II., and a Cabinet-councillor under William III., who in 1694 made him Marquis of Normandy. Anne made him Duke of Buckinghamshire (1703); but for his opposition to Godolphin and Marlborough he was deprived of the Seal (1705). After 1710, under the Tories, he was Lord Steward and Lord President till the death of Anne, when he lost all power, and intrigued for the restoration of the Stuarts. He wrote two tragedies, a metrical "Essay on Satire," an "Essay on Poetry," &c.—PATRICK AND GROOME, *eds.,* 1897, *Chambers's Biographical Dictionary, p.* 849.

PERSONAL

He had a piercing wit, a quick apprehension, an unerring judgment; that he understood critically the delicacies of poetry, and was as great a judge as a patron of learning.—DUNTON, JOHN, 1705, *Life and Errors, p.* 422.

"The nobleman-look."—Yes, I know what you mean very well: that look which a noble man should have; rather than what they have generally now. . . . The Duke of Buckingham (Sheffield) was a genteel man; and had a great deal the look you speak of.—POPE, ALEXANDER, 1742–43, *Spence's Anecdotes, ed. Singer, p.* 215.

The life of this peer takes up fourteen pages and a half in folio in the General Dictionary, where it has little pretensions to occupy a couple. But his pious relict was always purchasing places for him, herself and their son, in every suburb of the temple of fame,—a tenure, against which, of all others, quo-warrantos are sure to take place.—WALPOLE, HORACE, 1758, *A Catalogue of the Royal and Noble Authors of England, Scotland and Ireland, vol.* IV, *p.* 99.

His character is not to be proposed as worthy of imitation. His religion he may be supposed to have learned from Hobbes; and his morality was such as naturally proceeds from loose opinions. His sentiments with respect to women he picked up in the court of Charles; and his principles concerning property were such as a gaming-table supplies. He was censured as covetous, and has been defended by an instance of inattention to his affairs, as if a man might not at once be corrupted by avarice and idleness. He is said, however, to have had much tenderness, and to have been very ready to apologise for his violences of passion.—JOHNSON, SAMUEL, 1779–81, *Sheffield, Lives of the English Poets.*

As far as posterity has the means of judging, we can only come to the conclusion, that he was characterized by many vices, and, apparently, by scarcely a single virtue. The best that can be said of him is, that he was a brave man, and an agreeable companion. His laugh is described as having been the pleasantest in the world; and though his temper was passionate, his disposition is said to have been a forgiving one.—JESSE, JOHN HENEAGE, 1843, *Memoirs of the Court of England from the Revolution in 1688 to the Death of George the Second, vol.* II, *p.* 14.

He was, by the acknowledgment of those who neither loved nor esteemed him, a man distinguished by fine parts, and in parliamentary eloquence inferior to scarcely any orator of his time. His moral character was entitled to no respect. He was a libertine without that openness of heart and hand which sometimes makes libertinism amiable, and a haughty aristocrat without that elevation of sentiment which sometimes makes aristocratical haughtiness respectable. The satirists of the age nicknamed him Lord Allpride, and pronounced it strange that a man who had so exalted a sense of his dignity should be so hard and niggardly in all pecuniary dealings. He had given deep offence to the royal family by venturing to entertain the hope that he might win the heart and hand of the Princess Anne. Disappointed in this attempt, he had exerted himself to gain by meanness the favour which he had forfeited by presumption. His epitaph, written by himself, still informs all who pass through Westminster Abbey that he lived and died a sceptic in religion; and we learn from his memoirs, written by himself, that one of his favourite subjects of mirth was the Romish superstition. Yet he began, as soon as James was on the throne, to express a strong inclination towards Popery, and at length in private affected to be a convert.—MACAULAY, THOMAS BABINGTON, 1849, *History of England, ch.* VIII.

ESSAY ON SATIRE

I cannot think that any part of the "Essay on Satire" received additions from his [Dryden's] pen. Probably he might contribute a few hints for revision; but the author of "Absalom and Achitophel" could never completely disguise the powers which were shortly to produce that brilliant satire. Dryden's verses must have shone among Mulgrave's as gold beside copper. The whole Essay is a mere stagnant level, no one part of it so far rising above the rest as to bespeak the work of a superior hand. The thoughts even when conceived with some spirit, are clumsily and unhappily brought out,—a fault never to be traced in the beautiful language of Dryden, whose powers of expression were at least equal to his force of conception. —SCOTT, SIR WALTER, 1808–21, *Life of Dryden.*

Mulgrave affects ease and spirit; but his "Essay on Satire" belies the supposition that Dryden had any share in it.—HALLAM, HENRY, 1837–39, *Introduction to the Literature of Europe, pt.* iv, *ch.* v, *par.* 47.

ESSAY ON POETRY
1682

Yet some there were, among the sounder few
Of those who less presum'd, and better knew,
Who durst assert the juster ancient cause,
And here restor'd Wit's fundamental laws.
Such was the Muse, whose rules and practice tell,
"Nature's chief Master-piece is writing well."

—POPE, ALEXANDER, 1709, *Essay on Criticism, v.* 719–724.

This work by the Duke of Buckingham, is enrolled among our great English productions. The precepts are sensible, the poetry not indifferent, but it has been praised more than it deserves.—GOLDSMITH, OLIVER, 1767, *The Beauties of English Poetry.*

His "Essay on Poetry," to which Pope has given an undeserved immortality, is a short and tolerably meager performance, in which a variety of disjointed rules are applied to the principal species of poetic composition. It contains however some vigorous lines and some sensible observations of individual criticism.—WARD, ADOLPHUS WILLIAM, 1869, *ed., Poetical Works of Alexander Pope, p.* 68, *note.*

Mulgrave's "Essay on Poetry" contains some terse and effective lines, one or two of which have passed into current use. He lays down sensible rules for practitioners in the various departments of poetic art, but he was not very successful himself in the composition of odes, tragedies, and epistles.—GOSSE, EDMUND, 1888, *A History of Eighteenth Century Literature, p.* 31.

As a poet his reputation rests entirely upon his "Essay on Poetry," which contains many just thoughts expressed in pleasing numbers, although the author's deference to the conventional dicta of criticism leads him into idolatry, not only of Homer and Virgil, but of Bossu.—GARNETT, RICHARD, 1895, *The Age of Dryden, p.* 48.

GENERAL

When noble Sheffield strikes the trembling strings,
The little loves rejoice and clap their wings,
Anacreon lives, they cry, th' harmonious swain
Retunes the lyre, and tries his wonted strain.
—GAY, JOHN, 1714, *To Bernard Lintot, Poems.*

The Duke of Buckingham was superficial in everything; even in poetry, which was his *fort.*—POPE, ALEXANDER, 1742–43, *Spence's Anecdotes, ed. Singer, p.* 195.

I can recollect no performance of Buckingham that stamps him a true genius; his reputation was owing to his rank.—WARTON, JOSEPH, 1756, *Essay on the Genius and Writings of Pope.*

It is certain that his grace's compositions in prose have nothing extraordinary in them; his poetry is most indifferent, and the greatest part of both is already fallen into total neglect. It is said that he wrote in hopes of being confounded with his predecessor in the title; but he would more easily have been mistaken with the other Buckingham, if he had never written at all.—WALPOLE, HORACE, 1758, *A Catalogue of the Royal and Noble Authors of England, Scotland and Ireland,* vol. IV, p. 99.

He is introduced into this collection only as a poet; and, if we credit the testimony of his contemporaries, he was a poet of no vulgar rank. But favour and flattery are now at an end; criticism is no longer softened by his bounties, or awed by his splendour, and, being able to take a more steady view, discovers him to be a writer that sometimes glimmers, but rarely shines, feebly laborious, and at best but pretty. His songs are upon common topicks; he hopes, and grieves, and repents, and despairs, and rejoices, like any other maker of little stanzas; to be great, he hardly tries; to be gay, is hardly in his power. . . . His verses are often insipid; but his memories are lively and agreeable; he had the perspicuity and elegance of an historian, but not the fire and fancy of a poet.—JOHNSON, SAMUEL, 1779–81, *Sheffield, Lives of the English Poets.*

Mulgrave wrote verses which scarcely ever rose above absolute mediocrity; but as he was a man of high note in the political and fashionable world, these verses found admirers. Time dissolved the charm, but, unfortunately for him, not until his lines had acquired a prescriptive right to a place in all collections of the works of English poets. To this day accordingly his insipid essays in rhyme and his paltry songs to Amoretta and Gloriana are reprinted in company with "Comus" and "Alexander's Feast." The consequence is that our generation knows Mulgrave chiefly as a poetaster, and despises him as such.—MACAULAY, THOMAS BABINGTON, 1849, *History of England, ch.* VIII.

The Duke of Buckinghamshire's two plays of "Caesar" and "Brutus," a feeble execution of a not incorrect idea.—WARD, ADOLPHUS WILLIAM, 1875–99, *A History of English Dramatic Literature, vol.* II, *p.* 141.

Several of Sheffield's prose works are valuable historically, particularly his "Account of the Revolution;" but his statements have to be received with caution when he is personally concerned.— CARLYLE, E. IRVING, 1897, *Dictionary of National Biography, vol.* LII, *p.* 15.

Wrote couplets inferior to Roscommon's, and lyrics very inferior to Rochester's, yet some of these latter are not despicable. An "Essay on Satire," which is attributed to the joint efforts of Mulgrave and Dryden, is too rude, as well as mostly too rough, for the poet, and too clever for the peer; it contains perhaps the best satiric couplet in the English language, outside of Dryden and Pope—

Was ever prince by two at once misled,
False, foolish, old, ill-natured, and ill-bred?
—SAINTSBURY, GEORGE, 1898, *A Short History of English Literature, p.* 482.

Matthew Prior

1664–1721

Born, probably in Dorsetshire, 21 July 1664. Educated at Westminister School; King's Scholar, 1681. To St. John's Coll., Camb., as Scholar, 1682; B. A., 1686; Fellow, April 1688. For a short time tutor to sons of Lord Exeter. Gentleman of Bedchamber to the King. In Holland, as Sec. to Lord Dursley, 1690 [?]–97. Sec. of State in Ireland, 1697. Sec. to English Embassy in Paris, 1698. Returned to England, Nov. 1699; appointed Under-Sec. of State. Hon. M. A., Camb., 1700. Commissioner of Trade, 1700–07. M.P. for East Grinstead, Feb. to June, 1701. Commissioner of Customs, 1711–14. In Paris, 1711, and 1712–14. Imprisoned on political charge, March 1715 to 1717. Presented by Lord Harley with property of Down-Hall, Essex, 1720 [?]. Died, at Wimpole, 18 Sept. 1721. *Works:* "The Hind and the Panther transversed" (anon.), 1687; "Hymn to the Sun," 1694; "To the King: an Ode," 1695; "An English Ballad" (anon.), 1695; "Verses on the death of Queen Mary," 1695; "Carmen Seculare for the year 1700" (anon.), 1700; "Letter to Monsieur Boileau Despréaux" (anon.), 1704; "An Ode . . . to the Queen" (anon.), 1706; "Pallas and Venus" (anon.), 1706; "Poems," 1707 (unauthorised); "Poems," 1709; "A Fable of the Widow and her Cat" (with Swift), 1711; "Poems," 1716 (unauthorised); "The Dove" (anon.), 1717; "Poems," 1718; "The Conversation" (anon.), 1720; "The Curious Maid" (anon.), 1720. *Posthumous:* "Down Hall,"1723; "The Turtle and the Sparrow," 1723; "The Unequal Match" (anon.), 1737; "History of his Own Time," 1740; "Miscellaneous Works" (2 vols.), 1740. *Collected Works:* ed. by R. B. Johnson (2 vols.), 1892.—SHARP, R. FARQUHARSON, 1897, *A Dictionary of English Authors,* p. 232.

PERSONAL

Yet counting as far as to fifty his years,
  His virtue and vice were as other men's
    are,
High hopes he conceived and he smothered
  great fears,
  In a life party-coloured—half pleasure,
    half care.
Nor to business a drudge, nor to faction a
  slave,
  He strove to make interest and freedom
    agree;
In public employments industrious and grave,
  And alone with his friends, lord, how
    merry was he!
Now in equipage stately, now humbly on
  foot,
  Both fortunes he tried, but to neither
    would trust;
And whirled in the round as the wheel
  turned about,
  He found riches had wings, and knew man
    was but dust.
—PRIOR, MATTHEW, c 1708, *For My Own Monument.*

It is near three o'clock in the morning, I have been hard at work all day, and am not yet enough recovered to bear much fatigue; excuse therefore the confusedness of this scroll, which is only from Harry to Matt, and not from the secretary to the minister. Adieu, my pen is ready to drop out of my hand, it being now three o'clock in the morning; believe that no man loves you better, or is more faithfully yours, &c.—BOLINGBROKE, LORD, 1712, *Letter to Matthew Prior, Sept.* 10.

One Prior, who had been Jersey's secretary.—BURNET, GILBERT, 1715–34, *History of My Own Time.*

Our friend Prior not having had the vicissitude of humane things before his eyes, is likely to end his days in as forlorn a state as any other poet has done before him, if his friends do not take more care of him than he did of himself. Therefore to prevent the evil which we see is coming on very fast, we have a project of printing his "Solomon" and other poetical works by subscription; one guinea

to be paid in hand, and the other at the delivery of the book. He, Arbuthnot, Pope, and Gay are now with me, and remember you. It is our joint request that you will endeavour to procure some subscriptions. . . . There are no papers printed here, nor any advertisements, for the whole matter is to be managed by friends in such a manner as shall be least shocking to the dignity of a plenipotentiary.—LEWIS, ERASMUS, 1716–17, *Letter to Swift, Jan.* 12.

There is great care taken, now it is too late, to keep Prior's will secret, for it is thought not to be too reputable for Lord Harley to execute this will. Be so kind as to say nothing whence you had your intelligence. We are to have a bowl of punch at Bessy Cox's. She would fain have put it upon Lewis that she was his Emma; she owned Flanders Jane was his Chloe.—ARBUTHNOT, JOHN, 1721, *Letters to Mr. Watkins, Oct.* 10.

Prior was not a right good man. He used to bury himself, for whole days and nights together, with a poor mean creature, and often drank hard. He turned from a strong whig (which he had been when most with Lord Halifax) to a violent tory; and did not care to converse with any whigs after, any more than Rowe did with tories.—POPE, ALEXANDER, 1728–30, *Spence's Anecdotes, ed. Singer,* p. 2.

The same woman who could charm the waiter in a tavern, still maintained her dominion over the embassador at France. The Chloe of Prior, it seems, was a woman in this station of life; but he never forsook her in the height of his reputation. Hence we may observe, that associations with women are the most lasting of all, and that when an eminent station raises a man above many other acts of condescension, a mistress will maintain her influence, charm away the pride of greatness, and make the hero who fights, and the patriot who speaks, for the liberty of his country, a slave to her. One would imagine however, that this woman, who was a Butcher's wife, must either have been very handsome, or have had something about her superior to people of her rank: but it seems the case was otherwise, and no better reason can be given for Mr. Prior's attachment to her, but that she was his taste. Her husband suffered their intrigue to go on unmolested; for he was proud even of such a connexion as this, with so great a man as Prior; a singular instance of good nature.—CIBBER, THEOPHILUS, 1753, *Lives of the Poets, vol.* IV, *p.* 47.

Is it surprising that the works of a poet once so popular, should now be banished from a Lady's library?—a banishment from which all his sprightly wit cannot redeem him.—But because Prior's love for this woman was real, and that he was really a man of feeling and genius, though debased by low and irregular habits, there are some sweet touches scattered through his poetry, which show how strong was the illusion in his fancy.—JAMESON, ANNA BROWNELL, 1829, *Prior's Chloe, The Loves of the Poets, p.* 238.

We find him neither gay enough nor refined enough. Bolingbroke called him wooden-faced, stubborn, and said he had something Dutch in his appearance. His manners smacked very strongly of those of Rochester, and the well-clad refuse which the Restoration bequeathed to the Revolution. He took the first woman at hand, shut himself up with her for several days, drank hard, fell asleep, and let her make off with his money and clothes. Amongst other drabs, ugly enough and always dirty, he finished by keeping Elizabeth Cox, and all but married her; fortunately he died just in time.—TAINE, H. A., 1871, *History of English Literature, tr. Van Laun, vol.* II, *bk.* iii, *ch.* vii, *p.* 214.

Apparently he was not designed by nature or tastes for a professional statesman, as was Montague. As a writer, he had not genuis, like Addison's, to compel the world to accept as truths of human nature the humours of a special period. Yet, by tempering literature with politics, and politics with literature, he made a high reputation among his contemporaries, and won lofty official rank. By the mere weight of the frequent repetition of his name, in one relation or another, in the records of the period when he flourished,

his fame, as a diplomatist and poet, has descended to an age which recollects little of the circumstances of his negotiations, and not much more, in reality, of his muse. . . . In the unique social epoch of Queen Anne's reign, he occupies no place apart, no individual position among the many luminaries with whom he familiarly consorted. Scarcely an idea has been handed down to us of his demeanour and general appearance. He did, said, and wrote many things which are remembered; he himself is not. A nation did not mourn for him as for Cowley; and the grief of his other old friends was as well under control as Atterbury's, who was content to be kept away from his funeral by a cold. He had to remind posterity by a bequest for a sumptuous monument in the Abbey who he was, and what he had been.—STEBBING, WILLIAM, 1887, *Some Verdicts of History Reviewed, pp.* 87, 121.

Who was this fair rival of Venus, Prior's Chloe? Spence in his anecdotes asserts that she was a woman of the lowest class. Others say she was ideal. "I know the contrary," says John Wesley—an unexceptionable witness. "I have heard my eldest brother say her name was Miss Taylor; that he knew her well, and that she once came to him in Dean's Yard, Westminster, purposely to ask his advice. She told him. 'Sir, I know not what to do. Mr. Prior makes large professions of his love, but he never offers me marriage.' My brother advised her to bring the matter to a point at once. She went directly to Mr. Prior and asked him plainly, 'Do you intend to marry me or no?' He said many soft and pretty things, on which she said, 'Sir, in refusing to answer you do answer. I will see you no more.' " And she did see him no more to the day of his death. But afterwards she spent many hours standing and weeping at his tomb in Westminster Abbey. There let her stand, ye inquisitive critics, the true Chloe as we would fain picture her.—MANSON, EDWARD, 1896, *Matthew Prior, Temple Bar, vol.* 108, *p.* 535.

SOLOMON

Mr. Prior, by the suffrage of all men of taste, holds the first rank in poetry, for the delicacy of his numbers, the wittiness of his turns, the acuteness of his remarks, and, in one performance, for the amazing force of his sentiments. The stile of our author is likewise so pure, that our language knows no higher authority, and there is an air of original in his minutest performances. It would be superfluous to give any detail of his poems, they are in the hands of all who love poetry, and have been as often admired, as read. The performance however, for which he is most distinguished, is his "Solomon;" a Poem in three Books, the first on Knowledge, the second on Pleasure, and the third on Power. We know few poems to which this is second, and it justly established his reputation as one of the best writers of his age.—CIBBER, THEOPHILUS, 1753, *Lives of the Poets, vol.* IV, *p.* 53.

"Solomon" is the work to which he entrusted the protection of his name, and which he expected succeeding ages to regard with veneration. His affection was natural; it had undoubtedly been written with great labour; and who is willing to think that he has been labouring in vain? He had infused into it much knowledge and much thought; had often polished it to elegance, often dignified it with splendour, and sometimes heightened it to sublimity: he perceived in it many excellences, and did not discover that it wanted that without which all others are of small avail, the power of engaging attention and alluring curiosity. . . . Yet the work is far from deserving to be neglected. He that shall peruse it will be able to mark many passages, to which he may recur for instruction or delight; many from which the poet may learn to write, and the philosopher to reason.— JOHNSON, SAMUEL, 1779-81, *Prior, Lives of the English Poets.*

The poem has distinct merits; it is perhaps more "correct," in Walsh's sense, than any other in the language; but it cannot be read. This was the case in Prior's own day, and he fretted against the neglect of his masterpiece.—GOSSE, EDMUND, 1888, *A History of Eighteenth Century Literature, p.* 134.

If readers like John Wesley and Cowper thought highly of "Solomon," it must be concluded that what they admired was rather the wise king's wisdom than Prior's rendering of it. Johnson himself admits that it is wearisome, and Johnson, whose "lax talking" and perverse criticism have done Prior so much wrong, may, upon this point of wearisomeness, be admitted to speak with some authority.—DOBSON, AUSTIN, 1889, *Selected Poems of Matthew Prior, Introduction, p.* liv.

Is in heroic couplets of a rather Drydenian than Popian cast, with frequent Alexandrines. Here too the poem is much better worth reading than is usually thought; but the author's inability to be frankly serious again shows itself. His treatment of Vanity has neither the bitter quintessence of Swift, nor the solemn and sometimes really tragic declamation of Young, nor that intense conviction and ethical majesty which make Johnson's "Vanity of Human Wishes" almost a great poem, and beyond all question a great piece of literature.—SAINTSBURY, GEORGE, 1898, *A Short History of English Literature, p.* 557.

ALMA
1718

"Alma" is written in professed imitation of "Hudibras," and has at least one accidental resemblance: "Hudibras" wants a plan, because it is left imperfect; "Alma" is imperfect, because it seems never to have had a plan. Prior appears not to have proposed to himself any drift or design, but to have written the casual dictates of the present moment.—JOHNSON, SAMUEL, 1779-81, *Prior, Lives of the English Poets.*

What suggested to Johnson the thought that the "Alma" was written in imitation of "Hudibras," I cannot conceive. In former years they were both favourites of mine, and I often read them; but never saw in them the least resemblance to each other; nor do I now, except that they are composed in verse of the same measure. —COWPER, WILLIAM, 1784, *Letter to Unwin, March* 21

It is not to be read for its argument, or for that meaning which Goldsmith failed to grasp, but for its delightfully-wayward digressions, its humour and its good-humour, its profusion of epigram and happy illustration. Butler, though Cowper doubted it, is plainly Prior's model, the difference being in the men and not in the measure. Indeed, the fact is evident from the express reference to Butler in the opening lines of Canto ii.—DOBSON, AUSTIN, 1889, *Selected Poems of Matthew Prior, Introduction, p.* lvii.

HENRY AND EMMA

I was so much charmed at fourteen with the dialogue of "Henry and Emma," I can say it by heart to this day. . . . This senseless tale is, however, so well varnished with melody of words and pomp of sentiment, I am convinced it has hurt more girls than ever were injured by the worst poems extant.—MONTAGU, LADY MARY WORTLEY, 1755, *Letters to the Countess of Bute.*

A dull and tedious dialogue, which excites neither esteem for the man, nor tenderness for the woman.—JOHNSON, SAMUEL, 1779-81, *Prior, Lives of the English Poets.*

In this effort Prior elaborated and spoilt the fine ballad of the "Nut-Brown Maid." Assuredly "Emma and the Nut-Brown Maid" are not "one," as Prior said.—AITKEN, GEORGE A., 1890, *Matthew Prior, Contemporary Review, vol.* 57, *p.* 727.

GENERAL

Let Prior's Muse with soft'ning accents move,
Soft as the strains of constant Emma's love:
Or let his fancy choose some jovial theme,
As when he told Hans Carvel's jealous dream;
Prior th' admiring reader entertains,
With Chaucer's humour, and with Spencer's strains.
—GAY, JOHN, 1714, *To Bernard Lintot, Poems.*

While he of pleasure, power and wisdom sang,
My heart lap high, my lugs wi' pleasure rang:
These to repeat, braid-broken I wad spill,
Altho' I should employ my utmost skill.
He towr'd aboon: but ah! what tongue can tell
How high he flew? how much lamented fell?
—RAMSAY, ALLAN, 1728, *A Pastoral on the Death of Matthew Prior.*

Lord Bathurst used to call Prior his verseman, and Lewis his proseman.— Prior, indeed, was nothing out of verse: and was less fit for business than even Addison, though he piqued himself much upon his talents for it.—What a simple thing was it to say upon his tombstone, that he was writing a history of his own times!—He could not write in a style fit for history; and, I dare say, he never had set down a word toward any such thing. —POPE, ALEXANDER, 1734-36, *Spence's Anecdotes, ed. Singer, p.* 132.

That Matthew's numbers ran with ease
Each man of common-sense agrees; . . .
"Matthew," says Fame, "with endless pins
Smoothed and refined the meanest strains,
Nor suffered one ill-chosen rhyme
To escape him at the idlest time;
And thus o'er all a lustre cast,
That while the language lives shall last."
—COWPER, WILLIAM, 1754, *An Epistle to Robert Lloyd.*

Prior, lively, familiar, and amusing.— SMOLLETT, TOBIAS GEORGE, 1757-58, *History of England, George I., notes.*

This Bagatelle, ["Hans Cravel"] for which, by-the-by, Mr. Prior has got his greatest reputation, was a tale told in all the old Italian collections of jests; and borrowed from thence by Fontaine. It had been translated once or twice before into English, yet was never regarded till it fell into the hands of Mr. Prior. A strong instance how much every thing is improved in the hands of a man of genius. —GOLDSMITH, OLIVER, 1767, *The Beauties of English Poetry.*

What he has valuable he owes to his diligence and his judgement. His diligence has justly placed him amongst the most correct of the English poets; and he was one of the first that resolutely endeavoured at correctness. He never sacrifices accuracy or haste, nor indulges himself in contemptuous negligence, or impatient idleness: he has no careless lines, or entangled sentiments; his words are nicely selected, and his thoughts fully expanded. . . . His phrases are original, but they are sometimes harsh; as he inherited no elegances, none has he bequeathed. His expression has every mark of laborious study; the line seldom seems to have been formed at once; the words did not come till they were called, and were then put by constraint into their places, where they do their duty, but do it sullenly. . . . His numbers are such as mere diligence may attain; they seldom offend the ear, and seldom sooth it; they commonly want airiness, lightness, and facility: what is smooth, is not soft. His verses always roll, but they seldom flow.—JOHNSON, SAMUEL, 1779-81, *Prior, Lives of the English Poets.*

The best of what we copied from the Continental poets, on this desertion of our own great originals, is copied in the lighter pieces of Prior. That tone of polite raillery,—that airy, rapid, picturesque narrative, mixed up of wit and naïveté,—that style, in short, of good conversation, concentrated into flowing and polished verses,—was not within the vein of our native poets, and probably never would have been known among us if we had been left to our own resources. It is lamentable that this, which alone was worth borrowing, is the only thing which has not been retained. The tales and little apologues of Prior are still the only examples of this style in our language.— JEFFREY, FRANCIS LORD, 1811-44, Contributions to the Edinburgh Review.

To us the poet Prior is better known than the placeman Prior; yet in his own day the reverse often occurred. Prior was a State Proteus. . . . The Solomon of Bards.—DISRAELI, ISAAC, 1812- 13, The Illusions of Writers in Verse, Calamities of Authors.

Prior's writings evince less disposition to literary jealousy than those of any author of the age.—SCOTT, SIR WALTER, 1814, Life of Jonathan Swift.

Lord L[ansdowne] asked me what was the poem of Prior's I had once mentioned to him as very pretty; he had been often trying to recollect it. It was "Dear Chloe, how blubbered," &c., &c. We took it down and read it. Nothing can be more gracefully light and gallant than this little poem. I mentioned Lowth's objections to the last two lines as ungrammatical, correctness requiring "than she" and "than I;" but it is far prettier as it is.—MOORE, THOMAS, 1818, Diary, Nov. 21.

Prior has left no single work equal to Gay's "Fables," or the "Beggars' Opera." But in his lyrical and fugitive pieces he has shown even more genius, more playfulness, more mischievous gaiety. No one has exceeded him in the laughing grace with which he glances at a subject that will not bear examining, with which he gently hints at what cannot be directly insisted on, with which he half conceals, and half draws aside, the veil from some of the Muse's nicest mysteries. His Muse is, in fact, a giddy wanton flirt, who spends her time in playing at snap-dragon and blind-man's buff, who tells what she should not, and knows more than she tells. She laughs at the tricks she shows us, and blushes, or would be thought to do so, at

what she keeps concealed. . . . Some of Prior's bon-mots are the best that are recorded. His serious poetry, as his "Solomon," is as heavy as his familiar style was light and agreeable. His moral Muse is a Magdalen, and should not have obtruded herself on public view.—HAZLITT, WILLIAM, 1818, Lectures on the English Poets, Lecture vi.

Prior was one of the last of the race of poets who relied for ornament on scholastic allusion and pagan machinery; but he used them like Swift, more in jest than in earnest, and with good effect. In his "Alma" he contrives even to clothe metaphysics in the gay and colloquial pleasantry, which is the characteristic charm of his manner.—CAMPBELL, THOMAS, 1819, Specimens of the British Poets.

I believe that one chief reason for his (John Wesley's) high estimation of Prior among English poets was that he gives so many vivid sketches of man's wretchedness, in spite of all possible contrivances to enjoy life.—SOUTHEY, ROBERT, 1820, Life of John Wesley, vol. II, p. 498.

With the exception of his "Edwin and Emma," founded on the old ballad of the "Nut Brown Maid:" of which it were difficult to say, whether the original or the copy be the more remarkable for its insipidity, Prior seems to be well nigh forgotten; but he was a scholar, and a man of taste, and an "influential personage" in his day.—DIBDIN, THOMAS FROGNALL, 1824, The Library Companion, p. 727.

A poet now-a-days too much neglected. —LAMB, CHARLES, 1834, Table Talk by the Late Elia, Athenæum, p. 447.

Had he stated facility to be his aim, ["Ode on the Battle of Ramillies"] he had shown more honesty. He has escaped the difficulties of Spenser's stanza, but at the same time has sacrificed all its science and not a little of its beauty.—GUEST, EDWIN, 1838, A History of English Rhythms, vol. II, p. 394.

Johnson speaks slightingly of his lyrics; but, with due deference to the great Samuel, Prior's seem to me amongst the easiest, the richest, the most charmingly humorous of English lyrical poems. Horace is always in his mind, and his song and his philosophy, his good sense, his happy easy turns and melody, his loves, and his epicureanism, bear a great resemblance to that most delightful and accomplished master. In reading his works, one is struck with their modern air, as well as by their happy similarity to the songs of the charming owner of the Sabine farm.—THACKERAY, WILLIAM MAKEPEACE, 1853, *The English Humourists of the Eighteenth Century.*

Perhaps no one of the minor wits and poets of the time has continued to enjoy higher or more general favor with posterity. Much that he wrote, indeed, is now forgotten; but some of the best of his comic tales in verse will live as long as the lanugage, which contains nothing that surpasses them in the union of ease and fluency with sprightliness and point, and in all that makes up the spirit of humorous and graceful narrative. They are our happiest examples of a style that has been cultivated with more frequent success by French writers than by our own. In one poem, his "Alma, or The Progress of the Mind," extending to three cantos, he has even applied this light and airy manner of treatment with remarkable felicity to some of the most curious questions in mental philosophy. In another still longer work, again, entitled "Solomon on the Vanity of the World, in three Books," leaving his characteristic archness and pleasantry, he emulates not unsuccessfully the dignity of Pope, not without some traces of natural eloquence and picturesqueness of expression which are all his own.—CRAIK, GEORGE L., 1861, *A Compendious History of English Literature and of the English Language, vol.* II, *p.* 263.

His style was like his manners. When he tried to imitate La Fontaine's "Hans Carvel," he made it dull, and lengthened it; he could not be piquant, but he was biting; his obscenities have a cynical crudity; his raillery is a satire; and in one of his poems, "To a Young Gentleman in Love," the lash becomes a knocking-down blow. On the other hand he was not a common roysterer. Of his two principal poems, one on "Solomon" paraphrases and treats of the remark of Ecclesiastes, "All is vanity." From this picture you see forthwith that you are in a biblical land: such an idea would not then have occured to a friend of the Regent of France, the Duke of Orleans.

Solomon relates how he in vain "proposed his doubts to the lettered Rabbins," how he has been equaly unfortunate in the hopes and desires of love, the possession of power, and ends by trusting to an "omniscient Master, omnipresent King." Here we have English gloom and English conclusions. Moreover, under the rhetorical and uniform composition of his verses, we perceive warmth and passion, rich paintings, a sort of magnificence, and the profusion of a surcharged imagination.—TAINE, H. A., 1871, *History of English Literature, tr. Van Laun, vol.* II, *bk.* iii, *ch.* vii, *p.* 214.

In the strangely opposed characteristics of his intellectual and moral nature, in his brightness of wit and grace of expression, his insincerity, impurity, unspirituality, callousness, and bad taste, as well as in his geniality and *esprit de corps,* Prior seems to furnish a very truthful reflection of the age which produced him.—HEWLETT, HENRY G., 1872, *Poets of Society, Contemporary Review, vol.* 20, *p.* 248.

As a writer his longer poems have not many claims to a lasting remembrance; but his shorter pieces justly deserve all the fame they have acquired. They come barely short of perfection; Prior strives hard after obtaining a classic grace and just misses it. . . . Mat. Prior was held in high esteem by the most competent of his contemporaries, with whom he lived on excellent terms. But the judgment upon him must be that he faithfully represented in himself the follies of his time. His verse is flexible, sparkling, and flowing; at times, but very seldom, it merits higher praise; yet there was no one in his own day who wrote such verse so well. His views of woman, society, life, and pleasure were those almost of the lowest stratum, though his power over his art was so great that he could frequently counterfeit sentiments of a higher order.—SMITH, GEORGE BARNETT, 1875, *Poets and Novelists, pp.* 392, 394.

As a writer of what are called, not altogether happily, *vers de société,* Prior takes high rank. He has all the grace and lightness of touch, all the ease and ingenuity of Horace, though he wants that deeper and more serious tone which sometimes tempers the gaiety of the Latin poet. He was the first in the field which

Praed and Dobson and Locker have since so successfully cultivated; a field in which we trace the influence not only of Latin but of French predecessors. But besides those qualities which he had in common with other poets, he had a charm of his own which is rather to be felt than described.—ADAMS, W. H. DAVENPORT, 1886, *Good Queen Anne, vol. II, p. 282.*

Prior is probably the greatest of all who dally with the light lyre which thrills to the wings of fleeting Loves—the greatest English writer of *vers de société;* the most gay, frank, good-humoured, tuneful and engaging.—LANG, ANDREW, 1889, *Letters on Literature, p.* 153.

Almost all that is good in Moore may be found in Prior, and much besides, but Prior had one great accidental advantage over Moore. To write good society verse the social tone of the time must be good and artificial and complex, for the verse reflects the talk of the town or it is nothing worth. Society was never so much all this as in Queen Anne's day, when Prior mainly wrote, and never, for at least two hundred years previously, so bad or so brutal as in the day of King George IV., when Moore wrote his love songs.—CRAWFURD, OSWALD, 1896, *ed., Lyrical Verse from Elizabeth to Victoria, note, p.* 429.

What he considered to be his most successful efforts are at present, as it often happens, the least valued. His three books on "Solomon on the Vanity of the World," of which he himself ruefully admitted in "The Conversation,"

Indeed, poor Solomon in rhyme
Was much too grave to be sublime,

although they once found admirers in John Wesley and Cowper, find few readers today; and his paraphrase of the fine old ballad of "The Nut-Brown Maid" as "Henry and Emma" shares their fate. His "Alma," which he regarded as a "loose and hasty scribble," is, on the contrary, still a favourite with the admirers of Butler, whose "Hudibras" is its avowed model—a model which it perhaps excels in facility of rhyme and ease of versification. In Prior's imitations of the "Conte" of La Fontaine this metrical skill is maintained, and he also shows consummate art in the telling of a story in verse. Unhappily, in spite of Johnson's extraordinary dictum that "Prior is a lady's book" his themes are not equally commendable. But he is one of the neatest of English epigrammatists, and in occasional pieces and familiar verse has no rival in English.—DOBSON, AUSTIN, 1896, *Dictionary of National Biography, vol.* XLVI, *p.* 401.

Although Prior was neither a very great nor perhaps, in some respects, a very wise man, he had, at all events, what much greater men have often lacked, an excellent knowledge of books, the reading of which failed to make him a dull man.—ROBERTS, W., 1897, *Matthew Prior as a Book-Collector, The Athenæum, June 19, p.* 811.

Charles Leslie
1650–1722

Charles Leslie, or Lesley. Born at Dublin, Ireland, July 17, 1650: died at Glaslough, Monaghan, Ireland, April 13, 1722. A British nonjuror (Jacobite) and controversialist. He was an opponent of William III. whom he attacked in a pamphlet "Gallienus Redivivus, or Murther will out" (1695; a principal authority on the Glencoe massacre), of Burnet ("Tempora mutantur," 1689), Tillotson, and others. He also attacked the Quakers ("The Snake in the Grass, or Satan transformed into an Angel of Light" (1696), and other pamphlets) and the Jews, and engaged in political controversies. His best-known work is "A Short and Easy Method with the Deists" (1698). He was obliged to leave England (1711) to avoid arrest on account of his political opinions, and later joined the household of the Pretender, whom he ardently supported.—SMITH, BENJAMIN E., 1894–97, *The Century Cyclopedia of Names, p.* 606.

GENERAL

Leslie, a pert writer, with some wit and learning, insulted the government every week with the grossest abuse. His style and manner, both of which were illiberal, was imitated by Ridpath, De Foe, Dunton, and others of the opposite party.—GOLDSMITH, OLIVER, 1759, *The Bee, No.* 8, *Nov.* 24.

Leslie was a reasoner, and a reasoner

who was not to be reasoned against.—
JOHNSON, SAMUEL, 1784, *Life by Boswell.*

Leslie had much learning, but more
faction; some wit, but more scurrility.—
NOBLE, MARK, 1806, *A Biographical History of England, vol.* I, *p* 140.

A contemporary of Tillotson, but possessed of greater acumen, and exhibiting
a more condensed and logical style, he
was perhaps the ablest defender of orthodoxy at the close of the seventeenth century. Ever ardent and active in what he
conceived to be the cause of vital religion,
his heart and head were constantly excited
to the bringing forth of those admirable
works which appear to bear the stamp of
immortality. No single theological work
has perhaps received so much applause as
his "Short and Easy Method with the
Deists."—DIBDIN, THOMAS FROGNALL,
1824, *The Library Companion, p.* 62.

No book at this period, among many
that were written, reached so high a reputation in England as Leslie's "Short
Method with the Deists," published in
1694; in which he has started an argument, pursued with more critical analysis
by others, on the peculiarly distinctive
marks of credibility that pertain to the
scriptural miracles. The authenticity of
this little treatise has been idly questioned
on the Continent, for no better reason
than that a translation of it has been published in a posthumous edition (1732) of
the works of Saint Real, who died in
1692. But posthumous editions are never
deemed of sufficient authority to establish
a literary title against possession; and
Prosper Marchand informs us that several
other tracts, in this edition of Saint Real,
are erroneously ascribed to him. The
internal evidence that the "Short Method"
was written by a Protestant should be
conclusive.—HALLAM, HENRY, 1837–39,
*Introduction to the Literature of Europe,
pt.* iv, *ch.* ii, *par.* 44.

An acute controversialist in favour of
the Church of England.—BICKERSTETH,
EDWARD, 1844, *The Christian Student.*

His abilities and his connections were
such that he might easily have obtained
high preferment in the Church of England.
But he took his place in the front rank of
the Jacobite body, and remained there
steadfastly, through all the dangers and
vicissitudes of three and thirty troubled
years. Though constantly engaged in

theological controversy with Deists, Jews,
Socinians, Presbyterians, Papists, and
Quakers, he found time to be one of the
most voluminous political writers of the
age. Of all the nonjuring clergy he was
the best qualified to discuss constitutional
questions. For before he had taken
orders, he had resided long in the Temple,
and had been studying English history and
law, while most of the other chiefs of the
schism had been pouring over the Acts of
Chalcedon, or seeking for wisdom in the
Targum of Onkelos.—MACAULAY, THOMAS
BABINGTON, 1855, *History of England,
ch.* xiv.

The works of this remarkable man have
been collected in seven volumes (Oxford
1832), and it must be allowed that they
place their author very high in the list of
controversial writers, the ingenuity of the
arguments being only equalled by the keenness and pertinacity with which they are
pursued.—CHAMBERS, ROBERT, 1876, *Cyclopædia of English Literature, ed. Carruthers.*

Leslie was pronounced by Johnson to
have been the only nonjuror who could
reason. He was, in fact, no despicable
master of the art of expressing pithy arguments in vigorous English. His honourable independence of character attached
him to the fortunes of a small and declining party; whilst his pugnacity plunged
him into controversies with almost every
section of the majority. Besides numerous political skirmishes, he found time to
carry on operations against Quakers,
Deists, Socinians, Jews, and Papists. The
far more surprising circumstance is stated,
that he had the almost unique honour of
converting several of his antagonists.
Amongst those who surrendered to his
prowess was Gildon, who put forth his
recantation some years afterwards in a
flabby repetition of the regular commonplaces, called the "Deist's Manual." The
pleasure of dragging a captive infidel in
triumph must have been diminished by the
consciousness that he was so poor a creature; but we might turn over a long list
of controversial writers without finding
one who had even a Gildon to boast of.—
STEPHEN, LESLIE, 1876, *History of English
Thought in the Eighteenth Century, vol.* I,
p. 195.

Leslie wrote an easy and lively style,
had some learning and wit, and more

scurrility, and was adroit at logical fence. He was a most unsparing controversialist. Swift, while professing abhorrence of his political principles, warmly praised his services to the Anglican church. Johnson declared him the only reasoner among the nonjurors, and "a reasoner who was not to be reasoned against."—RIGG, J. M., 1893, *Dictionary of National Biography*, vol. XXXIII, p. 82.

John Toland
1670–1722

Born in Ireland, in 1669, of Roman Catholic parents, but became a zealous opponent of that faith before he was sixteen; after which he finished his education at Glasgow and Edinburgh; he retired to study at Leyden, where he formed the acquaintance of Leibnitz and other learned men. His first book, published in 1696, and entitled "Christianity not Mysterious," was met by the strongest denunciation from the pulpit, was "presented" by the grand jury of Middlesex, and ordered to be burnt by the common hangman by the Parliament of Ireland. He was henceforth driven for employ to literature; and in 1699 was engaged by the Duke of Newcastle to edit the "Memoirs of Denzil, Lord Hollis;" and afterwards by the Earl of Oxford on a new edition of Harrington's "Oceana." He then visited the courts of Berlin and Hanover. He published many works on politics and religion, the latter all remarkable for their deistical tendencies, and died in March, 1722.—DISRAELI, BENJAMIN (LORD BEACONSFIELD), 1881, *ed., Calamities of Authors, by Isaac Disraeli, note.*

PERSONAL

If his exceeding great value of himself do not deprive the world of that usefulness that his parts, if rightly conducted, might be of, I shall be very glad.—The hopes young men give of what use they will make of their parts is, to me, the encouragement of being concerned for them; but, if vanity increases with age, I always fear whither it will lead a man. —LOCKE, JOHN, 1697? *Letters.*

A lover of all literature,
and knowing more than ten languages;
a champion for truth,
an assertor of liberty,
but the follower or dependant of no man;
nor could menaces nor fortune bend him;
the way he had chosen he pursued,
preferring honesty to his interest.
His spirit is joined with its ethereal father
from whom it originally proceeded;
his body likewise, yielding to Nature,
is again laid in the lap of its mother:
but he is about to rise again in eternity,
yet never to be the same Toland more.
—TOLAND, JOHN, 1722, *Epitaph.*

The name of Toland is more familiar than his character, yet his literary portrait has great singularity; he must be classed among the "Authors by Profession," an honour secured by near fifty publications; and we shall discover that he aimed to combine with the literary character one peculiarly his own. With higher talents and more learning than have been conceded to him, there ran in his mind an original vein of thinking. Yet his whole life exhibits in how small a degree great intellectual powers, when scattered through all the forms which Vanity suggests, will contribute to an author's social comforts, or raise him in public esteem. Toland was fruitful in his productions, and still more so in his projects; yet it is mortifying to estimate the result of all the intense activity of the life of an author of genius, which terminates in being placed among these Calamities. . . . He was so confirmed an author, that he never published one book without promising another. He refers to others in MS.; and some of his most curious works are posthumous. He was a great artificer of title pages, covering them with a promising luxuriance; and in this way recommended his works to the booksellers. He had an odd taste for running inscriptions of whimsical crabbed terms; the gold-dust of erudition to gild over a title.—DISRAELI, ISAAC, 1812–13, *The Victims of Vanity, Calamities of Authors.*

From his earliest days Toland was a mere waif and stray, hanging loose upon society, retiring at intervals into the profoundest recesses of Grub Street, emerging again by fits to scandalise the whole respectable world, and then once more sinking back into tenfold obscurity. His career is made pathetic by his incessant efforts to clutch at various supports, which always gave way as he grasped them. The illegitimate son, as it was said, probably out of mere malice, of an Irish priest, he became a convert to Protestantism at sixteen, and was supported by certain dissenters at Glasgow, Leyden, and Oxford. He repaid their generosity by acquiring a considerable amount of learning, and then by suddenly firing "Christianity not Mysterious" in their faces. It was a luckless performance so far as his temporal interests were concerned. The Grand Jury of Middlesex presented it as a nuisance; the uproar which it excited followed him to Dublin; there for a time he braved the storm, and was foolish enough to maintain his opinions at "coffee-houses and public tables;" whereas infidelity, till a much later period, was, like hair-powder, an acknowledged perquisite of the aristocracy. Poor Toland fell into debt; it became dangerous to speak to him; and as South triumphantly declared, whilst wishing that English zeal were equally warm, "the (Irish) parliament, to their immortal honour, sent him packing, and, without the help of a faggot, soon made the kingdom too hot to hold him."—STEPHEN, LESLIE, 1876, *History of English Thought in the Eighteenth Century, vol.* I, *p.* 101.

GENERAL

His "Christianity not Mysterious," 1696, caused none the less excitement than its quarrel with orthodoxy was chiefly concerning the word "mysterious." He accepted the Bible theory of the origin of sin, only labouring to make out that there was nothing mysterious about it. He did not repudiate miracles; he only held that there was nothing mysterious in an all powerful Being breaking through the order of nature. Professor Ferrier styles him "but a poor writer," and charges him with "dulness, pedantry, vanity, and indiscretion."—MINTO, WILLIAM, 1872–80, *Manual of English Prose Literature, p.* 399.

His works were never collected, and are now forgotten.—CHAMBERS, ROBERT, 1876, *Cyclopædia of English Literature, ed.* Carruthers.

Toland was evidently a man of remarkable versatility and acuteness, and his first book struck the keynote of the long discussions as to the relation between the religion of nature and the accepted doctrines. He showed also an acute perception of the importance of historical inquiries into the origin of creeds, though his precarious circumstances prevented him from carrying out continuous studies. His contemporaries held that vanity led him to a rash exposition of crude guesses. Allowance must be made for the unfortunate circumstances which compelled him to make a living in the ambiguous position of a half-recognised political agent and a hack-author dependent upon the patronage of men in power. Some of his writings were respectfully criticised by Leibnitz, and he was in intercourse with some of the ablest men of his time. He is generally noticed along with Collins and Tindal as the object of the contempt of respectable divines, but deserved real credit as a pioneer of freethought. He had read widely and knew many languages, including Irish, which he had learned in his infancy (see his "History of the Druids"), and some of the Teutonic languages.—STEPHEN, LESLIE, 1898, *Dictionary of National Biography, vol.* LVI, *p.* 441.

Susannah Centlivre

1667?–1723

Mrs. Susannah Centlivre, 1667 [?]–1723. Born [Susanna Freeman? or Rawkins?], in Ireland [?] 1667 [?]. Is said to have run away from home on father's second marriage, and lived in Cambridge with Anthony Hammond; in London, for about a year, with a nephew of Sir Stephen Fox; and subsequently with a Capt. Carroll, for about eighteen months. Plays produced at Drury Lane, 1700–22; others occasionally at Lincoln's Inn Fields and Haymarket. First appeared as an actress at Bath, in her "Love at a Venture," 1706. Joined company of strolling players. Married to Joseph Centlivre, head cook to Queen Anne and George I., 1706 [?]. Died in London, 1 Dec. 1723. Buried in St. Martin's-in-the-Fields, and afterwards transferred to St. Paul's Covent Garden. *Works:* "The Perjur'd Husband," 1700 (produced at Drury Lane,

1700); "Love at a Venture," 1706 (prod. at Bath, 1706 [?]); "The Beau's Duel," 1702 (prod. Lincoln's Inn Fields, 1702); "The Stolen Heiress" (anon.), [1703] (prod. Lincoln's Inn Fields, 1702); "Love's Contrivance" (anon.), 1703 (prod. Drury Lane, 1703); "The Gamester" (anon.), 1705 (prod. Lincoln's Inn Fields, 1705 [?]); "The Bassett Table" (anon.), 1706 (prod. Drury Lane, 1705); "The Platonick Lady" (anon.), 1707 (prod. Drury Lane, 1706); "The Busy Body," 1709 (prod. Drury Lane, 1709); "The Man's Bewitched," [1710] (prod. Haymarket, 1709); "A Bickerstaff's Burial," [1710?] (prod. Drury Lane, 1710); "Marplot," 1711 (prod. Drury Lane, 1710); "The Perplex's Lovers," 1712 (prod. Drury Lane, 1712); "The Wonder!" 1714 (prod. Drury Lane, 1714); "A Gotham Election," 1715 (not acted; 2nd edn., called "Humours of Elections," 1737); "A Wife Well Managed," 1715 (prod. Drury Lane, 1715 [?]); "A Poem, humbly presented to . . . George, King of Great Britain, upon his Accession to the Throne," 1715; "The Cruel Gift" (with Rowe), 1717 (prod. Drury Lane, 1716); "A Bold Stroke for a Wife" (with Mottley), 1718 (prod. Drury Lane, 1718); "The Artifice," 1721 (prod. Drury Lane, 1722). *Collected Works:* in 3 vols., with *life*, 1761 (2nd edn., 1872).—SHARP, R. FARQUHARSON, 1897, *A Dictionary of English Authors*, p. 50.

PERSONAL

The world seemed disposed to take Susannah's word; but even good-nature must grant, that there are many breaks and chasms in her story. Indigent and friendless, lively and engaging, we reluctantly excuse where it is impossible to approve. It would, perhaps, be very difficult to find the marriage certificate for her second union.—NOBLE, MARK, 1806, *A Biographical History of England, vol.* II, p. 264.

In Spring Gardens, originally a place of public entertainment, died Mrs. Centlivre, the sprightly authoress of the "Wonder," the "Busy Body," and the "Bold Stroke for a Wife." She was buried at St. Martin's. She is said to have been a beauty, an accomplished linguist, and a good-natured friendly woman. Pope put her in his "Dunciad," for having written, it is said, a ballad against his "Homer" when she was a child! But the probability is that she was too intimate with Steele and other friends of Addison while the irritable poet was at variance with them. It is not impossible, also, that some raillery of hers might have been applied to him, not very pleasant from a beautiful woman against a man of his personal infirmities, who was naturally jealous of not being well with the sex.—HUNT, LEIGH, 1856, *The Town*, p. 368.

A sad lot were all these early feminine intruders into the field of letters,—Aphra Behn, Mrs. Manley, Mrs. Pilkington, and the rest. Mrs. Centlivre was the boldest of them. Almost the first of her sex to adopt literature as a calling, she may well

be regarded as an unconscious reformer, the leader of a forlorn hope against that literary fortress which was so long defended by the cruel sneers of its masculine garrison. She fell upon the glacis. But over her body the Amazons have marched on to victory.—HUNTINGTON, H. A., 1882, *Mrs. Centlivre, Atlantic Monthly, vol.* 49, p. 764.

The place of Mrs. Centlivre's burial has been for many years undetermined, many of the older authorities—among others, the "Biographia Dramatica"—placing it in the Church of St. Martin-in-the-Fields, in which parish she died. But search of the Register of St. Paul's, Covent Garden, shows that she was buried in that church, "Decemb'r 4th, 1723." The date of her birth or the position of her grave is not recorded.—HUTTON, LAURENCE, 1885, *Literary Landmarks of London*, p. 41.

THE BUSY BODY
1709

On Saturday last was presented the "Busy Body," a comedy, written (as I have heretofore remarked) by a woman. The plot and incidents of the play are laid with that subtlety of spirit which is peculiar to females of wit, and is very seldom well performed by those of the other sex, in whom craft in love is an act of invention, and not, as with women, the effect of nature and instinct.—STEELE, SIR RICHARD, 1709, *The Tatler*, No. 19, *May* 24.

"The Busy Body" is inferior, in the interest of the story and characters, to the "Wonder," but it is full of bustle and gaiety from beginning to end. The plot never stands still; the situations succeed one another like the changes of scenery in a pantomime. The nice dove-tailing of the incidents, and cross-reading in the situations, supplies the place of any great force of wit or sentiment. The time for the entrance of each person on the stage is the moment when they are least wanted, and when they arrive make either themselves or somebody else look as foolish as possible. The laughableness of this comedy, as well as of "The Wonder," depends on a brilliant series of mistimed exits and entrances. Marplot is the whimsical hero of the piece, and a standing memorial of unmeaning vivacity and assiduous impertinence.—HAZLITT, WILLIAM, 1818, *Lectures on the English Comic Writers, Lecture* viii.

"The Busy Body" still keeps the stage; for, though many years have elapsed since its performance in London, where various circumstances combine to limit the regular stock pieces within very narrow bounds, it continues to find favour in the country, being not unfrequently acted at some of the most distinguished of the provincial theatres.—DUNHAM, S. ASTLEY, 1838, *ed., Literary and Scientific Men of Great Britain and Ireland, vol.* III, *p.* 315.

THE WONDER
1714

The "Wonder" is one of the best of our acting plays. The passion of jealousy in Don Felix is managed in such a way as to give as little offence as possible to the audience, for every appearance combines to excite and confirm his worse suspicions, while we, who are in the secret, laugh at his groundless uneasiness and apprehensions. The ambiguity of the heroine's situation, which is like a continued practical *equivoque*, gives rise to a quick succession of causeless alarms, subtle excuses, and the most hair-breadth 'scapes. The scene near the end, in which Don Felix, pretending to be drunk, forces his way out of Don Manuel's house, who wants to keep him a prisoner, by producing his marriage-contract in the shape of a pocket-pistol, with the terrors and confusion into which the old gentleman is thrown by this sort of *argumentum ad hominem*, is one of the richest treats the stage affords, and calls forth incessant peals of laughter and applause.—HAZLITT,

WILLIAM, 1818, *Lectures on the English Comic Writers, Lecture* viii.

The busy, bustling nature of the plot, the excellence of the situations which it affords, and the skilful portraiture of the characters, have, in themselves, without much assistance from the dialogue, which, though pertinent and lively, has little or no pretensions to wit, enabled this play to keep the stage down to the present day.—DUNHAM, S. ASTLEY, 1838, *ed., Literary and Scientific Men of Great Britain and Ireland, vol.* III, *p.* 316.

In the elegance and brilliancy of its dialogue, and in the effectiveness of its situations, no comedy of Mrs. Centlivre's approaches "The Wonder." This is perhaps best shown by the fact that its chief character, so often played by him, was chosen by Garrick for his last appearance on the stage. He had thought of making his farewell in Richard III., but he dreaded the fight and the fall, and on reflection preferred to be remembered associated with the mad gayety of the jealous and choleric Don Felix, rather than with the sombre villainy of the crook-backed king.—HUNTINGTON, H. A., 1882, *Mrs. Centlivre, Atlantic Monthly, vol.* 49, *p.* 762.

A BOLD STROKE FOR A WIFE
1718

A truly excellent comedy.—ARNOLD, THOMAS, 1862–87, *A Manual of English Literature, p.* 246, *note.*

The "Bold Stroke for a Wife" is entirely her own, and has had a wonderful succession of Colonel Feignwells, from C. Bullock down to Mr. Graham! This piece, however, was but moderately successful; but it has such vivacity, fun, and quiet humor in it, that it has outlived many a one that began with greater triumph, and in "the real Simon Pure," first acted by Griffin, it has given a proverb to the English language.—DORAN, JOHN, 1863, *Annals of the English Stage, vol.* I, *p.* 168.

GENERAL

From a mean parentage and education, after several gay adventures (over which we shal draw a veil), she had, at last, so well improv'd her natural genius by reading and good conversation, as to attempt to write for the stage, in which she had as good success as any of her sex before her. Her first dramatic performance was a tragi-comedy called "The Perjur'd

Husband," but the plays which gained her most reputation were two comedies, "The Gamester" and "The Busy Body." She writ also several copies of verses on divers subjects and occasions, and a great many ingenious letters, entitled "Letters of Wit, Politics, and Morality," which I collected and published about twenty-one years ago.—BOYER, ABEL, 1729? *Political State, vol.* XXVI, *p.* 670.

Almost the last of our writers who ventured to hold out in the prohibited track was a female adventurer, Mrs. Centlivre, who seemed to take advantage of the privilege of her sex, and to set at defiance the cynical denunciations of the angry puritanical reformist. Her plays have a provoking spirit and volatile salt in them, which still preserves them, from decay. Congreve is said to have been jealous of their success at the time, and that it was one cause which drove him in disgust from the stage. If so, it was without any good reason, for these plays have great and intrinsic merit in them, which entitled them to their popularity . . . and besides, their merit was of a kind entirely different from his own. —HAZLITT, WILLIAM, 1818, *Lectures on the English Comic Writers, Lecture* viii.

Mrs. Centlivre had unobtrusive humor, sayings full of significance rather than wit, wholesome fun in her comic, and earnestness in her serious, characters. Mrs. Centlivre, in *her* pictures of life, attracts the spectator. There may be, now and then, something, as in Dutch pictures, which had been as well away; but this apart, all the rest is true, and pleasant, and hearty; the grouping perfect, the color faithful, and enduring too —despite the cruel sneer of Pope, who, in the "Life of Curll," sarcastically alludes to her as "the Cook's wife in Buckingham Court." — DORAN, JOHN, 1863, *Annals of the English Stage, vol.* I, *p.* 168.

Her comedies, whether original or not; —for several of these borrow their plots from foreign sources,—bear all an unmistakable family likeness to one another. Their authoress needed no indulgence as a playwright on the score of her sex; for not one among the dramatists contemporary with her better understood the construction of light comic actions, or the use of those conventional figures of comedy which irresistibly appeal to the mirthful instincts of a popular audience. Inasmuch as she had no hesitation in resorting to the broadest expedients of farce, she was sure of the immediate effect which was all that her ambition desired; for she never flattered herself, as she confesses, "that anything she was capable of doing could support the Stage." In one instance, however, she virtually invented a personage of really novel humour; and in another she devised a character to which the genius of a great actor ensured a long-enduring life on the boards. Marplot in "The Busy-Body" and Don Felix in "The Wonder" are creations upon which any comic dramatist might look back with satisfaction; and on the former, indeed, Mrs. Centlivre relies as conferring a real title to popular favour. As a rule, however, her characters are little more than thin outlines left to the actor to fill up. This cavil applies particularly to those of her comedies which are to all intents and purposes mere pictures of manners.— WARD, ADOLPHUS WILLIAM, 1875–99, *A History of English Dramatic Literature, vol.* III, *p.* 488.

The comedies of Mrs. Centlivre are often ingenious and sprightly, and the comic scenes are generally brisk. Mrs. Centlivre troubled herself little about invention, "A Bold Stroke for a Wife," being the only work for which she is at the pains to claim absolute originality. So far as regards the stage, she may boast a superiority over almost all her country-women, since two of her comedies remain in the list of acting plays. More than one other work is capable, with some alterations, of being acted. A keen politician, she displays in some of her dramatic writings a strong whig bias, which was in part responsible for their success.— KNIGHT, JOSEPH, 1887, *Dictionary of National Biography, vol.* IX, *p.* 422.

The best of her plays are "The Busy-body" and "A Bold Stroke for a Wife," from the last of which comes at least one universally known and quoted phrase, "the real Simon Pure." They are nearer literature than Cibber's, but they are chiefly interesting because they show the change of taste. The theme is still intrigue, but it is almost always unsuccessful.—SAINTS-BURY, GEORGE, 1898, *A Short History of English Literature, p.* 496.

Thomas D'Urfey

1653–1723

Thomas D'Urfey, born in Devonshire about 1630, lived to be very old, was known in the reign of George I. as one of the wits of the time of Charles II., and was "Tom" to the last, so that even the stone over his grave recorded of him "Tom D'Urfey: died February 26, 1723." He wrote plays, operas, poems, and songs, and was a diner-out among great people, whom he entertained by singing his own songs to his own music. That was his chief title to honour, and he was so well known that a country gentleman who came to London must not go home till he was able to say that he had met Tom D'Urfey. In 1676, D'Urfey began with "Archery Revived," a heroic poem; a tragedy, "The Siege of Memphis;" and a comedy, "The Fond Husband; or, The Plotting Sister." Comedies, with an occasional tragedy or tragicomedy, then followed one another fast. In 1682, D'Urfey, who had nothing of Butler's substance in him, published a satire, called "Butler's Ghost; or, Hudibras, the Fourth Part: with Reflections on these Times." A volume of songs by D'Urfey appeared in 1687, and the collection made from time to time was completed in six volumes by the year 1720, as "Wit and Mirth; or, Pills to Purge Melancholy: being a large Collection of Ballads, Sonnets, etc., with their Tunes."—MORLEY, HENRY, 1879, *A Manual of English Literature*, ed. Tyler, p. 422.

PERSONAL

The two poets I have mentioned, are Pindar and Mr. D'Urfey. The former of these is long since laid in his urn, after having, many years together, endeared himself to all Greece by his tuneful compositions. Our countryman is still living, and in a blooming old age, that still promises many musical productions; for if I am not mistaken, our British swan will sing to the last. . . . I myself remember King Charles the Second leaning on Tom D'Urfey's shoulder more than once, and humming over a song with him. It is certain that monarch was not a little supported by "Joy to great Cæsar," which gave the whigs such a blow as they were not able to recover that whole reign. . . . As my friend, after the manner of the old lyrics, accompanies his works with his own voice, he has been the delight of the most polite companies and conversations, from the beginning of King Charles the Second's reign to our present times. Many an honest gentleman has got a reputation in his country, by pretending to have been in company with Tom D'Urfey. . . . I must not omit that my old friend angles for a trout the best of any man in England. May-flies come in late this season, or I myself should, before now, have had a trout of his hooking.—ADDISON, JOSEPH, 1713, *The Guardian, No.* 67.

Mr. Rowe, the poet laureate, is dead, and has left a damned jade of a Pegasus. I'll answer for it, he won't do as your mare did, having more need of Lucan's present than Sir Richard Blackmore. I would fain have Pope get a patent for life for the place, with a power of putting in Durfey his deputy.—ARBUTHNOT, JOHN, 1718, *Letter to Swift, Dec.* 11.

D'Urfey, Thomas, the poet, ingenius for witty madrigals, buried Tuesday 26 day of February, 1722-3, in St. James' Church in Middlesex, *at the charge of the Duke of Dorset.*—NEVE, PETER LE, 1723, *Diary.*

Here lies the Lyrick, who, with tale and song,
Did life to three score years and ten prolong;
His tale was pleasant and his song was sweet,
His heart was cheerful—but his thirst was great.
Grieve, Reader, grieve, that he too soon grown old,
His song has ended, and his tale is told.
—ANON, 1726, *Epitaph on Tom D'Urfey, Miscellaneous Poems, vol.* I, *p.* 6.

He existed, or rather, I might say, flourished for forty-six years or more, living chiefly on the bounty of his patrons. He was always a welcome guest wherever he went, and even though stuttering was one of his failings, he could sing a song right well, and greatly to the satisfaction of the Merry Monarch. His publications are numerous; but Tom, it may be surmised, did not make much by his "copy." The chance profits of benefit nights brought more into his pockets than the sale of his plays to the booksellers. Tom was at home—perfectly at his ease—in three noble houses: Knowle, in Kent, the princely seat of the witty Earl of Dorset; Leicester House, in Leicester Square; and Winchendon, in Bucks, the stately residence of the licentious but gifted Philip, Duke of Wharton. Many are the stories on record of his sayings and doings at these places, and the revelry that took place at the jovial meetings of Tom and his great companions must have been of rich order.—RIMBAULT, EDWARD F., 1866, *Notes and Queries, Third Series, vol.* 10, *p.* 465.

And this it is to be an immortal bard! For bays so perishable and laurels that withered so soon, Tom gave up the labours of a long and industrious life. He discounted his own glory, it is true, and had that enjoyment of fame in his lifetime which many a better bard only gets after death. It is something, even if you are put away on the shelves and forgotten as soon as the funeral-service has been read over you, to have been compared by Addison with Pindar, and honourably mentioned in the same sentence with Terence and Horace. Very few of his contemporaries were so fortunate, and most of them cultivated the divine art without meeting any such reward either in life or after it. It is thus that Tom had one immense advantage over his fellows: he made the world laugh, while they only made the world yawn. . . . In Tom D'Urfey's nature there was not an ounce of malice; little as we know of him, there is yet enough to justify, amply and entirely, Addison's recommendation, that the world could not possibly do kindness to a more diverting companion, to a more cheerful, honest, and good-natured man. With lower aims and lower ideas he was the Hood of his period. It is well for our age, that modern humorists have discovered the art of promoting laughter by the employment of drugs less noxious than those with which poor Tom was fain to compound his "Pills." And after all, as we need not take this medicine of his, and there is no fear that it will ever be prescribed to melancholy boys and girls, it really doesn't matter any longer.—BESANT, WALTER, 1872, *Tom D'Urfey, Belgravia, vol.* 18, *pp.* 429, 436.

GENERAL

I have not quoted one Latin author since I came down, but have learned without book a song of Mr. Thomas Durfey's, who is your only poet of tolerable reputation in this country. He makes all the merriment in our entertainments. . . . Any man, of any quality, is heartily welcome to the best toping-table of our gentry, who can roundly hum out some fragments or rhapsodies of his works. . . . Dares any one despise him who has made so many men drink? . . . But give us your ancient poet Mr. Durfey. —POPE, ALEXANDER, 1710, *Letter to Henry Cromwell, April* 10, *Works, ed. Elwin, vol.* VI, *pp.* 91, 92.

A judicious author some years since published a collection of sonnets, which he very successfully called "Laugh and be Fat; or, Pills to purge Melancholy." I cannot sufficiently admire the facetious title of these volumes, and must censure the world of ingratitude, while they are so negligent in rewarding the jocose labours of my friend Mr. D'Urfey, who was so large a contributor to this treatise, and to whose humorous productions so many rural squires in the remotest parts of this island are obliged for the dignity and state which corpulency gives them. The story of the sick man's breaking an imposthume by a sudden fit of laughter, is too well known to need a recital. It is my opinion, that the above pills would be extremely proper to be taken with asses' milk, and mightily contribute towards the renewing and restoring decayed lungs.—STEELE, RICHARD, 1713, *The Guardian, No.* 29.

Nothing distinguishes his songs more than the uncouthness and irregularity of the metre in which they are written; the modern Pindaric odes, which are humorously resembled to a comb with the teeth broken by frequent use, are nothing to them. Besides that he was able to set English words to Italian airs, as in the instance of "Blouzabella my buxom doxy," which he made to an air of Bononcini, beginning "Pastorella che trà le selve," he had the art of jumbling long and short quantities so dexterously together, that they counteracted each other, so that order resulted from confusion. Of this happy talent he has given us various specimens, in adapting songs to tunes composed in such measures as scarce any instrument but the drum would express; and, to be even with the musicians for giving him so much trouble, he composed songs in metres so broken and intricate, that few could be found that were able to suit them with musical notes. It is said that he once challenged Purcell to set to music such a song as he would write, and gave him that well-known ballad "One long Whitsun holiday," which cost the latter more pains to fit with a tune than the composition of his Te Deum.—HAWKINS, SIR JOHN, 1776, *A General History of the Science and Practice of Music*, ch. clxxiii, *p.* 818.

His plays are numerous, his poems less so: the former have not been acted for many years, and the latter are seldom read.—NOBLE, MARK, 1806, *A Biographical History of England*, vol. I, *p.* 258.

The secret of D'Urfey's popularity as a song-writer, lay in his selection of the tunes. He trenched upon the occupation of the professed ballad-writers, by adopting the airs which had been their exclusive property, and by taking the subjects of their ballads; altering them to give them as his own.—CHAPPELL, WILLIAM, 1845–59, *Popular Music of the Olden Time*, vol. II, *p.* 623.

The procession, as it marched, sang "Joy to Great Cæsar," a loyal ode, which had lately been written by Durfey, and which, though, like all Durfey's writings, utterly contemptible, was, at that time, almost as popular as Lillibullero became a few years later.—MACAULAY, THOMAS BABINGTON, 1849, *History of England*, ch. iv.

It is singular, when we consider the boldness and uncompromising audacity of Addison's comparison of D'Urfey with Pindar, to observe how completely posterity has forgotten all about him. He wrote operas which were never sung after his death; comedies which could not hold the stage; tragedies which I believe—for I have actually read one—never did or could please; congratulatory verses which of course no man living or dead ever did read; satires of which the edge is taken off and the point blunted; stories "tragical, moral, and comical," which are very very dreary; and songs—songs patriotic, humourous, erotic, and anacreontic—still to be read in his famous collection. As it is difficult to pick out his own from the rest, some of his making may yet survive, if only one could recognise them.—

BESANT, WALTER, 1872, *Tom D'Urfey Belgravia*, vol. 18, *p.* 429.

He seems to have derived from his French blood a persistent amiability, which Tom Brown failed to upset and Jeremy Collier could scarcely disturb. Nor can it be denied that his songs amused four successive monarchs and their lieges, in the houses of the nobility, on the race-course, in the tavern, and in the theatre. His dramatic activity proper, however, calls for no detailed review. He adapted, or borrowed from, Shakspere, Chapman, Marston, Beaumont and Fletcher, Shirley, Marmion, Dryden, and doubtless many others, besides occasionally attempting original works; and he wrote altogether twenty-nine plays which were acted, and three which were not, comprising tragedies, comedies, operas serious and comical, and burlesques and extravaganzas under divers designations. He appears to have given a large amount of pleasure to great and small in his day—which was a long one—and to have been no very conspicuous sinner against a propriety which could hardly be expected to form part of his stock-in-trade.—WARD, ADOLPHUS WILLIAM, 1875–99, *A History of English Dramatic Literature*, vol. III, *p.* 454.

Three editions of it appeared in his lifetime, but no modern reprint of his dramas has been attempted, the contemporary issue having been large enough to keep the market supplied. His songs have never lost popularity, and many are still sung throughout Scotland under the belief that they were native to the soil.—EBSWORTH, J. W., 1888, *Dictionary of National Biography*, vol. XVI, *p.* 254.

Collier has not the slightest difficulty in proving the veteran Dryden and the new, brilliant, uncompromising Vanbrugh guilty of an infinite number of breaches of decorum. What is more surprising is that he should have thought it worth while to criticise Tom D'Urfey's twentieth play, when the nineteen that preceded it did but combine to prove him a scurrilous and witless buffoon, on whose shoulder the king might lean to hum over a song, but whom it was needless to discuss in any grave examination of British dramatic literature.—GOSSE, EDMUND, 1888, *Life of William Congreve (Great Writers)*, *p.* 110.

Below mediocrity.—GARNETT, RICHARD, 1895, *The Age of Dryden*, *p.* 119.

Increase Mather

1639–1723

Increase Mather, clergyman, born Dorchester, Mass., 21 June, 1639. Son of Richard. Graduated at Harvard and at Trinity College, Dublin. After preaching in various parts of England and in the island of Guernsey, he returned to America in 1661 on account of the Restoration, being unwilling to conform. He divided his time between the North Church at Boston and his father's church at Dorchester until 1664, when he was regularly ordained pastor of the former, holding the position until his death. He was elected president of Harvard in 1681, but did not accept. Was elected acting president, 1685, became president in 1692 and served until 1701. By his own statement, he concurred in the opinion of the twelve clergymen who advised Gov. William Phips to proceed with the witchcraft trials in June, 1692, but having become convinced of the unreliability of the so-called "spectre-evidence," he published a book called "Cases of Conscience concerning Witchcrafts and Evil Spirits personating Men" (1693), deprecating convictions for this alone. In this book, however, he expressed his approval of his son Cotton's "Wonders of the Invisible World." He had meanwhile rendered the colony valuable services in England. Originally a leader in the opposition to the surrender of the colony's charter, demanded by Governor Andros in 1687, he was sent to England the year after to plead the colony's cause. He obtained a new and fairly satisfactory charter from William and Mary, and returned with it in 1692. This instrument united the colonies of Massachusetts and Plymouth under one jurisdiction, and remained in force up to the Revolution. The list of his published volumes numbers one hundred and thirty-six, some of which are "The Life and Death of Rev. Richard Mather" (1670), "Heavens Alarm to the World" (1681), and "An Essay for the Recording of Illustrious Providences" (1684), also known as "Remarkable Providences." Died, Boston, Mass., 23 Aug., 1723.—STEDMAN, ARTHUR, 1890, *A Library of American Literature, ed. Stedman and Hutchinson, vol. XI, p. 551.*

PERSONAL

In the morning, repairing to his study (where his custom was to sit up very late, even until midnight and perhaps after it) he deliberately read a chapter, and made a prayer, and then plied what of reading and writing he had before him. At nine o'clock, he came down and read a chapter, and made a prayer with his family. He then returned unto the work of the study. Coming down to dinner, he quickly went up again, and begun the afternoon with another prayer. There he went on with the work of the study till the evening. Then with another prayer he again went unto his Father; after which he did more at the work of the study. At nine o'clock, he came down to his family sacrifices. Then he went up again to the work of the study, which anon he concluded with another prayer; and so he betook himself unto his repose.—MATHER, COTTON, 1725, *Parentator, p.* 181.

He lived to see wonderful changes in the political hemisphere. The Mathers were a race of puritans; he knew the strict sect first in his native plains of North America; but wishing to have a nearer view of it, he came to Britain when it was in its meridian splendor, in the reign of Charles I. The saints could do no other than find employment for the talents of so far-famed an apostle. He settled at Gloucester, where he remained until the brightest plumage of this sect had faded away. Leaving the city of Gloucester, he retired to Guernsey, where he acted as chaplain to a regiment; but the violence which had expelled him from Gloucester followed him even there, so that he applied himself again to the favourite seat of his beloved system of Gospel grace. There new honours, greater than Britain would have bestowed upon him: he was elevated to the highest seat of learning, being elected president of Harvard college in Cambridge, in New England. As an American author he has done credit to the appointment.—NOBLE, MARK, 1806, *A Biographical History of England, vol.* I, *p.* 136.

During his presidency of Harvard College, Mr. Mather received the title of Doctor in Divinity from the faculty of that institution. His diploma was the first of the kind issued in America, and he was a worthy recipient of that honor.—LOSSING, BENSON J., 1855–86, *Eminent Americans, p.* 48.

Probably he came nearer than any other man of modern times to the apostle's requisition, of "praying always, with all prayer and supplication in the spirit." In addition to mental ejaculations—those arrows of which his biographer tells us his quiver was full—he was habitually on his knees six times a day, in his family and closet prayers!—CLARK, JOSEPH S., 1861, *Increase Mather, The Congregational Quarterly, vol. 3, p.* 328.

Here, then, was a person, born in America, bred in America,—a clean specimen of what America could do for itself in the way of keeping up the brave stock of its first imported citizens; a man every way capable of filling any place in public leadership made vacant by the greatest of the Fathers; probably not a whit behind the best of them in scholarship, in eloquence, in breadth of view, in knowledge of affairs, in every sort of efficiency. As to learning, it has been said that he even exceeded all other New-Englanders of the colonial time, except his own son, Cotton. On the day when he was graduated at our little rustic university, he had the accomplishments usual among the best scholars of the best universities of the old world; he could converse fluently in Latin, and could read and write Hebrew and Greek; and his numberless publications in after life bear marks of a range of learned reading that widened as he went on in years, and drew into its hospitable gulf some portions of nearly all literatures, especially the most obscure and uncouth. His habits as a student were those of the mighty theologians and pulpit-orators among whom he grew up. He had the appalling capacity of working in his study sixteen hours a day.—TYLER, MOSES COIT, 1878, *A History of American Literature,* 1676–1765, *vol.* II, *p.* 69.

GENERAL

But though less learned than his son, and possessing less exuberance of fancy,

he had more sound, practical judgment—more common sense. His publications many of them are still extant. The style will compare with that of the best authors of the seventeenth century. As a preacher, Dr. Mather was at the head of his profession in this country.— POND, ENOCH, 1847, *Life of Increase Mather, p.* 142.

Mather was a learned man, and a solid and (we are told) effective sermonizer, whose printed discourses have a wide range, abound in quotations, after the fashion of the time, served their purpose, and really were not worth typographical perpetuation. Most printed sermons are like letter-files or bound volumes of daily newspapers, never referred to, save for a date, and for controversial purposes, and those of this great Boston figure are not exceptions. Increase Mather apparently had a deeper knowledge than that of Cotton, with less facility, less fondness for display, and less bungling inaccuracy. —RICHARDSON, CHARLES F., 1887, *American Literature,* 1607–1885, *vol.* I, *p.* 126.

He was learned, sober, and accurate; and curiously bound up in his massive character was a taste for the supernatural, which found literary expression in the only noticeable work of his that has reached our day, "An Essay for the Recording of Illustrious Providences." It is a bundle of strange coincidences, escapes, punishments and ghost-stories, each bearing an obstrusive moral. The book served as a sort of introduction to the Salem witchcraft delusion, which ran its course a few years later. In modern aftertype, without the morals, is the "Phantasms of the Living," recently published by the English Society for Psychical Research. — HAWTHORNE, JULIAN AND LEMMON, LEONARD, 1891, *American Literature, p.* 10.

The last of the clerical autocrats.— BATES, KATHARINE LEE, 1897, *American Literature, p.* 42.

Elkanah Settle

1648–1724

Born at Dunstable, went from Oxford to London to make a living by his pen. In 1671 he made a hit by his tragedy of "Cambyses." To annoy Dryden, Rochester got his "Empress of Morocco" played at Whitehall by the court lords and ladies. In "Absalom and Achitophel" Dryden scourged "Doeg" with his scorn, and Settle speedily relapsed into obscurity. In 1718 he was admitted to the Charterhouse.— PATRICK AND GROOME. eds., 1897, *Chambers's Biographical Dictionary, p.* 843.

PERSONAL

Doeg, though without knowing how or why,
Made still a blundering kind of melody;
Spurred boldly on, and dashed through thick
and thin,
Through sense and nonsense, never out nor
in;
Free from all meaning, whether good or bad,
And, in one word, heroically mad,
He was too warm on picking-work to dwell,
But faggoted his notions as they fell,
And, if they rhymed and rattled, all was
well.
Spiteful he is not, though he wrote a satire,
For still there goes some thinking to ill-
nature;
He needs no more than birds and beasts to
think,
All his occasions are to eat and drink.
If he call rogue and rascal from a garret,
He means you no more mischief than a par-
rot;
The words for friend and foe alike were made,
To fetter them in verse is all his trade.
For almonds he'll cry whore to his own
mother
And call young Absalom King David's
brother.
—DRYDEN, JOHN, 1682, *Absalom and
Achitophel*, pt. ii.

If Settle was capable of these mean
compliances of writing for, or against a
party, as he was hired, he must have
possessed a very sordid mind, and been
totally devoid of all the principles of
honour; but as there is no other authority for it than Wood, who is enthusiastic
in his temper, and often writes of things,
not as they were, but as he would wish
them to be, the reader may give what
credit he pleases to the report.—CIBBER,
THEOPHILUS, 1753, *Lives of the Poets*,
vol. iii, *p.* 350.

Elkanah Settle was so systematically
visited with damnation, that he was at
last compelled to bring out his plays
under fictitious names, and during the
long vacation, lest when the town was
full, some enemy should discover him.—
DORAN, JOHN, 1863, *Annals of the English
Stage, vol.* ii, *p.* 152.

GENERAL

An Author now living, whose *Muse* is
chiefly addicted to Tragedy; and has been
tragically dealt withal by a Tyranical
Laureat; which has somewhat eclips'd
the glory he at first appeared in: But
Time has her vicissitudes; and he has lived
to see his Enemy humbled, if not justly
punished; for this Reason, I shall not
afresh animadvert upon his fault, but
rather bury them in Oblivion; and without any Reflections on his Poetry, give a
succinct Account of those Plays, which
he has published, being Nine in Number.
—LANGBAINE, GERARD, 1691, *An Account
of the English Dramatick Poets*, p. 439.

Settle, in his Anti-Achitophel, was
assisted by Matthew Clifford, Sprat, and
several of the best hands of those times.
—LOCKIER, DR., DEAN OF PETERBOROUGH,
1730–32, *Spence's Anecdotes, ed. Singer*,
p. 51.

"The Empress of Morocco, a Tragedy;"
acted at the Duke of York's Theatre.
This play was likewise acted at court, as
appears by the two Prologues prefixed,
which were both spoken by the Lady Elizabeth Howard; the first Prologue was
written by the Earl of Mulgrave, the other
by Lord Rochester, when it was performed
at court, the Lords and Ladies of the Bedchamber played in it. Mr. Dryden, Mr.
Shadwell, and Mr. Crowne, wrote against
it, which began a famous controversy
betwixt the wits of the town, wherein,
says Jacob, Mr. Dryden was roughly
handled, particularly by the lord Rochester, and the duke of Buckingham, and
Settle got the laugh on his side.—CIBBER,
THEOPHILUS, 1753, *Lives of the Poets*,
vol. iii, *p* 350.

Elkanah Settle, who had answered
"Absalom," appeared with equal courage
in opposition to "The Medal," and published an answer called "The Medal
reversed," with so much success in both
encounters, that he left the palm doubtful, and divided the suffrages of the
nation. Such are the revolutions of fame,
or such is the prevalence of fashion, that
the man whose works have not yet been
thought to deserve the care of collecting
them, who died forgotten in an hospital,
and whose latter years were spent in contriving shews for fairs, and carrying an
elegy or epithalamium, of which the
beginning and end were occasionally
varied, but the intermediate parts were
always the same, to every house where
there was a funeral or a wedding, might
with truth have had inscribed upon his
stone,
Here lies the Rival and Antagonist of Dryden.
—JOHNSON, SAMUEL, 1779–81, *Dryden,
Lives of the English Poets*.

This poor wight had acquired by practice, and perhaps from nature, more of a poetical ear than most of his contemporaries were gifted with.—SCOTT, SIR WALTER, 1808-21, *The Life of John Dryden*.

In 1676 was performed his "Ibrahim, the Illustrious Bassa," of which I can give an account at first hand, and which is interesting as founded on Madeleine de Scudéry's "Ibrahim, ou l'Illustre Bassa," which her brother Georges had reproduced as a play. It must in candour be allowed that Settle's tragedy furnishes a fair example of a heroic play on a French love-story of the accepted type, written in rime, devoid of any trace of poetic afflatus, but on the whole (though exceptions might no doubt be here and there noted) free from rant. In spite of the accumulation of deaths in the last act, and of the pathetically conceived character of the self-sacrificing Asteria, the whole, however, leaves but a tame and commonplace impression behind it. The result is due above all to the flooding of both action and characters by the resistless waters of "heroic love," which take every trace of distinctive colour or complexion out of Turk and Persian, Mussulman Roxana and Christian Isabella, alike.— WARD, ADOLPHUS WILLIAM, 1875-99, *A History of English Dramatic Literature*, *vol.* III, *p.* 397.

Settle's character was beneath contempt, and his works are of a piece with his character; the first was a compound of flighty imbecility and grotesque presumption, and the second are a compound of sordid scurrility and soaring nonsense. —COLLINS, JOHN CHURTON, 1878-95, *Dryden, Quarterly Review; Essays and Studies*, *p.* 46.

Elkanah Settle was one of Rochester's innumerable led-poets, and was too utterly beneath contempt to deserve even Rochester's spite. The character of Doeg, ten years later, did Settle complete justice. He had a "blundering kind of melody" about him but absolutely nothing else. However, a heroic play of his, the "Empress of Morocco," had considerable vogue for some incomprehensible reason.—SAINTS-BURY, GEORGE, 1881, *Dryden (English Men of Letters)*, *p.* 53.

Settle was a smaller foe than Shadwell, although as a dramatist he had gained fame enough to make Dryden envious.

The quarrel between them was pitiful enough, and Dryden lowered himself to Settle's level. He could not well have sunk lower; but the marvel is, that when these poets were living the gulf that separates them was by no means so evident as it is to us. Settle, in some of his writings, divided with Dryden, as Johnson observes, the suffrages of the nation; yet he was both a mean poet and a mean man. —DENNIS, JOHN, 1883, *Heroes of Literature*, *p.* 176.

This absurd creature lives embalmed in the anger of Dryden, but he had a moment of not illegitimate success. . . . For a moment Settle was at the top of the fashion, but he had neither talent nor principle, and he soon sank into contempt.— GOSSE, EDMUND, 1888, *A History of Eighteenth Century Literature*, *p.* 59.

Miserable as his lampoons are, a line here and there is not destitute of piquancy; and if his "Empress of Morocco" (1673) has no literary pretensions, it is important in literary history for having so moved the wrath of Dryden, and in the history of the drama for having been issued with plates which contribute greatly to our knowledge of the internal arrangements of the Restoration Theatre. By a singular irony of fortune, his fate bears some analogy to that of his mighty antagonist. Settle lost caste by changing his politics at the wrong time, as Dryden his religion; but while Dryden bore up against the storm of adversity, Settle sunk into obscurity, and ultimately into the Charter House. Of his twenty plays none but "The Empress of Morocco" is now ever mentioned, unless an exception be made in favour of "Ibrahim, the Illustrious Bassa."—GARNETT, RICHARD, 1895, *The Age of Dryden*, *p.* 118.

Settle was not deficient in promise as scholar, rhymester, and wit; but he wrecked his career by his tergiversation and by his inept efforts to measure his mediocre capacity against the genius of Dryden. He soon became a butt for caricature as a voluminous and reckless dunce. "Recanting Settle," wrote a critic, when his tragedies and libels could no more yield him penny loaves and ale, "bids our youth by his example fly, the Love of Politics and Poetry."—SECCOMBE, THOMAS, 1897, *Dictionary of National Biography*, *vol.* LI, *p.* 274.

Mrs. Mary de la Riviere Manley
1672?-1724

Mrs. De la Riviere Manley, novelist and dramatist (born 1672, died 1724), wrote "Secret Memoirs and Manners of several Persons of Quality of both Sexes from the New Atalantis" (1736); also "The Royal Mischief" (1696); "The Lover Lost" (1696); "Lucius" (1717); "Bath Intrigues;" "A Stage Coach Journey to Exeter;" "The Secret History of Queen Zarah;" "The Adventures of Rivella;" "Memoirs of Europe;" "Court Intrigues;" and other works. Her "Memoirs" were published in 1717.— ADAMS, W. DAVENPORT, 1877, *Dictionary of English Literature*, p. 414.

PERSONAL

I am heartily sorry for her; she has very generous principles for one of her sort, and a great deal of good sense and invention; she is about forty, very homely and very fat.—SWIFT, JONATHAN, 1711-12, *Letter to Stella*, Jan. 28.

Being advanced to the autumn of her charms, she conversed with the opposite sex, in a manner very delicate, sensible, and agreeable, and when she felt that time had left his impression upon her brow, she did not court praise and flattery. The greatest genius's of the times conversed freely with her, and gave her daily proofs of esteem, and friendship, except Sir Richard Steele, with whom it seems she was at variance; and indeed Sir Richard sufficiently exposed himself by his manner of taking revenge; for he published to the world that it was his own fault he was not happy with Mrs. Manley, for which omission he publickly, and gravely asked her pardon. These are the most material incidents in the life of our poetess; a lady, who was born with high powers from nature, which were afterwards cultivated by enjoying the brightest conversation; the early part of her life was unfortunate, she fell a sacrifice to a seducer, who laid the foundation for those errors she afterwards committed, and of those sufferings she underwent; she had a high relish for the pleasures of life; she was extremely susceptible of the passion of love, and treated it with a peculiar vivacity.—CIBBER, THEOPHILUS, 1753, *Lives of the Poets*, vol. IV, p. 18.

This demirep—to give her a name exactly as much above her deserts as it is below those of an honest woman.—DE MORGAN, AUGUSTUS, 1856, *The New Atalantis, Notes and Queries, Second Series*, vol. 2, p. 265.

Except that he was a scoundrel, there is, I believe, little known of the individual who was the (pretended) husband of Mrs. Manley. If it had not been for his villany, Mrs. De la Rivière Manley might have borne a name among the most virtuous, as she was one of the wittiest, of women. . . . She never recovered the downfall which she owed to that heartless ruffian her cousin. Men were afraid of her wit, and ladies talked of, at, and against her, behind their fans, as a dreadfully intriguing hussey, who ruined the men out of revenge for the outrage by which one man had embittered her whole life. All the miseries and vices of that life (which terminated in 1734, [?] at the house of Alderman Barber, when she was about threescore and a few odd years), were owing to her wretched betrayer. She was betrayed, not seduced; and *she* who had qualities which, properly developed, might have rendered her name an honoured name on the roll of virtuous and accomplished women, is remembered with a sort of scorn, because our memories more easily hold on to her faults than to the wrongs by which she was led into error. I once met, in an old paper, with the name of Manley among some convicts sent to execution: I hope, with all my heart, that CL. HOPPER, in his farther inquiries, may discover that the atrocious miscreant who ruined Miss Manley, body and soul, who abandoned her to misery, drove her into vice, and made of her name a by-word of scorn, was, as he deserved to be, hanged like a dog.—DORAN, JOHN, 1857, *The Husband of Mrs. Manley, Notes and Queries, Second Series*, vol. 3, pp. 350, 351.

NEW ATALANTIS
1709

As long as "Atalantis" shall be read.
—POPE, ALEXANDER, 1712-14, *The Rape of the Lock*, v, 165.

The testimony of Mrs. Manley is of course wholly valueless except as an indication that scandal was current.—

ASPLAND, R. BROOK, 1856, *Lord Halifax and Mrs. Barton, Notes and Queries, Second Series, vol. 2, p. 390.*

Thus does the same conjectural fact, or figment, afford either a field for the cultivation of the choicest fruits, or a waste place for the reception of the vilest refuse.—WILLIAMS, JANE, 1861, *The Literary Women of England, p. 155.*

One of the worst books I know—the worst in style and worst in morals, and fully deserves the oblivion into which it has fallen. It is impossible to read it through; and that it should ever have been popular—the edition I have before me is the seventh—notwithstanding Pope's line,

"As long as Atalantis shall be read,"

is almost incredible, and denotes a taste utterly depraved. To a certain extent, however, this may be accounted for by the fact that it is a scandalous chronicle of persons in high life under thinly disguised names, and reveals or invents their amours and intrigues.—FORSYTH, WILLIAM, 1871, *Novels and Novelists of the Eighteenth Century, p. 197.*

That "cornucopia of scandal" "The New Atalantis," in which almost every public character of the day had his or her niche. This scurrilous book passed through a great number of editions; it amused Swift, who determined to make use of the author. . . . We would willingly give a page from "The New Atalantis," but unfortunately it is precisely where Mrs. Manley is most picturesque that it is least possible to quote from her.—GOSSE, EDMUND, 1888, *A History of Eighteenth Century Literature, p. 206.*

GENERAL

It appears from the preface ["Lost Lover"] that it was unsuccessful—Mrs. Manley was very imprudent in allowing a play to be acted, which she says she wrote in 7 days.—GENEST, P., 1832, *Some Account of the English Stage, vol. II, p. 75.*

The great society novelist of an age to which she should not be too severely condemned for having held up a mirror. Of her cleverness there can be no doubt, and if she had little consideration for the good fame of others, she had at least the courage of her intentions, and held her own not only by the fear she inspired.—WARD, ADOLPHUS WILLIAM, 1875-99, *A*

History of English Dramatic Literature, vol. III, p. 432.

While young she was basely tricked out of her character; but the prurience of her compositions must suggest to her readers that her virtue hung rather loosely about her, and would, even under favourable circumstances, have been a possession difficult to retain. She earned her living partly by a profession which the refinement of the present age forbids naming, and partly by writing romances and plays which, being among the most licentious works in the English language, had of course a considerable sale. In 1709 appeared her "Memoirs from the New Atlantis," a long series of anecdotes, in which lawless desire is depicted with a warmth of colouring which only female genius can give, but which to a reader not utterly depraved in taste, becomes monotonous from the apparent inability of the authoress to treat of any other theme. It was principally designed as a satire upon the Whigs all round, and excited no little indignation in a number of grave statesmen, who found themselves to their astonishment figuring, under thinly-disguised names, as heroes in all sorts of amorous tales.—WYON, FREDERICK WILLIAM, 1876, *The History of Great Britain During the Reign of Queen Anne, vol. II, p. 325.*

The one fact that she was the first woman of her country to support herself entirely by the pen, itself establishes her right to a certain place in the long line of female writers who have since her day done so much for literature.—HUDSON, WILLIAM HENRY, 1897, *Two Novelists of the English Restoration, Idle Hours in a Library, p. 155.*

Nobody can peruse the pages of Mrs. Manley herself, despite their coarseness and violence, without recognising a literary gift. She was a political caricaturist, but she had a talent for her trade.

"She seemed to laugh and squall in rhymes,
And all her gestures were lampoons."

And the frailties of her life were imposed by her surroundings. It is hard that such a woman should have been forced into Lintot's protection, and have ended an unaided struggle in want and illness.—SICHEL, WALTER, 1901, *Bolingbroke and His Times, p. 86.*

Henry Sacheverell

1674?–1724

Henry Sacheverell. Born at Marlborough, England, 1672; died at London, June 5, 1724. An English clergyman and Tory politician. He studied at Magdalen College, Oxford, and was associated there with Addison, with whom he shared his rooms. He came into notice as preacher of St. Saviour's, Southwark. For two sermons criticizing the Whig ministry, preached Aug. 14 and Nov. 5, 1709, he was prosecuted at the instigation of Godolphin, and March 23, 1710, suspended for three years. He was reinstated by the Tory ministry, April 13, 1713.—SMITH, BENJAMIN E., 1894–97, *The Century Cyclopedia of Names, p.* 878.

PERSONAL

Dr. Sacheverel came this morning, to give me thanks for getting his brother an employment. It was but six or seven weeks since I spoke to lord-treasurer for him. Sacheverel brought Trap along with him. . . . Trap is a coxcomb, and the other is not very deep; and their judgment in things of wit and sense is miraculous.—SWIFT, JONATHAN, 1711–12, *Journal to Stella, March* 17.

An ignorant and impudent incendiary, the scorn of those who made him their tool.—MARLBOROUGH, SARAH DUTCHESS, 1724, *Account of her Conduct, p.* 247.

On Friday, June 5, in the evening, Dr. Henry Sacheverell, rector of St. Andrews, Holburn, (worth about 700 libs. per an.) departed this life at Highgate. . . . He was a bold man, and of a good presence, and delivered a thing better than a much more modest man, however preferable in learning, could do. He was but an indifferent scholar, but pretended to a great deal of honesty, which I could never see in him, since he was the forwardest to take the oaths, notwithstanding he would formerly be so forward in speaking for, and drinking the health of, king James III. He hath printed several things; but that which is really good, *viz.* his speech at his tryal, was none of his own, but was penned by Dr. Francis Atterbury, the deprived bishop of Rochester. He died very rich. He had a complication of disorders.—HEARNE, THOMAS, 1724, *Reliquiæ Hearnianæ, ed. Bliss, June* 14, *vol.* II, p. 202.

Was bred at the public school at Marlborough, at the charge of one Edward Hearst, an apothecary, whose wife surviving him, continued his charity to Sacheverell, and sent him to Oxford. . . . He had not been long at Oxford before she discovered his turbulent, violent, and imperious temper,—the more ill-becoming in him, because he subsisted by charity. He was remarkable for his disrespectful behaviour to his superiors and his insolence to his equals. The very make and look of him were an index to his character. . . . Having a small benefice given him in Staffordshire, he gave great scandal to the sober and religious people in his neighbourhood by his immoralities, which are set forth in a treatise entitled "Peril of being zealously, but not well-affected," written by a minister of the Church of England, one of the brotherhood of St. Katharine's. While he was at his parish, or Oxford, he fell in with the most furious of the Jacobite party, made scurrilous reflections on the death of King William and the Hanover succession; and when the queen appeared against the High-Church memorial, he had the impudence to call her a "waxen queen," "whereby," says the annalist, "he alluded to or gave the hint of the tacit jest that was put upon her at Oxford, by those who put her motto of *semper eadem* on the vane of a weathercock."—OLDMIXON, JOHN, 1730–39, *History of England, vol.* II, p. 429.

Dr. Henry Sacheverell was a man of a large and strong make, with a good symmetry of parts, of a livid rather than a ruddy complexion, and an insolent overbearing front, with large staring eyes, but no life in them,—a manifest indication of an envious, ill-natured, proud, sullen, and ambitious temper.—CHAMBERLEN, PAUL, 1738, *History of the Life and Reign of Queen Anne, p.* 331.

It is difficult to say which is most worthy of ridicule—the ministry, in arming all the powers of government in their attack upon an obscure individual, or the public in supporting a culprit whose doctrine was more odious than his insolence, and his principles yet more contemptible than his parts.—MACAULAY, CATHERINE, 1763–83, *History of England*.

His enemies triumphed, yet dared not venture abroad. He was disgraced by the legislature; but tens of thousands bent as lowly before him, as the Thibetians to the Grand Lama. He went on a tour of triumph through the country; and was received with splendid, respectful pomp, at every place he visited: magistrates, in their formalities, welcomed him into their corporations; and his guard of honour, was frequently, a thousand gentlemen on horseback. At Bridgenorth he was met by Mr. Creswell, at the head of four thousand horse; and the same number of persons on foot, wearing white knots edged with gold, and three leaves of gilt laurel in their hats. The hedges, for several miles, were dressed with garlands of flowers; and the steeples covered with flags. In this manner he passed through Warwick, Birmingham, Bridgenorth, Ludlow, and Shrewsbury, on his way to his Welch living, with a cavalcade better suited to a prince than a priest. Ridiculous as this farce was, it did some good; as it kept up the respect due to the national church, by engaging the voice of the people at large in its favor; and discouraging any attempts to lower or innovate upon it, in the smallest degree. After the three years suspension had expired, a printer gave him £100 for his first sermon; and the house of Commons, *his prosecutors*, ordered him to preach before them; thanked him for his discourse; and he was presented to the valuable rectory of St. Andrew's, Holborn. Had the ministry remained in power, he might, probably, have beeen honoured with a mitre.—NOBLE, MARK, 1806, *A Biographical History of England, vol.* II, *p.* 128.

It is a strange conclusion to the enthusiastic championship of Sacheverell in his day, that he stands alone among the objects of great popular contests, as one who has had no historical vindicator. Whatever may be said of the folly, the tyranny, or the dishonesty of his opponents, no one has a good word to say for Sacheverell himself. Nay, he gets wounded in the assault on his enemies; for a chief characteristic in their offences is that they should have made war on a creature so despicable. This view of his character and position is perhaps the reason why there seems to have been a reluctance to open up the question, by a search through the rich and curious materials left in the impeachment and the controversy. The story as it was originally told by Burnet and Tindal has been repeated over and over. And yet writers who have thus carelessly dealt in it, have attributed to Sacheverell alone the great events of the later years of Queen Anne's reign—events produced by operative causes of which the Sacheverell affair was a mere superficial phenomenon.—BURTON, JOHN HILL, 1880, *A History of the Reign of Queen Anne, vol.* II, *p.* 293.

He had a fine presence and dressed well. He was an indifferent scholar and had no care for learning, was bold, insolent, passionate, and inordinately vain. His failings stand in a strong light, because the whigs, instead of treating him and his utterances with the contempt they deserved, forced him to appear as the champion of the church's cause, a part which, both by mind and character, he was utterly unfitted to play even respectably, yet the eager scrutiny of his enemies could find little of importance to allege against his conduct, though the charge that he used profane language when irritated seems to have been true.—HUNT, REV. WILLIAM, 1897, *Dictionary of National Biography, vol.* L, *p.* 83.

GENERAL

Nay, the Tatler, the immortal Tatler, the great Bickerstaff himself was fain to leave off talking to the ladies, during the Doctor's trial, and turn his sagacious pen to the dark subject of death, and the next world; though he has not yet decided the ancient debate, whether Pluto's regions were, in point of government, a kingdom or a commonwealth.—DEFOE, DANIEL, 1710, *The Review.*

A sudden conflict rises from the swell
Of a proud slavery met by tenets strained
In Liberty's behalf. Fears, true or feigned,
Spread through all ranks; and lo! the
　　　　　　Sentinel
Who loudest rang his pulpit 'larum bell,
Stands at the Bar, absolved by female
　　　　　　eyes
Mingling their glances with grave flatteries
Lavished on *Him*—that England may rebel
Against her ancient virtue.
—WORDSWORTH, WILLIAM, 1822–23, *Ecclesiastical Sonnets, pt.* iii, *No.* xi.

So superior was this speech [before the

Lords] in composition to any thing which Sacheverell had hitherto produced, that it was well understood to be no offspring of his brain. Its merit was in general and probably with reason ascribed to Atterbury.—STANHOPE, EARL, 1870, *History of England Comprising the Reign of Queen Anne until the Peace of Utrecht, p.* 414.

His literary skill was of the most mechanical kind.—MINTO, WILLIAM, 1879, *Daniel Defoe (English Men of Letters), p.* 80.

Humphrey Prideaux
1648–1724

In the year after Queen Anne's death, Dr. Humphrey Prideaux, born in 1648, published the first part of his very useful and valuable treatise on "The Connection of the History of the Old and New Testaments;" the second part appeared in 1717. It is still held in high estimation for the care and accuracy with which the events of the Old and New Testaments are synchronised. His "Life of Mahomet" (1697), though it has necessarily been superseded by Mure and other authorities, was a meritorious work, written with much seriousness and moderation. Prideaux was a native of Cornwall. He was educated at Westminster School and Christ Church, Oxford. When about thirty, he was preferred to the living of St. Clement's, Oxford; in 1681, he obtained a prebend in Norwich Cathedral: and in 1702 he was made Dean of Norwich. Scholarly studies seem favourable to longevity; the good Dean at his death, in 1724, was seventy-six years of age.—ADAMS, W. H. DAVENPORT, 1886, *Good Queen Anne, vol.* II, *p.* 155.

PERSONAL

The late Dr. Henry Aldrich, dean of Christ Church, had but a mean opinion, and used to speak slightingly, of Dr. Humphrey Prideaux, dean of Norwich, as an unaccurate muddy headed man. Prideaux's chief skill was in Orientals, and yet even there he was far from being perfect in either, unless in Hebrew, which he was well versed in. In 1677 he was preparing for the press an edition of Dionysius Halicarnasseus, to be printed at the Theatre, but it came to nothing, I know not for what reason, unless because it was found that 'twould be as uncorrect as his "Marmora Oxoniensia," and that he would do little or nothing to it, besides heaping up notes; and yet from a letter in his own hand I gather, that he intended to be short in them, and to make them consist only of references to other authors, where the several stories were also told. As for MSS., I perceive from that letter that he would not trouble himself about any, but rest wholly upon what had been done to his hands by former editors.—HEARNE, THOMAS, 1734, *Reliquiæ Hearnianæ, ed. Bliss, Oct.* 15, *vol.* III, *p.* 157.

He endured the most dreadful maladies that can afflict the human frame, for a series of years, with a patience and resignation without a parallel. He had a strong constitution; a firm mind, and a body, able to undergo great labour, until subdued by the stone, and its dreadful consequences. At ten o'clock he retired to rest; at five he renewed his studies.—NOBLE, MARK, 1806, *A Biographical History of England, vol.* II, *p.* 109.

GENERAL

Prideaux [in "The Life of Mahomet"] and the authors of the "Modern History" you will probably think unreasonably eager to expose the faults of the prophet, and you will surely be attracted to a second consideration of the work (Koran) of Sale by the candour, the reasonableness, and the great knowledge of the subject, which that excellent author appears everywhere to display. — SMYTH, WILLIAM, 1840, *Lectures on Modern History, Lecture* iii.

Prideaux's "Connection" is a work of great research, connecting the Old with the New Testament by a luminous historical summary. Few books have had a greater circulation, and it is invaluable to all students of divinity. Its author was highly respected for his learning and piety.—CHAMBERS, ROBERT, 1876, *Cyclopædia of English Literature, ed. Carruthers.*

Prideaux's literary reputation rests on his "Life of Mahomet" (1697) and his "Connection" (1716-18). Of each of these the story has been told that the bookseller to whom he offered the manuscript said he "could wish there were a little more humour in it." No sign of humour was ever shown by Prideaux, except in his proposal (26 Nov. 1715) for a hospital in each university, to be called "Drone Hall," for useless fellows and students. The "Life of Mahomet" was in fact pointed as a polemical tract against the deists. As a biography it is valueless from the point of view of modern knowledge.—GORDON, ALEXANDER, 1896, *Dictionary of National Biography, vol.* XLVI, *p.* 353.

Jeremy Collier

1650–1726

Born, at Stow Qui (or Quire), Cambridgeshire, 23 Sept. 1650. Educated at his father's school at Ipswich. To Caius Coll., Cambridge, as "poor scholar," 10 April 1669; B.A., 1672; M.A., 1676; Ordained Deacon, 24 Sept., 1676; Priest, 24 Feb. 1677. Chaplain to Dowager Countess of Dorset at Knowle, 1677–79. Rector of Ampton, Suffolk, 25 Sept. 1679 to 1685. Lecturer at Gray's Inn, 1685 [or 1686?]. Took up definite position as non-juror. Imprisoned for three months in Newgate owing to political pamphlet, 1688. Another short imprisonment, Nov. 1692. Much controversial writing on political and religious topics. Attack on stage begun, 1698. Consecrated as nonjuring bishop, 1713. Religious controversy; and abortive attempt to form union with Eastern Church. Died, in London, 26 April 1726. Buried in churchyard of St. Pancras. *Works:* "The Difference between the Present and Future State of our Bodies," 1686; "The Comparison between Giving and Receiving," 1687; "The Office of a Chaplain" (anon.), 1688; "The Disertion discuss'd" (anon.), 1688; "Vindiciæ Juris Regni" (anon.), 1689; "Animadversions upon the Modern Explanation of . . . a king *de facto*" (anon.), 1689; "A Caution against Inconstancy" (anon.), 1690; "A Dialogue concerning the Times," 1690; "To the Right Hon. the Lords and the Gentlemen," 1690; "Dr. Sherlock's Case" (anon), 1691; "A Brief Essay concerning the Independency of Church Power" (anon.), 1692; "The Case of giving Bail," 1692; "A Reply" (to remarks on preceding), 1693; "A Persuasive to Consideration tendered to the Royalists" (anon.), 1693; "Remarks upon the 'London Gazette,'" 1693; "Miscellanies" (afterwards pt. i. of "Essays upon several Moral Subjects"), 1694; "A Defence of the Absolution," 1696; "A further Vindication of the Absolution," 1696; "A Reply to the Absolution of a Penitent," 1696; "An Answer to the Animadversions" (on preceding; anon.), 1696; "The Case of the two Absolvers," 1696; "Essays upon several Moral Subjects," 1697; "A Short View of the Immorality and Profaneness of the English Stage," 1698; (2nd and 3rd edns. same year); "A Defence of the Short View," 1699; "A Second Defence," 1700; "The Great Historical, Geographical, Genealogical, and Poetical Dictionary," vol. i., 1701; vols. ii., iii., 1705; vol. iv., 1721; "A Letter to a Lady concerning the New Playhouse" (anon.), 1706; "A Further Vindication of the Short View," 1708; "An Ecclesiastical History of Great Britain," vol. i., 1708; vol. ii., 1714; "An Answer to some Exceptions" (to preceding), 1715; "Some Remarks on Dr. Kennet's . . . Letters," 1717; "Reasons for restoring some Prayers" (anon.), "A Defence of the Reasons" (anon.), 1718; "A Vindication of the Reasons and Defence" (anon), pt. i., 1718; pt. ii., 1719; "A Further Defence" (anon.), 1720; "Essays" (collected), 1722; "Several Discourses upon Practical Subjects," 1725; "God not the Author of Evil," 1726. Collier *translated:* "Sleidan's Commentaries," bks. ix.–xii., 1689; Marcus Aurelius' "Meditations," 1701; Gregory of Nazianzus "Upon the Maccabees," 1716; and wrote prefaces to: translation of Cicero "De Finibus" by S. Parker, 1702; and "Human Souls naturally Immortal," 1707. *Life:* by T. Lathbury, in 1852 edn. of "Ecclesiastical History." —SHARP, R. FARQUHARSON, 1897, *A Dictionary of English Authors, p.* 60.

PERSONAL

I shall say the less of Mr. Collier, because in many things he has taxed me justly; and I have pleaded guilty to all thoughts and expressions of mine which can be truly argued of obscenity, profaneness, or immorality, and retract them. If he be my enemy, let him triumph; if he be my friend, as I have given him no personal occasion to be otherwise, he will be glad of my repentance.—DRYDEN, JOHN, 1700, *Fables, Preface.*

He is well entitled to grateful and respectful mention; for to his eloquence and courage is to be chiefly ascribed the purification of our lighter literature from that foul taint which had been contracted during the Antipuritan reaction. He was, in the full force of words, a good man. He was also a man of eminent abilities, a great master of sarcasm, a great master of rhetoric. His reading, too, though undigested, was of immense extent. But his mind was narrow; his reasoning, even when he was so fortunate as to have a good cause to defend, was singularly futile and inconclusive; and his brain was almost turned by pride, not personal, but professional. In his view, a priest was the highest of human beings, except a bishop. Reverence and submission were due from the best and greatest of the laity to the least respectable of the clergy. However ridiculous a man in holy orders might make himself, it was impiety to laugh at him. So nervously sensitive indeed was Collier on this point that he thought it profane to throw any reflection even on the ministers of false religions. He laid it down as a rule that Muftis and Augurs ought always to be mentioned with respect. He blamed Dryden for sneering at the Hierophants of Apis. He praised Racine for giving dignity to the character of a priest of Baal. He praised Corneille for not bringing that learned and reverend divine Tiresias on the stage in the tragedy of Œdips. The omission, Collier owned, spoiled the dramatic effect of the piece; but the holy function was much too solemn to be played with. Nay, incredible as it may seem, he thought it improper in the laity to sneer even at Presbyterian preachers. . . . In parts Collier was the first man among the nonjurors.—MACAULAY, THOMAS BABINGTON, 1855, *History of England, ch.* xiv.

VIEW OF THE ENGLISH STAGE
1698

Being convinced that nothing has gone further in Debauching the Age than the Stage-Poets and Play-House; I thought I could not employ my Time better than in writing against them. These men, sure, take Virtue and Regularity for Great Enemies; why else is their disaffection so very remarkable? It must be said,

they have made their attack with great Courage, and gained no very inconsiderable Advantage. But it seems, Lewdness without Atheism is but half their Business. Conscience might possibly recover, and Revenge be thought on; and therefore like Foot-Pads, they must not only Rob but Murther. . . . I confess I have no Ceremony for Debauchery. For to Complement Vice, is but one Remove from worshipping the Devil.—COLLIER, JEREMY, 1698, *A Short View of the Immorality and Profaneness of the English Stage, together with the Sense of Antiquity upon this Argument, Preface.*

It goes for current authority round the whole town that Mr. Dryden himself publicly declared [the "Short View"] unanswerable, and thanked Mr. Collier for the just correction he had given him; and that Mr. Congreve and some other great authors had made much the same declaration; which is all so notoriously false, so egregiously a lie, that Mr. Dryden particularly always looked upon it as a pile of malice, ill-nature, and uncharitableness, and all drawn upon the rack of wit and invention.—FILMER, EDWARD, 1698, *A Further Defence of Dramatic Poetry.*

If I do not return him civilities in calling him names, it is because I am not very well versed in his nomenclatures. . . . I will only call him Mr. Collier, and that I will call him as often as I think he shall deserve it. The corruption of a rotten divine is the generation of our sour critic. . . . The greater part of those examples which [Mr. Collier] has produced are only demonstrations of his own impurity, they only savour of his utterance, and were sweet enough till tainted by his breath.—CONGREVE, WILLIAM, 1698, *Amendments of Mr. Collier's False and Imperfect Citations.*

He is too much given to horse-play in his raillery, and comes to battle like a dictator from the plough. I will not say "the zeal of God's house has eaten him up;" but I am sure it has devoured some part of his good manners and civility. It might also be doubted, whether it was altogether zeal which prompted him to this rough manner of proceeding; perhaps, it became not one of his function to rake into the rubbish of ancient and modern plays: a divine might have employed his pains to better purpose, than in the nastiness of Plautus and Aristophanes, whose examples, as they excuse not me, so might be possibly supposed, that he read it them not without some pleasure. They who have written commentaries on those poets, or on Horace, Juvenal, and Martial, have explained some vices, which, without their interpretation, had been unknown to modern times. Neither has he judged impartially betwixt the former age and us.—DRYDEN, JOHN, 1700, *Fables, Preface.*

However just his charge against the authors that then wrote for it might be, I cannot but think his sentence against the stage itself is unequal; reformation he thinks too mild a treatment for it, and is therefore for laying his axe to the root of it. . . . Nevertheless, Mr. Collier's book was upon the whole thought so laudable a work, that king William, soon after it was published, granted him a *nolo prosequi,* when he stood answerable to the law for his having absolved two criminals just before they were executed for high treason. And it must be farther granted, that his calling our dramatic writers to this strict account had a very wholesome effect upon those who wrote after this time.—CIBBER, COLLEY, 1739, *An Apology for His Life.*

He was formed for a controvertist: with sufficient learning; with diction vehement and pointed, though often vulgar and incorrect; with unconquerable pertinacity; with wit in the highest degree keen and sarcastick; and with all those powers exalted and invigorated by just confidence in his cause. Thus qualified, and thus incited, he walked out to battle, and assailed at once most of the living writers, from Dryden to Durfey. His onset was violent; those passages, which, whilst they stood single, excited little notice, when they were accumulated and exposed together, excited horror; the wise and the pious caught the alarm; and the nation wondered why it had so long suffered irreligion and licentiousness to be openly taught at the publick charge.—JOHNSON, SAMUEL, 1779–81, *Congreve, Lives of the English Poets.*

It is no disgrace to the memory of this virtuous and well-meaning man, that, to use the lawyer's phrase, he pleaded his cause too highly; summoned unnecessarily, to his aid the artillery with which the Christian fathers, had fuminated against the Heathen Drama· and, pushing his arguments to extremity, directed it as well against the use as the abuse of the stage. Those who attempted to reply to him, availed themselves, indeed, of the weak parts of his arguments; but upon the main points of impeachment, the poets stood self-convicted.—SCOTT, SIR WALTER, 1814–23, *Essay on the Drama, vol.* VI, *p.* 363.

In his "View of the English Stage," frightened the poets, and did all he could to spoil the stage by pretending to reform it; that is, by making it an echo of the pulpit, instead of a reflection of the manners of the world. . . . It seems that the author would have been contented to be present at a comedy or a farce, like a Father Inquisitor, if there was to be an *auto da fé* at the end, to burn both the actors and the poet. This sour, nonjuring critic has a great horror and repugnance at poor human nature in nearly all its shapes, of the existence of which he appears only to be aware through the stage: and this he considers as the only exception to the practice of piety, and the performance of the whole duty of man; and seems fully convinced, that if this nuisance were abated, the whole world would be regulated according to the creed and the catechism.—HAZLITT, WILLIAM, 1818, *Lectures on the English Comic Writers, Lecture* iv.

Collier's famous "View of the Immorality and Profaneness of the English Stage" came out in March 1697-8—and it did not come before it was wanted—things had gotten to such a pitch that Ladies were afraid of venturing to a new play, till they were assured that they might do it, without risking an insult on their modesty—or if their curiosity was too strong for their patience, they generally came in masks. . . . Collier had great merit, but he frequently goes too far—he has such a bias on his mind that he sees Profaneness where there is none.—GENEST, P., 1832, *Some Account of the English Stage, vol.* I, *pp.* 123, 125.

There is hardly any book of that time from which it would be possible to select specimens of writing so excellent and so various. To compare Collier with Pascal would indeed be absurd. Yet we hardly know where, except in the "Provincial Letters," we can find mirth so harmoniously and becomingly blended with solemnity as in the "Short View." In truth, all the modes of ridicule, from broad fun to polished and antithetical sarcasm, were at Collier's command. On the other hand, he was complete master of the rhetoric of honest indignation. We scarcely know any volume which contains so many bursts of that peculiar eloquence which comes from the heart, and goes to the heart. Indeed, the spirit of the book is truly heroic. In order fairly to appreciate it, we must remember the situation in which the writer stood. He was under the frown of power. His name was already a mark for the invectives of one half the writers of the age; when, in the case of good taste, good sense, and good morals, he gave battle to the other half. Strong as his political prejudices were, he seems on this occasion to have entirely laid them aside. He has forgotten that he was a Jacobite, and remembers only that he is a citizen and a Christian Some of his sharpest censures are directed against poetry which had been hailed with delight by the Tory party, and had inflicted a deep wound on the Whigs. It is really inspiriting to see how gallantly the solitary outlaw advances to attack enemies, formidable separately, and it might have been thought, irresistible when combined —distributes his swashing blows right and left among Wycherley, Congreve, and Vanbrugh—treads the wretched D'Urfey down in the dirt beneath his feet—and strikes with all his strength full at the towering crest of Dryden.—MACAULAY, THOMAS BABINGTON, 1841, *Comic Dramatists of the Restoration, Edinburgh Review; Critical and Miscellaneous Essays.*

The force of much of Jeremy Collier's invective, which was impaired neither by intemperance of language nor by any other symptom of inferior breeding, was irresistible; and although few literary manifestoes of the kind have been more abundantly answered, or answered by abler pens, the strength of his case was such that it may be said to have ensured him the victory at the outset.—WARD, ADOLPHUS WILLIAM, 1875-99, *A History of English Dramatic Literature, vol. III, p.* 511.

It would be foolish to attribute the influence exerted by the "Short View" to Collier's ability alone. It owed its success in great measure to the fact that it chimed in with a wide-spread public

sentiment. — NICOLL, HENRY J., 1882, *Landmarks of English Literature, p.* 150.

Jeremy Collier did infinite service to our Restoration Drama, but his was not the service of a scientific critic.—MOULTON, RICHARD G., 1885, *Shakespeare as a Dramatic Artist, p.* 35.

The reader who expects to find Collier's book a piece of ranting pharisaism, or full of the cant of a literary Tartuffe, will be disappointed. The treatment of the subject is severe, but reasonable; the tone is that of a man of the world. Collier— who afterwards, it is only fair to admit, lost his temper and wrote like a fanatic— remains, in the "Short View," temperate and even gay. He has no objection to poetry in general, or even, theoretically, to drama. . . . Is certainly the brightest prose pamphlet of its time, when he records his impression of its vivacity, variety, and glow. . . . The sensation which it caused was unparalled. No purely literary event—not even the publication of "Absolom and Architophel," which was not purely literary—had awakened anything like so great an excitement since the Restoration. The books sold like wild-fire, and it may be interesting to note, from more than one source, that Collier was paid £50 for the first edition. For the next twelve months the town was convulsed with pamphleteers attacking and defending the "Short View," sometimes in books longer than the original. In 1699 the controversy began to slacken, but the fire of answering pamphlets went sullenly on for many years, nor can be properly said to have closed until William Law brought the whole controversy to a climax, in 1726, with his "Absolute Unlawfulness of the Stage Entertainment fully demonstrated." —GOSSE, EDMUND, 1888, *Life of William Congreve (Great Writers), pp.* 102, 103, 111.

As the adversary of men of wit and genius, Collier has become obnoxious to their representatives, and has been unfairly reviled as a sour fanatic. In fact he is very moderate, admits that the stage may be a valuable medium of instruction, and only denounces its abuse. . . . His wit as unquestionable as his zeal, but his argument is not everywhere equally cogent. On the chapter of profaneness he is fantastic and straitlaced, and so

tender of dignities that he will not allow even the god Apis to be disrespectfully mentioned. On that of immorality he is unanswerable, and unless the incriminated dramatists were prepared to say, "Evil, be thou my good," they could but own
"Pudet haec opprobria nobis
Et dici potuisse, et non potuisse refelli."
—GARNETT, RICHARD, 1895, *The Age of Dryden, p.* 153.

Collier, academic or nothing, is also as full of familiar contractions and cant phrase, as little regardful of formal and scholastic graces, as any gutter-scribbler of the time.—SAINTSBURY, GEORGE, 1898, *A Short History of English Literature, p.* 526.

ECCLESIASTICAL HISTORY OF GREAT BRITAIN

1708-14

There appeared to me quite through the second volume, such a constant inclination to favour the popish doctrine, and to censure the reformers, that I should have had a better opinion of the author's integrity, if he had professed himself to be not of our communion, nor of the communion of any other protestant church. —BURNET, GILBERT, 1715, *History of the Reformation of the Church of England, Preface, vol.* III.

I said, that Mr. Collier's "History" was very well done, and that he was a clear-headed man. *He writes without rec-* ords, says the master, *and does not understand them, whereas Dr. Kennett is a master in these things.* I said, that there was no comparison between Dr. Kennett and Mr. Collier, the latter being much superior to him in learning and judgment; and as to his "History," I said it was compiled from records and the best authorities.— HEARNE, THOMAS, 1717, *Reliquiæ Hearnianæ, ed. Bliss, April 24, vol.* II, *p.* 45.

It is a work of great learning, the first of its kind that had appeared, save Fuller's "Church History," and in spite of the advance of historical scholarship, it has not lost its value.—HUNT, REV. WILLIAM, 1887, *Dictionary of National Biography, vol.* XI, *p.* 344.

GENERAL

His labours were always well meant; and, it is certain that, as a censor, he did much good. The learned and the pious of Europe bore witness to his merit as a writer; and his contemporaries and posterity unite in commending him as an excellent Christian, who sacrificed every thing to that which he thought his duty. —NOBLE, MARK, 1806, *A Biographical History of England, vol.* II, *p.* 144.

The name of Collier, a worthy, truly honourable man, who suffered for his conscience, deserves higher reputation than it has received.—FITZGERALD, PERCY, 1882, *A New History of the English Stage, p.* 192.

Sir John Vanbrugh

1664-1726.

Born, in London, Jan. 1664; baptized, 24 Jan. Probably spent some time in Paris in youth; afterwards served in Army. Play, "The Relapse," performed at Drury Lane, Dec. 1696; "Æsop," Drury Lane, Jan. 1697; "The Provok'd Wife," Lincoln's Inn Fields, May 1697; "The False Friend," Drury Lane, Jan. 1702. Practised as an architect. Built Castle Howard, Blenheim, and other important houses. Appointed Controller of Royal Works, 1702. Play, "Squire Trelooby" (written with Congreve and Walsh), produced at Lincoln's Inn Fields, 30 March 1704; "The Country House," 1705. Built a theatre in the Haymarket. His play, "The Confederacy," produced there, 30 Oct. 1705; "The Mistake," 27 Dec. 1705. Clarencieux King-at-Arms, 1705-26. To Hanover, on embassy to convey Order of Garter to the Elector, May 1706. Knighted, 19 Sept. 1714. Surveyor of Gardens and Waters, 1715. Surveyor of Works, Greenwich Hospital, 1716. Member of Kit-Kat Club. Married Henrietta Maria Yarburgh, 14 Jan. 1719. Died, in London, 26 March 1726. Buried in St. Stephen's, Walbrook. *Works:* "The Relapse" (anon.), 1697 (afterwards known, in Sheridan's adaptation, as "A Trip to Scarborough"); "The Provok'd Wife" (anon.), 1697; "Æsop," 1697; "A Short Vindication of 'The Relapse' and 'The Provok'd Wife' " (anon.), 1698; "The Pilgrim" (adapted from Dryden; anon.), 1700; "The False Friend" (anon.), 1702; "The Confederacy" (anon.), 1705; "The Mistake" (anon.), 1706; "The Country House" (trans. from the French of Carton D'Ancourt), 1715. *Posthumous:* "The Provok'd Husband" (completed by Cibber from Vanbrugh's "A Journey to London"), 1728; "The Cornish Squire" (trans. from Molière), 1734. *Collected Works:* in 2 vols., ed. by W. C. Ward, 1893.—SHARP, R. FARQUHARSON, 1897, *A Dictionary of English Authors*, p. 288.

PERSONAL

Under this stone, reader, survey
Dead Sir John Vanbrugh's house of clay:
Lie heavy on him, Earth, for he
Laid many a heavy load on thee.

—EVANS, ABEL, C 1699, *On Sir John Vanbrugh.*

A silly fellow, who is the architect at Woodstock. — HEARNE, THOMAS, 1714, *Reliquiæ Hearnianæ, ed. Bliss, Sept. 25, vol. I, p. 310.*

The only architect in the world who could have built such a house, and the only friend in the world capable of contriving to lay the debt upon one to whom he was so highly obliged.—MARLBOROUGH, SARAH DUTCHESS, 1718, *Case of the Duke of Marlborough and Sir John Vanbrugh.*

THE RELAPSE
1697

The character of Amanda is interesting, especially in the momentary wavering and quick recovery of her virtue. This is the first homage that the theatre had paid, since the Restoration, to female chastity; and notwithstanding the vicious tone of the other characters, in which Vanbrugh has gone as great lengths as any of his contemporaries, we perceive the beginnings of a re-action in public spirit, which gradually reformed and elevated the moral standard of the stage.—HALLAM, HENRY, 1837–39, *Introduction to the Literature of Europe, pt. iv, ch. vi, par. 53.*

We know of no better comic writing in the world than the earlier scenes of Lord Foppington in the "Relapse."—HUNT, LEIGH, 1840, *ed., The Dramatic Works of Wycherley, Congreve, Vanbrugh and Farquhar.*

Of Vanbrugh's ten or eleven plays, that which has longest kept the stage is the "Relapse," still acted, in its altered form, by Sheridan, as the "Trip to Scarborough." The piece was produced at the Theatre de l'Odeon, in Paris, in the spring of 1862, as a posthumous comedy of Voltaire's! It was called the "Comte de Boursoufle," and had a "run." The story ran with it that Voltaire had composed it in his younger days for private representation, that it had been more than

once played in the houses of his noble friends, under various titles, that he had then locked it up, and that the manuscript had only recently been discovered by the lucky individual who persuaded the manager of the Odeon to produce it on his stage? The bait took. All the French theatrical world in the capital flocked to the Faubourg St. Germain to witness a new play by Voltaire. Critics examined the plot, philosophized on its humor, applauded its absurdities, enjoyed its wit, and congratulated themselves on the circumstances that the Voltairean wit especially was as enjoyable then as in the preceding century! Of the authorship they had no doubt whatever; for, said they, if Voltaire did not write this piece, who *could* have written it? The reply was given at once from this country; but when the mystification was exposed, the French critics gave no sign of awarding honor where honor was due, and probably this translation of the "Relapse" may figure in future French editions as an undoubted work of Voltaire.—DORAN, JOHN, 1863, *Annals of the English Stage, vol. I, p. 158.*

"The Relapse" is a delightful play to read; its spirit is sustained without effort to the end; and although the characters are somewhat farcical, yet are they more so than many an anomaly we all and each of us meet in every day life? Lord Foppington, for instance, is a delicious coxcomb; but that man must be deaf, blind and insensible, who cannot in his own experience verify a Lord Foppington in absurdity, conceit, and stolid selfishness. This character is perhaps a reflex of the Sir Fopling Flutter of Etheredge; more so however in the externals than in the inner structure of the specimen.— CLARKE, CHARLES COWDEN, 1872, *On the Comic Writers of England, Gentleman's Magazine, n. s., vol. 8, p. 39.*

"The Relapse" must, I think, be pronounced Vanbrugh's best comedy. Lord Foppington is a humorous conception, and the whole dialogue is animated and to the point. One sees where Sheridan got his style. There are more brains, if less sparkle, in Vanbrugh's repartees than in Sheridan's.—BIRRELL, AUGUSTINE, 1894, *Men, Women and Books, p.* 102.

The play remained a prime favourite with the public throughout the eighteenth century, and has passed through several transformations. A three-act farce, called "The Man of Quality," was carved out of it by Lee and given at Covent Garden in 1776; and in the following year Sheridan, reflecting that it was "a pity to exclude the productions of our best writers for want of a little wholesome pruning," recast it as "A Trip to Scarborough." The original play was seen at the Olympic in 1846, and at the Strand as late as 1850. A version by Mr. John Hollingshead, also called "The Man of Quality," was produced at the Gaiety on 7 May 1870 with Miss Nellie Farren as Miss Hoyden, a part in which Mrs. Jordan had excelled; and another, called "Miss Tomboy," by Mr. Robert Buchanan, at the Vaudeville on 20 March 1890.—SECCOMBE, THOMAS, 1899, *Dictionary of National Biography, vol.* LVIII, *p.* 87.

THE PROVOKED WIFE
1697

In 1725 we were called upon, in a manner that could not be resisted, to revive the "Provoked Wife," a comedy which, while we found our account in keeping the stage clear of those loose libertines it had formerly too justly been charged with, we had laid aside for some years. The author, sir John Vanbrugh, who was conscious of what it had too much of, was prevailed upon to substitute a new written scene in the place of one in the fourth act, where the wantonness of his wit and humour had (originally) made a rake talk like a rake, in the borrowed habit of a clergyman; to avoid which offence, he clapt the same debauchee into the undress of a woman of quality. Now the character and profession of a fine lady not being so indelibly sacred as that of a churchman, whatever follies he exposed in the petticoat, kept him at least clear of his former profaneness, and were now innocently ridiculous to the spectator.—CIBBER, COLLEY, 1739, *An Apology for His Life.*

Has some merit as a comedy; it is witty and animated, as Vanbrugh usually was; the character of Sir John Brute may not have been too great a caricature of real manners, such as survived from the debased reign of Charles; and the endeavor to expose the grossness of the older generation was itself an evidence, that a better polish had been given to social life.—HALLAM, HENRY, 1837–39, *Introduction to the Literature of Europe, pt.* iv, *ch.* vi, *par.* 53.

The characters in this play, especially that of sir John Brute, are drawn with consummate skill, and the dialogue is easy, brilliant, and natural: but the plot is more licentious in its conduct and situations than any contemporary production with which we are acquainted, and absolutely demoralising in the principle of domestic retaliation it attempts to justify. A surly and unfeeling husband is here retorted upon by his wife, who sacrifices her own honour by way of taking revenge upon him for his ill-treatment of her: and this mode of avenging herself is admitted by the catastrophe to be perfectly reasonable and correct.—DUNHAM, S. ASTLEY, 1838, *ed., Literary and Scientific Men of Great Britain and Ireland, vol.* III, *p.* 216.

"The Provoked Wife," to my own feelings and taste, is a nauseous production. Sir John Brute, the chief person, is a monster-curiosity, and fit only for a museum. There are anomalies in the world, it is true, and Sir John Brute is one: he is an awful hog. His wife is an natural character, and tells her own tale clearly and well. The other characters, Belinda (her niece), Constant, Heartfree, and Lady Fanciful, are little better than common stock from the dramatic warehouse. The play is considerably licentious, and yet the spirit of its moral is less revolting, from the tone of unselfishness and an unconsciously developed tone of justice towards the party against whom the question is always begged, a frankness and liberality of sentiment that one may look for in vain in the heartless and passionless intrigueries of Congreve.—CLARKE, CHARLES COWDEN, 1872, *On the Comic Writers of England, Gentleman's Magazine, n. s., vol.* 8, *p.* 42.

A licentious comedy in which Betterton created, with great success, the role of *Sir John Brute,* and which was later to be revived by Garrick so that he might delight his admirers in the same character. It was a scandalous piece, yet it had so much genuine humor that Garrick ventured to add it to his repertoire, with some of the original grossness left out.—ROBINS,

EDWARD, JR., 1895, *Echoes of the Playhouse, p.* 98.

THE CONFEDERACY
1705

A more hopeless crew of unprincipled riff-raff surely never were assembled in any single list of *dramatis personæ.* Not one individual has the least claim upon our respect, nor is it looked for or required; not one even upon our interest, beyond the amusement of watching their escapes from their rascally slip-shod contrivances; and, really, these are sustained with considerable humour. — CLARKE, CHARLES COWDEN, 1872, *On the Comic Writers of England, Gentleman's Magazine, n. s., vol.* 8, *p.* 44.

The dialogue is distinguished by the author's usual vivacity. Dick Amlet and his mother make a choice pair, and Flippanta the lady's-maid is a fine specimen of the effrontery of her kind. The morality of this comedy is on Vanbrugh's usual level, which may be described as about the lowest to which English comedy has ever sunk; and the rascally Dick is made perfectly happy at the close.—WARD, ADOLPHUS WILLIAM, 1875–99, *A History of English Dramatic Literature, vol.* III, *p.* 479.

ARCHITECTURE

For building famed, and justly reckon'd
At court, Vitruvius the Second:
No wonder, since wise authors shew,
That best foundations must be low:
And now the duke has wisely ta'en him
To be his architect at Blenheim.
But, raillery for once apart,
If this rule holds in every art;
Or if his grace were no more skill'd in
The art of battering walls than building,
We might expect to see next year
A mouse-trap man chief engineer.
—SWIFT, JONATHAN, 1708, *Works.*

Belongs only to this work in a light that is by no means advantageous to him. He wants all the merit of his writings to protect him from the censure due to his designs. What Pope said of his comedies is much more applicable to his buildings—
"How Van wants grace!"—
Grace! He wanted eyes, he wanted all ideas of proportion, convenience, propriety. He undertook vast designs, and composed heaps of littleness. The style of no age, of no country, appears in his works; he broke through all rule, and compensated for it by no imagination.

He seems to have hollowed quarries rather than to have built houses; and should his edifices, as they seem forced to do, outlast all record, what architecture will posterity think was that of their ancestors? The laughers, his contemporaries, said, that having been confined in the Bastile, he had drawn his notions on building from that fortified dungeon.—WALPOLE, HORACE, 1762–86, *Anecdotes of Painting in England, p.* 310.

"We staid two nights in Woodstock; but there was an order to the servants, *under her grace's own hand, not to let me enter Blenheim!* and lest that should not mortify me enough, she having somehow learned that my *wife* was of the company, *sent an express the night before we came there,* with orders that if *she* came with the Castle Howard ladies, the servants should not suffer her to see either house, gardens, or even to enter the park: so she was forced to sit all day long and keep me company at the inn!" This was a *coup-de-théâtre* in this joint comedy of Atossa and Vanbrugh! The architect of Blenheim, lifting his eyes towards his own massive grandeur, exiled to a dull inn, and imprisoned with one who required rather to be consoled, than capable of consoling the enraged architect.—DISRAELI, ISAAC, 1791–1824, *Secret History of the Building of Blenheim, Curiosities of Literature.*

Vanbrugh's attempt, therefore, seems to have been an effort of genius: and if we can keep the imagination apart from the five orders, we must allow that he has created a magnificent whole; which is invested with an air of grandeur seldom seen in a more regular style of building. Its very defects, except a few that are too glaring to be overlooked, give it an appearance of something beyond common; and as it is surrounded with great objects, the eye is struck with the whole, and takes the parts upon trust. What made Vanbrugh ridiculous, was his applying to small houses a style of architecture which could not possibly succeed but in a large one.—GILPIN, WILLIAM, 1804? *Observations on the Mountains and Lakes of Cumberland and Westmoreland.*

There is, however, no doubt but that Vanburgh was justly accused by the Duchess of extravagance in many instances, and of exceeding his commission in others. She even taxed him with building one entire court at Blenheim without the Duke's knowledge. She detected his bad taste and grasping spirit, and despised his mismanagement,—of which latter the best proof was, that when, upon the death of the Duke, the whole charge of the building fell into her hands, she completed it in the manner, and at the reduced expense, which has been described. That "wicked woman of Marlborough," as Sir John- Vanbrugh termed the Duchess, had perhaps no greater error in his eyes than the penetration with which she discovered his narrow pretensions, his inadequacy, and wanton waste, not to say peculation. —THOMSON, KATHERINE, 1838, *Memoirs of Sarah Jennings, Duchess of Marlborough*, vol. II, p. 458.

Sir John Vanbrugh's merits as an architect—his fire, his daring, his picturesqueness, his solidity and grandeur—have been recognised and very handsomely acknowledged by the best judges of art. Sir Joshua Reynolds's judgment of him, though often quoted, may be quoted once again:—"In the buildings of Vanbrugh, who was a poet as well as an architect, there is a greater display of imagination than we shall find perhaps in any other; and this is the ground of the effect we feel in many of his works, notwithstanding the faults with which many of them are charged." It was the peculiarity of Vanbrugh's genius that he was a poet even more than a builder, and designed a palace as he designed a play—in masses, with so much unity of thought in the stone construction as he would have studied in his action and dialogue, the whole relieved and enlivened by artistic contrasts and surprises. No man, probably, not a slave of rules, will deny to Blenheim and to Castle Howard a certain splendour and originality not to be seen in the works of common men. Seen from the bridge, or from the grassy upland above the bridge, what secular edifice in England will compare in force, solidity, and cheeriness, with the front of Blenheim? Is it not wonderfully bright, and bold, and various, striking in the detail and in the mass? Does it not gloriously cap and adorn the voluptuous site on which it stands? Does not the work, too, thoroughly embody the idea out of which it grew—the memorial of a nation's

gratitude and of a hero's deeds?—MANCHESTER, DUKE OF, 1864, *Court and Society from Elizabeth to Anne*, p. 226.

The year 1702 presents our author in a new character. Of his architectural studies we know absolutely nothing, unless we may accept Swift's account, who pretends that Vanbrugh acquired the rudiments of the art by watching children building houses of cards or clay. But this was probably ironical. However he came by his skill, in 1702 he stepped into sudden fame as the architect of Castle Howard.—WARD, W. C., 1893, *ed. Vanbrugh's Collected Works*.

The verdict of Vanbrugh's literary rivals as to the architectural merit of Blenheim was wholly unfavourable. In the minds of less prejudiced critics there has been great divergence of opinion; but it must be conceded that Vanbrugh hardly rose to his opportunities. The general plan of a grand central edifice, connected by colonnades with two projecting quadrangular wings, and of the approaches (including the "Titanic bridge"), is admirable in its way. The sky-line is broken in a picturesque fashion, and the light and shade are balanced and contrasted in a manner which envoked the enthusiastic eulogy of Sir Joshua Reynolds, Uvedale Price, Allan Cunningham, and other connoisseurs of scenic effect. On the other hand, the ornament, when not positively uncouth, is unmeaning and there is a sensible coarseness in matters of detail throughout the work. Voltaire remarked upon Blenheim that if the rooms were as wide as the walls were thick, the château would be convenient enough. The last thing that Vanbrugh had in his mind was personal comfort for his clients. —SECCOMBE, THOMAS, 1899, *Dictionary of National Biography*, vol. LVIII, p. 91.

GENERAL

Sir *John Vanbrugh* has writ several comedies which are more humourous than those of Mr. *Wycherley*, but not so ingenious. Sir *John* was a man of pleasure, and likewise a poet and an architect. The general opinion is, that he is as sprightly in his writings as he is heavy in his buildings.—VOLTAIRE, FRANÇOIS MARIE AROUET, 1732? *Letters Concerning the English Nation*, p. 147.

How Van wants grace, who never

wanted wit!—POPE, ALEXANDER, 1733, *First Epistle of the Second Book of Horace*.

Though to write much in a little time is no excuse for writing ill, yet sir John Vanbrugh's pen is not to be a little admired for its spirit, ease, and readiness, in producing plays so fast upon the neck of one another; for notwithstanding this quick despatch, there is a clear and lively simplicity in his wit, that neither wants the ornament of learning, nor has the least smell of the lamp in it. As the face of a fine woman, with only her locks loose about her, may be then in its greatest beauty, such were his productions only adorned by nature. There is something so catching to the ear, so easy to the memory in all he wrote, that it has been observed by all the actors of my time, that the style of no author whatsoever gave their memory less trouble than that of sir John Vanbrugh; which I myself, who have been charged with several of his strongest characters, can confirm by a pleasing experience. And indeed his wit and humour were so little laboured, that his most entertaining scenes seemed to be no more than his common conversation committed to paper. Here I confess my judgment at a loss, whether in this I give him more or less than his due praise.— CIBBER, COLLEY, 1739, *An Apology for His Life*.

Sir John Vanbrugh, it is said, had great facility in writing, and is not a little to be admired for the spirit, ease, and readiness, with which he produced his plays. Notwithstanding his extraordinary expedition, there is a clear and lively simplicity in his wit, that is equally distant from the pedantry of learning, and the lowness of scurrility. As the face of a fine lady, with her hair undressed, may appear in the morning in its brightest glow of beauty; such were the productions of Vanbrugh, adorned with only the negligent graces of nature.—CIBBER, THEOPHILUS, 1753, *Lives of the Poets, vol.* IV, *v.* 103.

Sir John Vanburgh has spirit, wit, and ease; but he is, to the last degree, gross and indelicate. He is one of the most immoral of all our comedians. His "Provoked Wife" is full of such indecent sentiments and allusions, as ought to explode it out of all reputable society. His "Relapse" is equally censurable; and

these are his only two considerable pieces. —BLAIR, HUGH, 1783, *Lectures on Rhetoric and Belles-Lettres, ed. Mills, Lecture* xlvii, *p.* 542.

He is no writer at all, as to mere authorship; but he makes up for it by a prodigious fund of comic invention and ludicrous description, bordering somewhat on caricature. Though he did not borrow from him, he was much more like Moliere in genius than Wycherley was, who professedly imitated him. He has none of Congreve's graceful refinement, and as little of Wycherley's serious manner and studied insight into the springs of character; but his exhibition of it in dramatic contrast and unlooked-for situations, where the different parties play upon one another's failings, and into one another's hands, keeping up the jest like a game of battledore and shuttlecock, and urging it to the utmost verge of breathless extravagance, in the mere eagerness of the fray, is beyond that of any other of our writers. . . . He has more nature than art; what he does best, he does because he cannot help it. He has a masterly eye to the advantages which certain accidental situations of character present to him on the spot, and executes the most difficult and rapid theatrical movements at a moment's warning.— HAZLITT, WILLIAM, 1818, *Lectures on the English Comic Writers, Lecture* iv.

Is as appalling a Satirist as Swift. His pictures of human nature are hideously like; they are true to the very wrinkle. Swift said that he hated the Ourang Outang, because it was so like us; and so we may say of Vanbrugh's delineations of character. All the vices of humanity are treasured up in them; yet they are not natural delineations. They are the bad parts of human nature picked out and separated from those redeeming qualities, which scarcely the vilest of mankind are not without.—NEELE, HENRY, 1827–29, *Lectures on English Poetry, p.* 149.

No man who has been satirized by Swift, and praised by Reynolds, could have much chance of being forgotten; but the fame of him who was at once the author of "The Relapse" and "The Provoked Wife," and the architect of Castle Howard and Blenheim, stands independent of even such subsidiaries.—CUNNINGHAM, ALLAN, 1829–33, *Lives of the Most*

Eminent British Painters, Sculptors and Architects, vol. IV, *p.* 253.

The wit of Vanbrugh flows rather than flashes; but in its copious stream may vie in its own way with the dazzling fire-shower of Congreve's; and his characters have much more of real flesh and blood in their composition, coarse and vicious as almost all the more powerfully drawn among them are.—CRAIK, GEORGE L., 1861, *A Compendious History of English Literature and of the English Language, vol.* II, *p.* 274.

Less brilliant than Congreve, and altogether his inferior both as a dramatist and as a wit, Sir John Vanbrugh is in my opinion unsurpassed by any of our post-Restoration writers of comedy in the vivacity, gaiety, and ease of his prose dialogue. Moreover, he enriched the comic stage by one supremely ludicrous character which, except in so far as Etheredge's Sir Fopling Flutter may have a claim to its parentage, may fairly be called new, viz. the admirable Lord Foppington of "The Relapse;" and he invented some others which are almost equally extravagant and almost equally true to life. He borrowed with skill while he constructed with ease, and must altogether be allowed to be one of the most entertaining dramatists of his age. His morality might be averred to sink below that of Congreve—could it be said to sink at all; for such is the levity of this author that it is difficult to weigh even his sins in any very serious balance. The utter frivolity of the later Stuart comedy has no more signal representative than Vanbrugh, though, as it happened, he was very far from being a mere man of pleasure.—WARD, ADOLPHUS WILLIAM, 1875-99, *A History of English Dramatic Literature, vol.* III, *p.* 477.

Of the four great Restoration playwrights, Vanbrugh had most of the "trick of the stage." Like Wycherley, he has the rare and great merit that he wrote to be acted, not to be read. He is less cynical than Wycherley, more civilized and human in his satire, and far less gross. He lacks the wit and style of Congreve, but has greater natural flow and natural ease; the players are said to have found his pieces particularly easy to get by heart, and this would seem to be a proof that he spoke the language natural

to his day. Vanbrugh goes further afield for his plots than his contemporaries, and brings more than mere fine ladies and gentlemen on to the stage.—CRAWFURD, OSWALD, 1883, *ed., English Comic Dramatists, p.* 84.

This very clear and original writer had, indeed, erred by an extraordinary licence, and owes to his coarseness the obscurity into which his plays have fallen. . . . Where Congreve is volatile and sparkling, Vanbrugh does not attempt to compete with him, but reserves himself for carefully studied effects, for passages where every touch is marked by the precision and weight of the author's style. He is perhaps more like Molière than any other English dramatist; he is like him in the abundance of his stage-knowledge, and in the skill he shows in rapid and entertaining changes of situation. At the same time he is English to a fault, saturated with the brutality of the fox-hunting squire of the period. This very coarseness of fibre, added to Vanbrugh's great sincerity as a writer, gives his best scenes a wonderful air of reality.—GOSSE, EDMUND, 1888, *A History of Eighteenth Century Literature, p.* 67.

As for Sir John Vanbrugh, his two well-known plays, "The Relapse" and "The Provok'd Wife," are most excellent reading, Jeremy Collier notwithstanding. They must be read with the easy tolerance, the amused benignity, the scornful philosophy of a Christian of the Dr. Johnson type. You must not probe your laughter deep; you must forget for awhile your probationary state, and remember that, after all, the thing is but a play. Sir John has a great deal of wit of that genuine kind which is free from modishness. He reads freshly. He also has ideas.—BIRRELL, AUGUSTINE, 1894, *Men, Women and Books, p.* 100.

Vanbrugh's scenes stand on nothing but their biting and extravagant sarcasm. As Congreve's characters are indiscriminately witty, so Vanbrugh's are universally and wearisomely cynical, and at the expense of themselves and all society.—GUINEY, LOUISE IMOGEN, 1894, *A Little English Gallery, p.* 139.

His comedies are more natural than either Congreve's or Wycherley's.—SWAEN, A. E. H., 1896, *ed., The Plays of Sir John Vanbrugh.*

William Wotton
1666-1726

Born at Wrentham, Suffolk, England, Aug. 13, 1666: died at Buxted, Essex, Feb. 13, 1726. An English clergyman and scholar. He was educated at Cambridge, where he was admitted in his tenth year. He was a remarkable instance of precocity. When only twelve years old he was noted for his skill in Hebrew, Greek, Latin, three or four of the Eastern tongues, philosophy, mathematics, etc.; took his degree of B.A. in Jan., 1679, then knowing 12 languages; and became a fellow of St. John's College, Cambridge, in 1685. He became chaplain to the Earl of Nottingham and rector of Middleton Keynes, Buckinghamshire, in 1693, and prebendary of Salisbury in 1705. He is best known from his "Reflections upon Ancient and Modern Learning" (1694).—SMITH, BENJAMIN E., 1894-97, *The Century Cyclopedia of Names*, p. 1071.

PERSONAL

Last night I was with Mr. Wotton (who writ the "Essay on Ancient and Modern Learning") at the tavern, together with Mr. Thwaites, and Mr. Willis. Mr. Wotton is a person of general learning, a great talker and braggadocio, but of little judgment in any one particular science.—HEARNE, THOMAS, 1705, *Reliquiæ Hearnianæ*, ed. Bliss, Sept. 21, vol. I, p. 38.

Is perhaps the most remarkable of well-authenticated cases of intellectual precocity. When five years of age, he translated chapters and psalms from Hebrew, Greek, and Latin into English; in his tenth year he was admitted of Catherine Hall, Cambridge, and Dr. John Eachard, Master of the College, declared that "Gulielmus Wottonus, infra decem annos, nec Hammondo nec Grotio secundus," (April 1, 1676:) at twelve years of age his skill in Hebrew, Arabic, Syriac, Chaldee, Greek, and Latin, arts and sciences, geography, logic, philosophy, mathematics, and chronology, was celebrated in an elegant copy of verses (In Gulielmum Wottonum stupendi ingenii et incomparabilis spei puerum vixdum duodecim annorum) by the learned Dr. James Duport, Master of Magdalene College and Dean of Peterborough; when twelve years and five months old, (in Jan. 1679), then being acquainted with twelve languages, he was made Bachelor of Arts,—a case unparalleled before or since; in the next winter, at the invitation of Gilbert (afterwards Bishop) Burnet, was brought to London, where he was introduced to the learned, and astonished Dr. Lloyd, the Bishop of St. Asaph, (he often accomplished similar feats), by repeating *verbatim* one of his lordship's sermons after one hearing from the pulpit; in 1683 took the degree of M.A., and in 1685, at nineteen, became a Fellow of St. John's College, Cambridge. —ALLIBONE, S. AUSTIN, 1871, *Dictionary of English Literature*, vol. III, p. 2854.

He retained a powerful memory throughout life, his learning was always ready, and he helped many other scholars, among them Browne Willis. His hand writing was of fine strokes and very clear. He was of a genial disposition and fond of smoking.—MOORE, NORMAN, 1900, *Dictionary of National Biography*, vol. LXIII, p. 63.

GENERAL

If some kind genius had not in pity directed the most learned Mr. Wotton to give us a visit, and an inestimable present too, his "Reflections on the Ancient and Modern Learning;" which, in recognition of yours, I should have sent you, but that I was confident you must ere this have seen it, and been entertained with as much delight and satisfaction as universally learned, and indeed extraordinary person, is able to give the most refined taste. This is he whom I have sometimes mentioned to you, for one of the miracles of this age, for his early and vast comprehension. Set him down, then, in your Albo, among the Gales and the Bentleys, as you will certainly do as soon as you know him.—EVELYN, JOHN, 1694, *Letter to Pepys, July 7.*

Wotton argues with solid sense against the lively exotic fancies of Sir William Temple.—GIBBON, EDWARD, 1776-78, *Decline and Fall of the Roman Empire.*

Of his literary character he supported the reputation which he had so early acquired by a variety of learned publications. Of these, one of the best known and the most remarkable is his "Reflections upon Ancient and Modern Learning," first published in 1694, and intended as a refutation of Sir William Temple's celebrated essay on the same subject. To the second edition of his book, which appeared in 1697, Wotton annexed, by way of appendix, the elaborate "Dissertations upon Phalaris" by Bentley, a proceeding which not only involved him in the far-famed dispute with Boyle, but exposed him to the irony and sarcastic ridicule of Swift; who, in his "Tale of a Tub," and in his "Battle of the Books," has omitted no opportunity of placing our author in a ludicrous light. Wotton endeavoured to reply and recriminate by a "Defence of the Reflections," and by "Observations upon the Tale of a Tub," but in vain; for the satire is preserved and the answers are forgotten. The "Reflections" of Wotton, which were written in his twenty-ninth year, display much literature and research, and are, at the same time, free from all traces of asperity or ostentation.—DRAKE, NATHAN, 1804, *Essays Illustrative of the Tatler, Spectator and Guardian, vol.* III, *p.* 276.

Wotton executed his work ably and judiciously: wide as the proposed range is, his inquiry proceeds with calmness and caution into every part, and evinces not only more candour, but a more extensive acquaintance with the topics under discussion, than had previously been exhibited in this controversy. This must have made his "Reflections" very edifying, after the loose and declamatory tracts which preceded them, and even now renders their perusal interesting and useful. Though

professing the character of an umpire, he more frequently resists the arguments of Sir W. Temple; and this he does in the most efficacious manner, by destroying the premises upon which they are built, by giving a just view of the authorities for the alleged vast acquisitions of the ancient sages, and showing how ill they will bear the test of investigation.—MONK, JAMES HENRY, 1830–33, *Life of Richard Bentley, vol.* I, *p.* 61.

The most solid book that was written in any country upon this famous dispute. William Wotton published in 1694 his "Reflections on Ancient and Modern Learning." He draws very well in this the line between Temple and Perrault; avoiding the tasteless judgment of the latter in poetry and eloquence, but pointing out the superiority of the moderns in the whole range of physical science.—HALLAM, HENRY, 1837–39, *Introduction to the Literature of Europe, pt.* IV, *ch.* vii, *par.* 47.

He died in 1726, leaving behind him no competitor, perhaps, in variety of acquisitions as a linguist.—CUNNINGHAM, G. G., 1840, *ed., Lives of Eminent and Illustrious Englishmen, vol.* IV, *p.* 241.

Unlike most controversial writings it is chiefly devoted to the clear statement of facts, and may still be read as the best summary of the discoveries in nature and physical science up to its date.—MOORE, NORMAN, 1900, *Dictionary of National Biography, vol.* LXIII, *p.* 62.

Sir Isaac Newton

1642–1727

Born, at Woolsthorpe, Lincolnshire, 25 Dec. 1642. At Grantham Grammar School, 1654–56, 1660–61. Matric., Trin. Coll., Camb., as Subsizar, 5 June 1661; Scholar 28 April 1664; B.A., Jan. 1665. Occupied in mathematical investigations. First idea of law of Universal Gravitation, 1665. At Woolsthorpe, 1665–67; Returned to Cambridge, 1667; Fellow of Trin. Coll., 1 Oct. 1667; Lucasian Professor, 1669–1701. F.R.S., 11 Jan. 1672; Member of Council, 1699. M.P. for Cambridge Univ., 1689. Warden of the Mint, March 1696; Master, 1699. Foreign Associate of French Academy, 1699. M.P. for Cambridge Univ., Nov. 1701 to July 1702. Pres. of Royal Soc., 1703–27. Knighted, 15 April 1705. Died, at Kensington, 20 March, 1727. Buried in Westminster Abbey. *Works:* Newton's published works number upwards of 230. A full list is given in G. J. Gray's "Bibliography of the Works of Sir Isaac Newton," 1888. The "Principia" was published in 1687. *Collected Works:* ed. by S. Horsley, (incomplete), in 5 vols., 1779–85. *Life:* by Sir David Brewster, 2nd edn. 1860.—SHARP, R. FARQUHARSON, 1897, *A Dictionary of English Authors, p.* 213.

PERSONAL

What I heard to-day I must relate. There is one Mr. Newton (whom I have

very often seen), Fellow of Trinity College, that is mighty famous for his learning, being a most excellent mathematician,

GILBERT BURNET

*Painting by John Riley.   Engraving by
R. A. Muller, from Mezzotint by John Smith.*

SIR ISAAC NEWTON

*Painting by Sir Godfrey Kneller.
Engraving by Robert C. Bell.*

philosopher, divine, &c. . . . Of all the books he ever wrote there was one of colours and light, established upon thousands of experiments, which he had been twenty years making, and which had cost him many hundreds of pounds. This book, which he valued so much, and which was so much talked of, had the ill-luck to perish and be utterly lost, just when the learned author was almost at pushing a conclusion to the same, after this manner: —In a winter's morning, leaving it among his other papers on his study table, whilst he went to chapel, the candle, which he had unfortunately left burning there too, catched hold by some means of other papers, and they fired the aforesaid book, and utterly consumed it and several other valuable writings, and, which is most wonderful, did no further mischief. But when Mr. Newton came from chapel, and had seen what was done, every one thought he would have run mad; he was so troubled thereat that he was not himself for a month after.—PRYME, ABRAHAM DE LA, 1692, *Diary, Feb.* 3.

I have been, ever since I first knew you, so entirely and sincerely your friend, and thought you so much mine, that I could not have believed what you tell me of yourself, had I had it from any body else. And, though I cannot but be mightily troubled that you should have had so many wrong and unjust thoughts of me, yet next to the return of good offices, such as from a sincere good will I have ever done you, I receive your acknowledgement of the contrary as the kindest thing you have done me, since it gives me hopes I have not lost a friend I so much valued.—LOCKE, JOHN, 1693, *Letter to Newton, Oct. 5th.*

Sir,—Upon hearing occasionally that you had sent a letter to Dr. Wallis about the parallax of the fixed stars to be printed, and that you had mentioned me therein with respect to the theory of the moon, I was concerned to be publicly brought upon the stage about what, perhaps, will never be fitted for the public, and thereby the world put into an expectation of what, perhaps, they are never like to have. I do not love to be printed upon every occasion, much less to be dunned and teased by foreigners about mathematical things, or to be thought by our own people to be trifling away my time about them, when I should be about the King's business; and, therefore, I desired Dr. Gregory to write to Dr. Wallis against printing that clause, which related to that theory, and mentioned me about it. You may let the world know, if you please, how well you are stored with observations of all sorts, and what calculations you have made towards rectifying the theories of the heavenly motions. But there may be cases wherein your friends should not be published without their leave; and therefore I hope you will so order the matter, that I may not, on this occasion, be brought upon the stage.—I am your humble servant,—NEWTON, ISAAC, 1698-9, *Letter to John Flamsteed, Jan.* 6.

I have had another contest with the President of the Royal Society, who had formed a plot to make my instruments theirs, and sent for me to a Committee, where only himself and two physicians (Dr. Sloane, and another as little skilful as himself) were present. The President ran himself into a great heat, and very indecent passion. I had resolved aforehand his kn——sh talk should not move me; showed him that all the instruments in the observatory were my own—the mural arc and voluble quadrant having been made at my own charge, the rest purchased with my own money, except the sextant and two clocks, which were given me by Sir Jonas Moore, with Mr. Townley's nicrometer, his gift some years before I came to Greenwich. . . . I complained then of my Catalogue being printed by Raymer (Dr. Halley) without my knowledge, and that I was *robbed of the fruits of my labours.* At this he fired, and called me all the ill names, puppy, &c. that he could think of. All I returned was, I put him in mind of his passion, desired him to govern it and keep his temper. This made him rage worse: and he told me how much I had received from the Government in 36 years I had served. I asked what he had done for the L.500 per annum that he had received ever since he settled in London. This made him calmer. . . . Dr. Sloane had said nothing all this while; the other Doctor told me I was proud, and insulted the President, and ran into the same passion with the President. At my going out, I called to Dr. Sloane, told him he had behaved himself civilly, and thanked him for it. I saw Raymer after, drank a dish of coffee with him, and told him, still calmly, of the villany of his conduct, and called it *blockish.* Since then they let me be quiet; but how long will they do so I know not, nor am I solicitous.—FLAM-STEED, JOHN, 1711, *Letter to Sharpe, Dec. 22, Baily's Life of Flamsteed, pp.* 294, 295.

The corpse of sir Isaac Newton, which was buried on Tuesday (March 28) in the abbey, from the Jerusalem chamber, was followed to the grave by a great many persons of quality and distinction, to shew the respect they bore to that unquestion-ably great man, and six noble peers sup-ported the pall. Yesterday (March 29) John Conduit, esq., M.P. for Whitchurch, received his patent constituting him master worker of his majesty's mint in the Tower, in the room of sir Isaac Newton deceased.—READING POST, 1727, *April 3rd.*

I hear sir Isaac Newton died intestate, tho,' besides a considerable paternal estate, he was worth in money twenty-seven thousand pounds. He had promised to be a benefactor to the Royal society, but failed. Some time before he died, a great quarrel happened between him and Dr. Halley, so as they fell to bad language. This, 'tis thought, so much discomposed sir Isaac as to hasten his end. Sir Isaac died in great pain, though he was not sick, which pain proceeded from some inward decay, as appeared from opening him. He is buried in Westminster abbey. Sir Isaac was a man of no promising aspect. He was a short well-set man. He was full of thought, and spoke very little in company, so that his conversa-tion was not agreeable. When he rode in his coach one arm would be out of the coach on one side, and the other on the other. He hath left behind him a MS. chronology compleat, and ordered it to be printed. Some years ago sir Isaac was much troubled with a lethargy, occa-sioned by too much thinking, but he had got it off pretty well before he died.— HEARNE, THOMAS, 1727, *Reliquiæ Hearn-ianæ, ed. Bliss, April 4, vol.* II, *p.* 311.

I also conversed at different times with the illustrious Newton, who died in the month of March at the age of eighty-five. He read manuscript without spectacles, and without bringing it near his eyes.

He still reasoned acutely as he was wont to do, and told me that his memory only had failed him. . . . A few weeks before his death he threw into the fire many manuscripts written in his own hand. . . . He was not only deeply versed in mathematics and philosophy, but like-wise in theology and ecclesiastical his-tory.—CRELL, SAMUEL, 1727, *Letter to Lacroze, July* 17.

Say, ye who best can tell, ye happy few,
Who saw him in the softest lights of life,
All unwithheld, indulging to his friends
The vast unborrowed treasures of his mind,
Oh, speak the wondrous man! how mild,
        how calm,
How greatly humble, how divinely good;
How firm stablished on eternal truth;
Fervent in doing well, with every nerve
Still pressing on, forgetful of the past,
And panting for perfection; far above
Those little cares, and visionary joys,
That so perplex the fond impassioned heart
Of ever-cheated, ever-trusting Man.
—THOMSON, JAMES, 1727, *To the Memory of Sir Isaac Newton.*

His carriage then was very meek, sedate, and humble, never seemingly angry, of profound thought, his countenance mild, pleasant, and comely. I cannot say I ever saw him laugh but once. . . . Oftimes he has forgot to eat at all, so that, going into his chamber, I have found his mess untouched, of which when I have reminded him he would reply, "Have I?" and then, making to the table, would eat a bit or two standing, for I cannot say I ever saw him set at table by himself. . . . He very rarely went to bed till *two* or *three* of the clock, sometimes not till *five* or *six*, lying about *four* or *five* hours. . . . He very rarely went to dine in the hall, except on some public days, and then, if he has not been minded, would go very carelessly with shoes down at heels, stockings untied, surpliced on, and his head scarcely combed.—NEWTON, HUM-PHREY, 1727–28, *Letters to Mr. Conduitt, Jan.* 27.

I have heard my father often say that he has been a witness of what the world has so often heard of,—Sir Isaac's for-getfulness of his food when intent upon his studies; and of his rising in a pleasant manner with the satisfaction of having found out some proposition, without any concern for a seeming want of his night's sleep, which he was sensible he had lost thereby.—WICKINS, NICOLAS, 1727–28, *Letter to Prof. Smith, Jan. 16th.*

As he sat alone in a garden, he fell into a speculation on the power of gravity, that as this power is not found sensibly diminished at the remotest distance from the centre of the earth to which we can rise . . . it appeared to him reasonable to conclude that this power must extend much farther than is usually thought. Why not as high as the moon? said he to himself, and, if so, her motion must be influenced by it; perhaps she is retained in her orbit thereby.—PEMBERTON, HENRY, 1728, *A View of Sir Isaac Newton's Philosophy, Preface.*

Sir Isaac Newton, a little before he died, said: "I don't know what I may seem to the world, but, as to myself, I seem to have been only like a boy playing on the seashore, and diverting myself in now and then finding a smoother pebble or a prettier shell than ordinary, whilst the great ocean of truth lay all undiscovered before me."—RAMSAY, CHEVALIER, 1728–30, *Spence's Anecdotes, ed. Singer, p. 40.*

It is not at all improbable that Sir Isaac Newton, though so great a man, might have had a hankering after the French prophets. There was a time when he was possessed with the old fooleries of astrology; and another when he was so far gone in those of chemistry, as to be upon the hunt after the philosopher's stone.—LOCKIER, DR. DEAN OF PETERBOROUGH, 1730–32, *Spence's Anecdotes, ed. Singer, p. 54.*

ISAACUS NEWTONUS:
Quem Immortalem
Testantur *Tempus, Natura, Cœlum:*
Mortalem
Hoc marmor fatetur.
Nature and Nature's Laws lay hid in Night:
God said, *Let Newton be!* and all was Light.
—POPE, ALEXANDER, 1732, *Intended for Sir Isaac Newton, In Westminster Abbey.*

Here Lies
Sir Isaac Newton, Knight,
Who, by a vigour of mind almost supernatural,
First demonstrated
The motions and Figures of the Planets,
The Paths of the Comets, and the Tides of the Ocean.
He diligently investigated
The different refrangibilities of the Rays of Light,

And the properties of the Colours to which they give rise.
An Assiduous, Sagacious, and Faithful Interpreter
of Nature, Antiquity, and the Holy Scriptures,
He asserted in his Philosophy the Majesty of God,
And exhibited in his Conduct the simplicity of the Gospel
Let Mortals rejoice
That there has existed such and so great
AN ORNAMENT OF THE HUMAN RACE.
Born 25th Dec., 1642, Died 20th March, 1727.
—INSCRIPTION ON MONUMENT, WESTMINSTER ABBEY, 1731, *tr. Brewster.*

Sir Isaac Newton, though so deep in Algebra and Fluxions, could not readily make up a common account: and, when he was Master of the Mint, used to get somebody to make up his accounts for him.—POPE, ALEXANDER, 1734–36, *Spence's, Anecdotes ed. Singer, p. 132.*

Sir Isaac Newton's house at Coldsworth is a handsome structure.—His study boarded round, and all jutting out. We were in the room where he was born. Both of as melancholy and dismal an air as ever I saw. Mr. Percival, his tenant, who still lives there, says he was a man of very few words; that he would sometimes be silent and thoughtful for above a quarter of an hour together, and look all the while almost as if he was saying his prayers: but that when he did speak, it was always very much to the purpose. —SPENCE, JOSEPH, 1755, *Anecdotes, Supplement, May* 14.

The want of a life of Newton, on a scale and of a character commensurate with the dignity and importance of the subject, cannot but be regarded as a reproach to our national literature.
We cannot, however, help observing as somewhat singular, that in Newton's own university, where his name is, not unjustly, idolized, and his works have long furnished the established studies of the place— where, moreover, there exist valuable materials and a multitude of local traditions and associations—and where there have not been wanting a succession of men, since his death, possessed of the highest qualifications for the task, not one should have been found to pay this tribute to his memory.—POWELL, B., 1843, *Sir Isaac Newton and his Contemporaries, Edinburgh Review, vol. 78, pp.* 402, 403.

Right or wrong, Newton never faced

opinion. As soon as he found that publication involved opposition, from that time forward he published only with the utmost reluctance, and under the strongest persuasions; except when, as in the case of some of his theological writings, he confided the manuscript to a friend, to be anonymously published abroad. The "Principia" was extorted from him by the Royal Society; the first publication on fluctions was under the name of Wallis; the "Optics" were delayed until the death of Hooke; the first appearance against Leibnitz was anonymous; the second originated in a hint from the King. This morbid fear, which is often represented as modesty, would have made him, had he acted a part with regard to his niece which he could not avow, conduct it with the utmost reserve.—DE MORGAN, AUGUSTUS, 1853, *Lord Halifax and Mrs. Catherine Barton, Notes and Queries, First Series, vol. 8, p.* 432.

To-day I told the driver to take me to St. Martin's, where the guide-book says that Newton lived. He put me down at the Newton Hotel, but I looked in vain to its top to see anything like an observatory. I went into a wine-shop near, and asked a girl, who was pouring out a dram, in which house Newton lived. She pointed, not to the hotel, but to a house next to a church, and said, "That's it—don't you see a place on the top? That's where he used to study nights." It is a little, oblong-shaped observatory, built apparently of wood, and blackened by age. The house is a good-looking one—it seems to be of stone. The girl said the rooms were let for shops.—MITCHELL, MARIA, 1857, *Life, Letters and Journals, p.* 103.

In raising the statue which preserves his likeness, near the place of his birth, on the spot where his prodigious faculties were unfolded and trained, we at once gratify our honest pride as citizens of the same State, and humbly testify our grateful sense of the Divine goodness which deigned to bestow upon our race one so marvellously gifted to comprehend the works of Infinite Wisdom, and so piously resolved to make all his study of them the source of religious contemplations, both philosophical and sublime.—BROUGHAM, HENRY LORD, 1858, *Memorial to Sir Isaac Newton, Inaugural Address, Grantham.*

On March 28, 1727, the body of Sir Isaac Newton, after lying in state in the Jerusalem Chamber, where it had been brought from his deathbed in Kensington, was attended by the leading members of the Royal Society, and buried at the public cost in the spot in front of the Choir, which, being "one of the most conspicuous in the Abbey, had been previously refused to various noblemen who had applied for it." Voltaire was present at the funeral. The selection of this spot for such a purpose marks the moment at which the more sacred recesses in the interior of the church were considered to be closed, or to have lost their special attractions, whilst the publicity of the wide and open spaces hitherto neglected gave them a new importance. On the gravestone are written the words, which here acquire a significance of more than usual solemnity—"*Hic depositum quod mortale fuit Isaaci Newtoni.*"—STANLEY, ARTHUR PENRHYN, 1867–96, *Historical Memorials of Westminster Abbey, p.* 293.

He was not a simple-minded man in the sense propounded: he was not like the old philosopher who knocked his foot against a stone while he was looking at the stars. Though not learned in human nature, he was very much the man of the world; he stuck to the main chance, and knew how to make a cast. He took good care of his money, and left a large fortune, though very—even magnificently—liberal on suitable occasions, especially to his family. He was observant of small things, as are all men of suspicious temperament; and he had a strong hatred of immorality, whether in word or deed, which, no doubt, would have turned his acuteness of observation, and his tendency to suspicion, upon anything from which inference could have been drawn. Those who imagine that Newton was always thinking of gravitation might just as well imagine that Wellington was always thinking of strategy.— DE MORGAN, AUGUSTUS, 1871–85, *Newton: His Friend and his Niece, p.* 70.

It was here [St. Martin's Street] that the antiquary Dr. Stukely called one day, by appointment. The servant who opened the door said that Sir Isaac was in his study. No one was permitted to disturb him there; but as it was near his dinner-time the visitor sat down to wait for him. In a short time a boiled chicken under cover was brought in for dinner. An hour passed, and Sir Isaac did not appear. The doctor then ate the fowl, and, covering up the empty dish, desired the servant to get another dressed for his master. Before that was ready, the great man came down. He apologised for his delay, and added: "Give me but leave to take my short dinner, and I shall be at your service. I am fatigued and faint." Saying this, he lifted up the cover, and without emotion turned about to Stukely with a smile. "See," he said, "what we studious people are; I forgot that I had dined."—WALFORD, EDWARD, 1875, *Old and New London, vol.* III, *p.* 172.

Newton's marvellous insight into the order of Nature increased his reverence for the Creator. He spent much time in study of the Bible; and when he became foremost in fame among philosophers, and there was wonder at the comprehensive character of his discoveries, he said only: "To myself I seem to have been as a child picking up stones on the sea-shore, while the great ocean of truth lay unexplored before me."—MORLEY, HENRY, 1879, *A Manual of English Literature, ed. Tyler, p.* 471.

Most of the great predecessors of Newton passed through the ordeal of misfortune and failed not. His own lot was far different. And yet, perhaps, his trial was even more searching. To emerge at the end of a long life of unbroken success, of continuous prosperity, with heart still warm; to endure for half a century wealth and honours, the enthusiasm of his countrymen, the admiration of all men, and still to keep sympathy alive, and still to hold fast his faith, is a stronger test of the stuff a man is made of than the steadfast endurance of suffering or the dangerous witness to truth.—MORTON, E. J. C., 1882, *Heroes of Science, p.* 233.

Sir Isaac Newton is a remarkable instance of a distinguished man who never travelled. Whilst in mind he surveyed the heavens and journeyed to the remotest stars, he traversed in body but a tiny portion of the earth.—COPNER, JAMES, 1885, *Sketches of Celibate Worthies, p.* 207.

Many of the greatest men of genius have doubtless been single men, their passion of knowledge absorbing all other passions. Probably Newton never knew love, nor even the love of fame.—SMILES, SAMUEL, 1887, *Life and Labour, p.* 383.

Here is a man sent by Heaven to do certain things which no man else could do, and so long as he is comparatively unknown he does them; but so soon as he is found out, he is clapped into a routine office with a big salary: and there is, comparatively speaking, an end of him. It is not to be supposed that he had lost his power, for he frequently solved problems very quickly which had been given out by great Continental mathematicians as a challenge to the world. . . . I expect your truly great man never realizes how great he is, and seldom knows where his real strength lies. Certainly Newton did not know it. He several times talks of giving up philosophy altogether; and though he never really does it, and perhaps the feeling is one only born of some temporary overwork, yet he does not sacrifice everything else to it as he surely must had he been conscious of his own greatness. No; self-consciousness was the last thing that affected him.—LODGE, OLIVER, 1892, *Pioneers of Science, pp.* 198, 199.

The story that this train of thought was aroused by seeing an apple fall is due to Voltaire, and is given in his "Philosophie de Newton," 3me partie, chap. iii. Voltaire had it from Newton's step-niece, Mrs. Conduitt. For many years tradition marked the tree in the garden at Woolsthorpe; it was shown to Sir D. Brewster in 1814, and was taken down in 1820.—GLAZEBROOK, R. T., 1894, *Dictionary of National Biography, vol.* XL, *p.* 372.

LEIBNITZ CONTROVERSY

The celebrated Leibnitz may perhaps inquire how I became acquainted with the calculus which I use. About the month of April, and the following months in the year 1687, and subsequent years, when nobody, as I thought, used such a calculus but myself, I invented its fundamental principles, and several of its rules. Nor would it have been less known to me if Leibnitz had never been born. He may, therefore, boast of other disciples, but certainly not of me. And this would be sufficiently evident if the letters which passed between me and the illustrious Huygens were given to the public. Compelled by the evidence of facts, I hold Newton to have been *the first inventor* of the calculus, and the earliest by several years: And whether Leibnitz, *its second inventor*, has borrowed anything from him, I would prefer to my own judgment that of those who have seen the letters of Newton and copies of his other manuscripts. Nor will the silence of the more modest Newton, or the active exertions of Leibnitz in everywhere ascribing the invention of this calculus to himself, impose upon any person who shall examine these documents as I have done.—DUILLIER, NICOLAS FACIO, 1699, *Geometrical Investigation of the Solid of least Resistance, p.* 18.

We have consulted the letters and letterbooks in the custody of the Royal Society, and those found among the papers of Mr. John Collins, dated between the years 1669 and 1677 inclusive; and showed them to such as knew and avouched the hands of Mr. Barrow, Mr. Collins, Mr. Oldenburg, and Mr. Leibnitz; and compared those of Mr. Gregory with one another, and with copies of some of them taken in the hand of Mr. Collins; and have extracted from them what relates to the matter referred to us; all which extracts herewith delivered to you, we believe to be genuine and authentic; and by these letters and papers we find,—

I. That Mr. Leibnitz was in London in the beginning of the year 1673; and went thence, in or about March, to Paris; where he kept a correspondence with Mr. Collins, by means of Mr. Oldenburg, till about September 1676, and then returned by London and Amsterdam to Hanover: and that Mr. Collins was very free in communicating to able mathematicians, what he had received from Mr. Newton and Mr. Gregory.

II. That when Mr. Leibnitz was the first time in London, he contented for the invention of another differential method properly so called, and notwithstanding that he was shown by Dr. Pell, that it was Mouton's method, he persisted in maintaining it to be his own invention, by reason that he had found it by himself, without knowing what Mouton had done before, and had much improved it. And we find no mention of his having any other differential method than Mouton's, before his letter of 21st June 1677, which was a year after a copy of Mr. Newton's letter, of the 10th December 1672, had been sent to Paris to be communicated to him; and above four years after, Mr. Collins began to communicate that letter to his

correspondent; in which letter the method of fluxions was sufficiently described to any intelligent person.

III. That by Mr. Newton's letter of the 13th June 1676, it appears that he had the method of Fluxions above five years before the writing of that letter, and by his Analysis, *per Æquationes numero Terminorum Infinitas*, communicated by Dr. Barrow to Mr. Collins in July 1669, we find that he had invented the method before that time.

IV. That the differential method is one and the same with the method of fluxions, excepting the name and mode of notation; Mr. Leibnitz calling those quantities differences, which Mr. Newton calls moments or fluxions; and marking them with the letter *d*, a mark not used by Mr. Newton. And therefore we take the proper question to be, not who invented this or that method, but who was the first inventor of the method; and we believe, that those who have reputed Mr. Leibnitz the first inventor, knew little or nothing of his correspondence with Mr. Collins and Mr. Oldenburg long before; nor of Mr. Newton's having that method above fifteen years before Mr. Leibnitz began to publish it in the "Acta Eruditorum" of Leipsic. For which reasons we reckon Mr. Newton the first inventor; and are of opinion that Mr. Keill, in asserting the same, has been noways injurious to Mr. Leibnitz. And we submit to the judgment of the Society, whether the extracts, and letters, and papers, now presented, together with what is extant to the same purpose, in Dr. Wallis's third volume, may not deserve to be made public.—COMMITTEE OF ROYAL SOCIETY, 1712, *Report, April* 24.

I confess to you sincerely that till we had seen the "Commercium Epistolicum," it was commonly believed here that Leibnitz was the first inventor of the Differential Calculus, or at least the first publisher of it, though it was as well known that Sir Isaac Newton was master of the secret at the same time; but as he did not challenge it, we could not be undeceived, and what I said concerning it was upon the credit of the common belief, which I did not find contradicted. But since it is so now, I promise you I will change my language whenever there is an opportunity, for I do assure you that it has been my study all my lifetime, to keep myself free from any partiality, whether national or personal, nothing being my concern but truth.—FONTENELLE, BERNARD LE BOVYER, 1717, *Letter to Mr. Chamberlayne, Feb. 5th.*

It was long disputed whether the honour of inventing the method of Fluxions belonged to Newton or to Leibnitz. It is now generally allowed that these great men made the same discovery at the same time. Mathematical science, indeed, had then reached such a point, that if neither of them had ever existed, the principle must inevitably have occurred to some person within a few years.—MACAULAY, THOMAS BABINGTON, 1828, *Dryden, Edinburgh Review; Critical and Miscellaneous Essays.*

The verdict is universal and irreversible that the English preceded the German philosopher, by at least ten years, in the invention of fluxions. Newton could not have borrowed from Leibnitz; but Leibnitz might have borrowed from Newton. —CHITTENDEN, N. W., 1846, *ed., Newton's Principia, Life, p.* 50.

As both of these illustrious men could justly claim the honour of the disputed invention, so both, in the conduct of the controversy, and in the virulence of expression to which they were carried, in their reciprocal charges and accusations, exhibit themselves in much the same sorry light as the Philosopher in *Le Bourgeois Gentilhomme*, who begins to lecture the rival masters of dancing and fencing out of Seneca, and ends by forgetting that he is a philosopher altogether. The controversy is indeed an instructive spectacle of human infirmity—showing how passion can cloud the serenest intellects, and inflame the most philosophic temperaments; that its thunder-storms may be found in the highest latitudes—disturbing the frigid poles as well as the burning tropics; that there is no domain of speculation, however remote, or purely abstract, into which it cannot intrude; and that the Mathematician, as well as the Theologian, can exhibit all the rancour of the most vulgar controvertists. There is probably nothing parallel in history, except the controversy between the Nominalists and Realists, who actually began to fight for and against their shadowy universals.— ROGERS, HENRY, 1846, *Life and Genius of Leibnitz, Edinburgh Review, vol.* 84, *p.* 44.

It is not easy to penetrate into the motives by which this great man was actuated. If his object was to keep possession of his discoveries till he had brought them to a higher degree of perfection, we may approve of the propriety, though we cannot admire the prudence, of such a step. If he wished to retain to himself his own methods, in order that he alone might have the advantage of them, in prosecuting his physical inquiries, we cannot reconcile so selfish a measure with that oppenness and generosity of character which marked the whole of his life, nor with the communications which he so freely made to Barrow, Collins, and others. If he withheld his labours from the world in order to avoid the disputes and contentions to which they might give rise, he adopted the very worst method of securing his tranquility. That this was the leading motive under which he acted, there is little reason to doubt. The early delay in the publication of his method of fluxions, after the breaking out of the plague at Cambridge, was probably owing to his not having completed the whole of his design; but no apology can be made for the imprudence of withholding it any longer from the public,—an imprudence which is the most inexplicable, as he was repeatedly urged by Wallis, Halley, and his other friends, to present it to the world. Had he published the noble discovery previous to 1673, when his great rival had made but little progress in those studies which led him to the same method, he would have secured to himself the undivided honour of the invention, and Leibnitz could have aspired to no other fame but that of an improver of the doctrine of fluxions. But he unfortunately acted otherwise. He announced to his friends that he possessed a method of great generality and power: He communicated to them a general account of its principles and applications; and the information which was thus conveyed, might have directed the attention of mathematicians to subjects to which they would not have otherwise applied their powers. The discoveries which he had previously made were made subsequently by others; and Leibnitz, instead of appearing on the theatre of science as the disciple and the follower of Newton, stood forth with all the dignity of a second inventor; and, by the early publication of his discoveries, had nearly placed himself on the throne which Newton was destined to ascend. . . . In adjudicating on a great question like the present, surrounded as it has been with national sympathies, we are compelled to look into the character of the parties at our bar. We cannot commend the conduct of Newton in concealing from Leibnitz, in transposed letters, the discoveries which he had made, nor can we justify his personal retreat from the battle-field, and his return under the vizor of an accomplished champion. His representatives, however, were men of station and character, who gave their names, and staked their reputation in the contest; while Leibnitz and his disciples wielded the anonymous shafts of the slanderer, denied what they had written, and were publickly exposed through the very rents which they had left in their masks.—BREWSTER, SIR DAVID, 1855, *Memoirs of the Life, Writings and Discoveries of Sir Isaac Newton, vol.* II, *pp.* 22, 81.

The controversy was decided in favor of Newton by a committee appointed by the Royal Academy of Sciences, whose report was read on the 24th of April, 1713, [?] and published in the same year. This decision was partly just, and partly unjust. It was just, in so far as the two methods are identical, since Newton actually made his discovery before Leibnitz, while Leibnitz, not perhaps, altogether independently of Newton, made the same discovery again after Newton, and only preceded him in giving the method to the public. But the decision was unjust, in so far as the methods are not identical, the method of Leibnitz being more perfect and finished than that of Newton; in particular, the terminology adopted by Leibnitz is more pertinent to the subjects in hand and better adapted for use than Newton's, while the most fruitful development of the fundamental idea of the method was discovered, not by Newton, but partly by Leibnitz, and partly by the brothers Jacob and Johann Bardouilli (with especial reference to transcendent functions), who adopted Leibnitz' method. . . . To Leibnitz belongs the glory of an ingenious and relatively independent discovery, subsequent to that of Newton, but to which his own earlier investigations respecting series of differences were also influential in leading

him, and which conducted him to a form of the Infinitesimal Calculus materially superior to that discovered by Newton. But in casting on Newton the suspicion of plagiarism, he conducted the priority controversy (which in itself, in the interest of historical truth, was necessary and unobjectionable), in the later period of that controversy, with means which scarcely admit of excuse.—UEBERWEG, FRIEDRICH, 1871, *History of Philosophy, tr. Morris, vol.* II, *pp.* 99, 100.

PRINCIPIA
1687

In the publication of this work the most acute and universally learned Mr. Edmund Halley not only assisted me with his pains in correcting the press and taking care of the schemes, but it was to his solicitations that its becoming public is owing; for when he had obtained of me my demonstrations of the figure of the celestial orbits, he continually pressed me to communicate the same to the "Royal Society," who afterwards, by their kind encouragement and entreaties, engaged me to think of publishing them. But after I had begun to consider the inequalities of the lunar motions, and had entered upon some other things relating to the laws and measure of gravity, and other forces; and the figures that would be described by bodies attracted according to given laws; and the motion of several bodies moving among themselves; the motion of bodies in resisting mediums; the forces, densities, and motions, of mediums; the orbits of the comets, and such like; I deferred that publication till I had made a search into those matters, and could put forth the whole together. What relates to the lunar motions (being imperfect), I have put all together in the corollaries of Prop. 66, to avoid being obliged to propose and distinctly demonstrate the several things there contained in a method more prolix than the subject deserved, and interrupt the series of the several propositions. Some things, found out after the rest, I chose to insert in places less suitable, rather than change the number of the propositions and the citations. I heartily beg that what I have here done may be read with candour; and that the defects in a subject so difficult be not so much reprehended as kindly supplied, and investigated by new endeavours of my readers.—NEWTON, ISAAC, 1686, *The Principia, Preface.*

Certainly to use Cartesian fictitious hypotheses at this time of day, after the principal parts of Sir Isaac Newton's certain system have been made easy enough for the understanding of ordinary mathematicians, is like the continuing to eat old acorns after the discovery of new wheat, for the food of mankind.—WHISTON, WILLIAM, 1730, *Historical Memoirs of the Life and Writings of Dr. Samuel Clarke.*

Isaac Newton, whom that innate modesty which usually attends on true genius had restrained from displaying his mighty talents, broke forth from his obscurity in the reign of James II. Then it was that he published his "Principia," a work that occasioned the greatest revolution that was ever made in the world of science. This performance is an illustrious proof of the power of the human mind; it being the highest instance that can, or probably ever will be given of the exertion of it.—GRANGER, JAMES, 1769-1824, *Biographical History of England, vol.* VI, *p.* 143.

The importance and generality of the discoveries, and the immense number of original and profound views which have been the germ of the most brilliant theories of the philosophers of this century, and all presented with much elegance, will ensure to the work on the "Mathematical Principles of Natural Philosophy" a pre-eminence above all the other productions of human . genius.—LAPLACE, PIERRE SIMON, 1796-99, *Système du Monde, bk.* v, *ch.* v.

The Theory of the Moon, which crowns his immortal "Principia," is a production of genius, sagacity, and invention almost superhuman. He ascends with admirable order from the easier to the more difficult problems, reducing them always to greater simplicity; he pursues his approximations with consummate address, and, seldom passing the clear bounds of geometry or entangling his demonstrations in the labyrinth of algebraical *formulæ,* he advances with elegance and apparently without effort to the disclosure of the most recondite truths.—LESLIE, SIR JOHN, 1821, *Fourth Dessertation to Encyclopædia Britannica,* 7th ed., *p.* 663.

It is universally known, that Newton composed his wonderful work in a very hasty manner, merely selecting from a huge mass of papers such discoveries as would succeed each other as the connecting link of one vast chain, but without giving himself the trouble of explaining to the world the mode of fabricating those links. His comprehensive mind could, by the feeblest exertion of its powers, condense into one view many syllogisms of a proposition even heretofore uncontemplated. What difficulties, then, *to him* would seem his own discoveries? Surely none; and the modesty for which he is proverbially remarkable, gave him in his own estimation so little the advantage of the rest of created beings, that he deemed these difficulties as easy to others as to himself: the lamentable consequence of which humility has been, that he himself is scarcely comprehended at this day—a century from the birth of the "Principia."—WRIGHT, J. M. F., 1833, *A Commentary on Newton's Principia, Preface, p.* vii.

The reader of the "Principia," if he be a tolerably good mathematician, can follow the whole chain of demonstration by which the universality of gravitation is deduced from the fact, that it is a power acting inversely, as the square of the distance to the centre of attraction. Satisfying himself of the laws which regulate the motion of bodies in trajectories around given centres, he can convince himself of the sublime truths unfolded in that immortal work, and must yield his assent to this position, that the moon is deflected from the tangent of her orbit round the earth, by the same force by which the satellites of Jupiter are deflected from the tangent of theirs, the very same force which makes a stone unsupported fall to the ground. The reader of the "Mécanique Céleste," if he be a still more learned mathematician, and versed in the modern improvements of the calculus which Newton discovered, can follow the chain of demonstration by which the wonderful provision made for the stability of the universe, is deduced from the fact, that the direction of all the planetary motions is the same—the eccentricity of their orbits small, and the angle formed by the plane of their orbits with the ecliptic acute. Satisfying himself of the laws which regulate the mutual actions of those bodies, he can convince himself of a truth yet more sublime than Newton's discovery, though flowing from it, and must yield his assent to the marvellous position, that all the irregularities occasioned in the system of the universe, by the mutual attraction of its members, are periodical, and subject to an eternal law which prevents them from ever exceeding a stated amount, and secures through all time the balanced structure of a universe composed of bodies, whose mighty bulk and prodigious swiftness of motion mock the utmost efforts of the human imagination. All these truths are to the skilful mathematician as thoroughly known, and their evidence is as clear, as the simplest proposition in arithmetic is to common understandings. But how few are there who thus know and comprehend· them! Of all the millions that thoroughly believe those truths, certainly not a thousand individuals are capable of following even any considerable portion of the demonstrations upon which they rest, and probably not a hundred now living have ever gone through the whole steps of those demonstrations.— BROUGHAM, HENRY LORD, 1839, *Natural Theology, Works, vol.* VI, *p.* 404.

A work which will be memorable not only in the annals of one science or of one country, but which will form an epoch in the history of the world, and will ever be regarded as the brightest page in the records of human reason,—a work, may we not add, which would be read with delight in every planet of our system,— in every system of the universe. What a glorious privilege was it to have been the author of the "Principia!" There was but one earth upon whose form and tides and movements the philosopher could exercise his genius,—one moon, whose perturbations and inequalities and actions he could study,—one sun, whose controlling force and apparent motions he could calculate and determine,—one system of planets, whose mutual disturbances could tax his highest reason,—one system of comets, whose eccentric paths he could explore and rectify,—and one universe of stars, to whose binary and multiple combinations he could extend the law of terrestrial gravity. To have been the chosen sage summoned to the study of that earth, these systems, and that universe,—the favoured lawgiver to worlds unnumbered, the high-priest in the temple of boundless space,—was a privilege that could be

granted but one member of the human family;—and to have executed the task was an achievement which in its magnitude can be measured only by the infinite in space, and in the duration of its triumphs by the infinite in time. That Sage—that Lawgiver—that High-priest was Newton.—BREWSTER, SIR DAVID, 1855, *Memoirs of the Life, Writings and Discoveries of Sir Isaac Newton, vol* I, *p.* 318.

This immortal work not only laid the foundation of Physical Astronomy, it also carried the structure thereof very far towards its completion. . . . Taking the theory of gravitation in its universal acceptation, Newton, in a manner that looks as if he were divinely inspired, succeeded in demonstrating the chief inequalities of the moon and planetary bodies; in determining the figure of the earth—that it is not a perfect sphere, but an oblate spheroid; in explaining the precession of the equinoxes and the tides of the ocean. To such perfection have succeeding mathematicians brought his theory, that the most complicated movements and irregularities of the solar system have been satisfactorily accounted for and reduced to computation. . . . It adds to our admiration of the wonderful intellectual powers of Newton to know that the mathematical instrument he used was the ancient geometry.—DRAPER, JOHN WILLIAM, 1876, *History of the Intellectual Development of Europe, vol.* II, *pp.* 272, 275.

We hardly know whether to admire more the sublime discoveries at which Newton arrived, or the extraordinary character of the intellectual processess by which those discoveries were´ reached. Viewed from either standpoint, Newton's "Principia" is incomparably the greatest work on science that has ever yet been produced.—BALL, SIR ROBERT, 1895, *Isaac Newton, Good Words, vol.* 36, *p.* 115.

Though belonging to an earlier period, the full meaning of Newton's work has only been recognised in the course of our century. In fact the Newtonian philosophy can be said to have governed at least one entire section of the scientific research of the first half of this period: only in the second half of the period have we succeeded in defining more clearly the direction in which Newton's views require to be extended or modified. Newton's greatest achievements was to combine the purely mechanical laws which Galileo and Huygens had established with the purely physical relations which Kepler—following Copernicus and Tycho—had discovered in the planetary motions, and to abstract in so doing the general formula of universal attraction or gravitation. . . . Newton did not publish his "Principia" till 1687. The work, however, was conceived in the highest philosophic spirit, inasmuch as the enunciation of the so-called law of gravitation required the clear expression of the general laws of motion. In the first and second parts of the work the discoveries of Galileo and Huygens were absorbed, generalised, and restated in such terms as have up to our age been considered sufficient to form the basis for all purely mechanical reasoning. In the latter part the new rule, corresponding to Kepler's empirical laws, is represented as a key to a system of the universe. The great outlines of this system are boldly drawn, and the working out of it is left as the great bequest of Newton to his successors.—MERZ, JOHN THEODORE, 1896, *A History of European Thought in the Nineteenth Century, vol.* I, *p.* 317.

GENERAL

'Tis given out at Oxford, that Mr. Newton has improved his doctrine of gravity so far, that he can answer all my lunar observations exceeding nearly; and that now there is little need of them, since all the inequalities of the moon's motions may be discovered by the sole laws of gravitation without them. I said nothing of this, because I have moved him enough with what I have said about the comets: but to the honest man that told me of it, with some indignation I answered that he had been as many years upon this thing as I had been on the constellations and planets altogether; that he had made lunar tables once to answer his conceived laws,—but when he came to compare them with the heavens (that is, the moon's observed places), he found he had mistook, and was forced to throw them all aside; that I had imparted above 200 of her observed places to him, which one would think should be sufficient to limit any theory by; and since he has altered and suited his theory till it fitted these observations, 'tis no wonder that it represents them: but still he is more beholden to them

for it than he is to his speculations about gravity, which had misled him. Mr. Hobbs boasted that his laws were agreeable to those of Moses. Dr. Eachards tells him he doubted not of it; for being drawn from Moses' works, and copied into his, he might be sure they would agree, except the laws of Moses were flown, which he was sure they were not.—FLAMSTEED, JOHN, 1700, *Letter to Lowthorp, May* 10, *Baily's Life of Flamsteed, p.* 176.

Newton's harangue amounts to no more than that gravity is proportional to gravity.—BERKELEY, GEORGE, c 1705, *Commonplace Book, Life and Letters, ed. Fraser, vol.* IV, *p.* 497.

This I know, that he was much more solicitous in his inquiries into religion than into natural philosophy, and that the reason of his shewing the errors of Cartes' philosophy was because he thought it was made on purpose to be the foundation of infidelity. . . . It's hoped that the worthy and ingenious Mr. Conduitt will take care that they (his theological writings) be published, that the world may see that Sir Isaac Newton was as good a Christian as he was a mathematician and philosopher.—CRAIG, JOHN, 1727, *Letter to Mr. Conduitt, April* 7.

The French philosophers at present chiefly follow Malebranche. They admire Sir Isaac Newton very much, but don't yet allow of his great principle: it is his particular reasonings, experiments, and penetration, for which they so much admire him. — RAMSAY, CHEVALIER, 1728-30, *Spence's Anecdotes, ed. Singer, p.* 28.

Superior beings, when of late they saw
A mortal man unfold all Nature's law,
Admir'd such wisdom in an earthly shape,
And shew'd a Newton as we shew an Ape.
—POPE, ALEXANDER, 1733-34, *Essay on Man.*

And yet so incurable is the love of detraction, perhaps beyond what the charitable reader will easily believe that I have been assured, by more than one creditable person, how some of my enemies have industriously whispered about, that one Isaac Newton, an instrument-maker, formerly living near Leicester-Fields, and afterwards a workman in the Mint at the Tower, might possibly pretend to vie with me for fame in future times. The man, it seems, was knighted for making sun-dials better than others of his trade, and was thought to be a conjuror, because he knew how to draw lines and circles upon a slate, which nobody could understand. But adieu to all noble attempts for endless renown, if the ghost of an obscure mechanic shall be raised up to enter into competition with me, only for his skill in making pothooks and hangers with a pencil; which many thousand accomplished gentlemen and ladies can perform as well with pen and ink upon a piece of paper, and in a manner as little intelligible as those of Sir Isaac. —SWIFT, JONATHAN, ? 1738, *Complete Collection of Genteel and Ingenious Conversation by Simon Wagstaff, Introduction.*

God speaks, and the chaos at his voice subsides;
In various orbs the mighty mass divides;
At once they gravitate, they strive to fall,
One center seeking which attracts them all.
That soul of nature, that all moving spring,
Lay long conceal'd, an unregarded thing;
Till Newton's compass moving through the space
Measures all nature, and discovers place.
The famous laws of motion are survey'd,
Drawn back the veil, the heav'ns are all display'd.
—VOLTAIRE, FRANÇOIS MARIE AROUET, 1738, *Elements of Newton's Philosophy*, p. 79.

That wonder of our age and nation, Sir Isaac Newton.—WATTS, DR. ISAAC, 1741? *Improvement of the Mind.*

With respect to the primary planets, the attraction of the sun only is sufficient to oblige them to describe ellipses, but as they ought also to attract each other, there was some room to apprehend that the regularity of their motion might be thereby somewhat disturbed. We ought, however, to take Sir Isaac Newton's word upon this head, since we shall presently see from what he has done, that there is no reason to be in pain upon this account. According to his observation, bodies attract each other in a direct proportion of the quantities of matter they contain, and the converse proportion of the squares of their distances, and in this proportion it is that the planets affect each other. Now if the Newtonian Philosophy be true, there is a certain method of knowing the quantity of matter in the planets, and consequently of calculating the force of their impressions; such a calculation being made, it appears that Mars, our Earth, Venus and Mercury, attract each other so little in proportion to the force with which they are attracted by the sun, that the disorder arising from thence must be altogether imperceptible in many revolutions; and hence there appears a wonderful agreement between the principles of this philosophy and the phænomena. But this agreement appears still more clearly in what happens with respect to Jupiter and Saturn; the quantity of matter in Jupiter is so great, that the calculation demonstrates the effects of its attraction upon Saturn ought to be very sensible in the time of their conjunction. Sir Isaac Newton predicted this to the Astronomers Flamsteed and Halley, but the former of these great men gave no credit at all to that prediction. However, the conjunction of those two planets approaching, this singular observation was made for the first time, and the consequence was, that the calculation was exactly verified. This procured the Newtonian Philosophy the approbation of so great an Astronomer as Flamsteed; indeed it would have been very difficult for him to have denied it.—SIGORGNE, PIERRE, 1747, *Institutions Newtoniennes, Preface, p. XVII.*

He saw that it was necessary to consult nature herself, to attend carefully to her manifest operations, and to extort her secrets from her by well chosen and repeated experiments. He would admit no objections against plain experience from metaphysical considerations, which, he saw, had often missed philosophers, and had seldom been of real use in their enquiries. He avoided presumption, he had the necessary patience as well as genius; and having kept steadily to the right path, he therefore succeeded. Experiments and observations, 'tis true, could not alone have carried him far in tracing the causes from their effects, and explaining the effects from their causes: a sublime geometry was his guide in this nice and difficult enquiry. This is the instrument, by which alone the machinery of a work, made with so much art could be unfolded; and therefore he sought to carry it to the greatest height. Nor is it easy to discern, whether he has shewn greater skill, and been more successful, in improving and perfecting the instrument, or in applying its use.—MACLAURIN, COLIN, 1748-50, *An Account of Sir Isaac Newton's Philosophical Discoveries, p. 8.*

In Newton this island may boast of having produced the greatest and rarest genius that ever rose for the ornament and instruction of the species. Cautious in admitting no principles but such as were founded on experiment; but resolute to adopt every such principle, however new or unusual: from modesty, ignorant of his superiority to the rest of mankind; and thence less careful to accommodate his reasonings to common apprehensions: more anxious to merit than acquire fame: he was, from these causes, long unknown to the world; but his reputation at last broke out with a lustre which scarce any writer, during his own lifetime, had ever before attained. While Newton seemed to draw off the veil from some of the mysteries of nature, he showed at the same time, the imperfections of the mechanical philosophy; and thereby restored her ultimate secrets to that obscurity in which they ever did and ever will remain.—HUME, DAVID, 1762, *The History of England, James II.*

In a Latin converse with the Père Boscovitch, at the house of Mrs. Cholmondeley, I heard him maintain the superiority of Sir Isaac Newton over all foreign philosophers, with a dignity and eloquence that surprised that learned foreigner.—JOHNSON, SAMUEL, 1770, *Life by Boswell, ch.* xviii.

Both Newton and Bacon would have turned away in disgust from those who idolized them in the eighteenth century. In the case of the former, his strong attachment to Christianity and to the Bible was often pitied and deplored by his philosophic successors as the peculiar weakness of a mind naturally strong. In many of his expressions respecting the relations of the Diety to nature, or the starry heavens as the laboratory and reflex of the Divine glory, there is not merely a substratum of enthusiasm, but also of earnest conviction, bearing a peculiar impress, and proving that he had often deliberated on the supreme object of all contemplation, even though he was not actually a philosopher, and knew nothing of metaphysics.—SCHLEGEL, FREDERICK, 1815, *Lectures on the History of Literature, Lecture* xiii.

No one ever left knowledge in a state so different from that in which he found it. Men were instructed not only in new truths, but in new methods of discovering

truth: they were made acquainted with the great principle which connects together the most distant regions of space, as well as the most remote periods of duration; and which was to lead to future discoveries, far beyond what the wisest or most sanguine could anticipate.—PLAYFAIR, JOHN, 1816-19, *Preliminary Dissertation, Encyclopædia Britannica.*

All subsequent commentators are largely indebted to the labours of Sir Isaac Newton.—HORNE, THOMAS HARTWELL, 1818-39, *A Manual of Biblical Bibliography.*

This almost superhuman genius, whose powers and attainments at once make us proud of our common nature, and humble us with our disparity.—BROWN, THOMAS, 1820, *Lectures on the Philosophy of the Human Mind, Lecture* ii.

We praise Newton's clearness and steadiness. He *was* clear and steady, no doubt, whilst working out, by the help of an admirable geometry, the idea brought forth by another. Newton had his ether, and could not rest in—he could not conceive—the idea of law. He thought it a physical thing after all. As for his chronology, I believe those who are most competent to judge, rely on it less and less every day. His lucubrations on Daniel and the Revelations seem to me little less than mere raving.—COLERIDGE, SAMUEL TAYLOR, 1830, *Table Talk, ed. Ashe, Oct.* 8, *p.* 115.

Newton *was* a great man, but you must excuse me if I think that it would take many Newtons to make one Milton.—COLERIDGE, SAMUEL TAYLOR, 1833, *Table Talk, ed. Ashe, July* 4, *p.* 240.

The doctrine of universal gravitation, like other great steps in science, required a certain time to make its way into men's minds; and had to be confirmed, illustrated, and completed, by the labors of succeeding philosophers. As the discovery itself was great beyond former example, the features of the natural sequel to the discovery were also on a gigantic scale; and many vast and laborious trains of research, each of which might, in itself, be considered as forming a wide science, and several of which have occupied many profound and zealous inquirers from that time to our own day, come before us as parts only of the verification of Newton's Theory. Almost everything that has been done, and is doing, in astronomy, falls inevitably under this description; and it is only when the astronomer travels to the very limits of his vast field of labor, that he falls in with phenomena which do not acknowledge the jurisdiction of the Newtonian legislation.—WHEWELL, WILLIAM, 1837-57, *History of the Inductive Sciences*, *vol.* I, *p.* 420.

Newton's religious writings are distinguished by their absolute freedom from prejudice. Everywhere, throughout them, there glows the genuine nobleness of soul. To his whole life, indeed, we may here fitly extend the same observation. He was most richly imbued with the very spirit of the Scriptures which he so delighted to study and to meditate upon. His was a piety, so fervent, so sincere and practical, that it rose up like a holy incense from every thought and act. His a benevolence that not only willed, but endeavoured the best for all. His a philanthropy that held in the embracings of its love every brother-man. His a toleration of the largest and the truest; condemning persecution in every, even its mildest, form; and kindly encouraging each striving after excellence:—a toleration that came not of indifference—for the immoral and impious met with their quick rebuke —but a toleration that came of the wise humbleness and the Christian charity, which see, in the nothingness of self and the almightiness of TRUTH, no praise for the ablest, and no blame for the feeblest in their strugglings upwards to light and life.—CHITTENDEN, N. W., 1846, *ed., Newton's Principia, Life, p.* 41.

I cannot but fancy the shade of Newton blushing to reflect that, among the many things which he professed to *know not,* poetry was omitted, of which he knew nothing. Great as he was, he indeed saw nothing in the face of nature but its lines and colors; not the lines and colors of passion and sentiment included, but only squares and their distances, and the anatomy of the rainbow. He thought the earth a glorious planet; he knew it better than any one else, in its connection with other planets; and yet half the beauty of them all, that which sympathy bestows and imagination colors, was to him a blank. He took space to be the sensorium of the Deity, (so noble a fancy could be struck out of the involuntary encounter between

his intense sense of a mystery and the imagination he despised!) and yet this very fancy was but an escape from the horror of a vacuum, and a substitution of the mere consciousness of existence for the thoughts and images with which a poet would have accompanied it. He imagined the form of the house, and the presence of the builder; but the life and the variety, the paintings, the imagery, and the music —the loves and the joys, the whole riches of the place, the whole riches in the distance, the creations heaped upon creation, and the particular as well as aggregate consciousness of all this in the great mind of whose presence he was conscious—to all this his want of imagination rendered him insensible. The "Fairy Queen" was to him a trifle; the dreams of Shakspeare "ingenious nonsense." But courts were something, and so were the fashions there. When the name of the Deity was mentioned, he took off his hat!—HUNT, LEIGH, 1847, *Fiction and Matter of Fact; Men, Women and Books, vol.* I, *p.* 8.

In Isaac Newton two kinds of intellectual power, which have little in common, and which are not often found together in a very high degree of vigour, but which nevertheless are equally necessary in the most sublime departments of physics, were united as they have never been united before or since. There may have been minds as happily constituted as his for the cultivation of pure mathematical science; there may have been minds as happily constituted for the cultivation of science purely experimental; but in no other mind have the demonstrative faculty and the inductive faculty coexisted in such supreme excellence and perfect harmony. Perhaps in the days of Scotists and Thomists even his intellect might have run to waste, as many intellects ran to waste which were inferior only to his. Happily the spirit of the age on which his lot was cast, gave the right direction to his mind; and his mind reacted with tenfold force on the spirit of the age.—MACAULAY, THOMAS BABINGTON, 1849, *History of England, ch.* iii.

They who have overlooked or disregarded the proofs of the connexion between what Bacon enjoined and Boyle performed, are not likely to have recognized any traces of the lights held out by the former, in the philosophy of Newton.

Yet it appears undeniable that the latter was guided by principles which Bacon alone had taught; and that his philosophy derives an imperishable character from its rigid adherence to them.—NAPIER, MACVEY, 1853, *Lord Bacon and Sir Walter Raleigh, p.* 43.

We think of Euclid as of fine ice; we admire Newton as we admire the peak of Teneriffe. — BAGEHOT, WALTER, 1856, *Thomas Babington Macaulay, Works, ed. Morgan, vol.* II, *p.* 59.

A genius of the very highest order, a type of genius in science, if ever there was one.—ARNOLD, MATTHEW, 1865, *The Literary Influence of Academies, Essays in Criticism.*

Newton's merit consisted in this, that he applied the laws of dynamics to the movements of the celestial bodies, and insisted that scientific theories must be substantiated by the agreement of observations with calculations.—DRAPER, JOHN WILLIAM, 1874, *History of the Conflict Between Religion and Science, p*ι 237.

Our national reverence for Newton's scientific achievements has deterred us from laughing at his dabblings in the interpretation of prophecy; and, indeed, sighs rather than smiles should greet the melancholy spectacle of a noble intellect running to waste in puzzling over meaningless riddles.—STEPHEN, LESLIE, 1876, *History of English Thought in the Eighteenth Century, vol.* I, *p.* 212.

In the possession of five healthy senses he regarded himself as the centre of all phenomena, and asserted that what was discernible to the *unassisted human eye* was the real standard for everything. This was the reason why he found no pleasure in astronomy, for which he needed a telescope, or in microscopic investigations. He even cherished a prejudice against Newton from the one circumstance that he operated with a prism instead of making a sufficient instrument of his healthy human eye.— GRIMM, HERMAN, 1880, *The Life and Times of Goethe, tr. Adams, Lecture* xxiii.

That Kant was considerably influenced by Locke is evident from his numerous references to him; but in his earlier years, at least, he was much more indebted to Newton. This is not only seen in his work on cosmogony, but also in his first metaphysical dissertation, which aims to show that metaphysic is not in conflict with the natural philosophy of Newton. Locke's influence began later. While it may be impossible to trace the direct influence of Newton on the "Kritik," indirectly it was great.—STUCKENBERG, J. H. W., 1882, *The Life of Immanuel Kant, p.* 230.

The greatest of natural philosophers.— TAYLOR, H. M., 1884, *Encyclopædia Britannica, Ninth ed., vol.* XVII.

Sir Isaac Newton's great discovery was not of gravitation, but of the Unity which furnishes the proof of God's existence.— BRAY, CHARLES, 1884, *Phases of Opinion and Experience During a Long Life, p.* 231.

In Locke's famous countryman, Isaac Newton, the modern investigation of nature attains the level toward which it has striven, at first by wishes and demands, gradually, also, in knowledge and achievement, since the end of the mediæval period. . . . Newton resembles Boyle in uniting profound piety with the rigor of scientific thought. He finds the most certain proof for the existence of an intelligent creator in the wonderful arrangement of the world-machine, which does not need after-adjustment at the hands of its creator, and whose adaption he praises as enthusiastically as he unconditionally rejects the mingling of teleological considerations in the explanation of physical phenomena.—FALCKENBERG, RICHARD, 1885-93, *History of Modern Philosophy, tr. Armstrong, pp.* 181, 182.

Newton has with regard to our subject two great merits. Firstly, he has greatly enlarged the horizon of mechanical physics through the discovery of universal gravitation. Further, he has also completed the enunciation of the principles of mechanics as we now accept them. After him an essentially new principle has not been established. What after him has been done in mechanics refers to the deductive, formal, and mathematical development of mechanics on the ground of Newton's principles. . . . Newton's principles are sufficient without the introduction of any, new principle to clear up every mechanical problem which may present itself, be it one of statics or dynamics. If difficulties present themselves, they are always only mathematical, formal, not fundamental.—MACH, ERNST, 1889-93, *Mechanik in ihrer Entwickelung, historisch-kritisch dargestellt, tr. M'Cormack, pp.* 174, 239.

Newton has indeed but little direct claim to rank among the masters of English prose. With the exception of a few letters and theological pamphlets, his writings are all in Latin, academic instincts teaching him the inestimable value of that language as an instrument of definite and precise statement. Nor are the subjects such as to leave much room for beauty of form in their exposition. Order, lucidity, and a reverence for the syllogism—you can expect no more from a mathematician. And those same virtues of clear and cogent reasoning, are the chief qualities which Newton carries with him when he ventures into his mother tongue, and beyond the sphere of physics. Indirectly, however, he must have had a considerable influence upon the subsequent course of literature. The impulse of the scientific spirit is among the principal factors to be taken account of in examining the problem of the eighteenth century mind; and no one had a greater share in the propagation of this impulse than Newton.—CHAMBERS, E. K., 1894, *English Prose, ed. Craik, vol.* III, *p.* 311.

An estimate of his genius is impossible. "Sibi gratulentur mortales tale tantumque extitisse Humani generis Decus" are the words on his monument at Westminster, while on Roubilica's statue in Trinity College chapel the inscription is "Newton qui genus humanum ingenio superavit." All who have written of him use words of the highest admiration. On a table in the room in which Newton was born at Woolsthrop manorhouse is inscribed the celebrated epitaph written by Pope:

Nature and Nature's laws lay hid in night:
God said, "Let Newton be," and all was light.

Laplace speaks of the causes "which will always assure to the 'Principia' a pre-eminence above all other productions of the human intellect." Voltaire, who was present at Newton's funeral, and was profoundly impressed by the just honours paid to his memory by "the chief men of the nation," always spoke of the philosopher with reverence—"if all the geniuses of the uinverse assembled, he should lead the band."—GLAZEBROOK, R. T., 1894, *Dictionary of National Biography, vol.* XL, *p.* 392.

Had Newton done nothing beyond making his wonderful discoveries in light, his fame would have gone down to posterity as one of the greatest of Nature's interpreters. . . . Though Newton lived long enough to receive the honour that his astonishing discoveries so justly merited, and though for many years of his life his renown was much greater than that of any of his contemporaries, yet it is not too much to say that, in the years which have since elapsed, Newton's fame has been ever steadily advancing, so that it never stood higher than it does at this moment. We hardly know whether to admire more the sublime discoveries at which he arrived, or the extraordinary character of the intellectual processes by which those discoveries were reached. Viewed from either standpoint, Newton's "Principia" is incomparably the greatest work on science that has ever yet been produced.—BALL, SIR ROBERT S., 1895, *Great Astronomers, pp.* 131, 146.

His reputation spread more slowly than that of the great High Chancellor; but it rests on a surer foundation, which baffles every attempt to shake it, and will outlast all coming changes of thought. The beginnings of modern scientific thought are thus to be found in this country. Lord Bacon foretold prophetically the great change which the new philosophy was destined to work. Newton more patiently drew up the first simple rules and gave the first brilliant application. More than the unfinished and wearisome pages of Bacon's "Novum Organum" does the "Principia" deserve to be placed on a line with Aristotle and Euclid as a model work of scientific inquiry.—MERZ, JOHN THEODORE, 1896, *A History of European Thought in the Nineteenth Century, vol.* I, *p.* 95.

It has been said that the history of Sir Isaac Newton is also the history of science; yet the character of his life and the work does not entirely exclude him from the category of men of letters. . . . Milton and Dante dealt with the spiritual order of creation, Sir Isaac Newton with the material; yet to those who perceive an almost mystical significance in numbers,—to whom mathematics are, in a sense, gateways to the unseen,—the author of the "Principia" and of the "Treatise on Optics" will seem scarcely less a teacher than the poets.—WARNER, CHARLES DUDLEY, 1897, *ed., Library of the World's Best Literature, vol.* XVIII, *p.* 10619.

Cotton Mather
1663-1728

Son of Increase Mather. A famous Congregational clergyman of Boston, pastor of the North Church, 1683-1728, and his father's colleague for the greater part of that period. He was a prolific author, publishing nearly four hundred works, large and small, but it is upon the "Magnalia Christi Americana" that his reputation rests. Among other works are "Wonders of the Invisible World;" "Christian Philosopher;" "Psalterium Americanum;" "Manductio ad Ministerium;" "Memorable Providences Relating to Witchcraft;" "Essays to Do Good;" "The Armour of Christianity;" "Batteries upon the Kingdom of the Devil;" "Death made Easie and Happy." His style is disfigured by pedantry and strained analogies, and is at all times far removed from simplicity, but the author is nevertheless easily seen to be intensely earnest in his endeavours to be of service to his generation.—ADAMS, OSCAR FAY, 1897, *A Dictionary of American Authors, p.* 249.

PERSONAL

Dr. Cotton Mather is intombed. Bearers, the Rev'd Mr. Colman, Mr. Thacher; Mr. Sewall, Mr. Prince; Mr. Webb, Mr. Cooper. The Church went before the Corpse; first, Rev. Mr. Gee in mourning, alone; then three deacons; then Capt. Hutchinson, Adam Winthrop, Esq., Col. Hutchinson. Went up Hull street. I went in a coach. All the council had gloves. I had a pair. . . . Mr. Walter prayed excellently.— SEWALL, SAMUEL, 1728, *Diary, Feb.* 19.

By his learned works and correspondence, those who lived at the greatest distance might discern much of his superior light and influence; but they could discern these only by a more mediate and faint reflection. These could neither see nor well imagine that extraordinary luster of pious and useful literature, wherewith we were, every day, entertained, surprised, and satisfied, who dwelt in the directer rays, in the more immediate vision.— PRINCE, THOMAS, 1729, *Life and Times of Cotton Mather, by Marvin, p.* 575.

When I was a boy, I met with a book, entitled "Essays to do Good," which I think was written by your father. It had been so little regarded by a former possessor, that several leaves of it were torn out; but the remainder gave me such a turn of thinking, as to have an influence on my conduct through life. . . . It is now more than sixty years since I left Boston: but I remember well both your father and grandfather, having heard them both in the pulpit, and seen them in their houses. The last time I saw your father was in the beginning of 1724, when I visited him after my first trip to Pennsylvania. He received me in his library, and on my taking leave, showed me a shorter way out of the house through a narrow passage, which was crossed by a beam overhead. We were still talking as I withdrew, he accompanying me behind, and I turning partly towards him, when he said hastily, "Stoop, stoop!" I did not understand him, till I felt my head hit against the beam. He was a man that never missed any occasion of giving instruction, and upon this he said to me, "You are young, and have the world before you; stoop as you go through it, and you will miss many hard thumps." This advice, thus beat into my head, has frequently been of use to me; and I often think of it, when I see pride mortified, and misfortunes brought upon people by their carrying their heads too high.—FRANKLIN, BENJAMIN, 1784, *Letter to Samuel Mather, May* 12.

His early reputation, and the prominent part he took in the ecclesiastical affairs of New England; the great and long-continued consideration which he enjoyed with the people at large; his literary attainments and unquestionable ability of a certain kind; the contributions he made to the materials of our early history, ample at least, if not so exact as might be desired; and last, though not least, his grievous errors of conduct, on several important occasions, give him an undoubted eminence above most of his contemporaries, and make him one of the most remarkable characters that belong to the early period of New England.—PALFREY, JOHN GORHAM, 1836, *Spark's American Biography, North American Review, vol.* 43, *p.* 518.

In summing up the character of Cotton Mather, we should say, that he was a man of superior general ability, without the advantage of any leading intellectual tendencies, and that his warm and benevolent feelings were not sufficiently guarded by reserve, or qualified by worldly shrewdness. By nature and education he was unfortunately subject to conceit and self-complacency, which he had not tact enough to conceal. This infirmity was evidently the real cause of his misfortunes during life, and its influence has followed his reputation, and obscured his merits with posterity.—HAVEN, S. F., 1840, *Cotton Mather, North American Review, vol.* 51, *p.* 22.

To cover his confusion, Cotton Mather got up a case of witchcraft in his own parish. . . . Was Cotton Mather honestly credulous? . . . He is an example how far selfishness, under the form of vanity and ambition, can blind the higher faculties, stupefy the judgment, and dupe consciousness itself.—BANCROFT, GEORGE, 1840, *History of the United States, vol.* III.

He incurred the responsibility of being its chief cause and promoter. In the progress of the superstitious fear, which amounted to frenzy, and could only be satisfied with blood, he neither blenched nor halted; but attended the courts, watched the progress of invisible agency in the prisons, and joined the multitude in witnessing the executions.—QUINCY, JOSIAH, 1840, *History of Harvard University, vol.* I, *p.* 63.

The suggestion, that Cotton Mather, for purposes of his own, deliberately got up this witchcraft delusion, and forced it upon a doubtful and hesitating people, is utterly absurd. . . . Mather's position, convictions, and temperament alike called him to serve on this occasion as the organ, exponent, and stimulator of the popular faith.—HILDRETH, RICHARD, 1849, *History of the United States of America, vol.* II, *p.* 151.

As Cotton Mather was a very distinguished man, Grandfather took some pains to give the children a lively conception of his character. Over the door of his library were painted these words, BE SHORT,—as a warning to visitors that they must not do the world so much harm as needlessly to interrupt this great man's wonderful labors. On entering the room you would probably behold it crowded, and piled, and heaped with books. They were huge, ponderous folios, and quartos, and little duodecimos, in English, Latin, Greek, Hebrew, Chaldaic, and all other languages that either originated at the confusion of Babel or have since come into use. All these books, no doubt, were tossed about in confusion, thus forming a visible emblem of the manner in which their contents were crowded into Cotton Mather's brain. And in the middle of the room stood a table, on which, besides printed volumes, were strewn manuscript sermons, historical tracts, and political pamphlets, all written in such a queer, blind, crabbed, fantastical hand, that a writing-master would have gone raving mad at the sight of them. By this table stood Grandfather's chair, which seemed to have contracted an air of deep erudition, as if its cushion were stuffed with Latin, Greek, and Hebrew, and other hard matters. In this chair, from one year's end to another, sat that prodigious bookworm, Cotton Mather, sometimes devouring a great book, and sometimes scribbling one as big. In Grandfather's younger days there used to be a wax figure of him in one of the Boston museums, representing a solemn, dark-visaged person, in a minister's black gown, and with a black-letter volume before him.—HAWTHORNE, NATHANIEL, 1850, *Grandfather's Chair, ch.* iv.

Mather was always exercising his ingenuity to contribute something useful to the world. He was one of the first to employ the press extensively in the dissemination of tracts; he early lifted his voice in favor of temperance; he preached and wrote for sailors; he instructed negroes; he substituted moral and sagacious intellectual restraints with his children for flogging; conversation he studied and practised as an art; and he was a devoted historiographer of his country for posterity—besides his paramount employment, according to the full measure of his day and generation, of discharging the sacred duties of his profession. Pity that any personal defects of temperament or "follies of the wise" should counterbalance these noble achievements—that so well freighted a bark should at times experience the want of a rudder. Good sense was the one stick occasionally missing from the enormous faggot of Mather's studies and opinions. . . . One thing he never could attain, though he nearly inherited it, though his learning almost irresistibly challenged it, though he spiritually anticipated it—the prize of the Presidency of Harvard College. One and another was chosen in preference to him. The ghostly authority of the old priestly influence was passing away. Cotton Mather was, in age a disheartened and disappointed man. The possession, in turn, of three wives had proved but a partial consolation. One of his sons he felt compelled to disown; his wife was subject to fits of temper bordering on insanity; the glooms of his own disposition grew darker in age as death approached, a friend whom he was glad to meet, when he expired, at the completion of his sixty-fifth year, the 13th February, 1728. His last emphatic charge to his son Samuel was, "Remember only that one word, 'Fructuosus.' "—DUYCKINCK, EVERT A. AND GEORGE L., 1855-65-75, *Cyclopædia of American Literature*, ed. Simmons, vol. I, p. 67.

He is the greatest of American scholars. It is doubtful if any one in the New World has ever equalled his acquaintance with theological and classic literature, his readiness in using his knowledge, his wonderful industry, his intense literary ardor. No moment of his life was wasted, and all his life was given to study.—LAWRENCE, EUGENE, 1880, *A Primer of American Literature*, p. 20.

He became the greatest pulpit power in his day, and unsurpassed since, unless, perhaps, by a very few in later generations. During the week he made the most faithful preparation by reading, meditation, prayer, and writing. Study of the Bible in the original languages kept his mind fresh and unhackneyed. Praying as he wrote, he went into the house of God surcharged with God's truth and spirit. Nothing was left till Saturday night or Sunday morning to tax his strength by way of mental toil and worry over a sermon. Saturday evening and Sunday morning were sacred to devotions. He went to the sanctuary as to the "gate of heaven." Full of matter and fervent in prayer, he was like a charged battery, and he represented Christ as he stood before his auditory. They were instructed, they were aroused, their consciences were quickened, their affections were kindled, their reason was satisfied by the words spoken, and all was sent home by the intense spiritual energy with which he spoke and prayed.—MARVIN, ABIJAH P., 1892, *The Life and Times of Cotton Mather, p. 58.*

It was, perhaps, fear that the belief in the supernatural, and notably in the supernatural agency of the Evil One, was dying out which led Cotton Mather, a minister of prodigious though ill-digested learning and at the same time full of spiritual self-conceit, to countenance the horrible delusion of Salem Witchcraft which has left a dark stain on New England history, as readers of Hawthorne's "House of the Seven Gables" know. . . . Cotton Mather afterwards partly redeemed himself by countenancing, at a great sacrifice of his popularity and at some risk of his life, the introduction of inoculation, which excited the ignorant fury of the mob. Even in him learning begot something of liberality.—SMITH, GOLDWIN, 1893, *The United States, An Outline of Political History*, 1492-1871, pp. 37, 38.

On February 15, 1728, the Reverend Benjamin Colman, first minister of the Brattle Street church, preached the Boston lecture in memory of Cotton Mather, who had died two days before. Cotton Mather had lived all his life in Boston; there is no record, they say, of his ever having travelled farther from home than Ipswich or Andover or Plymouth. Of sensitive temperament, and both by constitution and by conviction devoted to the traditions in which he was trained, he certainly presented, to a degree nowhere common, a conveniently exaggerated type of the characteristics that marked the society of which he formed a part.—WENDELL, BARRETT, 1893, *Stelligeri and other Essays Concerning America, p. 47.*

In the old burying-ground on Copp's Hill is a table-like monument bearing the names of Increase Mather and Cotton Mather. The names on the moss-covered stones are almost illegible, and the memory of them has also grown dim in men's minds; but no two men ever had greater influence in Boston than the two who lie in this forgotten grave.—WARD, MAY ALDEN, 1896, *Old Colony Days, p. 114.*

MAGNALIA CHRISTI AMERICANA
1702

As for *my self*, having been, by the mercy of God, now above *sixty-eight years* in New-England, and served the Lord and his people in my weak measure _sixty years_ in the ministry of the gospel, I may now say, in my old age, _I have seen all that the Lord hath done for his people in New England_, and have known the beginning and progress of these churches unto this day; and, having read over much of this _history_, I cannot but in the love and fear of God bear witness to the _truth of it ; viz._ : that this present _church-history_ of New-England, compiled by Mr. Cotton Mather, for the substance, end, and scope of it, is, as far as I have been acquainted therewithall, _according to truth._—HIGGINSON, JOHN, 1702, _ed. Magnalia._

One of the most singular books in this or in any other language. Its puns and its poems, its sermons and its anagrams, render it unique in its kind. The author not unfrequently reminds us of our own church-historian Fuller; but circumstances counteracted the resemblance of their natural disposition.—SOUTHEY, ROBERT, 1813, _History of Dissenters, Quarterly Review, vol._ 10, _p._ 113.

As Chateaubriand boasts in his "Itinerary" that he was the _last_ Frenchman who would ever make a pilgrimage to Jerusalem, so it may hereafter be said that the writer of this was the _last_ (and possibly the first) individual who, _bona fide_, perused in regular course the whole of Mather's "Magnalia"; and, if any doubts had existed that great toil was necessary to the acquisition of fame, they would have been dispelled by this exertion. This book is worth consulting by those who wish to become acquainted with the character of our forefathers. Many of the author's faults were those of his age; and, if he has not left us the best, he has at least furnished the largest, work appertaining to our early history. . . . To those who are interested in the early history of our country, it may be well to remark that, for accuracy in historical occurrences, they will do well to rely upon other authorities; but, if they wish to obtain a general view of the state of society and manners, they will probably nowhere find so many materials for this purpose as in the work of this credulous, pedantick, and garrulous writer.—TUDOR, WILLIAM, 1818, _North American Review, vol._ 6.

No man since Dr. Mather's time has had so good an opportunity as he enjoyed to consult the most authentic documents. The greater part of his facts could be attested by living witnesses and the shortest tradition, or taken from written testimonies, many of which have since perished. The situation and character of the author afforded him the most favourable opportunities to obtain the documents necessary for his undertaking; and no historian would pursue a similar design with greater industry and zeal. . . . The work is both a civil and an ecclesiastical history. The large portion of it devoted to _Biography_ affords the reader a more distinct view of the leading characters of the times, than could have been given in any other form. — ROBBINS, THOMAS, 1820, _Magnalia, Preface._

His works are of a kind, which were attractive and interesting in their day, but now sleep in repose, where even the antiquary seldom disturbs them. He will be remembered, however, as the author of the "Magnalia," a work, which, with all its faults, will always find interested readers; as a man, too, of unexampled industry, and unrivalled attainments in curious rather than useful learning.—PEABODY, WILLIAM B. O., 1836, _Cotton Mather, Library of American Biography, ed. Sparks, vol._ VI, _p._ 349.

A most interesting and edifying work, with some peculiarities.—BICKERSTETH, EDWARD, 1844, _The Christian Student._

A monstrous mass of information and speculation, of error and gossip, of biography and history, of italics and capitals, of classical quotations, Latin and Greek, and of original epitaphs, Latin and English, in prose and in verse, which, as old Polonius said of Hamlet's actors, "either for tragedy, comedy, history, pastoral, pastoral-comical, historical-pastoral, tragical-comical, scene individable or poem unlimited," has hardly a parallel in the world! Let me not seem to disparage or undervalue Cotton Mather,—a perfect Dr. Pangloss, as he was in many particulars, —for with all his foibles and all his faults, all his credulity and all his vanity, it cannot be denied that he did a really great work for New England history. The lives of our Worthies could not have been written without him; while his "Essay to do Good" is known to have given the earliest incentive to the wonderful career of New England's most wonderful son,—Benjamin

Franklin.—Winthrop, Robert C., 1869, *Massachusetts and its Early History, Addresses and Speeches on Various Occasions, vol.* III, *p.* 20.

Cotton Mather's "Ecclesiastical History of New England," better known as his "Magnalia," from the head-line of the title page, "Magnalia Christi Americana," was published in London in 1702, in folio. Although relating generally to New England, it principally concerns Massachusetts. While the book is filled with the author's conceits and puns, and gives abundant evidence of his credulity, it contains a vast amount of valuable historical material, and is indispensable in any New England library. It is badly arranged for consultation, for it is largely a compilation from the author's previous publications, and it lacks an index.—Winsor, Justin, 1884, *Narrative and Critical History of America, vol.* III, *p.* 345.

The "Magnalia," despite its inclusiveness and augustness, its awe-inspiring quotations and allusions, is an untidy piece of literature,—inexcusably so when we consider its author's ability, training, and opportunities.—Richardson, Charles F., 1887, *American Literature,* 1607–1885, *vol.* I, *p.* 134.

The name is much more attractive than the interior.—Watkins, Mildred Cabell, 1894, *American Literature, p.* 12.

Mather wrote in the full and pregnant style of Taylor, Milton, Brown, Fuller, and Burton, a style ponderous with learning and stiff with allusions, digressions, conceits, anecdotes, and quotations from the Greek and the Latin. A page of the "Magnalia" is almost as richly mottled with italics as one from the "Anatomy of Melancholy," and the quaintness which Mather caught from his favorite Fuller disports itself in textual pun and marginal anagram and the fantastic sub-titles of his books and chapters.—Beers, Henry A., 1895, *Initial Studies in American Letters, p.* 29.

The prose epic of New England Puritanism it has been called, setting forth in heroic mood the principles, the history, and the personal characters of the fathers. The principles, theologic and disciplinary alike, are stated with clearness, dignity, and fervour. The history, though its less welcome phases are often lightly emphasised, and its details are hampered by deep regard for minor accuracy, is set forth with a sincere ardour which makes its temper more instructive than that of many more trustworthy records. And the life-like portraits of the Lord's chosen, though full of quaintly fantastic phrases and artless pedantries, are often drawn with touches of enthusiastic beauty.—Wendell, Barrett, 1900, *A Literary History of America, p.* 50.

GENERAL

What numerous volumes scatter'd from his hand,
Lighten'd his own, and warm'd each foreign land?
What pious breathings of a glowing soul
Live in each page, and animate the whole?
The breath of heaven the savory pages show,
As we Arabia from its spices know.
The beauties of his style are careless strew'd,
And learning with a liberal hand bestow'd:
So, on the field of Heav'n, the seeds of fire
Thick-sown, but careless, all the wise admire.
—Adams, John, 1728, *On the Death of Cotton Mather.*

If, as Mather would say, our little scrap of literary history need a moral, it shall be addressed to men of his own profession. Here is one man whom the world ranks as an ass, and another whom the world ranks as its most useful practical genius. The first was a preacher; and the second says, that, for any use he has been to the world, it may thank that preacher. Why is the man called an ass to whom the world owes its most useful practical genius? Because he could not omit his own prefaces. Because he overlaid everything with such a farrago of introduction. He could not begin at the beginning, and end at the end.—Hale, Edward Everett, 1859, *What made Franklin? The Christian Examiner, vol.* 66, *p.* 274.

The true place of Cotton Mather in our literary history is indicated when we say, that he was in prose writing, exactly what Nicholas Noyes was in poetry,—the last, the most vigorous, and, therefore, the most disagreeable representative of the Fantastic school in literature; and that, like Nicholas Noyes, he prolonged in New England the methods of that school even after his most cultivated contemporaries there had outgrown them, and had come to dislike them. The expulsion of the beautiful from thought, from sentiment, from language; a lawless and a merciless

fury for the odd, the disorderly, the grotesque, the violent; strained analogies,
unexpected images, pedantries, indelicacies, freaks of allusion, monstrosities
of phrase;—these are the traits of Cotton
Mather's writing, even as they are the
traits common to that perverse and detestable literary mood that held sway in different countries of Christendom during
the sixteenth and seventeenth centuries.
Its birthplace was Italy; New England
was its grave; Cotton Mather was its last
great apostle. His writings, in fact, are
an immense reservoir of examples in Fantastic prose. Their most salient characteristic is pedantry,—a pedantry that is
gigantic, stark, untempered, rejoicing in
itself, unconscious of shame, filling all
space in his books like an atmosphere.
The mind of Cotton Mather was so possessed by the books he had read, that his
most common thought had to force its way
into utterance through dense hedges and
jungles of quotation.—TYLER, MOSES COIT,
1878, *A History of American Literature,
1676–1765, vol.* II, *p.* 87.

Aptly styled by the historian of American literature "the literary behemoth"
of New England. . . . Cotton Mather
was a man of undoubted ability and vast
erudition, and much of his work may still
be read with curiosity and interest; but
as a historian he was untrustworthy, and
his style, overcharged and involved, was
the worst, as it was the last, in the fantastic fashion of the seventeenth century.
—LODGE, HENRY CABOT, 1881, *A Short
History of the English Colonies in America, pp,* 469, 470.

A very night-mare of pedantry.—LOW-
ELL, JAMES RUSSELL, 1886, *Harvard
Anniversary; Prose Works, Riverside ed.,
vol.* VI, *p.* 150.

His work can be reckoned up, but the
worker eludes comprehension. It is easier
to misjudge than to judge him. His mind
was pendulous, as one of his most discriminating biographers has observed, and
though attached at its highest point to
eternal justice, it was ever swaying over
a wide range of notions and impulses.
Oftentimes a riddle to himself, it is no
wonder that the measuring of him must
still be so largely conjectural with us.—
LORD, ELIOT, 1893, *Harvard's Youngest
Three, New England Magazine, vol.* 13,
p. 645.

His "Memorable Providences Relating
to Witchcraft," written apparently with
perfect honesty and published in 1789,
served as a fan for the fire smouldering
in Salem. Four years later, when men
like Justice Sewall were bitterly repenting
of their part in the terrible tragedy,
Mather published his "Wonders of the
Invisible World," a cold-blooded account
of the trials and executions at Salem, every
word pregnant with the belief that devils
and not human beings had been dealt with.
That he was intensely honest in all this
need not be said. His terrible convictions
triumphing over his naturally kind heart
would not have allowed him to hesitate
even had the evidence involved his son
Samuel.—PATTEE, FRED LEWIS, 1896, *A
History of American Literature, p.* 47.

Though not a man of great original
genius, his mind was massive and strong.
He had the quality which some have held
to be the essential thing in genius,—
the power of indomitable and systematic industry. — PAINTER, F. V. N.,
1897, *Introduction to American Literature,
p.* 30.

More precocious than his father, more
prolific in books and pamphlets, he illustrates nevertheless the decline of the
clergy both in outward power and in
actual sanity and breadth of thought.—
BATES, KATHARINE LEE, 1897, *American
Literature, p.* 43.

The book ["Magnalia"] has some historical value, because the writer was so near to
the events narrated; but it is careless, fantastic, and full of pedantry, the pages
being crammed with Latin, Greek, and
Hebrew, learned digressions, and abominable puns. Yet the narrative portions
sometimes have considerable interest, anecdotes frequently enliven an otherwise dull
passage, and the whole book is impressive
by its bulky strength. Cotton Mather's
contemporary reputation in America was
very great, and it even extended to the
Old World. He lives still, after a fashion,
as the most conspicuous American writer
of the seventeenth century. Yet on the
whole his life was a failure, and has the
pathos of failure, for he fought on the
side of a doomed cause. Puritanism was
passing away, never to return, and even
Cotton Mather battled for it in vain.—
BRONSON, WALTER C., 1900, *A Short History of American Literature, p.* 31.

William Congreve

1670–1729

Born, at Bardsey, near Leeds, Jan. [?] 1670. Soon after his birth, family removed to Lismore. Educated at Kilkenny School. To Trinity Coll., Dublin, 5 April 1685; M.A., 1696. Entered Middle Temple, but soon abandoned law. Play, "The Old Batchelor," produced, Jan. 1693; "The Double Dealer," Nov. 1693; "Love for Love," 30 April 1695; "The Mourning Bride," 1697; "The Way of the World," 1700. Commissioner for Licensing Hackney Coaches, July 1695 to Oct. 1707. Abandoned playwriting. Joined Vanburgh in theatrical management for short time in 1705. Commissioner of Wine Licenses, Dec. 1705 to Dec. 1714. Appointed Secretary for Jamaica, Dec. 1714. Member of Kit-Cat Club. Intimacy with Duchess of Marlborough in later years of life. Died, in London, 19 Jan. 1729. Buried in Westminster Abbey. *Works:* "The Mourning Muse of Alexis," 1659; "The Old Batchelor," [1693]; "The Double Dealer," [1694]; "A Pindarique Ode, humbly offer'd to the King," 1695; "Love for Love," [1695]; "Amendments upon Mr. Collier's false and imperfect Citations" (anon.), 1698; "The Birth of the Muse," 1698; "The Mourning Bride," 1697 (2nd edn. same year); "Incognita" (anon.), 1700; "The Way of the World," 1700; "The Judgment of Paris," 1701; "A Pindarique Ode, humbly offer'd to the Queen," 1706; "Works" (3 vol.), 1710; "A Letter to . . . Viscount Cobham," 1729. He *translated:* Book III. of Ovid's "Art of Love," 1709; Ovid's "Metamorphoses" (with Dryden, Addison, etc.), 1717; La Fontaine's "Tales and Novels" (with other translators), 1762: and assisted Dryden in revision of translation of Virgil, 1697. He *edited:* Dryden's "Dramatick Works," 1717. *Collected Works:* 1731, etc.—SHARP, R. FARQUHARSON, 1897, *A Dictionary of English Authors,* p. 65.

PERSONAL

I have a multitude of affairs, having just come to town after nine weeks' absence. I am growing fat, but you know I was born with somewhat of a round belly. . . . Think of me as I am, nothing extenuate. My service to Robin, who would laugh to see me puzzled to buckle my shoe, but I'll fetch it down again.—CONGREVE, WILLIAM, 1704, *Letter to Keally.*

Be pleased to direct your eyes toward the pair of beaux in the next chariot. . . . He on the right is a near favourite of the Muses; he has touched the drama with truer art than any of his contemporaries, comes nearer nature and the ancients, unless in his last performance, which indeed met with most applause, however least deserving. But he seemed to know what he did, descending from himself to write to the Many, whereas before he wrote to the Few. I find a wonderful deal of good sense in that gentleman; he has wit without the pride and affectation that generally accompanies, and always corrupts it. His Myra is as celebrated as Ovid's Corinna, and as well known. How happy is he in the favour of that lovely lady! She, too, deserves applause, besides her beauty, for her gratitude and sensibility to so deserving an admirer. There are few women, who, when they once give in to the sweets of an irregular passion, care to confine themselves to him that first endeared it to them, but not so the charming Myra. —MANLEY, MRS. MARY DE LA RIVIERE, 1709, *The New Atalantis.*

I was to-day to see Mr. Congreve, who is almost blind with cataracts growing on his eyes; and his case is, that he must wait two or three years, until the cataracts are riper, and till he is quite blind, and then he must have them couched; and besides he is never rid of the gout, yet he looks young and fresh, and is as cheerful as ever. He is younger by three years or more than I, and I am twenty years younger than he. He gave me a pain in the great toe, by mentioning the gout I find such suspicions frequently, but they go off again.—SWIFT, JONATHAN, 1710, *Journal to Stella,* Oct. 26.

The uncommon praise of a man of wit, always to please, and never to offend. No one, after a joyful evening, can reflect upon an expression of Mr. Congreve's that dwells upon him with pain.—STEELE, RICHARD, 1713, *Poetical Miscellanies, Dedication.*

Lame Congreve, unable such things to en-
dure,
Of Apollo begged either a crown or a cure;
To refuse such a writer Apollo was loath,
And almost inclined to have granted him
both.
—SHEFFIELD, JOHN (DUKE OF BUCKING-
HAM), 1719, *The Election of a Poet Laureat.*

Instead of endeavouring to raise a vain
monument to myself, . . . let me leave
behind me a memorial of my friendship
with one of the most valuable of men, as
well as finest writers of my age and country.
One who has tried, and knows by his own
experience, how hard an undertaking it
is to do justice to Homer, and one who
I'm sure sincerely rejoices with me at the
period of my labours. To him, therefore, having brought this long work to a
conclusion, I desire to dedicate it, and
have the honour and satisfaction of placing together in this manner, the names
of Mr. Congreve and of—POPE, ALEX-
ANDER, 1720, *Homer's Iliad, Postscript,
March 25.*

Mr. William Congreve died Jan. the
19th, 1728, aged fifty-six, and was buried
near this place; to whose most valuable
memory this monument is set up by Henrietta, Duchess of Marlborough, as a
mark how deeply she remembers the happiness and honour she enjoyed in the
sincere friendship of so worthy and honest
a man, whose virtue, candour, and wit
gained him the love and esteem of the
present age, and whose writings will be
the admiration of the future.—MARL-
BOROUGH, HENRIETTA DUCHESS OF, 1729,
Inscription on Tomb, Westminster Abbey.

Mr. *Congreve* had one defect, which was,
his entertaining too mean an idea of his
first profession, (that of a writer) tho'
'twas to this he owed his fame and fortune.
He spoke of his works as of trifles that
were beneath him; and hinted to me, in
our first conversation, that I should visit
him upon no other foot than that of a
gentleman, who led a life of plainness
and simplicity. I answered, that had he
been so unfortunate as to be a mere gentleman I should never have come to see him;
and I was very much disgusted at so
unseasonable a piece of vanity.—VOL-
TAIRE, FRANÇOIS MARIE AROUET, 1732?
*Letters Concerning the English Nation,
p.* 148.

I never knew anybody that had so much

wit as Congreve.—MONTAGU, LADY MARY
WORTLEY, 1740–41, *Spence's Anecdotes,
ed. Singer, p.* 175.

His place in the custom-house, and his
office of secretary in Jamaica, are said to
have brought him in upwards of 1200 *l.*
a year; and he was so far an œconomist, as
to raise from thence a competent estate.
No man of his learning ever pass'd thro'
life with more ease, or less envy; and as
in the dawn of his reputation he was very
dear to the greatest wits of his time, so
during his whole life he preserved the
utmost respect of, and received continual
marks of esteem from, men of genius and
letters, without ever being involved in
any of their quarrels, or drawing upon
himself the least mark of distaste, or even
dissatisfaction. The greatest part of the
last twenty years of his life were spent
in ease and retirement, and he gave himself no trouble about reputation.—CIB-
BER, THEOPHILUS, 1753, *Lives of the Poets,
vol.* IV, *p.* 93.

Congreve was very intimate for years
with Mrs. Bracegirdle, and lived in the
same street, his house very near hers;
until his acquaintance with the young
Duchess of Marlborough. He then quitted
that house. The duchess showed me a
diamond necklace (which Lady Di. used
afterwards to wear) that cost seven thousand pounds, and was purchased with the
money Congreve left her. How much
better would it have been to have given
it to poor Mrs. Bracegirdle.—YOUNG,
EDWARD, 1757, *Spence's Anecdotes, ed.
Singer, p.* 286.

Congreve was "the fashion," and could
do almost anything. That he was an
abandoned and dissolute rake was a matter of course. To be so was one of the
main accomplishments of a fine gentleman
of the period; and the women could not
endure a man who lay under horrid suspicion of being virtuous. He had the run of
the green rooms, and what they were, and
are, and always will be, every man about
them knows, and everybody not about
them may guess. He raked until he got
blind; now with Mrs. Bracegirdle, now
with Nan Jallett, now with Madame Ber-
enger, now with Madame Marlborough.
His middle age was cursed with the memorials of his excesses.—MONTAGU, EDWARD
WORTLEY, 1776? *An Autobiography, vol.*
I, *p.* 107.

Among his friends was able to name every man of his time whom wit and elegance had raised to reputation. It may be therefore reasonably supposed that his manners were polite and his conversation pleasing. . . . His studies were in his latter days obstructed by cataracts in his eyes, which at last terminated in blindness.—JOHNSON, SAMUEL, 1779–81, *Congreve, Lives of the English Poets.*

The charms of his conversation must have been very powerful, since nothing could console Henrietta, Duchess of Marlborough, for the loss of his company, so much as an automaton, or small statue of ivory, made exactly to resemble him, which every day was brought to table. A glass was put in the hand of the statue, which was supposed to bow to her grace and to nod in approbation of what she spoke to it.—DAVIES, THOMAS, 1784, *Dramatic Micellanies, vol.* III, *p.* 382.

Congreve has the solid reputation of never having forgotten any one who did him a service.—HUNT, LEIGH, 1840, *ed., The Works of Wycherley, Congreve, Vanbrugh and Farquhar.*

The body lay in state in the Jerusalem Chamber and was buried with great pomp in Westminster Abbey. A monument was erected in the abbey by the Duchess of Marlborough, with an inscription of her own writing, and a hideous cenotaph was erected at Stowe by Lord Cobham. It was reported that the duchess afterwards had a figure of ivory or wax made in his likeness, which was placed at her table, addressed as if alive, served with food, and treated for "an imaginary sore on its leg." The story, if it has any foundation, would imply partial insanity. —STEPHEN, LESLIE, 1887, *Dictionary of National Biography, vol.* XII, *p.* 8.

No defence can serve for our poet's abandonment of Mrs. Bracegirdle with the paltry legacy, and nothing can extenuate the mortal comedy of his end as *bon viveur* when the Duchess of Marlborough, whom he had made his heir, placed his waxen effigy at her table, so contrived as to nod when she spoke to it, wrapped its feet in cloths, and had a physician to attend upon it and render a daily diagnosis. With the seven thousand pounds remaining from the legacy, after this pleasant whim was satisfied, the young Duchess bought a diamond necklace.

Mrs. Bracegirdle, the favorite of his early years, the woman for whom he had written the best of his characters and who shares his theatrical fame, was poor, but she shielded Congreve's memory by her silence, while the Duchess blazoned his infatuation by her diamonds. This was a death scene for a comic dramatist to observe.—WOODBERRY, GEORGE EDWARD, 1888, *The Nation, vol.* 47, *p.* 256.

Congreve was within less than two months of sixty at the time of his death. The inscription on his monument in this same abbey declares him to have been then only fifty-six years old. The memorial in this case was set up by his intimate friend, Henrietta, Duchess of Marlborough, to whom he had bequeathed the bulk of his fortune.—LOUNSBURY, THOMAS R., 1892, *Studies in Chaucer, vol.* I, *p.* 27.

THE OLD BACHELOR
1693

Mr. Congreve was of the Middle Temple, his first performance was an Novel, call'd incognita, then he began his Play the old Batchelor, haveing little Acquaintance withe the traders in that way, his Cozens recommended him to a friend of theirs, who was very usefull to him in the whole course of his play, he engag'd Mr. Dryden in its favour, who upon reading it sayd he never saw such a first play in his life, but the Author not being acquainted with the stage or the town, it would be pity to have it miscarry for want of a little Assistance: the stuff was rich indeed, it wanted only the fashionable cutt of the town. To help that Mr. Dryden, Mr. Manwayring, and Mr. Southern red it with great care, and Mr. Dryden putt it in the order it was playd, Mr. Southerne obtaind of Mr. Thos: Davenant who then governd the Playhouse, that Mr. Congreve should have the privilege of the Playhouse half a year before his play was playd, wh. I never knew allowd any one before: it was playd with great success that play made him many friends.—SOUTHERNE, THOMAS, 1735–36? *Add. MSS.,* 4221, *British Museum.*

The age of the writer considered, it is indeed a very wonderful performance; for, whenever written, it was acted (1693) when he was not more than twenty-one [four] years old.—JOHNSON, SAMUEL, 1779–81, *Congreve, Lives of the English Poets.*

Was written, it should seem, when the author was under age, and a very extraordinary work of precocity it is. He started at once into a full knowledge of the world of artificial life: at eighteen his appreciation of his mother's sex was precisely that of a worn-out *roué* of fifty. —CLARKE, CHARLES COWDEN, 1871, *On the Comic Writers of England, The Gentleman's Magazine, n. s., vol. 7, p. 836.*

The writing here is already excellent, and distinguished, especially by its lightness, from anything that had preceded it in the post-Restoration drama. The majority of the leading characters, however, contain nothing quite original; it would be easy to find in Molière or elsewhere prototypes or analogues of Heartwell, who sets up for a misogynist but is in reality a victim to female wiles, of the blustering coward, Captain Bluffe, and of the demure but deep Mrs. Fondlewife. Yet these in company with a number of other personages furnish an abundant variety, and the action is both brisk and diverting. Morally, both the plots of which the play is composed are objectionable; but the dramatic life in this comedy is unmistakable, and more than any other quality justified a success so rarely achieved by the work of a novice hand.—WARD, ADOLPHUS WILLIAM, 1875-99, *A History of English Dramatic Literature, vol. III, p. 471*

The success of "The Old Bachelor" was the most rousing event in our literary history between the Revolution and the accession of Anne. Seldom has a new luminary appeared so vast and so splendid as its orb first slipped above the horizon. . . . We read "The Old Bachelor" with interest, and return to it with pleasure, but to the critic its main attraction is that it marks the transition between the imitation of Wycherley and Congreve's complete confidence in his own powers.— GOSSE, EDMUND, 1888, *Life of William Congreve (Great Writers), pp.* 40, 42.

THE DOUBLE DEALER
1694

But there is one thing at which I am more concerned than all the false criticism that are made upon me; and that is, some of the ladies are offended. I am heartily sorry for it; for I declare, I would rather disoblige all the critics in the world than one of the fair sex. They are concerned that I have represented some women vicious and affected. How can I help it? It is the business of a comic poet to paint the vices and follies of human kind. . . . I should be very glad of an opportunity to make my compliments to those ladies who are offended. But they can no more expect it in a comedy, than *to be tickled by a surgeon when he is letting their blood.*— CONGREVE, WILLIAM, 1693, *Double-Dealer, Epistle Dedicatory.*

Congreve's "Double Dealer" is much censured by the greater part of the town, and is defended only by the best judges, who, you know, are commonly the fewest. Yet it gains ground daily, and has already been acted eight times. The women think he has exposed their witchery too much, and the gentlemen are offended with him for the discovery of their follies and the way of their intrigue under the notions of friendship to their ladies' husbands. My verses, which you will find before it, were written before the play was acted; but I neither altered them, nor do I alter my opinion of the play.—DRYDEN, JOHN, 1793, *Letter to Walsh.*

Some of the characters, though rather exaggerated, are amusing: but the plot is so entangled towards the conclusion, that I have found it difficult, even in reading, to comprehend it.—HALLAM, HENRY, 1837-39, *Introduction to the Literature of Europe, pt. iv, ch. vi, par. 52.*

The "Double Dealer," with the solemn reciprocities of *Lord* and *Lady Froth,* and the capital character of *Lady Plyant,* "insolent to her husband, and easy to every pretender," is far superior to the "Old Bachelor." Congreve excels in mixtures of impudence, hypocrisy, and self-delusion. The whole of the fifth scene of the second act, between *Lady Plyant* and *Mellefont,* is exquisite for the grossness of the overtures made under pretence of a delicacy in alarm. But it is no wonder a comedy did not succeed that has so black a villain in it as *Maskwell,* and an aunt who has a regularly installed gallant in her nephew. *Sir Paul Plyant* also says things to his daughter, which no decent person could hear with patience between father and child. The writer's object might have been a good one; but it is of doubtful and perilous use to attempt to do good by effrontery.—HUNT, LEIGH, 1840, ed., *The Works of Wycherley, Congreve, Vanbrugh and Farquhar.*

Notwithstanding certain repulsive features in the action, this is undoubtedly one of the best comedies in our dramatic literature.—WARD, ADOLPHUS WILLIAM, 1875-99, *A History of English Dramatic Literature, vol.* III, *p.* 472.

LOVE FOR LOVE
1695

This play is as full of character, incident, and stage-effect, as almost any of those of his contemporaries, and fuller of wit than any of his own, except perhaps the "Way of the World." It still acts, and is still acted well. The effect of it is prodigious on the well-informed spectator. In particular, Munden's Foresight, if it is not just the thing, is a wonderfully rich and powerful piece of comic acting. His look is planet-struck; his dress and appearance like one of the signs of the Zodiac taken down. Nothing can be more bewildered; and it only wants a little more helplessness, a little more of the doating, querulous garrulity of age, to be all that one conceives of the superannuated, star-gazing original.—HAZLITT, WILLIAM, 1818, *Lectures on the English Comic Writers, Lecture* iv.

Congreve has never any great success in the conception or management of his plot; but in this comedy there is least to censure: several of the characters are exceedingly humorous; the incidents are numerous and not complex; the wit is often admirable. Angelica and Miss Prue, Ben and Tattle, have been repeatedly imitated; but they have, I think, a considerable degree of dramatic originality in themselves.—HALLAM, HENRY, 1837-39, *Introduction to the Literature of Europe, pt.* iv, *ch.* vi, *par.* 51.

The most amusing of all Congreve's plays, and the characters the least unpleasant. There are no revolting scoundrels: and the lovers really have some love. *Jeremy* is most improbably witty, for a servant; even though he once "waited on a gentleman at Cambridge." *Miss Prue* is not so naturally cunning as Wycherley's *Country Wife,* nor such a hearty bouncer as Vanbrugh's *Hoyden;* but she is a very good variety of that genus.—HUNT, LEIGH, 1840, *ed., The Works of Wycherley, Congreve, Vanbrugh, and Farquhar.*

The comedy of "Love for Love" has been commonly accounted Congreve's masterpiece, and perhaps with justice. It is not quite so uniformly brilliant in style as "The Way of the World," but it has the advantage of possessing a much wholesomer relation to humanity than that play, which is almost undiluted satire, and a more theatrical arrangement of scenes. In "Love for Love" the qualities which had shown themselves in "The Old Bachelor" and "The Double Dealer" recur, but in a much stronger degree. The sentiments are more unexpected, the language is more picturesque, the characters have more activity of mind and vitality of nature. All that was merely pink has deepened into scarlet; even what is disagreeable,—the crudity of allusion and the indecency of phrase,—have increased. The style in all its parts and qualities has become more vivid. We are looking through the same telescope as before, but the sight is better adjusted, the outlines are more definite, and the colours more intense. So wonderfully felicitous is the phraseology that we cannot doubt that if Congreve could only have kept himself unspotted from the sins of the age, dozens of tags would have passed, like bits of Shakespeare, Pope, and Gray, into habitual parlance. In spite of its errors against decency, "Love for Love" survived on the stage for more than a century, long after the remainder of Restoration and Orange drama was well-nigh extinct.—GOSSE, EDMUND, 1888, *Life of William Congreve (Great Writers), p.* 69.

THE MOURNING BRIDE
1697

The incidents succeed one another too rapidly. The play is too full of business. It is difficult for the mind to follow and comprehend the whole series of events; and, what is the greatest fault of all, the catastrophe, which ought always to be plain and simple, is brought about in a manner too artificial and intricate.—BLAIR, HUGH, 1783, *Lectures on Rhetoric and Belles-Lettres, ed. Mills, Lecture* xlv.

Written in prolix declamation, with no power over the passions.—HALLAM, HENRY, 1837-39, *Introduction to the Literature of Europe, pt.* iv, *ch.* vi, *par.* 46.

The "Mourning Bride" is not uninteresting in its story, nor so bad in its poetry as one might expect from the want of faith and passion natural to a town-wit of that age. . . . If the tragedy were revived now, the audience would laugh at the inflated sentences and unconscious prose. The revival of old English literature, and the tone of our best modern poets, have accustomed them to a higher and truer spirit. Yet some of the language of *Almeria*, as where, for instance, she again meets with *Osmyn*, is natural and affecting; and it is pleasing to catch a man of the world at these evidences of sympathy with. what is serious. Nor are sensible and striking passages wanting.—HUNT, LEIGH, 1840, *ed., The Works of Wycherley, Congreve, Vanbrugh and Farquhar*.

In general, being unequaled to really sustained flights of passion, the author has to take refuge in rant, and Lee himself could hardly have surpassed some of his attempts of this description. In brief, we may agree with Lessing, that Congreve's solitary attempt in tragic poetry proves this field to have lain outside the natural range of his talents; or, if we prefer to put it so, we may assent to the opinion of Swift's *quidnunc* (rather than to that of Swift himself), that tragic composition "quite lost" so essentially comic a genius.—WARD, ADOLPHUS WILLIAM, 1875–99, *A History of English Dramatic Literature, vol.* III, *p.* 477.

It has been the habit to quote "The Mourning Bride" as the very type of bad declamatory tragedy. No doubt Dr. Johnson did it harm by that extravagant eulogy in which he selected one fragment as unsurpassed in the poetry of all time. But if we compare it, not with those tragedies of the age of Elizabeth, studded with occasional naïve felicities, which it is just now the fashion to admire with some extravagance, but with what England and even France produced from 1650 to the revival of romantic taste, "The Mourning Bride" will probably take a place close after what is best in Otway and Racine. It will bear comparison, as I would venture to assert, with Southerne's "Fatal Marriage" or with Crébillon's "Rhadamiste et Zénobie," and will not be pronounced inferior to these excellent and famous tragedies in dramatic interest, or genuine grandeur of sentiment, or beauty of language. It has done what no other of these special rivals has done, outside the theatre of Racine, it has

contributed to the everyday fashion of its country several well-worn lines. But it is not every one who says that "Music has charms to soothe a savage breast" or that "Hell knows no fury like a woman scorn'd," who would be able to tell where the familiar sentiment first occurs.— GOSSE, EDMUND, 1888, *Life of William Congreve (Great Writers), p.* 87.

THE WAY OF THE WORLD
1700

The "Way of the World" was the author's last and most carefully finished performance. It is an essence almost too fine; and the sense of pleasure evaporates in an aspiration after something that seems too exquisite ever to have been realised. After inhaling the spirit of Congreve's wit, and tasting "love's thrice reputed nectar" in his works, the head grows giddy in turning from the highest point of rapture to the ordinary business of life; and we can with difficulty recall the truant Fancy to those objects which we are fain to take up with here, *for better, for worse.*—HAZLITT, WILLIAM, 1818, *Lectures on the English Comic Writers, Lecture* iv.

The great art of Congreve is especially shown in this, that he has entirely excluded from his scenes,—some little generosities in the part of Angelica perhaps excepted,—not only anything like a faultless character, but any pretensions to goodness or good feelings whatsoever. Whether he did this designedly, or instinctively, the effect is as happy, as the design (if design) was bold. I used to wonder at the strange power which his "Way of the World" in particular possesses of interesting you all along in the pursuits of characters, for whom you absolutely care nothing—for you neither hate nor love his personages—and I think it is owing to this very indifference for any, that you endure the whole. He has spread a privation of moral light, I will call it, rather than by the ugly name of palpable darkness over his creations; and his shadows flit before you without distinction or preference. Had he introduced a good character, a single gush of moral feeling, a revulsion of the judgment to actual life and actual duties, the impertinent Goshen would have only lighted to the discovery of deformities, which now are none, because we think them none.—LAMB,

CHARLES, 1824? *On the Artificial Comedy of the Last Century.*

The coquetry of Millamant, not without some touches of delicacy and affection, the impertinent coxcombry of Petulant and Witwood, the mixture of wit and ridiculous vanity in Lady Wishfort, are amusing to the reader. Congreve has here made more use than, as far as I remember, had been common in England, of the all-important soubrette, on whom so much depends in French comedy.—HALLAM, HENRY, 1837–39, *Introduction to the Literature of Europe, pt.* iv, *ch.* vi, *par.* 52.

The "Way of the World" is an admirable comedy, it must be confessed, especially for the sovereign airs and graces of *Millamant;* yet it is tiresome in its very ingenuity, for its maze of wit and intrigue; and it has no heart, therefore wants the very soul of pleasure.—HUNT, LEIGH, 1840, *ed., The Works of Wycherley, Congreve, Vanbrugh and Farquhar.*

I do not think it too much to say in its praise, that it comprises the most quintessentialised combination of qualities requisite to compound an artificially legitimate comedy to be found in the whole range of our dramatic literature. I do not say, the comedy of *primitive* and *natural* life; but the comedy of the furbelows and flounces; of powder and essences; of paint and enamelling; of high-heels, hoops, and all hideous artificialities, concealments, intrigues, plots, and subterfuges. In reading the play, one's faculties are retained in a perpetual suspension of pleasure at the unabating and highly sustained succession of flights of wit, gaily tinctured imageries, flashing repartees, and skilfully contrasted characters on the scene.—CLARKE, CHARLES COWDEN, 1871, *On the Comic Writers of England, The Gentleman's Magazine, n. s., vol.* 7, *p.* 842.

"The Way of the World" impresses the modern reader as a bitter satire, though the author was true to himself in the elegance of his handling. If the character of Lady Wishfort is almost too offensive for comedy, Witwould is as diverting as he is original—a man afflicted by a perfect cacoëthes of feeble repartee—"I cannot help it, madam," he says, "though it is against myself." And in Millamont and Mirabell he has excelled the brilliancy of all his previous raillery of social types and their deviations from sense and law, giving the place of distinction to the lady.—WARD, ADOLPHUS WILLIAM, 1875–99, *A History of English Dramatic Literature, vol.* III, *p.* 475.

The comic work of Congreve, though different rather in kind than in degree from the bestial and blatant license of his immediate precursors, was inevitably for a time involved in the sentence passed upon the comic work of men in all ways alike his inferiors. The true and triumphant answer to all possible attacks of honest men or liars, brave men or cowards, was then as ever to be given by the production of work unarraignable alike by fair means or foul, by frank impeachment or furtive imputation. In 1700 Congreve thus replied to Collier with the crowning work of his genius,—the unequalled and unapproached master-piece of English comedy. The one play in our language which may fairly claim a place beside or but just beneath the mightiest work of Molière is "The Way of the World."—SWINBURNE, ALGERNON CHARLES, 1877, *Encyclopædia Britannica, vol.* VI.

Successive critics, seeing, what we must all acknowledge, the incomparable splendour of the dialogue in "The Way of the World," have not ceased to marvel at the caprice which should render dubious the success of such a masterpiece on its first appearance. But perhaps a closer examination of the play may help us to unravel the apparent mystery. On certain sides, all the praise which has been lavished on the play from Steele and Voltaire down to Mr. Swinburne and Mr. George Meredith is thoroughly deserved. "The Way of the World" is the best-written, the most dazzling, the most intellectually accomplished of all English comedies, perhaps of all the comedies of the world. But it has the defects of the very qualities which make it so brilliant. A perfect comedy does not sparkle so much, is not so exquisitely written, because it needs to advance, to develop. To "The Way of the World" may be applied that very dubious compliment paid by Mrs. Browning to Landor's "Pentameron" that, "were it not for the necessity of getting through a book, some of the pages are too delicious to turn over."—GOSSE, EDMUND, 1888, *Life of William Congreve (Great Writers), p.* 135.

GENERAL

Our builders were with want of genius
　　cursed;
The second temple was not like the first;
Till you, the best Vitruvius, come at length,
Our beauties equal, but excel our strength.
Firm Doric pillars found your solid base,
The fair Corinthian crowns the higher space;
Thus all below is strength, and all above is
　　grace.

. . . .

Great Johnson did by strength of judgment
　　please,
Yet, doubling Fletcher's force, he wants his
　　ease.
In differing talents both adorned their age,
One for the study, t'other for the stage.
But both to Congreve justly shall submit,
One matched in judgment, both o'ermatched
　　in wit.
In him all beauties of this age we see,
Etherege his courtship, Southern's purity,
The satire, wit, and strength of manly Wych-
　　erly.
All in this blooming youth you have achieved;
Nor are your foiled contemporaries grieved.
So much the sweetness of your manners
　　move,
We cannot envy you, because we love.
Fabius might joy in Scipio, when he saw
A beardless Consul made against the law,
And join his suffrage to the votes of Rome,
Though he with Hannibal was overcome.
Thus old Romano bowed to Raphael's fame,
And scholar to the youth he taught became.
—DRYDEN, JOHN, 1693, *To My Dear
Friend, Mr. Congreve.*

　　Never did poetic mind before
　　Produce a richer vein, or cleaner ore.
—SWIFT, JONATHAN, 1693, *To Mr. Con-
greve.*

Congreve! whose fancy's unexhausted store
Has given already much, and promised more.
Congreve shall still preserve thy fame alive,
And Dryden's muse shall in his friend sur-
　　vive.
—ADDISON, JOSEPH, 1694, *An Account of
the Greatest English Poets.*

As tuneful Congreve tries his rural strains,
Pan quits the woods, the list'ning fawns the
　　plains;
And Philomel, in notes like his, complains.
—GARTH, SAMUEL, 1699, *The Dispensary,
canto* iv.

If thou wouldst have thy volume stand the
　　test,
And of all others be reputed best,
Let Congreve teach the list'ning groves to
　　mourn,
As when he wept o'er fair Pastora's urn.
—GAY, JOHN, 1714, *To Bernard Lintot,
Poems.*

　　　　. . . pens,
Powerful like thine in every grace, and
　　skilled
To win the listening soul with virtuous
　　charms.
—THOMSON, JAMES, 1729, *To the Memory
of Mr. Congreve.*

The late Mr. *Congreve* raised the glory
of Comedy to a greater height than any
English writer before or since his time.
He wrote only a few plays, but they are
all excellent in their kind. The laws of
the drama are strictly observed in them;
they abound with characters all which are
shadowed with the utmost delicacy, and
we do not meet with so much as one low,
or coarse jest.—VOLTAIRE, FRANÇOIS
MARIE AROUET, 1732? *Letters Concerning
the English Nation, p.* 148.

Among all the efforts of early genius
which literary history records, I doubt
whether anyone can be produced that
more surpasses the common limits of
nature than the plays of Congreve. . . .
Congreve has merit of the highest kind,
he is an original writer, who borrowed
neither the models of his plot, nor the
manner of his dialogue. Of his plays I
cannot speak distinctly; for since I
inspected them years have passed; but
what remains upon my memory is, that
his characters are commonly fictitious and
artificial, with very little of nature and
not much of life. . . . Of his miscellaneous poetry, I cannot say anything very
favourable. The powers of Congreve
seem to desert him when he leaves the
stage.—JOHNSON, SAMUEL, 1779-81, *Congreve, Lives of the English Poets.*

The poetry of Mr. Congreve was as much
disliked, as his plays were admired; and
his odes on the death of Queen Mary, and
the Marquis of Blanford, are such wailings,
or mere whining numbers, as too often
disfigure these memorials of the illustrious
dead. Yet he received 1000£. for the former from William III. more through respect
for the memory of his royal consort than
his love of poetry, and still less from its
merits.—NOBLE, MARK, 1806, *A Biographical History of England, vol.* II, *p.* 244.

The comedies of Congreve contain probably more wit than was ever before
embodied upon the stage; each word was
a jest, and yet so characteristic, that the
repartee of the servant is distinguished
from that of the master; the jest of the

coxcomb from that of the humorist or fine gentleman of the piece. Had not Sheridan lived in our own time, we could not have conceived the possibility of rivaling the comedies of Congreve.—Scott, Sir Walter, 1814–23, *Essay on the Drama*.

Congreve is the most distinct from the others, and the most easily defined, both from what he possessed, and from what he wanted. He had by far the most wit and elegance, with less of other things, of humour, character, incident, &c. His style is inimitable, nay perfect. It is the highest model of comic dialogue. Every sentence is replete with sense and satire, conveyed in the most polished and pointed terms. Every page presents a shower of brilliant conceits, is a tissue of epigrams in prose, is a new triumph of wit, a new conquest over dulness. The fire of artful raillery is nowhere else so well kept up. . . . . Sheridan will not bear a comparison with him in the regular antithetical construction of his sentences, and in the mechanical artifices of his style, though so much later, and though style in general has been so much studied, and in the mechanical part so much improved since then.—Hazlitt, William, 1818, *Lectures on the English Comic Writers*, *Lecture* iv.

If Congreve can dazzle by his brilliant dialogue, and his smart repartee, he does not shrink from putting the most splendid wit into the mouths of his fools, and exhibiting characters who are sunk in the depths of disaster, full of sprightliness and merriment. Shakspeare makes us forget the Author; Congreve makes us think of no one else. We rise from the scenes of the first, overwhelmed with the sorrows of *Hamlet*, or of *Othello*, or of *Lear*. We close the pages of the second, charmed with the wit, the sprightliness, and the vivacity of Congreve. I have chosen Congreve as the champion and exemplar of the second School, because he is, in many particulars, the most eminent Scholar which it has produced. Wit was it's grand distinguishing feature, and Congreve was one of the wittiest writers that, perhaps, any age or nation has given birth to. But the Dramatist has to paint character, and he who has only one colour in which to dip his pencil, Wit, cannot produce a true, a natural, or even a permanently pleasing picture. We may gaze

upon the Sun till we see nothing but darkling motes; and so Congreve's scenes fatigue us by their very brilliancy. All his characters are like himself, witty.—Neele, Henry, 1827–29, *Lectures on English Poetry*, p. 146.

They are too cold to be mischievous: they keep the brain in too incessant inaction to allow the passions to kindle. For those who search into the powers of intellect, the combinations of thought which may be produced by volition, the plays of Congreve may form a profitable study. But their time is fled—on the stage they will be received no more; and of the devotees of light reading such as could read them without disgust would probably peruse them with little pleasure.—Coleridge, Hartley, 1833, *Biographia Borealis*, p. 693.

Congreve's merit as a poet lies wholly in his dramas. His pieces in all other walks are affected and laboured. His comedies alone constitute that claim upon the admiration of his countrymen, which is never likely to be disputed. The school of comedy he may be said to have formed, has no foundation in actual life, but derives its charm exclusively from the perfection of an artificial style. His comedies are wanting in traits of real nature, in simplicity, in individual character subsisting by its intrinsic force, and in broad effects; but they exhibit, in a higher state of excellence than can be found anywhere else, a perpetual vein of wit, which glows in such incessant flashes over the surface, that we cannot, if we could, penetrate beneath to examine the slight *matériel* it conceals. With Congreve every thing is artificial—his fops, sharpers, coquettes, libertines; they are all drawn in excess, to afford a wider scope to the play of the brilliant dialogue.—Dunham, S. Astley, 1838, ed., *Literary and Scientific Men of Great Britain and Ireland*, vol. iii, p. 249.

Congreve is the most distinct from the others, and the most easily defined, both from what he possessed, and from what he wanted. He had by far the most wit and elegance, with less of other things, of humour, character, incident, &c. His style is inimitable, nay perfect. It is the highest model of comic dialogue. Every sentence is replete with sense and satire, conveyed in the most polished and pointed terms. Every page presents a shower of brilliant conceits, is a tissue of epigrams in prose, is a new triumph of wit, a new conquest over dullness.— HUNT, LEIGH, 1840, *ed., The Dramatic Works of Wycherley, Congreve, Vanbrugh and Farquhar.*

We believe that no English writer, except Lord Byron, has, at so early an age, stood so high in the estimation of his contemporaries. . . . There can be no stronger illustration of the estimation in which Congreve was held, than the fact that Pope's Iliad, a work which appeared with more splendid auspices than any other in our language, was dedicated to him. There was not a duke in the kingdom who would not have been proud of such a compliment.—MACAULAY, THOMAS BABINGTON, 1841, *Comic Dramatists of the Restoration, Edinburgh Review; Critical and Miscellaneous Essays.*

The patient glitter of Congreve.— WHIPPLE, EDWIN P., 1845–71, *Wit and Humor, Literature and Life, p.* 88.

Whose comedies, the admiration of their own age, for their fertility of fantastically gay dialogue, bright conceits, and witty repartees, are still read for their abundance of lively imagery and play of language, the "reciprocation of conceits and the clash of wit,"—although the personages of his scene, and all that they do and think, are wholly remote from the truth, the feeling, and the manners of real life. These productions, so remarkable in their way, were written before Congreve's twenty-fifth year; and his first and most brilliant comedy ("The Old Bachelor") was acted when he was yet a minor. His talent, thus early ripe, did not afterwards expand or refine itself into the nobler power of teaching "the morals of the heart," nor even into the delightful gift of embodying the passing scenes of real life in graphic and durable pictures. But his writings afford a memorable proof how soon the graces and brilliant effects of mere intellect can be acquired, while those works of genius which require the co-operation and the knowledge of man's moral nature are of a slower and later growth. —VERPLANCK, GULIAN CROMMELIN, 1847, *ed., The Illustrated Shakespeare, vol.* II.

I cannot pretend to quote scenes from the splendid Congreve's play—which are undeniably bright, witty, and daring,— any more than I could ask you to hear the dialogue of a witty bargeman and a brilliant fish-woman exchanging compliments at Billingsgate; but some of his verses, —they were amongst the most famous lyrics of the time, and pronounced equal to Horace by his contemporaries,—may give an idea of his power, of his grace, of his daring manner, his magnificence in compliment, and his polished sarcasm. He writes as if he was so accustomed to conquer, that he has a poor opinion of his victims. Nothing is new except their faces, says he; "every woman is the same." He says this in his first comedy, which he wrote languidly in illness, when he was an "excellent young man." Richelieu at eighty could have hardly said a more excellent thing.—THACKERAY, WILLIAM MAKEPEACE, 1853, *The English Humourists of the Eighteenth Century.*

To my remembrance Congreve is but a horrible nightmare, and may the fates forbid I should be forced to go through his plays again.—THOMSON, KATHERINE AND J. C. (GRACE AND PHILIP WHARTON), 1860, *The Wits and Beaux of Society.*

His comedies are steeped in vice.— COLLIER, WILLIAM FRANCIS, 1861, *A History of English Literature, p.* 252.

The comedy of Congreve has not much character, still less humor, and no nature at all; but blazes and crackles with wit and repartee, for the most part of an unusually pure and brilliant species,—not quaint, forced, and awkward, like what we find in some other attempts, in our dramatic literature and elsewhere, at the same kind of display, but apparently as easy and spontaneous as it is pointed, polished, and exact. His plots are also constructed with much artifice.—CRAIK, GEORGE L., 1861, *A Compendious History of English Literature and of the English Language, vol.* II, *p.* 274.

The fame of Congreve, notwithstanding the predictions of even such a judge as Dryden, has been evanescent, though the wit remains as bright as ever, but it is a wit aimless and objectless, and which ends in itself. The brilliancy dazzled his contemporaries and prevented them seeing clearly, as in the case of Swift with St. John, whose fame in a different field was very much of the same order. The whole merit of Congreve lay in his dialogue. His plots are obscure and intricate to a degree, his characters uninteresting, except as brilliant talkers, but there the wit blazed and sparkled with a continuous brightness that has never been surpassed, and rarely equalled.—MONTGOMERY, HENRY R., 1862, *Memoirs of the Life and Writings of Sir Richard Steele, vol.* I, *p.* 187.

Congreve was the key-stone to the arch of this conventional and artificial school of the comic drama. He was the flowery capital to its Corinthian column—the capstone and ornamented apex to the whole structure. In mind, constitution, habits, and manners Congreve was essentially the hollow fine gentleman. He carried his gentility into his genius, and it became the mainspring, the life-staff of his intellectual, as of his social existence.——CLARKE, CHARLES COWDEN, 1871, *On the Comic Writers of England, The Gentleman's Magazine, n. s., vol.* 7, *p.* 834.

Congreve is far above the others in talent and success; his comedies are sparkling with wit and eloquence, and they are particularly attractive for his diction, which possesses a certain artistic repose. —SCHERR, J., 1874–82, *A History of English Literature, p.* 124.

Congreve is indisputably one of the very wittiest of English writers. No doubt, even when this praise has been unreservedly accorded to a comic dramatist— for it is as such alone that Congreve can be held to have really excelled—the highest praise has not been given. . . . It should at the same time not be overlooked that Congreve's grace and ease of style, as distinguished from its brilliancy and wittiness, contribute to the charm of his prose and make it enjoyable like that of only the very best of contemporary English writers; and that, though these qualities are not always separable from, they should not in consequence be confounded with, one another. In brilliancy of wit he is the superior of all his predecessors and contemporaries of the post-Restoration period, among whom Dryden and perhaps Vanbrugh alone approached him, and Sheridan is his only successor. In ease of dialogue he far surpasses Wycherley; Vanbrugh, and still more Farquhar, lack the element of grace which he possesses; while Etheredge and the rest —even Dryden—fall short of him in polish as writers of comic prose. Congreve is therefore to be regarded as an artist of

rare as well as genuine gifts—the more so that he understood how to conceal his art.—WARD, ADOLPHUS WILLIAM, 1875– 99, *A History of English Dramatic Literature, vol.* III, *pp.* 468, 469.

Congreve's muse was about as bad as any muse that ever misbehaved herself— and I think, as little amusing.—TROLLOPE, ANTHONY, 1879, *Thackeray (English Men of Letters), p.* 159.

The poetical remains of Congreve, especially when considered in connection with those remarkable dramatic works which achieved for him so swift and splendid a reputation, have but a slender claim to vitality. His brilliant and audacious Muse seems to have required the glitter of the foot-lights and the artificial atmosphere of the stage as conditions of success; in the study he is, as a rule, either trivial or frigidly conventional.—DOBSON, AUSTIN, 1880, *English Poets, ed. Ward, vol.* III, *p.* 10.

It is not the least of Lord Macaulay's offences against art that he should have contributed the temporary weight of his influence as a critic to the support of so ignorant and absurd a tradition of criticism as that which classes the great writer here mentioned with the brutal if "brawny" Wycherley—a classification almost to be paralleled with that which in the days of our fathers saw fit to couple together the names of Balzac and of Sue. Any competent critic will always recognise in "The Way of the World" one of the glories, in "The Country Wife" one of the disgraces, of dramatic and of English literature. The stains discernible on the masterpiece of Congreve are trivial and conventional; the mere conception of the other man's work displays a mind so prurient and leprous, uncovers such an unfathomable and unimaginable beastliness of imagination, that in the present age at least he would probably have figured as a virtuous journalist and professional rebuker of poetic vice or artistic aberration.—SWINBURNE, ALGERNON CHARLES, 1880, *A Study of Shakespeare, p.* 42, *note.*

What makes Congreve hold so high a place among comic dramatists is not so much that naturalness which is the distinguishing characteristic of his school, nor his insight, nor his breadth; it is his style that gives him his pre-eminence, that "subtle turn and heightening" which makes the sentences of his dialogue shine like well-faceted precious stones. The polish and elaboration he gives would be excessive were his wit less hard and pure and bright. Congreve has numerous obvious drawbacks, his outlook is not a broad one upon human nature, but upon "the town" only —his sympathies are narrow, his morality on the wrong side of tolerable. A more technical objection to him as a playwright is that there is too much ingenuity, too much complexity, and too little true art in his plots; they do not move us, and they hardly interest us. Nevertheless, there are qualifications in Congreve for a great, almost the greatest, place in our literature as a comic dramatist besides this one of consummate wit and consummate style. One of these is his marvellous faculty of characterization. Mirabell, the fine gentleman lover, is not the mere "walking gentleman" of most playwrights, but manly, lover-like, readyspoken, and most witty on occasion. Lady Wishfort, Mincing, Foible, Lord Froth, the coxcomb, and that most entertaining of sots and country louts, Sir Wilfull Witwould, are all personages with the stamp of humanity upon them, and Millamant is by common consent the most delightful of fine ladies that the world has ever known. Congreve's supremacy in the domain of comedy is to a great extent due to this, that he was an accomplished fine gentleman in the first place, and an accomplished *littérateur* in the second. —CRAWFURD, OSWALD, 1883, *ed., English Comic Dramatists, p.* 130.

French authors are his masters, and experience supplies the colors of his portraits, which display both the innate baseness of primitive instincts, and the refined corruption of worldly habits.—WELSH, ALFRED H., 1883, *Development of English Literature and Language, vol.* II, *p.* 17.

Congreve's defects are to be sought not so much in the external blemishes pointed out by Collier as in the absence of real refinement of feeling. His characters, as Voltaire observes, talk like men of fashion, while their actions are those of knaves. Lamb's audacious praise of him for excluding any pretensions to good feeling in his persons might be accepted if it implied (as he urges) a mere "privation of moral light." But, although a "single gush of cynical sentiment is quite in

harmony," his wit is saturnine, and a perpetual exposition of the baser kind of what passes for worldly wisdom. The atmosphere of his plays is asphyxiating. There is consequently an absence of real gaiety from his scenes and of true charm in his characters, while the teasing intricacy of his plots makes it (as Hunt observes) impossible to remember them even though just read and noted for the purpose. It is therefore almost cruel to suggest a comparison between Congreve and Molière, the model of the true comic spirit. The faults are sufficient to account for the neglect of Congreve by modern readers in spite of the exalted eulogies not too exalted for the purely literary merits of his pointed and vigorous dialogue—bestowed upon him by the best judges of his own time and by some over-generous critics of the present day.—STEPHEN, LESLIE, 1887, *Dictionary of National Biography, vol.* XII, *p.* 8.

Congreve's literary influence, although it must be acknowledged that the next age in poetry remembered him only to improve upon him, was far from insignificant, and he little deserved the contempt he has sometimes received. Nevertheless, the impression one has of him is of a genius which made only an imperfect expression of itself; of a man with more mind than his few comedies could hold, with tastes, culture, curiosity, a naturally fertile nature richly developed, but leaving no memorial of itself equal to its value.—WOODBERRY, GEORGE EDWARD, 1888, *The Nation, vol.* 47, *p.* 255.

Nothing was too good for Mr. Congreve; he had patronage and great gifts; it seemed always to be raining roses on his head. The work he did was not great work, but it was exquisitely done; though, it must be said, there was no preserving savor in it but the art of it. The talk in his comedies, by its pliancy, grace, neat turns, swiftness of repartee, compares with the talk in most comedies as goldsmith's work compares with the heavy forgings of a blacksmith. It matches exquisitely part to part, and runs as delicately as a hair-spring on jewelled pinions. —MITCHELL, DONALD G., 1890, *English Lands Letters and Kings, From Elizabeth to Anne, p.* 270.

Congreve was essentially a man of letters; his style is that of a pupil not of

Molière but of the full, the rich, the excessive, the pedantic Jonson; his Legends, his Wishforts, his Foresights, are the lawful heirs—refined and sublimated but still of direct descent—of the Tuccas and the Bobadils and the Epicure Mammons of the great Elizabethan; they are (that is) more literary than theatrical —they are excellent reading, but they have long since fled the stage and vanished into the night of mere scholarship.—HENLEY, WILLIAM ERNEST, 1890, *Views and Reviews*, p. 206.

Was the first to teach the English writer how to impart somewhat of that point and balance to the prose epigram in which he may approach, though the genius of our language forbids him to rival, the French. —TRAIL, H. D., 1894, *Social England, Introduction, vol.* I, *p.* xli.

Whatever the cause, he was lost to the stage at thirty, and his occasional poetical productions, the most important of which have been already noticed, were far from qualifying him to sit in the seat of Dryden. He enjoyed, nevertheless, supremacy of another kind. Regarded as an extinct volcano, he gave umbrage to no rivals; his urbane and undemonstrative temper kept him out of literary feuds; all agreed to adore so benign and inoffensive a deity, and the general respect of the lettered world fitly culminated in Pope's dedication of his *Homer* to him, the most splendid literary tribute the age could bestow.—GARNETT, RICHARD, 1895, *The Age of Dryden*, p. 126.

Whose well-bred ease is almost as remarkable as his brilliant wit.—BROOKE, STOPFORD A., 1896, *English Literature*, p. 194.

No one, perhaps, in any country, has written prose for the stage with so assiduous a solicitude for style. Congreve balances, polishes, sharpens his sentences till they seem like a set of instruments prepared for an electrical experiment; the current is his unequalled wit, and it flashes and leaps without intermission from the first scene to the last. The result is one of singular artificiality; and almost from the outset—from the moment, at all events, that Congreve's manner ceased to dazzle with its novelty—something was felt, even by his contemporaries, to be wanting. The something, no doubt, was humanity, sympathy, nature. — GOSSE,

EDMUND, 1897, *Short History of Modern English Literature*, p. 191.

Where Congreve excels all his English rivals is in his literary force, and a succinctness of style peculiar to him. He had correct judgment, a correct ear, readiness of illustration within a narrow range, in snap shots of the obvious at the obvious, and copious language. He hits the mean of a fine style and a natural in dialogue. He is at once precise and voluble. If you have ever thought upon style you will acknowledge it to be a signal accomplishment. In this he is a classic, and is worthy of treading a measure with Molière. . . .—MEREDITH, GEORGE, 1897, *An Essay on Comedy and the Uses of the Comic Spirit, pp.* 32, 33.

Probability and strict stage construction are still as much to seek here as elsewhere, and no one of the characters is a whole live personage like those of Shakespeare in the drama before, and those of Fielding in the novel later. But, on the other hand, there is hardly one who, as a personage of artificial comedy, is not a triumph, from Sir Sampson Legend, the testy father, through his sons Valentine (spendthrift and rake, but a better fellow than most of them) and Ben, the simple sailor, who was now becoming a stock stage figure; through the sisters Foresight and Frail, whose simultaneous discovery of each other's slips is one of the capital moments of English comic literature; and the foolish astronomer, Foresight; and Tattle, the frivolous beau; and Jeremy, the impossibly witty servant; and Angelica, giving us the contemporary notion of a heroine who is neither heartless nor a fool; and Prue, the hoyden. All these are, for purely theatrical flesh and blood, perfect triumphs in their kind, and they move throughout in a perfect star-shower of verbal fireworks.—SAINTSBURY, GEORGE, 1898, *A Short History of English Literature*, p. 493.

As pictures of manners Congreve's comedies are valuable, since they undoubtedly give a lively presentation of the fashionable society of his day. . . . Congreve is a much more important figure in the history of the theatre than in the history of the drama.—JOHNSON, CHARLES F., 1900, *Outline History of English and American Literature, pp.* 236, 237.

Sir Richard Blackmore

1650?-1729.

Poetaster, was born at Corsham, Wilts, and educated at Westminster and Oxford, taking his B. A. in 1674. First a schoolmaster, and then a London physician (1687 1722), he was knighted in 1697, and died at Boxted, Essex, in 1729. He wrote six epics in sixty books (all on the loftiest themes), besides versions of various books of the Bible, and theological, medical and miscellaneous treatises.—PATRICK AND GROOME, eds., 1897, Chambers's Biographical Dictionary, p. 102.

Wrote "Prince Arthur' (1695); "King Arthur" (1697); "Pharaphrases of the Book of Job, &c." (1700); "A Satire upon Wit" (1700); "Eliza" (1705); "Creation" (1712); "The Lay Monk" (1713); "King Alfred" (1713); "The Accomplished Preacher" (1729); and other works.—ADAMS, W. DAVENPORT, 1877, Dictionary of English Literature, p. 89.

PERSONAL

'Twas in his carriage the sublime
Sir Richard Blackmore used to rhyme,
  And (if the wits don't do him wrong)
'Twixt death and epics passed his time
  Scribbling and killing all day long.
—MOORE, THOMAS, 1850? Epigrams.

He was a commonplace man with an amiable faith in himself, and without intellect to distinguish between good and bad in poetry. His religious purpose was sincere, and it gave dignity to his work in the eyes even of Locke and Addison.—MORLEY, HENRY, 1879, A Manual of English Literature, ed. Tyler, p. 511.

GENERAL

The two elaborate poems of Blackmore and Milton, the which, for the dignity of them, may very well be looked upon as the two grand exemplars of poetry, do either of them exceed, and are more to be valued than all the poets, both of the Romans and the Greeks put together.—HOWARD, EDWARD, 1695, Essay on Pastoral, and Elegy on Queen Mary, Proem.

Quack Maurus, though he never took degrees
In either of our universities,
Yet to be shown by some kind wit he looks,
Because he played the fool, and writ three books.
But if he would be worth a poet's pen,
He must be more a fool, and write again:
For all the former fustian stuff he wrote
Was dead-born dog'rel, or is quite forgot.
—DRYDEN, JOHN, 1700, Prologue to the Pilgrim.

'Tis strange that an author should have a gamester's fate, and not know when to give over. Had the City Bard stopped his hand at "Prince Arthur," he had missed knighthood, 'tis true, but he had gone off with some applause.—BROWN, TOM, 1709, Laconics, Works, note.

It ["The Creation."] deserves to be looked upon as one of the most useful and noble productions in our English verse. The reader cannot but be pleased to find the depths of philosophy enlivened with all the charms of poetry, and to see so great a strength of reason, amidst so beautiful a redundancy of the imagination.—ADDISON, JOSEPH, 1712, The Spectator, No. 339.

Unwieldy pedant, let thy awkward muse
With censures praise, with flatteries abuse;
To lash, and not be felt, in thee 's an art,
Thou ne'er mad'st any but thy school-boys
  smart.
Then be advised and scribble not again—
Thou 'rt fashioned for a flail and not a pen.
If B——l's immortal wit thou wouldst decry,
Pretend 'tis he that wrote thy poetry.
Thy feeble satire ne'er can do him wrong
Thy poems and thy patients live not long.
—GARTH, SIR SAMUEL, 1715, To the Merry Poetaster, at Saddler's-Hall, in Cheapside.

Far o'er all, sonorous Blackmore's strain;
Walls, steeples, skies, bray back to him again.
In Tot'nham fields, the brethren, with amaze,
Prick all their ears up, and forget to graze;
Long Chanc'ry-lane retentive rolls the sound,
And courts to courts return it round and
  round;
Thames wafts it thence to Rufus' roaring
  hall,
And Hungerford re-echoes bawl for bawl.
All hail him victor in both gifts of song,
Who sings so loudly, and who sings so long.
—POPE, ALEXANDER, 1724-43, The Dunciad, pt. ii, v. 259-268.

Boileau can write upon a Lutrin what one can read with pleasure a thousand times, and Blackmore cannot write upon the "Creation" any thing that one shall not yawn ten times over, before one has read it once.—HERVEY, LORD JOHN, 1728, Letter to Lady Mary Wortley Montagu, Oct. 28.

'Tis true, sir Richd. was a poet, but he is not placed by the best judges at the top head, notwithstanding Molyneux says in his Letters in Locke's works, p. 568, that "all our English poets (except Milton) have been ballad makers, in comparison to him."—HEARNE, THOMAS, 1734, *Reliquiæ Hearnianæ, ed. Bliss, Nov. 22, vol. III, p. 163.*

Mean circumstances in solemn description seem ridiculous to those who are sensible of the incongruity, except where the effect of that incongruity is counteracted by certain causes to be specified hereafter. Of this blunder in composition the poetry of Blackmore supplies thousands of examples. The lines on Etna quoted in the treatise on the Bathos, are well known. By his contrivance, the mountain is made to labour, not with a subterraneous fire and external conflagration, but with a fit of the colic; an idea, that seems to have been familiar to him (for we meet with it in other parts of his work); whether from his being subject to that distemper, or, as a physician, particularly successful in curing it, I cannot say. This poet seems to have had no notion of any thing more magnificent, than the usages of his own time and neighbourhood; which, accordingly, he transfers to the most awful subjects, and thus degrades into burlesque what he meant to raise to sublimity.—BEATTIE, JAMES, 1776–9, *Essays, p. 357.*

Blackmore's prose is not the prose of a poet, for it is languid, sluggish, and lifeless; his diction is neither daring nor exact, his flow neither rapid or easy, and his periods neither smooth nor strong. . . . Of his four Epick Poems, the first had such reputation and popularity as enraged the criticks; the second was at least known enough to be ridiculed; the two last had neither friends nor enemies. . . . He depended with great security on his own powers, and perhaps was for that reason less diligent in perusing books. His literature was, I think, but small. What he knew of antiquity, I suspect him to have gathered from modern compilers: but, though he could not boast of much critical knowledge, his mind was stored with general principales, and he left minute researches to those whom he considered as little minds.—JOHNSON, SAMUEL, 1779–81, *Blackmore, Lives of the English Poets.*

The author's good intentions cannot be denied; but good intentions do not make poetry; and we feel, with Cowper, that the pious Knight has committed "more absurdities in verse than any writer of our country."—ADAMS, W. H. DAVENPORT, 1886, *Good Queen Anne, vol. II, p. 323.*

The most notorious verse-writer, after Garth, of the interregnum between Pope and Dryden was the luckless Sir Richard Blackmore, one of the small and curious company who have been made immortal by their satirists. . . . "Creation," however, was highly praised, not merely by Addison, to whom piety and Whiggery combined would have been an irresistible bribe, but by Johnson, to whom the second quality would have neutralised the first. It is difficult for a reader of the present day to share their admiration. "Creation" supplies (as, for the matter of that, do the other poems, so far as the present writer knows them) tolerable rhetoric in verse occasionally not bad. But this is a different thing from poetry. Blackmore's couplets are often enjambed. SAINTSBURY, GEORGE, 1898, *A Short History of English Literature, p. 555.*

Samuel Clarke
1675–1729.

Born at Norwich, England, Oct. 11, 1675; died at London, May 17, 1729. A celebrated English divine and metaphysical writer, son of an alderman of Norwich. He was a graduate of Cambridge (Caius College), and was successively rector of Drayton, near Norwich; of St. Bennet's, London, in 1706; and of St. James's, Westminster, in 1709. He was also one of the chaplains of Queen Anne. His most celebrated work is his "Boyle Lectures" (1704-05), published as "A Discourse concerning the Being and Attributes of God, the Obligations of Natural Religion, and the Truth and Certainty of the Christian Revelation, in answer to Mr. Hobbes, Spinoza, etc." His metaphysical argument for the existence of God is especially famous, and he also holds a high place in the history of the science of ethics.—SMITH, BENJAMIN E., 1894–97, *The Century Cyclopedia of Names, p. 256.*

PERSONAL

Innocence is playful: Dr. Clarke not only loved to show his agility, by jumping over chairs and tables, but he would often unbend himself with his own or other children, in a way that would disgust austerity; but he would instantly stop if he saw a weak person approaching them, giving himself, the watchward, "Be grave, here comes a fool."—NOBLE, MARK, 1806, *A •Biographical History of England, vol.* III, *p.* 120.

Almost the only personal anecdotes to be found were printed in the "Gentleman's Magazine" for 1783 from notes by the Rev. Mr. Jones of Welwyn. They seem to show that Clarke was generally courtier-like and cautious in his conversation, but that he became playful in the intimacy of a few friends. He remonstrated impressively with his children for killing flies. Thomas Bott once found him "swimming on a table," and on the approach of a solemn coxcomb on some such occasion heard him say, "Boys, be wise, here comes a fool!" Warton, in his "Essay on Pope," says that Clarke would amuse himself by jumping over tables and chairs, and he appears to have been fond of cards. He was remarkable for his careful economy of time. He always had a book in his pocket, and is said never to have forgotten anything that he onced learned. At Norwich he preached extempore, but afterwards took great pains in the composition of his sermons.—STEPHEN, LESLIE, 1887, *Dictionary of National Biography, vol.* X, *p.* 445.

GENERAL

One of the most accurate, learned, and judicious writers this age has produced. —ADDISON, JOSEPH, 1712, *The Spectator, No.* 367.

Now I perceive that in these Sermons he had dealt a great deal in abstract and metaphysical reasonings. I therefore asked him how he ventured into such subtilties, which I never durst meddle with? And shewing him a nettle, or the like contemptible weed, in my garden, I told him, that weed contained better arguments for the Being and Attributes of God, than all his metaphysicks. He confessed it to be so; but alleged for himself, that, since such philosophers as Hobbes and Spinoza had made use of those kind

of subtilties *against,* he thought proper to shew, that the like way of reasoning might be better made use *on the side of,* religion. Which reason, or excuse, I allowed not to be inconsiderable.—WHISTON, WILLIAM, 1730, *Historical Memoirs of the Life and Writings of Dr. Samuel Clarke.*

Dr. Clarke was as bright a light and masterly a teacher of truth and virtue as ever yet appeared among us. . . . His sentiments and expressions were so masterly, his way of explaining the phraseology of Scripture by collecting and comparing together the parallel places, so extraordinary and convincing, as to make his method of preaching so universally acceptable, that there was not a parishioner who was not always pleased at his coming into their Pulpit, or who was ever weary of his instruction. His works must last as long as any language remains to convey them to future times.— HOADLY, BENJAMIN, 1738, *Life, Clarke's Works, vol.* I.

Even our better models are very defective. I have lately turned over Dr. Clarke's large collection, for the use of my parish; and yet, with much altering, and many additions, I have been able to pick out no more than eight or ten that I could think passable for that purpose. He is clear and happy enough in the explication of Scripture; but miserably cold and lifeless; no invention, no dignity, no force; utterly incapable of enlarging on a plain thought, or of striking out new ones: in short, much less of a genius than I had supposed him.—HURD, RICHARD, 1761, *Letter to Warburton, Letters from a Late Eminent Prelate, Dec.* 25, *p.* 331.

Everywhere abounds in good sense, and the most clear and accurate reasoning; his applications of scripture are pertinent; his style is always perspicuous, and often elegant; he instructs and he convinces; in what then is he deficient? In nothing except in the power of interesting and seizing the heart. He shows you what you ought to do; but he excites not the desire of doing it; he treats man as if he were a being of pure intellect without imagination or passions.—BLAIR, HUGH, 1783, *Lectures on Rhetoric and Belles-Lettres, ed. Mills, Lecture* XXIX.

After Locke and Newton, the most distinguished of the English philosophers.

—TENNEMANN, WILLIAM GOTTLIEB, 1812, *A Manual of the History of Philosophy,* tr. *Johnson,* ed. *Morell, p.* 331.

The chief glory of Clarke, as a metaphysical author, is due to the boldness and ability with which he placed himself in the breach against the Necessitarians and Fatalists of his times. With a mind far inferior to that of Locke, in comprehensiveness, in originality, and in fertility of invention, he was nevertheless the more wary and skillful disputant of the two; possessing, in a singular degree, that reach of thought in grasping remote consequences, which effectually saved him from those rash concessions into which Locke was frequently betrayed by the greater warmth of his temperament and vivacity of his fancy. This logical foresight (the natural result of his habits of mathematical study) rendered him peculiarly fit to contend with adversaries eager and qualified to take advantage of every vulnerable point in his doctrine; but it gave, at the same time, to his style a tameness and monotony, and want of colouring, which never appear in the easy and spirited, though often unfinished and unequal, sketches of Locke. Voltaire has somewhere said of him, that he was a mere reasoning machine, (*un moulin à raisonnement*), and the expression (though doubtless much too unqualified) possesses merit, in point of just discrimination, of which Voltaire was probably not fully aware. — STEWART, DUGALD, 1815-21, *First Preliminary Dissertation, Encyclopædia Britannica.*

Dr. Clarke was a superior scholar, and a man who studied the Bible with attention, though some of its grand doctrines were not correctly understood by him. . . . Those who are partial to paraphrases of the Bible, which the author of this work is not, will find Clarke and Pyle not inferior to the generality of paraphrasts. — ORME, WILLIAM, 1824, *Bibliotheca Biblica.*

The characteristic excellence of Dr. Clarke as a writer, consists in the vigour and clearness of his understanding. As a metaphysician, he has, we think, been greatly overrated. His abstruser speculations remind us rather of the intricate and unmeaning subtilities of the schoolmen, than of the depth and comprehensiveness of Bacon, Leibnitz, Locke, or Edwards.

But when a sound and manly sense is all that is required to elucidate a question, there Dr. Clarke appears almost without a rival. He appears, as a writer, entirely destitute of imagination and sensibility. His theological system was, in one point, as we have already seen, very erroneous. In other respects he appears, though an Arminian, to have held the leading principles of the gospel. His sermons are clear and well-arranged: but, on the whole, much inferior to the best of his other works. In life and warmth of evangelical sentiment they are especially defective. — CUNNINGHAM, G. G., 1840, ed., *Lives of Eminent and Illustrious Englishmen, vol.* IV, *p.* 253.

Whatever may be thought of the *à priori* argument, as it is called, for the being of God, it is certain that Clarke has based his ethical system on a just foundation: morality is in his view acting and feeling in harmony with the relations of things. Right reason is on its side, though probably most men will reach moral duties more easily in the method adopted by Butler. It is also to his honour that he defended the doctrine of moral liberty against the Fatalist school which Hobbes had fostered. — ANGUS, JOSEPH, 1865, *The Handbook of English Literature, p.* 381.

The most illustrious of all, the learned Clarke, a mathematician, philosopher, scholar, theologian. — TAINE, H. A., 1871, *History of English Literature,* tr. *Van Laun, vol.* II, *bk.* iii, *ch.* iii, *p.* 68.

Sir Isaac Newton's chief contribution to metaphysics was in the form of 'a scholium to the second edition of the "Principia," 1713, respecting Space and Duration, which was subsequently expanded into an *à priori* argument by Dr. S. Clarke and the philosophers of his school. It is singular, yet true, that the subsequent deviation from Locke's principles and method, or more properly, the recognition of an appropriate sphere for *à priori* truth, for which Locke's analysis had failed to provide, should have been largely owing to the influence of these two eminent physicists. The fact cannot be questioned that speculative philosophy asserted a wider range of inquiry for itself under the impulse given to it by Dr. Samuel Clarke and the theologians and philosophers of his school. — UEBERWEG, FRIEDRICH, 1871,

History of Philosophy, tr. Morris, vol. II, *p.* 370.

As regards style, Clarke's sermons may almost be said to have been the models of the Scotch "moderate" school of preachers—heavy, prolix, argumentative, full of practical good sense, and possessing more of the ardour familiar to us under the name "Evangelical."—MINTO, WILLIAM, 1872–80, *Manual of English Prose Literature, p.* 398.

Homer has never had a more judicious or acute commentator. . . . As a metaphysician, he was inferior to Locke in comprehensiveness and originality, but possessed more skill and logical foresight, the natural result of his habits of mathematical study; and he has been justly celebrated for the boldness of ability with which he placed himself in the breach against the Necessitarians and Fatalists of his times.—CHAMBERS, ROBERT, 1876, *Cyclopedia of English Literature, ed. Carruthers.*

Samuel Clarke was a man of sufficient intellectual vigour to justify a very high reputation, and his faults were those which are less obvious to the eyes of contemporaries than of posterity. He was deficient in originality and acuteness. He had perspicuity enough to avoid some of the extravagances of the school to which he belonged, but not enough to detect its fundamental fallacies. His contemporaries might therefore regard him as a bold, yet wary, logician; to us he appears to be a second-rate advocate of opinions interesting only in the mouths of the greater men who were their first and ablest advocates. He somewhat resembles a more recent Cambridge philosopher, Dr. Whewell, and stands to Leibnitz in the same sort of relation which Whewell occupied to modern German philosophers. In softening the foreign doctrines to suit English tastes, he succeeds in enervating them without making them substantially more reasonable. Clarke was the great English representative of the *à priori* method of constructing a system of theology. He was sufficiently tainted by rationalism to fall into certain errors in regard to the doctrine of the Trinity; and his incipient heterodoxy has caused later theologians to look upon him with suspicion, and has helped to reduce his name to a humble position in the list of eminent defenders of the faith. A more special characteristic resulted from his being regarded by himself and others as a theological lieutenant of Newton. In defence of that great name he plunged into a remarkable controversy with Leibnitz, from which he was held to have emerged with honour. The whole tone of his writings is coloured by the same influence. His ambition apparently was to compose a work which should be to Christianity what the "Principia" was to astronomy. More than any English writer he clothes his arguments with that apparatus of quasimathematical phraseology which was common to most of the followers of Descartes.—STEPHEN, LESLIE, 1876, *History of English Thought in the Eighteenth Century, vol.* I, *p.* 119.

If these editions [of Homer] had appeared before the age of Bentley, they might have had some prospect of more durable reputation; but the rapid advance of modern scholarship has left them far behind; and they now remain chiefly as witnesses of the large and liberal culture of mind more scientific than critical.—MARTINEAU, JAMES, 1885, *Types of Ethical Theory, vol.* II, *p.* 429.

The clear and solid reasonings of Samuel Clarke.—ABBEY, CHARLES J., 1887, *The English Church and Its Bishops, 1700–1800, vol.* I, *p.* 41.

With much convincing force, but in a cold, mathematical style.—ROBERTSON, J. LOGIE, 1894, *A History of English Literature, p.* 252.

Clarke's style is not particularly attractive. It is usually intelligible and fairly clear, but it inclines to be ponderous, and is marred by too plentiful sprinklings of Scripture texts. He has no humour, no imagination, and no great depth or originality of thought. In his philosophical writings he sought to introduce the truths of other men in plain and simple language and succeeded fairly well. His sermons are clear, forcible and well sustained. They exhibit great commonsense and moderation, and though far from beautiful, are dignified and in good taste. His Paraphrases of the Gospels are very able. The language is vigorous and fairly natural. They are colloquial, without irreverence or undue familiarity. —FITZROY, A. I., 1894, *English Prose, p.* 537.

KATHERINE PHILIPS

Drawing by J. Thurston.
Engraving by W. Finden.

SIR RICHARD STEELE

From Mezzotint by Simon.   Painting
by Sir Godfrey Kneller.

Sir Richard Steele

1672–1729.

Born, in Dublin, March 1672. Early education at Charterhouse, Nov. 1684 to Nov. 1689. Matric., Ch. Ch., Oxford, 13 March 1690; Postmaster Merton Coll., 1691. Left Oxford, 1694. Took no degree. Entered the army, 1695. Priv. Sec. to Lord Cutts, 1696-97. Commission in the Guards, 1697. Play, "The Funeral," produced at Drury Lane, Dec. 1701; "The Lying Lover," Dec. 1703; "The Tender Husband," April 1705. Married (i) Mrs. Margaret Stretch, 1705. Gentleman-Waiter to Prince George of Denmark, Aug. 1706 to Oct. 1708. Wife died, Dec. 1706. Gazetteer, May 1707 to Oct. 1710. Married (ii) Mary Scurlock, Sept. 1707. Contrib. to "The Muses Mercury," 1707; to "Spectator," March 1711 to Dec. 1714; to "Guardian," March to Oct. 1713; to "The Englishman," Oct. 1713 to Nov. 1715. Commissioner of Stamp Office, Jan. 1710 to June 1713. M. P. for Stockbridge, 1713; expelled from House of Commons on account of passages in writings, 1714. Surveyor of Royal Stables at Hampton Court, 1714. Lieutenant for County of Middlesex, and J. P., 1714. Governor of Royal Company of Comedians, 1715-20. Knighted, 1715. M. P. for Boroughbridge, 1715. Commissioner of Forfeited Estates in Scotland, 1715. Edited "The Theatre" (under pseud. "Sir John Edgar"), Jan. to April 1720. M. P. for Wendover, March 1722. Comedy, "The Conscious Lovers," produced at Drury Lane, Nov. 1722. Later years spent in retirement, mainly in Wales. Died at Carmarthen, 1 Sept. 1729. *Works:* "The Procession" (anon.), 1695; "The Christian Hero," 1701; "The Funeral," 1702; "The Lying Lover," 1704; "The Tender Husband," 1705; "Letter to Dr. Sacheverell" (under pseud, "Isaac Bickerstaff"), 1709; "The Tatler" (under pseud. "Isaac Bickerstaff," 4 vols.), 1709-11; Contributions to "The Spectator," 1711-14; to "The Guardian," 1713; to "The Englishman," 1713-15; "The Importance of Dunkirk Considered," 1713; "The Englishman's Thanks to the Duke of Marlborough" (anon.), 1712; "The Crisis," 1713; "Letter to the Tongue-loosed Doctor" (under pseud. "Isaac Bickerstaff") 1713; "Speech on the proposal of Sir T. Hanmer for Speaker," 1714; "Letter to a Member of Parliament," 1714; "Apology for Himself and his Writings," 1714; "A Defence for drinking to the pious memory of K. Charles I.," 1714; "Romish Ecclesiastical History of Late Years," 1714; "Letter from the Earl of Mar to the King," 1715; "The Lover; to which is added, the Reader," 1715; "Political Writings," 1715; "Town-Talk" (9 nos.), 1715-16; "Chit-Chat" (under pseud. "Humphrey Philroye"), 1716; "The British Subjects' Answer to the Pretender's Declaration," 1716; "Speech for Repealing of the Triennial Act," 1716; "The Tea Table," 1716; "An Account of the Fish-Pool" (with J. Gilmore), 1718; "Letter to the Earl of O——d," 1719; "The Spinster," 1719; "The Antidote" (2 nos.; anon.), 1719; "Inquiry into the Manner of Creating Peers" (anon.), 1719; "The Plebeian" (anon.), 1719; "The Theatre" (under pseud. "Sir John Edgar"), 1720; "The Crisis of Poverty," 1720; "A Nation a Family," 1720; "The D——n of W——r still the same" (anon.), 1720; "State of the Case between the Lord Chamberlain, etc.," 1720; "The Conscious Lovers," 1723; "Dramatick Works, 1723; "Woods' Melancholly Complaint" (anon.), 1725. *Posthumous:* "Epistolary Correspondence," ed. by J. Nichols, 1787. He *translated:* Cerri's "Account of the State of the Roman Catholic Religion," 1715; and *edited:* "Poetical Miscellanies," 1714; "The Ladies' Library," 1714. *Life:* by G. A. Aitken, 1889.—SHARP, R. ARQUHARSON, 1897, *A Dictionary of English Authors,* p. 267.

PERSONAL

On Sunday night last, Captain Keely and one Mr. Steele, an officer of the Guards, fought a duel in Hide-Park, in which the latter was mortally wounded, and some say he is since Dead.—FLYING POST, 1700, *June* 18-20.

After the first Bottle he is no disagreeable Companion. I never knew him taxed with Ill-nature, which hath made me wonder how Ingratitude came to be his prevailing Vice; and I am apt to think it proceeds more from some unaccountable sort of Instinct, than Premedtiation. Being the most imprudent Man alive, he never follows the Advice of his Friends, but is wholly at the mercy of Fools or Knaves, or hurried away by his own Caprice; by which he hath committed more Absurdities in Oeconomy, Friendship, Love, Duty, good Manners, Politics, Religion and Writing, than ever fell to one Man's share.—SWIFT, JONATHAN, 1713, *The Importance of the Guardian Considered.*

D'ye see that black beau (stuck up in a pert chariot), thickset, his eyes in his head with hanging eyebrows, broad face, and tallow complexion. . . . I long to inform myself if that coach be his own. . . . He is called M. L'Ingrate. . . . Though he's a most incorrect writer, he pleases in spight of his faults. . . . I remember him almost t'other day but a wretched common trooper. He had the luck to write a small poem, and dedicated it to a person he never saw. . . . His morals were loose.—MANLEY, MRS. MARY DE LA RIVIERE, 1709, *New Atalantis, vol.* I, *p.* 131.

Richard Steel, esq., member of parliament, was on Thursday last, about 12 o'clock at night, expelled the house of commons for a roguish pamphlett called "The Crisis," and for several other pamphletts, in which he hath abused the queen, &c. This Steel was formerly of Christ Church in Oxford, and afterwards of Merton college. He was a rakish, wild, drunken spark; but he got a good reputation by publishing a paper that came out daily, called "The Tatler," and by another called "The Spectator;" but the most ingenious of these papers were written by Mr. Addison, and Dr. Swift, as 'tis reported. And when these two had left him, he appeared to be a mean, heavy, weak writer, as is sufficiently demonstrated in his papers called "The Guardian," "The Englishman," and "The Lover." He now writes for bread, being involved in debt. —HEARNE, THOMAS, 1713-14, *Reliquiæ Hearnianæ, ed. Bliss, March* 23, *vol.* I, *p.* 296.

Sir John Edgar is of a middle stature, broad shoulders, thick legs, a shape like the picture of somebody over a farmer's chimney—a short chin, a short nose, a short forehead, a broad flat face, and a dusky countenance. Yet with such a face and such a shape, he discovered at sixty that he took himself for a beauty, and appeared to be more mortified at being told that he was ugly, than he was by any

reflection made upon his honour or understanding. . . . He is a gentleman born, witness himself, of very honourable family; certainly of a very ancient one, for his ancestors flourished in Tipperary long before the English ever set foot in Ireland. He has testimony of this more authentic than the Herald's Office or any human testimony. For God has marked him more abundantly than he did Cain, and stamped his native country on his face, his understanding, his writings, his actions, his passions, and, above all, his vanity. The Hibernian brogue is still upon all these, though long habit and length of days have worn it off his tongue. —DENNIS, JOHN, 1720, *The Character and Conduct of Sir John Edgar.*

Sir Richard Steele was a very good-natured man.—MONTAGU, LADY MARY WORTLEY, 1740-41, *Spence's Anecdotes, ed. Singer, p.* 175.

Sir Richard Steele having one day invited to his house a great number of persons of the first quality, they were surprised at the number of liveries which surrounded the table; and after dinner, when wine and mirth had set them free from the observations of a rigid ceremony, one of them inquired of Sir Richard how such an expensive train of domesticks could be consistent with his fortune. Sir Richard very frankly confessed that they were fellows of whom he would willingly be rid. And then, being asked why he did not discharge them, declared that they were bailiffs, who had introduced themselves with an execution, and whom, since he could not send them away, he had thought it convenient to embellish with liveries, that they might do him credit while they staid. — JOHNSON, SAMUEL, 1744, *Life of Richard Savage.*

Our author was a man of the highest benevolence; he celebrates a generous action with a warmth that is only peculiar to a good heart; and however he may be blamed for want of œconomy, &c., yet was he the most agreeable, and if we may be allowed the expression, the most innocent rake that ever trod the rounds of indulgence.—CIBBER, THEOPHILUS, 1753, *Lives of the Poets, vol.* IV, *p.* 116.

There was a great similitude between his [Fielding] character and that of Sir Richard Steele. He had the advantage both in learning, and, in my opinion, genius : they both agreed in wanting money in spite of all their friends, and would have wanted it, if their hereditary lands had been as extensive as their imagination.—MONTAGU, LADY MARY WORTLEY, 1755, *Letter to the Countess of Bute, Sept.* 22.

I was told he retained his cheerful sweetness of temper to the last; and would often be carried out in a summer's evening, when the country lads and lasses were assembled at their rural sports, and with his pencil give an order on his agent, the mercer, for a new gown to the best dancer.—VICTOR, BENJAMIN, 1776, *Original Letters, Dramatic Pieces, and Poems, vol.* I, *p.* 330.

He was one of those whose hearts are the dupes of their imaginations, and who are hurried through life by the most despotic volition. He always preferred his caprices to his interests; or, according to his own notion, very ingenious, but not a little absurd, "he was always of the humour of preferring the state of his mind to that of his fortune."—DISRAELI, ISAAC, 1812–13, *Genius the Dupe of Its Passions, Calamities of Authors.*

The privilege [expulsion from Parliament] was far more unwarrantably exerted by the opposite party in 1714, against sir Richard Steele, expelled the house for writing "The Crisis," a pamphlet reflecting on the ministry. This was, perhaps, the first instance wherein the house of commons so identified itself with the executive administration, independently of the sovereign's person, as to consider itself libelled by those who impugned its measures.—HALLAM, HENRY, 1827–41, *The Constitutional History of England, vol.* II, *ch.* xvi, *p.* 470.

Steele is said to have behaved to Addison in society with a marked deference, very uncommon and striking between old comrades, equal in age, and nearly so in all things excepting genuis and conduct. In private, however, there can be little doubt that they associated together on terms of great familiarity and confidence, and were frequent depositaries of the literary projects of each other.—AIKIN, LUCY, 1843, *Life of Addison, ch.* vii.

He was one of those people whom it is impossible either to hate or to respect. His temper was sweet, his affections warm, his spirits lively, his passions strong, and his principles weak. His life was spent in sinning and repenting, in inculcating what was right, and doing what was wrong. In speculation, he was a man of piety and honour ; in practice, he was much of the rake and a little of the swindler. He was, however, so good-natured that it was not easy to be seriously angry with him, and that even rigid moralists felt more inclined to pity than to blame him, when he diced himself into a sponging-house, or drank himself into a fever.—MACAULAY, THOMAS BABINGTON, 1843, *Life and Writings of Addison, Edinburgh Review ; Critical and Miscellaneous Essays.*

If there were no worse men in the world than Steele, what a planet we should have of it ? Steele knew his own foibles as well as any man. He regretted, and made amends for them, and left posterity a name for which they have reason to thank and love him.—HUNT, LEIGH, 1849, *A Book for the Corner, vol.* II, *p.* 40.

He had survived much, but neither his cheerful temper nor his kind philosophy. He would be carried out in a summer's evening, where the country lads and lasses were at their rural sports, and with his pencil give an order on his agent for a new gown to the best dancer. That was the last thing seen of Richard Steele. And the youths and maidens who saw him in his invalid-chair, enfeebled and dying, saw him still as the wits and fine ladies and gentlemen had seen him in his gaiety and youth, when he sat in the chair of Mr. Bickerstaff, creating pleasure for himself by the communication of pleasure to others, and in proportion to the happiness he distributed increasing his own.—FORSTER, JOHN, 1855, *Sir Richard Steele, Quarterly Review, vol.* 96, *p.* 568.

Who has not heard of Sir Richard Steele ? Wordsworth says of one of his characters—

"She was known to every star,
     And every wind that blows."

Poor Dick was known to every sponging-house, and to every bailiff that, blowing in pursuit, walked the London streets. A fine-hearted, warm-blooded character, without any atom of prudence, self-control, reticence, or forethought; quite as destitute of malice or envy; perpetually sinning and perpetually repenting;

never positively irreligious, even when drunk; and often excessively pious when recovering sobriety,—Steele reeled his way through life, and died with the reputation of being an orthodox Christian and a (nearly) habitual drunkard; the most affectionate and most faithless of husbands; a brave soldier, and in many points an arrant fool; a violent politician, and the best natured of men; a writer extremely lively, for this, among other reasons, that he wrote generally on his legs, flying or meditating flight from his creditors; and who embodied in himself the titles of his three principal works— "The Christian Hero," "The Tender Husband," and the "Tatler;"—being a "Christian Hero," in intention, one of those intentions with which a certain place is paved; a "Tender Husband," if not a true one, to his two ladies; and a "Tatler" to all persons, in all circumstances and at all times.—GILFILLAN, GEORGE, 1859, *ed., Poetical Works of Joseph Addison, etc., Life, p.* xiv.

From the time of his leaving college without a degree, to the day of his death on the banks of the Towy, at the age of 58, an old man before his time, he was the victim of his own temperament. He was completely incapable of restraining himself. He was genial, good-natured to excess, fond of good society, and, to use the words of Lady Mary W. Montagu, like Fielding, so made for happiness, that it is a pity he was not immortal. But happiness never came. In politics and in the business of life he was equally unsuccessful. Even in affairs of the heart, in which, as might be supposed, he had his share, he does not seem to have prospered. The "perverse" widow (widows, as De Coverley and more of us have experienced, are too often "perverse") left a wound in his heart that, we suspect, was never quite healed. Indeed, as Charter-house boy, collegian, soldier, lover, pamphleteer, gazetteer, Parliament man, patentee, inventor of fish machines, and father of a family, poor Sir Richard failed to reach the personal success he promised himself. He was a brave adventurer, but he never had the luck to secure a great prize; or, having secured it, he was unable to retain it. And the reason is plain. He failed, as all others have failed who attempted to eat the grape and drink the wine.

—PURNELL, THOMAS, 1867, *Literature and Its Professors, p.* 202.

Was it not in this age that loose Dick Steele paid his wife the finest compliment ever paid to woman, when he said "that to love her was a liberal education?"— LOWELL, JAMES RUSSELL, 1871–90, *Pope, Prose Works, Riverside ed., vol.* IV, *p.* 49.

That bundle of failings and weaknesses. . . . It was surface wickedness with Steele entirely: His heart was tender, and his character simple as a child's.— SMITH, GEORGE BARNETT, 1875, *Poets and Novelists, p.* 43.

He had two wives, whom he loved dearly and treated badly. He hired grand houses, and bought fine horses for which he could never pay. He was often religious, but more often drunk. As a man of letters, other men of letters who followed him, such as Thackeray, could not be very proud of him. But everybody loved him; and he seems to have been the inventor of that flying literature which, with many changes in form and manner, has done so much for the amusement and edification of readers ever since his time.—TROL-LOPE, ANTHONY, 1879, *Thackeray (English Men of Letters), p.* 162.

Dick Steele may have had many weaknesses and some vices, but we could forgive a good deal of both to a man who could write so tenderly to a woman as he writes to his "dear Prue." . . . After marriage Steele's gayety, his conviviality, and his recklessness about getting into debt, must often have made trouble for Mrs. Steele, and she must have had much cause to reproach him. Yet he almost disarms censure by his penitent acknowledgement of his faults and by his constant affection.—RICHARDSON, ABBY SAGE, 1882, *ed., Old Love-Letters, p.* 61.

I am confident that the result of the fuller study of his life, which is now rendered practicable, will be the conviction that, in spite of weaknesses, which are among the most apparent of all those to which mortals are liable, Steele's character is more attractive and essentially nobler than, perhaps that of any of the greatest of his contemporaries in the world of letters.—AITKEN, GEORGE A., 1889, *The Life of Richard Steele, vol.* I, *Preface.*

We have a characteristic glimpse of him in his later years—for he lived far down into the days of the Georges (one of whom gave him his knighthood and title)—when he is palsied, at his charming country home in Wales, and totters out to see the village girls dance upon the green, and insists upon sending off to buy a new gown for the best dancer; this was so like him! And it would have been like him to carry his palsied steps straight thereafter to the grave where his Prue and the memory of all his married joys and hopes lay sleeping.—MITCHELL, DONALD G., 1890, *English Lands Letters and Kings, From Elizabeth to Anne, p.* 287.

That Steele was an undetected hypocrite and a sentimental debauchee is now no longer maintained, although it cannot be denied that his will was often weaker than his purpose; that he was constitutionally improvident and impecunious; and that, like many of his contemporaries in that hard-drinking century, he was far too easily seduced by his compliant good-fellowship into excess in wine. "I shall not carry my humility so far as to call myself a vicious man," he wrote in "Tatler" No. 271, "but must confess my life is at best but pardonable." When so much is admitted, it is needless to charge the picture, though it may be added that, with all his faults, allowed and imputed, there is abundant evidence to prove that he was not only a doting husband and an affectionate father, but also a loyal friend and an earnest and unselfish patriot.—DOBSON, AUSTIN, 1898, *Dictionary of National Biography, vol.* LIV, *p.* 136.

Steele was not cast in the heroic mould. He was a man of many weaknesses, inconsistencies—careless, improvident, foolishly sanguine; and easy prey to the temptations of conviviality; often reckless in word and deed. But his personality is none the less a singularly attractive one. He was full of the milk of human kindness. With the defects of his Irish blood, he had its good qualities as well—its warmth, sympathy, buoyant courage. Often as he fell short of his own ideals, he honestly loved what was true, pure, and good. He was a loyal friend and a devoted husband and father. But nowhere is his thorough manliness exhibited more fully than in his chivalrous treatment of women. In that age of coarseness and frivolity, he spoke of them always with genuine admiration and respect; and were there no reason

for it but this, we ought to hold his name in kindly remembrance. Other men of his time may make larger claims upon our attention; for none do we conceive so deep an affection. Perhaps our feeling toward him is best illustrated by the fact that, despite the dignity of knighthood bestowed upon him by George I., we still find ourselves constantly thinking and speaking of him as "Dick" Steele.—HUDSON, WILLIAM HENRY, 1899, *ed., The Sir Roger De Coverley Papers, Introduction, p.* xi.

Dick Steele, who did so love his wife and friend,
Who gave to Addison of praise no end,
   And wrote his Prue such tender letters daily
I like and love. What though he took life gaily
And sometimes did strict laws of right offend?
His sins are free from guile. His deeds portend
No serpent's craft: he crawls not, is not scaly.
No faults of his could land him in Old Bailey.
High spirits and warm heart; a wit as sweet
   As it was shining; courage as high as any;
And civic virtue, giving to his seat
   In Parliament a fortress for the many—
Say, are not these a character complete,
   And need we care for wasted pound or penny?
—HUTSON, CHARLES WOODWARD, 1899, *The Bookman, August.*

Steele himself was no model of propriety like Addison. Indeed, he resembled Hogarth's "bad apprentice" in comparison. He had been a shuttlecock on the battledore of chance. He had dabbled in lotteries, in the philosopher's stone, in political intrigue, in what you will. He was fond of pleasure and display; he was indiscreet; he was ever falling, and always repenting. Debt, and even dissipation, were his concomitants. But nevertheless he loved his home and humbly adored his God. He was human to the core, in frailty as in generous aspiration. Politics drummed him out of his office, as his patron, Mainwaring, had drummed him in. He was no politician, and in this sphere merely a mouthpiece. He was intemperate in his quarrels, especially with Swift. He lacked self-control. But he was irrepressible and inexhaustible. — SICHEL, WALTER, 1901, *Bolingbroke and His Times, p.* 118.

THE CHRISTIAN HERO
1701

Steele began his career as a writer, with a poem, his "Christian Heroes," which justified no great expectations. This poem could have little of soul or of nature in it, because the contents stood in a most surprising contradiction with Steele's scandalous and dissolute course of life.— SCHLOSSER, FRIEDRICH CHRISTOPH, 1823-43, *History of the Eighteenth Century*, vol. I, p. 102.

Breathes the very spirit of piety.— MORRIS, EDWARD E., 1876, *The Age of Anne (Epochs of Modern History)*, p. 239.

One would hardly have looked to him for any early talk about the life of a true *Christian Hero*. But he did write a book so entitled, in those wild young days, as a sort of kedge anchor, he says, whereby he might haul out from the shoals of the wicked town, and indulge in a sort of contemplative piety. It was and is a very good little book, but it did not hold a bit, as an anchor.—MITCHELL, DONALD G., 1890, *English Lands Letters and Kings, From Elizabeth to Anne*, p. 281.

A manual of ethics; pious, but dull.— EMERY, FRED PARKER, 1891, *Notes on English Literature*, p. 62.

It differs considerably both in style and teaching from the ordinary devotional manual, and without much straining may be said to exhibit definite indications of that faculty for essay-writing which was to be so signally developed in the "Spectator," in which indeed certain portions of it were afterwards embodied.—DOBSON, AUSTIN, 1898, *Dictionary of National Biography*, vol. LIV, p. 131.

THE FUNERAL
1702

Nothing can establish a better proof of the admirable merit of this play . . . than the diligence with which the critics have attempted, to no purpose, to discover that it is not genuine; for the plot and the style are unquestionably the author's own, and the last is so peculiar, which is indeed the characteristic of Steele's writings, that nothing can be more difficult to get by heart; but when attached to the memory, nothing can be more easy to retain. . . . Every thing is perfectly in nature, and the moral is complete.— DIBDIN, CHARLES, 1795, *A Complete History of the Stage*, vol. IV, pp. 307, 308.

Very sprightly and pleasant throughout, it was full of telling hits at lawyers and undertakers, and, with a great many laughable incidents, and no laugh raised at the expense of virtue or decency, it had one character (the widow on whom the artifice of her husband's supposed death is played off) which is a masterpiece of comedy.—FORSTER, JOHN, 1855, *Sir Richard Steele, Quarterly Review*, vol. 96, p. 540.

His sense of humour enlivens some of the scenes, and is, perhaps, chiefly visible in "The Funeral;" but for the most part dulness is in the ascendant, and the sentiment is frequently mawkish.—DENNIS, JOHN, 1894, *The Age of Pope*, p. 137.

THE TENDER HUSBAND
1705

In the "Tender Husband" he seems to have contented himself with the more modest aim of being harmless, instead of didactic,—in other words, he tried to be simply amusing.—DOBSON, AUSTIN, 1886, *Richard Steele (English Worthies)*, p. 45.

In this play he gave unmistakable evidence of his happy genius for conceiving and embodying humorous types of character, putting on the stage the parents or the grandparents of Squire Western, Tony Lumpkin, and Lydia Languish.—MINTO, WILLIAM, 1887, *Encyclopædia Britannica, Ninth ed.*, vol. 22, p. 555.

The "Tender Husband," though not so good as the "Funeral," contains a great deal of genuine comedy. The weakness of the play lies in the "moral" scenes in which Clerimont, senior, makes trial of his wife by means of Fainlove. This part of the story, together with Fainlove's marriage with Humphery Gubbin, is far-fetched and out of place.—AITKEN, GEORGE A., 1889, *The Life of Richard Steele*, vol. I, p. 109.

The appropriateness of the title is a little open to question. The pair of innocents, the romantic heiress Biddy Tipkin and the clumsy heir Humphrey Gubbin, are really diverting, and in the first case to no small extent original; while they have furnished hints to no less successors than Fielding, Goldsmith, Sheridan, and Miss Austen. The lawyer and the gallant are also distinctly good, and the aunt has again furnished hints for Mrs. Malaprop, as Biddy has for Lydia. Steele, who always confessed, and probably as a rule exaggerated, his debts to Addison, acknowledges them here; and there is a certain Addisonian tone about some of the humours, though Steele, was quite able to have supplied them.—SAINTSBURY, GEORGE, 1898, *A Short History of English Literature, p.* 535.

THE TATLER
1709-11

But hitherto your Miscellanies have safely run the gauntlet, through all the coffee-houses; which are now entertained with a whimsical new newspaper, called the "Tatler," which I suppose you have seen. This is the newest thing I can tell you of.—WYCHERLEY, WILLIAM, 1709, *Letter to Pope, May* 19.

I really have acted in these cases with honesty, and am concerned it should be thought otherwise: For wit, if a man had it, unless it be directed to some useful end, is but a wanton, frivolous quality; all that one should value himself upon in this kind is, that he has some honourable intention in it.—STEELE, RICHARD, 1710, *The Tatler, Preface.*

It must, indeed, be confessed that never man threw up his pen under stronger temptations to have employed it longer; his reputation was at a greater height than, I believe, ever any living author's was before him. . . There is this noble difference between him and all the rest of our polite and gallant authors: the latter have endeavoured to please the age by falling in with them, and encouraging them in their fashionable vices and false notions of things. It would have been a jest some time since, for a man to have asserted that anything witty could be said in praise of a married state; or that devotion and virtue were anyway necessary to the character of a fine gentleman. . . . It is incredible to conceive the effect his writings have had on the town; how many thousand follies they have either quite banished, or given a very great check to; how much countenance they have added to virtue and religion; how many people they have rendered happy, by showing them it was their own fault if they were not so; and, lastly, how entirely they have convinced our fops and young fellows of the value and advantages of learning. —GAY, JOHN, 1711, *Present State of Wit.*

Steele appears to have begun the paper without any concert, or hope of other assistance than what come spontaneously. His chief dependence was on his intelligence, which gave him a superiority over his contemporaries, who were merely news-writers, and had never discovered that a periodical paper might furnish instruction of a better and more lasting kind. In the other parts of the "Tatler," he was at first less careful; his style had a familiar vulgarity not unlike that of the journalists of the age, which he adopted either in compliance with the prevailing manner, or by way of disguise. In one paper he acknowledges "incorrectness of style," and writing "in an air of common speech." All this however became a *Tatler,* and for some time he aimed at no higher character. But when associated with Addison, he assumed a tone more natural to a polished and elegant mind, and dispersed his coarser familiarity among his characteristic correspondents. If he did not introduce, he was the first who successfully employed the harmless fiction of writing letters to himself, and by that gave a variety of amusement and information to his paper, which would have been impracticable had he always appeared in his own character. All succeeding Essayists have endeavoured to avail themselves of a privilege so essential to this species of composition, but it requires a mimicry of style and sentiment which few have been able to combine.— CHALMERS, ALEXANDER, 1803, *ed., The Tatler, Biographical Preface, p.* 44.

I have . . . always preferred the "Tatler" to the "Spectator." Whether it is owing to my having been earlier or better acquainted with the one than the other, my pleasure in reading these two admirable works is not at all in proportion to their comparative reputation. The "Tatler" contains only half the number of volumes, and, I will venture to say, at least an equal quantity of sterling wit and sense. "The first sprightly runnings" are there—it has more of the original spirit, more of the freshness and stamp of nature. The indications of character and strokes of humour are more true and frequent; the reflections that suggest themselves arise more from the occasion, and are less spun out into regular dissertations. They are more like the remarks which occur in sensible conversation, and less like a lecture. Something is left to the understanding of the reader. Steele seems to have gone into his closet chiefly to set down what he observed out of doors. Addison seems to have spent most of his time in his study, and to have spun out and wire-drawn the hints, which he borrowed from Steele, or took from nature, to the utmost. I am far from wishing to depreciate Addison's talents, but I am anxious to do justice to Steele, who was, I think, upon the whole, a less artificial and more original writer. The humorous descriptions of Steele resemble loose sketches, or fragments of a comedy; those of Addison are rather comments, or ingenious paraphrases, on the genuine text.—HAZLITT, WILLIAM, 1818, *Lectures on the English Comic Writers, Lecture* v.

This paper was written for ladies, . . no flash of genius, no kindling fire, no kernel, no strength.—SCHLOSSER, FREIDRICH CHRISTOPH, 1823–43, *History of the Eighteenth Century, vol.* I, *pp.* 102, 103.

Why, as we turn over the papers preceding that number 81 which must be said to have begun the regular contributions of Addison, there is hardly a trait that does not flash upon us of the bright wit, the cordial humour, the sly satire, the subtle yet kindly criticism, the good-nature and humanity, which have endeared this delightful book to successive generations of readers. There is, indeed, not less prominent at the outset than it continued to the close, the love of theatrical representations, and no doubt actors are criticised and preachers too; but we require no better proof than the very way in which this is done, of the new and original spirit that entered with it into periodical literature. . . , At a time in no way remarkable for refinement, Steele's gallantry to women, thus incessantly expressed in "The Tatler" to the last, was that of a Sir Tristan or Sir Calidore; and in not a small degree, to every household into which it carried such unaccustomed language, this was a ground of its extraordinary success. Inseparable always from his passion is the exalted admiration he feels; and his love is the very flower of his respect.—FORSTER, JOHN, 1855–58, *Sir Richard Steele, Quarterly Review; Biographical Essays, vol.* II, *pp.* 119, 122.

It is fortunately not necessary nowadays to argue as to the comparative merits of the papers by Steele and Addison, and such a discussion would be the last thing that Steele would wish; but this may be said, that Steele was the originator of nearly every new departure in the periodicals which the two friends produced; and if Steele had not furnished Addison with the opportunity for displaying his special power, Addison would in all probability have been known to us only as an accomplished scholar and poet of no great power. The world owes Addison to Steele. . . . It is just because the "Tatler" is more thoroughly imbued with Steele's spirit than the "Spectator," that many competent judges have confessed that they found greater pleasure in the earlier periodical than in its more finished and more famous successor.—AITKEN, GEORGE A., 1889, *The Life of Richard Steele, vol.* I, *pp.* 248, 249.

He paints as a social humourist the whole age of Queen Anne—the political and literary disputes, the fine gentlemen and ladies, the characters of men, the humours of society, the new book, the new play; we live in the very streets and drawing-rooms of old London.—BROOKE, STOPFORD A., 1896, *English Literature, p.* 191.

Steele has the merit of having been the first to feel the new intellectual cravings of his day and to furnish what proved to be the means of meeting them. His "Tatler" was a periodical of pamphlet form, in which news was to be varied by short essays of criticism and gossip. But his grasp of the new literature was a feeble grasp. His sense of the fitting form for it, of its fitting tone, of the range and choice of its subjects, were alike inadequate. He seized indeed by a happy instinct on letter-writing and conversation as the two molds to which the essay must adapt itself; he seized with the same happy instinct on humour as the pervading temper of his work and on "manners" as its destined sphere. But his notion of "manners" was limited not only to the external aspects of life and society, but to those aspects as they present themselves in towns; while his humor remained pert and superficial. The "Tatler," however, had hardly been started when it was taken in hand by a greater than Steele.— HALE, SUSAN, 1898, *Men and Manners of the Eighteenth Century, p.* 76.

The "Tatler"—Swift's own suggestion to Steele—is full of happy illustration and communication of ideas. Dated from coffee-houses, it was the first paper to unite the record of news with the portrayal of manners, to disseminate at once fact and fiction, to publish Whig principles and puff friendly authors. How good is his description of the "Club!" Sir Geofrey Notch, who appropriates the "right-hand" chair, and "calls every thriving man a pitiful upstart;" Major Matchlock, who "has all the battles by heart . . . and brags every night of his having been knockt off his horse at the rising of the London apprentices." Dick Reptile, the "good-natured indolent man, who speaks little himself, but laughs at our jokes;" the Bencher, who is "the greatest wit next to myself," and "shakes his head at the dullness of the present age." They meet at six and disperse at ten. The maid comes with a lantern "to light me home." Literature for the first time descends to the people. Not without reason does Swift, under the *nom de plume* of Humphry Wagstaffe, boast that the Staffian style is *"to describe things exactly as they happen."* Realism made its bow to the world; and, then, too, for the first time women claimed the lion's share of attention, and button-holed mankind. Steele's letters from flirts and prudes, scolds and shrews, languishers and rebels, are the lineal precursors of the "Spectator." Children, too, win an audience. That really wonderful essay (which Thackeray has mentioned), where Steele records the impressions of his early fatherlessness, abounds in pathetic touches—the same that soften us in his "Spectator" paper about the poor Anonyma in the Piazza of Covent Garden. Does not the sentence of his "delight in stealing from the crowd" reveal the whole nature of the sensitive lad? There is a sob in the style. To Steele and Prior belong the domain of childhood.—SICHEL, WALTER, 1901, *Bolingbroke and His Times, p.* 116.

THE SPECTATOR
1711–14

Memorandum, That there is a daily paper comes out, called "The Spectator," written, as is supposed, by the same hand that writ the "Tatler," viz. Captain Steel. In one of the last of these papers is a letter from Oxon at four o'clock in the morning, and subscribed *Abraham Froth.* It ridicules our hebdomadal meetings. The *Abraham Froth* is designed for *Dr. Arthur Charlett,* an empty, frothy man, and indeed the letter personates him incomparably well, being written, as he uses to do, upon great variety of things, and yet about nothing of moment. It brings in his cronys, George Clarke, of All Souls, Dr. William Lancaster, provost of Queen's, and Dr. Gardiner, warden of All Souls. Dr. Lancaster is called in it *Sly-Boots,* and Dr. Gardiner is called in it *Dominick.* Queen's people are angry at it, and the common-room say there, 'tis silly, dull stuff, and they are seconded by some that have been of the same college. But men that are indifferent commend it highly, as it deserves.—HEARNE, THOMAS, 1711, *Reliquiæ Hearnianæ, ed. Bliss, April 22, vol.* I, *p.* 218.

The "Guardian" had but scant success. Its characters were ill-drawn and feebly supported, and the decline of the publication was decided ere Addison's help arrived. Only by party aid and by a larger infusion of party spirit did it carry into the autumn months its lingering existence. It was seen that the "Spectator" could not be rivalled—not even by the writers of the "Spectator" themselves. Still less was it rivalled in the ensuing age, even although the great genius of Dr. Johnson produced "The Rambler," and a whole cluster of wits combined to illustrate "the World." —STANHOPE, EARL, 1870, *History of England, Comprising the Reign of Queen Anne Until the Peace of Utrecht, p.* 564.

There is scarcely a department of essay-writing developed in the "Spectator" which does not trace its origin to Steele. It is Steele who first ventures to raise his voice against the prevailing dramatic taste of the age on behalf of the superior morality and art of Shakespeare's plays. . . . Steele, too, it was who attacked, with all the vigor of which he was capable, the fashionable vice of gambling. . . . The practice of duelling, also, which had hitherto passed unreproved, was censured by Steele. . . . The sketches of character studied from life, and the letters from fictitious correspondents, . . . appear roughly, but yet distinctly, drafted in the "Tatler." Even the papers of literary criticism, afterward so fully elaborated by Addison, are anticipated by his friend, who may fairly claim the honor to have been the first to speak with adequate respect of the genius of Milton. In a word, whatever was perfected by Addison was begun by Steele.—COURTHOPE, W. J., 1884, *Addison (English Men of Letters)*, *pp.* 98, 99, 100.

I happen to be the owner of a very old edition of these latter essays, in whose "Table of Contents" some staid critic of the last generation has written his (or her) comments on the various topics discussed; and I find against the papers of Addison, such notes as—*"instructive, sound, judicious;"* and against those of Steele, I am sorry to say, such words as *"flighty, light, witty, graceful, worthless;"* and I am inclined to think the criticisms are pretty well borne out by the papers: but if *flighty* and *light*, he was not unwholesome; and he did not always carry the rollicking ways of the tavern into the little piquant journalism, where the grave and excellent Mr. Addison presided with him.—MITCHELL, DONALD G., 1890, *English Lands Letters and Kings, From Elizabeth to Anne*, p. 285.

THE GUARDIAN
1713

The character of Guardian was too narrow and too serious: it might properly enough admit both the duties and the decencies of life, but seemed not to include literary speculations, and was in some degree violated by merriment and burlesque. What had the Guardian of the Lizards to do with clubs of tall or of little men, with nests of ants, or with Strada's prolusions? Of this paper nothing is necessary to be said, but that it found many contributors, and that it was a continuation of the Spectator, with the same elegance, and the same variety, till some unlucky sparkle from a Tory paper set Steele's politicks on fire, and wit at once blazed into faction. He was soon too hot for neutral topicks, and quitted the "Guardian" to write the "Englishman."—JOHNSON, SAMUEL, 1779–81, *Addison, Lives of the English Poets*.

CONSCIOUS LOVERS
1723

Parson Adams—"I never heard of any plays fit for a Christian to read but 'Cato' and the 'Conscious Lovers,' and I must own in the latter there are some things

almost solemn enough for a sermon."—FIELDING, HENRY, 1742, *Joseph Andrews*.

In the year 1722, he brought his "Conscious Lovers" on the stage, with prodigious success. This is the last and most finished of all Sir Richard's Comedies, and 'tis doubtful if there is upon the stage, any more instructing; that tends to convey a finer moral, or is better conducted in its design. We have already observed, that it is impossible to witness the tender scenes of this Comedy without emotion; that is, no man of feeling and humanity, who has experienced the delicate solicitudes of love and affection, can do it.—CIBBER, THEOPHILUS, 1753, *Lives of the Poets, vol.* IV, *p.* 119.

Steele's "Conscious Lovers" is the first comedy which can be called moral.—HALLAM, HENRY, 1837–39, *Introduction to the Literature of Europe, pt.* iv. *ch.* vi, *par.* 53, *note*.

Steele had all the brilliancy, and many of the failings, of his gifted countrymen. That his mind was never debased by the irregular pursuits and dissolute society to which he gave his time, is apparent from the beautiful sentiments which pervade that exquisite comedy, the "Conscious Lovers," one of the most elegant delineations of that species of love which borders on romance, in the range of our dramatic literature.—THOMSON, KATHERINE, 1838, *Memoirs of Sarah Jennings, Duchess of Marlborough, vol.* II, *p.* 433.

Nor can it be doubted that it was with Steele the unlucky notion began, of setting comedy to reform the morals, instead of imitating the manners, of the age. Fielding slily glances at this when he makes Parson Adams declare the "Conscious Lovers" to be the only play fit for a Christian to see, and as good as a sermon; and in so witty and fine a writer as Steele, so great a mistake is only to be explained by the intolerable grossness into which the theatre had fallen in his day.—FORSTER, JOHN, 1848–54, *The Life and Times of Oliver Goldsmith, vol.* II, *p.* 93.

LETTERS

These Letters manifest throughout, with irresistible conviction, the very many excellent and amiable qualities, which greatly endeared this public Benefactor to society; and, in proof of their authenticity, we see in them with regret, indubitable marks of "that imprudence of generosity, or vanity of profusion, which kept Steele always incurably necessitous," and shaded his fine character. Considering the constant vexation and serious inconveniences of which it was the cause or the occasion, to himself and his family, nothing can be said to excuse Steele's inattention to œconomy; it was however more pardonable, and the less reproachable, as in the end he did ample justice to his creditors. Our regret on every instance which these Letters afford of this indiscretion, is very greatly augmented, by our admiration and love of that extensive and indefatigable philanthropy, to which we are principally indebted for a long series of well-written papers, fraught with valuable lessons of morality and good-breeding, which have doubtless contributed very much to the intellectual improvement, and moral refinement, of both sexes, in this country. Excepting however what refers in these Letters to the lamentable failure of conduct above mentioned, too well ascertained before; no publication of Steele redounds more to his honour as a man, than the present. It shews him to have been a firm and conscientious patriot; a faithful affectionate husband; a fond, indulgent parent; and, even at this period, if it does not illustrate, it very much enhances the value of his writings, both moral and political, to know with certainty, that the salutary instructions and sublime preceps, so much admired, and so well received, from the fictitious Isaac Bickerstaff, esq., were no other than the genuine sentiments, and habitual practice, of the real Sir Richard Steele.—NICHOLS, JOHN, 1787–1809, ed., *The Epistolary Correspondence of Sir Richard Steele, Preface, p. vi.*

The earliest letters we have from Steele to Miss Scurlock are supposed to have been written in August 1707, and the marriage seems to have taken place on the 9th September following. Steele's wife treasured up the letters and notes she received from her husband, and for the next eleven years we have a record of events, passing troubles, successes, hopes and fears, such as cannot be paralleled in all literature. Swift's "Journal" is to some extent a similar unfolding of private thoughts and feelings, but Steele was entirely exempt from the limitations imposed upon Swift by his relations towards his correspondents. In judging of these letters it must be remembered that they were meant only for a wife's eye. In one of the earliest in the series Steele said expressly: "I beg of you to show my letters to no one living, but let us be contented with one another's thoughts upon our words and actions without the intervention of other people, who cannot judge of so delicate a circumstance as the commerce between man and wife." But, notwithstanding this, the whole series of 400 notes was published in 1787, without any suppressions, by John Nichols, who purchased the originals from Mr. Scurlock, next of kin to Steele's daughter, Lady Trevor, who had received them from her mother. Steele himself, it should be remembered, published some of these letters in the "Tatler" (No. 35) and "Spectator" (No. 142). Few men's character and innermost life have been exposed to anything approaching such a searching scrutiny, and very few could have passed through the ordeal with the honour that attaches to Steele. The marriage was one of affection, and it remained so on both sides until the end. There were, of course, defects of charcter in each; it would be absurd to contend that Steele was not faulty in many ways, and the faults were such as are seen most easily, especially by those who read to prove to their own satisfaction that the noblest of men fall short even as they; but the great fact remains that during all the years of married life Steele retained the affection of his wife unimpaired. At the end she was still his "dear Prue" and "dear Wife." —AITKEN, GEORGE A., 1889, *The Life of Richard Steele, vol. I, p. 172.*

The "fond fool of a husband," writing while his ragged boy tumbles on the floor, or the "brats his girls" stand on either side of the table, presents a picture which one would not exchange for all the immaculate primness of Joseph Addison. The letters to "Prue" should be read side by side with the "Journal to Stella." Both have the supreme merit of perfect sincerity, simplicity and devotion. The difference between them is the difference between the strongly contrasted natures of the two writers. No one can doubt which was the more lovable, any more than which was the greater. man.—POOLE,

STANLEY LANE–1898, *Eighteenth Century Letters*, ed. *Johnson, Introduction, p.* xxvii.

GENERAL

He's a poet too, and was very favourably received by the Town especially in his first performance, where, if you'll take my opinion, he exhausted most of his stock; for what he has since produced seem but faint copies of that agreeable original. Tho' he's a most incorrect writer, he pleases in spite of the faults we see and own. Whether application might not burnish the defect, or if those very defects were brightened, whether the genuine spirit would fly off? are queries not so easily resolved.—MANLEY, MARY DE LA RIVIERE, 1709, *New Atalantis, vol.* I, *p.* 187.

To take the height of his Learning, you are to suppose a Lad just fit for the University, and sent early from thence into the wide World, where he followed every way of Life that might least improve, or preserve the Rudiments he had got. He hath no Invention, nor is Master of a tolerable Style; his chief Talent is Humor, which he sometimes discovers both in Writing and Discourse.—SWIFT, JONATHAN, 1713, *The Importance of the Guardian Considered.*

Steele, who in his comedies successfully engrafted modern characters on the ancient dramas. — SMOLLETT, TOBIAS GEORGE, 1757-58, *History of England, George I.,* notes.

Though Sir Richard Steele's reputation as a public writer was owing to his connexions with Mr. Addison, yet, after their intimacy was formed, Steele sunk in his merit as an author. This was not owing so much to the evident superiority on the part of Addison, as to the unnatural efforts which Steele made to equal or eclipse him. This emulation destroyed that genuine flow of diction which is discoverable in all his former compositions. —GOLDSMITH, OLIVER, 1759, *The Bee, No.* 8, *Nov.* 24.

There is great regularity in the fable of all his plays, and the characters are well sketched and preserved; but in the dialogue he is sometimes tedious. He wants the quick repartee of Congreve; and though possessed of humour, falls into the style rather of an essay than a drama. Much of that point which appears in his Tatlers may be discovered in his. Comedies.—CHALMERS, ALEXANDER, 1803, ed., *The Tatler, vol.* I, *p.* 37.

Steele will be found in purity and simplicity inferior to Tillotson; to Temple in elegance and harmony; to Dryden in richness, mellowness, and variety. To the two former, however, he is equal in correctness; to the latter in vivacity; and with all he is nearly on a level as to ease and perspicuity. Steele's great misfortune has ever been the comparison, so perpetually drawn with regard to style, between himself and Addison. The proximity of their productions have naturally led to the consideration of their respective merits in point of composition; and though it must be allowed that from the best manner of Addison Steele stands widely apart, yet are there several papers which, having been written by Sir Richard with more than usual care, and with evident marks of emulation, appear to have imbibed a portion of Addisonian grace.— DRAKE, NATHAN, 1804, *Essays Illustrative of the Tatler, Spectator and Guardian, vol.* I, *p.* 201.

I question if his works, detached from those of his illustrious coadjutor, would find many purchasers. His "Christian Hero" is more talked of than read.— DIBDIN, THOMAS FROGNALL, 1824, *The Library Companion, p.* 606, *note.*

The utmost sweetness and love breathe through his moral speculations. How tender his remembrance of affecting scenes and incidents in his childhood. How lively his sense of the beauty of a sound, honest heart; of the dignity and benign power of woman, in her several relations and proper sphere; of the claims, confidence, and rewards of friendship; of the deference we owe to others in the smallest things. We are drawn near to him, and breathe the air of benevolence and courtesy, and love him the more that he is not perfect, if only for sympathy. . . . Steele never writes as if he had a literary character to support, or indeed any character but that of the good old gentleman who has taken our morals into keeping. . . . If we have read Steele much, and turn to him yet again, every new reading seems more like an act of meditation or memory than receiving another's thoughts. We have no surprises, no admiration. We do not need them. We do not feel that we are engaged with a memorable work of literature, which we are to compare with others. We do not say a word to ourselves about its merit. All that we are conscious of is, a succession of familiar, agreeable images which we begin to value as part of ourselves; an easy, natural humor which never quite runs over and never loses its charm, and an early companion, who is so visible and intelligible in every word, that he is at our side and talking with us.—Channing, William Ellery, 1838, *Periodical Essays of the Age of Anne, North American Review, vol.* 46, *pp.* 353, 357, 358.

He knew the town, and had paid dear for his knowledge. He had read much more than the dissipated men of that time were in the habit of reading. He was a rake among scholars, and a scholar among rakes. His style was easy and not incorrect; and though his wit and humour were of no higher order, his gay animal spirits imparted to his compositions an air of vivacity which ordinary readers could hardly distinguish from comic genius. His writings have been well compared to those light wines, which, though deficient in body and flavour, are yet a pleasant small drink, if not kept too long, or carried too far.—Macaulay, Thomas Babington, 1843, *Life and Writings of Addison, Edinburgh Review.*

For, though a man of greater intellectual activity than Addison, he had immeasurably less of genius.—De Quincey, Thomas, 1847–58, *Schlosser's Literary History, Works, ed. Masson, vol.* xi, *p.* 19.

I must own that I prefer open-hearted Steele with all his faults, to Addison with all his essays.—Hunt, Leigh, 1850, *Autobiography, ch.* ii.

The great charm of Steele's writing is its naturalness. He wrote so quickly and carelessly, that he was forced to make the reader his confidant, and had not the time to deceive him. He had a small share of book-learning, but a vast acquaintance with the world. He had known men and taverns. He had lived with gownsmen, with troopers, with gentlemen ushers of the Court, with men and women of fashion; with authors and wits, with the inmates of the spunging houses, and with the frequenters of all the clubs and coffee houses in the town.

He was liked in all company because he liked it; and you like to see his enjoyment as you like to see the glee of a box full of children at the pantomime. He was not one of those lonely ones of the earth whose greatness obliged them to be solitary; on the contrary, he admired, I think, more than any man who ever wrote; and full of hearty applause and sympathy, wins upon you by calling you to share his delight and good humour. His laugh rings through the whole house. He must have been invaluable at a tragedy, and have cried as much as the most tender young lady in the boxes. He has a relish for beauty and goodness wherever he meets it. —Thackeray, William Makepeace, 1853, *The English Humourists of the Eighteenth Century.*

I would rather have written what is here quoted from Steele than all the criticisms and philosophy of all the Edinburgh Reviewers. What a good critic he was! I doubt if he has ever been surpassed. Somehow I cannot but connect Steele and Goldsmith, as I do Cowper and Southey. Of all our literary men, they interest me the most. . . . Dear good faulty Steele!—Landor, Walter Savage, 1855, *Silent Companions, Works by Forster, vol.* i, *p.* 500.

We have already called Steele's wit fresh and natural. It came with no stinted flow. He wrote as he lived, freely and carelessly, scattering the coinage of his brain, as he did his guineas, with an unsparing hand. All who read his papers, or his letters to Prue, cannot help seeing the good heart of the rattle-brain shining out in every line. We can forgive, or at least forget, his tippling in taverns and his unthinking extravagance, bad as these were, in consideration of the loving touch with which he handles the foibles of his neighbours, and the mirth without bitterness that flows from his gentle pen.— Collier, William Francis, 1861, *A History of English Literature, p.* 271.

To him perhaps much can be traced that we find in Sterne, Fielding, Richardson, Thackeray, Dickens, and many of our humorous novelists.—Friswell, James Hain, 1869, *Essays on English Writers, p.* 114.

In opposition to his imprudences and irregularities, a noble catalogue of virtues can be recorded to Steele's honour.

Through all his writings he appears always to have entertained the purest and most transparent principles of religion and morals. . . . Steele possessed a high sense of propriety in language, too, as well as in conduct, and he appears to have had an absolute aversion to gross vices, as compromising the temporal if not the eternal welfare of man. He strenuously opposed—and, it is said, not without personal risk—the insane and wicked practice of duelling, that was so prevalent in his day. Upon this topic he wrote with bitterness, because he himself, in endeavouring to disarm an opponent who had forced him into a contest, wounded his adversary to death. . . . Steele was also constantly and uniformly vehement in his denunciations of gambling, and of women gamesters in particular. His sentiments, also, upon the passion of love are pure, generous, ardent, and graceful, and few writers have given vent to more cordial thoughts upon the blessings of a real love-marriage. There is a plainness, a sort of brotherly confidence, in his manner upon this question—particularly towards the women—that never can be mistaken for the lip-deep mouthing of the mere essayist. —CLARKE, CHARLES COWDEN, 1871, *On the Comic Writers of England, The Gentleman's Magazine, n. s., vol.* 7, *pp.* 338, 339.

He was a genial critic. His exuberant wit and humor reproved without wounding; he was not severe enough to be a public censor, nor pedantic enough to be the pedagogue of an age which often needed the lash rather than the gentle reproof, and upon which a merciful clemency lost its end if not its praises. He deserves credit for an attempt, however feeble, to reward virtue upon the stage, after the wholesale rewards which vice had reaped in the age of Charles II. Steele has been overshadowed, in his connection with Addison, by the more dignified and consistent career, the greater social respectability, and the more elegant and scholarly style of his friend; and yet in much that they jointly accomplished, the merit of Steele is really as great, and conduces much to the reputation of Addison. The one husbanded and cherished his fame; the other flung it away or lavished it upon his colleagues. As contributors to history, they claim an equal share of our gratitude and

praise.—COPPÉE, HENRY, 1872, *English Literature, p.* 267.

His intellect was of a rougher cast than his friend's. It is the emotional character of the man that renders him interesting, and entitles him to a good secondary place among our great writers of prose. Probably a large fraction of his energy was spent in the rollicking enjoyment of existence; otherwise his rank would have been higher than it is. His contributions to the "Spectator" and allied periodicals take their distinction from his prevailing tenderness of heart and wide acquaintance with human life. To him these papers owe their pathos, their humour, and their extraordinary variety of characters.

In command of words he is not equal to Addison; his choice is much less felicitous. His sentence composition is irregular and careless, often ungrammatical: writing in the character of a Tatler, he thought it incumbent to assume "incorrectness of style, and an air of common speech"—a style very agreeable to his own inclinations. He has not the polished and felicitous melody of Addison. His language and sentiments are much more glowing and extravagant; his papers may be distinguished by this feature alone. . . . Steele is one of the most touching of our writers. Himself of a nature the reverse of melancholy, he yet at certain seasons "resolved to be sorrowful;" and when the sorrowful mood was upon him, the incidents that he recalled or imagined were of the most heartrending character. The kind of pathos that we find in him would not be pathetic at all, in a poetic sense, to the more delicate order of sensibilities: it would be a pain, and not an æsthetic pleasure.—MINTO, WILLIAM, 1872-80, *A Manual of English Prose Literature, pp.* 389, 390.

The cardinal quality of these papers is their good sense; this never forsakes them. Their philosophy presents it in a penetrative, their humor in a pungent, form. Their criticisms on society are as just as they are amiable. Their analysis is correct and practical, their moral reflections, impressive and natural. This good sense was most effective in securing uniform success. It gave a restraint and proportion to what was said that made it difficult to be resisted, and impossible to be controverted. Whatever the object of satire, the pedantry of learning, the conceit of rank, the foppishness of dress, the frivolity of etiquette, the prejudice of partisanship, the same sober, sound opinion underlay and sustained the attack. Moderation was even more worthy of commendation then than now. The art of achieving a true success is found very much in tempering zeal to a just moderation. Steel that is too hard is fractured at every blow; draw the temper too much and it becomes iron. The Damascus blade, with its tough and steady edge clings to that nice line that divides excess and deficiency. From this middle region, Steele seems to have been inclined to range upward, and Addison downward. He complains of Addison, that "he blew a lute when he should sound a trumpet;" yet the lute notes of the one went farther than the trumpet tones of the other.— BASCOM, JOHN, 1874, *Philosophy of English Literature, p.* 174.

In pursuing the moral and social aims of which, to his enduring honour, he never allowed himself to lose sight, Steele as a dramatist came to mistake the true means and methods of the comic drama. His own comic genius lacked the sustained vigour which is required by the stage; and his artistic sense was too keen altogether to have left him unconscious of his inability to satisfy his moral purpose by holding up to ridicule with unflagging persistence those human vices and follies which are the proper subjects of comedy. He therefore called in sentiment to the aid of humour. Availing himself of the reaction against the grosser methods of provoking laughter and amusement which had set in as part of the general reaction against the licence of the Restoration age, he took a hint from Colley Cibber, who so carefully watched the currents of the public taste, and became the real founder of that Sentimental Comedy which during a period lying beyond the range of these volumes exercised so strong and, on the whole, so far from salutary an influence upon the progress of our dramatic literature. There is no reason for attributing Steele's innovation to any foreign literary influence; on the other hand it would be unjust to hold his tentative beginnings responsible for the futility of successors who, being altogether deficient in any

kind of comic power, in the end came to abandon even the semblance of true comic intention. In so far however as their aberrations followed the lines into which he was the first to cause English comedy consciously to deviate, Steele must be held to have contributed to the decline of the English drama, and in particular to the sinking of the sap in that branch of it to which his plays both nominally and in their general design belong.—WARD, ADOLPHUS WILLIAM, 1875–99, *A History of English Dramatic Literature, vol.* III, *p.* 493.

For the sake of his reputation, Steele is unfortunate in having constantly to be contrasted with Addison. His motives in writing for the "Tatler" and "Spectator" were identical with Addison's; both wished to improve the manners and morals of the day; and though Steele's papers do not always compare favorably with those of Addison, there are some of them which Addison could scarcely excel. Unlike his partner, he was without a settled literary style; but in whatever manner he wrote, he never neglected to display a great amount of spirit and excellent taste.— HABBERTON, JOHN, 1876, *ed., The Spectator, Selected Papers, p.* xix.

Steele's hearty interest in men and women gave life to his essays. He approached even literature on the side of human fellowship; talked of plays with strong personal regard for the players; and had, like Addison, depths of religious earnestness that gave a high aim to his work. He sought to turn the current of opinion against duelling. Some of his lightest papers were in accordance with his constant endeavor to correct the false tone of society that made it fashionable to speak with contempt of marriage. No man laboured more seriously to establish the true influence of woman in society.— MORLEY, HENRY, 1879, *A Manual of English Literature, ed. Tyler, p.* 525.

What ruled writer and reader alike was the new-found pleasure of talk. The use of coffee had only come in at the close of the civil wars; but already London and the bigger towns were crowded with coffee-houses. The popularity of the coffee-house sprang not from its coffee, but from the new pleasure which men found in their chat over the coffee-cup. And from the coffee-house sprang the

Essay. The talk of Addison and Steele is the brightest and easiest talk that was ever put in print: but its literary charm lies in this, that it is strictly talk. The essayist is a gentleman who chats to a world of gentlemen, and whose chat is shaped and coloured by a sense of what he owes to his company. He must interest and entertain, he may not bore them; and so his form must be short; essay or sketch, or tale or letter. So too his style must be simple, the sentences clear and quotable, good sense ready packed for carriage. Strength of phrase, intricacy of structure, height of tone were all necessarily banished from such prose as we banish them from ordinary conversation. There was no room for pedantry, for the ostentatious display of learning, for pompousness, for affectation. The essayist had to think, as a talker should think, more of good taste than of imaginative excellence, of propriety of expression than of grandeur of phrase. The deeper themes of the world or man were denied to him; if he touches them it is superficially, with a decorous dulness, or on their more humorous side with a gentle irony that shows how faint their hold is on him.—GREEN, JOHN RICHARD, 1880, *History of the English People, vol. IV, p. 113.*

However wild his conduct may have occasionally been, in his writings he never swerved from upholding the cause of purity and goodness; and in many respects his moral precepts were of a less conventional kind, and reached a higher spiritual level than Addison's.—NICOLL, HENRY J., 1882, *Landmarks of English Literature, p. 183.*

He excelled as a satirist, a humorist, and a storyteller, who must, like the poet, be born. He had a knowledge of the world, and a dramatic skill by which the serials profited largely. Some of his papers equal anything Addison ever wrote. Occupying a more elevated plane than many of his contemporaries, he is paled in his powers by the overshadowing presence of his illustrious friend. His writings have been compared to those light wines which, though deficient in body and flavor, are yet a pleasant small drink, if not kept too long or carried too far. . . . While his purpose (more or less vaguely realized) was reformatory and corrective, his service was chiefly indirect, in calling to the support and

development of his enterprises Addison, to whom it was reserved to make the periodical a true revolutionary power in literature and society. What shall we expect of a man who forever gathers the pleasures that lie on the border-land of evil, tearfully casts them away, then recklessly gathers them again?—WELSH, ALFRED H., 1883, *Development of English Literature and Language, vol. II, p. 79.*

Steele's humour is that of a full and impulsive nature, careless and frank, and too warm-hearted to be very satirical. It comes with the extemporaneous freshness of the man's character. It seems even sincerer from its want of polish; and though the writer touches off human weaknessess, he never forgets that he is only human himself.—DOW, JOHN G., 1885, *The Academy, vol. 28, p. 233.*

He ranks first among English humourists for geniality without boisterousness, and sentiment without gush.—SAINTSBURY, GEORGE, 1886, *Specimens of English Prose Style, p. 144.*

What strikes us first in his writing is its spontaneity. He wrote because he had something to say, and could not help saying it. He had seen much, and reflected much, though he had read little; and there were few subjects to the discussion of which he could not contribute something valuable from his stores of thought or observation. His exceeding naturalness is a characteristic remark by Thackeray; but at least as conspicuous is his sympathetic temper. He does not look upon his fellow-creatures with the austere gaze of the philosopher; but with the kindly eyes of a friendly onlooker, who knows that he is one of themselves, and not wholly free from the failings and foibles which he so good-naturedly chastises. It is no whip of scorpions that "Sir Richard" handles; the lash is of silk, and the touch light though smart. —ADAMS, W. H. DAVENPORT, 1886, *Good Queen Anne, vol. II, p. 117.*

His style presents less material for study than that of Addison, because it is itself unstudied. When Addison was so delicately weighing and polishing his sentences, Steele was pouring out what he saw or what he felt. He is very incorrect, sometimes downright ungrammatical. When he preaches, as he is very apt to do, we fall to nodding in his face.

But we wake again when he returns to the subject he knows best, the shifting pictures of human life, with its hopes and disappointments, its laughter and its tears. When he talks to us about the beauty of virtuous women, the loneliness of orphan children, the innocent conversation of old men, any of the single human topics which literature had so long time thought below her dignity, we are fascinated and bewitched; his style takes fire, "the motion doth dilate the flame," and Steele becomes a great writer.— GOSSE, EDMUND, 1888, *History of Eighteenth Century Literature, p.* 195.

The writings of Steele have never lost their interest for students of English literature. During the eighteenth century his works were constantly passing through new editions. One marked difference between the periodicals of the present day and those of the early eighteenth century is, that whereas the former are readily consigned to dealers in waste paper, the latter were carefully treasured and so continually sought after that new editions were a profitable investment for publishers. The "Tatler" and the "Spectator" appeared again and again in new dress. During the present century it may be that the writings of Steele have gone a little out of fashion; but it cannot for a moment be said with any truth that their author has been forgotten.—PICTON, J. ALLANSON, 1889, *Good Words, vol.* 30. *p.* 736.

The best work of Steele is in his "Essays," and his chief praise is in the elevating tone of his teaching. He brought back decency to the comic drama, and in his periodicals he set himself the task of improving the morals and manners of society. His style is natural and lively, less graceful than Addison's, and his taste is less refined; but he is his equal in inventiveness and in knowledge of the world. —ROBERTSON, J. LOGIE, 1894, *A History of English Literature, p.* 213.

Sir Richard's pathetic touches and artless turns of expression come from the heart. He is the most natural of writers, but does not seem to be aware that nature, in order to be converted into good literature, needs a little clothing. His essays have often a looseness or negligence of aim unpardonable in a man who can write so well.—DENNIS, JOHN, 1894, *The Age of Pope, p.* 147.

Yet when everything is allowed to Addison that can reasonably be conceded to him, and when everything has been said, that can be said, of Steele's slapdash method, impulsive judgment, and careless style, it must be admitted that Steele brought some gifts to his work for which one may seek in vain in the work of his coadjutor. If he was less literary, he was more earnest; if he was more hasty, he was sometimes more happy. The very energy of his indignation, pity, or enthusiasm frequently taught him those short cuts to his reader's sympathy, which neither art nor artifice can teach; and he often becomes eloquent by the sheer force and sincerity of his emotion. Like Addison, he is occasionally hortatory and didactic; but his sermons, though at times excellent, are not his best work. His true school is human nature. As a genial and kindly commentator upon the men and women about him; as a humane and an indulgent interpreter of their frailties; as a generous and an ungrudging sympathiser with their feeblest better impulse—he belongs to the great race of English humourists.—DOBSON, AUSTIN, 1894, *English Prose, ed. Craik, vol.* III, *p.* 472.

Phrases such as "Addison's *Spectator*" or "Addison's *Sir Roger*" are entirely question-begging phrases, and do a manifest injustice to the originality of Steele. If Addison be allowed to have been the more brilliant contributor, yet to Steele must be given all the credit of having been the projector and editor; and, whatever his literary deficiencies, it is his name that must rank the higher, if regard be had merely to the development of the English essay. In Steele there was a strange blending of a cute enterprise and boyish thoughtlessness, and it is the fate of all authors who have a special place in their readers' affections that the latter side of their character should be unduly emphasized. A claim to pity, even if it be a loving pity, is a dangerous attribute for an author to possess, and it has militated against Steele's purely literary reputation that he is thought of as being, like his friend Gay, "in wit a man, simplicity a child." So enamoured of Addison's "elegance" were his earlier editors that they rather grudged Steele any share of his fame, and it is unfortunate that some of the absurdities of Hurd should have been endorsed by the eloquence of Macaulay. Nor are some of Steele' sincerest admirers free from blame. Perhaps there is no more stimulating introduction to the literature of last century than Thackeray's lectures—or "Esmond;" but it is well in approaching Steele's writings to recognize that Thackeray's lovable Dick Steele is not altogether the same man as the founder of the English Essay.—Lobban, J. H., 1896, *English Essays*, ed. Herford, Introduction, p. xxiii.

The manly tenderness of Steele.—Bates, Arlo, 1897, *Talks on the Study of Literature*, p. 66.

The so-called Essay which Steele launched in the "Tatler," which was taken up and perfected in the "Spectator," which had numerous immediate followers, and a succession of the greatest importance at intervals throughout the century, and which at once expressed and influenced the tone and thought of that century after a fashion rarely paralleled, was not originally started in quite the form which it soon assumed, and never, for the greater part of a hundred years, wholly lost. . . . Steele, always zealous and always generous, but a little wanting in criticism, not infrequently diverged into sentimentality. Addison's tendency, though he, too, was unflinchingly on virtue's side, was rather towards a very mellow and not unindulgent but still distinctly cynical cynicism—a smile too demure ever to be a grin, but sometimes, except on religious subjects, faintly and distantly approaching a sneer. This appears even in the most elaborate and kindly of the imaginative creations of the double series, Sir Roger de Coverley, whom Steele indeed seems to have invented, but whom Addison adopted, perfected, and (some, perhaps without reason, say) even killed out of kindness, lest a less delicate touch should take the bloom off him. This great creation, which comes nearer than anything out of prose fiction or drama to the masterpieces of the novelists and dramatists, is accompanied by others hardly less masterly; while Addison constantly, and Steele not seldom, has sketches or touches as perfect in their way, though less elaborate. It is scarcely too much to say that these papers, and especially the "Spectator," taught the eighteenth century how it

should, and especially how it should not, behave in public places, from churches to theatres; what books it should like, and how it should like them; how it should treat its lovers, mistresses, husbands, wives, parents, and friends; that it might politely sneer at operas, and must not take any art except literature too seriously; that a moderate and refined devotion to the Protestant religion and the Hanoverian succession was the duty, though not the whole duty, of a gentleman. It is still a little astonishing to find with what docility the century obeyed and learnt its lesson. . . . Steele, though he has some rarer flights than his friend, is much less correct, and much less polished; while, though he had started with equal chances, his rambling life had stored him with far less learning than Addison possessed.—Saintsbury, George, 1898, *A Short History of English Literature*, pp. 537, 538, 539.

In this ["The Conscious Lovers"], as in his former plays, he broke entirely away from the profligate traditions of the restoration drama, and kept close to what he conceived to be the high moral purpose of the stage. But in his earnestness he too often forgot that the first object of comedy is to amuse and not to preach; and his plays, though occasionally enlivened with humour, are on the whole dull and insipid.—Hudson, W. H., 1899, ed. *The Sir Roger de Coverley Papers*, Introduction, p. x.

Everybody liked him, and even to this day it is natural to speak of him as "Dick" Steele. Without him it is doubtful if Addison would have developed his talent in the society essay. Like Addison he earned political preferment by his pen though the offices he held were of inferior dignity.—Johnson, Charles F., 1900, *Outline History of English and American Literature*, p. 256.

Steele's writings have not the polish or delicate humor of Addison's, but they have more strength and pathos. From the neglect of Steele and the enduring interest in Addison, the student should learn the valuable lesson that artistic finish, as well as excellence of subject matter, has become almost a necessity for a prose writer who would not be soon neglected. — Halleck, Reube Post, 1900, *History of English Literature*, p. 249.